THE WILEY-BLACKWELL COMPANION TO SOCIOLOGY

WILEY-BLACKWELL COMPANIONS TO SOCIOLOGY

The Wiley-Blackwell Companions to Sociology provide introductions to emerging topics and theoretical orientations in sociology as well as presenting the scope and quality of the discipline as it is currently configured. Essays in the Companions tackle broad themes or central puzzles within the field and are authored by key scholars who have spent considerable time in research and reflection on the questions and controversies that have activated interest in their area. This authoritative series will interest those studying sociology at advanced undergraduate or graduate level as well as scholars in the social sciences and informed readers in applied disciplines.

THE WILEY-BLACKWELL COMPANION TO

Sociology

EDITED BY

GEORGE RITZER

WILEY-BLACKWELL

A John Wiley & Sons, Ltd., Publication

This edition first published 2012
© 2012 Blackwell Publishing Ltd

Blackwell Publishing was acquired by John Wiley & Sons in February 2007. Blackwell's publishing program has been merged with Wiley's global Scientific, Technical, and Medical business to form Wiley-Blackwell.

Registered Office
John Wiley & Sons Ltd, The Atrium, Southern Gate, Chichester, West Sussex, PO19 8SQ, UK

Editorial Offices
350 Main Street, Malden, MA 02148-5020, USA
9600 Garsington Road, Oxford, OX4 2DQ, UK
The Atrium, Southern Gate, Chichester, West Sussex, PO19 8SQ, UK

For details of our global editorial offices, for customer services, and for information about how to apply for permission to reuse the copyright material in this book please see our website at www.wiley.com/wiley-blackwell.

The right of George Ritzer to be identified as the author of the editorial material in this work has been asserted in accordance with the UK Copyright, Designs and Patents Act 1988.

Wiley also publishes its books in a variety of electronic formats. Some content that appears in print may not be available in electronic books.

Designations used by companies to distinguish their products are often claimed as trademarks. All brand names and product names used in this book are trade names, service marks, trademarks or registered trademarks of their respective owners. The publisher is not associated with any product or vendor mentioned in this book. This publication is designed to provide accurate and authoritative information in regard to the subject matter covered. It is sold on the understanding that the publisher is not engaged in rendering professional services. If professional advice or other expert assistance is required, the services of a competent professional should be sought.

Library of Congress Cataloging-in-Publication Data

The Wiley-Blackwell companion to sociology / edited by George Ritzer.
　　p. cm. – (Wiley-Blackwell companions to sociology)
　Includes bibliographical references and index.
　ISBN 978-1-4443-3039-7 (hardback : alk. paper) – ISBN 978-1-4443-4735-7 (ePDF) –
ISBN 978-1-4443-4738-8 (Wiley Online Library) – ISBN 978-1-4443-4736-4 (ePub) –
ISBN 978-1-4443-4737-1 (Mobi)
　　1. Sociology.　I. Ritzer, George.
　HM585.W55 2011
　301–dc23

　　　　　　　　　　　　　　　　　　　　　　　　　　　　　　　　　　2011020599

A catalogue record for this book is available from the British Library.

This book is published in the following electronic formats: ePDFs 9781444347357; Wiley Online Library 9781444347388; ePub 9781444347364; Mobi 9781444347371

Set in 10/12.5 pt Sabon by Toppan Best-set Premedia Limited
Printed and bound in Singapore by Markono Print Media Pte Ltd

1　2012

Contents

Contributors

Graham Allan is Emeritus Professor of Sociology at Keele University, UK. His main research interests concern the sociology of informal relationships, particularly family sociology and the sociology of friendship. His recent publications include *Stepfamilies* (2011), co-authored with Graham Crow (Southampton University, UK) and Sheila Hawker, and *The End of Children? Changing Trends in Childbearing and Childhood* (2011), co-edited with Nathan Lauster (University of British Columbia).

Robert J. Antonio teaches social theory at the University of Kansas. He has been interested in theories and processes of modernization, anti-modernization, postmodernization, neomodernization, and globalization. Currently, he is focusing on the impact of the global system of production and consumption on the throughput of resources and production of waste and especially on the sustainability of the economic and cultural imperative of unplanned, exponential growth, central to modern capitalism and especially to today's neoliberal regime of accumulation.

Nachman Ben-Yehuda's work focuses on how, why, where, and when challenges to the status quo emerge and function as catalysts for processes of social change or stability. His books focus on betrayal and treason, the Masada myth, political assassinations, politics and deviance, the European witchcraze, deviant sciences and scientists, using archaeology for national purposes, and (with Erich Goode) moral panics. His 2010 book *Theocratic Democracy* examines public constructions of unconventional behavior amongst fundamentalists. His current work examines the culture of submarine warfare and atrocities. Ben-Yehuda is in the Department of Sociology and Anthropology at the Hebrew University, Jerusalem.

Suzanne M. Bianchi is Dorothy Meier Chair in Social Equities and Distinguished Professor of Sociology at the University of California, Los Angeles. She is a past

President of the Population Association of America. Her research focuses on time use, gender equality in American families and workplaces, and intergenerational family ties and population aging.

Stewart R. Clegg is Research Professor and Director of the Centre for Management and Organization Studies Research at the University of Technology, Sydney; Visiting Professor of Organizational Change Management, Maastricht University Faculty of Business; Visiting Professor and International Fellow in Discourse and Management Theory, Centre of Comparative Social Studies, Vrije Universiteit of Amsterdam; and he is also a Visiting Professor at Copenhagen Business School and EM-Lyon. A prolific publisher in leading academic journals in social science, management, and organization theory, he is also the author and editor of many books, including *Power and Organizations* (Clegg, Courpasson and Phillips 2006) and *Frameworks of Power* (1989).

William C. Cockerham is Distinguished Professor of Sociology and Chair of the Department of Sociology and Social Work at the University of Alabama at Birmingham, with secondary appointments in medicine and public health. Among his recent books are *Health and Globalization* (2010), *The New Blackwell Companion to Medical Sociology* (2010), and *Medical Sociology*, 12th edition (2012). He is the former President of the Research Committee on Health Sociology of the International Sociological Association (2006–10) and a former member of the Editorial Board of the *American Sociological Review* (2008–11).

Remy Cross is an Assistant Professor in the Department of Criminology at the University of South Florida. His areas of interest include social movements, radical activism, and the effects of new communication technologies on political behavior. His dissertation examines the decision-making and organization of grassroots anti-authoritarian movements on both the political right and left. His published work has appeared in the *Journal of Social Structure*, the *Journal of Mathematical Sociology*, and the *Encyclopedia of Social and Political Movements*.

Paul Dean is a PhD candidate in Sociology at the University of Maryland. His dissertation research explores movements that seek to regulate corporations through social certifications (e.g., Fair Trade) and socially responsible investments by examining how standards for socially responsible practices are constructed. He is also a Lilly Graduate Teaching Fellow and co-creator/co-editor of "The Sociological Cinema: Teaching Sociology Through Video," an online teaching resource for sociology instructors (www.thesociologicalcinema.com).

Mitchell Duneier is Maurice P. During Professor of Sociology at Princeton. He is the author of *Sidewalk, Slim's Table, and Ghetto* (with Alice Goffman, forthcoming 2011).

Riley E. Dunlap is Regents Professor of Sociology at Oklahoma State University and one of the founders of the field of environmental sociology. He has served as Chair of the environmental sociology groups within the American Sociological

Association, the Rural Sociological Society, and the Society for the Study of Social Problems, as well as President of the International Sociological Association's Research Committee on Environment and Society. He is currently chairing the American Sociological Association's Task Force on Sociology and Global Climate Change. Dunlap is senior editor of the *Handbook of Environmental Sociology* and *Sociological Theory and the Environment*.

Mark Erickson is Reader in Sociology at the University of Brighton, and his publications include *Science, Culture and Society: Understanding Science in the 21st Century* (2005), *Business in Society* (co-author, 2009), and *Myths at Work* (co-author, 2001).

Joe R. Feagin, Ella C. McFadden Professor at Texas A&M University, acquired his PhD in Sociology at Harvard University in 1966. Feagin has served as the Scholar-in-Residence at the US Commission on Civil Rights and has written 57 scholarly books in his research areas, one of which (*Ghetto Revolts*) was nominated for a Pulitzer Prize. He is the 2006 recipient of a Harvard Alumni Association lifetime award and was the 2000 President of the American Sociological Association.

Ge Liu earned her PhD in Sociology in the Department of Sociology of the University of Notre Dame in April 2011. Her main fields of research interest are sociology of education, stratification, economic sociology, and quantitative methods. Her dissertation is on peer influence on adolescents' academic outcomes, and in it she examines friendship networks and racial/ethnic differences in academic outcomes, US-East Asian differences in peer influence, and long-term peer influence.

Kevin Fox Gotham has research interests in real estate and housing markets, urban redevelopment, and the political economy of tourism. He is currently writing a book with Miriam Greenberg (University of California-Santa Cruz) on the federal response to the 9/11 and the Hurricane Katrina disasters. He is author of *Race, Real Estate, and Uneven Development* (2002) and *Authentic New Orleans: Race, Culture, and Tourism in the Big Easy* (2007).

Barbara Gurr's research highlights the intersections of race, class, gender, sexuality, and citizenship. She is the former Director of Women's Studies at Southern Connecticut State University and the former Assistant Director of Women's Studies at the University of Connecticut, where she is currently a graduate student in Sociology. Her dissertation, "Restrictive Relations: Native American Women, Reproductive Justice, and the Indian Health Service," utilizes a reproductive justice perspective to examine the failure of the federal government and the Indian Health Service to provide safe, adequate reproductive healthcare for Native American women.

Maureen T. Hallinan is the White Professor of Sociology at the University of Notre Dame. Her primary research interests are in the effects of the formal and informal organization of schools on students' cognitive and social development. Currently, she is investigating the effects of the school sector on student academic achievement. She is a past President of the American Sociological Association and the Sociological Research Association and a member of the National Academy of Education. She served as editor of *The Sociology of Education* and the *Handbook of Sociology of Education*.

Emma Head has been a Lecturer in Sociology at Keele University, UK, since 2006. She was awarded her PhD in Sociology from the University of Bristol in 2005. She then took up a postdoctoral fellowship at Leeds University. Her research interests are in the sociology of the family, particularly in the areas of parenting, early childhood, and policy.

Nathan Jurgenson is a PhD student in Sociology at the University of Maryland where he is working with George Ritzer on topics surrounding new technologies, especially social media. Nathan has focused on the topic of prosumption (that is, how people are increasingly producers of what they consume and vice versa), the blurring of the on- and off-line worlds, and how new possibilities of self-documentation via social media impact the way we live our everyday lives. All of this has vast consequences for identity, power and domination, surveillance, and much else.

Meyer Kestnbaum is Associate Professor of Sociology at the University of Maryland College Park. Kestnbaum's research focuses on warfare and the state, examining historical transformations in war making and their consequences. He has published on a variety of issues in this domain, including "Mars Revealed: The Entry of Ordinary People into War among States" in Adams, Clemens, and Orloff (eds.), *Remaking Modernity* (2005), and "The Sociology of War and the Military", *Annual Review of Sociology* (2009). His work highlights patterns of inclusion and exclusion and processes of meaning-making bound up with the organization and use of coercive force.

Nancy A. Naples is Professor of Sociology and Women's Studies at the University of Connecticut. She is author of *Grassroots Warriors: Activist Mothering, Community Work and the War on Poverty* (1998) and *Feminism and Method: Ethnography, Discourse Analysis and Activist Scholarship* (2003); editor of *Community Activism and Feminist Politics: Organizing Across Race, Class, and Gender* (1998); and co-editor of *Women's Activism and Globalization: Linking Local Struggles with Transnational Politics* (with Manisha Desai, 2002) and *The Sexuality of Migration: Border Crossing and Mexican Immigrant Men* (with Salvador Vidal-Ortiz, 2009). Her current work includes a study of racialization and social regulation of citizenship in the Midwest and a comparative study of sexual citizenship.

Angela M. O'Rand is Professor of Sociology and Dean of Social Sciences at Duke University. She has published research on aspects of the life course for over 30 years. Based primarily on diverse longitudinal datasets, her research has identified linkages between married couples' careers and retirement patterns; childhood adversity and later life outcomes in health and wealth; and childhood educational attainment and educational careers across midlife. A unique focus on the impact of retirement institutions (e.g., pension systems and related income security programs) on career trajectories and labor exits has distinguished her work.

John Durham Peters is A. Craig Baird Professor of Communication Studies at the University of Iowa. He is the author of *Speaking into the Air: A History of the Idea of Communication* (1999) and *Courting the Abyss: Free Speech and the Liberal Tradition* (2005). His scholarship traces out broad historical, philosophical, religious, cultural, legal, and technological contexts for the study of communication.

Ken Plummer is Emeritus Professor of Sociology at the University of Essex and the founder editor of the journal *Sexualities*. His works include *Sexual Stigma* (1975), *Telling Sexual Stories* (1995), and *Intimate Citizenship* (2003). His most recent book is *Sociology: The Basics* (2010).

Jefferson D. Pooley is Associate Professor of Media and Communication at Muhlenberg College in Allentown, Pennsylvania. He is co-editor, with David W. Park, of *The History of Media and Communication Research*. His research centers on the history of communication studies as the field's emergence has intersected with the twentieth-century rise of the other social sciences.

P. J. Rey is a PhD student in the Department of Sociology at the University of Maryland. His research is primarily concerned with understanding the social implications of the emergence of the internet. Specifically, his work explores shifting economic relations in the age of digital abundance and the consequences of the constant visibility that is encouraged and facilitated by social media. Additionally, he holds an MA in Philosophy from Duquesne University and maintains an interest in French and German philosophy – particularly the Frankfurt School and post-structuralism.

George Ritzer is Distinguished University Professor at the University of Maryland. Among his awards are an Honorary Doctorate from La Trobe University, Melbourne, Australia and the American Sociological Association's Distinguished Contribution to Teaching Award. He has chaired the American Sociological Association's Section on Theoretical Sociology, as well as the Section on Organizations and Occupations and History of Sociology, and he was the first Chair of the section-in-formation on Global and Transnational Sociology. Among his books in metatheory are *Sociology: A Multiple Paradigm Science* (1975/1980) and *Metatheorizing in Sociology* (1991). In the application of social theory to the social world, his books include *The McDonaldization of Society* (6th edn., 2011), *Enchanting a Disenchanted World* (3rd edn., 2010), and *The Globalization of Nothing* (2nd edn., 2007). His most recent book is *Globalization: A Basic Text* (2010). He is currently working on *The Outsourcing of Everything* (with Craig Lair, forthcoming). He was founding editor of the *Journal of Consumer Culture*. He also edited the 11-volume *Encyclopedia of Sociology* (2007) and the two-volume *Encyclopedia of Social Theory* (2005) and is currently editing the *Encyclopedia of Globalization* (forthcoming). He is editing a special issue of the *American Behavioral Scientist* on prosumption. His books have been translated into over 20 languages, with over a dozen translations of *The McDonaldization of Society* alone.

Kimberly B. Rogers is a doctoral candidate in the Department of Sociology at Duke University. She received her BA in Psychology from Randolph-Macon Woman's College in 2003, and her MA in Psychology from Wake Forest University in 2005. While at Wake Forest, her research explored American and Japanese thresholds for emotion recognition and use of contextual information in emotion perception. Since beginning her doctoral studies at Duke, her research has centered on the behavioral significance of cultural affective meaning. Her dissertation examines the social structural predictors of cultural meaning formation, and the processes that shape meaning and impression formation in dynamic social context.

Russell K. Schutt (BA, MA, PhD, University of Illinois at Chicago; postdoc, Yale University) is Professor and Chair of Sociology at the University of Massachusetts, Boston, and Lecturer on Sociology in the Department of Psychiatry at the Harvard Medical School. His many books, peer-reviewed articles, and book chapters concern research methods, social policy, mental health, law, organizations, and occupations, including *Investigating the Social World: The Process and Practice of Research* and *Homelessness, Housing and Mental Illness*. His research has been funded by the National Cancer Institute, National Institute of Mental Health, and state agencies.

Jane Sell is Professor of Sociology and a Cornerstone Faculty Fellow at Texas A&M University. She is presently doing research in two areas: the conditions under which racial inequality might be disabled in task groups, and how sudden changes in events can modify cooperation in social dilemmas.

Alan Sica is Professor of Sociology and Founder of the Social Thought Program at Pennsylvania State University. He was editor and publisher of the journal *History of Sociology*, editor of the ASA journal *Sociological Theory*, and is currently editor of another ASA journal, *Contemporary Sociology*. His books include: *Hermeneutics: Questions and Prospects*; *Weber, Irrationality, and Social Order*; *What Is Social Theory?*; *The Unknown Max Weber*; *Max Weber and the New Century*; *Max Weber: A Comprehensive Bibliography*; and *Social Thought: From the Enlightenment to the Present*. He has been publishing about social theory and the history of sociology since 1978.

Beverley Skeggs is the author of *The Media* (with John Mundy, 1992), *Feminist Cultural Theory* (1995), *Formations of Class and Gender* (1997), *Transformations: Thinking Through Feminism* (with Sara Ahmed, Jane Kilby, Celia Lury, and Maureen McNeil, 2000); *Class, Self, Culture* (2004); *Sexuality and the Politics of Violence and Safety* (with Les Moran, Paul Tyrer, and Karen Corteen, 2004); and *Feminism After Bourdieu* (with Lisa Adkins, 2005). She is a series editor of the Transformations: Thinking Through Feminism book series (published by Routledge). She is Professor of Sociology at Goldsmiths, University of London, previously at the University of Manchester, and before that Director of Women's Studies at the University of Lancaster. She has also taught at the universities of Keele and York.

Brittany Chevon Slatton earned her PhD from Texas A&M University, College Station, and is currently Assistant Professor of Sociology at Texas Southern

University. Her work examines the intersection of race, gender, class, and sexuality, and relationship dynamics. She recently completed a study documenting white men's contemporary perspectives on black women. Currently, she is working on an interdisciplinary study with Kamesha Spates on the intersection of masculinity and sexuality among men of color.

Christian Smith is the William R. Kenan, Jr. Professor of Sociology at the University of Notre Dame, Director of the Center for the Study of Religion and Society, Director of the Notre Dame Center for Social Research, Principal Investigator of the National Study of Youth and Religion, and Principal Investigator of the Science of Generosity Initiative. Smith worked at the University of North Carolina at Chapel Hill from 1994 to 2006, where he served as Associate Chair of the Department of Sociology from 2000 to 2005. Smith holds an MA (1987) and PhD (1990) in Sociology from Harvard University and has studied Christian historical theology at Harvard Divinity School and other Boston Theological Institute schools. He has directed more than $14 million in grant-funded research projects. Smith's BA is in Sociology (1983), from Gordon College, Wenham, Massachusetts. Before moving to UNC Chapel Hill in 1994 and prior to moving to Notre Dame, Smith taught for six years at Gordon College (1988–94). Smith is the author, co-author, or editor of numerous books, including *What is a Person?: Rethinking Humanity, Social Life, and the Moral Good from the Person Up*; *Souls in Transition: The Religious and Spiritual Lives of American Emerging Adults*; *Soul Searching: The Religious and Spiritual Lives of American Teenagers*; *Passing the Plate: Why American Christians Don't Give Away More Money*; *Moral, Believing Animals: Human Culture and Personhood*; *The Secular Revolution: Power, Interests, and Conflict in the Secularization of American Public Life*; *American Evangelicalism: Embattled and Thriving*; *Resisting Reagan: Radical Religion and Social Movement Theory*; *Disruptive Religion: The Force of Faith in Social Movements*; and *The Emergence of Liberation Theology: Radical Religion and Social Movement Theory*. He is also author or co-author of numerous journal articles. Smith's scholarly interests focus on American religion, cultural sociology, adolescents, generosity, sociological theory, and philosophy of social science.

Lynn Smith-Lovin is Robert L. Wilson Professor of Arts and Sciences in the Department of Sociology (with secondary appointments in Psychology and Neuroscience and in Women's Studies) at Duke University. She received the 2006 Cooley-Mead Award for lifetime achievement in social psychology from the American Sociological Association Section on Social Psychology and the 2005 Lifetime Achievement Award from the ASA Section on Sociology of Emotions. Her research examines the relationships among identity, action, and emotion. Her current projects involve (1) an experimental study of justice, identity, and emotion (funded by the National Science Foundation), (2) research with Miller McPherson on an ecological theory of identity (also funded by the National Science Foundation), and (3) a study of event processing in Arabic (funded by the Office of Naval Research). She has served as President of the Southern Sociological Society, Vice-President of the American Sociological Association, and Chair of the ASA Sections on the Sociology of Emotion and on Social Psychology.

David A. Snow is a Chancellor's Professor of Sociology at the University of California, Irvine. He has authored numerous articles and chapters on social movements, religious conversion, framing processes, identity, homelessness, and qualitative field methods, and has co-authored or co-edited *Down on Their Luck: A Study of Homeless Street People* (with Anderson), *The Blackwell Companion to Social Movements* (with Soule and Kriesi), *Together Alone: Personal Relationships in Public Places* (with Morrill and White), *Analyzing Social Settings: A Guide to Qualitative Observation and Analysis* (with Lofland, Anderson, and Lofland), *Readings in Social Movements* (with McAdam), *A Primer on Social Movements* (with Soule), and the *Blackwell Encyclopedia of Social and Political Movements* (with della Porta, Klandermans, and McAdam).

John Tomlinson is Professor of Cultural Sociology and Director of the Institute for Cultural Analysis, Nottingham (ICAn) at Nottingham Trent University. His many publications on the themes of globalization, cosmopolitanism, cultural modernity, and mediated cultural experience include *Cultural Imperialism* (1991), *Globalization and Culture* (1999), and *The Culture of Speed* (2007). He is currently writing *Culture and Virtue: Capitalism, Media and the Fragmentation of Public Value* (forthcoming).

Stephen Turner is Graduate Research Professor in Philosophy at the University of South Florida. His books include writings on explanation, such as *Sociological Explanation as Translation* (1980), issues of theory construction and statistical approaches to causality, including *Causality in Crisis? Statistical Methods and Causal Knowledge in the Social Sciences* (co-edited with Vaughn McKim, 1997). He has dealt with methodological issues in such fields as Organization Studies and International Relations. He has also written extensively on the history of methodology, especially of statistics and probabilistic thinking, including writings on Comte, Mill, Quetelet, and Durkheim, and on the origins of quantitative sociology in the United States. His most recent book, *Explaining the Normative* (2010), is a critique of the philosophical arguments for a normativity beyond ordinary social science explanation.

Steven P. Vallas has written widely in the sociology of work, authoring articles in the leading sociology journals. Much of his work has used ethnographic methods to explore the social bases of worker consent and resistance in various branches of the US economy. He is also the author of *Work: A Critique* (forthcoming). He is currently examining the shifting discourse found in popular management books, while also conducting research on the tensions and contradictions manifest within transnational movements to defend workers' rights, both in the US and abroad.

Frank Webster is Professor of Sociology and Head of Department, City University London. He has written extensively on informational developments. Recent books include: *Theories of the Information Society*, 3rd edn. (2006); *Journalists under Fire: Information War and Journalistic Practices* (with Howard Tumber, 2006); and *Anti-War Activism: New Media and Politics* (with Kevin Gillan and Jennifer Pickerill, 2008).

Murray Webster, Jr., is Professor of Sociology at the University of North Carolina, Charlotte. He conducts experimental and natural settings research on the operation of status processes, and writes on experimental design and sociological theory construction. He is co-editor of *Laboratory Experiments in the Social Sciences* (with Jane Sell, 2007).

Charles F. Wellford is Professor of Criminology and Criminal Justice at the University of Maryland, College Park. He was the founding director of the Office of International and Executive Programs (2005–7). From 1984 to 2007 he was Director of the Maryland Justice Analysis Center. He was Chair of the Department of Criminology and Criminal Justice (formerly the Institute of Criminal Justice and Criminology) from 1981 to 1995 and from 1999 to 2004. From 1992 to 1998 he was Director of the Office of Academic Computing Services in the College of Behavioral and Social Sciences. For 1998 he was Acting Associate Provost and Dean of Continuing and Extended Education, and in 1998–9 he was Interim Associate Provost for Research and Dean of the Graduate School. He serves on numerous state and federal advisory boards and commissions. He is a past (1995–6) President of the American Society of Criminology (ASC) and in 1996 was elected a Fellow of the ASC; in 2001 he was selected to be a lifetime National Associate of the National Academy of Sciences (NAS). He chaired the NAS Committee on Law and Justice from 1998 to 2004 and recently chaired the NAS panel on pathological gambling, the panel on research on firearms, and the panel to assess the National Institute of Justice. In Maryland he currently serves on the Maryland Sentencing Policy Commission. From 1976 to 1981 Dr. Wellford served in the Office of the United States Attorney General where he directed the Federal Justice Research Program. The author of numerous publications on criminal justice issues, Dr. Wellford's most recent research has focused on the determinants of sentencing, and the correlates of homicide clearance.

Vanessa Wight is a family demographer at the National Center for Children in Poverty, Columbia University Mailman School of Public Health. Her research focuses on child poverty and its implications for family processes and child well-being.

Robert D. Woodberry is Director of the Project on Religion and Economic Change and Assistant Professor of Sociology at the University of Texas at Austin. His current research uses both historical and statistical methods to analyze the long-term impact of Protestant and Catholic missions on education, civil society, economic development, and democracy. Other interests include comparative colonialism and the spread of religious liberty. His articles – one of which won the Outstanding Article Award from the ASA Sociology of Religion Section in 2001 – appear in the *American Sociological Review, Social Forces, JSSR, Teaching Sociology,* and elsewhere.

William Yagatich is currently earning his PhD in Sociology in the Department of Sociology at the University of Maryland, College Park. He is also working on publishing the main findings of his Master's thesis, where he examined the pressures of McDonaldization on the tattoo industry via the increasing popularity of American tattooing. His main research focus concerns the intersection of physical spatial structures, consumer behaviors, and power/knowledge. More specifically, in future work he will examine how spatial structures not only serve to control patterns of bodily movement but how these structures often serve to encourage consumption.

Richard York is Associate Professor of Sociology and Environmental Studies, Graduate Program Director of Sociology, and the Richard A. Bray Faculty Fellow at the University of Oregon. He has published over 50 articles in journals including *American Sociological Review*, *Conservation Biology*, *Sociological Theory*, and *Theory and Society*. He is co-editor of the journal *Organization & Environment*. He has also published three books: *The Critique of Intelligent Design* and *The Ecological Rift: Capitalism's War on the Earth* (both with John Bellamy Foster and Brett Clark) and *The Science and Humanism of Stephen Jay Gould* (with Brett Clark). He has twice (2004 and 2007) received the Outstanding Publication Award from the Environment and Technology Section of the American Sociological Association.

Introduction

GEORGE RITZER

Sociology is a highly diverse and ever-changing field. As a result, different observers of the field will necessarily see somewhat different realities. In part, this is a function of the different orientations of the observers. In addition, it is also related to the point in time at which the observations take place. Since the field is continually changing – at least in part because the social world is in constant flux – observations about sociology at one point in time will be different, perhaps very different, from those at another point in time. These thoughts are very relevant to a discussion of the relationship between this *Companion to Sociology* and its predecessor edited by Judith Blau. In a nutshell, because of the different orientations of the editors, and because of the passage of time (a decade since the first edition of Blau's *Companion* was published in 2001), there are huge differences between the two volumes.

This is clear, most obviously, in the fact that there are few carryovers from the previous version in this *Companion* and those that are carried over have been revised, in some cases extensively. There were 31 chapters in the Blau volume, as well as an Appendix; there are 33 chapters in this volume. Of the chapters included in the Blau *Companion*, only the following are included in this volume: Media and Communications (with a new co-author), Sociology of Religion, Sociology of Education (also with a new co-author), and Social Psychology (now entitled "Action, Interaction, and Groups" and with a new co-author). While many other chapters in this volume cover the same topics (e.g., inequality, the environment, social movements) as in the previous edition, the authors are different and the discussion is, in most cases, enormously different. Again, this is in part due to differences in the orientations of the authors involved and in part a result of the passage of a decade and the production of a decade's worth of new work.

The Wiley-Blackwell Companion to Sociology, First Edition. Edited by George Ritzer.
© 2012 Blackwell Publishing Ltd. Published 2012 by Blackwell Publishing Ltd.

While in some cases I have included essays on the same topic by a different author, in other cases I have chosen not to include a given topic in this *Companion*. In some instances I thought Blau's choices were idiosyncratic (of course many of my own choices reflect my idiosyncratic interests). Thus, I have not included entries on time and space (although I have great personal interest in this topic), human rights, codependence, and immigrant women and domestic work. Other topics covered in the Blau volume are touched on in chapters included here, or subsumed under broader headings (for example intimacy in the chapter on families and civil society under the heading of globalization).

More positively, the chapters included in this volume reflect a variety of factors. First, I thought it necessary to have chapters on the most basic topics in sociology, indeed the topics covered in an introduction to sociology text and course, but here dealt with in a more sophisticated and advanced manner and written more for professional sociologists and graduate students. This led to the inclusion of all of the chapters in Part Two of this volume. Many of the topics in this part of the book were not included in the Blau volume, at least as independent chapters, including criminology, deviance, organizations, culture, the life course, families, medical sociology, population, and urbanization.

Second, there were no chapters devoted explicitly to theory or methods in the Blau volume, but I have opted to give great attention to these basic matters. Thus, Part One includes no fewer than six chapters, beginning with one on philosophy and sociology and followed by a selective history of sociology, two chapters on methods (quantitative and qualitative) as well as two chapters on theory (classical and contemporary). This reflects my views on the continuing importance of these basics to sociology.

Third, there are a number of chapters that reflect my sense of what are, or should be, new and hot topics in sociology. These include chapters on consumption, globalization, neoliberalism and its relationship to contemporary capitalism, and the internet, especially Web 2.0.

I do not want to suggest that my choices in these or any other topics are somehow better than those of Blau, or even that this is a better book (although I would like to think it is) than the previous *Companion*. It is simply a very different book reflecting differences in the orientations of the editors and changes over time in the nature of sociology and in the world they study.

This brings me back to the new and hot topics mentioned above. The fact is that a decade ago it would have been difficult or impossible for Blau to have included these topics in her volume. They were not issues of nearly the same magnitude in the social world and sociologists had not devoted nearly as much attention to them then as they have in the last decade. Let me look at the topics involved, at least in brief. What they reflect is the changing nature of the social world, the changing nature of sociology as a result of such social changes, as well as the fact that volumes such as this must change to reflect such changes. That means that if there is another volume like this a decade from now, it will be different from this one in a number of unforeseeable ways.

Before getting to the topics in question, I should say that the first edition of this *Companion* had its share of essays that anticipated topics that continue to be cutting edge, including those on space and place, human rights, and civil society. Of special note are the three separate chapters that dealt in one way or another with immigration. I don't know that the topic deserved about a tenth of the book's chapters, but clearly such attention was way ahead of its time and immigration is even more relevant today than it was a decade ago.

In terms of the hot topics covered here, I begin with consumption. While this has been an important topic in many places in the world (especially Great Britain) for decades, it has not been a major concern elsewhere, most notably in the United States. This is particularly striking because the US is generally seen as the ultimate consumer society. Many major consumer goods, brands, types of consumption sites, methods of consumption, and innumerable other aspects of consumer society have their roots in the US and find their ultimate expression there. Furthermore, consumption is essential to the American (and global) economy with it often being argued that 70 percent, or even more, of the American economy is attributable to consumption. In addition, consumption in much of the world, especially the developed world, is heavily influenced by innovations in consumption in the US. Finally, production in much of the rest of the world is oriented to providing what is demanded by American consumers.

In spite of all of this, and much more, sociologists, again especially Americans, have devoted relatively little attention to consumption. It is not an important part of the broader field of economic sociology and is greatly subordinated to issues relating to production and work. More generally, American sociologists tend to have a productivist bias when they think about and study the economy. This is true today, but it was even more the case when Blau's volume first appeared.

A decade ago there was no central outlet for sociological work on consumption, but beginning in 2001 I began editing (at first with Don Slater as co-editor) the *Journal of Consumer Culture* (*JCC*). While the *JCC* was certainly not restricted to work done by sociologists, many of the articles throughout the journal's first decade were authored by sociologists, or inspired by their ideas and works. While there is greater interest in consumption in American sociology today than previously, it remains the case that it is a topic of greater sociological interest elsewhere in the world. Why that is the case remains a mystery, but it would be surprising if American sociologists do not devote more attention to this important social phenomenon in the coming years. I fully expect that it will be as important, and probably of increasing importance, to sociologists elsewhere in the world. For example, as China begins to move more toward a consumer society, Chinese sociologists (and others) will almost certainly devote more attention to the topic.

Neoliberalism, as well as the closely related "Washington Consensus," was still at its peak a decade ago, although it has since declined in importance and come under increasing attack as a result of the Great Recession (or is it a more structural change?) that began in late 2007. In fact, the first part of the title of Robert J. Antonio's chapter is, perhaps over-optimistically as far as the critics of neoliberalism are concerned, "After Neoliberalism." Neoliberalism is not a topic that would, itself, have necessarily attracted sociological attention a decade ago (it would have been seen more as a subject best left to economists). However, Antonio's subtitle dealing with capitalism and its future would certainly have been of great interest a decade ago, although it is not accorded chapter-length treatment in the Blau volume.

Given the continuing impact of the Great Recession brought about by capitalistic excesses, interest in that topic is very high today.

Neoliberalism (and capitalism) is also related to the third of the hot topics dealt with here – globalization. This, too, was not covered in the Blau volume. Although that omission (like that of capitalism) is a bit mystifying, globalization is another topic area that has a much longer history of popularity in many other parts of the world than in American sociology. Thus, as was the case for consumption, there was no American Sociological Association section devoted to globalization a decade ago. However, while there is still no section that focuses on consumption, there is now one devoted to globalization that came into existence in 2010. Globalization is with us to stay and will expand rapidly, as will sociological interest in the topic. The hegemony of neoliberalism within the global capitalist economy is a central concern to sociologists, and others, interested in globalization. It is also the case that the globalization of consumption is of interest to those who focus on globalization. However, globalization is far broader than that, encompassing almost every conceivable sociological concern.

Finally, it would have been difficult, if not impossible, to anticipate the growth of the internet, and of sociological interest in it, in 2001. The internet was a much smaller and less significant phenomenon than it has become in the last decade. Of particular interest to sociologists are user-generated sites on the internet, the so-called Web 2.0. Yet, user-generation barely existed in 2000 (Friendster began in 2002; Myspace started in late 2003; Facebook was launched in early 2004; Twitter commenced operations in mid-2006). In 2001 the internet was defined by Web 1.0 sites in which content was generated by those who controlled the sites and users could do little more than consume what they were offered. In contrast, Web 2.0 sites allow for at least some, if not a great deal of, user-generation and control. Among the user-generated sites, the most significant to sociologists are the social networking sites mentioned above (others are Wikipedia and Amazon. com). Of these, by far the most important is Facebook, now with over 750 million users worldwide. These sites clearly represent something of great importance and worthy of great sociological attention. It seems clear that a sociology of the internet and of related phenomena will expand dramatically in the years to come.

The internet is also related to the other distinctive concerns in this volume. There are, for example, great efforts to find increasing ways of advertising on the internet in order to increase consumption. Capitalists are constantly seeking to find new ways to gain control over, and earn profits from, the internet. The internet is certainly global in scope (although the digital divide means that large numbers of people in the less-developed world have little or no access to it), as are many of the sites on it, most notably Facebook.

Beyond these general areas, it is also the case that changes are afoot in many areas within sociology and they are dealt with throughout this book. Let me close this introduction by highlighting only a few of them:

- Increasing recognition of the fact that important theoretical ideas were developed before the "holy trinity plus one" – Marx, Weber, Durkheim, plus Simmel – developed their theories.

- New developments in sociological theory, as well as the continued existence of "zombie theories."
- In social psychology there are the new control theories of social interaction, which have revolutionized the symbolic interactionist tradition, and concern with the impact of group structures on the development of meaning, commitment, and group identity.
- Increased attention to social processes and social structures that occur in groups and institutions.
- The centrality of power to organizations and their study.
- The eruption of interest in culture in sociology and many other fields.
- Changes in the life course as a result of such factors as increased life expectancy, declining fertility, and the increasing variability in the timing of education, family, and work patterns.
- The changing nature of deviance and of the sociological approach to it.
- The emergence of a separate field of criminology with an interdisciplinary approach to the study of crime.
- Explosive change in sexuality and the development of new, more critical approaches to its study.
- The emergence of dynamic and performative understandings of social classes in the making, ranging from the global to the intimate.
- The emergence of a critical approach to race and ethnicity.
- Gender in an increasingly intersectional, cross-cultural, and global context.
- The growing complexity of the family.
- The gap between what sociologists know about education and the reforms undertaken on the basis of recommendations from educational policymakers.
- Seismic global changes in religion and the renewal of sociological interest in that topic.
- The distinctive contributions of medical sociology to such issues as social stress, health-related lifestyles, social capital, and the social determinants of disease.
- A variety of dramatic changes in the media including the increasing mediation of interpersonal interaction by phone, email, and social networks.
- The need for a multi-leveled approach to the study of work that examines the interrelationships among the nature of work, inequalities, and organizations.
- The new population problems in the developed world of very low levels of fertility, rapid aging, and population decline.
- Urbanization as a global trend (over 50 percent of the world's population now live in cities) that is taking place at different speeds on different continents.
- The emergence of a "movement society" and the development of a sociology of social movements in order to study it more adequately.
- The changing nature of armed conflict.
- The interrelationship among new theoretical approaches to the study of science and technology.
- The expansion of potentially catastrophic, global-level, human-generated environmental problems.

This is quite a provocative list of changes in both the social world and the sociological study of that world. Nonetheless, it is a foregone conclusion that a similar enumeration of such a list in the third iteration of this *Companion* a decade from now will look very different. That is both the lure of, and challenge to, a sociology that needs to change to keep pace with a rapidly changing social world.

Part I
Introduction

1

Philosophy and Sociology

Stephen Turner

Sociology is a discipline based on a philosophical idea: that there could be a science of social life. Beyond this bare thought there is a great deal of dispute. The disputes range from the question of whether it is true in any sense that there can be a science of the social, to the question of what kind of science it could be, to what "the social," "social life," "society" (or the many variants on this term) could be. The idea of a social science was born not in an empty field, but in a domain that was already crowded – with fields like philosophy, religion, ethics, legal science, and various other disciplines and sciences which had claims to explain or correctly describe this domain. There is no well-defined boundary to sociology as a discipline. Different national traditions have managed the relation to other disciplines differently, and operated in the context of disciplines that were and still are different. The term science and the German term *Wissenschaft* take in different territory. *Wissenschaft* includes any organized body of knowledge – and, in the hands of the neo-Kantian philosophers who dominated at the time of the birth of German sociology, the logical organization of the field in terms of fundamental concepts had special implications. In this chapter I will discuss both philosophical sources of sociology: the law and cause tradition begun by Comte and Mill and the tradition that develops from Kant.

Complexity: The Core Issue

John Stuart Mill grasped a basic issue with the idea that social science could be composed of causal laws, as the rest of science was: the complexity of the causes that work together to produce social consequences. Indeed, causal complexity is at

The Wiley-Blackwell Companion to Sociology, First Edition. Edited by George Ritzer.
© 2012 Blackwell Publishing Ltd. Published 2012 by Blackwell Publishing Ltd.

the historical center of discussions of the problem of social science knowledge: too many variables, too many interacting causes, and no good way to untangle these causes. The key problem arises from the addition and mixture of causal effects: unless the scientist is in a position to calculate the joint effects of two causes, and to extend the calculations to the addition of other causes, prediction of outcomes involving multiple causes is impossible. But the identification and discovery of predictive laws faces the same problem: the actual causal facts or relationships which appear empirically are already compounded of a long list of mixed-up causes, from which laws must be extracted and discovered. In a very simple case, one might be able to hypothesize both the laws and the mathematical nature of the additive relationship and find that one set of laws and one rule for combination of causes actually predicted the outcomes. But such simple cases are never found (Mill [1843] 1974: 591–603; Turner 1986: 40–59).

The most sophisticated American enthusiasts of the idea of science, including those who influenced "mainstream sociology," such as Franklin Giddings, understood by 1901 that sociology was not going to consist of laws (Giddings 1901). The causal knowledge of sociology would consist, they thought, of correlations, and, at best, sociology would discover a set of variables whose correlations persisted in a variety of circumstances (Giddings 1924: 33). There was a difficult philosophical problem with this answer. What is the relation between cause and correlation? Karl Pearson, who was the source for Giddings, took the view that the distinction between correlation and cause was bogus, and that the laws of physics themselves were correlations, just strong ones, and that there was no intrinsic or special connection between the two variables in the correlation other than one coming before the other (Pearson [1892] 1911). Applying this to social science knowledge was problematic. When the correlations were represented by the kind of scattergrams found in the social sciences, with their wide dispersion around a regression line, it was less clear that one knew what the correlations meant, or that they meant anything at all. One of the main sociologists in this tradition, W. F. Ogburn (1934), compared the interpretation of these scattergrams to interpreting an editorial cartoon in a newspaper – meaning that the scattergrams were objective, but the interpretations were subjective and not part of science at all. This was an extreme view, but as we will see, it points to a problem shared with other accounts of the meaning of correlational sociology, and points to the larger problem of subjectivity and objectivity in relation to the project of interpretive sociology.

The correlational tradition evolved in an odd way. The basic ideas of correcting a correlation by partialing, by determining whether the causal effect went through another variable, and the addition of multiple variables in order to see if adding a variable influenced outcomes were there very early. The classic papers by G. U. Yule in the 1890s asked the question of whether providing public relief for the poor outside the poorhouse helped alleviate poverty or generated more poverty (Yule 1896, 1899). This was a typical multi-variate problem: one could look at rates of poverty across many administrative districts, but this alone would not prove anything. Districts also differed in many other characteristics, many of which might also affect the level of poverty. Moreover, a simple correlation would not suffice: the interesting question was change. Does the introduction of outdoor relief – that is to say aid other than in the poorhouse – have the consequence of changing the number of poor people? Yule found that it did – that making it easier to be poor meant that more people chose to be poor – and that if one added other variables to correct for their effect, the basic results did not change, indicating that this cause could not have been spurious or a matter of confounding, and also, to the extent that the added causes represented the possible causes, there could be no cause that would make it spurious. By the 1920s, American sociologists were using methods involving partialing with intervening variables to determine whether schooling or Mexican background was the cause of illiteracy in the Southwest, and whether the influence was expressed through the lack of schooling or was a consequence of Mexican descent, which suggested language issues (Ross 1924).

These methods worked because they could rely on background knowledge about cause – the knowledge that such things as schooling and Mexican descent might have causal effects on literacy, or that making it easier to avoid work would lead to people avoiding work. This was not knowledge derived from the data. All the data allowed for was correlations. The pictures, the scattergrams, could have been interpreted by Martians having no background knowledge as having no causal significance, or as showing that literacy caused schooling or Mexican descent. Nor was it "subjective" in any usual sense. But it did not fit into the paradigm of "science" either.

So these methods were a puzzle: they made sense, but not in terms of the usual ideas of science. There was a strong temptation to assimilate them to the idea of experiment, through the notion of natural experiment, but this merely had the effect of highlighting the problem of assumptions. The result of this comparison was depressing: if one could correctly assume that the situation was like an experiment, meaning that all the relevant variables were included and randomization was approximated so that there were no spurious relations, one could draw causal conclusions. But these things were precisely what was not known and was difficult to warrant by background knowledge. Nevertheless, background knowledge provided a solution of sorts to the problem of cause: it could at least say what a possible causal relation was.

This tradition did produce a philosophy of science, both within sociology and within the larger methodological literature. It had an idea of what science consisted in: the discovery of quantitative relations. The available relations, in a world of overwhelming causal complexity, were correlations between quantitative variables that could be concocted to stand in for the kinds of facts that interest sociologists – facts about labor unrest, class, or attitudes toward different immigrant groups. The strategy was to look at what is objectively determinable, find the objectively determinable connections between them – which are correlations or associations rather than laws – and hope that the results add up to something. It was nevertheless evident very early that what it would add up to was not "science" in any familiar sense, and certainly not physics. But the pill was bitter, and there was no easy alternative model of science which fit the situation of sociology.

Cause was difficult to abolish by philosophical fiat, as Pearson tried to do. It came back under "Logical" positivism in the guise of the distinction between "genuine" laws and accidental laws. In the example of Ernest Nagel, the generalization "all the screws in this car are rusty" explains nothing, even though it is a true generalization (Nagel 1961: 49–52). Nor would it explain anything if it was stated in general form – if we invented a term "scarscrews" for the screws in this particular car, and said, "all scarscrews are rusty." But this distinction was easier to make and imagine than to put into practice. In the natural sciences, it was generally only necessary to place the generalization – for example about rusty screws – into a structure of larger generalizations, in terms of which the original generalization could be explained, such as, "screws with iron content that are exposed to oxygen and moisture rust." In the social sciences, there were no such true generalizations.

THE POSITIVISM DISPUTE

What in the 1960s came to be called, and reviled as, "positivism" was a strange amalgam: it was on one side a celebration and defense of the kind of statistical sociology which was concerned with the problem of cause and in particular the problems of distinguishing causal and spurious relations which, on the other side, employed the language that the Logical Positivists had developed to account for physics and then extended to explanation in all science. The two were incompatible. The Logical Positivist model of explanation needed genuine laws. The methods of statistical sociology produced something different, namely correlations or associations.

This fundamental conflict was obvious enough to the more sophisticated participants. Hans Zetterberg, whose *On Theory and Verification in Sociology* (1963) was the most influential text on "theory construction" of its time, argued that the laws of sociology could only be probabilistic laws. There were also attempts to construe the statistical material, the early forms of causal modeling, in terms of laws (e.g., Simon 1954). None of this worked. The problem for the attempt to construe causal modeling in terms of laws was the status of the assumptions needed to draw causal conclusions from the models, notably the uncorrelated error terms assumption. Simon argued that this assumption was "empirical." But it was not an assumption that could be tested – either directly or indirectly – in a definitive way (since any test using similar models would need to make new assumptions of the same kind). The problems for the idea that the laws of sociology were probabilistic were insurmountable. First, there were no such laws to be found, for reasons familiar since Mill: complexity meant that they would be hidden and impossible to discern, even if they were there. Second, it was impossible to derive these laws from one another in the kinds of hierarchical structures of laws. This is what the Logical Positivist approach to distinguishing genuine laws from accidental laws required.

The later history of this problem in philosophy takes a surprising twist, to be discussed below. But this twist came too late to stave off the long and confusing discussion of "Positivism" that occupied the decades of the 1960s, 1970s, and beyond. The profitable part of this discussion requires some background, which will be given in the next section. The unprofitable part concerned the long attempt to evade the message that there were to be no laws of sociology and the equally relentless effort by the critics of scientism to refute the evaders. The evasions mostly originated in the writings of Columbia sociologists associated with Merton and Lazarsfeld. Zetterberg came from this milieu as well, but was trained by F. Stuart

Chapin, who was himself trained in the earlier Pearson-Mach tradition applied to sociology by his own mentor, Franklin Giddings.

The primary source of the evasions was Robert Merton's influential writings on the relation of theory and method and middle-range theory, along with Lazarsfeld's ideas about the generalization of the findings of localized studies into higher-level generalizations (Merton [1957] 1968: 39–171; Turner 2009a, 2009b). This same idea of generalization was taken up by Glaser and Strauss in their book *The Discovery of Grounded Theory* (1967), which taught that one could generate theory by giving an explanation of findings in ordinary non-theoretical terms, and turning them into theory by substituting more general terms in the place of these terms. Merton made many gestures to the idea of sociology as a theoretical science and the idea of science as a body of propositions which could be derived from one another, but never addressed the question of how the dross of ordinary statistical association could be converted into this kind of gold. Instead he vaguely appealed to the idea that the accumulation of the kinds of statistical results Lazarsfeld and his students generated would, at some point in the future, become the basis for genuine theories unified into deductive wholes.

The discussion was fruitless because the model of science was incoherent. There was no way to get from statistical associations to "theory" in the sense of science – deductive theory in which one derived laws from one another. The relationship that virtually all these theory construction accounts relied on was the idea that a correlation between A and B and B and C warranted the claim that A and C were correlated. This warrant helped only under special circumstances (of particular combinations of relatively high correlations) and could not be relied on to continue to work to predict, for example, that A and other correlates of C, such as D, would be correlated, or that the correlates of D would be. The warranting relation was genuine, but very weak, and insufficient for anything like the long chains of deduction necessary for the deductive theory that was supposed to be the goal of this activity.

Nor were there any theories in the sense of science available in sociology to be critiqued. The actual Logical Positivists said almost nothing that supported the idea that "positivistic" social science as practiced by statistical sociologists would lead to genuine theories either. They did attempt to give philosophical analyses of such things as functional explanation, on the assumption that this is what sociologists were actually offering. But the analyses consistently showed that the extant examples of functional analysis were far from adequate or complete, and indeed were little more than empty speculation. One of the few philosophers to write extensively on social science who could be associated with "positivism" was Karl Popper. But Popper argued for a form of social science explanation involving rational reconstruction of situations of action, not the construction of deductive theory ([1957] 1961: 140–52).

In the German-speaking world, Popper became the subject of the *Positivismusstreit* or Positivist Dispute (Adorno, Albert, Dahrendorf, Habermas, Pilot & Popper [1969] 1976). Popper, however, was not (and insisted he was not) a positivist, and his actual writings on social science, including the idea of rational construction of situations of action, derived more or less directly from Weber ([1968] 1978: 6), and much of his work challenged the idea that there could be meaningful social science explanations of such things as science. So this extensive discussion, which ranged over many topics, never engaged the issues with statistical sociology and the idea of generating a science out of these materials. It nevertheless raised interesting questions about the necessary role (and character) of interpretation in the face of meaningful social action, to which we will return.

THREE PATHS FROM KANT

The problem of interpretation has an autonomous history, which requires its own background. Interpretation is usually thought to be subjective, and thus antithetical to science. We have already encountered Ogburn making the sharp contrast between the objective scattergram and its interpretation, which is as subjective as interpreting a newspaper editorial cartoon. But what if science itself is an interpretation? Kant is esteemed as the greatest modern philosopher for his insight that our world is understood by us not as it is, but as we ourselves organize it intellectually, into categories and objects. The core idea was expressed nicely by Georg Simmel in the opening lines of his classic paper, "How Is Society Possible?"

> Kant could propose and answer the fundamental question of his philosophy, How is nature possible?, only because for him nature was nothing but the representation (*Vorstellung*) of nature. . . . As the elements of the world are given to us immediately, there does not exist among them, according to Kant, that coherence (*Verbindung*) which alone can make out of them the intelligible regular (*gesetzmassig*) unity of nature; or rather, which signifies precisely the being-nature (*Natur-Sein*) of those in themselves incoherently and irregularly emerging world-fragments. (1910–11: 372)

If this account is correct, even making a scattergram into a fact requires the organizing activity of the mind. And the objectivity of the scattergram itself, in this account, comes from the fact that the organizing structures of the mind are shared with others. Neo-Kantianism salvaged from this problematic theory the idea that intellectual domains were constituted conceptually but added the idea that different domains were constituted conceptually by different presuppositions or guiding concepts.

This was an idea that proved to be extremely fecund, in three ways. The first is simply in the idea that groups have shared presuppositions. The idea that different groups have different worldviews, standpoints, and so forth is a staple of present sociology. It is familiar to us today in the form of such notions as paradigm, worldview, basic assumptions, and is part of the background to Michel Foucault's use of the concept of episteme (1980: 197) for what he called "the historical *a priori*" ([1966] 1970: xxiv), Bourdieu's concept of *habitus* (1977: 16–20), Mannheim's concept of ideology ([1929] 1936), Ludwig Fleck's thought styles ([1935] 1979), and so forth.

The interpretation by sociologists of "lay" concepts, the concepts which actors themselves use to constitute their own social worlds and interpret one another, is a characteristic activity of the social sciences: they must reinterpret and theorize the frameworks which lay actors use to interpret one another. Thus the social sciences depend on lay frameworks, and are forced to do so because the conceptualization, framing, and interpretation of people by one another is a basic part of social life, social action, and social interaction – a resource, in the terms of Harold Garfinkel (1967), which the social scientist must also use to make sense of action, but must then turn into a topic, in order to analyze and account for the ways people organize their world conceptually. These social science concepts, as Anthony Giddens points out, can become lay ideas and thus part of the culture. Indeed, this is also the source of the value of the social sciences, for, as Giddens says, "The best and most original ideas in the social sciences, if they have any purchase on the reality it is their business to capture, tend to become appropriated and utilized by social actors themselves" (1987: 19).

It is difficult to overstate the influence and usefulness of the idea of a worldview. The general Kantian image of a world of presupposed symbols or concepts that organized reality was a handy explainer and means of interpretation in the face of differences of opinions, perceptions, focuses of interest and concern, and so forth. And this very abstract theoretical idea had a strong empirical element when it was closely associated with ideas about community. Fleck wrote about thought collectives and thought communities, which captures this connection. We could think of thought in the Kantian sense of conceptually organizing the world to make the world into a set of cognizable experiences and objects – into the familiar world of daily life – and make this into a fact about community life that could be studied and treated more or less like an empirical fact itself.

This gets us two paths from Kant: the idea that each of us depended on and shared the worldview or fundamental presuppositions of our society, and the idea that understanding the worldview of other people required us to conceptually organize or construct the phenomenon of communities possessing worldviews. Contemporary "cultural sociology" depends entirely on this image. The "culture" that makes up its subject matter is exactly this conceptually-organizing stuff that is shared by a community and produces its characteristic experiences of the world. What makes cultural sociology an empirical subject is the fact that it can study the outward manifestations of this stuff: books, television shows, movies, rap songs, and the like.

But there is an ambiguity here, which shows up especially in relation to other cultures. What is the framework from within which we interpret other cultures? Is it the framework of our own culture? And could it be otherwise? If we are explaining the theory of mind of the Akan in Ghana, how could we do it without reference to and comparison to, or translation into, our theory of mind? If this is the case, interpreting is more like translation from one language to another than the production of facts that are the same for everyone. If science is that which is the same for everyone, it must depend on universally shared presuppositions. What is social science then? Is it a universal set of organizing concepts, or is it an extension of our own lay concepts that clarifies distinctions that are already part of our own culture? Weber would have answered this question by saying that the clarity we seek is clarity for us, in our own historical situation. Durkheim and Parsons would have insisted that we must analyze in terms of universal concepts to be scientific (Wearne 1989).

The idea that sociology can provide a universally valid single conceptual scheme is the third path from Kant. It is historically important in sociology, and is important today in philosophy. It is also one of the topics that divides contemporary sociology from contemporary philosophy. The third path from Kant goes back to Kant's original aim: to describe the conceptual conditions of natural science and therefore scientific truth, truth about the physical world, itself. Kant thought Newton was right about the physical world, but that the philosophical task of accounting for the truth of Newton's physics could not be completed by an empiricist account of knowledge. No collection of experiences or experiments could add up to the concepts of space and time: physical evidence, for example measurements, presupposed these concepts. So the task of the philosopher was to describe these concepts and account for their unique validity. The emphasis was on the uniqueness of the solution: there was one set of presuppositions that made physics valid. The presuppositions were thus a part of the science itself, inseparable from it and from its validity.

This general idea was turned into a formulaic method by the neo-Kantians. To have a science, one needed a single set of presuppositions in terms of which the concepts of the science could be validated and the statements within the science could be understood to be true. The formula was this: one science, one set of constitutive presuppositions organized hierarchically into a unified conceptual whole that accounted for and shows the logical or conceptual connections between all the concepts that defined the content of the science. This was a formula that could be made to work for all manner of sciences. The organizing conceptual principle of legal science was the concept of justice; for theology, God; for biology, life; and so forth. To be a science (or rather to be a science in the sense of the more expansive German notion, a *Wissenschaft*) for the neo-Kantians was to be a domain conceptually organized in this way.

This idea had a direct implication for sociology: if sociology was to be a science, the first order of business was to get its domain conceptually organized, and in the same way – as a hierarchical structure of concepts topped off by a single organizing idea. But this strategy of choosing a fundamental idea, as Simmel himself saw, ran into a serious problem. One could choose other organizing ideas, and one's choice of organizing idea was often ideological, or associated with a party position. In German sociology there was a flood of attempts to provide similar organizing structures for sociology, based on different ideas.

Neo-Kantianism in Trouble

Although the pervasive image of the two worlds of nature and the symbolic, meeting to constitute our experienced world, is a compelling one, it is also one fraught with trouble. These troubles eventually became apparent within neo-Kantianism itself, and they were apparent to critics all along. One problem was the kind of relativism noted in the last paragraph: there seem to be many possible conceptual starting points, and no grounds on which to choose. This problem was "solved" in a way that proved to be historically important, in the middle of the twentieth century, by Talcott Parsons. Parsons combined the basic idea of neo-Kantianism with other arguments. He used the model of the physicist Willard Gibbs to answer the problem of complexity: Gibbs was famous for constructing an approximation of a thermodynamic system seeking equilibrium. The model was rigorous, but it worked by ignoring variables. This suggested to Parsons that a simplification based on a short list of central variables could produce an approximation to the goal of a scientific theory consisting of differential equations. Instead of trying to ground his choice of an organizing idea phenomenologically or by some other means, he based it on a functional argument: that society would not be able to solve the Hobbesian problem of the war of all against all without norms. He then argued that a normative aspect was an essential feature of human action. Normativity or the valuative was the key aspect of action that none of the other social sciences had claimed. Hence it was the appropriate basis for a conceptual scheme that would make sociology a science.

In this way the problem of neo-Kantianism has reproduced itself in the history of sociology: as a problem of competing perspectives versus overarching claims for a single unifying or genuinely scientific perspective. But this is not simply a problem of pluralism. The problem involves the nature of the alternatives. If they are simply different means – different methodological approaches, for example, to the end of scientific truth – we may find that pluralism is irreducible in fact, because each means produces results that contribute to the goal of truth without any other means being decisively superior or encompassing the results. But we face a different problem using approaches with different fundamental presuppositions, for example, about what objects, such as "society," exist. If the presuppositions are really fundamental, there is no basis on which to judge them. By definition, we have reached the end of the chain of justification.

The claim that there are alternative fundamental presuppositions that cannot be decided between is relativism. Underdetermination is something different: in cases of the underdetermination of theory by data, the data cannot decide between alternative theories, because the data are consistent with both theories. Underdetermination is a kind of factual situation that could be otherwise – it could be that there were no alternative theories that fit the data (though one of the important discoveries in twentieth-century philosophy in the wake of positivism was that it was possible to generate alternative theories with different ontologies, that is, different lists of things that exist, by varying the theories that already fit the data by providing alternatives to the theoretical terms of the theories which made different things "real"). One can speak of the presuppositions or even the ontological presuppositions of alternative theories, but in these cases the theories are themselves tested against the data, a test they may fail (Quine 1970; Gibson 1982: 84–90).

Underdetermination is not neutral between existence claims (Quine & Ullian [1970] 1978: 64–73). If one gets the same predictions with a theory that uses the term "society" and one that does not, there is a presumption that there is no such thing as society. "Society exists" is not the same as "a theory that employs the term 'society' is consistent with the data." It is more a claim that one cannot account for the data without reference to society. The term "fundamental" has different implications. It means that the presuppositions are beyond correction entirely – by data or anything else. There is no test that fundamental presuppositions can fail.

There is an important issue here, and it bears on the problem of relativism. What is the status of the following ideas: that one selects between theories on the basis of how well they fit the data and that one would prefer the theory that does not require us to believe in unnecessary entities – such as "society"? These belong to the realm of reason, not fact or data. An argument for the idea that there are conflicting fundamental presuppositions, the key notion behind relativism, is also an idea in the realm of reason – universal reason. Claims about this sort of thing are universal appeals. So even the relativist must concede that there is something universal and rational. Hence relativism is self-contradictory and untenable. "Fundamental presuppositions" are themselves only intelligible as presuppositions if we assume some sort of universal rationality, with binding norms of reason that govern our inferences.

If this is true, which most contemporary philosophy takes for granted, then not only is relativism false, but there is a distinction between two senses of normativity. There is "sociological" normativity, which is to say the norms observed in fact in a given society or social setting, and "genuine" normativity, the normativity of reason itself, or of the universal community of rational beings (cf. DeVries 2005: 262–8). To even talk about other presuppositions requires us to speak rationally – rationally in a universal sense that applies to the people we are discussing and their presuppositions – as well as discussing the topic sociologically.

THE STATUS OF THE PROBLEMS TODAY

Reason and normativity

This reasoning sounds very esoteric, but it is at the heart of contemporary Anglo-American philosophy. Is all reasoning "cultural" and thus culture-relative, or is there something in the way of universal reason or even morality that is beyond the reach of sociological or any other kind of natural explanation that binds people normatively? Is any rejection of the idea of universal reason a descent into irrationalism and an example, as a recent book title puts it, of the *Fear of Reason* (Boghossian 2007; see also Searle 2009)? This deep problem is the legacy of Kant and neo-Kantianism. Sociology, by employing the useful notions of worldviews, paradigms, and so forth, brings this problem on itself.

The most dramatic form of the problem in sociology is in the sociology of scientific knowledge, which attempts to explain scientific beliefs causally and sociologically (Barnes, Bloor & Henry 1996). Sociologists of this kind account for the development, acceptance, and the appearance of the truth of scientific claims in terms of the thinking of a specific community, a community of a particular kind, with its own distinct practices and worldview. Does this conflict with the idea that the results are rational, in accordance with the truths of the natural world? One answer is this: how could it not conflict? The idea of universal norms of binding rational justification is the basis of the claims of science to intellectual authority and universal validity. The sociologist of scientific knowledge depicts these results as the product of a historically contingent, non-universal, set of distinctive practices and presuppositions in terms of which the results are "true" for the members of the community. This is relativism plain and simple, because it denies universal validity, relativizing scientific truth to local practices.

Is there a way out of this problem? One way is to separate the problem into two aspects: the question of whether the science is correct and the problem of explaining why the scientists came to these beliefs. The two, it can be argued, are completely separate questions. Claims about genuine truth, claims about what should be believed, belong in the domain of genuine norms, while explanations of what scientists actually believe come from the domain of sociological norms, norms that hold for a community. But for a believer in the idea that there is a universal rational framework which binds all rational persons – a Kantian in the primary sense – it is this framework that is supposed to explain rational behavior, not local frameworks of the kind appealed to by sociologists of science. "Binding" is an explanatory idea.

The sociologist's explanation competes with the Kantian account that claims to be an explanation of rationality. And the sociological account has to be wrong, because it is a denial that the binding framework of rationality is actually doing its job of binding – if it were not the case that we experienced the binding character of rationality, there would be no such thing as a genuine norm of rationality. So Kantianism is a theory of the mind and its relation to the world as well as a theory about rational standards. The sociologist cannot deny this, because after all the sociologist is also trying to persuade us that the claims of sociology are true and not merely a result of local presuppositions – including when the claims of the sociologist *are* about local presuppositions!

But there is a complication. Where do the norms of rationality come from? Evolution? If so, no one can explain how, and in any case it is common to explain our deviations from rationality by appealing to evolution. More important, we need a general account of norms, not just an account of rationality. Some "genuine" norms are clearly local – linguistic norms, for example, the norms that determine what words and sentences really mean. For these we need explainers that are specific to the community of language users – which is to say we need something like a sociological explanation. But standard sociology has no such explanations, because the concept of genuine normativity is not a concern to sociology, and one needs to go back to classical social theory to find serious discussions of this problem at all.

The standard philosophical solution to these issues has been this: we need some kind of sociology – a philosophical one. Durkheim, with his appeals to the collective consciousness, was close to a solution, but his idea that there was a real mind-like entity out there causally influencing our thinking and binding us was problematic. If we could keep the idea of binding, we could keep the distinction between what is binding as a norm and what people actually do. And we could do this if we could find an unproblematic ground for this distinction. The solution is the idea of collective intentionality – that the binding comes from shared intentions which individuals may deviate from while still sharing in the collective sense – we might steal, but still be aware of and share in the collective disapproval of stealing (Searle 1995; cf. Gilbert 1989; Turner 2002: 35–57).

Are there such things as collective intentions? Or is this merely a bizarre philosophical invention? If the idea of collective intentionality made sense, it would provide an instant explanation and alternative account of the social world to sociological theory – notions like culture could be replaced by appeals to collective intention, and similarly for appeals to norms. Yet this seems to be explanation by philosophical fiat. Collective intentions are not part of the ordinary explained human or empirical world. Their existence – the existence of genuine norms behind actual usage – is inferred from supposed necessities of reasoning, for example from the "fact" that sentences have meanings, or that there is a "correct" way to continue the series 2, 4, 6, 8.

Understanding

Worldviews, paradigms, and the like are not empirical facts in any normal sense: they are theoretical ideas that attempt to make sense of a very complex phenomenon of thinking, experiencing, feeling, and so forth. They have a purpose: making sense of behavior and beliefs that are otherwise puzzling. Is there a way to accomplish this purpose, and explain our capacity to understand, without appealing to these problem "facts"? One way out is to reject this whole line of theorizing. There is a long tradition in American sociology, rooted in the thought of George Herbert Mead, which does reject it. Herbert Blumer thought of symbolic interactionism as not merely a perspective like other perspectives within sociology, but as a complete alternative to sociology, psychology, *and* cultural anthropology. The reason anthropology is on this list is that Blumer rejected the idea of culture. The kind of understanding between people which is produced by taking the role of the other does not require a fixed set of cultural assumptions.

Mead and many of his philosophical and sociological contemporaries at the turn of the nineteenth century were inspired and fascinated by James Mark Baldwin's account of child development. They reasoned that whatever the child got in the way of understanding the world and the social world had to make sense in terms of actual developmental processes, including social interaction. The idea that there was a culture which was out there to be "introjected," as the mythological Freudian language had it, was not consistent with this idea: what one saw in observing children was the development of the self, as Cooley put it, through the looking-glass of other people's reactions and perceptions, and the child learning roles and about roles, and coming to understand others by enacting them.

This mode of thinking about interaction has recently acquired a surprising set of philosophical allies in the philosophy of cognitive science and in neuroscience itself. There was, in the 1990s, an elaborate controversy over the way in which children acquired a concept of mind or a sense of the mindedness of other people (Stone & Davies 1995). One answer was that they acquired a "theory of mind" just as people acquire a culture. The other answer was that simulation was a basic mental process, and that in interaction we routinely simulate other people's actions in our own mind in order to understand them. This reasoning received powerful support with the discovery of mirror neurons in monkeys (Gallese & Goldman 1998), and the development of a large experimental literature showing that our perceptions of the particular actions of others – dancing, for example – employed the same neurons that we would employ in performing the same acts (Calvo-Merino, Grèzes, Glaser, Passingham & Haggard 2006; Cross, Hamilton & Grafton 2006).

Simulation allows for an understanding of human understanding of other people and their actions that does not depend on the whole machinery of culture, assumptions, introjection, and the rest of it. And the fact that this kind of understanding is rooted in actual neuronal processes brings the whole problem of interpretation down from the clouds of hermeneutics. Hermeneutics modeled human interactional understanding on the interpretation of texts. And this is what gave it a non-objective character. Ogburn's example of the newspaper cartoon and its interpretation comes to mind. For him it was the very model of subjectivity. Although simulation does not guarantee objective results, rooting it in a natural process changes things. It allows us to see how data can be used to correct initial errors, producing a better understanding (Ickes 2009; Nickerson, Butler & Carlin 2009).

Objectivity and subjectivity in causal models and elsewhere

The "positivism" debate ended in a muddle over the idea of laws and deductive theory. But the discussion of causality in social science that developed in philosophy took off in a different direction. In a 1983 paper, "Social Science and Social Physics," Clark Glymour argued that the obsession of social science with imitating physics was a mistake, and that causal modeling provided an appropriate and adequate approach to social science causality that did not depend on laws. Causal models were not like laws because laws hold unconditionally and in all circumstances. Causal models hold under conditions that are unknown and perhaps unknowable, and fail to hold when these conditions change. Nevertheless, where the conditions hold, the relations of causality captured by the models are real (cf. Glymour, Scheines, Spirtes & Kelly 1987).

In addition, Glymour pioneered, with several collaborators and alongside Judea Pearl (2000), an approach to the discovery of causal structures that used computer search methods to eliminate possible causal models, and detect spurious relationships and hidden variables. One of Glymour and his associates' most striking findings using these techniques was that the iconic quantitative study of 1970s sociology, Peter Blau and O. D. Duncan's *The American Occupational Structure* (1967), consisted entirely of spurious correlations (Glymour 1997: 222–3; Freedman 1983).

This new philosophical literature was very slow to penetrate sociology. But it changed the problem of objectivity in a special way. The aim of this approach would have been familiar to Ogburn: to come to conclusions with a minimum of subjectivity. But to make the search process work, it was necessary to proceed by elimination. If one could use one's background knowledge to eliminate a large number of potential causal connections, it would be possible to generate smaller sets of possible causal structures in a given domain. If the background knowledge in question was truly innocuous – for example that the number of years a parent spent in school could influence whether a child smoked, but not the other way around – one could eliminate many possible models with very little subjectivity.

A similar strategy, of minimizing reliance on all but the most innocuous background knowledge, is central to various forms of network analysis, from the kind popular in American sociology to the Actor Network Theory of Bruno Latour (1987). The idea in each case is that knowledge about people's intentions, beliefs, and motivations, which is "subjective," can be minimized, with the result that any findings will be "objective." The differences, however, are differences of degree. Even the placing of objective labels on network objects requires some degree, however minimal, of background knowledge or "subjective" understanding.

CONCLUSION

The early relation of sociology to philosophy was one in which philosophy supplied methodological ideals, and in which sociology competed with philosophy over subject matter, such as the nature of morality. The slow demise of the idea that sociology could be a physics-like science freed sociology from this relationship of subordination, and allowed its methods (especially in relation to causality) to gain recognition as valid in their own right. But the competition over subject matter remains, with philosophers increasingly inclined to attempt to take back subject matter that was earlier conceded to sociology. Anti-relativism has been the main motive for this attempt, and its main strategy has been to provide or defend alternative "philosophical" explanations of sociological facts, using such concepts as collective intentionality, rationality, and normativity.

References

Adorno, T. W., H. Albert, R. Dahrendorf, J. Habermas, H. Pilot, and K. Popper ([1969] 1976) *The Positivist Dispute in German Sociology*. Trans. G. Adey and D. Frisby. London: Heinemann.

Barnes, B., D. Bloor, and J. Henry (1996) *Scientific Knowledge: A Sociological Analysis*. Chicago: University of Chicago Press.

Blau, P. and O. Duncan (1967) *The American Occupational Structure*. New York: Wiley.

Boghossian, P. (2007) *Fear of Knowledge: Against Relativism and Constructivism*. Oxford: Clarendon Press.

Bourdieu, P. (1977) *Outline of a Theory of Practice*. Trans. Richard Nice. Cambridge: Cambridge University Press.

Calvo-Merino, B., J. Grèzes, D. E. Glaser, R. Passingham, and P. Haggard (2006) "Seeing or Doing? Influence of Visual and Motor Familiarity in Action Observation." *Current Biology* 16: 1905–10.

Cross, E. S., A. F. de C. Hamilton, and S. Grafton (2006) "Building a Motor Simulation De Novo: Observation of Dance by Dancers." *NeuroImage* 31: 1257–67.

DeVries, W. (2005) *Wilfrid Sellars*. Chesham, UK: Acumen Publishing.

Fleck, L. ([1935] 1979) *The Genesis and Development of a Scientific Fact*. Ed. T. J. Trenn and R. K. Merton. Foreword by Thomas Kuhn. Chicago: University of Chicago Press.

Foucault, M. ([1966] 1970) *The Order of Things: An Archaeology of the Human Sciences*. New York: Random House.

Foucault, M. (1980) *Power/Knowledge: Selected Interviews and Other Writings, 1972–1977*. Ed. and trans. C. Gordon. New York: Pantheon Books.

Freedman, D. (1983) "Structural-Equation Models: A Case Study." Report, Department of Statistics, University of California, Berkeley.

Gallese, V. and A. Goldman (1998) "Mirror Neurons and the Simulation Theory of Mind-Reading." *Trends in Cognitive Sciences* 2(12): 493–501.

Garfinkel, H. (1967) *Studies in Ethnomethodology*. Englewood Cliffs, NJ: Prentice Hall.

Gibson, R. F. (1982) *The Philosophy of W. V. Quine: An Expository Essay*. Tampa: University Presses of Florida.

Giddens, A. (1987) *Social Theory and Modern Sociology*. Oxford: Polity Press.

Giddings, F. H. (1901) *Inductive Sociology: A Syllabus of Methods, Analyses and Classifications, and Provisionally Formulated Laws*. New York: Macmillan.

Giddings, F. H. (1924) *The Scientific Study of Human Society*. Chapel Hill, NC: University of North Carolina Press.

Gilbert, M. (1989) *On Social Facts*. London: Routledge.

Glaser, B. G. and A. Strauss (1967) *The Discovery of Grounded Theory: Strategies for Qualitative Research*. Chicago: Aldine Publishing Company.

Glymour, C. (1983) "Social Science and Social Physics." *Behavioral Science* 28(2): 126–33.

Glymour, C. (1997) "A Review of Recent Work on the Foundations of Causal Inference." In V. McKim and S. Turner (eds.), *Causality in Crisis: Statistical Methods and the Search for Causal Knowledge in the Social Sciences*. Notre Dame, IN: University of Notre Dame Press, pp. 201–48.

Glymour, C., R. Scheines, P. Spirtes, and K. Kelly (1987) *Discovering Causal Structure: Artificial Intelligence, Philosophy of Science, and Statistical Modeling*. Orlando, FL: Academic Press.

Ickes, W. (2009) "Empathic Accuracy: Its Links to Clinical, Cognitive, Developmental, Social, and Physiological Psychology." In J. Decety and W. Ickes (eds.), *The Social Neuroscience of Empathy*. Cambridge, MA: MIT Press, pp. 57–70.

Latour, B. (1987) *Science in Action: How to Follow Scientists and Engineers through Society*. Cambridge, MA: Harvard University Press.

Mannheim, K. ([1929] 1936) *Ideology and Utopia: An Introduction to the Sociology of Knowledge*. Trans. L. Wirth and E. Shils. New York: Harcourt, Brace and World.

Merton, R. ([1957] 1968) *Social Theory and Social Structure*, enlarged edn. New York: Free Press.

Mill, J. S. ([1843] 1974) *A System of Logic: Ratiocinative and Inducted, Collected Works*, Vol. VII, Books I–III. Toronto: Toronto University Press.

Nagel, E. (1961) *The Structure of Science: Problems in the Logic of Scientific Explanation*. New York: Harcourt, Brace and World.

Nickerson, R. S., S. F. Butler, and M. Carlin (2009) "Empathy and Knowledge Projection." In J. Decety and W. Ickes (eds.), *The Social Neuroscience of Empathy*. Cambridge, MA: MIT Press, pp. 43–56.

Ogburn, W. F. (1934) "Limitations of Statistics." *American Journal of Sociology* 40: 12–20.

Pearl, J. (2000) *Causality: Models, Reasoning, and Inference*. Cambridge: Cambridge University Press.

Pearson, K. ([1892] 1911) *The Grammar of Science*, 3rd edn. London: A. & C. Black.

Popper, K. ([1957] 1961) *The Poverty of Historicism*, 3rd edn. New York: Harper and Row.

Quine, W. V. O. (1970) *Philosophy of Logic*. Englewood Cliffs, NJ: Prentice Hall.

Quine, W. V. O. and J. S. Ullian ([[1970] 1978) *The Web of Belief*, 2nd edn. New York: Random House.

Ross, F. A. (1924) *School Attendance in 1920: An Analysis of School Attendance in the United States and in the Several States, with a Discussion of the Factors Involved*. Washington: Government Printing Office.

Searle, J. (1995) *The Construction of Social Reality*. New York: Free Press.

Searle, J. (2009) "Why Should You Believe It?" *New York Review of Books* 56(14): 88–92. www.nybooks.com/articles/article-preview?article_id=23077

Simmel, G. (1910–11) "How Is Society Possible?" *American Journal of Sociology* 16(3): 372–91.

Simon, H. (1954) "Spurious Correlation: A Causal Interpretation." *Journal of the American Statistical Association* 49: 407–79.

Stone, T. and M. Davies (eds.) (1995) *Mental Simulation: Evaluations and Applications*. Oxford: Blackwell.

Turner, S. (1986) *The Search for a Methodology of Social Science: Durkheim, Weber, and the Nineteenth Century Problem of Cause, Probability, and Action*. Dordrecht: Reidel.

Turner, S. (2002) *Brains/Practices/Relativism: Social Theory after Cognitive Science*. Chicago: University of Chicago Press.

Turner, S. (2009a) "Many Approaches, But Few Arrivals: Merton and the Columbia Model of Theory Construction." *Philosophy of the Social Sciences* 39(2): 174–211.

Turner, S. (2009b) "Shrinking Merton." *Philosophy of the Social Sciences* 39(3): 481–9.

Wearne, B. (1989) *The Theory and Scholarship of Talcott Parsons to 1951: A Critical Commentary*. Cambridge: Cambridge University Press.

Weber, M. ([1968] 1978) *Economy and Society: An Outline of Interpretive Sociology*, 3 vols. Ed. G. Roth and C. Wittich. Berkeley, CA: University of California Press.

Yule, G. U. (1896) "On the Correlation of Total Pauperism with Proportion of Out-Relief." *The Economic Journal* 6(24): 613–23.

Yule, G. U. (1899) "An Investigation into the Causes in Pauperism in England, Chiefly During the Last Two Intercensal Decades." Part I. *Journal of the Royal Statistical Society* 62(2): 249–95.

Zetterberg, H. (1963) *On Theory and Verification in Sociology*, rev. edn. Totowa, NJ: Bedminster Press.

2

A Selective History of Sociology

ALAN SICA

The history of sociology can be presented in several ways, each version bearing compelling evidence to support its claimed correctness. Thus, sociology's beginnings, depending on how the word is interpreted, lie with those earliest systematic reflections about social behavior of which we still have record; or it began "officially" on Saturday, April 27, 1839 when Auguste Comte invented the word itself (Pickering 1993: 615); or the discipline has not yet properly begun to be a "real" science because it fails to imitate the natural sciences with sufficient precision – each position depending on whom one is reading and what perspective they want to establish as superior. Sociology's past can also be viewed as the creation of a few nineteenth-century geniuses or as the collective achievement of bureaucratized academics in the drab confines of the mid-twentieth century, the world of "organization man" (Whyte 1956). When Harry Elmer Barnes edited *An Introduction to the History of Sociology* in 1948, he found scholars to fill the thousand pages of that book with chapters on Lewis Henry Morgan, Ludwig Gumplowicz, Wilhelm Wundt, Leopold von Wiese, Franz Oppenheimer, Alfred Weber, Hans Freyer, Gustav Ratzenhofer, Othmar Spann, Ludwig Stein, Jacques Novicow, Maksim Kovalevsky, Alfred Fouillée, Guillaume de Greef, and many others, whom almost no American sociologist today could or would identify as a precursor of the discipline (Barnes 1948). So definitions of what is historically important vary from time to time when dealing with sociology as with any field of learning. And given the familiar comfort that temporocentrism (hodiecentrism) confers on its believers – people's natural hope that their own epoch is culturally preeminent – the distant past is often dismissed as the weak rehearsal for one's glorious present. But in the case of sociology's development over several millennia, such a posture is indefensible.

The Wiley-Blackwell Companion to Sociology, First Edition. Edited by George Ritzer.
© 2012 Blackwell Publishing Ltd. Published 2012 by Blackwell Publishing Ltd.

Confucius, who was "charitable, just, modest, kindly, earnest, sincere, and courageous" (Becker & Barnes 1961: 58), wrote his *Analects* and *The Doctrine of the Mean* around 500 BCE, both of them loaded with sociological observations which the Chinese have found societally useful ever since, e.g., "The superior man undergoes three changes. Looked at from a distance, he appears stern; when approached, he is mild; when he is heard to speak, his language is firm and decided" (Confucius 1893: 342). Unpacked, this could have appeared in *The Presentation of Self in Everyday Life* (Goffman 1959), 2,500 years later. More broadly, "The preservation of the family virtues and relations where they are still intact, and their restoration where they are not, is the essence of Confucius's program of social reconstruction" (Becker & Barnes 1961: 59). Modern "family sociology" remains concerned with identical issues, even if its policy recommendations are more hesitantly expressed than were those of Confucius. Similarly, from around 100 BCE *The Laws of Manu* (*Manu Smriti*) advised Hindu believers of India in great detail about how to interact and what norms were binding in their daily lives, e.g., "77. For one year let a husband bear with a wife who hates him; but after (the lapse of) a year let him deprive her of her property and cease to cohabit with her" (Bühler 1886: 341) – an arrangement that could profitably be compared with today's attempts to handle marital failure.

Lynn McDonald, a Canadian sociologist and former Member of Parliament, propounds the view of sociology's ancient origins in her account of the field's methodological developments, when she says that "Most of the history of the social sciences consists of variations on themes developed in the sixth and fifth centuries B.C. . . . By the fifth century B.C. there was a fairly sophisticated understanding of many methodological issues. The earliest surviving book of social science, *The Peloponnesian Wars* [by Thucydides, c. 400 BCE] dates from this time" (McDonald 1993: 19). Indeed, a typical passage from Thucydides presages a great deal of modern research in social psychology, political science, law, and sociology:

> But our subjects [comparing Athenians with Spartans] are so habituated to associate with us as equals, that any defeat whatever that clashes with their notions of justice, whether it proceeds from a legal judgment or from the power which our empire gives us, makes them forget to be grateful for being allowed to retain most of their possessions, and more vexed at a part being taken, than if we had from the first cast law aside and openly gratified our covetousness. If we had done so, they would not have disputed that the weaker must give way to the stronger. *Men's indignation, it seems, is more excited by legal wrong than by violent wrong; the first looks like being cheated by an equal, the second like being compelled by a superior.* (1.77.5–16; Thucydides 1996: 44; emphasis added)

This lucid analysis of how legitimate power is exerted between superordinate and subordinate parties anticipates by 2,200 years the political motivation for the American Revolution, and by 2,300 years the theories of Georg Simmel which are parallel in their interests, if not in approach (Simmel 2009). Since Thucydides continues to be studied avidly, one must wonder if sociological research will be equally well attended to in the centuries to come.

McDonald is not the first scholar to claim that the Greeks are correctly understood as the earliest sociologists (see also McCarthy 2003). The learned, nearly forgotten American sociologist, Charles Ellwood (at one point internationally famous; Turner 2007), had this to say about this very topic in 1902 in the opening paragraph of "Aristotle as a Sociologist," an article of continuing utility:

> Sociology is ordinarily spoken of as a "new science." In a certain sense this is true; yet social thought is as old as history, and social philosophy as an organized discipline has existed, at least, since Aristotle. Only in a very special sense, therefore, is it right to speak of sociology as a new science. If we understand by sociology merely the effort to apply to social phenomena the method of quantitative measurement, and to interpret these phenomena as merely the most complex manifestation of the forces of the physical universe, then we are justified in regarding it as a new science; for sociology in this sense is the product of modern positivism. But those who reject the mechanical theory of society, together with the idea that the scientific interpretation of society must be limited thereto, have no right to speak of sociology as a new science. *When we regard modern sociology as "the more critical, more systematized study of the social reality," we do not make it a "new" science, but rather a renovated and reorganized science.* The beginnings of sociology as a science in this sense certainly lie far back of the modern scientific era. (Ellwood 1902; emphasis added)

Thus, we see that the question of where precisely sociology's roots lie is difficult to answer definitively.

Another early historian of the discipline, Floyd Nelson House, had this to say in 1936 about Plato while opposing Albion Small's dismissal of *The Republic*:

> It is, then, unfair to say in response to the question "What did Plato contribute to the development of modern social science?" "He contributed nothing" [Small 1925]. The reflective and critical approach to human problems was a relatively new thing in the time of Plato; and from the merely speculative and dialectic attack upon such problems to the systematic labor of checking concepts and theories against all available empirical evidence was a long road to travel. It has required over two thousand years for the thinkers of the Western world to travel as far as they have traveled on this road. (House 1936: 15–16)

Or, if one wishes while hunting for sociology's historical trail to wander away from the well-worn path that arrives at Plato's and Aristotle's "academy," there is always Polybius (c. 200–118 BCE):

> Polybius . . . is usually overlooked . . . but he is, nevertheless, one of the most important figures in the early development of [social thought]. His conception of social evolution was, in the main, accurate. He explained the aggregation and association of primitive men as resulting from a sense of weakness and a perception of likeness. Government, he believed, arose in force and was rendered permanent by the reflective action of the social mind, as it gradually perceived more clearly the utility of political relations. This was the argument advanced by Hume, nineteen centuries later, in his assault upon the doctrine of a social contract. [Polybius] also made an important

contribution in explaining the origin of morality and justice as due to group approval
or disapproval of social practices and modes of conduct. (Barnes 1948: 10)

Thus, as documented in enormous detail by Harry Elmer Barnes and Howard
P. Becker between 1938 and 1961, the origins of sociology lie very deep in human
consciousness and social organization, and if there is truly *nil novi sub sole* (nothing
new under the sun), as is claimed in Ecclesiastes, then it becomes difficult indeed to
establish an undebatable "start-up date" for sociology.

Still another notable precursor of sociology's pre-Comtean period is Muhammad
ibn Khaldun from Tunis (1332–1406), a statesman, political prisoner, judge, warrior,
and extraordinary scholar whose *History* was the most sophisticated comparative
sociology written to that point, retaining that distinction until the twentieth century.
(The *Muqaddimah* or "prolegomenon" is its best-known section.) This long work
is an extraordinary study (written during seven years of politically enforced calm
in the midst of a tumultuous life) and influenced every Western social thinker who
read it following its French translation in 1863; not until 1958 was the work entirely
rendered into English. Arnold Toynbee, the most ambitious English-language historian of the modern age, famously ranked it as "undoubtedly the greatest work of
its kind that has ever been created by any mind in any time or place" (Khaldun
1967: xiv).

Khaldun analyzed everything then known about northern African, Spanish, Egyptian, and Middle Eastern societies, from the largest to the smallest topic, including,
for instance, corporal punishment in schools, under the heading "Severity to Students Does Them Harm":

> Severe punishment in the course of instruction does harm to the student, especially to
> little children . . . Students, slaves, and servants who are brought up with injustice and
> (tyrannical) force are overcome by it. It makes them feel oppressed and causes them
> to lose their energy. It makes them lazy and induces them to lie and be insincere. That
> is, their outward behavior differs from what they are thinking, because they are afraid
> that they will have to suffer tyrannical treatment (if they tell the truth). Thus, they are
> taught deceit and trickery. This becomes their custom and character. They lose the
> quality that goes with social and political organization and makes people human,
> namely, (the desire) to protect and defend themselves and their homes, and they become
> dependent on others. Indeed, their souls become too indolent to (attempt to) acquire
> the virtues and good character qualities. Thus they fall short of their potentialities and
> do not reach the limit of their humanity. As a result, they revert to the stage of "the
> lowest of the low." (Khaldun 1958, Vol. 3: 305)

This adumbrates not only the famous section in Hegel's *Phenomenology of Spirit*
concerning "lord and bondsman," but also Marx's understanding of the condition
of workers under industrialized exploitation, plus many twentieth-century conceptualizations of how oppressive, authoritarian social relationships operate. And it is
one tiny part of the *Muqaddimah*.

In his understanding of how urban life and luxury lead to personal immorality
and the degeneration of citizenship, Khaldun anticipated the twentieth-century work
of Pitirim Sorokin; in his portrait of how "advanced" societies fail to cohere, he

anticipated Durkheim's theory of anomie; when he analyzed how groups of varying natures cycle in and out of leadership positions over time, he anticipated Vilfredo Pareto's "circulation of elites" in 1900; and when his analysis of the politics he witnessed is laid beside Machiavelli's *The Prince* (1513) or *Discourses* (1517), they share objectivity, realism, and secular beliefs that were far ahead of their times (Becker & Barnes 1961: 266–79).

And it is for a well-known sociological reason that his work, unlike that of other brilliant scholars from his epoch, was able to open new doors of cultural and political awareness. As the English translator of his great work explains:

> This background helps to explain the ease with which Ibn Khaldun shifted his loyalties through his life. No matter how high his own position or that of his ancestors before him at one or another northwest African court, no matter how close he was to a ruler, he did not feel bound by "group feeling," as he might have called it or by the ties of a common cultural heritage . . . it gave him a remarkable detachment with respect to the historical events that took place before his eyes. In a sense, it enabled him to view them as an impartial observer, even when he was deeply involved personally. This peculiar division in Ibn Khaldun's physical and spiritual ties seems to have been the decisive factor in his ability to abstract general reflections about history from observed facts, in his ability, that is, to write the *Muqaddimah*. (Khaldun 1958: xxxvi)

It has long been an axiom of sociological analysis that the best work done in the name of the discipline has often been carried out by people "at the margins," the outsiders, the un-belongers, those with nothing to gain or lose by telling the truth, a theme thoroughly explored by Georg Simmel (2009). This is not always a comfortable position for people to endure, but under the right conditions – in Khaldun's case, coming from an aristocratic lineage filled with scholars – it can give rise to exceptional societal analysis. In summary, it is fair to say that had Ibn Khaldun's masterpiece been translated into European languages earlier, sociology (and political science) would surely have progressed more quickly into a coherent body of thinking and research.

Other famous precursors of modern sociology ("proto-sociologists") include Niccolo Machiavelli (1469–1527), Thomas Hobbes (1588–1679; "the father of social psychology" [Wallas 1914: 191]), Giambattista Vico (1668–1744), Montesquieu (1689–1755), Adam Smith (1723–90), and Condorcet (1743–94), to name only a few. (For a more encompassing offering, see Sica 2005.) Their myriad fruitful observations, spurred in most cases as much by their lived experiences as by their scholarly work, point to manifold directions in twentieth-century sociological research.

Machiavelli, for instance, had this to say about rulership in *The Discourses*, a more important book for its sociological content than the much more famous and infamous *The Prince*:

> As every republic was composed of nobles and people, the question arose as to whose hands it was best to confide the protection of liberty . . . the Venetians gave it into the hands of the nobility; but the Romans entrusted it to the people. We must examine, therefore, which of these republics made the best choice. There are strong reasons in

favor of each, but, to judge by the results, we must incline in favor of the nobles, for the liberties of Sparta and Venice endured a longer space of time than those of Rome. But to come to the reasons, taking the part of Rome first, I will say, that one should always confide any deposit to those who have least desire of violating it; and doubtless, if we consider the objects of the nobles and the people, we must see that the first have a great desire to dominate, whilst the latter have only the wish not to be dominated, and consequently a greater desire to live in the enjoyment of liberty; so that when the people are entrusted with the care of any privilege or liberty, being less disposed to encroach upon it, they will of necessity take better care of it; and being unable to take it away themselves, will prevent others from doing so.

On the contrary, it is said, in favor of the course adopted by Sparta and Venice, that the preference given to the nobility, as guardians of public liberty, has two advantages: the first, to yield something to the ambition of those who, being more engaged in the management of public affairs, find, so to say, in the weapon which the office places in their hands, a means of power that satisfies them; the other, to deprive the restless spirit of the masses of an authority calculated from its very nature to produce trouble and dissensions, and apt to drive the nobles to some act of desperation, which in time may cause the greatest misfortune. (Machiavelli 1882, Vol. 2: 107–8)

Notice that Machiavelli counterposes "reason" or what we might call "plausible social action" against the actual historical record, of which he, like so many proto-sociologists, was a keen student. He accepts without question that every society features an upper class full of privilege and desirous of power, lording over those many "plebs" who do their best not to be manipulated by them. In the US today arbiters of political rhetoric have ruled that "class warfare" is an unwelcome term within electoral speech, despite the fact that ever larger percentages of income and wealth resolutely make their way into the hands of a tiny minority – a process explicitly initiated by Ronald Reagan 30 years ago through strategic changes in tax policy. Announcements that a handful of hyper-rich "citizens" are bankrolling pseudo-grassroots right-wing political parties seem to do little to dissuade ordinary citizens that the US is a "classless society." Machiavelli would not have been fooled for an instant.

He also thought about how to arrange governments within the limitations set by "equality and privilege," two central concerns of modern sociologists. When the Italian republics needed money for public works, they would proclaim a small tax on the value of property, and citizens would present themselves in public and pay the tax without complaint – in some quarters, at least. They would not be monitored for fraud, and thus embodied "a good deal of the goodness of ancient times" (Machiavelli 1882, Vol. 2: 244). Machiavelli wondered why this occurred, especially also in Germany, but less so in France and Spain, "the source of world-wide corruption." His answer is entirely sociological and fits well with studies carried out today:

honesty . . . is found only in that country [in Germany, as opposed to Spain or France]; and this results from two causes. The one is, that the Germans have no great commerce with their neighbors, few strangers coming amongst them, and they rarely visit foreign countries, but being content to remain at home and to live on what their country produces, and to clothe themselves with the wool from their own flocks, which takes

away all occasion for intimate intercourse with strangers and all opportunity of corruption . . . The other cause is, that those republics which have thus preserved their
political existence uncorrupted do not permit any of their citizens to be or to live in
the manner of gentlemen, but rather maintain amongst them a perfect equality, and
are the most decided enemies of the lords and gentlemen that exist in the country; so
that, if by chance any of them fall into their hands, they kill them, as being the chief
promoters of all corruption and troubles. (Machiavelli 1882, Vol. 2: 210)

Worries about the effect of luxurious living on republican virtue were uppermost
in the minds of many eighteenth-century social thinkers (e.g., Adam Smith, Adam
Ferguson, John Millar, and Etienne de Condillac; see Sica 2005), which led directly
to similar concerns harbored by the US Founders (most notably Ben Franklin, John
Adams, and Thomas Jefferson). Machiavelli does not rail against those "virtuous"
citizens who murder nobles they perceive to be corrupt, probably because he understood the ethical basis of these acts. Perhaps the principal difference between such
political action in sixteenth-century Italy and the more circumspect interaction
typical in today's nations between the wealthy and the ordinary is the size and
armaments of police forces who protect wealth and privilege.

Thomas Hobbes continues to inspire political scientists and sociologists of power;
his *Leviathan* (1651), still a canonical text, is based in part on the psychological
theory of Thucydides. Hobbes' experiences as the victim of capricious political
power were unhappy, which prompted him in part to see social life in dark terms,
as in this passage:

Nature has made men so equal in the faculties of body and mind as that, there be
found one man sometimes manifestly stronger in body or of quicker mind than another,
yet when all is reckoned together the difference between man and man is not so considerable as that one man can thereupon claim to himself any benefit to which another
may not pretend [claim] as well as he . . . From this equality of ability arises equality
of hope in the attaining of our ends. And therefore, if any two men desire the same
thing, which nevertheless they cannot both enjoy, they become enemies, and in the way
to their end, which is principally their own conservation, and sometimes their delecta-
tion [pleasure] only, endeavor to destroy or subdue one another. And from hence it
comes to pass that, where an invader has no more to fear than another man's single
power, if one plant, sow, build or possess a convenient seat, others may probably be
expected to come prepared with forces united, to dispossess and deprive him, not only
of the fruit of his labor, and also of his life and liberty. (Hobbes 1994: 74–5)

Shortly after this passage Hobbes refers to the inevitable outcome of this "normal"
human capacity for violent reappropriation of another's possessions – that is, war
– during which there are "no arts, no letters, no society, and which is worst of all,
continual fear and danger of violent death, and the life of man solitary, poor, nasty,
brutish, and short" (Hobbes 1994: 76). This is Hobbes' most famous line, but his
solution to this condition, a "social contract" guaranteed by an absolute monarch
that protects all against all, is far more important, and has served as the starting
point for every discussion of political power since it was published 360 years ago.
If one reflects on current war-making in the world – one respected source recently
counted "365 overall conflicts, 31 of which are . . . highly violent . . . seven are

classified as wars" (HIIK 2009) – Hobbes' concerns do not seem nearly so anti-quated as his writing style might lead one to believe.

The perpetual war between Islamic and Christian nations, though currently involving relatively few people in the combatant countries, has been ongoing for 1,500 years. Montesquieu's *The Spirit of the Laws* (1748) is an enormous compendium of early "social science," just as important as the works of Machiavelli or Hobbes, and includes a section which has been reinvigorated by current events: "That Modern Government is Better Suited to the Christian Religion, and Despotic Government to Mohammedanism." Montesquieu observes that, "The Christian religion is remote from pure despotism, the gentleness so recommended in the gospel stands opposed to the despotic fury with which a prince would mete out his own justice and exercise his cruelties" (Montesquieu [1748] 1989: 461). Leaving aside the political incorrectness of these sentiments, and even their question-able historical basis, it is nevertheless instructive that world religions continue to inspire bitter warfare 250 years after Montesquieu analyzed the problem. He continues:

> As this religion [Christianity] forbids more than one wife, princes here are less confined, less separated from their subjects, and consequently more human; they are more dis-posed to give laws to themselves, and more capable of feeling that they cannot do everything.
>
> Whereas Mohammedan princes constantly kill or are killed, among Christians religion makes princes less timid and consequently less cruel. The prince counts on his subjects, and the subjects on the prince. Remarkably, the Christian religion, which seems to have no other object than the felicity of the other [after-] life, is also our happiness in this one! . . . The Mohammedan religion, which speaks only with a sword, continues to act on men with the destructive spirit that founded it. (Montes-quieu [1748] 1989: 461–2)

Montesquieu was not a Christian apologist; he prided himself on his cosmo-politan view of the world, and he was lionized by Jefferson, Monroe, Adams, and other pivotal ideologists of the American Revolution. The fact that he could write in such bald terms about the superiority of Christianity indicates how difficult it remains for holders of these two worldviews to interpret each other in sympathetic terms. One must also remember that no less a sociological titan than Max Weber routinely referred to Islam as "the warrior religion," not out of disrespect, but as an accurate historical marker (see Huff & Schluchter 1999).

One could easily continue illustrating the extent to which sociological concerns of today were adumbrated by a succession of Western scholars, especially beginning with the eighteenth-century Enlightenment. Turgot's theory of progress (Meek 1973) was influential, as were the ideas of Condorcet (Baker 1976), Comte's mentor, Saint-Simon (Durkheim 1958), and dozens of others. For the most part these were "lone wolf" thinkers who did not have the desire or opportunity to establish "schools of thought." Even Marx claimed not to be a "Marxist," never wishing to surround himself with adoring acolytes (McLellan 1973; Wheen 1999). The history of *modern* sociology as we have come to know it is an entirely different creature, and of very recent origin.

As mentioned above, Auguste Comte (1798–1857) named the discipline in 1839. With invaluable inspiration from his theoretical predecessors, he slowly constructed an elaborate, historically based scheme whereby humanity could rid itself of prescientific notions, the kind that gave rise to violence and irrationality, by accepting the tenets of his "positivist" utopia. Convinced of his own genius, he anointed himself "the first sociologist." Like many in his generation, his dread of social and political violence arose from being born in the aftermath of the bloody French Revolution, but unlike moralizers who merely complained about human iniquities, Comte offered a "scientific" way out of the morass. He was a gifted mathematician, but more importantly a self-trained historian and philosopher, which led him to republican beliefs that were unusual for his social class. He was famously rebellious, hoping at one point to emigrate to the US so he could work in a country without a monarch.

In 1826 he started lecturing (for fees) on his *Course of Positive Philosophy*, eventually attracting the notice of no less a figure than John Stuart Mill, who supported him financially while publicizing his work by means of a small book. Like most of Comte's friends, Mill patiently tolerated Comte's mental instability and astonishing egocentrism. The noted, deaf British feminist, Harriet Martineau, heroically translated his work into digestible English. Through her work, Comteanism (or "Comtism") became a respectable affiliation, recognized worldwide among those interested in political and cultural change. His works were studied in Brazil, Mexico, Turkey, India, and elsewhere, and the Brazilian flag features the phrase *Ordem e Progresso*, which is condensed from Comte's own positivist motto.

The stimuli for Comte's development as an intellectual historian and theorist, as "the first sociologist," were proudly eclectic, or what might today be called "broadgauged." This set a pattern that remained in place for the century after his death, with early sociologists migrating to their new field from theology, social work, economics (Young 2009), philosophy, history, and other fields (Small 1916; Gillin 1927; Bernard & Bernard 1943; Odum 1951; Furner 1975; Haskell 1977; Ross 1991). Like most French intellectuals in the tradition of Pascal and Descartes, Comte venerated the Gallic tradition, but managed to go far beyond it in his search for "universal" knowledge. For example, David Hume was not only Comte's favorite historian, but also by his own admission his "principal philosophical predecessor" (Pickering 1993: 313, 306–8, 600), rather than the usual French standard-bearers (as textbooks sometimes claim, e.g., Turner, Beeghley & Power 1989: 7–13). Yet Comte's enthusiastic embrace of religio-positivism made it impossible for him to "grasp the depth of Hume's skepticism and relativism" (Pickering 1993: 312) – which was typical of his style of incorporating others' ideas into his own sprawling architectonic. Comte also claimed Turgot, Condorcet, the German phrenologist and biologist Franz Joseph Gall, and the arch-conservative Joseph de Maistre, as his major influences (Pickering 1993: 263).

Though he was loath to admit it, even the most cursory glance at Comte's road to the creation of "sociology," by name if not by practice, must give pride of place to Henri-Claude de Saint-Simon (1760–1825), for whom Comte served as a research associate from the summer of 1817 until March 1824. If the Marx/Engels relationship seems the least troubled, most productive, and most "brotherly" of all such team-efforts, it could be said that Saint-Simon and Comte's relationship – they were

respectively 47 and 19 when they met – represents the "dysfunctional family" of
early sociology. What began as worshipful attention of the younger for the elder
ended as a paranoid tragedy in which Comte repudiated everything good about
Saint-Simon's ideas and person, then pretended the older man's ideas were his own.
The parallels between the pair's ideas have become increasingly obvious since their
feuding bands of followers disappeared. Unlike Comte, who presented himself in
logorrheic fashion, Saint-Simon's ideas were best presented by his disciples (e.g.,
Amand Bazard's *Exposition de la doctrine de St Simon*, 2 volumes, 1828–30), and
not in Saint-Simon's own 47 volumes of collected writings (1865–78).

The belief Comte adopted, that science would guide "industrial society" toward
universal prosperity and freedom, and that superstitious beliefs would be left behind,
is indeed Saint-Simon's. The latter thought that industrialists could be trusted to
organize and run modern society (one is reminded of Thorstein Veblen's paean a
century later to a guiding "soviet of engineers" [Veblen 1921]), and that a Christian-
ized socialism would evolve from their efforts. A utopian condition would then
obtain in which the worst features of human behavior would "naturally" evaporate.
Ironically, it was Saint-Simon's late injection of religiosity into his program for social
change that alienated Comte, who would himself late in life make almost precisely
the same move when he fashioned his "Religion of Humanity."

In *The New Christianity* (1825), Saint-Simon held that the ultimate goal of his
utopian society would be to eliminate poverty and to elevate what Marx would call
"the proletariat" to a healthy and respectable condition. He envisioned the elimination of war, anarchy, and the egotistical impulses which gave rise to both, when his
religiously-based social order had been born, one built upon the conventional
Catholic virtues of obedience and devotion to a larger, collective good. Saint-Simon
had suffered imprisonment and near-execution during the Revolution, so he feared
organized aggression. Similarly, Comte grew up with family stories of The Terror,
so like many of their countrymen, including rightists such as de Maistre, he posited
the elimination of war and anarchic brutality as the supreme societal virtue. Saint-
Simon's utopia would give women the vote and abolish inheritance, themes picked
up by many revolutionary groups that followed him. His high regard for females is
another theme adopted by Comte as the latter entered his concluding years of creative work, around 1852.

The case of Turgot is also interesting and illustrative, not only as it was inserted
into Comte's project, but also as revealing the way early social theorists routinely
turned speculative ideas to their own more "policy-oriented" purposes. Turgot
proposed a three-stage theory of historical change in his famous 1750 address, "A
Philosophical Review of the Successive Advances of the Human Mind" (Meek 1973:
41–59), which won high praise from Condorcet and others whom Comte also
admired. One could therefore surmise (as did the noted chronicler, Harry Elmer
Barnes [1948: 72]) that Turgot's ideas directly influenced Comte when, 72 years
later in 1822, he created his own tripartite theory of cultural "advance" (the
theological-metaphysical-positivist eras). Yet according to Pickering, this is not
likely, because Comte apparently read Turgot only in 1852 or 1853, long after his
own theory had been formulated (Pickering 1993: 200, n.32). Moreover, his library
contained none of Turgot's own works, but instead, a well-used copy of Condorcet's
Vie de Monsieur Turgot (1787).

An intriguing intersection among the three thinkers occurs at the beginning of Condorcet's "Essay on the Application of Mathematics to the Theory of Decision-Making" (1785), which opens with what from our vantage point can only seem poignant hopefulness:

> A great man, Monsieur Turgot . . . was convinced that the truths of the moral and political sciences are susceptible of the same certainty as those forming the system of the physical sciences, even those branches like astronomy which seem to approach mathematical certainty. This opinion was dear to him, because it led him to the consoling hope that the human race will necessarily progress toward happiness and perfection, as it has done in the knowledge of truth. (Baker 1976: 33)

Such happy thoughts are virtually identical with Comte's, and continue even now to inspire a significant portion of modern sociological labors, even if in more circumspect terms, chastened by postmodern reflexivity and the failure of various large-scale social programs that were based on positivistic research (e.g., James Coleman's tragic "busing report" of 1966).

Working slavishly for decades, Comte vigorously pursued a piratical version of what Merton dubbed OBI – "obliteration by incorporation" (Merton 1968: 27–8, 35–7). He read so widely, even maniacally, that virtually any thinker of the Enlightenment figured positively or negatively in his *Cours de philosophie positive* (6 volumes, 1830–42) and his *Système de politique positive* (4 volumes, 1851–4), even if often only in caricature. As Pickering put it, "It is evident that Comte had absorbed the ideas of Montesquieu and Condorcet and was influenced by Constant, Staël, Say, Cabanis, and Destutt de Tracy" (Pickering 1993: 241) – among many others. This tendency to vacuum up scraps from whatever field seemed useful as a way of expanding sociology's grasp has continued into the present time among Comte's disciplinary descendants.

Sociology's troubled epistemological future was already latent in Comte, since he combined top-level mathematical and scientific capacities with a passionate commitment to history, propelled by an unconstrained desire to aid liberating social change. This problematic posture – bridging what the Germans later called the *Naturwissenschaften* (natural sciences) and the *Geisteswissenschaften* (human sciences) – has plagued sociology ever since Comte's day, but has also, despite the grumbling of purists, managed to produce vital scholarship that would not otherwise have been possible. Comte was not as economically skilled as Marx or Vilfredo Pareto were to become, and less well schooled in philosophical argument than were Weber, Durkheim, or Simmel. Nevertheless, he expanded on the teaching of his sometime employer and confederate, Saint-Simon, and laid out a form of methodological positivism which prompted generations of researchers during the ensuing century to adopt "sociology" as their identity, even when in quotation marks (as Weber did). They turned their backs on Comte's grandiose pronouncements about sociology being the "queen of the sciences," capable of saving global society from its self-immolating tendencies. But they accepted his larger goal, to purge the collective human life of folly through scientific analysis.

Comte believed that humankind had progressed from theological entrapment in myth and fetish-worship to a metaphysical stage of skilled speculation, finally achieving maturity in his own positivist era, which would use evidence and reasoned argument to establish truth. Comte's vision led him to argue that once sociologists had been installed as the secular priests of the social order, social and political calamities would be obviated, as he explained in "The Intellectual Character of Positivism":

> To effect this necessary intervention is the proper sphere of politics. But a right conception cannot be formed of it without the aid of the philosopher [i.e., the sociologist/"priest"], whose business it is to define and amend the principles on which it is conducted. With this object in view, the philosopher endeavors to co-ordinate the various elements of man's existence, so that it may be conceived of theoretically as an integral whole. (Lenzer 1975: 320)

Comte's legacy lives on mostly unperceived in modern social science, since the unspoken assumption underlying today's research restates his fondest hope: once the unvarying "laws" of social behavior are uncovered through rigorous positivistic research, behavior can be tailored to fit society's and individuals' needs, and socio-political miseries of the kind he knew about firsthand would no longer characterize the human condition. Comte's simple notion of positivism, his theory of the three stages of human thought, and the so-called "religion of humanity" over which he and other "sociologist-priests" would preside via scientific method no longer appeal in the way they did among J. S. Mill's peers. Yet this does not detract from Comte's singular role in the early legitimation of sociology.

Unsurprisingly, Comte was rediscovered during the 1960s and 1970s, the "Age of Aquarius," since he introduced his "religion of humanity" this way: "Love, then, is our principle; order our basis; and progress our goal" ("*L'amour pour principe et l'ordre pour base; le progrès pour but*") (Lenzer 1975: 381). Late in life he had learned, by meeting a sympathetic woman who too quickly died, that love is the great motivating force in social life, and "reason" alone cannot inspire humans to develop a "religion of humanity" of the sort he envisioned for a trouble-free world.

The intimate lineage connecting Saint-Simon, Comte, and the founder of modern French sociology, Emile Durkheim (1858–1917), is recorded in Durkheim's *Socialism and Saint Simon*, based on his 1895–6 lectures at Bordeaux and assembled posthumously in 1928 by his famous nephew, Marcel Mauss (Durkheim 1958). Durkheim intended to write a history of socialism by means of a set of courses on Saint-Simon, Proudhon, Lasalle, Marx/Engels, and others, but his ever-expanding duties prevented him from going beyond the first course. Many of Durkheim's students and colleagues were committed leftists, and even though he sympathized with their goal of ameliorating the grim lives of the working classes, he stood back from the fray and evaluated this broad movement "scientifically," following his usual tack. This "value-free" quality gave French sociology a particular flavor that distinguished it from US, German, and British variants, all of which were in the *fin de siècle* wrapped up in larger programs of socio-economic uplift. In 1892 Weber worked with the *Verein für Sozialpolitik*, a group of well-intentioned ministers worried about agrarian workers; the early Chicago School had close links with Jane Addams and other parties tied to social policy issues in the city's ethnic communities, to which George Herbert Mead also gave serious attention;

and British sociologists, despite Herbert Spencer's loud objection, were connected with the Fabians and other constituencies more committed to benefiting the poor than creating a value-free "social science." But French sociology maintained its Durkheimian remove from the mundane concerns of social work, probably in an effort to legitimize its status as an academic field worthy of a Sorbonne professorship.

Durkheim prized Saint-Simon's ideas, and pointed out the relative weakness of Comte's theorizing and its heavy reliance on the older man's more fundamental innovations: "Comte owed him much more than he acknowledged" (Durkheim 1958: 86). Moreover, "Durkheim firmly denies to Comte, and bestows on Saint-Simon, the 'honor' of having founded both positivist philosophy and sociology" (Gouldner in Durkheim 1958: ix). This claim hinges on the 1813 *Mémoire sur la science de l'homme* by Saint-Simon, published in 1859, where the lineaments of a positivist social science are clearly laid out. Saint-Simon's "socialism" may have ideologically discredited the "sociology" to which Comte laid claim, and early historians of the field distanced themselves from appearing to be leftist sympathizers by choosing to honor Comte rather than his mentor as the discipline's true father. In any case, sociology of the complex French variety fused aspects of Enlightenment secularism, newly formed positivism, and latent idealism.

Durkheim also knew that Saint-Simon had received encouragement and refinement from his youthful acquaintance with Jean D'Alembert, fueling his desire to update the great *Encyclopedia* by including advances in the natural sciences (Durkheim 1958: 82). This general ambition, to advance the "science" of human relations, was never far from Durkheim's plans for the sociological school he organized in Paris. Yet for all his apparent materialism, Saint-Simon's positivism rests, so says Durkheim, on an idealist base: "knowledge . . . according to him is the moving power of progress . . . For it is the positive source of all social life. A society is above all a community of ideas" (Durkheim 1958: 91). This notion, contradicting Marx's materialist view, saturated twentieth-century sociology through terms like "norms," "value consensus," and "societal belief-systems." All this clearly began with Saint-Simon's unique transformation of Enlightenment skepticism and materialism. In fact, Saint-Simon claimed that "philosophy appears as a branch of sociology" (Durkheim 1958: 93), another notion deftly exploited by Comte.

Durkheim thought that he was in serious intellectual competition with Herbert Spencer, but prior to battling his British foil, he first needed to trump Comte's prescription for the discipline as he advanced his own. He believed that Comte misunderstood, perhaps by minimizing Saint-Simon's insights, the actual conditions within industrializing Europe. For Durkheim modern life's multiplying interdependencies were not pathological, since it meant that philosophic and practical differences between individuals and their affiliated groups would "naturally" diminish over time. As population and socio-cultural "density" escalated, so too would the virtuous commonality of ever thicker interaction. There was therefore no need, so thought Durkheim, for a Comtean priesthood of propagandizing sociologists "tasked" with controlling the unruly masses. The irrepressible "division of labor" would resolve whatever residual tensions remained after the stunning transformation of village "mechanical solidarity" into the steely social structures of modern, urban life which constituted "organic solidarity."

This profound rearrangement of human life was most memorably analyzed by Durkheim's German competitor, Ferdinand Tönnies (1855–1936), whose *Gemeinschaft und Gesellschaft* (1887) gave sociology two of its immortal and most contested terms. Tönnies (associate of Weber and Simmel) understood that small-town life (*Gemeinschaft*) was made up of "community" relations, a naturally formed face-to-face intimacy which humans had perfected over millennia to meet the exigencies of everyday life, whereas urban existence (*Gesellschaft*) bore within it an unavoidably alienating set of forces that typifies modern existence, leading to a great number of "dysfunctions" (famously portrayed in Georg Simmel's "The Metropolis and Mental Life" [1903; in Simmel 1971: 324–39). Problems with *anomie*, which Comte described without using the term itself, would vaporize, as Durkheim argued in his opposition to Tönnies, when modern citizens assembled into professional groups that would restructure morality along "organic" rather than "mechanical" lines. All these standpoints came into play as French and German sociology separately matured, in conflict as usual. The Rhine so divided these sociological worldviews that neither Durkheim nor Weber ever referred to each other in print, though fully aware of each other's writings (Tiryakian 1966; see also Sica 1979). The fate of each nation's sociological enterprise would have been far different had they joined forces rather than ignored each other, since the strength of each would have secured the other.

The next indispensable character who brought sociology to life was the British autodidact and polymath, Herbert Spencer (1820–1903), who visited Comte in Paris with unhappy results. In a letter to his mother from Paris (October 20, 1856), Spencer wrote: "I called on Comte yesterday to give him a remittance from Chapman [his British publisher]. He is a very undignified little old man. My French sufficed me to carry on an argument with him in a very slipshod style." And to a friend on July 29, 1853: "The topic to which I refer is the 'Positive Philosophy.' Miss Martineau's translation of Comte will be out probably by Christmas; and having much to say on his system – mainly antagonism to it – I am desirous of reviewing this forthcoming English edition of his works" (Duncan 1908: 82, 72). As already mentioned, important early theorists practiced "mental hygiene" whereby they would assiduously avoid studying any opponent's works lest their own path be unwittingly modified. Spencer took this practice to its most extreme, yet one cannot read his *Principles of Sociology* (1876–96) without sensing an urgent need to triumph over Comte, perhaps because the latter had so many followers in Britain at the very time Spencer was fighting to establish his own way of thinking.

During his prime Spencer was held in awe on both sides of the Atlantic, but he is now mostly known as a propagator of "social Darwinism" (Bannister 1979). His massive *Autobiography* (2 volumes, 1,258 pages) and *The Life and Letters* detail his search for a "synthetic philosophy" that could arrange all natural and social data into a meaningful pattern, with sociology the centerpiece.

From these sources one learns, for instance, that Spencer's relation with philosophical thought (like Comte's and Marx's) was antinomically creative. He readily dismisses Kant:

I found in Mr. Wilson's house . . . a copy of a translation of Kant's *Critique of Pure Reason* . . . This I commenced reading, but did not go far. The doctrine that Time and

Space are 'nothing but' subjective forms, – pertain exclusively to consciousness and have nothing beyond consciousness answering to them, – I rejected at once and absolutely; and, having done so, went no further. Being then, as always, an impatient reader, even of things which in large measure interest me and meet with a general acceptance, it has always been out of the question for me to go on reading a book the fundamental principles of which I entirely dissent from. (Spencer 1904, Vol. 1: 289)

(Saint-Simon was similarly inclined to ignore his predecessors; he admitted in a letter to M. de Redern, "to have thought a great deal and to have read very little to produce really new ideas" [*Oeuvres*, 1.1.110], a fairly common sentiment among early sociologists.) Spencer also repudiates Comte and the numerous "Comtists" who labeled him a follower of Comte regarding sociology, which Spencer vigorously denied repeatedly (e.g., 1904, Vol. 1: 292n, 518).

Like Darwin, his confederate in evolutionary theory, Spencer began life in the midst of an intensely religious family, and carried with him into the study of the natural and social worlds a heavy load of religio-philosophical baggage – another parallel with early sociology in the United States (Vidich & Lyman 1985). Thus, "the Unknowable" figures prominently in his early work, *First Principles* (1862), since Spencer believed there were metaphysical questions humans could not possibly answer, and which should best be left to some external power beyond their secular sphere.

If Spencer had died at 32, he would already have established himself as a minor speculative thinker, but he persisted through 50 more years of rigorous, solitary study as an autodidact, probing and amalgamating biology, education, sociology, political theory, psychology, ethics, and comparative anthropology. By inventing the phrase "survival of the fittest" (*Principles of Biology*, 1864) he forever connected himself with the Darwinian camp of his walking partner, T. H. Huxley, and others. Yet one cannot view Spencer's gigantic *Synthetic Philosophy* (16 volumes) without realizing that the merely empirical, measurable, and palpable operated in his system under the sign of a theoretical commitment tending towards the teleological, which surely inspired him in his tireless pursuit of data. He was attacked late in life by "Spencer smashers" for being insufficiently devout, which prompted Lester Frank Ward, first president of the American Sociological Association (ASA), to defend him in 1894 against a phalanx of uncomprehending theologians (Anonymous 1894).

Spencer is now known as a champion of laissez-faire government (*Man Versus the State* [1884]), evolutionary progress, and industrial versus militaristic social organization. His materialist view of the physical world, alternating between decomposition and reconstitution toward some desirable evolutionary end, expressed via a special lexicon (persistence of force; necessary rhythm; evolution versus dissolution; instability of the homogeneous; et cetera), revealed his determination to grant sociology a firm epistemological and ontological base. His mixture of philosophical speculation, voiced or silent, and a rabid subsumption of data from every field of learning, created a legacy for sociology that commanded the field between 1875 and the First World War.

Spencer's *Life and Letters* (600 pages), assembled by an acolyte in 1908, illustrates the astonishing dimensions of nineteenth-century thought at its most accomplished, and helps explain how sociology was created. Comte, Marx, Spencer, and their intellectual kin did not suffer imprisonment within the narrow disciplinary identities that trap most scholars today, and they gloried in their ability to move freely among whatever fields of learning they found useful to their self-assigned tasks. It is therefore unsurprising that Spencer in his prime was often named "the nineteenth century's Aristotle," which seemed as plausible to his contemporaries as it appears preposterous now (Peel 1971; Francis 2007; Shapin 2007; Werth 2009).

From solo virtuosi of sociological reasoning, we move to the slightly less enchanting but equally important period of sociology's "institutionalization" – its shift from brilliant inventors to more rationalized practitioners within stable academic settings. The United States – and not England, Germany, or France – accepted the new discipline much more readily than did the rest of the world. This was partly because of the nation's religious heritage, which found sociology useful to its goal of ameliorating human misery, and also because of the experimental nature of American society, its unique polyglot culture, and the problems to which this ethnic mixture gave rise (Bannister 2003).

Sociology following Spencer's texts was first taught at Yale by William Graham Sumner around 1875, and a course in what was called sociology was offered at Indiana University in 1885. But the first "department of sociology" at an American university was founded in Kansas in 1889 (Sica 1983, 1990). Emile Durkheim taught the first courses in sociology in France in 1887 (Lukes 1972), but mostly taught pedagogy to future high school teachers; the German Sociological Society was launched in 1910 through the efforts of Weber, Simmel, and Tönnies (Käsler 1988: 16), was destroyed by the Nazis by 1938, then rebuilt in 1946; Princeton University did not have a free-standing sociology department until 1960 (Page 1982: 149), and shortly thereafter sociology finally landed at Oxford and Cambridge universities (Bannister 2003: 348–52). When these few facts are considered against the antiquity of sociology's theoretical predecessors, outlined above, one could argue that its institutionalized form is still in its infancy, especially when contrasted with the study of law, astronomy, mathematics, or medicine.

Early American sociologists were intent on highlighting their lineage to legitimate their claims on resources, often contested by rival disciplines, and to gain scholarly respect (Sica 2007: 726–31). When Albion Small (1854–1926) was called to the University of Chicago from the presidency of Colby College, he was given a very large salary and budget provided by its founder, John D. Rockefeller, and set about hunting for the best men (*sic*) he could find to fill his new department of sociology. By chance he also found money to start the *American Journal of Sociology* (*AJS*) in 1895. So, as the first well-endowed sociology department with multiple faculty, it was Small's unembarrassed grandiloquence that set the tone for the field for its first decades, e.g., "We do not fully take in [today's] problems as problems, unless to a certain extent we have put ourselves back into the state of mind of people before our time who were pioneering through blind trails that opened at last upon the problems of our own time, and were experimenting with devices for dealing with pioneering difficulties" (Small 1924: 325). Small was well aware of his central role in the beginnings of American sociology, and the "pioneering difficulties" he and his few colleagues would have to overcome to prove to skeptical colleagues that sociology was worth its keep.

Yet it should not be thought that sociology's acceptance on the American college scene was a simple or guaranteed matter, despite Small's good fortune at Chicago. Its bold sponsors faced numerous, stubborn obstacles on the road to legitimation. Their first statements of intent often took a cheering, celebratory form, a trope at which Small was expert, e.g., his opening blast in the *American Journal of Sociology*: "Sociology has a foremost place in the thought of modern men. Approve or deplore the fact at pleasure, we cannot escape it" (Small 1895: 1). He and others expressed themselves this way in order to announce a newcomer which scholars from competing fields disparaged from its very beginnings (at Johns Hopkins in the late 1880s). Similarly in the inaugural *AJS* issue, Lester Ward surveys the development of sociology through Comte, Spencer, and Mill, then has this to say: "We come to the last and highest of the sciences, viz., sociology . . . an advanced study, the last and latest in the entire curriculum . . . it involves high power of generalization, and what is more, it absolutely requires a broad basis of induction" (Ward 1895: 22, 25). Yet he also noted a few years later, delivering the first ASA presidential address in December 1906, "a retiring dean . . . in a public address . . . said, among other things, that 'Sociology, far from being a science, was little more than empty verbiage'" (Ward 1907: 582). And Edward Cummings confided to Small that prior to 1891/2, when he taught "the first sociology course offered at Harvard . . . no one had given me the slightest encouragement to believe there was any 'academic future' for 'sociological' work" (Small 1916: 761–2). Aspersions of this type became common, and in fact continued into the 1950s, it becoming a platitude in the academy that those adventurers who embraced sociology as a profession were setting out to sea in a fragile craft, without maps, and with no discernible destination. That "sociology" and "socialism" were chronically conflated in the popular mind did not help the discipline's advancement, either (see, *inter alia*, Gillin 1927: 24).

Nevertheless, legislatures across the Midwest were far more interested in establishing sociology in their state universities than were the Ivy League colleges, a strength in the discipline that persists until today. The first doctorates in sociology were granted at Chicago and Columbia in the 1890s, so before that sociologists came from a range of sister disciplines. The early practitioners were learned in the characteristic Victorian sense, including knowledge of multiple languages, history, political-economics, and literature, some of which they learned in Germany during what became a standard student sojourn. The quality of their formal writings, discussions (preserved stenographically), and letters is typically very high when compared to today's efforts, driven as much by elevated moral purpose as by scientific and historical literacy (e.g., the Small-Ross-Ward collections edited by Bernard Stern: 1932, 1933, 1935, 1936, 1937, 1938, 1946a, 1946b, 1947, 1948, 1949).

For example, in the foundational work by Small, "Fifty Years of Sociology in the United States (1865–1915)" (published twice in *AJS*), he offers the entire course guide to the "plan of instruction in the Columbia School of Political Science, as it was projected in 1892." This he viewed as "certainly the best considered, most comprehensive, and most coherent attempt up to that time in the United States to organize team-work in the social sciences so as to cover all the ground which needs to be surveyed in that field" (Small 1916: 737–8). The program "stimulated the inevitable demand for general sociology," which is why Small valued it. It was designed to be Germanically thorough and demanding, clearly imitating the universities where its professors had studied abroad: "The student is supposed to be familiar with the outlines of European history, ancient and modern . . . It is presumed that students possess a knowledge of the general principles of political economy as laid down in the ordinary manuals by Walker or Mill" (Small 1916: 739, 743); reading lists were in English, German, and French. Such scholars' strong training in rhetoric and argumentation makes it apparent that debating the future of sociology was not for them an idle hobby, but in fact defined their intellectual being. They staked out sociology's intellectual and political terrain in vigorous opposition not only to other academics, but also to a public which remained ambivalent about the connotative and denotative meanings of "social science" in general, and "sociology" in particular.

The American Sociological Association celebrated its centennial in 2005, an achievement that would have seemed improbable and unnecessary to most other members of the academy when it was first organized. It began humbly enough:

> During the summer of 1905, Professor C. W. A. Veditz, of the George Washington University, wrote to a number of the well-known sociologists of the United States with a view to securing an expression of opinion with regard to the desirability and feasibility of forming some sort of an organization of sociologists. This correspondence indicated, among those who participated in it, a unanimous desire for such an organization. Dr. Lester F. Ward, of Washington, believed that there is certainly need for a national sociological association . . . (Anonymous [probably Albion Small] 1906: 555)

The possible need for such a group, one that distinguished itself from psychology, political-economics, or history, was thoroughly discussed soon thereafter at Johns Hopkins University, "by some fifty persons, among whom were a number particularly interested in the practical aspects of sociology" (Anonymous 1906: 557). The attendees came from social work, social philosophy, practical theology, journalism, economics, and other fields (Rhoades 1981: 1). Many of the actual and virtual participants (by letters of intent) soon became iconic figures in US sociology's history. Optimism for the discipline's future was palpable: "Professor Giddings, of Columbia University, pointed out that probably in no country in the world is there so much interest in the problems of sociology, whether theoretical or practical, as in the United States. Many, if not most, of our colleges and universities offer courses in sociology" (Anonymous 1906: 561).

Within several years of that modest beginning, Theodore Roosevelt addressed the Society when it met in Washington, apparently the only time a US President has spoken to the ASA's annual meeting. From this humble origin the Society steadily grew, with membership rising to 1,021 by 1920, 1,530 in 1930 (when the Society's entire annual budget came to $9,160), and 3,241 by 1950. In sharp contrast, the annual meeting held in Atlanta in 2010 involved over 5,000 participants from around the globe, which represents only about 40 percent of the Association's total membership.

Despite intermittent, heroic efforts by scholars like Luther Bernard, Albion Small, Howard Odum, and Harry Elmer Barnes, sociology has not been especially well treated as a topic worthy of historical research by members of its own guild. The fact that younger social historians (most of whom are *not* formally trained sociologists, since no American sociology doctoral program currently offers specialization in the history of sociology) have over the last two decades or so vigorously pursued American sociology's origins and development (e.g., Bannister 1987; Igo 2007; Haney 2008) does not challenge my argument: today's sociologists are in general ignorant about their field's past, and are quite content to remain so, and surely do not wish to study the historical record itself. The "history of sociology" section of the American Sociological Association is very small relative to others, and limps along from year to year in search of permanence. The *Journal of the History of Sociology* existed for a few years in the 1980s through private efforts of a few supporters, and has not been succeeded by another of similar provenance.

Not surprisingly, Albion Small published the first attempt, *Origins of Sociology* (1924), to specify the beginnings of the field. He observes upon completing his survey (which in fact dealt mostly with German historiography), with a sentiment which has by now become familiar:

> The book sustains the main thesis that during the nineteenth century the social sciences were half-consciously engaged in a drive from relatively irresponsible discursiveness toward "positivity" or "objectivity"; and that, at its time, the initiation of the American Sociological Movement was as truly a lineal continuance from the previous tradition of social interpretation as was any other of the tendencies which varied the technique of historiography, or economics, or political science . . .
>
> All that has been said in this survey thus far might be compressed into the single sentence which has been repeated in various versions, viz. *Sociology has a venerable genealogy*. Sociology was not like Topsy, not even like Minerva, born in complete maturity from a single creative brain. Sociology is a branch of the great trunk of social science . . . Why is it worth while to dig up the record of all these people who are no more to us than we to them? This is the answer: Whatever we may construct as a logical statement of what ought to be true, it is true that *we cannot be as intelligent as we might be about the present problems or the present processes of any science, unless, among other things, we have joined company with the people who have at length differentiated the processes; in other words, unless we have acquired our sense of the present condition of that branch of knowledge in part by the historical approach*. (Small 1924: 324–5, emphasis in original)

Small's pivotal role as sociology's US co-founder (along with Franklin Giddings at Columbia) and chief propagandist reveals itself in this excerpt, which makes poignant the rapid eclipse of his reputation upon his death.

A vigorous history of US, European, then global sociology will eventually be composed, but it will likely come from outside ASA membership since there are few scholarly or material rewards for research of this kind within the discipline itself. Many of the raw materials are already in place and archives do exist which can be mined, as exemplified in a few recent works (e.g., Halsey 2004; Blasi 2005; Backhouse & Fontaine 2010). There are new avenues to be explored, as well, for instance, "transformative moments" in the discipline's history. Sociology's history has often been told through the biographies of famous men (*sic*) (Odum 1927) and/ or small-scale studies of individual departments (especially those at Chicago,

Harvard, Columbia, and Berkeley). There are more macro-oriented ways of understanding sociology's role in academic and extra-academic life, e.g., how wars have affected the discipline, how funding for large-scale research began in the 1920s (Turner & Turner 1990), how minorities began to have a voice within the discipline for the first time during the Depression, the remarkable role of European ethnic groups as "stars" of post-Second World War sociology, how external political forces (e.g., Nazism, McCarthyism, Reaganism, Thatcherism) have affected the field, and vice versa, to name only a few routes which new modes of research could take. Whether the future will find scholars ready to take up these tasks is another question.

Further Reading

Abbott, Andrew (1999) *Department and Discipline: Chicago Sociology at One Hundred.* Chicago: University of Chicago Press.

American Sociological Society (1907a) [Announcement of the formation of the ASS in December, 1905.] *American Journal of Sociology* 12(5): 579–80.

American Sociological Society (1907b) "Constitution of the American Sociological Society." *American Journal of Sociology* 12(5): 735–6.

American Sociological Society (1907c) "List of Members." *American Journal of Sociology* 12(5): 736–8.

Anonymous (1895) "Sociological Miscellany." *American Journal of Sociology* 1(2): 231–6.

Bernard, Jesse (1929) "The History and Prospects of Sociology in the United States." In George Lundberg, Read Bain, and Nels Anderson (eds.), *Trends in American Sociology.* New York: Harper and Brothers, pp. 1–71.

Bernard, Luther L. (1909) "The Teaching of Sociology in the United States." *American Journal of Sociology* 15(2): 164–213.

Bernard, Luther L. (1918) "The Teaching of Sociology in Southern Colleges and Universities." *American Journal of Sociology* 23(4): 491–515.

Bernard, Luther L. (ed.) (1934) *The Fields and Methods of Sociology.* New York: Farrar and Rinehart, Inc. [copyright by the American Sociological Society].

Bernard, Luther L. (1936) "Henry Hughes, First American Sociologist." *Social Forces* 15(2): 154–74.

Bierstedt, Robert (1981) *American Sociological Theory: A Critical History.* New York: Academic Press.

Bottomore, Tom and Robert Nisbet (eds.) (1978) *A History of Sociological Analysis.* New York: Basic Books.

Bramson, Leon (1961) *The Political Context of Sociology.* Princeton: Princeton University Press.

Branford, Victor V. (1903) "On the Origin and Use of the Word 'Sociology.'" *American Journal of Sociology* 9(2): 145–62.

Branford, Victor V. (1904) "The Founders of Sociology." *American Journal of Sociology* 10(1): 94–120 (discussion, 120–6).

Bulmer, Martin (1984) *The Chicago School of Sociology: Institutionalization, Diversity, and the Rise of Sociological Research.* Chicago: University of Chicago Press.

Burgess, Ernest W. (1939) "The Influence of Sigmund Freud upon Sociology in the United States." *American Journal of Sociology* 45(3): 356–74.

Calhoun, Craig (ed.) (2007) *Sociology in America: A History*. Chicago: University of Chicago Press.

Calverton, V. F. (1929) "The Sociological Aesthetics of the Bolsheviki." *American Journal of Sociology* 35(3): 383–92.

Camic, Charles (1995) "Three Departments in Search of a Discipline: Localism and Interdisciplinary Interaction in American Sociology." *Social Research* 62: 1003–33.

Camic, Charles and Yu Xie (1994) "The Statistical Turn in American Social Science: Columbia University, 1890–1915." *American Sociological Review* 59: 773–805.

Carver, T. N., John B. Clark, David Kinley, E. A. Ross, Lester F. Ward, Hutton Webster, and Albion W. Small (1907) "The Relations of the Social Sciences: A Symposium." *American Journal of Sociology* 13(3): 392–401.

Chapin, F. Stuart (1934) "The Present State of the Profession." *American Journal of Sociology* 39(4): 506–8.

Chugerman, Samuel (1939) *Lester F. Ward: The American Aristotle: A Summary and Interpretation of His Sociology*. Durham, NC: Duke University Press.

Commons, John R. (1899) "A Sociological View of Sovereignty. I." *American Journal of Sociology* 5(1): 1–15.

Comte, Auguste (1886) *The Positivist Library*. Trans. Frederic Harrison. London: Reeves and Turner. Reissued 1971. New York: Burt Franklin.

Comte, Auguste (1891) *The Catechism of Positive Religion*, 3rd edn., revised and corrected. Trans. Richard Congreve. London: Kegan Paul, Trench, Trübner and Co. Ltd. Reprinted 1973. Clifton, NJ: Augustus Kelley.

Converse, Jean M. (1987) *Survey Research in the United States: Roots and Emergence, 1890–1960*. Berkeley: University of California Press.

Cooley, Charles Horton (1907) "Social Consciousness." [Proceedings of the first ASS meeting.] *American Journal of Sociology* 12(5): 675–87 (comments by Edwin Earp, Alvan Tenney, Charlotte Perkins Gilman, C. W. A. Veditz, James Minnick, E. A. Ross: 687–94).

Cooley, Charles Horton (1920) "Reflections upon the Sociology of Herbert Spencer." *American Journal of Sociology* 26(2): 129–45.

Dealey, James Quayle (1910) "The Teaching of Sociology." *American Journal of Sociology* 15(5): 657–71.

Durkheim, Emile (1898) "Minor Editorials [a letter in French]." *American Journal of Sociology* 3(6): 848–9.

Durkheim, Emile (1983) *Pragmatism and Sociology*. Trans. J. C. Whitehouse. New York: Cambridge University Press.

Durkheim, Emile (2004) *Durkheim's Philosophy Lectures*. Trans. N. Gross and R. A. Jones. New York: Cambridge University Press.

Eliaesen, Sven (2002) *Max Weber's Methodologies: Interpretation and Critique*. Oxford: Polity Press.

Ellwood, Charles A. (1899) "Prolegomena to Social Psychology. IV. The Concept of the Social Mind." *American Journal of Sociology* 5(2): 220–7.

Ellwood, Charles A. (1907) "How Should Sociology Be Taught as a College or University Subject?" [Proceedings of the first ASS meeting.] *American Journal of Sociology* 12(5): 588–96; discussion by William Graham Sumner (596–9), Morgan Davenport (600–2), Jeffrey Brackett (602–3), Robert Chapin (603–4), Elbert Cutler (604–6).

Ellwood, Charles A. (1907) "Sociology: Its Problems and Its Relations." ["This paper constitutes the first four chapters of a text in sociology which Professor Ellwood has in preparation."] *American Journal of Sociology* 13(3): 300–48.

Ellwood, Charles A. (1908) "Review of Jerome Dowd, *The Negro Races: A Sociological Study, Vol. 1.* (New York: Macmillan, 1907)." *American Journal of Sociology* 13(6): 855–8.

Ellwood, Charles A. (1909) "The Science of Sociology: A Reply [to Henry Jones Ford]." *American Journal of Sociology* 15(1): 105–10.

Faris, Robert E. L. (1967/70) *Chicago Sociology 1920–1932.* Chicago: University of Chicago Press.

Fiamingo, G. (1895) "Sociology in Italy: The Sociological Tendency of Today." *American Journal of Sociology* 1(3): 334–52.

Fine, Gary Alan (ed.) (1995) *A Second Chicago School? The Development of a Postwar American Sociology.* Chicago: University of Chicago Press.

Fine, William F. (1979) *Progressive Evolutionism and American Sociology 1890–1920.* Ann Arbor, MI: UMI Research Press.

Ford, Henry Jones (1909) "The Pretensions of Sociology." *American Journal of Sociology* 15(1): 96–104. [Response by Charles Ellwood in following pages.]

Ford, Henry Jones (1909) "The Claims of Sociology Examined." *American Journal of Sociology* 15(2): 244–59.

Galton, Francis (1904) "Eugenics: Its Definition, Scope and Aims." *American Journal of Sociology* 10(1): 1–6 (discussion with Karl Pearson, H. G. Wells, Benjamin Kidd, Lady Welby, Mr. Hobhouse, G. Bernard Shaw, W. Bateson, et al.: 7–25).

Giddings, Franklin Henry (ed.) ([1906] 1923) *Readings in Descriptive and Historical Sociology.* New York: Macmillan.

Giddings, Franklin Henry (1912) "The Quality of Civilization [ASS Presidential Address]." *American Journal of Sociology* 17(5): 581–9.

Gouldner, Alvin (1965) *Enter Plato: Classical Greece and the Origins of Social Theory.* New York: Basic Books.

Halsey, A. H. and W. G. Runciman (eds.) (2005) *British Sociology Seen from Without and Within.* Oxford: British Academy/Oxford University Press.

Hankins, F. H. (1931) "Franklin Henry Giddins, 1855–1931: Some Aspects of His Sociological Theory." *American Journal of Sociology* 37(3): 349–67.

Hardin, Bert (1977) *The Professionalization of Sociology: A Comparative Study, Germany – USA.* Frankfurt: Campus Verlag.

Henderson, C. R. (1896) "Business Men and Social Theorists." *American Journal of Sociology* 1(4): 385–97.

Henderson, C. R. (1896a) "Rise of the German Inner Mission." *American Journal of Sociology* 1(5): 583–95.

Henderson, C. R. (1896b) "The German Inner Mission. II. The Experimental Stage." *American Journal of Sociology* 1(6): 674–84.

Hinkle, Roscoe C. (1980) *Founding Theory of American Sociology 1881–1915.* Boston: Routledge & Kegan Paul.

Hinkle, Roscoe C. (1994) *Developments in American Sociological Theory 1915–1950.* Albany, NY: SUNY Press.

Hinkle, Roscoe C., Jr. and Gisela J. Hinkle (1954) *The Development of Modern Sociology: Its Nature and Growth in the United States.* New York: Random House.

House, Floyd (1926) "A List of the More Important Published Writings of Albion Woodberry Small." *American Journal of Sociology* 32(1): 49–58.

Howard, George Elliott (1908) "Is the Freer Granting of Divorce an Evil?" *Papers and Proceedings of the American Sociological Society* 3 (December): 150–60, plus discussion.

Jones, Robert Alun (1983) "The New History of Sociology." *Annual Review of Sociology* 9: 447–69.

Judson, Harry Pratt (1895) "Is Our Republic a Failure?" *American Journal of Sociology* 1(1): 28–40.

Keller, Albert G. (1903) "Sociology and Homer." *American Journal of Sociology* 9(1): 37–45.

Kurtz, Lester R. (1984) *Evaluating Chicago Sociology: A Guide to the Literature, with an Annotated Bibliography*. Chicago: University of Chicago Press.

Lundberg, George A., Read Bain, and Nels Anderson (eds.) (1929) *Trends in American Sociology*. New York: Harper and Brothers.

Lundberg, George A., Read Bain, and Nels Anderson (1931) "The Interests of Members of the American Sociological Society, 1930." *American Journal of Sociology* 37(3): 458–60.

Marx, Karl and Friedrich Engels (1975–2010) *The Marx/Engels Collected Works*. New York: International Publishers.

Mathews, Shailer (1895a) "Christian Sociology: Introduction." *American Journal of Sociology* 1(1): 69–78.

Mathews, Shailer (1895b) "Christian Sociology. I. Man." *American Journal of Sociology* 1(2): 182–94.

Mathews, Shailer (1895c) "Christian Sociology. II. Society." *American Journal of Sociology* 1(3): 359–80.

Mathews, Shailer (1896a) "Christian Sociology. III. The Family." *American Journal of Sociology* 1(4): 457–72.

Mathews, Shailer (1896b) "Christian Sociology IV. The State." *American Journal of Sociology* 1(5): 604–17.

Mathews, Shailer (1896c) "Christian Sociology V. Wealth." *American Journal of Sociology* 1(6): 771–84.

Matthews, Fred H. (1977) *Quest for an American Sociology: Robert E. Park and the Chicago School*. Montreal: McGill-Queen's University Press.

Meroney, W. P. (1931) "The Membership and Program of Twenty-Five Years of the American Sociological Society." *Publications of the American Sociological Society* 25: 55–67.

Mill, John Stuart and Auguste Comte (1995) *The Correspondence of John Stuart Mill and Auguste Comte*. Ed. Oscar Haac. New Brunswick, NJ: Transaction Publishers.

Muensterberg, E. (1897) "Principles of Public Charity and Private Philanthropy in Germany." *American Journal of Sociology* 2(4): 589–605; 2(5): 680–98.

Odenwald-Unger, Mrs. J. (1907) "The Fine Arts as a Dynamic Factor in Society." [Proceedings of the first ASS meeting.] *American Journal of Sociology* 12(5): 656–65 (comments by George Cooke, Lester Ward, Franklin Sargent, Charles Moore: 665–74).

Odum, Howard W. (1937) "The Errors of Sociology." *Social Forces* 15(3): 327–42.

Olson, Richard (1993) *The Emergence of the Social Sciences, 1642–1792*. New York: Twayne Publishers.

Page, Charles H. ([1940] 1969) *Class and American Sociology: From Ward to Ross*. New York: Schocken Books.

Parsons, Talcott (1937) *The Structure of Social Action*. New York: McGraw-Hill Publishers.

Porter, Theodore and Dorothy Ross (eds.) (2003) *The Cambridge History of Science*, Vol. 7, *The Modern Social Sciences*. Cambridge: Cambridge University Press.

Pritchett, Henry (1914) "Reasonable Restrictions upon the Scholar's Freedom." *Papers and Proceedings of the American Sociological Society* 9: 150–9.

Rafferty, Edward C. (2003) *Apostle of Human Progress: Lester Frank Ward and American Political Thought, 1841–1913*. Lanham, MD: Rowman and Littlefield.

Rice, Stuart A. (ed.) (1931) *Methods in Social Science: A Case Book*. Compiled under the Direction of the Committee on Scientific Method in the Social Sciences of the Social Science Research Council. Chicago: University of Chicago Press.

Ross, Dorothy (1993) "An Historian's View of American Social Science." *Journal of the History of the Behavioral Sciences* 29(2): 99–112.

Ross, Dorothy (ed.) (1994) *Modernist Impulses in the Human Sciences 1870–1930*. Baltimore, MD: Johns Hopkins University Press.

Ross, Edward Alsworth (1896) "Social Control." *American Journal of Sociology* 1(5): 513–35.

Ross, Edward Alsworth (1945) "Fifty Years of Sociology in the United States." *American Journal of Sociology* 50: 489–92.

Russell, Bertrand (1939) "The Role of the Intellectual in the Modern World." ["An Address to the Sociology Club at the University of Chicago."] *American Journal of Sociology* 44(4): 491–8.

Salmon, Lucy M. (1912) "Democracy in the Household." *American Journal of Sociology* 17(4): 437–57.

Schwendinger, Herman and Julia R. Schwendinger (1974) *The Sociologists of the Chair: A Radical Analysis of the Formative Years of North American Sociology (1883–1922)*. New York: Basic Books.

Shanas, Ethel (1945) "The *American Journal of Sociology* Through Fifty Years." *American Journal of Sociology* 50(6): 522–33.

Sica, Alan (1986) "Impulses in Sociological Thought." [Review-essay on Arthur Vidich and Stanford Lyman, *American Sociology*.] *Science* 229(4719): 1255–7.

Sica, Alan (1995) "A Sociology Archive and the Discipline's Future." *American Sociologist* 26(2): 70–7.

Sica, Alan (1997) "Acclaiming the Reclaimers: The Trials of Writing Sociology's History." In C. Camic (ed.), *Reclaiming the Sociological Classics*. Oxford: Blackwell, pp. 283–98.

Sica, Alan (1998) "The Dire Need for History: Amnesia and Sociology in the U.S." *Swiss Journal of Sociology/Schweizerische Zeitschrift für Soziologie* 24(2): 191–8.

Simmel, George (1977) *The Problem of the Philosophy of History: An Epistemological Essay*. Trans. Guy Oakes. New York: Free Press.

Simmel, George (1990) *The Philosophy of Money*, 2nd edn. Trans. David Frisby. London: Routledge.

Small, Albion (1895) "Static and Dynamic Sociology." *American Journal of Sociology* 1(2): 195–209.

Small, Albion (1896) "Scholarship and Social Agitation." *American Journal of Sociology* 1(5): 564–82.

Small, Albion (1897) "Review of Herbert Spencer, *The Principles of Sociology*, Vol. III." *American Journal of Sociology* 2(5): 741–2.

Small, Albion (1897) "Review of Frank Wilson Blackmar, *The Story of Human Progress*." *American Journal of Sociology* 2(5): 745–6.

Small, Albion (1897) "Some Demands of Sociology upon Pedagogy." *American Journal of Sociology* 2(6): 839–51.

Small, Albion (1900) "The Scope of Sociology. I. The Development of Sociological Method." *American Journal of Sociology* 5(4): 506–26.

Small, Albion (1903) "What Is a Sociologist?" *American Journal of Sociology* 8(4): 468–77.

Small, Albion (1905) "A Decade of Sociology." *American Journal of Sociology* 11(1): 1–10.

Small, Albion (1907) "Points of Agreement Among Sociologists." [Proceedings of the first ASS meeting.] *American Journal of Sociology* 12(5): 633–49 (with comments by James Hagerty, J. Q. Dealey, and E. C. Hayes: 649–55).

Small, Albion (1908) "The Meaning of Sociology." *American Journal of Sociology* 14(1): 1–14.

Small, Albion (1909) "The Vindication of Sociology." *American Journal of Sociology* 15(1): 1–15.

Small, Albion (1910) "The Sociological Stage in the Evolution of the Social Sciences." *American Journal of Sociology* 15(5): 681–97.

Small, Albion (1913) "The Present Outlook of Social Science. Presidential Address [American Sociological Society]." *American Journal of Sociology* 18(4): 433–69.

Small, Albion (1921) "Evolution of Sociological Consciousness in the United States." *American Journal of Sociology* 27(2): 226–31.

Small, Albion and Lester F. Ward (1933/1935) "The Letters of Albion W. Small to Lester F. Ward." Ed. Bernhard J. Stern. *Social Forces* 12(2): 163–73; 13(3): 323–40.

Smith, Roger (1997) *The Norton History of the Human Sciences*. New York: W. W. Norton.

Sorokin, Pitirim (1928) *Contemporary Sociological Theories*. New York: Harper and Brothers.

Spencer, Herbert (1882–9) *Principles of Sociology*, 3 vols. London: Williams and Norgate.

Sumner, William Graham (1909) "The Family and Social Change." *American Journal of Sociology* 14(5): 577–91.

Thomas, William Isaac (1907) "The Significance of the Orient for the Occident." *Publications of the American Sociological Society* 2: 111–24 (plus discussion, through 137).

Thon, O. (1897) "The Present Status of Sociology in Germany." Trans. Albion Small. *American Journal of Sociology* 2(4): 567–88.

Thon, O. (1897) "The Present Status of Sociology in Germany. II." Trans. Albion Small. *American Journal of Sociology* 2(5): 718–36.

Thon, O. (1897) "The Present Status of Sociology in Germany. III." Trans. Albion Small. *American Journal of Sociology* 2(6): 792–800.

Tolman, Frank L. (1902) "The Study of Sociology in Institutions of Higher Learning in the United States. A Report of an Investigation Undertaken by the Graduate Sociological League of the University of Chicago." *American Journal of Sociology* 7(6): 797–838.

Tolman, Frank L. (1902) "Part II." *American Journal of Sociology* 8(1): 85–121.

Tolman, Frank L. (1902) "Part III." *American Journal of Sociology* 8(2): 251–72.

Tolman, Frank L. (1903) "Part IV." *American Journal of Sociology* 8(4): 531–58.

Tucker, Robert (1961) *Philosophy and Myth in Karl Marx*. Cambridge: Cambridge University Press.

Tufts, James H. (1896) "Recent Sociological Trends in France." *American Journal of Sociology* 1(4): 446–56.

Vandenberghe, Frédéric (2009) *A Philosophical History of German Sociology*. Trans. Carolyn Shread. London: Routledge.

Veditz, C. W. A. (1906) "The American Sociological Society." [Announcement of organizational meeting, December 1905, Baltimore.] *American Journal of Sociology* 11(1): 681–2.

Vincent, George E. (1896) "The Province of Sociology. Syllabus of a Course Occupying Four Hours Per Week during Twelve Weeks: Given by the Author at the University of Chicago in the Autumn Quarter, 1895." *American Journal of Sociology* 1(4): 473–91.

Vincent, George E. (1904) "The Development of Sociology." *American Journal of Sociology* 10(2): 145–60.

Wallis, Louis (1908–11) "Biblical Sociology. I." *American Journal of Sociology* 14(2): 145–70; "Biblical Sociology. II." *American Journal of Sociology* 14(3): 306–28; "Biblical Sociology. III." *American Journal of Sociology* 14(4): 497–533; "Biblical Sociology. IV." *American Journal of Sociology* 15(2): 214–43; "Biblical Sociology. V." *American Journal of Sociology* 16(3): 392–419; "Biblical Sociology. VI." *American Journal of Sociology* 17(1): 61–76; "Biblical Sociology. VII." *American Journal of Sociology* 17(3): 329–50. (Reissued as *The Sociology of the Bible*. Chicago: University of Chicago Press, 1912.)

Ward, Lester F. (1895) "Contributions to Social Philosophy. II. Sociology and Cosmology." *American Journal of Sociology* 1(2): 132–45.

Ward, Lester F. (1895) "Contributions to Social Philosophy. Sociology and Biology." *American Journal of Sociology* 1(3): 313–26.

Ward, Lester F. (1896) "Contributions to Social Philosophy. IV: Sociology and Anthopology." *American Journal of Sociology* 1(4): 426–33.

Ward, Lester F. (1896) "Contributions to Social Philosophy. V: Sociology and Psychology." *American Journal of Sociology* 1(5): 618–32.

Ward, Lester F. (1896) "Contributions to Social Philosophy. VI. The Data of Sociology." *American Journal of Sociology* 1(6): 738–52.

Ward, Lester F. (1896) "Contributions to Social Philosophy. VII. The Social Forces." *American Journal of Sociology* 2(1): 82–95.

Ward, Lester F. (1896) "Contributions to Social Philosophy IX. The Purpose of Sociology." *American Journal of Sociology* 2(3): 446–60.

Ward, Lester F. (1897) "Contributions to Social Philosophy. XI. Individual Telesis." *American Journal of Sociology* 2(5): 699–717.

Ward, Lester F. (1900) "Review-essay on Thorstein Veblen, *The Theory of the Leisure Class*." *American Journal of Sociology* 5(6): 829–37.

Ward, Lester F. (1902) "Contemporary Sociology. III." *American Journal of Sociology* 7(6): 749–62.

Ward, Lester F. (1909) "Ludwig Gumplowicz." *American Journal of Sociology* 15(3): 410–13.

Weber, Max (1946) *From Max Weber*. Trans. Hans Gerth and C. Wright Mills. New York: Oxford University Press.

Wells, D. Collin (1907) "Social Darwinism." [Proceedings of the first ASS meeting.] *American Journal of Sociology* 12(5): 695–708 (comments by Lester Ward, Carl Kelsey, William Allen, Mrs. Charlotte Perkins Gilman, G. W. Cooke, E. A. Ross; response by Wells: 709–16).

Windelband, Wilhelm (1893) *A History of Philosophy*. Trans. James H. Tufts. New York: Macmillan.

Wright, Carroll D. (1895) "Contributions of the United States Government to Social Science." *American Journal of Sociology* 1(3): 241–75.

Zetterberg, Hans L. (1956) *Sociology in the United States of America: A Trend Report*. Paris: UNESCO.

References

Anonymous (1894) "Spencer-Smashing at Washington." *Popular Science Monthly*, February: 856–7.

Anonymous (1906) "Organization of the American Sociological Society." *American Journal of Sociology* 11(4): 555–69.

Backhouse, Roger E. and Philippe Fontaine (eds.) (2010) *The History of the Social Sciences Since 1945*. Cambridge: Cambridge University Press.

Baker, Keith (ed.) (1976) *Condorcet: Selected Writings*. Indianapolis, IN: Bobbs-Merrill Corp.

Bannister, Robert C. (1979) *Social Darwinism*. Philadelphia, PA: Temple University Press.

Bannister, Robert C. (1987) *Sociology and Scientism: The American Quest for Objectivity, 1880–1940*. Chapel Hill, NC: UNC Press.

Bannister, Robert C. (2003) "Sociology." In Theodore M. Porter and Dorothy Ross (eds.), *The Cambridge History of Science*, Vol. 7, *The Modern Social Sciences*. Cambridge: Cambridge University Press, pp. 331–53.

Barnes, Harry Elmer (ed.) (1948) *An Introduction to the History of Sociology*. Chicago: University of Chicago Press.

Becker, Howard P. and Harry Elmer Barnes (1961) *Social Thought from Lore to Science*, 3rd edn., 3 vols. New York: Dover Publications.

Bernard, Luther L. and Jessie Bernard (1943) *Origins of American Sociology: The Social Science Movement in the United States*. New York: Thomas Y. Crowell.

Blasi, Anthony (ed.) (2005) *Diverse Histories of American Sociology*. Leiden: Brill.

Bühler, G. (trans.) (1886) *The Laws of Manu: Translated with Extracts from Seven Commentaries by G. Bühler*. Oxford: Clarendon Press.

Confucius (1893) *Confucian Analects, The Great Learning, and The Doctrine of the Mean*. Trans. and intro. James Legge. Oxford: Clarendon Press.

Duncan, David (1908) *The Life and Letters of Herbert Spencer*. London: Methuen.

Durkheim, Emile (1958) *Socialism and Saint-Simon*. Trans. Charlotte Sattler from the edition originally edited with an Introduction by Marcel Mauss. Ed. and intro. Alvin W. Gouldner. Yellow Springs, OH: Antioch Press.

Ellwood, Charles A. (1902) "Aristotle as a Sociologist." *Annals of the American Academy of Political Science* 19: 63–74.

Francis, Mark (2007) *Herbert Spencer and the Invention of Modern Life*. Ithaca, NY: Cornell University Press.

Furner, Mary O. (1975) *Advocacy and Objectivity: A Crisis in the Professionalization of American Social Science, 1865–1905*. Lexington, KY: University Press of Kentucky.

Gillin, John Lewis (1927) "The Development of Sociology in the United States." *Publications of the American Sociological Society* 21: 1–25.

Goffman, Erving (1959) *The Presentation of Self in Everyday Life*. Garden City, NY: Doubleday.

Halsey, A. H. (2004) *A History of Sociology in Britain: Science, Literature, and Society*. Oxford: Oxford University Press.

Haney, David Paul (2008) *The Americanization of Social Science: Intellectuals and Public Responsibility in the Postwar United States*. Philadelphia, PA: Temple University Press.

Haskell, Thomas L. (1977) *The Emergence of Professional Social Science: The American Social Science Association and the Nineteenth Century Crisis of Authority*. Urbana, IL: University of Illinois Press.

HIIK (Heidelberg Institute for International Conflict Research) (2009) Press Release: "Conflict Barometer 2009, December 15, 2009."

Hobbes, Thomas ([1651] 1994) *Leviathan or the Matter, Forme, and Power of a Commonwealth Ecclesiasticall and Civil*. Ed. Edwin Curley. Indianapolis, IN: Hackett Publishing Co.

House, Floyd (1936) *The Development of Sociology*. New York: McGraw-Hill Book Co., Inc.

Huff, Toby and Wolfgang Schluchter (eds.) (1999) *Max Weber and Islam*. New Brunswick, NJ: Transaction Publishers.

Igo, Sarah (2007) *The Averaged American: Surveys, Citizens, and the Making of a Mass Public*. Cambridge, MA: Harvard University Press.

Käsler, Dirk (1988) *Max Weber: An Introduction to His Life and Work*. Trans. Philippa Hurd. Oxford: Polity Press.

Khaldun, Ibn (1958) *The Muqaddimah: An Introduction to History*, 3 vols. Trans. Franz Rosenthal. New York: Bollingen Foundation/Pantheon Books.

Khaldun, Ibn (1967) *The Muqaddimah: An Introduction to History*. Trans. Franz Rosenthal. Ed. and abridged N. J. Dawood. Chicago: University of Chicago Press.

Lenzer, Gertrude (ed.) (1975) *Auguste Comte and Positivism*. New York: Harper & Row.

Lukes, Steven (1972) *Émile Durkheim, His Life and Work: A Historical and Critical Study*. New York: Harper and Row.

Machiavelli, Niccolo ([1517] 1882) *The Discourses*. In *The Historical, Political and Diplomatic Writings of Niccolo Machiavelli*, 4 vols. Trans. Christian E. Detmold. Boston: James R. Osgood and Company.

McCarthy, George E. (2003) *Classical Horizons: The Origins of Sociology in Ancient Greece*. New York: State University of New York Press.

McDonald, Lynn (1993) *The Early Origins of the Social Sciences*. Montreal: McGill-Queen's University Press.

McLellan, David (1973) *Karl Marx: His Life and Thought*. New York: Simon and Schuster.

Meek, Ronald L. (ed. and trans.) (1973) *Turgot on Progress, Sociology and Economics: A Philosophical Review of the Successive Advances of the Human Mind, on Universal History [and] Reflections on the Formation and the Distribution of Wealth*. Cambridge: Cambridge University Press.

Merton, Robert K. (1968) *Social Theory and Social Structure*, enlarged edn. New York: Free Press.

Montesquieu, Charles de Secondat ([1748] 1989) *The Spirit of the Laws*. Trans. and ed. A. Cohler, B. C. Miller, and H. S. Stone. Cambridge: Cambridge University Press.

Odum, Howard W. (comp.) (1927) *American Masters of Social Science: An Approach to the Study of the Social Sciences through a Neglected Field of Biography*. New York: Henry Holt and Co.

Odum, Howard W. (1951) *American Sociology: The Story of Sociology in the United States through 1950*. New York: Longmans, Green, and Co.

Page, Charles H. (1982) *A Lucky Journey: Fifty Years in the Sociological Enterprise*. Amherst, MA: University of Massachusetts Press.

Peel, J. D. Y. (1971) *Herbert Spencer: The Evolution of a Sociologist*. New York: Basic Books.

Pickering, Mary (1993) *Auguste Comte: An Intellectual Biography*, Vol. 1. Cambridge: Cambridge University Press.

Pickering, Mary (2009) *Auguste Comte: An Intellectual Biography*, Vols. 2 and 3. Cambridge: Cambridge University Press.

Rhoades, Lawrence J. (1981) *A History of the American Sociological Association 1905–1980*. Washington, DC: American Sociological Association (90-page pamphlet).

Ross, Dorothy (1991) *The Origins of American Social Science*. Cambridge: Cambridge University Press.

Saint-Simon, Claude-Henri, comte de (1966) *Oeuvres*, 6 vols. Paris: Anthropos; Geneva: Slatkine Reprints, 1977.

Shapin, Steven (2007) "Man with a Plan: Herbert Spencer's Theory of Everything." *The New Yorker*, August 13, 75–9.

Sica, Alan (1979) "Received Wisdom versus Historical Fact: On the Mutual Awareness of Weber and Pareto." *Journal of the History of Sociology* 1(2): 17–34.

Sica, Alan (1983) "Sociology at the University of Kansas, 1889–1983." *Sociological Quarterly* 24(4): 605–23.

Sica, Alan (1990) "A Question of Priority: Small at Chicago or Blackmar at Kansas?" *Social Thought and Research* 14(1/2): 1–12.

Sica, Alan (ed.) (2005) *Social Thought: From the Enlightenment to the Present*. Boston: Allyn and Bacon/Pearson Education.

Sica, Alan (2007) "Defining Disciplinary Identity: The Historiography of U.S. Sociology." In Craig Calhoun (ed.), *Sociology in America: A History*. Chicago: University of Chicago Press, pp. 713–31.

Simmel, George (1971) *George Simmel on Individuality and Social Forms*. Trans. Donald Levine. Chicago: University of Chicago Press.

Simmel, George (2009) *Sociology: Inquiries into the Construction of Social Forms*, 2 vols. Trans. and ed. Anthony J. Blasi et al. Leiden: Brill.

Small, Albion (1895) "The Era of Sociology." *American Journal of Sociology* 1(1): 1–15.

Small, Albion (1916) "Fifty Years of Sociology in the United States (1865–1915)." *American Journal of Sociology* 21(6): 721–864. (Reprinted with the *AJS* index to volumes 1–51 (1947), pp. 177–281.)

Small, Albion (1924) *Origins of Sociology*. Chicago: University of Chicago Press.

Spencer, Herbert (1904) *An Autobiography*, 2 vols. London: Williams and Norgate.

Spencer, Herbert ([1884] 1981) *The Man Versus the State: With Six Essays on Government, Society and Freedom*. Ed. Eric Mack. Intro. Albert Jay Nock. Indianapolis, IN: Liberty Classics.

Stern, Bernhard J. (1932) "Giddings, Ward, and Small: An Interchange of Letters." *Social Forces* 10(3): 305–18.

Stern, Bernhard J. (1933) "The Letters of Albion W. Small to Lester F. Ward: I." *Social Forces* 12(2): 163–73.

Stern, Bernhard J. (1935) "The Letters of Albion W. Small to Lester F. Ward: II." *Social Forces* 13(3): 323–40.

Stern, Bernhard J. (1936) "The Letters of Albion W. Small to Lester F. Ward: III." *Social Forces* 15(2): 174–86.

Stern, Bernhard J. (1937) "The Letters of Albion W. Small to Lester F. Ward: IV." *Social Forces* 15(3): 305–27.

Stern, Bernhard J. (1938) "The Ward-Ross Correspondence 1891–1896." *American Journal of Sociology* 3(3): 362–401.

Stern, Bernhard J. (1946a) "The Ward-Ross Correspondence II 1897–1901." *American Journal of Sociology* 11(5): 593–605.

Stern, Bernhard J. (1946b) "The Ward-Ross Correspondence II 1897–1901." *American Journal of Sociology* 11(6): 734–48.

Stern, Bernhard J. (1947) "The Ward-Ross Correspondence III 1902–1903." *American Journal of Sociology* 12(6): 703–20.

Stern, Bernhard J. (1948) "The Ward-Ross Correspondence III, 1904–1905." *American Journal of Sociology* 13(1): 82–94.

Stern, Bernhard J. (1949) "The Ward-Ross Correspondence IV, 1906–1912." *American Journal of Sociology* 14(1): 88–119.

Thucydides ([400 BCE] 1996) *The Landmark Thucydides: A Comprehensive Guide to the Peloponnesian War*. Ed. Robert B. Strassler. New York: Free Press.

Tiryakian, Edward (1966) "A Problem for the Sociology of Knowledge: The Mutual Unawareness of Each Other's Work." *Archives européennes de sociologie* 7: 330–6.

Tönnies, Ferdinand ([1887] 2001) *Community and Civil Society*. Trans. J. Harris and M. Hollis. Cambridge: Cambridge University Press.

Turner, Stephen (2007) "A Life in the First Half-Century of Sociology: Charles Ellwood and the Division of Sociology." In Craig J. Calhoun (ed.) *Sociology in America: A History*. Chicago: University of Chicago Press, pp. 115–154.

Turner, Jonathan, Leonard Beeghley, and Charles Power (1989) *The Emergence of Sociological Theory*, 2nd edn. Chicago: Dorsey Press.

Turner, Stephen Park and Jonathan H. Turner (1990) *The Impossible Science: An Institutional Analysis of American Sociology*. Newbury Park, CA: Sage Publications.

Veblen, Thorstein (1921) *The Engineers and the Price System*. New York: Viking Press.

Vidich, Arthur J. and Stanford M. Lyman (1985) *American Sociology: Worldly Rejections of Religion and Their Directions*. New Haven, CT: Yale University Press.

Wallas, Graham (1914) *The Great Society: A Psychological Analysis*. New York: Macmillan.

Ward, Lester F. (1895) "The Place of Sociology Among the Sciences." *American Journal of Sociology* 1(1): 16–27.

Ward, Lester F. (1907) "The Establishment of Sociology [includes excerpt from the First Presidential Address to the ASS, December 27, 1906]." *American Journal of Sociology* 12(5): 581–7.

Werth, Barry (2009) *Banquet at Delmonico's: Great Minds, the Gilded Age, and the Triumph of Evolution in America*. New York: Random House.

Wheen, Francis (1999) *Karl Marx: A Life*. New York: W. W. Norton.

Whyte, William (1956) *Organization Man*. New York: Doubleday.

Young, Cristobal (2009) "The Emergence of Sociology from Political Economy in the United States: 1880–1940." *Journal of the History of the Behavioral Sciences* 45(2): 91–116.

3

Quantitative Methods

Russell K. Schutt

It is hard to overemphasize the importance of quantitative methods in sociology and impossible to describe all of the specific methods that can reasonably be termed "quantitative." Given its importance and scope, it is tempting to enter the universe of quantitative methods and never look back, outside, or into the future. There is more than a lifetime of quantitative methods to review. But to ignore the history and philosophy of quantitative methods, to overlook current debates and emerging trends, is to fail to understand the nature of quantitative methods. By understanding how quantitative methods arose, what problems they have sought to solve and how well they have done so, and what new directions have emerged, we can better understand quantitative methods themselves. So before reviewing different quantitative methods and the problems they have both solved and overlooked, this essay will begin with a review of the history and philosophy of quantitative methods and an overview of the major goals and strategies by which quantitative methods can be distinguished. In addition, after reviewing specific techniques of each type, selected new developments will be considered.

History and Philosophy

Quantitative methods are a collection of techniques that rely on numbers to represent empirical reality and that presume a positivist philosophy in which it is presumed that the social world is knowable by observers who quantify its characteristics. Quantitative methods were part of sociology at its inception, infusing the discipline with the prevailing spirit of discovery and situating it within the historical advance of science. That advance can fairly be linked to the Renaissance, with its willingness to challenge prevailing orthodoxies and its spirit of discovery.

The Wiley-Blackwell Companion to Sociology, First Edition. Edited by George Ritzer.
© 2012 Blackwell Publishing Ltd. Published 2012 by Blackwell Publishing Ltd.

For the purpose of understanding the subsequent privileged role of quantitative methods in the advance of science, one event stands out above all others. With the development and (nearly) posthumous publication of his heliocentric theory of the solar system, Nicolaus Copernicus shattered the prevailing assumptions that either common sense or traditional beliefs were reliable guides to understanding the world in which we live (Tarnas 1991). Copernicus's *De Revolutionibus* ([1543] 1978), by contrast, demonstrated that years of careful quantitative measurement of the physical world and commitment to a theory that best explained those measurements could reveal fundamental principles about how the world operates – socially as well as physically – irrespective of the preferences of its human occupants (Adamczewski 1974).

It was not that Copernicus's theory immediately transformed understanding, for it was almost two centuries before religious opposition finally abated. What Copernicus succeeded in doing was to change the focus of debate about the physical world from what was most consistent with Church teachings or prevailing philosophies to what best predicted observable phenomena. The positivist spirit had triumphed; the Scientific Revolution had begun and quantitative methods were its foundation (Tarnas 1991: 248–71).

The equation of science with quantitative methods did not diminish for 300 years. Speaking to the Institution of Civil Engineers in London in 1883, William Thomson Kelvin explained:

> I often say that when you can measure what you are speaking about, and express it in numbers, you know something about it; but when you cannot measure it, when you cannot express it in numbers, your knowledge is of a meager and unsatisfactory kind; it may be the beginning of knowledge, but you have scarcely in your thoughts advanced to the state of Science, whatever the matter may be. (Scripture 1892: 127)

Sir Francis Galton translated Lord Kelvin's enthusiasm into a simple maxim for scientists: "Whenever you can, count" (Newman 1956: 1169). Social scientists were advised to resist the tendency "to rest contented with merely qualitative results where quantitative measurements could be made with the exercise of brains and patience" (Scripture 1892: 127).

Neither the triumph of the scientific worldview in the West nor its expression in quantitative methods was universal or permanent. Philosophers were troubled by the realization that human observations of the world could not be free of imposed conceptual judgments, that causal effects could not actually be observed (Tarnas 1991: 368). Certainty that empirical investigation in general and quantitative methods in particular could yield a verifiable understanding of the natural world also began to erode in the twentieth century due to the advance of science itself. Einstein's (1921) recognition of the interchangeability of matter and energy and of the relativity of space and time (Calder 1979), as well as Heisenberg's identification in the subatomic world of the impossibility of measuring simultaneously the position and momentum of a particle – the famous "uncertainty principle" – forever called into question the belief that quantitative measurement provides the necessary foundation for explaining natural phenomena (Reece 1977). Thomas Kuhn's (1970) reconceptualization of scientific progress as successive "revolutions" that overthrow prevailing paradigms further undermined the positivist belief that scientific methods were gradually increasing understanding of the world as it "really is."

These professional developments and philosophical debates both laid the foundation for quantitative methods in sociology and infused its subsequent construction. Two trends emerged. First, positivists continued to extend the reach of quantitative methods so as to describe an ever larger fraction of the social world in ways that reflected growing awareness of its complexity. Their efforts often took account of less quantifiable social phenomena and accepted a "post-positivist" assumption that the observations – including numbers – recorded by human beings inevitably will reflect to some extent the subjective orientations of the observers, but they remained committed to the core positivist belief in a knowable, objective external reality.

Relativist challenges to positivism encouraged some qualitative researchers to adopt an alternative "interpretivist" approach that focused on understanding the meanings people attached to their experiences and abjured the concept of an objective "real world." Quantitative methodologists rejected this trend, but some began to incorporate qualitative techniques, developing "mixed methods" that promised to yield greater insight into subjective as well as objective social phenomena.

GOALS AND STRATEGIES

Specific quantitative research methods can be classified by the primary goal they are designed to achieve and by the general strategy they employ.

Research goals

A positivist perspective on the social world privileges one paramount goal for quantitative research: to understand the external world as it "really" is. This is the goal of validity and it presumes that each methodological technique should be evaluated by its ability to reveal empirical phenomena without distortion. It has three aspects – measurement validity, generalizability, and causal validity – which themselves each subsume multiple quantitative techniques (Schutt 2009).

Measurement validity is achieved when data collected with the specified operational procedures reflect the empirical status of or variation in the phenomenon that the measure was designed to capture. Measurement validity is the cornerstone for quantitative methods, since unless the researcher has measured what he or she thinks has been measured, all analyses and statements based on those measures will mischaracterize empirical reality. Developing valid measurement begins with conceptualization – defining clearly what is meant by the term of interest – and then continues with operationalization – the process of specifying the operations that will yield empirical evidence of variation in a particular aspect of that concept.

Generalizations about findings based on a sample of observed units are valid if they apply to the larger population or collection of units about which they are made. Of course this aspect of validity is not a concern if we have collected data about every unit of interest and make no attempt to generalize findings about these units to some larger population. But this limited purpose is rarely the case in quantitative research. Whether they have collected data from a small group of college students, a large sample of employed persons, or a census of an entire nation, researchers usually want to draw conclusions about larger populations, a more complete collection of units, and sometimes other times and nations than those from which data were actually obtained. The likelihood of such generalizations being valid is related to the specific methods used.

Causal validity is achieved when conclusions about causal effects – what causes variation in the empirical phenomenon of interest – reflect the operation in empirical reality of the influence understood as causal. So, for example, the conclusion that receiving more education results in higher income would be causally valid if, among the persons studied, those who received more education earned higher income as a result. By contrast, the same conclusion would be invalid if higher parents' education led to higher respondents' education and to higher respondents' income, but higher respondents' education itself had no bearing on respondents' income once parents' education was taken into account.

Research strategies

Specific quantitative methods also differ in their research strategy. A *deductive* research project begins with a formal theory: a set of logically interrelated propositions about empirical reality. A specific hypothesis – a tentative statement about empirical reality involving the relations among two or more variables – is deduced from that theory and then tested. If the results of the test support the hypothesis, then the theory from which the hypothesis was deduced is considered to be on stronger ground. If the test does not support the hypothesis, then the theory from which the hypothesis was deduced is considered to have been weakened. This *hypothetico-deductive* mode of inquiry is considered by many to be the quintessential scientific method.

An *inductive* research project differs from a deductive project first and foremost in terms of its starting point. Inductive research begins with observations about empirical reality – observations that may include both empirical phenomena and relations between them. An explanatory framework is then induced from what has been observed. Many inductive research projects stop at this point, but some generate new propositions that are subsequently tested using a deductive strategy.

Purely *descriptive* research involves a more limited research strategy. If the goal of a research project is only to describe the empirical phenomena of interest, the project may be concluded when the phenomena of interest have been measured and the findings reported. No attempt is made to relate the observations to a general explanatory framework or even to evaluate the support for any specific predictions.

Although these three strategies can be viewed as alternatives, they may be combined in research projects. In fact, most quantitative research projects include an element of descriptive research, since what has been measured is often reported as a description of the setting and/or people studied. In addition, many quantitative projects designed with a deductive research strategy add an inductive component as the researchers try to make sense of unanticipated patterns they observe in their data.

SPECIFIC QUANTITATIVE METHODS

Specific quantitative methods are presented in the following sections in relation to the aspect of validity on which they focus. After the aspect of validity is introduced, the problem that achieving this aspect of validity poses for researchers is discussed and the traditional solution or solutions to this problem offered by specific quantitative methods are explained. Finally, new directions being taken to achieve the goal are highlighted. The new approaches often reflect more of an inductive strategy as compared to the deductive strategy underlying the traditional solutions.

Measurement

Quantitative measurement was a key element in the Scientific Revolution and many of that era's scientists as well as subsequent historians emphasized its singular importance: "it is possible that the deepest meaning and aim of . . . the whole scientific revolution of the seventeenth century . . . is just to abolish the world of the 'more or less,' the world of qualities and sense perception . . . and to replace it by the . . . universe of precision, of exact measures" (Koyré 1965: 4–5). Three hundred years after the Scientific Revolution, still associating a positivist philosophy with enthusiasm about quantitative measurement, Nobel laureate Max Planck declared, "An experiment is a question which science poses to nature, and a measurement is the recording of Nature's answer" (1949: 110).

Hubert M. Blalock, Jr. (1982: 7), one of sociology's foremost quantitative methodologists in the late twentieth century, tied sociological research methods directly to this tradition: "there is a sufficient number of commonalities so that we can hardly afford to throw away whatever success models may be available to us." He defined measurement as "the general process through which numbers are assigned to objects in such a fashion that it is also understood just what kinds of mathematical operations can legitimately be used, given the nature of the physical operations that have been used to justify or rationalize the assignment of numbers to objects" (Blalock 1982: 11).

The problem

It is at the point of measurement that fundamental differences between the physical and social sciences are most apparent. Whereas in the physical sciences, the properties of measured phenomena – whether atoms of carbon or cords of wood – are often homogeneous, key phenomena in the social sciences are notoriously variable – whether people in different cultures, or people in the same culture at different times. As a result, it cannot be assumed that a measure will perform in the same way across different studies. The complications that this measurement heterogeneity creates are legion (Blalock 1982: 17–20).

In practical terms, recognizing the challenge posed by the goal of measurement validity has meant focusing attention on the inability of the researcher to observe directly what he or she seeks to measure. The problem that this creates is represented in classical test theory as the difference between the variation captured by a specific measure and the underlying phenomenon – the true score or latent variable – that it is designed to measure. In algebraic form, this problem is captured as the size of the error term in the following classical equation:

$$\text{Observed Score} = \text{True Score} + \text{Error}$$

The larger the error term relative to the true score, the less the observed score tells us about the phenomenon of interest. Since there is no *a priori* way to distinguish the true score from the error component of an observed score, and since there are many sources of error, from systematic bias in response to misleading questions to random variation in response to unclear terms, improving and confirming measurement validity – that an observed score reflects what it is intended to measure (the true score) – becomes a central methodological concern (Viswanathan 2005).

In survey research, for example, to generate a quantitative measurement by asking a single question is to do what comes naturally in the course of conversation and thus to engage in what might seem an effortless task. Yet the inherent appeal of this straightforward measurement approach is also its Achilles' heel, for too many survey instruments are constructed without considering the many ways in which questions can be poorly constructed and the multiple adverse consequences of poor question design.

The problem with approaching the design of survey questions as if it was no more demanding than formulating conversational questions is that every survey respondent must interpret each survey question in the same way. If questions or their response choices include ambiguous words or phrases, or convey biased sentiments, the odds increase that different respondents will interpret them differently. The more heterogeneous the sample of survey respondents, the greater the problem is likely to be.

The solution

How can the size of the error term be reduced relative to that of the true score component in obtained measures? In survey research, question wording can be improved through pretesting strategies and systematic experimentation. Questions designed to measure the same concept can also be combined so that the resulting composite index scores represent better the corresponding latent trait, or true score.

Single questions

Pretesting methods can reveal problems with question wording and response choices. Simply asking experienced interviewers to administer a planned questionnaire to a small number of respondents similar to those to be included in a study can identify difficulties that cause hesitancy or confusion. A more systematic technique such as cognitive interviewing can reveal the extent to which potential respondents may adduce different meanings from key questions than the meanings intended by the researcher. In cognitive interviewing, the interviewer asks a question of one respondent and then probes with follow-up questions to elucidate the respondent's interpretation of the question and response choices (Schaeffer & Presser 2003: 82). Respondents may also be asked to "think aloud" as they answer questions in order to determine their mental operations as they formulate an answer.

Pretesting methods should result in greater question clarity through a process of successive refinement of question wording, but they are not a panacea for survey design. Research on cognitive interviewing and other pretesting methods indicates inconsistent results. There is no one method that seems most able to identify problems with questions and so there is no assurance that any particular method will eliminate most of the problems in question design or suggest changes that actually will improve the subsequent responses (Presser, Couper, Lessler, et al. 2004). Although much has been accomplished in improving methods of pretesting, progress continues to be inadequate.

Systematic experiments by Stanford's Jon Krosnick (1999) and others have advanced considerably awareness of the consequences of different ways of wording and organizing key questions and their response choices. The resulting improved guidelines range from choices for wording responses to achieve equal intensity intervals between them to cautions against using so-called Likert-style response choices ("strongly agree," "agree," "disagree," "strongly disagree") which elicit agreement bias and so lead to a 10–20 percent overestimate of the level of agreement.

Indexes

Writing clear and unambiguous questions is a sufficient challenge to provide limitless headaches for survey researchers. Nonetheless, it is only the starting point for concern when designing question-based measures. Single questions are simply not sufficient for measuring many of sociology's most important concepts. How satisfied are respondents with their marriage? To what extent are citizens alienated from conventional politics? What is the level of delinquency in a sample of juveniles? To what extent do respondents support abortion rights? For these and many other abstract concepts, no single question will suffice as an adequate measure.

An *index* combines responses to questions or other measures that are each indicators of a common concept. The logic of index construction from the standpoint of classical test theory is that a person's test (or index) score represents some combination of their true score, or value on the underlying latent variable, and an error component. Given assumptions about the error term (that errors will be normally distributed and independent of each other and the true scores), the more items included in an index, the more the errors will cancel each other out and the closer the average score will be to the subject's true score (Viswanathan 2005: 16–18).

The traditional solution to the problem of measurement can end at this point, following the construction of a multi-question index with a test for the measure's reliability – a test-retest evaluation or an inter-item correlation test – and for its validity, using a criterion validation or a construct validation approach (Schutt 2009: 132–41). However, index construction often includes an inductive stage in which the researcher analyzes inter-item correlations for evidence of multiple dimensions within the index. For example, an index measuring job satisfaction may include some questions that focus on intrinsic sources of satisfaction and so are more highly inter-correlated and other questions that focus on extrinsic sources of satisfaction. Different approaches to identifying subdimensions include exploratory factor analysis, multidimensional scaling, and cluster analysis (Jacoby 1991).

New directions

Classical test theory provides a conceptual framework within which measures can be developed, tested, and refined. Such work continues to dominate measurement textbooks, research protocols, and review standards. However, belief in the value of Classical Test Theory (CTT) rests on acceptance of the reasonableness of its assumptions. With respect to the error term, these assumptions require that the expected value of the error terms is zero, that they are uncorrelated with the true scores, that they are uncorrelated over successive observations, and that they are uncorrelated with all other variables in whatever system of equations is being investigated (such as a multiple regression model) (Blalock 1982: 31). Are these assumptions reasonable? Some investigators have concluded that they are not and so have turned to alternative approaches. The most prominent alternative approach is item response theory (IRT), with Rasch models as the most common such technique (Embretson & Hershberger 1999).

IRT focuses attention on differences between items in a test or index. Rather than treating all items as equivalent and creating a total score by adding them together, IRT distinguishes items in terms of their difficulty with respect to the latent trait that is being measured. The expectation is that fewer respondents will be able to pass more difficult items (or, similarly, fewer respondents will answer positively to items at a more extreme position on the underlying trait). Estimating a respondent's trait level thus depends on the characteristics of the items included in a test or index.

If items can be graded by their difficulty, testing can then be made more efficient by varying the items presented depending on responses to preceding items. There is no point in asking more "easy" questions of a respondent who has already answered a more difficult question; more accurate measurement will come from presenting such a respondent with more questions that are difficult to answer. Conversely, presenting difficult questions to a respondent who has difficulty answering easier questions is pointless (Embretson & Hershberger 1999: 9–10).

Computerized testing facilitates measurement based on IRT principles by making it easier to use adaptive testing, in which the presentation of items varies with responses to preceding items. As a result, fewer questions can be asked yet still provide a reliable assessment of the respondent's level on the latent trait. In contrast to CTT, which leads to the conclusion that longer tests are more reliable, shorter IRT-based tests can be more reliable because items are selected at the appropriate difficulty level for respondents. A related contrast is that while CTT presumes that test parallelism is required for comparing test scores across multiple forms, IRT presumes that different forms of a test developed through adaptive testing and administered to persons with different levels of a trait will maximize testing accuracy (Embretson & Hershberger 1999: 11–14).

The logic of IRT also suggests that the difficulty level of items within a test (or index) can be determined by the fraction of respondents who answer correctly (or in one direction). This in turn makes it possible to specify the numerical difference in difficulty between any two items, thus measuring the variation in true scores in terms of an interval scale. For example, Woodcock (1974) constructed a "word recognition ruler" using IRT principles. Words on a reading mastery test can be placed on this ruler and compared in standard intervals in terms of difficulty:

"away" is one unit less difficult than "drink," while "equestrian" is two units more difficult (Wright 1999).

IRT focuses attention on the possibility of differential functioning of items between different populations and provides a means for identifying such differences. As an example, Rania Tfaily (2010) estimated the extent to which different questions about the acceptability of family dissolution were understood differently by respondents of different gender, ethnicity, and nationality in 56 communities in South and Southeast Asia. Wives and then husbands were asked whether a husband (and then wife) is justified in leaving his wife given conditions ranging from infertility to infidelity. Statistical analysis identified several items as lacking measurement equivalence for respondents across regions and nations. The seriousness of behaviors like alcoholism or infidelity was viewed differently by respondents in some countries and with respect to wives compared to husbands, even among those with the same trait level (acceptance of family dissolution). Items about such behaviors should not be used in cross-country comparative studies with the assumption that their meaning is constant.

The IRT approach to measurement design thus reflects an inherently inductive strategy, in which the methodologist learns from research how to construct an efficient instrument and how to alter that instrument for different contexts.

Generalization

Quantitative methods begin with measurement and it might be said that they end with generalization. The best measures are of little use if the descriptions they provide cannot be generalized to the people, groups or other entities about which the researcher had hoped to learn. Of course if it were possible to measure every entity of interest, there would be no need to consider methods for improving researchers' ability to generalize their findings, but that is rarely – and, practically speaking, never – the case.

The problem

We need go no further than the US Constitution to begin to understand the problem. The decennial census is mandated by article 1, section 1 of the Constitution of the United States of America; it is planned and administered by a massive government agency, citizens are legally required to complete their census form, and there are tangible benefits to census completion in the resulting allocation of government services and political representatives. Yet in the 2010 US Census, only 67 percent of US households returned their mailed census form, leaving the rest of the population's participation to be elicited by 635,000 temporary workers (US Census Bureau 2010). In 2000, a comparable army of employees missed an estimated 3.3 million persons, compared to 281.4 million who were counted (ESCAP, US Census Bureau 2001). It is not certain what the future holds: the mailback response rate declined from 78 percent in 1970 to 65 percent in 1990, but regained some of that lost ground due to an extensive mobilization campaign in Census 2000 (Hillygus, Nie, Prewitt & Pals 2006: 20).

If the $4.5 billion spent to count almost every person in the 2000 US Census – about $15 per person – still leaves some uncertainty about generalizability to groups that fail to respond at high rates, what can researchers do who have only a tiny fraction of the resources of the US government at their disposal (Gauthier 2002: A1)? One response is to rely on Census data itself when planning analyses of sociological research questions. This is a very reasonable option for those whose research questions can be addressed with Census data, and there are also many datasets available for reanalysis from other government and private data collection efforts (Schutt 2009: ch. 13). However, in the usual circumstance when new data must be collected to answer previously unaddressed questions or to study different populations, researchers must rely on samples – subsets of the population – to which they can devote many more resources in order to achieve a higher rate of response.

The solution

The methodology of random sampling and associated statistics provides a means both for selecting a sample that is likely to be representative of the population from which it was selected and for estimating how probable it is that findings obtained with the sample are true for the larger population. A truly random sampling process results in the selection of cases without bias from the population of interest. In other words, each element in the population has an equal probability of selection in a simple random sample: no particular types of elements are more or less likely to be selected. More complex sampling strategies may involve stratifying the population in terms of key characteristics, such as income or race, and then sampling randomly within strata in order to ensure appropriate representation of each stratum, or sampling first clusters of elements, such as states, cities or blocks, and then sampling elements within those clusters. These strategies may be combined and they may be adjusted so as to over-represent within a sample elements in relatively small strata or clusters, but even in these samples the probability of selection of each element is known and can be adjusted *ex post facto* to yield a representative sample of the larger population.

Mastering the methods of probability-based sampling is the most important step to achieve generalizable results, but three problems remain. First, random selection of elements from a population will not itself produce a representative sample if many of those elements decline to participate in the survey or otherwise are unavailable to the researcher. Second, the method of statistical inference allows estimation of the odds that a statistical finding is due to chance, but it can be and is frequently misunderstood and misused. Third, researchers often seek to generalize beyond the population from which their samples were drawn and so the methods of statistical inference do not apply.

The problem of survey nonresponse is a major impediment to confident generalization of results obtained with an otherwise randomly selected sample. A typical mailed survey will elicit at best a response from 30 percent of the selected respondents, unless extensive follow-up efforts are made with nonrespondents and the survey is designed to exacting specifications so that it is clear, attractive, and credible. Phone surveys used to elicit a much higher rate of response, but the growth of cell phone-only households, the use of answering machines and caller ID as screening devices, and the negative penumbra emanating from excessive telemarketing have combined to drastically reduce the telephone survey response rate: from 80 percent in 1979 to 60 percent in 2003 for the general population, and from 35 percent in 1990 to 20 percent in 2006 among those aged 18 to 34 years (Keeter 2008; Rainie 2010). Response rates remain high for in-person interview studies, but costs are prohibitive for all but well-funded projects.

Once data have been collected with a probability sampling strategy and a reasonable response rate achieved, the process of statistical inference begins with the recognition that the value of a statistic calculated with the obtained sample – such as a mean (arithmetic average) – is only one of an infinite number of values for the statistic that would have been obtained if random samples were selected from the population, *ad infinitum* (presuming replacement of all elements back to the population after each random sample is drawn). Just by chance, some of these sample statistics will have a value close to the true value of the statistic in the population – the population parameter – and others will be far from that value. The hypothetical distribution of all possible values of a statistic for samples of a particular size is termed a sampling distribution.

Recognition of the inherent uncertainty in knowing that a sample statistic comes from an unknown point on a sampling distribution would paralyze efforts to generalize from random samples were it not for the discovery that the sampling distribution for each statistic with a sample of a particular size has a characteristic, and knowable, shape. For the mean and many other statistics, that shape is a normal distribution. Since the normal distribution has a known shape and properties – particularly, the area under the normal curve is invariant with respect to multiples of the sampling distribution's standard deviation (termed the "standard error") and the standard error decreases as sample size increases – knowing that the sample statistic comes from a distribution of known shape means knowing a lot. Armed with this knowledge, a statistician can then estimate the degree of confidence that can be placed in an estimate that the population parameter falls within a particular range of values. Thus does a statistical description of a sample become a generalization to a population: "We can be 95 percent confident that the mean level of anxiety in the population is between 3.7 and 5.2." Bertrand Russell (1962: 63–4) expressed the paradoxical result: "Although this may seem a paradox, all exact science is dominated by the idea of approximation. When a man tells you that he knows the exact truth about anything, you are safe in inferring that he is an inexact man. Every careful measurement in science is always given with the probable error . . . every observer admits that he is likely to be wrong, and knows about how much wrong he is likely to be."

A similar inferential process occurs when statistics are compared between two or more groups, or in fact whenever a statistic is used to characterize the relationship between two or more variables. Could the difference in means between two (or more) groups have been due to chance? Could the increasing average income that was observed as the average level of education increased have been a chance association?

Tests of significance are used to answer such questions. They proceed in three stages: first, specify what a truly random process would produce, such as no divergence between the means of two groups. Second, calculate a statistic capturing the difference between that result and what was actually obtained (such as a difference of 17.5 between the two groups rather than a difference of 0). Third, locate the value of the obtained statistic on the sampling distribution for that statistic (given the number of cases and the variability of the sample) and determine how likely it is that the obtained value of the statistic could have diverged as much as it did from the value expected on the basis of chance. Seeking to avoid a rush to the conclusion that a difference – that is, "something" – has been found, quantitative methodologists have settled on a convention that a difference is not considered "statistically significant" unless it is likely to have occurred on the basis of chance no more than five times in 100. However, even when used appropriately, inferential statistics cannot support generalizations to populations that have not been sampled: a study of students at one school cannot be generalized with any knowable degree of confidence to all students, nor a sample of residents of one city to all urban residents, or a sample from one nation to all nations. Perhaps the results in such situations are generalizable in the way desired, but that possibility cannot be estimated from the sample results themselves.

New directions

One might easily conclude, after reading many (although not all) quantitative research articles, that that is all there is to it. In other words, once the data analyst knows whether the possibility that a given result is due to chance can safely be rejected, the story is finished. We conclude that there is (or is not) a difference between two means, a relationship between two variables, perhaps a divergence between two trend lines. But such a result, stopping with the establishment (or not) of statistical significance, is a mistake. To maintain a singular focus on whether an effect "exists" in the probabilistic sense while ignoring the magnitude of that effect is to neglect substantive results and turn sociology and other social sciences into a "sizeless science." "To cease measuring *oomph* [or effect size; emphasis added] and its relevant sampling and nonsampling error is to wander off into probability spaces, forgetting – commonly forever – that your interest began in a space of economic or medical or psychological or pharmacological [or sociological] significance" (Ziliak & McCloskey 2008: 9). Growing recognition of the problem of overlooking the strength of relationships in quantitative research has led to more attention to "effect size" statistics – standardized estimates of the amount of change or difference (Lipsey & Wilson 2001).

New directions are also being charted in the effort to improve survey participation rates. As the percentage of households without internet access continues to drop (it was about one-quarter of households in the US in 2009), web-based surveys have become an increasingly attractive alternative to phone and mailed designs (Rainie 2010). The most rigorous web-based survey method involves samples of respondents who are recruited at the household level without regard to internet access and then provided with a free computer and internet access if they are not already connected (Couper 2000; Heeren, Edwards, Dennis, Rodkin, Hingson & Rosenbloom 2008). Internet-based surveys of populations in which internet use is almost universal, such as college students, can also be very successful (Dillman 2007). The increasing numbers of international surveys and the growing number of available datasets collected in diverse countries are improving the possibilities for research whose results can be generalized beyond traditional boundaries.

Causation

The central task of science is to explain how the natural world works and many quantitative methodologists in sociology accept this same causal mandate to guide their research and theorizing. More specifically, quantitative researchers develop and test "nomothetic causal explanations," in which a common influence is identified on variation in some phenomenon across a number of cases. From this standpoint, a causal effect occurs when variation in an independent variable is followed by variation in a dependent variable, *ceteris paribus* (all else being equal). Learning how to formulate hypotheses positing causal influences of an independent variable on a dependent variable is an essential part of any sociology research methods course.

The problem

What makes establishing causal effects a challenge – and even an impossibility, from the perspective of some philosophers of science – is the stipulation that a causal effect has only been identified when all else that might have caused variation in the phenomenon of interest is equal. This *ceteris paribus* assumption presumes a "counterfactual" situation that can only exist hypothetically. Whatever the posited cause of an outcome, the other circumstances associated with its occurrence cannot be replicated in exactly the same place, at exactly the same time, with exactly the same people, but now without that cause being present.

Lacking a perfect counterfactual comparison, most quantitative methodologists accept a causal assertion as being justified if the evidence meets three criteria: *association* – there must be an association between the presumed cause and effect; *time order* – variation in the presumed cause must occur prior to the variation in its presumed effect; *non-spuriousness* – the variation in the effect must not be due to some influence other than the presumed cause. The extent to which each of these criteria can be met is determined by the research design and the statistical procedures used to analyze data collected with that design.

The solution

Experimental design is widely accepted as the "gold standard" for meeting the three criteria for confirming a causal effect. In a true experimental design, two (or more) groups are assigned to receive different levels of the independent variable, or hypothesized cause (often treatment compared to no treatment), and after the treatment their scores are measured on the dependent variable of interest. Thus, the criterion of an association between the presumed cause and effect can be achieved. Scores on the dependent variable are measured in the different groups both before and after the treatment, thus allowing determination of whether the criterion of time order has been met. Most importantly, cases are assigned randomly to the two (or more) groups, thus allowing confidence that nothing but chance has influenced the value of the independent variable experienced by each case – thus ensuring (within a margin of statistical error) that there is no "selection bias" in assignment to the groups, so any association found between the independent variable and the dependent variable is not spurious due to the effect of some preexisting difference between the groups.

Of course many sociological hypotheses that involve causal relationships cannot be tested with a true experiment. People cannot be randomly assigned to a race or gender, or to have a specific income or to have been abused as children. In lieu of control for potential sources of spuriousness through experimental design, quantitative methodologists often turn to survey designs and multivariate statistical analyses to reduce the threat of spuriousness. The basic approach is to measure the other variables that may affect the causal relation of interest and then to hold variation in these variables constant while testing the relationship between the independent variable of interest and the dependent variable.

There are many multivariate statistical techniques that can be used for this purpose, with their appropriateness depending on the particular characteristics of the variables and the specific analytic problem. Multiple regression analysis is the most widely used multivariate statistical approach in sociology and it is the foundation for many more advanced techniques.

New directions

As quantitative methods for identifying causal effects, both experimental design and multivariate statistics have been extended with approaches that focus on two additional factors in addition to the three traditional criteria for establishing causality: causal mechanism and causal context. Causal mechanism can be defined as the process by which a treatment has its effect on a dependent variable, and with respect to experimental research it is often termed "opening the black box" of the treatment–outcome relationship. For example, reanalysis of qualitative observational data collected in the experimental study by Sherman and Berk (1984) of the police response to domestic violence allowed them to identify how police officers' interactions with the suspect influenced the extent to which the "treatment" imposed by the police officer (arresting or warning the suspect) changed the suspect's likelihood of reoffending (Paternoster, Brame, Bachman & Sherman 1997).

The effect of context can be evaluated in experimental research by replicating an experiment in diverse contexts. Again, the Sherman and Berk research provides a useful example. In order to determine whether the beneficial effect on recidivism of mandatory arrest in cases of domestic violence occurred in other contexts, the original study in Minneapolis was replicated in five other cities (Sherman 1992). The disparate results obtained made it clear that requiring arrest rather than less severe punishment in domestic violence cases did not have a consistent effect on recidivism. Thus, this variation in police practices could not be understood as by itself a cause of variation in recidivism; other conditions had to be met.

"Intervening variable" is the term used in multivariate statistics for what is called "causal mechanism" in experimental research. In multivariate non-experimental studies, the effort to identify variables that transmit a causal effect from an independent to a dependent variable can lead to complex causal models in which one or more paths of influence are proposed and then statistically tested. Path analysis apportions correlations between hypothesized causal variables between direct paths that lead to one or more dependent variables and indirect paths through hypothesized intervening variables to those same dependent variables. Structural equation modeling proposes latent variables to capture the shared variation between multiple indicators and then tests the relations between these latent variables (Goldberger & Duncan 1973).

Multilevel modeling, or hierarchical linear models, is an increasingly popular multivariate statistical method that takes account of clustering of individuals within groups and improves estimates of effects of context. The primary motivation for multilevel modeling is the realization that individuals who are clustered together in such units as schools, classes, or blocks will tend to be more similar to each other than to individuals in other such clusters. When a random sample of individuals is selected through a multistage process in which first the clusters and then individuals within the clusters are randomly sampled, this clustering must be taken into account when calculating significance tests (inferential statistics). If ordinary multiple regression analysis is used to estimate effects with such multilevel samples, the results can be totally misleading (Hox 1998).

Propensity score methods are also gaining in popularity as a quantitative approach to lessening the risk of selection bias in non-experimental research. An individual's propensity score is "the conditional probability of being treated given the individual's covariates" (D'Agostino 1998: 2265). The propensity score is calculated for each individual using discriminant analysis or logistic regression to estimate the likelihood that individuals would be in the treatment group or control group based on their characteristics ("covariates"). Once the propensity scores are calculated, they can be used to equate individuals in the treatment and control groups using techniques such as matching pairs of cases in the two groups or controlling for the propensity scores in a regression analysis. The result can be a closer equivalence of the treatment and control groups than otherwise is obtained, with a concomitant reduction of the risk of spurious conclusions about the treatment effect. However, the propensity score can only take into account potential influences on treatment selection that have been measured, so it is not a substitute for careful design of the original research.

CONCLUSIONS

Quantitative methods continue to play a central role in sociological research, but without the unfettered adulation of quantification that characterized the Scientific Revolution and much of American sociology in the early to mid-twentieth century. Increasingly sophisticated approaches have been developed in response to recognition of the limitations of what previously were considered to be adequate solutions to research problems. Recognition of non-homogeneity of measured units is increasing attention to item response theory as a guide in quantitative measurement; the limitations of tests of statistical significance fuel growing attention to effect size statistics; awareness of the inherent ambiguity of causal assertions has resulted in greater attention to causal mechanisms and causal context; evidence of misleading results due to common violations of multivariate statistical assumptions has led to greater use of multilevel modeling and other more sophisticated analytic techniques.

The growth and formalization of qualitative research methods and greater acceptance of mixed methods have also infused quantitative methods with greater sensitivity to the importance of inductive research strategies and the potential contribution of in-depth qualitative data for improving measures and specifying causal influences (Clark & Creswell 2008).

Increasingly powerful computational facilities, more sophisticated statistical procedures, and the challenges of investigating an increasingly diverse and interconnected social world will continue to fuel these trends. There is no more hope in the twenty-first century than there was in the twentieth that quantitative methods in general or statistics in particular will provide the key envisioned by Florence Nightingale to "the plan of God" (McDonald 2003: 74), but it is certain that they will continue to enrich sociology's contributions to understanding the social world.

References

Adamczewski, Jan (1974) *Nicolaus Copernicus and his Epoch*. In cooperation with Edward J. Piszek. New York: Scribner.

Blalock, Hubert M., Jr. (1982) *Conceptualization and Measurement in the Social Sciences*. Beverly Hills: Sage.

Calder, Nigel (1979) *Einstein's Universe*. New York: Viking Press.

Clark, Vicki L. Plano and John W. Creswell (2008) *The Mixed Methods Reader*. Thousand Oaks, CA: Sage.

Copernicus, Nicholas ([1543] 1978) *Nicholas Copernicus Complete Works*, Vol. II, *Nicholas Copernicus On the Revolutions*. Ed. Jerzy Dobrzycki. Trans. with commentary Edward Rosen. Warsaw-Cracow: Polish Scientific Publishers.

Couper, Mick P. (2000) "Web Surveys: A Review of Issues and Approaches." *Public Opinion Quarterly* 64: 464–94.

D'Agostino, Ralph B., Jr. (1998) "Tutorial in Biostatistics: Propensity Score Methods for Bias Reduction in the Comparison of a Treatment to a Non-Randomized Control Group." *Statistics in Medicine* 17: 2265–81.

Dillman, Don A. (2007) *Mail and Internet Surveys: The Tailored Design Method*, 2nd edn. Update with New Internet, Visual, and Mixed-Mode Guide. Hoboken, NJ: Wiley.

Einstein, Albert (1921) *Relativity: The Special and General Theory*. Trans. Robert W. Lawson. New York: Henry Holt.

Embretson, Susan E. and Scott L. Hershberger (eds.) (1999) *The New Rules of Measurement: What Every Psychologist and Educator Should Know*. Mahwah, NJ: Lawrence Erlbaum Associates.

Gauthier, Jason G. (2002) *Measuring America: The Decennial Censuses from 1790–2000*. Washington, DC: Department of Commerce, US Bureau of the Census.

Goldberger, Arthur S. and Otis Dudley Duncan (eds.) (1973) *Structural Models in the Social Sciences*. New York: Seminar Press.

Heeren, Timothy, Erika M. Edwards, J. Michael Dennis, Sergei Rodkin, Ralph W. Hingson, and David L. Rosenbloom (2008) "A Comparison of Results from an Alcohol Survey of a Prerecruited Internet Panel and the National Epidemiologic Survey on Alcohol and Related Conditions." *Alcoholism: Clinical and Experimental Research* 32: 222–9.

Hillygus, D. Sunshine, Norman H. Nie, Kenneth Prewitt, and Heili Pals (2006) *The Hard Count: The Political and Social Challenges of Census Mobilization*. New York: Russell Sage Foundation.

Hox, Joop (1998) "Multilevel Modeling: When and Why." In Ingo Balderjahn, Rudolf Mathar, and Martin Schader (eds.), *Classification, Data Analysis, and Data Highways*. New York: Springer Verlag, pp. 147–54.

Jacoby, William G. (1991) *Data Theory and Dimensional Analysis*. Thousand Oaks, CA: Sage.

Keeter, Scott (2008) "Survey Research and Cell Phones: Is There a Problem?" Presentation to the Harvard Program on Survey Research Spring Conference, New Technologies and Survey Research. Cambridge, MA: Institute of Quantitative Social Science, Harvard University, May 9.

Koyré, Alexandre (1965) *Newtonian Studies*. Cambridge, MA: Harvard University Press.

Krosnick, Jon A. (1999) "Survey Research." *Annual Review of Psychology* 50: 537–67.

Kuhn, Thomas (1970) *The Structure of Scientific Revolutions*, 2nd edn. Chicago: University of Chicago Press.

Lipsey, Mark W. and David B. Wilson (2001) *Practical Meta-Analysis*. Thousand Oaks, CA: Sage.

McDonald, Lynn (ed.) (2003) *Florence Nightingale on Society and Politics, Philosophy, Science, Education and Literature*. Waterloo, Ontario: Wilfrid Laurier University Press.

Newman, James R. (1956) "Commentary on Sir Francis Galton." In James R. Newman (ed.), *The World of Mathematics*, Vol. 2. New York: Simon and Schuster, pp. 1167–72.

Paternoster, Raymond, Robert Brame, Ronet Bachman, and Lawrence W. Sherman (1997) "Do Fair Procedures Matter? The Effect of Procedural Justice on Spouse Assault." *Law and Society Review* 31: 163–204.

Planck, Max (1949) *Scientific Autobiography and Other Papers*. Trans. Frank Gaynor. New York: Philosophical Library.

Presser, Stanley, Mick P. Couper, Judith T. Lessler, Elizabeth Martin, Jean Martin, Jennifer M. Rothgeb, and Eleanor Singer (2004) "Methods for Testing and Evaluating Survey Questions." *Public Opinion Quarterly* 68: 109–30.

Rainie, Lee (2010) *Internet, Broadband, and Cell Phone Statistics*. Pew Internet and American Life Project. www.pewinternet.org/~/media//Files/Reports/2010/PIP_December09_update.pdf (accessed June 24, 2010).

Reece, Gordon (1977) "In Praise of Uncertainty." In William C. Price and Seymour S. Chissick (eds.), *The Uncertainty Principle and Foundations of Quantum Mechanics: A Fifty Years' Survey*. New York: John Wiley and Sons, pp. 7–12.

Russell, Bertrand (1962) *The Scientific Outlook*. New York: Norton.

Schaeffer, Nora Cate and Stanley Presser (2003) "The Science of Asking Questions." *Annual Review of Sociology* 29: 65–88.

Schutt, Russell K. (2009) *Investigating the Social World: The Process and Practice of Research*, 6th edn. Thousand Oaks, CA: Pine Forge Press/Sage.

Scripture, E. W. (1892) "The Need of Psychological Training." *Science* 19: 127–8.

Sherman, Lawrence W. (1992) *Policing Domestic Violence: Experiments and Dilemmas*. New York: Free Press.

Sherman, Lawrence W. and Richard A. Berk (1984) "The Specific Deterrent Effects of Arrest for Domestic Assault." *American Sociological Review* 49: 261–72.

Tarnas, Richard (1991) *The Passion of the Western Mind: Understanding the Ideas That Have Shaped Our World View*. New York: Ballantine Books.

Tfaily, Rania (2010) "Cross-Community Comparability of Attitude Questions: An Application of Item Response Theory." *International Journal of Social Research Methodology* 13: 95–110.

US Census Bureau, ESCAP (2001) http://govinfo.library.unt.edu/cmb/cmbp/reports/final_ report/fin_sec3_evaluation.pdf

US Census Bureau (2002) Census 2000 Basics. www.census.gov/mso/www/c2000basics/ 00Basics.pdf

US Census Bureau (2010) "The Numbers Are In." www.census.gov/newsroom/releases/ archives/2010_census/cb10-cn61.html

Viswanathan, Madhu (2005) *Measurement Error and Research Design*. Thousand Oaks, CA: Sage.

Woodcock, Richard W. (1974) *Woodcock Reading Mastery Tests*. Circle Pines, MN: American Guidance Service.

Wright, Benjamin D. (1999) "Fundamental Measurement for Psychology." In Susan E. Embretson and Scott L. Hershberger (eds.), *The New Rules of Measurement: What Every Psychologist and Educator Should Know*. Mahwah, NJ: Lawrence Erlbaum Associates, pp. 65–104.

Ziliak, Stephen T. and Deirdre N. McCloskey (2008) *The Cult of Statistical Significance: How the Standard Error Costs Us Jobs, Justice, and Lives*. Ann Arbor, MI: University of Michigan Press.

4

Qualitative Methods

Mitchell Duneier

Within the field of sociology, qualitative methods tend to refer to ethnography, interviewing, and historical sociology. Ethnography involves an investigator's in-depth immersion in the world of the people he or she studies and delineates a relationship between what people say and what they do; interviewing – conducted over an extended period or on a one-shot basis – privileges actors' subjectivities and definition of the situation; and whereas ethnography and interviewing tend to rely on actors of the present moment, historical sociology mainly focuses on past events using written records contained in archives.

These three areas of research sometimes overlap (such as when historical sociologists use oral histories to get their data, or when interviewers live in a community and allow their ethnography to inform their questions), but on the whole they form distinct traditions and have different pivotal agendas. Historical sociologists tend to evaluate work on the basis of its success in making causal explanations on the basis of systematic comparisons. On the other hand, ethnographers and interviewers find that while the subjectivities they gain access to may help them to make valid causal claims, such claims are not the great strength of these methodologies and usually form the weakest parts of otherwise useful qualitative studies. Thus, it may be the case that due to differences in the priority given to causal understanding, historical sociology may be more akin to quantitative sociology, with interviewing and ethnography constituting the core areas of the qualitative tradition that is more distinct from quantitative sociology.

Qualitative modes of inquiry emerged in dialogue with more quantitative methods as the discipline of sociology made a transformation from being an almost completely theoretical field. From the turn of the nineteenth century to the publication

The Wiley-Blackwell Companion to Sociology, First Edition. Edited by George Ritzer.
© 2012 Blackwell Publishing Ltd. Published 2012 by Blackwell Publishing Ltd.

of W. I. Thomas's (1918–20) work on Polish immigrants, there was a lot of armchair speculating, and many notions were developed about how the world worked that were not really grounded in a great deal of evidence. But sometime around the 1920s in American sociology, largely at the University of Chicago, there developed a more intense commitment to the idea that these theoretical speculations were not enough, that sociology as a discipline needed to ground its concepts and theories in facts and data.

This goal for sociology was represented by two figures who were both professors at the University of Chicago: Robert Park and William Ogburn. Park was an ex-newspaper man before he became a sociologist. He had studied philosophy in Europe, but he had also worked for the *Minneapolis Star* as a reporter. His beliefs about how to make social research more scientific really came from a combination of those backgrounds. He was interested in developing theories, but he wanted those ideas to relate directly to the actual lives of people, and to be based on the careful accumulation of evidence about their lives. He told his students that they needed to get the seat of their pants dirty and wear out their shoes in real research. In other words, he was a believer in shoe leather as a means of discovering the truth.

Park thought that the most important thing for a sociologist was to go around the city, into all of the nooks and crannies, and find out what was going on by meeting the people who were the subjects of sociological theories. Following Park's lead, the University of Chicago's sociology department used the city as a laboratory. These early sociologists took on roles in the communities to see how they lived, they did interviews with them, and they did a great deal of firsthand observation. Their research reports tended to be highly systematic, well written, and oriented toward improving conditions in the city and the country.

At the same time, another prominent sociologist at the University of Chicago in that era was William Ogburn. He did not believe that the future of sociology could lie in shoe leather, in well-written books, in findings that could not be quantified, or in efforts to influence public policy. He believed that these aspirations were the domains of ethics, religion, journalism, and propaganda. In his 1929 presidential address to the American Sociological Society, he argued that sociology needed to become a science. The goal, he argued, was not "to make the world a better place to live," or to set forth "impressions of life" or "guiding the ship of state," but only "discovering new knowledge" (Ogburn 1930). Ogburn wanted sociology to be a much more boring discipline than it was in the work of Park. He wanted it to be a field that would look a lot more like the natural sciences in the way it was presented and the way it was oriented. Whereas Park had clear ideas about what the subject matter of sociology should be – immigration and the life of the city – Ogburn did not. He was much more focused on studying anything that could be measured with numbers.

These two figures – Park and Ogburn – coexisted at the University of Chicago for many years and both of them had a clear vision for what sociology could be. Whereas both were committed to the idea that sociology needed to be a science, this meant different things for each of them. For Park and his students, the up close, personal, emotional, and scientific side of sociology coexisted with the aspiration to develop explanations about the social world. These explanations needed to be in dialogue with the experiences of actual living, breathing human beings. The fundamental idea was to find out whether or not the things that we learn in interacting with people can help improve the dominant sociological theories about them.

Ever since Park and Ogburn sat at opposite ends of the Chicago department, there has always been a danger that the division between qualitative methods and quantitative could be too strongly marked. For many years, there was a division between scholars who were trained in statistics and others who were not; quantitative and qualitative sociologists believed their work was governed by completely different assumptions about how to study the social world. The two kinds of researchers looked with suspicion on one another. Within some departments, it was typical for scholars in different camps to persecute one another by holding up promotions or maintaining feuds and alliances that were determined by membership in the qualitative or quantitative camp. Alternatively, it was typical for departments to be strong in one or the other of the approaches. Thus, from 1950 to 1990, the Wisconsin sociology department was known as the premier center for quantitative methods, and departments like Santa Barbara and San Diego were known for their prowess in qualitative methods.

What a difference a few decades make! Today in the field of sociology, almost all students are trained in statistics and those interested in using methods that are not statistics-based go on to receive additional training. During the 1980s and 1990s, US sociology underwent a sea change such that departments like Santa Barbara became as well known for some of their quantitative research. Thus William Bielby, a sociologist of labor markets and culture who used statistical methods to study discrimination, served as chair of the UCSB department, and went on to become President of the American Sociological Association. Likewise, during the 1980s and 1990s, the demographers in the Wisconsin department made a conscious decision to diversify their famous quantitative faculty by hiring a number of people known for doing qualitative work. By the end of the first decade of the new century, a conversation analyst, Douglas Maynard, had served as chair at Wisconsin and nobody in US sociology thought that was strange.

A context for this transformation was the rise of postmodernism, an intellectual movement that rejected the possibility that "any of us can know an 'out there,' a real object of investigation existing apart from the systems of signification through which the world is described and understood" (Smith 1992: 498). In studying the social world, postmodernists believed there was no such thing as real facts of life and that the idea of science holding a mirror up to society to show how it works was nothing less than naïve. Science was not merely a way of revealing social relations (including power relations), but also a modality through which power is exercised. The rise of such concerns, particularly those elements that appeared to reduce "the terrain of knowledge and meaning in the social and human sciences" to "pure subjectivity" (Smith 1992: 499), may have had the effect of uniting quantitative and qualitative researchers who did not share these concerns as pivotal agenda. Thus, the attack on realism which came from postmodernism tended to make most qualitative and quantitative scholars feel they had something significant in common. A smaller subset of qualitative sociologists who embraced postmodernism remained outside of this consensus and tended not to have access to posts in the leading sociology departments. The result was that the postmodern critique was rendered more peripheral than it was in anthropology where it came to dominate ethnographic and historical studies.

To what extent has the emerging consensus been based on an idea that qualitative and quantitative methods have the same logic of inference? During the 1990s, King, Keohane, and Verba laid out this perspective in the influential *Designing Social Inquiry: Scientific Inference and Qualitative Research* (a book known as KKV), which would go on to become one of the most widely cited methodological statements on qualitative methods. According to these authors, the criteria for good research are the same for either type, and this view has come to be accepted by many researchers (especially quantitative researchers) who found KKV compelling.

King, Keohane, and Verba are political scientists, and though their work has been adopted by many sociologists, the concerns of the book are driven by the discipline of political science in which comparative historical work and historical case studies are the core of qualitative work, whereas ethnography and even interviewing are less central. As a result, KKV's emphasis on causal inference as the dominant agenda of good qualitative research may have greater application in political science than in sociology where the pivotal agenda of non-historical qualitative work is not necessarily the working out of causal mechanisms.

There are differences between interviewing and participant observation on the one hand, and quantitative sociology on the other. First, the fact of the former's contact with human subjects means that these methodologies are inherently at risk of being exploitative. Those who work with statistical data rarely have to worry that the people from whom the data are derived will feel manipulated or have a sense that the researcher has benefited at their expense. The subjects of qualitative research frequently live with memories of the way they were treated for years into the future. Part of the scientific imperative of qualitative research is an ethical dimension which quantitative researchers can easily sidestep.

Second, there is constant demand upon qualitative sociologists to be reflexive about their own social position, such that the grounds of their action are made explicit. While it is likely the case that such attentiveness would be beneficial to quantitative social science, it is not a normal part of quantitative studies. Whereas there is a tendency in quantitative studies for authors to let the data "speak for itself," the tendency in qualitative work is usually the opposite: making sure the lens through which the reality is refracted is made explicit. In a sense, this is one of a number of ways that qualitative researchers meet the demand upon quantitative researchers to be "public about procedures" (King, Keohane & Verba 1994).

Third, the possibility of investigator effects is a particular danger of qualitative research. Due to their contact with the subjects of their studies, interviewers and ethnographers must always be concerned about the possibility of bringing about the conditions they are trying to explain. This happens through leading questions, but it also occurs by spending long periods of time with subjects who can engage in behaviors in response to the fieldworker's presence. It is frequently very difficult for consumers of qualitative research to judge the extent to which this has occurred.

Fourth, whereas quantitative research has ways of being clear about uncertainty built into its confidence intervals, qualitative research has no agreed upon procedures for achieving such a sense on the part of readers.

Although quantitative research is also defined in contrast to qualitative research, the end of the age of conflict between the two styles was accompanied by a widespread belief that research that mixes quantitative and qualitative data has the potential to provide the special kind of understanding that occurs when biases of one method are highlighted and counterbalanced by the biases of a totally different method. Yet, this often repeated claim tends not to hold true much of the time. All too frequently, when one mixes the two kinds of work, one gets the kind of understanding that one would expect when the biases of one method are *reinforced* by the biases of a very similar method.

One typical procedure in such work is for an investigator to begin by using the things learned from large surveys to conduct in-depth structured interviews with a sub-sample of the original population, in some cases conducting multiple in-depth interviews with the very same people. In these interviews, the topics are predetermined on the basis of what is already known from the larger survey, where the topics were, in turn, predetermined on the basis of whatever the investigator thought was important (only in rare instances ethnography). In other words, whereas in the best qualitative research there are many things we don't know about but are told anyway (Becker 1996), in mixed method research of the type described here, the types of things we learn but did not know are of a very restricted kind – namely directly related to the statistical patterns of the larger survey. The procedure becomes one of cherry-picking quotations from statements by subjects about their personal experiences in order to illustrate the findings.

Many quantitative researchers who take this approach think that they are benefiting from qualitative data, but the first question they should ask themselves is whether the materials contain the kind of surprises that are the hallmark of an ethnographic encounter. Whereas the survey researcher or the experimenter has a pretty good idea of the kinds of things he or she will learn about by dint of a questionnaire, the ethnographer who puts him or herself in natural settings is going to be confronted by aspects of social life that he or she didn't ask about but learns about anyway. The point is that what makes ethnography particularly rigorous is that we do not "insulate" ourselves from data, but, by putting ourselves in the field for long stretches of time, we confront "surprise data, things you didn't ask about but were told anyway" (Becker 1996).

The second question a quantitative researcher using data in this way might ask is: when looking for quotations that support the quantitative findings, what is there in the interviews that the reader is not getting to see? Ethnographers know that if you spend enough time with subjects, they frequently say contradictory things, and what they say is heavily influenced by the questions that they are asked, as well as the stage in their life that they are at. Has the researcher cherry-picked a statement that illustrates the quantitative finding whereas later in the interview the subject said something contradictory? Does the researcher know the data well enough to make such a judgment, or was the quotation pulled from the document by a research assistant who was sent on a mission to find the relevant evidence? In collaborative research, was there a division of labor in which qualitative researchers pulled the quotes without all authors seeing the full transcript? With all the pages of interview transcripts generated, did anyone ever get to know the data well enough to understand all the contradictions? It is usually much simpler to find a quote that matches up with a predetermined finding than to depict the complexity that exists within the same groups or individuals.

Another important reason that mixed method work frequently makes it seem as though the biases of one method are reinforcing the biases of another is that the two methods which get mixed both rely on asking questions. In a sense, they are essentially the same. Ethnographers who rely on participant observation share with Oscar Lewis the fundamental concern that "the structured one shot interview does not give us some of the kinds of information that we sorely need [in low-income family research] . . . Right now . . . there is a crying need to be aware of – and to try to record and interpret – the complexity, change and variability in [low-income] family life and organization" (Lewis, quoted in Liebow 1968: 9). Within ethnography, for example, by contrast to the interview method, fieldwork seeks to make ghetto domestic life intelligible through observations of residents *in* the context of their kin- and non-kin-based networks. In the work of such scholars, unlike those who rely on surveys and interviews, one gets a sense that talk can be cheap, or at least not fully adequate for making valid inferences. By looking at such studies we see what has been lost as interviews have become the dominant form of qualitative evidence in poverty research.

In *Tally's Corner*, for example, Elliot Liebow regards talk and action as dissimilar units that can only be understood in comparison to one another. His book is a project in comparative sociological explanation, whereby the major strategy is to compare what his subjects say against the wider context of what he has learned about them. He focuses not merely on what they talk about, but also on what they don't say, which topics don't come up, what kinds of things don't get referred to in a spontaneous way, and what they won't admit. He contrasts what people say they want to do against a more realistic appraisal of what is possible in their lives, given their particular abilities. He assesses subjects' interpretations at a moment in time by looking at how events unfolded later. He is perceptive about the ways that subjects' explanations for their behavior are public presumptions and common narratives which do not bear upon the actual lives of the people who use them. He compares what people say in one conversation against what they say in another. He is sensitive to the way that both boasting and modesty can be self-serving. He compares declarations of intent against what subjects actually do later on. He speaks with both male and female partners, gauging what his male subjects say about their relationships against the views of their wives and lovers.

With the proliferation of ethnographic interviewing today, there is a danger of forgetting how cheap talk can be. Researchers increasingly use interviews to try to discover the reasons that people did things in their lives, to discover motivation. They let their subjects' attributions of cause and effect stand, as they take explanations of why things happened to them at face value. They write as if there is a clear correspondence between confident statements by subjects and reality, rather than understanding how what their subjects tell them are actually public poses, public displays, or public fictions. These interview studies are usually based on anywhere from a dozen to a couple of hundred respondents. Investigators tend to use the data to tell readers the specific or rough percentage of people who characterize their experiences in a particular way. Treating data in such a manner would be appropriate if it were generated by a simple random sample from a well-defined population.

Yet, respondents in these interview-based studies are almost always chosen through snowball samples. Nor are scholars who employ these contemporary approaches to qualitative work able to take the time to follow individuals in their networks, groups, and communities. There have, of course, been some real achievements with interviews. Here I think of the work of Kathryn Edin, who asked welfare and working mothers the basic question, "How much money do you spend in an average month on different goods and services, and how do you pay your bills?" (Edin & Lein 1997). Piecing the story together took considerable shoe leather, including many interviews spread over several months, and eventually her subjects provided budgets that more or less balanced, showing that none lived on Aid to Families with Dependent Children (AFDC) alone, and that none reported all of their income to the welfare department, findings consistent with Carol Stack's earlier observation to that effect (Stack 1974). But despite such outstanding exceptions, I believe that the kind of depth we saw in the studies of Liebow and Stack is getting lost in contemporary poverty research. As Edin and Lein wrote in *Making Ends Meet*, it is possible that because they observed the behavior of mothers at a point in time, they found little of the mutual exchange between kin that Stack did. "Had we been able to follow mothers over time, we might have seen some of our mothers move into a position to help others in their network" (Edin & Lein 1997).

Instead of trying to use interviews to illustrate central tendencies with ethnographic data, quantitative researchers should be more open to finding the evidence which points out the biases inherent in their quantitative work. This will lead to moving away from the interview in mixed method work and to highlighting the ways in which people speak against the main perspectives identified by the survey. Such information is very valuable not only if it adds up to represent a significant number of people, but also because all neighborhoods and communities are constituted of relations between the different kinds of people. The goal should be to place perspectives in a context by illuminating connections between various elements or kinds of people in a community or setting. Likewise, another goal of good ethnographic work is not to simply report upon what people say, but to highlight the connection between what people say and what they do, and demonstrating the relationship between how subjects define situations and what they take for granted. Much mixed method work takes the statements of subjects at face value rather than evaluating what they say against what they do. An interesting juxtaposition of observational and interview data on the same topic can be found in a recent study by Andrew Cherlin, Caitlin Cross-Barnet, Linda Burton, and Raymond Garrett-Peters (2008). They conducted longitudinal interviews *and* observations of a sample included in a larger survey and demonstrated that over time more respondents were in marital and cohabiting relationships than said they were, and many said they were not interested in having romantic relationships, even though it turned out they were involved in a wide variety of relations, which would not have been detected from the answers to the interviews. In Cherlin et al.'s mixed methods, the methods really were different (observation and interviewing), so the biases of one method did not end up reinforcing the biases of the other.

Carol Stack's *All Our Kin* (1974) provides an early model of mixed method research because she constantly kept her eye on the importance of using her qualitative data to provide a better context for the quantitative data. The research for

All Our Kin was conducted only after a review of the AFDC case files for the county she studied, enabling her to determine the typical patterns before she chose Ruby Banks as her key subject. Yet, Stack did not begin by assuming that the quantitative data could tell the whole story. She described a phenomenon whereby children end up living with adults who are not their biological parents, showing the ways that close kin cooperate in childcare and domestic activities. Stack reveals how the processes that determine where children live are not random, but "the outcome of calculated exchanges of goods and services between kinsmen" (1974: 67). She begins by looking at the data from the program on AFDC which shows how common fosterage is and suggests that 20 percent of dependent children were living with a woman other than their mother. She goes on to show that these statistics are "much lower than actual instances" as her research shows "disagreement between the record and the actual residency patterns . . . In the process of switching the residence of children, mothers or grantees rarely report these residence changes to the welfare office" (1974: 68). Based on her observations and detailed life histories of adults and children, Stack estimates that at least one-third of children have been kept by family members other than their mothers once or twice during their childhood.

In and of itself, this would have been interesting, but Stack takes it one step further. If one goes by data alone, the assumption might be that these dispersed children are not actually living with their biological mother. Stack uses ethnography as a tool to uncover the underlying patterns which show with whom the children are actually living. Her field observations demonstrated that of 139 dependent children who were reassigned to a grantee other than their mother, about half of those children's mothers resided in the same home as their children. Many of these mothers were teenagers when their first child was born, and their own mother (the child's grandmother) was the welfare grantee for purposes of receiving benefits from public aid.

Stack creates several dialogues between numbers and patterns on the ground. When she observed that children were cared for or informally fostered by their *father's* mother or sisters (a pattern in contrast to stereotypes of the commitment of fathers and fathers' families to their children), she returned to the county AFDC data once again. She discovered that when mothers were officially asked by the welfare agency who they would want to raise their child in the event of their own death, more than a quarter named the child's father's kin, rather than their own. This observation disrupts the characterization of urban black families as uniformly matrifocal in that "both a child's mother's and father's socially recognized kinsmen are expected to assume parental rights and duties" (Stack 1974: 73).

Today in the study of poverty, all too often the essential function of qualitative data is to serve or assist quantitative studies by putting a human face on the numbers produced by economists and demographers, or else qualitative data is seen as most useful when it is shown to be typical or representative of larger macro-level trends or populations. While Stack frequently uses quantitative data to place her ethnographic findings in the proper context, she is also sensitive to the "confusion that can arise when statistical data is interpreted out of context" (1974: 71). As she shows, ethnography has the possibility of unearthing culturally meaningful questions that can inform the ways in which surveys ask questions, and can give meaning when relevant to quantitative findings.

References

Becker, Howard S. (1996) "The Epistemology of Qualitative Research." In R. Jessor, A. Colby, and R. Shweder (eds), *Ethnography and Human Development: Context and Meaning in Social Inquiry*. Chicago: University of Chicago Press, pp. 53–71.

Cherlin, Andrew, Caitlin Cross-Barnet, Linda Burton, and Raymond Garrett-Peters (2008) "Promises They Can Keep: Low Income Women's Attitudes toward Marriage and Motherhood." *Journal of Marriage and Family* 70(4): 919–33.

Edin, Kathryn and Laura Lein (1997) *Making Ends Meet: How Single Mothers Survive Welfare and Low-Wage Work*. New York: Russell Sage Foundation.

King, Gary, Robert Keohane, and Sidney Verba (1994) *Designing Social Inquiry: Scientific Inference and Qualitative Research*. Princeton: Princeton University Press.

Liebow, Elliot (1968) *Tally's Corner: A Study of Negro Streetcorner Men*. Boston: Little, Brown.

Ogburn, William F. (1930) "The Folkways of a Scientific Sociology." 1929 Presidential Address, American Sociological Association. *The Scientific Monthly* 30(4): 300–6.

Smith, Michael Peter (1992) "Postmodernism, Urban Ethnography, and the New Social Space of Ethnic Identity." *Theory and Society* 21(4): 493–531.

Stack, C. (1974) *All Our Kin: Strategies for Survival in a Black Community*. New York: Harper and Row.

Thomas, W. I. (1918–20) *The Polish Peasant in Europe and America: Monograph of an Immigrant Group*, Vol. 1, *Primary-Group Organization* (1918). Chicago: University of Chicago Press; Vol. 2, *Primary-Group Organization* (1918). Chicago: University of Chicago Press; Vol. 3, *Life Record of an Immigrant* (1919). Boston: Badger; Vol. 4, *Disorganization and Reorganization in Poland* (1920). Boston: Badger; Vol. 5, *Organization and Disorganization in America* (1920). Boston: Badger.

5

Classical Sociological Theory

ALAN SICA

The definition of which bodies of writing should constitute "classical" social theory regularly changes, reflecting alterations in the intellectual and political goals of those who create theory, as well as those who teach it. Only recently has it become the case that "The Holy Trinity: Marx-Weber-Durkheim" is widely viewed as a convenient surrogate for "classical theory" *in toto*. That these three titans are essential to this tradition is undebatable, but the supposition that they adequately represent "everything still worth knowing" from the history of sociological theory is unsupportable. When Pitirim Sorokin, the first sociologist ever hired by Harvard University, published his *Contemporary Sociological Theories* in 1928 (two years before he left Minnesota for Harvard), his index named over 1,000 scholars whom he showed had contributed to its development. Other important textbooks of the period were similarly generous in their portrayal of who should be included in social theory's past and its consequent present (e.g., Becker & Barnes 1938; Bogardus 1940).

In a field often organized for pedagogical purposes around "great thinkers," favored names come and go with almost seasonal predictability. For example, during the Great Depression, major US publishers reissued the works of Karl Marx in student editions, while during the 1950s, it was dangerous to teach his work in US colleges for fear of becoming subject to politically motivated punishment. Similarly, the Italian economist and political theorist, Vilfredo Pareto, was widely known to the literate public in the 1930s, and regarded as an indispensable social theorist for scholars who worked in this area. Yet following the Second World War, after his name had been incorrectly linked to Benito Mussolini, he was promptly and permanently banished from "the canon." The Italian fascist dictator was portrayed as

The Wiley-Blackwell Companion to Sociology, First Edition. Edited by George Ritzer.
© 2012 Blackwell Publishing Ltd. Published 2012 by Blackwell Publishing Ltd.

Pareto's "student," whereas in fact he attended a few of Pareto's lectures on economics around 1900, encouraged to do so by his Russian lover, Angelica Balbanoff (Mussolini 1928: 14).

The case of Georg Simmel was less subject to gross political forces, yet his reputation waxed, waned, and waxed again in what has become a familiar pattern. He was interjected into American sociology during the 1890s by his American student, Albion Small, editor of the *American Journal of Sociology*, and for the next 20 years became the most often translated European theorist of his generation (Levine, Carter & Gorman 1976). His ideas played an essential role in the creation of social psychology, exchange theory, and urban sociology, yet from the 1930s through the 1970s, he took a back seat to other theorists. When Talcott Parsons set about reshaping sociology's theoretical foundation in the 1930s, he omitted a chapter on Simmel, already written, when assembling his transformative book, *The Structure of Social Action*. He realized that Simmel was incommensurable with the other figures he chose to analyze, that his way of theorizing did not mesh well with the story Parsons wished to tell regarding an alleged "convergence" among Weber, Durkheim, Pareto, and Alfred Marshall, the economist (Parsons 1937; Levine 1957). Although important textbooks continued to include chapters on Simmel (e.g., Ashley & Orenstein 1985; Ritzer 1988), he was not generally viewed as a member of that small group of theorists who were indispensable to an understanding of the discipline's legacy. Only in the 1990s, with the rise of postmodernism as a school and methodology, was he rediscovered, and in some ways redefined, and he now seems again as "contemporary" as ever (among many, see Frisby & Featherstone 1997).

Examples of this kind abound, of course, since styles change in the academic world just as they do in any other human endeavor. History shows that genuine permanency is impossible to maintain in any sphere of human learning or the arts; it is worth remembering that Plato, Shakespeare, Bach, and Vivaldi were all neglected for long periods of cultural history, and other iconic presences in our own time will surely fall from view before the end of our century. Someday the Beatles' music will likely become a small footnote to cultural history, and the novels of Kurt Vonnegut will seem as old-fashioned and "unreadable" as today do those of dozens of Victorian novelists who were household names in their time, yet are now wholly forgotten.

Not only has the theoretical pantheon seen significant repositionings regarding its "personnel" during the last half-century, but the range of learning that scholars agree to identify as "social theory" has also undergone continual refashioning. Unlike today, between the two world wars a US college student might well have been introduced to social theory of the classical mode by examining the ancient Egyptians, Persians, or Greeks (e.g., Hertzler 1936; Becker & Barnes 1938; Ellwood 1938; Bogardus 1940). For instance, consider Joyce Hertzler's unique volume, *The Social Thought of the Ancient Civilizations*, published in 1936 by McGraw-Hill, still today a major source of sociology textbooks. This 400-page work, written by a Nebraska sociologist, begins with the Egyptians ("Imhotep and His Philosophy: 'Eat, Drink and Be Merry'"), moves to Babylonian (now Iraqi) thought, then through Hittite, Persian, and Indian ideas, concluding with investigations of Chinese and Hebrew social analysis. Hertzler closes by providing the student with a summary of the lastingly important notions offered by proto-sociologists in these major civilizations, and argues that knowing about these systems of thought achieves two major goals.

First, it demonstrates that "there is nothing new under the sun" when it comes to the most critical matters facing humans in social groups: how to control misbehavior and encourage normatively approved behavior, how to distribute goods and services fairly, how to maintain stable, satisfying families, how to encourage social cohesion rather than dispersion, how to use supernatural events and sentiments, and so on. Second, the proverbs and morality tales that circulated among all ancient civilizations, the purpose of which was always to transmit "social theory" to ordinary people, were far more entertaining and provocative than modern social science and sociological theory. This is in part why they were so well regarded, even cherished, for so many centuries in ways that today's social science arguments seldom are. If one compares the contents, say, of the *King James Bible* or the *Bhagavad Gita* with current articles in any social science journal, substantive parallels can surely be drawn, yet these "holy books" inspire people with emotionally satisfying narratives in ways that "bloodless" social science cannot. The rhetoric of storytelling and moralizing, the creation of appealing parables, shares very little with the "objective" language adopted during the twentieth century by social scientists in their effort to emulate the imagined "objectivity" of the natural sciences, and the technology they made possible. Hertzler was surely correct in these claims, and he wrote the book in part to substantiate them, probably reflecting his own broad educational and cultural background that no longer characterizes sociological "training."

The well-known sociologist, Emory Bogardus, offered the first edition of *The Development of Social Thought* a few years later, in 1940. After racing through the same historical texts and personalities in a few pages which Hertzler had required an entire book to traverse, he launches into the sociological ideas of Plato, Aristotle, Aurelius, early Christian thinkers, the Middle Ages, and then shifts into what we now regard as the "early modern period." He writes about Thomas More's *Utopia* (the predecessor to Orwell's *1984*, Huxley's *Brave New World*, plus dozens of other dystopian novels), the Enlightenment *philosophes*, and Thomas Malthus (founder of demography), consuming a third of his long book before arriving at Auguste Comte – who invented the term "*sociologie*" in 1839 (Pickering 1993: 615).

From here Bogardus pursues a long list of thinkers who no longer appear in any textbooks of "classical" social theory, but who were at that time still regarded as vital figures in the history of societal analysis. After an obligatory chapter on Marx (whose place in the pantheon remains secure despite political events since 1989), he allocates chapters to "[Henry] Buckle and Geographic Social Thought," Herbert Spencer, Lester Frank Ward (first president of the American Sociological Society in 1905), William Graham Sumner (first teacher of sociology at Yale), Francis Galton and eugenics, now entirely repudiated in sociological circles, Ludwig Gumplowicz and conflict theory, Peter Kropotkin on cooperation and anarchism, Gabriel Tarde on imitation, the indispensable Emile Durkheim, and the founder of Chicago Sociology, Albion Small. Bogardus then produced chapter-length treatments of Franklin Giddings, Georg Simmel, Max Weber, Charles Horton Cooley, Vilfredo Pareto,

Edward A. Ross, W. I. Thomas, Robert E. Park, Charles Ellwood, Karl Mannheim, Howard Odum, and Radhakamal Mukerjee.

With the solid exceptions of Marx, Durkheim, Weber, and Simmel, none of these thinkers is any longer considered critically necessary for inclusion in the basic sociological theory course taught in every US sociology department, and even specialists in the field likely know little about them. There are niche enthusiasms for Cooley and Thomas, honorable memorialization of Comte and Sumner, occasional textual reference to Tarde and Mannheim. Yet 90 percent of Bogardus's textbook treatment (which went through four editions in the next 20 years) has been sloughed off in today's "marketplace of ideas." The reasons for this diluting of theory's past are many, some obvious, some not. Yet it is undeniably true that a very great deal of serious thinking about social life, individual or collective, has been thrown into the "dustbin of history" (Marx's phrase) without benefit of scholarly scrutiny.

It is surely comforting, if delusory, to believe that sociological theory, like physics or chemistry, has "moved beyond" its founders' plethora of notions, hunches, hypotheses, and arguments – that we no longer should study their writings, any more than today's astronomers need to master Copernicus's work before advancing their field. Were this true, it would surely ease the labors required to become expert in the study of social theory. Those who adhere to a natural science model of sociology make exactly this claim, and have been doing so at least since the days of the "social physicist," George Lundberg, in the 1930s (Lundberg 1939; see also Lundberg 1947). In fact, the lineage of this belief-system goes back to the seventeenth century and exploded in the nineteenth – that earnest longing to launch social science into the same high regard the natural sciences have enjoyed since the seventeenth century when Newton showed the way. Sorokin's treatment of what he calls "the mechanistic school" begins with the philosophers Descartes, Spinoza, Leibniz, Grotius, Malebranche, and others, all of whom aimed during the seventeenth century to create a "social mechanics" (Sorokin 1928: 2–62).

> The social physicists of the 17th century tried to do the same as the physicists themselves. In the first place they constructed the conception of a *moral or social space* in which social, and moral, and political movements go on. It was a kind of space analogous to physical space and superposed upon it. To the *position* of a material object in physical space, there corresponded, in social space, the conception of *status*, as of sex, age, occupation, freedom, religion, citizenship, and so on. In this way they constructed a system of social coordinates, which defined the position of man in this moral space as exactly as the system of geometrical coordinates defines the position of a material object in physical space. Physical mechanics explains the motions, also, of physical objects by the principles of inertia and gravitation. Similarly, social mechanics regarded the social processes as a result of the gravitation and inertia of human beings or groups. . . . The social power and authority were interpreted as resultants of the pressures of "social atoms" (individuals) and "social molecules" (groups). (Sorokin 1928: 8–9)

This mode of analysis continued into the eighteenth century with the philosopher George Berkeley and others. It blossomed in the nineteenth century in the work of H. C. Carey, whose *Principles of Social Science* (1858) preceded the more celebrated writings of Herbert Spencer (*First Principles*, 1862), and claimed that "the laws which govern matter in all its forms, whether that of coal, clay, iron, pebble stones, trees, oxen, horses, or men," are the same; "man is the molecule of society"; and social interaction operates under the "great law of molecular gravitation" (Carey 1858, cited in Sorokin 1928: 13). These were heady arguments in the mid-nineteenth century, and Carey was not alone in proposing programs of social analysis built upon them. But in the end, as Sorokin points out, these "childish mechanical analogies" (1928: 39) did not pan out since the built-in irrationalities of human life are impossible to model, even with sophisticated math.

There were other, competing approaches dealing with the problem of human action in somewhat less "childish" ways, less tied to the belief that *Homo sapiens* could be understood by means of mechanical or molecular imagery. A few examples from a large pool of possible instances might illustrate how eager were gifted thinkers to make use of scientific reasoning, even if physics was not their preferred model. Marquis de Condorcet (1743–94) came up with a "jury theorem" in 1785 based on simple probability reasoning which shows, given strict assumptions, the likelihood of a small group arriving at a "correct" decision. He also invented "Condorcet's paradox" (or voting paradox), which demonstrates that majority preferences can be undone under certain conditions involving what is now called "non-transitivity," so that the "correct" outcome is impossible to attain (Baker 1975: 197–263).

In the same era Henri Saint-Simon (1760–1825), Comte's mentor and competitor, even while developing a so-called "new religion" in the 1820s, nevertheless concurred that social life could be organized around indubitable "laws" of industrial life. He persuaded his followers that correct analysis of social processes would allow society at large to avoid the many miseries that inspired Marx and Engels to create their emancipatory theories (as in Engels 1845). Like the Marxists, but much earlier, he believed that through scientific reorganization and management of industrialization, the poor could be protected from the ravages of factory life, proposing that the welfare of the weakest should be a society's highest goal. (A similar argument was considered "new" in 1971 when John Rawls published his *Theory of Justice*, long after Saint-Simon had been forgotten.) Very unlike Marx and Engels, though, he thought that industrial "managers" could combine their technical administrative skills with high moral reasoning, thereby emancipating the working class from the chains which Marx claimed were the unavoidable accompaniment to industrial life. For all their differences, they agreed that Science as a slogan and practice was the road to societal salvation, one which sidestepped the ideological and spiritual battles that always seemed to surround religiously-motivated programs for social change.

The most scientifically accomplished of these early proto-sociologists was Adolphe Quetelet (1796–1874), gifted mathematician and official Belgian astronomer. He invented the "body-mass index" measurement still used avidly by weightwatchers and athletes. While compiling statistics and observations relating to shooting stars, celestial movement, and seasonal vegetation changes, Quetelet found time to propose a "social physics" in 1835 (as well as the first "scientific" criminology; Quetelet 1835) that Lundberg and other twentieth-century theorists regarded as the foundation of their positivism. By using a statistical construct which he called the "average man," Quetelet was able to employ Dutch and Belgian data to show that certain human behaviors followed recognizable patterns, and deviated more or less predictably from what we now call "the normal curve." He was particularly successful in correlating certain social characteristics with particular types of criminal behavior, coming up with 17 statements that summarized his findings, e.g., "1. *Age* is without contradiction the cause which acts with the most energy to develop or moderate the propensity for crime" (Quetelet 1984; in Sica 2005: 166–8). From this work Durkheim and subsequent researchers took their lead when studying what has since come to be called "deviance."

For example, in his most successful demonstration of "empirical" sociology, *On Suicide* (1897), Durkheim notes:

> When Quetelet directed the attention of philosophers to the surprising regularity with which certain social phenomena are repeated in identical periods of time, he thought that he could explain it by his theory of the "ordinary man," which has in fact remained the only systematic explanation of this remarkable feature of societies. According to him, there is a definite type in each society which the majority of individuals reproduce more or less exactly, with only a minority deviating from it under the influence of disruptive force. (Durkheim 2006: 332–3)

After mentioning Quetelet's name in the body of his text, Durkheim added a knowing footnote:

> Notably in his two works, *Sur l'homme de la développement de ses facultés ou Essai de physique sociale*, 2 vols., Paris, 1835, and *Du système social et des lois qui le régissent*, Paris, 1848. While Quetelet was the first to try to explain this regularity in a scientific manner, he was not the first to observe it. The real founder of moral statistics was Pastor Süssenlich, in his work *Die Göttliche Ordnung in den Veränderungen des menschlichen Geschlechts, aus der Geburt, dem Tode und der Fortpflanzung desselben erwiesen*, 3 vols., 1742.

Nowadays no one remembers or reads Pastor Süssenlich, who lives on only in Durkheim's footnote. But it is instructive to realize that a search for precursors – or "adumbrationists," as Pitirim Sorokin named them in his classic work – seldom fails to find someone who thought of a technique of analysis or an illuminating idea before those who are currently most often credited with a specific intellectual "discovery."

These early proponents of a scientific sociology – Condorcet, Saint-Simon, and Quetelet – were the best known exemplars of what more recently has been named "humanothermodynamics." The central tenet of this field is that people can be portrayed for analytic purposes as "molecules" in a vast social system, and therefore studied in the same way physicists explore the subatomic world. Naively perceived, it makes sense to some optimistic thinkers that human action should be "model-able" in ways similar to techniques of analysis so successful in chemistry and physics. The goal, of course, ever since the eighteenth century, has been to *predict* human action in order to propel people into behavior which strengthens rather than endangers social order, or to provide them with more pleasurable individual lives by helping them avoid pathological conditions of their own making. The idea behind this is always the same: social life is difficult to interpret, so scientific reduction is necessary in order to clarify the consequences of various actions or lack of actions. "Laws" of social life have thus been sought ever since the *philosophes* saw what the natural sciences had achieved after they determined how the "laws of nature" functioned (Mirowski 1989; Urry 2004). A famous modern example of this tendency came from Charles Darwin's grandson, C. G. Darwin, who published *The Next Million Years* in 1952, where he proposed that "statistical mechanics" be used to study human behavior by conceiving of individuals as "human molecules" in a "conservative dynamical system" (Darwin 1952). More alarmingly, he predicted that humans would run out of food by 2000. Even though this school of thinking has found few followers within the ranks of American sociologists, the latent notion – that social laws ought to be discoverable through quantitative investigation and the application of probability – runs deep among many social researchers, even in unspoken form. Almost all "quantitative" research clings to this "domain assumption" (Gouldner 1970) in an unquestioning, unstated way, since without it there would be little justification in carrying out thousands of studies each year that portray human behavior as meaningfully reducible to correlation coefficients.

Another vital inspiration for classical social theory came from Scotland during the mid-eighteenth century, where a talented, interpersonally connected group of men composed literate, even entertaining, treatises which shared very little with the French *philosophes'* view of human society and their utopian recommendations for its restructuring along modern lines. Inspired in part by the philosophy of Francis Hutcheson (1694–1746), including his *Essay on the Nature and Conduct of the Passions with Illustrations of the Moral Sense* (1728), the so-called "Scottish moralists" wrote clear prose about socially important issues which gives their work continuing importance (see Broadie 1997). Those who participated in what has been called "the Scottish Enlightenment" (Camic 1983) included Adam Smith (1723–90), Adam Ferguson (1723–1816), John Millar (1735–1801), and others like Millar's friend, the great philosopher David Hume (1711–76).

Millar, a law professor, was more a sociologist than a philosopher, writing about what we now call "social stratification" in *The Origin of the Distinction of Ranks* (1771), one part of which was "Of the Rank and Condition of Women in Different Ages." He also managed to anticipate Emile Durkheim's famous dissertation (Durkheim 1893) by more than a century with "Social Consequences of the Division of Labour" (Millar 1806). His observations gave rise to what is now called "comparative sociology," as in this passage from his 1771 book:

> In the most rude and barbarous ages, little or no property can be acquired by particular persons; and consequently, there are no differences of rank to interrupt the free intercourse of the sexes. The pride of family, as well as the insolence of wealth, is unknown; and there are no distinctions among individuals, but those which arise from their age and experience, from their strength, courage, and other personal qualities. The members of different families, being all nearly upon a level, maintain the most familiar intercourse with one another, and when impelled by natural instinct, give way to their mutual desires without hesitation or reluctance. They are unacquainted with those refinements which create a strong preference of particular objects, and with those artificial rules of decency and decorum which might lay a restraint upon their conduct. (Millar 1806; in Sica 2005: 55)

A common thread through all the Scottish moralists' writings was an overriding concern for the ways that industrialization, beginning to interject itself into quiet rural Scotland, was threatening to corrode interpersonal trust and the many societal virtues associated with it. Millar clearly argues in this passage that an "arcadian" condition of tranquility preceded modern, capitalist interactions, likely a reflection of comparing his life in Glasgow with work on his 30-acre farm. From this basic idea he adumbrates Thorstein Veblen's *The Theory of the Leisure Class* by 130 years in pointing out that "preference of particular objects" – what Veblen called "conspicuous consumption" (Veblen 1899: 68–101) – would also work to destabilize that "familiar intercourse with one another" which in pre-industrial, pre-urbanized societies promoted harmonious interactions. He is not, like Rousseau or Hobbes, offering a utopian or dystopian vision of humankind's imagined history, but instead is simply reporting what he has seen in historical documents as well as everyday life in Scotland. It was this "common sense" philosophy that endeared Millar (the most popular law professor of the era) and his confederates to generations of readers.

The most famous of the Scots was Adam Smith, whose *An Inquiry into the Nature and Causes of the Wealth of Nations* (1776) has formed the backbone of what Marx called "bourgeois economics" ever since it was published. But for social theorists, his more important book was *The Theory of Moral Sentiments* (1759). It is difficult for some readers to reconcile the dog-eat-dog ethics which today's economists claim they see in Smith's book on wealth creation with the soft-hearted portrait of humankind he champions in his moral theory, though surely for Smith they were all of a piece. Smith's professor at Glasgow University, Francis Hutcheson, gave him the philosophic tools to consider the fundamental nature of humans as they interact. Anticipating Wilhelm Dilthey (1833–1911), who inspired Max Weber and Georg Simmel, Smith proposed that sympathy and empathy for another person's suffering or experiences are the hallmark of humanity's peculiar and unique condition of being. He opens the book with this famous paragraph:

> How selfish soever man may be supposed, there are evidently some principles in his nature which interest him in the fortune of others and render their happiness necessary to him, though he derives nothing from it except the pleasure of seeing it. Of this kind is pity or compassion, the emotion which we feel for the misery of others when we either see it or are made to conceive it in a very lively manner. (Smith 1761: 1)

These observations, basic to Smith's worldview, are worlds removed from the fierce "survival of the fittest" ethic that pervades modern capitalism in the global economy, where no quarter is given to one's competition, and their suffering is a source of joy – and profits.

According to Smith, and contrary to raw capitalist motivations, in order for civilized society to function properly, its citizens must be able to judge the "propriety or impropriety" of one another's actions. This capacity turns around correct appraisals of gratitude, resentment, and other typical responses to social action, and Smith believed that a key measure of societal sophistication lay in being able to interpret accurately the interactional repertoire of responses people give to one another, and which are witnessed by others. When today people sometimes say about a given event or condition, "It may be legal, but it's just not *right*!" – say, regarding Wall Street salaries compared with those of factory workers or teachers – they are registering exactly the emotions and analyses that Smith so skillfully catalogued in 1759, when evaluating the underside of capitalist accumulation. Not surprisingly, the book has been continuously in print ever since, and has served as a beacon of sanity among competing ideologies, each trying to explain or justify the modern world.

Auguste Comte created and noted the word "*sociologie*" in his notebooks on Saturday, April 27, 1839, because others had coined the expression "social physics" and he wished to distinguish himself from all his predecessors, including especially his former friend and employer, Saint-Simon (Pickering 1993: 615; with the recent completion of Pickering's monumental biography of Comte, more information is now accessible concerning him and his setting than for any other classical social theorist except for Marx; there is no equivalently detailed work for Durkheim, Weber, Simmel, or any other social theorist of note). Comte embodied all the sterling qualities of early "social science" and in equal measure all its foibles. A precocious and gifted mathematician who tutored in this field when young, he turned his back on math to embrace history and philosophy as he created his multi-volume works, *The Positive Polity* (6 volumes, 1830–42) and *The System of Positive Polity* (4 volumes, 1851–4). In this he imitated Turgot, Condorcet, and other *philosophes* who believed that history, carefully studied, revealed patterns of rise and fall, stasis and change, which could be systematized and turned into roadmaps for the human future. Comte loathed the Catholic Church's hierarchy, patriarchalism, and medievalism in the France of his day, yet he understood the centrality of belief-systems for human populations generally, and the role that unthinking acceptance of dogma played in controlling large groups. His hope was to link science with a particular reading of the historical record so that societies which in the past had been ruled by authoritarian violence could be guided instead by "sociological priests." Their authority would be linked in the popular mind with specialized knowledge of how societies can and should operate, that is, from the *sociologie* he proposed.

The story of Comte's following in Britain and the US is a long tale, which includes heroic translating labors by the novelist and travel-writer, Harriet Martineau, and earnest propagandizing from the world-class philosopher, John Stuart Mill. A sense for this cult can be gained from a pamphlet published in New York in 1856, the year before Comte's death, called *A Book for the Times: To Exterminate Political Vermin and Moral Quacks. Social Physics; From the Positive Philosophy of Auguste Comte*. This is actually a retitled excerpt from Comte's *Positive Philosophy* (1856: 399–440). The title page quotes Comte:

> By including social science in the scientific hierarchy, the positive spirit admits to success in this study only well-prepared and disciplined minds, so trained in the preceding department of knowledge as to be fit for the complex problems of the last. The long and difficult preliminary elaboration must disgust and deter vulgar and ill-prepared minds, and subdue the most rebellious. This consideration, if there were no other, would prove the eminently organic tendency of the new political philosophy. (1856: 434)

All this for a mere 25 cents ($6.63 today). Comte's characterization of the past was not charitable, and his hope for a positivist future of his own design must seem from our vantage point deliriously optimistic. Yet he proposed with endless energy and repetition a program of planned social change which he thought would eliminate most of humanity's discomforts, political and otherwise, and would bring human behavior into line with the latest scientific achievements and ways of thinking.

As he explained:

> The theories of Social science are still, even in the midst of the best thinkers, completely implicated with the theologico-metaphysical philosophy . . . The philosophical procedure which I have undertaken to carry through becomes more difficult and bold, from this point onward, without at all changing its nature or object; and it must so far present a new character as it must henceforth be employed in creating a wholly new order of scientific conceptions, instead of judging, arranging, and improving such as already existed . . . In its scientific connection with the rest of this work, all that I can hope to do is to exhibit the general considerations of the case, so as to resolve the intellectual anarchy which is the main source of our moral anarchy first, and then of the political . . . I propose to state, first, how the institution of a science of Social Physics bears upon the principal needs and grievances of society, in its present deplorable state of anarchy . . . [thus] society is preserved from chimerical and mischievous schemes . . . there is a deep and widely-spread anarchy of the whole intellectual system, which has been in this state of disturbance during the long interregnum, resulting from the decline of theological-metaphysical philosophy. At the present time, the old philosophy is in a state of imbecility . . . we shall see the necessity of introducing an entirely new spirit into the organization of society, by which the useless and passionate struggles may be put an end to, and society led out of the revolutionary state in which it has been tossed about for three centuries past. (Comte 1856: 399–400)

This fiery rhetoric, so remote from the calmly measured tones that typify today's social science writing, is nevertheless the direct progenitor of all the social sciences that have followed. In his detailed attack on the "theological-metaphysical" ways of thinking – by which he meant in short the ancient and medieval worldviews – and his protracted celebration of positivism (the "scientific method" still universally taught as good), he laid a broad path for sociology which has never been questioned. The unspoken assumption of all modern Comteans, even those who know nothing of his work, is that "objective" appraisal of society, however it is carried out or defined, will "naturally" lead to improved social life once its denizens recognize the folly of their ways. Comte assigned to sociologically alert priests the task of persuading, not forcing, the masses to obey "laws" of social behavior which their research had unearthed. It was an article of faith for him that the "modern mind" would respond with alacrity to intellectual arguments based on scientifically gleaned findings. Growing up in the shadow of the French Revolution, he knew of course that "the madness of crowds" was a real danger to social order, yet he thought his system could end wanton violence and the terrors it brings. He also believed that in the modern world the condition of women would be vastly improved, and in this one notion, at least for women in the richest societies, his hopes have been well founded. Very little of the history of humanity's last century supports his most cherished beliefs, yet they live on, just as Comte thought they should, in the unexamined hearts of social scientists everywhere. Like it or not, know it or not, they are all Comteans.

We arrive at five thinkers whose claim to "permanent" residence in the pantheon of social theory is as firm as can be imagined given current norms of intellectual lineage-formation: Karl Marx (1818–83), Herbert Spencer (1820–1903), Emile Durkheim (1858–1917), Georg Simmel (1858–1918), and Max Weber (1864–1920). Without each of their unique visions of how industrialized society functioned in the mid- to late nineteenth century, we could hardly speak a line of modern sociology, since they gave us a vocabulary that remains indispensable. Many of their ideas have steadily migrated from the lecture hall to newspapers and then into common parlance, e.g., "rationalization," "division of labor," "anomie," "marginality," "survival of the fittest," "class warfare," "the Protestant ethic," "charisma," and so on.

The literature on Marx has for decades operated within an international frame of reference that continues, even after official communism's apparent demise, to produce thousands of new entries per annum. Not long ago the venerable British firm, Routledge, published *Karl Marx's Grundrisse: Foundations of the Critique of Political Economy 150 Years Later* (Musto 2010), a collection of 32 Marxological studies which probe a compendium of working papers from 1857–8, preparatory to *Das Kapital*, which Marx never published. It remained unknown until 1939 when a German edition was published in Russia, and was unavailable in English until the 1970s. The clothbound version of this new commentary sold well enough to justify a paperback edition. This is roughly equivalent to a book being offered today which at length and with utmost seriousness would investigate unpublished working drafts of Brahms' symphonies from the 1870s. Yet the Marx volume "still sells," whereas the imagined Brahms volume would surely not.

So long as contemporary societies produce conditions of "alienation" and "reification," operate through "the cash nexus" and "commodification," "immisserate" laborers while capitalists flourish, destroy the global environment in pursuit of profits, and subordinate broad groups of people to elite control, Marx and Engels' works will be studied, taught, and elaborated. *The Economic and Philosophic Manuscripts* (1844) of the youthful Marx, the "Communist Manifesto" (1848), and *The German Ideology* (1845–6) advance insights and arguments which have played well in existential philosophy and psychology as well as literature and drama. They capture graphically and with memorable rhetoric the powerless and hopeless sensations experienced by that great majority of humanity who work for capital but do not own it – who have nothing to sell but their "labor power." The "late Marx" of *Theories of Surplus Value* (3 vols., 1861–3), *Capital* (Vol. 1, 1867), and *The Civil War in France* (1871), to name but a few, are works that speak more to political-economic and governmental issues, and exhibit more utility when analyzing global trade, war, and the systematic exploitation of labor, both domestic and international. Marx's proudest analytic achievement, the "Law of the Tendency of the Rate of Profit to Fall" (*Capital*, Vol. 3, Book III, Part 3), and its associated labor theory of value, continues to fascinate analysts who are not mesmerized by the limiting parameters of "capitalist logic." And without Marx's notion of "commodity fetishism," students of consumer culture would lack a fundamental analytic tool. Sociologically, Marxist ideas have become the bedrock of research in social stratification, gender relations, political sociology, and other subfields, even including the sociology of culture. The works that Marx and Engels created during their 40-year partnership, and which Engels continued alone for another 12 years, will continue to inform, correct, and inspire social theory until such time that a post-exploitative utopia can be formed, or until people no longer care to interpret the meaning of social relations that function within the strictures of "private property."

Born two years after Marx, but into an entirely different intellectual and political orbit, as shy about public appearances as Marx was bold, as afraid of familial complications as Marx was intrepid, Herbert Spencer was invited to New York City's Delmonico's Steak House for a grand dinner on November 8, 1882, where Andrew Carnegie and a host of politicians, religious leaders, intellectuals, and businessmen feted him, to his astonishment and discomfort. They ate a 12-course dinner with a dozen wines which began at 6:00 and ended at 9:30 with cigars, followed by speeches about Spencer's greatness – they called him "the Aristotle of our age" – and their own, which his ideas, so they thought, explained and justified (Werth 2009: 276–95). In "The Theory of Population" (1852), Spencer invented the phrase "survival of the fittest," seven years prior to Darwin's *Origin of Species*, and thus became a favorite of the Robber Barons, especially Carnegie, since it seemed to justify their plutocratic control of the American economy during the late nineteenth century. They comforted themselves with this denatured Spencerianism: since they had all the money and power, they must *ipso facto* be "the best." Yet Spencer emphasized in his *Principles of Biology* (1872) that "fittest" did not mean best or most desirable in moral or societal terms. As in Darwin, it simply denoted creatures who, given their environment, were most likely to survive. That this situation when applied to human arrangements can result in some of the "worst" people thriving – consider heartless marauders during war – was perfectly obvious to Spencer, but much less so to the capitalists of his period for whom any governmental regulating of their activities was anathema, and any labor organizing a destabilizing force to be destroyed at once.

Without realizing it while he created his "organic analogy" between the physical and social bodies, he became the intellectual symbol for laissez-faire government. Yet his *Principles of Sociology* (1896) offered far more than a simple-minded legitimation of "Wild West Capitalism" of the kind typified by Carnegie, J. P. Morgan, John D. Rockefeller, and their peers. Spencer was first of all a dedicated scientist who studied as much natural history as he failed to study human history (which separates him distinctly from Comte, Marx, and Weber), or literature, art, music, and philosophy. His forte was careful observation, not scholarly analysis of previous authors' works. By drawing careful, even exhausting, analogies between the structure of the human body and the various social institutions and social structures of all the societies he could find, he believed he had discovered the same "laws" of social organization that Comte and Marx had pursued by other means.

Spencer was not a moralist; in fact, his closest associates often remarked on his "total lack of sensuality" and "lack of emotional depth" (Collier in Royce 1904: 188). British capitalist society, from which he was insulated in his study, did not offend him, as it did Marx and Engels, due to its systematic oppression of workers, and the cyclical collapses of its finances. Instead he was keen to understand what central principle organized all natural life, human included, and he decided that "evolution" was the correct answer, a set of immutable forces that must be left free to do its worst or best without any governmental intrusion. During the late twentieth century Spencer's name was dusted off from library neglect and inserted, often incorrectly, into debates about "socio-biology." But as with Comte, for all the curt references to his name in this literature, very few scholars bothered to read Spencer to find out what he was truly doing. If his multi-volume studies of biology and psychology were out of date even before they appeared, his three fat books called *The Principles of Sociology* (1876–96) showed Spencer at his best, along with his *The Study of Sociology* (1873). He not only argued strenuously for the legitimacy of this "new-fangled" field, but also showed in enormous detail that an evolutionary theory of societal development could make sense of the anthropological record as it was then known. Using information systematically compiled and organized by three research assistants whom he hired (who over 20 years and at great cost produced the 12-volume *Descriptive Sociology*), he decided that societies went through periods of increased differentiation of functions as they "matured," and that military societies necessarily gave way to industrial societies. The former are authoritarian, brutal, hold women in low esteem, and do not invite innovation, whereas the latter tend toward democracy, the equalization of gender roles, the rich economic fruits of peace rather than war, and an opportunity for continued positive development. It was for arguments like these that Spencer's books were used as required textbooks in sociology courses throughout England and the US well into the twentieth century.

About Durkheim, Weber, and Simmel, a very great deal has been written in all the major languages; entire scholarly journals are dedicated now to each of them separately, and hundreds of monographs, textbooks, and summaries of their work are readily available. Analyzing their works and lives has become an academic "industry"; one recent bibliography concerning Weber lists nearly 5,000 items in English alone (Sica 2004). There are interesting links and differences among them, particularly in view of the fact that their lives almost perfectly overlapped. Durkheim wrote an unflattering review of a book written by Marianne Weber, Max Weber's wife and intellectual partner, but otherwise never referred to Weber himself in his own works. Durkheim's nephew, the anthropologist Marcel Mauss, testified that Weber had in his personal library a complete set of scholarly journals which Durkheim founded and edited, yet he never cited Durkheim's work in any of his own. Simmel did not refer to Durkheim, but was a frequent houseguest of Weber's, and a recipient of Weber's personal and professional kindness. Simmel, an unorthodox scholar and talented lecturer, was not offered a professorship in Germany, in part due to anti-Semitism, despite Weber's vigorous sponsorship, and the fame Simmel enjoyed at Berlin University. Yet Durkheim's profoundly Jewish identity did not stop him from creating French sociology from nothing, rising to the top academic position in the nation, even in a society with deeply anti-Semitic tendencies (witness the Dreyfus affair).

Durkheim seldom invoked historical data in his work, but wrote a long book about aboriginal religion in Australia called *The Elementary Forms of the Religious Life* (1911), which has become a classic. He did no fieldwork, and relied on others' reports. Weber was formally educated both as an attorney and a historian (ancient as well as medieval), and once spent a summer in a relative's textile mill carrying out a "time and motion study." His major work was entitled posthumously by his wife *Economy and Society*, which reflects the centrality that economic relationships always had in Weber's sociology. Simmel did no fieldwork in a formal sense, but so keenly studied Berlin society, where he was a lifelong resident, that he was able to formulate the principles of social psychology without access to a lab for experiments. From Durkheim we get a solidly "sociologistic" worldview, where "personality" is an illusion and social organization dictates the structures and functions of human life, individually and collectively. He also wrote the first manual on sociological methods, the most important study of suicide by a sociologist, and propelled Spencer into continuous use by including his ideas in his dissertation, *The Division of Labor in Society* (1893). Weber's sociology (a term he refused to use until very late in life) was comprised of sociologies of law, of music, of ancient and modern economic institutions, of bureaucracy, of comparative religions, of political power, and many more ingredients, surely the broadest and most encompassing portrayal of what sociology could accomplish when in the right hands. Simmel helped Americans, especially at Chicago, legitimate sociology as a new field in the 1890s through translations of his essays. More importantly, his social psychological perceptions linked young Marx's understanding of alienation and reification with recent postmodern "interventions" regarding identity, sexuality, and marginality. None of the other classical theorists shared Simmel's philosophically astute rendering of private consciousness as it tries to negotiate the difficulties as well as the opportunities of the modern metropole. Taken together, these classical theorists, and their predecessors, set a high standard of insights and ideas for their sociological descendants which, some would argue, has not yet been surpassed. Yet with new biographies of Max and Marianne Weber now available (Radkau 2009; Meurer 2010), a new Durkheim biography in French (Fournier 2007), a new complete translation of Simmel's *Soziologie* (1908) finally available (Simmel 2009), the Marx/Engels *Collected Works* completed (Marx & Engels 1975–2010), perhaps the time will soon come when contemporary sociologists will be able to come to terms with their past in a more complete and satisfactory way.

References

Ashley, David and David Michael Orenstein (1985) *Sociological Theory: Classical Statements*. Boston: Allyn and Bacon.

Baker, Keith Michael (1975) *Condorcet: From Natural Philosophy to Social Mathematics*. Chicago: University of Chicago Press.

Becker, Howard P. and Harry Elmer Barnes (eds. and comps.) (1938) *Social Thought from Lore to Science*. New York: D. C. Heath and Co.

Bogardus, Emory (1940) *The Development of Social Thought*. New York: Longmans, Green, and Co.

Broadie, Alexander (ed.) (1997) *The Scottish Enlightenment: An Anthology*. Edinburgh: Canongate Books.

Camic, Charles (1983) *Experience and Enlightenment: Socialization for Cultural Change in Eighteenth Century Scotland*. Chicago: University of Chicago Press.

Comte, Auguste (1856) *Social Physics from the Positive Philosophy of Auguste Comte*. New York: Calvin Blanchard.

Darwin, C. G. (1952) *The Next Million Years*. London: Rupert Hart-Davis.

Durkheim, Emile ([1893] 1984) *The Division of Labor in Society*. Trans. W. D. Halls. New York: Free Press.

Durkheim, Emile ([1897] 2006) *On Suicide*. Trans. Robin Buss. New York: Penguin Books.

Ellwood, Charles (1938) *A History of Social Philosophy*. New York: Prentice Hall.

Engels, Friedrich ([1845] 1987) *The Condition of the Working Class in England*. New York: Penguin Books.

Fournier, Marcel (2007) *Emile Durkheim: 1858–1917*. Paris: Fayard.

Frisby, David and Mike Featherstone (eds.) (1997) *Simmel on Culture: Selected Writings*. London: Sage.

Gouldner, Alvin (1970) *The Coming Crisis of Western Sociology*. New York: Basic Books.

Hertzler, Joyce (1936) *The Social Thought of the Ancient Civilizations*. New York: McGraw-Hill Book Co.

Levine, Donald (1957/1980) *Simmel and Parsons: Two Approaches to the Study of Society*. New York: Arno Press.

Levine, Donald, Ellwood B. Carter, and Eleanor Miller Gorman (1976) "Simmel's Influence on American Sociology." *American Journal of Sociology* 81: 813–45, 1112–32.

Lundberg, George (1939) *Foundations of Sociology*. New York: Macmillan Publishing Co.

Lundberg, George (1947) *Can Science Save Us?* New York: Longmans, Green, and Co.

Marx, Karl and Friedrich Engels (1975–2010) *Collected Works*, 51 vols. New York: International Publishers.

Meurer, Bärbel (2010) *Marianne Weber: Leben und Werk*. Tübingen: Mohr Siebeck.

Millar, John (1806) *The Origin of the Distinction of Ranks or, An Inquiry into the Circumstances Which Give Rise to Influence and Authority in the Different Members of Society*, 4th edn. London: Longman, Hurst, Rees, and Orme.

Mirowski, Philip (1989) *More Heat Than Light: Economics as Social Physics, Physics as Nature's Economics*. Cambridge: Cambridge University Press.

Mussolini, Benito (1928) *My Autobiography*. New York: Charles Scribner's Sons.

Musto, Marcello (ed.) (2010) *Karl Marx's Grundrisse: Foundations of the Critique of Political Economy 150 Years Later*. London: Routledge.

Parsons, Talcott (1937) *The Structure of Social Action*. New York: McGraw-Hill.

Pickering, Mary (1993) *Auguste Comte: An Intellectual Biography*, Vol. 1; Vol. 2 (2009), Vol. 3 (2009). Cambridge: Cambridge University Press.

Quetelet, Adolphe (1835) *Sur l'homme et le Développement de ses Facultés, ou Essai de Physique Sociale*, 2 vols. Paris: Imprimeur-Libraire.

Quetelet, Adolphe (1984) *Adolphe Quetelet's Research on the Propensity for Crime at Different Ages*. Trans. Sawyer Sylvester. New York: Anderson Publishing Company.

Radkau, Joachim (2009) *Max Weber: A Biography*. Trans. Patrick Camiller. Cambridge: Polity Press.

Ritzer, George (1988) *Sociological Theory*, 2nd edn. New York: Knopf.

Royce, Josiah (1904) *Herbert Spencer: An Estimate and Review, Together with a Chapter of Personal Reminiscences by James Collier [his secretary]*. New York: Fox, Duffield, and Co.

Sica, Alan (2004) *Max Weber: A Comprehensive Bibliography*. New Brunswick, NJ: Transaction Publishers.

Sica, Alan (ed.) (2005) *Social Thought: From the Enlightenment to the Present*. Boston: Pearson/Allyn and Bacon.

Simmel, Georg (2009) *Sociology: Inquiries into the Construction of Social Forms*, Vols. 1 and 2. Trans. and ed. Anthony Blasi et al. Boston: Brill.

Smith, Adam (1761) *The Theory of Moral Sentiments*, 2nd edn. London: A. Millar.

Sorokin, Pitirim (1928) *Contemporary Sociological Theories*. New York: Harper and Brothers.

Urry, John (2004) "Small Worlds and the New 'Social Physics'." *Global Networks* 4(2): 109–30.

Veblen, Thorstein (1899) *The Theory of the Leisure Class*. New York: Macmillan Company.

Werth, Barry (2009) *Banquet at Delmonico's: Great Minds, the Gilded Age, and the Triumph of Evolution in America*. New York: Random House.

6

Contemporary Sociological Theory

George Ritzer and William Yagatich

There was a time in the recent history of sociology (roughly 1930 to 1980), especially in the United States, when it was relatively easy to be a sociological theorist, or at least it seemed that way, especially compared to the situation today. There were graduate departments of sociology that specialized in specific theories. They were likely to have *the* thinker associated with that theory, or at least students, or disciples, of that theorist. The paradigm case was, of course, structural functionalism, but symbolic interactionism, ethnomethodology, critical theory, world system theory, the Birmingham School, and others were organized in a somewhat similar manner. In structural functionalism's case, the place to be was Harvard, where the acknowledged leader of the perspective, Talcott Parsons, reigned supreme. His students went off to schools like Columbia (Robert Merton), Cornell (Robin Williams), Princeton (Marion Levy), and so on. As a result, if you were a graduate student interested in structural functionalism, it was relatively easy to know where you did, or did not, want to study.

Of course, the situation was far less clear-cut in most graduate programs. Various theoretical perspectives were likely to be represented (although it was possible that there was no dedicated theorist, or not much theory at all, in a given program). However, even in this case it was not difficult for a budding theorist to discern who worked within a given theory and whether or not one wanted to work with that person and in that theoretical tradition.

There were people involved in all of this so the situation could get quite messy. A student could be drawn to a particular perspective, but not to the professor representing it, or vice versa. However, the discipline as a whole seemed much neater

The Wiley-Blackwell Companion to Sociology, First Edition. Edited by George Ritzer.
© 2012 Blackwell Publishing Ltd. Published 2012 by Blackwell Publishing Ltd.

because there were simply different sets of abstract ideas that one could decide to resonate with or resist. For most sociologists, the leaders associated with a particular set of ideas (e.g., Talcott Parsons, Herbert Blumer, Immanuel Wallerstein, Herbert Marcuse, Stuart Hall) were just as distant and abstract as the ideas themselves. In fact, for most sociologists thinkers themselves were in many ways little more than sets of ideas.

Eventually, a number of theoretical categories emerged and they became increasingly standard fare in most courses and textbooks in sociological theory. Every basic textbook included chapters, or at least parts of chapters, devoted to structural functionalism, conflict theory, neo-Marxian theory, systems theory, symbolic interactionism, ethnomethodology, exchange theory, and so on. The eighth edition of Ritzer's (2010b) basic textbook in sociological theory retains many of the same general theory categories used in the first edition of that book published nearly three decades ago. Over the years, various categories of theory have been added (e.g., globalization theory, feminist theory, queer theory, critical race theory). (A smaller number of theoretical categories have come and, for the most part, gone, including sociobiology, behavioral sociology, and phenomenological sociology.) In the end, there are more neat theoretical boxes even though it has become increasingly clear to most students of theories that such categories no longer make much sense. Interestingly, there have been perspectives that have challenged this category system – micro-macro integration, agency-structure integration, and postmodern theory are the best known of these. However, in most cases they have been co-opted into mainstream sociological theory, and theory textbooks, and have simply become new categories of theory.

The need to categorize theories, as well as the theoretical categories themselves, has come to be reified in sociology. They have been passed down from generation to generation of sociologists and have come to be seen as necessities by publishers, sociologists, teachers, authors, and students. This is especially clear in textbooks in introductory sociology, which not only almost always use, but are built on a base of, such categories of theory. Most introductory textbooks use the same limited number of categories – structural functionalism, conflict theory, and symbolic interactionism – that were used over a half-century ago. The categories, in introductory sociology textbooks as well as elsewhere, are handy, but they are inaccurate depictions of sociological theory today, or at any given moment in time.

This neat categorization system, as well as the categories that were produced, represented a very modern orientation. They were being produced and reproduced at the height of the modern era. Furthermore, they were being created for, and imposed upon, a set of theorists who for the most part considered themselves modernists. They were not only producing modern theories, but they were quite proud of it. And they were doing so in a field that considered itself to be very modern in its pursuit of a, or perhaps the, grand theory, as well as a science of society.

While categorization, and even many of the specific theoretical categories mentioned above (and others), continue to be widely used, there is an increasing realization on the part of virtually everyone in the field that these categories are mythological in themselves and represent mythological realities. Even introductory sociology texts are finally beginning to move away from the rigid three-category theoretical system that dominated them for decades. The lines of demarcation among and between theories were never real and there is a wide-ranging and growing realization of that fact. Furthermore, much of the theoretical content that made up these categories has changed, eroded, or perhaps even passed into the discipline's ancient history, as have the thinkers (such as Parsons) most associated with the categories.

CHALLENGES FROM WITHIN MODERNITY

One set of challenges to these categories and this categorization system came from modernists themselves. As early as 1975 the senior author of this essay sought to deal with this way of categorizing theory in the context of an effort to delineate sociology's major paradigms (Ritzer 1975). As a modernist, using a modernist approach derived from the work of Thomas Kuhn ([1962] 1963) on the paradigmatic structure of science, Ritzer came up with three new and somewhat broader categories – the social facts, social definition, and social behavior paradigms. However, this enabled him to see that at least some perspectives (e.g., structural functionalism and conflict theory; symbolic interactionism and ethnomethodology) that were thought of as distinct theoretical categories in fact shared many characteristics and were part of the same paradigm. This demonstrated that the dividing lines between them were not as clear-cut as many thought. More importantly, Ritzer ended his 1975 book with an argument for the need for a paradigm that cut across extant paradigms and their theories and dealt with their diverse concerns in a more integrated manner. That perspective was more fully developed in *Toward an Integrated Sociological Paradigm* (Ritzer 1980). While this had the unfortunate consequence of suggesting yet another paradigm, or category, the main thrust was to argue for a more fluid (see below), less differentiated type of theory. In fact, beginning about that time there was movement toward such theorizing both in the US (micro-macro theory) and in Europe (agency-structure theory). However, as pointed out above, these, too, quickly became new categories rather than approaches that broke down the barriers between theoretical categories.

This way of thinking about sociological theory as a set of categories fits well with Zygmunt Bauman's (2000) thinking on the relationship between modernity and solidity. That is, modernists tend to think in terms of, and more importantly to construct, solid structures, both in the material world (e.g., border fences between the US and Mexico; Israel and the West Bank) and in the realm of ideas. In the case of sociological theory, this took the form of solid structures (e.g., "schools" such as those at Harvard or the University of Chicago) and, more importantly, categories of sociological theory that seemed solid to both insiders and outsiders. Insiders sought in various ways to solidify the theory (e.g., by making its basic assumptions more consistent or even by creating jargon impenetrable to outsiders) and, at least in the heyday of such theories, outsiders found them and their "borders" to be largely unassailable.

If such solidity describes sociological theory between about 1930 and 1980, the new theoretical reality since 1980 and to this day is captured well by Bauman's notion of liquidity, an idea he associates with late modernity. Rather than being treated and seen as solid structures, sociological theories are increasingly treated and seen as highly fluid and as, themselves, a part of a highly fluid world. In fact, it is likely that sociological theory was always better thought of in terms of liquidity than solidity, and it is the case that theory is far more fluid today than it ever was in the past. Conceiving of theories as liquid has a number of important implications.

First, theories are not, and should not be seen as being, fixed in time; they are constantly changing and in flux over time. For example, even though we may use the same label today as we did a half-century, or more, ago, symbolic interactionism (to take one example) today is very different from what it was then and will be still more different in the decades to come (Fine 1993). Thus, within a seemingly fixed theoretical category, ideas are changing over time. Furthermore, the relationship among and between theories within sociology is also changing over time.

Second, and more important for our purposes, is the fact that theories are not fixed in space. On a tangible level, this means that theories can no longer (if they ever could) be identified with physical locales as was the case with structural functionalism with Harvard, symbolic interactionism with Chicago, critical theory with Frankfurt (although the current leading active figure in critical theory, Axel Honneth, is located there; see below), world system theory with Binghamton, or the Birmingham School with, well, Birmingham. More importantly, on an ideational level this means that we cannot differentiate between types of theory as if they occupied entirely different intellectual spaces. There are no solid lines between such spaces and ideas are constantly flowing between them, making the idea that there are borders between them seem silly.

Third, theoretical ideas, as ideas, are liquid phenomena and this means that they have always moved about easily. However, today, especially in the era of jet travel (with ideas borne by theorists) and the internet, they are able to move about far more easily and quickly than ever before. Furthermore, once on the move, especially at warp speed on the internet, those ideas are nearly impossible to slow down, let alone stop. In any case, in the liquid age, few want to slow down the flow of theoretical ideas, let alone stop it.

Fourth, liquids in general, especially liquid ideas, tend to melt whatever solid structures or barriers stand in their way. In the mid-twentieth century, theoretical ideas were just as liquid as they are today but they were artificially contained by physical barriers around universities and departments (e.g., admission standards), as well as ideational barriers around theoretical schools. Of course, those barriers, especially the latter, existed far more in the minds of social theorists, and those of metatheorists who studied theory (Mullins 1983), than as real structures that succeeded in impeding the flow of ideas. In any case, whatever the realities in the mid-twentieth century, those ideas have long since overflowed and/or dissolved those barriers and now flow more freely than ever in every conceivable direction.

Bauman's work takes on modernity in general, and modern sociological theory in particular, from within the context of a modern paradigm. A similarly modern challenge comes from Anthony Giddens (1990) and Ulrich Beck (1992) and their argument that we live in an era that can be thought of as being characterized by reflexivity; we live in the era of "reflexive modernization." In terms of social theory, this means that social theorists have come to be increasingly reflexive about the theoretical categories (as well as the whole idea of a theoretical category) which they choose for themselves or into which they have been thrust by what may have been the accidental choice of a particular graduate program or thesis advisor. More generally, it means that social theorists are growing much more reflexive about the whole idea of solid structures and barriers, especially in the context of this discussion as they relate to theory. This kind of theoretical solidity could not survive careful reflection. After all, it really made no sense in the first place. More generally, such reflexivity means that theorists are going to reflect continually on ideas and to move on readily when the ideas no longer stand up to close scrutiny. This serves to give theory even greater fluidity.

Also emanating from within the modernist perspective was the rise of a number of alternative theories – especially feminist, critical race, and queer theories. These theories challenged the hegemony of the dominant theories and schools in various ways. However, they were themselves modernist in many ways (e.g., scientific, seeking the betterment of society) and therefore did not challenge modernism as a whole. For one thing, they pointed out that women (and men who were feminists), blacks (and other minorities), and gays (especially those who wrote about gay issues) were largely excluded from the dominant departments that focused on theory. For another, the theories themselves accorded relatively little room to the issues of concern to these minorities (among the exceptions was Miriam Johnson [1989] who focused on issues of concern to feminists from within a structural functional approach). Furthermore, when the dominant theories did concern themselves with these issues, it was largely the dominant white males (e.g., Parsons or Everett Hughes on race) who examined them, inevitably at a distance and with a "god's eye" perspective on the matter. Such thinking was largely unacceptable not only to minority scholars, but to many members of the majority group, as well.

Those who became the leaders in these theoretical perspectives (e.g., Dorothy Smith, Patricia Hill Collins, Eduardo Bonilla-Silva, Chela Sandoval, Howard Winant) were not likely to have come out of the major sociology departments, the dominant theoretical perspectives, or to be trained by the leading sociological theorists. In fact, many (e.g., Judith Butler, Audre Lorde, Dawne Moon, David Theodore Goldberg, Eva Kosofsky-Sedgwick) were not even sociologists. The interdisciplinary character of these perspectives also reflected the increasingly fluid character of theory as ideas flowed easily not only across theoretical, but also across the often seemingly much more solid disciplinary, boundaries (Abbott 2001). The fact that so many leading thinkers did not come from the dominant schools and were not associated with the leading perspectives was an indication of the weakness of both. It demonstrated the increasing fluidity of theory as those associated with less prestigious graduate schools and seemingly marginal perspectives were able to rise to centrality in sociological theory. At the same time, it showed the even greater fluidity of theory as their ideas rose to prominence and were barely affected by the solid structures put in place by the dominant theories, schools and even academic fields to protect their ideas and their positions. In fact, the barriers may have aided the rise of the new ideas by causing increasing resentment against those creating the barriers and greater efforts to overcome them and their barriers. Worse, the growth of these alternative perspectives demonstrated the irrelevance of the dominant perspectives to theory, especially to the most important cutting-edge developments in theory.

CHALLENGES FROM POSTMODERNITY

To Bauman (2000), Giddens (1990), Beck (1999), and others we live in a late modern age that is different from the modern age that dominated the golden years of sociological theory. However, in the end they still offer modern perspectives on the world. Others see this more radically as postmodernists who argue that we have moved beyond modernity into a postmodern age. Whether or not we see the current era as a postmodern epoch, this brings us to the paradoxical role that postmodern social theory has played in the changing nature of sociological theory. To put it succinctly, sociological theorists, especially in the United States, paid little or no serious attention to postmodern theory even though postmodern theory played a major role in changing the practice of sociological theory in very profound ways. Interestingly, much the same thing can be said about sociological methods (see Duneier, Chapter 4).

First, postmodern thinkers tended to reject the idea of putting solid barriers between such things as "culture and life, fiction and theory, image and reality," and academic disciplines (Rosenau 1992: 6). This prohibition could easily be extended, and was in fact extended, to surrounding social theories with such barriers.

Second, postmodern theorists devoted to the idea of deconstruction could easily turn their attention to deconstructing the major sociological theories as well as the solid barriers that surrounded them. Tearing down those barriers, like tearing down the Berlin Wall, came to be seen as a blow against the failed modern project. Deconstructionists were not only devoted to tearing down barriers, but they were also opposed to the creation of new "walled" theories.

Third, postmodern theorists were, above all, critical of modernity, and sociological theory was seen as a modern undertaking. Modern sociological theories were seen as not having delivered on their promises and, worse, as having contributed to the worst excesses of the twentieth century (e.g., the Holocaust and the Gulag archipelago). While sociological theory was not directly implicated in these excesses, it was tarred by the same brush that adversely affected various social theories (e.g., of Heidegger) and more applied theories (e.g., communism) that wreaked so much havoc in the world.

Relatedly, much of sociological theory was scientific in its orientations, or at least it was not hostile to science. Of course, postmodernists viewed science as one of the major contributions of modernity and it, too, came under assault. The most scientific of sociological theories created hypotheses (e.g., George Homans' [1974] exchange theory; Randall Collins' [1975] conflict theory), or were easily reducible to seemingly testable hypotheses (see any of Jonathan Turner's frequent efforts to do so). However, all of this scientific theory created neither generally agreed-upon theories nor breakthroughs that revolutionized the impact that theory had on the social world (through, for example, the amelioration of various social problems).

Fourth, each of the solid barriers that characterized sociological theory encompassed a theory that offered a totalizing view of the world. Such totalizing views were associated with modernity and they came to be rejected in favor of more local, even micro-, narratives. Such perspectives did not lend themselves well to, or even suggest the need for, solid barriers.

Fifth, postmodernists rejected the essentialism that lay at the core of modern sociological theories and in the center of the stockades that protected those essentialist ideas from close, less sympathetic, critical scrutiny.

Finally, while modern social theories were oriented around a center, as well as to getting at the center or core of a social issue or even of the social world, postmodern social theorists were much more oriented to looking toward the periphery in an effort to find new ways of thinking about the social world. Thus the postmodernist would examine the borders of the boxes or, better, tear down those borders and go outside the boxes altogether. It was there in the netherworld beyond modernist borders that true insight was to be found. Much of Jean Baudrillard's work on death and symbolic exchange ([1976] 2002), seduction ([1979] 1990), and simulations (1983) exemplified this approach.

Thus, there is much about postmodern social theory that suggests the rejection and the end of solid theoretical categories or well-differentiated theoretical schools. While there is an elective affinity between the end of modern theory and postmodern social theory, it is difficult to assert a causal relationship between the two even though the decline of modern theory coincided more or less with the rise of postmodern theory. The problem is that theorists, especially those in the United States, showed a marked disinclination to study, or perhaps even read, the works of the premier postmodern theorists including Baudrillard, Deleuze and Guattari, Lyotard, and many others. Michel Foucault was at least an exception to this, perhaps because he was more of a post-structuralist than a postmodernist. It is also the case that his major substantive works on prisons (Foucault [1977] 1995), medicine ([1973] 1994), madness ([1965] 1998), and sexuality ([1978] 1990) were not as unfamiliar substantively, or as difficult to decipher, as the work of the postmodern theorists mentioned above (and many others). Not only did most American theorists not want to engage seriously with postmodern theory in a scholarly way, they also didn't want to teach the theory to either their graduate or undergraduate students. The senior author of this essay can attest to this personally since his *Postmodern Social Theory* (Ritzer 1997) was the only one of his several theory textbooks to fail and to be put out of print by the publisher a few years after it was published. Thus, it could not have been the substantive ideas associated with postmodern theory that caused the weakening of modern theories, but it could well have been the mood that was created by postmodernism, not only in theory, but in society as a whole, that made the continuation of business-as-usual in sociological theory (and, as we have seen, sociological methods) impossible.

Even greater threats to the idea of solid, modern social theory were posed by a series of theories that arose in the wake of postmodern theory. Post-postmodern theory came to focus, among many other things, on fashion and consumption (Lipovetsky [1987] 2002, 2005), challenging the tendency of the established theories to focus on issues relating to production; to operate with a productivist bias. Furthermore, it tended to focus on the seemingly trivial periphery (e.g., fashion) rather than the "serious" and more central issues (e.g., work) of concern to modern theorists. Actor network theory (Latour 1999; Law 1999) threatened the dominant theories in various ways, including the effort to include inanimate objects, even animals, as part of social networks and more generally of the social world. The idea of a post-social (Franklin 2007), even a post-human, sociology (Knorr-Cetina 2001) constituted a powerful threat to established theories wedded to sociologies that focused on humans in the social world.

"ZOMBIE THEORIES"

In spite of all of the changes and critiques, much of the focus remains on traditional theories and theoretical perspectives. Following Ulrich Beck's frequent discussion (see, for example, Beck 2007) of "zombie concepts," we would like to argue that many, but not all, of the traditional theoretical approaches might better be seen as "zombie theories."

For example, Beck discusses the nation-state as a zombie concept. It was a perfectly appropriate concept a few decades ago before the rise of globalization, but the latter has progressively reduced its significance. That is because the nation-state is unable to stem or control a wide array of global flows, many of which freely pierce its borders. Further, many global flows (e.g., those associated with finance) are now arguably of far greater importance than the nation-state. However, a great deal of attention continues to be devoted to the concept (and phenomenon), especially in fields such as international relations and political sociology, even though the nation-state, at least as we have traditionally conceived it, has been dealt what, in the eyes of many observers, is a mortal blow by globalization.

It is possible to think of many theories as zombie theories, or at least as in the process of dying and moving toward a zombie-like state. That is, the theories seem alive to many, especially supporters and textbook authors, but in fact, if they are not yet dead, there is only the faintest of pulses reflecting a bare minimum of life.

Interestingly, the theories that dominated American sociology a half-century ago, and that are still seen as central by the writers of basic textbooks in sociology in general, and sociological theory in particular, can be put in this category. This is particularly true of structural functionalism and conflict theory even though they are still seen by many as the polar types (consensus and conflict) that define sociological theory. The best example of a zombie theory is the one-time giant of American sociological theory, structural functionalism. This is striking because there was a time when structural functionalism was not only thought of as the most important sociological theory, but seen as more or less synonymous with (American) sociology (Davis 1959). However, it is difficult to find anyone in sociology today who would even admit to being a structural functionalist and it is even more difficult to find any significant new contributions to that theory. Conflict theory existed largely as an alternative to structural functionalism and with the latter's demise, its *raison d'être* disappeared. It, too, can be seen as a zombie theory. This is the case even though many still see society as defined by conflict (and others persist in emphasizing consensus, even if they are not structural functionalists), but merely seeing society in that way does not mean that one is a conflict theorist. The other major sociological theory of the mid-twentieth century, symbolic interactionism, is clearly still alive and kept that way by a number of supporters, especially in the US. However, if it is not yet a zombie theory, it is clearly on life-support and heading in that direction.

Marxian theory is still quite vibrant and has even been given a boost by the Great Recession (see Rey and Ritzer, Chapter 24), but a number of its major sub-theories (economic determinism, Hegelian Marxism) can be placed in the category of zombie theories. This is especially true of structural Marxism which had a large following, especially in Europe, a half-century ago. Just as one might ask who now reads the structural functionalism of Talcott Parsons, it is also possible to ask who now reads the structural Marxism of Louis Althusser and Nicos Poulantzas.

Among the more micro-theories, phenomenological sociology, existential sociology, and behavioral sociology can all be considered zombie theories.

The point here is not to enumerate all of the theories that can be seen as zombie theories (or the many others that are simply dead and buried – although they can always return as theoretical zombies), but to note that there are a number of zombie theories that still get a great deal of attention in sociology even though they are among the "living dead." There are few sociologists today who would identify themselves with the theories mentioned in the last few paragraphs, and it is difficult to point to many, if any, important recent developments in these theories. It is clear in the practice of sociological theory that these are zombie theories. However, one gets a very different impression from the textbooks in the courses that deal with them.

The Liveliness of Traditional Theories

In contrast to the dead and zombie theories, as well as those that are on some sort of life-support, there are some more traditional theories that continue to show signs of life, if not continuing to be quite vibrant. To illustrate this, we will focus here on recent work in critical theory as well as in structuralism and post-structuralism.

Critical theory and the work of Axel Honneth

The leading contemporary figure in critical theory is, of course, Jürgen Habermas, but he is in retirement. The mantle of leading critical theorist has passed to Axel Honneth who is the current Director of the Frankfurt Institute of Social Research. To achieve the status of leading critical theorist, Honneth has developed a theoretical position that builds on, but critiques, the work of the critical school as well as that of Habermas in particular (Honneth [1985] 1997, [1990] 1995, [1992] 1996, [2000] 2007, 2008).

Honneth's critique of his predecessors, as well as his own theoretical perspective, is based on his fundamental views on the requirements of a critical theory. For one thing, it must be done "in such a way that a practical dimension of critique emerges as a constitutive requirement for critical understanding" (Honneth [1990] 1995: xii). For another, a critical theory must not only be based on critiques that exist in the everyday world, but it must also have an interest in emancipating people from the domination and oppression that they experience in (that is immanent in) the real world. That is, critical theory must have an integrative interest in both theory *and* practice. It must seek the "determination of the driving forces of society which locates in the historical process itself the impetus both to critique as well as to overcome established forms of domination" (Honneth [1990] 1995: xii).

The basic problem with classic critical theory, especially that of Horkheimer and Adorno, is that its totally administered view of the capitalist world led to negativism; it left no hope for practical critique and emancipatory possibilities in the everyday world and in critical theory itself. Of critical theory, Honneth ([1990] 1995: xii) said that it supposed a "closed circle between capitalist domination and cultural manipulation, that there could remain within the social reality of their time no space for a zone of moral-practical critique." This leads him to the conclusion that the key problem for critical theory today is how to come "to grips with the structure of social domination as well as with identifying the social resources for its practical transformation" (Honneth [1990] 1995: xiii).

In this context, Honneth sees Habermas's communication theory as a step forward because it offered us a way of dealing with, getting at, offering an immanent critique of, and transcending, the everyday lifeworld (Honneth [1990] 1995: xiii). It is the everyday social world that provides "social criticism with a moral foothold" (Honneth [1990] 1995: xv). In that world, Honneth comes to focus on the recognition of identity claims made by individuals and collectivities. Consistent with critical theory, he wants to deal with the violence committed against those claims for recognition and the injuries and pathologies that result for the claimants. Individuals and groups come to engage in political resistance not because of some abstract moral principles, but because of the "experience of violence to intuitively presupposed conceptions of justice" (Honneth [1990] 1995: xiv). That is, they feel that they deserve recognition and when they do not get it, their sense of fair play is upset, and they come to resist those who are seen as being unfair to them. And, "it is principally violence to individual or collective claims to social recognition within the lifeworld which will be experienced as moral injustice" (Honneth [1990] 1995: xv).

At the heart of Honneth's work is the idea of "the struggle for recognition." While people have historically often felt that they did not get the recognition they deserved, it is possible, even likely, that there is an increasing crisis of recognition in contemporary society. For example, it is difficult to get recognition for one's work (especially for women; see Rossler 2007). More generally, there has been a decline in the ability of various institutions – e.g., family, work – to create the kinds of recognition people need.

More specifically, people are seen as needing three forms of recognition from others. The first is *love*, or caring for a person's needs and emotions. People gain self-confidence when they receive such recognition. The second is *respect* for a person's moral and legal dignity and this leads to self-respect. Finally, there is *esteem* for a person's social achievements and this leads to self-esteem (Van den Brink & Owen 2007a). These forms of recognition are acquired and maintained intersubjectively. That is, in order to relate to themselves in these ways (and to have self-confidence, self-respect, and self-esteem), people must receive recognition from others. Ultimately, "[r]elations of recognition are a necessary condition of our moral subjectivity and agency" (Van den Brink & Owen 2007b: 4–5). It is only with adequate recognition that people can realize their full autonomy as human beings.

Disrespect occurs when people do not receive the recognition they feel they deserve, and this adversely affects their ability to form appropriate identities. Feelings of a lack of respect are not unverifiable feelings, but are based on a normative standard that people deserve certain forms of recognition; most generally, they deserve love, respect, and esteem. Conflict and resistance are likely to result when they do not get the recognition the normative system says they should. The existence of such a normative standard not only lies at the base of such actions, but it allows outsiders (including critical theorists) to utilize established norms to evaluate those actions, and the concrete claims for recognition on which those actions are based. That is, Honneth offers us an Archimedean point from which to evaluate claims for recognition; our judgments of the legitimacy of those claims need not be arbitrary.

There are at least four major criticisms of Honneth's critical theory. First, there are those who question the placement of recognition at the heart of a social and ethical theory. Is recognition as important as Honneth suggests? Is it as important as work and labor in Marx's theory or communication in Habermas's theory? Second, there are doubts about the kind of monistic theory created by Honneth; is recognition all that matters? Third, there are those who question whether there are three bases of recognition – why not more or less? Finally, it is hard to discern the operations of power in Honneth's theory. Nonetheless, Honneth has created a distinctive form of critical theory that demonstrates the continued liveliness of that theory.

Structuralism, post-structuralism: Foucault and Agamben

Michel Foucault developed his theories in the context of structuralism in France and the efforts to move beyond it in post-structuralism. Foucault is generally seen as a post-structuralist, although he developed his own very distinctive theoretical approach. This involved the creation of a new method, purged of individuals, which focused on the practice of discourse. Foucault's work has a powerful influence on sociological theory today. It is especially through his work that structuralism and post-structuralism continue to be lively, even powerful, presences in contemporary theory.

We cannot offer an overview of Foucault's numerous theoretical ideas in the context of this relatively brief chapter. Rather, we will focus on his work on the penal system since it is, at least in part, on the basis of that work that Giorgio Agamben develops his critique of Foucault, as well as his own ideas on the "camp."

Foucault makes it clear that the purpose of *Discipline and Punish* is to provide "a correlative history of the modern soul and of a new power to judge; a genealogy of the present scientifico-legal complex from which the power to punish derives its bases, justifications and rules, from which it extends its effects and by which it masks its exorbitant singularity" ([1977] 1995: 23). In that context, Foucault traces the development of the modern penal system. In the process, Foucault demonstrates how "knowledge and power directly imply one another" ([1977] 1995: 27). Power in the prison system, and elsewhere, is based on, and expressed in, observation, normalizing judgments, and the use of examination. They are used to produce docile bodies subjected to the discursive regime. The key to this analysis is Foucault's concept, based on the work of Jeremy Bentham, of the panopticon.

In this case, the panopticon is a tower in the center of the prison yard. This allows guards within the tower to see into the individual prison cells that are arrayed around the tower. Inmates could be viewed, or at least they thought they could be watched, at any given time. At the same time, the tower windows are designed in such a way that inmates cannot see inside the tower. Thus, whether or not anyone is really inside the tower, it is possible to maintain at least the illusion, if not the fact, that an inmate is being watched: "The panopticon is a machine for dissociating the see/being seen dyad: in the peripheric ring, one is totally seen, without ever seeing; in the central tower, one sees everything without ever being seen" (Foucault [1977] 1995: 201–2). The panopticon is used "to induce in the inmate a state of conscious and permanent visibility that assures the automatic functioning of power" (Foucault [1977] 1995: 20). More generally, the panopticon is the paradigmatic example of surveillance, and surveillance was, in Foucault's view, coming to be manifest across and throughout the social body.

From this, Foucault developed the idea of the carceral archipelago, where the methods of discipline and surveillance developed in the prison swarmed throughout the social body. This resulted in "a great carceral continuum that diffused penitentiary techniques into the most innocent disciplines." It produced a "subtle, graduated carceral net, with compact institutions, but also separate and diffused methods" (Foucault [1977] 1995: 297). The production of docile bodies through the disciplines and the use of surveillance became the dominant focus of institutions throughout society.

Ultimately, Foucault is highly critical of the new means of punishment. For one thing, it has become the dominant mode of power throughout the social body (schools, hospitals, etc.), resulting in a carceral archipelago from which it is increasingly difficult to escape. For another, it is not just the body that is disciplined but also the soul.

Agamben has built on Foucault's theories by, for example, contesting his ideas on the prison and substituting, instead, the camp. Agamben ([1995] 1998: 122) is interested in the biopolitics (which he defines in his own terms [Foucault had no sense of "bare life"] as the "care, control, and use of bare life") of the Nazi concentration camp, and the camp more generally, as well as the larger society that has become a camp. It is in his thinking on biopolitics that Agamben was most influenced by Michel Foucault and his seminal work on that topic. As Agamben saw it, biopolitics, as the concept was developed by Foucault, involved "the species and the individual as a simple living body becom[ing] what is at stake in a society's political strategies" ([1995] 1998: 3). However, while to Foucault this development was relatively recent, to Agamben it is an ancient phenomenon (DeCaroli 2007: 53; for other differences[1] between the two thinkers, see Mills 2007). To Agamben:

> The decisive fact is that, together with the process by which the exception everywhere becomes the rule, the realm of bare life – which is originally situated at the margins of the political order – gradually begins to coincide with the political realm, and exclusion and inclusion, outside and inside, *bios* and *zoe*, right and fact, enter into a zone of irreducible indistinction. At once excluding bare life from and capturing it within the political order, the state of exception actually constituted, in its very separateness, the hidden foundations on which the entire political system rested . . . the bare

life . . . becomes . . . the one place for the organization of State power and emancipation from it. ([1995] 1998: 9)

In the above, bare life becomes the objective of biopolitics and the linkage between the work of Foucault and Agamben.

However, while Foucault focused on the prison as the key site for the practice of biopolitics, Agamben argued that that site was the camp, "not the prison" ([1995] 1998: 20). Thus, Agamben critiques Foucault because he "never brought his insights to bear on what could well have appeared to be the exemplary place of modern biopolitics: the politics of the great totalitarian states of the twentieth century" ([1995] 1998: 119). Foucault should have seen, for example, that Nazism and the concentration camps were the "point at which the integration of medicine and politics, which is one of the essential characteristics of modern biopolitics, began to assume its final form . . . the physician and the sovereign seem to exchange roles" (Agamben [1995] 1998: 143).

Agamben also differs from Foucault in terms of his outlook for the future. Foucault has a reasonably optimistic outlook involving the future emergence of a "different economy of bodies and liberation" (Agamben [1995] 1998: 187). Agamben is more cautious, even pessimistic, about the future because he believes that we will never again be able to integrate our biological and political bodies.

RECENT DEVELOPMENTS IN THE SOCIAL WORLD *AND* IN SOCIOLOGICAL THEORY

Rather than survey and take the temperature of all of the theories in contemporary sociology, we close this chapter with a brief overview of a series of relatively new theoretical developments. We can be brief since the major areas covered – globalization, consumption, and the internet – are also the subject of separate essays in this volume and theorizing in these areas has been at least touched on in each of them. Many other recent developments, and the new theorizing they helped spawn, are detailed in many of the other substantive chapters in this volume.

The key point to be made here is that developments in contemporary sociological theory are driven more by developments in the social world than they are by those taking place within sociological theory itself. This, of course, is nothing new. In fact, the classic theorists were much more likely to develop their theories out of an engagement with the social world, especially changes in that world. It is also true, of course, that their thinking was shaped by the ideas of other theorists. For example, Marx's ideas were famously developed in dialogue with the thinking of Hegel, Smith, Ricardo, and others. However, no one would disagree with the idea that Marx's thinking was shaped much more by developments in the social world, especially the rise of capitalism, than it was by the theories of others. Furthermore, the work of many neo-Marxists, while certainly not unmindful of the contributions of other theorists, was shaped far more heavily by the changing character of the social world, especially capitalism. One notable example (of many) is the growing importance of culture in the early twentieth century and the effort by the critical theorists to shift the focus of Marxian analysis from the economic base to the cultural superstructure.

While there are certainly many exceptions, and almost all theorists attend to *both* developments in theory *and* in the social world, it can be argued that much of sociological theory from roughly 1930 to 1970 focused more on other theories than on the social world. To put this another way, metatheorizing was more important in the development of theory than was theorizing about the social world (Ritzer 1991). Metatheorizing involves thinking about theory, especially the work of other theorists, and the major goal of such work is the development of new theory. The examples of this are legion and they include conflict theory (especially the major example created by Dahrendorf), developed in reaction to the work of the structural functionalists (who tended to develop their ideas through a metatheoretical analysis of their own theories), neofunctionalism, based on an analysis and a critique of structural functionalism, systems theory (especially Luhmann's), developed at least in part out of the weaknesses of Parsons' systems theory, both exchange theory and ethnomethodology in reaction to the macro-excesses of Parsons' theories (and others), micro-macro theory and agency-structure theory out of a frustration with the excesses of *both* macro- and micro-theories, and post-structuralism because of the extremes of structuralism and existentialism.

This is not to say that all theory in this era was largely metatheoretical in character. C. Wright Mills' radical sociology was much more shaped by the nature of the society in which he lived, although his ideas were shaped at least negatively, as well, by theoretical inputs (for example, his famous dismissal of Talcott Parsons' thinking). Structural functionalists were certainly aware of developments in the social world and those developments played a role in their thinking (e.g., the effect of Nazism on Parsons). Most neo-Marxists were attuned to changes in capitalism (e.g., the need to update Marxian theory to take into consideration increasing monopolization, as well as the shift from Fordism to post-Fordism). Rational choice theorists, although they were largely metatheoretical in their orientation, were not unaware of the developments in the social world (the growing power of corporate over human actors).

Nevertheless, theory circa 1930 to 1970 tended to develop more on the basis of metatheoretical than theoretical analyses. In roughly the last 40–50 years the pendulum has swung and the focus of theorists has tended to be more on the social world than on other theories. While postmodern theorists do metatheoretical work (e.g., Baudrillard on Marx), their overwhelming focus is on what they perceive to be a dramatic change in the social world from the modern to the postmodern. Even modern theorists such as Bauman are highly attuned to such changes, which Bauman, for example, saw as characterized by the change from solidity to liquidity, or Beck described as the shift from industrial to risk society. However, the best examples are cutting-edge developments in, for example, feminist theory, critical theories of race and racism, and queer theory. Clearly, the overwhelming focus of those developing these theories is on the social world, especially the problems confronting racial and sexual minorities.

Of course, the preceding is describing theory with very broad brush strokes. It is clear that *all* theorists attend, as they should, to *both* the work of other theorists *and* events, especially changes, in the social world. In spite of its limitations, the need to attend to *both* developments in theory and changes in the social world provides a useful context for examining the three areas of theoretical development of concern here. These are three areas of the social world that have experienced major changes in the last two decades. While observers disagree on when it began (as if such dating is even possible), it seems clear that the great boom in globalization occurred around 1990. The internet, as we now know it, did not even exist in the early 1990s and it is today a, if not *the*, major force in the social world. Consumption is nothing new, but what Baudrillard first called the "consumer society" is new, as is consumerism, hyperconsumption, and an American society whose economy is dominated by consumption (the usual estimate is that at least 70 percent of the US economy is accounted for by consumption). The point is that theorizing in these areas is much more shaped by the changing nature of the social world than it is by the nature of other theories. However, the latter is far from non-existent. For example, Sklair's (2002) neo-Marxian theory of globalization is shaped, in part, by a reaction against world system theory because it is not sufficiently global and because it takes the nation-state as its basic unit of analysis.

Globalization

There are many different types of theory in the study of globalization, with political (political realism and alternatives to it such as complex interdependence), economic (e.g., neoliberalism and the heated debate that surrounds it), and cultural theories showing the greatest vibrancy. We will briefly discuss the range of cultural theories of globalization, both because they are the most sociological of the theories (the others are dominated by political scientists and economists) and because of limitations in terms of space.

Cultural theories of globalization can be grouped under three broad headings – cultural differentialism, cultural hybridization, and cultural convergence (Pieterse 2004). Representative of cultural differentialism is Samuel Huntington's (1997) *The Clash of Civilizations and the Remaking of World Order*. Huntington contends that cultures, understood in the broadest sense as civilizations, are the fundamental arenas of identity and social relations. He believes that the differences among civilizations will persist and be the cause of world tensions (especially economic and political/military) in the global age. To Huntington, there are irreconcilable differences among civilizations. These differences serve as barriers to flows of all manner of things among and between cultures. This argument has drawn criticism not only from those who support other theoretical perspectives, but also because Huntington operates from a West-centered perspective. In addition, he is seen as making gross generalizations about civilizations that do not hold up well in the light of empirical analyses (Gray 1998; Matlock 1999). Furthermore, most observers would contend that culture is much more fluid and amorphous than Huntington suggests.

Representative of cultural hybridization, the work of Jan Nederveen Pieterse (2004) goes to great lengths to describe cultures as products of long historical processes where cultures are continually interwoven and reconfigured over time to form new cultures. Cultural hybridization is not a new phenomenon but an ongoing process that continues to interweave different cultures and, in the process, to create new cultural configurations.

The third perspective, cultural convergence, contends that cultural differences are dissipating and that cultures are increasingly growing to resemble one another as a result of the global flows of cultural, especially consumer, practices and ideologies. Cultural convergence, buttressed by the efforts of multinational corporations, serves to refashion local cultures and, in the process, make them increasingly alike (Waters 1996; Bryman 2003; Ritzer 2006).

There are heated debates among the adherents of each of the three cultural theories. The cultural differentialists see cultures as resistant both to external cultures that would produce hybrids, as well as to those external cultures that seek to impose themselves on others and in the process create convergent cultures. Those who operate from the perspective of cultural hybridity reject the static, essentialistic views of those who accept cultural differentialism, as well as the notion that cultures are converging. Those who adopt a convergence perspective reject the largely antithetical view of the cultural differentialists and they see cultural hybridicists as overemphasizing the power of the local to resist the global.

Whatever the debates, and one's position on them, it is clear that globalization has generated a number of new theories, especially those that relate to culture and globalization.

The internet

Even more recent is the explosion of the internet and of issues of concern to all sociologists, including theorists and especially network theorists. Wellman et al.'s (1996) article, "Computer Networks as Social Networks: Collaborative Work, Telework, and Virtual Community," recognizes the dearth of sociological work (at least at the time) on the topic, and, almost prophetically, the authors state: "Research in this area engages with important intellectual questions and social issues at all scales, from dyadic to world system. It offers stimulating collaborations with other disciplines, industry, labor, and government" (Wellman, Salaff, Dimitrova, Garton, Gulia & Haythornthwaite 1996: 232). Sociological attention devoted to the topic has boomed not only in books and journal articles, but on innumerable internet blogs.

Of special interest, and an important link to the next new topic (consumption), is thinking on prosumption on the internet, especially Web 2.0. Early sociological theorists, as well as many of today's theorists, have focused on myriad issues relating to production. Beginning in the 1960s, a shift began to take place in the direction of focusing on consumption (see below). Key theoretical works appeared soon after, including Daniel Bell's *The Cultural Contradictions of Capitalism* ([1976] 1996) and especially Jean Baudrillard's *The Consumer Society* ([1970] 1998). As consumption boomed, and production, especially in the US, declined, increasing attention came to be focused on consumption. However, this continued the historical tendency to set up a false distinction between production and consumption.

Ritzer (2009) has recently argued that the focus on either production or consumption has always been misplaced and that all acts always involve both. That is, all acts of production and consumption are fundamentally acts of prosumption. The assembly-line worker is always consuming all sorts of things (parts, energy, tools) in the process of production, and conversely the consumer in, for example, a fast-food restaurant is always producing (garnishes for a sandwich, soft drinks from the self-serve dispenser, the disposal of debris derived from the meal). This suggests a dramatic reorientation of theorizing about the economy away from production or consumption and in the direction of prosumption.

Prosumption is not only a historical reality, but it is becoming increasingly ubiquitous with the emergence on the internet of Web 2.0. Web 1.0 (e.g., AOL) typically involved sites that were created and managed by producers and used more or less passively by separable consumers. The latter not only did not produce the websites, but usually could not alter their content in any meaningful way. In contrast, Web 2.0 is defined by sites (e.g., Facebook, blogs) the contents of which are produced, wholly (blogs) or in part (Facebook), by the user. While everything about some 2.0 sites (a blog, for example) is likely produced by those who also consume them, on others (the Facebook page) the basic structure of the site is created by the producer, while all of the content comes from the consumer(s). Even though something of the distinction between producer and consumer remains in the latter case, it is clear that Web 2.0 is the paradigmatic domain of the prosumer. As the internet continues to evolve, we can expect to see more and more user-generated content and therefore an even greater role for the prosumer.

Of course, this shift to prosumption does not mean that sociological theorists should ignore production (the production end of the prosumption continuum) or consumption (the consumption end of that continuum). On the production side, there is certainly no end of issues to concern the theorist. Among others, there is David Harvey's (2005) interest in, and critique of, neoliberalism, as well as Hardt and Negri's (2000) interest in the transformation of the capitalist and proletariat into Empire and Multitude in the global age.

Consumption

While much theoretical (and empirical) attention will be paid to production (that is, the production end of the prosumption continuum), it is consumption (or the consumption end of the prosumption continuum) that is likely to receive the lion's share of attention. That is due, in part, to less of a focus in the past on consumption and the fact that the realm of consumption is both so vast and expanding so rapidly. We will see more and more theorizing on consumers (Gabriel & Lang [1995] 2006), the consumption process (Miller 1998; Zukin 2005), goods and services (Molotch 2005; Miller 2009a, 2009b; Molotch & Noren 2010), and consumption settings (Zukin 1993; Ritzer 2010a).

Of course there is much else to theorize in the realm of consumption. One such topic is credit, which is important not only because of the key role it plays in consumption, but also because of its role in the Great Recession. One particularly good example of theorizing consumption, credit in particular, especially from a Foucauldian perspective, is Donncha Marron's (2009) *Consumer*

Credit in the United States: A Sociological Perspective from the 19th Century to the Present.

While we have focused on three areas in which we can expect to see significant further theoretical development, there are many other areas (for example, the body, "queerness," social geography) that are, and will continue to be, sites of considerable theorizing.

CONCLUSION

Much has been covered in this chapter, but this only scratches the surface of contemporary theories and of the issues that relate to them. If there is one overarching conclusion to this analysis, it is that sociological theory has historically been too "rigid"; it has not been flexible, fluid, enough. That has created great problems for sociological theory, but the hope is for greater fluidity associated, at least in part, with more inter-paradigmatic and inter-disciplinary theorizing (Abbott 2001). The areas outlined above – globalization, consumption (and prosumption), and the internet – are characterized by multi-disciplinary and inter-disciplinary theory and research. They relate to a fluid world and demand intellectual and theoretical fluidity. These realities and demands may augur the beginning of a new age of theorizing in sociology.

Note

1   For example, Foucault did a genealogical analysis, while Agamben was more ontological in his approach (although Agamben [[2002] 2005: 50] did do genealogical analyses of his own, but not on the core issue of biopolitics).

References

Abbott, Andrew (2001) *Chaos of Disciplines*. Chicago: University of Chicago Press.

Agamben, Giorgio ([1995] 1998) *Homo Sacer: Sovereign Power and Bare Life*. Trans. D. Heller-Roazen. Reprint. Stanford, CA: Stanford University Press.

Agamben, Giorgio ([2002] 2005) *State of Exception*. Trans. K. Attell. Reprint. Chicago: University of Chicago Press.

Baudrillard, Jean ([1970] 1998) *The Consumer Society: Myths and Structures*. Trans. C. Turner. Reprint. London: Sage.

Baudrillard, Jean ([1976] 2002) *Symbolic Exchange and Death*. Trans. I. H. Grant. Reprint. London: Sage.

Baudrillard, Jean ([1979] 1990) *Seduction*. Trans. B. Singer. Reprint. New York: St. Martin's Press.

Baudrillard, Jean (1983) *Simulations*. Trans. P. Foss, P. Patton, and P. Beitchan. Cambridge, MA: MIT Press.

Bauman, Zygmunt (2000) *Liquid Modernity*. Malden, MA: Polity Press.

Beck, Ulrich (1992) *Risk Society: Toward a New Modernity*. London: Sage.

Beck, Ulrich (1999) *World Risk Society*. Cambridge, MA: Polity Press.

Beck, Ulrich (2007) "Cosmopolitanism: A Critical Theory for the Twenty-First Century." In George Ritzer (ed.), *Blackwell Companion to Globalization*. Malden, MA: Blackwell, pp. 162–76.

Bell, Daniel ([1976] 1996) *The Cultural Contradictions of Capitalism*. New York: Basic Books.

Bryman, Alan (2003) "Global Implications of McDonaldization and Disneyization." *American Behavioral Scientist* 47: 154–67.

Collins, Randall (1975) *Conflict Sociology: Toward an Explanatory Science*. New York: Academic Press.

Davis, Kingsley (1959) "The Myth of Functional Analysis as a Special Method in Sociology and Anthropology." *American Sociological Review* 24: 757–72.

DeCaroli, Steven (2007) "Giorgio Agamben and the Field of Sovereignty." In Steven DeCaroli and Matthew Calarco (eds.), *Sovereignty and Life*. Stanford, CA: Stanford University Press, pp. 43–69.

Fine, Gary Alan (1993) "The Sad Demise, Mysterious Disappearance, Glorious Triumph of Symbolic Interactionism." *Annual Review of Sociology* 19: 61–87.

Foucault, Michel ([1965] 1998) *Madness and Civilization: A History of Insanity in the Age of Reason*. Trans. R. Howard. Reprint. New York: Vintage Books.

Foucault, Michel ([1973] 1994) *The Birth of the Clinic: An Archaeology of Medical Perception*. Trans. A. M. Sheridan Smith. Reprint. New York: Vintage Books.

Foucault, Michel ([1977] 1995) *Discipline and Punish: The Birth of the Prison*. Trans. A. Sheridan. Reprint. New York: Vintage Books.

Foucault, Michel ([1978] 1990) *The History of Sexuality*, Vol. 1, *An Introduction*. Trans. R. Hurley. Reprint. New York: Vintage Books.

Franklin, Adrian (2007) "Posthumanism." In George Ritzer (ed.), *The Blackwell Encyclopedia of Sociology*. Oxford: Blackwell, pp. 3548–50.

Gabriel, Yiannis and Tim Lang ([1995] 2006) *The Unmanageable Consumer*. Reprint. London: Sage.

Giddens, Anthony (1990) *The Consequences of Modernity*. Stanford, CA: Stanford University Press.

Gray, John (1998) "Global Utopias and Clashing Civilizations: Misunderstanding the Present." *International Affairs* 74: 149–63.

Hardt, Michael and Antonio Negri (2000) *Empire*. Cambridge, MA: Harvard University Press.

Harvey, David (2005) *A Brief History of Neoliberalism*. Reprint. Oxford: Oxford University Press.

Homans, George (1974) *Social Behavior: Its Elementary Forms*, rev. edn. New York: Harcourt Brace Jovanovich.

Honneth, Axel ([1985] 1997) *The Critique of Power: Reflective Stages in a Critical Social Theory*. Trans. K. Baynes. Reprint. Cambridge, MA: MIT Press.

Honneth, Axel ([1990] 1995) *The Fragmented World of the Social: Essays in Social and Political Philosophy*. Ed. C. W. Wright. Reprint. Albany, NY: State University of New York Press.

Honneth, Axel ([1992] 1996) *The Struggle for Recognition: The Moral Grammar of Social Conflicts*. Trans. J. Anderson. Reprint. Cambridge, MA: MIT Press.

Honneth, Axel ([2000] 2007) *Disrespect: The Normative Foundations of Critical Theory*. Reprint. Cambridge: Polity Press.

Honneth, Axel (2008) *Reification: A New Look at an Old Idea*. Ed. M. Jay. Oxford: Oxford University Press.

Huntington, Samuel (1997) *The Clash of Civilizations and the Remaking of World Order*. Reprint. New York: Simon and Schuster.

Johnson, Miriam (1989) "Feminism and the Theories of Talcott Parsons." In R. A. Wallace (ed.), *Feminism and Sociological Theory*. Newbury Park, CA: Sage, pp. 101–18.

Knorr-Cetina, Karin D. (2001) "Postsocial Relations: Theorizing Sociality in a Postsocial Environment." In George Ritzer and Barry Smart (eds.), *Handbook of Social Theory*. London: Sage, pp. 520–37.

Kuhn, Thomas S. ([1962] 1963) *The Structure of Scientific Revolutions*. Reprint. Chicago: University of Chicago Press.

Latour, Bruno (1999) "On Recalling ANT." In John Law and John Hassard (eds.), *Actor Network Theory and After*. Oxford: Blackwell, pp. 15–25.

Law, John (1999) "After ANT: Complexity, Naming and Topology." In John Law and John Hassard (eds.), *Actor Network Theory and After*. Oxford: Blackwell, pp. 1–14.

Lipovetsky, Gilles ([1987] 2002) *The Empire of Fashion: Dressing Modern Democracy*. Trans. C. Porter. Reprint. Princeton, NJ: Princeton University Press.

Lipovetsky, Gilles (2005) *Hypermodern Times*. Trans. A. Brown. Malden, MA: Polity Press.

Marron, Donncha (2009) *Consumer Credit in the United States: A Sociological Perspective from the 19th Century to the Present*. New York: Palgrave Macmillan.

Matlock, Jack F., Jr. (1999) "Can Civilizations Clash?" *Proceedings of the American Philosophical Society* 143: 428–39.

Miller, Daniel (1998) *A Theory of Shopping*. Ithaca, NY: Cornell University Press.

Miller, Daniel (2009a) *The Comfort of Things*. Reprint. Cambridge: Polity Press.

Miller, Daniel (2009b) *Stuff*. Cambridge: Polity Press.

Mills, Catherine (2007) "Biopolitics, Liberal Eugenics, and Nihilism." In Matthew Calarco and Steven DeCaroli (eds.), *Sovereignty and Life*. Stanford, CA: Stanford University Press, pp. 180–202.

Molotch, Harvey (2005) *Where Stuff Comes From: How Toasters, Toilets, Cars, Computers, and Many Other Things Come to Be as They Are*. Reprint. New York: Routledge.

Molotch, Harvey and Laura Noren (eds.) (2010) *Toilet: Public Restrooms and the Politics of Sharing*. New York: New York University Press.

Mullins, Nicholas (1983) "Theories and Theory Groups Revisited." In Randall Collins (ed.), *Sociological Theory*. San Francisco: Jossey-Bass, pp. 319–37.

Pieterse, Jan Nederveen (2004) *Globalization and Culture: Global Mélange*. Lanham, MD: Rowman and Littlefield.

Ritzer, George (1975) *Sociology: A Multiple Paradigm Science*. Boston: Allyn and Bacon.

Ritzer, George (1980) *Toward an Integrated Sociological Paradigm*. Boston: Allyn and Bacon.

Ritzer, George (1991) *Metatheorizing in Sociology*. Lexington, MA: Lexington Books.

Ritzer, George (1997) *Postmodern Social Theory*. New York: McGraw-Hill.

Ritzer, George (2006) *The Globalization of Nothing 2*. Thousand Oaks, CA: Pine Forge Press.

Ritzer, George (2009) "Focusing on the Prosumer: On Correcting an Error in Social Theory." Paper presented at conference on the Prosumer, Frankfurt, Germany, April.

Ritzer, George (2010a) *Enchanting a Disenchanted World: Continuity and Change in the Cathedrals of Consumption*. Thousand Oaks: Pine Forge Press.

Ritzer, George (2010b) *Sociological Theory*, 8th edn. New York: McGraw-Hill.

Rosenau, Pauline Marie (1992) *Post-modernism and the Social Sciences: Insights, Inroads, and Intrusions*. Princeton, NJ: Princeton University Press.

Rossler, Beate (2007) "Work, Recognition, Emancipation." In Bert van den Brink and David Owen (eds.), *Recognition and Power: Axel Honneth and the Tradition of Critical Theory*. Cambridge: Cambridge University Press, pp. 135–65.

Sklair, Leslie (2002) *Globalization: Capitalism and Its Alternatives*. Oxford: Oxford University Press.

Van den Brink, Bert and David Owen (eds.) (2007a) *Recognition and Power: Axel Honneth and the Tradition of Critical Theory*. Cambridge: Cambridge University Press.

Van den Brink, Bert and David Owen (2007b) "Introduction." In Bert van den Brink and David Owen (eds.), *Recognition and Power: Axel Honneth and the Tradition of Critical Theory*. Cambridge: Cambridge University Press, pp. 1–30.

Waters, Malcolm (1996) "McDonaldization and the Global Culture of Consumption." *Sociale Wetenschappen* 39: 17–28.

Wellman, Barry, Janet Salaff, Dimitrina Dimitrova, Laura Garton, Milena Gulia, and Caroline Haythornthwaite (1996) "Computer Networks as Social Networks: Collaborative Work, Telework, and Virtual Community." *Annual Review of Sociology* 22: 213–38.

Zukin, Sharon (1993) *Landscapes of Power: From Detroit to Disney World*. Berkeley: University of California Press.

Zukin, Sharon (2005) *Point of Purchase: How Shopping Changed American Culture*. Reprint. New York: Routledge.

Part II

Basic Topics in Sociology

7

Action, Interaction, and Groups

Kimberly B. Rogers and Lynn Smith-Lovin

People have a natural tendency to sort the social world into categories (Allport 1954). Schema-based processing contributes to the fluidity of perception, simplifies interpretations of others' behavior, and prompts accurate and coordinated action, while minimizing the expenditure of cognitive resources (Barresi & Moore 1996). Recent studies suggest that cognitive responses to the social world are primarily determined by situational factors beyond our awareness rather than the intentional choices we make, as the human capacity for conscious self-regulation is surprisingly limited (Bargh & Chartrand 1999).

Because people respond to self and other as members of social categories and thus carry non-conscious category-based expectations for situated behavior, identity is a core concept in understanding action, interaction, and group processes. Sociologists use the term "identity" to refer to the many meanings attached to a person, both by the self and by others. The concept embraces structural features such as group affiliations, role occupancy, and category memberships as well as character traits that individuals display or that others attribute to them (Smith-Lovin 2007). While research on identity was historically isolated from studies of social structure and groups, more recent research has produced cross-fertilization between the three faces of sociological social psychology: symbolic interaction, group processes, and social structure and personality (Cook, Fine & House 1995). Identity processes are increasingly featured in research from all three domains, forming a common ground upon which we can integrate knowledge.

Rather than providing an encyclopedic review of sociological social psychology, this chapter will concentrate on developments in two areas where major advances

The Wiley-Blackwell Companion to Sociology, First Edition. Edited by George Ritzer.
© 2012 Blackwell Publishing Ltd. Published 2012 by Blackwell Publishing Ltd.

have come in the past three decades, and where controversies still brew: (1) the new control theories of social interaction, which have revolutionized the symbolic interactionist tradition, and (2) the impact of group structures on the development of meaning, commitment, and group identity. In recent years, scholars have begun to examine how instrumental and affective processes are interrelated. The chapter will end by reviewing this convergence and highlighting some new areas for development.

MEANING AND EMOTION IN SOCIAL INTERACTION

The symbolic interactionist tradition in sociology has at its root three principles: (1) people act toward things, including each other, on the basis of the meanings that those things hold for them; (2) the primary source of these meanings is social interaction; and (3) meanings are managed and transformed through an interpretative process (Snow 2000). The fundamental conception of the actor is that of a meaning-creator, who actively works to interpret what is happening around him or her in terms of meanings accrued from past interactions, and who actively generates new lines of action to maintain a coherent, meaningful view of self and others. Historically a heavily cognitive perspective, symbolic interaction has turned its eye toward affective meaning and emotion in the past 20 years (MacKinnon 1994).

There has historically been some tension between two types of symbolic interactionists: those who focus on the creative, actively negotiated process through which people make their identities within social interaction, and those who emphasize the extent to which people's identities are shaped by the social structures in which they live (see Stryker [1980, 2008] and Snow [2000] for an overview). In recent years, theoretical thinking in the latter camp – often called structural symbolic interactionism – has been dominated by a control system model that makes it much more dynamic, creative, and processual. This theoretical advance has generated some convergence in the two symbolic interactionist frameworks. Presently, most research in this domain draws upon two closely related models: affect control theory and identity theory.

Affect control theory

David Heise (1979) initially developed a control system view of social interaction, borrowing a conceptual model from engineering and measurement technology from psychology. His affect control theory represented a major sociological development by offering insight into the processes by which culturally acquired meanings are maintained over time through social interaction (Heise 1979; Smith-Lovin & Heise 1988; MacKinnon 1994; Heise 2007). In keeping with much structural symbolic interactionist theory (e.g., McCall & Simmons 1966; Stryker 1980), affect control theory holds that "the structural features of society are translated into interactional settings through widely shared cultural beliefs and meanings," referred to as *fundamental sentiments* (Ridgeway & Smith-Lovin 1994: 220). Sentiments about identities and actions remain stable over long periods of time, but are not always confirmed *in situ* – the *transient impressions* generated within interaction may or may not align with fundamental meanings (Heise 1979, 2007). Instead, the two sets of social meanings – stable, culturally held sentiments and transient, situated impressions – relate to one another through a cybernetic control process.

Fundamental sentiments act as a social reference point. People engaged in social interaction compare them to transitory, situational impressions regarding self-identities, social actions, and the identities of others implicated in social events. Fundamental sentiments are compared to transient impressions on the basis of three parsimonious affective dimensions (e.g., Osgood 1962; Osgood, May & Miron 1975): evaluation (good–bad), potency (strong–weak), and activity (lively–quiet). For example, a woman who sees herself as a mother interacting with a daughter will do things that maintain the good, powerful, and lively meanings associated with that identity, and will expect her daughter to do things that maintain her somewhat less potent but livelier identity. When these meaning sets are incongruent, an inter-actant will experience *deflection*, conceptualized as a shift on the dimensions of meaning described above, and will respond emotionally to this deflection in certain predictable ways (Heise 2007). In other words, deflection and its associated emotional response are produced when a person's definition of the situation is not upheld – when culturally acquired sentiments toward the actors, behaviors, and objects in a given interaction are disconfirmed (Smith-Lovin & Heise 1989). Emotional response provides a visceral signal of the discrepancy, and an incentive for restoring the fundamental affective order.

As a result, interactants commonly behave in such a way as to bring fundamental sentiments and transient impressions from a situation back into line with one another, regardless of whether the emotional consequences of deflection are positive or negative on any of the three dimensions (Heise 1979; Robinson & Smith-Lovin 1992, 2006; Heise 2007). For instance, a mother who has just been appreciated by her daughter would be likely to feel relieved and merely supervise her child in a second interaction, while a mother who has just been ignored might instead feel apprehensive and discipline her child. The earlier interaction would result in a daughter who is relaxed, and the latter a daughter who is tense, but both place her back into a less powerful role position. Alternatively, interactants will avoid situations likely to be deflecting (Robinson & Smith-Lovin 1992), or seek to prevent deflection by controlling the definition of the situation through means such as self-presentation (Goffman 1959; Hochschild 1979; Smith-Lovin & Heise 1988). Thus, behavioral control is a mechanism that functions to maintain congruency between fundamental ("ought") and transient ("actual") affective meanings, through the maintenance or restoration of cultural standards.

Based on extensive empirical research (e.g., Smith-Lovin & Heise 1988; Heise 2007), affect control theorists have developed structural equations to predict how social interaction will change meanings. These models allow mathematical expression of the theory's control assumptions (as the minimization of the squared difference between the fundamental and transient meanings) and the prediction of three-number numerical values (representing evaluation, potency, and activity, or EPA) that describe behavioral and emotional outcomes of a given interaction (Smith-Lovin & Heise 1982; Heise 1991). The program INTERACT (Heise 1988) is a computer interface developed for the simulation of social interaction according to these models (Heise 1979, 2007). Interaction is simulated through a series of Actor-Behavior-Object (ABO) sentences, as behaviors are traded between interactants.

For instance, in American culture, the identity *manager* has an EPA value of (0.98, 1.57, 1.34), implying that managers are seen as somewhat good (0.98), and quite powerful (1.57) and active (1.34). Behaviors seen as fitting to a manager, such as *supervising* (1.30, 1.30, 1.14) or *transacting business* (1.56, 1.39, 1.25), share comparable EPA profiles to the identity itself. The identity *receptionist* (1.00, 0.37, 0.16), on the other hand, is seen as somewhat good (1.00), but fairly neutral in power (0.37) and activity (0.16). Such a person is expected to engage in fairly passive behaviors, such as *requesting something* (0.51, -0.08, -0.05) or *concurring* (1.27, 1.06, 0.34). Given their similarity in evaluation and discrepancy in power and activity, a common interaction between two people carrying the identities *manager* and *receptionist* would involve ABO sentences like *manager supervises receptionist* or *receptionist requests something from manager*. Such interactions produce low levels of deflection, and result in structural emotions that have an affective character similar to that of the identity profiles.

There are several important ways in which affect control theory represents a major advance over earlier symbolic interactionist formulations. The model focuses explicitly on the relational context of interaction, with events (an actor–behavior–object combination) rather than individuals as the unit of analysis. The use of standard, universal dimensions of meaning allows all types of social entities (actors, behaviors, emotions, traits, social settings) to be characterized within the same system. Using an impression formation paradigm from psychology, the theory specifies exactly how the elements of a situation combine to form a situation-specific meaning. That situated meaning is then compared to fundamental sentiment to ascertain how well events are maintaining meanings. Most importantly, the control view of the relationship between role identity and social action represents the extraordinary flexibility of actors' application of cultural information as they move through varying situations. Role occupants do not follow a simple, static script of role expectations for a particular interaction partner. Their behavior is powerfully shaped by the events that occur and their interpretation of them. A final insight from affect control theory is the sense in which cognition and affect are intertwined inexorably. One cannot process an interpersonal situation cognitively without responding to it emotionally, and emotion is unlikely to occur in any but the simplest stimulus-response modes without the active work of defining the situation.

Identity theory

Burke (1991) later developed an alternative control model initially called identity control theory. Burke and Stets (2009) have since dropped the "control" part of the label and combined their theoretical work with Stryker's earlier efforts to call the combination "identity theory." Much like affect control theory, Burke's approach views behavioral choice as a mechanism by which situationally generated meanings (inputs) are kept in line with broader self-sentiments for a particular identity (the *identity standard*). A process called the *comparator* evaluates the discrepancy between input and standard, and (as with affect control theory's deflection) behavioral responses are selected to reduce the difference. Thus, the control system mechanism at the foundation of identity theory shares many commonalities with processes described by affect control theory. However, the two theories can be distinguished on the basis of three key differences: the measurement of meaning, the location of the reference standard, and the predicted valence of emotion. Each of these differences will be discussed in turn.

First, Burke's theory employs a more intricate, role-specific method of measuring meaning. Rather than using common dimensions to interpret all identities, behaviors, and settings under study, identity theorists select a set of dimensions determined to predict the majority of variation in meaning within the given institution. These dimensions are derived through discriminant function analysis, which identifies the set of adjectives that most clearly differentiate the groups under study within the sample population (Burke & Tully 1977). For instance, the *student* identity has been measured on dimensions like academic responsibility, intellectual curiosity, sociability, and personal assertiveness (Reitzes & Burke 1980), while the *feminine* identity has been measured on dimensions like non-competitiveness, passivity, and ease of having feelings hurt (Burke & Cast 1997). While this approach can provide greater specificity within a given social context, it limits comparisons of meaning across role domains.

Second, identity control theory focuses on meaning processes operating at the level of the individual actor. Theorists view the behavioral outputs of a given situation as the direct result of a process that compares situational feedback with self-meanings, seeking to minimize dissonance and ultimately social stress (Burke 1991). However, the maintenance of one's own identity is of primary significance, and the identities of others are of concern only to the extent that they impact self-meanings. In contrast, meaning maintenance in affect control theory is thought to operate across all elements of a situation, including the identities of others and the meanings of actions or even behavioral settings. Although affect control theorists also view people as motivated to verify their self-identities, the control system primarily functions to maintain a stable definition of the situation. As a result, the behavioral choices of each member of a given interaction are part of a control system functioning to maintain a stable situation, given that actors come from the same culture and share an institutional definition for the situation.

The third and perhaps most pronounced difference between the two control models is in their view of emotion (see Robinson and Smith-Lovin [2006] for a more complete discussion). According to affect control theory, emotions can signal deflections above *or* below the reference standard. While people are predicted to act in ways that bring situated meanings back into line with reference signals across interactions, people may feel more or less good, potent, or lively than anticipated if their immediate experiences deflect them upward or downward on one or more affective dimensions. Thus, an employee who receives an unexpectedly good performance evaluation might feel "high as a kite," whereas an employee receiving an unexpectedly bad one may feel "down in the dumps." In contrast, failure to confirm meanings in identity control theory is always assumed to produce negative emotions or distress, regardless of whether the disconfirmation is positive or negative (Burke & Stets 1999, 2009).

Empirical tests of the control theories

Researchers have tested the control theories successfully using a wide array of experimental, survey, and qualitative methods (see reviews in Heise 2007 and Burke & Stets 2009). Experimental research suggests that affect control theory does a good job of predicting the emotions of actors and the recipients of actions, as well as the behavioral outcomes of interaction (Smith-Lovin 1988). For instance, predictions about behaviors generated from the sentiments of members of a religious group have demonstrated general congruence with group members' predicted event likelihoods (Smith-Lovin & Douglass 1992). Experiments have also confirmed the counterintuitive prediction that self-verification motives hold up for negative identities; people will choose to interact with others who confirm a negative self-identity even when the alternative interaction partner evaluates them more positively than they evaluate themselves (Robinson & Smith-Lovin 1992).

Burke and his colleagues have tested their control theory extensively using a three-year study of newly married couples in Washington state. This research demonstrates that gender identities, personal identities about control, and parental/spousal identities are quite stable over time and across a variety of situations. This stability is associated with self-verification processes as well as structural anchors like biological sex (Burke & Cast 1997). For marriages in which the spousal identity is not verified, dysfunction is introduced into partners' patterns of interaction and the stability of both self-meanings and the relationship structure is placed at risk (Stets & Burke 2005). Another study confirms that control system processes function to maintain the structural arrangements within which they operate. Spouses with lower status tend to defer to judgments made about them by spouses of higher status, measured by occupational status and years of education (Cast, Stets & Burke 1999).

With regard to the theories' discrepant predictions on emotion, research findings generally support the expectations of affect control theory. Positive identity deflection produces higher levels of positive emotion and lower levels of negative emotion than feedback in congruence with the reference standard (Stets 2005, 2006). Counter to the expectations of identity control theorists, emotional experiences are most positive when feedback is considerably more positive than expected (Clay-Warner, Robinson & Smith-Lovin 2010). Only in long-term marital relationships do we see that lack of identity verification in a positive direction causes stress and mental distress (Burke & Harrod 2005), supporting identity theory's emotion predictions. Upcoming research by Robinson, Smith-Lovin, and Clay-Warner will investigate the emotional and behavioral implications of receiving overly positive feedback in situations where this feedback is explicitly social (e.g., when another group member will be informed of the feedback) or its effects are zero-sum (e.g., when a reward will be distributed across the group based on feedback).

Other new research focuses on the enactment of multiple identities. These studies deal with the salience of identities within a relatively stable self-structure (Stryker 1980, 2008) and the parallel processing of multiple identities that may be evoked within a single situation (Smith-Lovin 2007; Burke & Stets 2009). MacKinnon and Heise (2010) have incorporated a model of self-hierarchy into the affect control model, to demonstrate how people integrate multiple identities and yet maintain a fundamental self-image. We now turn to a discussion of this exciting new work.

Multiple identities

Theorists have taken great interest of late in the significance of multiple-identity enactments for the organization of the self, and for the stability of self and identity meanings over time. Structural symbolic interactionists tend to conceive of the self as comprised of multiple identities that are organized hierarchically according to their prominence or salience among all the identities activated as people move through various social situations (McCall & Simmons 1978; Stryker 1980). Identity salience hierarchies are generally stable over time (Serpe 1987); even when placed into new settings people seek out relationships that preserve the preeminence of highly salient identities (Serpe & Stryker 1987). However, identities carry an inherent periodicity. The extent to which certain identities are engaged can vary depending on the nature of the identity and social context in question, as well as characteristics of the person engaging that identity (Burke 1991). A person's position in the social structure or life course and the trajectory of events which they have experienced to that point can all contribute to the determination of which identity will be engaged in a social encounter.

The simultaneous enactment of multiple identities can have varying consequences. In many situations, the specific identity by which a person is recognized entails other, more generalist identities; for example, being a neurosurgeon also implies one's identity as a physician (MacKinnon & Heise 2010). In cases like this the engagement of multiple identities can be cooperative; roles with shared meanings are likely to be engaged simultaneously, pose no real threat to identity verification, and may even enhance the likelihood of mutual confirmation (Burke & Stets 2009). Often, such identities comprise a salient part of the self, meaning they are more readily activated in a diverse array of situations (Deaux 1992). In fact, research suggests that identities routinely activated together are likely to increase in salience (Burke & Stets 2009) and to acquire shared meanings, even for identities with meanings that would otherwise be unrelated (Burke 2003). These mechanisms function to maintain our sense of a uniform self.

In other instances, the identities engaged in a particular situation may be at odds, and confirmation of one identity may occur at the expense of another. To understand this phenomenon, theorists have looked at the effects of a changing social structure on the structure of the self. As patterns of affiliation and social engagement become more diversified, selves have generally become more complex and less stable (Smith-Lovin 2007). Individuals more frequently find themselves to be bridging ties between otherwise non-overlapping social groups (McPherson 2000; Pescosolido and Rubin 2000), performing distinct roles in different social contexts (MacKinnon & Heise 2010). Accordingly, the self has come to incorporate a variety of role identities, though the prevalence of complex selves and the situational likelihood of multiple-identity enactment are thought to vary considerably across the social structure. For instance, due to an increased likelihood of affiliating with out-group alters, high-status social actors (Lin 2001) and members of social categories that are numerically small (Blau 1977) are considered more likely to experience a complex, differentiated

self than their counterparts (Smith-Lovin 2007). Additionally, certain types of interactions or interaction partners may be more likely to generate complex selves. For
example, multiple-identity enactment is likely more prevalent for interaction partners with relationships spanning a variety of role identities, or for those with a long
history of interaction (McPherson & Smith-Lovin 2002; Smith-Lovin 2007).

Researchers have also begun to consider how the identity verification process
might be affected when identities with divergent meanings are enacted simultaneously. Identity salience and commitment have been identified as significant factors
in determining which identities are likely to take precedence (Burke & Stets 2009).
Identity salience refers to the probability that a given identity will be invoked and
shape behavior across a wide variety of social situations, while commitment is the
degree to which membership in certain networks is contingent on identity performance (Stryker & Burke 2000). Commitment, through its association with our
social relationships, influences the salience of an identity and, accordingly, our enactment of certain identities more than others. For example, commitment to relationships based on religion predicts the salience of religious identities, which in turn
predicts the amount of time spent in religious identities (Stryker & Serpe 1982).

Research suggests that people are likely to engage in behavior that supports
identities to which they are highly committed (Burke & Reitzes 1991), although no
research to date has empirically examined whether commitment processes drive
behavioral choice in cases of multiple-identity enactment. Thus, in the event that
identities carrying different meanings are activated simultaneously in intersecting
groups, the meanings for the identity that is most salient or to which there is the
most commitment would shift the least, while meanings for identities with lower
salience and commitment would be expected to shift more. Burke and Stets (2009)
offer an example: a child has her friends over for a visit, while her parents are also
present for the interaction. While the *daughter* identity implies a certain amount of
weakness or naïvety, the *friend* identity entails somewhat more power and sophistication. Since these identities carry distinct meanings, only one can be successfully
verified in a given interaction; commitment is one indicator of which identity is most
likely to be verified. The association of certain identities with one's position in the
social structure (Stryker 1980) is another key predictor of selective verification, as
the disconfirmation of structural identities can lead to distress from role conflict or
status inconsistency (Burke & Stets 2009).

When salient and distinct identities to which people are highly committed are
simultaneously enacted, verification of one identity is likely to result in deflection
on others, and the experience of mixed emotions (Smith-Lovin 2007). When this
occurs routinely, people tend to make one of two behavioral choices. First, re-
identification of the self can allow for an alternative contextualization of the situation that generated conflicting enactments. If one can apply an alternate label to
one of the conflicting identities that reduces the difference in meaning, deflection
on the previously unconfirmed identity is minimized. Second, modifying the social
situations that are regularly engaged offers two potential alternatives to conflicting
enactments. If actors are able to maintain separate social networks for the conflicting identities, they are likely to avoid their simultaneous engagement and, thus,
conflicts in identity verification. Alternatively, if actors are able to surround themselves with a set of individuals who hold non-normative but more compatible mean-

ings for the two identity sets, they can sustain modified identity beliefs by which meanings do not conflict. For example, qualitative data from two church congregations demonstrated how gay Christians created new identities and rituals to generate positive emotions and thwart identity conflicts in a religious context; more traditional identity meanings for homosexual and religious identities would have generated negative emotion (Smith-Lovin & Douglass 1992).

SOCIAL STRUCTURAL INFLUENCES ON MEANING

Another active area of study links affective meaning to the interactional structures in which people are embedded. It is a core tenet of symbolic interactionist thought that meanings develop through social interaction (Snow 2000; Stryker 2008), but theorists have seldom accepted the challenge of identifying the process by which this occurs. Network analysis and other conceptual innovations have only recently given theorists considerable traction on the problem.

Noah Friedkin's network theory of social influence has explored how consensus of opinion is reached within networks containing a distinct array of initial opinions and varying amounts of social influence and susceptibility to this influence (Friedkin 2005). Researchers in this tradition propose that norm formation occurs as members of a given network seek to cognitively integrate a set of disparate opinions, using a weighted average of influential views to reach consensus through the iterative revision of attitudes (Friedkin 2001). Thus, the network members most consistently deemed influential play the largest role in determining normative consensus.

According to Friedkin (2005), social influence is determined by interpersonal visibility and salience. While the social precondition of visibility is met when one actor has some information about another, numerous conditions are contingent on a person's salience, including status characteristics and the social power drawn from one's network position (Friedkin 1993; Friedkin & Johnsen 2003). As demonstrated by research on expectation states, group members who are accorded high status commonly have this status legitimated within interaction (Berger, Cohen & Zelditch 1972; Berger 1988). High-status group members are often given greater time and attention by the group and tend to receive deference and support for their ideas (Berger, Rozenholtz & Zelditch 1980; Gould 2002), rendering them more influential than low-status members. Thus, over the course of multiple interactions, interpersonal sentiments contribute to the weighting of group members' opinions, such that group consensus disproportionately represents the initial views of highly influential members (Friedkin & Johnsen 2003).

In short, research on social influence networks indicates that flows of interpersonal influence within social networks affect network members' opinions on a variety of issues (Friedkin & Johnsen 1999). Above and beyond preexisting group norms, decision rules, and the persuasiveness of group members' arguments, the perceived salience of a social contact affects the degree to which their opinion contributes to group consensus on a given issue (Friedkin 1999). Influential actors' attitudes, preferences, and behavior all contribute to symbolic interaction within networks, shaping the attitudes and behavior of their less influential contacts (Friedkin 2010). Current research by Rogers (2011) combines theories of social influence and affect control to explore the mechanisms through which social influence occurs in interaction. This research examines group consensus following a deliberation task, as well as change in affective meanings for a set of identities relevant to both the discussion issue and the identities engaged during group interaction. It is expected that people modify not only their opinions but also their identity sentiments on the basis of influential others' responses to the actors, behaviors, and objects in a given social situation (Friedkin & Johnsen 2003).

In another research paradigm, an exploratory study by Thomas and Heise (1995) identified clustering in sentiments toward certain social identities measured using the methods of affect control theory. *Post hoc* interviews led the researchers to hypothesize that both the extensiveness and stability of a person's social ties are potential predictors of their identity and emotion meanings. These expectations are being tested in current research by Rogers (2011), which explores whether social position and connectedness predict subcultural clustering in affective meaning, and whether the structural predictors of clustering hold up cross-culturally.

GROUP PROCESSES AND THE DEVELOPMENT OF MEANING

Historically, the group processes tradition within sociological social psychology has concentrated on instrumental action within group structures. Research has focused on how status and power develop within groups, usually with the scope condition that group members are trying to maximize their outcomes. In fact, most of this theory has its roots in the exchange traditions of Homans and Emerson. Here, rather than attempting a comprehensive review (see Molm and Cook [1995] for such a review), we focus on the aspects of group processes that operate to create categorizations, identities, and meaning. It is this work that connects the group processes tradition with the structural symbolic interactionist work described above.

Expectation states theory as an identity theory

One major research tradition spawned by the early exchange theorists, but moved far from its roots, is expectation states theory. Influenced by Homans' early exchange theory (1961) and by Bales' (1950) observations of behavior in small task groups, Joseph Berger and his colleagues (Berger, Conner & Fisek 1974) proposed a theory to explain how observable status hierarchies develop within groups. Research in expectation states suggests why a large number of group behaviors like talking, being spoken to, evaluating the ideas of others, and receiving positive evaluations from others all tend to occur together in a *power and prestige order*. Under certain conditions – namely, a collective task orientation where all group members stand to gain from better performance on a group enterprise – inequalities in task-related behaviors develop out of group members' expectations about the value of their own and others' contributions to the group task. The exchange process occurs as deference is granted to group members in exchange for the recipient engaging in behaviors that produce rewards for the other group members.

Performance expectations are the central concept in the theory. Group members form expectations about others' relative capabilities to contribute to task completion, then give or take requests for assistance (*action opportunities*) and opportunities to engage in task-related behavior (*performance outputs*) to produce the best group outcome. In spite of the fact that expectations are formed by individuals, the interactional encounter is the unit of analysis in the theory; comparing the expectations of two group members allows for the prediction of the behavior that they will engage in *vis-à-vis* one another. Thus, in expectation states theory, status is a relational concept rather than an individual characteristic.

Performance expectations can arise from several sources. In a group of highly similar people, behavioral cues early in the interaction can be crucial. People who engage in positive task behaviors, seizing early action opportunities, generate high performance expectations. Additionally, status characteristics valued in society at large are often used to differentiate group members. When people differ on some evaluated characteristic, the characteristic becomes salient in forming performance expectations. Unless there is evidence to the contrary, the group member carrying the more valued status characteristic will be presumed by group members to have higher competence at the group task than someone with a less valued status.

Berger and his colleagues isolate status processes from other small group dynamics by using a standardized experimental setting, within which a subject interacts with a simulated actor and both make judgments about an ambiguous stimulus while motivated to be accurate. Individual judgments are then reported back to the subject, who is given a chance to change his or her decision if the two disagree. The proportion of "stay" responses – sticking with one's own opinion in the face of disagreement from the simulated other – is the key dependent variable. Independent variables typically include characteristics like gender, race, ethnicity, personal attractiveness, or education that are evaluated in our society and are assigned to the simulated actor in order to produce status advantage or disadvantage for the subject.

Importantly, status characteristics (for example, being male as opposed to female) are *not* seen as directly determining task behavior. Instead, the theory predicts that these characteristics will determine the power and prestige order only when they differentiate group members and are linked to expectations about the task in particular ways. For example, men are generally presumed in our society to be more competent than women, but this has only an indirect link to a non-gendered task. If the task is male-stereotypic, the link could be stronger; if it is female-stereotypic, the link could be reversed in direction, with women receiving higher performance expectations. Researchers have devoted many studies to exploring how different types of information combine to form performance expectations (see review in Ridgeway & Walker 1995).

Expectation states theory has been very successful in applied research as well. A number of experiments demonstrate how initial status differences, imported from the external societal structure, can be reduced or eliminated by employing interventions that shape group members' expectations. Elizabeth Cohen (1982), for example, showed how group tasks and strategic interventions can help racial minorities become more active in school settings. Others have demonstrated how gender inequalities can be reduced or reversed (Wagner, Ford & Ford 1986). Additional studies have moved from the rigorously controlled standardized experiment to the analysis of small group interaction. For example, Cathy Johnson (1993) has explored how being assigned to a managerial or worker role in a simulated work environment influences conversational behaviors such as interruption and suggesting ideas. Event history methods have enabled researchers to determine how information imported from outside status structures combines with information that unfolds as the group interacts to form a cumulating status structure (Fararo & Skvoretz 1986).

Recent research has increasingly employed expectation states theory outside of its scope conditions, demonstrating that in some cases cooperative, task-oriented behavior is not a precondition to the predictive capacities of the theory. For example, Cast and colleagues suggest that higher-status group members garner more influence even for groups with a long history of interaction across a variety of contexts (e.g., marriage partners), and for expectation judgments about self rather than task alone (Cast, Stets & Burke 1999). Thus, in its modern incarnations, with the exchange foundations of the theory removed, expectation states theory is often treated as a situational identity theory. In this context, expectation states are the meanings associated with an actor in a group setting, and the status that actor is accorded is a situated identity (Ridgeway & Smith-Lovin 1994).

Status value theory

An even more direct example of how group processes can create identity meaning is Cecilia Ridgeway's theory of status value (Ridgeway 1991). Ridgeway asked the question: How do nominal characteristics (social categories like male/female, young/old, black/white) acquire consensual status value (evaluative connotation) in society? Using expectation states' logic, she argued that if a nominal characteristic is correlated initially with some material resource, interactions between people who differ on both resource levels and the nominal characteristic will lead to inferences about performance that will eventually diffuse through the society, thereby creating status value for the nominal categories. Simulation work by Mark, Smith-Lovin, and Ridgeway (2009) indicates that, in small societies, a correlation between resources and nominal characteristics is not necessary for the creation of status value. Random differential performance is sufficient to create status value which then can diffuse through the system. This result makes it more difficult to explain why everything does *not* become a status characteristic, than to explain why identifiable characteristics become consensually evaluated in society.

Social exchange, affect, and the creation of meaning

While research on social exchange, identity, and emotional processes proceeded without much cross-fertilization for many years, several research streams have recently developed to examine how instrumental exchanges affect emotional outcomes, sometimes leading to the formation of commitment and group identity. The oldest and most developed stream focuses on how perceptions of justice, equity, or fairness develop from exchange interactions (see review in Hegtvedt & Markovsky 1995). Indeed, this was a central concern of the original exchange theorists – Homans, Blau, and Emerson. Not surprisingly, people feel they have been unjustly treated and express anger when their rewards are lower than their investments. However, past reward experiences, status structures, power structures, and reference groups all serve to complicate this process. People quickly acclimate to any given levels of rewards (or a stable trajectory, like steadily rising rewards) and experience outcomes that fall below that expected level with a sense of distressing loss (Molm 1997). Moreover, they tend to expect congruence between their status value within a group and the level of rewards they receive. Therefore, people perceive fairness and are satisfied with their outcomes "when you and I receive what people like us generally get" (Hegtvedt & Markovsky 1995: 269). Therefore, the evaluation of fairness and equity is inherently tied to identity processes that determine to whom people compare themselves.

A more recent research thread in social exchange deals with the related question of how trust and affective commitment build up in exchange relationships. Edward Lawler and his colleagues have posited a model through which repeated exchanges each create small amounts of positive emotion, cumulating over time to create a positive attitude toward the exchange partner and behavioral commitment to the exchange relationship (Lawler & Yoon 1998). Perceptions of network cohesion mediate this relationship; affective commitment is highest in exchange structures like productive exchange, where shared responsibility and perceived cohesion are high (Lawler, Thye & Yoon 2008, 2009). Other network theorists have concentrated on the link between uncertainty, behavioral commitment, and trust. Basically, these researchers show that trust can only develop when an exchange is risky (i.e., the situation allows for untrustworthy behavior) *and* the trading partner acts in a reliable, trustworthy manner. Kollock (1994), for example, showed that trust and behavioral commitment develop more quickly when the quality of the traded good is difficult to determine, and therefore the opportunity to deceive is present. Molm (2000) showed that trust and affective commitment develop to their highest levels in reciprocal exchange (where partners did not negotiate binding agreements) when the power structure made behavioral commitment advantageous for both.

Just as exchange researchers have shown how emotions are embedded in exchange structures, expectation states researchers have looked at how identity meanings and emotions can shape status processes. When status hierarchies form in small, task-oriented groups, high-status group members often experience more positive emotions, since they are more often encouraged to make contributions and their contributions are more often marked by positive evaluation. Conversely, lower-status group members often feel negative emotions about being ignored or having their contributions commented on negatively. Lovaglia and Houser (1996) demonstrated that these emotions tend to mute the status structure; lower-status group members are resistant to influence because of their negative emotion, while higher-status members may be unusually accepting because of their positive feelings. Exchange researchers have noted a similar dynamic in the interaction of power, influence, and emotion: the negative emotion felt by low-power group members makes them much less likely to accept influence from high-power members for whom they would normally hold high expectations (Willer, Lovaglia & Markovsky 1997).

Group processes researchers are also beginning to explore how identity interacts with status and power processes. Identity that links low- and high-power positions seems to mute power use in exchange networks (Lawler & Yoon 1998). If the subject in an expectation states experiment shares an identity with a simulated actor, that piece of positive identity information seems to combine just like other status information to form performance expectations (Kalkhoff & Barnum 2000).

FUTURE POTENTIAL FOR LINKAGE

The research strategy chosen by the major theoretical programs in sociological social psychology has paid off handsomely. Isolating power, status, and identity processes so that they could be studied in pure form led to a dramatic growth of theoretical knowledge in the second half of the twentieth century. Indeed, we have progressed so far that researchers are only starting to put the picture back together again. In just the last decade, several studies have appeared that examine how status, power, identity, and emotion interact in more complex situations. Our growing understanding of these interactions has also increased the interplay between experimental, survey, and ethnographic research. As experimentalists, who primarily test theories, develop more complex views of how basic processes interact, their theories become more useful to survey and ethnographic researchers who necessarily deal with a more complex social situation.

It is, of course, more difficult to say where we are going than to say where we have been. One expects the current trend toward studying the interactions between status, power, identity, and emotion to continue. But advances will certainly come *within* the faces of social psychology as well. In social exchange, people are beginning to think about how exchange networks change. Studies of network dynamics – how networks evolve – are effectively studies of identity change. Since our conception of identity is that of a social position, defined by its relationship to other positions, any change in the network involves the creation or decay of identities over time. Social positions acquire meanings by virtue of their structure. People learn and act on those meanings and have emotional responses to them, structuring interactions. In extensions of Noah Friedkin's work, we will need to see if structures reach equilibrium and, if so, whether they create consensual culture or stable, conflicting views of reality.

The study of identity and emotion must focus to some degree on exploring the differences between the Heise and Burke models that now dominate the field. There also may be a return to the more network-ecological view of the self that characterized the structural symbolic interactionists' early efforts (Stryker 1980). Once we understand how the social actor attempts to maintain identity meanings through social interaction and emotion display, we can return to the central question of how those identities and their meanings are obtained, and what evokes them in one situation as opposed to another.

References

Allport, G. (1954) *The Nature of Prejudice*. Reading, MA: Addison-Wesley.
Bales, R. F. (1950) "A Set of Categories for the Analysis of Small Group Interaction." *American Sociological Review* 15: 257–63.

Barresi, J. and C. Moore (1996) "Intentional Relations and Social Understanding." *Behavioral and Brain Sciences* 19: 107–22.

Bargh, J. and T. L. Chartrand (1999) "The Unbearable Automaticity of Being." *American Psychologist* 54: 462–79.

Berger, J. (1988) "Directions in Expectation States Research." In M. Webster, M. Foschi, et al. (eds.), *Status Generalization: New Theory and Research*. Stanford, CA: Stanford University Press, pp. 269–89.

Berger, J., B. P. Cohen, and M. Zelditch, Jr. (1972) "Status Characteristics and Social Interaction." *American Sociological Review* 37: 241–55.

Berger, J., T. L. Conner, and H. Fisek (1974) *Expectation States Theory: A Theoretical Research Program*. Cambridge, MA: Winthrop.

Berger, J., S. J. Rosenholtz, and M. Zelditch, Jr. (1980) "Status Organizing Processes." *Annual Review of Sociology* 6: 470–508.

Blau, P. M. (1977) *Inequality and Heterogeneity*. New York: Free Press.

Burke, P. J. (1991) "Identity Processes and Social Stress." *American Sociological Review* 56: 836–49.

Burke, P. J. (2003) "Relationships among Multiple Identities." In P. J. Burke, T. J. Owens, R. T. Serpe, and P. A. Thoits (eds.), *Advances in Identity Theory and Research*. New York: Kluwer Academic/Plenum, pp. 195–214.

Burke, P. J. and A. D. Cast (1997) "Stability and Change in the Gender Identities of Newly Married Couples." *Social Psychology Quarterly* 60: 277–90.

Burke, P. J. and M. M. Harrod (2005) "Too Much of a Good Thing?" *Social Psychology Quarterly* 68: 359–74.

Burke, P. J. and D. C. Reitzes (1991) "An Identity Theory Approach to Commitment." *Social Psychology Quarterly* 54: 239–51.

Burke, P. J. and J. E. Stets (1999) "Trust and Commitment through Self-Verification." *Social Psychology Quarterly* 62: 347–66.

Burke, P. J. and J. E. Stets (2009) *Identity Theory*. New York: Oxford University Press.

Burke, P. J. and J. C. Tully (1977) "The Measurement of Role Identity." *Social Forces* 55: 881–97.

Cast, A. D., J. E. Stets, and P. J. Burke (1999) "Does the Self Conform to the Views of Others?" *Social Psychology Quarterly* 62: 68–82.

Clay-Warner, J., D. T. Robinson, and L. Smith-Lovin (2010) "Responding to Over-Reward: Tests of Equity Theory Predictions." Paper presented at the Meetings of the International Society for Justice Research, Banff, BC, Canada.

Cohen, E. G. (1982) "Expectation States and Interracial Intervention in the Classroom." *Annual Review of Sociology* 8: 209–35.

Cook, K. S., G. A. Fine, and J. S. House (eds.) (1995) *Sociological Perspectives on Social Psychology*. Boston: Allyn and Bacon.

Deaux, K. (1992) "Personalizing Identity and Socializing Self." In G. M. Blackwell (ed.), *Social Psychology of Identity and the Self-Concept*. London: Surrey University Press, pp. 9–33.

Fararo, Thomas J. and John Skvoretz (1986) "E-state Structuralism: A Theoretical Method." *American Sociological Review* 51: 591–602.

Friedkin, N. E. (1993) "Structural Bases of Interpersonal Influence in Groups." *American Sociological Review* 58: 861–72.

Friedkin, N. E. (1999) "Choice Shift and Group Polarization." *American Sociological Review* 64: 856–75.

Friedkin, N. E. (2001) "Norm Formation in Social Influence Networks." *Social Networks* 23: 167–89.

Friedkin, N. E. (2005) *A Structural Theory of Social Influence*. New York: Cambridge University Press.

Friedkin, N. (2010) "The Attitude-Behavior Linkage in Behavioral Cascades." *Social Psychology Quarterly* 73: 196–213.

Friedkin, N. E. and E. C. Johnsen (1999) "Social Influence Networks and Opinion Change." *Advances in Group Processes* 16: 1–29.

Friedkin, N. E. and E. C. Johnsen (2003) "Attitude Change, Affect Control, and Expectation States in the Formation of Influence Networks." *Advances in Group Processes* 20: 1–29.

Goffman, E. (1959) *The Presentation of Self in Everyday Life*. New York: Overlook Press.

Gould, R. V. (2002) "The Origins of Status Hierarchies: A Formal Theory and Empirical Test." *American Journal of Sociology* 107: 1143–78.

Hegtvedt, K. A. and B. Markovsky (1995) "Justice and Injustice." In K. S. Cook, G. A. Fine, and J. S. House (eds.), *Sociological Perspectives on Social Psychology*. Boston: Allyn and Bacon, pp. 257–80.

Heise, D. R. (1979) *Understanding Events*. New York: Cambridge University Press.

Heise, D. R. (1988) *Programs INTERACT and ATTITUDE*. Dubuque, IA: William C. Brown Publishers.

Heise, D. R. (1991) "OLS Equation Estimations for Program Interact." www.indiana.edu/~socpsy/papers/EQ_Estimations.pdf

Heise, D. R. (2007) *Expressive Order: Confirming Sentiments in Social Actions*. New York: Springer.

Hochschild, A. R. (1979) "Emotion Work, Feeling Rules and Social Structure." *American Journal of Sociology* 85: 551–75.

Homans, G. C. (1961) *Social Behavior: Its Elementary Forms*. New York: Harcourt, Brace & World.

Johnson, C. (1993) "Gender and Formal Authority." *Social Psychology Quarterly* 56: 193–210.

Kalkhoff, W. and C. Barnum (2000) "The Effects of Status-Organizing and Social Identity Processes on Patterns of Social Influence: Experimental Data and Conclusions." *Social Psychology Quarterly* 63: 95–115.

Kollock, P. (1994) "The Emergence of Exchange Structures: An Experimental Study of Uncertainty, Commitment and Trust." *American Journal of Sociology* 100: 313–45.

Lawler, E. J. and J. Yoon (1998) "Network Structure and Emotion in Exchange Relations." *American Sociological Review* 63: 871–94.

Lawler, E. J., S. R. Thye, and J. Yoon (2008) "Social Exchange and Micro Social Order." *American Sociological Review* 73: 519–42.

Lawler, Edward J., Shane R. Thye, and Jeongkoo Yoon (2009) *Social Commitments in a Depersonalized World*. New York: Russell Sage Foundation.

Lin, N. (2001) "Building a Network Theory of Social Capital." In N. Lin (ed.), *Social Capital: Theory and Research*. New Brunswick, NJ: Transaction Publishers, pp. 3–30.

Lovaglia, M. and J. Houser (1996) "Emotional Reactions, Status Characteristics and Social Interaction." *American Sociological Review* 61: 867–83.

MacKinnon, N. J. (1994) *Symbolic Interactionism as Affect Control*. New York: SUNY Press.

MacKinnon, N. J. and D. R. Heise (2010) *Self, Identity, and Social Institutions*. New York: Palgrave.

Mark, N., L. Smith-Lovin, and C. L. Ridgeway (2009) "Why Do Nominal Characteristics Acquire Status Value? A Minimal Explanation for Status Construction." *American Journal of Sociology* 115: 832–62.

McCall, G. J. and J. L. Simmons (1966) *Identities and Interactions*. New York: Free Press.

McCall, G. J. and J. L. Simmons (1978) *Identities and Interactions: An Examination of Human Association in Everyday Life*, 3rd edn. New York: Free Press.

McPherson, M. (2000) "Modeling Change in Fields of Organizations: Some Simulation Results." In D. R. Ilgen and C. L. Hulin (eds.), *Computational Modeling of Behavioral Processes in Organizations*. Washington, DC: American Psychological Association Press, pp. 134–44.

McPherson, M. and L. Smith-Lovin (2002) "Cohesion and Membership Duration: Linking Groups, Relations and Individuals in an Ecology of Affiliation." In S. R. Thye and E. J. Lawler (eds.), *Group Cohesion, Trust, and Solidarity*. New York: Elsevier Science/JAI Press, pp. 1–36.

Molm, L. D. (1997) *Coercive Power in Social Exchange*. New York: Cambridge University Press.

Molm, L. D. (2000) "Risk and Trust in Social Exchange: An Experimental Test of a Classical Proposition." *American Journal of Sociology* 105: 1396–427.

Molm, L. D. and K. S. Cook (1995) "Social Exchange and Exchange Networks." In K. S. Cook, G. A. Fine, and J. S. House (eds.), *Sociological Perspectives on Social Psychology*. Boston: Allyn and Bacon, pp. 209–35.

Osgood, C. H. (1962) "Studies on the Generality of Affective Meaning Systems." *American Psychologist* 17: 10–28.

Osgood, C. H., W. H. May, and M. S. Miron (1975) *Cross-Cultural Universals of Affective Meaning*. Urbana, IL: University of Illinois Press.

Pescosolido, B. A. and B. A. Rubin (2000) "The Web of Group Affiliations Revisited: Social Life, Postmodernism, and Sociology." *American Sociological Review* 65: 52–76.

Reitzes, D. C. and P. J. Burke (1980) "College Student Identity: Measurement and Implications." *Pacific Sociological Review* 23: 46–66.

Ridgeway, C. L. (1991) "The Social Construction of Status Value: Gender and Other Nominal Characteristics." *Social Forces* 70: 367–86.

Ridgeway, C. L. and L. Smith-Lovin (1994) "Structure, Culture and Action: Comparing Two Generative Theories." *Advances in Group Processes* 11: 213–39.

Ridgeway, C. L. and H. A. Walker (1995) "Status Structures." In K. S. Cook, G. A. Fine, and J. S. House (eds.), *Sociological Perspectives on Social Psychology*. Boston: Allyn and Bacon, pp. 281–310.

Robinson, D. T. and L. Smith-Lovin (1992) "Selective Interaction as a Strategy for Identity Negotiation." *Social Psychology Quarterly* 55: 12–28.

Robinson, D. T. and L. Smith-Lovin (2006) "Affect Control Theory." In P. Burke (ed.), *Contemporary Social Psychological Theories*. Stanford, CA: Stanford University Press, pp. 137–64.

Rogers, K. B. (2011) "Mapping the Social Ecology of Culture: Social Position, Connectedness, and Influence as Predictors of Systematic Variation in Affective Meaning." Unpublished manuscript.

Serpe, R. T. (1987) "Stability and Change in Self: A Structural Symbolic Interactionist Explanation." *Social Psychology Quarterly* 50: 44–5.

Serpe, R. T. and S. Stryker (1987) "The Construction and Reconstruction of Social Relationships." In E. Lawler and B. Markovsky (eds.), *Advances in Group Processes*. Greenwich, CT: JAI Press, pp. 41–66.

Smith-Lovin, L. (1988) "Affect Control Theory: An Assessment." *Journal of Mathematical Sociology* 13: 171–92.

Smith-Lovin, L. (2007) "The Strength of Weak Identities: Social Structural Sources of Self, Situation and Emotional Experience." *Social Psychology Quarterly* 70: 106–24.

Smith-Lovin, L. and W. Douglass (1992) "An Affect Control Analysis of Two Religious Subcultures." In V. Gecas and D. Franks (eds.), *Social Perspectives on Emotions*, Vol. 1. Greenwich, CT: JAI Press, pp. 217–48.

Smith-Lovin, L. and D. R. Heise (1982) "A Structural Equation Model of Impression Formation." In N. Hirschberg and L. G. Humphreys (eds.), *Multivariate Applications in the Social Sciences*. Hillsdale, NJ: Lawrence Erlbaum, pp. 195–222.

Smith-Lovin, L. and D. R. Heise (1988) *Analyzing Social Interaction: Advances in Affect Control Theory*. New York: Gordon and Breach.

Smith-Lovin, L. and D. R. Heise (1989) *Affect Control Theory: Research Advances*. London: Gordon and Breach.

Snow, D. A. (2000) "Symbolic Interactionism." In N. J. Smelser and P. B. Baltes (eds.), *International Encyclopedia of the Social and Behavioral Sciences*, Sociology vol. London: Elsevier Science.

Stets, J. E. (2005) "Emotions in Identity Theory." *Social Psychology Quarterly* 68: 39–56.

Stets, J. E. (2006) "Identity Theory." In P. J. Burke (eds.), *Contemporary Social Psychological Theories*. Palo Alto, CA: Stanford University Press, pp. 88–110.

Stets, J. E. and P. J. Burke (2005) "Identity Verification, Control, and Aggression in Marriage." *Social Psychology Quarterly* 68: 160–78.

Stryker, S. (1980) *Symbolic Interactionism*. Menlo Park, CA: Benjamin/Cummings.

Stryker, S. (2008) "From Mead to a Structural Symbolic Interactionism and Beyond." *Annual Review of Sociology* 34: 15–31.

Stryker, S. and P. J. Burke (2000) "The Past, Present, and Future of an Identity Theory." *Social Psychology Quarterly* 63: 284–97.

Stryker, S. and R. T. Serpe (1982) "Commitment, Identity Salience, and Role Behavior: A Theory and Research Example." In W. Ickes and E. S. Knowles (eds.), *Personality, Roles, and Social Behavior*. New York: Springer-Verlag, pp. 199–218.

Thomas, L. and D. R. Heise (1995) "Mining Error Variance and Hitting Pay-Dirt: Discovering Systematic Variation in Social Sentiments." *Sociological Quarterly* 36: 425–39.

Wagner, D. G., R. S. Ford, and T. W. Ford (1986) "Can Gender Inequalities Be Reduced?" *American Sociological Review* 51: 47–61.

Willer, D., M. Lovaglia, and B. Markovsky (1997) "Power and Influence: A Theoretical Bridge." *Social Forces* 76: 571–603.

8

Groups and Institutions, Structures and Processes

MURRAY WEBSTER, JR. AND JANE SELL

Human life is distinctly social. Except in rare instances, people pass their time in the company of others, and even in solitude they carry memories and imaginations of others that affect thoughts and action (Simmel [1908] 1950: 118–20). The mix of physical association and mental images ordinarily defines "group" as the term is used in sociology. People in a group notice that they have something in common, even when that commonality may be minimal and temporary (for example, a group of students waiting in the hall outside their professor's office).

Situations in which people lack coordinating awareness, such as people at a bus stop, each in his or her own world of thoughts, cell phone, or MP3 player, are usually called "collectivities." People in collectivities act differently from people in groups, and different phenomena are studied there. For instance, the study of panics and the study of propaganda generally presume collectivities. On the other hand, status hierarchies and network power positions are usually studied in groups where individuals orient themselves to each other in thoughts and actions. This entry limits attention to actions.

Social structure refers to patterned relationships, roles, rules governing individuals and behavior, and informal or formal agreements affecting individuals in groups. Institutions are the more or less enduring structures in which we spend our lives, including families, schools, corporations, clubs, political parties, and many others. In most cases structures precede individuals – that is, we move into an existing set of structural arrangements – though as research described below shows, people will create structures in initially undefined situations such as that of the autokinetic experiments. Institutions, like all social structures, permit, organize, and constrain action; in addition, they often define the meanings of various acts. Thus they create social realities for individuals.

The Wiley-Blackwell Companion to Sociology, First Edition. Edited by George Ritzer.
© 2012 Blackwell Publishing Ltd. Published 2012 by Blackwell Publishing Ltd.

Institutions constrain and enable differing types of interactions within and between groups. As Hodgson (2006) noted, discussion of the roles of institutions dates back at least to Giambattista Vico in *Scienza Nuova* in 1725. While the concept of institution is central to sociology, it is frequently undefined. Sociologists have traditionally talked of the important empirical institutions of family, education, religion, economics, and politics. But while those settings do enable different kinds of group interactions, it is theoretically more useful to analyze how and why the theoretical properties of institutions shape behavior. Thus groups, like individuals, are not independent from the institutional structures in which they are embedded.

Institutions generally are analyzed as distinct from their participants (North 1990: 3), and while institutions "depend upon the thoughts and activities of individuals," they "are not reducible to them" (Hodgson 2006: 2). Institutional rules have long been the subject of study in political science and economics, but have only recently been incorporated into group studies in sociology. Lovaglia, Mannix, Samuelson, Sell & Wilson (2004) and Sell, Lovaglia, Mannix, Samuelson, Sell & Wilson (2004) argue that interdisciplinary groups research might explicitly include institutional rules. They identify four types of institutional rules as particularly important: *boundary rules* which define group membership, *aggregation rules* which specify how individual decisions result in group decisions, *position rules* which specify rights and responsibilities by position, and *information rules* which specify who has what information. (Crawford and Ostrom's 1995 formulation of institutional grammar is an elegant approach to formalizing components of institutions by sorting the components into three types of statements: rules, norms, and shared strategies.) To illustrate ways in which these institutional rules might change the ways in which groups interact, we consider some examples below.

THEMES AND CONTRASTS

While earlier research often studied the groups or institutions themselves (for instance, describing what a gang or a school looked like and what happened there), most contemporary research can better be described as studying phenomena that occur in groups and institutions. Put differently, contemporary research usually focuses on social processes and social structures that occur in groups and institutions. This different focus might seem trivial, but actually it constitutes an important change. The study of a group or an institution is concrete and descriptive: it tells what the case is like, and the more detail it gives, the better it fulfills the descriptive task. Describing a gang, for instance, is tied to a particular setting. In contrast, studies of processes and structures are abstract and general. Such research studies processes and structures that may be seen in a given group or institution, and elsewhere. For instance, conformity processes occur in small groups, and they also occur in settings such as large corporations and schools.

Second, group research is coming to focus more on artificial groups rather than on natural groups. The same is true for institutions, which may be created in a laboratory. The reason is that for theory testing an artificial case provides a better place to study processes and structures than does a natural case. Natural cases are complex, and many factors affect any observations that a researcher might make.

Artificial instances are simpler and a researcher has much more flexibility to design them so that they contain all of the independent variables of interest, and fewer confounding variables. In addition, artificial settings may be designed to make observation and data collection easier. It often makes sense to create groups for the purpose of research rather than searching for a naturally occurring group meeting the needs of the research questions and measurement requirements. Webster and Sell (2007: ch. 1) discuss experimental artificiality and its relation to theory testing.

A third distinction is whether research is purely observational or whether it includes some applications or even interventions. Purely scientific research is observational. Researchers are interested in what happens under certain conditions. Applied research is conducted for some purpose beyond simply adding to knowledge. Thus most businesses and political organizations now use "focus groups" – small groups whose members are asked to describe their reactions to ideas and products while observers note the content and process of their discussions, to assess the appeal of new products, television programs, and political policies. Interventions are devised for producing changes a researcher desires, such as reducing interaction disabilities produced by racial differences in schools, or implementing policies making it easier for corporate employees to balance work and family tasks. Webster and Whitmeyer (2001) offer a typology of theoretical applications, along with examples.

A fourth distinction is whether research focuses on *processes* or *structure*; that is, whether researchers are studying what goes on among people when they meet or whether they study how certain practices and norms affect processes and outcomes. Though the classifications overlap – studies of process are conducted with certain structural conditions and studies of structure involve processes as independent or dependent variables – the terms capture whether researchers are primarily interested in the processes or whether the effects of social arrangements are of primary concern. The distinction of process and structure is one of naming rather than a natural separation because interaction processes lead to formation of structures, and structures affect interaction processes. The value of any research appears in its contributions to knowledge, which includes both what the groups and institutions are like (structure) and how they function (process). Sewell (1992) and Turner (2006: 360–1) provide a more complete discussion of "structure" in sociology.

We begin by reviewing historical foundations for the study of groups. Next we describe research on group processes and structures within institutions. Our review is not exhaustive, but reflects some of the significant programs of research conducted over the past 100 years or so.

THEORETICAL AND EMPIRICAL FOUNDATIONS IN THE STUDY OF GROUPS

Probably every social thinker has considered the significance of groups, but two in the early twentieth century identified themes that persist to the present. In Germany, Georg Simmel (1858–1918) lectured and wrote about group affiliation, the social nature of isolation, conflict, secrets, and many other themes. Simmel's work appears in English translations, including those of Wolff (Simmel 1950, 1964) and Levine

(1971). Wolff (Simmel 1950) first used the terms *dyad* and *triad* in place of the awkward phrases of a literal translation. In the US, Charles Horton Cooley (1864–1929) lectured and wrote about forms of social organization and formation of the self.

The most enduring of Simmel's insights probably appear in his distinction of the *dyad* from the *triad*, detailing ways in which two-person groups are distinct from larger sizes. Dyadic relations are marked by intense emotions (including love and hate), uniqueness (every dyad has more differences than it has similarities with other dyads), and fragility (either member can destroy a dyad by leaving). A triad or larger group shows emotional modulation and other social influences such as unequal power; its similarities with other groups can outnumber its unique characteristics; and the group can persist even if a member leaves and is replaced. Simmel's insight that simple numbers could be important – without taking into account factors such as personalities of the individuals or their history – was foundational for the new field of sociology. In contemporary terms, triads and larger groups have similarities, no matter which particular individuals compose the groups. Social structure becomes important by itself.

At the University of Michigan, Charles Horton Cooley adopted the term *primary groups* ([1909] 1956) to mean those characterized by intimacy and close association, including the family, children's play groups, and neighborhoods. Cooley's best-known work is *Human Nature and the Social Order* ([1902] 1956), though he wrote many other books and journal articles, including topics in economics, in which he had earned his PhD. An overarching theme of Cooley's sociological work was the importance of social context in formation and change of the self.

The family, of course, is the primary or first group of which one is a member. Primary groups are sometimes contrasted to *secondary groups* such as formal organizations. Primary groups, as Cooley used the term, resemble *gemeinschaft* relations, which Ferdinand Tönnies (1887) contrasted to *gesellschaft* relations. Tönnies defined the types as found, respectively, in informal community and formal economic relationships.

Contemporary usage often treats primary groups as those in which members interact as individuals rather than as role occupants; that is, in which they attend to each other's individual characteristics. Sociological study of groups focuses on those small enough that members treat each other as individuals, though these groups often do not display the strong intimacy of a family. Because of the limits of attention, research groups are limited in size, perhaps to 15 or 20 members. Beyond that size, the meaning of interaction differs; for instance, audience phenomena appear and interaction is mostly one-way. Contemporary study of groups is thus limited in size, determined by practical limitations on the number of individuals a researcher can directly observe, and more importantly by the number of individuals that group members can interact with and distinguish as individuals.

Empirical study of groups has almost as long a history as the theoretical work of Simmel, Cooley, and others. Much of the early research was conducted to study processes occurring in natural groups. A foundational reader, called *Small Groups* (Hare, Borgatta & Bales 1965), contains reports from studies of schoolchildren (Terman 1904), gangs (Thrasher 1927), a telephone assembly factory (Turner 1933), and even a college poker game (Riddle 1937). The widespread usage of the term "small groups" can be traced to that book's title. A second collection of research papers, *Group Dynamics* (Cartwright & Zander 1960), brought a second widely used term to sociological language.

"Small groups" and "group dynamics" both originated in interdisciplinary programs, including sociologists, psychologists, anthropologists, and mathematicians. At Harvard University in the 1940s and 1950s, R. F. Bales and his students and colleagues studied task groups, still often called "Bales Groups." Dorwin P. Cartwright and his collaborators at the University of Michigan, including the mathematician Frank Harary, were more interested in change (process) than in composition (structure) of the groups, and thus their preferred term "group dynamics." Research represented in those two collections from the 1960s, including research by the editors, fostered the development of the contemporary study of groups, shaping the approach and choice of research problems even more than they shaped terminology.

TWO EARLY RESEARCH PROGRAMS: STRUCTURING AND CONFORMITY

Some early research addressed the meaning of group influence and how group influence might be different from individual influence. Muzafer Sherif (1936; Sherif & Sherif 1956) developed an elegantly simple design to study ways people influence each other in understanding minimal situations. In a completely dark room, a stationary pinpoint of light will appear to move. A person in this situation will generally develop a characteristic mean and range of movement. If people participate together, they come to share a mean and range; and if people who have previously developed their own beliefs about movement come together, they influence each other in their beliefs. Furthermore, if group members are replaced one by one, the arbitrary group traditions about movement will persist, with attenuation, through as many as eight "generations" of replacements (Jacobs & Campbell 1961). This line of research shows the process of structuring, reaching common definitions of an undefined situation, and it also shows that the structures thus created are the basis for influence among group members.

A dramatic demonstration of group influence occurs in a design developed by Solomon Asch (1952, 1953) to study conformity processes. Here, a lone individual is unknowingly placed in a group of others, all of whom are confederates of the experimenter. They are asked to judge line lengths, a task for which right answers are easy and obvious. However the confederates unanimously give an incorrect answer on every decision trial, and the naïve subject is faced with either telling what he sees (and so differing from the group) or saying what the others say (and conforming to something he knows is incorrect). The surprising finding is that about one-third of answers in this situation are conforming. People vary widely in their propensities to conform and responses vary widely on individual trials, but overall, about one-third of answers are conforming. Participants evidence considerable stress: they squint, fidget, sweat, and afterwards report feeling pressure to conform. The experiment shows that influence processes can overcome obvious reality, even when nobody makes arguments or tries physical coercion. It would not be correct to interpret these results as showing that people "always conform," or that conformity is the main force governing behavior in other situations. Cohen (1963) and Cohen and Lee (1975) developed theoretical explanations for behavior in this situation, including variants of it, and they discuss natural analogues of the processes involved. Results of the conformity experiments show that social influence processes operate powerfully in a minimal situation. Together, the autokinetic experiments and the conformity experiments show that individuals in groups develop characteristic opinions and behavior, and that they can have great effects on each other's opinions and actions.

CONTEMPORARY RESEARCH PROGRAMS

Leadership and legitimation

Much of early small groups research in the years following the Second World War was concerned with leadership, how it emerges and is maintained, and how to identify potential leaders (e.g., Berkowitz 1953; Borgatta, Couch & Bales 1954). More recent research has studied leadership as a social position rather than as a cluster of individual traits (Dornbusch & Scott 1975), and treats legitimation as an essential feature of leadership (Berger, Ridgeway, Fişek & Norman 1998). Generally, of course, legitimate structures are stable and illegitimate are less stable; this is consistent with Max Weber's (1922) analysis that authority depends on consent of the governed. Evan and Zelditch (1961) investigated authorization as a source of legitimation and distinguished the *legal* and *rational* components of Weber's theory of bureaucratic authority, finding that the source of legitimation was more important than competence of the authority when it came to eliciting compliance. Other research (Zelditch & Walker 1984; Thomas, Walker & Zelditch 1986; Walker, Thomas & Zelditch 1986; Zelditch 2001; Walker, Rogers & Zelditch 2002; Johnson, Dowd & Ridgeway 2006) continues to refine the theoretical foundations and explore empirical consequences of legitimation.

Read (1974) showed that group members often prefer an elected leader over a more talented appointed leader, illustrating the importance of legitimacy in stable leadership. Unchallenged rituals can maintain leadership, even when it is not beneficial to the group (Knottnerus 1997; Sell, Knottnerus, Ellison & Mundt 2000); the process may be involved when individuals eventually come to support leadership that was initially coercively introduced. Lucas and Lovaglia (2006) propose that legitimation works through an intervening mechanism, promoting trust in the leader.

Groups, identity, and group identity

The book *Folkways* (1906), by anthropologist William Graham Sumner, provided the impetus for studies of how group members form alliances and respond more favorably to those who share their group membership. Social psychologists (Tajfel 1970; Tajfel, Billig, Bundy & Flament 1971; Fiske & Neuberg 1990; Fiske & Taylor 1991; Fiske 1992, 1998; Fiske, Cuddy, Glick & Xu 2002) have demonstrated that mere classification on an arbitrary category is enough to create in-group bias. This bias creates higher regard and higher reward allocations for those within one's own group than those outside one's group (Brewer 1979; Brewer & Kramer 1986). However, in a recent discussion of in-group bias, Brewer (2007) notes that in-group favoritism does not necessarily create out-group harm.

Identity – cognitions and affect regarding oneself – is of continuing interest to many scholars. Several theoretical research programs have investigated how identity develops and changes, and how a person's identity affects behavior. Peggy Thoits (1983, 1986, 1991, 2003) has emphasized multiple identities and factors associated with choosing to enact one or another of them. Depending on other factors, activating multiple identities can either protect against stress from social isolation, or it can generate stress from conflicting demands. Sheldon Stryker and his associates (Stryker 1968; Stryker & Macke 1978; Stryker 1980; Stryker & Serpe 1982; Stryker 1987; Stryker & Serpe 1994; Stryker 1997, 2000; Stryker & Vryan 2003; Stryker 2004, 2008) study effects of the salience of different identities, assuming the existence of a hierarchy from which individuals select identities from among those available. A representative study (Serpe & Stryker 1987a, 1987b), for instance, describes the process by which students come to see themselves as members of a university rather than as members of their high schools and hometowns during their first year of college.

Two influential research programs have developed: identity theory (e.g., Burke 1980; Stets 1993, 1995, 1997; Burke 2004; Stets 2004; Burke 2006, 2007, 2008; Stets & Asencio 2008; Burke & Stets 2009) and affect control theory (e.g., Smith-Lovin & Heise 1988; Smith-Lovin 2003; Rogers & Smith-Lovin, Chapter 7, this volume). Smith-Lovin and Robinson (2006) delineate similarities and differences in the affect control theory and identity theory research programs. Stryker and Burke (2000) present a comparable comparison of Stryker's and Burke's research programs on identity. Both of these programs treat identity as the central concept in a homeostatic control process. Individual behavior is largely (not exclusively) the result of attempts to get confirmatory feedback from the social environment, and stress results when evidence shows that others do not share the individual's view of himself or herself.

A large body of literature examines how group memberships shape individual identity and how individual identities shape group identities (Brewer 2007). Research in this area has been directed at examining when particular identities become most salient (Stryker 2008) and how interruption in the identity maintenance process can be stressful (Burke 1991) or lead to disruption (Smith-Lovin 2003) and instigate changes in perceptions or behavior. This literature has prompted investigations especially of categories linked to ethnic or national identity (see Campbell 1958; Phinney 2000).

Two recent studies of the significance of race in identity show how important societal context is in molding interpretations and actions, and how the processes differ or are similar in different countries. Kruttschnitt and Hussemann (2008) compared the views of long-term women prisoners in California and in England. In California, where white ethnics are a minority, race is highly significant in coping with the adversities of life. In England, the minority of foreign nationality view race as highly significant. The significance of racial identity thus becomes most salient under conditions of disadvantaged minority position. Faas (2009) measured racial identity among teenagers in Stuttgart and London. He found hybrid ethnic and national identities, and showed that the components of identities are associated with social class, with cosmopolitan identities being more common among advantaged youth, and ethnicity (Turkish origins) being more significant among working-class youth.

Institutional changes in boundary conditions obviously can change group identity and the subsequent processes that result. The boundary institutions are rules about how group membership is defined, maintained, and changed. As an example, there are institutional rules that define who can be a member of a professional association or organization and who cannot. In a study of differing forestry groups in Nepal, Varughese and Ostrom (2001) detail ways that many differences among group members can be overcome to enable cooperation if the people develop an overarching group identity tied to the forest.

Role differentiation and expectation state structures

As noted above, the study of small groups is usually traced to the laboratory discussion groups studied by Bales and his students and associates. One of the earliest findings from that work was that, when group members are task-focused and collectively oriented, they rapidly develop inequality when they meet. That is, when the purpose of meeting is to solve a problem or a set of problems (task-focused) and everyone's ideas must be considered (collectively oriented), group members participate different amounts and exert different influence over the group outcome. Participation and influence are correlated; the most active members are also the most influential. Further, participation and influence also correlate with group members' perceptions of specific task skill, leadership, and general problem-solving ability (Bales 1950; Bales, Strodtbeck, Mills & Roseborough 1951; Bales 1970, 1999).

The regular emergence of inequality and its association with ability perceptions led to development of a large research program by Joseph Berger and associates (Berger & Snell 1961; Berger, Fişek, Norman & Zelditch 1977; Berger & Webster 2006). In this view, the behavioral and perceptual inequalities are produced by an underlying structure of *performance expectation states* that form during the interaction process. That is, features of group interaction create relative expectations for the quality of each member's performance, and once those form, they govern behavior (such as chances to perform and evaluations of performances) and cognitions (such as perceived leadership). Where do expectations come from? Problem-solving interactions include suggestions and evaluations ("good idea," "bad idea"), and those generalize to individuals ("knows how to do this," "doesn't understand"). That generalization creates expectations for individuals, which govern future interaction inequality. Individuals need to take advantage of good ideas and avoid being misled by bad ideas, so one of their "sub-tasks" is to form expectations for everyone in the group. Task-focused interaction therefore leads to inequality.

Status organizing effects

In the Bales groups, performance expectations form among individuals who were initially undifferentiated. More commonly, however, individuals come to task-focused groups with many differentiating characteristics: age, education, gender, race, and socio-economic status, among others. Those characteristics confer status advantages and disadvantages in the larger society. A jury is like a Bales group except that individuals are differentiated by status characteristics. When that is true, a process called *status generalization* causes expectation formation without any interaction. Individuals are likely to form high expectations for those with status advantages and low expectations for those whose characteristics disadvantage them in the outside society. Thus, for instance, men participate more, exert more influence, and are more likely to be chosen as jury foreperson than women – despite the absence of any evidence that men are actually more competent on juries than women. Generally, in task-focused collectively oriented groups, status generalization "imports" the society's inequality to the small group and allows it to produce a corresponding interaction inequality.

Constraints to preferences

Shelly Correll (2004; Correll & Benard 2006) has traced effects of status generalization processes from the characteristic of gender, showing ways that they may affect fields of study and occupational specialization. This work shows how gender status beliefs affect career aspirations and decisions of men and women: if women are thought less capable of mathematical tasks, they are likely to "prefer" non-mathematical college majors and careers. Thus status-based stereotypes can channel people differentially into occupations. More generally, status-based stereotypes can bias many task-related activities and bias interaction in ways that perpetuate gender inequality and gender stereotypes (Ridgeway 2011).

Research in Scandinavian countries shows similar processes to those that Correll finds in the US, despite the European countries' greater gender equality and more egalitarian norms. In Sweden, one of the most gender-equal societies, teenage boys and girls still display gender differentiation in household chores (girls do more housework), though gender neutrality is improved by modeling processes when the parents engage more equally in tasks (Evertsson 2006). Norwegian women government workers apply for promotion to managerial positions less frequently than do men, perhaps fearing discrimination – a fear that may or may not be justified (Storvik & Schone 2008). Other Swedish research shows that girls' choice of a science and technology program in high school is more likely when highly educated fathers, even stepfathers and absent fathers, encourage it (Laftman 2008). Structural factors affect preferences also. Halrynjo and Lyng (2009) found that women professionals in Norway, a country with a well-developed welfare state, often lower their career aspirations as their family demands increase following childbirth.

Overcoming status effects

Several studies have investigated ways to intervene to affect undesirable outcomes of status generalization. Techniques include adding more status characteristics and other information, and task definition. Webster and Driskell (1978) showed that the negative effects of race on expectations could be overcome by adding status information. White women working in biracial dyads formed low expectations for their black partner, reflected in behavior and perceptions of ability. When positively valued status characteristics were introduced for the black woman, the white partner formed higher expectations for her, again reflected in behavior and perceptions. In classrooms, Cohen and Lotan (1997) developed several techniques to overcome interaction disabilities associated with ethnicity (Hispanic/white) and economic status. These included adding characteristics as Webster and Driskell had done in the laboratory, introducing role relationships, and defining task complexity. This last technique, defining a task as complex and requiring a variety of skills, tends to block simple status generalization. Goar and Sell (2005) showed that it worked to overcome undesirable status generalization from race in groups of college women. In general, this research points to ways of using analysis of structural factors – race, gender, and other characteristics – to intervene in the processes for desirable ends.

Institutional rules can create a status characteristic, strengthen an existing status characteristic, or nullify its effects. So, for example, if institutional rules specify a seniority rule, a particular kind of status is legitimated within the group and hierarchy will generally follow the rule. Berger, Ridgeway, Fişek, and Norman (1998) specify how legitimating structures (institutional rules) intervene in group settings to create stronger or weaker status processes within the group. This formulation draws attention to the nested nature of institutional rules. Such rules sanction certain behaviors; organizations often (although not always) reflect those rules, and small groups also often (although not always) reflect those same rules.

There have been some analyses of how status organizing processes might be diminished that can be conceptualized as using institutional rule interventions. Lucas (2003) varied institutional rules defining the meaning of the leader's gender and the way in which the leader was chosen, to create a laboratory organization. When a female leader was appointed on the basis of ability *and* organizational rules endorsed female leaders, then the leader was able to influence her team. Without that normative support, however, women leaders seldom attempted influence and were usually unsuccessful when they did attempt to guide the group. This research shows how groups and institutional rules are nested; that is, that they must be translated from the institutional level to the individual level to be effective.

Additional research emphasizing institutional rules in status organizing processes includes research by E. G. Cohen and her associates within school settings (Cohen & Lotan 1997). One of the institutional rules shown to intervene in stereotyping on the basis of race was the introduction of behavioral norms in classrooms. The norms specified that all the children should participate in the class activities. Those norms are institutional rules about position; that is, that everyone has an equal position in terms of participation. It should be noted that this is another example of how an institutional rule for the group has effects even if it is not consistent with general societal rules. In this case, the participation equality rule was counter to the usual participation inequality rule in the outside society.

Social exchange processes

Georg Simmel, already mentioned, and, more recently, George C. Homans (1910–1989) saw exchange processes as fundamental in social life. Informal language – "I got a lot out of meeting her"; "What's the profit in doing that?" – illustrates an exchange view. Interaction is analyzed in terms of the rewards and costs of alternatives. Homans first presented the ideas in an "essay that will hope to honor the memory of Georg Simmel." He continued, "I have come to think that [the main jobs facing sociology] would be furthered by our adopting the view that interaction between persons is an exchange of goods, material and nonmaterial" (Homans 1958: 597). He later presented an explicit theory of social exchange (Homans 1961), and Peter M. Blau (1964) and many others have elaborated the basic insights to explore how variations in exchange affect group processes.

Combining insights from social exchange and operant learning theory, Richard M. Emerson (1925–82) founded an important line of research with two papers (1962, 1964) clarifying the relationship of power and dependence. The more dependent Person B is upon Person A for some resource, the greater A's power over B; or $P_{A|B} = D_{B|A}$. That relationship underlies nearly all contemporary research on exchange processes in groups and social networks. During their research together, Emerson and Karen S. Cook laid the foundations for several branches of contemporary research in exchange processes. Cook and Emerson (1978, 1984) describe representative work on power and commitment. Summaries of the large literature are available in Molm and Cook (1995) and Molm (2006).

One of the larger research programs on exchange processes has been developed by Linda D. Molm and her associates (Molm 1994, 1997; Molm, Peterson & Takahashi 1999; Molm 2003). In *coercive exchange*, individuals have the capacity to punish others by taking away resources for non-compliance. As might be expected, coercion produces negative emotional responses, and it also reduces cohesiveness of the exchange relationship. Perhaps because individuals anticipate negative effects of coercion, Molm and her associates found that most individuals were hesitant to employ coercion even when they stood to gain large rewards from doing so.

Molm's research team has identified four types of exchange relationships, and described different behavioral processes produced in each.

- In *negotiated exchange*, parties bargain over the exchange terms, and reach agreement only when both of them are satisfied. Buying a car or signing a legal contract are instances of negotiated exchange.
- In *reciprocal exchange*, one party gives something to the other without guarantee of any value in return. Giving a birthday present or extending a dinner invitation are instances.
- In *generalized exchange*, a party gives to a group in anticipation of someone in the group returning equal value. Donating blood and "secret Santa" programs at work are examples.
- In *productive exchange*, parties contribute jointly and perhaps unequally to an outcome that rewards them both. Co-authoring a book or participating in a work team or a sports team are examples.

Negotiated and reciprocal exchanges have been studied the most. People report greater satisfaction from reciprocal exchanges, and, perhaps surprisingly, they find them to be more fair, despite the fact that they have not previously agreed on terms, as they would have done in negotiated exchanges. Generalized exchanges seem to produce social solidarity and feelings of similarity to others, and they are also pleasanter than negotiated exchanges.

Exchange, affect, and group cohesion

Exchanges can lead to feelings of attachment to exchange partners and to the group. From a basic insight that exchange processes can be rewarding or pleasant, Edward J. Lawler, Shane R. Thye, and Jeongkoo Yoon have developed an elaborate theory of how exchange generates emotions, how emotions become associated with exchange partners and with groups, and consequences of emotions generated in exchange, including cohesion and identification with groups (Lawler, Thye & Yoon 2009). In this theory, different forms of exchange are differentially effective at generating the emotions that produce cohesion.

As mentioned, there are many varieties of exchange theories. But for all of these theories, institutional rules can be exceptionally important. For example, the work on relational cohesion (Lawler & Yoon 1996) demonstrates that when an institutional rule results in equal power among individuals, more positive emotions and perceptions result than when the rule produces unequal power. The central role of power position, decision-making, and allocation of resources, which are all types of institutional rules, highlights the importance of their specification for understanding social exchanges.

Networks and power

Several programs have studied how an actor's position in a social network affects power to negotiate successfully, or, when possible, to change the network. In a network structure, connections between actors permit them to exchange with each other, while lack of connections prevents exchanges. In general, having many connections gives power, while having few is to be powerless. To see this, imagine a simple line network with three actors, A, B, and C, and A–B and B–C connections. In this case, B can exchange with either A or C, while they can only exchange with B. Thus B has greater power than either of them to demand favorable negotiation outcomes. David Willer and his associates (Lovaglia, Skvoretz, Willer & Markovsky 1995; Willer 1999; Willer & Emanuelson 2008) have developed formal theoretical analyses of power in networks, along with supporting experimental tests.

Heckathorn and his colleagues (Heckathorn, Broadhead, Anthony & Weakliem 1999) have used network analyses to reach the "invisible population" of injecting drug users and have shown that the techniques can bring many of them to outreach clinics at low cost. The method involves giving small rewards to individuals in the group for reaching others in the group, thus biasing the flow of rewards and influence in the social structure. Heckathorn et al. (1999) note that this method could be used to reach other sociologically important but hard to reach invisible populations, including the homeless, income tax cheats, street prostitutes, and gay members of the military. In both laboratory and naturally occurring networks, the flow of rewards and punishments through the network is what leads to power and influence, as well as to accumulating differential shares of negotiated rewards.

Trust

Much recent research has considered the meaning of interpersonal trust, and its sources and consequences in groups. Karen S. Cook (2005) treats trust as a specific relation: Actor A trusts Actor B with respect to x in a particular situation. Thus someone might trust another with money but not with a child. The key to understanding trust in this view is the presence of risk; without risk, talk of trust is meaningless. Thus trust emerges and has effects under conditions of uncertainty, as, for instance, where someone initiates a reciprocal exchange without certainty of reciprocation (Cook, Rice & Gerbasi 2004). Nickel (2009) analyzed various cases of trust, showing that many can be seen as situations in which moral normative expectations get activated: when Actor A trusts Actor B, that entails both of them acknowledging norms of moral behavior, and when A's trust is particularly strong, B may decide to avoid the relationship rather than incur the associated obligations. Kramer and Cook (2004) summarize research on trust in organizations. Cook, Hardin, and Levi (2005) consider the relationship of trust and cooperation, and describe conditions under which trust complements cooperation and other conditions under which lack of trust facilitates cooperative behavior. Gambetta and Hamill (2005) describe the situational and behavioral cues taxi drivers use to assess the trustworthiness of strangers who might be either legitimate fares or murderous criminals.

Trust and trustworthiness has been an active area of investigation across disciplines (Eckel 2007). Institutional rules about who has information about what seem to be important in whether people might even invoke trust. So, for example, when boundary rules specify that people cannot just exit a group, but rather must interact for longer time periods, trust is affected. Under such conditions, people develop reputations for their trustworthiness and these reputations become important in group behavior and strategies. In ongoing exchange, trust is fostered by experience of reciprocation or of fair negotiation, and it leads to commitment to dyadic relationships (Yamagishi, Cook & Watabe 1998). In natural settings, many authors treat generalized social trust as a measure of the "health" of a community or of a democracy. It is associated with social capital, such as contacts and voluntary associations (Paxton 1999; Putnam 2000; Robinson & Jackson 2001). Li, Savage, and Warde (2008) refined this analysis, showing that among British service workers, especially second-generation workers, many cross-class associations exist, and that having cross-class associations was linked, perhaps causally, with expressing high levels of generalized social trust.

Cooperation and social dilemmas

A social dilemma is any setting in which there is a conflict between individual short-term incentives and overall group incentives (Dawes 1980). Common examples include civil rights movements and the protection of fragile ecosystems. Because social dilemmas are so pervasive, most of the social sciences have investigated them. As a result, there is an especially rich cross-disciplinary literature. Many solutions to social dilemmas involve changing the basic structure of the dilemma and thereby affecting incentives (Messick & Brewer 1983; Samuelson & Messick 1995); for instance, punishment mechanisms for not cooperating (one class of which includes "trigger strategies"), and incentives for cooperating (Sato 1987; Yamagishi 1988; Ostrom, Gardner & Walker 1994; Sell & Wilson 1999). Other solutions to social dilemmas have focused on "social" factors, that is factors affected by group interaction. Communication among group members facilitates cooperation (Sally 1995). The reasons include the creation of commitments (Orbell, Van de Kragt & Dawes 1988; Kerr & Kaufman-Gilleland 1994) and the development of in-group identity (Brewer & Kramer 1986). However, simply sending signals of intention, or "cheap talk," is not enough to increase cooperation (Wilson & Sell 1997). Recently, Sell and Love (2009) have posited that "transformative crises," disruptions that temporarily create uncertainty from lack of information, can either increase prosocial behavior or increase selfish behavior, depending on which sorts of information a crisis disrupts. Generally, strong group identity tends to bring out the best in people in crises, while not knowing how others are acting promotes individualistic behavior. Simpson and Willer (2008) attribute the activation of prosocial or selfish behavior to prior traits (egoism and altruism) that get activated in such situations. Similarly, Haski-Leventhal (2009) sees altruism and volunteerism as both produced by "alter-centricity," that is, by a moral concern for the welfare of others, a view similar to that proposed by Skitka, Bauman, and Mullen (2008). Conditions under which structural factors or individual factors trigger prosocial action are a crucial topic for further investigation.

Partly because social dilemmas have been the topic of interdisciplinary research, institutional rules have been articulated in some research areas related to cooperation. So, for example, institutional rules about information have received scrutiny (e.g., Binmore 2007; Holt 2007). Social dilemmas with asymmetrical information (meaning that only some people have information while others do not) promote different kinds of interaction than social dilemmas with symmetrical information. Ostrom (1998) argues that communication between group members promotes sharing of information, a way to modify asymmetrical information, and, most importantly, the opportunity to develop contingent agreements, informal contracts specifying how participants will act. These examples demonstrate how the participants might modify the institutional rules (informational rules and position rules for example) and thereby create different group conditions over time.

Justice

Aspects of justice or fairness have been studied for centuries in natural settings (e.g., Solomon & Murphy 2000). In groups, contemporary research focuses on *distributive justice*, whether people get fair benefits and burdens, and *procedural justice*, whether outcome decisions have been made fairly (Hegtvedt & Markovsky 1995; Hegtvedt 2006). Among other types of justice that have been identified, Colquitt, Conlon, Wesson, Porter, and Ng (2001) also discuss "interactional" and "informational" justice, and Okimoto and Wenzel (2008) explore "restorative" justice. Retributive justice is often studied in criminology.

Distributive justice research attracted considerable attention through some ingenious experiments reported by Adams (1965). In certain conditions, participants were told that they were overpaid for a proofreading task, based on their supposed lack of qualifications. In those conditions, they responded by working harder, proofing more pages and finding more errors and non-errors (e.g., marking as misspelled a word that actually was spelled correctly). Those experiments demonstrated that unfair distributions, over- as well as under-reward, produce distress and attempts to restore justice. Researchers at the time adapted a relationship first proposed by Homans (1961), in which two people compare their outcomes (e.g., wages) divided by their inputs (e.g., years of education) in a ratio: $O_A / I_A = O_B / I_B$. An equality sign between the ratios constitutes justice; inequality is injustice. Berger, Zelditch, Anderson, and Cohen (1972) improved the theory in two ways: (1) by expanding the referent from a single other actor to a group sharing characteristics with the individual (for example, "college graduates"), and (2) by incorporating status valued rewards (for example, a reserved parking space).

A series of papers by Jasso (1978, 1980, 2001) further improve the theoretical foundation of distributive justice by incorporating a logarithmic function, the effect of which is to capture the common observation that people feel injustice to their detriment more acutely than to their benefit; for instance, a small salary differential favoring oneself is mildly pleasant, while a small differential favoring a co-worker can be strongly unpleasant. Jasso's theory is a general theory of comparison processes, of much wider scope than distributive justice cases, though it incorporates them. Jasso (2006) provides a general introduction to the theory, and Jasso (2008) provides a more technical explication.

As an example, Jasso's theory has been used to document changes in perceived fair wages for women and men between 1977 and 1997 (Jasso & Webster 1999), and Jasso and Webster's findings in the US have been replicated in Germany (Sauer 2009). Mueller and Kim (2008) describe "the paradox of the contented female worker" (that is, that in 43 countries surveyed, women were just as satisfied with their jobs as men, despite the women's lower material rewards) as potentially understandable with Jasso's theory of comparison processes because women compare themselves to other women, and men compare themselves to other men.

Procedural justice

Thibaut and Walker's (1975) research generally treats fair procedures as pleasant because they signal that a person is a valued member of a group (Clay-Warner 2006). Clay-Warner, Hegtvedt & Roman (2005) studied procedural and distributive justice effects among workers in firms where downsizing removed many of them from their jobs. They found that procedural justice affected commitment to the firm among those who survived the downsizing; that is, those who felt the downsizing followed fair procedures remained committed to their firms, while those who felt that fairness had been violated were less likely to remain committed. Among those who suffered layoffs, distributive justice concerns were more important in their emotional responses. These findings are consistent with earlier research showing that strong group identification reduces self-interested views of fairness (Wenzel 2002). Wenzel, Okimoto, Feather, and Platow (2008) argue that a preference for *restorative* justice over *retributive* justice (punishment) requires perception of a shared identity with the rule-breaker.

CONCLUSION

The study of groups, structures, and institutions has a long history within sociology. The study has evolved from observing groups and group behavior in specific settings such as poker games or religious meetings to focusing on what sets of theoretical principles lead to what kinds of structures and processes within groups. Such a theoretical strategy makes cumulative development possible because the emphasis is upon predicting and explaining the conditions under which interaction occurs rather than dissecting specific groups one at a time, and emphasizing particulars. We argue that one way to further this approach might be to emphasize theoretical principles of institutions and how differing institutions might modify groups.

A second evolution in the study of groups has been an emphasis upon how groups are nested or embedded in other settings such as institutions. This recognition has encouraged researchers to look at the effects differing groups have on one another. It is possible then to examine issues of legitimation, justice, and trust within one group and analyze how these are affected by other groups. Thus the study of groups is not necessarily the study of "small." As an illustration, the investigation of groups of internet users (which could well be millions of people) can be examined as well as the institutions that constrain and enable them. The co-orientation and interdependence of participants, rather than size, define the group.

References

Adams, J. Stacy (1965) "Inequity in Social Exchange." *Advances in Experimental Social Psychology* 2: 267–99.

Asch, Solomon E. (1952) *Social Psychology*. Englewood Cliffs, NJ: Prentice Hall.

Asch, Solomon E. (1953) "Effects of Group Pressure upon the Modification and Distortion of Judgments." In Eleanor Maccoby, Theodore M. Newcomb, and Edward Hartley (eds.), *Readings in Social Psychology*. New York: Holt, Rinehart and Winston.

Bales, R. F. (1950) "The Analysis of Small Group Interaction." *American Sociological Review* 15: 257–64.

Bales, R. F. (1970) *Personality and Interpersonal Behavior*. New York: Holt, Rinehart and Winston.

Bales, R. F. (1999) *Social Interaction Systems: Theory and Measurement*. New Brunswick, NJ: Transaction.

Bales, R. F., Fred L. Strodtbeck, Theodore M. Mills, and Mary E. Roseborough (1951) "Channels of Communication in Small Groups." *American Sociological Review* 16: 461–8.

Berger, Joseph and J. Laurie Snell (1961) "A Stochastic Theory for Self-Other Expectations." Technical Report #1, Laboratory for Social Research, Stanford University.

Berger, Joseph and Murray Webster, Jr. (2006) "Expectations, Status, and Behavior." In Peter J. Burke (ed.), *Contemporary Social Psychological Theories*. Stanford, CA: Stanford University Press, pp. 268–300.

Berger, Joseph, Hamit Fişek, Robert Z. Norman, and Morris Zelditch, Jr. (1977) *Status Characteristics and Social Interaction: An Expectation States Approach*. New York: Elsevier.

Berger, Joseph, Cecilia Ridgeway, M. Hamit Fisek, and Robert Z. Norman (1998) "The Legitimation and De-legitimation of Power and Prestige Orders." *American Sociological Review* 63: 379–405.

Berger, Joseph, Morris Zelditch, Jr., Bo Anderson, and Bernard P. Cohen (1972) "Structural Aspects of Distributive Justice: A Status Value Formulation." In Joseph Berger, Morris Zelditch, Jr., and Bo Anderson (eds.), *Sociological Theories in Progress*, Vol. 2. Boston: Houghton Mifflin, pp. 119–46.

Berkowitz, Leonard (1953) "Sharing Leadership in Small, Decision-Making Groups." *Journal of Abnormal and Social Psychology* 48: 231–8.

Binmore, Kenneth (2007) *Playing for Real – A Text on Game Theory*. New York: Oxford University Press.

Blau, Peter M. (1964) *Exchange and Power in Social Life*. New York: Wiley.

Borgatta, Edgar F., Arthur S. Couch, and Robert F. Bales (1954) "Some Findings Relevant to the Great Man Theory of Leadership." *American Sociological Review* 19: 755–9.

Brewer, Marilynn B. (1979) "In-Group Bias in the Minimal Intergroup Situation: A Cognitive-Motivational Analysis." *Psychological Bulletin* 86: 307–24.

Brewer, Marilynn B. (2007) "The Importance of Being We: Human Nature and Intergroup Relations." *American Psychologist* 62(8): 728–38.

Brewer, Marilynn B. and Roderick M. Kramer (1986) "Choice Behavior in Social Dilemmas: Effects of Social Identity, Group Size and Decision Framing." *Journal of Personality and Social Psychology* 50: 543–9.

Burke, Peter J. (1980) "The Self: Measurement Implications from a Symbolic Interactionist Perspective." *Social Psychology Quarterly* 43: 18–29.

Burke, Peter J. (1991) "Identity Process and Social Stress." *American Sociological Review* 56: 159–69.

Burke, Peter J. (2004) "Identities and Social Structure: The 2003 Cooley-Mead Award Address." *Social Psychology Quarterly* 67: 5–15.

Burke, Peter J. (2006) "Identity Change." *Social Psychology Quarterly* 69: 81–96.

Burke, Peter J. (2007) "Identity Control Theory." In George Ritzer (ed.), *Blackwell Encyclopedia of Sociology*. Oxford: Blackwell, pp. 2202–7.

Burke, Peter J. (2008) "Identity, Social Status, and Emotion." In Jody Clay-Warner and Dawn T. Robinson (eds.), *Social Structure and Emotion*. San Diego, CA: Elsevier, pp. 75–93.

Burke, Peter J. and Jan E. Stets (2009) *Identity Theory*. New York: Oxford University Press.

Campbell, Donald T. (1958) "Common Fate, Similarity, and Other Indices of the Status of Aggregates of Persons as Social Entities." *Behavioral Science* 3: 14–25.

Cartwright, Dorwin and Alvin F. Zander (1960) *Group Dynamics: Research and Theory*. New York: Harper and Row.

Clay-Warner, Jody (2006) "Procedural Justice and Legitimacy: Predicting Negative Emotional Reactions to Workplace Injustice." In Shane R. Thye and Edward J. Lawler (eds.), *Advances in Group Processes*, Vol. 23. San Diego, CA: JAI Press, pp. 207–77.

Clay-Warner, Jody, Karen Hegtvedt, and Paul Roman (2005) "Procedural Justice, Distributive Justice: How Experiences with Downsizing Condition Their Impact on Organizational Commitment." *Social Psychology Quarterly* 68: 89–102.

Cohen, Bernard P. (1963) *Conflict and Conformity: A Mathematical Model*. Cambridge, MA: MIT Press.

Cohen, Bernard P. and Hans E. Lee (1975) *Conflict, Conformity, and Social Status*. Amsterdam: Elsevier.

Cohen, Elizabeth G. and Rachel A. Lotan (1997) *Working for Equity in Heterogeneous Classrooms*. New York: Columbia University Teachers Press.

Colquitt, Jason A., Donald E. Conlon, Michael J. Wesson, Christopher O. L. H. Porter, and K. Yee Ng (2001) "Justice at the Millennium: A Meta-Analytic Review of 25 Years of Organizational Justice Research." *Journal of Applied Psychology* 86: 425–45.

Cook, Karen S. (2005) "Networks, Norms and Trust: The Social Psychology of Social Capital." *Social Psychology Quarterly* 68: 4–14.

Cook, Karen S. and Richard M. Emerson (1978) "Power, Equity, and Commitment in Exchange Networks." *American Sociological Review* 43: 721–39.

Cook, Karen S. and Richard M. Emerson (1984) "Exchange Networks and the Analysis of Complex Organization." In Samuel B. Bacharach and Edward J. Lawler (eds.), *Research in the Sociology of Organizations*. Greenwich, CT: JAI Press, pp. 1–30.

Cook, Karen S., Russell Hardin, and Margaret Levi (2005) *Cooperation Without Trust?* New York: Russell Sage.

Cook, Karen S., Eric R. W. Rice, and Alexandra Gerbasi (2004) "The Emergence of Trust Networks under Uncertainty: The Case of Transitional Economies – Insights from Social Psychological Research." In Susan Rose-Ackerman, Bo Rothstein, and Janos Kornai (eds.), *Creating Social Trust in Post-Socialist Transition*. New York: Macmillan, pp. 193–212.

Cooley, Charles Horton (1956) *Two Major Works: Social Organization [1909] and Human Nature and the Social Order [1902]*. With an introduction by Robert Cooley Angell. Glencoe, IL: Free Press.

Correll, Shelley J. (2004) "Constraints into Preferences: Gender, Status and Emerging Career Aspirations." *American Sociological Review* 69: 93–113.

Correll, Shelley J. and Stephen Benard (2006) "Biased Estimators? Comparing Status and Statistical Theories of Gender Discrimination. " In Shane R. Thye and Edward J. Lawler (eds.), *Advances in Group Processes*, Vol. 23. New York: Elsevier, pp. 89–116.

Crawford, Sue E. S. and Elinor Ostrom (1995) "A Grammar of Institutions." *American Political Science Review* 89: 582–600.

Dawes, R. M. (1980) "Social Dilemmas." *Annual Review of Psychology* 31: 169–93.

Dornbusch, Sanford M. and W. Richard Scott (1975) *Evaluation and the Exercise of Authority*. San Francisco: Jossey-Bass.

Eckel, Catherine (2007) "Economic Games for Social Scientists." In Murray Webster and Jane Sell (eds.), *Laboratory Experiments in the Social Sciences*. Amsterdam: Elsevier, pp. 497–515.

Emerson, Richard M. (1962) "Power-Dependence Relations." *American Sociological Review* 27: 31–41.

Emerson, Richard M. (1964) "Power-Dependence Relations: Two Experiments." *Sociometry* 27: 282–98.

Evan, William M. and Morris Zelditch, Jr. (1961) "A Laboratory Experiment on Bureaucratic Authority." *American Sociological Review* 26: 883–93.

Evertsson, Marie (2006) "The Reproduction of Gender: Housework and Attitudes towards Gender Equality in the Home among Swedish Boys and Girls." *British Journal of Sociology* 57: 415–36.

Faas, Daniel (2009) "Turkish Youth in Germany and England." *British Journal of Sociology* 60: 299–320.

Fiske, Susan (1992) "Thinking Is for Doing." *Journal of Personality and Social Psychology* 63: 877–89.

Fiske, Susan T. (1998) "Stereotyping, Prejudice, and Discrimination." In D. T. Gilbert, S. T. Fiske, and G. Lindzey (eds.), *The Handbook of Social Psychology*, 4th edn., Vol. 2. Boston: McGraw-Hill, pp. 357–411.

Fiske, Susan and Steven Neuberg (1990) "A Continuum of Impression Formation, from Category-Based to Individuating Processes: Influences of Information and Motivation on Attention and Interpretation." In Mark Zanna (ed.), *Advances in Experimental Social Psychology*. New York: Academic Press, pp. 1–73.

Fiske, Susan and Shelley Taylor (1991) *Social Cognition*. New York: McGraw-Hill.

Fiske, Susan T., Amy J. C. Cuddy, Peter Glick, and Jun Xu (2002) "A Model of (Often Mixed) Stereotype Content: Competence and Warmth Respectively Follow from Perceived Status and Competition." *Journal of Personality and Social Psychology* 82: 878–902.

Gambetta, Diego and Heather Hamill (2005) *Streetwise: How Taxi Drivers Establish Customers' Trustworthiness*. New York: Russell Sage.

Goar, Carla and Jane Sell (2005) "Using Task Definition to Modify Racial Inequality within Task Groups." *Sociological Quarterly* 46: 525–43.

Halrynjo, Sigtona and Selma Therese Lyng (2009) "Preferences, Constraints or Schemas of Devotion? Exploring Norwegian Mothers' Withdrawals from High-Commitment Careers." *British Journal of Sociology* 60: 321–43.

Hare, A. Paul, Edgar F. Borgatta, and Robert F. Bales (1965) *Small Groups: Studies in Social Interaction*, rev. edn. New York: Alfred A. Knopf.

Haski-Leventhal, Debbie (2009) "Altruism and Volunteerism: The Perceptions of Altruism in Four Disciplines and Their Impact on the Study of Volunteerism." *Journal for the Theory of Social Behaviour* 39: 271–99.

Heckathorn, Douglas D., Robert S. Broadhead, Denise L. Anthony, and David L. Weakliem (1999) "AIDS and Social Networks: Prevention through Network Mobilization." *Sociological Focus* 32: 159–79.

Hegtvedt, Karen A. (2006) "Justice Frameworks." In Peter J. Burke (ed.), *Contemporary Social Psychological Theories*. Stanford, CA: Stanford University Press, pp. 46–69.

Hegtvedt, Karen A. and Barry M. Markovsky (1995) "Justice and Injustice." In Karen S. Cook, Gary A. Fine, and James S. House (eds.), *Sociological Perspectives on Social Psychology*. Boston: Allyn and Bacon, pp. 257–80.

Hodgson, Geoffrey M. (2006) "What Are Institutions?" *Journal of Economic Issues* 40: 1–25.

Holt, Charles A. (2007) *Markets, Games, and Strategic Behavior*. Boston: Pearson.

Homans, George C. (1958) "Social Behavior as Exchange." *American Journal of Sociology* 63: 597–606.

Homans, George C. (1961) *Social Behavior: Its Elementary Forms*. New York: Harcourt, Brace and World.

Jacobs, R. C. and D. T. Campbell (1961) "The Perpetuation of an Arbitrary Tradition through Several Generations of a Laboratory Microculture." *Journal of Abnormal and Social Psychology* 62: 649–58.

Jasso, Guillermina (1978) "On the Justice of Earnings: A New Specification of the Justice Evaluation Function." *American Journal of Sociology* 83: 1398–415.

Jasso, Guillermina (1980) "A New Theory of Distributive Justice." *American Sociological Review* 45: 3–32.

Jasso, Guillermina (2001) "Comparison Theory." In Jonathan H. Turner (ed.), *Handbook of Sociological Theory*. New York: Kluwer Academic/Plenum, pp. 669–98.

Jasso, Guillermina (2006) "The Theory of Comparison Processes." In Peter J. Burke (ed.), *Contemporary Social Psychological Theories*. Stanford, CA: Stanford University Press, pp. 165–93.

Jasso, Guillermina (2008) "A New Unified Theory of Sociobehavioral Forces." *European Sociological Review* 24: 411–34.

Jasso, Guillermina and Murray Webster, Jr. (1999) "Assessing the Gender Gap in Just Earnings and Its Underlying Mechanisms." *Social Psychology Quarterly* 62: 367–80.

Johnson, Cathryn, Timothy J. Dowd, and Cecilia L. Ridgeway (2006) "Legitimacy as a Social Process." *Annual Review of Sociology* 32: 53–78.

Kerr, N. L. and C. M. Kaufman-Gilleland (1994) "Communication, Commitment, and Cooperation in Social Dilemmas." *Journal of Personality and Social Psychology* 66: 513–29.

Knottnerus, J. David (1997) "The Theory of Structural Ritualization." In Barry Markovsky, Michael J. Lovaglia, and Lisa Troyer (eds.), *Advances in Group Processes*, Vol. 14. Greenwich, CT: JAI Press, pp. 257–79.

Kramer, Roderick and Karen S. Cook (2004) *Trust and Distrust in Organizations: Dilemmas and Approaches*. New York: Russell Sage.

Kruttschnitt, Candace and Jeanette Hussemann (2008) "Micropolitics of Race and Ethnicity in Women's Prisons in Two Political Contexts." *British Journal of Sociology* 59: 709–28.

Laftman, Sara Brolin (2008) "Parent Presence and Gender-Typicalness of Educational Choice." *British Journal of Sociology* 59: 757–82.

Lawler, Edward J. and Jeongkoo Yoon (1996) "Commitment in Exchange Relations: Test of Relational Cohesion." *American Sociological Review* 61: 89–108.

Lawler, Edward J., Shane R. Thye, and Jeongkoo Yoon (2009) *Social Commitments in a Depersonalized World*. New York: Russell Sage.

Levine, Donald N. (trans. and ed.) (1971) *On Individuality and Social Forms: Selected Writings of Georg Simmel*. Chicago: University of Chicago Press.

Li, Yaolin, Mike Savage, and Alan Warde (2008) "Social Mobility and Social Capital in Contemporary Britain." *British Journal of Sociology* 59: 391–411.

Lovaglia, Michael J., Elizabeth Mannix, Charles Samuelson, Jane Sell, and Rick K. Wilson (2004) "Conflict, Status and Power in Groups." In M. S. Poole and A. Hollingshead (eds.), *Theories of Small Groups: Interdisciplinary Perspectives*. Thousand Oaks, CA: Sage, pp. 139–84.

Lovaglia, Michael J., John Skvoretz, David Willer, and Barry B. Markovsky (1995) "Negotiated Exchanges in Social Networks." *Social Forces* 74: 123–55.

Lucas, Jeffrey W. (2003) "Status Processes and the Institutionalization of Women as Leaders." *American Sociological Review* 68: 464–80.

Lucas, Jeffrey W. and Michael Lovaglia (2006) "Legitimation and Institutionalization as Trust-Building: Reducing Resistance to Power and Influence in Organizations." In Shane R. Thye and Edward J. Lawler (eds.), *Advances in Group Processes*, Vol. 23. San Diego, CA: JAI Press, pp. 229–52.

Messick, David M. and Margaret B. Brewer (1983) "Solving Social Dilemmas: A Review." In Ladd Wheeler and Phillip Shaver (eds.), *Review of Personality and Social Psychology*. Beverly Hills, CA: Sage.

Molm, Linda D. (1994) "Dependence and Risk: Transforming the Structure of Social Exchange." *Social Psychology Quarterly* 57: 163–76.

Molm, Linda D. (1997) *Coercive Power in Social Exchange*. Cambridge: Cambridge University Press.

Molm, Linda D. (2003) "Theoretical Comparisons of Forms of Exchange." *Sociological Theory* 21: 1–17.

Molm, Linda D. (2006) "The Social Exchange Framework." In Peter J. Burke (ed.), *Contemporary Social Psychological Theories*. Stanford, CA: Stanford University Press, pp. 24–45.

Molm, Linda D. and Karen S. Cook (1995) "Social Exchange and Exchange Networks." In Karen S. Cook, Gary Alan Fine, and James S. House (eds.), *Sociological Perspectives on Social Psychology*. Boston: Allyn and Bacon, pp. 209–35.

Molm, Linda D., Gretchen Peterson, and Nobuyuki Takahashi (1999) "Power Use in Negotiated and Reciprocal Exchange." *American Sociological Review* 64: 876–90.

Mueller, Charles W. and Sang-Wook Kim (2008) "The Contented Female Worker: Still a Paradox." In Karen A. Hegtvedt and Jody Clay-Warner (eds.), *Advances in Group Processes*, Vol. 25. Bingley: Emerald Group Publishing, pp. 117–49.

Nickel, Philip J. (2009) "Trust, Staking, and Expectations." *Journal for the Theory of Social Behaviour* 39: 345–62.

North, Douglass C. (1990) *Institutions, Institutional Change, and Economic Performance*. Cambridge: Cambridge University Press.

Okimoto, Tyler G. and Michael Wenzel (2008) "The Symbolic Meaning of Transgressions: Towards a Unifying Framework of Justice Restoration." In Karen A. Hegtvedt and Jody Clay-Warner (eds.), *Advances in Group Processes*, Vol. 25. Bingley: Emerald Group Publishing, pp. 291–326.

Orbell, John M., Alphons J. C. van de Kragt, and Robyn M. Dawes (1988) "Explaining Discussion Induced Cooperation." *Journal of Personality and Social Psychology* 54: 811–19.

Ostrom, Elinor (1990) *Governing the Commons: The Evolution of Institutions for Collective Actions*. Cambridge: Cambridge University Press.

Ostrom, Elinor (1998) "Rational Choice Theory of Collective Action." *American Political Science Review* 92: 1–22.

Ostrom, Elinor, Roy Gardner, and James Walker (1994) *Rules, Games, and Common Pool Resources*. Ann Arbor, MI: University of Michigan Press.

Paxton, Pamela (1999) "Is Social Capital Declining in the United States? A Multiple Indicator Assessment." *American Journal of Sociology* 105: 88–127.

Phinney, J. (2000) "Identity Formation Across Cultures: The Interaction of Personal, Social and Historical Change." *Human Development* 43: 27–31.

Putnam, Robert D. (2000) *Bowling Alone: The Collapse and Revival of American Community*. New York: Simon and Schuster.

Read, Peter B. (1974) "Sources of Authority and the Legitimation of Leadership in Small Groups." *Sociometry* 37: 189–204.

Riddle, Ethel M. (1937) "Aggressive Behavior in a Small Social Group." In Gardner Murphy, Lois B. Murphy, and Theodore M. Newcomb, *Experimental Social Psychology: An Interpretation of Research upon the Socialization of the Individual*. New York: Harper and Brothers.

Ridgeway, Cecilia L. (2011) *Framed by Gender: How Gender Inequality Persists in the Modern World*. New York: Oxford University Press.

Robinson, Robert V. and Elton F. Jackson (2001) "Is Trust in Others Declining in America? An Age-Period-Cohort Analysis." *Social Science Research* 30: 117–45.

Sally, D. (1995) "Convention and Cooperation in Social Dilemmas: A Meta-Analysis of Experiments from 1958 to 1992." *Rationality and Society* 7: 58–92.

Samuelson, Charles D. and D. M. Messick (1995) "Let's Make Some New Rules: Social Factors That Make Freedom Unattractive." In R. Kramer and D. M. Messick (eds.), *Negotiation as a Social Process*. Thousand Oaks, CA: Sage, pp. 48–68.

Sato, Kaori (1987) "Distribution of the Cost of Maintaining Common Resources." *Journal of Experimental Social Psychology* 31: 19–31.

Sauer, Carsten (2009) "Gender Differences in Just Earnings – the Just Gender Pay Gap."
   Working Paper #7, Factorial Survey Research Group. Bielefeld, Germany: Universität
   Bielefeld.
Sell, Jane and Tony P. Love (2009) "Common Fate, Crisis, and Cooperation in Social Dilemmas." In Shane R. Thye and Edward J. Lawler (eds.), *Advances in Group Processes*, Vol.
   26. Bingley: Emerald Group Publishing, pp. 53–79.
Sell, Jane and Rick K. Wilson (1999) "The Maintenance of Cooperation: Expectations
   of Future Interaction and the Trigger of Group Punishment." *Social Forces* 77:
   1551–70.
Sell, Jane, J. David Knottnerus, Christopher Ellison, and Heather Mundt (2000) "Reproduc-
   ing Social Structure in Task Groups: The Role of Structural Ritualization." *Social Forces*
   79: 453–75.
Sell, Jane, Michael J. Lovaglia, Elizabeth A. Mannix, Charles D. Samuelson, Jane Sell, and
   Rick K. Wilson (2004) "Investigating Conflict, Power, Status Within and Among
   Groups." *Small Group Research* 35: 44–72.
Serpe, Richard T. and Sheldon Stryker (1987a) "Stability and Change in Self: A Structural
   Symbolic Interactionist Explanation." *Social Psychology Quarterly* 50: 44–55.
Serpe, Richard T. and Sheldon Stryker (1987b) "The Construction of Self and Reconstruction
   of Social Relationships." In Edward J. Lawler and Barry Markovsky (eds.), *Advances in
   Group Processes*, Vol. 4. Greenwich, CT: JAI Press, pp. 41–66.
Sewell, William H., Jr. (1992) "A Theory of Structure: Duality, Agency, and Transformation."
   American Journal of Sociology 98: 1–29.
Sherif, Muzafer (1936) *The Psychology of Social Norms*. New York: Harper and Row.
Sherif, Muzafer and Carolyn W. Sherif (1956) *An Outline of Social Psychology*. New York:
   Harper.
Simmel, Georg (1950) *The Sociology of Georg Simmel*. Trans., ed., and intro. Kurt H. Wolff.
   New York: Free Press.
Simmel, Georg (1964) *Conflict/The Web of Group Affiliations*. Trans. Kurt H. Wolff and
   Reinhard Bendix. New York: Free Press.
Simpson, Brent and Robb Willer (2008) "Altruism and Indirect Reciprocity: The Interaction
   of Person and Situation in Prosocial Behavior." *Social Psychology Quarterly* 71: 37–52.
Skitka, Linda J., Christopher W. Bauman, and Elizabeth Mullen (2008) "Morality and Justice:
   An Expanded Theoretical Perspective and Empirical Review." In Karen A. Hegtvedt and
   Jody Clay-Warner (eds.), *Advances in Group Processes*, Vol. 25. Bingley: Emerald Group
   Publishing, pp. 1–27.
Smith-Lovin, Lynn (2003) "Self, Identity, and Interaction in an Ecology of Identities." In
   Peter J. Burke, Timothy J. Owens, Richard T. Serpe, and Peggy Thoits (eds.), *Advances
   in Identity Theory and Research*. New York: Kluwer Press, pp. 167–78.
Smith-Lovin, Lynn and David Heise (1988) *Analyzing Social Interaction: Advances in Affect
   Control Theory*. New York: Gordon and Breach Scientific Publishers.
Smith-Lovin, Lynn and Dawn T. Robinson (2006) "Affect Control Theory." In Peter J. Burke
   (ed.), *Contemporary Social Psychological Theories*. Stanford, CA: Stanford University
   Press, pp. 137–64.
Solomon, Robert C. and Mark C. Murphy (eds.) (2000) *What Is Justice? Classic and Con-
   temporary Readings*, 2nd edn. New York: Oxford University Press.
Stets, Jan E. (1993) "Control in Dating Relationships." *Journal of Marriage and the Family*
   55: 673–85.
Stets, Jan E. (1995) "Role Identities and Person Identities: Gender Identity, Mastery Identity,
   and Controlling One's Partner." *Sociological Perspectives* 38: 129–50.

Stets, Jan E. (1997) "Status and Identity in Marital Interaction." *Social Psychology Quarterly* 60: 185–217.

Stets, Jan E. (2004) "Emotions in Identity Theory: The Effects of Status." In Shane R. Thye and Edward J. Lawler (eds.), *Advances in Group Processes*, Vol. 21. San Diego, CA: JAI Press, pp. 51–76.

Stets, Jan E. and Emily K. Asencio (2008) "Consistency and Enhancement Processes in Understanding Emotions." *Social Forces* 86: 1055–78.

Storvik, Aagoth Elise and Pal Schone (2008) "In Search of the Glass Ceiling: Gender and Recruitment to Management in Norway's State Bureaucracy." *British Journal of Sociology* 59: 729–55.

Stryker, Sheldon (1968) "Identity Salience and Role Performance." *Journal of Marriage and the Family* 4: 558–64.

Stryker, Sheldon (1980) *Symbolic Interactionism: A Social Structural Version*. Caldwell, NJ: Blackburn Press.

Stryker, Sheldon (1987) "Identity Theory: Developments and Extensions." In K. Yardley and T. Honess (eds.), *Self and Identity: Psychological Perspectives*. Chichester: Wiley, pp. 89–104.

Stryker, Sheldon (1997) "In the Beginning There Is Society: Lessons from a Sociological Social Psychology." In C. McGarty and S. A. Haslam (eds.), *The Message of Social Psychology: Perspectives on Mind in Society*. Malden, MA: Blackwell, pp. 315–27.

Stryker, Sheldon (2000) "Identity Competition: Key to Differential Social Movement Participation?" In Sheldon Stryker, Timothy J. Owens, and Robert W. White (eds.), *Self, Identity, and Social Movements*. Minneapolis: University of Minnesota Press, pp. 21–40.

Stryker, Sheldon (2004) "Integrating Emotions into Identity Theory." In Shane R. Thye and Edward J. Lawler (eds.), *Advances in Group Processes*, Vol. 21. San Diego, CA: JAI Press, pp. 1–23.

Stryker, Sheldon (2008) "From Mead to Structural Symbolic Interactionism and Beyond." *Annual Review of Sociology* 34: 15–31.

Stryker, Sheldon and Peter J. Burke (2000) "The Past, Present and Future of an Identity Theory." *Social Psychology Quarterly* 63: 284–97.

Stryker, Sheldon and Anne S. Macke (1978) "Status Inconsistency and Role Conflict." *Annual Review of Sociology* 4: 57–90.

Stryker, Sheldon and Richard T. Serpe (1982) "Commitment, Identity Salience, and Role Behavior: A Theory and Research Example." In W. Ickes and E. S. Knowles (eds.), *Personality, Roles, and Social Behavior*. New York: Springer-Verlag, pp. 199–218.

Stryker, Sheldon and Richard T. Serpe (1994) "Identity Salience and Psychological Centrality: Equivalent, Overlapping, or Complementary Concepts?" *Social Psychology Quarterly* 57: 16–35.

Stryker, Sheldon and Kevin D. Vryan (2003) "The Symbolic Interactionist Frame." In John DeLamater (ed.), *Handbook of Social Psychology*. New York: Kluwer Academic/Plenum, pp. 3–28.

Sumner, William G. (1906) *Folkways*. New York: Ginn.

Tajfel, H. (1970) "Experiments in Intergroup Discrimination." *Scientific American* 223: 96–102.

Tajfel, H., M. G. Billig, R. P. Bundy, and C. Flament (1971) "Social Categorization and Intergroup Behavior." *European Journal of Social Psychology* 1: 149–78.

Terman, Lewis M. (1904) "A Preliminary Study of the Psychology and Pedagogy of Leadership." *Pedagogical Seminary* II: 413–51.

Thibaut, John and Laurens Walker (1975) *Procedural Justice: A Psychological Analysis.* Hillsdale, NJ: Erlbaum.

Thoits, Peggy A. (1983) "Multiple Identities and Psychological Well-Being: A Reformulation and Test of the Social Isolation Hypothesis." *American Sociological Review* 49: 174–87.

Thoits, Peggy A. (1986) "Multiple Identities: Examining Gender and Marital Status Differences in Distress." *American Sociological Review* 51: 259–72.

Thoits, Peggy A. (1991) "On Merging Identity Theory and Stress Research." *Social Psychology Quarterly* 54: 101–12.

Thoits, Peggy A. (2003) "Personal Agency in the Accumulation of Role-Identities." In Peter J. Burke, Timothy J. Owens, Peggy A. Thoits, and Richard T. Serpe (eds.), *Advances in Identity Theory and Research.* New York: Kluwer Academic/Plenum, pp. 179–94.

Thomas, George M., Henry A. Walker, and Morris Zelditch, Jr. (1986) "Legitimacy and Collective Action." *Social Forces* 65: 378–404.

Thrasher, Frederic M. (1927) *The Gang.* Chicago: University of Chicago Press.

Tönnies, Ferdinand ([1887] 1963) *Community and Society (Gemeinschaft und Gesellschaft).* Trans. and ed. Charles P. Loomis. New York: Harper and Row.

Turner, C. E. (1933) "Test Room Studies in Employee Effectiveness." *American Journal of Public Health* 23: 577–84.

Turner, Jonathan H. (2006) "The State of Theorizing in Sociological Social Psychology: A Grand Theorist's View." In Peter J. Burke (ed.), *Contemporary Social Psychological Theories.* Stanford, CA: Stanford University Press, pp. 353–73.

Varughese, George and Elinor Ostrom (2001) "The Contested Role of Heterogeneity in Collective Action: Some Evidence from Community Forestry in Nepal." *World Development* 29: 747–65.

Walker, Henry A., Larry Rogers, and Morris Zelditch, Jr. (2002) "Acts, Persons, and Institutions: Legitimating Multiple Objects and Compliance with Authority." In Sing C. Chew and J. David Knottnerus (eds.), *Structure, Culture, and History: Recent Issues in Social Theory.* Oxford: Rowman and Littlefield, pp. 323–39.

Walker, Henry A., George M. Thomas, and Morris Zelditch, Jr. (1986) "Legitimation, Endorsement and Stability." *Social Forces* 64: 620–43.

Weber, Max ([1922] 1968) *Economy and Society.* Ed. Hans Gerth and C. Wright Mills. New York: Oxford University Press.

Webster, Murray, Jr. and James E. Driskell, Jr. (1978) "Status Generalization: A Review and Some New Data." *American Sociological Review* 43: 220–36.

Webster, Murray, Jr. and Jane Sell (2007) *Experimental Methods in the Social Sciences.* San Diego, CA: Academic Press.

Webster, Murray, Jr. and Joseph Whitmeyer (2001) "Applications of Theories of Group Processes." *Sociological Theory* 19: 250–70.

Wenzel, Michael (2002) "What Is Social about Justice? Inclusive Identity and Group Values as the Basis of the Justice Motive." *Journal of Experimental Social Psychology* 38: 205–18.

Wenzel, Michael, Tyler G. Okimoto, Norman T. Feather, and Michael J. Platow (2008) "Retributive and Restorative Justice." *Law and Human Behavior* 32: 375–89.

Willer, David (ed.) (1999) *Network Exchange Theory.* Westport, CT: Praeger.

Willer, David and Pamela Emanuelson (2008) "Testing Ten Theories." *Journal of Mathematical Sociology* 32: 165–203.

Wilson, Rick K. and Jane Sell (1997) "Cheap Talk and Reputation in Repeated Public Goods Settings." *Journal of Conflict Resolution* 41: 695–717.

Yamagishi, Toshio (1988) "The Provision of a Sanctioning System in the United States and Japan." *Social Psychology Quarterly* 51: 265–71.

Yamagishi, Toshio, Karen S. Cook, and Motoku Watabe (1998) "Uncertainty, Trust and Commitment Formation in the United States and Japan." *American Journal of Sociology* 104: 165–94.

Zelditch, Morris, Jr. (2001) "Processes of Legitimation: Recent Developments and New Directions." *Social Psychology Quarterly* 64: 4–17.

Zelditch, Morris, Jr. and Henry A. Walker (1984) "Legitimacy and the Stability of Authority." In Edward J. Lawler (ed.), *Advances in Group Processes*, Vol. 1. Greenwich, CT: JAI Press, pp. 1–25.

Zelditch, Morris, Jr. and Henry A. Walker (1997) "Legitimacy and the Stability of Authority." In J. Szmatka, J. Skvoretz, and J. Berger (eds.), *Status, Network and Structure*. Stanford, CA: Stanford University Press.

9

The Sociology of Organizations

Stewart R. Clegg

Introduction

The sociology of organizations is very largely a post-Second World War American invention but it built, initially, on Max Weber's work as it was translated in the post-war era. At the outset the sociological classics were a potent source of inspiration, especially Weber: today that is no longer the case (Adler 2009: 5). The critical function of the classics as being a signifier for disparate worldviews that encapsulate deep and compelling insights into the human condition has been largely abandoned (Alexander 1987). One refreshing sign of the times, however, is the recent publication of *The Oxford Handbook of Sociology and Organization Studies*, edited by Paul Adler, in 2009. The usual candidates, Marx, Weber, and Durkheim, are considered, as well as many others (some of whom might have been surprised to be called sociologists).

The Oxford Handbook of Sociology and Organization Studies is a singular exercise: on the whole, the classics are far less likely to be engaged with in the material that fills the contemporary journals. It was not always the case. For instance, one might characterize the period from the 1940s to the mid-1960s as largely a debate with the ghost of Max Weber, conducted by scholars such as Merton (1940), Gouldner (1954), Selznick (1949, 1957), Blau (1965), and Crozier (1963). By the mid-1960s, however, it would be fair to say that the lead in the sociology of organizations passed to the United Kingdom, where the Aston School (Pugh & Hickson 1976) set the standard for empirical research in the field, investigating the structural contingency features of organizations, and in the process claiming to replace the Weberian typology with an empirically grounded taxonomy. In retrospect, however, it is evident that the taxonomy owed a great deal to Weber's

The Wiley-Blackwell Companion to Sociology, First Edition. Edited by George Ritzer.
© 2012 Blackwell Publishing Ltd. Published 2012 by Blackwell Publishing Ltd.

typology (see Clegg & Dunkerley 1980; Clegg 1990). However, it was embedded in a framework distinctly non-Weberian: a systems-based contingency theory. There were three key texts in the framing of this systems approach: Parsons' (1951) *The Social System*, March, Simon, and Guetzkow's (1958) *Organizations*, and Thompson's (1967) *Organizations in Action*. Parsons was the fount; March and Simon codified much of the sociological work of the 1950s, from authors such as Merton and Gouldner, around the idea of a "need for control" generating various dysfunctions of bureaucracy exemplified in vicious circles; while Thompson (1967) also drew on March. He did so using Cyert and March's (1963) *A Behavioral Theory of the Firm*, to position analysis of organizations as dealing with what was posed as a fundamental ontological issue – "coping with uncertainty" – a billing in which Crozier's (1963) work also assumed prominent position.

As Reed (2009) has argued, these attempts at synthesis and codification, to the extent that they related to sociological problematics, did so very much in relation to functionalism and its problem of order. Such formulations did not go unopposed. From the late 1960s onwards there was a steady stream of work that was much closer to the antithetical axis of a conflict sociology (Albrow 1970; Silverman 1970; Clegg & Dunkerley 1980; Perrow 1986), as well as a notable attempt at mapping the field in terms of the axes of order and conflict cross-cut with those of system and actor in Burrell and Morgan (1979). What united these conflict-oriented writers was a stress on organizations not so much as orderly systems of authority with occasional dysfunctional problems but as structures of dominancy that are perpetually troubled by the human agency they strive to contain: in short, a radical Weberian problematic (Clegg 1975). In the 1970s this was closely allied to a labor process perspective, developed under the tutelage of Braverman (1974), which reintegrated Marx into sociological perspectives on organizations. The more phenomenological and agentic-centered of the conflict perspectives largely mutated into a concern with subjectivity from the 1980s onwards, and after a brief liaison, as a result of misgivings, with the structuralism of the labor process perspective, there developed a critical management studies or CMS (Grey & Willmott 2005) perspective that certainly drew on sociology but was not itself an explicit part of sociology. Internal tensions arose among people committed to labor process theory, as factions developed in what had been a broad-based critical approach. Some adherents, who were more focused on the classical texts of Marxism and its more recent development in Braverman (1974), were aghast at the incorporation of fashionable French theory from evident non-Marxist scholars such as Foucault (Thompson 1990; Thompson & Ackroyd 1995). From this split came the genesis of CMS as a platform and legitimate interest area (Fournier & Grey 2000: 9). Thus, in the UK CMS was a platform for developing theoretical issues alien to more orthodox labor process approaches. In particular, there was a concern with issues of subjectivity and identity, conceived in much broader terms than those of class identity and class politics, to which Knights and Willmott (1989) and Willmott (1997) provide good guides.

The last paragraph, with the exception of Perrow's (1986) and Braverman's (1974) work, refers to UK sources. By the 1980s it was evident that more than the Atlantic divided US and UK approaches to organizations in English-language scholarship, for if we crossed the Atlantic to the US, the picture would seem quite different. Three emergent theoretical currents held sway from the late 1970s alongside the continuing popularity of structural contingency theory (see Donaldson 1996): population ecology, which focused on the population-level analysis of organizations (Hannan & Freeman 1977); resource dependency theory (Pfeffer & Salancik 1978), the focus of which was relations between organizations and their environments; and institutional theory, which once more turned to Weber for its initial inspiration as a sociology of culture. Of these three streams, at the current time it is undoubtedly institutional theory that seems to have become the new "normal" frame for the sociology of organizations.

In order to contain the focus of the chapter I have adopted some self-denying ordinances: first, I have focused largely on intra-organizational accounts of contemporary sociology of organizations rather than follow much of the considerable work in organization studies (a more business school categorization of the field as more broadly interdisciplinary, including elements from areas such as economics, ecology, psychology, etc.); second, I have confined the chapter to addressing the most explicitly sociological approaches in current work, which are those associated with institutional theory; third, I have chosen to focus only on those currents of research within these ordinances that are most active at the time of writing; fourth, following the line of argument advanced by Hinings and Greenwood (2002) that what characterizes the sociology of organizations, as opposed to broader organization studies or theory, is a concern with power, the theme of institutional sociology and the subject of power will form the spine of the essay. Doing this enables one to bring Foucault's work on power back into the canon. Although Scott (1987) brought Foucault's work into the fold of the sociology of organizations pursued from an institutional perspective at an early stage in its development, Foucault's potential has since been very largely neglected. Hence, the chapter will conclude with an account of what Foucault can offer the sociology of organizations.

EXPLORING THE FOUNDATIONS

Few works in the sociology of organizations can be positioned as citation classics but Meyer and Rowan's (1977) "Institutionalized Organizations: Formal Structure as Myth and Ceremony" and DiMaggio and Powell's (1983) "The Iron Cage Revisited: Institutional Isomorphism and Collective Rationality in Organizational Fields" are undoubtedly such works. The resonances with Weber were evident from the title through to the cultural orientation of the text (see Clegg 1995). DiMaggio and Powell drew on the new institutional theory pioneered by Meyer and Rowan in 1977 and were influenced by Bourdieu's (1977) ideas about practice, applied to a consideration of how rationalized myths lodged in institutional settings, conceived in terms of rules, norms, and ideologies, shape organizational action to the extent that they can secure semblances of organizational legitimacy in order to capture resources and mobilize support. Much of this institutional work is concerned with ceremonial ordering, a theme that was especially stressed in early work focused on non-market organizations. For such organizations, the need for legitimacy was seen to be much greater than for those that were market players, as they had no sources of market evaluation to which they could refer to establish legitimacy.

Quite what an institution was remained implicit in the early accounts but the core idea seems to be that it is a pattern of social action anchored by normative assumptions and framed in more-or-less shared cognitive understandings which sustains social ordering and its reproduction in significant social spheres. Typically, these spheres were conceptualized either at the level of the organization or at the level of the organizational field – a rather fuzzy concept for capturing the organization's environment as a field of other organizations. The organizational field was defined by DiMaggio and Powell in relational terms as "those organizations that, in the aggregate, constitute a recognized area of institutional life: key suppliers, resource and product customers, regulatory agencies, and other organizations that produce similar services or products" (1983: 148). Later they add that the field includes all those who have "voice" as well as those who do not – picking up on Bachrach and Baratz's (1962, 1970) influential critique of Robert Dahl's (1961) work by stressing non-action, or absence from a field, as a significant form of presence. On the whole, as I shall argue, this element of power has been largely absent from engagement with DiMaggio and Powell's work.

To be institutionalized is to have undergone a process of institutionalization – in Berger and Luckman's (1967) terms, ideas achieve this state when they are held to be social factual, that is, when they are exteriorized and objective. While institutional isomorphism has become, perhaps, the key concept for much mainstream organization studies work of the past decade, and three ideal-type mechanisms of organizational change by institutional isomorphism have been sketched, not all have seemed as compelling to researchers. The mechanisms identified were categorized as follows: coercive (when external agencies impose changes on organizations – most obviously through practices of state regulation), normative (when professionalization projects shape entire occupational fields), and mimetic mechanisms (essentially the copying of what is constituted as culturally valuable ways of doing or arranging things – cultural capital). Interest in mimetic mechanisms has far outweighed interest in coercive and normative mechanisms in US empirical studies, as Greenwood and Mayer (2008) note, while European researchers have been more oriented to the role of the state and other regulatory agencies, such as standards-setting bodies (see Higgins & Hallström 2007).

Many of the concerns of institutional theory achieved institutionalization, if one may say so, with the integrative and synthetic account of the approach provided by Scott in 1995. In his book, *Institutions and Organizations*, he distinguished three "pillars" that grounded institutions and made them possible. These corresponded to the regulative, normative, and cultural-cognitive emphases that had been found in the literature to that date. Of these, it was argued by Scott (and others such as Phillips & Malhotra 2008) that the cultural-cognitive pillar had the deepest foundations, as it was upon these that norms and rules rested. Implicitly, this is a conservative position because it assumes that there is, indeed, a taken-for-granted and shared understanding that provides social arrangements with their legitimacy. For instance, if we return to the example presented earlier of the institutionalization of a deregulated account of the market, it would assume that the rationalized myth took hold because it was one widely shared. In a famous turn of phrase, Zucker concluded that institutionalization means that "alternatives may be literally unthinkable" (1983: 5). Tolbert and Zucker (1983: 25) suggested three indicators of institutionalized practices: they are widely followed, without debate, and exhibit permanence. Sociological institutional theory had some conservative biases implanted in it early on: DiMaggio and Powell proposed that within organizational fields, "there is an inexorable push towards homogenization" (1983: 148), a process that was interpreted by subsequent researchers overwhelmingly in terms of mimetic isomorphic pressures. Mimesis became increasingly seen as the dominant ideal type for institutional transmission. Ideal types tend to reification and institutional isomorphism mechanisms are no exception. It is this reification that makes many institutional analyses so mechanical; as a theory designed to explain how things got to be the way they are, it does not really handle discontinuous change very well. Indeed, its most significant theoretical innovation has been the development of the idea of the institutional entrepreneur, designed to save the theory from its implicit functionalism. The implicit functionalism of the perspective becomes evident when we look at the problem that the theory's most productive category was designed to solve. The problem was that if it was assumed, with DiMaggio and Powell, that there is a "startling homogeneity of organizational forms and practices" (1983: 147), how was it possible for change or innovation to occur if all the pressures, institutionally, were towards conformity? In other words, where was sociological agency in the midst of all this structural determination?

INSTITUTIONAL ENTREPRENEURS

If actors are institutionally embedded, how is it that things change? Institutional theory, as largely functionalist, had to invent the over-used category of institutional entrepreneur to "save" the theory and include an account – amongst all the stasis, conformity, and legitimacy – that things and times change. The institutional entrepreneur is the category that institutionalism's functionalism requires in order to make change from isomorphized regimes possible. The category of the institutional entrepreneur was introduced by DiMaggio in terms of "organized actors with sufficient resources (institutional entrepreneurs)" who see "an opportunity to realize interest that they value highly" (1988: 14). If so much energy goes into being similar to culturally valued organizations through mimesis, how is it possible that organizations can change? This is the question the institutional entrepreneur is designed to answer. Yet it is an answer that focuses overly on a few champions of change and neglects the wider social fabric in which they are embedded. As Hardy and Maguire acknowledge, too many accounts of institutional entrepreneurship are actor-centric; instead we should seek "images of activism, collective action and struggle [which] may be more appropriate" (2008: 213) and are more likely to be found in process accounts. However, these process accounts are largely presented in terms of struggles over meaning, a bias that is explicable in terms of the cultural-cognitive foundations that institutional approaches have assumed. The underlying focus of institutional approaches within the sociology of organizations, in short, was the role of shared meanings, institutional processes (such as cultural prescriptions [Zucker 1977]), and institutional conformity. Hence, it is not surprising to find that legitimacy is the key category of this sociological institutionalism.

LEGITIMACY

Institutional theories' key category is legitimacy. From nearly all perspectives in recent sociology, it has emerged that legitimacy itself is a problematic category, in which domination may well be present. If we look to Lukes' (1974) third dimension of power, Foucault's (1977) power/knowledge hypothesis, the various traditions of power analysis that build upon the Gramscian (1971) concept of hegemony and Bourdieu's (1990) concept of symbolic violence, etc., what lies at the centre of all these perspectives is the image of social actors acquiescing in their own domination. One way of theorizing this is to argue that these individuals perceive certain exercises of power, and structured relations of authority, as legitimate, but (for various reasons) the observing sociologist or political theorist/scientist believes that the actors in question should not view them in this manner. In Lukes, actors consider power legitimate because they do not know what their real interests are. In Foucault they consider their objectification as subjects as legitimate because it is derived from some locally perceived concept of truth. In Gramsci, the subaltern classes accept bourgeois domination because they have internalized the latter's interpretative horizon; and in Bourdieu, symbolic violence makes people "misrecognize" reality. In all these versions of power and domination actors view social relations as legitimate due to some kind of cognitive shortcoming; the granddaddy of these accounts, of course, is Marx (and Engels). If it were not for the cognitive shortcoming, the very same social relations would appear straightforwardly as domination. If this is the case, then it is unhelpful to separate power from authority because the very separation is actually central to the efficacy of this form of domination, changing the conception of legitimacy in important ways. One consequence is that what was once regarded as legitimate can be rapidly and radically reframed as illegitimate once actors' cognitive shortcomings are rectified.

Institutionalized myths by themselves are insufficient to create institutionalization, the social processes by which obligations or actualities come to take on a rule-like status in social thought and action. On the contrary, they will only be likely to achieve this outcome where there exists regulated conflict leading to a fair degree of cooperation creating a ceremonially observed social ordering. Where the sources of such conflict are excluded then tensions will be raised, ordering diminished, and institutionalization limited. If organizations become *isomorphic* with their institutional context in order to secure social approval (*legitimacy*), which provides survival benefits, then this requires that the institutional context is already secured and is seen as such a sign of legitimacy. Perhaps scholars disinclined to comparative or historical analysis might imagine that these are somehow universal standing conditions, but we should be well aware that they are not.

Legitimacy has hardly been treated in relation to power theories in the sociology of organizations (see Deephouse & Suchman 2008). Instead, it has been treated as a variable conferring taken-for-grantedness on organizations, with little or no interrogation of whether or not that taken-for-grantedness is itself legitimate. For instance, Meyer and Scott's oft-cited definition of legitimacy suggests that it "refers to the degree of cultural support for an organization" (1983: 201). For any social order to be established as "the way we do things around here" – as obligatory passage points that become institutionalized – a great deal of strategic agency has to be carried out, which means that social structures and practices are always up for grabs. The type of strategic agency required has been identified by Vaara, Tienari, and Laurila (2006) as consisting of normalization, authorization, rationalization, moralization, and narrativization. Thus, from this perspective a de-stabilization of any one or more of these would threaten legitimacy. Such an emphasis is more sociologically useful than the previous accounts of legitimacy because it does not trade off the tacit assumption of legitimacy as an effect of members' practices, as do Suchman (1995) and Meyer and Scott (1983). Instead, the orientation is to the social practices that produce legitimacy effects, bracketing the question of legitimacy itself.

INSTITUTIONAL LOGICS AND TRANSLATION

Categories for making sense derive from the specific forms of discursive practice that are institutionalized within specific fields, such as professions, industries, and sectors. Making sense implies communicative competence premised on reciprocally meaningful speaking and hearing constituted by norms of mutual intelligibility. Hence, it is correct to see a central sociological element of an institution as a cognitive construction, whether they are infused with value, in Selznick's (1957: 16) terms, or merely procedurally accepted scripts, rules, and classifications (DiMaggio & Powell 1991). To the extent that these sociological elements of an institution are transcendent across organizational contexts rather than immanent to specific contexts they may be said to form an institutional logic (Alford & Friedland 1985; Friedland & Alford 1991). For instance, if we were to think of the widespread translation of the terms of Osborne and Gaebler's (1992) espousal of the new public management into many spheres of public service organizations internationally, we would be dealing with an institutional logic of managerialism. Managerialism is one of those central institutions of contemporary advanced societies which operate as a higher-order societal institutional logic, instantiations of which can be found at the level of many specific organizations. Friedland and Alford (1991) see specific societies as constituted by a number of key institutional sectors, in a regulatory sense, such as the economy, families, the state, and so on, with each of the core institutions having a central logic that is both constraining and enabling of individual and collective actions. In what is the most complete definition of an institutional logic, Thornton and Ocasio define the concept in terms of the "socially constructed, historical patterns of material practices, assumptions, values, beliefs, and rules by which individuals produce and reproduce their material subsistence, organize time and space, and provide meaning to their social reality" (1999: 804). What institutional logics provide are more or less tightly coupled, embedded, and nested logics for action or modes of rationality that provide for institutional sense-making by individuals competing and negotiating, organizations conflicting and collaborating, and institutions contradicting and cohering. Institutional logics are tangled up in each other: for instance, a field such as healthcare is riven by logics derived from managerialism, various clinical professionalisms, notions of state citizenship entitlements, and consumer preferences in healthcare markets. These enable various forms of taken-for-granted discourse to be translated from context to context by actors and organizations according to their sense of the logic of appropriateness (March & Olsen 1989).

Institutional logic analysis explains change not only through institutional entrepreneurs and translators as (scholars such as Osborne and Gaebler [1992] have been in the field of public management, for instance) but also through mechanisms of structural overlap, event sequencing, and the presence of competing institutional logics. Structural overlap occurs where previously distinct and differentiated individuals and organizations are forced to engage with each other, perhaps as a result of a restructuring, merger, or acquisition. Where such events occur, as Thornton and Ocasio (2008: 116) suggest, differentiated logics create contradictions in organizations and organizational fields, facilitating not only entrepreneurial but also translation opportunities that can lead to institutional change, whether deliberative or not. An example of these mechanisms at work is Stovel and Savage's (2005) analysis of "how a merger wave exposed competing institutional logics and triggered the elaboration of the modern, mobile, bureaucratic career in the financial sector" (Thornton & Ocasio 2008: 116). A similar process occurred when consulting and accounting practices became lodged in the largest international accounting firms and accounting became an instrument for on-selling consultancy services (Thornton, Jones & Kury 2005). Greenwood and Suddaby (2006) note that elite business service organizations are more likely to come into competing and contradictory logics because they bridge different organizational fields; here innovation occurs through the structural overlaps being translated from one setting to another.

Event sequencing occurs when there is a "temporal and sequential unfolding of unique events that dislocate, rearticulate, and transform the interpretation and meaning of cultural symbols and social and economic structures (Sewell 1996: 844)," as Thornton and Ocasio (2008: 116) propose. Where such sequencing occurs, events can rupture normalcy and create multiple changes and dramatically transform previous modes of categorizing phenomena: 9/11 is the perfect example. Here, a shift in the symbolic interpretation of events about the meaning of national security was locked in place by a simultaneous shift in resources so that they now focused on the problem of Islamist terrorism – albeit that some of the signifiers of the latter became confused with questions concerning Iraq. Institutional ordering is modular, decomposable, contiguous, and contested. Consequently, translations can occur down or across any cell in the matrix of different institutional logics and individual, organizational, and societal instantiations, as can colonization attempts by competing logics, such as medical professionalism versus business-like healthcare in Canada, as studied by Reay and Hinings (2005: 375).

The powerful actors, in terms of institutional isomorphism, are the professions, according to Scott (2008). Professions, Scott maintains, define, interpret, and apply institutional elements such that they are the most influential contemporary creators of institutions. Perhaps. In arguing this he is at odds with other sociological accounts, such as Bauman's (1987) analysis of a historical shift in liquid modernity from legislators to interpreters; in this view, the professions' power to legislate interpretations has declined markedly and we now live in an age in which every person potentially becomes their own authority on matters of diet, health, lifestyle, and general management of their selves, matters that in an earlier era would have been the preserve of professionals. Views allied with Bauman would expect to see a weakening of professional institutionalization rather than a tightening as the plurality of interpretive sources available in liquid modernity overtake authoritative legislative knowledge, which, comparatively, declines in importance. In Scott's view, professions as institutions rest on three different pillars: the regulative, normative, and cultural-cognitive pillars, familiar from DiMaggio and Powell (1983). Two views are contrasted concerning how these pillars emerge. One stresses *naturalistic evolution* while the other, *agent-based view* emphasizes power and intentional design. In practice, Scott suggests, the two accounts become tangled up; agency has unintended effects, creates routines, and is not always self-interested, such that action becomes quasi-naturalized.

INSTITUTIONALISM'S OPPOSITION

There are elements of radical opposition that have been incorporated into sociological institutionalism but that have not been fully developed within the corpus. For instance, Alvesson and Willmott focus on the idea of emancipation, which they define as "the process through which individuals and groups become freed from repressive social and ideological conditions, in particular, those that place socially unnecessary restrictions upon the development and articulation of human consciousness" (1992: 432). For Alvesson and Willmott (1992), emancipation is the result of a struggle for self-determination and a protracted and often painful process of self-reflection and change. The concern with engagement, the recognition of a conflict of interests, and a focus on emancipation all stem directly from the work of the Frankfurt School.

While Alvesson and Willmott (1992) focused on emancipation, Jermier (1985) focuses on the concept of alienation. In his early writings, Marx introduced the concept of alienation as the necessary result of the private appropriation of labor value under capitalist modes of production. But in early capitalism, the shared awareness of the class-based oppression experienced by workers prevented their separation from their true selves. Workers were therefore objectively alienated but subjectively remained aware of their condition. But later conceptualizations of alienation had to deal with the reality of the loss of awareness of workers. To the objective alienation that results from the capitalist system was added the subjective alienation of workers who were not aware of their own situation. Two different approaches were developed to explain this situation. Lukacs (1972) argued that the system becomes mystified and workers, while experiencing the oppression of the system, are unable to understand it. For Critical Theory of the Frankfurt School, the blame lies in the intensity of consumption made possible by the material success of capitalism and the effects of the cultural industries together resulting in a mirage of well-being in the midst of capitalist oppression. Jermier (1985) represents these two very different conceptualizations of alienation in two different short stories. Jermier's study provides a challenging view of work, and particularly the subjective experience of work. His discussion of alienation challenges researchers to look at the broader context of work, rather than just the narrow conditions of work, in thinking through the subjective experience of work.

Michael Burawoy is a British-trained anthropologist who moved from researching labor in copper mines in Africa to researching labor in a plant in Chicago, which turned out to be the same plant in which Donald Roy (1959) had done his pioneering ethnographic work. Burawoy's theoretical inspiration is drawn from the work of the Italian theorist Antonio Gramsci (1971) and his theory of hegemony. Gramsci sought to account for the collapse of the Western working-class movements during the post-First World War years. The reason, he concluded, could not be found within either the state or the capitalist economy; rather, the key lay in the institutional fabric of civil society, which in the West succeeded in eliciting the "spontaneous consent of the masses" to the status quo (Gramsci 1971: 12). Burawoy took from Gramsci the importance of "managing consent" for maintaining orderly legitimated power relations in organizations. In essence, the research question was why the Western working classes had not revolted, as Marxist theory would have expected them to, under the burden of exploitation and the economic contradictions of late capitalism. The answer, said Burawoy, was that in their everyday working lives managers and workers manufactured consent to the dominant relations of production. Of course, the question only makes sense if one assumes that the hypotheses of Marxist theory are correct: that is, if one assumes that what needs to be explained is something that should have happened but did not. The question then becomes why it did not happen. It was not a unique question: earlier versions of it had been asked by a number of industrial sociologists, but their answers were a little different from Burawoy's. For instance, the emphasis on cultural or normative domination is to be found in the classic text of William Whyte, *The Organization Man* (1960). Corporations no longer sought merely the worker's labor (the main concern of industrial and organizational analysis at that point) but also their lifeworld.

British researchers had developed the theory of embourgeoisement, which saw the Western working classes as adopting middle-class values of acquisitiveness and individualism in place of an older class-based culture (Goldthorpe, Lockwood, Bechhofer & Platt 1969; Abercrombie, Hill & Turner 1980). Burawoy introduced a new spin on these accounts by hooking up these "dominant ideology" accounts to Braverman's (1974) labor process analysis. He sought to identify the labor control systems that elicited workers' consent. Burawoy (1979, 1985) discerned several species of hegemonic factory regime, each of which invites workers to align their interests with those of their employers; closely related, Richard Edwards (1979) saw corporations maintaining control over white-collar workers and increasingly manual employees through the spread of "bureaucratic controls" encouraging workers to identify with the organization to a greater extent than any union or class affiliation (Joyce 1980; Vallas 1991). In particular, Burawoy stressed the importance of small everyday things in the life of the factory, the rituals and games that made work tolerable and allowed the employees to distantiate themselves from the mind-numbing ordinariness of work. Thus, rather than see the explanation for their attitudes to work as arising from the orientations they brought to work, as did the Cambridge researchers of the embourgeoisement thesis (Goldthorpe, Lockwood, Bechhofer & Platt 1969), Burawoy, following Roy (1958), saw their attitudes as arising from the nature of social relations in work.

The hegemonic thesis has been developed further by a number of people. For example, Guillermo Grenier (1988) conducted fieldwork at Johnson and Johnson's medical instruments plant in Albuquerque, New Mexico. He saw that initiatives such as quality circles, by imbuing work relations with the trappings rather than the substance of participation, dissipated dissent and implicated workers in enforcing managerial norms as a part of their everyday work. Barker (1993) provides an ethnographic account of ISE, a small electronics assembly plant spun off from a large corporation which adopted self-managed teams to ensure its competitive success. Workers were encouraged to embrace team principles and willingly assumed responsibility for mutual discipline and control. Kunda (1992) provides an ethnographic account of a computer engineering organization which systematically developed a system of "normative control," which it used to gain the professional employees' consent. In all these studies, the manufacture of consent is seen to be an important aspect of what is done as a normal part of everyday work, as it is shaped by various managerial devices, such as teams, quality circles, and so on. Thus, the focus on power is dedicated to explaining the relative quiescence of employees and the ways in which their goals become closely aligned with those of management.

More recent writers have sought to combine institutional theory with Gramsci. Levy and Scully (2007) develop a strategic theory of power that enhances understanding of institutional entrepreneurship. They build on Gramsci's account of the "war of position" led by "organic intellectuals" of the working class against the structures dominating the institutional field. The account drops the class rhetoric from Gramsci but retains the politics translated into an organizations and institutions framework, using the case of the international distribution of AIDS drugs to developing countries. Strategic action by institutional entrepreneurs demonstrates a strategic face of power reliant on skilled analysis, deployments, and coordination grounded in local knowledge with which to outflank dominant actors with superior resources. In turn, these dominant actors are able to exercise hegemony over the field with which accommodation is necessary.

WHITHER FOUCAULT'S POWER?

Scott's (1987) adolescence of organization theory included Foucault, but, for all intents and purposes, as with other theorists who have resisted splitting the world into *a priori* theoretical binaries, such as Garfinkel (1967), Sacks (1972, 1992), and Goffman (1959, 1961), Foucault has been strangely neglected by institutional theory. Foucault's work is usually divided into three distinct preoccupations: with archeology, with genealogy, and with the care of the self. Rather than being three distinct approaches these represent different emphases that are more or less predominant at different stages in Foucault's work. In his discussion of governmentality he seeks to bring these different accounts into a patterned relation with each other. Nonetheless, there are distinct emphases: the archeological approach seeks to demonstrate the arbitrary nature of that which confronts us as the assumed nature of everyday life; in Bauman's (1976) words, the present way of seeing the world seems to us to be almost a second nature, as overwhelmingly there, as something natural. The discourses with which, in their assemblage and grammar, we render the world as something knowable and as true provide us with the means to make the facticity of the world. It is not that the world we experience in some way denies a human essence – because it represses us through unreal interests (Lukes 1974) – or can be remade in a more ideal or utopian form in which discourse will be less distorted.

In *Discipline and Punish* (1977), Foucault introduces a view of power as productive, as creative, as much closer to the "power to" conception than that of "power over." Here the concern is less with power as something that is distributed, so that some have it, or have more or less of it than others, but instead the concern is with how the techniques and practices of power are normalized into ways of being in and thinking of the world that we share discursively, and which structure conduct in the world – including resistance to these techniques and practices. Such resistance merely serves to demonstrate the necessity for the further application or refinement of those techniques and practices so that, in future, resistance will be overcome. Power feeds on its failures to achieve those ends that those who wield it desire. In fact, failure is its most essential ingredient as it continually demonstrates to the elites of power the necessity of the power they invariably exercise imperfectly.

The phase of Foucault's work indicated by the publication of *Discipline and Punish* centered on the "explicit recognition that meanings are central to the constitution of social life as a complex set of petty and ignoble power relations" (Haugaard 1997: 43). So it is not just that our sense of the world in which we live is embedded in our institutionalized conventions for making sense of it; these also form the warp and weft of everyday power relations. We cannot understand our present without knowing its history; a history of the present is the first step to rethinking the pasts we might imagine, to see "how that-which-is has not always been" (Foucault 1988: 37). Thus, from this perspective, power is always at work. It is both inescapable and also something active, something done, something exercised. "Power is the consequence of petty confrontations between actors fighting within or over a regime of truth production," as Haugaard (1997: 69) suggests. It is produced through the strategies and tactics of local conflicts "carried out by actors with specific strategies and objectives," rather than being the effect of some capacities to access resources, or real interests, or ideologies that obscure these. Power is always embedded in those forms of rationality with which actors will be held accountable.

Foucault introduced the term governmentality in a series of lectures that he gave at the Collège de France on the "Birth of Biopolitics" in 1979 (Marks 2000: 128). These lectures engaged with the changing face of liberalism as a political project in the Reagan and Thatcher administrations. In this later work, Foucault used the notion of "governmentality" to connect the idea of "government" with that of "mentality," producing new and different forms of rationality to conduct the art of governing, an idea that he introduced to deal with changing conceptions of governmental bureaucracy that emerged as a part of the swing to neoliberal forms of economic governance from the 1980s onwards. Foucault was pointing to a fusion of new *technologies* of government with a new political *rationality*. "Governmentality" refers both to the new institutions of governance in bureaucracies as well as their effects. These effects are to make problematic whole areas of government that used to be accomplished through the public sector, seamlessly regulated by bureaucratic rules; now they are moved into calculations surrounding markets. Foucault defines government as a specific combination of governing techniques and ratio-nalities, typical of the modern, neoliberal period.

For Foucault governmentality meant both strategies of organizational gover-nance, in a broad sense, as well as self-governance by those who are made subjects of organizational governance. The concept of governmentality sought to capture new liberal approaches to political management. The focus was on "the totality of practices, by which one can constitute, define, organize, instrumentalize the strate-gies which individuals in their liberty can have in regard to each other" (Foucault 1988: 20). As du Gay (2000: 168) suggests, governmentality "create[s] a distance between the decisions of formal political institutions and other social actors, conceive[s] of these actors as subjects of responsibility, autonomy and choice, and seek[s] to act upon them through shaping and utilizing their freedom." What is novel about liberal forms of governance is that the personal projects and ambitions of individual actors become enmeshed with, and form alliances with, those of orga-nization authorities and dominant organizations. With the exception of du Gay (2000), Jackson and Carter (1998), and van Krieken (1996), few Foucauldian theorists of governmentality have explicitly addressed organizational issues (e.g., Burchell, Gordon & Miller 1991; Miller 1992; Hunter 1993).

In Jackson and Carter's (1998) terms, governmentality means that "people should voluntarily and willingly, delegate their moral autonomy and moral responsibility to obedience to the rules, to being governed in their conduct by a 'moral' force . . . which is external to the 'self'." As they go on to note, the requirement for obedience "usually is rationalized and justified in terms of a greater collective interest" (Jackson & Carter 1998: 51). Or, as Townley suggests, "before a domain can be governed or managed it must first be rendered knowable in a particular way" (1998: 193). Governmental power operates largely through facilitative rather than prohibitory mechanisms, using forms of institutionalized regulation to achieve their effects, through "the continuous and relatively stable presence of a series of ideals, expectations, received 'truths', standards and frameworks which provoke individu-als to govern their lives in quite particular ways" (Allen 2003: 82).

CONCLUSION

For many initiates into the sociology of organizations today, institutional theory is the main game. In the super league of the game as it is played in key contributions, some of which have been reviewed here (and many more of which are visited in Greenwood, Oliver, Sahlin, and Suddaby 2008), some basic institutional elements seem to have gone missing, notably discussion of power. There are contributions that run counter to this assessment but on the whole they have been fairly marginal to the mainstream of sociological institutionalism (but see Lawrence 2008). Largely they have derived from the incorporation of more classical theorists such as Marx, Gramsci, and Foucault. These theorists add a much needed power perspective to sociological institutional theories of organizations. Organizations, sociologically, are machines for domination and discipline, as Weber (1978), Marx (1976), and Gramsci (1971) argued; moreover, as Foucault (1977) suggests, they can be seen not just as repressive machinery but also as productive. Nonetheless, in recent sociology of organizations what seems to have gone out of focus is any account of how organizations as normative orders are also simultaneously structures of dominancy. By heeding Scott's (1987) inclusion of Foucault as a part of the adolescence of sociological institutionalism, we can recover some sense of the central role of power in organizations.

References

Abercrombie, N., S. Hill, and B. S. Turner (1980) *The Dominant Ideology Thesis*. London: Allen and Unwin.

Adler, P. S. (2009) "Introduction: A Social Science Which Forgets Its Founders Is Lost." In P. S. Adler (ed.), *The Oxford Handbook of Sociology and Organization Studies: Classical Foundations*. Oxford: Oxford University Press, pp. 3–19.

Albrow, M. (1970) *Bureaucracy*. London: Pall Mall Press.

Alexander, J. C. (1987) "The Centrality of the Classics." In A. Giddens and J. Turner (eds.), *Social Theory Today*. Palo Alto, CA: Stanford University Press.

Alford, R. R. and R. Friedland (1985) *Powers of Theory: Capitalism, the State, and Democracy*. Cambridge: Cambridge University Press.

Allen, J. (2003) *Lost Geographies of Power*. Oxford: Blackwell.

Alvesson, K. and H. Willmott (1992) 'On the Idea of Emancipation in Management and Organization Studies.' *Academy of Management Review* 17(3): 432–64.

Bachrach, P. and M. S. Baratz (1962) "Two Faces of Power." *American Political Science Review* 56: 947–52.

Bachrach, P. and M. S. Baratz (1970) *Power and Poverty: Theory and Practice*. New York: Oxford University Press.

Barker, J. (1993) "Tightening the Iron Cage: Concertive Control in Self Managing Teams." *Administrative Science Quarterly* 38: 408–37.

Bauman, Z. (1976) *Towards a Critical Sociology: An Essay on Common-sense and Emancipation*. London: Routledge & Kegan Paul.

Bauman, Z. (1987) *Legislators and Interpreters*. Cambridge: Polity Press.

Berger, P. and T. Luckman (1967) *The Social Construction of Reality: A Treatise in the Sociology of Knowledge*. Harmondsworth: Penguin.

Blau, P. M. (1965) "The Comparative Study of Organizations." *Industrial and Labor Relations Review* 18: 323–38.

Bourdieu, P. (1977) *Outline of a Theory of Practice*. Cambridge: Cambridge University Press.

Bourdieu, P. (1990) *A Theory of Practice*. Stanford, CA: Stanford University Press.

Braverman, H. (1974) *Labor and Monopoly Capital: The Degradation of Work in the Twentieth Century*. New York: Monthly Review Press.

Burawoy, M. (1979) *Manufacturing Consent: The Labour Process under Monopoly Capitalism*. Chicago: University of Chicago Press.

Burawoy, M. (1985) *The Politics of Production*. London: Verso.

Burchell, G., C. Gordon, and P. Miller (1991) *The Foucault Effect: Studies in Governmentality: With Two Lectures by and an Interview with Michel Foucault*. London: Harvester Wheatsheaf.

Burrell, G. and G. Morgan (1979) *Sociological Theories and Organizational Paradigms*. London: Heinemann.

Clegg, S. R. (1975) *Power, Rule and Domination*. London: Routledge and Kegan Paul.

Clegg, S. R. (1995) "Weber and Foucault: Social Theory for the Study of Organizations." *Organization* 1: 149–78.

Clegg, S. R. (1990) *Modern Organizations: Organization Studies in the Post Modern World.* London: Sage.

Clegg, S. R. and D. Dunkerley (1980) *Organization, Class and Control.* London: Routledge & Kegan Paul.

Crozier, M. (1963) *The Bureaucratic Phenomenon.* Chicago: University of Chicago Press.

Cyert, R. and J. G. March (1963) *A Behavioral Theory of the Firm.* Englewood Cliffs, NJ: Prentice Hall.

Dahl, R. A. (1961) *Who Governs?* New Haven, CT: Yale University Press.

Deephouse, D. L. and M. Suchman (2008) "Legitimacy in Organizational Institutionalism." In R. Greenwood, C. Oliver, K. Sahlin, and R. Suddaby (eds.), *The Sage Handbook of Organizational Institutionalism.* London: Sage, pp. 49–77.

DiMaggio, P. J. (1988) "Interest and Agency in Institutional Theory." In L. G. Zucker (ed.), *Institutional Patterns and Organizations: Culture and Environment.* Cambridge, MA: Ballinger, pp. 3–22.

DiMaggio, P. J. and W. W. Powell (1983) "The Iron Cage Revisited: Institutional Isomorphism and Collective Rationality in Organizational Fields." *American Sociological Review* 48: 147–60.

DiMaggio, P. J. and W. W. Powell (1991) "Introduction." In P. J. DiMaggio and W. W. Powell (eds.), *The New Institutionalism in Organizational Analysis.* Chicago: University of Chicago Press, pp. 1–38.

Donaldson, Lex (1996) "The Normal Science of Structural Contingency Theory." In S. R. Clegg, C. Hardy, and W. Nord (eds.), *The Handbook of Organization Studies.* London: Sage, pp. 1–108.

Du Gay, P. (2000) *In Praise of Bureaucracy: Weber, Organization, Ethics.* London: Sage.

Edwards, R. (1979) *Contested Terrain: The Transformation of the Workplace in the Twentieth Century.* London: Heinemann.

Foucault, M. (1977) *Discipline and Punish: The Birth of the Prison.* London: Allen and Lane.

Foucault, M. (1988) "The Care of the Self as a Practice of Freedom." In J. Berbauer and D. Rasmussen (eds.), *The Final Foucault.* Cambridge, MA: MIT Press, pp. 1–20.

Foucault, M. and L. D. Kritzman (1988) *Politics, Philosophy, Culture: Interviews and Other Writings, 1977–1984.* London: Routledge.

Fournier, V. and C. Grey (2000) "At the Critical Moment: Conditions and Prospects for Critical Management Studies." *Human Relations* 53(1): 7–32.

Friedland, R. and R. R. Alford (1991) "Bringing Society Back in: Symbols, Practices, and Institutional Contradictions." In Walter W. Powell and Paul J. DiMaggio (eds.), *The New Institutionalism in Organizational Analysis.* Chicago: University of Chicago Press, pp. 232–63.

Garfinkel, H. (1967) *Studies in Ethnomethodology.* Englewood Cliffs, NJ: Prentice Hall.

Goffman, E. (1959) *The Presentation of Self in Everyday Life.* Harmondsworth: Penguin.

Goffman, E. (1961) *Asylums.* Harmondsworth: Penguin.

Goldthorpe, J., D. Lockwood, F. Bechhofer, and J. Platt (1969) *The Affluent Worker in the Class Structure.* London: Cambridge University Press.

Gouldner, A. W. (1954) *Patterns of Industrial Bureaucracy.* Glencoe, IL: Free Press.

Gramsci, A. (1971) *From the Prison Notebooks.* London: Lawrence and Wishart.

Greenwood, R. and R. E. Meyer (2008) "Influencing Ideas: A Celebration of DiMaggio and Powell (1983)." *Journal of Management Inquiry* 17(4): 258–64.

Greenwood, R. and R. Suddaby (2006) "Institutional Entrepreneurship in Mature Fields: The Big Five Accounting Firms." *Academy of Management Journal* 49(1): 27–48.

Greenwood, R., C. Oliver, K. Sahlin, and R. Suddaby (eds.) (2008) *The Sage Handbook of Organizational Institutionalism*. London: Sage.

Grenier, G. J. (1988) *Inhuman Relations: Quality Circles and Anti-Unionism in American Industry*. Philadelphia, PA: Temple University Press.

Grey, C. and H. C. Willmott (2005) *Critical Management Studies: A Reader*. Oxford: Oxford University Press.

Hannan, M. T. and J. Freeman (1977) "The Population Ecology of Organizations." *American Journal of Sociology* 82: 929–64.

Hardy, C. and S. Maguire (2008) "Institutional Entrepreneurship." In R. Greenwood, C. Oliver, K. Sahlin, and R. Suddaby (eds.), *The Sage Handbook of Organizational Institutionalism*. London: Sage, pp. 198–217.

Haugaard, M. (1997) *The Constitution of Power*. Manchester: Manchester University Press.

Higgins, W. and K. T. Hallström (2007) "Standardization, Globalization and Rationalities of Government." *Organization* 14(5): 685–704.

Hinings, C. R. and R. Greenwood (2002) "Disconnects and Consequences in Organization Theory?" *Administrative Science Quarterly* 47: 411–21.

Hunter, I. (1993) "Subjectivity and Government." *Economy and Society* 22(1): 123–34.

Jackson, N. and P. Carter (1998) "Labour as Dressage." In A. McKinley and K. Starkey (eds.), *Foucault, Management, and Organization Theory: From Panopticon to Technologies of Self*. London: Sage, pp. 49–64.

Jermier, J. (1985) "When the Sleeper Awakens: A Short Story Extending Themes in Radical Organization Theory." *Journal of Management* 11(2): 67–80.

Joyce, P. (1980) *Work, Society, and Politics: The Culture of the Factory in Later Victorian England*. Brighton: Harvester Press.

Knights, D. and H. Willmott (1989) "Power and Subjectivity at Work: From Degradation to Subjugation in Social Relations." *Sociology* 23(4): 535–58.

Kunda, G. (1992) *Engineering Culture: Control and Commitment in a High-Tech Corporation*. Philadelphia, PA: Temple University Press.

Lawrence, T. (2008) "Power, Institutions and Organizations." In R. Greenwood, C. Oliver, K. Sahlin, and R. Suddaby (eds.), *The Sage Handbook of Organizational Institutionalism*. London: Sage, pp. 170–93.

Levy, D. and M. Scully (2007) "The Institutional Entrepreneur as Modern Prince: The Strategic Face of Power in Contested Fields." *Organization Studies* 28: 971–91.

Lukacs, G. (1972) *History and Class Consciousness*. Boston: MIT Press.

Lukes, S. (1974) *Power: A Radical View*. London: Macmillan.

March, J. G., H. A. Simon, and H. S. Guetzkow (1958) *Organizations*. New York: John Wiley & Sons Inc.

March, J. G. and J. P. Olsen (1989) *Rediscovering Institutions: The Organizational Basis of Politics*. New York: Free Press.

Marks, J. (2000) "Foucault, Franks, Gauls: Il faut défendre la société: The 1976 Lectures at the Collège de France." *Theory, Culture and Society* 17(5): 127–47.

Marx, K. (1976) *Capital*, Vol. 1. London: NLR.

Merton, R. K. (1940) "Bureaucratic Structure and Personality." *Social Forces* 18(4): 560–8.

Meyer, J. W. and B. Rowan (1977) "Institutionalized Organizations: Formal Structure as Myth and Ceremony." *American Journal of Sociology* 83: 340–63.

Meyer, J. W. and W. R. Scott (1983) "Centralization and the Legitimacy Problems of Local Government." In J. W. Meyer and W. R. Scott (eds.), *Organizational Environments: Ritual and Rationality*. Beverly Hills, CA: Sage, pp. 199–215.

Miller, P. (1992) 'Accounting and Objectivity: The Invention of Calculating Selves and Calculable Spaces.' *Annals of Scholarship* 9(1/2): 61–86.

Miller, P. (1994) "Accounting and Objectivity: The Invention of Calculating Selves and Calculable Spaces." In A. Megill (ed.), *Rethinking Objectivity*. Durham, NC: Duke University Press, pp. 239–64.

Osborne, D. and T. Gaebler (1992) *Re-Inventing Government: How the Entrepreneurial Spirit Is Transforming the Public Sector*. Reading, MA: Addison-Wesley.

Parsons, T. (1951) *The Social System*. New York: Free Press of Glencoe.

Perrow, C. (1986) *Complex Organizations: A Critical Essay*. Glenview, IL: Scott, Foresman.

Pfeffer, J. and G. R. Salancik (1978) *The External Control of Organizations: A Resource Dependence Perspective*. New York: Harper and Row.

Phillips, N. and N. Malhotra (2008) "Taking Social Construction Seriously: Extending the Discursive Approach in Institutional Theory." In R. Greenwood, C. Oliver, K. Sahlin, and R. Suddaby (eds.), *The Sage Handbook of Organizational Institutionalism*. London: Sage, pp. 702–20.

Pugh, D. S. and D. J. Hickson (1976) *The Aston Programme: Organizational Structure in Its Context*. London: Saxon House.

Reay, T. and C. R. Hinings (2005) "The Recomposition of an Organizational Field: Health Care in Alberta." *Organization Studies* 26: 351–84.

Reed, M. (2009) "Bureaucratic Theory and Intellectual Renewal in Contemporary Organization Studies." In P. S. Adler (ed.), *The Oxford Handbook of Sociology and Organization Studies: Classical Foundations*. Oxford: Oxford University Press.

Roy, D. F. (1959) "Banana Time: Job Satisfaction and Informal Interaction." *Human Organization* 18(4): 158–68.

Sacks, H. (1972) "An Initial Investigation of the Usability of Conversational Data for Doing Sociology." In *Studies in Social Interaction*. New York: Free Press, pp. 31–74.

Sacks, H. (1992) *Lectures on Conversations*. Oxford: Blackwell.

Scott, W. R. (1987) "The Adolescence of Institutional Theory." *Administrative Science Quarterly* 32: 493–511.

Scott, W. R. (1995) *Institutions and Organizations*. Thousand Oaks, CA: Sage.

Scott, W. R. (2008) "Lords of the Dance: Professionals as Institutional Agents." *Organization Studies* 29: 219–38.

Selznick, P. (1949) *TVA and the Grass Roots: A Study in the Sociology of Formal Organization*. Berkeley, CA: University of California Press.

Selznick, P. (1957) *Leadership and Administration*. Berkeley, CA: University of California Press.

Sewell, W. H., Jr. (1996) "Historical Events as Transformations of Structures: Inventing Revolution at the Bastille." *Theory and Society* 25: 841–81.

Silverman, D. (1970) *The Theory of Organization*. London: Heinemann.

Stovel, K. and M. Savage (2005) "Mergers and Mobility: Organizational Growth and Origins of Career Migration at Lloyds Bank." *American Journal of Sociology* 111: 1080–121.

Suchman, M. C. (1995) "Managing Legitimacy: Strategic and Institutional Approaches." *Academy of Management Review* 20(3): 571–611.

Thompson, J. D. (1967) *Organizations in Action: Social Science Bases of Administrative Theory*. New York: McGraw-Hill.

Thompson, P. (1990) "Crawling from the Wreckage: The Labour Process and the Politics of Production." In D. Knights and H. Willmott (eds.), *Labour Process Theory*. Basingstoke: Macmillan, pp. 95–125.

Thompson, P. and S. Ackroyd (1995) "All Quiet on the Workplace Front?" *Sociology* 29: 615–33.

Thornton, P. and W. Ocasio (1999) "Institutional Logics and the Historical Contingency of Power in Organizations: Executive Succession in the Higher Education Publishing Industry 1958–1990." *American Journal of Sociology* 105: 801–43.

Thornton, P. and W. Ocasio (2008) "Institutional Logics." In R. Greenwood, C. Oliver, K. Sahlin, and R. Suddaby (eds.), *The Sage Handbook of Organizational Institutionalism*. Los Angeles: Sage, pp. 99–129.

Thornton, P., C. Jones, and K. Kury (2005) "Institutional Logics and Institutional Change: Transformation in Accounting, Architecture, and Publishing." In C. Jones and P. Thornton (eds.), *Research in the Sociology of Organizations*. London: JAI Press, pp. 125–70.

Tolbert, P. S. and L. G. Zucker (1983) "Institutional Sources of Change in the Formal Structure of Organizations: The Diffusion of Civil Service Reform, 1880–1935." *Administrative Science Quarterly* 28: 22–39.

Townley, B. (1998) "Beyond Good and Evil: Depth and Division in the Management of Human Resources." In A. McKinley and K. Starkey (eds.), *Foucault, Management, and Organization Theory: From Panopticon to Technologies of Self*. London: Sage, pp. 191–210.

Vaara, E., J. Tienari, and J. Laurila (2006) "Pulp and Paper Fiction: On the Discursive Legitimacy of Global Industrial Restructuring." *Organization Studies* 27: 789–810.

Vallas, S. P. (1991) "Workers, Firms, and the Dominant Ideology: Hegemony and Consciousness in the Monopoly Core." *Sociological Quarterly* 32: 61–83.

Van Krieken, R. (1996) "Proto-Governmentalization and the Historical Formation of Organizational Subjectivity." *Economy and Society* 25(2): 195–221.

Weber, M. (1978) *Economy and Society: An Outline of Interpretive Sociology*. Berkeley, CA: University of California Press.

Whyte, W. (1960)*The Organization Man*. Harmondsworth: Penguin.

Willmott, H. (1997) "Rethinking Management and Managerial Work: Capitalism, Control, and Subjectivity." *Human Relations* 50(11): 1329–59.

Zucker, L. G. (1977) "The Role of Institutionalization in Cultural Persistence." *American Sociological Review* 42: 726–43.

Zucker, L. G. (1983) "Organizations as Institutions." In Samuel B. Bacharach (ed.), *Advances in Organizational Theory and Research*, Vol. 2. Greenwich, CT: JAI Press, pp. 1–43.

10

Cultural Analysis

JOHN TOMLINSON

INTRODUCTION: THE PROLIFERATION OF THE CULTURAL

In 1984 four American sociologists, Robert Wuthnow, James Davidson Hunter, Albert Bergesen, and Edith Kurzweil, published a book called *Cultural Analysis*. This is their assessment of the state of play, nearly 30 years ago:

> While theories, methods and research investigations in other areas of the social sciences have accumulated at an impressive pace over the past several decades, the study of culture appears to have made little headway. The major theorizing, as well as the bulk of empirical work, that has been done in the social sciences since the Second World War has tended to pay little attention to the cultural factor . . . With only a few exceptions, this field remains an impoverished area in the social sciences . . . On the whole it may be only slightly presumptuous to suggest that the social sciences are in danger of abandoning culture entirely as a field of enquiry. (Wuthnow, Davidson Hunter, Bergesen & Kurzweil 1984: 1–3)

This bleak assessment looks almost incredible today, given the current huge attention given to cultural matters across the social sciences. Was it accurate? Well, judging this would depend partly on how narrowly one defined the social sciences and partly on which side of the Atlantic one happened to be. After all, the Centre for Contemporary Cultural Studies in Birmingham had been established in 1964 (albeit originally in an English department) and during the intervening 20 years had already generated what was to become perhaps the most influential cross-disciplinary program of theoretical, textual-analytical, and ethnographic research in Cultural Studies (see, for example, Hall, Hobson, Lowe & Willis 1980). Curiously,

---

Wuthnow and his colleagues make no mention of the project of Cultural Studies, nor of its key thinkers and influences – for instance Richard Hoggart, Raymond Williams, and Stuart Hall.

If the authors had paid some attention to this current they might have produced a rather different assessment, but what they could not have predicted was the way in which the discourse of the cultural was, within a few years, to erupt across all fields of the social sciences and humanities in what has been loosely described as the "cultural turn" (Chaney 1994; Jameson 1998; Ray & Sayer 1999). Always a rather ambiguous formulation, the idea of the cultural turn nonetheless points us to one of the key outcomes of the theoretical ferment in the academy from the late 1980s onwards. A combination of the impact of iconoclastic theories such as post-structuralism and postmodernism, along with the more directly political agendas of gender, sexuality, and post-colonialism, led virtually all disciplines towards a process of interrogation of their fundamental conceptualizations and operational principles. Out of this process emerged the preoccupation with the cultural dimension – that is, with questions of representation, discourse, experience, subjectivity, identity, and diversity, and the politics attaching to all this – that has been a feature of so much academic attention in the intervening years.

It is not too fanciful, then, to say that today we are faced with almost the opposite problem to the one Wuthnow and his colleagues identified: too much culture. By this I mean two things. First, with the cultural inflection of work in so many disciplines and fields – from international relations and geography to art history and business studies – it becomes more problematic than it seemed in 1984 to attempt to define a single unified approach to cultural analysis – and even more presumptuous to locate this within sociology. Secondly, the sheer amount of "cultural discourse" circulating – not only in the academy, but in journalism, in the representational sphere of new media defined by internet search engines, blogs, and social networking sites, in marketing, and in various agencies of the nation-state – has done little to sharpen the soft definitional edges of the concept of culture.

When Wuthnow and his colleagues were writing, the problem seemed to be to rescue the domain of culture either from the obscurity of subjectivity or from various forms of reductionism, and to constitute it as "a distinct aspect of social reality, the patterns of which are subject to observation and theoretical interpretation [and thus] as a systematic body of enquiry . . . distinct from related disciplines such as social psychology or sociology . . . " (Wuthnow, Davidson Hunter, Bergesen & Kurzweil 1984: 259). Their strategy to achieve this was to bring together four different theoretical approaches to the analysis of culture: critical theory, as represented by Jürgen Habermas; cultural anthropology, in the work of Mary Douglas; phenomenology (Peter Berger); and "neo-structuralism" (what we would today more commonly call post-structuralism), in the person of Michel Foucault.

What is interesting here is the rationalist assumption that the various insights of these very different perspectives could somehow be "consolidated" to forge a unitary approach to the analysis of culture in general. With the benefit of hindsight we can see that this was never on the cards: instead, as Foucault (1981) might have warned them, the unruly discourse of the cultural has "proliferated to infinity," both within and beyond the academy. Ironically, then, the constitution of culture as "a distinct aspect of social reality" has been achieved more or less independently of the efforts of academics. It has been thrust upon us all by a complicated combination of the "aestheticization of everyday life" (Featherstone 2007) produced by an ever-expanding consumer culture and the establishment of political agendas and the assertion of claims in relation to various aspects of cultural identity.

The problem for us today then is absolutely not one of academic pioneering – of staking a claim for a recognized analytic terrain for cultural analysis. Nor is it really the old and still unresolved definitional issue of what is to count as "culture" (Williams 1981; Eagleton 2000; Inglis 2004). It is, rather, one of how to get some analytic grip on an enormous unruly field of modern public cultural discourse in which systematic intellectual analysis, cultural-political lobbying, the institutional discourses of the state and the market-place, and the vast and near-chaotic sphere of individual cultural opinion and intervention of the "blogosphere" (Rettberg 2008) all jostle and blur.

My approach to this rather daunting task will be both modest and practical. Wuthnow and his colleagues chose to discuss theoretical approaches. I shall address three *contexts* within which we might begin to address these complex discursive entanglements. Or at least begin to identify and explore some of the most significant forces shaping cultural practice and experience today. These contexts are, first, the impact of globalization; second, the commodification of culture; and third, the influence of ubiquitous media technologies in cultural life.

Given the limitations of a short chapter there will only be space to sketch these contexts – and we will have to add the qualification that these are contexts most readily applied to the analysis of culture in developed industrial economies or, more accurately, to the developed industrial sectors of globalized economies.

GLOBALIZATION

It is salutary to reflect that when Wuthnow and his colleagues were writing in 1984, the term globalization was virtually unheard of. Once the term became established, it seemed difficult – rather like in the case of mobile (cell) phones, Google, or disposable nappies – to imagine how we ever managed without it. The point is, I think, that the concept of globalization grasps a range of *new* political, economic, and cultural phenomena that make themselves evident at the start of the new millennium, and, at the same time, force us to re-assess some of our conventional ways of understanding the social world (Beck 2002; Urry 2003; Held & McGrew 2007; Tomlinson 2007b).

This is nowhere more apparent than in the domain of culture. Globalization – understood in the broadest way as the rapidly expanding network of social, economic, and cultural connectivity across the globe (Giddens 1990; Castells 1996; Held, McGrew, Goldblatt & Perraton 1999; Beck 2000) – has forced analysts of culture to re-assess traditional assumptions about the defining relationship between culture and geographical place. In a world in which distant events and influences so easily "reach into" our localities, it becomes much more difficult precisely to trace the formative influence of local conditions on cultural experience.

Cultural experience – particularly in locales which have a high degree of global connectivity – thus becomes "deterritorialized," lifted off its anchorings in geographical place (Garcia Canclini 1995; Tomlinson 1999). Deterritorialization makes itself felt in different modalities. Most spectacularly, perhaps, in a techno-logical mode: in the routine delivery of information and entertainment into our homes via globalized electronic media systems and institutions; in the now almost ubiquitous use of mobile communications technologies enabling more or less instant contact across continents; in the dramatically rapid desertion of local physical stores of information (libraries, archives, information centers) in favor of internet search engines like Google. But it is also found in a globalized set of consumption practices: as people in developed economies are exposed to wider and wider varieties of "global goods" in their stores; in food culture, as the choice to eat at their "local" Italian, French, Chinese, Thai, Indian, Turkish, American, Mexican, or Japanese restaurant becomes a commonplace of globalized urban life. And it is present in the spontaneous popular-cultural activities of local communities: from tai chi to karaoke to salsa dance classes. These examples of the permeable texture of everyday experi-ence, now so taken for granted in the advanced economies and growing at such a pace in the urban sectors of the developing world, are amongst the most salient indicators of cultural globalization. But they are also the indices of deeper transfor-mations in culture, as globalization reaches into individual phenomenal "worlds," complicating our understanding of what *counts* as home and abroad, expanding our horizons of cultural and moral relevance, and adding layers to our sense of cultural belonging (Tomlinson 2003, 2007b).

One of the striking things about this process is the divergence in the response to it as between ordinary people – who have tended on the whole to take these changes in their stride – and cultural critics – who have generally been pessimistic and on occasions apocalyptic in their assessments. The key issue here has been the proposition that cultural globalization must present a general threat to global cultural diversity. This is not a new idea: fears of Western cultural imperialism, or more specifically "Americanization," were voiced by cultural critics for most of the second half of the twentieth century. Although the cruder formulations of the idea of cultural imperialism have been heavily criticized within sociology and cultural studies (Tomlinson 1991; Thompson 1995; Lull 2000; Beck, Sznaider & Winter 2003), the debate over the threat to cultural diversity has lost none of its vigor, particularly as conducted in relation to cultural policy within institutional frameworks like that of UNESCO (UNESCO 2000; UNDP 2004; UNESCO 2009).

Perhaps the main reason why this debate continues to elude clear resolution is the inherent difficulty in eliciting clear empirical evidence and relating this, causally, to the globalization process. If we take a relatively simple case, that of the demon-strable loss of particular global languages in recent decades (Crystal 2000; Nettle & Romaine 2000), the case against globalization might appear a strong one. However it becomes a more complicated task to gather such particulars into a general thesis about the *overall* loss of cultural diversity, given the fact that new cultural practices, new language variants, new hybrid cultural forms, and new phe-nomena afforded by media technologies are constantly being generated (Cowen 2002; Moore 2008). The result of this lack of hard evidence has been that, in general, claims over the loss of global diversity in culture have been based on impres-sions, anecdotal evidence, and speculation.

Recently, however, some clear evidence has begun to emerge in at least one area of cultural production and circulation. In their study of the cultural impact of global news media, Norris and Inglehardt (2009) argue that the threats to cultural diversity have commonly been exaggerated. Drawing on data collected on cultural values across 93 countries between 1981 and 2007, their survey represents the best data available so far on the relationship between globalized media use and the constitution of cultural values.

Norris and Inglehardt find a much more complex picture of cultural interaction than can be accommodated in the view of globalization as the enemy of cultural diversity. In particular, they demonstrate the existence of a series of intervening factors at institutional, economic and social-psychological levels that serve significantly to *moderate* the influence of cultural imports on national cultures, particularly those outside of the affluent West – those societies generally judged to be at risk from the culturally homogenizing effects of globalization. Thus, they argue that the low levels of trade integration with the global market, low levels of economic development and investment in communications systems, and accompanying limited access to information and media freedom that characterize many of the poorer countries of the world, combine to reduce the impact of the global media on these populations. Added to this political-economic insulating effect, they point to the existence of what they refer to as social-psychological "firewalls" in the shape of "socialization filters involved in the acquisition and transmission of core attitudes and enduring values. These firewalls, individually and in combination, help protect national cultural diversity from foreign influence" (Norris & Inglehardt 2009: 30).

What Norris and Inglehardt confirm in their empirically based study, then, are two arguments that have been leveled against the "globalization-as-cultural-imperialism" thesis. First, that there is a clear contradiction between the (compelling) claim that at the political-economic level globalization is uneven and excluding in the distribution of cultural goods and technologies, and the claim that *at the same time* it is drawing economically marginalized cultures into a homogenized global culture. And secondly, that the deep grammar of local meaning systems is unlikely to collapse entirely in face of the mere distribution of globalized cultural goods.

They go on, indeed, to demonstrate that even in those nation-states having the lowest levels of institutionalized "firewalls" – that is to say the most affluent, high-connectivity, liberal democracies – an emerging consensus on a certain range of cosmopolitan values does not signal the collapse of cultural particularity:

> even amongst post-industrial societies such as the United States and Britain, Sweden and Germany, and Japan and South Korea, which are tightly interconnected through communications networks, trade flows, and economic interdependence, having the greatest share of cultural trade in audiovisual programs, there remain distinctive and persistent cultural differences that show no signs of disappearing. These societies do not share a monolithic Western culture toward which developing societies are converging. Instead, both developing societies and western societies are changing in ways shaped by broad forces of modernization, while retaining distinctive national cultures. (Norris & Inglehardt 2009: 209)

Interaction with news media is of course only one aspect of the complex cultural flows generated by globalization. But the example is sufficiently generalizable to suggest that we should view the issue of cultural diversity under globalization rather differently. If we understand it more broadly in terms of the deterritorializing transformation of localities that I mentioned earlier, then the effects of the "reaching in" of a range of different cultural experiences, along with a plurality of value perspectives, suggest an expansion in the cultural horizons of people in high-connectivity societies. The overall impact of globalization is thus likely to be an increase rather than a decrease in the global sum of cultural diversity.

Thus, through routine experience of a global media, greater opportunities for travel, increased interaction with other cultures within multicultural urban settings, more globally aware educational programs in schools and universities, and so on, the positive potential of deterritorialization is that it weakens the tendency to ethnocentrism that has been pretty much a historical constant of cultural outlook. To this extent, deterritorialization may contribute in the long term to the shaping of attitudes of cultural openness and tolerance, pluralism, and the celebration rather than the suspicion of difference. Deterritorialization may thus eventually provide the cultural conditions for the emergence of a progressive cosmopolitan culture (Cheah & Robbins 1998; Tomlinson 2002; Vertovek & Cohen 2002; Beck 2006). But on the other hand, it carries with it a uniquely modern cultural burden in the instabilities and anxieties that proceed from routine exposure to the world beyond the locality. This irrevocable transformation of the relationship between culture and geographical place that we have seen in the past few decades of human history sets an agenda for cultural analysis that we have only begun to address.

COMMODIFICATION

One of the major underlying questions posed by globalization is that of the commodification of culture within global market capitalism. Some anthropologists argue that commodification of culture is not peculiar to capitalist-modern societies, but can be found in the exchange relations of pre-modern cultures, for example those of pre-colonial Melanesia (Moore 2008). However true this may be, there can be little doubt that the commodification of culture to be found in contemporary capitalist cultures is of a quite different scale and order. It is less a matter of the practices of exchange involved, than the fact that so many expressions of meaning – or simple routine recreational activities of daily life – have become transformed into entities having an intrinsic market value which comes to redefine them. Culture then becomes increasingly understood in a different register: less as practice and process and more as a set of "things" that are bought and sold. And not only cultural artifacts – books, films, recorded music – but in a curious sort of reification, even cultural activities like academic courses or holidays become described as "products." Indeed the activity of shopping itself is now undoubtedly one of the most popular cultural practices in developed industrial societies and is structured into almost any contemporary cultural activity (Rojek 2000; Bauman 2005).

Commodification is without doubt one of the most striking features of the organization of contemporary cultural practice and experience. But how should it be regarded critically? There is of course a long tradition, dating back at least to the work of Herbert Marcuse (1964) and Erich Fromm (1955) in the 1950s and 1960s, which regards consumer culture as an aspect of the alienation of life in capitalist societies. And, despite the considerable sophistications that have been achieved in the analysis of consumer culture since the 1990s (Slater 1997; Miller, Jackson, Thrift, Holbrook & Rowlands 1998; Ritzer 2001; Warde 2002; Featherstone 2007), a deep strain of pessimism still persists amongst some major cultural critics. Take, for example, Zygmunt Bauman's description of the "consumerist syndrome":

> a batch of variegated yet closely interconnected attitudes and strategies, cognitive dis-
> positions, value judgements and prejudgements, explicit and tacit assumptions about
> the ways of the world . . . It colours inter-human relations at work and at home, in
> public as well as in the most intimate private domains. It rephrases and recasts the
> destinations and itineraries of life pursuits so that not one of them bypass the shopping
> malls . . . it casts the gigantic shadow of consumerism on the whole of the Lebenswelt.
> It relentlessly hammers home the message that everything is or could be a commodity,
> or if it is short of becoming a commodity, that it should be handled like a commod-
> ity . . . (Bauman 2005: 83–8)

Bauman is quite right of course to point out how relentless are the concerted efforts by capitalist-inflected modern institutions – not merely commercial enter-prises but all the institutions of the modern nation-state – towards expanding con-sumption. But a problem with such analyses (see also Lipovetsky 2005) is the implication that compliance on the part of consumers with these efforts involves either a state of systematic ideological deception or indeed (a more dispiriting thought) a condition of deep existential commitment to endless consumerism. Com-modification of culture demands vigorous critique at an *institutional* level for all sorts of good reasons – not least being the shrinking of the free public cultural sphere that it entails. But what also needs to be problematized is the assumption that this institutional pressure translates into attitudes symmetrically obedient to the system needs of contemporary capitalism. There are two main reasons to distrust this implication.

The first is a familiar objection to "ideological manipulation" critiques of con-sumerism. It is that human beings, in their actions as consumers as in every other sphere, are knowledgeable agents. This means they are likely to possess a broad reflexive understanding of consumption practices: of their increasing centrality in everyday life; of the strategies of marketing and advertising; of the significance of increasing consumption in the overall system of capitalism; and, most importantly, of the potential and limitations of consumer goods to bring different levels and orders of satisfaction. This sort of everyday understanding arises from a variety of sources. It comes from accumulated stocks of knowledge produced in previous consumer activity; it is familiarized through a host of media representations; and of course it derives from the roles many consumers *themselves* occupy within the marketing and retailing sectors. If modern culture is saturated with advertising imagery and marketing discourse, it is also replete with common-sense understand-ings and popular interpretations of consumer culture. This does not, of course, imply that average consumers have a developed theoretical-critical attitude to consumer culture, but it does suggest that they are by no means "cultural dopes" in the process.

The second reason relates more specifically to the idea of consumers being caught up in an accelerating and endlessly repeated cycle of stimulation and frustration. This is a key idea in Zygmunt Bauman's critique. He claims: "the consumerist syndrome has degraded duration and elevated transience . . . it has sharply shortened the timespan separating . . . the birth of wanting and its demise . . . it has put appropriation, quickly followed by waste disposal, in the place of possessions and enjoyments that last . . . " (Bauman 2005: 83–4).

Again, Bauman identifies a significant feature of contemporary cultural practice and experience. The argument that the focus of consumption activities has shifted from long-term possession to immediate, recurrent appropriation is a persuasive one. However, again, we need to handle the inferences we draw from this with care. In particular we need to avoid being pushed towards implausible explanations of the increased frequency of this cycle of consumption. One such would be that, not only are consumers routinely deceived by the promises of consumer goods, but that, in the triumph of hope over experience, they just blindly keep coming back for more. (A good simple test of the plausibility of this scenario is to ask ourselves if we would recognize our *own* routine consumption behavior in this pattern.) It is indeed rather difficult to *imagine* the sort of general cultural attitude – in the sense of a broad narrative of meaning – that would actually correspond to this state of affairs.

If we reject ideas of repetition-compulsion, sustained and comprehensive deception, or some version of general human incorrigibility, this does not mean we have exhausted ways of interpreting the perplexing cultural phenomenon that Bauman describes. Indeed it may be interpretable by considering an almost *opposite* general cultural attitude to consumption. This is that, far from having consistently high expectations of the capacity of consumer goods to provide satisfaction – expectations that are routinely (indeed, systematically) dashed – the great majority of people actually have rather *low* expectations of what consumer goods can and should provide.

Put in another way, it is plausible that there exists a widespread *disbelief* in the capacity of consumer goods to provide profound satisfactions; but that this exists alongside an expectation that the capitalist system will – and indeed should – continue to deliver the goods. These two attitudes are not necessarily contradictory. One way of reconciling them is to say that contemporary consumption is characterized by the expectation of the continual *delivery* of goods rather than of their providing satisfaction (Tomlinson 2007a).

Understood in this way, "delivery" becomes the *telos* of consumption, the termination of the implicit social contract between consumer and consumer capitalism, the point at which (both economic and cultural) liability ceases. Modern populations have refined expectations of consumer goods: that they be either functional or novel or amusing; that they exhibit style and quality; that they afford value for money. But also – and this is part of the sophisticated knowledgeability of contemporary consumers – that they will provide a "lifestyle semiotic" function – as markers of taste, as indicators of cultural capital – that the marketing strategies promise. All these are aspects of the social compact implicit in consumer culture.

But here the compact ends. In the vast majority of cases it is plausible to argue that these expectations stop short of a conviction that commodities will, in any profound sense, satisfy our deepest desires. This is not however an obstacle to continued consumption, particularly since it is combined with the happy expectation that something new is always around the corner.

This characterization is quite the opposite of the assumption that consumers are endlessly hopeful of existential fulfillment, and in this sense deeply emotionally invested in the system. However it is not without its own ambiguities. It is not quite the idea that modern consumers are simply cynical in their attitudes – because this would not account for the levels of positive engagement involved. Nor is it that consumers typically display what Georg Simmel famously described as the "blasé attitude," a relative detachment from the pleasures and novelties of consumer goods, "an incapacity to react to new sensations with the appropriate energy" ([1903] 1997: 178).

One way of making sense of it is as a condition of *reciprocally low horizons of expectation*. What this means is that the intrinsically prosaic nature of consumer goods and the transparently disingenuous nature of the claims made for them are matched by a low level of what we could call "fulfillment-demand" by consumers on the system itself.

This interpretation can make intelligible some puzzling aspects of the shift Bauman identifies from possession to appropriation. For instance, it helps explain the popular acceptability of contrived redundancy in certain consumer goods: for example, mobile (cell) phones, which have an average shelf life per model of around six months. The toleration of such examples of high-frequency obsolescence is made easier if we focus on the idea of delivery. The expectation of recurrent episodes of "delivery" corresponds to an imagination of consumption as linear rather than as punctual – as a process strung out across the individual's biography and stretching into the future. This contrasts with an imagination of possession as, as it were, an end-state of satisfaction, of imagined contentment. Understood in this context – in the light of the expected continual flow and affordability of new goods from the future – inbuilt redundancy in a product might seem less unreasonable – if not actually less objectionable in terms of the waste of resources involved.

The tolerance of contrived redundancy also serves to remind us of something which is often overlooked in the critique of consumerism: the basic human delight in novelty. This characteristic is often absorbed by critics of consumerism into the more negatively marked categories of capriciousness, faddism, and whimsy, and thence into the general idea of the manipulation of desires. But thinking about consumerism in terms of delivery recovers some of the innocence of the attraction of novelty. For a delight in new experiences is something which, of its nature, matches the repeated events of consumer delivery, and which cannot be understood in terms of enduring satisfactions. It is, of course, immensely convenient to the system demands of capitalism that such a desire exists, and there is ample scope for its exploitation. But it is by no means obviously a vicious element of the human constitution. In fact, as Karl Marx understood, it is consistent with a view of full human development ("Bildung") as constituted by the emergence of new radical needs related to the "education of the senses" (Marx 1992). Recognizing the legitimacy of the desire for novelty casts a different light on the open-ended nature of consumer demand. It serves to remind us that the model of a rational, proportionate culture of consumption against which we can criticize the irrationality and excesses of contemporary capitalism cannot be one that imagines satisfaction as some punctual end-state, as the terminus of aspiration. To consume rationally does not mean to extinguish the restlessness that is inherent in human existence.

To summarize then, the profound reach of commodification into everyday practice and experience must be counted as one of the fundamental contexts in which to understand contemporary culture. It establishes an agenda for analysis which extends beyond simple individual acts of consumption to embrace the institutionalized worldviews within which collective meaning is now constructed. High on this agenda is certainly the potential for commodification to produce a narrowing and convergence of cultural action experience: a marshaling of "what we do" into one particular form of doing it. And this is a particular worry in relation to the fate of a free public cultural sphere separate from the state and the market (Habermas 1989; Goode 2005).

But at the same time it is important not to exaggerate the commodification thesis so as to lose sight of the many areas of everyday cultural experience which escape the grip of the market: deeply-structured senses of national or ethnic identity, a whole range of activities related to religious observance, local communal activities such as amateur dramatics or music making, volunteering and charity work, the culture developed within educational contexts and institutions, and so forth. These and many other common practices are not negligible exceptions to an iron rule of market control: as they are enacted and experienced within different local contexts and traditions they produce the "thickening" of cultures (Geertz 1973) that in various ways preserves cultural distinctions and chafes against the smooth advance of a uniform capitalist culture. They are reminders that we must approach commodification – however powerful it has become in inflecting contemporary culture – as but one aspect of a complex and often contradictory "totality."

MEDIATIZATION AND THE CULTURE OF IMMEDIACY

The final context I want to consider arises from the fact that so much of modern cultural experience comes to us in mediatized form. I use the rather ungainly term "mediatized" to distinguish this process from the more general process of mediation. All cultural experience is mediated, if we mean by this that it is given to human beings through the symbolic orders of language and other representational systems. Mediatization points us to the increasing implication of electronic communications and media systems in the delivery of culture.

This context is, of course, a wide one, raising a range of different issues and levels of analysis. Amongst these, the ones that have received most attention within the field of media studies are: the institutional structures of the media; its political economy; the professional practices and informing ideologies of its practitioners; its relationship to the political process; its technological ramifications; and the analysis of the impact of media "texts" on consumers and audiences. But here I shall focus on a more general question: how should we regard the influence of mediatization itself – as a distinct *modality* of everyday popular-cultural engagement?

Consider then the range of commonplace mediatized practices and experiences: watching television, films or DVDs; typing, scrolling, clicking, browsing, and gaming at the computer screen; talking, texting, sending and receiving emails and pictures on a mobile (cell) phone. What unites these various activities is that they are all historically new ways in which representations are configured, and experience presented to consciousness. They occupy a space in the everyday flow of experience within the individual's life-world that is distinct, yet fully integrated with face-to-face interactions of physical proximity, and with the routine mobility of modern cultures.

Mediatized practices and experiences are now so much a taken-for-granted aspect of everyday life in developed societies that they can appear almost transparent. Yet once we "make strange" these familiar aspects of the social-technological interface, they are revealed in all their complexity and variety. Consider the differences between these three everyday activities: the communal family viewing of a TV serial; the focused attention of web-searching; the interruption of a face-to-face conversation as one person breaks off to answer their mobile (cell) phone. Each of these utterly mundane occurrences re-orders the cultural environment of the participants in quite different ways. In the first example, it introduces a sort of imaginary "annex" to domestic life – a world of familiar characters whose lives we track almost as intimates within our living rooms. In the second, it involves a summoning of infinite presence: a sense of the ubiquity of the world's resources gathered and laid out for our instant attention. And in the third, it dissolves assumptions of priority given to corporeal presence in social interactions. None of these experiences have any counterpart beyond the last few decades of world history, and each of them helps to define what it is to exist as a social being in the modern world.

Mediatization thus establishes a crucial agenda for cultural analysis in (at least) the following terms: the transformations which ubiquitous media technologies produce in our experience and interaction in time and space; the implications of this transformation for our emotional sensibilities and perhaps the extension of our ethical horizons; the significance of this transformation for debates about the cultural and political public spheres.

There is not space here to begin to explore this broad agenda. (For some interesting recent interventions, see Morley 2007; van Loon 2007; Dreyfus 2008.) Instead I shall conclude by raising one issue that has perhaps received too little attention within cultural analysis. This is the contribution which routine mediatization makes to the general acceleration of the pace of life in modern cultures. To approach this I shall employ the idea of "immediacy" (Tomlinson 2007a). The attraction of this term is that it has two related meanings which between them have particular relevance to the accelerating properties of media technologies.

First, in relation to *time*, immediacy means, "occurring without delay or lapse in time; instant." This connotes ideas of the acceleration of the pace of life and a culture of instantaneity, adapted and accustomed to the rapid delivery of goods and (particularly) information. And underpinning this, a capitalist economy and an associated work and consumption culture geared not just to sustaining, but to constantly increasing this tempo of life (Agger 1989; Brennan 2003).

And secondly, in relation to *space*, it means "proximate, nearest, close" – implying a sense of directness, of cultural *proximity*. Etymologically this is actually the primary sense: from the Latin "immediatus," "not separated." So immediacy suggests not just an acceleration in the pace of everyday life, but a distinct *quality* to the resulting cultural experience. What is central to this shift in the "texture" of culture is an increasing routine connectedness both with other people and with the access points (increasingly now, websites) of the institutions that afford and govern modern social existence. As daily life becomes increasingly saturated in communicational practices and increasingly dependent on the ubiquitous availability, via electronic media, of informational and human resources, so the pace of life seems inexorably to increase.

There may be a temptation for cultural critics to read in this process various elements of cultural degradation or even pathology: to view contemporary mediatized culture – particularly in its prevalent commodified form – as impatient with the values of endurance and commitment of time, dominated by the obsessive pursuit of rapidly shifting sensations and instant gratification. Indeed recent years have seen the emergence of a globally spread social movement – the "slow movement" – based precisely in the perception of the need to decelerate technologically driven culture (Eriksen 2001; Honoré 2004).

But it is wise not to rush to judgment. It may be that we are witnessing in the emergence of "immediacy" a cultural sensibility that is quite new, not easily accommodated to traditional understandings of the speed of events and processes, and thus not yielding to interpretation in terms of familiar values. The cultural interpretations of speed that we have been accustomed to until quite recently draw on some of the core themes and values of industrial modernity, in particular, functional rationality, social regulation, the idea of progress, the emancipatory potential of machine power, and the "heroic" nature of human effort and endeavor in the control of the natural world – particularly in the overcoming of distance. But we now inhabit a different era of modernity and there is some doubt that these themes and values speak to our present accelerating cultural condition.

The concept of immediacy offers us a different approach both to the lived experience of mediatized speed and to the values by which we can judge it. Most specifically it grasps a cultural contrast that Zygmunt Bauman (2000, 2005) has famously made between the hard, heavy "solid" modernity of the era of machine technology and the lightness and fluidity of contemporary "liquid modernity." The technologies of communication through which we now routinely interact seem central to the constitution of liquid modernity. They create a *modality* of experience characterized by a general lightness, effortlessness, and ubiquity of contact, which seems to be quite distinct from the serious purposiveness of mechanically accomplished speed.

This experience derives from reiterated communicational routines which are at the same time cognitive-communicational and *bodily* practices – linking representations on screens to the touch on keyboards, keypads, and handsets. These manipulations are deft and smoothly choreographed into our working (and playing) rhythms, seeming almost less physical operations than gestures. And this lightness of touch is closely associated with the perception of immediate and ubiquitous access to the world. Information, consumer goods – people themselves – appear to be constantly and immediately available – summoned simply by the lightest pressure on a keypad. This association of physical lightness and effortlessness in the operation of media technologies with a tacit assumption of the instant and constant availability of things and people – of a world, as it were, waiting to be accessed – is characteristic of the experience of immediacy.

But this perceived ubiquity – what Paul Virilio has called "the *generalized arrival of data*" (Virilio 1997: 56) – has entailments that cannot be grasped merely in terms of a critique of the shallowness of popular cultural practices or anxieties over diminishing attention spans in children. The coming of cultural immediacy also brings with it all manner of new demands and obligations: for example the assumption – structured into both the work process and wider social etiquette – that we all as citizens have a social *obligation* to be skilled users of media technologies. And more than this, that we should be almost constantly *accessible* as social actors – available, that is, for communicational purposes and desires of others.

Most significantly, the condition of immediacy confronts us with a world in which some of the core ontological assumptions of social life seem to begin to dissolve: the constraints of situated embodiment, the concrete realities of physical distance, the disciplines of time. And along with these, a set of stable distinctions that up until now have provided the underpinnings of cultural value: the distinctions between here and elsewhere, now and later, desire and its fulfillment.

One of the major challenges facing cultural analysis today, then, is to come to terms with this sudden and dramatic eclipse of these profound implicit cultural parameters, and to explore what is replacing them in the collective cultural narratives through which people render their existence meaningful.

A final thought. In sketching these three contexts for contemporary cultural analysis – the impact of globalization, the consolidated reach of commodification into virtually every aspect of public and private life, and the profound re-ordering of cultural experience presented by ubiquitous mediatization – we are describing a world which would have been – in some of its aspects at least – only at the margins of imagination for the readers of *Cultural Analysis* less than 30 years ago. This suggests a final requirement for contemporary cultural analysis and critique: that it be constantly tuned to the rapidity of cultural change and reflexively supple in the generation of its interpretations and conceptualizations. As William Connolly puts it: "it becomes wise to fold the expectation of surprise and the unexpected into the very fabric of our explanatory theories, interpretative schemes . . . and ethical sensibilities. And to work on ourselves subtly to overcome existential resentment of these expectations" (Connolly 2002: 145).

References

Agger, B. (1989) *Fast Capitalism*. Urbana, IL: University of Illinois Press.
Bauman, Z. (2000) *Liquid Modernity*. Cambridge: Polity Press.
Bauman, Z. (2005) *Liquid Life*. Cambridge: Polity Press.
Beck, U. (2000) *What Is Globalization?* Cambridge: Polity Press.
Beck, U. (2002) "The Cosmopolitan Society and Its Enemies." In M. Featherstone, H. Patomäki, J. Tomlinson, and C. Venn (eds.), *Theory, Culture and Society: Special Issue on Cosmopolis* 19(1–2): 17–44.
Beck, U. (2005) *Power in the Global Age*. Cambridge: Polity Press.

Beck, U. (2006) *Cosmopolitan Vision*. Cambridge: Polity Press.

Beck, U., N. Sznaider, and R. Winter (2003) *Global America?* Liverpool: University of Liverpool Press.

Brennan, Teresa (2003) *Globalization and Its Terrors: Daily Life in the West*. London: Routledge.

Castells, M. (1996) *The Rise of the Network Society*. Oxford: Blackwell.

Chaney, D. (1994) *The Cultural Turn*. London: Routledge.

Cheah, P. and B. Robbins (eds.) (1998) *Cosmopolitics: Thinking and Feeling Beyond the Nation*. Minneapolis: University of Minnesota Press.

Connolly, William (2002) *Neuropolitics: Thinking, Culture, Speed*. Minneapolis: University of Minnesota Press.

Cowen, Tyler (2002) *Creative Destruction: How Globalization Is Changing the World's Cultures*. Princeton: Princeton University Press.

Crystal, D. (2000) *Language Death*. Cambridge: Cambridge University Press.

Dreyfus, H. (2008) *On the Internet*, 2nd edn. London: Routledge.

Eagleton, T. (2000) *The Idea of Culture*. Oxford: Blackwell.

Eriksen, Thomas Hylland (2001) *Tyranny of the Moment*. London: Pluto Press.

Featherstone, M. (2007) *Consumer Culture and Postmodernism*, 2nd edn. London: Sage.

Foucault, M. (1981) "The Order of Discourse." In R. Young (ed.), *Untying the Text*. London: Routledge and Kegan Paul, pp. 48–78.

Fromm, Erich (1955) *The Sane Society*. London: Routledge and Kegan Paul.

Garcia Canclini, N. (1995) *Hybrid Cultures: Strategies for Entering and Leaving Modernity*. Minneapolis: University of Minnesota Press.

Geertz, C. (1973) *The Interpretation of Cultures*. New York: Basic Books.

Giddens, A. (1990) *The Consequences of Modernity*. Cambridge: Polity Press.

Goode, L. (2005) *Jürgen Habermas: Democracy and the Public Sphere*. London: Pluto Press.

Habermas, J. (1989) *The Structural Transformation of the Public Sphere*. Cambridge: Polity Press.

Hall, S., D. Hobson, A. Lowe, and P. Willis (eds.) (1980) *Culture, Media and Language*. Centre for Contemporary Cultural Studies. London: Unwin-Hyman.

Held, D. and A. McGrew (eds.) (2007) *Globalization Theory: Approaches and Controversies*. Cambridge: Polity Press.

Held, D., A. McGrew, D. Goldblatt, and J. Perraton (eds.) (1999) *Global Transformations*. Cambridge: Polity Press.

Honoré, Carl (2004) *In Praise of Slow*. London: Orion Books.

Inglis, F. (2004) *Culture*. Cambridge: Polity Press.

Jameson, F. (1998) *The Cultural Turn: Selected Writings on the Postmodern 1983–1998*. London: Verso.

Lipovetsky, Gilles (2005) *Hypermodern Times*. Cambridge: Polity Press.

Lull, J. (2000) *Media, Communication, Culture: A Global Approach*. Cambridge: Polity Press.

Marcuse, Herbert (1964) *One Dimensional Man*. London: Abacus.

Marx, Karl (1992) *Early Writings*. Harmondsworth: Penguin.

Miller, Daniel, Peter Jackson, Nigel Thrift, Beverley Holbrook, and Michael Rowlands (1998) *Shopping, Place and Identity*. London: Routledge.

Moore, H. L. (2008) "The Problem of Culture." In David Held and Henrietta Moore (eds.), *Cultural Politics in a Global Age: Uncertainty, Solidarity and Innovation*. Oxford: Oneworld Publications, pp. 21–8.

Morley, D. (2007) *Media, Modernity and Technology*. London: Routledge.

Nettle, D. and S. Romaine (2000) *Vanishing Voices: The Extinction of the World's Languages*. New York: Oxford University Press.

Norris, P. and R. Inglehardt (2009) *Cosmopolitan Communications: Cultural Diversity in a Globalized World*. New York: Cambridge University Press.

Ray, L. and A. Sayer (1999) *Culture and Economy After the Cultural Turn*. London: Sage.

Rettberg, J. W. (2008) *Blogging*. Cambridge: Polity Press.

Ritzer, George (2001) *Explorations in the Sociology of Consumption: Fast Food, Credit Cards and Casinos*. London: Sage.

Rojek, Chris (2000) *Leisure and Culture*. London: Macmillan.

Simmel, Georg ([1903] 1997) "The Metropolis and Mental Life." In David Frisby and Mike Featherstone (eds.), *Simmel on Culture*. London: Sage, pp. 174–85.

Slater, Don (1997) *Consumer Culture and Modernity*. Cambridge: Polity Press.

Thompson, J. B. (1995) *The Media and Modernity*. Cambridge: Polity Press.

Tomlinson, J. (1991) *Cultural Imperialism: A Critical Introduction*. London: Cassell.

Tomlinson, J. (1999) *Globalization and Culture*. Cambridge: Polity Press.

Tomlinson, J. (2002) "Interests and Identities in Cosmopolitan Politics." In S. Vertovek and R. Cohen (eds.), *Conceiving Cosmopolitanism*. Oxford: Oxford University Press, pp. 240–53.

Tomlinson, J. (2003) "Globalization and Cultural Identity." In D. Held and A. McGrew (eds.), *The Global Transformations Reader*, 2nd edn. Cambridge: Polity Press, pp. 269–78.

Tomlinson, J. (2007a) *The Culture of Speed: The Coming of Immediacy*. London: Sage.

Tomlinson, J. (2007b) "Globalization and Cultural Analysis." In D. Held and A. McGrew (eds.), *Globalization Theory: Approaches and Controversies*. Cambridge: Polity Press, pp. 148–68.

UNDP (2004) *Human Development Report: Cultural Liberty in Today's Diverse World*. New York: United Nations Development Programme.

UNESCO (2000) *World Cultural Report: Cultural Diversity, Conflict and Pluralism*. Paris: UNESCO Publishing.

UNESCO (2009) *World Cultural Report: Investing in Cultural Diversity and International Dialogue*. Paris: UNESCO Publishing.

Urry, J. (2003) *Global Complexity*. Cambridge: Polity Press.

Van Loon, J. (2007) *Media Technologies: Critical Perspectives*. London: Open University Press.

Vertovek, S. and R. Cohen (eds.) (2002) *Conceiving Cosmopolitanism*. Oxford: Oxford University Press.

Virilio, Paul (1997) *Open Sky*. London: Verso.

Warde, Alan (2002) "Setting the Scene: Changing Conceptions of Consumption." In Steven Miles, Alison Anderson, and Kevin Meethan (eds.), *The Changing Consumer: Markets and Meanings*. London: Routledge, pp. 10–24.

Williams, R. (1981) *Culture*. London: Fontana.

Wuthnow, R., J. Davidson Hunter, A. Bergesen, and E. Kurzweil (1984) *Cultural Analysis*. London: Routledge and Kegan Paul.

11

The Changing Life Course

ANGELA M. O'RAND

The life course is changing across advanced and developing societies. Observable demographic shifts and institutional responses to globalization pressures are interacting to reconstruct the life course. Increased life expectancy, declining fertility, and the growing variability in the timing of education, family, and work patterns are challenging the (Western) sequential, age-graded conception of the life course, including its gendered differentiation, on which institutional arrangements have been predicated. Simultaneously, globalization pressures are impelling state and market institutions in late industrial and developing societies to reconsider, and renegotiate, their *social contracts*. The directions of these changes are strongly influenced by globalizing market forces and international governmental bodies, but also conditioned by the unique and distinctive histories of these contracts across countries, and thus preclude any near-term convergence across systems of policy changes. A product of these changes across societies – although to varying degrees – is increased economic inequality across the life span and a growing destandardization of the life course. As such, the life course and the welfare state are *interdependent works in progress*.

This chapter will first summarize the basic elements of the life course perspective which include key principles and mechanisms that organize lives over time. Then, the chapter will examine the life course implications of the dynamic and interdependent relationships between demographic changes, such as population aging and changing household structures, and recent and proposed shifts in the mix of market and state institutions that shape the life course in the twenty-first century, including

The Wiley-Blackwell Companion to Sociology, First Edition. Edited by George Ritzer.
© 2012 Blackwell Publishing Ltd. Published 2012 by Blackwell Publishing Ltd.

the shift across countries towards market solutions for social welfare problems. This intersection is serving to de-standardize the life course and to contribute to growing inequalities within and across cohorts.

The Life Course Perspective

The life course perspective is concerned with the intersection of biography and history (Mortimer & Shanahan 2005; Elder & Shanahan 2006). Biographies are variable sequences of social statuses and life conditions across the life span, some of which are correlated with age. History can influence biography by interrupting, delaying, precluding, or providing new opportunities for social transitions. And biography can filter the experience of history depending on the phase of the life course (or age) when individuals encounter historical events. Accordingly, the life course perspective examines life transitions and trajectories and the social circumstances that condition them, including life transitions experienced earlier in the life span as well as present personal and historical circumstances. The life course is a lifelong cumulative, multiplex process from birth to death, making life transitions in nearly any domain at risk across the life span.

Figure 11.1 adapts Riley and Riley's original model of the shift from an age-differentiated to an age-integrated life course (Riley, Kahn & Foner 1994). The figure is an expansion of that model. On the left is the standard (industrial)

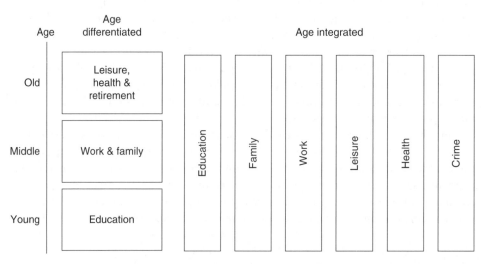

Figure 11.1 Expanded version of the Riley and Riley (1994) model of the changing life course
Note: The chart includes crime as a life domain. This is included here because in the United States a significant minority of the population is incarcerated, especially young men, and the life course implications of this are considerable (O'Rand 2007). Riley and Riley referred only to education, work, and leisure (Riley, Kahn & Foner 1994).

tri-phasic life course; on the right is a more age-integrated life course which depicts lifelong risks for transitions across life domains (Crosnoe & Elder 2004). It is cumulative insofar as earlier life circumstances constrain or bolster later circumstances. It is multiplex because transitions in one life domain such as education, family, work, or health can influence transitions in other domains. And, while some life transitions are highly correlated with age (e.g., education and retirement), changing historical conditions and demographic patterns are diminishing the correlations of specific life transitions such that transitions in all domains can occur across ages, and do. Riley and her colleagues argued that social policies are "lagging" behind demographic changes which include less age-differentiated behaviors over the life span. Population aging is accompanied by delays in the onset of functional limitations and disabilities – thus permitting individuals to sustain productive working lives well into their seventies. Transitions can occur across domains from life until death as a result of longer lives, changing historical conditions, and variable individual options spanning the life course. For example, education is no longer restricted exclusively to youth in the US and elsewhere. Formal education continues well into adulthood as some adults return to schooling to meet changing labor market conditions (Bernhardt, Morris, Handcock & Scott 2001) and in response to job insecurity or changing life circumstances such as divorce (Elman & O'Rand 2004). Similarly, family transitions can occur across the life span not just in midlife, with transitions observable among youth in cases of teenage pregnancy at younger and younger ages (McLanahan 2004), and among older populations as grandparents rear their grandchildren (Burton, Welsh & Destro, forthcoming) and reproductive technologies enable older women to conceive and give birth (Richards 2004).

The principles regulating these processes have been elaborated over the last 50 years, most extensively by the work of Glen H. Elder, Jr. and his colleagues (see Shanahan and Macmillan (2008) for an exhaustive review of this body of work). These principles identify how biography and history intersect and how biographies develop over time.

Historical time and place

The life course is organized differently across historical periods and geopolitical spaces. The life course depicted in the left panel of Figure 11.1 is probably most closely associated with industrial societies in which educational, employment, and familial institutions structure social transitions in an age-graded sequence. In post-industrial societies, social transitions are less age-graded and less normatively regulated, in part in response to globalization processes.

Situational imperatives

New situations can constrain individual options and alter the courses of lives. For example, the compelling severity of a large-scale event such as an economic depression or war, or of a disruptive proximate event such as severe illness, job loss, or incarceration, reorients the life course. The classic research study in this vein was Glen Elder's *Children of the Great Depression* (1974).

Life stage

The effects of an event depend on the age or phase of life of the individual. Social change or adverse events have enduring impact on those in vulnerable or transitional periods in life such as childhood or the transition to adulthood. This idea can be traced to Ryder's (1965) classic essay on cohorts and social change, which emphasized the impact of historical change on young populations entering adulthood. Elder's (1987) comparison of two cohorts' encounters with mobilization in World War II illustrates how the effects of mobilization were more disruptive of the lives of men who had already entered adult roles as fathers and workers than of their younger counterparts.

Linked lives

Social ties diffuse experiences such that the effects of these experiences are felt not only by those with direct exposure to them, but also by their families and associates. The experience of unemployment impacts families as well as individual workers. Elder's collaborative studies of the impact of the Midwestern farm crisis in the 1980s on rural families show how the crisis affected children indirectly through the experiences and coping styles of their parents (Elder & Conger 2000).

Agency

Individuals seek to manage their life circumstances and their biographies in an ongoing fashion. Disruptive life events present challenges and induce efforts to regain control. Social contexts can enable or disable action orientations, and the phase of life in the biography can define the salience of certain actions. An example of this process is identified in analyses of the Stanford-Terman data (drawn from a sample of gifted children born between 1900 and 1920 who were followed until the late 1970s and repeatedly queried about changes in their lives and political attitudes and identities), in which early planful actions in the life course were most influential on later achievements (Shanahan & Elder 2002), controlling for intervening actions and decisions.

Accentuation

Long-term habits and behavioral patterns are amplified in the context of social change, life transitions, or stressful life events. Individuals select environments that match their preferences and personal attributes, which in turn amplify their preferences and reinforce their attributes (Elder & Caspi 1990). The famous Bennington follow-up study identified this pattern among women whose college choice reflected preferences which became more pronounced through interactions with their similarly oriented peers; later these women married spouses with similar preferences (Alwin, Cohen & Newcomb 1991).

Varieties of time are central to these processes. *Biographical time*, measured as age and the timing, duration, and sequencing of life statuses or roles, and *historical time*, measured as events or periods with salient, though differential, social impact on lives, constitute the primary framework for life course research. *Age*, *period*, and *cohort* represent these varieties of time. Cohort lies at the intersection of biography (age or life phase) and history (period), since it refers to subgroups of the population who experience a particular event or live through a distinctive historical period at the same time in their lives. Persons born at the same time constitute a birth cohort (Hughes & O'Rand 2004). So, for example, members of the US baby boom cohort born between 1946 and 1964 have encountered historical events like the Vietnam War in young adulthood (for older baby boomers), and the economic crisis of 2008–10 in middle to late middle age, with presumably shared experiences and biographical consequences unlike those of other age groups at these times.

The varieties of time encompassing the life course perspective have distinctive general analytical requirements. Mayer (2009: 414) identifies three of these general requirements: (1) changes in human lives should be considered over long stretches of lifetime rather than limited to single transitions or shorter phases of biographies; (2) changes in human lives should be compared across multiple cohorts (synthetic and otherwise); and (3) changes in lives should be studied across domains, such as those identified in Figure 11.1 above.

Mayer also argues that comparisons across space (geographic or institutional context) are as important as those across time. Diverse macro cultural, institutional, and structural contexts that may coincide in historical time may nevertheless put different constraints on individual resources, opportunities, and preferences. Hence, for example, across countries or regions, diverse welfare institutions, educational opportunity structures, market environments, and ethnic/religious mixes can coexist in the same historical periods, with different effects on life courses. Meso-level contexts also affect biographies; families, couples, and cohorts influence individual resources, opportunities, and preferences. Along this line, Mayer adds that the intersection of time and context makes life course research particularly valuable for policy change and interventions of diverse kinds.

The next section of this chapter will examine the demographic and structural trends of the past three to four decades which have led to what some have referred to as the "individualization" or the "de-standardization" of the life course. These characterizations reflect the longitudinal and contextual observations, advocated by Mayer (2009) above, which have shown more diversity in biographies than the older age-graded conception of the life course afforded.

DEMOGRAPHIC CONTEXTS OF THE CHANGING LIFE COURSE

The de-standardization of the life course is driven by the weakening of the association of age with numerous life transitions. It is also a complex process wherein the decline of age-grading is associated with the interdependence of life transitions across domains. As stated earlier, the timing of educational, marital, work, health, and other transitions is a cumulative, manifold process: changes in one domain can produce changes in others. And, as men and women experience more individualized transitions across the life course, gender differentiation becomes less important. The tri-phasic life course was largely predicated on a traditional division of labor among men and women, i.e., on a breadwinner family model. This model is in decline across countries as women and men experience transitions in educational, familial, and labor market institutions across their lives following diverse schedules.

Demographic trends

Long-term and recent demographic trends have contributed to the changing life course. The long-developing demographic transition associated with declining fertility and mortality has spread to the developing world. In advanced countries, fertility has fallen below replacement levels and has been accompanied by declining mortality and increased life expectancies. The median age in the developed world is approximately 37 years, up from 29 years in 1950 (Bongaarts 2004).

An increase in "healthy" or active life expectancies – i.e., years free of disability over the life span – has also accompanied mortality declines (Land, Guralnik & Blazer 1994). Studies tracking multiple cohorts have documented this trend. Yang and Lee (2009) use the Americans' Changing Lives dataset to track inter- and intra-cohort changes in trajectories of disability, self-assessed poor health, and depressive symptoms over 15 years. They find declining levels of disability and self-assessed poor health across successive cohorts and narrowing disparities within cohorts by sex and race. However, they also observe the opposite patterns in depressive symptoms; that is, these symptoms increase across successive cohorts, and sex and race disparities widen within successive cohorts.

The identification of these cohort patterns in this study and others (e.g., Lynch 2003; House, Lantz & Herd 2005) provides two insights to the changing life course. The first is that better health across the life course may increase the options available to individuals in their day-to-day decisions. Healthy life expectancies with lower probabilities of the onset of disabilities across the life course enable life activities over the life span across domains, including education, work, family, and leisure, and permit their extension into later years. However, not all health outcomes over the life course have improved. Yang and Lee (2009) observe trends in depressive symptoms to be increasing, and increasing more among disadvantaged groups (nonwhites and women). Others have observed similar trends in disparities in depression (Kasen, Cohen, Chen & Castille 2003), smoking (Pampel 2005), and obesity (Flegal, Carroll, Ogden & Johnson 2002), with consequences for life course trajectories, including the timing of mortality (Land, Guralnik & Blazer 1994), and for the sense of well-being with age, including the prevalence of happiness across groups (Yang 2008).

This second set of findings provides the insight that inequalities in health over the life course constrain the life activities and sense of well-being of some social groups and lead to diverging life course trajectories. A very large and growing literature on the relationship between socioeconomic factors and health replicates a robust relationship between these two variables (e.g., Lynch 2003; House, Lantz & Herd 2005). This seemingly persistent association has raised questions regarding the relative importance of selection versus causation over time; the specific puzzle has been whether health selects individuals into socioeconomic statuses, or socioeconomic factors condition health. An exemplary study in this literature uses the panel from the Wisconsin Longitudinal Study followed between adolescence in 1957 and retirement age in 2005 (Warren 2009). This analysis examines self-assessed health, musculoskeletal disease, and depression over this extended period and finds that socioeconomic factors have a causal relationship to health at multiple points in the life course.

Another repeated observation, however, is that serious illness and economic adversity in childhood have long-term negative impacts on both socio-economic and health outcomes throughout the subsequent life course (Palloni 2006; O'Rand, Hamil-Luker & Elman 2009). A recent analysis using the Health and Retirement Study, based on a panel aged 51 to 61 in 1992 and followed until 2002, reports that poor childhood health and economic adversity (based on retrospective accounts) predict higher rates of growth in functional limitations in this aging cohort (Haas 2008). Using the same panel, followed until 2002, Hamil-Luker and O'Rand (2007) find that women experiencing illness and adversity in childhood have elevated risks for heart attack in later adulthood. The mechanisms driving these observations are not fully established. Some biological theories argue that long-term health outcomes can be traced to conditions as early as those found *in utero* which constrain hardiness at birth (e.g., birth weight, head circumference, etc.), subsequent development in childhood, and resilience in adulthood (Barker 1998). Recent research on gene–environment interactions in childhood finds that biological and social environments probably interact in fateful ways to influence development and long-term well-being. In this line of studies, Guo and his colleagues (Guo, Roettger & Cai 2008) use the Add Health data to examine such interactions and find, specifically, that genes related to risky (adolescent) behaviors can be "turned off" with effective parenting in early life.

The second demographic transition

Besides the long-term decline in mortality and increased active life expectancy, another demographic shift is influencing the structure of the life course by introducing diverse environments that create social inequalities. The "second demographic transition" refers to patterns emerging over the past four decades which are de-standardizing family and work role sequences that prevailed in the mid-twentieth century (Lesthaeghe 1995). The postponement of marriage and first births, the increase of childbearing outside of marriage, the increase in divorce rates, and the increase in the proportions of the never-married are among the demographic drivers of population aging (Kinsella and Phillips 2005) and have emerged so dramatically as to be identified by some scholars as constituting a new transition. These patterns have introduced complex heterogeneity in the organization of the life courses of men and women alike. In many respects, men's and women's lives are becoming more alike – with more extended educational careers, longer but interrupted labor market careers, and more compressed family (childrearing) careers than observed in preceding cohorts.

Sweeney (2002) argues that the gender-specific life course has changed primarily because the economic foundations of marriage have shifted. Both genders approach marriage in terms of its affordability and the resources that potential partners bring to such a union. Women's market values are as important as men's. And, in the absence of incentives to support a traditional breadwinner arrangement (especially in the US), women are motivated to remain relatively independent as a result of prolonged education, sustained labor market participation, the technological control of fertility, and the cultural acceptability of cohabitation and other nonstandard household structures.

However, these major trends interact with class and race origins in the US to produce two distinct intergenerational trajectories of parenting in the US which are amplifying patterns of social inheritance (McLanahan 2004). The first consists of patterns of delayed childbearing among women with higher levels of education, market employment, and marriage (and educationally homogamous marriage besides). These resources, which translate into money and time for children, afford their offspring greater advantages in the attainment of higher education, social skills and social capital, and other benefits (such as better health). The second trajectory is defined by patterns of lower educational attainment among women with higher rates of divorce and non-marital childbearing. This is a more disadvantageous parenting sequence that produces fewer resources, and the continuing risk of loss of resources. It reproduces poverty across generations.

Recent research suggests that marital status (marriage) probably matters more than gender in all aspects of inequality in the US. While women's well-being has improved across cohorts, the inequality among women has increased dramatically. Race, educational and occupational differences, and wage mobility are implicated in this respect. But marital histories are even more important. Patterns of marital homogamy coupled with spreading divorce rates stratify women's fortunes. Married-couple households have higher incomes and greater wealth, leading some to argue that marriage itself is becoming a class phenomenon in the US (Sweeney 2002). This trend accelerated after the 1960s, propelled first by the baby boom cohorts and sustained by later cohorts until well into the 1990s (Hughes & O'Rand 2004).

The extended educational career

The second demographic transition involves a wider range of changes than fertility and (non)marriage and divorce patterns which are weakening the age-based and gender-differentiated institutionalization of the life course. Educational careers are also changing. They do not end in late adolescence for a growing proportion of the population, especially in the US where secondary and post-secondary education is relatively more accessible to adults than in other countries. The extension of the educational career has occurred for men and women alike. Its effects have not only been to delay marriage and fertility among young adults; it has also become tightly coupled to employment stability in later adulthood in advanced industrial countries. The ascendance of the so-called "college premium" (the employment and wage advantages conferred by college degrees) in the US in the 1990s explains a significant share of the surge in job mobility, underemployment, and wage inequality (Bernhardt, Morris, Handcock & Scott 2001).

A non-trivial proportion of US men and women in recent cohorts have enrolled at successively increasing rates in post-secondary educational institutions after the age of 30 for mostly work-related reasons (Elman & O'Rand 2004). Yet, nearly all sociological research presumes that "years of schooling" measures an age-bound life phase that ends by young adulthood. By 2000 over 40 percent of college students were over the age of 24, more than twice the rate in 1980. But if all kinds of post-secondary schooling are considered, including junior colleges, vocational/technical schools, business and nursing schools, four-year colleges, and graduate/professional schools, a much larger proportion of adults are enrolled. A recent study by O'Rand, Hamil-Luker, and Elman (2009) uses the National Survey of Families and Households to track the educational careers of those aged 30 and older in 1987–8 until 2001–3. They estimate the probability of enrollment in all post-secondary institutions (listed above) by age. Enrollment is defined as enrollment in more than two courses or attendance for six weeks or more. They find that approximately 10 percent of adults aged 25–39 are enrolled in college, with an increase to 14 percent of those in their forties; 6 percent of adults aged between 25 and 49 are enrolled in graduate/professional schools. Approximately 8 percent of adults between the ages of 25 and 49 are enrolled in junior colleges. And another 6 to 7 percent of adults aged 25–49 are enrolled in business, nursing, and vocational/technical schools. Finally, approximately 15 percent of adults aged 49–59 are enrolled in some kind of post-secondary institution.

Clearly, educational participation is not strictly age-graded. Given available educational resources, adults return to school not only to complete unfinished degrees but to begin new degree or credential programs. They return primarily for job-related reasons and usually in response to a change in their lives such as job loss (or feared job loss), divorce, empty nest, and other transitions (Elman & O'Rand 2004). Hence, the educational career in the US is an exemplar of the changing life course. It spans the life course through adulthood and it is intertwined with other life domains.

Another notable recent trend contributing to the changing life course is the gender gap in college completion which favors women both in the US and in Europe. Women are completing college at higher rates than men in Western countries. DiPrete and Buchmann (2006) argue that this is occurring because women need these degrees more for labor market reasons, because the occupations and employment contexts that they aspire to require these credentials and because they perceive that the gender earnings gap can only be eased with these credentials. As such, between-gender differences in educational attainment are disappearing while within-gender differences are translating into class differences as marriage rates are higher among the most highly educated and as married partners tend to be at similar educational levels (Sweeney 2002).

SOCIAL CONTRACTS AND THE DEVOLUTION OF RISK

Social contracts refer to diverse national systems of interconnected state, market, and civil institutions that have developed since the nineteenth century to maintain economic and political stability (O'Rand, Isaacs & Roth 2009). They are based on varying levels of risk pooling and risk sharing to protect against individual life course risks related to educational attainment, income maintenance, health declines, and family stability. They are the result of the taxing and borrowing authority of the state. They are reflected in diverse welfare systems that define social and citizenship rights to education, health insurance, income insurance, and social retirement across countries.

The most popularly applied typology of these systems is Esping-Andersen's (1999) welfare states typology, including the liberal, corporatist, and social democratic models. The liberal model privileges market institutions and private mechanisms for individual security. Public programs serve a residual role, as safety nets beneath the market system. Anglo-American countries subscribe to this model, though their respective systems may vary with regard to specific policies related to public educational subsidies, support of dependent families, and retirement timing and benefits (O'Rand & Hamil-Luker, forthcoming). The corporatist model partitions social rights along institutional lines that preserve boundaries between market (occupational and sectoral) and familial institutions. This model is found in continental Europe, in countries such as Germany, the Netherlands, and France. The social democratic model of the Nordic states places citizenship first as the basis of social rights and entitlements, intervenes in the market through wage and active employment policies, and has the most extensive system of family support with gender-neutral policies.

Developing countries are adapting different aspects of these primary models. Some strong developing states, primarily located on the Pacific Rim, directly support national industries with subsidization and tariff protection and the construction of educational and familial systems to fit with economic development projects. Former Soviet socialist states (post-Soviet Eastern Europe and Asia) are undergoing rapid transformations in the direction of liberal reforms, adopting selected privatized and individualized insurance policies that follow the guidelines of the World Bank and other international organizations on which they depend for international credit (Bonoli 2003). And, some Latin American countries are adopting liberal reforms following World Bank guidelines (World Bank 1994). Chile, specifically, led the way with the implementation of mandatory individual retirement accounts. The Chilean model has diffused throughout the region (Sinha 2000).

Globalization processes and population aging are challenging all forms of welfare states (Bonoli 2003). Globalization has reorganized the production process to distribute capital and work beyond national borders. Multinational enterprises seek younger, cheaper labor forces, found principally in developing countries. This increases unemployment and underemployment in advanced countries. Some implications of globalization processes for the life course include the growth of job insecurity in advanced countries which, in turn, affects family stability and the demand for higher educational credentials in order to return to, or remain secure in, employment. Population aging also challenges all forms of the welfare state, as the ratio of retirees to workers shrinks, not only because of aging *per se* but also because of growing job insecurity among working-age populations in advanced countries (Bongaarts 2004; O'Rand & Hamil-Luker, forthcoming).

Welfare state reform across the world is moving in the direction of a more privatized and individualized system, closer to the liberal Anglo-American model (O'Rand, Ebel & Isaacs 2009). The shift is away from risk sharing to individualized risk – towards *the devolution of risk* (O'Rand 2003, 2006). This is currently and most publicly challenging social retirement systems, which cannot sustain their policies. The World Bank's (1994) three-pillar model of public sector (PAYGO – pay as you go), occupational sector, and private individual sector foundations for the support of retirement has more and more countries shifting away from traditional PAYGO plans to more privatized individualized savings schema for which individuals and their families are more and more responsible. These shifts also apply to health insurance systems which are under attack for similar reasons besides their accelerating costs.

The US has one of the most liberal models of retirement and health insurance coverage. It has moved rapidly since the 1970s towards individual savings for retirement, reflected in the replacement of traditional defined benefit pensions (DB) by defined contribution (DC) pensions (O'Rand, Ebel & Isaacs 2009). The former were developed and negotiated over the twentieth century by employers and unions to maintain stable workforces and to regulate retirement ages through incentives in the form of specific benefits payable for life. But, globalization and population aging have led employers to retreat from DB plans and embrace DC plans.

Defined contribution (DC) plans are quite different. They are investment accounts to which workers and (some) employers contribute. Their portability across employers, the loan options they offer, and their tax shelter component all appeal to workers. But, they assign the responsibility to workers to decide among investment options – company stocks and mutual funds of stocks and bonds that can be invested in an array of markets ranging from real-estate to emerging markets elsewhere in the world. At the time of retirement, workers then must often decide whether the balances of these accounts should be paid out as lump sums or following variable or fixed (or mixed) annuity arrangements.

The DC plans have come to be associated with delayed or interrupted retirement at the start of the twenty-first century (Quinn 1997). A new trend labeled "unretirement" is growing (Maestas 2005) as workers retire for a period of time only to return to work. Often their reasons are tied to pensions that have taken hits from economic cycles that diminish investment holdings. These cycles have become more frequent in the last decade, adding insecurity to retirement as well as to work. Accordingly, one life course implication of these changes is delayed retirement – or may very well be the erosion of the retirement transition as it was institutionalized in the last century.

CONCLUSIONS

The new model of the life course requires taking the "long view" and linking the varieties of social time that define the life course, which include biography and history. Arguably, welfare state institutions as they developed in the twentieth century contributed to the construction of the life course. Childhood, adulthood, and old age came to be defined in terms of economic roles sustained by the linkage of state and market structures. The growing wealth of industrializing societies raised the level of resources available across the society and afforded surpluses that could be redistributed across the population, in part, in accordance with age. Welfare states are comprised of "equalizing institutions" (Levy 1998) which provide structural supports that maintain middle classes with protections against life course risks emanating from educational opportunities, employment options, and family and health shocks, and buttress lower classes from dropping below levels of sustainability.

State, family, and market structures have regulated life course transitions. Public education systems with age requirements allocated the young to this sector and held them in place over a specific age-range. Employment insurance systems have protected workers and families from shocks that can precipitate situations of family dissolution. Education systems in some societies (like Germany) even channeled students into specific occupations, almost seamlessly, making the transition to adulthood relatively uniform. Similarly, retirement systems have regulated the end of work careers with mandatory exits and/or with benefit entitlements (incentives) linked to age. As such, the tri-phasic life course (in the left panel of Figure 11.1) once represented lives as they were normally (and normatively) lived in the recent past. However, these institutions no longer coincide with the reality of lives being lived under conditions of social change.

Population aging and changing institutional environments in the current context are differentiating the opportunities for and constraints on life courses across subgroups of the population. The result is the increasing individualization of the life course and growing inequalities based on the retreat of equalizing institutions and the unpredictable occurrence of global events that have differential impacts on advantaged and disadvantaged subgroups in the US and elsewhere.

References

Alwin, D. F., R. L. Cohen, and T. M. Newcomb (1991) *Political Attitudes Over the Life Span: The Bennington Women After Fifty Years*. Madison, WI: University of Wisconsin Press.

Barker, D. J. P. (1998) *Mothers, Babies and Health in Later Life*. Philadelphia, PA: Churchill Livingstone (Elsevier).

Bernhardt, A., M. Morris, M. S. Handcock, and M. A. Scott (2001) *Divergent Paths: Economic Mobility in the New American Labor Market*. New York: Russell Sage Foundation.

Bongaarts, J. (2004) "Population Aging and the Rising Cost of Public Pensions." *Population and Development Review* 30(1): 1–23.

Bonoli, G. (2003) "Two Worlds of Pension Reform in Western Europe." *Comparative Politics* 35: 399–416.

Burton, L.M., W. Welsh, and L. Destro (forthcoming) "Grandmothers' Differential Involvement with Grandchildren in Rural Multi-Partnered Fertility Family Structures." In M. Silverstein and R. Giarrusso (eds.), *From Generation to Generation: Continuity and Discontinuity in Aging Families*. Baltimore, MD: Johns Hopkins University Press.

Crosnoe, R. and G. H. Elder, Jr. (2004) "From Childhood to Later Years: Pathways of Human Development." *Research on Aging* 26: 623–54.

DiPrete, T. D. and C. Buchmann (2006) "Gender Specific Trends in the Value of Education and the Emerging Gender Gap in College Completion." *Demography* 43(1): 1–24.

Elder, G. H., Jr. (1974) *Children of the Great Depression*. Chicago: University of Chicago Press.

Elder, G. H., Jr. (1987) "War Mobilization and the Life Course: A Cohort of World War II Veterans." *Sociological Forum* 2: 449–72.

Elder, G. H., Jr. and A. Caspi (1990) "Studying Lives in a Changing Society: Sociological and Personological Explorations." In A. I. Rabin, R. A. Zucker, and S. Frank (eds.), *Studying Persons and Lives*. New York: Springer, pp. 201–47.

Elder, G. H., Jr. and R. Conger (2000) *Children of the Land: Adversity and Success in Rural America*. Chicago: University of Chicago Press.

Elder, G. H., Jr. and M. J. Shanahan (2006) "The Life Course and Human Development." In R. Lerner (ed.), *Handbook of Child Psychology*, Vol. 1, *Theory*. Hoboken, NJ: John Wiley & Sons, pp. 665–715.

Elman, C. and A. M. O'Rand (2004) "The Race is to the Swift: Socioeconomic Origins, Adult Education and Mid-life Economic Status." *American Journal of Sociology* 110: 123–60.

Esping-Andersen, G. (1999) *Social Foundations of Postindustrial Economies*. New York: Oxford University Press.

Flegal, K. M., M. D. Carroll, C. L. Ogden, and C. L. Johnson (2002) "Prevalence and Trends in Obesity Among U.S. Adults." *Journal of the American Medical Association* 288: 1723–7.

Guo, G., M. Roettger, and T. Cai (2008) "The Integration of Genetic Propensities into Social Control Models of Delinquency and Violence Among Male Youths." *American Sociological Review* 73: 543–68.

Haas, S. (2008) "Trajectories of Functional Health: The 'Long Arm' of Childhood Health and Socioeconomic Factors." *Social Science and Medicine* 66: 849–61.

Hamil-Luker, J. and A. M. O'Rand (2007) "Gender Differences in the Link Between Childhood Socioeconomic Conditions and Heart Attack Risk in Adulthood." *Demography* 44: 137–58.

House, J. S., P. M. Lantz, and P. Herd (2005) "Continuity and Change in the Social Stratification of Aging and Health Over the Life Course." *Journals of Gerontology*: Series B 60B (Special Issue II): 15–26.

Hughes, M. E. and A. M. O'Rand (2004) *The Lives and Times of the Baby Boomers*. Washington, DC/New York: Population Reference Bureau/Russell Sage Foundation.

Kasen, S., P. Cohen, H. Chen, and D. Castille (2003) "Depression in Adult Women: Age Changes and Cohort Effects." *American Journal of Public Health* 93: 2061–6.

Kinsella, K. and D. Phillips (2005) "The Demographic Drivers of Aging." *Population Bulletin*, March: 8–11.

Land, K. C., J. M. Guralnik, and D. G. Blazer (1994) "Estimating Increment-Decrement Life Tables with Multiple Covariates from Panel Data: The Case of Active Life Expectancy." *Demography* 31: 297–319.

Lesthaeghe, R. (1995) "The Second Demographic Transition in Western Countries: An Interpretation." In K. O. Mason and A.-M. Jensen (eds.), *Gender and Family Change in Industrialized Societies*. Oxford: Clarendon, pp. 17–62.

Levy, F. (1998) *The New Dollars and Dreams*. New York: Russell Sage Foundation.

Lynch, S. M. (2003) "Cohort and Life-Course Patterns in the Relationship Between Education and Health: A Hierarchical Approach." *Demography* 40: 309–31.

Maestas, N. (2005) *Back to Work: Expectations and Realizations of Work After Retirement*. RAND Labor and Population Working Paper WR-196-1. Santa Monica, CA.

Mayer, K. U. (2009) "New Directions in Life Course Research." *Annual Review of Sociology* 35: 413–33.

McLanahan, S. (2004) "Diverging Destinies: How Children are Faring Under the Second Demographic Transition." *Demography* 41: 607–27.

Mortimer, J. T. and M. J. Shanahan (eds.) (2005) *Handbook of the Life Course*. New York: Kluwer/Plenum.

O'Rand, A. M. (2003) "The Future of the Life Course: Late Modernity and Life Course Risks." In J. T. Mortimer and M. J. Shanahan (eds.), *Handbook of the Life Course*. New York: Kluwer/Plenum, pp. 693–701.

O'Rand, A. M. (2006) "Stratification and the Life Course: Life Course Capital, Life Course Risks and Social Inequality." In R. H. Binstock and L. K. George (eds.), *Handbook of Aging and the Social Sciences*. Boston: Elsevier, pp. 146–65.

O'Rand, A. M. (2007) "Theories of Aging and the Life Course." In G. Ritzer (ed.), *Blackwell Encyclopedia of Sociology*, Vol. I. Oxford: Blackwell, pp. 73–7.

O'Rand, A. M. and J. Hamil-Luker (forthcoming) "Late Employment Careers, Transitions to Retirement, and Retirement Income in the U.S." In H.-P. Blossfeld, S. Buchholz, and K. Kurz (eds.), *Ageing Populations, Globalization and the Labor Market: Comparing Late Working Life and Retirement in Modern Societies*. Cheltenham: Edward Elgar.

O'Rand, A. M., D. Ebel, and K. Isaacs (2009) "Private Pensions in International Perspective." In P. Uhlenberg (ed.), *The International Handbook of Population Aging*. Dordrecht: Springer-Verlag, pp. 429–43.

O'Rand, A. M., J. Hamil-Luker, and C. Elman (2009) "Childhood Conditions, Educational Trajectories and Midlife Health in the U.S." In H.-P. Blossfeld and J. Baumert (eds.), *Zeitschrift für Erziehungswissenschaft: Special Issue on Aging and Education* 12: 409–36.

O'Rand, A. M., K. Isaacs, and L. Roth (2009) "Age and Inequality in a Global Context." In D. Dannefer and C. Philipson (eds.), *International Handbook on Social Gerontology*. Thousand Oaks, CA: Sage, pp. 127–36.

Palloni, A. (2006) "Childhood Health and the Reproduction of Inequalities." *Demography* 43: 587–615.

Pampel, F. C. (2005) "Diffusion, Cohort Change, and Social Patterns of Smoking." *Social Science Research* 34: 117–39.

Quinn, J. (1997) "Retirement Trends and Patterns in the 1990s: The End of an Era?" In *National Academy on Aging, Public Policy and Aging Report*. Washington, DC: National Academy on Aging, pp. 10–14.

Richards, M. (2004) "Assisted Reproduction, Genetic Technologies and Family Life." In J. Scott, J. Treas, and M. Richards (eds.), *The Blackwell Companion to the Sociology of Families*. Oxford: Blackwell, pp. 478–98.

Riley, M. W. and J. W. Riley (1994) "Age Integration and the Lives of Older People." *The Gerontologist* 24: 110–15.

Riley, M. W., R. L. Kahn, and A. Foner (1994) *Age and Structural Lag: Society's Failure to Provide Meaningful Opportunities in Work, Family and Leisure*. New York: Wiley.

Ryder, N. B. (1965) "The Cohort as a Concept in the Study of Social Change." *American Sociological Review* 30: 843–61.

Shanahan, M. J. and G. H. Elder, Jr. (2002) "History, Agency and the Life Course." In L. J. Crockett (ed.), *Agency, Motivation and the Life Course*. Lincoln, NE: University of Nebraska Press, pp. 145–85.

Shanahan, M. J. and R. Macmillan (2008) *Biography and the Sociological Imagination: Contexts and Contingencies*. New York: W. W. Norton and Company.

Sinha, T. (2000) *Pension Reform in Latin America and Its Lessons for International Policymakers*. Boston: Kluwer Academic.

Sweeney, M. (2002) "Two Decades of Family Change: The Shifting Economic Foundations of Marriage." *American Sociological Review* 67: 132–47.

Warren, R. W. (2009) "Socioeconomic Status and Health Across the Life Course: A Test of the Social Causation and Health Selection Hypotheses." *Social Forces* 87: 2125–53.

World Bank (1994) *Averting the Old Age Crisis: Policies to Protect the Old and Promote Growth*. Oxford: Oxford University Press.

Yang, Y. (2008) "Social Inequalities in Happiness in the U.S., 1972–2004: An Age-Period-Cohort Analysis." *American Sociological Review* 73: 204–26.

Yang, Y. and L. C. Lee (2009) "Sex and Race Disparities in Health: Cohort Variations in Life Course Patterns." *Social Forces* 87: 2091–124.

12

Deviance

A Sociology of Unconventionalities

Nachman Ben-Yehuda

I am that part of the power that eternally wants bad and eternally does only good.

Goethe's Faust

What Is Deviance?

The word deviance conjures up many associations. Imagine, for example, a road. People travel along that road but it is not difficult to observe that quite frequently travelers deviate from the road. Having this imagery in mind yields some intriguing questions such as: who made this road? Where is it coming from? Where is it leading to? Do travelers who deviate from the road do it alone? Together with others? How do travelers on the road react to the deviance? Do these deviating travelers pave a new road?

To understand better the nature of deviance we need to take what may appear as a simple concept and examine it as a potentially problematic concept, which indeed it is.

In the 1930s, some sociologists posed an intriguing question. Prostitution, they pondered, was a behavior that did not require a great investment to learn. Most sexual behavior is straightforward and women who want to become prostitutes do not need to spend a great deal of time in acquiring complex skills. Economically, becoming a prostitute has a promise of a potentially high income. Why, then, they asked, do most women not become prostitutes? The answer was that this dilemma reflects a clash between two social systems – morality and economy. Economically

The Wiley-Blackwell Companion to Sociology, First Edition. Edited by George Ritzer.
© 2012 Blackwell Publishing Ltd. Published 2012 by Blackwell Publishing Ltd.

speaking, prostitution could yield a high income with a low investment. Morally, becoming a prostitute meant acquiring a stigma, damaging one's self-esteem, and basically being involved in an immoral behavior. The clash between these two social systems ends with morality gaining the upper hand, and thus, most women do not become prostitutes.

This interpretation brings forth one of the two essential elements in deviance: morality. Simply put, morality is a social system which we acquire in various processes of socialization, and which tells us what is right and what is wrong, what is beautiful and what is ugly, what is allowed and what not. Moral guidelines are not simple and social systems may have a few such guidelines, some even incommensurable one with another. Moreover, as we pass through such various stages in our life as professional training, jobs, aging, we may experience various – sometimes contradictory – moral guidelines. Nevertheless, the first element to define deviance is morality. It is not too difficult to realize that because morality is not a simple entity, we already have in-built into deviance an unstable (and sometimes vague) element of uncertainty and ambiguity.

Morality, in and by itself, is insufficient to turn any behavior into deviance. There are many people who feel that some behaviors are deviant and many others who disagree. There is a second element missing here. This is the element of power. That is, the ability to force a specific definition of behavior as deviant, even against opposition. Alas, social and political power can be just as ambiguous and shaky as morality – perhaps even more so. Nevertheless, it is the combination of these two elements – morality and power – that will dictate who and what will be defined as deviant.

We need to keep in mind that the very definition of what deviance is depends on two variables that can in essence be ambiguous and uncertain. Indeed, Downes and Rock (2007) emphasize that deviance eludes definitions and that much of it has to do with the difficulties involved in predicting and controlling the implications of moral rules. Looking from this perspective, deviance seems to be characterized by its relative nature and changing character. One of the instructive illustrations for this is Robert R. Bell's 1971 textbook on deviance. Following an introductory conceptual section, the second part of the book presents – in different chapters – various cases of deviance. Obviously, it should not be too difficult to view these chapters as presenting what the field of deviance views as deviance. Moreover, one can infer that the order of the presentation of the cases may have something to do with the importance of the topics. How then did Bell in 1971 present the empirical bread and butter of the field? The *first* empirical chapter which presents a case of deviance, 24 pages long, is devoted to and focused on – you better believe this – "premarital sex." The last three chapters of the book are on "militant women," "militant students," and "the Hippie movement," respectively. Furthermore, if one looks at the development of one of the long-lasting and established textbooks on deviant behavior, that of Erich Goode (now in its ninth edition, all published by Prentice Hall), one can see that from its second edition (1984; the first 1978 edition was packaged in a symbolic interactionism perspective), such cases of deviance as drug usage, homosexuality, violent behavior (including homicide and rape), property crimes, and mental disorders, featured in the book (as well as in the various editions of another established textbook – by Alex Thio, published by different publishers).

However, in its fifth edition (1997), but much more forcefully in its sixth (2001) and seventh (2005) editions, a chapter on ideological, ethical, and moral implications of studying deviance was added, and the sixth and seventh editions also had chapters on cognitive deviance (focusing on religious deviance, parapsychology, UFOlogy, and urban legends – a category which, by the way, had appeared in Jack D. Douglas and Frances C. Waksler's textbook in 1982) and physical aberrations, as a result of which, previous subjects were condensed and presented in a much more concise manner. The seventh edition even had a chapter on the "death" of the sociology of deviance. Moreover, such deviancies as shoplifting and massage parlors which appeared quite saliently in the 1978 edition disappeared completely in the 2005 edition.

To go beyond this illustration let me use a few others. We consider incest as a most serious offense. However, Cleopatra's first marriage was to her younger brother. She herself was the result of her mother's marriage to her brother. In fact, we have historical accounts which reveal that sexual relations and marriages between siblings were, in some ancient cultures, a privilege of upper, nobility, and royalty classes. In certain situations of war, rape is a practice not punished by combatants. Sometimes it is even encouraged. Killing people is not always forbidden and there are situations when killing people becomes mandatory. Sometimes it is even rewarded. When examining acts we consider "deviant" it is always a good idea to separate the act and the cultural interpretation of the act (for example, what we call it), and to look for similar acts and cultural interpretations in both history and other cultures.

Clearly, deviance is a relative phenomenon, among cultures and over time within cultures. Researchers of deviance have known, discussed, and written about this for dozens of years.

SOME CONTEMPORARY DEBATES

In recent years, the sociology of deviance has become a focus for four different debates. The first has probably to do with the fact that since the late 1960s to 1970s, no major theoretical or paradigmatic shifts have been introduced. The last analytical upheaval was the introduction of labeling theory and since then nothing of that magnitude or caliber has taken place. One of the results is that some works have been published about the "death" of deviance (Sumner 1994a, 1994b; Bendle 1999; Miller, Wright & Dannels 2001; Best 2004, 2005; for counter-arguments see Goode 2002, 2004a, 2004b).

One needs to be aware that declarations of "death" have become rather popular: the death of history, the novel, sociology, the city, the suburbs, crime, love, sex, religion, God, the nation-state, friendship, and more. These proclamations have become a fashionable, provocative, and headline-grabbing popular activity. Deviance, obviously, is not dead. Behavior that violates moral codes and is reacted to by powerful enforcers is not, and will not be, dead. The question of whether to refer to these behaviors as "deviance" remains open.

This brings us to the next debate, and that is whether there is something we can refer to as "positive deviance." Some sociologists who have studied and written about deviance, for example Erich Goode, feel very strongly that the very essence that defines deviance is that it elicits negative responses. Such gatekeepers would not allow any expansion or re-interpretation of the concept of deviance in non-negative terms (see Ben-Yehuda 1990a). This debate about the nature of the concept naturally directs us to two other related and relevant debates, this time from two supposedly opposing political views.

The ascendance of postmodern and politically correct criticisms and influences has made hurling stones at the study of deviance a common practice for some. This practice challenges the very definition of some behaviors as "deviance" and accuses sociologists who study deviance of being part of helping to oppress cultural variance and support hegemonic repressive powers to suppress and delegitimize suffering minorities. The claim is made that the study of deviance itself reifies cultural power relationships and moral perceptions that in turn define deviance (typically a claim from the radical left side of the political spectrum). In no other current behaviors is this claim clearer than in discussions about homosexuality. In fact, the attack is so severe that we should not be surprised to see the category of "homosexuality" being phased out from textbooks on deviant behavior. Moreover, Dombrink and Hillyard (2007) point out that as moralities changed in the USA, gambling went through a process of normalization. They suggest that more normalization processes will probably occur in relation to abortion, assisted suicide, and stem cell research. Legalizing the usage of psychoactive substances may be on the horizon as well.

The last challenging attack on the study of deviance comes from the opposite side of the political map. This conservative criticism maintains that the way we define and study deviance somehow degrades American society by challenging the validity of its moral claims and relativizing morality to a point where morality itself may disappear. A good illustration for this position can be found in Hendershott's (2002) book which argues that deviance is an absolute term, and represents an essential phenomenon.

This claim which comes from the right side of the map – if taken seriously – requires that we shrink the variance with which we conceptualize "deviance," abandon the idea and empirical findings that deviance is a relative phenomenon, and conceptualize deviance according to strict black-and-white boundaries, like in a good old western à la John Wayne, Gary Cooper, Sergio Leone, or Clint Eastwood. This morality, undoubtedly informed by religious standards, stands a pretty good chance of throwing us back to deviant behavior perspectives of the 1950s when – supposedly – it was very clear what was and what was not deviance. As an antidote to the politically correct postmodernists, this is a powerful potion. However, because it is so radical, and constructs complex realities in such simplified terms, it shrinks the variance of social phenomena and creates an unnecessary, and empirically wrong, extremism. And yet a danger lurks here. The danger is that with the ascendance of religious fundamentalism, moral majorities, and conservatism generally, this radical view may find strong political (ergo, budgetary as well) and academic support.

Given that deviance is a relative, sometimes ambiguous, phenomenon, how is it best to conceptualize it? I believe that it is best approached if we take the formulations of Emile Durkheim as our starting point.

ENTER DURKHEIM

Emile Durkheim first set out to establish that deviance is an inevitable aspect of all societies: "Crime . . . is . . . an integral part of all healthy societies . . . Crime is . . . necessary; it is bound up with the fundamental conditions of all social life, and . . . is useful" (1938: 67, 70). Next, Durkheim attempted to specify exactly why this is so. His answer consists of two interconnected foci. In *The Rules of Sociological Method*, he argues that:

> Crime is normal because a society exempt from it is utterly impossible . . . Crime implies not only that the way remains open to necessary changes, but that in certain cases it directly prepares these changes. Where crime exists, collective sentiments are sufficiently flexible to take on a new form, and crime sometimes helps to determine the form they will take. (1938: 65–73)

This formulation implies that crime is a necessary and vital part of social systems because it can create and sustain the flexibility necessary for the social system to adapt itself to varying conditions. Crime and deviance are thus viewed as mechanisms for social change. Durkheim offers as evidence the example of a renowned criminal, Socrates. "According to Athenian law Socrates was a criminal, and his condemnation was no more than just. However, his crime, namely the independence of his thought . . . served to prepare a new morality and faith" (1938: 73).

However, in *The Division of Labor in Society*, Durkheim adds that:

> The only common characteristic of all crimes is that they consist . . . in acts universally disapproved of by members of each society . . . An act is criminal when it offends strong and defined states of the collective conscience . . . Crime is everywhere essentially the same, since it everywhere calls forth the same effect . . . Its primary and principal function is to create respect for . . . beliefs, traditions, and collective practices . . . Crime damages . . . unanimity [and] since it is the common conscience which is attacked, it must be that which resists, and accordingly the resistance must be collective. [Punishment's] true function is to maintain social cohesion intact. ([1933] 1964: 70–110)

Even more specifically, Durkheim notes that:

> Crime brings together upright consciences and concentrates them. We have only to notice what happens, particularly in a small town, when some moral scandal has just been committed. They stop each other on the street, they visit each other, they seek to come together to talk of the event and wax indignant in common. From all the similar impressions which are exchanged, for all the temper that gets itself expressed, there emerges a unique temper – which is everybody's without being anybody's in particular. That is the public temper. ([1933] 1964: 102)

What Durkheim implies in these passages is that crime threatens the moral core of society. Crime's main role is therefore to invoke punishment, which in turn facilitates cohesion and maintains societal boundaries. That is, crime helps to maintain stability. The idea that deviance helps to solidify symbolic-moral boundaries was echoed by quite a few sociologists.

IMPLICATIONS OF DURKHEIM'S IDEAS

Durkheimian formulations give us some interesting insights into the nature of deviance, reactions to it, and its complex cultural role.

The first insight is that to understand the way cultures and societies work, we need to understand the symbolic order of these societies. At the core of these symbolic orders lies morality. Acts that challenge this core stand a good chance of being defined as crime or deviance. However, such challenges are far from being simple on at least two accounts. First, they open the way for two contradictory paths. One, the challenge may succeed and the result could be social change. Two, the challenge may fail and the result could be a stronger ossification of the culture. Second, although Durkheim's formulations about morality are basic and important, our understanding of morality has developed much further (see, for example, Boltanski & Thévenot 2006; Lowe 2006). The idea that societies are structured from different, often competing, symbolic-moral universes takes us away from Durkheim's concept of coherency in societal moral systems, which are – supposedly – internalized in more or less uniform processes of socialization. Durkheim did not give too much weight to the role of power either. But, certainly, power plays a major role in deciding which one of the two paths will be chosen. This is not to say that deviants are always agents for social change, romantic, or rebellious (Kooistra 1989). On the contrary.

However, the idea that deviance is connected to morality and power gives us an interesting clue to a possibility to interpret deviance within a broader context – that of change and stability. Let us examine these two routes.

DEVIANCE AND SOCIAL CONTROL

Negative responses to nonconformity and deviance tend to neutralize the challenge in such behaviors and re-affirm boundaries of symbolic-moral universes. Such responses can be conceptualized under the heading of social control. Social control theoreticians tend to assume that, given a chance and an opportunity, humans will deviate. Contrary to the main question asked by many scholars working on deviance – "Why does deviance occur?" – scholars working in social control reverse the question. Their main question is "Why does deviance not occur more, lots more?" Their answer is that the reason most people do not deviate is because they are influenced by mechanisms of social control. Typically, researchers tend to detail two types of such mechanisms. First are inner mechanisms – in such forms as conscience or internalization and absorption of values and norms acquired during various socialization processes. Second are external mechanisms such as parents, teachers, police officers, courts. The various combinations of internal and external mechanisms have provided a basis to quite a few theories and concepts on how we can conceptualize control. A contemporary influential theory is that of Gottfredson and

Hirschi (1990) who argue that an ineffective socialization process breeds low self-control which in turn allows the pursuit of immediate and simple gratifications. Involvement in deviance and committing crimes is not far behind.

Influenced by Foucault's ideas, a new approach to control – sometimes referred to as "controlology" – was developed by such scholars as Stanley Cohen, Jason Ditton, and others. It views societies as control organs that apply coercive and repressive measures in a systematic and continuous fashion to keep citizens docile and conformist.

The other possibility is that challenges to the status quo will produce cultural and social change. Examining this possibility will take us to the next section of this chapter.

MORAL ENTREPRENEURSHIP

In relatively non-complex cultures, there is a fairly good chance that similar moral perceptions characterize the entire culture and are accepted by most if not all of its members. Processes of differentiation and the creation of morally and culturally fragmented cultures – or multi-culturalism – gave rise to societies where morality itself is chronically contested and negotiated, thus enabling room for, and empowering, the activities of multiple moral entrepreneurs.

Moral crusades, as a form of moral enterprise (Becker 1963), mean that some social agents, feeling committed and dedicated to a specific morality, typically present such motivational accounting systems as "cause" or "justice." These crusaders begin to be socially and culturally active and rally support in order to generate social power and use it to try to steer a culture in a direction they feel is right. These activities are typically characterized as a moral crusade. Such crusades, for example, were easy to discern in the attempt on the part of the feminist movement to try to make pornography illegal (e.g., Goode & Ben-Yehuda 2009: ch. 13), and in the moral crusades in the early part of the twentieth century which brought about the criminalization of the use of various consciousness-altering substances (including – for a short period – alcohol).

MORAL PANICS

Perhaps the most dramatic of all moral enterprises and crusades is the moral panic (Young 1971; Cohen 1972; Goode & Ben-Yehuda 2009). Based mainly on symbolic interaction and labeling theory, but having its eyes on some other areas such as collective behavior, social problems, and social movements, the concept and theory of moral panics present us with a large base of analytical power and flexibility allowing us to examine a sizeable variety of cultural happenings with a theoretically integrated apparatus. In essence, moral panics refer to the creation of a situation where exaggerated fear is manufactured about topics that are moral in essence and nature. Moral panics have to create, focus on, and sustain powerfully persuasive images of folk devils that can serve as the heart of moral fears. Such imaginary and highly overstated fears characteristically focus on gang activities, youth, illicit psychoactive drug usage, pornography, prostitution, witchcraft, satanic kidnapping of children, but not only on these.

Researchers interested in moral panics tend to examine people's cognitive maps (how they construct their worldviews and behavior), and how and where the symbolic nature of cultures materializes. The role moral panics play lies in their ability to help draw the moral boundaries among the different symbolic-moral universes that make up complex cultures and societies. Moral panics have always been the occasion for bearers of different moralities to clash, negotiate, and end the panic, either with a continued process of social change or by re-affirming existing moral boundaries. The volatile nature of moral panics need not mislead us. Like the routinization of charisma, moral panics may leave in their wake a trail of new institutional arrangements and bureaucratic structures. Once such social arrangements come into being, their vested interest will continue to influence actions. One of the best historical illustrations of this process is the criminalization of the use of a variety of consciousness-altering chemicals. Moreover, even if a specific moral panic does not seem to leave immediate routinization traces, its very occurrence tends to leave memories and cognitive sediments that may make the next moral panic more successful in achieving longer-lasting effects.

Moral panics are therefore not marginal or trivial events. They represent central challenging processes of change and stability in the symbolic realm of cultures. While not exclusively so, it is through these moral panics that we are made to understand and construct the social and cultural ambience in which we choose – or are made – to live. As Stanley Cohen (1972) compellingly pointed out, moral panics are about representations: which sector of the society has the power to represent itself and its interests to others as legitimate and valid. In this sense, moral panics touch some most central and profound social processes. The popularity and widespread usage of the concept is thus easily understood.

What happens to moral panics in multicultural societies where morality itself is constantly contested and negotiated? Consensus about morality in such societies is not a simple or taken-for-granted issue and, therefore, the entire issue of launching moral panics within more general processes of moral entrepreneurship, legislation, policing, and regulation has had to be re-conceptualized. For instance, it is reasonable to assume that the number of moral panics in multicultural societies will increase. Such societies are likely to experience many small-scale moral panics, launched by various moral entrepreneurs, some of whom may even compete for the moral hearts and minds of different cultural groups. Moral panics, after all, are intended to help specific moral perceptions dominate.

When different moral ideas and concepts compete for attention and domination in a social and cultural landscape that allows and tolerates such rivalry, indeed more moral panics can be expected to occur. Thus, in a recent augmentation of moral panic theory, modern theories of risk have prompted some researchers to try to conceptualize moral panics within theorizations of moral risk. Furthermore, researchers interested in the media as creator and spreader of fear (following the newsroom slogan, "if it bleeds it leads") have also focused on moral panics as an important mechanism for creating and sustaining cultures of fear.

It is thus not too difficult to realize that moral entrepreneurs are engaged in moral crusades that sometimes develop into moral panics, the goal of which is to change the moral landscape of a culture. These attempts are not always successful because in multicultural societies these moral entrepreneurships may encounter resistance and the result may be no change in the moral landscape. Moral entrepreneurships typically involve constructions and manipulations of social memories. These activities ultimately aim to alter the social identity of persons and cultures.

Deviance, Change, and Stability[1]

Examining deviance from a revised Durkheimian perspective implies that we can look at deviance as part of processes of cultural change and stability. This perspective leads us to a conceptual model.

As many researchers of deviance have pointed out, deviance is not a rare occurrence. When acts of deviance occur, the next question is: how are they reacted to? A successful harsh squelching response will annul the challenge to the status quo and maintain moral and symbolic stability. This, I suspect, is the more frequent scenario. However, a different scenario may take place. Some moral entrepreneurs may unleash a moral crusade, accompanied by moral panics, and manage to achieve significant cultural changes. Douglas's 1977 analysis suggests the term "creative deviance" and argues that "deviance is the mutation that is generally destructive of society, but it is also the only major source of creative adaptations of rules to new life situations" (1977: 60). Consequently, he suggests that entire cultures and societies can change through deviance. To have a better understanding of how this can happen, some discussion of deviance and power is necessary.

Politics and Deviance

Who defines what (and who) as deviance? Who has the power to enforce such a definition? Two main possibilities exist here. The first consists of types of deviance where the issues of power and morality are explicitly at the forefront as the challenge (and potential threat) to the status quo. The second consists of deviancies where this challenge is implicit. Many deviant acts which are referred to as "political" are in the first category. Roebuck and Weeber (1978) suggested three categories in this area: first, crimes against the state such as assassination, political bombing, bribery, tax and/or tax evasion, conscientious objection, spying; second, crimes against society such as false advertisements, medical fraud, environmental pollution, occupational hazards, unsafe machines; third, crimes committed by the government such as police corruption and/or violence, violation of human rights, genocide, discrimination. Ross (2002) focuses on such topics as sabotage, treason, terror, state crimes (torture, genocide), corruption, illegal surveillance, and human rights violation. My previous work on betrayal and treason (Ben-Yehuda 2001) indicated that invocation of the term betrayal, or treason, always involved violations of the moral codes associated with loyalty and trust. Such violations, however, were not enough. Invoking treason or betrayal and enforcing its acceptance required the use of power. Moreover, in cases of terror and the media, morality and especially power play a major role (Ben-Yehuda 2005).

Politics and deviance can be classified into three basic types of deviance which come from: (1) the periphery and are aimed at the center; (2) the center and are aimed at the periphery; (3) either the center or the periphery and are aimed at the same level (center to center, periphery to periphery). These forms of deviance are always connected to issues of political justice, political trials, criminals as heroes, and political criminals.

POLITICAL DEVIANCE VS. POLITICAL JUSTICE

Strong feelings of injustice could motivate people into actions aimed to rectify what they feel is unjust. Criteria for these feelings and actions are not, and cannot be, objective or absolute. Many deviant acts classified as "terror" may use the language of justice/injustice in justifying or condoning these acts. And, indeed, rhetorics capitalizing on "victim accounts (or narratives)" have become quite popular in justifying some nasty and problematic behaviors. Such behaviors may challenge (or threaten) the foundations of a social order. A closely related issue is that of using processes of deviantization (sometimes by the criminal justice system itself) for political purposes – for example, police involvement in riot control, capture and trials of terrorists, enforcement of immigration laws, or treating political opponents as criminals. My previous work on political assassinations (Ben-Yehuda 1993) documented how assassinations can be conceptualized as an alternative system of justice. A sharp decrease in assassinations could be observed when formal mechanisms of justice were introduced.

POLITICAL TRIALS AND JUDGING DEVIANTS

Characterizing political trials is not a simple undertaking because their nature is not entirely clear. In essence, such trials tend to involve those who are accused, directly and explicitly, of threatening and/or challenging the legitimacy of a regime: treason, sedition, mutiny, civil unrest. Political trials may produce political prisoners, which in turn may lead to another interesting process – politicization of prisons.

Political deviance always entails some form of conflict which is presented as a conflict between two, or more, symbolic-moral universes: that of the challengers (real or imaginary) and that of those being challenged. Therefore, the history of political deviance is also, in an inverse fashion, the history of morality and the distribution of power. However, in the popular and older professional literature, political deviance was usually taken to mean challenges against the power and legitimacy of the rulers, and not vice versa. In the culture where Socrates lived, his persecutors had more legitimized power, so that when the two symbolic-moral universes and opposing systems of vocabularies of motives collided, Socrates lost. In today's liberal democratic societies, freedom of thought and speech are hailed as primary virtues. In other regimes, individuals who exercise freedom of thought, or challenge the "order," are liable to find themselves imprisoned or committed to an insane asylum. Science is no exception. Giordano Bruno died for challenging the

Ptolemaic worldview and the morality which supported it; Galileo as well suffered because of this worldview.

Judging, one needs to note, need not be done only in courts. Freud's theory which revolutionized psychology and psychiatry and enriched other disciplines was originally criticized heavily on moral grounds. Likewise, the first innovators in radio astronomy and the developers of some of the most central concepts in astronomy (e.g., black holes, the Big Bang theory, or background microwave radiation) were isolated and kept away from the main halls of science. It is not too difficult to find cases of innovations, some quite significant, in the sciences and the arts, which were reacted to as deviance, and the innovators treated as deviants – deviantized, ostracized, stigmatized, and ridiculed. Discovery of the role of the bacterium Helicobacter pylori in the development of peptic ulcers is a good and recent illustration. While laughed at and ridiculed initially, this discovery ended up with a Nobel Prize in 2005.

The question of who interprets and judges whose behavior, why, where and when, is crucial because it gives us strong clues as to who will be judged by whom. Pat Lauderdale's insightful observation is very relevant here:

> Is, for example, the leader of loose-knit bands of hit-and-run killers of British soldiers a "homicidal maniac," a "crazed cult killer," or a "bandit"? Or is George Washington a revolutionary hero? Is Nat Turner, who executed Virginia slave owners and their families in 1830, in the same category? Is the Jewish terrorist in Palestine in 1948 distinguishable from the Palestinian terrorist in Israel in 1978? (2003: 5)

CRIMINALS AS HEROES AND POLITICAL CRIMINALS

History teaches us that on many occasions deviants and criminals were treated as heroes. The famous Robin Hood syndrome received a strong validation in Kooistra's (1989) work where he examined a large variety of such cases. However, the existence of this category also raises the reverse possibility – of politicians as criminals. Suffice it to point out that some of the vilest and most despicable mass murderers of the twentieth century (and perhaps in history) were politicians – for example, Adolf Hitler, Mao Zedong, Pol Pot, and Joseph Stalin.

POWER AND MORALITY IN REGULAR DEVIANCE

The second possibility consists of regular forms of deviance which, prima facie, do not seem to present any explicit challenge to the status quo. Finding out the implicit power/morality challenge in these forms of behavior requires some digging. Doing this may mean following different, yet complementary, routes – for example, examining the ways in which criminal laws are created, passed, and enforced. The very act of defining a particular behavioral pattern as deviant is inherently political – it uses power to impose the view of a specific symbolic-moral universe upon other universes. This process, referred to by Schur (1980) as "deviantization" and consisting of stigma contests, typically begins when some moral entrepreneurs try to change public attitudes and law. Processes of deviantization play key roles in the social stratification order because they intervene in processes of resource allocation. A process of deviantization may involve shaming (Braithwaite 1989), vilification, degradation ceremonies (Garfinkel 1950), and stigmatization (Goffman 1963). Since power and morality are the basis of these deviantization processes, reversal can be achieved by using the same resources (Ben-Yehuda 1990b: 221–50). Thus, actors in societal centers who negotiate power and morality, attempting to define particular patterns of behavior as deviant (or non-deviant), are necessarily engaged in constructing the boundaries of symbolic-moral universes and affecting processes of change or stability. These moral entrepreneurs, or agents of moral claims, seek constantly to manipulate political, as well as moral, symbols in order to mobilize support, generate power, and control or influence public opinion. Some interesting insights may be gained here by examining how specified behaviors once considered "deviant" or "criminal" become legitimized at other times and vice versa. There are some good examples of this. For instance, Gusfield's (1963) work on the Temperance Movement's anti-liquor struggle illustrates this:

> What prohibition symbolized was the superior power and prestige of the old middle class in American society. The threat of decline in that position had made explicit actions of government necessary to defend it. Legislation did this in two ways. It demonstrated the power of the old middle classes by showing that they could mobilize sufficient political strength to bring it about, and it gave dominance to the character and style of old middle-class life in contrast to that of the urban lower and middle classes. The power of the Protestant, rural, native American was greater than that of the Eastern upper classes, the Catholic and Jewish immigrants, and the urbanized middle class. (Gusfield 1963: 122–3)

What Gusfield's work implies is that a contemporary "problem," perceived as excessive use of alcohol, was socially constructed. Zurcher, Kirkpatrick, Cushing & Bowman (1971) showed that in two cases of anti-pornography campaigns, the moral crusaders emphasized a general lifestyle and set of values instead of the specific steps they demanded in order to abolish pornography. Kuzmarov's (2009) meticulous historical research indicates that the claim that American soldiers in Vietnam used drugs ("the addicted army") and that this practice was one of the causes of losing the war there is a myth. His work shows that this claim has no basis in reality and that it was used by the American war hawks to justify the failure of that war. The mythical "addicted army" was used, according to this work, to alter perceptions about that war, and it was based on falsehoods.

Parties to a potential moral-political conflict, and therefore to negotiations, are typically engaged in efforts to create or maintain a collective identity by defining the moral boundaries of the symbolic-moral universe of that collective. Hence, collective definitions of deviance always result in stigma contests and in deviantization processes. The creation of rules and punishments implies that the lifestyle, values, and morality of specific social groups has gained ascendancy over those of other groups, often at the other groups' expense (Gusfield 1963). Two examples followed by two illustrations will suffice.

First, until the first two decades of the twentieth century many psychoactive drugs were freely available in commercial and medical markets. Then, during these first two decades an effective campaign of various moral entrepreneurs made us all experience an interesting exercise in criminalization as slowly but surely most psychoactive substances were defined as dangerous and their use as criminal. Only towards the end of the century did some loud voices begin to be heard demanding a re-evaluation of this criminalization and its results, and that a "harm reduction" policy be introduced instead and that decriminalization, and even full legalization, be considered. Second, rape, which for so many decades was considered as a "sexual deviance," was re-interpreted as a crime which has sexual tones, but which is primarily a crime of violence reflecting an unequal distribution of power between the sexes.

TWO ILLUSTRATIONS

The first illustration is the European witch craze of the fourteenth to sixteenth centuries (Ben-Yehuda 1980, 1985). During this time, hundreds of thousands of innocent victims, the vast majority of whom were women, were defined as "witches" who conspired with Satan in order to have Satanic rule over the earth. Using torture, hearsay, dubious confessions, and kangaroo courts, tormented victims were convicted on phony charges and sentenced to a horrendous death: burning alive on the stake. Prior to this fateful time, witchcraft was perceived as a complex phenomenon. There were supposed to be good and bad witches, and a cosmic conspiracy by Satan and women to corrupt the world was not part of the phenomenon. Thus, a new form of crime had to be invented – witchcraft. This new crime was invented, developed, and defined by Dominican friars, and – using political power and influence – they managed to get it accepted. It is instructive to remember that the development of this new form of crime took place while European culture and society were undergoing a significant change – from the medieval social order to the Renaissance and beyond. This transition led to momentous changes in the status of women, the economy, the beginnings of the separation of the state from religion, different forms of religion coming to prominence, and more. The old, medieval culture and social order was crumbling and a new social order and culture was emerging. New modes of thinking and behavior, as well as new identities, were slowly replacing the old. Facing these changes, old elites were trying to re-establish the previous cultural hegemony, using their moral beliefs as well as considerable power, and they introduced a new and invented form of crime. The essence of this new crime, witchcraft, was that it explained the social, cognitive, and political upheavals in terms of a cosmic struggle between Satan and the Almighty. Moreover, Satan recruited humans in this struggle and those humans who were aware of this struggle must identify Satan's servants and eliminate them before it was too late. As the cultural and social changes continued, eventually the steam that drove the machinery that persecuted witches evaporated, and the persecutions and executions ended. A new cultural and social order came into being and the ferocious attempt to reinstate older symbolic-moral boundaries failed – at the terrible price of hundreds of thousands of innocent victims who were tortured to a horrific death.

The second illustration is focused on deviance within contemporary ongoing processes of social change and stability (Ben-Yehuda 2010a). Cultural conflicts can take place between and within societies. One of the arenas where such conflicts are played out is the media. Examining more than 50 years of media-reported unconventional and deviant behavior by the fundamentalist ultra-orthodox – *Haredi* – counter-cultural community in Israel yields some surprising results. To begin with, relying on *Haredi* culture's insistence on a policy of the "right of the people not to know," its media under-reports infractions and comparisons of them between *Haredi* and secular media tend to rely more on secular media. *Haredi* infractions reveal a pattern. They have increased over the years and the most salient feature of them is violence. This violence is not random or precipitated by some situational emotional rage. It is planned and aims to achieve political goals. Using verbal and non-verbal violence in the form of curses, intimidations, threats, setting fires, throwing stones, beatings, staging mass violations, and more, *Haredi* (and other theocratic) activists try to drive Israel to present more of a theocratic ambience. Most of the struggle is focused on feuds around the state-religion status quo and the public arena. Driven by a theological notion that stipulates that all Jews are mutually responsible and accountable to the Almighty, these activists believe that the sins of the few are paid by the many. Making Israel a theocracy will, they believe, reduce the risk of transcendental penalties. An interesting idea indeed for criminal justice theorists. Like other democracies in the global village, Israel has had to face both theocratic and secular pressures on a significant level of intensity. The political structure that accommodates these contradicting pressures is the theocratic democracy. This structure is characterized by chronic negotiations, tensions, and accommodations, and is based on dexterity of politicians. While by nature it is an unstable structure, it allows citizens with different worldviews to live under the umbrella of a nation-state without tearing the social fabric apart.

Cultural Criminology

Works like those of Kooistra (1989), Black (1984), or Heckert (1989) give deviants a role as potential shapers and manipulators of social realities. A new cultural criminology (Ferrell, Hayward & Young 2008) suggests examining deviants as rebels and searching for moments and incidences where deviants were effective in promoting cultural alternatives.

Concluding Summary

Deviance can be an elusive entity. Its essence is based on morality and power, two concepts that are themselves problematic. That there is a significant ambiguous layer in deviance need not surprise us.

Thus, instead of exhausting ourselves on definitional and characterization issues, it may be more effective and productive to try to understand the cultural and social role of deviance. Doing that leads us to classical formulations by Emile Durkheim and to examine deviance within the context of social change and stability.

Complex societies are composed of a number of symbolic-moral universes that compete and clash in terms of attractiveness for inhabitants. Each of these universes has moral codes and power structures. Moral activists in these universes may launch moral crusades and/or moral panics and use power so that their moral codes become hegemonic. This conceptualization has a few implications. One is that deviance and reactions to it can become important symbolic tools in processes that preserve symbolic stability or that cause change. In most cases, it is stability that is achieved by exposing and reacting to deviants. There have been many cases, though, where deviance and reactions to it led to changes. Understanding this analytical framing inevitably directs us to examine the area of politics and deviance.

The analytical perspective presented here also provides a clue to another question – are there challenges, and, if so, what is the direction of the challenges? Societies and cultures are constantly faced with challenges to the status quo that emerge from individualistic ideas in a large number of spheres: the arts, sciences, religion, politics, family life, the nature of work, gender, wealth, etc. Many of these challenges are formulated within the context of moral reactions and enterprises. Some of these ideas will be accepted and will promote significant changes in the boundaries of societal symbolic-moral universes. Others will be pushed away; no change in boundaries will take place and in fact the older boundaries will be re-affirmed. Because we know how and from where challenges come, we can analyze these challenges, one by one, and examine their impact. What we cannot do, given our present state of knowledge in social science, is to predict which challenges will be accepted and what will be the direction(s) of change, if any. That is, we can tell where challenges come from and how, but we cannot tell where they are going.

If this formulation sounds like Darwin's theory of survival of the fittest, it is because it does indeed resemble it. However, the significant differences between the two make the comparison and analogy valid only on a superficial, imagery, level. Evolution assumes the emergence of various genetic mutations, some or one of which will give a mutated species a survival advantage in a given environment in terms of offspring's adaptability to a changing environment. The conceptualization presented here focuses on non-biologically transmitted ideas and behaviors, and the fact that some of these ideas have the capacity to actually *change* (not adapt to given) social and physical ecologies. These are very significant differences as compared to evolutionary theory.

Note

1   This section is based on Ben-Yehuda 1990b, 2006, 2010b.

References

Becker, Howard S. (1963) *Outsiders*. New York: Free Press.
Bell, Robert R. (1971) *Social Deviance: A Substantive Analysis*. Homewood, IL: Dorsey Press.
Bendle, Mervyn (1999) "The Death of the Sociology of Deviance?" *Journal of Sociology* 35(1): 42–59.

Ben-Yehuda, Nachman (1980) "The European Witchcraze of the Fifteenth–Seventeenth Centuries: A Sociologist's Perspective." *American Journal of Sociology* 86(1): 1–31.

Ben-Yehuda, Nachman (1985) *Deviance and Moral Boundaries: Witchcraft, the Occult, Science Fiction, Deviant Sciences and Scientists*. Chicago: University of Chicago Press.

Ben-Yehuda, Nachman (1990a) "Positive Deviance: More Fuel for a Controversy." *Deviant Behavior* 11(3): 221–43.

Ben-Yehuda, Nachman (1990b) *The Politics and Morality of Deviance*. Albany, NY: State University of New York Press.

Ben-Yehuda, Nachman (1993) *Political Assassinations by Jews: A Rhetorical Device for Justice*. Albany, NY: State University of New York Press.

Ben-Yehuda, Nachman (2001) *Betrayals and Treason: Violations of Trust and Loyalty*. Boulder, CO: Westview Press.

Ben-Yehuda, Nachman (2005) "Terror, Media and Moral Boundaries." *International Journal of Comparative Sociology* 46(1–2): 33–53.

Ben-Yehuda, Nachman (2006) "Contextualizing Deviance within Social Change and Stability, Morality and Power." *Sociological Spectrum* 26(6): 559–80.

Ben-Yehuda, Nachman (2010a) *Theocratic Democracy: The Social Construction of Religious and Secular Extremism*. New York: Oxford University Press.

Ben-Yehuda, Nachman (2010b) "Social Change and Deviance." In Clifton D. Bryant (ed.), *Handbook on Deviant Behavior*. London: Sage.

Best, Joel (2004) *Deviance: Career of a Concept*. Belmont, CA: Thompson/Wadsworth.

Black, Donald (ed.) (1984) *Toward a General Theory of Social Control*. New York: Academic Press.

Best, Joel (2005) "Greatly Exaggerated? The Reports of Deviance's Death." Paper delivered at the 100th annual meeting of the American Sociological Association, Philadelphia, August 16.

Boltanski, Luc and Laurent Thévenot (2006) *On Justification: The Economies of Worth*. Princeton, NJ: Princeton University Press.

Braithwaite, John (1989) *Crime, Shame, and Reintegration*. New York: Cambridge University Press.

Cohen, Stanley (1972) *Folk Devils and Moral Panics*. London: MacGibbon and Kee.

Dombrink, John and Daniel Hillyard (2007) *Sin No More: From Abortion to Stem Cells, Understanding Crime, Law, and Morality in America*. New York: New York University Press.

Douglas, Jack (1977) "Shame and Deceit in Creative Deviance." In Edward Sagarin (ed.), *Deviance and Social Change*. Beverly Hills, CA: Sage, pp. 59–86.

Durkheim, Emile ([1933] 1964) *The Division of Labor in Society*. New York: Free Press.

Durkheim, Emile (1938) *The Rules of Sociological Method*. New York: Free Press.

Ferrell, Jeff, Keith Hayward, and Jock Young (2008) *Cultural Criminology: An Invitation*. London: Sage.

Garfinkel, Harold (1950) "Conditions of Successful Degradation Ceremonies." *American Journal of Sociology* 61: 420–4.

Goffman, Erving (1963) *Stigma*. Englewood Cliffs, NJ: Prentice Hall.

Goode, Erich (2002) "Does the Death of the Sociology of Deviance Claim Make Sense?" *American Sociologist* 33(3): 107–18.

Goode, Erich (2004a) "Is the Sociology of Deviance Still Relevant?" *American Sociologist* 35(4): 46–57.

Goode, Erich (2004b) "The 'Death' MacGuffin Redux: Comments on Best." *Deviant Behavior* 25(5): 493–509.

Goode, Erich and Nachman Ben-Yehuda (2009) *Moral Panics. The Social Construction of Deviance*. Chichester: Wiley-Blackwell.

Gottfredson, Michael M. and Travis Hirschi (1990) *A General Theory of Crime*. Stanford, CA: Stanford University Press.

Gusfield, J. R. (1963) *Symbolic Crusade: Status Politics and the American Temperance Movement*. Chicago: University of Illinois Press.

Heckert, Maria Druann (1989) "The Relativity of Positive Deviance: The Case of the French Impressionists." *Deviant Behavior* 10(2): 131–44.

Hendershott, Ann (2002) *The Politics of Deviance*. San Francisco: Encounter Books.

Kooistra, Paul (1989) *Criminals as Heroes: Structure, Power and Identity*. Bowling Green, OH: Bowling Green State University Popular Press.

Kuzmarov, Jeremy (2009) *The Myth of the Addicted Army*. Amherst, MA: University of Massachusetts Press.

Lauderdale, Pat (ed.) (2003) *A Political Analysis of Deviance*. Toronto: De Sitter Publications.

Lowe, Brian M. (2006) *Emerging Moral Vocabularies: The Creation and Establishment of New Forms of Moral and Ethical Meanings*. Oxford: Lexington Books.

Miller, J. Mitchell, Richard A. Wright, and David Dannels (2001) "Is Deviance Dead? The Decline of a Sociological Research Specialization." *American Sociologist* 32(2): 43–59.

Roebuck, J. and S. C. Weeber (1978) *Political Crime in the United States*. New York: Praeger.

Ross, Jeffrey Ian (2002) *Dynamics of Political Crime*. Thousand Oaks, CA: Sage.

Schur, Edwin M. (1980) *The Politics of Deviance*. Englewood Cliffs, NJ: Prentice Hall.

Sumner, Colin (1994a) *The Sociology of Deviance: An Obituary*. Buckingham: Open University Press.

Sumner, Colin (1994b) "The Social Nature of Crime and Deviance." In John Curra (ed.), *Understanding Social Deviance: From the Near Side to the Outer Limits*. New York: HarperCollins, pp. 3–31.

Young, Jock (1971) *The Drugtakers*. London: MacGibbon and Kee.

Zurcher, Louis A. Jr., George R. Kirkpatrick, Robert G. Cushing, and Charles K. Bowman (1971) "The Anti-Pornography Campaign: A Symbolic Crusade." *Social Problems* 19(2): 217–38.

13

Criminology

CHARLES F. WELLFORD

INTRODUCTION

Ask a student majoring in sociology the name of the founder of their major and undoubtedly they will respond Auguste Comte. Every sociology textbook identifies Comte as the founder of sociology because of the central role that he played in laying the foundation for that discipline. Ask a student majoring in criminology to name the founder of that discipline and you are likely to get first a pause and then the name Beccaria and then Lombroso. This reflects the fact that criminology actually has two beginnings, one in the late 1700s and one in the late 1800s. These two beginnings mean that criminology has two sometimes divergent intellectual traditions: a focus on the criminal justice system and a focus on the causes of crime. Far too frequently these two dimensions of the field are treated not only as separate intellectual traditions but as antagonistic ones. In this chapter I trace the development of these two traditions in criminology and describe their current status, with particular emphasis on the increasing convergence between the two. The classic definition of criminology offered by Sutherland (1924) is that criminology is the scientific study of the making of law, the breaking of law, and society's reaction to law breaking. This definition describes the foundations of criminology, with Beccaria primarily addressing the making of law and how society should react to law breaking, and Lombroso primarily focusing on the causes of crime. While other social sciences have contributed greatly to each of these areas during the last 50 years, it has been the emergence of a separate discipline of criminology that has resulted in the greatest contributions to our understanding.

The Wiley-Blackwell Companion to Sociology, First Edition. Edited by George Ritzer.
© 2012 Blackwell Publishing Ltd. Published 2012 by Blackwell Publishing Ltd.

THE MAKING OF LAW

Cesare Beccaria was a little known Italian lawyer whose work, *Essays on Crime and Punishment*, published in 1764, made him famous and fundamentally changed how scholars and governments approached legal reform. This work offered a theory of the origins of law, a structure of government derived from that theory, and a criminal justice system that was to be grounded in science. Beccaria's ([1764] 1963: 10–13) theory of law contains five fundamental propositions:

1   "No man ever freely sacrificed a portion of his personal liberty merely in behalf of the common good."
2   "Laws are the conditions under which independent and isolated men united to form a society."
3   Punishments are necessary to prevent the "despotic spirit, which is in every man" from seeking to maximize his pleasure at the expense of fundamental liberties of others.
4   Therefore, men give up some of their liberty to the state so that society can function.
5   Excessive punishments are in themselves unjust – they must be severe enough to prevent law violations and no more.

Obviously influenced by Montesquieu, this theory of the origins of law became the intellectual foundation for the American Revolution and Constitution and the reform of legal systems throughout Europe.

For Beccaria, governments founded with this understanding of the source of law must: have a publicly known and understandable system of laws that prescribe specific punishments; be characterized by a separation of powers between the executive, legislative, and judicial branches; and with "geometric precision" (scientifically established) demonstrate that punishments are certain, quick, and minimally severe. Numerous leaders (including Blackstone, Adams, and Jefferson) noted the importance of these ideas to their efforts to create a new system of laws and new governments.

However, note that for Beccaria the explanation of law did not require great scholarship. The only laws that should exist are those that are necessary for the protection of individual liberties. Murder, sexual assault, kidnapping, and theft were illegal because if these behaviors were not controlled society could not function to protect the liberty interests of its citizens. These behaviors would be universally proscribed. The only issue for science was how to set the punishment for each and how to increase the certainty that those who violated these laws were fairly apprehended, tried, and punished. So although criminology includes the science of law making as a central issue, the question of why these behaviors are defined as crimes everywhere and at all times (see Linton 1954) is not central to the discipline. Rather the central questions are about fair, effective, and just police, court, and correctional systems and the setting of penalties that are consistent with Beccaria's theory of law.[1]

For many years the position of criminology was that the discipline had little to offer to the question of the effectiveness of the criminal justice system. For example,

David Bailey, as recently as 1994, observed that, "repeated analysis has consistently failed to find any connection between the number of police officers and crime rates . . . [and] the primary strategies adopted by modern police have been shown to have little or no effect on crime" (1994: 3). This statement by a leading police scholar reflects well the notion that criminology had little to offer to our understanding of how police reduce crime. More recently this position has changed, beginning with the pioneering work in 1999 on homicide investigations (Wellford & Cronin 1999). This work for the first time demonstrated that certain steps taken by the police during homicide investigations could significantly improve the ability of police to make correct arrests in these cases. In 2004 the National Academy of Sciences' report on policing concluded that criminological research on police deployment had clearly demonstrated that deploying police in areas of high crime and utilizing a research-based approach to police activities were highly effective in reducing crime in those areas without displacement to other portions of cities or jurisdictions. Approaches developed by criminologists labeled "hotspots policing" (e.g., Sherman, Gartin & Buerger 1989) and "evidence-based policing" along with crime mapping are now standard activities for police agencies. These developments from criminology are widely thought to have contributed to the substantial decline in crime since the early 1990s (National Academy of Sciences 2004). These approaches have also led to research which has identified best police practices for reducing a wide range of criminal activities. Today the conclusions drawn by Bailey nearly 20 years ago are no longer supported and are called into question by a body of research that demonstrates how well criminologists have been able to improve the operations of police agencies.

The question of the fairness of the justice system continues to be a central focus for criminology. Early research demonstrated a strong racial bias in the operation of the criminal justice system (Green 1970). However, as research methodologies improved and our understanding of criminal justice procedures advanced, the strength of the association between race and criminal justice outcomes diminished (Zatz 1987). While the estimates of racial impacts on criminal justice operations were reduced, the fact that any impact remained, even in sophisticated research models, increased concern about fairness in the criminal justice system. Criminologists sought to address this residual but not inconsequential flaw in the justice system by trying to identify ways in which the methods of criminology could be used to further reduce the impact of race on criminal justice outcomes. While research on the death penalty which demonstrated a clear impact of race on the imposition of the most serious punishment (Paternoster 2001) was not accepted by the courts (McKlesskey v. Georgia), the development of sentencing guidelines systems has profoundly changed sentencing in the United States.

It has long been known that the race of the defendant, particularly in crimes of violence when combined with the race of the victim, is correlated with the sentences given in criminal courts. As criminologists demonstrated this fact in a continuing body of research, judges and others began to call for changes in sentencing that would address this issue. In some jurisdictions this was accomplished through the passage of laws that mandated specific sentences for specific types of offenses and offenders (determinate sentencing). These approaches proved relatively unworkable because they resulted in such an absence of discretion in the judicial process that outcomes were felt to be unfair and unsustainable. Another approach to reducing racial disparity in sentencing was the development of sentencing guidelines systems (Frankel 1974). Today 23 states operate with sentencing guidelines systems that involve substantial involvement of criminologists. Guidelines systems, although differing in important ways, all involve the conduct of research to describe past sentencing in terms of the offense for which one is convicted and the criminal history characteristics of the offender (the two most agreed-upon legal sentencing criteria). These historical descriptions are then adjusted to achieve appropriate symmetry in the establishment of sentencing guidelines that specify ranges of punishments for specific offenses and offenders. These guidelines can be presumptive or voluntary but in all cases they have been found to be used by judges extensively. While judges have been upset by guidelines systems because they limit their discretion, and the Supreme Court has recently called into question the constitutionality of requiring that judges use guidelines (United States v. Booker 2005), voluntary systems that allow judges to benefit from a better understanding of past sentencing have proven to be quite successful in further reducing the impact of race on judicial outcomes and allowing jurisdictions that wish to do so to make greater use of alternatives to incarceration and maintain or reduce their prison populations (Baumer 2010).

Similarly, in the area of arrest decisions by police, research has demonstrated a continuing racial effect in these decisions (Walker 2010). This research has prompted the police and the courts to be much more concerned about racial components of police actions. This has become most prominent in the area of racial profiling for motor vehicle violations (sometimes referred to as the offense of "driving while black"). Racial profiling and the role of race in decisions to issue citations, to search cars and persons, and to effectuate arrest as a result of traffic stops have been studied in great detail. This research has resulted in numerous administrative actions and court decisions which have sought to reduce this form of racial discrimination in our justice system. While it is too early to tell if these have substantially reduced the role of race in all police actions, it is clear that the impact on traffic law enforcement has been substantial.

Finally, in studies of the correctional system and parole release decisions criminologists have sought to document the extent of racial disproportionality in decisions about the allocation of correctional resources. Since Beccaria called for a criminal justice system that was effective and just, criminologists have sought to use their research approaches to document the role of race in criminal justice decision-making. Where the best research has demonstrated a continuing indication of race effects, criminologists have sought to develop research-based strategies to address these concerns. In summary, over the last 250 years criminology has advanced Beccaria's notion of the need for a fair system by using social science research strategies to first document the problems of racial and other disparity in criminal justice processing and then develop techniques for reducing this impact. Finally, criminologists have been at the forefront of identifying effective police deployment and investigative strategies to improve the fairness and efficiency of police operations and investigations in reducing crime. The goal of effective and just systems of criminal justice that was central to Beccaria and the emerging democracies he influenced continues to motivate and direct criminology today.

The influence of Beccaria can be seen in the continuing focus of criminology on the issue of deterrence – that is, establishing penalties that are just severe enough to offset the benefits of engaging in crime. Beccaria called on criminology to identify with "geometric precision" the appropriate punishment for each offense and offender. While some early criminology contended that criminals were "born" criminal and thus could not be deterred, the reality of punishment in the justice system prompted criminologists to continue to focus on this issue. No matter what theories of crime might say, the justice system assigns punishments.

Beccaria postulated that the deterrence capacity of a punishment was determined by its certainty, celerity, and severity – in that order. While punishments should not be too severe, they must be certain and quickly applied. Two hundred years of experience and 100 years of research have demonstrated that the American system of justice is low in certainty, slow in application, and more severe than that of any other Western democracy. As a result, the deterrent effect of the American system is called into question by critics and some research. It is very clear that the American criminal justice system is low in certainty. The probability of being arrested if you commit homicide is approximately 60 percent; for burglary it is less than 15 percent; and for drug offenses below 1 percent. The mean time from arrest to imposition of sentence for those found guilty of committing serious crimes is 14 months. Thus, combining certainty and celerity characteristics, you would predict low levels of deterrence. On the other hand, American retention of the death penalty, levels of use of imprisonment, and length of sentences result in the United States being the most punitive society amongst Western democracies.

But punishments can deter those who have not committed a crime (general deterrence) or those who are being punished (special deterrence). Those punished may be deterred but may also learn new crime skills during their punishment or be further disaffected from society, resulting in even more crime than they would have committed if not punished. Those punishments that remove offenders from their communities may also result in collateral consequences for their children, spouses or partners, and communities (Rose & Clear 1998). So estimating the deterrent effect of punishment requires measures of the impact of the punishment on the person punished; those not punished but who might commit the crime; and those not punished who are connected to the offender. This is much more complicated than Beccaria anticipated. It is this more complex notion of deterrence that underlies contemporary criminological research. In a recent review of the full body of research, Durlauf and Nagin (2011) conclude that current punishments have a deterrent effect but that we could achieve the same levels of crime control with less punishment and more certainty. As summarized by Paternoster: "although there may be some dispute as to how large an effect formal sanctions may have on crime, there is little dispute that formal punishments . . . do seem to lower crime" (2009: 240).

In summary, criminology has had profound impacts on the nature of our criminal justice system by focusing on two issues of importance to Beccaria: creating a fair system of justice, and maximizing the deterrent effect of punishments while not violating the principle that the pains of punishment should just exceed the benefits of committing the crime. The next steps are to focus on increasing certainty and celerity of punishment consistent with our notions of individual rights and the rule of law.

THE BREAKING OF LAW

In 1876 another Italian, this time a physician, published a book that was to transform how we think about criminals. Cesare Lombroso wrote *The Criminal Man* in which he reported on his observations of criminals while working as a doctor at a local prison. In the first edition of this work (only 252 pages in length) he observed that criminals had physical characteristics that more closely resembled animals lower in the evolutionary chain than humans. Writing just 17 years after Darwin's *On the Origin of Species* (1859), which introduced the notion of evolution into scientific and popular thinking, Lombroso explained crime as the behavior of humans who were "throwbacks" to earlier developmental forms. Their physical appearance signaled their inferior intellectual and moral development. Crime was a product of this inferior development. For 30 years the biological causes of crime heavily influenced thinking about crime causation.[2] The most forceful rejection of this particular approach to crime causation came with the publication of a large-scale empirical test of Lombroso's theory, *The English Convict* (1913). The author, Charles Goring, using the emerging statistical techniques that now form the basis of social science empirical research, tested convicts and non-convicts and demonstrated that the physical differences that Lombroso described did not differentiate between these groups. In fact, by the time this work was published Lombroso had published the fifth edition of his book, each edition getting longer and noting other possible explanations of crime (the fifth edition had grown to 1,903 pages and listed hundreds of causes of crime).

SINGLE FACTOR REDUCTIONISM

In his initial formulation, Lombroso argued that all crime could be explained by one factor – a failure of evolution. No other variable or dimension needed to be considered to understand the range of crimes and/or the types of criminals. The theory was parsimonious to the extreme; this single factor could explain crime. Soon others began to identify other single factor explanations for crime; mental illness (or as it was called then, "feeblemindedness" [Dugdale 1877]), bad families, the loss of faith or religion, and other explanations were offered, not as parts of a comprehensive explanation but as *the* explanation of crime – all influences reduced to this one factor. This approach quickly collapsed as the study of those who committed crime began to identify a wide range of characteristics that appeared to distinguish criminals from non-criminals.[3] This led to the next two approaches to developing theories of criminal behavior: systemic reductionism and multidisciplinary approaches. While they occurred simultaneously, systemic reductionism had the greater influence, for reasons I now discuss.

SYSTEMIC REDUCTIONISM

As noted earlier, there was a period of over 50 years between the time when criminology emerged as a field of study and when it was institutionalized in universities and with its own professional organizations. During this period, in the United States,[4] criminology was contained in almost all instances in sociology departments. As such, during this period the explanation of crime causation was constrained by the sociological system of knowledge. Systemic reductionism expanded beyond sociology but it was the sociological perspective that dominated criminological theory for many years, and even today it is the dominant theoretical perspective. The importance of systemic reductionism can be seen in many criminological textbooks where the discussion of crime causation is organized in a series of sections – sociological explanations, psychological explanations, and biological explanations – each presented as if these systems of knowledge were unrelated to each other and they provided competing ways of explaining crime.

Why did the study of crime, which all the early thinkers recognized as having a multitude of explanations, become the exclusive domain of sociology? Most likely because of the way sociology developed at the University of Chicago – the birthplace of American sociology. Here sociology (the Chicago School) was the study of urban development and the problems associated with such development. It made perfect sense to locate the study of crime in such a field of study, and once located there it is not surprising that the theories that came to dominate criminology were sociological in nature. The biology and psychology of crime were greatly minimized and instead crime was seen as a function of community, family, school, and the other socializing institutions. The explanation of crime became the explanation of crime rate differences within the city, across class levels, and between recent immigrants and less recent immigrants. Criminals were disproportionately found in poverty and in homes and friendships that saw criminal behavior as a reasonable response to their social location. As Dennis Wrong (1961) would observe near the end of this period of theory in criminology, sociological systemic reductionism presented an "oversocialized conception" of human behavior, largely ignoring personality and biology.

This is not to suggest that this period made no contributions to understanding crime. The focus on variation in crime rates introduced issues of critical importance to understanding crime. Theories like differential association (Sutherland 1924; which offered a social learning explanation), anomie (Merton 1938; which explained crime concentrations in the lower class as a result of a cultural condition), culture conflict (Sellin 1938; which suggested that crime clustered in groups going through a transition from one culture to another), social disorganization (Shaw & McKay 1942; which explained crime in poor areas as a result of the relative absence of family and community controls on behavior), and labeling (Schur 1971; Lemert 1972; which argued for the criminogenic effect of designating people as criminals) have proven to be valuable in the development of more comprehensive theories of crime and theory-based crime interventions. All of these approaches persist today in only slightly modified form or as part of more complex explanations. The essential element in sociological systemic reductionism is that crime is clustered in the lower class and therefore there is something about this social situation that accounts for the higher rates of crime. The individual offender is a reflection of his or her social situation.

Multidisciplinary Approaches

Of course sociologists were not the only ones interested in the causes of crime. While sociology was dominating the study of crime in universities, psychologists, biologists, and others were considering how their disciplines or theoretical perspectives would explain such behavior. Furthermore, it became clear that these other perspectives offered reasonable approaches and research that demonstrated that the approaches had some level of empirical support. Gradually, a model of crime explanation emerged that is still with us today, especially in standard criminological texts – the multidisciplinary explanation of criminal behavior. This approach argues that there is a set of explanations for the causes of criminality, drawn from all of the social and behavioral sciences, including biology, psychology, anthropology, economics, and sociology. Only by using all of these perspectives can one understand criminal behavior. This can be seen in contemporary criminological texts which have separate chapters on each of these approaches to explaining crime. Of course, multidisciplinary approaches are not theories at all but rather the search for the set of causal variables that explain the greatest amount of variation in the occurrence of criminal behavior.

The most prominent practitioners of multidisciplinary criminology were Sheldon and Eleanor Glueck (1968). In a series of longitudinal studies they sought to find the factors that "unraveled" juvenile delinquency and adult criminal behavior. Sheldon Glueck was a lawyer with little advanced education in the social and behavioral sciences. While Eleanor had that education, it was Sheldon who formulated their approach to research and theory. Working in a law school setting they pursued an empirically based way to predict and explain criminal law violations of juveniles and adults. In a particularly clear statement of their position and their rejection of systemic reductionism, the Gluecks observed that:

> It is common knowledge that the great majority of children growing up in urban slums do not become delinquents despite the deprivations of a vicious environment, despite the fact that they and their parents have not had access to fruitful economic opportunities, despite the fact that they are swimming around in the same antisocial subculture in which delinquents and gang members are said to thrive. Why? (Glueck & Glueck 1968)

Their position was that the then dominant sociological approach could not explain the empirical reality that most of those who grow up in high crime areas are not criminal. Their focus was on explaining why a few in those areas became, and in some cases remained for many years, offenders while others did not. To answer this question they sought to find out what distinguished the law violator from the non-law violator when both came from the same deprived social conditions. To do this they studied similarly socially situated individuals, looking for shared characteristics that distinguished them. Drawing on what they considered the best possible sources of explanation, they considered biological factors (e.g., body type), psychological differences, family structure, parent behavior differences, and school factors, in an effort to predict and understand the occurrence of delinquent and criminal behaviors. In all of their works the Gluecks sought to identify the specific set of factors that accounted for the fact that individuals faced with the same difficult social conditions would behave differently.

Sheldon and Eleanor Glueck sought to move the study of criminal behavior out of the sole domain of sociology and make it at least multidisciplinary. They did this by showing the empirical relationship between criminal behavior and a number of factors drawn from a variety of disciplines and perspectives. However, their work did not produce a coherent theory of crime that went beyond their empirical results – it did produce a scale that was widely used (for a time) to predict delinquency and focus prevention and intervention efforts and it did force criminologists to begin to recognize that disciplines other than sociology would be needed to develop a comprehensive explanation of the criminal behavior of individuals.

INTERDISCIPLINARY EXPLANATIONS

Criminology as a separate field of study emerges when the model underlying the explanation of criminal behavio\r becomes interdisciplinary. Only then does an intellectual justification for a separate field of study in universities exist that is compelling enough to support such a development. Today, the leading journal in criminology – the journal of the American Society of Criminology – has as its subtitle "An Interdisciplinary Journal": a clear statement of the importance of this perspective to criminology.

But what do we mean by inte rdisciplinary theory? Most obviously, this approach assumes that more than one discipline is needed to explain criminal behavior. Any approach to explanation that is built on one discipline is by definition incomplete. But if we only have explanations based on the accumulation of variables from different disciplines we have what the Gluecks proposed – multidisciplinary explanations. So an interdisciplinary theory goes beyond the assembly of contributions of different disciplines and integrates the contributions of these different disciplines into a coherent theory of criminal behavior. This approach emphasizes bringing perspectives together, not the competition of perspectives to see which one is "right."

In interdisciplinary theory it is assumed that there is a role for biological, psychological, social, and cultural explanations but that the relationship between these perspectives is as important and that no perspective can totally explain the influence of another perspective. Thus, interdisciplinary theory can be expected to contain elements of all of the explanatory perspectives but also to go beyond that to identify how each level of explanation influences, but does not eliminate, the other levels of explanation. For example, the question is not whether nature or nurture causes crime but how they interact to account for individual variations in criminal behavior. It is not a question of why poverty seems to be associated with higher crime rates, but how individual development and poverty interact to explain why some are delinquent and others are not. Each dimension of explanation is to a degree irreducible and each is related to and influences the other.

One of the most influential theories in criminology today is developmental or life course theory.[5] This is a good example of how interdisciplinary theory is emerging as the dominant paradigm in the field. Robert Sampson (2001) suggests that this approach to theory is "best introduced by considering the questions it asks," which he identifies as including:

- Why and when do most juveniles stop offending?
- What factors explain desistance?
- Are some delinquents destined to become persistent criminals in adulthood?
- Is there in fact such a thing as a life-course persistent offender?
- What explains the stability of offending?

One of the early contributors to this approach, Terrie Moffitt (2001), addressed these questions by hypothesizing that there were two patterns of antisocial behavior: life-course persistent – those who started early and maintained involvement in antisocial behavior throughout the life course – and adolescent-limited – those whose antisocial behavior emerges and ends during that period of the life course. Moffitt (2001: 34) observes that the persistent pattern results from "childhood neuropsychological problems interacting cumulatively with their criminogenic environments producing a pathological personality." With the adolescent-limited pattern, "a contemporary maturity gap encourages teens to mimic antisocial behavior in ways that are normative and adjustive." Clearly, biological, psychological, and social levels of explanation are evident even in this summary statement of her work. This is characteristic of efforts to answer the questions posed by Sampson, and it is a central characteristic of life course theory. For this reason, this approach offers a framework for criminology to move closer to an interdisciplinary theory of criminal behavior that will more fully justify the emergence of the field as a new discipline in the social and behavioral sciences.

For almost two centuries after Beccaria, criminologists did not pay consistent and organized attention to the criminal justice system. Rather, the tradition of criminology begun by Lombroso – the search for the causes of crime – was the focus of criminology until the last half of the twentieth century. This period of searching for the causes of crime passed through four distinct phases of theoretical development:[6] single factor reductionism; systemic reductionism; multidisciplinary theories; and interdisciplinary theory. Today, interdisciplinary theory stands as the dominant model for explaining crime (and other human behaviors). Criminology today rests on two foundations: the interdisciplinary explanation of crime, and the analysis of the fairness and effectiveness of the criminal justice system. Both of these fundamental aspects of criminology are informed by the application of scientific methods (as called for by Beccaria, Lombroso, and Sutherland).

SOCIETY'S REACTION TO LAW BREAKING

But what of the other focus of criminology – how societies react to law breaking? As Ingraham (1987) observed, following his comparative analysis of criminal procedure, all systems of justice are organized to apprehend offenders, determine guilt, and impose punishments. Though the means to do this may vary in time and space, the functions are always performed. While police and prosecution practices are heavily influenced by what we know about how these work best in the United States, no country seeks to emulate our approach to punishment. The high rate of use of imprisonment and the length of sentences given in the United States are not the standards for effective and fair justice systems around the world. In fact, many contend that US punishment practices are more like those of a developing, non-democratic country than those of a highly industrialized, Western democracy. This aspect of US reaction to crime has sparked much discussion and some research.

For much of the twentieth century the rate of imprisonment in the United States hovered around 100 inmates per 100,000. This rate was so stable that Blumstein and Cohen (1973) developed a theory of punishment that argued this level would always remain, even in periods of high crime, because the system would adjust by shortening sentences or accelerating release from prison. Less than two years after this publication, imprisonment rates increased rapidly to current levels of about 500 per 100,000. Today in the United States there are over 2 million people in prison and another 4 million under community supervision by the criminal justice system. Why this has occurred and with what impact are important questions for criminologists and policymakers. While some will always offer a conflict or Marxist interpretation of such changes (e.g., prison populations increase to control the "dangerous classes"), the focus in criminology has been to better understand the increases before offering an explanation.

The increase in prison populations has been the result of increased sentence lengths, slower rates of release from prison, and higher rates of return to prison for violation of conditions of release. Increases in the rate of commitment have only minimally contributed to the increase in prison populations (Blumstein & Beck 1999). Changes in criminal justice processes account for this increase, not changes in demography or the extent or nature of crime. Why have these processes occurred? I suggest that three overriding factors have been most important in this shift in the American response to crime. First, crime became more of a national political issue than ever before in United States history; second, there was widespread acceptance of the apparent finding from research that criminal rehabilitation did not work (Martinson 1974); and, finally, there was widespread acceptance of the findings of research that a small number of persons (5 percent) accounted for a large portion of crime (over 50 percent) (Wolfgang, Figlio & Sellin 1972). Political and professional wisdom concluded that prisons could not change people, therefore we should keep offenders in as long as the law would allow, that the laws and/or sentences should be changed to make sure this happened, and since we could not accurately identify the 5 percent we should adopt incapacitation as a universal means of controlling crime. Today we are seeing the devastating consequences of this approach for individuals, communities, and government budgets. Since 2000 the increase in prison populations has been a factor in the reduction in crime (best estimates are that the increase in prison populations accounts for 5–20 percent of the crime drop [Levitt 1997]), but some argue that the costs associated with this strategy have not been worth the benefits. In any case, we are now in a period where society's reaction is changing to one that emphasizes risk assessment and the reservation of imprisonment for those who need to be incarcerated to protect the public.

In this new era criminology becomes even more prominent in the development of effective strategies. Research evaluating what works in corrections (MacKenzie 2008) is demanded by policymakers before they institute new programs. Cost-effectiveness studies are in great demand (Aos 2004). The development of risk assessment instruments for corrections is widespread. Just as in earlier times police and courts recognized the value of criminology, now correctional policymakers have turned to the social sciences to assist them in the task of "right-sizing" prisons and developing cost-effective correctional programs, especially for the 700,000 persons leaving prisons each year and reentering society (Travis 2005).

CONCLUSION

In almost 250 years criminology has emerged as a separate social science that focuses on three primary questions: why we have law, why people break the law, and how society does and should respond to law breaking. Great progress has been made in all of these areas. The next great stride in the discipline will see the closer alignment of our approach to these issues – mainly in the greater use of theory in addressing law making and responses to law breaking. This will require the development of much better understanding of the causes of crime than currently exists. Recently, Weisburd and Piquero (2008) asked the question: how good are our theories in explaining criminal behavior and the distribution of crime? Their answer, which was based on an analysis of tests of criminological theory published in the leading criminology journal between 1968 and 2005, was not encouraging. They found that the level of variation explained by the theories was low (80–90 percent unexplained); there was no improvement in explained variation over time; and the weakest theories were those trying to explain individual criminal behavior. This represents the greatest challenge to criminology – providing much better answers to the question asked by Lombroso: why do we have criminals?

Notes

1 Criminology's focus on the making of law has been on why certain behaviors that are not seen as so central to societies' functioning are criminalized. Chambliss's (1969) study of vagrancy laws, and the consideration of the impact of the criminalization of drug use and prostitution, are the most important of these efforts. Still they are not central to the discipline.

2 For a discussion of this criminological work during this period see Vold (1979), especially chs. 3 and 4.

3 This approach continues today in some public and political discourse. Too frequently we hear that crime is caused by "welfare moms," lead paint, unemployment, and a variety of other factors. Criminologists can usually respond, yes, but that is just one of a myriad of characteristics that may cause crime and the problem is that we do not know which is most important and how these many factors interact. This type of response reinforces the idea held by some that criminologists do not know much about crime.

4   In Europe and the rest of the world, criminology did not develop as rapidly as it did in the United States. In many ways, the history of criminology since the beginning of the twentieth century until quite recently has been written in the United States, hence the focus on crime and justice in the United States in this chapter.

5   As noted earlier, criminological theories do not easily disappear. The problem has been that these theories accumulate but are not cumulative. The issue addressed today in criminology is how to use an interdisciplinary framework to integrate these theories and develop cumulative knowledge.

6   While these themes were dominant during specific times, the development of theories of crime has not been so straightforward or developmental. In fact, all four approaches to explaining the causes of crime can still be found today.

References

Aos, Steven (2004) *Benefits and Costs of Prevention and Early Intervention Programs for Youths*. Olympia, WA: Washington State Institute of Public Policy.

Bailey, David (1994) *Police for the Future*. New York: Oxford University Press.

Baumer, Eric (2010) "Reassessing and Redirecting Research on Race and Sentencing." Paper presented at the Symposium of the Past and Future of Empirical Sentencing Research, Albany, NY.

Beccaria, C. ([1764] 1963) *Essays on Crime and Punishment*. Trans. Henry Paolucci. Indianapolis, IN: Bobbs-Merrill.

Blumstein, Alfred and Allen Beck (1999) "Population Growth in U.S. Prisons. 1980–1996." In M. Tonry (ed.), *Crime and Justice: A Review of Research*, Vol. 26. Chicago: University of Chicago Press, pp. 17–61.

Blumstein, Alfred and Jacqueline Cohen (1973) "A Theory of the Stability of Punishment." *Journal of Criminal Law and Criminology* 64: 198–207.

Chambliss, William (1969) *Crime and the Legal Process*. New York: McGraw-Hill.

Darwin, Charles (1859) *On the Origin of Species*. London: John Murray.

Dugdale, R. (1877) *The Jukes: A Study in Crime, Pauperism and Heredity*. New York: Putnam.

Durlauf, Steven and Daniel Nagin (2011) "Imprisonment and Crime: Can Both Be Reduced?" *Criminology and Public Policy* 10(1): 13–54.

Frankel, Marvin (1974) *Criminal Sentences: Law without Order*. New York: Hill and Wang.

Glueck, S. and E. Glueck (1968) *Delinquents and Nondelinquents in Perspective*. Cambridge, MA: Harvard University Press.

Goring, C. (1913) *The English Convict*. Reprinted 1972. Montclair, NJ: Patterson Smith.

Green, Edward (1970) "Race, Social State and Criminal Arrest." *American Sociological Review* 35: 476–90.

Ingraham, Barton L. (1987) *The Structure of Criminal Procedure*. New York: Greenwood Press.

Lemert, E. (1972) *Human Deviance, Social Problems and Social Control*, 2nd edn. Englewood Cliffs, NJ: Prentice Hall.

Levitt, Steven (1997) "Using Electoral Cycles in Police Hiring to Estimate the Effect of Police on Crime." *American Economic Review* 87(3): 270–90.

Linton, Ralph (1954) "The Problem of Universal Values." In Robert F. Spencer (ed.), *Method and Perspective in Anthropology (Papers in Honor of Wilson D. Wallis)*. Minneapolis: University of Minnesota Press, pp. 145–68.

Lombroso, C. (1876) *Criminal Man*. Milan: Hoepli.

MacKenzie, Doris (2008) *What Works in Corrections*. Cambridge: Cambridge University Press.

Martinson, Robert (1974) "What Works? – Questions and Answers about Prison Reform." *The Public Interest* 35: 22–54.

Merton, R. (1938) "Social Structure and Anomie." *American Sociological Review* 3: 672–82.

Moffitt, T. (2001) "Adolescence-Limited and Life Course Persistent Antisocial Behavior." In A. Piquero and P. Mazerolle (eds.), *Life-Course Criminology*. Belmont, CA: Wadsworth, pp. 91–145.

National Academy of Sciences (2004) *Fair and Effective Policing*. Washington, DC: National Academy Press.

Paternoster, Raymond ([1991] 2001) *Capital Punishment in America*. Lexington, MA: Lexington Books.

Paternoster, Raymond (2009) "Deterrence and Rational Choice Theories." In J. Mitchell Miller (ed.), *21st Century Criminology*. Thousand Oaks, CA: Sage, pp. 236–45.

Rose, Dina and Todd R. Clear (1998) "Incarceration, Social Capital and Crime: Examining the Unintended Consequences of Incarceration." *Criminology* 36(3): 441–79.

Sampson, R. (2001) "Foreword." In A. Piquero and P. Mazerolle (eds.), *Life-Course Criminology*. Belmont, CA: Wadsworth.

Schur, E. (1971) *Labeling Deviant Behavior*. Englewood Cliffs, NJ: Prentice Hall.

Sellin, T. (1938) *Culture Conflict and Crime*. New York: Social Science Research Council.

Shaw, C. and H. McKay (1942) *Juvenile Delinquency and Urban Areas*. Chicago: University of Chicago Press.

Sherman, Lawrence, Patrick Gartin, and Michael Buerger (1989) "Hot Spots of Predatory Crime." *Criminology* 27: 27–55.

Sutherland, E. (1924) *Principles of Criminology*. Philadelphia, PA: Lippincott.

Travis, Jeremy (2005) *But They All Come Back*. Washington, DC: Urban Institute Press.

Vold, G. (1979) *Theoretical Criminology*, 2nd edn. Prepared by T. Bernard. Oxford: Oxford University Press.

Walker, Samuel (2010) *The Color of Justice*. Belmont, CA: Wadsworth Press.

Weisburd, David and Alex Piquero (2008) "How Well Do Criminologists Explain Crime?" In M. Tonry (ed.), *Crime and Justice: A Review of Research,* Vol. 37. Chicago: University of Chicago Press, pp. 453–502.

Wellford, Charles and James Cronin (1999) "Factors Influencing the Clearance of Homicide Cases." *NIJ Journal* 1.

Wolfgang, Marvin, Robert Figlio, and Thorsten Sellin (1972) *Delinquency in a Birth Cohort*. Chicago: University of Chicago Press.

Wrong, Dennis (1961) "The Oversocialized Conception of Man." *American Sociological Review* 26: 183–93.

Zatz, Marjorie (1987) "The Changing Forms of Racial and Ethnic Bias in Sentencing." *Journal of Research in Crime and Delinquency* 24(1): 69–92.

14

Critical Sexualities Studies

KEN PLUMMER

As sex goes, so goes society. As society goes so goes sexuality.
Jeffrey Weeks (2003: 33)

For the first 150 years of its existence, sociologists paid very little serious attention to the study of human sexualities. True, Max Weber wrote a little about the rationalization of love, the Chicago School made some small forays into the sexual underworld of that city, and Kingsley Davis looked at the functions of prostitution (Heap 2003). But, as I documented 40 years ago in the early 1970s, in general, "sociologists have failed to study sex" (Plummer 1975, 1982). This is really surprising since we now know, from much social and cultural history, that far from this being a time of massive sexual repression, it appears to have been a moment when there was an incitement to a proliferation of discourses about sex (Foucault [1976] 1980). More and more people started to talk about their sexualities (albeit usually behind closed doors) as a new sexual world came into being. Sociologists must have known this but it must have been just too controversial and too difficult to study.

But that was then, and we have moved on. That was a world long before Viagra, AIDS, mediated cybersex, and the globalization of erotic spaces. Now, by contrast, we live in a time where new social structures of cyberspace, global order, and advanced capitalism have worked to reshape our sexual lives. For many, the Western world has moved from a great repression to a world which has been "made sexy" (Rutherford 2007). There has been a widespread sexualization of everyday life, the arrival of what Bauman calls "liquid love," the spread of commodification and commercialization of sex, and for some critics, "the demoralization of western

The Wiley-Blackwell Companion to Sociology, First Edition. Edited by George Ritzer.
© 2012 Blackwell Publishing Ltd. Published 2012 by Blackwell Publishing Ltd.

culture" (cf. Fevre 2000; Bauman 2003; Rutherford 2007; Attwood 2009). And along with this, over the past half-century, there has been a major development of a new and critical sociology of sexualities.

Starting with a trickle of papers in the 1960s, by 1994 the British Sociological Association could devote its entire annual conference to the theme "Sexualities in Social Context," with over 250 papers being presented (see Adkins & Merchant 1996; Holland & Adkins 1996; Weeks & Holland 1996). Two years later, the American Sociological Association set up its own section group for the study of sexualities. A sense of some of the new research and study that has been going on in this complex, rich, and varied field can be grasped through some of its key new journals such as *Sexuality and Culture, Culture, Health and Sexuality, GLQ*, and *Sexualities*. A review of the content of the first 10 years of the journal *Sexualities* (1997–2007) revealed that it had examined:

> Pornographies and erotica; sex work, sex industry and prostitution; commercial sex and sex entertainment; mediated sex; sado-masochism; cyber sexualities, internet and digital sexualities; heterosexuality; male rape, women rape, sexual violence and anti-rape education; female exhibitionism; HIV and sexual health; masturbation, intercourse, anal intercourse, fellatio, orgasm; dogging; bare backing; hints of pederasty and paedophilia; men/women/masculinity/femininity/ transgender/trans-women; inter-sexuality; the sexualities of the young and the old; married sex and single sex; sex tourism; sex education; strippers – men and women – and "exotic dance"; pregnant bodies and sexuality; city sex and rural sex; bisexualities and poly-amory; Viagra; lesbian, gay and queer studies; circumcision; children's sex books; migration; couples; gay and lesbian marriages; sluts; sexual dysfunction; bodies; cosmetic surgery; inter-racial intimacy; teenage mothers; contraception; celibacy; corporal punishment; professional wrestling and drag; fantasy; social movements around gender & sexuality; sexual politics; sexual citizenship; sexual meanings; sexuality and nationalism; sex hormones; safe spaces; post-modern sexualities; and sexualities in the primary school. (Plummer 2008: 11)

This is quite a syllabus for the new critical sexualities studies (CSS), and one which has established a massive diversity of specialized areas now being developed by a field of global researchers. It was also surely a sign of the times that, by the start of the twenty-first century, we could find a proliferation of journals, books, readers, conferences, and research on the multiplicities of all social aspects of sexuality. In this short chapter I plan to capture a little of its history, a few of its key themes, and a sense of the changes in the making.

HISTORY: THE EMERGING NEW CRITICAL SEXUALITIES STUDIES

The story is beginning to be told of this growing and shifting social understanding of sexuality during the mid-twentieth century. The earlier classic contributions of Ellis, Kinsey, Freud – even Masters and Johnson – should not be overlooked (Robinson 1976). Some works have brought together some of the key "sexual documents" of our time (Porter & Hall 1995; Bland & Doan 1998), others provided major reviews of ongoing development (e.g., Eriksen 1998; Weston 1998; Gamson & Moon 2004; Irvine 2005), and still others provide major readers and texts (e.g., Beasley 2005; Herdt & Howe 2007; Jackson & Scott 2010). With flourishing optimism about the progress of this work, Jeffrey Weeks (himself a pioneer in its development) has outlined many of the key changes of the past half-century in *The World We Have Won* (2007).

Early days

There are always difficulties in chronicling the plot-lines, progress, and narratives of time (Zerubavel 2003), and we know there are many world-historical antecedents to the Western sociological study of sex. But our contemporary field of sociological studies of the sexual is probably best seen to begin in the 1960s with John Gagnon and William Simon's key idea that *sexuality should be seen not as a biological drive but as a socially constructed script* (Gagnon & Simon 1973; Plummer 1975, 1982). In multiple papers theorizing the sexual in the mid-1960s, they aimed to bring the study of the sexual into the regular orbit of social structure and regular social learning. As John Gagnon said:

> In any given society, at any given moment in its history, people become sexual in the same way as they become everything else. Without much reflection, they pick up direction from their social environment. They acquire and assemble meanings, skills and values from the people around them. Their critical choices are often made by going along and drifting. People learn when they are quite young a few of the things they are expected to be, and continue slowly to accumulate a belief in who they are and ought to be throughout the rest of childhood, adolescence and adulthood. Sexual conduct is learned in the same ways and through the same processes; it is acquired and assembled in human interaction, judged and performed in specific cultural and historical worlds. (Gagnon 1977: 2)

Based at the Kinsey Institute, and hence grounded in a major empirical effort, Gagnon and Simon's theoretical work was paradigm-breaking in bringing the social to the forefront of thinking about sexuality. It moved sexuality from being seen as essentially biological and reproductive to the challenge of taking seriously its socially grounded multiple meanings.

Shortly after the publication of their key work, *Sexual Conduct*, in 1973, came the publication of Foucault's extraordinarily influential book, *The History of Sexuality*, which critiqued the old "repression hypotheses" and led to sexualities being seen as a discursive formation embodying power circuits. For Foucault, "Sexuality is the name given to a historical construct . . . a great surface network in which the stimulation of bodies, the intensification of pleasures, the incitement to discourse, the formation of knowledge, the strengthening of controls and resistances, are linked to one another, in accordance with a few major strategies of power" (Foucault [1976] 1980: 196).

Foucault's work – with all its challenging polemic – became the canonical text of the neophyte sexual studies. But this was also the period of gay liberation and second-wave feminism challenging the heterosexist and patriarchal orthodoxies of the time and producing their own analyses of sexuality, gender, and power. The women's movement generated an enormous and flourishing debate on sexuality in the 1970s. It started with Kate Millett's claim for a need for *Sexual Politics* (1969) and Adrienne Rich's (1981) critique of "compulsory heterosexuality" and went on to examine the history of rape (Brownmiller 1975) and ultimately the "feminization of sex" (Ehrenreich, Hess & Jacobs 1987). Most of all, by the early 1980s, the controversies of the "pleasure" and "danger" debate created abiding factions: prominent in their analysis was a focus on sexual violence and pornography contrasted with the potentials of female desire (Dworkin 1981; Vance 1984; Leidholdt & Raymond 1990; Jackson & Scott 1996). Likewise many ideas of identity, culture, and differences and the structuring of homohate and homophobia, sex negativism, and ultimately heteronormativity started to be fostered within the Gay and Lesbian Movement, a movement which has subsequently generated LGBTQ (Lesbian, Gay, Bisexual, Transgender, and Queer) Studies, with its own panoply of courses, writings, and histories (e.g., Abelove, Barale & Halperin 1993; Duberman 1997; Nardi & Schneider 1998; Aggleton & Parker 2010). Taken together, these movements and moments helped to shape what came to be known as the "essentialist-constructionist" debate – a debate which dominated sexualities studies from the mid-1970s to the mid-1990s, leading to major world conferences about the subject. Even today, its core debate hovers over much of the work in the field. I will not rehearse this here (see Altman et al. 1989; Fuss 1989).

From AIDS to postmodern queer

In the early 1980s, the world started to confront the pandemic of AIDS/HIV. Tragic and fearsome as it was, it had the curious side effect of generating a worldwide program of sex research, often with much furor over funding. Much of this research was indeed moribund, opportunistic, and limited to a very dull and expensive program of behavioral studies in classic positivist mold which revealed little; but some of it produced striking work on sexual differences and behavior – and in particular an awareness of how local knowledge, local communities, and local identities infuse sexual practices and generate new and changing sexual meanings and scripts. It established beyond doubt that sexual practices bring a variety of meanings; they differ from situation to situation; local communities generate different responses and epidemiologies. AIDS research became a global industry and through this we start to see a growing awareness of the differences of sexualities across cultures (now regularly revealed through papers in the journal *Culture, Health and Sexualities*). Sex research gained a funding, a professionalism, and a degree of legitimacy – even respectability – across the world.

Towards the end of the 1980s, a significant theoretical turn emerged through the amplification of postmodern theorizing and the development of queer theory. Building on the ideas of Gagnon and Simon, Foucault, and feminist theory, the notion of any one true sexuality was attacked, and binary systems of gender and sexuality and heterosexual dominance were challenged – ultimately urging more transgressive and postmodern readings of human sexualities. Here, as William Simon developed in his important book on *Postmodern Sexualities* (1996), the grand narrative of sexuality came to an end. "Sex" was no longer the source of truth, as it was for the moderns with their strong belief in science. Instead, human sexualities became destabilized, decentered, and de-essentialized: the sexual life could no longer be seen as harboring any essential unitary core locatable within a clear framework (like the nuclear family) with an essential truth waiting to be discovered; now there were only fragments. At this time philosophy, literature, cultural studies, and history took over the lead from sociology – and Queer Studies arrived in the academy. Whilst the ideas of Michel Foucault certainly loomed large in this (with his talk of "regimes of truth"), the roots of queer theory (if not the term) are usually seen to lie in the work of Eve Kasofsky Sedgwick (1991) and Judith Butler (1990). The former argued in *The Epistemology of the Closet* that:

> many of the major nodes of thought and knowledge in twentieth century Western culture as a whole are structured – indeed fractured – by a chronic, now endemic crisis of homo/heterosexual definition, indicatively male, dating from the end of the nineteenth century . . . any understanding of any aspect of modern Western culture must be, not merely incomplete, but damaged in its central substance to the degree that it does not incorporate a critical analysis of modern Homo/heterosexual definition. (Sedgwick 1991: 1)

"Queer" deconstructs discourses and creates a greater openness and fluidity by suggesting that very few people really fit into the straightjackets of our contemporary gender and sexual categories. It hence becomes a stark attack on "normal business in the academy" (Warner 1993: 25), challenging the thoroughly gendered mode of thinking behind much academic work. One early leading proponent, David Halperin, suggests that, "Queer is by definition whatever is at odds with the normal, the legitimate, the dominant. There is nothing in particular to which it necessarily refers" (1997: 62; see also Halperin 1993). For much of this work, a key theme became sexual transgression and sexual dissidence; ironically, many of its ideas have now become institutionalized in universities, readers, and careers (see Corber & Valocchi 2003; Lovaas, Elia & Yep 2006; Giffney & O'Rourke 2009). Transgression has become normalized. In sociology, the earliest contribution to this work was to be found in Steven Seidman's *Queer Theory/Sociology* (1996), and following a queer path has been one option open for critical sociologists. Many have followed. But equally many have not taken this route: queer theory is seen as following a path that is too literary, too philosophical, and lacking an adequate empirical analysis of comparative social structures (cf. Stein & Plummer 1994; Gamson & Moon 2004).

From sexual rights to global citizenship

During the 1990s, more and more thinkers moved to the idea of inclusion of sexual minorities through the development of ideas around sexual and reproductive rights, and their links to citizenship. David Evans' *Sexual Citizenship* (1993) pioneered the idea theoretically, whilst international campaigning started attempts at establishing gender and sexual rights on world agendas through the work of the United Nations, the world Women's Movement, UNICEF, and others, and the formation of the International Lesbian and Gay Movement (Plummer 1992, 1995; Adam, Duyvendak & Krouwel 1998; Richardson 1998; Weeks 1998; Petchesky 2000; Richardson

2000; Plummer 2001). Growing out of this, the even broader ideas of *intimate citizenship* have been developed (Plummer 2003). The emphasis is placed on citizenship as *the right to choose*: to choose your partner, your sexual activities, to have a child or not, or to control your own body. Couched in the language of "intimate citizenship" (Plummer 2003), it is a citizenship of "the right to choose" a personal life. All this, of course, raises the issue of whether citizenship can ever allow for a radical, transgressive, dissident, or queer citizenship (Phelan 1989; Bell & Binnie 2000): can you, in short, stay "queer and radical" and yet be a "good citizen"? All this talk of sexual citizens subsequently led to talk of dissident sexualities, showing how citizenship may well work directly against the "bad gays" and foster social exclusion processes.

These agendas became more and more prominent at a global level. Notably in Asia and Latin America, but also in Muslim countries and African nations, the human sexualities of every "imagined community" and nation-state – along with their control and regulation – became more and more an issue. Can (and should) Western sexualities and Western rights be transplanted across the world? By the turn of the millennium, we see a major trend to examine sexualities as they are refashioned across the globe. The *globalization of sexualities* became a major theme. Contemporary sexualities became *hybridic sexualities*, subject to wider processes of globalization and glocalization, in the process of which human sexualities became increasingly cosmopolitan (Binnie 2004). We enter the age of the *sexual diaspora*.

Dennis Altman's *Global Sex* (2001) was perhaps the pioneer of this approach but it has been joined now by a multitude of studies. In Muslim cultures, in Latin America, in South Africa, in India, and in Southeast Asia – in fact everywhere – studies have started to look at the shifting internal and external borders of the sexualities of nations and countries. In all this, there has been a recent flourishing of work by new scholars who reject the presumptions of much Western theorization about both queer and gay. In 2000, the International Association for the Study of Sexuality, Culture and Society (ASSCS) was established; and by 2005 the Asian Queer Studies Conference could bring together in Bangkok some 600 academics and activists, marking a turning point for all this challenging new work. (The most recent conference (in Hanoi in 2009) welcomed 432 delegates from 46 countries.) What is starting to be critically examined here is *hybridic* and *cosmopolitan* sexualities as they are lived in their political contexts. This research typically produces ethnographic work on the complexities and subtleties of grounded lives in specific locations which are always much more messy, contradictory, and ambiguous than wider theories or dogmatic positions allow for (e.g., Kulick 1998; Parker 1999; Manalansan 2003; Boellstorff 2005; Reddy 2005; Aoyama 2009; Zheng 2009; Kong 2010).

Sexual cosmopolitanism/sexual fundamentalism

In a sense much of the most recent work may be seen as investigating a kind of *sexual cosmopolitanism*: an awareness of, and a willingness to live with, human sexual variety both within and across cultures. (Cosmopolitan sexualities by contrast might be used to refer to the variety of sexual conducts.) The history of cosmopolitanism (like the history of sexualities) is a long, complex one. Holton's recent study (2009) has catalogued over 200 meanings. What I certainly do *not* mean is – as is often suggested in the use of the term, and in the magazine of that name – a kind of sophistication, even superior lifestyle (usually associated with metropolitan living), an elitist cosmopolitanism: the sort that we find in writings of metropolitan sexualities, where the world of the young and the hip is the focus. I am rather closer to the ideas of the Ghanaian-American Kwame Anthony Appiah (2006) – that it is a "universal concern and respect for legitimate difference." In some ways its oldest meaning works best: "citizens of the cosmos."

In the new sexualities studies, we might detect three strands of this cosmopolitanism: the political, the cultural, and the personal dimension. The strand of *cultural cosmopolitan sexualities* reveals the wide array of meanings and practices of human sexualities that form the ways of life under conditions of multiple modernities – a vast array of different sexual cultures of all sexual tastes and relationships. *Political sexual cosmopolitanism* takes us into debates about sexual rights and governance – about global intimate citizenship and ways of loving and living with differences in our lives. And *personal cosmopolitanism* suggests – following on from Ulrich Beck's influential study of *The Cosmopolitan Vision* (2006) – the ability or attitude to sense and empathize with a range of different positions in the world, many of which will be contested, and to seek out some common ways of living around them, and moving on. Sexual cosmopolitanism means that we look outwards globally and learn to empathize with the sexual worlds and perspectives of others (even those others who call themselves our enemies).

Sexual fundamentalism is the worldwide enemy of sexual cosmopolitanism. By this I mean those who (1) reject pluralistic views of sexuality; (2) promote conservative and traditional beliefs about sex in an absolute way, often critiquing all those aspects of modernity which foster diversity; and (3) usually refer to a time-honored (often sacred) text which gives a strict and single interpretation of what sex is about (e.g., the Bible, the Koran). At its most blatant, sexual fundamentalism calls for maintaining a strong divide between men and women, the overwhelming superiority of the heterosexual, and the extermination of all perversities. Just as we have seen the rise of sexual cosmopolitanism in recent decades, so we have also seen the continuing journey of sexual fundamentalism. This tension is a long historical one and it is not likely to go away or be easily resolved. It may indeed be a feature of social life that needs dealing with anew in each generation.

FRAMING CRITICAL SEXUALITY STUDIES: ESSENTIAL SOCIAL FEATURES OF THE HUMANLY SEXUAL

CSS claims that for human beings *sexuality is a profoundly social matter*: the simple reduction of it to a biological or psychological fixed feature is inadequate. Although CSS has grown through many twisting theoretical, empirical, and methodological turns, there is a common ground – an "essence" upon which all agree. In sum, I argue that human sexualities emerge through complex symbolic systems in specific social worlds (or cultures), grounded in material, biographical, and bodily lives and embedded in wider historical structures – themselves always on the move, shaped by time and space, and orchestrated through power and inequalities. Sexualities harbor few – if any – fixed or permanent forms but derive their essences from the structural and cultural milieu, historical moments, and relationships in which they are embedded. And within this, what all this thinking and researching has undoubtedly concluded is that *human sexualities are multiple, varied, and contradictory*.

There are roughly 7 billion people who live on the earth and their various sexual practices, meanings, identities, and worlds are mind-boggling. Whilst millions scarcely give sex a thought (from the abstinent to the asexual [Scherrer 2008]), many others probably spend all their lives dedicated to it (from the aficionados to the addicted [Irvine 2005]). Understanding this social complexity requires ways of slicing into this seething matrix of desire and practices. This was the project started by the pioneer sexological work of Krafft-Ebing, Hirschfield, Ellis, and Freud in the nineteenth century. The trouble is that their way into sexuality was through individuals and their desires. What sociologists are now trying to build is an understanding of the ways in which social patterns can be found in our worlds of sexualities: to put the social in the sexual. In what follows, I suggest a broad (incomplete) set of sensitizing terminologies that are helping to frame this understanding: sexual meanings, sexual selves, sexual cultures, sexual structures, sexual differences, sexual conflicts, sexual regulations, sexual embodiments, and sexual feeling worlds. There are others.

Sexual meanings/sexual selves

First, the foundational argument of CSS is very straightforward: what marks all human sexualities (from other animals) is that human sexualities are always symbolic and meaningful. These meanings are a core problematic to be puzzled: contrasting ideas of scripts, stories, narratives, discourses, subjectivities, and the "sexual metaphors we live by" have all been evoked to help do this. Gagnon and Simon's pioneer work argued that sexual conduct is always scripted conduct in three ways. *Personally*, it guides sexual thoughts, fantasies, feeling, and behaviors. *Interactionally*, it guides sexual encounters. And *cultural-historical-politically*, it lays down wider cultural codes and narratives: what Steven Epstein has called the "macro-structuring of scripts" (2007: 251). "Scripts," says Gagnon, "specify, like blueprints, the who's, the what's, the when's, where's and why's for given types of activities" (1977: 6). Other ideas have also been influential: Foucault's guiding imagery was that of discourse in a power/knowledge spiral, whereby new species – like the homosexual, the pervert, the masturbating child, the Malthusian couple, and the hysterical woman – had appeared as targets for study (Foucault [1976] 1980). On a much smaller scale, my own work suggested the importance of sexual stories (Plummer 1995). A very wide array of sexual meanings have now been studied, ranging from rape and gay youthful coming out, to sadomasochist practices, to the narratives of many books and films (see Kimmel [2007] for a selection of such articles). In these arguments, sexuality is rarely a simple biological release, but is engaged in for multiple social purposes (Plummer 1996).

Part of this "symbolicity" (as the critic Kenneth Burke called it) is that of our *public and private identities*: we have *sexual selves* (Kimmel 2007). This is central to the work of Charles Horton Cooley and William James, and their arguments have now for a century or so stressed that the self is a process, always subject to change, contingent upon contexts and others, multiple in its forms and embedded in shifting environments which give it its meanings. The search for a cosmopolitan self is even recognized in some of this earlier work (Aboulafia 2001). Indeed, CSS has been haunted by the identity problem since its earliest days. In studies like Carol Warren's (1974) *Identity and Community in the Gay World*, Barbara Ponse's (1978) *Identities in the Lesbian World*, and my own *Sexual Stigma* (Plummer 1975), a key concern was with the way gay identity works. A major research agenda emerged to ask about the nature of sexual categories and identities and to question how they came into being (personally and historically), their evolution, and ultimately their impact on both lives and cultures (see Plummer 1981). Here the problem was defined as the very social and complex nature of the category of the sexual: in this case what is the nature of the lesbian, gay, bisexual, transgendered identity? And, these days, just how is the category of masochist, pedophiliac, sex addict, sex worker, heterosexual, or asexual made to assume the nature of an identity? How do such identities work? Over time, of course, the notion of identity has become even more complex as stage models of identity were challenged, variations of ethnicity and sexualities were confronted, and a new politics of hybridic, diasporic, and global sexual identities was developed (Phelan 1989; Seidman 2002; Boellstorff 2005; Kong 2010). The making, transformation, and instability of emergent sexualized identities has been a recurrent theme of CSS for over 40 years.

Sexual cultures/sexual structures

A third, and loosely connected, theme suggests we can see that every kind of human sexuality is grounded in a social world. Sexualities can eventually be teased into *sexual cultures* as ways of human life. There is now a multiplicity of cultures which sociologists have studied: from weddings (Ingraham 2008) to multiple sex work worlds (Agustin 2007; Bernstein 2007; Sanders 2008); from drag and transgender worlds (Rupp & Taylor 2003; Ekins & King 2006) to pedophile and polyamory worlds (Klesse 2007; Goode 2010); from teenage worlds (Pascoe 2007) to BDSM (bondage, domination, submission, and masochism) worlds (Beckman 2009) – and, of course, the more routine worlds of mundane heterosexualities (Hockey, Meah & Robinson 2009). These multiple worlds have been characterized through theories as sexual worlds, sexual tribes, social movements, "counterpublics," and sexual networks (Plummer 1995; Maffesoli 1996; Warner 2002). And at the start of the twenty-first century, this cumulative research has clearly shown that these worlds are never unitary phenomena, but that each always exists in its own multiple varieties: each splinters into many linked worlds and remains in process, always segmenting, creating new forms. *Sexual cultures* are never harmonious, well ordered, or consensual wholes – they are *multi-layered, fluid, negotiable, and emerging*. Thus, there is no unified gay culture, sex-worker culture, drag culture, heterosexual culture, or sadomasochist culture: there are multiplicities of scenes. "Worlds" – often imagined – which are only momentarily held together before they splinter and fragment. There is, for instance, absolutely not *one* gay community or world. Gay cultures – like all cultures – exist in the plural. To enter a "gay world" is to stand on the brink of many possibilities: old and young, trendy and not so trendy, the "Faeries, Bears and Leathermen," the drag queens and the drag kings, the "butch in the hood" rappers, trans-butches, the bisexuals, the queers, the couples, the gay Christians, the cruisers, and the barebackers. There is absolutely no gay community or gay scene, only a vast web of conflicting and variable social worlds (e.g., Hennen 2008; Halberstam 1998, 2005).

Fourthly, and despite "liberationist" and "transgressive " talk, it is important to grasp that there is no such thing as "free love": human sexualities *never* function in a free-for-all – but depend upon, and are enabled by, human communities and structures. Human sexualities are fashioned by time and space, history and location – what we might indeed call *sexual structures*. Like all social structures, they are constituted through human negotiation yet give a society deep patterns which both enable and constrain social life. And over the past 30 years, social thought has unpacked more and more of these structuring processes. It has started to see how family processes and personal and friendship communities are lodged in structures of religion, economy, community, and organization – how intimacies are habitualized into social institutions and social practices through power relations and symbolic forms. CSS is starting to identify the ways in which sexualities are enmeshed in structures and intersecting stratification systems such as age, ethnicity, class, disability, nation, as well as gender – the key divisions of social life found across most if not all societies. As they change and move, so our sexualities are organized and shaped by them. Sociologists are compelled to ask how structures of family and relationship along with a matrix of inequalities interconnect, intersect, and weave their way into human sexualities. (The word and paradigm used most commonly now for this is *intersectionality*, as found in the work of Kimberlé Crenshaw [1991], Patricia Hill Collins [1990], Taylor, Hines, and Casey [2010], and others.) Already within this frame they have detected the structures of homophobia (Adam 1998), sex negativism (Davis 1983), sex hierarchy (Rubin 1984), compulsory heterosexuality (Rich 1981), a continuum of sexual violence (Kelly 1989), hegemonic masculinity (Connell [1995] 2005), the heterosexual imaginary (Ingraham 2008), heteronormativity (Warner 1993), and now even homonormativity (Duggan 2003). The term "heteronormativity," for example, was introduced by queer theorist Michael Warner, and defined as the practices and institutions that work to legitimize and privilege heterosexuality in a society – making it seem fundamental and "natural." All these ideas – and more – capture structures that are important in understanding sexuality.

Ultimately, these sexual structures are located in a matrix of inequalities embedded in power within systems of oppression, dominance, and exclusion organized through a set of structural arrangements centered around gender and sexuality (cf. Young 1990). The most apparent feature here is the structuring of sexualities through families. As Goran Therborn (2004) has shown in his history of twentieth-century families, they can be seen to be underpinned by patriarchy (and the relative rights and duties of parents and children, men and women), fertility and birth control (with implications for aging), and marriage systems. His own work charts five dominant world patterns (African, European, East Asian, South Asian, and West Asian/North African) and the sexual structures which differ in each. It is only in the European pattern (which includes New World settlements) that we see major changes in sexuality in the twentieth century, as family forms change.

So there are many structures to be analyzed here. Yet most of the key features of sexual life are organized through the binaries of male and female, though these very ideas are the products of historical forces (Lacqueur 1990) and subsequent daily performative reinforcement (Zimmerman & West 1987; Butler 1990). At the very least we have to ask why it is that women are *the most likely* to be abused, the victims of rape, the sellers of sex – and also *the least likely* to be the fetishists, the sex addicts, the sex offenders. There is also what Joane Nagel (2003) calls an "ethnosexuality at work" which considers how sex gets racialized and race gets sexualized. It is found in the construction of the boundaries of nations and communities and in the long history of conquest, rape, and sexual violence – in slavery and wars. These days it is to be found in widespread sex tourism and trafficking. Here the new CSS poses a massive research agenda asking about the global degradation, defilement, and terrorization of many women; the class organization, commodification, and exploitation of sex; the trafficking and scaling of sexed bodies; the pauperization of intimacies; the racialization of sex; inter-generational conflicts; the sexualities of disabilities; and the problem of migrating, border crossing, and diasporic sexualities (cf. Plummer 2005).

Sexual differences/sexual regulations

Sexual differences are a further essential hallmark of all societies and this difference is clearly visible in human patterns of sexual experience, though it is also present in much animal life too (Roughgarden 2004). From ancient texts to modern, it is not possible to travel far in the worlds of desire without encountering the documentation of massive human difference. There are multiplicities of sexual meanings, behaviors, identities, cultures, and politics, and all are routinely in contradiction and tension with each other. The (postmodern) world reveals this even more clearly: sexualities are never fixed or stable, they do not harbor one grand truth, and they do not reveal our essential nature. In all this change, we may well find a multiplication of desires and differences which may, as I suggest below, even be proliferating.

With these differences human sexualities dwell ubiquitously in *sexual conflicts*, *contradictions*, and *contestations*. Look at any area of sexual life and you will soon find disagreements. Unlike other animals, human cultures are riddled with sexual conundrums, found across and within cultures, across and within groups, and across and within people. The multiplicities of sexualities and their accompanying talks flow labyrinth-like perpetually into endless puzzles: scratch the surfaces of everyday life, and the contradictory puzzles of sexual life appear. People never agree about sexuality.

Given this, all societies proceed to channel and regulate human sexualities – through various laws, customs, and habits. The vast world of desire is always placed under certain sexual restrictions. The when, where, why, what, and how of sexualities are usually given scripts and rules which channel these puzzling complexities into patterns or structures. As a consequence, most social orders function with notions of good (or insider) sexualities, and bad (or outsider/transgressive) sexualities. They are mutually reinforcing: boundaries mark out the good and the bad. But there is a lot of range even here with both the varieties allowed and the conventions established. At the heart of all human sexualities lie human-made systems of *sexual regulations.* Unlike animal life which depends mainly on programmed instincts, all human societies necessarily develop their own systems of norms, rules, and laws which help to regulate, classify, order, and set boundaries to sexual behaviors. Such systems can move from the simplest to the most complex, from the most authoritarian to the most democratized, from the most formal to the most informal; but systems of regulation there will always be. The twenty-first century sees multiplicities of such systems at work – often clashing with each other and creating ceaseless contestations over the boundaries of sexualities organized through political crusades and moral panics (cf. Showalter 1991; Herdt 2009). Murray Davis's much neglected study of *Smut* (1983) draws out the basic contestation across modern societies as one between Jehovanists, who make strict divides between the normal and the abnormal, and the Gnostics and Naturalists who see sex in more open terms.

Sociologists know that differences cannot live in worlds without some kind of borders – however widely they may be stretched and negotiated. This is surely a sociological truism. As Alan Wolfe says: "It is impossible to imagine a society without boundaries" (1992: 323). I have argued in more detail elsewhere that classification systems are needed in order to make sense of the world and boundaries are needed to mark out "group belonging" (the we) from others (Plummer 2007a). If we accept this, then although we can certainly push and pull at sexual boundaries and indeed change them, we cannot get rid of them. Sexual transgressions meet sexual boundaries and this complex interchange at the borders of a society is an ongoing project for the sociology of sexualities.

Embodied sexualities/emotionalized sexualities

All of the above essential features of human sexualities highlight the significance of the social and it might be claimed that all this can lead to a minimizing of the importance of the biological and emotional worlds of sexualities. The meaningful world may indeed be what distinguishes us from most other animals, but we are also pumping fleshy biological creatures who heave and hump, sweat and slide, and deliver orgasmic frenzies. We also harbor deep emotional worlds and worlds of sexual feelings. CSS recognizes the centrality of this in what it analyzes – *sexual embodiment flows through sexual biographies and sexual subjectivities.* Here we have started to investigate *sex as body projects* (Schilling 1993), and Australian activist, sociologist, and AIDS researcher, Gary Dowsett (1996, 2000), has done more than most to bring this sexed body and "bodyplay" back into our studies. Elsewhere I have remarked on the significance of this return to the body for sex studies:

> We might start to speak of the embodiment of sexual practices; of doing body work around sex. "Sexualities" involve social acts through which we "gaze" at bodies, desire bodies, taste (even eat) bodies, smell bodies, fashion and adorn bodies, touch bodies, hear bodies, penetrate bodies, and orgasm bodies. These bodies can be our own or those of others. "Doing sex" means "doing erotic body work." Sex body projects entail, at the very least, presenting and representing bodies (as sexy, non-sexy – on the street, in the gym, in the porno movie), interpreting bodies and body parts ("the gaze"

and the "turn ons" and "turn offs" – sexual excitements of different kinds from voy-
eurism to stripping), manipulating bodies (through the use of fashion, cosmetics,
prosthetics), penetrating bodies (all kinds of intercourses from body parts like fingers
and penises to "sex toy objects"), transforming bodies (stages of erotic embodiment,
movements towards orgasms), commodifying bodies (in sex work, live sex acts, stripping, pornography and the like – Chapkis etc), ejecting and ejaculating bodies as all
kinds of bodily fluids – semen, blood, sweat, saliva – even urine and fecal matter – start
to commingle; possessing bodies (as we come to own or dominate others' bodies),
exploiting bodies (as we come to abuse or terrorize them), and transgressing bodies
(as we go to the extremes in the use of our erotic bodies). (Plummer 2003: 526)

But the body does not stand alone. There are also the socialized sexual emotions.
Human sexualities also deeply connect to *sexual feeling worlds*, the "structures
of feeling" and the "realm of the senses." Sociologists are starting to take this more
seriously though they have rarely confronted sex with emotion. They are much
more prone so far to look at love and relations and their feelings. Thus Ann Swidler's
Talk of Love (2001) suggests how people find "love" through a language of love
widespread in their culture; Giddens (1990) has famously suggested the emergence
of a "plastic sexuality" and a "pure relationship"; Eva Illouz (2007) has suggested
a "cold intimacy," Elizabeth Bernstein (2007) a new kind of "bounded intimacy,"
and Lynn Jamieson (1998) a "disclosing intimacy." More specific emotions such as
shame, and rage, have also been studied (e.g., Ahmed 2004; Stein 2006; Munt
2007).

CHANGE: TRANSFORMATIONS OF TWENTY-FIRST-CENTURY SEXUALITIES

All of the above flags the social constants and constraints of human sexualities: their
symbolic, material nature to be found in human subjectivities, sexual cultures, and
structural inequalities. But it also suggests ceaseless change: never fixed or stable,
human sexual life is persistently up for reworking and re-organizing; and the twenty-
first century appears to have been accelerating its pace of change. The old orders
have not gone – but new ones are certainly appearing alongside them. Hence we all
now live simultaneously in traditional, modern, and postmodern worlds (though at
different paces and to differing degrees). There are many terminologies and shifting
arguments about all this, but I think it provisionally useful to think of these as
multiple modernities where there are different routes back to the past and different
pathways into the future (Eisenstadt 2000).

In this final section, I want to briefly outline some of the sources of this continuing transformation of our sexualities. Some have already been located: the work of
social movements such as feminism and the queer movement, the significance of
globalization, the arrival of AIDS, and the development of cosmopolitanism. Here
I focus briefly on just eight key structural changes that are facilitating new sexual
forms. These are changes in capitalism (and the economy), in the new communications (old and new media), in technology, in the move from rural to urban, in the
creation of professions, and in individualization. Each in their own way works

towards a possibly even greater expansion of the variety of human sexualities – an increasing proliferation and multiplication of sexual diversities.

Globalization revisited

We have already seen some of these changes. The history of CSS is in fact an ongoing reflection on this change, suggesting shifting interests and concerns. A key dimension we have already touched upon is globalization and hybridization. Classical sociology has tended to read the wider world through "Western lenses" and it is only in recent years that the study of sexualities has broadened out to take on board the full range of sexualities across the world and to sense their differences and interconnections (cf. Connell 2007). To some extent, it was research on the global pandemic of AIDS and HIV which, as it seriously impacted the entire world, led to more and more research and thinking on the sexualities of different cultures across the globe. But theorizations from post-colonialism, world systems theory, and globalization theory, as well as the world activist movements of feminism, the LGBTQ movement, international sex workers, and others have started to put the interconnected wider worlds of sexualities firmly on the agenda.

From now on, then, the analysis of one isolated sexual culture on its own will prove very limited. Human sexualities have become embroiled with wider processes of globalization, glocalization, and transnationalism. The diversities and sexual organization of one culture now transforms itself into other cultures through a wide cluster of new processes which I outline below: mediatization, digitalization, commodification, consumption and global markets, urbanization, travel and global cities, as well as migration and tourism and travel. There are, as Weeks has so cogently listed, multiple "sexscapes" to facilitate the flows of sexualities through transnational friendships, global social movements (feminism, queer, transgender), global sex media (including porn and digital – see below), sex trafficking, sex tourism, gay global parties (the celebrated "white parties"), and the wider sexual diaspora with dialogues across the North and the South, and the East and the West (Weeks 2007: 206–9). We now have "queer diasporas" (Patton & Sánchez-Eppler 2000), "multiple queer modernities" (Jackson 2009), "lifestyle travel" (Frank 2007), "cross-border marriage" (Constable 2003), "unruly immigrants" (Das Gupta 2006), "mobile cultures" (Berry, Martin & Yue 2003) – and *Love and Globalization* (Padilla, Hirsch, Munoz-Laboy, Sember & Parker 2007), the title of a useful collection of readings. Throughout these studies the flow is not seen as one-way – the Americanization or Europeanization of sex. Rather, it is persistently seen within a frame of dynamic change. Martin Manalansan (2003), for example, shows that queer migrants do not simply assimilate to their new cultures, but bring their own experiences. New lives and new sexualities emerge. Likewise, James Farrer (2002) shows that Shanghai discos become Western-styled places for sexual encounters, but take on distinctive forms; whilst Travis Kong (2010) shows the complex movements of Chinese identities across London, Hong Kong, and Shanghai.

Against this background, I want to suggest a number of broader structural changes that appear to be fostering many changes in our sexualities – and usually in the direction of diversity.

Capitalism: commodification and market sex

Sex has always been open to a certain amount of selling – as histories of prostitution detail. Viviana Zelizer's provocative *The Purchase of Intimacy* (2005) has argued that intimate ties and connections are bounded by economic activity. Love, sex, and money are ultimately intertwined, and Zelizer develops an argument for connected lives – how lives bridge the public and the private, the personal and the economic. In the current moment, this means looking for the deep interconnection between money and sex under capitalist and neoliberal orders which form a ubiquitous (if highly differentiated and shaky) world economic system: sexualities are everywhere up for sale. Every aspect of sexual life has become commodified and turned into a sellable commodity. Sex is on sale in pornography, in strip clubs, in the army, in tourism, online – locally and globally (Jeffreys 2008). This is not just a world of sex workers or pornography, but a deeply pervasive market which will sell any kind of sex it can and use any sexual tricks to sell anything. Amongst other things we have seen, alongside sex work and international sex trafficking, are the growth and diversity of sexualized technologies (Viagra, contraceptives, cosmetic surgery); mail order brides; the pink economy; the sale of "sex toys," s&m costumes, nitrate inhalants ("poppers"), vibrators; and Ann Summers shops. And with this has come the massive commercial world where sex is used to sell anything and everything (Farrer 1999; Hennesy 2000; Storr 2004; Sender 2005; Plummer 2007b; Attwood 2009).

Elizabeth Bernstein (2007) has examined the broad trans-historical shifts in the sexual economy from pre-modern to post-modern societies and developed an overarching thesis about the changing nature of sex commerce in late modern society. She schematizes the differences between "early-modern sexual barter, modern-industrial prostitution and post industrial sexual commerce" (Bernstein 2007: 170). The latter she claims has a very different shape, and it is one which all studies from now on should have to engage. Yes, sex work and prostitution have become more diversified than ever before with a wider range of services; such work is dispersed everywhere – breaking down the old distinctions of private and public, and no longer necessarily locating itself within specially stigmatized areas or red light districts. New technologies have become endemic in much of its organization. But more telling still is the suggestion that there has started to be a real shift in the meaning of sexuality in these times – towards what Bernstein calls a "bounded authenticity." Here a new "relationship meaning" is evolving; and it is becoming more and more common. Sex is not just a sexual release (if it ever was), but is developing into a more complex relationship linked to intimacies. Bernstein claims that there is no longer a simple cash nexus and market relation, but increasingly a situation where many sex workers are paid to provide erotic acts premised upon the promise of an "authentic" interpersonal connection. The public/private boundaries between intimacy and commerce are being reworked in new and challenging ways.

Communications: mediated sex, digitalized sex

The historical evolution of societies has gradually moved sexuality into an electronic age where a great deal of sexuality becomes highly visible and "mediated" into our

lives: contemporary sexualities dwell in these new global media. Sex, once hidden
in private spaces, now proclaims its sexual stories loudly from traditional media
such as film, photographs, music, advertising, drama, radio, and television – but
also now the new media: websites, iPhones, blogs, Twitter. This new public telling
of sex invades what was once seen as private; what was once experienced as a very
personal and hidden sphere is now made accessible to all. The so-called "pluralistic
ignorance" of others in past times has now become public knowledge as human
sexualities become increasingly visible or prone to disclosure (Jamieson 1998). So
here we now see the massive development of pornographic photos and films ("por-
nographization," "pornification," and the "pornographication" of culture [McNair
2002; Passenen, Nikunen & Saaranemma 2007]), along with the widespread sexualization of media saturated with erotic availability. Elvis's hip wiggling in the 1950s
seems mild when compared with the remarkable inventory of full-scale sexual global
antics of Madonna in the 1980s and 1990s (and a string of women before her).
Look, for example, at Paul Rutherford's (2007) instructive detailed chronology of
Madonna's music videos (1984–95) which lists just what she did publicly over 10
years. In addition there was the bestselling book, *Sex* (Madonna 1992). Much contemporary media has become saturated with sex: what has been called sexualization
(Attwood 2009), a process which might have started in the nineteenth century
(Wouters 2004).

As the song in the musical *Avenue Q* goes, "The internet is for porn." All the
new digital media, from cell phones and games to webcams and chat rooms, have
been swamped globally by the erotic. Valid estimates of use are very hard to collect
– some suggest that up to 40 per cent of the male population in the UK use the
internet for porn (*Independent*, May 28, 2006); others suggest the figure is much
higher (especially organizations crusading against it). But porn is only one of many
possible ways the internet can be used for sex – a global and ubiquitous cyber-
sexual smorgasbord has developed, fostering new modes of sexual meeting and
communication on a truly massive scale: every desire charted by Krafft-Ebing in
the nineteenth century now has its own website followers! This has generated ubiquitous new ways of doing sex across groups and generations: e.g., self-made digital
porn; cybersex; webcam sex; cell phone sex; online dating; sex chat rooms for all
kinds of sexual tastes; and proliferation and ease of access to porn of all kinds. It
is the age of cyber-porn, cyber-queer, cyber-dating, cyber-stalking, cyber-rape, cyber-
victim, cybersex, and cyber grooming (cf. Waskul 2004; Attwood 2010). More than
this, new sexual cultures and new sexual knowledges become available (with different degrees of access) across the globe (cf. Berry, Martin & Yue 2003).

Science and the "technology fix": techno sex

Many developments in science have also transformed the sexual. Much of it has
had the consequence of disconnecting sexuality from its long presumed biological
essence and coupling with reproduction. With the new technologies and pharmaceuticals we have seen a reproductive sex under greater control as we move to a
sexuality that is more relational, representational, and recreational. Sex is no longer
"simply" needed for reproduction; and the life of a sexually active person has been
extended and diversified. Thus Viagra prolongs sex way beyond the reproductive

years; contraceptive pills, "morning after" pills (and condoms for men *and* women) facilitate sex without reproduction; the new reproductive technologies make pregnancy and childbirth possible without sex. Put these together and we have a heady mix: sex and reproduction are no longer linked (for the first time in history). On top of this, a whole array of new techno-fetishes have been developed around machines – with robots and cyborgs and electrical BDSM, as well as new materials like the fetish of plastic and leather; and the rise of pharmaceuticals, e.g., poppers, to enhance sex. There is also the new world of body enhancement – from breast enhancement surgery to transgender surgery. Some claim we are moving to the post-human (cf. Loe 2004; Tiefer 2006; Shapiro 2010).

From rural to urban: urban anonymity and sex in the city

As the scale of cities has grown from half a million in pre-industrial times to the current megacities of 17–20 million or more, so social life has gradually become more and more prone to segmentation, anonymity, and massness. It is easy to get lost in the city. And this in turn reworks sexual life as the city becomes divided into housing spaces for singles, sex zones, and ecologies of sexual markets and "lifestyle enclaves." Modern cities often bring gay networks and communities; neighborhoods of sex work; "no go" areas – safer and unsafe sex areas. The move to cities, global cities, and urban conglomerations links with the growth of singles, the rise of diverse urban enclaves, and the fostering of blasé attitudes. Social life can become more fleeting, transient, and many more places can develop for street sex, public sex, and anonymous encounters.

At the simplest level, sex is everywhere spatially organized but it is also on the move. As Laumann, Ellingson, Mahay, and Paik (2004) show in their survey of over 2,000 people in four Chicago neighborhoods, sex is significantly shaped by the neighborhood you live in, your ethnicity, your sexual preference, and the circle of friends to which you belong. Others have shown how small towns and commuter suburbs or rural areas can also bring distinctive patterns of, for example, gay life (Brekhus 2003; Gray 2009). But human sexualities are also open to flows, movements, mobilities. They are constantly being reworked, re-drawn, re-shaped – more and more subject to flows, fluidities, networks, contingencies, movement, scapes. John Urry's *Sociology Beyond Societies* (2000) talks of *mobilities*, and suggests that in such a world, borders and boundaries cannot remain fixed – they become a shifting presence as the edges are always being re-negotiated: in international trafficking, in the flows of sex tourism, in the movements from country to cities, in the flows of cyberspace. There are "sexscapes" at work, as Travis Kong (2010) has shown in his work on the mobilities across Hong Kong, London, and Shanghai. In recent works, then, there has been a major rethinking of sexual "spaces and places."

Professionalization and medicalization: sexperts

Contemporary social life is characterized by more and more specializations, divisions of labour and professions – in medicine, in law, in education, and even in sex itself. This is the age of "professional dominance," the audit culture, and the culture of the expert. Not surprisingly, the experts have invaded the zones of intimacy to capture the "sexual soul" – from the psychiatrists, the counselors, the sex therapists, and the sexologists through to the library of self-help books, self-help groups, agony aunt columnists, and TV confessionals (Plummer 1995; Illouz 2007, 2008). Every aspect of our sexualities has been documented, probed, and "therapized" by an army of "sexperts" – from the lowest of drives (the asexual and those lacking desire – now seen as suffering from medical disorders) to hypersexual sex addiction (which became a clinical entity in the early 1980s) (Levine & Troiden 1988; Irvine 2005). In a major way, every aspect of our sexual life has been placed in "expert" hands – from birth control to "death by Viagra." We have sexperts running education programs, couples visiting sex therapists, and a veritable "science/fiction" of sex has been constructed in sex guides and sex manuals (Potts 2002). There is even a "rescue industry" for sex workers (Agustin 2008).

Power, democratization, and the new social movements: sex rights

In tandem with these changes has been the rise of the ballot box, the search for democratic governments, and the development of social movements. Charles Tilley (2004) and others have shown how, over the past 200 years, social movements have evolved, developing claims, mobilizing resources, and shaping arenas of public discourse over many fields of social life. One of these has been the claims made by social movements over intimacy and sex – which can be traced back at least to the late eighteenth century, and is most clearly represented by the women's movement (with claims over birth control, abortion rights, sexual violence, and women's sexuality) and the gay movement (with claims of equality over sexuality). There are many others – protest movements over sex laws, purity crusades, erotic minorities, and tribes of all kinds have made sexual life the focus of public contestation. More and more, social movements have their role to play in the shaping of sex. And in recent decades, a major language and rhetoric of human sexual rights and the right to choose the nature of one's sexual life has become central to contemporary debates on human intimacy (Plummer 2006, 2010a). Here a major conflict usually appears. For gays, sex workers, the transgender movement, and the rest there has also been a history of conflict between assimilationists and radicals. The former argue that they are normal, deserve equal rights, and want to be "good citizens." They want to stay inside the boundaries set by a patriarchal and heteronormative society. By contrast, "radicals" argue that these sexualities are indeed invariably "outside." To get rights and become citizens is to become normalized and to reinforce the dominant values. Radicals usually celebrate sexual desire in all its hedonistic forms – providing a "seductive (and dangerous) vision of alternative possibilities." These are the sexual outlaws and sexual citizenship is not the name of their game (see Aggleton & Parker 2010).

Informalism, individualism, and the liquid society: the personalization of sexualities

Finally there is a large rag-bag of other changes that center around the re-organization of the personal life. There is a long history – from at least de Tocqueville – which has suggested how personal life has become more individualized and open to a sense of personal choice, which was not to be found in all societies. We have arrived at the time of impulsivity (Turner 1976), mutability (Zurcher 1977), narcissism (Lasch 1979), informalization (Wouters 2004), individualization (Beck & Gernsheim 2002), liquid life (Bauman 2003), and "the new individualism" (Elliott & Lemert 2010). These changes are not about sex *per se*, but they all touch on key themes about the personal life. They suggest how the formality of sexual emotions, manners, language, groups, and hierarchies of the past has become increasingly supplanted by more informal relations, so sexual patterns have been "deregulated." We now live in a world of sexual choices (Plummer 2003), pure relationships (Giddens 1990, 1992), cold intimacies (Illouz 2007, 2008), and disclosing intimacies (Jamieson 1998). Tight codes and formal rules have given way to more fluid rules and a highly questionable set of choices about the personal life. A seemingly "endless hunger for instant change," "self reinvention," and "short-term living" have become themes which characterize the new personal – read also sexual – life.

There are two rather different approaches to this increasing level of individual choice and the balance of individualism and individualization in these accounts. One is critical and suggests growing levels of narcissism, selfishness, and egoism. It is the view that prevails – speaking of how "togetherness is being dismantled" (Bauman 2003: 119). Indeed, for some it has led to the "breakdown of character" (Hunter 2000), and even "the demoralization of western culture" (Fevre 2000). The alternative approach suggests growing levels of autonomy, choice, and independence – much of the change has given greater scope to personal life. Carol Smart's *Personal Life* (2007), for example, draws from empirical research (something the theorists often ignore) to show the connectedness, relationality, and embeddedness of many personal relations today – rejecting many of the assumptions found in theories of individualization. As personal life goes, so go sexualities.

CONCLUSION: GENERATIONAL SEXUALITIES

This chapter has taken stock of a complex and quite vast new field of study which moves under many names and has many disagreements within itself. I call it Critical Sexualities Studies (CSS), and I have hardly been able to do justice to the labyrinth of complex inquiries it has generated over the past 50 years. It is now a large, lively, and distinctively challenging arena of global, cosmopolitan analysis, which is usually driven by a passionate concern for a better sexual world for all. Of course, in reality it has a very long history, and it bridges into key longstanding dilemmas of sociological analysis. And so a final issue: recently I have been exploring the importance of seeing sexualities as always generational (Plummer 2010b).

What I have been locating in this chapter are shifting generational sexualities. We see a new version of sexualities being created for twenty-first-century life by a questioning millennial, digital, and global generation, one that will not put up with the old orthodoxies that have created much sexual suffering in the past (though doubtless they will generate their own). A new world is in the making. At the same time, recent generations have been helping to make this new world – critical sexualities, for example, has a lineage going back a few decades and it brings to the forefront the deep ways in which our sexualities are structured by the social and the political. The old simple sense of any unified sexuality and the inevitable powerfulness of biology alone has been placed seriously under question since at least the generations of Ellis and Krafft-Ebing, even as such an idea still rages in popular culture. The constant struggles between difference and sameness, the unique and the general, the cosmopolitan and the fundamentalist – and the optimists and the pessimists – are all found here. Bridging human rights and intimate citizenship with sociology and queer theory, the personal with the political, and the local with the global, Critical Sexual Studies has established itself as a major field within sociology and the wider intellectual landscape.

References

Abelove, Henry, M. A. Barale, and D. Halperin (eds.) (1993) *The Lesbian and Gay Studies Reader*. New York: Routledge.

Aboulafia, Mitchell (2001) *The Cosmopolitan Self: George Hebert Mead and Continental Philosophy*. Urbana, IL: University of Illinois Press.

Adam, Barry (1998) "Theorizing Homophobia." *Sexualities* 1(4): 387–404.

Adam, Barry, J. W. Duyvendak, and A. Krouwel (eds.) (1998) *The Global Emergence of Gay and Lesbian Politics*. Philadelphia, PA: Temple University Press.

Adkins, Lisa and Vicki Merchant (eds.) (1996) *Sexualizing the Social: Power and the Organization of Sexuality*. New York: St Martin's Press.

Aggleton, P. and R. Parker (eds.) (2010) *Routledge Handbook of Sexuality, Health and Rights*. London: Routledge.

Agustin, Laura Maria (2007) *Sex at the Margins: Migration, Labour Markets and the Rescue Industry*. London: Zed Books.

Ahmed, Sara (2004) *The Cultural Politics of Emotion*. Edinburgh: Edinburgh University Press.

Altman, Dennis (2001) *Global Sex*. Chicago: University of Chicago Press.

Altman, Dennis et al. (1989) *Homosexuality? Which Homosexuality?* London: Gay Men's Press.

Aoyama, Kaoru (2009) *Thai Migrant Workers: From Modernisation to Globalisation*. Basingstoke: Palgrave Macmillan.

Appiah, Kwame Anthony (2006) *Cosmopolitanism: Ethics in a World of Strangers*. London: Allen Lane.

Attwood, Feona (ed.) (2009) *Mainstreaming Sex: The Sexualization of Western Culture*. London: I. B. Tauris.

Attwood, Feona (ed.) (2010) *Porn.Com*. New York: Peter Lang.

Bauman, Zygmunt (2003) *Liquid Love*. Cambridge: Polity Press.

Beasley, Chris (2005) *Gender and Sexuality: Critical Theories, Critical Thinkers*. London: Sage.

Beck, Ulrich (2006) *The Cosmopolitan Vision*. Cambridge: Polity Press.

Beck, Ulrich and Elizabeth Beck Gernsheim (2002) *Individualization*. London: Sage.

Beckman, Andrea (2009) *The Social Construction of Sexuality and Perversion: Deconstructing Sadomasochism*. Basingstoke: Palgrave.

Bell, David and Jon Binnie (2000) *The Sexual Citizen: Queer Politics and Beyond*. Cambridge: Polity Press.

Bernstein, Elizabeth (2007) *Temporarily Yours: Intimacy, Authenticity and the Commerce of Sex*. Chicago: University of Chicago Press.

Berry, C., F. Martin, and A. Yue (2003) *Mobile Cultures: New Media in Queer Asia*. Durham, NC: Duke University Press.

Binnie, Jon (2004) *The Globalization of Sexuality*. London: Sage.

Bland, Lucy and Laura Doan (1998) *Sexology Uncensored: The Documents of Sexual Science*. Cambridge: Polity Press.

Boellstorff, Tom (2005) *The Gay Archipelago: Sexuality and Nation in Indonesia*. Princeton, NJ: Princeton University Press.

Brekhus, Wayne H. (2003) *Peacocks, Chameleons, Centaurs: Gay Suburbia and the Grammar of Social Identity*. Chicago: University of Chicago Press.

Brownmiller, Susan (1975) *Against Our Will: Men, Women and Rape*. New York: Simon and Schuster.

Butler, Judith (1990) *Gender Trouble: Feminism and the Subversion of Identity*. London: Routledge.

Collins, Patricia Hill (1990) *Black Feminist Thought*. London: Routledge.

Connell, Raewyn (2007) *Southern Theory*. Cambridge: Polity Press.

Connell, Robert ([1995] 2005) *Masculinities*. Cambridge: Polity Press.

Constable, Nicole (2003) *Romance on a Global Stage: Pen Pals, Virtual Ethnography and Mail Order Magazines*. Berkeley, CA: University of California Press.

Corber, Robert J. and Stephen Valocchi (ed.) (2003) *Queer Studies*. Oxford: Blackwell.

Crenshaw, Kimberlé Williams (1991) "Mapping the Margins: Intersectionality, Identity Politics, and Violence Against Women of Colour." *Stanford Law Review* 43(6): 1241–99.

Das Gupta, Monisha (2006) *Unruly Immigrants: Rights, Activism, and Transnational South Asian Politics in the United States*. Durham, NC: Duke University Press.

Davis, Murray (1983) *Smut: Erotic Reality/Obscene Ideology*. Chicago: University of Chicago Press.

Dowsett, Gary (1996) *Practicing Desire: Homosexual Sex in an Age of AIDS*. Stanford, CA: Stanford University Press.

Dowsett, Gary (2000) "Bodyplay: Corporeality in a Discursive Silence." In Richard Parker, Regina Maria Barbosa, and Peter Aggleton (eds.), *Framing the Sexual Subject: The Politics of Gender, Sexuality and Power*. Berkeley, CA: University of California Press, pp. 29–45.

Duberman, Martin (ed.) (1997) *A Queer World*. New York: New York University Press.

Duggan, Lisa (2003) *The Twilight of Equality? Neoliberalism, Cultural Politics, and the Attack on Democracy*. Boston: Beacon Press.

Dworkin, Andrea (1981) *Pornography: Men Possessing Women*. New York: Perigee.

Ehrenreich, Barbara, Elizabeth Hess, and Gloria Jacobs (1987) *Remaking Love: The Feminization of Sex*. London: Fontana.

Eisenstadt, S. N. (2000) "Multiple Modernities." *Daedalus* 129: 1–29.

Ekins, Richard and Dave King (2006) *The Transgender Phenomenon*. London: Sage.

Elliott, Anthony and Charles Lemert (2010) *The New Individualism*, 2nd edn. London: Routledge.

Epstein, Steven (2007) "The Badlands of Desire." In Michael Kimmel (ed.), *The Sexual Self*. Nashville, TN: Vanderbilt University Press, pp. 249–64.

Eriksen, Julia (1998) *Kiss and Tell*. Cambridge, MA: Harvard University Press.

Evans, David (1993) *Sexual Citizenship*. London: Routledge.

Farrer, James (1999) "Disco Super-Culture: Consuming Foreign Sex in the Chinese Disco." *Sexualities* 2(2): 147–66.

Farrer, James (2002) *Opening Up: Youth Sex Culture and Market Reform in Shanghai.* Chicago: University of Chicago Press.

Fevre, R. W. (2000) *The Demoralization of Western Culture: Social Theory and the Dilemmas of Modern Living.* London: Continuum.

Foucault, M. ([1976] 1980) *The History of Sexuality*, Vol. 1, *An Introduction.* Trans. R. Hurley. New York: Vintage Books.

Frank, Katherine (2007) "Playcouples in Paradise: Touristic Sexuality and Lifestyle Travel." In Mark B. Padilla, Jennifer S. Hirsch, Miguel Munoz-Laboy, Robert E. Sember, and Richard G. Parker (eds.), *Love and Globalization: Transformations of Intimacy in the Contemporary World.* Nashville, TN: Vanderbilt University Press, pp. 163–85.

Fuss, Dianne (1989) *Essentially Speaking.* London: Routledge.

Gagnon, John (1977) *Human Sexualities.* New York: Scott, Foresman & Co.

Gagnon, J. H. and W. Simon (1973) *Sexual Conduct: The Social Sources of Human Sexuality.* Chicago: Aldine.

Gamson, J. and D. Moon (2004) "The Sociology of Sexualities: Queer and Beyond." *Annual Review of Sociology* 30: 47–64.

Giddens, Anthony (1990) *Modernity and Self-Identity.* Cambridge: Polity Press.

Giddens, Anthony (1992) *The Transformation of Intimacy.* Cambridge: Polity Press.

Giffney, Noreen and Michael O'Rourke (eds.) (2009) *The Ashgate Research Companion to Queer Theory.* Aldershot: Ashgate.

Goode, Sarah (2010) *Understanding and Addressing Adult Sexual Attraction to Children: A Study of Paedophiles in Contemporary Society.* London: Routledge.

Gray, Mary L. (2009) *Out in the Country: Youth, Media and Queer Visibility.* New York: New York University Press.

Halberstam, Judith (1998) *Female Masculinity.* Durham, NC: Duke University Press.

Halberstam, Judith (2005) *In a Queer Time and Place: Transgender Bodies and Subcultural Lives.* New York: New York University Press.

Halperin, David M. (1993) "Is There a History of Sexuality?" In Henry Abelove, Michèle Aina Barale, and David Halperin (eds.), *The Lesbian and Gay Studies Reader.* London: Routledge, pp. 416–31.

Halperin, David M. (1997) *Saint Foucault: Towards a Gay Hagiography.* Oxford: Oxford University Press.

Heap, Chad (2003) "The City as a Sociological Laboratory: The Queer Heritage of the Chicago School." *Qualitative Sociology* 26(4): 457–87.

Hennen, Peter (2008) *Faeries, Bears and Leathermen: Men in Community Queering the Masculine.* Chicago: University of Chicago Press.

Hennesy, Rosemary (2000) *Profit and Pleasure: Sexual Identities in Late Capitalism.* London: Taylor and Francis.

Herdt, G. (ed.) (2009) *Moral Panics, Sex Rights: Fear and the Fight over Sexual Rights.* New York: New York University Press.

Herdt, Gil and Cymene Howe (eds.) (2007) *21st Century Sexualities.* London: Routledge.

Hockey, J., A. Meagh, and V. Robinson (2009) *Mundane Heterosexualities: From Theory to Practices.* London: Palgrave.

Holland, Janet and Lisa Adkins (2006) *Sex, Sensibility and the Gendered Body.* New York: St Martin's Press.

Holton, Robert J. (2009) *Cosmopolitanisms: New Directions and New Thinking.* Basingstoke: Palgrave.

Hunter, James Davidson (2000) *The Death of Character.* New York: Basic Books.

Illouz, Eva (2007) *Cold Intimacies: The Making of Emotional Capitalism*. Cambridge: Polity Press.

Illouz, Eva (2008) *Saving the Modern Soul: Therapy, Emotions and the Culture of Self-Help*. Berkeley, CA: University of California Press.

Ingraham, Chrys (2008) *White Weddings: Romancing Heterosexuality in Popular Culture*, 2nd edn. London: Routledge.

Irvine, Janice (2005) *Disorders of Desire: Sexuality and Gender in Modern American Sexology*, 2nd edn. Philadelphia, PA: Temple University Press.

Jackson, Peter (2009) "Capitalism and Global Queering: National Markets, Parallels amongst Sexual Cultures, and Multiple Queer Modernities." *GLQ* 15(3): 257–395.

Jackson, Stevi and Sue Scott (eds.) (1996) *Feminism and Sexuality: A Reader*. Edinburgh: Edinburgh University Press.

Jackson, Stevi and Sue Scott (2010) *Theorising Sexuality*. Maidenhead: Open University Press.

Jamieson, Lynn (1998) *Intimacy: Personal Relationships in Modern Societies*. Cambridge: Polity Press.

Jeffreys, Sheila (2008) *The Industrial Vagina: The Political Economy of the Global Sex Trade*. London: Routledge.

Kelly, Liz (1989) *Surviving Sexual Violence*. Cambridge: Polity Press.

Kimmel, Michael (ed.) (2007) *The Sexual Self*. Nashville, TN: Vanderbilt University Press.

Klesse, Christian (2007) *The Spectre of Promiscuity: Gay Male and Bisexual Monogamies and Polyamories*. Aldershot: Ashgate.

Kong, Travis (2010) *Chinese Male Homosexualities*. London: Routledge.

Kulick, Don (1998) *Travesti: Sex, Gender and Culture amongst Brazilian Prostitutes*. Chicago: University of Chicago Press.

Lacqueur, Thomas (1990) *Making Sex*. Cambridge, MA: Harvard University Press.

Lasch, Christopher (1979) *The Culture of Narcissism: American Life in an Age of Diminishing Experience*. New York: W. W. Norton.

Laumann, Edward O., Stephen Ellingson, Jennay Mahay, and Anthony Paik (2004) *The Sexual Organization of the City*. Chicago: University of Chicago Press.

Leidholdt, Dorchen and Janice G. Raymond (1990) *The Sexual Liberals and the Attack on Feminism*. New York: Pergamon.

Levine, M. P. and R. R. Troiden (1988) "The Myth of Sexual Compulsivity." *Journal of Sex Research* 25: 347–63.

Loe, Meike (2004) *The Rise of Viagra*. New York: New York University Press.

Lovaas, Karen E., John P. Elia, and Gust A. Yep (eds.) (2006) *LGBT Studies and Queer Theory*. Binghamton, NY: Harrington Park Press.

Madonna (1992) *Sex*. London: Secker and Warburg.

Maffesoli, Michel (1996) *The Time of the Tribes: The Decline of Individualism in Mass Society*. London: Sage.

Manalansan, Martin F. (2003) *Global Divas*. Durham, NC: Duke University Press.

McNair, Bryan (2002) *Striptease Culture: Sex, Media and the Democratization of Desire*. London: Routledge.

Millett, Kate (1969) *Sexual Politics*. London: Granada.

Munt, Sally (2007) *Cultural Attachments: The Cultural Politics of Shame*. Aldershot: Ashgate.

Nagel, Joane (2003) *Race, Ethnicity and Sexuality: Intimate Intersections, Forbidden Frontiers*. Oxford: Oxford University Press.

Nardi, Peter N. and Beth E. Schneider (eds.) (1998) *Social Perspectives in Lesbian and Gay Studies*. London: Routledge.

Padilla, Mark B., Jennifer S. Hirsch, Miguel Munoz-Laboy, Robert E. Sember, and Richard G. Parker (eds.) (2007) *Love and Globalization: Transformations of Intimacy in the Contemporary World*. Nashville, TN: Vanderbilt University Press.

Parker, Richard (1999) *Beneath the Equator: Cultures of Desire, Male Homosexuality and Emerging Gay Communities in Brazil*. London: Routledge.

Parker, Richard and Peter Aggleton (eds.) (1999) *Culture, Society and Sexuality: A Reader*. London: Taylor and Francis.

Pascoe, C. J. (2007) *Dude You're a Fag*. Berkeley, CA: University of California Press.

Passenen, Susanna, K. Nikunen, and L. Saaranemma (2007) *Pornification: Sex and Sexuality in Media Culture*. Oxford: Berg.

Patton, Cyndy and Benigno Sánchez-Eppler (eds.) (2000) *Queer Diasporas*. Durham, NC: Duke University Press.

Petchesky, Rosalind (2000) "Sexual Rights: Inventing a Concept, Mapping an International Practice." In Richard Parker, Regina Maria Barbosa, and Peter Aggleton (eds.), *Framing the Sexual Subject: The Politics of Gender, Sexuality and Power*. Berkeley, CA: University of California Press, pp. 81–103.

Phelan, Shane (1989) *Identity Politics*. Philadelphia, PA: Temple University Press.

Plummer, Ken (1975) *Sexual Stigma: An Interactionist Account*. London: Routledge.

Plummer, Ken (ed.) (1981) *The Making of the Modern Homosexual*. London: Hutchinson.

Plummer, Ken (1982) "Symbolic Interaction and Sexual Conduct: An Emergent Perspective." In M. Brake (ed.), *Human Sexual Relations*. Harmondsworth: Penguin, pp. 223–41.

Plummer, Ken (ed.) (1992) *Modern Homosexualities*. London: Routledge.

Plummer, Ken (1995) *Telling Sexual Stories: Power, Change and Social Worlds*. London: Routledge.

Plummer, Ken (1996) "Symbols of Change." Introduction to William Simon, *Postmodern Sexualities*. London: Routledge.

Plummer, Ken (2001) "The Square of Intimate Citizenship: Some Preliminary Proposals." *Citizenship Studies* 5(3): 237–55.

Plummer, Ken (ed.) (2002) *Sexualities: Critical Assessments*, 3 vols. London: Routledge.

Plummer, Ken (2003) *Intimate Citizenship: Private Decisions and Public Dialogues*. Seattle: University of Washington Press.

Plummer, Ken (2005) "Intimate Citizenship in an Unjust World." In Mary Romero and Eric Margolis (eds.), *The Blackwell Companion to Social Inequality*. Oxford: Blackwell, pp. 75–100.

Plummer, Ken (2006) "Rights Work: Constructing Lesbian, Gay and Sexual Rights in Late Modern Times." In Lydia Morris (ed.), *Rights*. London: Routledge, pp. 152–67.

Plummer, Ken (2007a) "The Flow of Boundaries: Gays, Queers and Intimate Citizenship." In D. Downes, P. Rock, C. Chinkin, and C. Gearty (eds.) *Crime, Social Control and Human Rights: From Moral Panics to States of Denial*. Cullompton, Devon: Willan.

Plummer, Ken (2007b) "Sexual Markets, Commodification and Consumption." In G. Ritzer (ed.), *The Blackwell Encyclopedia of Sociology*, Vol. IX. Oxford: Blackwell, pp. 4242–4.

Plummer, Ken (2008) "Studying Sexualities for a Better World? Ten Years of Sexualities." *Sexualities* 11(1): 11–22.

Plummer, Ken (2010a) "The Social Reality of Sexual Rights." In P. Aggleton and R. Parker (eds.), *Routledge Handbook of Sexuality, Health and Rights*. London: Routledge, pp. 45–56.

Plummer, Ken (2010b) "Generational Sexualities, Subterranean Traditions and the Hauntings of the Sexual World: Some Preliminary Remarks." *Symbolic Interaction* 33(2): 163–90.

Ponse, Barbara (1978) *Identities in the Lesbian World*. Westport, CT: Greenwood Press.

Porter, Roy and Lesley Hall (1995) *The Facts of Life: The Creation of Sexual Knowledge in Britain 1650–1950*. New Haven, CT: Yale University Press.

Potts, Annie (2002) *The Science Fiction of Sex*. London: Routledge.

Reddy, Gayatri (2005) *With Respect To Sex: Negotiating Hijra Identity in South India*. Chicago: University of Chicago Press.

Rich, Adrienne (1981) *Compulsory Heterosexuality and Lesbian Existence*. London: Women Only Press.

Richardson, Diane (1998) "Sexuality and Citizenship." *Sociology* 32(1): 83–100.

Richardson, Diane (2000) "Constructing Sexual Citizenship: Theorizing Sexual Rights." *Critical Social Policy* 20(1): 105–35.

Robinson, Paul (1976) *The Modernization of Sex*. London: Paul Elek.

Roughgarden, Joan (2004) *Evolution's Rainbow: Diversity, Gender and Sexuality in Nature and People*. Berkeley, CA: University of California Press.

Rubin, Gayle (1984) "Thinking Sex." In Carol Vance (ed.), *Pleasure and Danger*. London: Routledge, pp. 143–78.

Rupp, Leila J. and Verta Taylor (2003) *Drag Queens at the 801 Cabaret*. Chicago: University of Chicago Press.

Rutherford, Paul (2007) *A World Made Sexy: Freud to Madonna*. Toronto: University of Toronto Press.

Sanders, Teela (2008) *Paying for Pleasure*. Cullompton, Devon: Willan.

Scherrer, Kristin S. (2008) "Coming to an Asexual Identity: Negotiating Identity, Negotiating Desire." *Sexualities* 11(5): 621–41.

Schilling, Chris (1993) *The Body and Social Theory*. London: Sage.

Sedgwick, Eve Kasofsky (1991) *The Epistemology of the Closet*. London: Harvester Wheatsheaf.

Seidman, Steven (1996) *Queer Theory/Sociology*. London: Routledge.

Seidman, Steven (2002) *Beyond the Closet*. London: Routledge.

Sender, K. (2005) *Business Not Politics: The Making of the Gay Market*. New York: Columbia University Press.

Shapiro, Eve (2010) *Gender Circuits: Bodies and Identities in a Technological Age*. London: Routledge.

Showalter, Elaine (1991) *Sexual Anarchy: Gender and Culture at the Fin de Siècle*. London: Bloomsbury.

Simon, William (1996) *Postmodern Sexualities*. London: Routledge.

Smart, Carol (2007) *Personal Life: New Directions in Sociological Thinking*. Cambridge: Polity Press.

Stein, Arlene (2006) *Shameless*. New York: New York University Press.

Stein, A. and K. Plummer (1994) "I Can't Even Think Straight: Queer Theory and the Missing Revolution in Sociology." *Sociological Theory* 12(2): 178–87.

Storr, Merl (2004) *Latex and Lingerie: Shopping for Pleasure at Ann Summers Parties*. Oxford: Berg.

Swidler, Ann (2001) *Talk of Love: How Culture Matters*. Chicago: University of Chicago Press.

Taylor, Yvette, Sally Hines, and Mark Casey (eds.) (2010) *Theorizing Intersectionality and Sexuality*. Basingstoke: Palgrave.

Therborn, Goran (2004) *Between Sex and Power: Family in the World 1900–2000*. London: Routledge.

Tiefer, L. (2006) "The Viagra Phenomenon." *Sexualities* 9(3): 273–94.

Tilley, Charles (2004) *Social Movements: 1768–2004*. Boulder, CO: Paradigm Press.

Turner, Ralph (1976) "The Real Self: From Institution to Impulse." *American Journal of Sociology* 81(5): 989–1016.

Urry, John (2000) *Sociology Beyond Societies: Mobilities for the Twenty-First Century*. London: Routledge.

Vance, Carol (ed.) (1984) *Pleasure and Danger*. London: Routledge.

Warner, Michael (1993) *Fear of a Queer Planet*. Minneapolis: University of Minnesota Press.

Warner, Michael (2002) *Publics and Counterpublics*. New York: Zone Books.

Warren, Carol (1974) *Identity and Community in the Gay World*. New York: Wiley.

Waskul, Dennis (ed.) (2004) *net.SeXXX: Readings on Sex, Pornography and the Internet*. New York: Peter Lang.

Weeks, Jeffrey (1998) "The Sexual Citizen." *Theory, Culture and Society* 15(3–4): 35–52.

Weeks, Jeffrey (2003) *Sexuality*, 2nd edn. London: Routledge.

Weeks, Jeffrey (2007) *The World We Have Won*. London: Routledge.

Weeks, Jeffrey and Janet Holland (eds.) (1996) *Sexual Cultures*. London: Macmillan.

Weston, Kath (1998) *Longslowburn*. London: Routledge.

Wolfe, A. (1992) "Democracy and Sociology: Boundaries and Their Consequences." In Michelle Lamont and Marcel Fournier (eds.). *Cultivating Differences*. Chicago: University of Chicago Press, pp. 309–26.

Wouters, Cass (2004) *Sex and Manners: Female Emancipation in the West 1890–2000*. London: Sage.

Young, Iris Marion (1990) *Justice and the Politics of Difference*. Princeton, NJ: Princeton University Press.

Zelizer, Viviana A. (2005) *The Purchase of Intimacy*. Princeton, NJ: Princeton University Press.

Zerubavel, A. (2003) *Time Maps: Collective Memory and the Social Shape of the Past*. Chicago: University of Chicago Press.

Zheng, Tiantian (2009) *Red Lights: The Lives of Sex Workers in Postsocialist China*. Minneapolis: University of Minnesota Press.

Zimmerman, Don and Candace West (1987) "Doing Gender." *Gender and Society* 1(2): 125–51.

Zurcher, L. A., Jr. (1977) *The Mutable Self*. London: Sage.

15

Feeling Class

Affect and Culture in the Making of Class Relations

BEVERLEY SKEGGS

INTRODUCTION

New understandings have developed recently in the analysis of class, emerging from understandings of culture and affect. These understandings expand the ways we recognize and make sense of class relations; they ask: what does the concept of class "do" and how does it do what it does? These are dynamic and performative understandings of class in the making that range in scale from the global to the intimate. They ask: how has the term class come into effect, by and for whom, and to whom does it apply? What purpose and interests does classification serve? And what significance does it hold for our understandings of social relations more generally?

For instance, affect is a highly recognizable but little discussed aspect of class relationships: fear, anxiety, and disgust have filled categorizations of class. The fear of the urban outcast or the contagious woman in the history of the UK or the "fear of the black planet" in the US have long been mobilized to generate political campaigns. Sonia Rose (1999) in a detailed historical analysis has shown how in moments of national economic crisis the figure of the "contagious dangerous woman" has been used to contain projections of British national anxiety. More positively, Barack Obama's electoral success in 2008 was put down to the mobilization of hope, a campaign built around affect that is now mobilized in the UK in "hope not hate" organization against racism. These mobilizations of hope took a very different form from the affects generated from class relations detailed by Tom Frank's (2004) analysis of the G. W. Bush presidential campaign, which worked to shape the resentment generated from unemployment and lack of hope into a national

The Wiley-Blackwell Companion to Sociology, First Edition. Edited by George Ritzer.
© 2012 Blackwell Publishing Ltd. Published 2012 by Blackwell Publishing Ltd.

resentment of the figure of the privileged liberal. Moreover, Linda Williams (2001) demonstrates how the affective technology of melodrama has established the tone and the terms by which race relations are understood in the US. Here I will argue that affect and culture shape how class relations are made, known, and lived in social encounters.

I begin with a brief outline of Bourdieu's (1985, 1987, 1989) use of capital metaphors to understand how people can move through social space. I then point to the "doing" power of the term class, outlining its different historical trajectories to show how class is made to perform through analysis. Detailing how it is always produced through associations with discourses of symbolic value and figures that condense moral value, I then suggest that if we add affect to understandings of composite value (economic, cultural, social) we increase our capacity to understand class relations.

Bourdieu demonstrates how class is shaped by access to different capitals which over time become literally embodied, that is lived as bodily dispositions: our bodily movement, speech, and actions (especially dispositions such as confidence and anxiety) are formed by class (and I would add gender, race, and sexuality) over time. Bourdieu develops a model of social topography to demonstrate how relative positions and the *relations* between these positions constitute forms of power, enabling bodies to move in social space. Bourdieu identifies four main types of capital: economic, cultural, social, and symbolic:

- *Economic capital*: this includes income, wealth, financial inheritances, and monetary assets: what one owns.
- *Cultural capital*: this can exist in three forms: in an embodied state, i.e., in the form of long-lasting dispositions of the mind and the body; in the objectified state, in the form of cultural goods; and in the institutionalized state, resulting in such things as educational qualifications. Bourdieu defines cultural capital as high culture.
- *Social capital*: resources based on connection, networks, and group membership: who you know, used in pursuit of favor and advancement.
- *Symbolic capital*: the form the different types of capital take once they are perceived and recognized as legitimate. Legitimation is the key mechanism in the conversion to power. Cultural capital has to be legitimated before it can have symbolic power. Capital has to be regarded as legitimate before it can be capitalized upon, before its value is realizable.

People are distributed in social space according to: the global *volume* of capital they possess; the *composition* of their capital; *evolution* of the volume and composition according to their *trajectory* in social space. It is not just the volume and composition of the right sort of cultural capital (for national belonging, for instance), but it is also *how* one accumulates one's capital that is significant to its capacity to be converted. Bourdieu distinguishes between those who only have to be *what they are* as opposed to those who *are what they do* and, therefore, have to constantly prove that they are capable of carrying symbolic value.

Bourdieu also notes how proximity to necessity is one of the key ways in which we measure class relations: proximity to life (life expectancy and mortality rates are probably the most extreme example of unequal class relations), but also proximity to basic resources such as food and water, and proximity to health care: see Wilkinson and Pickett (2010) for an extended analysis of global class inequalities. Thus class relations range in scale through possibilities for accumulation: for instance the rich North is able to accumulate wealth based on the dispossession of the poor South, what David Harvey (2007) calls "accumulation by dispossession" which can be seen to shape global as well as national class relations, as well as the micro-scale of bodily dispositions and how we encounter others. The possibilities for accumulation of value to the person begin at birth, as studies of childhood show, with middle-class parents trying to load their children with as many forms of capital as possible: Annette Lareau (2003) describes this process as one of "concerted cultivation," in opposition to those denied access to forms of capital and/or who cannot compete for limited resources, or are not interested in "growing" their children in ways that subject them to continual educative and improving activities (Lawler 2000; Gillies 2007). The pressure on middle-class "mums" to provide extracurricular activities points to the significance of the accumulation of capitals over time.

Forms of cultural taste are another mechanism by which class differences are established, enabling one group to claim rights to adjudication over what counts as taste and what is considered tasteless. In his classic study of "distinction" in France in the 1970s, Bourdieu details – quantitatively and qualitatively – how understandings of taste are established, institutionalized, paralleled by the education system, and maintained by those who are able to use access to symbolic power to preserve and reproduce their interests. Access to high culture enables people to develop dispositions and knowledge over time and space (refined and distanced contemplation for instance as opposed to expressions of hedonism). The ability to accrue high culture dispositions depends on exposure to social spaces, what Bourdieu calls "fields," abstract spaces in which the forces of history cohere, where battles for value and legitimacy are fought and where different forms of capital are converted (or not) into value over time. The symbolic system creates, circulates, and maintains distinctions from the perspective and interest of those with power (symbolic capital), enabling them to accrue value to themselves whilst keeping others contained in social spaces with little prospect of conversion, unable to access the capitals that have value to enable social movement to occur. Judgments of taste and classification are considered by Bourdieu to be acts of symbolic violence: "If there is any terrorism it is in the peremptory verdicts which, in the name of taste, condemn to ridicule, indignity, shame, silence . . . men and women who simply fall short, in the eyes of their judges, of the right way of being and doing" (1986: 511).

Social encounters are dialectical movements of value, whereby one may establish one's value at the expense of another (micro movements of accumulation by dispossession). Measures of cultural distinction also reveal how national culture shapes understandings of class relations. "Taste" in France is premised on cultural judgments reproduced by those with power, whereas in the US, as Michele Lamont (1991) demonstrates, it is less a matter of cultural judgment and more a matter of money that establishes national cultural worth. Interestingly, Bourdieu also considers these class-based taste judgments to be shaped by understandings of space: distanced speculation is (following Kant) a sign of good taste whereas immediate pleasure is considered to be vulgar. Proximity and distance inform very different understandings of scalar class relations in Bourdieu's class analysis.

CLASS PERFORMATIVITY

Drawing on the work of linguist Austin (1962) and making an argument similar to that of Judith Butler (1999), about how the term gender and the classification "woman" and "heterosexual" come into effect, Pierre Bourdieu (1992) argues that theory is performative, bringing into effect that which it names, hence class theorists bring into effect that which they name: class. This is not to suggest that relations of inequality only exist when they are named, rather that they are only known, recognized, and shaped in particular ways when given a name by academics (and others if circulated through popular culture, or used to organize resistance, as shown by E. P. Thompson, the English historian). The term class has very different historical trajectories and is highly disputed. Is it a term that was generated by what we now know to be "the working class" or "the middle class" (that is, did they generate the term to describe their own experiences)? Or was it a term applied to people that was not recognizable to those whom it was meant to describe? Or does it matter if people recognize the term, if it describes the relations they live? Bourdieu maintains that it is important to challenge descriptions that consist in treating classes on paper as real classes. Metaphors, he argues, allow us to move beyond the alternatives of realism and nominalism, enabling us to make abstractions about social relations, to think about how they are "made." He notes:

> The title of E. P. Thompson's book "*The Making of the English Working Class*" must be taken quite literally; the working class such as it appears to us today through the words meant to designate it, "working class", "proletariat", "workers", "labour movement", and so on, through the organizations that are supposed to express its will, through the logos, bureaus, locals, flags, etc., is a well founded historical artefact. (Bourdieu 1989: 16)

Thus the term "class" is performative, it brings perspectives, interests, and people into view in particular ways. As a performative classification it does things in two ways: first, to confirm the perspective of the classifier and, second, to capture the classified within discourse. As Bourdieu notes, "nothing classifies somebody more than the way he or she classifies" (1989: 19).

What is significant is the longevity of the term (stretching back to the Ancient Greeks, as Ste. Croix [1981] notes), is the way it is used as a way of explaining all social organization, how it is almost impossible to extract from the entwined condition of its utterance, how it is intimately tied to nation, sexuality, race, and gender, and how it has been known through proximity to labor. As a term like all other terms, it codifies histories and interests within its definition (Skeggs 2004). This is not to say that it is purely discursive, for it is a term that has very powerful material effects. As Mary Poovey (1995) notes, abstractions like "minorities" (however defined) receive differential symbolic and material treatment according to prevailing assumptions about their relative value to society as a whole.

DIFFERENT HISTORICAL TRAJECTORIES

There are two radically opposed trajectories to the historical emergence of the term class. The first, Marxist, prioritizes the role of exploitation and struggle in the making of classes and hence social relations more generally; the second focuses on class hierarchies and status without reference to struggle and exploitation (see Cannadine 1988) and is recognizable in studies of "social stratification," or Weberian understandings of class. For Marxists, class has a number of distinctive features: class is a *relationship* that is always relative to other groups and the relationship is *antagonistic* because it is always based on exploitation and control. The antagonism is always formed in the process of *production*; and class is an *objective* relationship. It does not matter what people think about their location (subjective class position, identity); rather, it is about the location of people according to economic relationships (Callinicos & Harman 1987). And just because somebody believes they are middle class does not mean that they stop being exploited through the economic system they inhabit, capitalism.

For Marx it is the bourgeoisie that calls into existence the modern working class – the proletarians – "who live only so long as they find work and who find work only so long as their labour increases capital" (Marx & Engels [1848] 1968: 51). The proletariat is "the special and essential product of the bourgeoisie." Class, for Marx and Engels, is a description of the conditions of existence of labor under capitalism.

This perspective could not be more different from the other major trajectory which concerns itself with the precise nature of classification, employment "aggregates," status, and how best to conceptualize occupational groups in a hierarchical order. It began in 1665 with William Petty, who set out to calculate the value of the "people" of England for taxation purposes. Petty is attributed with devising what is now known as the "political arithmetic" tradition of class analysis in which (associated with hierarchy rather than class struggle) the person was conceptualized as a quantifiable, knowable, hence *governable object*, tightly linked to national concerns and formation (Poovey 1995). James Thompson documents how, throughout the eighteenth century, there was a "drive towards an abstract and consistent and therefore predictable representation of exchange, that is, toward (new) scientific, quantitative, and mathematical modelling" (1996: 28). These processes involved the quantification of labor, making the person an object of calculation. Counting the worth of persons became institutionalized in the eighteenth century through the machinery of the New Poor Law (1834) which generated an avalanche of new information and mandated more and more far-reaching fact-gathering, inspection, and legislation.

The continued emphasis on measurement and calculation deflects attention away from the reasons for inequality into a methodological debate about how best to measure, into scientific calculus, as if divisions were the result of mathematical formulae. The significant difference between the two main perspectives is thus cause and effect: the first attempts to explain why classes come into effect, whilst the other measures the end product. However, central to both is work: labor as a force which shapes all relations and work as organized into occupations for measurement. Both definitions have been subject to feminist critiques which showed, first via Marxism, that paid labor was only one way in which capitalism operates, pointing instead to the significance of domestic labor for social reproduction, thus sustaining exploitation; and second, via feminist stratification critiques, that measuring women's social class on husband's and father's occupation was inadequate (see Stanworth 1984; Crompton 1993).

There is, however, one element still missing from the historical performative production of class, which is morality and how it was articulated culturally. Definitions of class often encode ideas of a person's moral worth. There have been certain periods when class was definable *primarily* by economic, monetary, and market value; at others it was defined in relation to moral behavior. During the 1850s and 1860s, for instance, there was less talk of working class and middle class, and more of deserving and undeserving poor, of "respectable artisans and 'gentlemen', as emphasis was placed on moral rather than economic criteria" (Crossick 1991). It was in the play for power and legitimation that morality became central to defining class. Adam Smith (1757), the proponent of political economy, for instance, advanced the concept of self-interest (and its according accrual of wealth) as a moral imperative, and the emergent bourgeoisie were concerned to legitimate their mercantile interests by differentiating themselves from the degenerate behavior of aristocrats via the use of religious justification.

However, it is not until the early nineteenth century that the term "class" appears regularly in discourse in England and is consolidated in descriptions of society. Some theorists argue that the term class emerged to coincide with the rise of the "middle sort" (Williams 1988). Dror Wahrman (1995) maintains that the crucial moment for fixing the idea of the middle class was around the time of the 1832 Reform Act when the need for political representation allowed the middle class to be consolidated as a group. Hence political interests brought the term into effect. Terry Eagleton notes how the middle class used the expression of "taste" and the generation of distinctive cultures: "the ultimate binding force of the bourgeois social order [was] habits, pieties, sentiments and affections" (1989: 22) to which they attributed higher moral value to legitimate their social position. The claims to high culture and taste continue to be a mechanism for promoting and legitimating distinction and enabling the recognition of class positions (see Bourdieu 1986).

The emergence of the term "working class" is a similarly contested and nationally specific debate. Lynette Finch (1993) documents how, in Australia, the idea of class emerged from the middle-class colonial welfare administrators as a category to define the urban poor. Carrying with them British imperial definitions, Finch illustrates how they developed their own interpretations and categorizations that were particularly gendered and moral, conceived through the interpretation of the behavior of women of urban slums. In an equally detailed historical analysis of British imperial discourse, Ann McClintock (1995) suggests that the concept of class has a historical link to more generalizable "others," who were known through the concept of degeneracy, a term applied as much to classifying racial "types" as to the urban poor.

Domestic servants, for instance, were often depicted using the racialized imagery of degradation – of contagion, promiscuity, and savagery. As Friedrich Engels notes of the working class: "a physically degenerate race, robbed of all humanity, degraded, reduced morally and intellectually to bestiality" ([1844] 1958: 33). What we see in Engels' comment is how a description, used in his case to advocate for social justice, is limited by the prevailing discourses of his time, which semiotically work to attach degeneracy to the working classes. In the bourgeois claim for moral legitimacy, domestic servants, in particular, became the projected object for dirt, and more explicitly were associated with the care of back passages, and the generalized poor came to be represented as excrement. Osbourne's pamphlet on "Excremental Sewage" in 1852 represents the working class as a problem for civilization, as sewage that contaminates and drains the nation (Yeo 1993). Moreover, hygiene became one of the first discourses to rely on marketing and commodities as a solution to the threat to the nation posed by those figured as decadent, degenerate, and unhygienic: washing the nation clean offered a defense to the threatening pollution of race, class, gender, and sexuality. Dirt and waste, sexuality and contagion, danger and disorder, degeneracy and pathology, became the moral evaluations by which the working class were coded and recorded in the discourses of the day (Nead 1988) – discourses not dissimilar to those reproduced today. Chris Haylett (2001), for instance, notes how in the 1990s in the UK the white working class were increasingly colored, coded as "dirty white" in government rhetoric; as degenerate, atavistic, and abject, surplus to the requirements of a vanguard bourgeois cosmopolitan nation.

Semiotic chains of association were established between already existing discourses such as hygiene, taste, and degeneracy and newly emergent terms such as middle and working class which enable them to develop associations that can be known, recognized, and established with value formations (lack and added value). If the Reform Law (political representation structured through property ownership) was key to the formation of the middle class, the Poor Law (basic economic subsistence) was significant to the establishment of the working class. In these differentially invested and incited formations – one that makes political claims for legitimated legal property ownership and one that forced recipients to perform their morality for the state legal/welfare system to stay alive – class differences come into effect.

Likewise, gender, race, and sexuality amalgamate in all class definitions. As McClintock puts it, "the invention of *racial* fetishism became central to the regime of sexual surveillance, while the policing of *sexual* fetishism became central to the policing of the 'dangerous classes'" (1995: 182). In most debates about the moral formation of the middle class, aristocratic women are seen to signal constitutive negative limits, particularly despised for their excessive and lascivious sexuality. Foucault (1979) argues that the middle class, struggling to find the means to define themselves, used reference to commodification to regulate sexuality as a means of social identification: "The middle-class thus defined itself as different from the aristocracy and the working-classes who spent, sexually and economically, without moderation . . . It differed by virtue of its sexual restraint, its monogamy and its economic restraint or thrift" (Foucault 1979: 100).

Capital metaphors – spent, restraint, thrift – shape the formation of moral class values. And just as Foucault identifies the four discourses that came to produce sexuality (the Malthusian couple, the masturbating child, the hysterical woman, the perverse adult), we can see a similar discursive production with class. The discourses of the dangerous outcast, the urban mass, the revolutionary alien, the contagious woman, and the dirty degenerate came to produce figures to which ideas about what was known as "working-classness" became attached (Skeggs 2004). Ideas about what constitutes different classes are often moral battlegrounds, as struggles over "dignity" demonstrate. The sexuality of working-class women became not just a reference to moral denigration but also a source of desire and "scientific" observation for the Victorian male reformers who tried to apply "scientific methods" to the study of their objects of fascination. Reformers attempted to justify their pursuits by claiming they were describing the absolute limits to morality. However, the outcome of this projected exclusion was to make the limit the site of all that was interesting and potentially desirable.

CLASS RECOGNITIONS AND JUDGMENT

Yet what is interesting in these different amalgamations and trajectories is how different classifications of class were recognized, used, or became attached to different bodies. Class became a performative statement of a person's value, still used in the present (Sayer 2005). The moral evaluation of the category draws attention away from economic inequality. But most historians of class debate whether the working class made the term, or willingly used the term, strategically to receive poor relief, or recognized themselves in the classification.

E. P. Thompson (1966) maintains that industrial workers and artisans learnt to organize politically around the term class. He details how the term working class came to have increasing significance for trade union organizing (Marx's combination groups, e.g., the Chartists) and the formation of political parties (the British Labour Party), offering a space for identification for those who could join, and there are substantive debates about the exclusion of women from trade union campaigns (Brenner & Ramas 1984).

The attempt to make the working class recognize their classification is also noted by Carolyn Steedman (1999, 2000) who introduces an important factor into the performative emergence of the category class. She traces how a working-class self as a moral categorization came into existence through the religious discourse of redemption, a self that had to be respectable and prove itself to be capable of narrating itself in the terms established by the state-legal interlocutor systems of poor relief. If they could not speak the narrative of redemption – an aspiration towards middle-class morality – they were unlikely to receive money for living – eating, safe water (beer), and sanitary conditions. Steedman's analysis is supported by David Vincent's (1981) extensive study of working-class autobiographies in England which details how specific narrative forms and techniques are used to tell the stories of a working-class life lived through narratives of redemption and dignity.

If we move into the present we can see how the same processes are in operation and come to shape different forms and figures; for instance in the UK at the moment the figure of the "Chav" follows in the tradition of the dangerous urban outcast and the contagious woman (Skeggs 2005). Chav is the symbolic condensation of all that is nationally negative attached to a body that is made recognizable as working-class. The recognition of the body and its lack of value comes into effect through symbolic repetition and figural circulation via the media. The Chav classification contains every negative national value: every benefit-claiming, smoking, pleasure-seeking, fake-buying, noisy, space-taking form of excess. Chav women, in particular, are subject to extensive symbolic violence as their bodies are represented as danger-ous and costly to the nation, excess personified through fecundity and obesity. The Chav figure was cited so much in British popular culture that the term became the *Oxford English Dictionary* word of 2004. As Bourdieu notes above, what it revealed was more about the class position and the perspectives of the classifiers, as they attempted to reach the moral high ground and draw distance from connotations of working-classness, than about the person to whom it was applied. The symbolic designation was an attempt by one privileged group (journalists, TV producers, writers, comedians) to denigrate another by turning them into a figure of contempt and ridicule, in which the classifier names their claim to moral and taste superiority whilst pretending it is an objective cultural judgment. The speaking of the term Chav reveals the snobbery of the speaker, as they attempt to name their social dis-tinction. In this way the speaking of the classification Chav is an example of how class relations are repeatedly enacted through culture, visualizing and legitimating judgment.

The Chav was a distinctly white figure, only enabled through the distance that was drawn via discourses of multi-culturalism from the black and South Asian working class in the UK. But as Chris Haylett (2001) has argued, through both popular culture *and* government policy rhetoric, the Chav represents the attempt to divide and rule the working class through ethnicity so that governmental responsi-bility to deal with economic inequality is eclipsed by the emphasis on individualized cultural difference. She demonstrates how government rhetoric was able to paint the white working class as dirty white, thus making its difference from the respect-able middle-class pure white clear and recognizable. In a reverse move, Cecily Forde-Jones (1998) shows how in an attempt to retain white power in Barbados in the Victorian period efforts were made to recuperate the dirty white population into the pure respectable whites *against* the black population. This re-allocation of value through associations between race and class exemplifies how those with power can use their access to the symbolic to organize, legitimate, and maintain their interests. The discourse of multi-culturalism and the morally loaded accusations of racism have partially protected the British working-class black and South Asian groups from similar morally denigrating figurations. They, however, have been defined as dangerous and threatening, not just as a national irritant subject to disdain and contempt, but as a threat to the core of the life of the nation itself.

Hence it is the adjective-value designations that are added to the term class that illustrate how structural inequalities of race, gender, and class are known and cir-culated through culture. Vicki Mayer (2011) demonstrates how in the US most people try to attach the term middle class to themselves in order to defend against accusations of lack of cultural value. The term middle class may have no relation-ship to their economic positioning but it represents how they want to enter inter-actions with others and be seen to have value. In a complete reversal of this imperative to claim value, Andrew Sayer (2002) demonstrates how in the UK middle-class people do not want to be attached to the term middle class, as they consider it to be the expression of privilege and snobbery, leading to the bizarre finding, in response to a MORI poll, that 76 percent of British people think they have "working-class feelings" (whatever these are is not defined). Applying the adjective "trash" to the term class means that no doubt is left as to the negative symbolic value loading: as Hartigan (1997) notes, to embrace the term "trash" would take considerable effort by those who want to be positioned as respectable, valuable, and part of the nation. The term itself signifies the impossibility of inclusion. But it also displays how significant judgment of a person's value is to understandings of class relationships.

When social inequalities become coded as moral positions, judgment of others' value may shape the form the social encounter takes, hence the insistence on drawing distance from certain groups – especially when, as Savage, Bagnall, et al. (2001) argue, the middle class have through their access to circuits of symbolic capital (media, popular culture, political rhetoric) been able to construct what counts as normative. The middle class may not want to name themselves as such, and Savage et al.'s research echoes that of Sayer, maintaining that middle-class people in the UK want to be considered "ordinary," but they certainly want to attach to themselves the moral values of the normative nation, and are able to do this by naming the constitutive outside, the working class, the white trash, the poor black, the dangerous Muslim, and the Chav.

But how do those who are positioned as the constitutive limit, subject to continual symbolic denigration, generate value for themselves?

One of the ways in which the working class "combined," which is often overlooked, is through their demands for decadence, for fun and pleasure; a necessary defense, Zizek (2000) argues, against the grim conditions endured. Through fun and pleasure they also found alternative ways of challenging the moral authority and legitimacy of the classifiers. Martha Vicinus reveals how the working class reversed moral judgments by heaping scorn on those with pretensions to gentility, by laughing at those who restrained their own pleasure, and by deriding those who tried to occupy the moral high ground: "Putting on airs was the greatest sin anyone could commit" (1974: 262–3), a statement still found in contemporary research on class relations (Walkerdine & Lucey 1989). A study of Victorian music-hall entertainment, and now contemporary entertainment, dramatizes a class struggle in which the working class challenge the moral authority that seeks to condemn them.

Paul Willis (1977) notes the hedonism, excitement, and defiance of authority achieved by working-class boys in the UK who invert the school's core values. American subculture theory from the 1950s (e.g., Cohen 1955) shows how boys disengage themselves from school rituals and values and re-orientate themselves instead around leisure activities. Walter Miller (1958) suggests that their behavior is not an inversion as such, but represents the focal concerns of masculine working-class culture – excitement, toughness, and luck. This "creative" analysis shows how dominant values are inverted, but I would argue with very different gender performances. In my ethnographic research (Skeggs 1997) of a group of working-class women I showed how they generated value for themselves by claiming to be the real and proper mothers *against* middle-class mothers who by "shopping out" their children (sending their children to private schools or to nursery at an early age) reveal themselves to be uncaring, unnatural, irresponsible, and ultimately immoral. My research respondents inverted class divisions and claimed *moral superiority* to the middle-class women. This inversion of value has also been documented in other research on motherhood (Reay 1998; Lawler 2000; Duncan 2005) and child development (Walkerdine & Lucey 1989). What we see is a continual struggle over withholding consent to the legitimating practices of moral judgment (in this case mothering, which is constantly subject to judgment *and* a claim for value).

If we apply Bourdieu's metaphor topology theory, we can see how gender enables different forms of value inversion fought on key sites of class performance: manual labor, pleasure, and motherhood. Lois Weis's (2004) longitudinal ethnography of the transition of "Freeway" in the US from an industrial steel town to a restructured service economy demonstrates what happens to the working class when traditional economies are destroyed and gender becomes detached from the sexual division of labor. Weis details how a considerable amount of class, race, and gender re-embedding occurs, with redundant men no longer able to fulfill their "hard work" ethos and unable to deal with domesticity. The women become more resourceful and creative in dealing with the new conditions, suggesting that irreverence and inversion are highly specific responses to changing capitalist relations.

The search for dignity beyond work, for value in conditions of devaluation, by both men and women, black and white, has also been charted by Mitch Duneier (1992) who illustrated how a group of black men in Chicago desired to be recognized as respectable and *not* as dangerous, criminal, or pathological, which (like the women above) was often how they were misrecognized and diminished in social encounters (Khanna 2007). Likewise, Michelle Lamont (2000) identifies a distinct moral code focusing on personal integrity and the quality of interpersonal relationships amongst both the white and black working-class men to whom she spoke. These were not responses of radical creativity (Willis) or antagonistic moral inversion (Skeggs) but straightforward attempts to claim worth and value for themselves. These studies, however, also point to the lack of antagonism present in generalized American class analysis and cultural theory, what bell hooks calls "the elephant in the room" – the unnamed subject that everybody knows is central to their lives but cannot be named as such; instead, "Race and gender are used as screens to deflect attention away from the harsh realities that class politics exposes" (hooks 2000: 7).

The next section explores how value judgments and the making of distinctions that eclipse inequalities through appearing as culture, but simultaneously make and legitimate those inequalities (circulating as forms of capital that cannot be easily separated as they cohere on the person), are actually experienced.

AFFECT AND SYMBOLIC VIOLENCE

Cultural analyses of class enable us to see how value is distributed and circulated through social spaces in which people are able or not to access moral and cultural value and convert it into legitimate symbolic value and economic resources. If a person is a composite package of capital value that circulates through the social and can increase or deplete their value through the possibilities for conversion, we can see how social encounters are important micro-spaces of exchange where value is made visible and evaluated. If judgment is one of the key behaviors that informs these encounters, which research into how class relations are lived demonstrates, we therefore also need to take into account how affect shapes these encounters.

We never enter an encounter without history or affect: every time we meet somebody we experience the encounter through different emotional responses such as disgust, horror, fear, anxiety, dignity, gravitas, pleasure, warmth, kindness. Even unoccupied spaces carry affects – such as houses and street spaces: we feel them. Our responses may be learnt from our inherited social position: for instance, we learn to fear and be disgusted by certain figures through repetitive symbolic loading. The figure of the contagious dangerous woman of the Victorian period was recognized through repeated visualizations (through newspapers, art, penny criminal stories, the media of the time), enabling even a slight resemblance to the figure to generate fear and disgust (Nead 1988).

If we add Spinoza's (1996) theory of affect to Bourdieu's spatial metaphors, we can see how what Spinoza terms "the force of existing" informs and shapes class relations. Seventeenth-century Spinoza maintains that when we come across somebody good, if they make us joyful, they increase our capacity/ability to act, whereas if we meet sadness, inhibition increases and it decreases our capacity to act. Spinoza was concerned to understand how people with power use sadness to affect us to increase their power and decrease the power of others (he studied priests). This continual variation experienced through all social encounters – increase–diminution or diminution–diminution or increase–increase – helps us understand why some people may, through repeated access to accruing, capital-converting spaces, learn to feel entitled to space and cultural resources, while others, due to lack of access and experience, feel constrained and limited in social space, where they may be subject to repeated judgment, subject to contempt, and humiliated (as were the women of my *Formations* ethnography). I would argue that the continual attachment of negative value to those recognized through prior symbolic figuring as working-class intensifies and increases the feeling of diminution over time and space as a metaphoric accumulation of negative capital – a disinvestment, a depreciation of value.

This is not just about individualized social encounters but how through repetition and performativity total social relations are shaped; affects arise from within the system of social relationships, institutions, and practices which exceed individuals. When one enters a social encounter with an awareness of the possibilities for denigration, a defensive response to the potential negative evaluation is prepared, as my ethnographic research demonstrated: defense against denigration was one of the main ways by which subjectivity was produced over time and space. The women of my research learnt not to enter certain social spaces for fear of contempt, misrecognition, and negative judgment. Institutions institutionalize symbolic value, they make people feel they *should not* belong. Spinoza and Bourdieu together offer us a way of understanding class relations as a moral topology of entitlement and constraint accumulating or depreciating over time. Together they show how culture and affect are materialized through bodily movement in social space.

Spinoza also notes how continuous variation in the force of existing is determined by the ideas one gives to the affects we feel. So if we feel diminished we may look for an idea to explain our diminution. If we look to the category of working-class to explain our negative evaluation, we may either be able to convert it into something positive, such as trade union activity, or be able to generate distance from it (such as white trash, Chav) in order to protect ourselves from its negative effects (feeling sad, diminished, under-valued, mis-recognized as having no value, and out of place). Likewise, if diminished by class we may be able to protect our value through other classificatory systems such as sexuality, gender, or race which have different potentials for re-signification and value attachment (e.g., "Black and Proud" or "Queer and Here"). Thus social encounters are dialectical movements of value.

Sara Ahmed (2004) suggests that we inhabit an affective economy where affects such as hate are economic; that is, hate circulates between signifiers in relationships of difference and displacement and is distributed across a variety of figures through the process of what she calls "metonymic slide." Figures such as Chavs (and in her example, "asylum seekers," a highly racialized negative term in the UK) become readable as nationally cancerous, as rotting the moral fabric of the nation. Hate, she maintains, cannot be found just in one figure, but works to create the very outline of different figures or objects of hate, a creation that crucially aligns the figures together and constitutes them as a "common" threat, but with different intensities (e.g., the female and male Chav). In such affective economies, Ahmed argues, emotions *do things*, they align individuals with communities – or bodily space with social space – through the very intensity of their attachments. For instance, the ex-Conservative Party advisor, Ferdinand Mount (2004), points to the "sustained programme of social contempt and institutional erosion which has persisted through many different governments and several political fashions," to which the working class in the UK has been subject.

However, even if the working class feel anger, resentment, and hate, it is unlikely that their expression of these emotions will be given legitimacy through access to symbolic power – they are more likely to be criminalized for their expression. Or as Sianne Ngai (2005) points out, they will be symbolically devalued as the expression of "ugly feelings" by "ugly people." She details how:

> While envy describes a subject's polemical response to a perceived inequality in the external world, it has been reduced to signifying a static subjective trait: the "lack" or "deficiency" of the person who envies. Hence, after a person's envy enters a public domain of signification, it will always seem unjustified and critically effete – regardless of whether the relation of inequality it points to (say, unequal ownership of a means of production) has a real and objective existence. Although envy begins with a clearly defined object – and it is the only negative emotion defined specifically by the very fact that it addresses forms of inequality – it denies the very objectivity of this object. Envy is in a sense an intentional feeling that paradoxically undermines its own intentionality. (Ngai 2005: 21)

Ngai charts a range of ugly feelings to demonstrate how justifiable responses to inequality are often read as a problematic pathology of the person who expresses them. Respondents from a recent research project noted how they thought it was unjust that they were constantly subject to blame for that which they could not control: being born into a working-class life, being sent to "dump" schools, or facing high unemployment on leaving school. They pointed out that when they

expressed these concerns at university to middle-class audiences they were repeatedly told to "get over it," and described as having "a chip on their shoulder." Their
experience of injustice was understood as a subjective trait, their own problem,
something they should transcend and entirely divorced from the conditions of production (Skeggs in press). What we see in the UK through the expression of such
dismissal of concerns about injustice and the "new" unadulterated contempt is a
public alignment of middle-class values *against* working-class lifestyles. The affects
of antagonism thus become central to how people express their social relations and
to how people are recognized, evaluated, and legitimated. Moreover, daily low-level
affects such as resentment against injustice hum away, shaping social encounters,
but they can be mobilized in different ways.

Tom Frank (2004) notes how in the US in the 1990s a disaffected, unemployed,
male working class were persuaded through anti-liberal populist public outrage
rhetoric to elevate "morality" via the protection of the family and the fetus, and
in so doing align themselves with a Republican Right that promoted the interests
of the super-rich. Part of the Right's rhetorical appeal was its ability to detach
already formed moral values such as unpretentiousness, authenticity, hard work,
and loyalty from the conditions of their original production (working-class life),
a space which was increasingly entrenched, and re-attach them to the interests
of an imaginary safe and secure, prosperous right-wing nation through the promise
of respect and respectability. The aim of such rhetoric, Frank maintains, was
to generate indignation by voicing the fury of the imposed-upon, enabling
diminished subjects to voice their indignation, not just through claims to respectability, but by revenge: deriding the denigrators. Contempt returns to contempt.
Cultural grievances and the challenges to authority are given national space and
credibility through a very specific form of symbolic conversion into a political
formation.

What we see from these different political mobilizations is how they are premised
on already structured class relations from which class antagonism can be activated.
The working-class men identified by Tom Frank (2004) in Kansas were ripe for
recruitment to moral causes, such as protecting the fetus, because it offered them
moral value whilst visualizing and naming an enemy which fitted their already existing class antagonisms based on their experience of inequality and injustice. Their
grievances were detached from source and they were offered an affective fantasy of
revenge to which they attached themselves, for a time. The moral struggles of the
women of my ethnography are like a microcosm of this process; they live the
antagonism and the diminishing, struggling to gain moral value through motherhood and respectability in an attempt to make their lives bearable and value-full.
Unlike the Kansas men they have not been mobilized around the visualization of
an enemy; instead they engage in minor battles in cramped spaces on a daily basis.
What we see in all the working-class ethnographies (from early subculture theory
to the contemporary, through race and gender) is a desire to be recognized as having
value, and thereby not denigrated, when one is repeatedly symbolically positioned
as valueless. Barack Obama's appeal to hope offered a much more positive shape
to the negative affects in circulation. In a period of working-class black and white
sub-prime economic devastation, he replaced hate with hope, suggesting that affects
can be channeled.

CONCLUSION

Class is a relationship between people who inherit not just different categories but the values the categories contain: the inequalities and injustices. To inherit inequalities which are then symbolically repeated as ugly feelings, as a moral measure of a person, leads to justifiable resentments. Those who are subject to the judgmental gaze of middle-class institutions and authority are fully aware of how cultural distinction and classification work in the interests of the powerful – legitimating inequalities so that privilege cannot be contested. Class relations still determine life chances, health, and wealth regardless of how people speak their relationship to them (see Wilkinson & Pickett 2010). Class relations are dynamic forces that underwrite all social encounters. Capitalism is the inequality generator shaping how people live, what they inherit, and how they move through social space. To understand this process fully we need an analysis of an "economy of personhood" (Skeggs 2011) within capitalism which can explain how different values – economic, cultural, symbolic, social, moral – can be accessed, attached, and utilized, and how they work through encounters that repeatedly enhance or diminish value in the person. The analysis of culture offers us ways to understand how perspective and performativity inform classifications, showing how moral value and judgment are key to how class is lived and cohere on the person. If we add affect to this analysis we can see in even more detail how class relations are experienced and felt as bodies move through social space and time as enhanced or cramped. Even when inversion, reversal, or challenge to legitimacy and inequality occurs, these responses are shaped by the terrain of the class-infused social encounter, an encounter which is always a performance generated from the affective structure of class relations, whether they sing loudly or hum quietly. As the super-rich become super-richer and the poor become sub-prime we should stop trying to pretend that inequality is just a matter of culture or subjectivity and understand how the very grounds for our constitution as persons are shaped always/already by class, constantly felt in the making.

References

Ahmed, S. (2004) "Affective Economies." *Social Text* 22(2): 117–39.

Austin, J. (1962) *How to Do Things with Words*. Oxford: Clarendon.

Bourdieu, P. (1986) *Distinction: A Social Critique of the Judgement of Taste*. London: Routledge.

Bourdieu, P. (1985) "The Social Space and the Genesis of Groups." *Theory and Society* 14: 723–44.

Bourdieu, P. (1987) "What Makes a Social Class? On the Theoretical and Practical Existence of Groups." *Berkeley Journal of Sociology* 32: 1–17.

Bourdieu, P. (1989) "Social Space and Symbolic Power." *Sociological Theory* 7: 14–25.

Bourdieu, P. (1992) *Language and Symbolic Power*. Cambridge: Polity Press.

Brenner, J. and M. Ramas (1984) "Rethinking Women's Oppression." *New Left Review* 144: 33–72.

Butler, J. (1999) "Performativity's Social Magic." In R. Shusterman (ed.), *Bourdieu: A Critical Reader*. Oxford: Blackwell, pp. 113–29.

Callinicos, A. and C. Harman (1987) *The Changing Working-Class: Essays on Class Structure Today*. London: Bookmarks.

Cannadine, D. (1988) *Class in Britain*. New Haven, CT: Yale University Press.

Cohen, A. K. (1955) *Delinquent Boys: The Culture of the Gang*. Chicago: Free Press.

Crompton, R. (1993) *Class and Stratification: An Introduction to Current Debates*. Cambridge: Polity Press.

Crossick, G. (1991) "From Gentlemen to the Residuum: Languages of Social Description in Victorian Britain." In P. J. Corfield (ed.), *Language, History and Class*. Oxford: Blackwell, pp. 150–78.

Duncan, S. (2005) "Mothering, Class, Rationality." *Sociological Review* 53(1): 50–76.

Duneier, M. (1992) *Slim's Table: Race, Respectability and Masculinity*. Chicago: University of Chicago Press.

Eagleton, T. (1989) "The Ideology of the Aesthetic." In P. Hernadi (ed.), *The Rhetoric of Interpretation and the Interpretation of Rhetoric*. Durham, NC: Duke University Press, pp. 75–86.

Engels, F. ([1844] 1958) *The Condition of the Working-Class in England*. St Albans: Panther.

Finch, L. (1993) *The Classing Gaze: Sexuality, Class and Surveillance*. Sydney: Allen and Unwin.

Forde-Jones, C. (1998) "Mapping Social Boundaries: Gender, Race and Poor Relief in Barbadian Plantation Society." *Journal of Women's History* 10(3): 9–31.

Foucault, M. (1979) *The History of Sexuality, Vol. 1, An Introduction*. London: Penguin.

Frank, T. (2004) *What's the Matter with America: The Resistable Rise of the American Right*. London: Secker and Warburg.

Gillies, V. (2007) *Marginalised Mothers: Exploring Working-Class Experiences of Parenting*. London: Routledge.

Hartigan, J. J. (1997) "Unpopular Culture: The Case of White Trash." *Cultural Studies* 11(2): 316–43.

Harvey, D. (2007) *The Limits to Capital*. London: Verso.

Haylett, C. (2001) "Illegitimate Subjects? Abject Whites, Neoliberal Modernisation and Middle Class Multiculturalism." *Environment and Planning D: Society and Space* 19: 351–70.

hooks, b. (2000) *Where We Stand: Class Matters*. New York: Routledge.

Khanna, R. (2007) "Indignity." *Ethnic and Racial Studies* 30(2): 257–81.

Lamont, M. (1991) *Money, Morals and Manners: The Culture of the French and the American Upper Middle Class*. Chicago: University of Chicago Press.

Lamont, M. (2000) *The Dignity of Working Men: Morality and the Boundaries of Gender, Race and Class*. Cambridge, MA: Harvard University Press.

Lareau, A. (2003) *Unequal Childhoods: Class, Race and Family Life*. Berkeley, CA: University of California Press.

Lawler, S. (2000) *Mothering the Self: Mothers, Daughters, Subjects*. London: Routledge.

Marx, K. and F. Engels ([1848] 1968) *Manifesto of the Communist Party*. London: Lawrence and Wishart.

Mayer, V. (2011) "Reality Television's 'Class' Rooms: Knowing, Showing and Telling about Social Class in Reality Casting Labour and the College Classroom." In H. Wood and B. Skeggs (eds.), *Reality TV and Class*. London: BFI/Palgrave.

McClintock, A. (1995) *Imperial Leather: Race, Gender and Sexuality in the Colonial Context*. London: Routledge.

Miller, W. B. (1958) "Lower Class Culture as a Generating Milieu of Gang Delinquency."
    Journal of Social Issues 15: 5–19.

Mount, F. (2004) *Mind the Gap: Class in Britain Now*. London: Short Books.

Nead, L. (1988) *Myths of Sexuality: Representations of Women in Victorian Britain*. Oxford:
    Blackwell.

Ngai, S. (2005) *Ugly Feelings*. Cambridge, MA: Harvard University Press.

Poovey, M. (1995) *Making a Social Body: British Cultural Formation 1830–1864*. Chicago:
    University of Chicago Press.

Reay, D. (1998) *Class Work: Mother's Involvement in Their Children's Primary Schooling*.
    London: UCL Press.

Rose, S. O. (1999) "Cultural Analysis and Moral Discourses: Episodes, Continuities and
    Transformations." In V. E. Bonnell and L. Hunt (eds.), *Beyond the Cultural Turn*. Berke-
    ley, CA: University of California Press, pp. 217–41.

Savage, M., G. Bagnall, et al. (2001) "Ordinary, Ambivalent and Defensive: Class Identities
    in the Northwest of England." *Sociology* 35(4): 875–92.

Sayer, A. (2002) "What Are You Worth? Why Class Is an Embarrassing Subject." *Socio-
    logical Research Online* 7(3).

Sayer, A. (2005) *The Moral Significance of Class*. Cambridge: Cambridge University
    Press.

Skeggs, B. (1997) *Formations of Class and Gender: Becoming Respectable*. London: Sage.

Skeggs, B. (2004) *Class, Self, Culture*. London: Routledge.

Skeggs, B. (2005) "The Making of Class and Gender through Visualising Moral Subject
    Formation." *Sociology* 39(5): 965–82.

Skeggs, B. (2011) "Imagining Personhood Differently: Person Value and Autonomist Working
    Class Value Practices." *Sociological Review* 59(3): 579–94.

Skeggs, B. (in press) "'Contingencies of Value': Doing Things Differently, Value Practies and
    Person-Value." *Sociology*.

Smith, A. (1757) *Theory of the Moral Sentiments*. London: Liberty Press.

Spinoza, B. de (1996) *Ethics*. London: Penguin.

Stanworth, M. (1984) "Women and Class Analysis: A Reply to Goldthorpe." *Sociology* 18(2):
    153–71.

Ste. Croix, G. de (1981) *The Class Struggle in the Ancient Greek World*. London: Duckworth.

Steedman, C. (1999) "State Sponsored Autobiography." In B. Conekin, F. Mort, and C.
    Waters (eds.), *Movements of Modernity: Reconstructing Britain 1945–1964*. London:
    Rivers Oram.

Steedman, C. (2000) "Enforced Narratives: Stories of Another Self." In T. Cosslett, C. Lury,
    and P. Summerfield (eds.), *Feminism and Autobiography: Texts, Theories, Methods*.
    London: Routledge, pp. 25–40.

Thompson, E. P. (1966) *The Making of the English Working Class*. Harmondsworth: Penguin.

Thompson, J. (1996) *Models of Value: Eighteenth Century Political Economy and the Novel*.
    Durham, NC: Duke University Press.

Vicinus, M. (1974) *The Industrial Muse: A Study of Nineteenth Century British Working
    Class Literature*. London: Croom Helm.

Vincent, D. (1981) *Bread, Knowledge and Freedom: A Study of Working-Class Nineteenth
    Century Autobiography*. London: Europa Publications.

Wahrman, D. (1995) *Imagining the Middle-Class: The Political Representation of Class in
    Britain, c. 1780–1840*. Cambridge: Cambridge University Press.

Walkerdine, V. and H. Lucey (1989) *Democracy in the Kitchen: Regulating Mothers and
    Socialising Daughters*. London: Virago.

Weis, L. (2004) *Class Reunion: The Remaking of the American White Working Class*. New York: Routledge.

Wilkinson, R. and K. Pickett (2010) *The Spirit Level: Why Equality Is Better for Everyone*. London: Penguin.

Williams, L. (2001) *Playing the Race Card: Melodramas of Black and White from Uncle Tom to O.J. Simpson*. Princeton, NJ: Princeton University Press.

Williams, R. (1988) *Keywords: A Vocabulary of Culture and Society*. London: Fontana.

Willis, P. (1977) *Learning to Labour: How Working Class Kids Get Working Class Jobs*. Farnborough: Saxon House.

Yeo, E. (1993) *The Contest of Social Science in Britain: Relations and Representations of Gender and Class*. Lancaster: Lancaster University.

Zizek, S. (2000) "Class Struggle or Postmodernism: Yes, Please!" In J. Butler, E. Laclau, and S. Zizek (eds.), *Contingency, Hegemony, Universality: Contemporary Dialogues on the Left*. London: Verso, pp. 90–136.

16

Racial and Ethnic Issues

Critical Race Approaches in the United States

Brittany Chevon Slatton and Joe R. Feagin

Introduction

On September 9, 2009, President Barack Obama presented a major speech on health-care reform to a joint session of Congress. As President Obama expressed to the audience that a government health-care plan would not apply to those living in the United States unlawfully, Republican Representative Joe Wilson yelled out, "you lie." Republicans also laughed when the President stated the health-care plan still needed to be worked on (Huffington Post 2009). Former President Jimmy Carter was one of few influential whites to publicly come forward and denounce this hostile treatment of President Obama as racist, for which he faced great criticism from other whites. The unprecedented lack of reverence and the crude belittling of the authority of the President of the United States, the first black President, likely reflected a deep-seated racism, which is part of the foundational structure of the United States. However, in contemporary times, mainstream politicians, media commentators, and social scientists – including conservatives and even some liberals – often cleverly claim that the state of the United States is one of colorblindness and "postraciality," thereby denying outright any form of racism that does not fall in line with the dominant white-constructed narrative.

In this chapter we provide a critical analysis of contemporary racial and ethnic issues, mainly by analyzing contemporary ways that whites engage in racism and by arguing for the continuing significance of "race," as evidenced by the critical research on race and racism that frequently utilizes new theoretical concepts. We divide this chapter into three sections. In the first section we critique mainstream

The Wiley-Blackwell Companion to Sociology, First Edition. Edited by George Ritzer.
© 2012 Blackwell Publishing Ltd. Published 2012 by Blackwell Publishing Ltd.

race and ethnicity theories, revealing how they are limited in analysis of race and racism and ultimately aid the maintenance of existing white racial-power structures. We then provide a detailed analysis of critical theoretical approaches in race and ethnic studies scholarship. Attention is given to theoretical underpinnings of major critical theorists from varying disciplines that advance Critical Race Theory. These theorists, in both law and social science, have provided powerful scholarship articulating new modes of thought which identify and challenge currently hegemonic notions of race and racism that mostly treat racism as "rare and aberrational rather than systemic and ingrained" (Crenshaw, Gotanda, Peller & Thomas 1995: xvi).

In the second section, we discuss important examples of racism experienced today by people of color, including effects of racism and its racial framing on Asian Americans and black women. We present critical research studies that employ new concepts to contemporary racism, which allow us to better grasp the deep foundation of racism and document the contemporary ways that whites engage and sustain racist thoughts, values, emotions, and actions.

Historically and in the present, people of color have not passively accepted systemic racism and its discrimination – including the ways in which they have been defined by whites in a system where they wield little or no power. They have always, in varying ways and degrees, fought back and attempted to redefine their own space and meaning in society. Hence, in the final section we discuss the centrality of resistance in critical racial theories and the resistance and *counter-frame* strategies actually used by people of color.

CRITICAL ANALYSIS OF RACE AND ETHNICITY THEORIES AND APPROACHES

Critique of mainstream race and ethnicity theories

Mainstream social science research on race and ethnicity has been inadequate in delineating theories and concepts on race that are outside of the hegemonic paradigm that privileges white ideals, culture, thoughts, and interpretations. Historically, these scholars have generally been influential white men, such as Gunnar Myrdal, Robert Park, and Milton Gordon – scholars who provided mid-twentieth-century theories on race that privilege a white male lens. Their limited and white-privileged theoretical approaches continue to be influential, and while their major concepts and theories have sometimes been updated, they often provide the theoretical and methodological agenda for much social science research on race and ethnicity today. These approaches have provided such concepts as "assimilation," "tolerance," "stereotypes," "prejudice," and "racial bigotry," which, while often helpful analytical concepts, are severely limited in capturing the full extent of a racialized society and how racism is a systemic, foundational framework of a country like the United States (Feagin 2010b).

A substantial proportion of contemporary work on race and racism in mainstream social science has focused on the actions of prejudiced individuals (e.g., "bigots"), thus placing the theoretical focus of racism at the micro (individual) level, rather than connecting how micro-level racism is rooted firmly in the deeper and broader systemic (macro) structures of racism (Feagin & Feagin 2008; Feagin 2010a). It is problematic when social scientists engage in research that focuses solely on individual racism, because it leads to several inaccurate assumptions. For example, numerous mainstream social scientists suggest that serious or blatant racism is dead or declining, because the instruments used to measure individual racism are usually a set of "standard questions" that do not change much over time (Bonilla-Silva 1997; Alba 2009). When social science researchers focus solely on individual racism, without a structural-historical analysis of institutional racist realities, they assume that social institutions in themselves are not racist and that studying contemporary racism is just a matter of measuring the percentage of people holding certain "racist beliefs" (Bonilla-Silva 1997). These scholars may represent individual racism as just "irrational thinking" – a problematic assumption because people who are overtly racist in their thinking are then defined as "pathological," while those who are "rational" are assumed to be "racism-free" (Bonilla-Silva 1997). What gets ignored in this analysis is that the structural foundation of racism has the *very rational basis* of providing and reproducing socio-economic privileges, benefits, and power to whites at the expense of, and exploitation of, people of color.

Ignoring white racial oppression as the foundation of the United States is a central problem of past and current social science research on race and ethnicity. Let us take for example the contemporary theory of racial formation, developed by pioneering social science scholars Michael Omi and Howard Winant (1986, 1994). The central point of this significantly race-critical theory is that racial formation is a process whereby racial projects or ideologies, explanations, interpretations, and representations of race are created, changed, destroyed, and historically situated (Omi & Winant 1994). This theory is more critical of existing institutions than mainstream approaches and has been especially influential in theorizing race and ethnicity and identifying the role of governments in racializing society through the creation of racial categories and racialized institutions (Feagin 2006, 2010b). However, despite this theory's analytical benefits, a critical problem is that it tends to view contemporary US racial groups – white, black, Latina/o, and Asian – as capable of developing racial projects that together can greatly or equally affect the major racial formation(s) in US society. This aspect of the theory is problematic, because it does not thoroughly address the undergirding structural foundation of the USA – a foundation of white-imposed racial oppression that continually provides greatly disproportionate privileges and benefits, some obvious but many hidden, for whites at the expense of Americans of color. Thus, contemporary black Americans can and do develop a series of "racial projects" and/or perspectives, but that does not mean that their projects or perspectives will carry determinative and central weight in a society where they do not wield much power because of centuries of deep-lying oppression and exclusion from major socio-economic resources. Elite and rank-and-file whites mostly decide the extent of the dominant racial discourse in US society, and even the extent to which the demands and perspectives of racially marginalized groups will be recognized and acted upon. Critical race legal scholar, Derrick Bell, developed the concept of interest-convergence, that is, racial progress is made only to the "extent that the divergence of racial interests [for whites] can be avoided or minimized" (Bell [1980] 1995: 24). Hence, elite whites, in particular, must agree for major racial change to take place in society.

Critical theoretical approaches to race and ethnicity: critical race theory

Critical scholarship on race offers a theoretical space where scholars can critique and analyze mainstream assumptions of race and ethnicity that either do not question the normativity of white power structures or do not provide a critical enough analysis of that power structure which aids in the continued subordination of people of color. The US analytical movement called Critical Race Theory initially developed as critical legal scholars and activists, and some other scholars (mostly scholars of color), were dissatisfied with the discourse and research of conventional legal scholarship as well as much social science scholarship (Crenshaw, Gotanda, Peller & Thomas 1995; Delgado & Stefancic 2001) because it failed to "examine racism as an ideological pillar upholding American society" (Crenshaw 1995: 110). Thus, Critical Race Theory seeks to transform the "relationship among race, racism, and power" (Delgado & Stefancic 2001: 2), "to understand how a regime of white supremacy and its subordination of people of color have been created and maintained," to change the "bond between law and racial power" (Crenshaw, Gotanda, Peller & Thomas 1995: xiii), and to adhere to an activist social-justice agenda. Although Critical Race Theory began in the law tradition, scholars of other disciplines, particularly the social sciences, have adopted various tenets of a critical theoretical approach to race scholarship in their respective disciplines. There are several foundational tenets that proponents of critically theorizing race generally follow. In this chapter, we present, non-exhaustively, a few of these key principles developed by social science scholars and related activists: (1) undergirding institutional/systemic racism (and other forms of subordination), (2) challenging hegemonic ideology such as colorblindness and postraciality, (3) centering the experiential voices of people of color in critical race scholarship.

Undergirding institutional/systemic racism

While mainstream analysts of race and ethnicity often focus their analysis on prejudiced individuals and assert an "American creed" of liberty and justice for all as central to the United States, critical theoretical approaches to race start by recognizing institutional racism as an essential concept. Stokely Carmichael (Kwame Ture) and Charles V. Hamilton in their work *Black Power* define institutional racism as "active" and "pervasive" racist attitudes and practices that permeate "the society on both the individual and institutional level, covertly and overtly" (Ture & Hamilton 1967: 5). Expanding on the influential theorizing of Carmichael, Hamilton, and other critical social scientists, Feagin (2006, 2010b) articulates a theory of *systemic racism*. Systemic racism involves the deep foundation and surface structures of racial oppression. It encompasses (1) the array of whites' discriminatory practices targeting black Americans and other Americans of color, (2) unjustly gained political-economic and other resource inequalities along racial lines, and (3) the emotion-laden racial framing long ago created by whites to rationalize their unjustly gained resources, privileges, and power. Systemic racism is a material, social, and ideological reality and is manifested in all major institutions. Systemic racism is foundational for what became US society. It began in the seventeenth century in the early

European exploitation and genocidal treatment of Native Americans and the domination and labor exploitation of enslaved Africans.

To rationalize whites' oppressive treatment of blacks and Native Americans, and later other groups of color, whites developed a *white racial frame*, which has been documented in American society as early as the seventeenth century. This frame includes an array of critical features, including racist ideas, stereotypes, racialized narratives, images, emotions, and inclinations to discriminate (Feagin 2006, 2010b). Whites draw upon this racialized knowledge to interpret, rationalize and legitimize oppression against people of color (Feagin 2006), and to legitimize their privileged positions. The white racial frame presents whiteness as the pinnacle of superiority and morality, and people of color, particularly blacks, as negative and inferior, often regardless of their adoption of white cultural norms. To a lesser extent, people of color often understand the world through the white racial frame as well (Picca & Feagin 2007; Feagin 2010b). This frame is pervasive in major institutions, and thus it is difficult to live in this society without adopting aspects of the racial frame, consciously or unconsciously.

While centering race is an integral component, critical theorists recognize that race does not operate as an exclusive form of subordination and that people of color experience overlapping categories of subordination. The intersecting effects of gender, class, and sexual orientation with race are integral in critically theorizing the oppression of people of color (King 1988; Crenshaw 1991a, 1991b; Collins 2000, 2005; Wingfield 2009).

Challenging hegemonic ideology of colorblindness and postraciality

Critical Race Theory is concerned with refuting hegemonic ideologies, such as contemporary white ideologies of colorblindness and postraciality. Mainstream analyses of race in legal and other influential institutions typically view racism as existing only when one can identify specific discriminators with intent to discriminate. Thus, US courts tend to ignore status-race and historical-race, that is, the historical reality behind dominant racial categories such as white, black, Latino, and so forth. Instead, they focus on formal race, treating racial categories as disconnected from North America's history of racial oppression (Gotanda 1995).This narrow and inaccurate view of racism has led to an espousal of colorblindness in mainstream legal thinking. Critical Race Theory acts as a theoretical framework to counter such contemporary judicial ideology:

> Critical Race Theory can be productively used to expose the irreducibly political character of the current Court's general hostility toward policies which would take race into account in redressing historic and contemporary patterns of racial discrimination . . . Critical Race Theory's deconstruction of color-blindness . . . show[s] that the current Supreme Court's expressed hostility toward race-consciousness must be deemed a form of race-consciousness in and of itself . . . (Crenshaw, Gotanda, Peller & Thomas 1995: xxviii)

The acknowledgment of systemic racism in legal and other important institutions is an essential component of providing atonement for past and present racial injustice. Ignoring the deep structures of racism just facilitates the continuation of contemporary discrimination against people of color and, thus, white power and privilege continue unchecked. The election of President Barack Obama and the subsequent distorted US media coverage of colorblindness and near postraciality – whereby race is no longer a necessary category for acknowledgment or analysis – is an example of such contemporary race-conscious ideologies in action. A critical race approach to social science research on racial matters provides the theoretical groundwork to combat such unsupported suppositions.

Experiential voices of people of color

To a large extent, mainstream approaches to race and racism privilege a white interpretation, and thus lack a serious in-depth analysis of the experiences of people of color. Thoroughly discussing the experience of racism through the voices of people of color also threatens white power structures and is consequently avoided in most mainstream approaches. Thus, to document the lived experiences of racism, to adequately understand racial oppression, and to develop the best ways to counteract it, critical theorizing engages experiential voices of people of color (Yosso & Daniel 2005: 123). According to Delgado and Stefancic, underscoring the voices of people of color "holds that because of their different histories and experiences with oppression, black, Indian, Asian, and Latino/a writers and thinkers may be able to communicate to their white counterparts matters that the whites are unlikely to know" (2001: 9). This experiential knowledge is often expressed in critical theory through the usage of storytelling, narratives, oral histories, and other forms of qualitative research techniques (Delgado 1995; Delgado & Stefancic 2001; Solorzano & Yosso 2002; Chou & Feagin 2008).

CONTEMPORARY EXAMPLES OF RACISM AND DISCRIMINATION

We provided above a critique of mainstream social science approaches to race and ethnicity issues. We have identified Critical Race Theory, the important tenets of critical racial theorizing, and concepts such as systemic racism, racial framing, and centering experiential voices as a more cogent and probing approach to identifying the white power structures that hide behind the ideological language and pseudo-science practices of colorblindness and postraciality. In this next section we discuss the continued and widespread experiences of racial hostility and discrimination faced by people of color, as revealed through research studies on racism that employ powerful critical-race concepts.

Asian Americans: the "model minority" myth

There has been little critical research that substantially documents Asian American experiences of systemic racism. Mainstream media and some social scientists have assumed Asian Americans do not experience the same racist stereotyping and imagery as other racial groups (Prashad 2003). To the contrary, Asian Americans have experienced longstanding anti-Asian racial framing by whites, which has rarely been addressed in social science research, yet is paramount to the experiences of racial hostility and discrimination Asian Americans face. Claire Jean Kim (1999, 2003) and Chou and Feagin (2008) are among the few researchers who have examined how racism affects the lives of Asian Americans, including the harsh effects of the white racial framing of Asian Americans as "model minorities." These social scientists have identified whites as major actors in constructing a racialized system that places whites at the top of a white-constructed racial hierarchy, while subordinating and placing Asian Americans in the middle of this hierarchy and at the same time using them as a measuring stick for other groups of color (especially black Americans) who are placed at the bottom.

The model minority myth, created during the 1960s by white politicians and commentators (Feagin 2010a), inaccurately portrays Asian Americans as the successful minority that is racially and socially "problem free" (Yu 2006). Although some Asian American groups have achieved significant economic success, this myth is a gross overgeneralization of the Asian American experience. In fact, many Southeast Asian ethnic groups, such as Laotians, Hmong, Cambodians, and Vietnamese, have relatively high numbers of families living below the US poverty line (Chang 2000). The different experiences among Asian ethnic groups are ignored by the model minority myth in order to extend a political agenda (Yu 2006). The original goal of this political agenda was to quiet and discredit black protest against racism during the 1960s. Since then, by claiming Asian Americans have been successful through hard work and without government aid, the myth has allowed whites to blame blacks (and Latinos) for their problems and chastise them for protesting discrimination rather than "working hard" like Asian Americans. Not only has this myth operated to counter black protests, but it has delegitimized Asian American protests against discrimination, and reduced the possibility that governments will take action to meet their social and economic needs (Feagin & Feagin 2008).

The myth created yet other problems for some Asian Americans who bought into the racialized ideals, believing the myth to be a positive representation of Asians, thereby limiting the relationships they form with other groups of color fighting against systemic racism (Chou & Feagin 2008). Additionally, many Asian Americans have tried to live up to this model minority myth, which places great pressure on them to succeed, resulting in serious health problems for some. For example, Asian American teenagers have the highest rate of depression (Center for Medicaid Services 2002). One recent report on young adults at Cornell University found that Asian American students committed half of all suicides at the university, although they made up only 17 percent of the student population (Harder 2005). Additionally, elderly Chinese American women have a substantially higher suicide rate than elderly white women (Browne & Broderick 1994), and Asian American women between the ages of 15 and 24 have the highest suicide rate of all racial groups. The high suicide rates among Asian American women may be a consequence of women experiencing even greater pressure to imitate the model minority myth than men (Amusa 2006; Cohen 2007).

In addition, Asian American communities are seriously impacted by other forms of anti-Asian stereotyping and discrimination. Common anti-Asian stereotyping and discrimination includes the enforcement of a "foreigner" status (Wu 2002; Tuan 2003; Chou & Feagin 2008) whereby Asian Americans are regularly considered outsiders and/or immigrants regardless of how many generations their families have lived in the US. In Chou and Feagin's (2008) recent research interviewing 43 Asian Americans on their experiences with racism, one respondent described an experience of an Asian American co-worker being treated as an outsider:

> I got into this disagreement with one of my coworkers because we have this person, she's rather old. She's from Cambodia. She is an assembler, so all she does is she comes to work for eight hours, she assembles some stuff. She goes home. Because her English is poor, he wouldn't say she's "American." I say she has American citizenship, she pays American taxes, you know, she does everything to be qualified to be American citizen. His argument is she doesn't speak the language well. I tried to tell him . . . that's just unfair because she did everything the American government asked her to obtain American citizenship. Now somebody said she's not American. (Chou & Feagin 2008: 129)

In this quote the respondent illustrates the reality of many Asian Americans, that regardless of American citizenship, Asian Americans will never truly be considered "American" by many whites and other non-Asians.

Not surprisingly, as a way to avoid this hostility, non-acceptance, and other forms of anti-Asian discrimination, some Asian Americans hyper-conform and buy strongly into the white-constructed racial hierarchy and racial frame. Since those groups at the bottom of the US racial hierarchy face added vilification, some Asian Americans fight hard to maintain their middle status in the hierarchy and thus aggressively adopt white ideals, values, and even stereotypes from the white racial frame (Chou & Feagin 2008).

Contemporary forms of white racism: frontstage and backstage racism

Today US society has moved away from a legalized acceptance of overt racial discrimination and segregation, a process that has resulted in contemporary whites using more subtle, covert, and backstage ways to maintain and enact racist beliefs and behaviors. According to mainstream media and social science analysts who accentuate the colorblind and postracial framing of society (see Alba 2009), blatantly racist and discriminatory attitudes of whites rarely exist anymore. However, such inaccurate conclusions are often based on survey research which use brief superficial questions to measure racial attitudes, and/or other research studies which do not adequately take into account social desirability bias. Research shows that discussing sensitive subjects, such as racial matters, often leads to socially desirable responses whereby respondents provide answers that fall in line with the (socially or publicly correct) temperature of the time. Thus, in today's society researchers may find that whites are "less" racist, because they may be inclined to provide "colorblind" or "postracial" responses to superficial survey questions that are asked of them by strangers (for example, survey researchers on the phone). Additionally, whites' responses to interviewers' questions on racial matters have been shown to be affected by the racial characteristics of the interviewer. Some time ago, research by Hatchett and Schuman (1975) found that whites were more likely to provide black interviewers with responses that were racially liberal, i.e., more colorblind, whereas their responses to white interviewers were more racist and frank. Studies that remove the social correctness and interviewer effects lessen the likelihood of social desirability bias in responses to questions on racial matters (Sudman & Bradburn 1982; Kellner 2004). Critical research on racism reveals, contrary to mainstream survey research findings, that much of the old-fashioned racist framing among whites has not dissipated. These old-fashioned racist views still exist, but have often moved in their routine expression to "backstage" settings, since many whites now realize that expressing strong racist views in the public "frontstage" is no longer socially acceptable.

For example, critical research by Picca and Feagin (2007) sheds light on the type of racial performances that whites commonly engage in while in such frontstage and backstage settings. Their research analyzes racial events that 626 white college students at more than two dozen colleges and universities reported in recent journals they kept for a few weeks. Most actors in the events were whites; the data show most whites know when and where to engage in openly racist performances. More than 7,000 backstage-racism and frontstage-racism events were reported in these diaries. Backstage racism is when whites engage in racist performances in settings with other whites (e.g., friends and relatives) among whom they feel comfortable and have little fear of being reprimanded. When in the frontstage, around people of diverse racial-ethnic backgrounds or with people who will not tolerate such racism, a great many white individuals will engage in racial performances of "colorblindness," hiding or playing down their racist views. Significantly, the majority of racist commentaries and performances the students reported, for backstage and frontstage settings, were directed at African Americans, showing the continuing centricity of blacks in the white racial frame.

In backstage settings many whites feel safe in making racist comments or telling racist jokes, a common backstage interaction and essential component of sustaining modern racism. For example, one white college student in Picca and Feagin's research described the racial joking of white fraternity members in the backstage:

> As I sit in a room with a bunch of frat guys, Phil walks in chanting "rotchie, rotchie, rotchie!!" I asked quietly what that term means and I am answered with a giggle and a quick "its slang for nigger like niggerotchie." . . . The guys I hang around (white college males) spend their "bored time" making up new ways to criticize each other, and the easiest way to do that is to call each other racial slurs when everyone is clearly white . . . If there happened to be people of a different color in the room, they would never say anything like that . . . I see that making racial slurs is only really "racial" when it is said to the person of the race. Otherwise, it is more of a term people use to define someone, where sometimes it has negative connotations. I just don't understand why people choose race as a means to make fun of other people. (Picca & Feagin 2007: 97)

In this diary entry the student reveals how white students use code language to express racial slurs in an exclusively white setting. Instead of saying "nigger" the students replace it with a code word, so if outsiders intrude into this space, they will not understand it. The central protagonist here was open to explaining the code meaning for "rotchie" to the student diarist because he was in a backstage setting. An important point represented in this diary entry, and found often in Picca and Feagin's (2007) data, is that whites easily rationalize other whites' racist behavior. Their friends and acquaintances are not "really racist," for in their view that phrase is reserved for Ku Klux Klan members. Here their use of racial slurs is not seen as racial if they are not addressed to people of color.

White men's deep frame and its impact on their perception of black women

As stated previously, many mainstream social scientists assume that race and racism are no longer central components of the everyday lives of whites and that whites are dramatically less racist than in the past. Downplaying the significance of racism can also be seen in current research and analysis of interracial relationships, such as white–black dating and marriage. A major problem in some interracial relationship literature is that once researchers have debunked the relevancy of exchange or caste theories in explaining the likelihood of interracial relationships, they assume that race and racism are no longer relevant to understanding these relationships. As a result, these analysts conclude that decisions regarding interracial marriage and dating are mainly based on love and common ideals or goals (Yancey & Yancey 1998; Rosenfeld 2005). However, this supposition is inaccurate and limited in explaining the longstanding exclusion of black women as relationship partners for white men, as well as for other non-black men.

Census data show a distinctive and persistent trend over time: black women are not intermarrying at significant rates with white men or men of other racial groups. The incidence of black women–white men marriage is not as positively influenced by education and class status as for other forms of intermarriage with whites (Lee & Edmonston 2005; Qian & Litcher 2007). Studies of online dating trends show that black women (and blacks in general) are a severely excluded dating group when whites are making such choices. A recent study of internet dating preferences by Feliciano, Robnett, and Komaie (2008) found that of the white men who specified a racial preference, 93 percent had excluded black women – indeed the most excluded racial group for these men. Although white men are less likely to indicate a racial preference in dating advertisements, their openness to interracial relationships is largely exclusive to *non-black women* (Phua & Kaufman 2005; Feliciano, Robnett & Komaie 2008).

These studies show that black women are persistently excluded as dating and marriage partners for white men yet do not provide an adequate and in-depth conceptual analysis to explain this phenomenon. However, the use of a critical theory that underscores how racism continues to act as a central societal structure and, thus, to affect decisions white men make regarding black women allows us to better analyze what is taking place. Slatton's (2011) recent qualitative research (using self-administered open-ended online questionnaires) has looked carefully and intensively at the longstanding exclusion of black women by white men. In this work she engages critical theory and uses the concepts of social construction and *deep framing*. According to her research analysis, influential white men have for centuries had the power to socially construct black female bodies in raced, gendered, and classed terms. Historically, elite white men constructed black female bodies as sexually licentious, naturally immoral, diseased, animalistic, and masculine (Hammonds 1997; St. Jean & Feagin 1998; Jones & Shorter-Gooden 2003; Collins 2005). Black women were and today still are considered everything that a white woman is not in terms of beauty, sexual morality, femininity, and womanhood.

This white male construction of black female bodies is representative of many white men's (as well as white women's and other men's) *deep framing*, which is our common-sense worldview and "cognitive infrastructure of the mind" (Lakoff 2006: 12). The deep frame of many white men contains white-constructed, racialized, gendered, and classed pseudo-knowledge of black women and is the lens through which a great many come to perceive, interpret, understand, emote, and engage in actions where black women are concerned. Slatton's (2011) study found that well over three-quarters of her 134 white male respondents – despite most having very little contact or experience with black women – defined black women as unwanted women and ascribed a bevy of white-constructed attributes to them.

For example, one respondent stated the following: "Just the term 'black women' conjures up thoughts of an overweight, dark-skinned, loud, poorly educated person with gold teeth yelling at somebody in public. I hope that doesn't make me racist but honestly that's the first thing I think of." This respondent described himself as having had little experience with black women, including no black female friends and rare interactions with black families growing up, yet he has a deeply entrenched view of black women. This is an example of the deep racist frame in operation, whereby whites do not need experiences with black women to have such views. Learned from white parents and friends and/or the mass media, their deep frame of white-constructed racialized knowledge acts as a cognitive, emotional, and action/reaction guide on how to think about, understand, define, and interact with black women and with black people generally (Slatton 2011).

RESISTANCE

Previous sections document some of the critical-racism research, revealing the contemporary ways whites engage in racism and documenting the continuing experiences of racial hostility and discrimination in the lives of people of color. However, in the past and present people of color have not just passively accepted racism and white domination, but in various forms and degrees have engaged in resistance strategies against this white oppression. A critical approach to race acknowledges the ways in which various groups of color fight back against white power structures that subsist on racial subordination. Critical race theorists have a rich history of providing insightful narratives and counter-stories (Ross 1989; Delgado 1995; Torres & Milun 1995) to engage in resistance and theorize how people of color create their own meaning systems in a white-normative society. Critical race theorists analyze narratives and counter-stories of people of color to reveal those resistance realities that have been ignored or marginalized, and they use counter-methods as tools to dispute the narratives and stories of the dominant white group (Yosso & Daniel 2005). According to Delgado, thus, the "stories or narratives told by the [dominant group] remind it of its identity in relation to outgroups, and provide it with a form of shared reality in which its own superior position is seen as natural. The stories of the outgroups aim to subvert that reality" (1995: 60).

Feagin (2010b) extends the literature on resistance with the concept of counter-framing, an interpretive tool many people of color use to resist the white racial frame's negative ideas, stereotypes, and images of them. The counter-frame provides a way for groups of color to fight back against oppression and to resist the way the white racial framing defines them as inferior and whites as superior. Generally, black Americans have a substantially more defined and effective counter-frame than other racial and ethnic groups of color, because they have had some four centuries in North America to develop it (Feagin & Feagin 2008; Feagin 2010b).

Consider briefly some resistance strategies of African Americans and Asian Americans. African Americans have a long history of resistance and counter-framing that traces back to centuries of slavery in North America. An integral component of resistance for enslaved Africans involved religion. White slaveowners taught enslaved Africans about Christianity to encourage docile acquiescence to slavery, teaching obedience and long-suffering. Many enslaved Africans, however, used this Christianity in an alternative form that linked it to their traditional African religions, including using biblical ideas in preaching deliverance from slavery. The valiant yet unsuccessful 1831 slave revolt of Nat Turner, a Baptist preacher, and 70 other enslaved Africans (Greenberg 2003), is but one example in a long tradition, to the present day, of the centrality of religion and religious leaders in black resistance and counter-framing.

Enslaved black Americans also resisted by counter-framing the white racial frame's definition of blacks as inhuman, dependent, and unworthy of liberty and justice. For example, the 1829 pamphlet, *To the Coloured Citizens of the World*, by David Walker, a young black abolitionist, provides one of the earliest counter-frames to the white racial framing of blacks. Walker refuted statements of influential whites, such as Thomas Jefferson, who framed blacks as inherently incompetent and incapable of learning. Walker asserted racial oppression to be the barrier to black learning. He aggressively identified white slaveowners as stifling black talents and self-actuation, as one of their means to sustain black subordination. Walker also asserted in his appeal a strong counter-frame to the white construction of blacks as inhuman; he proclaimed, "Are we MEN!! – I ask you, O my brethren! [A]re we MEN?" (Walker 1829: 36). Resisting white racism and oppression by claiming their humanity and right to be treated as "men," and not animals, has long been a key component of black resistance framing.

In more contemporary times, black resistance to legal segregation was observed in civil rights and black power movements of the 1960s to 1970s. In these movements, black men, women, and children resisted and emphasized their rights to liberty, justice, and *black power*. They counter-framed white definitions of them as unattractive by asserting "Black is Beautiful" (Ture & Hamilton 1967) and "I'm Black and I'm Proud." A central component of black resistance has been the passing on of a resistance or counter-frame to black children, generation after generation. Most black Americans today have some degree of a resistance frame that they can use when faced with white oppression. Indeed, Robinson and Ward (1991) note that contemporary black (particularly black women's) resistance strategies must be more than a resistance for survival, but also a resistance for liberation.

Other research shows that resistance to white racism by many Asian Americans takes the form of aggressively assimilating to dominant white ideals and values, such as by changing names to white Americanized names, in the hope of avoiding white hostility and discrimination (Chou & Feagin 2008). For example, some Japanese Americans' use of resistance through conformity may be rooted in the experiences of second-generation Japanese Americans forced by whites into US concentration camps during World War II. After their release from these camps, many second-generation Japanese Americans placed great pressure on themselves and their children to assimilate to white culture, ideals, and values (Tanaka 1999), including a strong adoption of elements of the white racial frame and racial hierarchy. These Japanese Americans adopted white values and orientations in the hope of preventing and avoiding present and future white racial discrimination.

Because Asian American groups have had fewer centuries of historical experience in dealing with white racism than African Americans, relatively few among them have as yet constructed as strong a counter-frame to the white racial frame as have African Americans. Nonetheless, some in Asian American groups have developed a strong counter-frame and engaged in more overt resistance against white racial framing. This includes the "yellow power" movements that took place alongside 1960s–1970s black power movements, as well as the relatively recent pan-Asian and other anti-discrimination organizations (Daniels 1988; Zhou & Gatewood 2000; Chou & Feagin 2008). Despite generally lacking a well-developed anti-racist counter-frame, most people in Asian American groups do have strong home-culture frames – frames predicated on important Asian American cultural and community beliefs and values – which allows them to engage in at least modest acts of resistance to anti-Asian racism. Through use of their home-culture frame, Asian American groups are able to maintain and assert their distinctive cultural perspectives that can offer strategies of resistance (Feagin 2010b).

CONCLUSION

Critical-racism research shows the continuing importance of understanding and analyzing racial matters in society. Mainstream race-ethnic theorists and many politicians and media commentators – especially those who are white – strategically push colorblindness and postraciality as the "new" signs of the times, thereby providing a convenient way to deny systemic racism and ignore the emotional, psychological, and economic effects of centuries-long oppression experienced by people of color. Colorblindness and postraciality allow whites to marginalize the experiences and claims of injustice of people of color. This reality has even played out on the largest political stage in the 2008 US presidential election. However, the adoption of critical theoretical concepts in approaching racial matters allows us to challenge this colorblind ideology with strong evidence.

The critical approach to racial matters is not just concerned with presenting data on systemic racism, but often takes an activist stand. "It not only tries to understand our social situation, but to change it; it sets out to ascertain how society organizes itself along racial lines and hierarchies, but to transform it for the better" (Delgado & Stefancic 2001: 3). The ability to bring about positive racial changes is greatly impeded by whites' racial framing of society, which rationalizes white dominance and privilege and the subordination of people of color as normative. Thus, a key component in evoking societal change is through the process of deframing and reframing a racialized society. This process is a difficult one, especially for whites, as the major components of the old racist frame are deeply embedded in societal institutions. In the white case, this deframing process means that a majority of whites must examine the deep-seated white-constructed thoughts, values, and emotions of the old white racial frame, and then reframe by accepting a framing that includes critical knowledge regarding systemic racism. For real change, reframing must include the adoption of anti-discrimination programs so that whites not only think differently about race, but also actively oppose white racism in all frontstage and backstage settings and thus engage in anti-racist activism (Feagin 2010b).

References

Alba, R. (2009) *Blurring the Color Line: The New Chance for a More Integrated America.* Cambridge, MA: Harvard University Press.

Amusa, M. (2006) "Asian Women Face 'Model Minority' Pressures." *Wenews*, September 18. http://www.womensenews.org/story/mental-health/060918/asian-women-face-model-minority-pressures (accessed December 16, 2009).

Bell, D. ([1980] 1995) "Brown v. Board of Education and the Interest Convergence Dilemma." In K. Crenshaw, N. Gotanda, G. Peller, and K. Thomas (eds.), *Critical Race Theory*. New York: New Press, pp. 20–9.

Bonilla-Silva, E. (1997) "Rethinking Racism: Toward a Structural Interpretation." *American Sociological Review* 62: 465–80.

Browne, C. and A. Broderick (1994) "Asian and Pacific Island Elders: Issues for Social Work Practice and Education." *Social Work* 39: 252–9.

Center for Medicaid Services (2002) *Medicaid Managed Care Enrollment Report: Depression for Adolescent Youth.* New York: Medicaid Statistics.

Chang, R. S. (2000) "Toward an Asian American Legal Scholarship: Critical Race Theory, Post-Structuralism, and Narrative Space." In R. Delgado and J. Stefancic (eds.), *Critical Race Theory: The Cutting Edge*, 2nd edn. Philadelphia, PA: Temple University Press, pp. 345–68.

Chou, R. S. and J. R. Feagin (2008) *The Myth of the Model Minority: Asian Americans Facing Racism.* Boulder, CO: Paradigm.

Cohen, E. (2007) "Push to Achieve Tied to Suicide in Asian American Women." *CNN*, May 16. http://www.cnn.com/2007/HEALTH/05/16/asian.suicides/index.html?eref=rss_top-stories (accessed December 16, 2009).

Collins, P. (2000) *Black Feminist Thought: Knowledge, Consciousness, and the Politics of Empowerment.* New York: Routledge.

Collins, P. (2005) *Black Sexual Politics: African Americans, Gender, and the New Racism.* New York: Routledge.

Crenshaw, K. (1991a) "Demarginalizing the Intersection of Race and Sex: A Black Feminist Critique of Antidiscrimination Doctrine, Feminist Theory, and Anti-Racist Politics." In K. T. Bartlett and R. Kennedy (eds.), *Feminist Legal Theory: Readings in Law and Gender*. Boulder, CO: Westview Press, pp. 57–80.

Crenshaw, K. (1991b) "Mapping the Margins: Intersectionality, Identity Politics, and Violence against Women of Color." *Stanford Law Review* 43: 1241–99.

Crenshaw, K. (1995) "Race, Reform, and Retrenchment: Transformation and Legitimation in Antidiscrimination Law." In K. Crenshaw, N. Gotanda, G. Peller, and K. Thomas (eds.), *Critical Race Theory: The Key Writings that Formed the Movement*. New York: New Press, pp. 103–22.

Crenshaw, K., N. Gotanda, G. Peller, and K. Thomas (eds.) (1995) *Critical Race Theory: The Key Writings that Formed the Movement*. New York: New Press.

Daniels, R. (1988) *Asian America: Chinese and Japanese in the United States since 1850*. Seattle: University of Washington Press.

Delgado, R. (1995) "Storytelling for Oppositionists and Others: A Plea for Narrative." In R. Delgado and J. Stefancic (eds.), *Critical Race Theory: The Cutting Edge*, 2nd edn. Philadelphia, PA: Temple University Press, pp. 60–70.

Delgado, R. and J. Stefancic (2001) *Critical Race Theory: An Introduction*. New York: New York University Press.

Feagin, J. R. (2006) *Systemic Racism: A Theory of Oppression*. New York: Routledge.

Feagin, J. R. (2010a) *Racist America: Roots, Current Realities, and Future Reparations*, 2nd edn. New York: Routledge.

Feagin, J. R. (2010b) *The White Racial Frame: Centuries of Racial Framing and Counter-Framing*. New York: Routledge.

Feagin, J. R. and C. B. Feagin (2008) *Racial and Ethnic Relations*, 8th edn. Upper Saddle River, NJ: Prentice Hall.

Feliciano, C., B. Robnett, and G. Komaie (2008) "Gendered Racial Exclusion among White Internet Daters." *Social Science Research* 38: 39–54.

Gotanda, N. (1995) "A Critique of 'Our Constitution is Color-Blind'." In K. Crenshaw, N. Gotanda, G. Peller, and K. Thomas (eds.), *Critical Race Theory: The Key Writings that Formed the Movement*. New York: New Press, pp. 257–75.

Greenberg, K. S. (ed.) (2003) *Nat Turner: A Slave Rebellion in History and Memory*. New York: Oxford University Press.

Hammonds, E. M. (1997) "Toward a Genealogy of Black Female Sexuality: The Problematic of Silence." In M. Jacqui Alexander and C. Mohanty (eds.), *Feminist Genealogies, Colonial Legacies, Democratic Futures*. New York: Routledge, pp. 170–82.

Harder, L. (2005) "Asian Americans Commit Half of All Suicides at Cornell." *Cornell Daily Sun*, March 29, p. 1.

Hatchett, S. and H. Schuman (1975) "White Respondents and Race-of-Interviewer Effects." *Public Opinion Quarterly* 39: 523–8.

Huffington Post (2009) "Rep. Joe Wilson Yells Out 'You Lie' During Obama Health Care Speech." *Huffington Post*, November 9. www.huffingtonpost.com/2009/09/09/gop-rep-wilson-yells-out_n_281480.html?page=2 (retrieved December 9, 2009).

Jones, C. and K. Shorter-Gooden (2003) *Shifting: The Double Lives of Black Women in America*. New York: HarperCollins.

Kellner, P. (2004) "Can Online Polls Produce Accurate Findings?" *International Journal of Market Research* 46: 3–22.

Kim, C. J. (1999) "The Racial Triangulation of Asian Americans." *Politics and Society* 27: 105–38.

Kim, C. J. (2003) *Bitter Fruit: The Politics of Black-Korean Conflict in New York City*. New Haven, CT: Yale University Press.

King, D. (1988) "Multiple Jeopardy, Multiple Consciousness: The Context of Black Feminist Ideology." *Signs* 14: 42–72.

Lakoff, G. (2006) *Whose Freedom? The Battle over America's Most Important Idea*. New York: Farrar, Straus and Giroux.

Lee, S. M. and B. Edmonston (2005) "New Marriages, New Families: U.S. Racial and Hispanic Intermarriage." *Population Reference Bureau* 60: 1–40.

Omi, M. and H. Winant (1986) *Racial Formation in the United States*. New York: Routledge.

Omi, M. and H. Winant (1994) *Racial Formation in the United States*, 2nd edn. New York: Routledge.

Phua, V. C. and G. Kaufman (2005) "The Crossroads of Race and Sexuality: Date Selection among Men in Internet 'Personal' Ads." *Journal of Family Issues* 24: 981–94.

Picca, L. J. and J. R. Feagin (2007) *Two-Faced Racism: Whites in the Backstage and Frontstage*. New York: Routledge.

Prashad, V. (2003) *The Karma of Brown Folk*. Twin Cities, MN: University of Minnesota Press.

Qian, Z. and D. T. Litcher (2007) "Social Boundaries and Marital Assimilation: Interpreting Trends in Racial and Ethnic Intermarriage." *American Sociological Review* 72: 68–94.

Robinson, T. and J. V. Ward (1991) "A Belief in Self Far Greater than Anyone's Belief: Cultivating Resistance among African American Female Adolescents." In C. Gilligan, A. Rogers, and D. Tolman (eds.), *Women, Girls, and Psychotherapy: Reframing Resistance*. New York: Haworth, pp. 87–103.

Rosenfeld, M. J. (2005) "A Critique of Exchange Theory in Mate Selection." *American Journal of Sociology* 110: 1284–325.

Ross, T. (1989) "The Richmond Narratives." *Texas Law Review* 68: 381–414.

Slatton, B. C. (2011) *Mythologizing Black Women: Unveiling White Men's Racist and Sexist Deep Frame*. Boulder, CO: Paradigm.

Solorzano, D. G. and T. J. Yosso (2002) "Critical Race Methodology: Counter-Storytelling as an Analytical Framework for Education Research." *Qualitative Inquiry* 8: 23–44.

St. Jean, Y. and J. R. Feagin (1998) *Double Burden: Black Women and Everyday Racism*. Armonk, NY: M. E. Sharpe.

Sudman, S. and N. M. Bradburn (1982) *Asking Questions: A Practical Guide to Questionnaire Design*. San Francisco: Jossey-Bass.

Tanaka, J. (1999) *When You're Smiling: The Deadly Legacy of Internment*. Los Angeles: Visual Communications.

Torres, G. and K. Milun (1995) "Translating Yunnondio by Precedent and Evidence: The Marshpee Indian Case." In R. Delgado and J. Stefancic (eds.), *Critical Race Theory: The Cutting Edge*, 2nd edn. Philadelphia, PA: Temple University Press, pp. 52–9.

Tuan, M. (2003) *Forever Foreigners or Honorary Whites? The Asian Ethnic Experience Today*. New Brunswick, NJ: Rutgers University Press.

Ture, K. and C. V. Hamilton (1967) *Black Power: The Politics of Liberation*. New York: Vintage Books.

Walker, D. (1829) *To the Coloured Citizens of the World: But in Particular, and Very Expressly, to those of the United States of America*. Baltimore, MD: Black Classic Press.

Wingfield, A. H. (2009) *Doing Business with Beauty: Black Women, Hair Salons, and the Racial Enclave Economy*. Lanham, MD: Rowman and Littlefield.

Wu, F. H. (2002) *Yellow: Race in America beyond Black and White*. New York: Basic Books.

Yancey, G. and S. Yancey (1998) "Interracial Dating: Evidence from Personal Advertisements." *Journal of Family Studies* 19: 334–48.

Yosso, T. J. and G. S. Daniel (2005) "Conceptualizing a Critical Race Theory in Sociology." In M. Romero and E. Margolis (eds.), *The Blackwell Companion to Social Inequalities*. Malden, MA: Blackwell, pp. 117–46.

Yu, T. (2006) "Challenging the Politics of the 'Model Minority' Stereotype: A Case for Educational Equality." *Equity and Excellence in Education* 39: 325–33.

Zhou, M. and J. V. Gatewood (2000) "Introduction: Revisiting Contemporary Asian America." In M. Zhou and J. V. Gatewood (eds.), *Contemporary Asian America: A Multidisciplinary Reader*. New York: New York University Press, pp. 27–35.

17

Genders and Sexualities in Global Context

An Intersectional Assessment of Contemporary Scholarship

Nancy A. Naples and Barbara Gurr

INTRODUCTION

On August 19, 2009, South African runner Caster Semenya won the women's 800m final race of the International Association of Athletics Federation (IAAF) World Championships. Several other runners immediately questioned her gender. Was she really a woman? The Federation called for gender testing and the leaked results concluded that she had both male and female sex organs. The public debate that resulted from this case indicates the cultural commitment to a binary gender construction as it shapes participation in sports and other institutions. In an interview with the Associated Press, IAAF Medical Commission chair Anne Ljungqvist explained that, "There are many, many other reasons why a woman looks male. Probably the most common has nothing to do with intersex: production of steroids from the adrenal gland. Most of the women you see who look like men are not intersexed. Some men have a very womanlike body shape" (Lehourites 2009).

Social constructions of what defines one as a man or a woman are linked to culturally diverse and changing constructions of masculinity and femininity. Consequently, sociological perspectives on gender have changed dramatically since the term "gender" was first used in the 1950s. Credit for the introduction of the term "gender" is given to psychologist John Money (1952) whose research on gender identity and sex reassignment was widely read, especially following the revelation that one of his patients, David Reimer, a biological male who was raised as a female following a botched circumcision, reclaimed a male identity at age 14 and committed suicide at age 38 (Colapinto 2001). This case is often used to illustrate the strong and determinant relationship between biological sex and gender. However, as this chapter illustrates, sociologists of gender offer a wide diversity of explanations to account for differences in gender and sexual identity which call into question strict biological explanations.

Sociologists have also focused attention on how gender and sexuality shape structures of inequality and power (see, for example, Land 1980; Bergmann 1986; Boris 1995; McCall 2001). This research highlights, among other structural dynamics, wage gaps between men and women and other forms of discrimination in the labor force (Weir & McIntosh 1982; Leidner 1991; Williams 1992; England 2005; Wharton 2006; Britton 2003; Winter 2010); gender and heteronormative assumptions embedded in science, law, and policy (see, for example, Joffe 1986; Skocpol 1995; Pierce 1996; O'Connor, Orloff & Shaver 1999; Sainsbury 2000; Mayberry, Subramaniam & Weasel 2001; Mezey 2007; Smith 2007; Barclay, Bernstein & Marshall 2009); and sexual violence (see, for example, Enloe 1983; Martin 2003; Sokoloff 2005; Villalón 2010). As a powerful illustration of the last point, according to Amnesty International (2007), in every armed conflict they investigated that occurred during 1999 and 2000, "the torture of women was reported, most often in the form of sexual violence." They explain that, "Rape, when used as a weapon of war, is systematically employed for a variety of purposes, including intimidation, humiliation, political terror, extracting information, rewarding soldiers, and 'ethnic cleansing'." Theories of gender and sexuality are central to understanding these practices as well as the intimate violence that shapes everyday lives of women and sexual minorities.

Sociologists of gender and sexuality have also addressed the dynamics of oppression and resistance. This research focuses on the diverse strategies that people use to negotiate and contest hegemonic and culturally reductive gender norms and heteronormativity (see, for example, Devor 1989; Lorber 1994; Altman 2002; Lorber 2005; Mamo 2007; Lal, McGuire, Steward, Zaborowska & Pax 2010; Thayer 2010a). This scholarship also explores the role of globalization and transnational women's, lesbian, gay, bisexual, and transgender (LGBT), and social justice movements that challenge gender oppression, sexual violence, and other human rights violations (see, for example, Adam, Duyvendak & Krouwel 1999; Naples & Desai 2002; Tripp & Ferree 2006; Lind 2010; Thayer 2010b; Zheng and Zhang 2010).

Organization of the chapter

Contemporary approaches to gender and sexuality are heavily influenced by postmodern perspectives that emphasize the fluidity of gender and sexual identity and argue against any grand or overarching explanation for gender differences and structural inequalities (see, for example, Foucault 1978; Butler 1990; Risman 2004; Greenberg 2006). The diversity of approaches to gender and sexuality is especially evident when the study of gender and sexuality is placed in a global context (see, for example, Grewal & Kaplan 1994; Herdt 1997; Lamphere, Ragone & Zavella 1997; Oyèwúmi 1997; Summerhawk, McMahill & McDonald 1998; Adam,

Duyvendak & Krouwel 1999; Kondo 1999; Chao 2000; Grewal & Kaplan 2001; Altman 2002; Chant & Craske 2002; Gopinath 2003; Binnie 2004; Whitaker 2006; Njambi & O'Brien 2007; Parker 2010). In this chapter, we consider these related trends in current sociological analyses of gender. The chapter is divided into four parts: we begin with a brief summary of the emergence of gender, first as a category of analysis then as a field of inquiry that is found within almost all subfields of sociology. We then filter the debates about the relationship between sex and gender through the lens of the gendered body and transgender scholarship and conclude with a discussion of gender as a social structure. In the second section, we highlight different approaches to understanding how gender and sexuality intersect with race, culture, ability, and power. The third section places the analysis of gender and sexualities in cross-cultural perspective. In the last section, we examine the production and reproduction of inequalities in the context of contemporary neoliberal globalization and conclude by discussing research on resistance strategies developed to contest gender oppression, heteronormativity, and sexual violence.

SOCIOLOGY OF GENDER AND SEXUALITY IN HISTORICAL PERSPECTIVE

Following Talcott Parsons' distinction between expressive and instrumental functions and his analysis of social roles, early sociological attention to gender included distinguishing between the personal characteristics and the social roles of women and men (Parsons & Bales 1953; see also Mead 1950). These approaches tended to treat gender as a fixed category. In this view, men and women performed different functions in society and their willingness to adopt different roles in the family and in other social institutions contributed to societal equilibrium. Boys and girls learned their social roles first in the family by watching how their mothers and fathers divided emotional and instrumental functions in the home (see, for example, Chafetz 1974). A child's understanding of gender roles expanded as he or she entered school and interacted with other institutions. Learning one's gender role included understanding dominant norms related to these roles. Beliefs about appropriate gender behavior were incorporated into law, medicine, religion, media, and education as well as early childhood socialization (see, for example, Ruether 1983; Fausto-Sterling 1985; Chapkis 1986; MacKinnon 1989).

Arlie Hochschild (1973) explains that by the mid-1970s, gender role research (which was alternately called sex roles research in the literature) relied on four primary perspectives: sex differences, sex roles, women as a minority group, and sex stratification (see, for example, McIntosh 1968). Socialist feminists focused on the relationship between capitalism and patriarchy as well as debated how white supremacy functioned to shape the lives of women of color (see, for example, Eisenstein 1979; Barrett 1980; Sokoloff 1980; Bose 1985). In the 1980s, scholarship focused on the social construction of normative masculinity and femininity and the gender division of labor and gendered assumptions in various social institutions such as the family (Risman & Schwartz 1988; Hochschild & Machung 1989; Risman 1998; Coltrane & Adams 2008), the workforce (Epstein 1981; Lorber

1984; Bergmann 1986; Ferree 1987; Eisenstein 1988), and other institutions (Fausto-Sterling 1985); the intersections of gender, race, and class (Davis 1983; Lorde 1984; Crenshaw 1989; Collins 1994); and how social actors resist or challenge dominant gender norms and institutional inequalities (Enloe 1983; Ferree & Hess 1985; Bookman & Morgen 1988).

Until the 1970s, sociologists who were interested in sexuality often took their lead from medical and legal constructions that defined sexual minorities as either psychologically unhealthy or criminally deviant (Chauncey 1989). In fact, the topics of homosexuality, sex work or prostitution, and androgynous gender presentation were more often found within the sociology of deviance than in any other subfield of sociology (see, for example, Sagarin 1972). However, John Gagnon and William Simon (1973), writing from the new field of sexuality studies, built on the interactionist tradition in sociology in their early work on sexuality and argued that "nothing is intrinsically sexual and that anything can be sexualized in a given social context" (Parker 2010: 59). Richard Parker points out that Gagnon and Simon's work opened the way for the examination of the politics of sexuality (see also Irvine 2005). However, by this time, feminists were already emphasizing the politics of gender as it shaped everyday life and social institutions (see, for example, Davis 1983; D. Smith 1987; Weiler 1987; Aptheker 1989). Traditional views generally understood gender and sexuality as co-determinative with heterosexuality, defined as the normative and healthy sexual identity for biologically distinct men and women. Feminist sociologists contested the biologically determinist and essentialist views of gender, while queer scholars argued against the privileging and presumption of heterosexuality in socialization, discourse, and social policy. Following Foucault's analysis of sexuality, queer theorists also "insisted on the impossibility of 'explaining' sexuality as a function of some other, ostensibly more fundamental, phenomenon" (Turner 2000: 46).

Sociologists of gender often distinguished between gender and biological sex. Gender was defined as a consequence of social and cultural constructions of differences between male-sexed and female-sexed bodies. This feminist approach included the premise that culture and society exert a greater influence than biology on gender identity, gendered behaviors, and gender stratification (Walters 1995; Balsamo 1996). In their materialist analyses, Nancy Chodorow (1978) and Sara Ruddick (1989) complicate the interactions between biology and society, arguing that the structural arrangement between twentieth-century US notions of motherhood and women's biological mothering interacts to produce and reproduce gendered effects. Ruddick's (1989) notion of the "ethics of care" that derive from women's social role contributes to findings that women are more oriented to peace and caring for the planet than men (see also Gilligan 1982; Belenky, Clinchy, Golberger & Tarule 1997). While Chodorow's and Ruddick's arguments are based on the social division of labor between men and women, critics argue that they neglect the diversity of family forms, household arrangements for care, and race, class, and cultural differences (see, for example, Lorber 1981; Collins 1994). In response to Chodorow's analysis, Adrienne Rich (1980) raises the question of "lesbian existence." If the bond between mothers and daughters is so strong, then what, Rich wonders, other than strong cultural pressure or "compulsory heterosexuality," could explain women's rejection of these emotional ties to form intimate relationships with men, who, Chodorow argues, hold negative views of women.

DESTABILIZING CATEGORIES

The distinction between gender and sex has been blurred by contemporary scholarship influenced by postmodern and queer analyses that argue that "sex" is also socially constructed (Nicholson 1994; Seidman 1996; Jagose 1997; Rupp & Taylor 2003). Linda Nicholson argues that "it is not enough to claim that the body always comes to us through social interpretation, that is, that sex is subsumable under gender," therefore, "we cannot look to the body to ground cross-cultural claims about the male/female distinction" (1994: 83). Gatens (1983) writes that the relationship between sex and gender is characterized by "contingency" and that "the sex/gender relationship is neither necessary nor arbitrary" (Bloodsworth-Lugo 2007: 4). Therefore, Bloodsworth-Lugo explains, "femininity does not have to attach to the female body at all (nor masculinity to the male body)" (2007: 4; see also Halberstam 1998).

Transgender scholarship offers another arena in which to explore the complex relationship between gender, sex, and sexuality (see, for example, Bolin 1994; Devor 1997; Fausto-Sterling 2000; Shapiro 2010). Transgender identity, in which an individual's physically sexed body is not congruent with their felt sense of gender identity, is defined by the American Psychiatric Association as a Gender Identity Disorder. Joan Roughgarden points out the limitations of medicalized perspectives which often conflate gender and sexuality, arguing that academic disciplines have defined cultural understandings of gender and sexuality, but "[t]he fundamental problem is that our academic disciplines are all rooted in Western culture, which discriminates against diversity" (2004: 3) and reproduces static notions of a gender/sex binary. Brill and Pepper point out, however, that gender identity and sexuality may be related, but are not necessarily predictive of each other, asserting that "gender variance is not a marker of sexual orientation" (2008: 33). A number of scholars argue that theorizing about gender from the social sciences neglects transgender experiences or even distances transgender experiences from more general theorizing about gender (see, for example, Halberstam 1998; Namaste 2000). Scholars such as David Valentine (2007) and transgender activist and performance artist Kate Bornstein (1995) offer increasingly complex perspectives on the interplay of genders, sexualities, the body, and society.

Sociological analyses emphasize how socialization processes draw on culturally dominant notions of gender and sexuality to reinforce masculinity, femininity, and heterosexuality (see, for example, Connell 1985, 1987; Kimmel 1990, 1996; Thorne 1997; Messner 2002; Lorber & Moore 2006; Kimmel 2007; Pascoe 2007). For example, drawing on data from a cross-cultural study of paths towards manhood, David Gilmore demonstrates how culturally produced "manhood scripts" contribute to "constructing an appropriate manhood" in different cultural contexts (1990: 11, 224; see also Plummer 1975, 1995; Parker 2010). Michael Kimmel (1990) analyzes the rules associated with appropriate masculinity in the US and demonstrates how they are incorporated into specific sexual scripts that are reinforced through sexual socialization. These scripts stress accumulating multiple sexual partners, rejection of caretaking behaviors, and sexuality without emotional bonding or sensuality. Kimmel explains that "masculine sexuality is not about mutual pleasuring but the confirmation of masculinity which is based on physical capacities. And these, in turn, require emotional detachment, a phallocentric world view of sexual pleasure, and self-objectification" (Kimmel 1990: 105). These forms of gender behavior lead to an exaggeration of masculinity, or hypermasculinity, which has negative social consequences including aggressive behaviors and violence against women (Connell 1987). A major component of these sexual scripts is hatred towards men who display any characteristics or behaviors associated with a culturally defined femininity (Pascoe 2007).

As C. J. Pascoe aptly demonstrates in *Dude, You're a Fag*, gender and sexuality are constructed through the interactive performances of active agents (West & Zimmerman 1987; West & Fenstermaker 1995; Butler 1997; Fenstermaker & West 2002). In her 1992 book, *Gender, Interaction, and Inequality*, a study in the status characteristic tradition, Cecilia Ridgeway analyzes the role of emotions and nonverbal behavior in perpetuating gender inequality. Ridgeway explains the persistence of gender inequality and the implications of gender for organizational leadership. Her research explores how gender inequalities are created, and sustained, and what strategies are effective in contesting the interactional processes that promote gender inequality (see also Ridgeway & Correll 2004).

In their influential article, "Doing Gender," Candace West and Don Zimmerman (1987) offer an interactionist approach to gender which is informed by ethnomethodology (Kessler & McKenna 1978; see also West & Fenstermaker 1995). This perspective shares some core theoretical premises with Goffman's (1976) theory of dramaturgy and his analysis of gender as a behavioral display. However, West and Zimmerman (1987) contend that gender, rather than merely a displayed behavior, is interactionally achieved and that this achievement shapes and is shaped by all social interactions. They understand gender as an interactional achievement through which individuals dynamically, though not always consciously, respond in collaboration with other individuals and social forces to present or perform particular aspects of gender.

Another influential social constructionist framework is offered by Judith Butler (1990) who draws on Michel Foucault's postmodern perspective to argue that gender is a social construction that is inscribed in the body. Butler argues that:

> According to the understanding of identification as an enacted fantasy or incorporation, however, it is clear that coherence is desired, wished for, idealized, and that this idealization is an effect of a corporeal signification. In other words, acts, gestures, and desire produce the effect of an internal core or substance, but produce this *on the surface* of the body, through the play of signifying absences that suggest, but never reveal, the organizing principle of identity as a cause. Such acts, gestures, enactments, generally construed, are *performative* in the sense that the essence or identity that they otherwise purport to express are *fabrications* manufactured and sustained through corporeal signs and other discursive means. (1990: 136)

The notion of "gendered bodies" provides a major analytic frame that derives from feminist efforts to analyze the social construction of gender and sexuality

(Balsamo 1996; Lorber & Moore 2006). This approach foregrounds how social norms shape bodies and how bodies that do not map onto normative constructions are stigmatized. These processes are filtered through cultural constructions of race, gender, sexuality, age, and ability. Approaches to gendered bodies examine, among other structural and institutional processes, the power of media representation and corporate strategies that construct desire through the purchase of fitness, food, and skin products, among others (B. Thompson 1996; Washington & Shaver 1997; Mamo & Fishman 2001; Fishman 2004; Loe 2006; Collins 2008). Gender becomes naturalized by filtering the construction of femininity and masculinity through the body. As Lorber and Moore point out,

> In Western societies, most people are persuaded to accept gender inequalities by a belief that they emerge from the body. This belief claims that it is our "natural differences" that explain why men and women have different roles and positions in work organizations, politics, education systems, and the other main areas of society, and why men predominate in positions of power and authority. These "natural" explanations are reinforced by culture, the mass media, religions, and knowledge systems and erase the ways in which social processes produce gendered bodies and behavior. (2006: 3)

Through the lens of the gendered body, feminist scholars demonstrate how, among other things, "conception, procreation, pregnancy, and childbirth, assumed to be natural, are socially constructed as gendered" (Lorber & Moore 2006: 8; see also Rothman 1991; Conboy, Medina & Stanbury 1997; Mamo 2007).

The social construction of gender and sexuality is accomplished through socialization and is infused in language and culture as well as in the social structures that contour everyday life, institutional practices, and knowledge production (see, for example, D. Smith 1987; Lorber 1994; Risman 2004). For example, in "The Egg and the Sperm: How Science Has Created a Romance Based on Stereotypical Male-Female Roles," Emily Martin (1991) demonstrates how cultural meanings are inscribed in scientific practices which serve to reinforce heteronormative constructions. Feminist science studies scholars also examine the discursive links between social constructions of gender and science (see, for example, Fox, Johnson & Rosser 2006; Loe 2006; Mamo 2007). In her article, "The Gender/Science System: Or, Is Sex to Gender as Nature Is to Science?", Keller illustrates the gender politics of scientific knowledge, including the complicated ways that gender meanings are infused into scientific findings, gender division of labor in the production of science, and gendered norms that are internalized by scientists (1987: 38). Sandra Harding (1991) illuminates this last point in her discussion of the limits of knowledge that is generated from social locations distant from women's lives and, as Dorothy Smith (2005) extends it, most men's lives. Harding and Smith argue for knowledge that is grounded in the everyday lives of people, rather than in abstract theories or in the limited perspectives of a small number of privileged knowers (see also Haraway 1988). According to Harding, "the problem is that knowledge that has been generated only from the lives of a small portion of the society (and, at that, the most powerful one) is not useful for most people's projects" (1991: 22–3). Instead, Harding argues for an approach grounded in women's lives which she terms feminist standpoint epistemology.

Feminist standpoint analysis has been taken up by sociologists of gender to further examine how knowledge about the social world and experiences differ based on social location of the knower and social actor. Feminist standpoint epistemology developed in dialogue with Marx's historical materialism and its stated goal is to explicate how relations of domination are gendered in particular ways (Hartsock 1998). Another influence on the development of this approach can be found in Third World and post-colonial feminist challenges to so-called dual systems analyses of patriarchy and capitalism (Eisenstein 1979; Rowbotham 1981; Young 1981). Third World and post-colonial feminist critics have pointed out the lack of attention paid by socialist feminist analyses to racism, white supremacy, and colonialism. Contemporary feminist standpoint theories call for an intersectional analysis of gender, race, ethnicity, class, and other social structural aspects of social life which do not privilege one dimension (Dill & Zambrana 2009).

INTERSECTIONAL ANALYSES OF GENDER AND SEXUALITIES

The term "intersectionality" is credited to legal theorist Kimberlé Crenshaw (1989, 1991), although theories of intersectionality were being developed and deployed at least as far back as the US Abolition movement (see hooks 1981; Brah & Phoenix 2004). Intersectional theories seek to highlight the ways in which gender is experienced, achieved, or performed simultaneously with other social identities and structures (Irvine 2005; Dill & Zambrana 2009; Kitch 2009). During the women's liberation movements of the 1970s, intersectionality was explicitly developed by Black feminist theorists such as Barbara Smith (1998) and activist organizations such as the Combahee River Collective ([1977] 1997), a Black lesbian organization which Smith helped to form in the mid-1970s. The origins of sustained intersectional theory are often located in the work of African American feminists; bell hooks wrote a foundational text on intersectionality titled *Ain't I a Woman? Black Women and Feminism* (1981) while still an undergraduate, and activist and writer Angela Davis (1983, 1990) further developed theories of intersectionality in her works through the 1980s and 1990s. Like many other women of color activists and scholars of the time, Davis traced micro-level experiences of intersecting oppressions to broader exploitative structures such as capitalism.

Although early intersectional work as it entered what Chela Sandoval (2000) calls "hegemonic feminism" derived primarily from African American women theorists and activists, intersectionality has, from its beginnings, included the analyses of women from multiple social locations who wrote against essentialist notions of women by insisting on recognition of multiple racial lenses (see, for example, Acosta-Belén 1986; Allen 1986; Moraga 1986; Anzaldúa 1987). Lesbian writers such as Audre Lorde, Merle Woo, Barbara Smith, and Beverly Little Thunder also worked to include sexualities in the dynamics of theorizing oppression (see Pillow & Mayo 2007). However, these voices were often muted in academic discourse; although one can cite Lorde (1984), Moraga (1983), Moraga and Anzaldúa (1981), and Anzaldúa (1987), for instance, for their insistence on inserting lesbian identities and experiences into larger discourses around gender, much of the intersectional work emerging from the 1970s and 1980s focused on the mutually productive oppressions found in race, class, and gender systems and neglected a sustained analysis of the roles of sexualities in matrices of oppression (see, for example, McCall 2001; Dill & Zambrana 2009).

Sociologists have also attempted to map the structural context for intersectional inequalities through quantitative analysis. One illustration of this approach is found in Leslie McCall's (2001) *Complex Inequality: Gender, Class and Race in the New Economy*. McCall uses the construct "configurations of inequality" in her analysis of the ways "in which race, gender, and class intersect in a variety of ways depending on underlying economic conditions in local economies" (2001: 6). She emphasizes the importance of regional variation, an emphasis that is also featured in Evelyn Nakano Glenn's (1992, 2002) historical analysis of gender, race, and class in three different regions of the US. While Glenn focuses on the relationships between white women and women of color in interdependent labor contexts, McCall uses quantitative data to examine the structure of inequality in the labor markets as they vary across different regions. Glenn's and McCall's analyses further highlight the importance of localized analyses of gender and sexuality (see also Massey 1994; Bulbeck 1998; Kaplan, Alarcón & Moallem 1999; Naples & Desai 2002; Moghadam 2003; Eisenstein 2004; Gunewardena & Kingsolver 2008).

Since the early 1990s, intersectional theorizing around gender has expanded to incorporate analyses of intersecting structures of oppression while also linking personal experience within macro-level interrogations. Crenshaw's (1989) discussion of intersectionality cautions against essentialist notions of "womanhood" in legal theorizing, and particularly highlights the interactions of race, class, and gender in the legal system. She argues that gender and gendered oppression can never be fully understood without adequate attention to the simultaneous role of race, and compares these interactive oppressions to a traffic intersection where accidents happen because of cars traveling to and from different directions. She asserts that "Black women can experience discrimination in ways that are both similar to and different from those experienced by white women and Black men" and that these differences produce "the combined effects of practices which discriminate on the basis of race, and on the basis of sex. And sometimes, they experience discrimination as Black women – not the sum of race and sex discrimination, but as Black women" (Crenshaw 1989: 149). Patricia Hill Collins further developed structural theories of intersectionality in her work on Black feminist thought and Black motherhood (see, for example, Collins 1994) and Black sexuality (Collins 2004).

Disabilities scholars argue that ability has been generally neglected in intersectional analyses of gender and that gender has been undertheorized within disabilities scholarship (see, for example, Mairs 1996; Wendell 1996; R. G. Thompson 1997; Gordon & Rosenblum 2001; Hans & Patri 2003; Mays 2006; Clare 2007). According to Eli Clare (2007), the latter neglect has contributed to a largely white Disability Studies agenda which further marginalizes non-white and queer-identified people. Carrie Sandahl extends the analysis of gender, sex, and ability in her use of the term "queercrip" to make explicit the ways in which hegemonic heterosexism intersects with "able-bodied assumptions and exclusionary effects" (2003: 37). Anna Stubblefield (2007) illustrates how racism and sexism intersected to construct "feeble-mindedness" in the first half of the twentieth century. Her analysis illustrates the ways in which notions of feeble-mindedness, derived from racialized constructions of intelligence, resulted in the coercive sterilization of thousands of people (disproportionately female), many of whom were also poor. Thus, the medical, legal, and social understanding of feeble-mindedness as racialized, hereditary, and predominantly a characteristic of the poor intersected with sexuality and gender to surgically advance a eugenicist project. Studies such as this highlight the social construction of dis/ability as it intersects with other social locations and with political agendas through medical institutions. The invisibility of dis/ability in intersectional theorizing is slowly being addressed in contemporary scholarship in gender, sexualities, and racialization studies (see, for example, Zitzelsberger 2005; Petersen 2006; Jitka 2008). For example, in 2003, *GLQ: A Journal of Lesbian and Gay Studies* devoted an issue to the intersections of queer theory and disability studies (McRuer & Wilkerson 2003), and in 2002 the first international Queer Disability conference was held in San Francisco. Disabilities scholars have also broadened the focus of their inquiry to address the cross-cultural differences in constructions of disability (see, for example, Charlton 1998; Islam 2008; Heap, Lorenzo & Thomas 2009).

Recent research by Native American theorists further highlights structural intersections by juxtaposing historic and contemporary colonialism with Native American tribal sovereignty (see, for example, A. Smith 2005; Simpson 2006; Ramirez 2007). Their work necessarily inserts notions of citizenship into the matrix of domination first described by Collins (1994), and ruptures the limited race/class/gender paradigm produced by early intersectional work. These ruptures are echoed and further developed in transnational intersectional theories of gender and sexuality (see, for example, Herdt 1997; Adam, Duyvendak & Krouwel 1999; Ong 1999; Eisenstein 2004; Whitaker 2006; Narrain 2007; Desai 2009; Naples 2009; Purkayastha 2010). These scholars trace shifting conceptualizations of gender and sexuality as these cross political and cultural borders (see also Anzaldúa 1987; Grewal & Kaplan 1994; Altman 2002; Cantú 2009). These scholars necessarily include consideration of the gendered body (as it crosses these borders) as well as the dynamic social expectations and uses of the gendered body in everyday interaction, culture, and social institutions.

An intersectional approach also attends to the multiple processes, social locations, and cultural practices that shape everyday life and structure social institutions. For example, in his book *Global Sex*, Dennis Altman calls for "a political economy of sexuality, one which recognizes the interrelationship of political, economic, and cultural structures, and avoids the tendency to see sexuality as private and the political and economic as public" (2001: 157). Lionel Cantú (2009) explains that "sexual identities, explicitly 'gay' identities, are linked to capitalist development and urban migration" among other political economic processes (see also D'Emilio [1983] 1993; Rubin 1984; Weeks 1996). Therefore, he argues for a queer materialist theoretical perspective that is informed by feminist standpoint and queer theories. His approach brings together cultural and political economic analyses to demonstrate how sexuality shapes immigration and, in turn, how immigration shapes sexuality (see also Luibhéid 2002; González-López 2005). In producing his perspective, Cantú demonstrates the power of an intersectional framework to illuminate the mutually constitutive construction of gender, sexuality, race, class, and culture of origin.

GENDER AND SEXUALITIES IN CROSS-CULTURAL CONTEXT

Constructions of gender and sexuality vary across cultures and historical period. In the case of Native American two-spirit-identified people, gender and sexuality were historically often constructed in tandem with each other but were understood to be more easily separated in practice than in many European-dominated cultures (Blackwood 1984; Roscoe 1997). Largely (though not universally) egalitarian gender roles in pre-contact and early-contact Native communities may have allowed greater maneuverability between male and female genders; according to Sabine Lang (1997), the emphasis on labor contributions in Native communities forged links between occupational roles and gender rather than between sexuality and gender (see also Blackwood 1984). Sexual relations between people of opposite genders (as these genders were expressed through occupational roles), regardless of body type, could be understood as "heterosexual"; sexual relations between people of the same gender, regardless of body type, could be understood as "homosexual." Lang (1997) asserts that this flexibility resulted in three or four identifiable "genders" in many Native communities. Epple (1998) explains that this de-coupling of sexuality and the body from gender and occupational roles extends to heterosexual-identified people who have sex with two-spirit-identified people; an erotic relationship with a two-spirit person does not automatically signify homosexuality, regardless of the body types involved.

However, the imposition throughout the last five centuries of Western conceptualizations of gender and sexuality as inherently and heteronormatively linked has severely restricted the abilities of Native two-spirit people to identify as anything other than homosexual, thus connecting gender and sexuality in Native American experiences in ways similar to the links found in mainstream heteronormative US culture. Further, Beatrice Medicine notes the location of this linkage within mental health services provided to Native people, thus inserting a historically recent "deviancy" into two-spirit expressions, a deviancy which derives from colonial definitions of gender and sexuality (2007: 152).

Similar liminal spaces of gender and sexuality are constructed and experienced throughout the world. For instance, across the Indian subcontinent *hijra* are understood as a sex/gender system which works outside of a sex/gender binary, and exist as a community which is simultaneously culturally specific and politically bounded. According to Nanda (1994), hijra communities include transvestites, castrated men, prostitutes, followers of the mother goddess, and non-menstruating or infertile women. Nanda argues that British colonialism, demographic changes in family size, and increasing Westernization have exerted profound influences on cultural understandings of hijra and their roles in society (see also Agrawal 1997; Roughgarden 2004). For instance, the Criminal Tribes Act of 1897, imposed by the colonial British government, criminalized the identity of "eunuch" which many hijra claimed. By specifically regulating gender/sex identities, the colonial project in India legally imposed a heteronormative binary which marginalized those who stepped outside of the legal bounds of gendered sexuality. Currently, according to Arvind Narrain (2007), hijra are economically, politically, and socially marginalized, and many earn their income as sex workers; therefore legal surveillance of hijra has evolved to include surveillance by public health officials, largely as a result of the global spread of HIV/AIDS and other sexually transmitted infections.

By many accounts, the *fa'afafine* of Samoa, biologically male-bodied persons who live as women, experience a greater social acceptance than hijra, although they similarly challenge a sex/gender binary system (see, for example, Schmidt 2003; Vasey & Bartlett 2007). However, according to Schmidt (2003), historically high rates of social acceptance have been mitigated recently by globalization and the encroachment of capitalist values into Samoan society. Similarly to Native American two-spirit people, fa'afafine were historically largely understood through occupational roles; Schmidt explains that the introduction of capitalism to Samoa instigated a cultural shift from family and community orientations toward more individualistic orientations; resulting changes in economic structures have impacted gendered divisions of labor and potentially undermined the social ease with which male-bodied persons could historically adopt female identities through occupational roles. The consequences of these changes may include a decreasing social acceptance of the fa'afafine experience. As Plante (2006) points out, there has been far less research on *fa'afatama*, female-bodied persons who occupy a male gender role in Samoa; however, the Samoa Fa'afafine Association Incorporated includes fa'afatama in their community of sexual and gender minorities in Samoa.

It is important to recognize that two-spirit, fa'afafine, and hijra identities are gendered and sexed, but also connected with cultural, national, and spiritual practices. As Yuval-Davis (1997) points out, intersecting social locations, including gender, sexuality, and spirituality, are crucial to conceptualizations and material constructions of citizenship; they are therefore not simply transferable between national and cultural contexts. Amongst the hijra, constructions of citizenship during the period of British colonialism legally excluded certain people from full citizenship statuses based on sexualized identities (Narrain 2007). The British colonial powers incorporated hijra into a grander, criminalized category which included all non-heterosexual identities without distinction. Although similar processes of exclusion by the state have occurred for two-spirit people in North America and fa'afafine people in Samoa, these exclusionary practices also differ significantly in some ways from those experienced by hijra. For instance, Native American two-spirit people have been defined by hegemonic Western notions of the gender/sex binary, but have simultaneously been racialized in a colonialist project which seeks the extermination of Native people as a whole. In addition, Schmidt (2003) argues that the encroachment of Western economic models has exerted a greater organizing force on the gender/sex system in Samoa than tactics of outright removal and conquest such as those experienced by Native Americans.

Two-spirit, hijra, and fa'afafine simultaneously embody several conceptualizations of genders and sexualities: for instance, gender as a binary system in which "male" or "female" does not necessarily align with biological assignment; gender as a fluid social category which does not necessarily adhere to one type of body, but can in fact migrate between body types; historical and tradition-oriented conceptualizations of gender and sexuality as these are subsumed by or stand in relation to Western conceptualizations of heteronormative, binary gender; and multiple conceptualizations of the links between gender, the body, and sexuality. Examination of these conflicts from a global perspective reveals the complexities of genders and sexualities, particularly as their constructions rely on the gendered and sexed body.

GENDER, SEXUALITY, AND GLOBALIZATION

Scholars have long recognized that culture is not a fixed or static phenomenon. Social location, political history, and economic factors all contribute to changes in cultural constructions of gender and sexuality. Colonialism, capitalism, and neoliberalism are three of the most powerful forces that serve to reshape social relations in different locales. For example, Tom Boellstorff demonstrates "how postcolonial heteronormative sexuality is shaped by the state, but is done so in ways specific to particular colonial legacies and national visions that therefore vary over time as well as space" (2007: 166). Boellstorff (2005) also effectively links the local and global processes that construct different sexualities.

As illustrated above, post-colonial and Native American scholars stress the importance of colonialism for imposing Western gender and sexual norms on non-Western cultures. As Jacqui Alexander and Chandra Mohanty (1997) argue, "located subjectivities" should be placed "against the backdrop of globalising capitalism and the complex, diffuse ways it builds upon and retrenches colonial relationships" (Eschle 1999; see also Sassen 1996). In a powerful example of these processes, Kathleen Staudt (2008) analyzes the rape and murder of women and girls along the US–Mexico border and demonstrates the interplay of neoliberal globalization and cultural context. Although misogyny and other forms of male power over women are not unique to Mexico, she notes that "Mexican myths about female betrayal and rage . . . morphed into a national hegemony and added an ugly legitimizing zest to male rage" (Staudt 2008: 144). However, Staudt challenges the view that explains violence against women primarily as a result of a particular culture's view of women, and highlights the role of "a neocolonial global economy" that contributes to "changes in gender power relations" which fueled "selective male backlash as a desperate and flawed strategy to regain power" (2008: 49).

Feminist scholars offer insights into the contradictions associated with globalization by exploring how market relations rely on and further contour social constructions and structures of gender, sexuality, racialization, and region. For example, as Lisa Lowe argues, "One of the distinct features of the global restructuring of capital is its ability to profit not through homogenization but through the differentiation of specific resources and markets that permit the exploitation of gendered and racialized labor within regional and national sites" (1996: 161; see also Mendez 1995; Crehan 1997; Fernandes 1997; Oyèwúmi 1997; Ong 1999; Moghadam 2003; Salzinger 2003). Ironically, she argues, "the very processes that produce a racialized feminized proletariat . . . displace traditional and national patriarchies," thus generating "new possibilities precisely because they have led to a breakdown and a reformulation of the categories of nation, race, class, and gender" (Lowe 1996: 161–2; see also Grewal & Kaplan 1994; Bulbeck 1998; Grewal & Kaplan 2001; Kelly, Bayes, Hawkesworth & Young 2001). Mary Meyer and Elisabeth Prugl also observe that "international economic and political crises destabilize entrenched institutions, including institutions of gender, thus opening up opportunities for emancipatory politics" (1999: 16).

Sociologists of gender and sexualities attend to the multiple ways that people actively challenge structural pressures that shape their everyday lives (see, for example, Naples & Desai 2002; Moghadam 2005). Within this field of inquiry, there is ongoing recognition of the dynamics of power and access to resources that affect the ability of women and sexual minorities from non-Western communities to participate in political organizing beyond their local communities (Moghadam 2008). Rural women are often left out of national organizing, although they do participate in the creation of "counterpublics" in which they appropriate and mobilize transnational gender and sexual frames and political strategies for their own activist purposes (see, for example, Thayer 2010a). However, inequalities of access and resources persist at all levels of organizing. Participation in cross-national meetings and other forms of political activism requires levels of funding that are often beyond the reach of most local groups. When funds are available through state or non-governmental organizations, they often require a shift in priorities that can take away from local organizing efforts (see, for example, Friedman 1999; Hrycak 2007). Funding may be tied to participation in transnational meetings such as the United Nations Conferences on Women. For example, Elisabeth Friedman (1999) notes that the US Agency for International Development (USAID) was the primary sponsor of the Latin American regional process which was put in place to provide a mechanism to link local NGOs to the UN Conference planning process. Friedman reports that: "Women's movements throughout the region debated whether or not to accept money from an agency with a history of promoting US interests to the detriment of those of Third World nations" (1999: 362).

Despite these concerns, "activists have taken the vision of a 'global civil society' to infuse local community organizing efforts with new strategies for linking community-based economic development and consumption practices with a sensitivity to the interdependence of the local and global dimensions of social life" (Naples 2002: 10). In a recent collaborative project designed to examine the diversity of women's activism, Jayati Lal and co-authors document "the extent to which women's movements in and feminist scholarship from different countries and regions have developed through transnational conversation and exchange" (Lal, McGuire, Steward, Zaborowska & Pax 2010: 36). Their findings "interrupt the expectations of either a universalizing global feminism or of uniquely disparate non-Western feminisms, because they show how dialogues with the West do not determine the outcomes of their interlocutors' politics or beliefs" (2010: 37).

The calls for gender justice, economic rights, and sexual citizenship are becoming increasingly salient in transnational organizing. The term "sexual citizenship" gained traction following the publication of David Evans' (1993) book. By the end of the 1990s the term had been taken up by both academic and LGBTQ activist organizations as a claims-making strategy to argue for a wide range of political, economic, and social rights. Ken Plummer, who questions whether or not the term "citizenship" forecloses discussion of "individual, intimate, and private worlds" (2003: 15), offers the construction of "intimate citizenship" to bridge the personal and the political. Diane Richardson argues that sexual rights should include "rights to various forms of sexual practice in personal relationships," "rights through self-definition and the development of individual identities," and "rights within social institutions: public validation of various forms of sexual relations" (2000: 108). She also asks whether or not we should "theorize sexual or intimate citizenship in terms of universalistic notions of 'the sexual citizen' or . . . embrace a gendered and sexually differentiated model which would allow for a specific notion of 'lesbian citizenship'" (Richardson 2000: 261).

One significant limitation in the literature on sexual citizenship has been the focus on Western countries and the relative lack of attention to or marginalization of non-Western countries (see, for example, Wintermute & Andenaes 2001). Post-colonial scholars argue that the heterosexuality/homosexuality binary and the "Western" construction of "gay and lesbian" that dominates in many social movement organizations, as post-colonial feminist and queer scholars caution, construct a much too narrow framework that does not capture the diversity of sexual identities and practices that are evident among people in diverse cultural contexts (see, for example, Morgan and Wierenga [2006] and Arnfred [2004] on African sexualities, Jacobs, Thomas, and Lang [1997] on Native American sexualities, and Summerhawk, McMahill, and McDonald [1998] on Japanese sexualities). A salient oppositional frame generated to deny sexual freedom to gay men and lesbians in many non-Western countries is the charge that homosexuality is a Western import, one designed to pollute the culture. Joseph Massad argues that the presumed liberatory discourse of the international gay rights groups "both produces homosexuals, as well as gays and lesbians, where they do not exist, and represses same-sex desires and practices that refuse to be assimilated into its sexual epistemology" (2002: 363). In contrast, as one observer notes (and Massad acknowledges), "the main force behind homophobic sentiments in many countries is often the Christian church, which is the true Western import" (Shand 2005: 3; see also Schmitt [2003] for a response to Massad).

Among the important factors that shape the complex landscape for sexual citizenship in post-colonial contexts is the extent to which religious law and cultural practices are recognized and protected by the state. Judith Stacey and Tey Meadow (2009) analyze the South African law which recognizes same-sex marriage as well as polygamy in the 1996 Constitution. As they demonstrate, "legal recognition for polygamy *preceded and facilitated* legal same-sex marriage, but the latter is likely to undermine the patriarchal practice of the former" (Stacey & Meadow 2009: 171). Furthermore, as Natalie Oswin argues, the lobbying efforts of the gay rights movement "took a deliberately conservative approach that has been characterized as elitist, unrepresentative, and male dominated" (2007: 650).

Hester Eisenstein (2009) identifies another process of cooptation in her assessment of "how global elites use women's labor and ideas to exploit the world." She argues that "feminist ideas, however watered down by fundamentalist forces, have become useful to the powerful industrialized countries, and their instruments in the World Bank and the other IFIs [international financial institutions], as a way of distracting attention from the devastation brought about by the policies of structural adjustment" (Eisenstein 2009: 168). For example, she points out "the Bush administration's embrace of women's rights as part of the justification for the war in Afghanistan" as an illustration of how feminism serves as one of the "constituent elements of the war on terror" (2009: 174).

Social justice claims and interventions on behalf of women and sexual minorities have been increasingly framed as "human rights" concerns (for examples, see Wilson 1996; Keck & Sikkink 1998). Scholars debate the limits and possibilities of the human rights framework for capturing the diverse demands and collective struggles of people across the globe. Inderpal Grewal (1999) notes that human rights as a neoliberal individualist framework does not provide the basis for group-based claims which is especially important for native Indian and indigenous peoples' struggles for land rights and political sovereignty . Furthermore, University of Delhi law professor Upendra Baxi argues that "the neoliberal frame, even when cloaked in 'people-friendly' global governance, is about creating . . . 'market-friendly NGOs' that can cooperate with, and be co-opted by, but do not oppose CSOs [civil society organizations], states, and international organizations that support a neoliberal agenda" (Runyan 1999: 211). Sexualities studies scholars also caution that "the deployment of rights in universal terms" (Binnie 2004: 148) inevitably renders invisible the specific circumstances and needs of different subjects and communities (see also Bell & Binnie 2000). Debates regarding the limits and possibilities of the rights frame reveal what Corrêa, Petchesky, and Parker explain as "the indispensability and insufficiency of human rights" (2008: 151; see also Karides 2002; Wing 2002).

CONCLUSION

The study of gender as a sociological unit of analysis has evolved tremendously since the early 1970s. Initially, the study of gender was largely organized around attempts to fill in the blanks where women had historically been excluded from sociological consideration. Bringing women into view also allowed scholars to critique the very nature of sociology itself by pointing out what had been missing in previous theories and methods of analysis, and thus the 1970s and 1980s also saw a burgeoning of critical gender studies. During the 1990s, scholars of gender and sexualities were drawn to the postmodern critiques of categories and grand narrative explanations of gender and sexual diversity. Feminist and queer theorists continue to draw on Foucault's analysis of "governmentality" and "biopower" to, among other things, situate discussion of how different nation-states and specific laws serve to regulate bodies and construct normative sexual citizens and explore how "bodies give substance to citizenship" and how "citizenship matters for bodies" (Beasley & Bacchi 2000: 337; see also Mamo 2007).

A focus on technologies of the body is gaining increasing attention, as evidenced by the establishment of the new section within the American Sociological Association, the Section on the Body and Embodiment. Two Sections-in-formation, one on Disability and Society and another focused on Global and Transnational Sociology, reflect the growing recognition of these subfields in which intersectional analyses of gender and sexualities should find new intellectual spaces to expand on current work in these areas. Contemporary analyses of gender and sexuality are further enriched by attention to intersectionality, cross-national and cross-cultural differences, and globalization. For example, intersectional analyses of violence against women which incorporate attention to global economic restructuring deepen understandings of the complex processes that shape women's lives and bring to light the experiences of social actors who were rarely the subjects of academic research a few decades ago (Staudt 2008; Villalón 2010).

Sociologists of gender and sexualities continue to stress the power of interactionist, social constructionist, and structural perspectives for revealing the complex ways that gender and sexual normativity and inequalities are produced, reproduced, and resisted. There is also growing attention to new technologies as they reshape the relationship between gender and sexuality. This avenue of research asks, among other questions, how are technologies gendered, racialized, and sexed; how, and in what ways, are new technologies shaping gender, race, sexuality, and social inequalities in different places; and can new technologies be used to promote "a practical emancipatory politics" (Wajcman 2004: 101)?

The social movement goal of an emancipatory politics that animates women's movements and LGBT politics remains central to feminist and queer scholarship. In one recent effort to imagine a world without gender, Judith Lorber calls for "a movement that acknowledges the continuing power of gender but looks for ways of dismantling it in the family and the workplace, the areas most significant for our daily lives" (2005: xiii). She also argues that, among other things, "intersecting identities can be a way of degendering, of undercutting the power of gender to structure women's and men's lives" (Lorber 2005: xviv). Therefore, an intersectional politics that is "panethnic, cross-racial, and transgendered" is required to undo gender (see also Butler 2004). Can gender and sexuality be "undone" or reperformed and represented in such a way that the inequalities, normative structures, and social regulatory processes no longer rely on these categories of difference? Given the persistence of inequality along the lines of gender and sexuality, it will take a worldwide movement of "gender troublemakers" (Lorber 2005: 21) to degender the structures that sustain these hierarchies of difference.

References

Acosta-Belén, Edna (ed.) (1986) *The Puerto Rican Woman's Perspectives on Culture, History and Society*, 2nd edn. New York: Praeger.

Adam, Barry D., Jan Willem Duyvendak, and André Krouwel (1999) *The Global Emergence of Gay and Lesbian Politics*. Philadelphia, PA: Temple University Press.

Agrawal, Anuja (1997) "Gendered Bodies: The Case of the Third Gender in India." *Contributions to Indian Sociology* 31(2): 273–97.

Alexander, Jacqui and Chandra Talpade Mohanty (eds.) (1997) *Feminist Genealogies, Colonial Legacies, Democratic Futures*. New York: Routledge.

Allen, Paula Gunn (1986) *The Sacred Hoop: Recovering the Feminism in American Indian Traditions*. Boston: Beacon Press.

Altman, Dennis (2002) *Global Sex*. Chicago: University of Chicago Press.

Amnesty International (2007) "Stop Violence Against Women: Rape as a Tool of War: A Fact Sheet." www.amnestyusa.org/women/rapeinwartime.html (accessed May 26, 2010).

Anzaldúa, Gloria (1987) *Borderlands/La Frontera: The New Mestiza*. San Francisco: Spinsters/Aunt Lute.

Aptheker, Bettina (1989) *Tapestries of Life: Women's Work, Women's Consciousness, and the Meaning of Daily Experience*. Amherst, MA: University of Massachusetts Press.

Arnfred, Signe (ed.) (2004) *Re-thinking Sexualities in Africa*. Uppsala: Nordic Africa Institute.

Balsamo, Anne (1996) *Technologies of the Gendered Body: Reading Cyborg Women*. Durham, NC: Duke University Press.

Barclay, Scott, Mary Bernstein, and Anna-Maria Marshall (2009) *Queer Mobilizations: LGBT Activists Confront the Law*. New York: New York University Press.

Barrett, Michèle (1980) *Women's Oppression Today*. London: Verso.

Beasley, Chris and Carol Bacchi (2000) "Citizen Bodies: Embodying Citizens – A Feminist Analysis." *International Feminist Journal of Politics* 2–3: 337–58.

Belenky, Mary, Blythe Clinchy, Nancy Golberger, and Jill Tarule (1997) *Women's Ways of Knowing: The Development of Self, Voice, and Mind, 10th Anniversary Edition*. New York: Basic Books.

Bell, David and Jon Binnie (2000) *The Sexual Citizen: Queer Politics and Beyond*. Cambridge: Polity Press.

Bergmann, Barbara R. (1986) *The Economic Emergence of Women*. New York: Basic Books.

Binnie, Jon (2004) *The Globalization of Sexuality*. London: Sage.

Blackwood, Evelyn (1984) "Sexuality and Gender in Certain Native American Tribes: The Case of Cross-Gender Females." *Signs: Journal of Women and Culture in Society* 10(1): 27–42.

Bloodsworth-Lugo, Mary K. (2007) *In-Between Bodies: Sexual Difference, Race, and Sexuality*. Albany, NY: SUNY Press.

Boellstorff, Tom (2005) *The Gay Archipelago: Sexuality and Nation in Indonesia*. Princeton, NJ: Princeton University Press.

Boellstorff, Tom (2007) *A Coincidence of Desires: Anthropology, Queer Studies, Indonesia*. Durham, NC: Duke University Press.

Bolin, Ann (1994) "Transcending and Transgendering: Male-to-Female Transsexuals, Dichotomy and Diversity." In Gilbert Herdt (ed.), *Third Sex, Third Gender: Beyond Dimorphism in Culture and History*. New York: Zone Books, pp. 247–86.

Bookman, Ann and Sandra Morgen (eds.) (1988) *Women and the Politics of Empowerment*. Philadelphia, PA: Temple University Press.

Boris, Eileen (1995) "The Racialized Gendered State: Constructions of Citizenship in the United States." *Social Politics* 2(2): 160–80.

Bornstein, Kate (1995) *Gender Outlaws: On Men, Women, and the Rest of Us*. New York: Vintage Books.

Bose, Christine E. (1985) *Jobs and Gender: A Study of Occupational Prestige*. New York: Praeger.

Brah, Avtar and Ann Phoenix (2004) "Ain't I a Woman? Revisiting Intersectionality." *Journal of International Women's Studies* 5(3): 75–86.

Brill, Stephanie A. and Rachel Pepper (2008) *The Transgender Child: A Handbook for Families and Professionals*. San Francisco: Cleis Press.

Britton, Dana M. (2003) *At Work in the Iron Cage: The Prison as Gendered Organization*. New York: New York University Press.

Bulbeck, Chilla (1998) *Re-Orienting Western Feminisms: Women's Diversity in a Postcolonial World*. Cambridge: Cambridge University Press.

Butler, Judith (1990) *Gender Trouble: Feminism and the Subversion of Identity*. New York: Routledge.

Butler, Judith (1997) "Performative Acts and Gender Constitution: An Essay in Phenomenology and Feminist Theory." In Katie Conboy, Nadia Medina, and Sarah Stanbury (eds.),

Writing on the Body: Female Embodiment and Feminist Theory. New York: Columbia University Press, pp. 401–18.

Butler, Judith (2004) *Undoing Gender*. New York: Routledge.

Cantú, Lionel (2009) *The Sexuality of Migration: Border Crossings and Mexican Immigrant Men*. New York: New York University Press.

Chafetz, Janet S. (1974) *Masculine/Feminine or Human? An Overview of the Sociology of Sex Roles*. Itasca, IL: F. E. Peacock.

Chant, Sylvia, with Nikki Craske (2002) *Gender in Latin America*. New Brunswick, NJ: Rutgers University Press.

Chao, Antonia (2000) "Global Metaphors and Local Strategies in the Construction of Taiwan's Lesbian Identities." *Culture, Health and Sexuality* 2(4): 377–90.

Chapkis, Wendy (1986) *Beauty Secrets: Women and the Politics of Appearance*. Boston: South End Press.

Charlton, James I. (1998) *Nothing About Us Without Us: Disability Oppression and Empowerment*. Berkeley, CA: University of California Press.

Chauncey, George (1989) "From Sexual Inversion to Homosexuailty: The Changing Medical Conceptualization of Female 'Deviance'." In Kathy Peiss and Christina Simmons, with Robert Padgug (eds.), *Passion and Power: Sexuality in History*. Philadelphia, PA: Temple University Press, pp. 87–117.

Chodorow, Nancy (1978) *The Reproduction of Mothering: Psychoanalysis and the Sociology of Gender*. Berkeley, CA: University of California Press.

Clare, Eli (2007) *Exile and Pride: Disability, Queerness, and Liberation*. Boston: South End Press.

Colapinto, John (2001) *As Nature Made Him: The Boy Who Was Raised as a Girl*. New York: Harper Perennial.

Collins, Patricia Hill (1994) "Shifting the Center: Race, Class, and Feminist Theorizing about Motherhood." In Donna Bassin, Margaret Honey, and Meryle Mahrer Kaplan (eds.), *Representations of Motherhood*. New Haven, CT: Yale University Press, pp. 56–74.

Collins, Patricia Hill (2004) *Black Sexual Politics: African Americans, Gender, and the New Racism*. New York: Routledge.

Collins, Patricia Hill (2008) "Color, Hair Texture, and Standards of Beauty." In Estelle Disch (ed.), *Reconstructing Gender: A Multicultural Anthology*. New York: McGraw-Hill, pp. 127–31.

Coltrane, Scott and Michele Adams (2008) *Gender and Families*. Lanham, MD: Rowman and Littlefield.

Combahee River Collective ([1977] 1997) "A Black Feminist Statement." In Linda Nicholson (ed.), *The Second Wage: A Reader in Feminist Theory*. New York: Routledge, pp. 63–70.

Conboy, Katie, Nadia Medina, and Sarah Stanbury (eds.) (1997) *Writing on the Body: Female Embodiment and Feminist Theory*. New York: Columbia University Press.

Connell, R. W. (1985) *Masculinities*. Berkeley, CA: University of California Press.

Connell, R. W. (1987) *Gender and Power: Society, the Person, and Sexual Politics*. Stanford, CA: Stanford University Press.

Corrêa, Sonia, Rosalind Petchesky, and Richard Parker (2008) *Sexuality, Health and Human Rights*. New York: Routledge.

Crehan, Kate (1997) *The Fractured Community: Landscapes of Power and Gender in Rural Zambia*. Berkeley, CA: University of California Press.

Crenshaw, Kimberlé (1989) "Demarginalizing the Intersection of Race and Sex: A Black Feminist Critique of Antidiscrimination Doctrine, Feminist Theory and Antiracist Politics." *University of Chicago Legal Forum*, 138–67.

Crenshaw, Kimberlé Williams (1991) "Mapping the Margins: Intersectionality, Identity Politics, and Violence Against Women of Color." *Stanford Law Review* 43(6): 1241–99.

Davis, Angela (1983) *Women, Race, and Class*. New York: Vintage Books.

Davis, Angela (1990) *Women, Culture, and Politics*. New York: Vintage Books.

D'Emilio, John ([1983] 1993) "Capitalism and Gay Identity." In W. B. Rubenstein (ed.), *Cases and Materials on Sexual Orientation and the Law: Lesbians, Gay Men, and the Law*. New York: New Press, pp. 132–4.

Desai, Manisha (2009) *Gender and the Politics of Possibility: Rethinking Globalization*. Lanham, MD: Rowman and Littlefield.

Devor, Holly (1989) *Gender Blending: Confronting the Limits of Duality*. Bloomington, IN: Indiana University Press.

Devor, Holly (1997) *FTM: Female-to-Male Transsexuals in Society*. Bloomington, IN: Indiana University Press.

Dill, Bonnie Thornton and Ruth Enid Zambrana (eds.) (2009) *Emerging Intersections: Race, Class, and Gender in Theory, Policy, and Practice*. New Brunswick, NJ: Rutgers University Press.

Eisenstein, Hester (2009) *Feminism Seduced: How Global Elites Use Women's Labor and Ideas to Exploit the World*. Boulder, CO: Paradigm.

Eisenstein, Zillah (ed.) (1979) *Capitalist Patriarchy and the Case for Socialist Feminism*. New York: Monthly Review Press.

Eisenstein, Zillah (1988) *The Female Body and the Law*. Berkeley, CA: University of California Press.

Eisenstein, Zillah (2004) *Against Empire: Feminisms, Racism, and the West*. London: Zed Books.

England, Paula (2005) "Gender Inequality in Labor Markets: The Role of Motherhood and Segregation." *Social Politics* 12: 264–88.

Enloe, Cynthia (1983) *Does Khaki Become You? The Militarisation of Women's Lives*. Boston: South End Press.

Epple, Carolyn (1998) "Coming to Terms with Navajo *Nadleehi*: A Critique of *Berdache*, 'Gay,' 'Alternate Gender,' and 'Two-Spirit'." *American Ethnologist* 25(2): 267–90.

Epstein, Cynthia (1981) *Women in Law*. Garden City, NY: Doubleday/Anchor.

Eschle, Catherine (1999) "Review Essay: Building Global Visions: Democracy and Solidarity in the Globalisation of Feminism." *International Feminist Journal of Politics* 1: 327–31.

Evans, David T. (1993) *Sexual Citizenship: The Material Construction of Sexualities*. New York: Routledge.

Fausto-Sterling, Anne (1985) *Myths of Gender: Biological Theories about Women and Men*. New York: Basic Books.

Fausto-Sterling, Anne (2000) *Sexing the Body: Gender Politics and the Construction of Sexuality*. New York: Basic Books.

Fenstermaker, Sarah and Candace West (eds.) (2002) *Doing Gender, Doing Difference: Inequality, Power, and Institutional Change*. New York: Routledge.

Fernandes, Leela (1997) *Producing Workers: The Politics of Gender, Class, and Culture in the Calcutta Jute Mills*. Philadelphia, PA: University of Pennsylvania Press.

Ferree, Myra Marx (1987) "She Works Hard for a Living." In Beth Hess and Myra Marx Ferree (eds.), *Analyzing Gender*. Newbury Park, CA: Sage, pp. 322–47.

Ferree, Myra Marx and Beth B. Hess (1985) *Controversy and Coalition: The New Feminist Movement*. Boston: Twayne.

Fishman, Jennifer R. (2004) "Manufacturing Desire: The Commodification of Female Sexual Dysfunction." *Social Studies of Science* 34(2): 187–218.

Foucault, Michel (1978) *The History of Sexuality*, Vol. I. New York: Random House.

Fox, Mary Frank, Deborah G. Johnson, and Sue V. Rosser (eds.) (2006) *Women, Gender and Technology*. Urbana, IL: University of Illinois Press.

Friedman, Elisabeth (1999) "The Effects of 'Transnationalism Reversed' in Venezuela: Assessing the Impact of UN Global Conferences on the Women's Movement." *International Feminist Journal of Politics* 1(3): 357–81.

Gagnon, John H. and William S. Simon (1973) *Sexual Conduct: The Social Sources of Human Sexuality*. Chicago: Aldine.

Gatens, Moira (1983) "A Critique of the Sex/Gender Distinction." In Judith Allen and Paul Patton (eds.), *Beyond Marxism: Interventions after Marx*. Leichhardt, NSW: Intervention Publications, pp. 143–60.

Gilligan, Carol (1982) *In a Different Voice*. Cambridge, MA: Harvard University Press.

Gilmore, David (1990) *Manhood in the Making: Cultural Concepts of Masculinity*. New Haven, CT: Yale University Press.

Glenn, Evelyn Nakano (1992) "From Servitude to Service Work: Historical Continuities in the Racial Division of Paid Reproductive Labor." *Signs: Journal of Women in Culture and Society* 18(1): 1–43.

Glenn, Evelyn Nakano (2002) *Unequal Freedom: How Race and Gender Shaped American Citizenship and Labor*. Cambridge, MA: Harvard University Press.

Goffman, Erving (1976) "Gender Display." *Studies in the Anthropology of Visual Communication* 3: 69–77.

González-López, Gloria (2005) *Erotic Journeys: Mexican Immigrants and Their Sex Lives*. Berkeley, CA: University of California Press.

Gopinath, Gayatri (2003) "Nostalgia, Desire, Diaspora: South Asian Sexualities in Motion." In Robert J. Corber and Stephen Valocchi (eds.), *Queer Studies: An Interdisciplinary Reader*. London: Wiley-Blackwell, pp. 206–17.

Gordon, Beth Omansky and Karen E. Rosenblum (2001) "Bringing Disability into the Sociological Frame: A Comparison of Disability with Race, Sex, and Sexual Orientation Statuses." *Disability and Society* 16(1): 5–19.

Greenberg, Julia A. (2006) "The Road Less Traveled: The Problem with Binary Sex Categories." In Paisley Currah, Richard M. Juang, and Shannon Price Minter (eds.), *Transgender Rights*. Minneapolis: University of Minnesota Press, pp. 51–73.

Grewal, Inderpal (1999) "On the New Global Feminism and the Family of Nations: Dilemmas of Transnational Feminist Practice." In Ella Shohat (ed.), *Talking Visions: Multicultural Feminism in a Transnational Age*. Cambridge, MA: New Museum of Modern Art and MIT Press, pp. 501–30.

Grewal, Inderpal and Caren Kaplan (eds.) (1994) *Scattered Hegemonies: Postmodernity and Transnational Feminist Practices*. Minneapolis: University of Minneapolis Press.

Grewal, Inderpal and Caren Kaplan (2001) "Global Identities: Theorizing Transnational Studies of Sexuality." *GLQ: A Journal of Lesbian and Gay Studies* 7(4): 663–79.

Gunewardena, Nandini and Ann Kingsolver (2008) *The Gender of Globalization: Women Navigating Cultural and Economic Marginalities*. Sante Fe, NM: School for Advanced Research Press.

Halberstam, Judith (1998) *Female Masculinity*. Durham, NC: Duke University Press.

Hans, Asha and Annie Patri (eds.) (2003) *Women, Disability and Identity*. New Delhi: Sage.

Haraway, Donna (1988) "Situated Knowledges: The Science Question in Feminism and the Privilege of Partial Perspective." *Feminist Studies* 14(3): 575–99.

Harding, Sandra (1991) *Whose Science? Whose Knowledge? Thinking from Women's Lives*. Ithaca, NY: Cornell University Press.

Hartsock, Nancy (1998) *The Feminist Standpoint Revisited and Other Essays*. Boulder, CO: Westview Press.

Heap, Marion, Theresa Lorenzo, and Jacky Thomas (2009) "'We've Moved Away from Disability as a Health Issue, It's a Human Rights Issue': Reflecting on 10 Years of the Right to Equality in South Africa." *Disability and Society* 24(7): 857–68.

Herdt, Gilbert (1997) *Same Sex, Different Cultures: Exploring Gay and Lesbian Lives*. Boulder, CO: Westview Press.

Hochschild, Arlie R. (1973) "A Review of Sex Roles Research." *American Journal of Sociology* 78: 1011–29.

Hochschild, Arlie R. and Anne Machung (1989) *The Second Shift*. New York: Penguin.

hooks, bell (1981) *Ain't I a Woman? Black Women and Feminism*. Boston: South End Press.

Hrycak, Alexandra (2007) "From Global to Local Feminisms: Transnationalism, Foreign Aid and the Women's Movement in Ukraine." In Sonita Sarker (ed.), *Sustainable Feminisms* (Advances in Gender Research, Vol. 11). Burlington, VT: Emerald Group Publishing, pp. 75–93.

Irvine, Janice M. (2005) *Disorders of Desire: Sexuality and Gender in Modern American Sexology*. Philadelphia, PA: Temple University Press.

Islam, Zoebia (2008) "Negotiating Identities: The Lives of Pakistani and Bangladeshi Young Disabled People." *Disability and Society* 23(1): 41–52.

Jacobs, Sue-Ellen, Wesley Thomas, and Sabine Lang (1997) *Gays, Transsexuals and Bisexuals, Two-Spirit People: Native American Gender Identity, Sexuality, and Spirituality*. Urbana, IL: University of Illinois Press.

Jagose, Annamarie (1997) *Queer Theory: An Introduction*. New York: New York University Press.

Jitka, Sinecka (2008) "'I Am Bodied'. 'I Am Sexual'. 'I Am Human'. Experiencing Deafness and Gayness: A Story of a Young Man." *Disability and Society* 23(5): 475–84.

Joffe, Carole (1986) *The Regulation of Sexuality: Experiences of Family Planning Workers*. Philadelphia, PA: Temple University Press.

Kaplan, Caren, Norma Alarcón, and Minoo Moallem (eds.) (1999) *Between Woman and Nation: Nationalisms, Transnational Feminisms, and the State*. Durham, NC: Duke University Press.

Karides, Marina (2002) "Linking Local Efforts with Global Struggle: Trinidad's National Union of Domestic Employees." In Nancy A. Naples and Manisha Desai (eds.), *Women's Activism and Globalization: Linking Local Struggles with Transnational Politics*. New York: Routledge, pp. 156–71.

Keck, Margaret E. and Kathyrn Sikkink (1998) *Activists Beyond Borders: Advocacy Networks in International Politics*. Ithaca, NY: Cornell University Press.

Keller, Evelyn Fox (1987) "The Gender/Science System: Or, Is Sex to Gender as Nature Is to Science?" *Hypatia* 2(3): 37–50.

Kelly, Rita Mae, Jane H. Bayes, Mary E. Hawkesworth, and Brigitte Young (eds.) (2001) *Gender, Globalization, and Democratizaion*. Lanham, MD: Rowman and Littlefield.

Kessler, Suzanne J. and Wendy McKenna (1978) *Gender: An Ethnomethodological Approach*. Chicago: University of Chicago Press.

Kimmel, Michael (1990) "After 15 Years: The Impact of the Sociology of Masculinity on the Masculinity of Sociology." In Jeff Hearn and David Morgan (eds.), *Men, Masculinities and Social Theory*. London: Unwin Hyman, pp. 97–109.

Kimmel, Michael (1996) *Manhood in America: A Cultural History*. New York: Free Press.

Kimmel, Michael (2007) *The Sexual Self: The Construction of Sexual Scripts*. Nashville, TN: Vanderbilt.

Kitch, Sally L. (2009) *The Specter of Sex: Gendered Foundations of Racial Formation in the United States.* Albany, NY: SUNY Press.

Kondo, Dorinne (1999) "Fabricating Masculinity: Gender, Race, and Nation in a Transnational Frame." In Caren Kaplan, Norma Alarcón, and Minoo Moallem (eds.), *Between Woman and Nation: Nationalisms, Transnational Feminisms, and the State.* Durham, NC: Duke University Press, pp. 296–319.

Lal, Jayati, Kristin McGuire, Abigail J. Steward, Magdalena Zaborowska, and Justine M. Pax (2010) "Recasting Global Feminisms: Toward a Comparative Historical Approach to Women's Activism and Feminist Scholarship." *Feminist Studies* 36(1): 13–39.

Lamphere, Louise, Helena Ragone, and Patricia Zavella (1997) *Situated Lives: Gender and Culture in Everyday Life.* New York: Routledge.

Land, Hilary (1980) "The Family Wage." *Feminist Review* 6: 55–77.

Lang, Sabine (1997) "Various Kinds of Two-Spirit People: Gender Variance and Homosexuality in Native American Communities." In Sue-Elen Jacobs, Wesley Thomas, and Sabine Lang (eds.), *Two-Spirit People: Native American Gender Identity, Sexuality, and Spirituality.* Chicago: University of Chicago Press, pp. 100–18.

Lehourites, Chirs (2009) "Semenya's Gender Test Results Are In." Associated Press, May 9. www.fanhouse.com/news/main/caster-semenya-gender-test-results/666103/ (accessed May 28, 2010).

Leidner, Robin (1991) "Serving Hamburgers and Selling Insurance: Gender, Work, and Identity in Interactive Service Jobs." *Gender and Society* 5(2): 154–77.

Lind, Amy (ed.) (2010) *Development, Sexual Rights and Global Governance.* New York: Routledge.

Loe, Meika (2006) *The Rise of Viagra: How the Little Blue Pill Changed Sex in America.* New York: New York University Press.

Lorber, Judith (1981) "Critical Symposium on *The Reproduction of Mothering.*" *Signs: Journal of Women in Culture and Society* 6(3): 482–6.

Lorber, Judith (1984) *Women Physicians: Careers, Status, and Power.* New York: Tavistock.

Lorber, Judith (1994) *Paradoxes of Gender.* New Haven, CT: Yale University Press.

Lorber, Judith (2005) *Breaking the Bowls: Degendering and Feminist Change.* New York: W. W. Norton.

Lorber, Judith and Lisa Jean Moore (2006) *Gendered Bodies: Feminist Perspectives.* Oxford: Oxford University Press.

Lorde, Audre (1984) *Sister Outsider: Essays and Speeches.* Berkeley, CA: Crossing Press.

Lowe, Lisa (1996) *Immigrant Acts: On Asian American Cultural Politics.* Durham, NC: Duke University Press.

Luibhéid, Ethiene (2002) *Entry Denied: Controlling Sexuality at the Border.* Minneapolis: University of Minnesota Press.

MacKinnon, Catherine (1989) *Toward a Feminist Theory of the State.* Cambridge, MA: Harvard University Press.

Mairs, Nancy (1996) *Waist-High in the World: A Life Among the Nondisabled.* Boston: Beacon Press.

Mamo, Laura (2007) *Queering Reproduction: Achieving Pregnancy in the Age of Technoscience.* Durham, NC: Duke University Press.

Mamo, Laura and Jennifer R. Fishman (2001) "Potency in All the Right Places: Viagra as a Technology of the Gendered Body." *Body and Society* 7(4): 13–35.

Martin, Emily (1991) "The Egg and the Sperm: How Science Has Constructed a Romance Based on Stereotypical Male-Female Roles." *Signs: Journal of Women in Culture and Society* 3(16): 485–501.

Martin, Patricia Yancey (2003) "'Said and Done' Versus 'Saying and Doing': Gendering Practices, Practicing Gender at Work." *Gender and Society* 17(3): 342–66.

Massad, Joseph (2002) "Re-Orienting Desire: The Gay International and the Arab World." *Public Culture* 14(2): 361–85.

Massey, Doreen (1994) *Space, Place and Gender*. Minneapolis: University of Minnesota Press.

Mayberry, Maralee, Banu Subramaniam, and Lisa Weasel (2001) *Feminist Science Studies: A New Generation*. New York: Routledge.

Mays, Jennifer M. (2006) "Feminist Disability Theory: Domestic Violence Against Women with a Disability." *Disability and Society* 21(2): 147–58.

McCall, Leslie (2001) *Complex Inequality: Gender, Class and Race in the New Economy*. New York: Routledge.

McIntosh, Mary (1968) "The Homosexual Role." *Social Problems* 16(2): 182–92.

McRuer, Robert and Abby Wilkerson (eds.) (2003) "Desiring Disability: Queer Theory Meets Disability Studies." *GLQ: A Journal of Lesbian and Gay Studies* 9(1–2).

Mead, Margaret (1950) *Male and Female: A Survey of the Sexes in a Changing World*. London: Gollancz.

Medicine, Beatrice (2007) "Changing Native American Roles in an Urban Context *and* Changing Native American Sex Roles in an Urban Context." In Sue-Elen Jacobs, Wesley Thomas, and Sabine Lang (eds.), *Two-Spirit People: Native American Gender Identity, Sexuality, and Spirituality*. Chicago: University of Chicago Press, pp. 145–55.

Mendez, Jennifer Bickham (1995) *From the Revolution to the Maquiladoras: Gender, Labor, and Globalization in Nicaragua*. Durham, NC: Duke University Press.

Messner, Michael (2002) *Taking the Field: Women, Men, and Sports*. Minneapolis: University of Minnesota Press.

Meyer, Mary K. and Elisabeth Prugl (eds.) (1999) *Gender Politics in Global Governance*. Lanham, MD: Rowman and Littlefield.

Mezey, Susan Gluck (2007) *Queers in Court: Gay Rights Law and Public Policy*. Lanham, MD: Rowman and Littlefield.

Moghadam, Valentine M. (2003) *Modernizing Women: Gender and Social Change in the Middle East*. Boulder, CO: Lynne Rienner.

Moghadam, Valentine M. (2005) *Globalizing Women: Transnational Feminist Networks*. Baltimore, MD: Johns Hopkins University Press.

Moghadam, Valentine M. (2008) *Globalization and Social Movements: Islamism, Feminism, and the Global Justice Movement*. Lanham, MD: Rowman and Littlefield

Money, John (1952) "Hermaphroditism: An Inquiry into the Nature of a Human Paradox." Unpublished PhD thesis, Harvard University, Cambridge, MA.

Moraga, Cherrie (1983) *Loving in the War Years*. Boston: South End Press.

Moraga, Cherríe (1986) "From a Long Line of Vendidas: Chicanas and Feminism." In Teresa de Lauretis (ed.), *Feminist Studies: Critical Studies*. Bloomington, IN: Indiana University Press, pp. 173–90.

Moraga, Cherríe and Gloria Anzaldúa (eds.) (1981) *This Bridge Called My Back: Writings by Radical Women of Color*. Watertown, MA: Persephone Press.

Morgan, Ruth and Saskia Wierenga (2006) *Tommy Boys, Lesbian Men, and Ancestral Wives*. Johannesburg: Jacana Media.

Namaste, Viviane K. (2000) *Invisible Lives: The Erasure of Transsexual and Transgendered People*. Chicago: University of Chicago Press.

Nanda, Serena (1994) "Hijras: An Alternative Sex and Gender Role in India." In Gilbert Herdt (ed.), *Third Sex, Third Gender: Beyond Sexual Dimorphism in Culture and History*. New York: Zone Books, pp. 372–417.

Nanda, Serena (2007) "Multiple Genders Among Native American Indians." In Joan Spade and Catherine G. Valentine (eds.), *Kaleidoscope of Gender*. Thousand Oaks, CA: Pine Forge Press, pp. 47–54.

Naples, Nancy A. (2002) "Changing the Terms: Community Activism, Globalization, and the Dilemmas of Transnational Feminist Praxis." In Nancy A. Naples and Manisha Desai (eds.), *Women's Activism and Globalization: Linking Local Struggles and Transnational Politics*. New York: Routledge, pp. 3–14.

Naples, Nancy A. (2009) "Crossing Borders: Community Activism, Globalization, and Social Justice." *Social Problems* 56(1): 2–20.

Naples, Nancy A. and Manisha Desai (eds.) (2002) *Women's Activism and Globalization: Linking Local Struggles with Transnational Politics*. New York: Routledge.

Narrain, Arvind (2007) "Rethinking Citizenship: A Queer Journey." *Indian Journal of Gender Studies* 14(1): 61–71.

Nicholson, Linda (1994) "Interpreting Gender." *Signs: Journal of Women in Culture and Society* 20: 79–105.

Njambi, Wairumū Ngarūiya and William O'Brien (2007) "Revisiting 'Woman-to-Woman Marriage': Notes on Gĩkũyũ Women." In Joan Spade and Catherine G. Valentine (eds.), *Kaleidoscope of Gender*. Thousand Oaks, CA: Pine Forge Press, pp. 127–36.

O'Connor, Julia S., Ann Shola Orloff, and Sheila Shaver (1999) *States, Markets, Families: Gender, Liberalism and Social Policy in Australia, Canada, Great Britain and the United States*. Cambridge: Cambridge University Press.

Ong, Aihwa (1999) *Flexible Citizenship: The Cultural Logics of Transnationality*. Durham, NC: Duke University Press.

Oswin, Natalie (2007) "Producing Homonormativity in Neoliberal South Africa: Recognition, Redistribution, and the Equality Project." *Signs: Journal of Women in Culture and Society* 32(3): 649–69.

Oyèwúmi, Ověrónké (1997) *The Invention of Women: Making an African Sense of Western Gender Discourses*. Minneapolis: University of Minnesota Press.

Parker, Richard (2010) "Reinventing Sexual Scripts: Sexuality and Social Change in the Twenty-First Century (The 2008 John H. Gagnon Distinguished Lecture on Sexuality, Modernity and Change)." *Sexuality Research and Social Policy* 7: 58–66.

Parsons, Talcott and Robert Bales (1953) *Family, Socialization, and Interaction Process*. Glencoe, IL: Free Press.

Pascoe, C. J. (2007) *Dude, You're a Fag: Masculinity and Sexuality in High School*. Berkeley, CA: University of California Press.

Petersen, Amy (2006) "An African-American Woman with Disabilities: The Intersection of Gender, Race and Disability." *Disability and Society* 21(7): 721–34.

Pierce, Jennifer (1996) *Gender Trials: Emotional Lives in Contemporary Law Firms*. Berkeley, CA: University of California Press.

Pillow, Wanda S. and Cris Mayo (2007) "Toward Understandings of Feminist Ethnography." In Sharlene Nagy Hesse-Biber (ed.), *Handbook of Feminist Research: Theory and Praxis*. Thousand Oaks, CA: Sage, pp. 155–71.

Plante, Rebecca (2006) *Sexualities in Context: A Social Perspective*. Boulder, CO: Westview Press.

Plummer, Ken (1975) *Sexual Stigma: An Interactionist Account*. London: Routledge and Kegan Paul.

Plummer, Ken (1995) *Telling Sexual Stories: Power, Change and Social Worlds*. London: Routledge.

Plummer, Ken (2003) *Intimate Citizenship: Private Decisions and Public Dialogues*. Seattle: University of Washington Press.

Purkayastha, Bandana (2010) "Interrogating Intersectionality: Contemporary Globalisation and Racialised Gendering in the Lives of Highly Educated South Asian Americans and Their Children." *Journal of Intercultural Studies* 31(1): 29–47.

Ramirez, Renya (2007) "Race, Tribal Nation, and Gender: A Native Feminist Approach to Belonging." *Meridians* 7(2): 22–40.

Rich, Adrienne (1980) "Compulsory Heterosexuality and Lesbian Existence." *Signs: Journal of Women in Culture and Society* 5(4): 631–60.

Richardson, Diane (2000) "Claiming Citizenship: Sexuality, Citizenship and Lesbian/Feminist Theory." *Sexualities* 3(2): 255–72.

Ridgeway, Cecilia (1992) *Gender, Interaction, and Inequality*. New York: Springer-Verlag.

Ridgeway, Cecilia and Shelley J. Correll (2004) "Unpacking the Gender System: A Theoretical Perspective on Gender Beliefs and Social Relations." *Gender and Society* 18(4): 510–31.

Risman, Barbara (1998) *Gender Vertigo: American Families in Transition*. New Haven, CT: Yale University Press.

Risman, Barbara (2004) "Gender as a Social Structure: Theory Wrestling with Activism." *Gender and Society* 18(4): 429–50.

Risman, Barbara J. and Pepper Schwartz (1988) *Gender in Intimate Relationships: A Micro-Structural Approach*. New York: Wadsworth.

Roscoe, Will (1997) "Gender Diversity in Native North America: Notes Toward a Unified Analysis." In Martin Duberman (ed.), *A Queer World*. New York: Center for Lesbian and Gay Studies, CUNY, pp. 65–86.

Rothman, Barbara Katz (1991) *In Labor: Women and Power in the Birthplace*. New York: W. W. Norton.

Roughgarden, Joan (2004) *Evolution's Rainbow: Diversity, Gender, and Sexuality in Nature and People*. Berkeley, CA: University of California Press.

Rowbotham, Sheila (1981) *Beyond the Fragments: Feminism and the Making of Socialism*. London: Merlin Press.

Rubin, Gayle (1984) "Thinking Sex: Notes for a Radical Theory of the Politics of Sexuality." In Carole S. Vance (ed.), *Pleasure and Danger: Exploring Female Sexuality*. London: Pandora, pp. 267–319.

Ruddick, Sara (1989) *Maternal Thinking: Towards a Politics of Peace*. Boston: Beacon Press.

Ruether, Rosemary Radford (1983) *Sexism and God-Talk: Towards a Feminist Theology*. Boston: Beacon Press.

Runyan, Anne Sisson (1999) "Women in the Neoliberal 'Frame'." In Mary K. Meyer and Elisabeth Prugl (eds.), *Gender Politics in Global Governance*. Lanham, MD: Rowman and Littlefield, pp. 210–20.

Rupp, Leila J. and Verta Taylor (2003) *Drag Queens at the 801 Cabaret*. Chicago: University of Chicago Press.

Sagarin, Edward (1972) *Odd Man In: Societies of Deviants in America*. New York: Quadrangle Books.

Sainsbury, Diane (ed.) (2000) *Gender and Welfare State Regimes*. New York: Oxford University Press.

Salzinger, Leslie (2003) *Genders in Production: Making Workers in Mexico's Global Factories*. Berkeley, CA: University of California Press.

Sandahl, Carrie (2003) "Queering the Crip or Cripping the Queer? Intersections of Queer and Crip Identities in Solo Autobiographical Performance." *GLQ: A Journal of Lesbian and Gay Studies* 9(1–2): 25–56.

Sandoval, Chela (2000) *Methodology of the Oppressed*. Minneapolis: University of Minnesota Press.

Sassen, Saskia (1996) "Cities and Communities in the Global Economy." *American Behavioral Scientist* 39(5): 629–39.

Schmidt, Johanna (2003) "Paradise Lost? Social Change and Fa'afafine in Samoa." *Current Sociology* 51(3–4): 417–32.

Schmitt, Arno (2003) "Gay Rights versus Human Rights: A Response to Joseph Massad." *Public Culture* 15(3): 587–91.

Seidman, Steve (ed.) (1996) *Queer Theory/Sociology*. Oxford: Blackwell.

Shand, Aimee (2005) "Invisibility, Globalization, and the Struggle for 'Lesbian' Rights in the Third World." Paper presented at Women's Studies Conference, Florida Atlantic University, Boca Raton, Florida, March 16–17.

Shapiro, Eve (2010) *Gender Circuits: Bodies and Identities in a Technological Age*. New York: Routledge.

Simpson, Leeann (2006) "Birthing an Indigenous Resurgence." In D. Memee Lavell-Harvard and Jeannette Corbiere Lavell (eds.), *"Until Our Hearts Are on the Ground": Aboriginal Mothering, Oppression, Resistance and Rebirth*. Toronto: Demeter Press, pp. 25–33.

Skocpol, Theda (1995) *Protecting Soldiers and Mothers: The Political Origins of Social Policy in the United States*. Cambridge, MA: Belknap Press of Harvard University Press.

Smith, Andrea (2005) *Conquest: Sexual Violence and American Indian Genocide*. Cambridge, MA: South End Press.

Smith, Anna Maria (2007) *Welfare Reform and Sexual Regulation*. New York: Cambridge University Press.

Smith, Barbara (1998) *The Truth That Never Hurts: Writings on Race, Gender, and Freedom*. New Brunswick, NJ: Rutgers University Press.

Smith, Dorothy E. (1987) *The Everyday World as Problematic: A Feminist Sociology*. Toronto: University of Toronto Press.

Smith, Dorothy E. (2005) *Institutional Ethnography: A Sociology for People*. Lanham, MD: AltaMira.

Sokoloff, Natalie J. (1980) *Between Money and Love: The Dialectics of Women's Home and Market Work*. New York: Praeger.

Sokoloff, Natalie J. (ed.) (2005) *Domestic Violence at the Margins: Readings in Race, Class, Gender, and Culture*. New Brunswick, NJ: Rutgers University Press.

Stacey, Judith and Tey Meadow (2009) "New Slants on the Slippery Slope: The Politics of Polygamy and Gay Family Rights in South Africa and the United States." *Politics and Society* 37(2): 167–202.

Staudt, Kathleen (2008) *Violence and Activism at the Border: Gender, Fear, and Everyday Life in Ciudad Juárez*. Austin, TX: University of Texas Press.

Stubblefield, Anna (2007) "Beyond the Pale: Tainted Whiteness, Cognitive Disability, and Eugenic Sterilization." *Hypatia* 22(2): 162–81.

Summerhawk, Barbara, Cheiron McMahill, and Darren McDonald (1998) *Queer Japan: Personal Stories of Japanese Lesbians, Gays, Transsexuals and Bisexuals*. Norwich, VT: New Victoria.

GENDERS AND SEXUALITIES IN GLOBAL CONTEXT 331

Thayer, Miller (2010a) *Making Transnational Feminism: Rural Women, NGO Activists, and Northern Donors in Brazil*. New York: Routledge.

Thayer, Millie (2010b) "Translations and Refusals: Resignifying Meanings as Feminist Political Practice." *Feminist Studies* 36(1): 200–30.

Thompson, Becky W. (1996) *Hunger So Wide and So Deep: A Multiracial View of Women's Eating Problems*. Minneapolis: University of Minnesota Press.

Thompson, Rosemarie Garland (1997) *Extraordinary Bodies: Figuring Physical Disability in American Culture and Literature*. New York: Columbia University Press.

Thorne, Barrie (1997) *Gender Play: Girls and Boys in School*. New Brunswick, NJ: Rutgers University Press.

Tripp, Aili and Myra Ferree (eds.) (2006) *Global Feminism: Transnational Women's Activism, Organizing, and Human Rights*. New York: New York University Press.

Turner, William B. (2000) *A Genealogy of Queer Theory*. Philadelphia, PA: Temple University Press.

Valentine, David (2007) *Imagining Transgender: An Ethnography of a Category*. Durham, NC: Duke University Press.

Vasey, Paul and Nancy Bartlett (2007) "What Can the Samoan Fa'afafine Teach Us about the Western Concept of Gender Identity Disorder in Childhood?" *Perspectives in Biology and Medicine* 50(4): 481–91.

Villalón, Roberta (2010) *Violence Against Latina Immigrants: Citizenship, Inequality, and Community*. New York: New York University Press.

Wajcman, Judy (2004) *Techno Feminism*. Cambridge: Polity Press.

Washington, Patricia A. and Lynda Dixon Shaver (1997) "The Language Culture of Rap Videos." In Joseph K. Adjaye and Adrianne R. Andrews (eds.), *Language, Rhythm and Sound: Black Popular Cultures into the Twenty First Century*. Pittsburgh, PA: University of Pittsburgh Press, pp. 164–77.

Walters, Suzanna (1995) *Material Girls: Making Sense of Feminist Cultural Theory*. Berkeley, CA: University of California Press.

Weeks, Jeffrey (1996) "The Idea of a Sexual Community." In *Making Sexual History*. Oxford: Polity Press, pp. 181–93.

Weiler, Kathleen (1987) *Women Teaching for Change: Gender, Class and Power*. Westport, CT: Bergin & Garvey.

Weir, Angela and Mary McIntosh (1982) "Towards a Wages Strategy for Women." *Feminist Review* 10: 5–20.

Wendell, Susan (1996) *The Rejected Body: Feminist Philosophical Reflections on Disability*. New York: Routledge.

West, Candace and Sarah Fenstermaker (1995) "Doing Difference." *Gender and Society* 9(1): 8–37.

West, Candace and Don H. Zimmerman (1987) "Doing Gender." *Gender and Society* 1: 125–51.

Wharton, Amy (2006) "Understanding Diversity of Work in the 21st Century and Its Impact on the Work-Family Area of Study." In Marcie Pitt-Catsouphes, Ellen Kossek, and Stephen Sweet (eds.), *The Work-Family Handbook: Multi-Disciplinary Perspectives and Approaches*. Mahwah, NJ: Lawrence Erlbaum Associates, pp. 17–40.

Whitaker, Brian (2006) *Unspeakable Love: Gay and Lesbian Life in the Middle East*. Berkeley, CA: University of California Press.

Williams, Christine L. (1992) "The Glass Escalator: Hidden Advantages for Men in the 'Female' Professions." *Social Problems* 39: 253–67.

Wilson, Richard A. (ed.) (1997) *Human Rights, Culture and Context: Anthropological Perspectives*. London: Pluto Press.

Wing, Susanna (2002) "Women Activists in Mali: The Global Discourse on Human Rights." In Nancy A. Naples and Manisha Desai (eds.), *Women's Activism and Globalization: Linking Local Struggles with Transnational Politics*. New York: Routledge, pp. 172–85.

Winter, Bronwyn (2010) "Preemptive Fridge Magnets and Other Weapons of Masculinist Destruction: The Rhetoric and Reality of 'Safeguarding Australia'." *Signs: Journal of Women in Culture and Society* 33(11): 25–51.

Wintermute, Robert and Mads Andenaes (2001) *Legal Recognition of Same-Sex Partnerships: A Study of National, European, and International Law*. Oxford: Hart Publishing.

Young, Iris (1981) "Beyond the Unhappy Marriage: A Critique of Dual Systems Theory." In Lydia Sargent (ed.), *Women and Revolution*. Boston: South End Press, pp. 71–90.

Yuval-Davis, Nira (1997) *Gender and Nation*. London: Sage.

Zheng, Wang and Ying Zhang (2010) "Global Concepts, Local Practice, Chinese Feminism Since the Fourth UN Conference on Women." *Feminist Studies* 36(1): 40–70.

Zitzelsberger, Hilde (2005) "(In)visibility: Accounts of Embodiment of Women with Physical Disabilities and Differences." *Disability and Society* 20(4): 389–403.

18

Changing Families

Fluidity, Partnership, and Family Structure

GRAHAM ALLAN AND EMMA HEAD

Over the last 30 years, patterns of family living have altered quite dramatically across a wide range of industrialized societies. Changes have affected many areas of family life including household composition, age and rates of marriage, patterns of childbearing, trends in cohabitation, the numbers of gay and lesbian partnerships, levels of separation, divorce, and remarriage/re-partnering, and the numbers of lone-parent households and stepfamilies (Teachman, Tedrow & Crowder 2000; Cherlin 2004; Seltzer, Bachrach, Bianchi, et al. 2005; Cherlin 2010). At the heart of many of these changes lie shifts in practices of family formation and dissolution, which in turn are linked to changes in socially acceptable ways of constructing and terminating committed domestic/sexual partnerships (Kiernan 2004; Le Bourdais & Lapierre-Adamcyk 2004; Smock 2004). For most of the twentieth century, these matters were comparatively uniform. A period of engagement was followed by a lifelong marriage, in which, typically, children were born. The marriage ended with the death of one of the spouses. By the turn of the twenty-first century, though, there was far more diversity in family pathways. Increasingly the family courses that individuals' lives now follow lack the clear-cut and predictable structure evident in earlier generations' experiences.

Numerous social theorists have linked this greater demographic complexity in domestic/sexual partnerships to changes in the structural characteristics of late modern societies (Giddens 1992; Beck & Beck-Gernsheim 1995; Bauman 2003). More specifically, contemporary social and economic conditions are seen as associated with a greater individualism and with fuller rights of citizenship. Key factors here include the impact of increased educational and employment opportunities for women, the growth of sexual freedoms and expression, and a greater acceptance of personal happiness as a legitimate goal for all. The evident diversity and greater freedom in the construction of family life has also had significant consequences for theorizing about family relationships. In the past, the focus tended to be on the characteristics of relatively static family forms, particularly the operation of the nuclear family. Increasingly, though, agency has come more to the fore. Family sociologists have needed to develop frameworks which examine processes of transition that are more varied and less predictable.

This is evident in two of the major developments that have influenced perspectives on family sociology over the last two decades. The first of these is an increased emphasis on the active construction of relationships. There has been a strong move away from viewing relationships as predominantly normative, whereby individuals are seen as uncritically and somewhat passively following a conventional social script that effectively structures their domestic/familial roles. Instead there has been increased focus on the flexibility there is in the ways individuals construct their different relationships. Attention is now more on the "doing" of family relationships (Nelson 2006), on "negotiating" them across time (Finch & Mason 1993), and on diversity of "family practices" (Morgan 1996, 2011).

The second development to underline here concerns shifts in social understandings of who comprises "family." There have been a number of issues that have given rise to these shifts, four of which warrant highlighting here. The first of these concerns recent increases in stepfamily membership. The question of who is and who is not "family," and what responsibilities are or are not entailed, is rarely straightforward (Ganong & Coleman 2004; Pryor 2008). Second, there has been the growth of cohabitation which also raises questions about the boundaries of family membership for both the cohabitees and for their other family members (Cherlin 2004; Kiernan 2004). Third, new quandaries about family relatedness have emerged as a result of developments in *in vitro* fertilization (Strathern 2005; Edwards & Salazar 2009). And fourth, research on gay and lesbian family commitment has opened up questions around the construction of "families of choice," whereby family membership is not understood as inevitably dependent on biological and/or marital connection, but more through the demonstration of commitment and solidarity within personal networks (Weston 1991; Weeks, Heaphy & Donovan 2001). Issues like these have made "family" seem far less "given" than was the case for much mid-twentieth-century family sociology, and have encouraged perspectives which embrace ideas of agency and diversity within the evidently *social* construction of family membership.

FLEXIBILITY AND CHOICE: THE EXAMPLE OF COHABITATION

In a chapter of this length it is not possible to consider all these issues fully. Instead we will illustrate some of the processes involved by concentrating on a small number of topics. We will begin with one of the most significant shifts that has been occurring over the last 30 years: the growth of cohabitation. This change in the social patterning of sexual/domestic partnership has been quite remarkable, not only representing a radical move in social mores but also encapsulating many of the main

drivers that have led to other shifts in familial and partnership behavior. In particular, the popularity of cohabitation as a mode of partnership reflects a decline in
the rigidity of social control exercised over couples and a growth in acceptance of
the personal realm as essentially a matter for those involved to determine. This is
not to argue that there are no social controls operating; it is merely to recognize
that the practice of sexual and domestic partnerships is increasingly understood to
be more a matter of private than public concern (Allan & Crow 2001; Lewis 2001).

As noted, cohabitation as a mode of relationship has become more common
across the Western or industrially advanced world. However, for much of the early
and middle parts of the twentieth century non-marital cohabitation was considered
socially deviant and morally disreputable. Marriage signified respectability for the
individual, and for his or her family, but also institutionally. Employers, financial
organizations and the like valued marriage as a symbol of adult stability and social
embeddedness. Indeed it was only as divorce became more acceptable that cohabitation began to increase. In both Europe and North America there was comparatively little cohabitation before the 1960s and that which there was tended to involve
people who were maritally separated or divorced. Even in the late 1960s, very few
never-married couples cohabited. In the UK, for example, at this time fewer than 5
percent of couples lived publicly together prior to their marriage. One reason for
this was that it was extremely difficult for them to acquire housing without the
social legitimacy of marriage. By the end of the 1970s, around 20 percent of couples
marrying for the first time had previously lived together, a significant change over
a decade (GHS 1992).

Over the next 30 years, changes in cohabitation behavior became even more
marked. By the late 1980s, in the UK, cohabitation had become the dominant route
into marriage, with over 50 percent of couples marrying for the first time having
previously lived together. In other words, by this time cohabitation had become the
normal form of "engagement" and/or preparation for marriage (GHS 1992). More
radically, though, by the end of the twentieth century, the connection between
cohabitation and marriage had been broken. What was until then seen as an appropriate way for couples to express commitment and use as a route into marriage
became more evidently an alternative form of partnership. Throughout Western
countries, cohabitation came to be accepted, whether or not there was an intention
to enter into marriage at some future date; it was, in other words, regarded socially
as an increasingly unremarkable way of being a couple (Cherlin 2004; Le Bourdais
& Lapierre-Adamcyk 2004; Manning & Smock 2005). In Britain, roughly a third
of all women between the ages of 18 and 49 were cohabiting in 2008 (ONS 2010a).
Similar shifts have emerged in other comparable countries (Kiernan 2004). For
example in the US approximately 17 percent of women aged 15–44 living in a
couple relationship in 2002 were cohabiting (Goodwin, Mosher & Chandra 2010),
while in Canada nearly a fifth of all couples were cohabiting in 2006 (Milan, Vézina
& Wells 2007). Of course there are cultural variations in the detailed patterns of
cohabitation change, influenced by ethnic, religious, and legal differences, but the
growth of cohabitation as a legitimate form of partnership is comparatively uniform
across Western societies.

This has created far greater diversity in partnership patterns than was previously
the case. Divorce and remarriage of course complicated the "partnership pathways"

different individuals experienced over time, but the growth of cohabitation has taken this a stage further. An important set of factors generating diversity concerns the level of commitment expressed and experienced by the couple, a factor which for many is likely to be emergent and, thus, liable to alter over the lifetime of the relationship. Some couples especially at the beginning may define their relationship as comparatively temporary, a "for now" or "until things change" arrangement. For others, the intention will be more "marriage-like," with the relationship being seen as committed in the long run (Jamieson, Anderson, McCrone, Bechhofer, Stewart & Yaojun 2002; Manning & Smock 2005).

With the more diverse commitments there are with cohabitation, so too the ways the relationships are constructed by those involved are more diverse. Some couples quite deliberately aim for their cohabitation to be different from marriage. They want to construct a tie that is not constrained by the social assumptions or legal rights that are constituent of marriage. They want, for example, to create a more equal union or one which has greater relational freedom for both individuals. Equally some do not wish to be trapped by existing gender presumptions or by ideas of shared material resources. Others may cohabit because they are not yet ready for marriage, but nonetheless want to create a "marriage-like" partnership that in most respects mirrors their understanding of what marriage entails. They may not have the legal rights and responsibilities of marriage, but they create a relationship that in terms of day-to-day organization is little different (Manning & Smock 2005; Goodwin, Mosher & Chandra 2010).

COHABITATION AND FAMILY RELATIONSHIPS

All this creates many fascinating questions for family sociologists. It not only highlights the flexibility there now is in the decisions couples make about the construction of their partnerships, and thus focuses the sociological gaze on the role of choice and agency in family matters. More substantively, it opens up a set of concerns about, *inter alia*, the nature of commitment, its different dimensions, and changes in social understandings of what commitment means. Similarly it shines a new light on other issues which have proved core to family sociology. For example, what patterns of money management are characteristic of cohabitation? How different is domestic abuse and its relational consequences outside of formal marriage? Do different divisions of labor emerge in cohabitation and are these sustained in the long run? What impact do children have on cohabiting partnerships, and does the formality of marriage make any real difference here? In raising such questions as these, the increased incidence and social acceptance of cohabitation has encouraged a fresh engagement with substantive issues that lie at the heart of much family sociology.

As mentioned earlier, the growth of cohabitation also connects with increased sociological debate about the constitution of family. In the past, these issues seemed relatively clear-cut, with blood connection and marriage defining common understandings of kinship. (See Schneider [1968], for the classic account of this.) The changes of the last 30 years have led to this being questioned. The increased prevalence of cohabitation has itself clearly been one of these changes. The simple question is: "When does a cohabitee come to be regarded as part of one's kinship?"

With marriage the issue is comparatively straightforward. The marriage ceremony itself, with its attached rights and obligations, is routinely taken as signifying the start of kinship. In a sense this is what marriage means, with the ceremony symbolizing the creation of the "new" family. With cohabitation, there typically is no ceremony; there is no symbolic moment when the creation of "family" is socially recognized, leaving the issue of family membership more fuzzy and indeterminate (Manning & Smock 2005).

The absence of ceremony does not rule out cohabitees being recognized as family, though some are clearly not. However, whether, when, and in what regard they are varies over time as well as with relational position. For the couple, it may be a matter of personal commitment. If commitment is experienced as high and long-term, then a sense of "family" may be recognized. For the couple's kin, on the other hand, determination of the cohabitees' family status may be more varied. It could, for example, depend on length of the relationship and its perceived stability; it may only develop with the birth of a child; or it may depend on issues of personal and family network compatibility. Moreover perceptions about family membership are likely to be influenced by legal constructions.

The growth of cohabitation has meant that different jurisdictions are having to consider adjusting their legislation governing partnership rights. Giving legal protections to couples who have chosen not to have their partnership legally recognized is a contentious and complex matter. The more a society assigns legal rights and obligations to cohabiting couples, the more similar from a legal perspective cohabitation becomes to marriage, an issue of consequence for those who are choosing to cohabit as a deliberate alternative (at least at this stage of their relationship) to marriage. Canada provides an interesting example, as federal legislation gives many of the rights attached to marriage to any couple who have cohabited for a year or more. In its extreme, such a treatment of cohabitation renders the distinction between marriage and cohabitation of little consequence, a practice that in turn is likely to influence everyday understandings of family membership (Le Bourdais & Lapierre-Adamcyk 2004; Kerr, Moyser & Beaujot 2006).

Equally, though, these changes are also wrapped up with changes in people's understandings of marriage (Cherlin 2004). The increased acceptance of cohabitation, along with that of divorce, has been integral to shifts in the "doing" of sexual and emotional intimacy and, in turn, to the expectations about what people can reasonably require of their marriages. Giddens (1992) was right to highlight the "transformation of intimacy," even if his analysis can be criticized for underplaying the material and emotional constraints of "family," especially when there are children involved (Jamieson 1999). Allowing for personal, socio-economic, and cultural differences, individuals are no longer as trapped in loveless or "empty-shell" marriages as they once were. Not only is there considerably less moral value now placed on staying in unhappy marriages than on ending them and attempting to rebuild happier futures, but, as importantly, what constitutes an unhappy marriage has itself been re-defined. Relational behavior that was once tolerated is no longer seen as acceptable, instead being taken as grounds for ending the tie. In this regard marriage has become increasingly personal. Culturally, the point of the relationship is defined as principally about personal satisfaction, or, in more romantic language, "love."

PARENTING

A second area that demonstrates the increasing levels of diversity and flexibility that have developed in family practices is that of parenting. One key issue to consider concerns the demographic changes that have been occurring in transitions to parenthood. There are three related elements of consequence here: the age at which people become parents for the first time; the partnership status of new parents; and increasing levels of intentional childlessness. As with cohabitation, these changes in patterns of childbearing reflect significant shifts in social understandings of the relationship between sex, marriage, and childbearing. In the early twenty-first century, norms and expectations around the demography of parenting are clearly quite different from those that were dominant throughout most of the previous century.

The age at which women first become mothers is one aspect of this. While there is a degree of class, ethnic, and educational variation here (Smock & Greenland 2010), across Western societies in general age at first birth has steadily increased since the 1970s. In the UK, for example, the average age of mothers giving birth to their first child in the mid-1970s was around 24 (Ruddock, Wood & Quinn 1998). By 2008, it had become 27.5 (ONS 2010b). In the US it was 25.0 in 2006, an increase of 3.6 years since 1970. However there are very clear ethnic differences in this. In 2006, the average age of non-Hispanic white American mothers having their first child was 26.0; for Hispanic mothers it was 23.1; and for Black American mothers it was 22.7 (Mathews & Hamilton 2009). It is also worth noting here that women in general are bearing fewer children than they did in the past, raising concerns within a number of Western societies about levels of replacement fertility (Lauster & Allan 2011).

Over the last 30 years or so there has also been a move away from the norm that couples should marry before the birth, and ideally before the conception, of their first child. There is now far greater social acceptance of unmarried childbearing, be the mothers involved cohabiting or single and unpartnered. In 2007, very nearly 40 percent of American women giving birth were unmarried; in 1980 the proportion had been less than half this (18.4 percent) (Ventura 2009). In 2007 around half of these unmarried mothers were cohabiting at the time of the birth, while the other half were unpartnered (Cherlin 2010). In the UK, 55 percent of births in 2008 were to married couples and 30 percent to cohabiting parents (ONS 2009). However, as with mother's age at first birth, these general trends mask a diversity of women's experiences linked to their ethnicity, place of birth, religion, and level of educational attainment (Smock & Greenland 2010). For example, some 98 percent of those women living in the UK but born in India, Pakistan, or Bangladesh who gave birth in 2008 were married (ONS 2009). This contrasts with just under 50 percent of UK-born women. Similarly in the US in 2006, the birth rate per 1,000 unmarried women was 32 for non-Hispanic white women, 72 for black women, and 106 for Hispanic women (Ventura 2009).

Whether married or not, the large majority of women do become mothers at some point in their lives. However, rates of childlessness have been increasing markedly in recent decades. In the US one in five women aged 40–44 years are currently childless, double the rate of childlessness of 30 years ago (Dye 2008). A number of factors have contributed to this rising rate of childlessness, including the increased education and employment opportunities for women and the greater control women have over their reproductive lives through the ready availability of effective contraception. As with the other changes we have discussed here, this also reflects the greater agency granted individuals in personal and family matters and, in turn, the increased flexibility now evident in life-course construction.

Becoming a parent, and especially a mother, at whatever age this takes place, represents what Umberson, Pudrovska and Reczek term "a pivotal life course transition" (2010: 614). However it was only in the 1970s that this transition began to be examined seriously by sociologists. In the UK, Oakley's (1974, 1980) early work on becoming and being a mother has proved to be of lasting influence. Oakley explored the experience of becoming a mother in the British context at a time when women tended to leave the labor market, often for an extended period, when their children were born. She identified a gap between the expectations that women had of pregnancy, childbirth, and motherhood and the reality of these experiences. In particular, her work highlighted both the joys and the dissatisfactions of motherhood and the contradictions that existed between the then dominant ideologies of motherhood and the impact mothering had on the structure of women's everyday lives.

More recent research in the sociology of motherhood continues to explore the impact on women's lives of becoming a mother and their experiences of mothering. A dominant theme in these more recent accounts is a focus on the way a woman's relationship to the labor market shapes her performance of motherhood. Of particular importance in this area has been Sharon Hays' (1996) work in which she identifies the "cultural contradictions" of being both a mother and an employee in a (North American) culture pervaded by what she terms an "ideology of intensive mothering." Hays argues that there are opposing logics at play in the separate worlds of business in the public sphere and childrearing in the private sphere. While business works on the principles of self-interest and profit maximization, the ideology of intensive mothering demands that the needs of children are prioritized. Additionally, this ideology of intensive mothering requires that mothers spend a "tremendous amount of time, energy, and money" on meeting the perceived – and culturally informed – "needs" of their children (Hays 1996: x).

Anita Garey (1999) contributes further to these discussions of motherhood and employment by critiquing the dominant cultural image of women in the US as being either work-oriented or family-oriented. Her empirical research powerfully dispels this notion. Garey's argument is that such an "either/or" model of orientation to work and family "obscures the integration and connectedness" (1999: 8) of women's involvement in both spheres – paid work and family life. Instead, Garey adopts the metaphor of "weaving" as a way to understand the lives of employed mothers, thereby bypassing the problematic oppositional construction of paid work and motherhood in women's lives.

Until recent times the relationship between work and family for men has been rather easier to characterize. The dominant construction of fatherhood for much of the twentieth century was as "breadwinner," so employment was seen as central to the role of fathers as the financial providers for their family. However, much current sociological work on fatherhood focuses on the ways in which change may be occurring. As Dermott comments, "[t]here is general agreement among researchers that fatherhood has altered over the last century but there is less consensus over the degree and way in which change has occurred" (2006: 619). In a US context, Cabrera, Tamis-LaMonda, Bradley, and Hofferth (2000) note that the greater participation of mothers in the labor market means that only around a quarter of children living in two-parent households are in families where fathers are the sole breadwinners.

In the light of higher levels of divorce and single motherhood, the role of men in family life has increasingly been debated by social commentators of different persuasions as well as in the media. As policy initiatives emphasizing the rights of separated fathers attest, there is increasing acceptance that fathers' participation in their children's lives results in beneficial outcomes for the children. However, the extent and nature of the changes there have been in men's involvement in family life can be difficult to assess and remain somewhat contentious among family sociologists. A key issue concerns whether fathers who are co-resident with their children have become more involved in the daily lives and direct care of their children. Implicit in these debates is the idea that there has been the emergence of the "new" father who is involved with the care of his children and challenges the traditional norms of masculinity and a fatherhood role based on discipline (Lupton & Barclay 1997).

A range of research data in the UK context confirms that the time fathers spend with their children increased appreciably between the 1970s and the first decade of the twenty-first century. However, as Featherstone (2009) indicates in her discussion of the research evidence in this area, the methodological problems involved in investigating time use, the complexity of the research data, and the diverse nature of change in different national contexts make generalization about the changes occurring difficult. Moreover, as might be expected, the nature and extent of change appears to vary within different national contexts and between fathers from different social and ethnic backgrounds. For example, Canadian and American fathers in full-time employment reported more daily involvement with their children than fathers employed full-time in Germany or Australia (Featherstone 2009). In addition, the changes in the demography of partnership discussed earlier in this chapter – and in particular the consequent prevalence of non-residential fathers and stepfathers – add further diversity to the ways in which fathering is done. As Cabrera et al. (2000) argue, any notion of a universal model of fatherhood is difficult to sustain, especially so if it involves a sense of uniform transition. As with other aspects of family life, the construction of fatherhood – and for that matter motherhood – is now characterized by greater flexibility and diversity than was the case in the past.

FLEXIBILITY AND FAMILY STRUCTURE

In discussing contemporary partnerships in the first part of this chapter we emphasized the increased choice and flexibility apparent in the ways in which people constitute their domestic and sexual relationships. We want to return to these issues here, though from the perspective of family structure rather than partnership behavior. For most of the twentieth century, the classic family structure within Western societies was taken to be the nuclear family. This form was legitimized as normative as well as normal. Increasingly, however, the changes there have been have led to greater social acceptance of alternative modes of family organization. Not only are lone-parent families, families co-parenting across different households, stepfamilies, and the like more common than they were, but, as importantly, these family forms are increasingly accepted as viable and legitimate alternatives to the standard nuclear family. Equally, there is now a much broader incidence of "child-free" families and households. These include both child-free heterosexual, gay, and lesbian families, whether based on marriage or cohabitation, and single person and other non-family households (Bulcroft & Teachman 2004; Rowland 2007; Jamieson, Wasoff & Simpson 2009).

However the key issue is not just that this range of family forms now occurs, or even that such forms are given greater legitimacy. Of equal importance is that individuals often experience a number of these family forms across their life course. Singlehood, cohabitation, marriage, stepfamily living can all occur and re-occur in diverse fashion as people's partnerships develop and wane. The majority pattern may still be for individuals to have a single "life partner," but, as discussed earlier, even when this is so, the routes into this lifelong partnership are far more varied than they were (Sassler 2010). This has significant consequences for family structure, not just in the obvious sense of who it is who lives with whom at any time, but more significantly in terms of the patterning of long-term kinship obligation and responsibility. Within the nuclear family model, especially that classically associated with the writings of Talcott Parsons (1959), the primary obligation was between spouses and their dependent children; other family ties were not unimportant but they were given lower priority. The shifts there have been in the temporal and moral construction of partnerships have rendered this prioritizing of commitment less dominant.

Indeed, in an important paper Vern Bengtson (2001) argues that the changes in partnership and childbirth there have been have resulted in a shift in the key structural bonds within the American family system. Rather than the emphasis being on marriage and dependent children, at a systemic level it is multi-generational ties that are increasingly important. Put a little over-simply, partners and spouses now offer less secure commitment and solidarity than they did when lifelong marriage was more clearly the norm. Instead the family ties that can be relied on most fully are generational ties of direct descent, ties between grandparents, parents, and (grand)children. In particular, it is relationships between grandmothers, mothers, and their children that, for many, provide the most enduring commitment and support and which are core to the contemporary kinship system. Whether or not this element of Bengtson's argument is accepted, it is certainly the case that in many families maternal grandparents, and grandmothers especially, are highly involved in sustaining and managing the routines of family living.

One aspect of this in the US is the number of grandparents who are involved in providing high levels of care for one or more of their grandchildren. Goodman and Silverstein (2002) estimated that more than 6 percent of all children in the US were being raised in grandparental households. Often this is a consequence of mothers being unable to provide adequately for their children, sometimes through illness, at other times through substance dependency or imprisonment. In such circumstances, grandmothers are frequently the ones who provide dependent children with stability, support, and security (Hayslip & Hicks Patrick 2006). However, grandparental participation in family matters is far wider than this; to perceive it solely as a response to problematic parenting is to misunderstand its basis. Central to these relationships is the diffuse and enduring solidarity which remains central to "blood" connection within US and other Western constructions of family. For many, grandparents routinely and willingly act as a flexible resource for material and emotional support for their adult children and, directly or indirectly, their grandchildren (Szinovacz 1998; Dench & Ogg 2002; Kemp 2007).

The specific involvement of grandparents in their grandchildren's lives of course varies significantly, depending in part on their particular circumstances. Some grandparents are comparatively young, some quite old. In the UK, for example, most people currently become grandparents for the first time in their early fifties (Clarke & Roberts 2004). Equally some live close to (some of) their grandchildren; others live considerable distances away. Many are juggling complex obligations and responsibilities independently of their grandparental status. In addition, some embrace the role of grandparent more actively than others. As a result the forms of participation that grandparents have with the second and third generation vary widely. In general, though, most feel a relatively strong sense of connection with their grandchildren, expressed in terms of enduring love and commitment. Although patterns of divorce and separation impact on this, these relationships are typically reported as being highly meaningful by grandparents, particularly grandmothers (Szinovacz 1998; Dench & Ogg 2002; Ochiltree 2006).

While this is so, the specific forms of participation, and consequently the modes of support provided across the generations, are not set in any standard way. Not only are the exchanges involved contextually specific and dependent on the circumstances of each party, but they also involve processes of agency and negotiation (Finch & Mason 1993; Nelson 2006). For reasons embedded in their own circumstances, lifestyle choices, or relational histories, grandparents may seek greater or lesser involvement, and their adult children will only be willing to accept certain levels of grandparental "interference." Nelson's (2006) research on how family, and particularly mothering, is negotiated when young single mothers live with their parents is particularly illuminating about the structural pressures that need managing when grandmothers are routinely and actively involved in childcare provision. Nonetheless, overall there is little doubt that in an era of high levels of marital and partnership separation, reliance on generational support is increasingly significant in the way Bengtson (2001) argues. Even allowing for the impact of paternal disengagement following separation and divorce, these family solidarities are typically "there" to be turned to when support is, for whatever reason, required (Mason, May & Clarke 2007).

The consequences of increased flexibility in the way familial relationships are now ordered are evident in other spheres aside from heightened prioritization of multi-generational ties. It is, for example, clearly reflected in the greater legal and social acceptance of the familial character of gay and lesbian relationships. This is most manifest in the acceptance of gay and lesbian marriage which assigns rights of kinship previously restricted to heterosexual unions. As importantly within the context of what "family" is taken to comprise, some gay and lesbian individuals have been at the forefront of critically questioning assumptions about the "givenness" of family networks. In essence, they have argued for a social rather than biological/legal understanding of what constitutes family. In other words, family comprises those people who have provided levels of solidarity and support that are recognized as "family apposite," irrespective of the genealogical connection there may or may not be (Weeks, Heaphy & Donovan 2001).

Thus, in this formulation, the traditional "givenness" of family membership has been replaced by an emphasis on choice; in Weston's (1991) phrase, "families of choice" consisted of those others who you defined as your family. These others may include some genealogically-based kin, but they could also include friends with no such connection. Family, in this way, becomes a personally selected set of others with whom you have a sufficiently significant relational history to warrant categorization as family. Leaving aside the issue of how readily different individuals do see friends without genealogical connection as family (Allan 2008), the idea of increased choice, flexibility, and individualization within the construction of family networks is an important one which is not limited solely to non-heterosexual lifestyles. While fictive kinship is recognized in many cultures, including Western ones, what is more novel in contemporary kinship constructions is the greater selectivity over who is granted the status of family connection, and in turn what this signifies. In this, family membership, as well as relational content, is negotiable. As a consequence, family structure itself needs to be seen as increasingly negotiated.

A further example of this concerns stepfamily kinship. As a result of other changes in family formation and dissolution, especially rises in divorce and unmarried parenthood, the number of stepfamilies has increased significantly since the mid-twentieth century. This has led to questions about the "relatedness" of different stepfamily members. To the fore here are the "family" connections of residential stepparents and stepchildren. But also relevant are the constructions of kinship ties between non-residential stepparents and stepchildren, between step-siblings, and between step-grandparents and step-grandchildren. There is a good deal of diversity in the involvement of these step-kin with one another, in part depending on the "biographical" pathways taken by each stepfamily, but also reflecting a level of flexibility over the manner in which people choose to develop their network of ties constituent of "family" (Schmeeckle, Giarrusso, Feng & Bengtson 2006; Allan, Hawker & Crow 2008; Allan, Crow & Hawker 2011).

CONCLUSION

In this chapter we have addressed a small number of important changes that have been occurring within the realm of family sociology. In particular, we have discussed the greater fluidity there now is in family patterns. Substantively we have addressed issues relating to partnership formation and dissolution, parenthood and family structure, but we could have chosen to focus on various other issues, such as stepfamily organization, work–life balance, or gendered divisions of paid, domestic, and caring labor. In discussing the issues we have, we also sought to illustrate the changing approaches there are to family sociology. Again we highlighted here the increased emphasis on choice and agency. Structural aspects within the analysis of family life clearly remain important, in particular with regard to the ways material circumstances and cultural expectations pattern the choices individuals make. But there has been an important shift from more traditional normative approaches to ones which highlight the routine yet active construction and achievement of family relationships. Terms like "negotiation," the "doing" of family, family "practices," and others which emphasize *process* play a larger part in the understandings family sociologists are now generating.

These changes in the theoretical perspectives informing much family sociology are, inevitably, part of a wider theoretical movement within sociology as a discipline. They also have implications for the methodologies that are used to research family relationships. To conclude this chapter we want to highlight two methodological approaches which have contributed much to recent understandings of family change. The first of these, most strongly represented in US family sociology, is the increasing use of longitudinal research. The main difficulty with undertaking such research is, of course, its costs, in terms of both money and time. However we now possess an increasing number of surveys which have been mapping how people's family circumstances and experiences have been altering over significant periods of time. This has enabled the emergence of a far better understanding of the impact of different family events than we previously had. Examples include the *National Survey of Families and Households*, *The Fragile Families and Child Well-Being Study*, and the *Marital Instability over the Life Course* surveys in the US and the Dutch *Longitudinal Aging Study Amsterdam*. There are numerous other data sets available which similarly facilitate an understanding of process rather than a given time-specific outcome.

Second, we want to argue for the importance of detailed qualitative research on family processes. Such research may not readily lend itself to generalization, but what it does do is enable researchers to comprehend more fully the detailed processes that generate or lie behind the outcomes that are captured by survey research. In a sense, qualitative research facilitates answers to the "why" or "how come" questions of family patterns in contrast to the "what is happening" questions and findings of more structured survey research. Much family behavior is routine and tacit, unexceptional, and taken for granted by those directly involved. The character of family practices is such that often they emerge without those party to them being fully conscious or aware of their construction. They just "are." Qualitative research allows some of these implicit processes to be uncovered and explored more fully than simply relying on respondents' relatively uncritical accounts in response to survey questioning. Observing family relations is problematic, though not impossible; much family behavior occurs in private settings, though not all of it. Moreover forms of family ethnography have been facilitated by new developments in recording technologies. Detailed qualitative interviewing allows the implicit to be made explicit, especially if it involves multiple interviews and, where feasible, interviews with more than one family member. Whatever the form of the research, though, such qualitative approaches facilitate a deeper understanding of how particular family relationships come to be established as they are.

References

Allan, G. (2008) "Flexibility, Friendship, and Family." *Personal Relationships* 15: 1–16.

Allan, G. and G. Crow (2001) *Families, Households and Society*. Basingstoke: Palgrave.

Allan, G., G. Crow, and S. Hawker (2011) *Stepfamilies*. Basingstoke: Palgrave Macmillan.

Allan, G., S. Hawker, and G. Crow (2008) "Kinship in Stepfamilies." In J. Pryor (ed.), *The International Handbook of Stepfamilies: Policy and Practice in Legal, Research, and Clinical Environments*. Hoboken, NJ: Wiley & Sons, pp. 323–44.

Bauman, Z. (2003) *Liquid Love: On the Frailty of Human Bonds*. Cambridge: Polity Press.

Beck, U. and E. Beck-Gernsheim (1995) *The Normal Chaos of Love*. Cambridge: Polity Press.

Bengtson, V. (2001) "Beyond the Nuclear Family: The Increasing Importance of Multigenerational Bonds." *Journal of Marriage and the Family* 63: 1–16.

Bulcroft, R. and J. Teachman (2004) "Ambiguous Constructions: Development of a Childless or Child-Free Life Course." In M. Coleman and L. Ganong (eds.), *Handbook of Contemporary Families*. Thousand Oaks, CA: Sage, pp. 116–35.

Cabrera, N., S. Tamis-LaMonda, R. Bradley, and S. Hofferth (2000) "Fatherhood in the Twenty-First Century." *Child Development* 71: 127–36.

Cherlin, A. (2004) "The Deinstitutionalization of American Marriage." *Journal of Marriage and Family* 66: 848–61.

Cherlin, A. (2010) "Demographic Trends in the United States: A Review of Research in the 2000s." *Journal of Marriage and Family* 72: 403–19.

Clarke, L. and C. Roberts (2004) "The Meaning of Grandparenthood and Its Contribution to the Quality of Life of Older People." In A. Walker and C. Hennessy (eds.), *Growing Older: Quality of Life in Old Age*. Maidenhead: Open University Press, pp. 188–208.

Dench, G. and J. Ogg (2002) *Grandparenting in Britain*. London: Institute of Community Studies.

Dermott, E. (2006) "What's Parenthood Got to Do with It? Men's Hours of Paid Work." *British Journal of Sociology* 57: 619–34.

Dye, J. (2008) "Fertility of American Women: 2006." www.census.gov/population/www/socdemo/fertility.html

Edwards, J. and C. Salazar (2009) *European Kinship in the Age of Biotechnology*. Oxford: Berghahn Books.

Featherstone, B. (2009) *Contemporary Fathering: Theory, Policy and Practice*. Bristol: Policy Press.

Finch, J. and J. Mason (1993) *Negotiating Family Responsibilities*. London: Routledge.

Ganong, L. and M. Coleman (2004) *Stepfamily Relationships: Development, Dynamics and Interventions*. New York: Kluwer Academic/Plenum.

Garey, A. (1999) *Weaving Work and Motherhood*. Philadelphia, PA: Temple University Press.

GHS (1992) *General Household Survey, 1990*. London: HMSO.

Giddens, A. (1992) *The Transformation of Intimacy*. Cambridge: Polity Press.

Goodman, C. and M. Silverstein (2002) "Grandmothers Raising Grandchildren: Family Structure and Well-Being in Culturally Diverse Families." *The Gerontologist* 42: 676–89.

Goodwin, P., W. Mosher, and A. Chandra (2010) "Marriage and Cohabitation in the United States: A Statistical Portrait Based on Cycle 6 (2002) of the National Survey of Family Growth." www.cdc.gov/nchs/data/series/sr_23/sr23_028.pdf

Hays, S. (1996) *The Cultural Contradictions of Motherhood*. New Haven, CT: Yale University Press.

Hayslip, B. and J. Hicks Patrick (2006) *Custodial Grandparenting: Individual, Cultural, and Ethnic Diversity*. New York: Springer.

Jamieson, L. (1999) "Intimacy Transformed? A Critical Look at the 'Pure Relationship'." *Sociology: The Journal of the British Sociological Association* 33: 477–94.

Jamieson, L., M. Anderson, D. McCrone, F. Bechhofer, R. Stewart, and L. Yaojun (2002) "Cohabitation and Commitment: Partnership Plans of Young Men and Women." *Sociological Review* 50: 356–77.

Jamieson, L., F. Wasoff, and R. Simpson (2009) "Solo-Living, Demographic and Family Change: The Need to Know More about Men." *Sociological Research Online* 14: 5.

Kemp, C. (2007) "Grandparent–Grandchild Ties." *Journal of Family Issues* 28: 855–81.

Kerr, D., M. Moyser, and R. Beaujot (2006) "Marriage and Cohabitation: Demographic and Socioeconomic Differences in Quebec and Canada." *Canadian Studies in Population* 33: 83–117.

Kiernan, K. (2004) "Redrawing the Boundaries of Marriage." *Journal of Marriage and Family* 66: 980–7.

Lauster, N. and G. Allan (2011) *The End of Children? Changing Trends in Childbearing and Childhood*. Vancouver: University of British Columbia Press.

Le Bourdais, C. and E. Lapierre-Adamcyk (2004) "Changes in Conjugal Life in Canada: Is Cohabitation Progressively Replacing Marriage?" *Journal of Marriage and Family* 66: 929–42.

Lewis, J. (2001) *The End of Marriage: Individualism and Intimate Relations*. Cheltenham: Edward Elgar.

Lupton, D. and L. Barclay (1997) *Constructing Fatherhood: Discourses and Experiences*. London: Sage.

Manning, W. D. and P. J. Smock (2005) "Measuring and Modeling Cohabitation: New Perspectives from Qualitative Data." *Journal of Marriage and Family* 67: 989–1002.

Mason, J., V. May, and L. Clarke (2007) "Ambivalence and the Paradoxes of Grandparenting." *Sociological Review* 55: 687–706.

Mathews, T. and B. Hamilton (2009) "Delayed Childbearing: More Women Are Having Their First Child Later in Life." Hyattsville, MD: National Centre for Health Statistics. www.cdc.gov/nchs/data/databriefs/db21.pdf

Milan, A., M. Vézina, and C. Wells (2007) "Family Portrait: Continuity and Change in Canadian Families and Households in 2006." 2006 Census. www12.statcan.gc.ca/english/census06/analysis/famhouse/pdf/97-553-XIE2006001.pdf

Morgan, D. H. J. (1996) *Family Connections*. Cambridge: Polity Press.

Morgan, D. H. J. (2011) *Rethinking Family Practices*. Basingstoke: Palgrave Macmillan.

Nelson, M. (2006) "Single Mothers 'Do' Family." *Journal of Marriage and Family* 68: 781–95.

Oakley, A. (1974) *The Sociology of Housework*. Oxford: Martin Robertson.

Oakley, A. (1980) *Women Confined: Towards a Sociology of Childbirth*. Oxford: Martin Robertson.

Ochiltree, G. (2006) *Grandparents, Grandchildren and the Generation in between*. Melbourne: ACER Press.

ONS (2009) "Statistical Bulletin: Who Is Having Babies? 2008." www.statistics.gov.uk/pdfdir/births1209.pdf

ONS (2010a) "Birth statistics." www.statistics.gov.uk/downloads/theme_population/FM1_37/FM1_37_2008.pdf

ONS (2010b) "General Lifestyle Survey, Overview Report, 2008." www.statistics.gov.uk/downloads/theme_compendia/GLF08/GLFoverview2008.pdf

Parsons, T. (1959) "The Social Structure of the Family." In R. Anshen (ed.), *The Family: Its Function and Destiny*. New York: Harper, pp. 241–74.

Pryor, J. (2008) *The International Handbook of Stepfamilies*. Hoboken, NJ: John Wiley & Sons.

Rowland, D. (2007) "Historical Changes in Childlessness." *Journal of Family Issues* 28: 1311–37.

Ruddock, V., R. Wood, and M. Quinn (1998) "Birth Statistics: Recent Trends in England and Wales." *Population Trends* 94: 12–18.

Sassler, S. (2010) "Partnering across the Lifecourse: Sex, Relationships and Mate Selection." *Journal of Marriage and Family* 72: 557–75.

Schmeeckle, M., R. Giarrusso, D. Feng, and V. L. Bengtson (2006) "What Makes Someone Family? Adult Children's Perceptions of Current and Former Stepparents." *Journal of Marriage and Family* 68: 595–610.

Schneider, D. (1968) *American Kinship: A Cultural Account*. Englewood Cliffs, NJ: Prentice Hall.

Seltzer, J. A., C. A. Bachrach, S. M. Bianchi, et al. (2005) "Explaining Family Change and Variation: Challenges for Family Demographers." *Journal of Marriage and Family* 67: 908–25.

Smock, P. J. (2004) "The Wax and Wane of Marriage: Prospects for Marriage in the 21st Century." *Journal of Marriage and Family* 66: 966–73.

Smock, P. J. and F. Greenland (2010) "Diversity in Pathways to Parenthood: Patterns, Implications, and Emerging Research Directions." *Journal of Marriage and Family* 72: 576–93.

Strathern, M. (2005) *Kinship, Law and the Unexpected: Relatives Are Always a Surprise*. Cambridge: Cambridge University Press.

Szinovacz, M. E. (1998) *Handbook on Grandparenthood*. Westport, CT: Greenwood Press.

Teachman, J., L. Tedrow, and K. Crowder (2000) "The Changing Demography of America's Families." *Journal of Marriage and Family* 62: 1234–46.

Umberson, D., T. Pudrovska, and C. Reczek (2010) "Parenthood, Childlessness and Well-Being: A Life Course Perspective." *Journal of Marriage and Family* 72: 612–29.

Ventura, S. (2009) "Changing Patterns of Nonmarital Childbearing in the United States." Hyattsville, MD: National Centre for Health Statistics. www.cdc.gov/nchs/data/databriefs/db18.htm

Weeks, J., B. Heaphy, and C. Donovan (2001) *Same Sex Intimacies: Families of Choice and Other Life Experiments*. London: Routledge.

Weston, K. (1991) *Families We Choose: Lesbians, Gays, Kinship*. New York: Columbia University Press.

19

Sociology of Education

Maureen T. Hallinan and Ge Liu

The number of studies in the sociology of education has been increasing exponentially over the past few decades. In the early years of the twentieth century, European sociologists were interested in abstract, theoretical ideas about how societal institutions, including education, function. During this period, American sociologists were oriented more toward the empirical study of schools. Applied research was common, examining topics such as leadership, teacher professionalism, and the curriculum.

American sociology of education established itself as a subfield of sociology only in the second half of the twentieth century. As the subfield matured, sociologists of education relied on general sociological theory developed primarily in Europe, to give studies of schools a theoretical foundation. They seldom attempted to formulate new theory specific to the schooling process. Even up to the present time, the primary contribution of sociologists of education in America has been empirical analyses of schooling. These empirical studies were informed by newly developed statistical methods for the analysis of experimental and survey data and, recently, by the availability of large nationally representative longitudinal data sets. This applied work led to progress in understanding how schools function, but shed less light on education as a unique societal institution that interacts with other societal institutions.

THEORETICAL APPROACHES TO THE STUDY OF SOCIOLOGY OF EDUCATION

Sociology of education does not have deep roots in theory. That is partly because sociology itself, as one of the youngest of the social sciences, has not yet

The Wiley-Blackwell Companion to Sociology, First Edition. Edited by George Ritzer.
© 2012 Blackwell Publishing Ltd. Published 2012 by Blackwell Publishing Ltd.

formulated a set of theories capable of explaining a wide array of social phenomena relevant to education. In addition, the attraction of sociologists of education to empirical analyses has directed their attention to basic and applied social problems rather than to grand or middle-range theories that identify and integrate a large number of social processes. Instead, following the lead of its sister disciplines, sociology of education makes reference to grand theories like structural functionalism and conflict theory but without using these theories to develop concepts and propositions specific to how schools work.

In the absence of abstract sociological theory to explain and predict empirical findings about schools, sociologists of education tend to borrow the theoretical frameworks developed in more longstanding social science disciplines. For example, research that analyzes student motivation and effort, attitudes and behavior, or self-confidence, may employ psychological explanations of the effects of context on individuals. Research on classroom behavior may borrow political science explanations of conflict and consensus to explain student interactions and peer influence. Research on school organization and governance may utilize concepts from the sociology of organizations to study leadership, faculty morale, norm formation, and school practices and policies. Relying on well-established middle-range theories and showing how their propositions can be applied to the study of schools would facilitate the efforts of sociologists of education to explain phenomena unique to schooling. Sociology of education would be a theoretically richer subfield with greater heuristic value if it had sociological theories designed specifically to explain the schooling process. Consequently, developing a stronger, theoretical foundation that specifically targets school organization and schooling processes would represent a major advance in the field of sociology of education.

School Organization and Student Achievement

One of the primary functions of schooling is to increase student learning. For this reason, sociologists of education focus more attention on the determinants of student achievement than on other outcomes of schooling, such as educational attainment, aspirations, and returns to schooling. As a result, this chapter is concerned primarily with determinants of academic performance.

One of the most frequently investigated factors affecting student achievement is a school's formal organization. An early conceptualization of the school as a formal organization was presented in Bidwell's (1965) seminal analysis of the school as a bureaucracy. This important work highlighted ways in which the authority structure of a school, with its rules and regulations governing the behavior of faculty and students, influences student outcomes. At the same time, Bidwell's analysis laid the groundwork for subsequent models of schools which demonstrate ways in which schools fail to have a strict bureaucratic structure. Since Bidwell presented his conceptualization, sociologists of education have given considerable attention to the formal organization of schools. Empirical analyses of the school as an organization began with Coleman, Campbell, Hobson, McPartland, Mood, and Weinfeld's (1966) studies of school effects on student achievement. Coleman's model of school effects on student achievement was referred to as an input-output model or a black box model, since virtually no attention was given to the processes that link school characteristics to test scores. Rather, it focused on exogenous school characteristics, such as size, racial/ethnic composition, and resources, as determinants of student achievement.

Dissatisfied with this conceptualization, sociologists of education proposed a nested layers model in which school characteristics are linked to what happens in school which then is related to student achievement. (A detailed discussion of this work appears in the comprehensive and insightful work of Gamoran, Secada, and Marrett [2007].) The nested layers model considered outputs at one hierarchical level of a school to be inputs at the next level. For example, characteristics of a school are seen as affecting classroom processes which produce variation in student learning. The nested layers model represented a paradigm shift for sociologists of education by redirecting interest from the effects of school characteristics to school and classroom processes.

Critics of the nested layers model argue that regardless of school-level regulations governing instructional time, the content of the curriculum, methods of assessment, and other instructional features, teachers still assume considerable discretion over how closely they adhere to school-level constraints on what they do in the classroom. Teacher autonomy increases the difficulty of linking classroom processes to student outcomes. Despite this criticism, the nested layers model provides some guidance in designing school effects studies.

The weakness of the nested layers model lies in its rigidity. Bidwell and Kasarda (1980) addressed this problem by suggesting that schools actually are loosely, not tightly, coupled, as the nested layers model indicates. Meyer and Rowan (1978) claim that schools are loosely connected in terms of their core technology. What is taught in the classroom and how it is taught depends more on the influence of a teacher's training program and socialization than a principal's decisions or school-level characteristics. Empirical work by Metz (1989) and Hemmings and Metz (1991) supports this contention.

The most recent conceptual work on school organization was developed by Rowan (1990) and Gamoran, Secada, and Marrett (2000). Their argument is that the organizational models to date assume that the teaching-learning process is asymmetrical, whereas, in actuality, it is reciprocal. The link between teaching and learning involves feedback and growth on both sides of the relationship. For example, the complexity of the learning process may lead to greater teacher interaction as faculty discuss effective pedagogical practices, which in turn may improve student learning.

Yet despite progress in understanding how the organization of a school affects student achievement, Gamoran (1996) argues that these studies have not been very successful in explaining variation in student outcomes. This is surprising since the study of school organization is one of the few areas which have shown consistent growth in conceptualization and it now provides the groundwork for a sociological theory of student learning. Further empirical work on organizational effects on student outcomes should benefit the study of student learning and provide new insights into how school organization influences and predicts student growth in achievement.

SCHOOL SECTOR AND STUDENT ACHIEVEMENT

School sector is one of the school characteristics that research in the sociology of education has found to affect student learning. Early studies of sector effects in the US involve analyses of the High School and Beyond (HSB) data (Coleman, Hoffer & Kilgore 1982; Hoffer, Greeley & Coleman 1985; Coleman & Hoffer 1987; Bryk, Lee & Holland 1993). These studies found that students in Catholic high schools achieved higher test scores than their counterparts in public high schools. This effect was referred to as the Catholic school advantage. They also found that the Catholic school advantage is greater for disadvantaged minority students (Hoffer, Greeley & Coleman 1985; Coleman & Hoffer 1987). That is to say, race/ethnicity and socioeconomic status matter less in Catholic schools than in public schools. Critics of these studies either found no such Catholic school effect or very small effects (Alexander & Pallas 1985; Willms 1985).

More recent school sector studies using the National Education Longitudinal Study (NELS) of 1988 replicated these results at the high school level. Hoffer (1998) reported significant Catholic school effects on high school achievement gains in math, reading, and history. Gamoran (1996) found greater math gains for students in urban Catholic schools than those in other urban schools. Morgan and Sorensen (1999) and Morgan (2001) also found positive Catholic school effects using the NELS data sets. Similarly, Carbonaro and Covay (2010) showed that students in Catholic and private-secular schools have higher gains in medium to advanced math skills from tenth to twelfth grade than those in other school sectors.

These studies were limited to high school students. Research using data from elementary schools had mixed results regarding a school sector effect. Carbonaro (2003) found that private school first-graders learned more in reading but less in math and general knowledge than their peers in public schools. Carbonaro (2006) also showed that kindergarteners in public and religious schools learned more than kindergarteners in private-secular schools. Lubienski and Lubienski (2006) reported that fourth and eighth graders in public schools scored higher in math than their private school counterparts. Reardon, Cheadle, and Robinson (2009) found that third and fifth graders in public schools had higher math scores than their peers in Catholic schools.

Sociologists of education offer several explanations for the Catholic school advantage in high schools. The most prominent of these is a favorable academic environment, including a rigorous academic curriculum, high teacher expectations, and strict discipline (Coleman & Hoffer 1987; Bryk, Lee & Holland 1993; Gamoran 1996; Lee, Chow-Hoy, Burkham, Geverdt & Smerdon 1998; Carbonaro & Covay 2010). Strong school community and collegiality (Bryk, Lee & Holland 1993) and close student-teacher-parent relationships (Coleman & Hoffer 1987) are also offered as explanations for the Catholic school effect. Most of these factors can be implemented in both private and public schools.

A favorable academic environment is one that offers all students a challenging curriculum. Catholic schools, in particular, are noted for requiring that all students take demanding courses. The practice of tracking or grouping students by ability for instruction was designed to match students to the highest-level courses they can master. However, some empirical studies report a negative impact of tracking on students assigned to low-ability groups or tracks, particularly in public schools with a wide distribution of student ability. Many studies claim that minority and low-income students are assigned disproportionately to lower tracks, controlling for previous academic achievement (Heyns 1974; Hauser, Sewell & Alwin 1976; Rosenbaum 1980; Alexander & Cook 1982; Gamoran & Mare 1989; Gamoran 1996; Lucas 1999). Despite these findings, Hallinan (1994) argues that assignment to tracks or ability groups can be neutral, if faculty make a concerted effort to avoid introducing extraneous considerations, such as personal characteristics, into the assignment process and if expert teachers are assigned to low-track classes.

One area of research that bears further study is whether moving a student from an assigned track or ability group level to a higher- or lower-level group affects student achievement. In one of the few studies of track reassignment, Hallinan (2003) showed that students attain higher test scores if they are moved to a higher ability group than if they remain at the group level to which they were originally assigned. Similarly, students perform more poorly if moved to a lower ability group. What is remarkable about this finding is that it holds regardless of the student's ability. This study raises critical questions about whether American schools sufficiently challenge students to attain optimal performance, and suggests a way to increase the achievement of all students, but especially slow learners. Since minority students tend to be assigned to lower ability groups or tracks, the research suggests that the achievement gap may be decreased by assigning minority students to more challenging instructional groups.

RACIAL/ETHNIC EFFECTS ON STUDENT ACHIEVEMENT

Racial/ethnic differences in academic achievement have long been a focus of research in the sociology of education. Although the gaps have been narrowed over the years, differences in academic achievement remain between white students and those from disadvantaged racial/ethnic groups.

Data from the 2008 long-term trend assessments of the National Assessment of Educational Progress (US Department of Education 2009), known as the nation's "report card," document long-term substantial black-white and Hispanic-white gaps in reading and math test scores for students at ages 9, 13, and 17 over the past 35 years. The magnitude of black-white and Hispanic-white gaps in grades is similar to that in test scores (Kao & Thompson 2003). Moreover, the 2009 Digest of Education Statistics (US Department of Education 2010) reports that the dropout rate for blacks and Hispanics (9.9 and 18.3 percent, respectively) remained higher than that for whites (4.8 percent) in 2008. Asian Americans have comparable or in some respects better educational outcomes than whites, while Native American students usually have similar achievement and attainment levels to black and Hispanic students (Kao & Thompson 2003).

Socioeconomic status (SES) explains the largest proportion of the differences in educational achievement outcomes between black and white and Hispanic and white students (Kao & Thompson 2003). Black and Hispanic students compare unfavorably to white students in terms of the three main aspects of SES – parental income, parental education, and parental occupation (Duncan, Featherman & Duncan 1972). Empirical research shows that SES is a critical determinant of academic achievement (Coleman, Campbell, Hobson, et al. 1966; Sirin 2005).

Researchers offer many reasons to account for the test score gap. Among these are genetics, culture, social capital, and school characteristics and organization (Hallinan 2001; Kao & Thompson 2003). Genetic determinism is a controversial explanation for the lower achievement of black students. Jensen (1973) claimed that, compared to whites, blacks have innate genetic inferiority in intelligence which accounts for their weaker academic performance, compared to white students. Herrnstein and Murray (1994) provide limited empirical support for this argument. Most social scientists, however, refute the genetic explanation, primarily on methodological grounds. They argue that social context, rather than genetics, is a major influence on the development of intelligence and ability (Sorensen & Hallinan 1984; Fischer, Hout, Jankowski, Lucas, Swidler & Voss 1996). Students of a disadvantaged racial or ethnic group have fewer resources and opportunities to nurture the development of their intelligence than more privileged white students.

Other social scientists focus on cultural explanations for racial/ethnic stratification in academic performance. Bourdieu's (1977) cultural capital theory argues that students from privileged families possess the cultural background, knowledge, disposition, and skills that facilitate study in school. Applying cultural capital theory, Lareau (2000) claims that middle-class parents have mindsets that align with school goals and that parental attitudes toward the importance of education benefit students of higher SES. Lareau (2003) further argues that middle-class parents tend to adopt a "concerted cultivation" in their rearing style, which supports academic development, while the "natural development" attitude found among lower-class parents leads to less cultural capital to promote success in education.

Two classic theories that provide insights into the lower achievement levels of black students are cultural deprivation theory and cultural difference theory. According to cultural deprivation theory, the negative and self-defeating attitudes of blacks are to blame for their failure to succeed in school (Loury 1985; Hunter 1986). Cultural difference theory states that the historic oppression of blacks by whites has resulted in their living in a culture that is in opposition to mainstream white culture (Ogbu 1978). Since academic success is part of mainstream middle-class values, black students do not want to be seen as acting white by doing well academically. (Research has found mixed results for Ogbu's theory [Mickelson 1990; Hauser & Anderson 1991; Ainsworth-Darnell & Downey 1998; Kao & Tienda 1998].)

Gibson and Ogbu (1991) add to the cultural difference theory by categorizing minority groups into "involuntary minorities" and "voluntary minorities." Due to their past experiences of being discriminated against, involuntary minorities, such as blacks and some Hispanic groups, have little belief in education as a means to achieve socioeconomic mobility. Voluntary minorities, on the other hand, who emigrated to the US by choice, tend to be more willing to believe in the value of education.

Steele and Aronson (1995) and Steele (1997, 1998) propose stereotype threat theory to explain the black-white achievement gap. They argue that during tests of ability blacks are anxious not to conform to the stereotype that they usually perform poorly, but their anxiety has a negative effect on their test scores. However, Downey and Gibbs (2007) find that the black-white achievement gap appears as early as 2 years of age. Children at this age could not be aware of the stereotype about black students in terms of their test performance.

The concept of social capital provides another explanation for the racial/ethnic differences in educational outcomes. Coleman (1988) defined social capital as a form of capital resulting from interpersonal relationships. Ties with others provide individuals with access to resources. Coleman named three specific forms of social capital: obligations and expectations, information channels, and social norms. The social capital of particular racial/ethnic groups could account partly for their academic success. Caplan, Choy, and Whitmore (1997) show that sibling tutoring after school is conducive to the better academic performance of Southeast Asian children from refugee families. Zhou and Bankston (1998) report that policing by parents helps prevent delinquent behavior for some Asian American youths. Kao (1995) and Zhou and Bankston (1998) cite the obligations felt by Asian American youths as one of the explanations for their doing well in school.

At the school level, social scientists find that certain school characteristics and organizational arrangements contribute to the racial/ethnic achievement gap. Among these are the SES and racial composition of the school. Many studies show that school SES composition is strongly and positively related to students' achievement (Coleman, Campbell, Hobson, et al. 1966; Chubb & Moe 1990; Jencks & Mayer 1990). Since students of a disadvantaged race or ethnicity attend schools that are lower in average SES level and higher in minority composition, they experience double jeopardy (Kahlenberg 2001). School racial composition also matters. It has long been established that racial segregation is detrimental to the achievement of black students (Coleman, Campbell, Hobson, et al. 1966; Crain & Strauss 1985; Wells & Crain 1994).

In addition, teacher quality and expectations are believed to be related to the academic achievement of disadvantaged minority students. Research reports that students of disadvantaged racial and ethnic minorities are more sensitive to teacher effects than advantaged students, yet they tend to have poorer quality teachers (Oakes 1990; Lankford, Loeb & Wyckoff 2002; Ingersoll 2004; Nye, Konstantopoulos & Hedges 2004). Teacher expectations are positively related to student achievement. Yet, research shows that teacher expectations are influenced by race and ethnicity. Entwisle and Alexander (1988) report that teacher expectations tend to be prejudiced against black students and have a significant, negative impact on their achievement. Other studies reveal that low expectations for students of disadvantaged racial and ethnic groups help perpetuate the achievement gap (Wigfield, Galper, Denton & Seefeldt 1999; McKown & Weinstein 2002; Ferguson 2003; Rubie-Davies, Hattie & Hamilton 2006).

Since structural and social factors explain a large proportion of the racial/ethnic stratification in academic achievement, educational policies should be able to narrow the achievement gap. Most academic learning takes place in school, implying that school-related programs can be implemented to help disadvantaged minority students. For example, since the achievement gap appears very early in a child's life, quality preschool programs should make a difference. Some programs, such as Head Start, have proven successful in reducing the gap (Currie 2001; Farkas 2003). Summer school and extended school hours/days also may be helpful for the disadvantaged. Finally, schools need to provide equal resources and learning opportunities in school for all students. Policies aimed at equalizing spending across school districts, placing and keeping good teachers in poor inner-city and rural schools, and making rigorous academic programs available for all students appear to be enlightened and effective policies to improve the learning outcomes of all students.

GENDER EFFECTS ON ACADEMIC ACHIEVEMENT

Social science research has paid relatively little attention to gender inequality in educational outcomes compared to racial/ethnic or social class inequality (Jacobs 1999). Part of the reason is that while women previously lagged behind men in terms of educational achievement, they have now caught up and in many cases surpassed men in academic achievement. Women have maintained a slight advantage over men in standardized test scores in reading while their math test scores are only slightly lower. The 2008 long-term trend assessments of the National Assessment of Educational Progress (NAEP) (US Department of Education 2009) show that female students outperform male students for all three age groups in reading. In math, female students outscored males in 1973, while males outscored females by slight margins in 2008. Other research (e.g., Nowell & Hedges 1998) shows patterns similar to NAEP long-term trend reports.

In terms of grades, research using high school data in the 1950s and 1960s demonstrates that females received higher grades (both in reading and in math) than males, had higher class standing, and took courses as rigorous as those taken by males (Alexander & Eckland 1974; Alexander & McDill 1976). More recent research supports these findings (e.g., Willingham & Cole 1997). Females also are better students than males, as measured by such indicators as repeating grades, number of students in special education classes, behavioral problems, being on the honor roll, and being elected as class officers (Hyde & Kling 2003).

Women's incentives to pursue academic goals are related to their perception of declining gender discrimination in the labor market and changing conceptions of the opportunity structure for women in society (Buchmann & DiPrete 2006). Women's advantage in academic performance is also related to the financial, social, and cultural resources that have become available to them through their families and schools. Over the past several decades, parents' investment in their children's education has changed gradually to the point where the sexes are now treated equally, or parents even favor daughters. Better-educated parents have more egalitarian values and invest in the education of daughters as well as sons, which explains the decreasing gap between men and women in educational achievement (Thornton & Freedman 1979; Cherlin & Walters 1981; Twenge 1997; Axinn & Thornton 2000).

Moreover, social and cultural resources are more readily available to women today than in the past. Downey and Powell (1993) and Powell and Downey (1997) argue that female students view their mothers as academic role models while male students imitate their fathers in their educational pursuits. With an increasing number of female-headed households, women are in a more advantaged position than men in terms of role models and parental support (Sommers 2000; Cancian & Reed 2001). Buchmann and DiPrete's (2006) analyses of the NELS data indicate that having a poorly educated or absent father disadvantages males, especially black males, in academic performance. Kalmijn (1994) and Korupp, Ganzeboom, and Van Der Lippe (2002) challenge these research findings, claiming that mother's level of education and occupation influences boys and girls equally. Buchmann and DiPrete (2006) offer an alternative explanation for the negative effect of an absent father on a male's academic achievement. They state that an absent father increases the likelihood of a male's misbehavior and delinquency which are detrimental to learning.

Gender differences in the effort students expend in learning and the nature of their social behavior in school also contribute to the gender gap in student outcomes. Analyzing the NELS data, Downey and Vogt Yuan (2005) find that teachers rate girls higher than boys in terms of effort to learn, but lower than boys in the amount of disruptive behavior they exhibit in high school. They argue that the primary reason that females earn higher grades than males in all subjects is that the class-room behavior of females is more acceptable to teachers than that of males. Extra-school activities are also believed to influence gender differences in test scores. Relying on a cultural capital perspective, Dumais (2002) claims that female students are more likely to participate in cultural activities than males, leading to higher grades.

Several empirical studies support these assumptions and propositions about a female academic advantage. Jacob (2002) finds that girls possess higher levels of non-cognitive skills, such as attentiveness and organizational ability, than boys, which may facilitate girls' learning. Condron (2007) shows that teachers evaluate girls' academic, social, and behavioral skills as being more favorable to learning than those of males in early childhood, leading to the assignment of males to lower-level reading groups. Similarly, Carbonaro (2005) reports that teachers rate the effort that female students expend in learning higher than that of male students in middle and high school, resulting in more female students being placed in higher academic tracks. Carbonaro also shows that females' superior performance at earlier stages of their schooling results in greater success in later stages.

Given the recent academic gains of female students relative to males, women have largely attained equality, and in some areas superiority, in academic achievement and attainment. However, concerns remain (Mickelson 1989; Mare 1995). A male academic advantage remains in certain areas of achievement, particularly areas that lead to more stable and higher salaried positions in the workforce. Labor market outcomes for women do not reflect their relatively stronger academic outcomes (Stockard 1985; Jacobs 1996). Women in the US still earn only 77.5 cents for every dollar men earn (Mickelson 2003). Policies aimed at fighting sex stereotypes in academic areas traditionally dominated by men, such as math, engineering, and physics, should help women gain greater returns on their academic performance. Only when women receive equal returns for their academic achievement and equal access to the labor market will gender equity be achieved.

POLICY IMPLICATIONS OF RESEARCH
IN THE SOCIOLOGY OF EDUCATION

The most recent national educational reform implemented in the US is the "No Child Left Behind" (NCLB) Act of 2001. The main goal of NCLB is to provide every child with a quality education by closing the achievement gap between high- and low-achieving students, minority and non-minority students, and advantaged and disadvantaged students. The law has five main requirements (Karen 2005). First, it mandates annual testing in reading and mathematics in grades 3–8, and testing once in grades 10–12. Second, states and districts must report data on student test performance by race, special education, limited English proficiency, and low income for each school in their jurisdiction. Third, states must establish adequate yearly progress (AYP) standards for each grade in each school, and 95 percent of students in each subgroup must participate in the testing. Fourth, schools that fail to meet their stated goals for two consecutive years are designated as in need of improvement, requiring them to allow students to either attend a different school or participate in a federally funded tutoring program. Failure to meet goals in a subsequent year subjects the school to restructuring. Fifth, schools must have highly qualified teachers in core academic subjects.

While sociologists generally applaud NCLB's focus on inequality, they question whether the Act focuses on the conditions necessary to improve student learning. In constructing NCLB requirements, the authors of the Act failed to take into account the wealth of information about how schools work provided by sociologists of education over the past few decades. The path NCLB takes to achieve its goals may not be effective since it is not informed by sociological research. Theoretical and empirical studies in sociology of education provide a basis for evaluating the strengths and weaknesses of NCLB.

A primary component of NCLB is its requirement of annual high-stakes testing of students. From the perspective of the loose-coupling model of school organization (Bidwell 1965; Weick 1982), high-stakes testing is an example of top-down accountability and, as such, is unlikely to influence the teaching and learning that occur in the classroom. Since teachers have considerable independence in the classroom, they are insulated from school-level rules and regulations such as those driving NCLB. Moreover, arguing from an institutional perspective, Meyer (1977) and Meyer and Rowan (1978) point out that standardized tests are merely symbolic labels that do not ensure educational quality. Moreover, Gamoran, Secada, and Marrett's (2007) insight that a symmetric relationship exists between school structure and instructional practices is missing from NCLB's testing requirement. This absence weakens NCLB by failing to take into account processes that influence teacher instruction and student learning in school.

Some empirical research provides evidence in favor of high-stakes testing. Toenjes and Dworkin (2002) report that the Texas accountability system has forced schools to attend to the educational needs of under-served student populations. Warren and Jenkins (2005) find no evidence of an increase in dropout rates in Texas and Florida since the implementation of the high-stakes graduation tests. However, these studies are confined to specific states and measure proficiency in taking standardized tests rather than learning. Other studies show unintended but anticipated negative effects of high-stakes testing. Heubert and Hauser (1999), McNeil (2000), and Nichols and Berliner (2007) report that reliance on standardized tests limits the curriculum to the material expected to be on a test, leads to teaching to the test, tempts school personnel and students to cheat, promotes the development of test-taking skills but not the actual learning of content, increases dropout rates, and discriminates against students who have difficulty with the multiple-choice form of testing.

NCLB's requirement of adequate yearly progress fails to take into account that schools are societal institutions in which adequate yearly progress has symbolic power that may conflict with the necessity of schools to set criteria for progress. Even the US Government Accountability Office (2004) raised doubts about whether states can correctly judge whether schools meet their proficiency goals.

Moreover, the organizational context for teaching and learning provided by the school predicts that when schools manipulate resources to maximize their chances of meeting AYP, teaching and learning will be affected in unexpected ways (Gamoran & Dreeben 1986; Gamoran, Secada & Marrett 2000). Dworkin (2005) raised concern that the AYP requirement could lead schools to focus exclusively on ways to maximize student passing rates on the tests. His research showed that instead of investing resources in the neediest students, that is, those scoring lower than the passing bar, some schools direct resources to the students who are most likely to pass the exam the following year.

According to NCLB, the consequences for a school's failing to meet AYP standards in two consecutive years are that students must be offered the opportunity to transfer to another public school or to participate in a federally funded tutoring program. Moreover, the schools must provide teachers with opportunities for professional development. If schools fail to improve for four years, they must take corrective action such as replacing key staff and employing outside consultants to advise on school management. Yet, the sociological nested layers model of school organization indicates that schools, teachers, and students are constrained by inputs over which they have limited control and the outcomes they produce. In addition, the loosely coupled model of schools suggests that schools have limited influence on classroom instruction, and student effort and ability. Therefore, punishing failing schools may not be the solution to achieving quality education. Empirical analyses support this conjecture. Dworkin (2005) reports that low-performing schools do not start on an equal footing with high-performing schools, and continue to lag behind over time. Offering public school choice to students may lead high performing students to transfer, leaving the failing school less able to meet the AYP goal the following year.

The fifth requirement of NCLB gives schools flexibility in defining highly qualified teachers. Most schools require a teacher to have a college degree, a teaching certificate, and certification in subjects taught (Ingersoll 2005). The institutional model of schools suggests that such symbolic requirements are not likely to ensure teacher quality. The Center on Education Policy (2006) points to widespread skepticism among state and district school officials about whether the NCLB teacher quality requirements are improving teaching quality. Moreover, Henig (2006) shows that variation in how states define teacher quality dilutes the high quality requirement. Relying on an organizational perspective, Ingersoll (1999, 2004) claims that NCLB's focus on training requirements for teachers or increasing teacher supply may not be the solution to teacher shortage and out-of-field teaching (Ingersoll 2005). He stresses the need to pay attention to the organizational and occupational contexts within which teachers teach. Changing organizational practices and professional-izing the teaching occupation likely are more effective ways to improve instructional quality and student learning (Ingersoll 2005).

Sociologists of education have identified several other factors that influence student academic performance but that are ignored in NCLB. Teacher relationships based on trust, shared responsibility, common values, and collective decision making lead to more successful teaching and learning (Rowan 1990), as does a strong pro-fessional community composed of technical knowledge, an ethic of service, and commitment to the profession (Talbert & McLaughlin 1994). Teacher collegiality also leads to higher student achievement (Bryk, Lee & Holland 1993). Moreover, sociologists of education demonstrate how the larger social context also influences student learning (Karen 2005). Without the support of social policies aimed at the disadvantaged, such as access to medical care, housing vouchers, community-based economic development, and school desegregation by race, ethnicity, and SES, the goal of NCLB to reduce educational inequality is not likely to be achieved. These sociological studies demonstrate that in order to increase student learning, far more is needed than NCLB requires.

Recent evaluations of the effectiveness of NCLB show that the Act is not meeting its goals. The Center on Education Policy (2006) reported that NAEP test scores showed no significant improvement five years after NCLB took effect. Similarly, Lee's (2006) analysis of NAEP scores in pre- and post-NCLB years reveals neither significant growth in achievement nor closure of the achievement gap following the implementation of NCLB. This is not surprising since the NCLB provisions lack solid theoretical and empirical support from research in sociology of education.

Conclusions

Dissatisfaction with the current educational enterprise has led to a plethora of school reforms that take various approaches to improving education. While the intention motivating these educational reforms is commendable, the success rate, in terms of improving learning opportunities for all students, is disappointing.

A major reason for the failure of many school reforms is the simple fact that policymakers continue to view school as a black box, based on an outdated input-output model of schooling. Ignoring the wealth of sociological studies of the learn-ing process, they focus on school inputs, such as resources, size, and racial/ethnic composition, and on student outputs, primarily academic achievement, measured by scores on standardized tests. Sociologists of education have yet to convince edu-cational policymakers that schooling is a far more complex enterprise than the input-output model assumes. Grounding school policy and practice in scientific studies of schools would greatly increase the success of reform efforts. Rather than concentrating primarily on different ways of structuring, governing, organizing, and resourcing schools, reforms need to incorporate what social science has learned about determinants and consequences of the learning process itself.

These conceptual models of schooling look at schooling as a dynamic process rather than a static program and see education as an interdependent societal institution rather than solely or mainly an effort to prepare students for adulthood. Research in other areas of sociology of education not discussed here, such as comparative cross-cultural and cross-national studies of schools, the global expansion of education, demographic influences on schooling, and access to higher education and its relationship to the job market, further broadens our understanding of schooling and leads to more enlightened school policies. Relying on insights from theoretical and empirical studies in sociology of education should enable policymakers to greatly improve reform efforts and finally move US schools to a new level of excellence.

References

Ainsworth-Darnell, J. M. and D. B. Downey (1998) "Assessing the Oppositional Culture Explanation for Racial/Ethnic Differences in School Performance." *American Sociological Review* 63: 536–53.

Alexander, K. L. and M. A. Cook (1982) "Curricula and Coursework: A Surprise Ending to a Familiar Story." *American Sociological Review* 47: 626–40.

Alexander, K. L. and B. E. Eckland (1974) "Sex Differences in the Educational Attainment Process." *American Sociological Review* 39: 668–82.

Alexander, K. L. and E. L. McDill (1976) "Selection and Allocation within Schools: Some Causes and Consequences of Curriculum Placement." *American Sociological Review* 41: 963–80.

Alexander, K. and A. Pallas (1985) "School Sector and Cognitive Performance: When Is a Little a Little?" *Sociology of Education* 58: 115–27.

Axinn, W. G. and A. Thornton (2000) "The Transformation in the Meaning of Marriage." In L. Waite, C. Bachrach, M. Hindin, E. Thompson, and A. Thornton (eds.), *The Ties that Bind: Perspectives on Marriage and Cohabitation*. New York: Aldine de Gruyter, pp. 147–65.

Bidwell, C. E. (1965) "The School as a Formal Organization." In J. G. March (ed.), *Handbook of Organizations*. Chicago: Rand McNally, pp. 922–1022.

Bidwell, C. E. and J. D. Kasarda (1980) "Conceptualizing and Measuring the Effects of School and Schooling." *American Journal of Education* 88: 401–30.

Bourdieu, P. (1977) *Reproduction in Education, Society, and Culture*. Beverly Hills, CA: Sage.

Bryk, A. S., V. E. Lee, and P. Holland (1993) *Catholic Schools and the Common Good*. Cambridge, MA: Harvard University Press.

Buchmann, C. and T. A. DiPrete (2006) "The Growing Female Advantage in College Completion: The Role of Family Background and Academic Achievement." *American Sociological Review* 71: 515–41.

Cancian, M. and D. Reed (2001) "Changes in Family Structure and Implications for Poverty and Related Policy." In S. H. Danziger and R. H. Haveman (eds.), *Understanding Poverty*. Cambridge, MA: Harvard University and Russell Sage Foundation, pp. 69–161.

Caplan, N., M. H. Choy, and J. K. Whitmore (1997) *Children of the Boat People: A Study of Educational Success*. Ann Arbor, MI: University of Michigan Press.

Carbonaro, W. (2003) "Sector Differences in Student Learning: Differences in Achievement Gains across School Years and during the Summer." *Journal of Catholic Education* 7: 219–45.

Carbonaro, W. (2005) "Tracking, Students' Effort, and Academic Achievement." *Sociology of Education* 78: 27–49.

Carbonaro, W. (2006) "Public-Private Differences in Achievement among Kindergarten Students: Differences in Learning Opportunities and Student Outcomes." *American Journal of Education* 113: 31–65.

Carbonaro, W. and E. Covay (2010) "School Sector and Student Achievement in the Era of Standards Based Reforms." *Sociology of Education* 83: 160–82.

Center on Education Policy (2006) "From the Capital to the Classroom: Year 4 of the No Child Left Behind Act." Washington, DC: Center on Education Policy. www.ctredpol.org/NCLB/Year4/CEP-NCLB-Report-4.pdf

Cherlin, A. and P. B. Walters (1981) "Trends in the United States Men's and Women's Sex-Role Attitudes: 1972–1978." *American Sociological Review* 46: 453–60.

Chubb, J. E. and T. M. Moe (1990) *Politics, Markets, and America's Schools*. Washington, DC: Brookings Institution Press.

Coleman, J. S. (1988) "Social Capital in the Creation of Human Capital." *American Journal of Sociology* 94: S95–S120.

Coleman, J. S., E. Q. Campbell, C. J. Hobson, J. McPartland, A. M. Mood, and F. D. Weinfeld (1966) *Equality of Educational Opportunity*. Washington, DC: US Department of Education, Government Printing Office.

Coleman, J. S. and T. Hoffer (1987) *Private and Public Schools*. New York: Basic Books.

Coleman, J. S., T. Hoffer, and S. Kilgore (1982) "Cognitive Outcomes in Public and Private Schools." *Sociology of Education* 55: 65–76.

Condron, D. J. (2007) "Stratification and Educational Sorting: Explaining Ascriptive Inequalities in Early Childhood Reading Group Placement." *Social Problems* 54: 139–60.

Crain, R. L. and J. Strauss (1985) *School Desegregation and Black Occupational Attainments: Results from a Long-term Experiment* (Rep. No. 359). Baltimore: Center for the Social Organization of Schools.

Currie, J. (2001) "Early Childhood Education Programs." *Journal of Economic Perspectives* 15: 213–38.

Downey, D. B. and B. Gibbs (2007) "When and Why Does the Black-White Gap in Cognitive Skills Emerge?" Presented at Annual Meeting of the American Sociological Association, New York, August 11.

Downey, D. B. and B. Powell (1993) "Do Children in Single-Parent Households Fare Better Living with Same-Sex Parents?" *Journal of Marriage and the Family* 55: 55–71.

Downey, D. B. and A. S. Vogt Yuan (2005) "Sex Differences in School Performance during High School: Puzzling Patterns and Possible Explanations." *Sociological Quarterly* 46: 299–321.

Dumais, S. A. (2002) "Cultural Capital, Gender, and School Success: The Role of Habitus." *Sociology of Education* 75: 44–68.

Duncan, O. D., D. L. Featherman, and B. Duncan (1972) *Socio-economic Background and Achievement*. New York: Seminar Press.

Dworkin, A. G. (2005) "The No Child Left Behind Act: Accountability, High-Stakes Testing, and Roles for Sociologists." *Sociology of Education* 78: 170–4.

Entwisle, D. R. and K. L. Alexander (1988) "Factors Affecting Achievement – Test Scores and Marks of Black and White 1st Graders." *Elementary School Journal* 88: 449–71.

Farkas, G. (2003) "Racial Disparities and Discrimination in Education: What Do We Know, How Do We Know It, and What Do We Need to Know?" *Teachers College Record* 105: 1119–46.

Ferguson, R. F. (2003) "Teachers' Perceptions and Expectations and the Black-White Test Score Gap." *Urban Education* 38: 460–507.

Fischer, C. S., M. Hout, M. S. Jankowski, S. R. Lucas, A. Swidler, and K. Voss (1996) *Inequality by Design: Cracking the Bell Curve Myth*. Princeton, NJ: Princeton University Press.

Gamoran, A. (1996) "Student Achievement in Public Magnet, Public Comprehensive, and Private City High Schools." *Educational Evaluation Policy Analysis* 18: 1–15.

Gamoran, A. and R. Dreeben (1986) "Coupling and Control in Educational Organizations." *Administrative Science Quarterly* 31: 612–32.

Gamoran, A. and R. D. Mare (1989) "Secondary School Tracking and Educational Inequality: Reinforcement, Compensation, or Neutrality?" *American Journal of Sociology* 94: 1146–83.

Gamoran, A., W. G. Secada, and C. B. Marrett (2000) "The Organizational Context of Teaching and Learning: Changing Theoretical Perspectives." In M. T. Hallinan (ed.), *Handbook of the Sociology of Education*. New York: Kluwer Academic/Plenum, pp. 37–63.

Gamoran, A., W. G. Secada, and C. B. Marrett (2007) "The Organizational Context of Teaching and Learning." In A. R. Sadovnik (ed.), *The Sociology of Education: A Critical Reader*. New York: Routledge.

Gibson, M. A. and J. U. Ogbu (1991) *Minority Status and Schooling: A Comparative Study of Immigrant and Involuntary Minorities*. New York: Garland.

Hallinan, M. T. (1994) "School Differences in Tracking Effects on Achievement." *Social Forces* 72: 799–820.

Hallinan, M. T. (2001) "Sociological Perspectives on Black-White Inequalities in American Schooling." *Sociology of Education*, Special Issue: S50–S70.

Hallinan, M. T. (2003) "Ability Grouping and Student Learning." In D. Ravitch (ed.), *Brookings Papers on Education Policy 2003*. Washington, DC: Brookings Institution, pp. 95–140.

Hauser, R. M. and D. K. Anderson (1991) "Post-High School Plans and Aspirations of Black and White High School Seniors: 1976–86." *Sociology of Education* 64: 263–77.

Hauser, R. M., W. H. Sewell, and D. F. Alwin (1976) "High School Effects on Achievement." In W. H. Sewell et al. (eds.), *Schooling and Achievement in American Society*. New York: Academic, pp. 309–43.

Hemmings, A. and M. H. Metz (1991) "Real Teaching: How High School Teachers Negotiate Societal, Local Community, and Student Pressures When They Define Their Work." In R. N. Page and L. Valli (eds.), *Curriculum Differentiation: Interpretive Studies in U.S. Secondary Schools*. Albany, NY: State University of New York Press, pp. 91–112.

Henig, S. (2006) "Back to School for Teachers: The No Child Left Behind Act Has Changed How Colleges Serve Classroom Practitioners." *Chronicle of Higher Education* 53(7): A20. http://chronicle.com.proxy.library.nd.edu/article/Back-to-School-for-Teachers/6756.

Herrnstein, R. J. and C. Murray (1994) *The Bell Curve: Intelligence and Class Structure in American Life*. New York: Free Press.

Heubert, J. P. and R. M. Hauser (1999) *High Stakes: Testing for Tracking, Promotion, and Graduation*. Washington, DC: National Academy Press.

Heyns, B. (1974) "Social Selection and Stratification within Schools." *American Journal of Sociology* 79: 1434–51.

Hoffer, T. (1998) "Social Background and Achievement in Public and Catholic High Schools." *Social Psychology of Education* 2: 7–23.

Hoffer, T., A. Greeley, and J. S. Coleman (1985) "Achievement Growth in Catholic and Public Schools." *Sociology of Education* 54: 74–97.

Hunter, A. (1986) *Children in the Service of Conservatism*. Madison, WI: Department of History, University of Wisconsin-Madison.

Hyde, J. S. and K. C. Kling (2003) "Women, Motivation, and Achievement." *Psychology of Women Quarterly* 25: 364–78.

Ingersoll, R. M. (1999) "The Problem of Under-Qualified Teachers in American Secondary Schools." *Educational Researcher* 28: 26–37.

Ingersoll, R. M. (2004) *Why Do High-Poverty Schools Have Difficulty Staffing Their Classrooms with Qualified Teachers?* Washington, DC: Center for American Progress.

Ingersoll, R. M. (2005) "The Problem of Under-Qualified Teachers: A Sociological Perspective." *Sociology of Education* 78: 175–8.

Jacob, B. A. (2002) "Where the Boys Aren't: Noncognitive Skills, Returns to School, and the Gender Gap in Higher Education." *Economics of Education Review* 21: 589–98.

Jacobs, J. A. (1996) "Gender Inequality and Higher Education." *Annual Review of Sociology* 22: 153–85.

Jacobs, J. A. (1999) "Gender and the Stratification of Colleges." *Journal of Higher Education* 70: 161–87.

Jencks, C. and S. Mayer (1990) "The Social Consequences of Growing up in a Poor Neighborhood." In L. Lynn, Jr. and M. G. H. McGeary (eds.), *Inner-City Poverty in the United States*. Washington, DC: National Academy Press, pp. 111–86.

Jensen, A. R. (1973) *Educability and Group Differences*. New York: Harper and Row.

Kahlenberg, R. D. (2001) *All Together Now: Creating Middle-Class Schools through Public School Choice*. Washington, DC: Brookings Institution Press.

Kalmijn, M. (1994) "Mother's Occupational Status and Children's Schooling." *American Sociological Review* 59: 257–75.

Kao, G. (1995) "Asian-Americans as Model Minorities? A Look at Their Academic Performance." *American Journal of Education* 103: 121–59.

Kao, G. and J. S. Thompson (2003) "Racial and Ethnic Stratification in Educational Achievement and Attainment." *Annual Review of Sociology* 29: 417–42.

Kao, G. and M. Tienda (1998) "Educational Aspirations of Minority Youth." *American Journal of Education* 106: 349–84.

Karen, D. (2005) "No Child Left Behind? Sociology Ignored!" *Sociology of Education* 75: 165–9.

Korupp, S., H. B. G. Ganzeboom, and T. Van Der Lippe (2002) "Do Mothers Matter? A Comparison of Models of the Influence of Mothers' and Fathers' Educational and Occupational Status on Children's Educational Attainment." *Quality and Quantity* 36: 17–42.

Lankford, H., S. Loeb, and J. Wyckoff (2002) "Teacher Sorting and the Plight of Urban Schools: A Descriptive Analysis." *Educational Evaluation and Policy* 24: 37–62.

Lareau, A. (2000) *Home Advantage: Social Class and Parental Intervention in Elementary Education*. Lanham, MD: Rowman and Littlefield.

Lareau, A. (2003) *Unequal Childhoods: Class, Race, and Family Life*. Berkeley, CA: University of California Press.

Lee, J. (2006) *Tracking Achievement Gaps and Assessing the Impact of NCLB on the Gaps: An In-Depth Look into National and State Reading and Math Outcome Trends*. Cambridge, MA: Civil Rights Projects, Harvard University.

Lee, V., T. Chow-Hoy, D. Burkham, D. Geverdt, and B. Smerdon (1998) "Sector Differences in High School Course Taking: A Private or Catholic School Effect?" *Sociology of Education* 71: 314–35.

Loury, G. C. (1985) "The Moral Quandary of the Black Community." *Public Interest* 79: 9–22.

Lubienski, S. and C. Lubienski (2006) "School Sector and Academic Achievement: A Multilevel Analysis of NAEP Data." *American Education Research Journal* 43: 651–700.

Lucas, S. R. (1999) *Tracking Inequality: Stratification and Mobility in American High Schools*. New York: Teachers College Press.

Mare, R. D. (1995) "Changes in Educational Attainment and Social Enrollment." In R. Farley (ed.), *State of the Union: America in the 1990s*. New York: Russell Sage Foundation, pp. 155–213.

McKown, C. and R. S. Weinstein (2002) "Modeling the Role of Child Ethnicity and Gender in Children's Differential Response to Teacher Expectations." *Journal of Applied Social Psychology* 32: 159–84.

McNeil, L. M. (2000) *Contradictions of School Reform: Educational Costs of Standardized Testing*. New York: Routledge.

Metz, M. H. (1989) "Real School: A Universal Drama amid Disparate Experiences." *Journal of Education Policy* 4: 75–91.

Meyer, J. W. (1977) "The Effects of Education as an Institution." *American Journal of Sociology* 83: 55–77.

Meyer, J. W. and Rowan, B. (1978) "The Structure of Educational Organizations." In M. Meyer & Associates (eds.), *Environments and Organizations*. San Francisco, CA: Jossey-Bass, pp. 78–110.

Mickelson, R. A. (1989) "Why Does Jane Read and Write So Well – The Anomaly of Women's Achievement." *Sociology of Education* 62: 47–63.

Mickelson, R. A. (1990) "The Attitude-Achievement Paradox among Black Adolescents." *Sociology of Education* 63: 44–61.

Mickelson, R. A. (2003) "Gender, Bourdieu, and the Anomaly of Women's Achievement Redux." *Sociology of Education* 76: 373–5.

Morgan, S. (2001) "Counterfactuals, Causal Effect Heterogeneity, and the Catholic School Effect on Learning." *Sociology of Education* 74: 341–74.

Morgan, S. and A. Sorensen (1999) "Parental Networks, Social Closure, and Mathematics Learning: A Test of Coleman's Social Capital Explanation of School Effects." *American Sociological Review* 64: 661–81.

Nichols, S. L. and D. C. Berliner (2007) *Collateral Damage: How High-Stakes Testing Corrupts America's Schools*. Cambridge, MA: Harvard Education Press.

Nowell, A. and L. V. Hedges (1998) "Trends in Gender Differences in Academic Achievement from 1960 to 1994: An Analysis of Differences in Mean, Variance, and Extreme Scores." *Sex Roles* 39: 21–43.

Nye, B., S. Konstantopoulos, and L. V. Hedges (2004) "How Large Are Teacher Effects?" *Educational Evaluation and Policy Analysis* 26: 237–57.

Oakes, J. (1990) *Multiplying Inequalities: The Effects of Race, Social Class, and Tracking on Opportunities to Learn Mathematics and Science*. R-39928-NSF. Santa Monica, CA: RAND.

Ogbu, J. U. (1978) *Minority Education and Caste: The American System in Cross-Cultural Perspective*. New York: Academic Press.

Powell, B. and D. B. Downey (1997) "Living in Single-Parent Households: An Investigation of the Same-Sex Hypothesis." *American Sociological Review* 62: 521–39.

Reardon, S., J. Cheadle, and J. Robinson (2009) "The Effect of Catholic Schooling on Math and Reading Development in Kindergarten through Fifth Grade." *Journal of Research on Educational Effectiveness* 2: 45–87.

Rosenbaum, J. E. (1980) "Social Implications of Educational Grouping." *Review of Research in Education* 8: 361–401.

Rowan, B. (1990) "Commitment and Control: Alternative Strategies for the Organizational Design of Schools." In C. Cazden (ed.), *Review of Research in Education*. Washington, DC: American Educational Research Association, pp. 353–89.

Rubie-Davies, C., J. Hattie, and R. Hamilton (2006) "Expecting the Best for Students: Teacher Expectations and Academic Outcomes." *British Journal of Educational Psychology* 76: 429–44.

Sirin, S. R. (2005) "Socioeconomic Status and Academic Achievement: A Meta-Analytic Review of Research." *Review of Educational Research* 75: 417–53.

Sommers, C. H. (2000) *The War against Boys: How Misguided Feminism Is Harming Our Young Men*. New York: Touchstone.

Sorensen, A. B. and M. T. Hallinan (1984) "Race Effects on Assignment to Ability Groups." In P. Peterson, L. C. Wilkinson, and M. T. Hallinan (eds.), *The Social Contest of Instruction: Group Processes*. San Diego, CA: Academic Press.

Steele, C. M. (1997) "A Threat in the Air – How Stereotypes Shape Intellectual Identity and Performance." *American Psychologist* 52: 613–29.

Steele, C. M. (1998) "Stereotyping and Its Threat Are Real." *American Psychologist* 53: 680–1.

Steele, C. M. and J. Aronson (1995) "Stereotype Threat and the Individual Test Performance of African Americans." *Journal of Personality and Social Psychology* 69: 797–811.

Stockard, J. (1985) "Education and Gender Equality: A Critical View." In *Research in Sociology of Education and Socialization*, Vol. 5. Greenwich, CT: JAI Press, pp. 299–326.

Talbert, J. E. and M. W. McLaughlin (1994) "Teacher Professionalism in Local School Context." *American Journal of Education* 102: 123–53.

Thornton, A. and D. Freedman (1979) "Changes in the Sex-Role Attitudes of Women, 1962–1977: Evidence from a Panel Study." *American Sociological Review* 44: 831–42.

Toenjes, L. A. and A. G. Dworkin (2002) "Are Increasing Test Scores in Texas Really a Myth?" Education Policy Analysis Archives. http://epaa.asu.edu/epaa/vl On17

Twenge, J. M. (1997) "Attitudes toward Women, 1970–1995: A Meta-Analysis." *Psychology of Women Quarterly* 21: 35–51.

US Department of Education, National Center for Education Statistics (2009) *The Nation's Report Card: Long-Term Trend 2008*. Washington, DC: US Government Printing Office. Publication # NCES 2009-479.

US Department of Education, National Center for Education Statistics (2010) *Digest of Education Statistics 2009*. Washington, DC: US Government Printing Office. Publication # NCES 2010-013.

US Government Accountability Office (2004) *No Child Left Behind Act: Improvements Needed in Education's Process for Tracking States' Implementation of Key Provisions*. Washington, DC: US Government Printing Office. Publication # GAO-04-734.

Warren, J. R. and K. N. Jenkins (2005) "High School Exit Examinations and High School Dropout In Texas and Florida, 1971–2000." *Sociology of Education* 78: 122–43.

Weick, K. E. (1982) "Administering Education in Loosely Coupled Systems." *Phi Delta Kappa* 63: 673–5.

Wells, A. S. and R. L. Crain (1994) "Perpetuation Theory and the Long-Term Effects of School Desegregation." *Review of Educational Research* 64: 531–55.

Wigfield, A., A. Galper, K. Denton, and C. Seefeldt (1999) "Teachers' Beliefs about Former Head Start and Non-Head Start First-Grade Children's Motivation, Performance, and Future Educational Prospects." *Journal of Educational Psychology* 91: 98–104.

Willingham, W. W. and N. S. Cole (1997) *Gender and Fair Assessment*. Mahwah, NJ: Lawrence Erlbaum Associates.

Willms, J. D. (1985) "Catholic School Effects on Academic Achievement: New Evidence from the High School and Beyond Follow-up Study." *Sociology of Education* 58: 98–114.

Zhou, M. and C. L. Bankston, III (1998) *Growing Up American: How Vietnamese Children Adapt to Life in the United States*. New York: Russell Sage Foundation.

20

Sociology of Religion

CHRISTIAN SMITH AND ROBERT D. WOODBERRY

Three decades ago, sociologists paid little attention to religion as an important force in social life, nor was religion considered to be very significant. Anthropologist Anthony Wallace summarized the then-prevailing view that, "The evolutionary future of religion is extinction. Belief in supernatural beings and supernatural forces that affect nature without obeying nature's laws will erode and become only an interesting historical memory . . . Belief in supernatural powers is doomed to die out, all over the world, as the result of the increasing adequacy and diffusion of scientific knowledge" (1966: 265). But affairs have changed dramatically in the few decades since then. Peter Berger, one of an earlier era's most eloquent theorists of secularization, now proclaims a shift "from the crisis of religion to the crisis of secularity" and "secularism in retreat" (1982, 1996), concluding that "those who neglect religion in their analyses of contemporary affairs do so at great peril" (1996: 12).

Sociologists' renewed interest in religion as a social factor is primarily the result of global events that spotlighted religion's vitality. Throughout the era of religion's academic neglect, there were sociologists who produced distinguished scholarship demonstrating religion's continued social significance. But it took a series of international political incidents to shock academia out of the old secularization paradigm. The crucial years were 1979 and 1980. In 1979, Muslim militants overthrew the Shah of Iran and installed an Islamic republic, which reverberated into a broad irruption of militant Islamic movements in many parts of the Middle East and beyond. At the same time, a Christian Right catapulted itself into American political attention, its members declaring themselves a "moral majority" to counteract the forces of secular humanism and reclaim a Christian America.

The Wiley-Blackwell Companion to Sociology, First Edition. Edited by George Ritzer.
© 2012 Blackwell Publishing Ltd. Published 2012 by Blackwell Publishing Ltd.

Then in 1980, Salvadoran Roman Catholic Archbishop Oscar Romero was assassinated while saying mass, because of his role in the Latin American liberation theology movement which committed the region's Church to progressive social activism and sometimes revolutionary insurrection on behalf of the poor; Romero's assassination was only the most prominent of tens of thousands of political abductions, tortures, and murders of Latin American Christian social activists in the 1970s. Only months later, the Roman Catholic-based Solidarity movement initiated a wave of protest strikes against Poland's communist government, winning unheard-of concessions from the state, culminating in Lech Walesa's signing of the Gdansk Accords with a Pope John Paul II souvenir pen and sporting a lapel pin of the Black Madonna of Czestochowa. Ensuing years witnessed a series of important religiously-based movements around the globe: the anti-Apartheid movement in South Africa, the anti-communist movement in East Germany, and the Central America peace movement in the United States. More recently, the role of Islam in the terrorist attacks of September 11, 2001 has underscored the continued public relevance of religion.

With new eyes to see religion's social and political significance, sociologists have noticed high-intensity Pentecostalism sweeping Latin America, Christianity spreading in Africa and parts of East and South Asia, a panoply of religions multiplying in the US through new immigration, the resurgence of religious identities in parts of post-communist Europe, and so on. By the 1990s, the University of Virginia's James D. Hunter (1991) was declaring a religiously-infused "culture war" in America, and Harvard's Samuel Huntington (1996) predicted a global clash of civilizations with religious differences at the heart. Overstated, perhaps, but the point remains: religion is back.

Academic scholarship is struggling to catch up with and make sense of the implications of these major events. For a long time, social scientists assuming secularization were lazy in thinking about religion. Now much empirical and theoretical work remains to bring our scholarship "up to speed" with our growing awareness of religion's social significance. This chapter is an attempt to map out some helpful recent work in that regard, and to suggest areas that need greater attention in future sociological scholarship on religion.

Much of the most interesting and important recent work in the sociology of religion has developed from engaging theories from other fields and in shifting levels of analysis. For example, stimulating debates have emerged by integrating insights from rational choice theory, cultural sociology, social psychology, institutional and organizational theory, studies of ethnicity, sociology of professions, and so on. The perceived failure of older categories of thought has given way to alternative conceptualizations of religion in social life. In the sections that follow, we discuss developments we believe are among the most valuable and interesting.

RETHINKING MICRO-LEVEL SECULARIZATION

One area of ferment in the sociology of religion in the 1990s was the reconsideration of secularization theory at the level of individual belief, consciousness, and practice. The apparent persistence of religious commitment and activity at the grassroots, particularly in the United States, spawned attempts to better theorize religious growth and strength. This revolved around two related theoretical approaches, both of which argued that religious and cultural pluralism does – or at least can – help religions to thrive.

One theoretical approach is the "religious economies" theory of Roger Finke, Rodney Stark, Laurence Iannaconne, and others (e.g., Finke & Stark 1992; Iannaconne 1994; Young 1997; Stark & Finke 2000; see also Warner 1993) which employs a rational choice framework to try to explain (1) the effects of religious competition and entrepreneurial mobilization on differential rates of church attendance; (2) the influence of religious capital formation on religious conversion and continuity; (3) the effect of religious strictness on church growth; and (4) the influence of the distribution of diverse religious products in a structured religious field on different religious organizations' ideologies, membership appeals, and growth and decline cycles. This theory's attempt to recast religion in economic terms has generated opposition from dissenting scholars. An annual review article by Chaves and Gorski (2001) and a methodological critique by Voas, Olson, and Crockett (2002) have dampened enthusiasm for the religious economies theory, although the larger debate is not entirely settled.

The second theoretical approach to rethinking micro-level secularization has been the "subcultural identity" theory of Christian Smith and colleagues (Smith, Emerson, Gallagher, Kennedy & Sikkink 1998). Rather than taking an economistic rational choice approach, this theory synthesizes insights from literature on moral identity, reference group theory, the social psychology of group identity, the social functions of inter-group conflict, and structural approaches to deviant subcultures. It uses these insights to explain the positive effects of modern pluralism on the identity-work and symbolic boundary maintenance of thriving religious subcultures. It suggests that religion survives and can thrive in pluralistic, modern society by embedding itself in subcultures that offer satisfying morally oriented collective identities which provide adherents with meaning and belonging; and that those religious subcultures will grow strong which possess and use the subcultural tools to create both clear distinction from and significant engagement and tension with relevant outgroups. Like the religious economies theory, the subcultural identity theory advances an explanation for traditional religion's persistence in the modern world that turns on its head secularization theory's premise that cultural and religious pluralism is detrimental to religion. However, more empirical research and theoretical refinement are needed to assess the subcultural identity theory's enduring contribution and limitations.

RELIGIOUS PLURALIZATION

The US is now undergoing a pluralization of religions, particularly in urban areas. This is made more complicated by issues of race, ethnicity, social class, and generational change. Waves of "new immigrant groups" have arrived in North America since the US and Canada lifted restriction on non-European immigration in the mid-1960s. These groups often carry with them their native (and sometimes missionary-planted) religions of their homelands. The substantially increased presence and visibility of Salvadoran Catholics, Indian Hindus, Korean Presbyterians, Cambodian Buddhists, Pakistani Muslims, and so on is transforming the US religious landscape and making it more complex. The simple days of Protestant-Catholic-Jew are gone. But a new surge of sociological research is examining the implications of this religious pluralization in the US (Warner & Wittner 1998; Yang 2001; Cadge 2004; Ecklund 2008).

This research suggests that religion plays a varied and vital role for new immigrants. The new immigration has brought visible religious pluralism to North America. Now mosques, temples, and ashrams sit alongside Protestant and Catholic churches in many parts of the country. However, it has not brought as much pluralism as many scholars suspect. This is partly because the vast majority of new immigrants to North America are at least nominally Christian. Much of this is because of the large waves of immigration from Latin America and the Philippines – both predominantly Catholic. But even immigrants from Korea, Vietnam, and the Middle East are disproportionately Christian (e.g., Yang & Zhai 2005). Persecuted religious minorities such as Jews, Ahmadia Muslims, and Bahais are also over-represented. Thus, even with the new immigration, the 2006 General Social Survey (GSS) found that 1.7 percent of Americans identify themselves as Jewish and only 1.4 percent identify with a specific non-Judeo-Christian religion (Muslim, Buddhist, Hindu, Native American, etc.). The Adolescent Health Survey of high school students gives similar results.

Religious affiliation helps immigrants adapt to US life and preserve key elements of their cultures. However, religious traditions also often transform in the process. In most groups, religiosity increases after immigration. Groups also generally increase lay involvement, become more congregational and text-based, and become more intentional in training congregants – for example, children do not automatically pick up Hinduism from North American culture and so must be carefully instructed (Yang 2001). Gender roles within religious groups also often change. In some groups (e.g., Latin American Pentecostal converts), women gain more functional power; in others, the involvement of women is restricted. For example, among Indian Thomas Christians, men often compensated for their decline in social status relative to their wives in the general society by maintaining stricter control of church leadership (Warner & Wittner 1998). One of the most difficult problems for immigrant congregations is bridging the gap between the first and second generations. In churches, mosques, and temples that do not successfully bridge this gap, the young often leave their parents' faith. Tensions also develop between earlier and later waves of immigrants and between immigrants and their host religious denominations (Yang 2001; Ecklund 2008). Thus immigrant congregations provide a fascinating laboratory to study cultural and institutional change, and the selective process of cultural resistance and assimilation.

Yet immigration is not just a North American issue. Many Muslims, Hindus, and Buddhists have migrated to Europe, Latin America, and former British colonies. Indian, Filipino, Korean, European, and North American workers also migrate to the oil-rich Middle East, and wars, famines, and natural disasters force major cross-national migrations around the world. However, it is still unclear if religious groups play a similarly vital role for these immigrants and migrants. Future research should analyze such things as religion's possible influence on who migrates and to where, and how the religious context of host societies influences immigrant response. Future research should also attempt to gather more regionally and nationally representative data and be more comparative – examining the same group of immigrants moving to two different countries, or going back to the immigrants' place of origin to see how their religious traditions have changed (but see Levitt 2009; Mooney 2009).

RELIGION AND HEALTH

Although long neglected, research on the relationship between religion and health is growing rapidly. Much research suggests that religiosity has a consistent, moderate, positive influence on life expectancy, health, psychological well-being, and recovery from illnesses and surgery (see, for example, Hummer, Rogers, Nam & Ellison 1999; Hummer, Ellison, Rogers & Moulton 2004; Wood, Williams & Chijiwa 2007; Woodberry 2008; Ellison & Hummer 2010). These salutary effects are consistent across several hundred studies and persist despite an impressive array of statistical controls for social ties, physical mobility, health behavior, and socio-demographics. They are consistent for a wide variety of illnesses and surgeries, for multiple age groups, social classes, races, ethnicities, and nationalities. The positive impact of religiosity seems greater for the elderly and African Americans, but does not vary much by gender. There may also be some variation by religious tradition, as some studies suggest that certain conservative religious groups have greater positive health outcomes and greater life satisfaction (Ellison & Levin 1998). Generally, church attendance has the greatest positive impact – although private prayer, subjective importance of religion, and religious coping strategies often have additional positive influence. Greater social support, more satisfying family relationships, and healthier behavior (e.g., less smoking, alcohol abuse, and risky sexual behavior) account for some, but not all, of this positive impact. Scholars have begun analyzing a number of other possible mechanisms, such as the possible impact of religious meaning systems on stress.

Of course, not all forms of religiosity promote health and psychological well-being. A significant amount of research focuses on bad pastors, abusive churches, "toxic faith," and maladaptive religious coping strategies (e.g., Stacey, Darnell & Shupe 2000). Similarly, theorists like Sigmund Freud (e.g., [1927] 1961), Albert Ellis (1992), and Nathaniel Branden (1994) have argued that religion is neurotic and damaging to self-esteem and self-efficacy. Most of this research, however, is based on anecdotal evidence and non-random samples. The overwhelming empirical evidence suggests that these cases are the exception rather than the rule (Gorsuch 1988; Ellison & Levin 1998).

However, there remain some important weaknesses in the field of health and religion. First, almost all this research has been done in North America and Europe, where Christianity and Judaism predominate. The minimal research conducted elsewhere suggests the association between religion and mental and physical health does not generalize easily to Eastern religious traditions (Krause, Liang, Shaw, Sugisawa, Kim & Sugihara 2002; Tarakeshwar, Pargament & Mahoney 2003; Roemer 2008). To the extent that different religious traditions do not have the same effects on health, it would require a significant reformulation of some theories.

Second, the generic religion questions on many surveys prevent scholars from modeling many possible causal mechanisms – although this is rapidly changing. Third, most of the research only looks at the direct impact of religiosity, while controlling for social support, health behavior, and so on. However, much of religion's impact may be indirect (e.g., through greater social support). With structural equations modeling, researchers could model both the direct and indirect impact of religiosity and use better latent measures of religious variables. Finally, because few longitudinal surveys include questions about religion on early waves, many of the conclusions are based on cross-sectional evidence or short time-lags. This makes it difficult to control for selection bias – perhaps the type of people who will be more healthy also choose to be more religious. It also means that researchers cannot measure the cumulative impact of religion well, since they only have snapshots of respondents' religiosity over a limited period of time. If religion's impact is so consistent with such weak measures of cumulative religiosity, it will likely be stronger with better measures.

ADOLESCENT RELIGION

One area that has recently seen a renewed focus of sociological research has been the religious lives of teenagers and emerging adults, spurred primarily by new high-quality data sets collected by the National Study of Youth and Religion (NSYR) and the National Longitudinal Study of Adolescent Health (Add Health). Some current studies have mapped the demographic and cultural landscape of youth religion in detail (Smith with Denton 2005; Smith with Snell 2009; Pearce & Denton 2010). Others have focused on how adolescent religion does and does not shape life behaviors and outcomes, such as teenage sexual practices (Regnerus 2007; Freitas 2008). Yet others have focused on cutting-edge trends in youth's engagements with the challenges of modernity (Flory & Miller 2008). Dillon and Wink (2007) examine religion in a life-course perspective across the twentieth century. Recent studies of youth and religion outside of the US (e.g., Mason, Singleton & Weber 2009; Collins-Mayo & Dandelion 2010) also provide helpful comparative perspectives.

CONSERVATIVE PROTESTANTISM IN THE UNITED STATES

Since the 1990s, scholars have carried out much interesting work about conservative Protestants (CPs) in the US – that is, evangelicals, fundamentalists, Pentecostals, and charismatics. To be clear about terms, "conservative" here refers to theological, not economic or political, conservativism – CPs are typically more economically liberal with regard to government spending for the poor, for example, than are theologically liberal Protestants (Iannaconne 1993; Clydesdale 1999; Davis & Robinson 1999). Long thought by scholars to be languishing in the backwaters of American religion, American CPs have become more socially mobile and culturally and politically visible since the 1970s. Inheritors of a religious tradition that consciously resisted the naturalism and liberalism of modernity, CPs represent an attempt to maintain a more intense religiosity and theological orthodoxy than much of American mainline religion. As a group, CPs have higher levels of church attendance, attach greater importance to faith, and also are more successful in membership recruitment and retention than most other American religious groups. These characteristics help make CPs significantly different in a variety of other ways. For example, when it comes to family, CPs are strict about premarital sex; generally marry earlier than other Americans; have higher marital fertility rates; and report higher levels of marital happiness and adjustment (Woodberry & Smith 1998; Waite & Lehrer 2003; Robbins 2004). CPs tend to emphasize well-defined, gendered, non-egalitarian parenting roles, and are more likely than other Americans to endorse and use corporal punishment of children. But they are also less likely to yell at, more likely to express verbal and physical affection to, and more likely to spend greater time with their children (Wilcox 1998). CPs are more likely to say they support patriarchal marital roles; but as a group they also exhibit greater diversity on gender attitudes than other Americans, and have more egalitarian marriages in practice than their ideology would suggest (Woodberry & Smith 1998; Gallagher & Smith 1999). Similarly, studies show CPs are also distinct when it comes to political attitudes and behaviors, workplace ethics, volunteering behavior, rates of giving to the poor, and other issues of social and policy importance (Smith 2000; Greeley & Hout 2006; Woodberry 2008). Beyond merely demonstrating the sustained social influence of a particular religious tradition, studies of American CPs reveal interesting and important larger processes of collective identity construction, subculture formation, and the selective resistance to modernity (Smith, Emerson, Gallagher, Kennedy & Sikkink 1998). Valuable work on improving measurement in studies of conservative Protestantism has been published recently (Steensland, Park, Regnerus, Robinson, Wilcox & Woodberry 2000; Hackett & Lindsay 2008; Hempel & Bartkowski 2008).

TOLERANCE AND PREJUDICE

As societies become increasingly globalized and pluralistic, religion's effects on tolerance and prejudice grow more important to understand. The general relationship between religiosity and racial prejudice in the US seems to be curvilinear. Those who are only peripherally involved in religion are the most racially prejudiced, and both the non-religious and those who are heavily involved in religion are among the least prejudiced. People's motivations for attending religious services are also important. Those who report attending for religious reasons are less prejudiced, while those who attend for social reasons are more prejudiced (Gorsuch 1988).

Most past research suggests that conservative Protestants are less tolerant than other North Americans. However, a number of scholars suggest that most tolerance scales (e.g., on the General Social Survey) are biased against conservative religionists because they primarily test tolerance for left-wing and secular groups (atheists, feminists, communists, homosexuals) and exclude most right-wing and religious groups (fundamentalists, anti-abortion protesters, gender-role traditionalists, "creationists"). Some evidence supports this claim. There seems to be strong intolerance of CPs by groups that rate well on standard tolerance scales (Bolce & De Maio 2008). Moreover, when respondents are asked which outgroups they most dislike and then are asked about tolerance for that group, CPs are just as tolerant as other religious and non-religious groups (Busch 1998; Eisenstein 2006). Certain groups within conservative Protestantism are extremely intolerant, but they are not large enough to influence significantly the overall CP mean.

However, while the extent of intolerance does not seem to vary by religious group, perhaps the breadth does, or at least CP intolerance seems to work against not only liberal and secular groups such as atheists, feminists, and homosexuals, but also some right-wing groups such as militarists and racists. Generally CPs are not less tolerant of Jews, blacks, Asians, Catholics, Hispanics, or immigrants than other Americans (Woodberry & Smith 1998; Smith 2000).

RELIGION AND SOCIAL JUSTICE

Much recent work in the sociology of religion has also focused on religion's role in movements for social justice. Moderns have inherited from the skeptical and revolutionary Enlightenment (May 1976) the view that religion is naturally conservative, defensive, and allied with ruling elites – as, for example, the French Catholic Church was in the eighteenth century. Certainly in many cases religion has proved to be conservative, elitist, and allied with forces of oppression. But religion can cut both ways. It also readily inspires, mobilizes, and supports movements for social justice and democratization (Smith 1996; Woodberry 2004; Etherington 2005). Historically, in the US, religious actors and organizations were crucial in the fight for religious freedom in the eighteenth century and against slavery in the nineteenth century. In the mid-twentieth century, the black church in America was central in mobilizing and sustaining the black civil rights movement. People and organizations of faith have also played crucial roles in the anti-Vietnam war movement, and in the Sanctuary movement to protect illegal Central American refugees, and were active in the nuclear freeze movement, the environmental movement, the Central America peace movement against Ronald Reagan's sponsored wars in El Salvador and Nicaragua, and in organizations such as Amnesty International, Habitat for Humanity, and the American Friends Service Committee, to name a few.

Around the world, religion has played a significant role in liberation theology; the overthrow of the Somoza dictatorship in Nicaragua in 1979; the insurrection against El Salvador's military regime in the 1970s; Solidarity's resistance to the Polish communist state; the toppling of the Marcos dictatorship in the Philippines; resistance to the Pinochet dictatorship in Chile; the anti-Apartheid movement in South Africa; and the fall of the East German regime in 1989. In many movements, religion has provided activists with sacred legitimation for protest; supplied insurgents with moral imperatives; and offered activists powerfully motivating icons, rituals, songs, testimonies, and oratory. Religion can foster self-discipline, sacrifice, and altruism; furnish movements with trained and experienced leadership and financial resources; and supply congregated participants and solidarity incentives.

Movements often reduce start-up costs by using pre-existing religious communication channels, authority structures, and social control mechanisms. Religion can also provide potential common identification among gathered strangers, and shared transnational identities beyond nation and language. Finally, religion can offer movements transnational organizational linkages; the protection of "open spaces" in civil society; and activists political legitimacy in public opinion (Smith 1996; Woodberry 2004).

Much work remains to explore religion's role in sometimes sustaining, but also often challenging, social injustice around the world. However, a number of recent publications point in helpful directions. For example, Warren (2001) and Wood (2002) examine the role of religion in grassroots social-justice community organizations. Young (2007) shows the crucial role played by antebellum evangelical reform movements in founding the American social movement sector. Bartkowski and Regis (2003) examine how religion and race interact in congregational social ministries targeting poverty (see also Bender 2003). Burdick (2004) explores the ongoing influence of liberation theology in Brazil. Nepstad (2008) analyzes the role of religion in war resistance in the Plowshares movement; and Woodberry (2004, 2006) shows the role of missionaries in reforming British colonialism and spurring immediate abolitionism.

IMPROVING RELIGION MEASURES

Many of the standard religion measures used in survey research are inadequate. For example, the significance of denominations in the US has changed such that many denominational questions have little use. Surveys often ask if respondents are Catholic, Protestant, or Jewish, but this distinction increasingly has little predictive power. Moreover, some standard theological indicators (e.g., "literal Bible") yield invalid estimates of what researchers want to study. Better measures of religious identity, practices, beliefs, and organizational location often exist, but need to be used more often. Most surveys – especially longitudinal surveys – have no questions on religion or only a few poorly constructed ones. Fortunately, this is beginning to change. High-quality data are increasingly becoming available and are transforming scholars' perceptions of religion. The greatest progress has been made in measuring Protestant groups; little progress has been made on differentiating types of Catholics (although see Leege & Welch 1988, 1991). Moreover, we still know little about how to differentiate types of Muslims, Buddhists, Hindus, and other religious groups on surveys (although see Tarakeshwar, Pargament & Mahoney 2003; Roemer 2008).

In North America, religious denomination is the most common way scholars identify religious groups. With good denominational lists and categorization schemes, scholars can effectively differentiate mainline-liberal and conservative Protestant denominations, as well as Pentecostals and black Protestants. Unfortunately, many denomination questions lack sufficient detail to distinguish subgroups within larger religious families – which causes major coding problems. For example, Lutherans are very heterogeneous – the Evangelical Lutheran Church of America tends to be liberal, while Missouri Synod Lutherans are conservative.

Fortunately, Steensland et al. (2000) have developed a useful scheme for recoding denomination lists.

Another way to differentiate religious groups is according to beliefs. In North America, "biblical literalism" or "biblical inerrancy" are the most common beliefs scholars use – in this case, to identify conservative Protestants. However, these Bible measures are crude. People vary widely in what they mean by "literal" and "without error." Moreover, because these measures exclude many better-educated evangelicals who are not literalists or inerrantists, it makes CPs appear less educated and from a lower class than other measures. Another problem is that scholars generally only use one belief measure to categorize religious respondents; this can cause significant measurement error and biased coefficients. Or they use belief measures additively, such as identifying conservative Protestants as people who are biblical literalists, *and* 'born again," *and* have shared their faith with others. But this stringent procedure can confound the problem, excluding respondents who actually belong. Ideally, researchers should use multiple beliefs as indicators of a *latent* belief system (Woodberry & Smith 1998).

Even so, denominational measures and most belief measures do not distinguish different subtypes of CPs or Catholics, although there are striking differences among them. Recently scholars have begun asking respondents which religious tradition or movement they identify with – fundamentalist, evangelical, Pentecostal, charismatic, traditionalist Catholic, liberal Catholic, etc. These generally predict attitudes and behaviors better than denomination or the religious belief measures. The way scholars measure CPs matters a lot – even using the same data set, denomination, belief, and identity measures capture distinct groups and shape scholar findings significantly (Alwin, Felson, Walker & Tufiş 2006; Hackett & Lindsay 2008).

To measure religiosity, scholars typically use church attendance, prayer, or subjective importance of religion. These religious measures work equally well for different groups of American Catholics, Protestants, and Jews (Woodberry 1998), though attendance typically has the strongest impact on people's beliefs and behavior. But it is not clear how well these measures work for non-Christian groups. As new surveys increasingly contact non-Christian respondents, scholars need to develop new measures that address other forms of religiosity (Roemer 2008).

Finally, several new techniques promise to enhance our study of religion. For example, past research tended to analyze differences between religious traditions, but neglected diversity within them. However, scholars have developed ways to test whether internal diversity is greater in some religious groups than in others (DiMaggio, Evans & Bryson 1996; Gay, Ellison & Powers 1996).

Scholars have also begun mixing qualitative and quantitative research more effectively. Past qualitative research suffered because it was difficult to determine how representative case studies, "insider documents," or interviews were. Conversely, survey research often missed important nuances, contradictions, and ambivalence in religious language and culture, and researchers often projected alien meanings onto their research subjects. Fortunately, several groups of scholars are beginning to bridge the gap between qualitative and quantitative research. For example, Christian Smith and colleagues (1998) conducted two-hour face-to-face interviews with a random sample of churchgoing Protestants they had contacted in a representative telephone survey. This directly linked national survey data with detailed information about how respondents understand concepts and the reasons they give for what they believe and do. Bradford Wilcox (1998) has combined broad reviews of religious family-advice books with careful quantitative analysis. These kinds of mixed-methods strategies hold much promise for advances in religion research.

Finally, religion research is also employing multi-level designs. The National Congregations Study (Chaves, Konieczny, Beyerlein & Barman 1999) and the Panel Study of American Religion and Ethnicity (Emerson, Sikkink & James 2010) both asked respondents where they attend church, and used this information to study a representative sample of US churches. This procedure could also be used to contact representative samples of religious-based schools, voluntary organizations, or political groups. Religion research will only improve by moving beyond simple cross-sectional surveys to creative mixed-methods, longitudinal, and multi-level designs.

GLOBALIZING RELIGION

Religious transformation is taking place on a global scale. In the past two centuries, and especially since World War II, Christianity has spread rapidly in Asia; Islam and Christianity in Africa; Protestantism in Latin America; and Hinduism, Buddhism, and Islam have spread to North America, Europe, and former British colonies. Many new religious movements (NRMs) have also sprung up by combining elements of different traditions. Population migrations with religious implications are underway, and old religious cleavages are reasserting themselves in places like Serbia, Palestine, India, and Indonesia. Meanwhile, Pentecostalism – a native of the early twentieth-century US West coast – is spreading rapidly in many parts of the world. Large segments of many societies have changed their religions, and members of these "imported" religions have been disproportionately influential in their home societies, both in the West and non-West (Jenkins 2002; Woodberry forthcoming).

We should remember that this process is not new. Religious traditions have always been in flux, and sociologists have extensive historical data about religious and societal change. For example, Christianity originated and had much of its early strength in the Middle East and North Africa. Yet with the rise of Islam, much of Christianity in the Middle East and North Africa disappeared. Buddhism developed in India, but was then re-absorbed into Hinduism and disappeared from most of the subcontinent. Important strands of Tantric and Mahayana Buddhism developed in Afghanistan and Pakistan, spreading from there to China and Tibet, and then on to Korea and Japan. But both traditions disappeared from Central Asia, replaced by Islam (Woodberry forthcoming). Nestorian Christianity entered China not long after Buddhism (circa AD 600) and both were initially banned and persecuted as foreign religions. But over time, Christianity faltered, and Mahayana Buddhism came to be viewed as an indigenous religion. Yet Christianity entered India by the second century AD and China by AD 635, well before it entered much of Northern or Eastern Europe (Moffett 1992; Jenkins 2002). Conversely, in this century Christianity is spreading rapidly in Mainland China and Buddhism is gaining influence in Europe. Everywhere, the great missionary traditions of Islam,

Buddhism, and Christianity have spread at the expense of indigenous and tribal religions, although often these indigenous religions persist as folk traditions within global religions.

This raises many interesting theoretical questions. Why do some groups radically change their religious traditions, while others preserve their traditions for millennia despite missionizing, invasion, and persecution – for example, Jews, Armenians, Coptic Christians, Parsis, and Thomas Christians of India. Why do some missionary efforts succeed and others fail? How and why do people come to see some foreign traditions as indigenous, while continuing to see others as foreign? How do particular religious traditions or the competition between multiple religious traditions shape society?

Religious globalization has profoundly shaped both "imported" and "indigenous" religious traditions. As people adopt new religions, they adapt them to their culture and use them to pursue their own interests. As dominant indigenous religions react to imported traditions and competition for adherents, they are transformed as well. For example, in South and East Asia, reaction to Protestant missions played a vital role in both the Hindu and Buddhist renaissances of the nineteenth and early twentieth centuries, and, in turn, neo-Hinduism and neo-Buddhism have influenced the West. Reaction to neo-Hindu thought, for example, played an important role in the development of the theology of universal salvation within liberal Protestantism (Welch 1968; Gombrich & Obeyesekere 1988; van der Veer 2001; Woodberry forthcoming). These interactions of religious traditions provide another ideal laboratory for the study of cultural change – for example, which parts of religious traditions are most malleable or resistant to change; which groups adopt or resist new religions, etc. This globalization of religious traditions also has important political and social implications. Imported religious traditions in various countries have influenced gender roles, the practice of slavery, drug and alcohol use, democratization, church–state relations, and concepts of political and religious rights. Whether religions spread along or across existing cleavages may also help stabilize or destabilize societies (Lutz 2002; Woodberry 2004, 2011, forthcoming).

Recently there has been growing interest in global civil society and international non-governmental organizations (INGOs). Yet this literature seldom mentions religious INGOs – in fact they are often excluded from consideration – despite the fact that they continue to both dwarf and pre-date most of their non-religious counterparts. The literature that does analyze religion suggests that religious groups were central to the rise of INGOs (Boli & Thomas 1999), as well as NGOs around the world; and that religious involvement is an important predictor for participating in both religious and non-religious voluntary associations. Moreover, comparative research suggests that religious context plays a substantial role in the number and type of voluntary associations around the world (James 1987; Anheier & Salamon 1998: 11–17, 354–6; Woodberry 2004, 2011).

One area inviting further research is missionaries and missionary organizations. For good or ill, they transferred a massive number of personnel and resources to developing nations; invested heavily in education and translation projects; created the first written form of most languages; and usually imported the first printing technology – they even spurred a print revolution in East Asia, which already had printing technology. Missionaries often established the first formal education for girls, and before the 1960s often provided the most widespread access to Western formal education. Well into the twentieth century, more Western missionaries went overseas than any other group other than tourists (if we exclude settlers in countries like New Zealand). Missionaries were also from among the most educated segments of North American and European society and their organizations dwarfed other NGOs in size. In 1900, for example, the American Federation of Labor had a budget of $71,000, but the missions board of Northern Methodists (a single US denomination) had a budget of over 1 million dollars (Hutchison 1987; Woodberry 2004, 2011).

Protestant and Catholic missionaries wanted to transform societies, and they usually did – some for the good, some for the bad – and changed themselves in these encounters as well. Moreover, the number of Christian missionaries increased substantially over the twentieth century. And now Muslim, Hindu, Buddhist, Bahai, and NRM missionaries compete with Christian groups in spreading their messages, and religious mission work is increasingly being done by people from the developing world. In the past 25 years historians have begun serious research on missions. But social science research on their impact is still extremely rare. However, the research that has analyzed them suggests they have powerfully shaped outcomes of interest to social scientists: e.g., education, economic development, health, political organization, political democracy, and possibly ethnic violence (Woodberry 2004; Wood, Williams & Chijiwa 2007; Trejo 2009; Woodberry 2011).

Religion and Economic and Political Outcomes

Finally, there is a rapidly growing literature on the economic and political impact of religion. Recent empirical work suggests the plausibility of Weberian-style arguments about Protestantism fostering economic growth and political democracy – through different mechanisms than Weber posited (Grier 1997; Treisman 2000; Woodberry 2004; Woodberry & Shah 2004; Becker & Woessman 2009; Young 2009; Woodberry 2011), although, through religious competition, religious differences seem to dissipate over time. Religiosity may also have an independent effect on the economy (Gruber 2005). While these arguments are not settled, they are reinvigorating old debates.

Conclusion

Social scientists have increasingly come to realize that religion is not going to disappear with the advance of modernity. Nor is it going to be confined to a mere privatized existence without public influence. Traditional forms of religious belief and practice have remained resilient in the modern world, and new religions continue to emerge and spread with regularity. All of this has important consequences in many areas of social life. This realization opens up a host of research opportunities which recent scholarship is beginning to explore. The field remains wide open for development in ways that will enhance our understanding of the social significance of the sacred in human consciousness and practice.

References

Alwin, D. F., J. L. Felson, E. T. Walker, and P. A. Tufiş (2006) "Measuring Religious Identity in Surveys." *Public Opinion Quarterly* 70: 530–64.

Anheier, H. and L. Salamon (eds.) (1998) *The Nonprofit Sector in the Developing World: A Comparative Analysis*. Manchester: Manchester University Press.

Bartkowski, J. P. and H. A. Regis (2003) *Charitable Choices: Religion, Race, and Poverty in the Post-Welfare Reform Era*. New York: New York University Press.

Becker, S. O. and L. Woessman (2009) "Was Weber Wrong? A Human Capital Theory of Protestant Economic History." *Quarterly Journal of Economics*: 531–96.

Bender, C. (2003) *Heaven's Kitchen: Lived Religion at God's Love We Deliver*. Chicago: University of Chicago Press.

Berger, P. (1982) "From the Crisis of Religion to the Crisis of Secularity." In M. Douglas and S. Tipton (eds.), *Religion and America*. Boston: Beacon Press, pp. 14–24.

Berger, P. (1996) "Secularism in Retreat." *The National Interest*: 3–12.

Bolce, L. and G. De Maio (2008) "A Prejudice for the Thinking Classes: Media Exposure, Political Sophistication, and the Anti-Christian Fundamentalist." *American Politics Research*: 155–85.

Boli, J. and G. M. Thomas (1999) *Constructing World Culture*. Stanford, CA: Stanford University Press.

Branden, N. (1994) *The Six Pillars of Self-Esteem*. New York: Bantam.

Burdick, J. (2004) *Legacies of Liberation: The Progressive Catholic Church in Brazil at the Start of a New Millennium*. Aldershot: Ashgate.

Busch, B. G. (1998) "Faith, Truth, and Tolerance: Religion and Political Tolerance in the United States." PhD dissertation, University of Nebraska, Lincoln, NE.

Cadge, W. Heartwood (2004) *The First Generation of Theravada Buddhism in America*. Chicago: University of Chicago Press.

Chaves, M. and P. Gorski (2001) "Religious Pluralism and Religious Participation." *Annual Review of Sociology*: 261–81.

Chaves, M., M. E. Konieczny, K. Beyerlein, and E. Barman (1999) "The National Congregations Study: Background, Methods, and Selected Results." *Journal for the Scientific Study of Religion*: 458–76.

Clydesdale, T. (1999) "Toward Understanding the Role of Bible Beliefs and Higher Education in American Attitudes toward Eradicating Poverty, 1964–1996." *Journal for the Scientific Study of Religion*: 103–18.

Collins-Mayo, S. and P. Dandelion (2010) *Religion and Youth*. Aldershot: Ashgate.

Davis, N. and R. Robinson (1999) "Their Brothers' Keepers? Orthodox Religionists, Modernists, and Economic Justice in Europe." *American Journal of Sociology*: 1631–65.

Dillon, M. and P. Wink (2007) *In the Course of a Lifetime: Tracing Religious Belief, Practice, and Change*. Berkeley, CA: University of California Press.

DiMaggio, P., J. Evans, and B. Bryson (1996) "Have Americans' Social Attitudes Become More Polarized?" *American Journal of Sociology*: 690–755.

Ecklund, E. (2008) *Korean American Evangelicals*. New York: Oxford University Press.

Eisenstein, M. A. (2006) "Rethinking the Relationship between Religion and Political Tolerance in the US." *Political Behavior*: 327–48.

Ellis, A. (1992) *Reason and Emotion in Psychotherapy*. Secaucus, NJ: Lyle Stuart.

Ellison, C. and R. Hummer (2010) *Religion, Families, and Health*. New Brunswick, NJ: Rutgers University Press.

Ellison, C. and J. S. Levin (1998) "The Religion-Health Connection: Evidence, Theory, and Future Directions." *Health Education and Behavior*: 700–20.

Emerson, M., D. Sikkink, and A. James (2010) "The Panel Study of American Religion and Ethnicity: Background, Methods, and Selected Findings." *Journal for the Scientific Study of Religion*: 162–71.

Etherington, N. (2005) *Missions and Empire*. New York: Oxford University Press.

Finke, R. and R. Stark (1992) *The Churching of America*. New Brunswick, NJ: Rutgers University Press.

Flory, R. and D. Miller (2008) *Finding Faith: The Spiritual Quest of the Post-Boomer Generation*. New Brunswick, NJ: Rutgers University Press.

Freitas, D. (2008) *Sex and the Soul: Juggling Sexuality, Spirituality, Romance, and Religion on America's College Campuses*. New York: Oxford University Press.

Freud, S. ([1927] 1961) *The Future of an Illusion*. New York: Norton.

Gallagher, S. and C. Smith (1999) "Symbolic Traditionalism and Pragmatic Egalitarianism: Contemporary Evangelicals, Families, and Gender." *Gender and Society*: 211–33.

Gay, D. A., C. Ellison, and D. A. Powers (1996) "In Search of Denominational Subcultures: Religious Affiliation and 'Pro-Family' Issues Revisited." *Review of Religious Research*: 3–17.

Gombrich, R. and G. Obeyesekere (1988) *Buddhism Transformed: Religious Change in Sri Lanka*. Princeton, NJ: Princeton University Press.

Gorsuch, R. L. (1988) "Psychology of Religion." *Annual Review of Psychology*: 201–21.

Greeley, A. and M. Hout (2006) *The Truth about Conservative Christians*. Chicago: University of Chicago Press.

Grier, R. (1997) "The Effect of Religion on Economic Development: A Cross National Study of 63 Former Colonies." *Kyklos* 50: 47–62.

Gruber, J. (2005) "Religious Market Structure, Religious Participation, and Outcomes: Is Religion Good for You?" NBER Working Paper #11377. Boston: National Bureau of Economic Research. www.nber.org/papers/w11377

Hackett, C. and D. M. Lindsay (2008) "Measuring Evangelicalism: Consequences of Different Operationalization Strategies." *Journal for the Scientific Study of Religion*: 499–514.

Hempel, L. and J. Bartkowski (2008) "Scripture, Sin, and Salvation: Theological Conservatism Reconsidered." *Social Forces*: 1647–74.

Hummer, R. A., C. G. Ellison, R. G. Rogers, and B. E. Moulton (2004) "Religious Involvement and Adult Mortality in the United States: Review and Perspective." *Southern Medical Journal*: 1223–30.

Hummer, R. A., R. G. Rogers, C. B. Nam, and C. G. Ellison (1999) "Religious Involvement and US Adult Mortality." *Demography*: 273–85.

Hunter, J. (1991) *Culture Wars*. New York: Basic Books.

Huntington, S. (1996) *The Clash of Civilizations and the Remaking of World Order*. New York: Simon and Schuster.

Hutchison, W. (1987) *Errand to the World: American Protestant Thought and Foreign Missions*. Chicago: University of Chicago Press.

Iannaconne, L. (1993) "Heirs to the Protestant Ethic? The Economics of American Fundamentalism." In M. Marty and S. Appleby (eds.), *Fundamentalism and the State*. Chicago: University of Chicago Press, pp. 342–66.

Iannaconne, L. (1994) "Why Strict Churches Are Strong." *American Journal of Sociology*: 1180–212.

James, E. (1987) "The Nonprofit Sector in Comparative Perspective." In W. Powell (ed.), *The Nonprofit Sector: A Research Handbook*. New Haven, CT: Yale University Press, pp. 397–415.

Jenkins, P. (2002) *The Next Christendom*. New York: Oxford University Press.

Krause, N., J. Liang, B. A. Shaw, H. Sugisawa, H. K. Kim, and Y. Sugihara (2002) "Religion, Death of a Loved One, and Hypertension among Older Adults in Japan." *Journal of Gerontology Series B: Psychological Sciences and Social Sciences*: S96–S107.

Leege, D. and M. Welch (1988) "Religious Predictors of Catholic Parishioners' Sociopolitical Attitudes." *Journal for the Scientific Study of Religion*: 536–52.

Leege, D. and M. Welch (1991) "Dual Reference Groups and Political Orientation." *American Journal of Political Science*: 28–56.

Levitt, P. (2009) *God Needs No Passport: Immigrants and the Changing American Religious Landscape*. New York: New Press.

Lutz, J. G. (2002) *Mission Dilemmas: Bride Price, Minor Marriage, Concubinage, Infanticide, and Education of Women*. New Haven, CT: Yale Divinity School Library.

May, H. (1976) *The Enlightenment in America*. New York: Oxford University Press.

Mason, M., A. Singleton, and R. Weber (2009) *The Spirit of Generation Y*. Mulgrave, Vic.: John Garrett.

Moffett, S. H. (1992) *A History of Christianity in Asia, Vol. 1, Beginnings to 1500*. San Francisco: Harper San Francisco.

Mooney, M. (2009) *Faith Makes Us Live: Surviving and Thriving in the Haitian Diaspora*. Berkeley, CA: University of California Press.

Nepstad, S. (2008) *Religion and War Resistance in the Plowshares Movement*. Cambridge: Cambridge University Press.

Pearce, L. and M. Denton (2010) *A Faith of Their Own: Stability and Change in the Religiosity of American Adolescents*. New York: Oxford University Press.

Regnerus, M. (2007) *Forbidden Fruit: Sex and Religion in the Lives of American Teenagers*. New York: Oxford University Press.

Robbins, J. (2004) "The Globalization of Pentecostal and Charismatic Christianity." *Annual Review of Anthropology*: 117–43.

Roemer, M. K. (2008) "Religiosity and Subjective and Psychological Well-Being in Contemporary Japan." PhD dissertation, University of Texas at Austin, Austin, TX.

Smith, C. (1996) *Disruptive Religion: the Force of Faith in Social Movement Activism*. New York: Routledge.

Smith, C. (2000) *Christian America? What Evangelicals Really Want*. Berkeley, CA: University of California Press.

Smith, C. with M. Denton (2005) *Soul Searching*. New York: Oxford University Press.

Smith, C. with T. Snell (2009) *Souls in Transition*. New York: Oxford University Press.

Smith, C., M. Emerson, S. Gallagher, P. Kennedy, and D. Sikkink (1998) *American Evangelicalism: Embattled and Thriving*. Chicago: University of Chicago Press.

Stacey, W., S. Darnell, and A. Shupe (2000) *Bad Pastors: Clergy Misconduct in Modern America*. New York: New York University Press.

Stark, R. and R. Finke (2000) *The Human Side of Religion*. Berkeley, CA: University of California Press.

Steensland, B. S., J. Park, M. D. Regnerus, L. D. Robinson, W. B. Wilcox, and R. D. Woodberry (2000) "The Measure of American Religion: Toward Improving the State of the Art." *Social Forces*: 291–318.

Tarakeshwar, N., K. I. Pargament, and A. Mahoney (2003) "Measures of Hindu Pathways: Development and Preliminary Evidence of Reliability and Validity." *Cultural Diversity and Ethnic Minority Psychology*: 316–32.

Treisman, D. (2000) "The Causes of Corruption: A Cross-National Study." *Journal of Public Economics*: 399–457.

Trejo, G. (2009) "Religious Competition and Ethnic Mobilization in Latin America: Why the Catholic Church Promotes Indigenous Movements in Mexico." *American Political Science Review*: 323–42.

Van der Veer, P. (2001) *Imperial Encounters*. Princeton, NJ: Princeton University Press.

Voas, D., D. Olson, and A. Crockett (2002) "Religious Pluralism and Participation: Why Previous Research Is Wrong." *American Sociological Review*: 212–30.

Waite, L. J. and E. L. Lehrer (2003) "The Benefits from Marriage and Religion in the United States." *Population and Development Review*: 255–75.

Wallace, A. (1966) *Religion: An Anthropological View*. New York: Random House.

Warner, R. S. (1993) "Work in Progress toward a New Paradigm for the Sociological Study of Religion in the United States." *American Journal of Sociology*: 1044–93.

Warner, R. S. and J. G. Wittner (eds.) (1998) *Gatherings in Diaspora: Religious Communities and the New Immigration*. Philadelphia, PA: Temple University Press.

Warren, M. (2001) *Dry Bones Rattling: Community Building to Revitalize American Democracy*. Princeton, NJ: Princeton University Press.

Welch, H. (1968) *The Buddhist Revival in China*. Cambridge, MA: Harvard University Press.

Wilcox, B. (1998) "Conservative Protestant Childrearing." *American Sociological Review*: 796–809.

Wood, C. H., P. Williams, and K. Chijiwa (2007) "Protestantism and Child Mortality in Northeast Brazil, 2000." *Journal for the Scientific Study of Religion*: 405–16.

Wood, R. (2002) *Faith in Action: Religion, Race, and Democratic Organizing in America*. Chicago: University of Chicago Press.

Woodberry, R. D. (1998) "Religiosity: Does One 'Size' Fit All?" Unpublished paper.

Woodberry, R. D. (2004) "The Shadow of Empire: Christian Missions, Colonial Policy and Democracy in Post-Colonial Societies." PhD dissertation, University of North Carolina, Chapel Hill, NC.

Woodberry, R. D. (2006) "Reclaiming the M-Word: The Consequences of Missions for Nonwestern Societies." *Review of Faith and International Affairs* 4: 3–12.

Woodberry, R. D. (2008) "Pentecostalism and Economic Development." In J. B. Imber (ed.), *Markets, Morals, and Religion*. New Brunswick, NJ: Transaction, pp. 157–77.

Woodberry, R. D. (2011) "Religion and the Spread of Human Capital and Political Institutions: Christian Missions as a Quasi-Natural Experiment." In R. McCleary (ed.), *The Oxford Handbook of the Economics of Religion*. Oxford: Oxford University Press, pp. 111–31.

Woodberry, R. D. (forthcoming) "World Christianity: Its History, Spread and Social Influence." In C. Farhadian (ed.), *Introducing World Christianity*. Oxford: Wiley-Blackwell.

Woodberry, R. D. and T. S. Shah (2004) "Christianity and Democracy: The Pioneering Protestants." *Journal of Democracy*: 47–61.

Woodberry, R. D. and C. S. Smith (1998) "Fundamentalism et al.: Conservative Protestants in America." *Annual Review of Sociology*: 25–56.

Yang, F. (2001) "Transformations in New Immigrant Religions and the Global Implications." *American Sociological Review* 66: 269–88.

Yang F. and J. E. Zhai (2005) "The Distorted Perception of Religious Pluralism: What Do Asian Americans Really Believe?" Presented at the National Meeting of the Association for the Sociology of Religion, Philadelphia, August.

Young, C. (2009) "Religion and Economic Growth in Western Europe: 1500–2000." Presented at the National Meeting of the American Sociological Association, San Francisco, August.

Young, L. (1997) *Rational Choice Theory and Religion: Summary and Assessment*. New York: Routledge.

Young, M. (2007) *Bearing Witness against Sin: The Evangelical Birth of the American Social Movement*. Chicago: University of Chicago Press.

21

Current Directions in Medical Sociology

WILLIAM C. COCKERHAM

The purpose of this chapter is to examine the current state of medical sociology. Over the past 60 years medical sociology has evolved from the status of a marginal field with tenuous links to mainstream sociology to become one of the largest and most important sociological specialties. This could be considered surprising, given its aberrant beginning. The classical theorists who founded sociology in the nineteenth century ignored health and medicine altogether and it was not until the late 1940s that medical sociology appeared in direct response to government efforts to advance the health of citizens after World War II. Medical sociology was a prime example of how Western governments attempted to utilize the social sciences to help solve the problems of industrial society and the welfare state in the postwar era (Gouldner 1970).

While this seemed a good idea about how to use medical sociology, there was not much in medical sociology to use. The field barely existed. A few studies on the patient–physician relationship and the social ecology of mental illness, along with early essays and books written about medical sociology, had been produced largely by physicians. This body of work had not provided the critical mass needed to establish a sociological subdiscipline (Bloom 2002). Nevertheless, public awareness that socially and economically disadvantaged people had shorter life spans and more health problems than their affluent counterparts stimulated interest in the field as Western governments turned their attention from fighting a world war to rebuilding society. A field like medical sociology seemed to be a potentially promising ally. Postwar government and private foundation funding for research and job positions thus provided the catalyst for the emergence of a new sociological specialty intended

The Wiley-Blackwell Companion to Sociology, First Edition. Edited by George Ritzer.
© 2012 Blackwell Publishing Ltd. Published 2012 by Blackwell Publishing Ltd.

to inform medical practice and policy. It was primarily through the stimulus of this external funding that sociologists and health professionals embraced medical sociology.

At its inception, however, medical sociology lacked trained practitioners. Moreover, some participants were not even sociologists; they had changed their affiliations to secure positions in a new field with funding and interesting challenges (Claus 1982). Others were sociologists but virtually none of them had formal training in the study of health, illness, or the medical profession (Bloom 2002: 131). Much of the research in medical sociology at this time was atheoretical, focused mostly on patients, and was open to criticisms that it was limited as an academic and policy science by a subordinate relationship with medicine (Gold 1977). As will be seen in this chapter, however, this situation no longer exists since medical sociology today is nothing like what has just been described.

The field today has a robust theoretical orientation, an extensive research literature on a variety of health-related topics, and a demonstrated professional independence from medicine. Rather than subservience, medical sociologists in the United States made the medical profession itself an object of study, focusing objectively on its core relationships with patients and other health-care providers and on the organizational structure of health-care delivery systems (Bloom 2002). The medical profession's efforts to maintain the fee-for-service system that discriminated against the poor, the weak professional sanctions for medical mistakes and malpractice, and opposition to national health insurance were all documented (Freidson 1970a, 1970b; Stevens 1971; Freidson 1975; Bosk 1979; Starr 1982). Medical sociologists also brought their own topics to the study of health, such as social stress, health-related lifestyles, social capital, and the social determinants of disease. This chapter will provide an overview of their work by reviewing medical sociology's evolution from the past to the present, with an emphasis upon current directions in research.

PARSONS AND THE ROLE OF THEORY

A major factor in medical sociology's evolution was the expanded utilization of sociological theory within an area of study initiated to produce knowledge that could be applied to solving health problems, not theorizing about them. The key figure in this development is Talcott Parsons, one of the twentieth century's leading theorists. Theory is critical to any academic discipline because it provides a systematic framework for conceptualizing, analyzing, and verifying knowledge. It is the use of sociological theory that binds medical sociology to the larger discipline of sociology more than any other feature of sociological work. Whereas seminal sociological contributions in quantitative and qualitative research methods, along with many fundamental concepts of social behavior, have been adopted by several fields, sociological theory allows medical sociology to remain unique among the various health-related disciplines (Cockerham & Scambler 2010).

Medical sociology's early deficit in theory was due to its origin in the late 1940s and 1950s in an intellectual climate far different from sociology's traditional specialties. Funding agencies that provided the field with its early support were not interested in theoretical work and generally sponsored only research that had some practical utility for policy or clinical practice. Sociological specialties like theory, social stratification, urbanization, social change, and religion, in contrast, had direct roots in nineteenth-century European social thought. Sociology's early theorists had ignored medicine, presumably because it was not an institution structuring society similar to religion, the rise of cities and industry, the distribution of wealth and power, and patterns of class divisions. An exception is sometimes claimed for Emile Durkheim's classic work *Suicide* ([1897] 1951) when it is cited as the first major work in the field. But this is perhaps reaching back too far as there is no evidence Durkheim saw any connection to something called "medical sociology."

Better candidates for the first major studies in medical sociology include the publication in 1957 of *The Student-Physician*, edited by Robert Merton, George Reader, and Patricia Kendall, and the 1958 book *Social Class and Mental Illness: A Community Study*, by August Hollingshead (a sociologist) and Frederick Redlich (a psychiatrist). Merton and his colleagues extended the structural-functionalist mode of analysis to the socialization of medical students, with Renée Fox's paper on training for uncertainty ranking as a major contribution. The Hollingshead and Redlich study, funded by the National Institute of Mental Health, was a landmark investigation. It produced lasting and important evidence that social class position was correlated with different types of mental disorders and the manner in which people received psychiatric care. The book remains the seminal study of the relationship between mental illness and social class. This study also played a key role in the debate during the 1960s leading to the establishment of community mental health centers in the United States.

The critical event bringing sociological theory into medical sociology and deflecting its orientation from purely applied matters was the publication in 1951 of Parsons' *The Social System*. Parsons had a longstanding interest in medicine, as seen in his training in psychoanalysis and as a student of Lawrence Henderson, a physician who taught sociology at Harvard in the 1930s. Henderson espoused structural-functionalist theory and published a 1935 work on the patient–physician relationship as a social system (Bloom 2002). Parsons' book, *The Social System*, written to explain a complex structural-functionalist model of society, contained his concept of the sick role. Parsons was a giant figure in sociology at the time and having a theorist of his stature provide a major theory to medical sociology called considerable attention to theoretical opportunities in the new field. Parsons may not have intended to have had such an important influence on medical sociology, but anything he published attracted interest among academic sociologists. Not only was his concept of the sick role a distinctly sociological analysis of sickness, but it was widely believed by many at the time that he was charting a future course for all of sociology through his theoretical approach. This did not happen because of subsequent criticisms by his detractors. Nevertheless, Parsons brought medical sociology the intellectual recognition that it needed in its early development, by endowing it with theory. Moreover, following Parsons, other leading sociologists of the day, such as Merton and Erving Goffman, published work in medical sociology that further promoted the academic legitimacy of the field.

The merit of Parsons' theory was that it described a patterned set of expectations explaining the norms, values, and roles appropriate for being sick, for the ill person and others who interact with that person. Additionally, the concept was grounded in the theories of Durkheim on moral authority and Max Weber on social values, thereby linking it to classical sociological theory.

The sick role concept stimulated considerable debate and research, and was criticized for not applying uniformly to all sick persons or to all patient–physician relationships, and for being more applicable to acute than chronic diseases and to the middle class rather than the lower class. But despite these criticisms, the theory has had lasting influence as an "ideal type" of sickness behavior that applies in many situations.

THE POST-PARSONS ERA (1952–69)

The next major area of research after Parsons introduced his sick role concept was medical education. First, Merton and his colleagues (1957) published their study of student physicians, followed by Howard Becker and his associates whose research was reported in *Boys in White* (Becker, Greer, Hughes & Strauss 1961). The latter was a study of medical school socialization conducted from a symbolic interactionist perspective which became a sociological classic. Becker and his research team spent one year at the University of Kansas Medical School and produced a detailed sociological account of their observations. Their book was important not only for its findings concerning medical training, but also for its theoretical and methodological content. The techniques in participant observation used in this study, for example, provided a basis for the work on death and dying and subsequent innovations in theory and methods by Barney Glaser and Anselm Strauss (1965, 1967).

With the introduction of symbolic interaction into a field that had been dominated for a short time by structural-functionalism, medical sociology became a major arena of conflict and debate between two of sociology's leading theoretical schools. This debate stimulated a virtual flood of publications in medical sociology in the 1960s. Also, the Medical Sociology Section of the American Sociological Association (ASA) was formed in 1959 and grew to become one of the largest and most active ASA Sections. American influence was also important in founding Research Committee 15 (Health Sociology) of the International Sociological Association in 1967 (Bloom 2002). The Medical Sociology Group of the British Sociological Association (BSA) was organized in 1964 and became the largest specialty group in the BSA, with its own annual conference.

In 1966 the *Journal of Health and Social Behavior*, founded in 1960, became an official ASA publication, making medical sociology one of the few sociological subdisciplines publishing its own journal under ASA auspices. In the meantime, in Great Britain, a new journal, *Social Science and Medicine*, was founded in 1967 which became an especially important journal for medical sociologists throughout the world. The growing literature in medical sociology also led to the publication of textbooks. The first textbook was Norman Hawkins' *Medical Sociology* (1958), but the early leaders were the first editions of books by David Mechanic (1968) and Rodney Coe (1970). Howard Freeman, Sol Levine, and Leo Reeder likewise made an important contribution by publishing the *Handbook of Medical Sociology* (1963), which contained summary essays on major topics by leading medical sociologists.

During the 1960s, the symbolic interactionist perspective temporarily dominated much of medical sociology's literature. One feature of this domination was the numerous studies conducted with reference to labeling theory and the mental patient experience. Sociologists expanded their work on mental health to also include studies of stigma, stress, families coping with mental disorder, and other areas of practical and theoretical relevance. For example, Goffman's *Asylums* (1961), a study of life in a mental hospital, presented his concept of "total institutions" which stands as a significant sociological statement about social life in an externally controlled environment. An abundant literature emerged at this time which established the sociology of mental disorder as a major subfield within medical sociology and eventually led to the formation of its own ASA Section, with its own journal, *Mental Health and Society*, approved in 2010.

THE PERIOD OF MATURITY (1970–2000)

Between 1970 and 2000 medical sociology emerged as a mature sociological sub-discipline. This period was marked by the publication of two especially important books, Eliot Freidson's *Professional Dominance* (1970a) and Paul Starr's *The Social Transformation of American Medicine* (1982). Freidson formulated his influential "professional dominance" theory to account for an unprecedented level of professional control by physicians over health-care delivery – something that was true at the time but is no longer the case. Starr's book won the Pulitzer Prize and countered Freidson's thesis by examining the decline in status and professional power of the medical profession as large corporate health-care delivery systems oriented toward profit effectively entered an unregulated medical market. Donald Light (1993) subsequently used the term "countervailing power" to show how the medical profession was but one of many powerful groups in society – including federal and state governments, employers, health insurance companies, patients, pharmaceutical and other companies providing medical products – all maneuvering to fulfill their interests in health care.

Another major work was Bryan Turner's *The Body and Society* (1984) which initiated the sociological debate on this topic. Theoretical developments concerning the sociological understanding of the control, use, and phenomenological experience of the body, including emotions, followed. Much of this work has been carried out in Great Britain and features social constructionism as its theoretical foundation. Social constructionism has its origins in the work of the French social theorist Michel Foucault and takes the view that knowledge about the body, health, and illness reflects subjective, historically specific human concerns and is subject to change and reinterpretation.

Other areas in which British medical sociologists have excelled include studies of medical practice, emotions, and the experience of illness. Medical sociology also became a major sociological specialty in Finland, the Netherlands, Germany, Italy, Spain, and Israel, and began to emerge in Russia and Eastern Europe in the 1990s after the collapse of communism. In the meantime, the European Society for Health and Medical Sociology was formed in 1983, which hosts a biannual conference for European medical sociologists. In Japan, the Japanese Society for Medical Sociology was established in 1974 and since 1990 has published an annual review of work in the field. Elsewhere in Asia, medical sociology is especially active in Singapore, Australia, Thailand, and India, and is beginning to appear in China. In Africa, medical sociology is strongest in South Africa. Medical sociology is also an important field in Latin America and because of its special Latin character many practitioners prefer to publish their work in books and journals in Mexico, Brazil, Argentina, and Chile (Castro 2005).

From the 1970s through the 1990s, medical sociology flourished as it attracted large numbers of practitioners in both academic and applied settings and its research literature exploded with publications. Major areas of investigation included stress, the medicalization of deviance, mental health, inequality and class differences in health, health-care utilization, managed care and other organizational changes, AIDS, and women's health and gender. Several books, edited collections of readings, and textbooks appeared. A new textbook was William Cockerham's *Medical Sociology* which was first published in 1978 and will appear in a twelfth edition in 2012. Another major medical sociology journal, *Sociology of Health and Illness*, was started in Britain in 1978, as was a new journal, *Health*, in 1999.

However, the success of medical sociology also brought problems in the 1980s. Research funding opportunities declined and the field faced serious competition for existing resources with health economics, health psychology, medical anthropology, health services research, and public health. These fields not only adopted sociological research methods in the form of social surveys, participation observation, and focus groups, but some employed medical sociologists in large numbers. While these developments were positive in many ways, the distinctiveness of medical sociology as a unique subdiscipline was nevertheless challenged as other fields moved into similar areas of research. Furthermore, some of the medical sociology programs at leading American universities had declined or disappeared over time as practitioners retired or were hired away. Yet the overall situation for medical sociology was positive as the job market remained good, almost all graduate programs in sociology offered a specialization in medical sociology, and sociologists were on the faculties of most medical schools in the United States, Canada, and Western Europe (Bloom 2002).

The 1990s saw medical sociology move closer to its parent discipline of sociology. This was seen in a number of areas with medical sociological work appearing more frequently in general sociology journals and the increasing application of sociological theory to the analysis of health problems. While medical sociology drew closer to sociology, sociology in turn moved closer to medical sociology as the field remained one of the largest and most robust sociological specialties.

THE PRESENT (2000–10)

The beginning of the twenty-first century witnessed further developments. Postmodern theory faltered, while medicalization, health lifestyles, social capital, and neighborhood disadvantage emerged as important areas of research. Moreover, in the US the Patient Protection and Affordable Care Act and the Health Care and Education Affordability Reconciliation Act, sponsored by the Obama administration and passed by Congress in 2010, open the need for new research in a variety of areas because of the many changes brought to health care in the US. The remainder of this chapter will discuss these current directions in medical sociology.

Postmodern theory

Postmodern theory seemed to be a promising approach for explaining the social changes accompanying the new century. There was considerable disagreement about the nature and definition of postmodernism, but a common theme was the disintegration of modernity and its post-industrial social system, leading to new social conditions. Postmodernism was generally ignored by sociologists until the mid-1980s when a few social scientists decided it was worthy of serious attention. Postmodernism emerged out of post-structuralism as a more inclusive critique of modern sociological theory and grand narratives making sweeping generalizations about society as a whole; it rejected notions of order and continuity with the past, calling for new concepts explaining the disruptions of late modern social change (Best & Kellner 1991). Postmodern theory itself posited that there was no single coherent rationality and that the framework for social life had become fragmented, diversified, and decentralized (Turner 1990). Its sociological relevance rested in its depiction of the destabilization of society and the requirement to adjust theory to new social realities. The advantage of postmodern theory is that modern society is undergoing a transition with social conditions different from the recent past (the latter part of the twentieth century) and the perspective provides a theoretical framework, despite its diffuse literature, for examining some of these changes.

The theory reached its highest level of popularity in sociology during the early 1990s and momentarily seemed poised to have an important future. But this did not occur. Use of the theory declined abruptly in the late 1990s and a strong foothold in medical sociology has yet to be achieved in the twenty-first century (Cockerham 2007b). There are several reasons for this. Postmodern theory turned out to have a number of shortfalls, including its failure to explain social conditions after the rupture with modernity is complete, the lack of an adequate theory of agency, being too abstract and ambiguous, not providing clear conceptualizations, an inability to account for social causation, not having empirical confirmation, and invariably featuring an obtuse jargon that only its dedicated adherents found meaningful and others came to regard as nonsense (Best & Kellner 1991; Pescosolido & Rubin 2000; Cockerham 2007a; Ritzer 2011). It is still popular in some circles although its influence has waned considerably in recent years and become less important.

At present, there is no dominant theoretical approach in medical sociology, nor has there ever been a leading theory since the early days of Parsons and structural-functionalism in the 1950s. Generally the field has been and remains eclectic in its use of theory. Although certain theories and theorists have remained important (Durkheim, Weber), fallen into disfavor (structural-functionalism, Marxism), had limited impact (conflict theory, rational choice, feminist theory, critical realism), started to fade (postmodernism), or become static (symbolic interaction, labeling theory), others are currently popular (social constructionism, Foucault) or are rising (Bourdieu). Some current theories are associated with substantive topics such as social capital, stress-process, the life course, fundamental cause theory, medicalization, and attribution. It is clear that for a theory to be a success in medical sociology it must meet two obvious and fundamental criteria: the theory must (1) relate to health matters and (2) be applicable to the empirical world. That is, the theory must specify a connection to the realm of health and disease that has some practical relevance for understanding the effects of these biological phenomena on the human social condition or, conversely, the effects of social factors on these phenomena (Cockerham 2007a).

Medicalization

Medicalization was an earlier development which continued to gain attention in the twenty-first century. Some medical sociologists expressed concern that the medical profession was taking responsibility for an increasingly greater proportion of deviant behaviors and bodily conditions by defining them as medical problems (Clarke, Shim, Mamo, Fosket & Fishman 2003; Conrad 2007). As Freidson (1970a) put it decades ago, medicine had established a jurisdiction over problems in living far wider than justified by its demonstrable capacity to "cure" those problems. Nevertheless, the medical profession has been successful in gaining authority to define aberrant behaviors and even naturally occurring physical conditions as illness, and thus problems best handled by physicians. We see this when hyperactivity at school by children is defined as Attention-Deficit/Hyperactivity Disorder (ADHD) and requires Ritalin; menopause is treated with estrogen replacement therapy, whose side effects have been shown to promote even greater risk from blood clots, stroke, heart disease, and breast cancer; being short in stature necessitates growth hormones for the person afflicted with below average height; and male baldness is slowed or prevented by using Propecia and lost hair is restored by surgical transplants (Conrad 2007). There was a time when hyperactivity, menopause, shortness, and baldness were not medical conditions, but they are today.

For some people, new medical treatments for previously untreated conditions were positive, such as the development of Viagra and similar drugs for erectile dysfunction. Success for some problems and hopeful expectations for others apparently stimulated an even greater expansion of the medicalization process. Whereas medicalization has traditionally been a means by which professional medicine acquires more problems to treat, Clarke, Shim, Mamo, Fosket & Fishman (2003) find that major technological and scientific advances in biomedicine are taking this capability even further and producing what Clarke and her colleagues refer to as biomedicalization. Biomedicalization consists of the capability of computer information and new technologies to extend medical surveillance and treatment interventions well beyond past boundaries through the use of genetics, bioengineering, chemoprevention, individualized drugs, patient data banks, digitized patient records, and other innovations. Also important in this process is the internet, advertising, consumerism, and the role of pharmaceutical companies in marketing their products to doctors and patients alike.

The increasing commercialization of health products and services in the expansion of the medical marketplace has been observed by other medical sociologists. Conrad (2007), for instance, argues that the forces pushing medicalization have changed, with biotechnology, consumers, and managed care now promoting the process. Conrad notes that biotechnology has long been associated with medicalization, with the pharmaceutical industry playing an increasingly central role; however, in the future the impact of genetics may be substantial. Managed care, in turn, has become the dominant form of health-care delivery in the US, which makes insurance companies as third-party payers important in both enabling medicalization through their coverage of health services and placing limitations on those services.

While medicalization is prevalent in the United States, observes Conrad, it is increasingly an international phenomenon with multinational drug companies leading the way in expanding its development. In the meantime, consumers have become major players in the health marketplace through their purchase of health insurance plans and health products. According to Conrad, consumer demand for these products fuels medicalization. "The Internet," says Conrad, "has become an important consumer vehicle" (2007: 9) as people search health-related websites for medical information and products. Public and professional medical concern about medicalization may be growing, but the process it represents remains a powerful influence on behavior and an important area of study.

Health lifestyles

Health lifestyles have become a relatively new area of research as the concept of what it means to be healthy has changed. Part of this change stems from the epidemiological transition in mortality from acute to chronic diseases that allow people to live longer but have their mortality more affected by their lifestyle. In the distant past, a person was either healthy or unhealthy and this situation was typically taken for granted. Now, with the increasing evidence that health-related behavior either promotes longevity or causes mortality, health has come to be regarded as something a person needs to work on in order to achieve (Clarke, Shim, Mamo, Fosket & Fishman 2003). This means that individuals (not physicians) are ultimately responsible for their own health, and the best option they have is a health-promoting lifestyle. Consequently, the study of health lifestyles is likely to be of greater importance in the present and future.

Health lifestyles are collective patterns of health-related behavior based on choices from options available to people according to their life chances (Cockerham 2005). A person's life chances are largely determined by their class position which either enables or constrains health lifestyle choices. The behaviors that are generated from these choices can have either positive or negative consequences for body and mind, but nonetheless form an overall pattern of health practices that constitute a lifestyle. Health lifestyles include contact with medical professionals for checkups and preventive care, but the majority of activities take place outside the health-care delivery system. These activities typically consist of choices and practices, influenced by the individual's probabilities for realizing them, which range from brushing one's teeth and using automobile seat belts to relaxing at health spas. For most people, health lifestyles involve decisions about food, exercise, relaxation, personal hygiene, risk of accidents, coping with stress, smoking, alcohol and drug use, as well as having medical checkups.

Drawing upon the work of Weber ([1922] 1978) and Pierre Bourdieu (1984), Cockerham (2005, 2007b) formulated an initial theory of health lifestyles which involves four categories of social structural variables that have the potential to shape such lifestyles: (1) class circumstances, but also (2) age, gender, and race/ethnicity, (3) collectivities (i.e., families, groups, organizations), and (4) living conditions. These structural variables provide the social context for an individual's socialization (upbringing) and experiences that influence his or her choices in life. These variables, especially class position, also influence a person's chances of reaching their health or other life goals. The choices available to an individual and their chances of realizing them interact to commission the formation of particular dispositions toward habitual ways of acting that Bourdieu describes as a habitus. The habitus generates dispositions toward engaging in certain practices, including such health-related actions as smoking or not smoking, using alcohol or avoiding it, watching or not watching one's diet, and similar activities. Health practices constitute patterns of health lifestyles whose reenactment results in their reproduction (or modification) through feedback. Consistent with Weber's thesis, this model views a person's life chances as socially determined and an individual's social structure as the arrangement of those chances. Choices and chances thus interact to determine a person's health lifestyle, as life chances either enable or constrain the choices made. Overall, this theory is an initial representation of the health lifestyle phenomenon and is intended to show how social structures influence individual participation in such lifestyles.

Social capital

Another relatively new area of research which is experiencing considerable attention is concerned with social capital. Turner defines social capital as "the social investments of individuals in society in terms of their membership in formal and informal groups, networks, and institutions" (2004: 13). He explains that the degree to which an individual is socially integrated in networks of family, neighborhood, community groups, churches and other places of worship, clubs, voluntary service organizations, and other social institutions provides an objective measure of that person's social capital. Nan Lin (2001) sees social capital as an investment in social relations that people can use as a buffer against stress and depression, while Bourdieu (1993) viewed it as a resource that people obtain through their memberships in social groups.

Yet social capital is not just a property of individuals, it is also a characteristic of social networks from which individuals draw psychological and material benefits. According to Bourdieu, one can get an intuitive idea of social capital by saying that it is what ordinary language calls "connections" (1993: 2). People have connections to other people and groups and can draw on the resources they represent to help them be healthy. While Bourdieu emphasizes the resources of networks, Robert Putnam (2000) emphasizes the cohesion of networks. Putnam defines social capital as a community-level resource reflected in social relationships involving not only networks, but also norms and levels of trust. He maintains that the positive influences of social capital on health are derived from enhanced self-esteem, sense of support, access to group and organizational resources, and its buffering qualities in stressful situations. Social connectedness, in Putnam's view, is one of the most powerful determinants of health. After reviewing several studies, he found that people who are socially disconnected are two to five times more likely to die from all causes when compared with similar individuals who have close ties to family and friends.

The importance of social capital in health outcomes is seen in studies showing that people embedded in supportive social relationships providing high levels of social capital have better health and longevity (Browning & Cagney 2002; Lochner, Kawachi, Brennan & Buka 2003). However, findings on the relationship between social capital and health outcomes have not always been consistent and are affected by the difficulty in measuring a variable with multiple – individual, group, community, and so on – conceptual levels. But the concept has grown in popularity and is a promising area of research in medical sociology.

Neighborhood disadvantage

Yet another new area of research emerging in medical sociology is that of "neighborhood disadvantage," which focuses on unhealthy urban living conditions. Cities contain the best that human society has to offer in terms of jobs, arts, entertainment, and other forms of culture and amenities, but they also include pockets of the worst social environments. Neighborhoods have resources needed to produce good health or, conversely, harm it. Examples of neighborhood characteristics that can be either health-promoting or health-damaging are found in the work of Macintyre and her colleagues (Macintyre, Ellaway & Cummins 2002) in the west of Scotland. They determined there are five features of neighborhoods that can affect health: (1) the physical environment; (2) surroundings at home, work, and play; (3) services provided to support people such as schools, street cleaning and garbage collection, police, hospitals, and health and welfare services; (4) the socio-cultural aspects of the neighborhood such as its norms and values, economic, political, and religious features, level of civility and public safety, and networks of support; and (5) the reputation of an area that signifies its esteem, quality of material infrastructure, level of morale, and how it is perceived by residents and nonresidents.

Ross (2000) observes that neighborhoods can be rated on a continuum in terms of order and disorder that are visible to its residents. Orderly neighborhoods are clean and safe, houses and buildings are well maintained, and residents are respectful of each other and each other's property. Disorderly neighborhoods reflect a breakdown in social order, as there is noise, litter, poorly maintained houses and buildings, vandalism, graffiti, fear, and crime. Many families with children in such neighborhoods are single-parent families headed by females. Ross asked whether people who live in disadvantaged neighborhoods suffer psychologically as a result of their environment and found the answer to be yes. Several studies find that the structural effects of neighborhoods promote ill health through long-term exposure to stress, depression, and unhealthy lifestyles and living conditions (Hill, Ross & Angel 2005; Wen & Christakis 2006). Conversely, residents of affluent neighborhoods rate their health significantly better than people in disadvantaged neighborhoods (Browning & Cagney 2002). This is not surprising because these neighborhoods have healthier living conditions and significantly better access to quality health care. Research on this topic illustrates the effects of the structural characteristics of neighborhoods on the physical and mental health of the people who live in them.

Socioeconomic status as a fundamental cause
of sickness and mortality

Studies of neighborhood disadvantage join with other research on the powerful effects of social class on health to illustrate the importance of social structural factors in disease causation. The enduring association of low socioeconomic status (SES) with illness, disability, and death has led Link and Phelan (1995, 2000; Phelan, Link, Diez-Roux, Kawachi & Levin 2004) to propose that SES is a "fundamental cause" of mortality. This is an important proposition because most researchers in the past viewed SES as a factor contributing to poor health and mortality, not as a direct cause. However, the persistent association of SES with a variety of disease patterns during changing historical periods increasingly identified SES as having a causal role. In order for a social variable to qualify as a cause of mortality, Link and Phelan (1995: 87) hypothesize that it must: (1) influence multiple diseases, (2) affect these diseases through multiple pathways of risks, (3) be reproduced over time, and (4) involve access to resources that can be used to avoid risks or minimize the consequences of disease if it occurs.

SES or social class meets all four of these criteria because a person's class position influences multiple diseases in multiple ways, the association has endured for centuries, and persons with higher SES have the resources to better avoid health problems or minimize them when they occur. Consequently, the degree of socioeconomic resources a person has or does not have, such as money, knowledge, status, power, and social connections, either protects health or causes premature mortality. According to Phelan, Link, Diez-Roux, Kawachi, and Levin (2004: 267), these resources directly shape individual health behaviors by influencing whether people know about, have access to, can afford, and are motivated to engage in health-enhancing behaviors. In addition, such resources shape access to neighborhoods, occupations, and social networks that vary dramatically in relation to risk and protective factors. Furthermore, living in a social context where neighbors, friends, family members, and co-workers generally look forward to a long and healthy life contributes to an individual's motivation to engage in health-enhancing behaviors.

In short, Phelan and her associates conclude that there is a long and detailed list of mechanisms linking socioeconomic status with mortality. Included is a sense of personal "control" over one's life because people with such control typically feel good about themselves, handle stress better, and have the capability and living situations to adopt healthy lifestyles. This situation may especially apply to people in powerful social positions. "Social power," state Link and Phelan, "allows one to feel in control, and feeling in control provides a sense of security and well being that is [health-promoting]" (2000: 37). Persons at the bottom of society are less able to control their lives, have fewer resources to cope with stress, live in more unhealthy situations, face powerful constraints in choosing a healthy way of life, and die earlier from diseases whose onset could have been prevented or delayed until old age (Phelan, Link, Diez-Roux, Kawachi & Levin 2004).

Given that the profile of socioeconomic inequalities in sickness and mortality has been virtually unchanged over the course of the twentieth century, class has emerged as a leading causal factor in relation to poor health (Warren & Hernandez 2007). This is particularly evident when social gradients in mortality universally display a hierarchical gradient from low to high in death rates along class lines. The *enduring* outcome of good health at the top of society and worse health in descending order toward the bottom marks class as a fundamental social cause of health, disease, and death (Cockerham 2007b). Recognition of the causal properties of social variables in health matters has been slow in coming, but there is growing evidence that such variables are highly significant.

HEALTH REFORM

The newest area of research in medical sociology – which will capture the interest of its practitioners for some time to come – pertains to the effects of the health reform legislation in 2010 on American society. Briefly stated, the legislation extended health insurance coverage to 32 million uninsured people, beginning in 2014, with tax credits currently approved to help small businesses give coverage to their employees. Medicaid coverage for the poor is also expanded to cover people with incomes up to 133 percent of the federal poverty line, which is currently $14,000 for an individual and $29,327 for a family of four. Nearly all Americans would be required by law to purchase health insurance, or pay a fine, while employers with more than 50 workers who do not provide coverage will pay significant fines. Persons who are exempt from this requirement are American Indians, those with religious objections, and those who can prove financial hardship. The legal mandate to purchase health insurance has been challenged by lawsuits in 26 states claiming such a requirement is unconstitutional as the federal government does not have the right to require people to buy any good or service as a condition of lawful residence in the US. The eventual success of such lawsuits, however, is questionable.

Persons who are not covered by their employer and earn too much to qualify for Medicaid can buy coverage through their state insurance exchange which will offer a variety of plans and costs for coverage. People who earn up to four times the poverty threshold ($88,200 for a family of four) will receive subsidies to help them pay for insurance. Individuals and families who presently purchase their own health insurance or have employer-sponsored coverage may keep their coverage or purchase coverage from state exchanges if their current policy covers less than 60 percent of their costs or they earn four times less than the poverty line. Individuals earning more than $200,000 or families earning more than $250,000 annually will see their Medicare taxes increase in 2013.

The health insurance industry would no longer be able to reject applicants with pre-existing conditions or charge them excessively high rates, or cancel policies after they become sick. All plans have to offer a minimum package of benefits defined by the federal government, including certain preventive measures at no cost. It is expected that by 2019 about 95 percent of all Americans will have health insurance. The cost of the program is supposed to be covered by revenues from new taxes and reductions in spending on Medicare and other government programs.

What this means is that the US will no longer be the only industrialized country in the world where many of its citizens lack health insurance. The impact of this historic legislation on medical sociology will be substantial. For example, much of the literature in medical sociology covers class disparities in health and highlights the plight of the poor and the uninsured. This would change as almost everyone would have at least a minimum basic level of benefits covering essential services. Whether or not health disparities between social classes will be reduced would be a major research topic. The probabilities, based on the British experience with national health care, are that the health of all would improve, but the gradient in mortality would remain because health-related differences in living conditions and lifestyles are not changed. Those lower on the social scale would still live in less healthy conditions, have poorer diets, smoke more, exercise less, exhibit more problem drinking, secure less preventive care even though covered by insurance, etc. What would have changed is the availability of health insurance coverage and easier, affordable access to health care for the formerly uninsured. It nevertheless moves the US much closer to having some type of national health insurance and a changed pattern of health services utilization.

Another likely change is a doctor shortage as more people seek their services and nurse practitioners assume an even greater role in health care. As nurse practitioners, pharmacists, physical therapists, and other health-care workers earn PhDs and add "Dr." to their titles, and federal government control of health care increases, the status and authority of physicians is likely to decrease even more than it has in recent decades. These and other developments associated with health reform will be major research topics.

FUTURE DIRECTIONS

Current studies of the relationship between health and medicalization, health life-styles, social capital, neighborhood disadvantage, and health-care reform, along with the increasing evidence of socioeconomic status as a fundamental cause of disease, are all part of the growing focus on the role of structure in health matters. This does not mean that micro-level methods and theories like symbolic interaction are obsolete. To the contrary, qualitative research provides some of the most insight-ful data available on social relationships. However, sociology, from its inception, has been oriented toward investigating the effects of structures – such as groups, communities, classes, institutions, or societies – on human social behavior. The ultimate goal of medical sociology, as with all of sociology, is an accurate assessment of social life at all levels, which is only possible by fully accounting for the effects of structure on individuals.

Recent developments in statistics currently make it possible to measure more accurately the effects of structure on individuals and assess structure's causal qualities. Hierarchical linear models now exist that provide efficient estimations for a wider range of applications than previously possible. Hierarchical linear modeling (HLM) makes it feasible to test hypotheses about relationships occurring at differ-ent social levels and assess the amount of variation explained at each level (Rauden-bush & Bryk 2002). Briefly stated, HLM tests the strength of the interaction between variables that describe individuals at level one, structural entities such as households or families at level two, and sequentially higher levels such as commu-nities, social classes, and nations depending on the variable's conceptual position in a structural hierarchy. By comparing changes in the regression equations, the relative effects of each level of variables on health outcomes can be simultaneously determined. What this forecasts is an emphasis upon fully investigating the effects of structural conditions on health which is increasingly appearing in medical sociology journals as the next methodological focus for the field.

CONCLUSION

Ultimately, what allows medical sociology to retain its unique character is (1) its utilization and mastery of sociological theory in the study of health, and (2) the sociological perspective that accounts for collective causes and outcomes of health problems and issues. No other field is able to bring these skills to health-related research and analysis. Today it can be said that medical sociology produces literature intended to inform medicine and policymakers, but research in the field is also grounded in examining health-related situations that inform sociology as well. Health sociology no longer functions as a field whose ties to the mother discipline are lax, nor has it evolved as an enterprise subject to medical control. It now works most often with medicine in the form of a partnership and, in some cases, as an objective critic. Moreover, medical sociology owes more to medicine than sociology for its origin and initial financial support, so the relationship that has evolved is essentially supportive. As medical sociology continues on its present course, it is emerging as one of sociology's core specialties as the pursuit of health increasingly becomes important in everyday social life.

References

Becker, Howard D., Blanche Greer, Everett C. Hughes, and Anselm Strauss (1961) *Boys in White: Student Culture in Medical School.* Chicago: University of Chicago Press.

Best, Steven and Douglas Kellner, (1991) *Postmodern Theory.* New York: Guilford Press.

Bloom, Samuel W. (2002) *The Word as Scalpel: A History of Medical Sociology.* New York: Oxford University Press.

Bosk, Charles L. (1979) *Forgive and Remember: Managing Medical Failure.* Chicago: University of Chicago Press.

Bourdieu, Pierre (1984) *Distinction.* Cambridge, MA: Harvard University Press.

Bourdieu, Pierre (1993) *Sociology in Question.* London: Sage.

Browning, Christopher R. and Kathleen A. Cagney (2002) "Neighborhood Structural Disadvantage, Collective Efficacy, and Self-Rated Health in a Physical Setting." *Journal of Health and Social Behavior* 43: 383–99.

Castro, Roberto (2005) "Medical Sociology in Mexico." In William Cockerham (ed.), *The Blackwell Companion to Medical Sociology.* Oxford: Blackwell, pp. 214–32.

Clarke, Adele E., Janet K. Shim, Laura Mamo, Jennifer Ruth Fosket, and Jennifer R. Fishman (2003) "Biomedicalization: Technoscientific Transformation of Health, Illness, and U.S. Biomedicine." *American Sociological Review* 68: 161–94.

Claus, Lisabeth (1982) *The Growth of a Sociological Discipline: On the Development of Medical Sociology in Europe,* Vols. I and II. Leuven, Belgium: Katholieke Universiteit.

Cockerham, William C. (2005) "Health Lifestyle Theory and the Convergence of Agency and Structure." *Journal of Health and Social Behavior* 46: 51–67.

Cockerham, William C. (2007a) "A Note on the Fate of Postmodern Theory and its Failure to Meet the Basic Requirements for Success in Medical Sociology." *Social Theory and Health* 5: 285–96.

Cockerham, William C. (2007b) *Social Causes of Health and Disease*. Cambridge: Polity Press.

Cockerham, William C. (2012) *Medical Sociology*, 12th edn. Upper Saddle River, NJ: Prentice Hall.

Cockerham, William C. and Graham Scambler (2010) "Medical Sociology and Sociological Theory." In William Cockerham (ed.), *The New Blackwell Companion to Medical Sociology*. Oxford: Blackwell, pp. 3–26.

Coe, Rodney (1970) *Sociology of Medicine*. New York: McGraw-Hill.

Conrad, Peter (2007) *The Medicalization of Society: On the Transformation of Human Conditions into Treatable Disorders*. Baltimore, MD: Johns Hopkins University Press.

Durkheim, Emile ([1897] 1951) *Suicide*. New York: Free Press.

Freeman, Howard, Sol Levine, and Leo Reeder (eds.) (1963) *Handbook of Medical Sociology*. Englewood Cliffs, NJ: Prentice Hall.

Freidson, Eliot (1970a) *Professional Dominance*. New York: Dodd, Mead.

Freidson, Eliot (1970b) *Profession of Medicine: A Study of the Sociology of Applied Knowledge*. Chicago: Aldine.

Freidson, Eliot (1975) *Doctoring Together*. New York: Elsevier-North Holland.

Glaser, Barney G. and Anselm M. Strauss (1965) *Awareness of Dying*. New York: Dodd, Mead.

Glaser, Barney G. and Anselm M. Strauss (1967) *The Discovery of Grounded Theory*. Chicago: Aldine.

Goffman, Erving (1961) *Asylums*. New York: Anchor.

Gold, Margaret (1977) "A Crisis of Identity: The Case of Medical Sociology." *Journal of Health and Social Behavior* 18: 160–8.

Gouldner, Alvin (1970) *The Coming Crisis of Western Sociology*. New York: Basic Books.

Hawkins, Norman (1958) *Medical Sociology*. Springfield, IL: Charles C. Thomas.

Hill, Terrence D., Catherine E. Ross, and Ronald J. Angel (2005) "Neighborhood Disorder, Psychophysiological Distress, Health." *Journal of Health and Social Behavior* 46: 170–86.

Hollingshead, August B. and Frederick C. Redlich (1958) *Social Class and Mental Illness: A Community Study*. New York: John Wiley.

Light, Donald (1993) "Countervailing Power: The Changing Character of the Medical Profession in the United States." In Fred Hafferty and John McKinley (eds.), *The Changing Medical Profession: An International Perspective*. New York: Oxford University Press, pp. 69–79.

Lin, Nan (2001) *Social Capital: A Theory of Social Structure and Action*. Cambridge: Cambridge University Press.

Link, Bruce G. and Jo Phelan (1995) "Social Conditions as Fundamental Causes of Disease." *Journal of Health and Social Behavior*, Extra Issue: 80–94.

Link, Bruce G. and Jo Phelan (2000) "Evaluating the Fundamental Cause Explanation for Social Disparities in Health." In Chloe Bird, Peter Conrad, and Allen Fremont (eds.), *Handbook of Medical Sociology*, 5th edn. Upper Saddle River, NJ: Prentice Hall, pp. 33–47.

Lochner, Kimberly A., Ichiro Kawachi, Robert T. Brennan, and Stephen I. Buka (2003) "Social Capital and Neighborhood Mortality Rates in Chicago." *Social Science and Medicine* 56: 1797–805.

Macintyre, Sally, Anne Ellaway, and Steven Cummins (2002) "Place Effects on Health: How Can We Conceptualise, Operationalise, and Measure Them?" *Social Science and Medicine* 60: 313–17.

Mechanic, David (1968) *Medical Sociology*. New York: Free Press.

Merton, Robert K., George G. Reader, and Patricia Kendall (eds.) (1957) *The Student-Physician*. Cambridge, MA: Harvard University Press.

Parsons, Talcott (1951) *The Social System*. New York: Free Press.

Pescosolido, Bernice A. and Beth Rubin (2000) 'The Web of Group Affiliations Revisited: Social Life, Postmodernism, and Sociology." *American Sociological Review* 65: 52–76.

Phelan, Jo C., Bruce G. Link, Ana Diez-Roux, Ichiro Kawachi, and Bruce Levin (2004) "'Fundamental Causes' of Social Inequalities in Mortality: A Test of the Theory." *Journal of Health and Social Behavior* 45: 265–85.

Putnam, Robert (2000) *Bowling Alone: The Collapse and Revival of American Community*. New York: Simon and Schuster.

Raudenbush, Stephen W. and Anthony S. Bryk (2002) *Hierarchical Linear Models: Applications and Data Analysis*, 2nd edn. Thousand Oaks, CA: Sage.

Ritzer, George (2011) *Sociological Theory*, 8th edn. New York: McGraw-Hill.

Ross, Catherine E. (2000) "Neighborhood Disadvantage and Adult Depression." *Journal of Health and Social Behavior* 41: 177–87.

Starr, Paul (1982) *The Social Transformation of American Medicine*. New York: Basic Books.

Stevens, Rosemary (1971) *American Medicine and the Public Interest*. New Haven, CT: Yale University Press.

Turner, Bryan (1984) *The Body and Society*. Oxford: Blackwell.

Turner, Bryan (1990) "The Interdisciplinary Curriculum: From Social Medicine to Post-Modernism." *Sociology of Health and Illness* 12: 1–23.

Turner, Bryan (2004) *The New Medical Sociology*. New York: Norton.

Warren, John Robert and Elaine M. Hernandez (2007) "Did Socioeconomic Inequalities in Morbidity and Mortality Change in the United States over the Course of the Twentieth Century?" *Journal of Health and Social Behavior* 48: 335–51.

Weber, Max ([1922] 1978) *Economy and Society*, Vol. 1. Berkeley, CA: University of California Press.

Wen, Ming and Nicholas Christakis (2006) "Prospective Effect of Community Distress and Subcultural Orientation on Mortality Following Life-Threatening Diseases in Later Life." *Sociology of Health and Illness* 28: 58–82.

22

Media and Communications

John Durham Peters and Jefferson D. Pooley

Communication and Social Theory: Legacy and Definitions

Of all the social sciences, sociology has the most distinguished record of contributions to the study of media and communications. Throughout every decade of the twentieth century, important sociologists have made it a central topic – Tarde, Park, Blumer, Ogburn, Lazarsfeld, Merton, Katz, Adorno, Habermas, Tuchman, Schudson, Gans, Luhmann, Bourdieu, among many others. Yet communication is not simply a specialty in sociology; it is in many ways the historical precondition of modern social theory. Its founding thinkers such as Tocqueville, Marx, Durkheim, Weber, Simmel, and Tönnies rarely mention communication by name, and yet their picture of modern society, with its individualism, participatory institutions, and new possibilities of large-scale social conflict, administration, and integration, centers on the symbolic coordination of individuals and populations. Concepts as diverse as Marx's class consciousness, Durkheim's collective representations, or Tönnies' *Gesellschaft* all point to social relationships that transcend the face-to-face. Neither ancient nor feudal society had any use for a notion of pluralistic, inclusive, and horizontal sociability. Modernity, with its political and transportation revolutions, foregrounds the symbolic aspect of social coordination. Communication becomes an axis of modern society. Association not anchored in place or in personal acquaintance is the central topic of both modern social theory and mass communication theory. Classic European social theory in this sense was always the study of communication without knowing it.

The Wiley-Blackwell Companion to Sociology, First Edition. Edited by George Ritzer.
© 2012 Blackwell Publishing Ltd. Published 2012 by Blackwell Publishing Ltd.

It was the Americans who made the explicit connection of sociology and communication. Drawing on German political economy and the evolutionary philosophy of Herbert Spencer, such first-generation American evolutionary sociologists as Lester Frank Ward and Franklin Giddings saw the movement of goods and ideas as the lifeblood of modern society. Even more emphatically, Charles Horton Cooley, Robert Ezra Park, and W. I. Thomas, along with their philosophical co-conspirators John Dewey and George Herbert Mead, saw society as a network of symbolic interactions. Communication was the secret of modern social organization. In Dewey's famous declaration, "Society not only continues to exist *by* transmission, *by* communication, but it may be fairly said to exist *in* transmission, *in* communication" ([1916] 1944: 4).

In its intellectual development, "communication" has meant many things (Peters 1999), and this was no less true in sociology. Communication's sense could include the dissemination of symbols, cultural transmission, and also more intimate processes as dialogue, socialization, or community-creation. For the Chicagoans, communication could mean the descriptive total of human relationships as well as an ideal of democratic participation. American democracy, they thought, depended on citizens becoming co-authors in the symbolic and material shaping of their worlds. Park and Burgess offer a characteristic pair of sentences: "[T]he limits of society are coterminous with the limits of interaction, that is, of the participation of persons in the life of society. One way of measuring the wholesome or the normal life of a person is by the sheer external fact of his membership in the social groups of the community in which his lot is cast" ([1921] 1924: 341). A straightforward descriptive statement (that communication defines social order) is followed by a normative one (that participation is the criterion of healthy social relations). This normative loading of communication persists in social theory to this day. For Jürgen Habermas, for instance, communication is not just linguistic exchange or social interaction, but a principle of rational intersubjectivity, even of social justice. For him, communication is much more than the sharing of information; it is the foundation of democratic deliberation. In seeing communication as the mesh of ego and alter, he is a clear heir to the early Chicago sociologists. "Communication" has always worn a halo, offering inklings of the good society.

Communication as a concept also splits along symbolic and material lines. In E. A. Ross's classic definition, "Communication embraces all symbols of experience together with the means by which they are swung across gulfs of space or time" (1938: 140). *Communications*, in contrast to *communication*, often makes just this distinction, referring to the institutions and practices of recording and transmitting symbols rather than to an ideal of community. It typically includes telecommunications such as the postal service, telegraph, telephone, satellite, and computer networks; sometimes railroads, highways, air and sea travel; sometimes also fundamental modes of human intercourse such as gesture, speech, writing, and printing.

We can also speak of these institutions and practices as *media*. The term has several senses. First, and least interesting, *media* in popular usage refers indiscriminately and often disparagingly to the personnel or institutions of the news media, taken as a lump. Second, *mass* media often refers to a complex of culture industries, especially the big five – radio, television, movies, newspapers, and magazines –

which share the features of being for-profit institutions that use industrial-era technology to engage in largely monologic transmission to massive audiences. Media sociology arose in the heyday of these media, roughly the 1920s through the 1960s or 1970s, but it is now clear that these definitional criteria may be valid only for a passing historical moment. Hence a third definition of media is needed: any vessel of cultural storage, transmission, or expression. In this sense, architecture, cities, sculpture, bumper stickers, skywriting, or the human body could be media, in the same sense that one speaks of artistic media such as oil, watercolor, or papier mâché. This expanded sense of *media* is used by thinkers outside of the mainstream of media sociology such as Harold Adams Innis, Lewis Mumford, and Friedrich Kittler (1999) who link basic media forms with larger civilizational consequences. Though less precise, this more open definition broadens the historical and comparative vistas of media studies. A more expansive definition is helpful for understanding current transformations in communications pushed by digital media.

Standardizing and localizing trends

In broad strokes, a fundamental task of twentieth-century media sociology has been to assuage the anxiety that modern communications homogenize culture and society. Sociological research has repeatedly minimized fears of media power. Though new communications media seemingly rupture social scale, local community life does not disappear, say most sociologists; rather, it takes different shapes.

In the early twentieth century, the main challenge came from the anxiety, deriving largely from crowd psychology and Tocqueville's notion of democratic leveling, that modern communication, thanks to its contagious sweep and increased radius of influence, would wash all personal, cultural, and geographic diversity into a standardized ocean of sameness. Cooley (1909: ch. 9) responded by arguing that improved communications enhance "choice" and weaken "isolation" as the basis of individuation. His point, familiar in turn-of-the-century social thought, was that communication had superseded geography as the chief constraint on human sociability. A community of isolation would differentiate, like Darwin's finches, in idiosyncratic directions, but a community of choice, one united by the interests rather than location of its participants, was a harbinger of a renewed democracy. In a sense Cooley theorized virtual communities by suggesting that new forms of communication allowed for remote associations based on interest rather than place. Thus Cooley, like his colleagues, identified countervailing tendencies against the supposed time- and space-destroying powers of new forms of communication. The first generation of American sociology answered the specter of uniformity with the hope of the great community.

Malcolm Willey and Stuart Rice, in a forgotten but highly suggestive early study of new transport and communication media, made a similar argument: "Contacts within the community are multiplied out of proportion to contacts at a distance" (1933: 57). Rather than eviscerating local life, cars and telephones actually multiplied the intensity of contacts. Though new means offered an unprecedented opportunity to escape locality, they were more often used to link familiar people and places. "Individuals north, south, east, and west, may all wear the garments of Hollywood. At the same time each may hold with undiminished vigor to certain local attitudes, traditions, and beliefs. An increase in overt standardization may be accompanied by retention of inward differences" (Willey & Rice 1933: 213–14). The Payne Fund studies were published around the same time: 13 book-length reports on cinema and children by sociologists such as Herbert Blumer and psychologists including L. L. Thurstone. The studies themselves, though undercut by an alarmist and moralizing popular summary volume, challenged the fear that America's children were altogether movie-made. One nearly forgotten Payne Fund sociologist, Paul Cressey, dismissed "sweeping statements about the motion picture's 'effect'": what the movie-goer "perceives or fails to perceive upon the screen, what he feels or does not feel, what he remembers or fails to remember, and what he does or does not imitate," wrote Cressey, "are inevitably affected by his social background and personality as much, or more than, by the immediate motion picture situation" (1938: 521).

In a somewhat similar way, the tradition of work on media effects associated with Columbia University sought to check the fear that media were bulldozing collective bonds and individual judgment. The hallmark of the research done by Paul F. Lazarsfeld and his students at Columbia in the 1940s and 1950s was the proposition that media have strong influence only when mediated by such psychological variables as selectivity or sociological variables as interpersonal relations. Work at the Columbia Bureau of Applied Social Research focused more on the short-term attitudinal effects of media campaigns than on the larger trends favored by the Chicagoans, although Lazarsfeld's blueprint, at least, of the mission of communications research did include the macro, long-term consequences of media for social organization.

The Columbia tradition's insight that the power of mediated messages is constrained by extant social-psychological conditions has proved remarkably influential and adaptable. Against the inflated fears (or hopes) of some propaganda analysts, Lazarsfeld and Robert Merton (1948) argued that mass communication could be persuasive only under special conditions such as the absence of counter-propaganda, the reinforcement of media messages by face-to-face discussion, and the strategic exploitation of well-established behaviors. The power of unaided mass media to win wars, sway voters, or sell soap was, they argued, overrated. In their 1955 book, *Personal Influence*, Lazarsfeld and Elihu Katz argued for the priority of personal over mediated influence. People, not radio or newspapers, turned out to be the key channels of communication. Opinion leaders first expose themselves to media, then talk to friends and family, thus serving as links in the larger network of communication, by dancing "the two-step flow" of communication. The "discovery of people" in the process of communication, as Katz and Lazarsfeld whimsically called it, was not only empirical; it was a gambit in the debate in 1950s sociology about whether postwar America had become a mass society of lonely crowds, disconnected from each other but connected by media. (In the same decade, however, Bureau researchers and many other media sociologists applied the "two-step flow" findings to the Cold War search for effective propaganda design, in sometimes-classified work for the military and other federal agencies.) In its front-stage, published work at least, Lazarsfeld's Bureau expounded people's immunity to media-induced atomization and assimilation, thus fitting the broader American legacy of understanding media as agents of social differentiation rather than homogenization. Localizing factors were again deemed as important as standardizing ones in the effects of mass communication.

The same argumentative logic appears in later work in the same tradition. In a study of the worldwide reception of the television program *Dallas*, Tamar Liebes and Katz (1990) argue against the widespread fear that a new imperialism of television, music, and film would lead to a global (American) monoculture. Instead, Liebes and Katz showed that different groups used their own cultural and ideological predispositions and resources to interpret *Dallas* in distinct ways. Russian Israelis, for instance, often read *Dallas* as a self-critical exposé of American capitalism while Israeli Arabs often focused on its intricate kinship structures and clan-loyalties. Against the classic fear of a powerful media stimulus, updated here to an international setting, Liebes and Katz affirmed the inevitability of diverse and local responses to a homogeneously disseminated text. (In this, they were in line with trends in literary and cultural studies work on audiences, even if the affinities were not often recognized.) Though the context was different from the founding generation of American sociology – electronic media threatening national diversity worldwide vs. national railroads and newspapers threatening island communities – the sociological response was similar: outward (media) standardization, inward (social) differentiation.

The critical tradition of media sociology contests this *Gemeinschaft*-after-all optimism. Though home-grown variants like C. Wright Mills (1956) emerged in the 1950s, the main body of critical sociology appeared in the United States during the aftermath of the New Left's self-immolation in the late 1960s. For theoretical coordinates, sociologists largely turned to the chastened Marxists of the post-1917 West, who decades before had sought to explain working-class consent to dominant class rule. Western Marxists like Antonio Gramsci, Georg Lukács, Max Horkheimer, and Theodor Adorno had grappled with the market's awesome staying power. They had identified culture and ideology as potent weapons in the capitalist arsenal, capable of convincing the masses to tighten their own chains. For Horkheimer and Adorno, the Frankfurt School scholars, the "might of industrial society is lodged in men's minds . . . Immovably, [the masses] insist on the very ideology which enslaves them" ([1944] 1991: 127, 133). Though Horkheimer and Adorno had clashed with Lazarsfeld (Adorno's erstwhile employer) during their New York exile in the 1940s, most of the Western Marxist canon – including the critical theorists' "The Culture Industry" essay – was not translated into English until the early 1970s. Gramsci's theory of hegemony left the strongest imprint on critical media sociology, in works like Todd Gitlin's *The Whole World Is Watching* (1980).

Lazarsfeld's tradition, like that of the Chicago school, ultimately sees the media as agents of social integration; the critical tradition agrees that media achieve integration – a forced reconciliation in the interest of a few. It is a remarkable irony, to recast the point, that Katz's "And Deliver Us from Segmentation" (1996) overlaps so much with a Marxist screed like Herbert Schiller's *The Mind Managers* (1973). The former, a homage to the nation-binding vitality of limited-channel TV, subscribes to Schiller's core thesis with a more voluntaristic twist: that mass communication acts as a societal glue, adhering its members to one another against a common, mediated horizon. Media sociology, whether critical or mainstream, has turned on the question of social homogenization and control.

CONTEMPORARY ISSUES

The national frame

All complex societies, ancient and modern, organize communications in various ways and to diverse ends. For much of the past century, communications generally and the mass media in particular were designed to link the nation-state with the household. In Habermas's language, media have been a chief agent in coupling "system" (the market and the state) and "lifeworld" (civil society and the family). Modern media history, especially that of the press and broadcasting, is an open book of large-scale social integration. Modern media have had the task of tying micro-level parts of social life (taste, consumption, the household) to macro-level cultural, political, and economic structures (corporations, the nation). Raymond Williams (1974) coined the suggestive term "mobile privatization" for the contradictory historical processes shaping the emergence of broadcasting: increased mobility in goods, people, and ideas, together with the solidification of the household as a site of entertainment and consumption. (Note too the hint of political pathos: this was not public mobilization!) Newspapers, realist drama, brand names, opinion polling, mail-order catalogs, soap operas, call-in shows, or TV guides are diverse examples of practices that mediate feeling and structure, household and society. As media always involve negotiations along the border of public and private, their study raises explicit questions about the constitution of social order (Carey 1989). What was significant about modern media was not only the pervasiveness of their reach, but also the intimacy of the site in which they touched us.

In Benedict Anderson's thesis (1991), the modern newspaper, even with local circulation, invited its readers to imagine themselves members in a vast national community. Network broadcasting, which did achieve national distribution, likewise operated in the frame of the nation-state. The national focus is clear in such names as NBC, CBS, ABC, BBC, and CBC, each of which indexes the polity: National, Columbia, American, British, and Canadian. Radio first established the crucial arrangements in the two decades between the world wars: nationwide distribution of programs to a domestic audience trained to simultaneous reception. Despite differences between the market-sponsored system in the United States and the state-sponsored systems of Europe and elsewhere, something sociologically remarkable was achieved in broadcasting: the coordination of national populations over time and space. Perhaps what emerged earlier on Sunday mornings in Protestant countries, with the whole population effectively tuned to the same "program" (the vernacular Bible), was similar, but broadcasting was new in the conjuring of a simultaneously co-oriented national populace and in its address of a listenership at home. Cinema too, from the First World War through the 1960s or so, was organized nationally in production, content, distribution, and exhibition. In their heydays, both broadcasting and cinema were at once a mode of production, a set of stylistic conventions, and a set of social relations involving audiences and cultural forms (though these, as we will see, were importantly different for the two media).

Due to technical, regulatory, and economic developments, the national frame for cinema and television has been waning in the past 35 years. (In some regions, such as sub-Saharan Africa, radio is still the medium of national integration, but for most industrialized countries it has long been the medium of musically differentiated taste cultures or "formats.") The domestic box office is only one important source of revenue for Hollywood films today, along with foreign box office sales, video sales, and merchandising. Instead of a studio system churning out variations on well-known genres for a national audience, one shift has been to blockbusters (genres based on a single case), from *Jaws* to *Avatar*, for distribution (and merchandising) across the globe. Television audiences, while often still huge in relative terms, are increasingly fragmented into demographic segments thanks to channel proliferation and the migration of programming onto the internet. Given the digital encoding of all content, media are increasingly inseparable from communications. The air once carried radio and television programming, but increasingly fiber-optic cables are the main medium for news and entertainment, just as the air is becoming the prime medium of voice and data transmission thanks to mobile telephony, in a rather stunning switch of the old order. In 1950, mail, telephones, phonographs, radios, televisions, and movie theaters were all separate platforms with distinct content such as print, interactive voice, sound, image, and money; now they are all carried on the internet in digital form. Broadcasting to a national audience, then, just like national cinema, may turn out to be a momentary historical deviation. When social scientists were minting concepts for media analysis at mid-century, mass communication had paradigmatic status. Today different conditions such as smaller audience size, differentiated niches, altered social norms, and user-generated content raise new questions.

One such question is the fate of social integration amidst the proliferation of channels and fragmentation of audiences. As recently as the 1970s, the three American television networks, NBC, CBS, and ABC, shared up to 95 percent of the viewing audience. That figure has dropped to just over 50 percent, shared among NBC, CBS, ABC, and Fox, owing to competition with cable services, but also satellite, video rentals, home computers, mobile devices, and the internet. Since the 1970s, advertisers have sought purer demographic segments (Turow 2006). This is clearly a radical shift from the national provision of news and entertainment – though not an utter meltdown. A common fear is that citizens will be mutually isolated by their idiosyncratic tastes. Instead of national newspapers people will read "the daily me"; identity politics will vanquish the common good. Yet the potential to fragment into a Babel of private cultural tongues is tempered by various attention-gathering exercises afforded by the internet. Overwhelmed consumers have in effect turned to each other: user-generated YouTube reviews, virally spread link-advice, micro-blogging endorsements, and even professional "curators" at the Huffington Post and elsewhere. To some extent, social networks have replaced the broadcast networks as the conveners of our attention. Clearly channel-multiplication has created neither cultural nor cognitive chaos, as some postmodern writers once feared (or celebrated). The statistical limits on human energy always centralize attention. Audiences still take shape, albeit smaller and asynchronous ones. The fear that media segmentation will cause citizens to retreat to a cocoon of private egoism (a fear in social theory that dates at least to Tocqueville) is checked by the habitual preferences of audiences for programming that engages a broader frame. Fragmentation has replaced homogenization as the chief fear aroused by media.

The shifting moral economy of media

The waning of a nationally organized schedule of programs as a cultural grid suggests a more significant, but more subtle transformation of the place of media in the general moral economy. Because it entered the homes of the nation, broadcasting historically accepted constraints on topics and forms of expression. Radio, like television, was painted as a guest in the family circle, and was hence pressured to embody a culture of middle-brow mundaneness and normality, a tonality that continued from early radio through much of television, though never with full compliance. From Mae West's banishment off the airwaves in 1938 for inviting the puppet Charlie McCarthy to play in her "wood pile," through the 1978 Supreme Court case *Pacifica* which found that broadcasting's "unique pervasiveness" justified tighter content controls than in other media, radio and television have been bound by a thick set of normative, if obviously ideologically loaded, constraints (the nation as patriarchal family). Because they spoke to the nation at home, radio and television in their heydays were regarded, for better or worse, as forums whose tone should be suitable to all.

Film, in contrast, never quite assumed the same burden of public decency as broadcasting, despite an even more intense history of attack by the guardians of public morals. The theatrical exhibition of movies took place outside the home, in dark spaces set apart for collective fantasy on extraordinary topics such as romance, sex, crime, and adventure. The dangers of such fantasy were buffered by collective viewing; the assembled peer group of fellow citizens, as Cantril and Allport (1935) argued, immunized against anti-social consequences. Wandering eyes and hearts were cathartically reserved to the film palace. For both film and broadcasting around mid-century, the audience experience was intensely normed: one watched movies collectively and took part in broadcasting with the awareness that one's reference groups were also simultaneously doing so.

The division of media labor – broadcasting as normalizing the family circle, film as fantasizing the collective psyche – has crumbled. The multiplication of channels and shifting modes of exhibition and delivery suggest shifting constraints on the audience experience. The old standard of broadcast decency has weakened, as has the sense of a simultaneous collectivity of fellow watchers. Katz (1996) argues that proliferation of channels breaks the collective norm of obligatory viewing. Viewing becomes an asocial experience, not a simultaneous communion of reference groups that sets the agenda for water-cooler discussions the next day. The very notion of a "Home Box Office," the first dominant cable channel (1975) and a leader in getting content hitherto allowed only in theaters onto television screens, signaled the beginning of these changes.

In an age of increased fragmentation, content once taboo for a national audience fills channels aimed at a few but available to many. Conservative backlash against cultural industries, and efforts to label, rate, or otherwise police the vast output of new film, television, and music commodities will likely remain part of the political landscape. Legislation like the Communications Decency Act (1996), the Child Online Projection Act (1998) – both found unconstitutional – and the Children's Internet Protection Act (2000) are state-sponsored answers to the decline of moral inhibitions in the wake of splintering audiences and globalized programming flows.

What some read as symptoms of large moral or civilizational decline reflects, in fact, changing industrial and technical conditions. As long as profit is the chief value that governs media production, new kinds of content will continue to appear that can make money from marginal audiences.

The normative frame of much American television programming has shifted from common culture to private club, allowing forms and contents of expression adapted to homogeneous in-groups. No longer under the ideological and economic constraint of reaching general audiences, American television today includes R-rated prime-time drama, explicitly indecent talk shows, and caught-on-tape programs featuring, for example, animals (or police officers) attacking people. As programs proliferated into niches, television lost its halo as the collective hearth, even if still viewed by a plurality of citizens. Nowhere is this loss clearer than on the internet. The invitation of YouTube, the Google-owned online video site, to "broadcast yourself" signals the shift in a single phrase. Once broadcasting was impersonal and collective; today it can be a project in self-expression bordering on narcissism. The blogosphere allows everyone with time, access, and skills to be a journalist, and Facebook allows users to personalize their content (and advertisers to specify their appeals). The internet has become the world's leading purveyor of pornography. What during the broadcast era was a niche medium available only through shops, the mail, or certain urban districts, now has a potential outlet at every computer screen connected to the internet. Totalizing pervasiveness is down, differentiated ubiquity is up.

Channel-multiplication creates a huge demand for content. Prime-time television drama is still sometimes lavishly or at least expensively produced, as in the case of *CSI* or *Lost*, but talk, game, and "reality" shows have the advantage of attracting saleable audiences with low production budgets. (For one thing, actors taken off the street do not charge huge fees.) The race for content also makes control over the rights to film, television, and music libraries industrially crucial (and worrisome to historians and purists, who fear such commercially-motivated tampering as the colorization of old black-and-white movies). The scarcest commodity today is not channel capacity, as it was when broadcasting emerged; it is desirable programming.

The proliferation of channels, then, does not imply social fragmentation; it implies a changed social place for the public delivery of content and an attendant loss of moral inhibitions. Nonetheless, live collective mass television viewing is likely to recur on an intermittent basis with "media events" such as royal funerals, sports extravaganzas, or natural or human disasters such as tsunamis and terrorist attacks (Katz & Liebes 2007).

Globalization

Media flows have long been conceived as threats to national culture. In the 1970s, the common critique was that American film and television were agents of cultural imperialism since national entertainment industries could not compete with their slick products. While such arguments could serve to fortify nationalist sentiments at home, they correctly saw Hollywood's comparative advantage in its production values and economies of scale. For the price of creating one hour of original TV, countries can lease from 10 to 100 times as much US prime-time drama. Audiences worldwide prefer local or national content, but the hitch is always production quality. Still, globalization and Americanization are not the same thing. Like everything else, media globalize unevenly. The media are not as American as they used to be (Tunstall 2008). Multiple centers of production trouble the old model of one center and one periphery: Brazilian telenovelas in Russia, Mexican programs in Latin America, Egyptian television in the Arab world, Bollywood movies in East Africa, Eastern Europe, and China, or Hong Kong action cinema in the US. There is important regionalization of media flows, often based on common language and culture, but also mixtures and pockets (Indian "Vedic" metal, karaoke in the Philippines, or the wild diversities of global hip hop, etc.). Even so, America remains the most dominant exporter. Compared to the vast majority of other nations, the US is ironically quite lacking in foreign media content. Countries average about one-third foreign TV programming, but the US has about 2 percent. The American market can absorb Power Rangers and Pokémon, but in entertainment, as in news, it remains isolated by its gigantism. It is strange indeed that the world's chief exporter of cultural matter is relatively blind to what every other nation sees constantly: media content from elsewhere.

States often seek to protect national culture by building dams for media flows. France, Canada, and New Zealand, for instance, all have quotas for the radio play of nationally produced music. States also find other motives for blockage, usually sex and politics. Some Muslim nations are nervous about satellite television. China continues to maintain its Great Firewall and censor online content. In all efforts to block media flows, the state walks a tightrope between global political-economic pressures (since regulation erects a statist obstacle to global capitalism) and national-political ones (preservation of national distinctness). Besides state intervention, there are other subtler impediments to media flows, such as cultural accessibility. Violence and sex may travel more readily across national and linguistic borders than culturally-specific and dialogue-heavy programming such as comedy and drama.

The miniaturization and cheapening of media production also fuels transborder media flows. Much can be done at a desktop, in a basement, or even on a phone. Email and other internet-based social networking tools are the bane of repressive governments from Tehran to Rangoon. The ease of citizen production (and piracy) bypasses traditional gatekeepers. *Titanic* was banned in Iran, and yet it was almost instantly available there in bootleg versions, recorded by hand-held video cameras in movie theaters abroad. Digital file-sharing sites make the process even easier (Cenite, Wang Wanzheng, Peiwen & Shimin Chan 2009). The heavy artillery of media once touted by modernization theory, which not only require capital investment but also a complex division of labor, have been outflanked by do-it-yourself media. As conceived by modernizers such as Rostow, Lerner, and Schramm, literacy, newspapers, and national broadcasting are the crown atop industrialization and infrastructural development such as roads, schools, and hydroelectric dams. Instead, relatively cheap, oral media such as mobile phones and radios have spread in such non-industrialized regions as Africa or the Middle East. If we count piracy, much of sub-Saharan African is well plugged into global cultural circulation (Larkin 2004). Media are a chief exhibit of the disjunctive character of globalization (Appadurai 1996). Clearly, modernity is not a package deal.

Given shrinking cost and access to media production, how to explain the persistent concentration in media corporations? The long muckraking tradition attacking media power that stretches from Upton Sinclair to Noam Chomsky to Robert McChesney, with its doctrine that concentration of control means uniformity in content, risks missing the curious ways that huge cultural industries have learned to allow, like the Catholic Church, all kinds of internal variety in cultural production. Likewise, Horkheimer and Adorno's classic analysis of the integrated culture industry was quite apt for Hollywood in the 1940s, when vertical integration of film production, distribution, and exhibition was at its height, but finds only partial resonance today. Corporate power should be a foremost issue on the agenda of media studies, but *modi operandi* have changed. The recording industry majors, for instance, are hardly the monolithic trusts of yore. Non-existent synergies, fragmenting audiences, and competition from digital upstarts have led the big conglomerates to sell off major units (Time Warner), split in two (Viacom), or get out of the media business altogether (GE). Rupert Murdoch's efforts to colonize Chinese TV screens by satellite went bust. The media barons are scrambling.

Implications of digital media

Driving much of the transformation of media is the growing power and shrinking size and cost of computing. The "convergence" of telephones, televisions, and computers on the internet creates both a new medium and a zoo of diverse media species – raising again the paradox of simultaneous bigness and smallness in media today. Marshall McLuhan argued that the content of a new medium is an old medium. The internet contains all previous media forms – telegraphy, telephony, phonography, radio, television, film, books, magazines, newspapers, and videogames – and, alas, advertising. Indeed, the internet has recapitulated radio's early transition from a culture of anarchic, technically minded renegades (amateurs/nerds) into a corporate engine of mass entertainment and commerce.

Like channel-multiplication in television, digitization raises questions of the public organization of cultural menus. What is to keep cultural consumption from being identical to cultural production, as people learn to treat digitized products as code to be manipulated? (The "mash-up" is a favored YouTube genre.) Again, the fear of private cocoons or the utopia of universal creativity should both be limited by the recognition of opportunity costs and the ongoing need for shared cultural experience. Information is not scarce in a digital world, but intelligence is – one reason why aggregation sites are proliferating. The packaging (pre-processing) of information is always crucial, especially in situations of programming abundance. Information bottlenecks make clear the principle that media are not just pipes, but have unanticipated consequences. As Innis (1950) insisted, new media create monopolies of knowledge and hence aid formation of new power-holding classes, such as search giant, Google, the world's *de facto* library.

The internet is a huge well of digitized code – sounds, texts, images – available for creative appropriation, raising fascinating questions for art and economics. One issue is the unprecedented manipulability of digital texts. Digital technology allows for editing *within* the frame, instead of between frames, blurring the formerly separate domains of production and post-production in film and video. The documentary or testimonial function of photography or sound recording is now more dubious. Probably the biggest issue arising from the plasticity of digital content is intellectual property rights. Advocates for the internet as a cultural commons and citizens as mash-up artists who remix culture to their own visions face uphill battles against corporate power and entrenched copyright law (Lessig 2008). A related issue is the infrastructural architecture of the internet. Will domain names continue to be assigned by the American ICANN or will a more global form of governance emerge? Do nation-states have a legitimate interest in regulating internet access? Google's agreement to do business in China at the price of censoring searches the Chinese state deemed sensitive was widely criticized, but few have complained about how Google.de regularly censors anti-Semitic sites in accordance with German laws against hate speech. What are the bounds of privacy in a time when massive amounts of personal information are collected from every move we make online? Every search and its subsequent "clickstream" ever made on Google is recorded on its computers, and even though that company still presents itself as a search utility, its corporate mission is data analysis, and on a peta-byte scale, something unprecedented in history. Questions about power and surveillance will continue to shape inquiry about the internet (Andrejevic 2007).

Digitization intensifies an old principle of electronic media: economies of scale. In contrast to print media, which always had steep unit costs (paper and ink), audiovisual media generally faced gigantic first-copy costs and cheap unit costs. Even a feature-film print, costing over 10,000 dollars, is inexpensive compared to the cost of the original; cutting a vinyl LP copy is even cheaper; but a digital copy costs next to nothing. Whereas analog media require a physical tie to the original, digital media can be transported anywhere with enough bandwidth. Media industries are today principally in the software business, spreading their goods across many platforms. Newspapers and magazines have watched their business models collapse as they migrate online, with new, revenue-siphoning advertising competition and a generation of consumers unwilling to pay for their now-ethereal products. Prominent scholars and journalists have answered the white-knuckled prophesies of doom with calls for nonprofit ownership and foundation-supported investigative journalism along the lines of the Pulitzer Prize-winning Pro Publica website (Downie & Schudson 2009). It is an index of print-media desperation that its fortunes are widely seen to rest on the success of Apple's media-on-a-screen mobile devices.

The dream of universal accessibility of culture, of an Alexandrine library on the wires, is nowhere in sight, Google Books notwithstanding. Consider how fragile – how fugitive – are the quanta of online expression. The valiant efforts of the Internet Archive and other digital preservationists have not solved the technological problems of incompatibility and turnover. All records are subject to degradation, but we have lots of experience with writing and printing, whose (not inconsiderable) decoding apparatus is literacy, and little experience with digital storage in an economy of planned obsolescence. This age, eager to record everything, could ironically be a sealed book in the future if playback machines are not preserved. Digitization may mean traffic jams as much as information flows. As always, the sociology of digital media should recognize centripetal as well as centrifugal trends.

The great communications switch

Perhaps one of the strangest and subtlest shifts of our time is the increasing mediation of interpersonal interaction – by phone, email, social networks, etc. At the same time, mass media discourse has grown increasingly conversational. In the 1940s, Adorno attacked "pseudo-individualization" in mass culture, the pretense of establishing one-on-one relationships with audiences in commercial forms of address like "especially for you"; and Merton attacked the "pseudo-*Gemeinschaft*" of media-promoted communities. Both grasped, from distinct positions on the theoretical compass, the ways that media imitated interpersonal styles and vice versa (Thompson 1995). Just as broadcasting and telephony have switched media (from air to wires), perhaps the richer nations of the planet are in the middle of a great communications switch: in face-to-face talk intimates broadcast at each other while media are full of strangers making peer-to-peer connections with us.

A hallmark of twentieth-century cinema, drama, and literature – and sociology – was the gaps between people, that is, the distortion and difficulty of dialogue. People were seen as sending messages to each other and never quite connecting. Broadcasting and the press, in contrast, have consistently imitated dialogical and intimate styles of talk, a development motivated by both domestic reception and commercial purpose (Scannell 1991). Though some scholars have treated "parasocial interaction" (the feeling that people have personal relationships with media figures) as a pathology, it is clear that most relationships, face-to-face or otherwise, are imagined in some sense. There are elements of fictionalization in interpersonal relationships, not only in fan clubs or the more prototypical kinds of parasocial interaction. Harvey Sacks's (1992) conversational analysis showed just how tortured and fraught – and intricately ordered – everyday dialogue could be. Knowing what is dialogue and what is broadcast in daily interactions is often difficult in an age when people routinely talk in public to an invisible partner (on their phones). The disembodiment of interaction represents a longer trend that theorists such as Luhmann and Giddens associate with modernity generally. There is, too, the calculated spontaneity of the Facebook status update – extroversion with a motive, to an audience of hundreds. Interaction has become precisely something to be managed, not a natural reciprocity.

While everyday speech has grown more fraught, public discourse has grown more personal. In the nineteenth century, it was considered undignified for presidential candidates to make personal campaign appearances. Aloofness was honorable. Today it is a truism that leaders project their sincerity to the camera. From Teddy Roosevelt onward, the personalization of political leaders has grown massively, thanks to developments in the audiovisual capacities of the press and a more general process of social informalization (Elias 1998), a process, once started, that did not stop with Reagan's smile and Clinton's tears, but made public the former's polyps and the latter's semen.

Sociologists in the sociology of media

A paradox of media sociology is that most of it, at least over the last 40 years, has been the work of non-sociologists. Sociology as an organized discipline largely abandoned the study of mass communication in the early 1960s, after three decades at the center of the interdisciplinary field. The reasons for the fall-off are complex, but two important factors stand out: a major shift in federal funding for social science after Sputnik, along with the emergence of the would-be discipline of communication. In effect, PhD-granting journalism schools took over the formal study of media, in part by drawing media sociologists into their well-off orbit (Pooley & Katz 2008). In *Social Theory and Social Structure* (1949), Merton had positioned the sociology of mass communication as the American answer to the European sociology of knowledge. As it turned out, schools of journalism supplied the answer, however ungainly.

The irony is that sociology, the only discipline with the ambition to understand social life as a whole, has for many decades neglected a central dimension of the modern experience. One consequence is that sociological theory, by now an established subdiscipline, touches on media questions only glancingly. Even the sociology of culture, gathering momentum since the mid-1970s, has largely sidestepped media institutions in its studies of expressive culture. There are exceptions, of course, including the efflorescence of newsroom sociology associated with Herbert Gans and Gaye Tuchman, among others, in the late 1970s and early 1980s. Looking back, however, this literature comes off more like a rule-proving interregnum. The neglect is mutual, as scholars of communication – beset by status anxieties and the taint of vocational instruction – are sealed off from sociology.

There is a final, happy irony. In the last decade or so, sociologists have been returning to communication questions – a gathering interest galvanized by the internet and other new media technologies. This sociology of the internet, epitomized by the work of Manual Castells and Barry Wellman, has its roots in the study of social networks and urban life. There is, in its motivating questions, more than an echo of Chicago. Castells and Wellman conceive of social networks, including but not limited to those afforded by the internet, as something like social structure – as the flexible sinew by which societies and institutions hold (and adjust) their shape. Recall Dewey's phrase: society exists *in* communication.

Acknowledgment

The authors would like to thank Benjamin Peters for helpful commentary.

References

Anderson, B. (1991) *Imagined Communities: Reflections on the Origins and Spread of Nationalism*, 2nd edn. London: Verso.

Andrejevic, M. (2007) *iSpy: Surveillance and Power in the Interactive Era*. Lawrence, KS: University Press of Kansas.

Appadurai, A. (1996) *Modernity at Large: Cultural Dimensions of Globalization*. Minneapolis: University of Minnesota.

Cantril, H. and G. W. Allport (1935) *The Psychology of Radio*. New York: Harpers.

Carey, J. W. (1989) *Communication as Culture: Essays on Media and Society*. Boston: Unwin Hyman.

Cenite, M., M. Wang Wanzheng, C. Peiwen, and G. Shimin Chan (2009) "More Than Just Free Content: Motivations of Peer-to-Peer File Sharers." *Journal of Communication Inquiry* 33(3): 206–21.

Cooley, C. H. ([1909] 1993) *Social Organization: A Study of the Larger Mind*. New Brunswick, NJ: Transaction.

Cressey, P. G. (1938) "The Motion Picture Experience as Modified by Social Background and Personality." *American Sociological Review* 3: 516–25.

Dewey, J. ([1916] 1944) *Democracy and Education*. New York: Free Press.

Downie, L., Jr. and M. Schudson (2009) *The Reconstruction of American Journalism*. New York: Columbia University Graduate School of Journalism.

Elias, N. (1998) "Informalization and the Civilizing Process." In Johan Goudsblom and Stephen Mennell (eds.), *The Norbert Elias Reader*. Oxford: Blackwell, pp. 325–35.

Gitlin, T. (1980) *The Whole World Is Watching: Mass Media in the Making and Unmaking of the New Left*. Berkeley, CA: University of California Press.

Horkheimer, M. and T. W. Adorno ([1944] 1991) *Dialectic of Enlightenment*. New York: Continuum.

Innis, H. A. (1950) *Empire and Communications*. Oxford: Clarendon Press.

Katz, E. (1996) "And Deliver Us from Segmentation." *Annals of the American Academy of Political and Social Science* 546(1): 22–33.

Katz, E. and T. Liebes (2007) "'No More Peace!': How Disaster, Terror and War Have Upstaged Media Events." *International Journal of Communication* 1: 157–66.

Kittler, F. (1999) *Gramophone, Film, Typewriter*. Stanford, CA: Stanford University Press.

Larkin, B. (2004) "Degraded Images, Distorted Sounds: Nigerian Video and the Infrastructure of Piracy." *Public Culture* 16(2): 289–314.

Lazarsfeld, P. F. and E. Katz (1955) *Personal Influence: The Part Played by People in the Flow of Mass Communications*. Glencoe, IL: Free Press.

Lazarsfeld, P. F. and R. K. Merton (1948) "Mass Communication, Popular Taste, and Organized Social Action." In L. Bryson (ed.), *The Communication of Ideas*. New York: Harper, pp. 95–118.

Lessig, L. (2008) *Remix: Making Art and Commerce Thrive in the Hybrid Economy*. New York: Penguin.

Liebes, T. and E. Katz (1990) *The Export of Meaning: Cross-Cultural Readings of Dallas*. New York: Oxford University Press.

Merton, R. K. (1949) *Social Theory and Social Structure*. Glencoe, IL: Free Press.

Mills, C. W. (1956) *The Power Elite*. New York: Oxford University Press.

Park, R. E. and E. W. Burgess ([1921] 1924) *Introduction to the Science of Sociology*. Chicago: University of Chicago Press.

Peters, J. D. (1999) *Speaking into the Air: A History of the Idea of Communication*. Chicago: University of Chicago Press.

Pooley, J. and E. Katz (2008) "Further Notes on Why American Sociology Abandoned Mass Communication Research." *Journal of Communication* 58: 767–86.

Ross, E. A. (1938) *Principles of Sociology*. New York: Appleton-Century.

Sacks, H. (1992) *Lectures on Conversation*, Vols. 1–2. Oxford: Blackwell.

Scannell, P. (1991) *Broadcast Talk*. London: Sage.

Schiller, H. I. (1973) *The Mind Managers*. Boston: Beacon Press.

Thompson, J. (1995) *The Media and Modernity*. Stanford, CA: Stanford University Press.

Tunstall, J. (2008) *The Media Were American: U.S. Mass Media in Decline*. New York: Oxford University Press.

Turow, J. (2006) *Niche Envy: Marketing Discrimination in the Digital Age*. Cambridge, MA: MIT Press.

Willey, M. M. and S. A. Rice (1933) *Communication Agencies and Social Life*. New York: McGraw-Hill.

Williams, R. (1974) *Television: Technology and Cultural Form*. New York: Schocken.

23

Work and Employment

STEVEN P. VALLAS

INTRODUCTION

Work and employment have been of central concern to virtually all major sociological thinkers since the very inception of the discipline. The classical theorists
emphasized the primacy of work organizations and occupational life in the production of modernity itself. In the United States, the Chicago School paid keen attention
to the relation between work and communities, and generally viewed work as a
"fateful" social tie (Hughes [1951] 1994). After World War II, a rich tradition of
ethnographic research emerged on the basis of such thinking, with major works
published by Chinoy (1955), Gouldner (1954), and Roy (1952). With the tumult
of the 1960s, Marxist work in particular asked probing questions about the establishment of managerial control over the labor process. Since that time, scholars have
contributed a vibrant literature on the social mechanisms that perpetuate both racial
and gender inequalities at work (with obvious implications for both management
practices and public policy as well). Equally pronounced has been an explosion of
research on the relationship between organizations and their wider environments.
Within each of these strands of theory and research, methodological innovations
have been developed that have made possible a level of sophistication that previous
studies could not attain.

Yet, as the field has evolved, it has increasingly found itself divided into a welter
of competing conceptual domains that lack any shared theoretical premises or
kindred methods of analysis. Indeed, perhaps the single most pronounced feature
of this field during the last half-century has been its marked centrifugal tendencies,

The Wiley-Blackwell Companion to Sociology, First Edition. Edited by George Ritzer.
© 2012 Blackwell Publishing Ltd. Published 2012 by Blackwell Publishing Ltd.

as a once-coherent field of "industrial sociology" gradually came apart, giving way to a balkanized terrain whose organizing principles are increasingly unclear. In place of a single analysis of labor, then, we have instead the study of jobs, workplaces, occupations, labor markets, organizations, and economic institutions as well. In all, not a propitious warrant for rich and meaningful conversation, whether within sociology or between us and the public as such.

This chapter can hardly provide the antidote. It can, however, survey the field, examine developments in various quarters, and critically assess places where integrative steps might be taken that can deepen our understanding of work and employment. With these goals in mind, this chapter explores three strands of analysis that have predominated in the field. Moving roughly from micro- to macro-social levels of analysis, the chapter begins with literature in the sociology of work, where scholars have focused on the labor process, on the social relations established among workers, and on the employment relationship as such. Next, the chapter discusses the main lines of analysis that have opened up with respect to ascriptive inequalities – those based on race and gender – in the distribution of job rewards. Finally, it examines recent developments in the sociology of organizations, where the dominant concern – especially as articulated by neo-institutionalist theory – has encompassed the relation between organizations and their social and political environments. The chapter concludes by exploring the conditions that might make it possible to pursue lines of analysis that cut across these three levels and strands of research, emphasizing issues of pressing concern to the public at large. This last goal seems especially urgent in the contemporary context, marked by far-reaching structural dislocations with respect to work, the distribution of economic opportunity, and the reconfiguration of economic sectors in an era of ongoing globalization.

THE SOCIOLOGY OF WORK

Sociologists of work have typically shared two orienting assumptions that have been foundational to this field. One, the primacy of production thesis, unites thinkers as disparate as Adam Smith, Karl Marx, Everett C. Hughes, and Melvin Kohn, all of whom contended that the work that people do inscribes itself on the very souls of the workers involved. A second assumption suggests that work cannot be understood as merely an economic transaction. Rather, the structure, allocation, and experience of work are always already embedded within webs of social obligation and meaning that inevitably complicate or over-determine the exchange of goods or commodities (Polanyi [1944] 2001; Block 1990).

Beyond these shared assumptions, however, sociologists of work have adopted widely divergent theoretical orientations. Perhaps the dominant line of demarcation lies between those adopting a "consensual" image of work organizations and those favoring a more "conflictual" approach. Indeed, it can be argued that the sociology of work constitutes one prolonged debate between advocates of these two competing views of work.

"Consensual" social science approaches found their first modern expression in the Human Relations school of thought, as formulated in the work of Mayo and his associates (e.g., Roethlisberger & Dickson 1939), which later gave rise to the classic 1950s studies of the management/worker relationship developed by Melville Dalton (1959) and Donald Roy (1952). Key to such approaches was their assumption that workers were not simply rationally acting individuals motivated by economic rewards (as the prevailing managerial wisdom then presumed). Instead, workers were inherently *social* beings who sought *symbolic* rewards, such as a sense of recognition and integration within groups and organizations larger than themselves. When industrial conflict arose, it typically occurred because management had naïvely imposed its own market-driven ethos on workers, inadvertently inducing them to find meaning and integration *in opposition to* the firm. The goal of Human Relations theory was to alert management to its role in the production of worker resistance, fostering a better pattern of communication between managers and employees, in this way restoring industrial peace. The Durkheimian assumptions that underlay this approach were nowhere more evident than in the work of Elton Mayo, for whom the workplace provided a social mooring for members of society seeking refuge from an era of depersonalized and disrupted social bonds. In the consensual view, then, the interests of management and workers were, save for instances of managerial failure, for the most part well aligned.

This consensual image of work has remained highly influential, although it has taken different forms. One especially influential development emerged in the form of Kerr's theory of industrial society (Kerr, Dunlop, Harbison & Meyers 1960), a form of modernization theory in which the values of achievement, mobility, and affluence overwhelmed earlier tendencies toward class conflict. Influenced by such thinking, Robert Blauner's *Alienation and Freedom* (1964) argued that the alienating and dehumanizing consequences of industrial capitalism, which reached their zenith under assembly-line production processes, would eventually be overcome as advanced technologies relieved workers of the most deadening forms of toil. More recent incarnations of this consensual view can be found in the work of Zuboff (1988), who speaks of the "post-hierarchical workplace"; in the influential theory of Piore and Sabel (1984), who argue that an increasingly communitarian logic has begun to govern contemporary economic institutions; and in the work of many neo-institutional theorists of work organizations, as is discussed further below.

Over against the consensual view stands a rival tradition which has adopted a fundamentally different image of the contemporary capitalist firm, which most often draws on either Weberian or Marxist theory (Mills 1951; Bendix 1956; Whyte 1956; Braverman 1974). The general notion here is one that views the workplace as an arena of ongoing contestation – not only *horizontally* (as different actors or departments within an organization vie for control), but also and especially along *vertical* lines (as owners and managers use normative constructs and material resources to legitimate their control over production). Workers are assumed to resist managerial prerogatives and to mobilize alternative norms and practices, fostering what Giddens (1982) has called the "dialectic of control." This, and not industrial peace, is regarded as the natural state of affairs under contemporary capitalism.

Perhaps the clearest and most consequential variant of the conflictual tradition emerged in the form of labor process theory, which drew on Marxist theory to identify the conditions that make possible managerial control over the capitalist firm. Though labor process theory has lost much of its early fervor as a distinct school of thought in the United States, it has left a substantial and enduring effect on the sociology of work more generally and thus warrants especially close consideration.

The labor process and beyond

In Marx's original formulation, any labor process was composed of three distinct elements: labor power (the capacity to produce), the instruments of labor (tools and machinery), and the object of labor (raw materials, to be transformed into finished goods or services). For Marx, the question was precisely how these three elements were combined under any given mode of production. Under capitalism, which pitted each capitalist against the others, Marx foresaw an inevitable trend toward the "real subordination" of labor to capital – i.e., a state in which the instruments and objects of labor came to dominate the physical movements of the worker. Operating on the assumption that "anarchy in the market begets tyranny in production," Marx's accounts of the labor process emphasized its uniformly coercive face.

Marx's concerns lay with the totality of capital accumulation and not with the actual state of the labor process in any given industry or region. It fell to later generations of labor process theorists to assess the applicability of Marx's general account, and to ask such questions as these: What types of institutional mechanisms do employers use in their effort to establish control over the workers they employ? What variations on the theme of labor control have existed, and with what effects on the course of workers' movements in particular societies? Braverman (1974) and many US labor historians (e.g., Montgomery 1979; Noble 1984) sought answers to these questions by fastening on the possession of strategic production knowledge and expertise. For them, the key to labor control rested in management's ability to introduce Taylorist models of work organization, which instituted a sharp division between the work of conception (redefined as a managerial function) and execution (the province of the workers). Consequently, this view envisioned a broad and deepening "deskilling" trend that cheapened work and emptied it of any autonomy, the better to design and control it from above.

Critical commentary on labor process theory quickly fastened on its many limitations: its highly deterministic view, its economistic tendencies, and its rigid adherence to traditional Marxist dichotomies (such as the distinction between class in- and for-itself). In response, and drawing on theories of economic segmentation, Edwards (1979) developed a sequential model of labor control systems that envisioned a historical progression from "simple" and "technical" to "bureaucratic" systems of control. Since each system persisted within distinct segments of the economy, the result generated a stratified working class rather than the homogeneous class deskilling theory expected. For his part, Burawoy (1979, 1985) pursued an even greater rejection of Braverman's approach by emphasizing the *politics* of production. Key here was Burawoy's argument that state intervention in the economy had altered the functioning of labor control systems. As the state established wage and hours standards and social insurance programs, in however limited a fashion, employers could no longer rely on mere *coercion*. Rather, they were compelled to embrace strategies aimed at eliciting worker *consent*. Developing these insights through ethnographic research in a machine tool shop in Chicago, Burawoy (1979) developed a theory of industrial games, in which workers' own cultural practices led them to consent to their own exploitation. Later (1985), on the basis of comparative and historical analysis, he developed a rich conceptual system with which to account for variations in the production regimes that emerged under given economic, social, and political conditions.

Influenced by Burawoy's thinking in particular, numerous studies have explored the social conditions that enable firms to elicit the consent of their employees. In his study of a high-tech engineering firm, Kunda (1992) emphasized management's elaboration of a rich organizational culture, which served to establish a system he termed "normative control." Studying the restructuring of a large California bank, Smith (1990) identified a contradictory phenomenon she dubbed "coercive autonomy." Here, headquarters appeared to give branch managers greater control over their internal operations, yet did so in ways that actually placed ever-sharper limits on the decisions which branch managers could make. In a study of a Japanese-owned assembly plant in Indiana, Graham (1995) concluded that the social production of worker consent began even before workers were hired. By selecting compliant workers, exposing them to managerial frameworks even during the selection process, and nurturing a culture of compliance, management established what Graham referred to as "post-Fordist hegemonic control" (see also Grenier 1988; Adler 1992; Barker 1993). The notion here is that a historical shift has occurred: where Fordist patterns of labor control focused on the effort to direct workers' *behavior*, the nascent post-Fordist regimes aim to shape workplace *culture*, now in accordance with management's needs.

Much of this literature has focused on manufacturing workers, begging the question of its relevance to other branches of the economy. For this reason, analysis of interactive service workers (where workers directly serve customers) has assumed particular importance. By very definition, service occupations of this sort are unique in several respects. First, the production and consumption of the "product" often must coincide in time and space. Second, the "product" is itself inextricably tied to the performative qualities of the service worker him or herself. And third, workers must respond to directives not only from managers but also from the customers with whom they interact (Sallaz 2002; Korczynski & MacDonald 2009). Perhaps the most important theme that has emerged from this strand of research has involved the ways in which organizational routines have gained purchase on the presentation of workers' identities. This point was first made by Hochschild (1983), in her highly influential study of the "emotional labor" in which flight attendants must engage. Drawing attention to the endless smiling and gestures of concern which these workers must provide, Hochschild makes the broader point that such emotional management practices had previously resided within the workers' private domain. Now, as emotional expression becomes an integral part of the "products" employers bring to market, the worker's identity has ceased to be her (or his) own. In her study of fast-food workers and insurance salesmen, Leidner (1993) expanded this analysis by comparing the different forms that interactive service work seems to assume under different economic and organizational conditions. Yet more recent studies have made the linkage between labor control and workers' identities even more forcefully.

Studying temporary workers struggling to retain a sense of dignity and integrity, Padavic (2005) documents the pressures workers impose on themselves to construct identities as "good workers." Casey (1995) argues that firms in the service sector often seek to select, train, and evaluate employees on the basis of their compliance with company-favored identity norms (yielding, at the extreme, what Casey dubs "designer selves"). In his study of retail service workers, du Gay (1996) argues that consumer culture has increasingly leached into the fabric of work organizations, generating a managerial discourse that conjures employees as active, energetic entrepreneurs, or "enterprising subjects" (see also Waring 2008). Extending this analysis further, Warhurst and Nickson (2001, 2007) find that in retail shops, restaurants, and bars, employers increasingly demand what they term "aesthetic labor." Here, managers select, train, and evaluate workers on their ability to affect the desired sense of fashion, physical appeal, linguistic skill, and bodily comportment needed to embody the organization's brand. The point of these and other studies is that labor control systems under contemporary capitalism have gained increasing purchase on workers' identities and styles of comportment. In effect, they now operate by fostering new identity norms that, reinforced by the wider culture of consumption, articulate with organizational needs.

Arguably, analysts such as du Gay and Casey have tended to reproduce the very determinism that characterized early labor process analysis. Over against this tendency, a growing number of scholars have emphasized the role of human agency – that is, the capacity of workers to resist managerial directives, or actively to negotiate the boundaries of managerial authority (Simpson 1989; Hodson 1995; Knights & McCabe 2000). Noteworthy here have been efforts to explore the social conditions that enable workers to challenge managerial edicts and prerogatives (Vallas 2003). Such resistance can at times be hidden (as when workers traffic in cynicism, destructive gossip, or humor, all of which can serve to level managerial pretensions; see Kunda 1992; Weeks 2003; Collinson & Collinson 2004). At other times resistance can be more openly expressed (as when "authority contests" develop, or when workers manage to appropriate organizational reforms and use them for their own ends; see V. Smith 2001; Vallas 2006).

Perhaps the most important analysis of the structure/agency question at work has emerged in the research of Hodson and his colleagues, who coded the population of book-length ethnographies of work published in the English language during the last several decades (Hodson, Welsh, Rieble, Jamison & Creighton 1993; Hodson 2001). Linking the structural conditions that obtain at work with the varying forms of worker response, Hodson et al. found that it was not the contours of the labor process (e.g., closeness of supervision or a lack of control) so much as violations of worker dignity that drove worker resistance. They also found that oppositional or defiant forms of consciousness and action have remained fairly pronounced among some occupational groups – especially among skilled manual workers, the very group which deskilling theory had declared to be extinct.

A further way in which the sociology of work has moved beyond labor process theory lies in its focal concerns. Analysts such as Braverman assumed that the key to managerial control hinged on the employer's ability to control the method and the pace of work, and in turn on the distribution of production knowledge and expertise (Spenner 1979, 1983; Vallas 1999; Levy & Murnane 2005; Handel 2005). This assumption eventuated in a broad debate over trends in skill requirements. Yet in retrospect, it has grown increasingly clear that debates concerning skill and control over the labor process took for granted what recent trends have shown to be increasingly problematic: the continued existence of the "standard" (full-time, permanent) employment relationship itself. The assumption here was that large, centralized hierarchies would continue to provide secure and stable full-time work with benefits, as the decades following World War II seemed to suggest. Yet, as a host of subsequent studies have shown, employers have increasingly tended to resort to forms of employment that accomplish two critical goals: they relieve employers of any legal commitment to the workers who toil on their behalf, and they provide employers with maximum discretion over staffing levels at any given moment. Part of the much-discussed notion of workplace flexibility (Vallas 1999), the new forms of employment typically include the use of temporary workers, independent contracting, part-time work, and the outsourcing or off-shoring of work to outside vendors, service providers, or temporary help firms – all of which lead to a massive trend toward the "externalization" of work (Pfeffer & Baron 1988; Gonos 1997; Kalleberg 2009).

A burgeoning literature has emerged on these developments which cannot be reviewed here in any detail (see V. Smith 1997; Vallas 1999). Several points can however be made. First, there is indeed a significant number of labor force participants (professionals and consultants of various sorts) who stand to benefit when centralized hierarchies externalize large swaths of functions previously performed in-house (Arthur & Rousseau 2001; Barley & Kunda 2004; Osnowitz 2010). Such workers – some proportion of whom may warrant the name "knowledge workers" (see Kleinman & Vallas 2001) – often strongly identify with their occupations rather than with the firm, or with an occupational community that provides important sources of knowledge and social solidarity. Such workers often enjoy job rewards that are both material (job opportunities, income) and symbolic (fulfillment, status, and a sense of self-efficacy). Yet, side by side with such a relatively privileged species of independent workers can be found the presumably more numerous groups of workers whose jobs are rendered increasingly precarious (Kalleberg, Reskin & Hudson 2000; Kalleberg 2009), or who are otherwise deprived of the orderly career trajectories and material benefits (such as health insurance and defined retirement plans) that a previous generation had come to expect.

Much remains unknown about how profoundly these shifts have altered the opportunity structures which large firms now provide. It is not known whether internal labor markets within large firms have become markedly less available to employees than before (Cappelli 1995). Although there is some evidence that workers within particular occupational or demographic categories suffer disproportionately from establishment closings, downsizing, and outsourcing (Kim 2010), the mechanisms that account for such disparities have remained obscure. One especially under-studied area is whether there has been a "student effect" in the labor market – that is, whether increasing labor force participation rates among college students, coupled with growing pressure to complete unpaid internships, have begun to erode the wages or labor market conditions that workers encounter more generally. A final point here concerns the ways in which structural changes in work and employment have begun to alter the meanings and aspirations workers hold with respect to their working lives. Suggestive, but as yet empirically unexamined, is Sennett's (1998) argument about the subjective or personal consequences of the new forms of work organization. In this view, work organizations are now so marked by instability and discontinuity as to undermine workers' ability to establish meaningful life narratives. In Sennett's view, workers now experience superficial forms of sociability and organizational expectations that place a premium on conformity to ever-changing management practices – developments Sennett finds to be hollow and empty substitutes for an older and presumably more authentic form of workplace life.

Sennett's argument has been criticized for its tendency to essentialize a form of labor that has rapidly fallen away. Indeed, some theorists have argued that the structural and cultural changes underway run deeper than Sennett realizes, and that his approach fails to see that the sphere of production no longer exerts the same gravitational pull as it previously did. Taken to its extreme, this argument suggests that what economic historian Sebastian de Grazia (1994) once termed the "work society" is increasingly being eclipsed by the spread of new media and consumption-based identities. In her recent, probing response to these arguments, Leidner (2006) allows that some cultural influences have indeed weakened the link between work and identity. But she also identifies numerous influences that have had the opposite effect, reinforcing the salience of work for contemporary forms of subjectivity. The influx of women into the paid labor force has had this effect, as has the expansion of professional occupations, the rising number of hours workers put in on the job, and the pervasive existence of the 24/7 economy.

Beyond these points, the argument can also be made that "work" does not exist within the material domain alone. Precisely because we are awash in media constructs of all types, we are often immersed in *symbolic* representations of work on television, in movies, and in magazines and other media. It is curious to see how much of the content of media programming in fact relies on the representation of work and the occupational communities that are sustained in hospitals, law firms, political institutions, and the criminal justice system. Interestingly, although there is some literature on media representations of work (Signorielli & Kahlenberg 2001; Massoni 2004), we know relatively little about how work is portrayed in particular venues, and with what effects on occupational aspirations or understandings of managerial authority and workers' rights. This is an unexplored terrain that holds substantial potential for future research.

It is possible to identify a further absence within the literature that is relatively surprising: the relation between work and new technology. This area of research was once a dominant concern, first in studies of organizational structure and later in the labor process school. Save for studies focused on call centers (see Ritzer & Lair 2009: 40–3) and on the adequacy of economic theories of wage inequality (Fernandez 2001), the relation between work and new technologies has received relatively little sociological attention of late. Indeed, the last major study in this area – that of Thomas (1994; cf. Orlikowski 2007) – was published nearly two decades ago, prior to the ubiquity of email, smartphones, webtools, teleconferencing, social networking websites, and electronic point-of-sale information systems. We therefore lack any developed understanding of how these and other technologies may have altered the fabric of workplace relations or, at a higher level of analysis, the spatial dispersion of the labor process (as with the logistics revolution that Wal-Mart has led) and the webs (or commodity chains) that increasingly link production processes on a global basis (Castells 1996; Salzinger 2010). Nor has research begun to explore how technology (e.g., the electronic handling of job applications) has altered the operation of labor markets (see especially Sharone 2011). Here too is a fertile area for future research.

ASCRIPTIVE INEQUALITY AT WORK

Gender, race, and work structures

Much but not all literature in the sociology of work is predicated on the link between work and class-based inequalities. Side by side with this literature, however, there has developed a long tradition of inquiry into the ways in which racial and gender influences differentially shape access to highly valued job rewards, quite apart from (or in interaction with) the impact of class-based inequalities. The point of departure for much of this literature has been a shared rejection of human capital theory, which views disparities in job rewards as a function of *supply*-side factors (e.g., differences in the worker's investment in education and labor market experience). While there are sharp variations among sociological thinkers in this field, virtually all fasten on the *demand* side of the equation, thus centering their analysis on the formal and informal aspects of work that impinge on the distribution of employment opportunity.

With respect to racial disparities, there can be little doubt (popular misconceptions aside) that minority workers remain disproportionately excluded from the most prestigious and high-paying occupational positions, even when educational attainment and labor market experience are held constant. Studies of the hiring process reveal a clear bias in favor of white employees, even when job-relevant qualifications are held constant. Audit studies (which simulate the hiring experience using experimental methods) reveal this, as do experimental studies that construct actual job applications using African American and Euro-American sounding names (Bertrand & Mullainathan 2004). Likewise, the experimental study by Pager, Bonikowski, and Western (2009) finds that white job-seekers with felony convictions stand better chances in the labor market than do African American and Latino job-seekers with clean records. The hiring process varies in subtle ways across racial lines, with whites more likely to find jobs through informal networks that place less emphasis on formal credentials. Black applicants tend to be more strictly evaluated on the basis of educational credentials and experience, and are expected to demonstrate their skills internally before gaining access to better jobs (Wilson 1997).

Once hired, minority workers have a lower probability of rising into supervisory positions than do whites with similar experience and credentials. This point was established in an early paper by Kluegel (1978), who estimated that one-third of the income disparity between white and black men stemmed from such unequal access to authority at work. More recently, studies by Smith (R. Smith 1997, 2001; Smith & Elliott 2002) demonstrate that minority workers are only half as likely to receive promotions as are similarly qualified whites, net of human capital variables. At least some of these barriers to promotion may stem from the nature of supervisory relations, as literature reveals that dominant group supervisors provide less

favorable evaluations to African Americans than to members of their own racial or
ethnic group (Tsui & O'Reilly 1989).

Literature on gender inequalities reports generally similar patterns, although
there are important substantive variations. Perhaps the single most influential contribution on this terrain has been Kanter's (1977) study of the organizational dynamics that exclude women from the most rewarding managerial and professional
positions. One such source of exclusion revolves around the phenomenon of
homophily (or same-group preference). Kanter reasoned that since managers confront high levels of uncertainty in their jobs, they understandably place a premium
on trust. This in turn inclines them to favor apprentices or assistants who share
their basic domain assumptions and dispositions, thus producing powerful pressures
toward in-group selection and thus toward "homosocial reproduction" – recruitment that perpetuates already established selection patterns. A substantial body of
literature suggests that hiring done along the lines of informal referrals and social
networks of affiliation also promotes gender and ethnic homogeneity (e.g., Mouw
2002).

A further contribution of Kanter's study fastened on the role played by relative
proportions, or variations in the social composition at the level of the work group.
While the *absolute* size of the firm had long been a major source of concern among
researchers, few had studied *relative* size – i.e., the contextual effects that flow from
the demographic mix of socially defined types of employees. Where women workers
accounted for only a small proportion of the groups and departments within a given
workplace (as in "skewed" groups), they were likely to experience three perceptual
tendencies: greater visibility (and thus more intense performance pressures), an
exaggeration of their differences from the dominant group (leading to heightened
boundaries), and an imposition of exaggerated images or perceptions on women
(despite their individual differences). These tendencies erected powerful impediments to women's success, in ways that the sheer passage of time was not likely to
erode. In organizations marked by the dynamics of tokenism, vicious cycles of disadvantage were likely to result, only perpetuating women's subordinate positions
within the firm.

Kanter's study was part of a broader public and policy-related discussion of the
subtle forms of exclusion that women and minorities encounter as they approach
the upper levels of managerial and professional occupations. Its structural orientation is at least partly responsible for the spread of the architectural metaphors that
have influenced subsequent research. One such instance is research on the "glass
ceiling," which gained currency within journalistic discourse (Hymowitz & Schellhardt 1986) and resulted in the 1991 establishment of a Federal Glass Ceiling
Commission (see 1995a, 1995b). Empirical studies using the glass ceiling construct
have often sought to determine whether "the disadvantages women [and minorities]
face relative to men *intensify* as they move up organizational hierarchies" (Baxter
& Wright 2000: 276, emphasis added). Results are as yet somewhat mixed. There
can be no question that women remain remarkably under-represented in the upper
reaches of the corporate and professional worlds, this despite their dramatically
increased numbers within law, medical, and business schools. Moreover, using the
Panel Study of Income Dynamics, Cotter, Hermsen, Ovadia & Vanneman (2001)
do find evidence of a glass ceiling among both white and black women, relative to

the trajectories of men. Yet Baxter and Wright (2000) found no evidence of an intensified disadvantage within the United States, and only limited support for the same hypothesis in Sweden and Australia. Methodological and measurement issues bedevil this area, as Gorman and Kmec note (2009; cf. Britton & Williams 2000). Indeed, in their carefully designed study of hiring patterns within private law firms, Gorman and Kmec find a complex pattern: women *do* encounter reduced opportunities as they seek senior promotions within the law firm, but these disparities do not operate when women pursue *lateral* moves at the senior level. The implication is that women *do* face a glass ceiling when they hold junior positions, but once they have broken through such barriers (and have had their professional abilities certified by another firm), they find it possible to compete with men on something approaching a more level playing field. This study demonstrates the need to consider the *differential* operation of gender biases within distinct labor markets even within the same occupational domain.

The theory of relative proportions initially claimed to encompass perceptual tendencies affecting all groups that were significantly outnumbered. Thus, the question quickly arose as to the experience of *men* who encounter the token situation. In this vein, Williams (1995) studied men and women who entered into careers as social workers, teachers, nurses, and librarians. She found that, unlike the experience of women, men seemed to derive significant *advantages* from being in the minority position, for they were more quickly elevated into administrative or managerial positions than were the women who outnumbered them. This finding led Williams to coin a further architectural trope, referring to a "glass escalator" effect, in which men, "despite their intentions . . . face invisible pressures to move up in their professions. Like being on a moving escalator, they have to work to stay in place" (1995: 87).

Subsequent research has qualified Williams' arguments in important respects. Using national data on the US nursing profession, Snyder and Green (2008) found that gender was salient in one important respect, in that it tends to segregate male and female nurses horizontally into distinct (and unequally rewarded) specialties. Yet gender did not facilitate the movement of men into administrative positions, raising questions about the "glass escalator" thesis as such. Other studies have suggested that any 'escalator' effect may implicitly hinge on racial privilege (a factor that Williams largely failed to explore). For example, in a study of African American men employed as nurses, Wingfield (2009) found that racial boundaries prevented black men in this occupation from establishing the same social networks and favorable ties with supervisors as their white male counterparts were able to do. In a similar vein, Smith and Elliott (2002) find that the promotion prospects of minority workers are often limited by processes of "ethnic matching," which limit minority supervisors to jobs overseeing members of their own racial group.[1] Clearly, research in this vein will need to examine the simultaneous effects of race *and* gender as they bear on access to supervisory and managerial posts.

Recent studies on gender and racial boundaries at work have begun to open up highly suggestive lines of analysis. For example, Blair-Loy's (2001) study of the financial industry speaks to some of the ways in which workplace culture may have begun to evolve beyond Kanter's own findings. The key to success in financial analysis lies in maintaining favorable relations with clients, which often demands of women that they develop skills in the negotiation of boundaries that men only rarely face. In their effort to do this, the women in Blair-Loy's study often invoked highly gendered strategies of self-presentation, whether acting as matrons, *femmes fatales*, or as "one of the boys." Each of these strategies tended to reproduce the very boundaries that Kanter had identified. Yet Blair-Loy *also* found a pronounced cohort effect: younger women in this industry found it increasingly possible to combine *multiple* strategies for survival, achieving more flexible forms of self-presentation than were possible in the past, and thus opening up possibilities to disrupt existing gender lines.

Equally suggestive research has opened up with respect to the concept of "diversity." In a qualitative study of three organizations providing professional services of different types, Ely and Thomas (2001) found sharp variations in the way the "diversity" concept was defined and used. Although some organizations used a "learning" conception of diversity (which was viewed as contributing to the well-being of all employees), others adopted a narrower, more instrumental conception that valued diversity for the market advantages it conferred (i.e., its ability to open up markets that firms could not otherwise tap). Not surprisingly, the latter, instrumental conception of diversity tended to confine minority employees within implicitly racialized functions (such as the handling of minority accounts), in turn generating resentment, blocked opportunity, and heightened racial hierarchies within professional settings. Interestingly, Edelman, Fuller, and Mara-Drita (2001) found patterns that closely resembled the narrow, instrumental usage that Ely and Thomas had found. According to the latter authors, the prevalence of the diversity construct signals a subtle shift on the part of American business, moving racial and ethnic policy *away* from a set of binding obligations (as under the civil rights frame), *toward* a looser and more discretionary discourse that provides management with a much freer hand. These studies begin to suggest some of the ways in which discourse about diversity can be consequential, shaping the social relations that surround workers and the opportunity structures that develop at the level of the workplace itself.

Job segregation by race and gender

As noted, until the 1980s, scholarly interpretations of job segregation were most often dominated by human capital theories, which fastened on individual-level explanations. With the advent of approaches appearing under the banner of the "new structuralism," however, research began to appear that compared the effects of individual-level characteristics with those rooted in organizational-level variables. Perhaps the best example of such research is that of Tomaskovic-Devey (1993), who used a state-wide study of workers and jobs in North Carolina to unpack the sources of earnings inequality by race and gender. The author distinguished two sources of such inequalities: "status closure" (exclusion from higher-paying jobs) and "status composition" (where the over-representation of women and minorities in certain jobs reduces the value accorded incumbents' skills). Careful quantitative analysis gave rise to several important findings.

First, little support emerged for human capital explanations of earnings inequalities. Second, racial and gender disparities in pay were driven by different sets of determinants. Whereas status closure effects did emerge with respect to black workers, there was no deeply entrenched status composition effect with respect to race. Among women workers, however, *both* sources of inequality exerted powerful effects, suggesting that women's lower pay stemmed not only from their exclusion from better-paying jobs but also from the devaluation of jobs that were disproportionately performed by women. Similar findings have since emerged in numerous additional studies as well (see Catanzarite 2003; Levanon, England & Allison 2009).

Methodological innovations since the 1990s have enabled researchers to disentangle trends in job segregation with greater specificity than before. Perhaps the most important innovation here has been the use of EEO-1 data, based on the employment information that larger firms must submit annually to the Equal Employment Opportunity Commission. These data have twin advantages: first, they support analysis of occupational differences at the establishment (workplace) level, rather than at the broader, firm-wide level. And second, they also make it possible to examine temporal shifts in job segregation by race, ethnicity, and gender. A number of important findings have emerged on the basis of these data. Stainback and Tomaskovic-Devey (2009) find that white men remain highly over-represented in managerial groups, relative to their proportions in local labor markets; indeed, within construction, manufacturing, and other long-established sectors of the economy, this over-representation has actually increased since 1966. These authors also find that a substantial share of the gains made by white women, black men, and black women have been confined to the growing service sectors, and that without such sectoral shifts in the economy, these groups would have made substantially fewer inroads with respect to management jobs.

In a highly inventive approach, Dobbin and his colleagues linked the EEO-1 data to a retrospective workplace survey at the establishment level, making it possible to examine the organizational conditions that account for any changes in the demographic composition of particular job categories over time. Using these data, Kalev (2009) found that workplace innovations that disrupt established forms of occupational boundaries (e.g., team systems that require cross-occupational collaboration) provide a powerful impetus toward desegregation, partly because they break down long-established assumptions about worker characteristics and enable women and minorities to establish social networks that link them to more powerful actors within the firm. Kalev, Dobbin, and Kelly (2006) also used these data to examine which of several leading diversity management practices actually foster more inclusive outcomes. They found that some of the most frequently used diversity practices (sensitivity training, mentoring) have little if any effect, and actually produce significant setbacks for some subgroups (such as black women). Significant gains do result, by contrast, when establishments tie the pursuit of inclusivity to powerful agencies or departments within the firm.

Perhaps the most ambitious and historically sensitive use of these data has been that of Dobbin (2010), who has sought to unpack the organizational and political dynamics that forged affirmative action policy in the United States. Dobbin finds that the Executive Orders of the 1960s and the judicial rulings that followed had highly complex effects: they fostered substantial uncertainty (since few guidelines existed regarding equal opportunity practices), and they emboldened personnel administrators (who gained authority by devising opportunity structures that could gain favor in the public arena and in the courts). Since courts were unable to define how equal opportunity should take shape, corporations provided the model on which affirmative action practices were eventually based.

The great strength of this developing literature on job segregation stems from its national scope, temporal reach, and ability to grasp change at the establishment level of analysis. Yet such analytic breadth comes at a price – here, in the form of distance from the informal mechanisms at hand (Reskin 2003), and in an overarching concern with numerical representation that too seldom explores the fabric of the workplace relations encountered by workers who do indeed gain access to particular jobs. On this score, qualitative studies such as those by Collins (1997), Ely and Thomas (2001), and Royster (2003) hold enduring value, in that they help to capture the organizational-level processes that underlie the perpetuation of racial and gender hierarchies. What is needed is research that can combine the richness of focused qualitative work and the temporal shifts which EEO-1 data support.

THE SOCIOLOGY OF ORGANIZATIONS

A third strand in the study of work and employment – organizational sociology – has undergone significant change in recent decades. Until the late 1970s, organizational analysts were primarily concerned with the "technical" features of organizational life, such as the firm's size, age, or technology (by which scholars meant the nature and sequencing of its tasks; see Thompson [1967] 2003). When attention was paid to the wider environment of the firm, most analysts emphasized the characteristics of markets, raw materials, and other material inputs.

Since that time, matters have changed a great deal. First, rather than viewing firms as independent entities, analysts have come to view the internal structure and operations of the firm as responses to the institutional environment in which the organization is lodged. It has increasingly been recognized, in other words, that environments "*penetrate* the organization, creating the lenses through which actors view the world and the very categories of structure, action, and thought" they use to carry out their functions (DiMaggio & Powell 1991: 13, emphasis added). Second, analysts have increasingly broadened their conception of the firm's environment to include social, political, and cultural influences that previously had gone ignored. In the words of Meyer and Scott: "Environments are more than stocks of resources and energy flows; they are cultural systems, defining and legitimating organizational structures and thus aiding in their creation and maintenance." In short, the tendency now is to view organizations as both "connected to" and "constructed by" their wider, societal environments (Meyer & Scott 1992: 1).

These shifts are especially apparent in the neo-institutionalist approach toward organizations, which has rapidly become the dominant paradigm within the field. In this perspective, managers and professional employees are perpetually faced with uncertainty, and thus motivated to find established models that promise to deliver a modicum of stability. Further, managers are keenly aware of the need to establish and maintain the firm's legitimacy in the eyes of various audiences, the most important of which reside outside the firm's boundaries. Applying these notions in an early instance of institutionalist theory, Meyer and Rowan (1977) argued that the technical features of a firm's internal operations are less important to its success than is the firm's ability to signal its conformity with widely accepted business practices. Organizations that do signal such conformity thereby "increase their legitimacy and their survival prospects, *independent* of the immediate efficacy of the acquired practices and procedures" (Meyer & Rowan 1977: 340). Indeed, because the advantages provided by established practices are often quite mythical, pragmatically-oriented managers must sometimes buffer the firm's internal operations from legitimacy-oriented change. Thus while the pursuit of legitimacy can deliver real resource advantages to firms, it may do so for reasons that have nothing to do with technical efficiency; indeed, the changes firms embrace may even stand at odds with effective operations.

In a subsequent, massively influential analysis, DiMaggio and Powell (1983) agreed that firms experience powerful legitimacy imperatives, but they extended this insight in ways that shifted the very problematic that informs the neo-institutional approach. The question that drives research in this area, they argued, can no longer be that of identifying the sources of *variation* among organization structures. To the contrary: the question becomes one of identifying the conditions that generate *homogeneity* – i.e., isomorphism – among the organizations within any given institutional domain. Following their lead, the great bulk of organizational research has sought to understand how and why given organizational arrangements become *doxic*, or taken-for-granted, practices that pervade broad swaths of the organizational terrain.

DiMaggio and Powell (1983) provided a conceptual platform for such analysis by identifying three mechanisms that invite isomorphism among the organizations in a given field – the now-famous triptych of coercive, mimetic, and normative influences. Briefly, by *coercive* influences, these authors meant stipulations rooted in regulatory or contractual obligations. By *mimetic* influences, DiMaggio and Powell meant band-wagon effects, or voluntary emulation. And by *normative* tendencies, these authors referred to influences exerted by professionals and their associations, whose cognitive orientations and practices spread rapidly across organizational fields, often borne by the mobility of professional employees.

Because analysts using the DiMaggio-Powell schema have proceeded somewhat selectively, fastening primarily on mimetic isomorphism, ensuing literature has acquired a one-sided character (Mizruchi & Fein 1999). Still, research in this vein has made several useful contributions, especially when set alongside rational actor or transaction cost approaches toward the firm (DiMaggio 1988; Schneiberg & Clemens 2006). Studies have repeatedly shown that technical and market conditions provide weak explanations of organizational structure, and that normative or institutional influences powerfully affect the diffusion of given organizational arrangements. This point has emerged in studies focusing on some of the major structural developments within the US economy and polity from the nineteenth century on, including the formation of modern industrial regulation in the late nineteenth century (Dobbin 1994), the adoption of the civil service model of public employment in the early twentieth century (Tolbert & Zucker 1983), the diffusion of the multi-divisional form of corporation organization throughout the twentieth century (Fligstein 1987), the spread of the internal labor market and due process provisions for personnel administration in the wake of the civil rights movement (Edelman

1990; Dobbin, Sutton, Meyer & Scott 1993; Sutton, Dobbin, Meyer & Scott 1994), and the adoption of downsizing as a means of enhancing shareholder value (Budros 2004). In all these cases, scholars have found that structural arrangements were more powerfully driven by mimetic processes (e.g., the pursuit of public legitimacy or pressures to conform to culturally prevalent expectations) than by such factors as transaction costs, labor market conditions, or considerations of efficiency.

Yet, while neo-institutionalist theory usefully challenges market-oriented, rational actor theories of the atomized firm, it has also suffered from important gaps and ambiguities, especially in its earlier formulations. For one thing, the great bulk of research in the institutionalist camp has viewed the achievement of isomorphism as a relatively simple and unproblematic process of organizational adaptation. Although some theorists have alluded to internal resistance and agency (Meyer & Rowan 1977; Fligstein 1987, 1990), many subsequent approaches tended to leave little room for agency, contestation, and change (DiMaggio 1991). Even more important has been the tendency to view normative or cultural influences as if they constituted a unitary set of expectations with which organizations were expected to conform. This, a kind of "looking glass self" theory of organizational development, rarely acknowledges the possibility that the mirror is often cracked, presenting organizations with a fragmented or contradictory array of images. This in fact is the point made by Friedland and Alford (1991), who emphasize the existence of a *multiplicity* of institutional logics in any given societal context, whose very combination gives rise to tensions and contradictions, whether within a given organizational field or even within the firm as such (Stark 2001; Vallas & Kleinman 2008). In a subtle way, much of the neo-institutionalist corpus has, however implicitly, assumed the existence of a Parsonian value consensus in modern organizational dress.[2]

The broader problem that institutionalist theory has encountered, then, is a failure to allow that institutionalized scripts and cognitive styles do not emerge or congeal in any simple or unproblematic way; rather, they typically reflect sharp contestation and mobilization, whether within the firm, the organizational field, the public arena, or the state apparatus itself. Environments are not seamlessly integrated entities, but manifest fault lines and diverging interests and orientations that (however obscured) must be taken into account (cf. DiMaggio 1988). Interestingly, older literatures such as Lawrence and Lorsch's *Organization and Environment* (1967) realized the contradictory ways in which different facets of the environment can impinge on the same firm, thus inviting organizational tensions with which management must cope. Recognition of this point has often been absent on the part of research within the institutionalist genre.

Mindful of these challenges, scholars have increasingly sought to develop models that include greater space for the workings of power, agency, and contestation (DiMaggio 1991; Haveman & Khaire 2006; Schneiberg & Clemens 2006). Although numerous examples of such research have begun to appear, the most creative and potential-laden are those that bring social movement theory into closer dialogue with organizational analysis (Schneiberg & Lounsbury 2008). This effort, which began decades ago (Zald & Berger 1978), has now given rise to important papers by a growing number of scholars. Examples include research highlighting the response of American universities to student movements demanding divestment from apartheid South Africa (Soule 2006), the efficacy of gay rights movements in expanding employee rights (Raeburn 2004), and the consequences of environmental movements for the social organization of waste management work (Lounsbury & Kaghan 2001). In much the same vein, Haveman, Rao, and Paruchuri (2007) have examined the impact of the Progressive movement on the structure of US banks at the turn of the twentieth century, and Schneiberg and Soule (2005) have examined the contentious political mobilization that shaped rate regulation in the fire insurance industry (see also Davis, McAdam, Scott & Zald 2005; Minkoff & McCarthy 2005). Although these are vibrant and suggestive studies that hold great promise, the question emerges as to how they might be squared with the premises that have guided the foundational statements of the neo-institutionalist corpus.

An example will perhaps help drive this last point home. A literature has begun to emerge that views Wal-Mart as providing the prevailing model of work organization in the retail sector, much as Fordism played this role in an earlier period of capitalist development. And indeed, there is little question but that big-box stores have had to embrace many of the same low-wage, lean retailing practices that Wal-Mart pioneered. Yet it would be hard to identify important ways in which the diffusion of the Wal-Mart model has hinged on the pursuit of organizational legitimacy, except perhaps if legitimacy is sought in the narrowest of audiences, as among investors and financial analysts. Apart from such domains, it would seem to be not legitimacy but sheer economic power that compels so many appliance, grocery, and apparel retailers to adopt the lean retailing approach. A similar argument can be made for the diffusion of the use of temporary employment and the legal, political, and organizational mobilization that made temporary work so prevalent (Gonos 1997). To cite these examples is to note how rarely institutionalist scholars have engaged questions of labor organization, or, for that matter, the expansion of social inequality within the firm. Indeed, it seems fair to characterize institutionalist theory as a latter-day instance of the consensual model of work and employment, as was discussed above.

CONCLUSION

Ex uno, plures. From the relatively unified corpus of writing on work and occupations that characterized sociology at the middle of the last century, we now confront a Babel of specialized literatures, each operating at a distinct level of analysis, using theories and concepts unique to its domain, and approaching distinct objects of analysis. There are, to be sure, shared concerns that connect these fields. Perhaps the most important of these is their shared rejection of economic approaches premised on the atomized worker and rationally-acting work organizations. Over against the latter models, the sociologies of work, ascriptive inequality, and organizations all insist on the social and cultural construction of economic arrangements. For sociologists of work, the nature of workers' tasks and the authority relations they confront often reflect class-based efforts to exercise control over labor, in turn fostering ongoing processes of contestation, negotiation, or acquiescence to managerial regimes. Likewise, students of racial and gender inequalities refuse supply-side approaches, and trace the distribution of job rewards to aspects of workplace structure that exclude women and minorities from employment opportunities, or devalue the work they are assigned. Finally, scholars concerned with organizations typically document the linkage tying organizational structures and practices not to market or technological imperatives but to normative and institutional features of the wider environment. One unifying trait that connects all these strands of theory and research, then, is that work structures – jobs, workplace cultures, occupations, internal labor markets, and institutionalized practices within the firm – are not driven by economic necessity. The corollary is important: precisely because they *are* social constructs, they should in theory be susceptible to social changes of one or another sort.

This point raises an important issue of interest to both academics and the public alike, especially at a time of economic disarray. How are outsourcing, downsizing, and globalization reshaping the job terrain that workers can expect to find in the coming years? How has the "financialization" of work – the growing power enjoyed by institutional investors and finance capital generally – reshaped the internal contours and managerial orientations found among work organizations in the contemporary setting? In what ways has the mobilization of women and minority workers within the legal and political arenas reshaped the race and gender hierarchies established within the firm itself? And how is the meaning of work changing in a period marked by precarious employment, changing prestige hierarchies, and globally ascendant neoliberalism? Questions such as these seek to open up the issue of the possible paths down which work can be led. They also frame our analyses in ways that seek to operate at multiple levels, breaching the lines that separate the three strands of research with which this chapter has been concerned. Finally, they link what might otherwise be purely academic concerns with matters that acquire great public urgency.

Answers to questions such as these are of course still evolving – and there are multiple obstacles in the way of such efforts. For one thing, sociological research on work structures does not occur in a vacuum. The questions which we pose are always already embedded within collectively defined contexts that govern what it seems legitimate to think. This is not an idle point, for the dominant culture has clearly affected the development of the strands of theory and research this chapter has addressed. Most notably perhaps, especially in the years since the dot-com boom, interest in the sociology of work has seemed to wane even as a veritable explosion of organizational research has occurred on the basis of the institutionalist paradigm. It is not difficult to see why this would be the case. The decline of organized labor and of the workers' movement more generally; adverse labor market conditions; the 'cultural turn' taken by growing numbers of scholars; and the growing prevalence of market fundamentalism within the wider culture – all these factors have combined to make it increasingly difficult for researchers to define "work" as a social and political issue in its own right.[3] The opposite conditions have affected organizational research, which has found steadily increasing demand for its products, especially within business schools, whose audience seems to favor its more consensual orientation toward organizational practices.[4]

Can multi-level analyses develop that cut across the seams that increasingly demarcate research on the nature of work, ascriptive inequalities, and organizational environments? Can sociologists in this field develop the reflexivity needed to act back on the anesthetizing effects the culture of consumption can impose on scholarly research? Beyond purely cultural influences, what structural factors contribute to the seeming acquiescence of the unemployed to their fate (Sharone 2007)? How can we use social science theory in such a way as to open up the space needed for public debate about the nature of work in the contemporary setting? Questions such as these promise to break down the divisions that plague sociological thinking about work and employment. They may also bring sociology into closer contact with the public at large.

Notes

1 Smith and Elliott (2002), drawing on Berheide (1992), develop another architectural metaphor, referring to the "sticky floor" processes that confine minority workers to positions of limited authority.
2 Interestingly, Dobbin's (1994) comparative study of the making of railway regulation emphasizes the importance of political culture as a determinant of organizational structure. But he conceives of political culture as a unitary force, specific to whole nation-states, and thus untethered to material interests or ideologies. For a similar formulation, see Hamilton and Biggart (1988).
3 One important expression of this declining attention to the nature of work has been the withering away of labor journalism in the mainstream press since the late 1980s, leaving the self-help columns, comic strips such as Dilbert, and TV shows such as *The Office* as the major sites of public discourse about the work experience.
4 Vidal (2010) presents data suggesting that a disproportionately large number of institutionalist articles are either published within management journals or else authored by scholars employed within business schools.

References

Adler, Paul (1992) "The 'Learning Bureaucracy': New United Motor Manufacturing, Inc. Research." *Organizational Behavior* 15: 111–94.
Arthur, Michael B. and Denise Rousseau (2001) *The Boundaryless Career: A New Employment Principle for a New Organizational Era*. London: Oxford University Press.
Barker, James R. (1993) "Tightening the Iron Cage: Concertive Control in Self-Managing Teams." *Administrative Science Quarterly* 38: 408–37.
Barley, S. R. and G. Kunda (2004) *Gurus, Hired Guns and Warm Bodies: Itinerant Experts in a Knowledge Economy*. Princeton, NJ: Princeton University Press.
Baxter, Janeen and Erik Olin Wright (2000) "The Glass Ceiling Hypothesis: A Comparative Study of the United States, Sweden, and Australia." *Gender and Society* 14: 275–95.
Bendix, Rinehard (1956) *Work and Authority in Industry*. Berkeley, CA: University of California Press.
Berheide, Catherine W. (1992) "Women Still 'Stuck' in Low-Level Jobs." *Women in Public Service* 3: 1–4.
Bertrand, Marianne and Sendhil Mullainathan (2004) "Are Emily and Greg More Employable than Lakisha and Jamal? A Field Experiment on Labor Market Discrimination." *American Economic Review* 94(4): 991–1013.

Blair-Loy, M. (2001) "It's Not Just What You Know, It's Who You Know: Technical Knowledge, Rainmaking, and Gender among Finance Executives." *Research in the Sociology of Work* 10: 51–83.

Blauner, Robert (1964) *Alienation and Freedom: The Factory Worker and His Industry*. Chicago: University of Chicago Press.

Block, Fred (1990) *Post-Industrial Possibilities: A Critique of Economic Discourse*. Berkeley, CA: University of California Press.

Braverman, Harry (1974) *Labor and Monopoly Capital*. New York: Monthly Review.

Britton, Dana M. and Christine L. Williams (2000) "Response to Baxter and Wright." *Gender and Society* 14: 804–8.

Budros, Art (2004) "Causes of Early and Later Organizational Adoption: The Case of Corporate Downsizing." *Sociological Inquiry* 74(3): 355–80.

Burawoy, Michael (1979) *Manufacturing Consent*. Chicago: University of Chicago Press.

Burawoy, Michael (1985) *The Politics of Production*. London: Verso.

Cappelli, Peter (1995) "Rethinking Employment." *British Journal of Industrial Relations* 33: 563–602.

Casey, Catherine (1995) *Work, Self, and Society: After Industrialism*. London: Sage.

Castells, Manuel (1996) *The Rise of the Network Society*, Vol. 1. Malden, MA: Blackwell.

Catanzarite, Lisa (2003) "Race-Gender Composition and Occupational Pay Degradation." *Social Problems* 50: 14–37.

Chinoy, Ely (1955) *Automobile Workers and the American Dream*. New York: Doubleday.

Collins, S. (1997) *Black Corporate Employees: The Making and Breaking of a Black Middle Class*. Philadelphia, PA: Temple University Press.

Collinson, David and Margaret Collinson (2004) "The Power of Time: Leadership, Management, and Gender." In Cynthia Fuchs Epstein and Arne Kalleberg (eds.), *Fighting for Time: Shifting Boundaries of Work and Social Life*. New York: Russell Sage Foundation, pp. 219–48.

Cotter, David A., J. M. Hermsen, S. Ovadia, and Reeve Vanneman (2001) "The Glass Ceiling Effect." *Social Forces* 80(2): 655–92.

Dalton, Melville (1959) "Men Who Manage." In Mark Granovetter and Richard Swedberg (eds.), *The Sociology of Economic Life*. Boulder, CO: Westview Press, pp. 315–44.

Davis, G. F., D. McAdam, W. R. Scott, and M. N. Zald (eds.) (2005) *Social Movements and Organization Theory*. Cambridge: Cambridge University Press.

De Grazia, Sebastian (1994) *Of Time, Work and Leisure*. New York: Vintage.

DiMaggio, Paul (1988) "Interest and Agency in Institutional Theory." In Lynne G. Zucker (ed.), *Research on Institutional Patterns: Environment and Culture*. Cambridge: Ballinger.

DiMaggio, Paul (1991) "Constructing an Organizational Field as a Professional Project: The Case of U.S. Art Museums." In P. DiMaggio and W. W. Powell (eds.), *The New Institutionalism in Organizational Analysis*. Chicago: University of Chicago Press, pp. 267–92.

DiMaggio, Paul and Walter W. Powell (1983) "The Iron Cage Revisited: Institutional Isomorphism and Collective Rationality in Organizational Fields." *American Sociological Review* 48: 147–60.

DiMaggio, Paul and Walter W. Powell (1991) "Introduction." In DiMaggio and Powell (eds.), *The New Institutionalism in Organizational Analysis*. Chicago: University of Chicago Press, pp. 1–40.

Dobbin, Frank (1994) *Forging Industrial Policy: The United States, Britain, and France in the Railway Age*. Cambridge: Cambridge University Press.

Dobbin, Frank (2010) *Inventing Equal Opportunity*. Princeton, NJ: Princeton University Press.

Dobbin, Frank, John R. Sutton, John W. Meyer, and Richard Scott (1993) "Equal Opportunity Law and the Construction of Internal Labor Markets." *American Journal of Sociology* 99: 396–427.

Du Gay, Paul (1996) *Consumption and Identity at Work*. Thousand Oaks, CA: Sage.

Edelman, L. (1990) "Legal Environments and Organizational Governance: The Expansion of Due Process in the American Workplace." *American Journal of Sociology* 95: 1401–40.

Edelman, L. B., S. R. Fuller, and I. Mara-Drita (2001) "Diversity Rhetoric and the Managerialization of Law." *American Journal of Sociology* 106: 1589–641.

Edwards, Richard (1979) *Contested Terrain: The Transformation of the Workplace in the Twentieth Century*. New York: Basic Books.

Ely, Robin J. and David A. Thomas (2001) "Cultural Diversity at Work: The Effect of Diversity Perspectives and Diversity Processes." *Administrative Science Quarterly* 46: 229–73.

Federal Glass Ceiling Commission (1995a) *Good for Business: Making Full Use of the Nation's Human Capital: The Environmental Scan; A Fact-Finding Report of the Federal Glass Ceiling Commission*. Washington, DC: Government Printing Office.

Federal Glass Ceiling Commission (1995b) *A Solid Investment: Making Full Use of the Nation's Human Capital; Recommendations of the Federal Glass Ceiling Commission*. Washington, DC: Government Printing Office.

Fernandez, Roberto M. (2001) "Skill-Biased Technological Change and Wage Inequality: Evidence from a Plant Retooling." *American Journal of Sociology* 107: 273–320.

Fligstein, Neil (1987) "The Intraorganizational Power Struggle: Rise of Finance Personnel to Top Leadership in Large Corporations, 1919–1979." *American Sociological Review* 52: 44–59.

Fligstein, Neil (1990) *The Transformation of Corporate Control*. Cambridge, MA: Harvard University Press.

Friedland, Roger and R. Alford (1991) "Bringing Society Back in: Symbols, Practices and Institutional Contradictions." In Walter W. Powell and Paul DiMaggio (eds.), *The New Institutionalism in Organizational Analysis*. Chicago: University of Chicago Press, pp. 232–63.

Giddens, Anthony (1982) "Power, the Dialectic of Control, and Class Structuration." In A. Giddens, G. MacKenzie, and Ilya Neustadt (eds.), *Social Class and the Division of Labor*. Cambridge: Cambridge University Press, pp. 29–46.

Gonos, George (1997) "The Contest over 'Employer' Status in the Post-War U.S.: The Case of Temporary Help Firms." *Law and Society Review* 31(1): 81–110.

Gorman, Elizabeth and Julie Kmec (2009) "Hierarchical Rank and Women's Organizational Mobility: Glass Ceilings in Corporate Law Firms." *American Journal of Sociology* 114: 1428–74.

Gouldner, Alvin (1954) *Patterns of Industrial Bureaucracy*. New York: Free Press.

Graham, Laurie (1995) *On the Line at Subaru-Isuzu*. Ithaca, NY: Cornell University Press.

Grenier, Guillermo (1988) *Inhuman Relations: Quality Circles and Anti-Unionism in American Industry*. Philadelphia, PA: Temple University Press.

Hamilton, Gary G. and Nicole Woosley Biggart (1988) "Market, Culture, and Authority: A Comparative Analysis of Management and Organization in the Far East." *American Journal of Sociology* 94(Suppl.): S52–S94.

Handel, Michael J. (2005) "Trends in Perceived Job Quality, 1989–1998." *Work and Occupations* 32: 66–94.

Haveman, Heather and Mukti Khaire (2006) "Organizational Sociology and the Analysis of Work." In Marek Korczynski, Randy Hodson, and Paul Edwards (eds.), *Social Theory at Work*. Oxford: Oxford University Press, pp. 272–98.

Haveman, Heather A., Hayagreeva Rao, and Srikanth Paruchuri (2007) "The Winds of Change: The Progressive Movement and the Bureaucratization of Thrift." *American Sociological Review* 72: 114–42.

Hochschild, Arlie (1983) *The Managed Heart*. Berkeley, CA: University of California Press.

Hodson, Randy (1995) "Worker Resistance: An Underdeveloped Concept in the Sociology of Work." *Economic and Industrial Democracy* 16: 79–110.

Hodson, Randy (2001) *Dignity at Work*. New York: Cambridge University Press.

Hodson, Randy, S. Welsh, S. Rieble, C. S. Jamison, and Sean Creighton (1993) "Is Worker Solidarity Undermined by Autonomy and Participation? Patterns from the Ethnographic Literature." *American Sociological Review* 58: 398–416.

Hughes, Everett C. ([1951] 1994) "Work and Self." In Hughes, *On Work, Race, and the Sociological Imagination*. Ed. Lewis A. Coser. Chicago: University of Chicago Press, pp. 57–66.

Hymowitz, Carol and Timothy Schellhardt (1986) "The Glass Ceiling: Why Women Can't Seem to Break the Invisible Barrier That Blocks Them from the Top Jobs." *Wall Street Journal*, March 24.

Kalev, Alexandra (2009) "Cracking the Glass Cages? Restructuring and Ascriptive Inequality at Work." *American Journal of Sociology* 114: 1591–643.

Kalev, Alexandra, Frank Dobbin, and Erin Kelly (2006) "Best Practices or Best Guesses? Assessing the Efficacy of Corporate Affirmative Action and Diversity Policies." *American Sociological Review* 71: 589–617.

Kalleberg, Arne L. (2009) "Precarious Work, Insecure Workers: Employment Relations in Transition." *American Sociological Review* 74: 1–22.

Kalleberg, Arne L., Barbara F. Reskin, and Ken Hudson (2000) "Bad Jobs in America: Standard and Nonstandard Employment Relations and Job Quality in the United States." *American Sociological Review* 65: 256–78.

Kanter, Rosabeth Moss (1977) *Men and Women of the Corporation*. New York: Basic Books.

Kerr, Clark, John T. Dunlop, Frederick C. Harbison, and Charles A. Meyers (1960) *Industrialism and Industrial Man: The Problems of Labor and Management in Economic Growth*. Cambridge, MA: Harvard University Press.

Kim, Soohan (2010) "Hard to Get, Easy to Lose: The Effects of Women and Minorities in Management on Establishment Closings, 1984–2002." Paper presented at the Annual Meetings of the Eastern Sociological Society, Boston, MA.

Kleinman, D. L. and S. P. Vallas (2001) "Science, Capitalism, and the Rise of the 'Knowledge Worker': The Changing Structure of Knowledge Production in the United States." *Theory and Society* 30(4): 451–92.

Kluegel, James R. (1978) "The Causes and Cost of Racial Exclusion from Job Authority." *American Sociological Review* 43: 285–301.

Knights, David and Darren McCabe (2000) "Ain't Misbehavin'? Opportunities for Resistance under New Forms of 'Quality' Management." *Sociology* 34(3): 421–36.

Korczynski, Marek (2009) "Understanding the Contradictory Lived Experience of Service Work: The Customer-Oriented Bureaucracy." In Marek Korczynski and Cameron Macdonald (eds.), *Service Work: Critical Perspectives*. New York: Routledge, pp. 73–90.

Korczynski, Marek and Cameron Macdonald (2009) "Critical Perspectives on Service Work: An Introduction." In Marek Korczynski and Cameron Macdonald (eds.), *Service Work: Critical Perspectives*. New York: Routledge, pp. 1–10.

Kunda, Gideon (1991) *Engineering Culture: Control and Commitment in a High-Tech Corporation*. Philadelphia, PA: Temple University Press.

Kunda, Gideon (1992) *Engineering Culture*. Cambridge, MA: MIT Press.

Lawrence, P. R. and J. W. Lorsch (1967) *Organization and Environment: Managing Differentiation and Integration*. Cambridge, MA: Harvard Business Press.

Leidner, Robin (1993) *Fast Food, Fast Talk: Service Work and the Routinization of Everyday Life*. Berkeley, CA: University of California Press.

Leidner, Robin (2006) "Identity and Work." In Marek Korczynski, Randy Hodson, and Paul Edwards (eds.), *Social Theory at Work*. Oxford: Oxford University Press, pp. 424–63.

Levanon, Asaf, Paula England, and Paul Allison (2009) "Occupational Feminization and Pay: Assessing Causal Dynamics Using 1950–2000 U.S. Census Data." *Social Forces* 88(2): 865–92.

Levy, Frank and Richard J. Murnane (2005) *The New Division of Labor: How Computers Are Creating the Next Job Market*. Princeton, NJ: Princeton University Press.

Lounsbury, Michael and Bill Kaghan (2001) "Organizations, Occupations and the Structuration of Work." In S. P. Vallas (ed.), *Research in the Sociology of Work* 10: 25–50.

Massoni, Kelley (2004) "Modeling Work: Occupational Messages in Seventeen Magazine." *Gender and Society* 18: 47–65.

Meyer, J. and B. Rowan (1977) "Institutional Organizations: Formal Structure as Myth and Ceremony." *American Journal of Sociology* 83: 340–63.

Meyer, J. and W. R. Scott (1992) *Organizational Environments: Ritual and Rationality*. Thousand Oaks, CA: Sage.

Mills, C. Wright (1951) *White Collar: The American Middle Classes*. New York: Oxford University Press.

Minkoff, Debra C. and John D. McCarthy (2005) "Reinvigorating the Study of Organizational Processes in Social Movements." *Mobilization: An International Journal* 10(2): 289–308.

Mizruchi, Mark S. and Lisa C. Fein (1999) "The Social Construction of Organizational Knowledge: A Study of the Uses of Coercive, Mimetic, and Normative Isomorphism." *Administrative Science Quarterly* 44: 653–83.

Montgomery, David (1979) *Workers' Control in America: Studies in the History of Work, Technology, and Labor Struggles*. New York: Cambridge University Press.

Mouw, Ted (2002) "Are Black Workers Missing the Connection? The Effect of Spatial Distance and Employee Referrals on Interfirm Racial Segregation." *Demography* 39: 507–28.

Noble, David (1984) *Forces of Production*. Oxford: Oxford University Press.

Orlikowski, Wanda (2007) "Sociomaterial Practices: Exploring Technology at Work." *Organization Studies* 28: 1435–48.

Osnowitz, Debra (2010) *Freelancing Expertise: Contract Professionals in the New Economy*. Ithaca, NY: ILR/Cornell University Press.

Padavic, Irene (2005) "Laboring Under Uncertainty: Identity Renegotiation among Contingent Workers." *Symbolic Interaction* 28(1): 111–34.

Pager, Devah, Bart Bonikowski, and Bruce Western (2009) "Discrimination in a Low-Wage Labor Market: A Field Experiment." *American Sociological Review* 74: 777–99.

Pfeffer, Jeffery and James Baron (1988) "Taking the Workers Back Out: Recent Trends in the Structuring of Employment." *Research in Organizational Behavior* 10: 257–303.

Piore, Michael and Charles Sabel (1984) *The Second Industrial Divide*. New York: Basic Books.

Polanyi, Karl ([1944] 2001) *The Great Transformation: The Political and Economic Origins of Our Time.* Boston: Beacon.

Raeburn, Nicole (2004) *Changing Corporate America from Inside Out: Lesbian and Gay Workplace Rights.* Minneapolis: University of Minnesota Press.

Reskin, B. (2003) "Including Mechanisms in Our Models of Ascriptive Inequality." *American Sociological Review* 68: 1–21.

Ritzer, George and Craig D. Lair (2009) "The Globalization of Nothing and the Outsourcing of Service Work." In M. Korczynski and Cameron Macdonald (eds.), *Service Work: Critical Perspectives.* New York: Routledge, pp. 31–50.

Roethlisberger, F. J. and William J. Dickson (1939) *Management and the Worker.* Cambridge, MA: Harvard University Press.

Roy, Donald (1952) "Quota Restriction and Goldbricking in a Machine Shop." *American Journal of Sociology* 57: 427–42.

Royster, Deirdre A. (2003) *Race and the Invisible Hand: How White Networks Exclude Black Men from Blue-Collar Jobs.* Berkeley, CA: University of California Press.

Sallaz, Jeffrey J. (2002) "The House Rules: Autonomy and Interests among Contemporary Casino Croupiers." *Work and Occupations* 29(4): 394–427.

Salzinger, Leslie (2010) "Who Done It? Or: Where Does 'Power' Fit in Global Currency Markets? A Shop Floor Ethnographer Moves to the Trading Floor." Paper presented at the Annual Meetings of the Eastern Sociological Society, Boston, MA.

Schneiberg, Marc and Elisabeth Clemens (2006) "The Typical Tools for the Job: Research Strategies in Institutional Analysis." *Sociological Theory* 3: 195–227.

Schneiberg, Marc and Sarah Soule (2005) "Institutionalization as a Contested, Multi-Level Process: Politics, Social Movements and Rate Regulation in American Fire Insurance." In Gerald Davis, Doug McAdam, W. R. Scott, and Mayer Zald (eds.), *Social Movements and Organizations.* Cambridge: Cambridge University Press, pp. 122–60.

Sennett, Richard (1998) *The Corrosion of Character: The Personal Consequences of the New Capitalism.* New York: Knopf.

Sharone, Ofer (2007) "Constructing Unemployed Job Seekers as Professional Workers: The Depoliticizing Work-Game of Job Searching." *Qualitative Sociology* 30(4): 403–16.

Sharone, Ofer (2011) "Unemployment and Job Seeking in the Great Recession: A Cross-Class Comparison of American Job Seekers." Paper presented at the Annual Meetings of the Eastern Sociological Society. Philadelphia, PA.

Signorielli, Nancy and Susan Kahlenberg, (2001) "Television's World of Work in the Nineties." *Journal of Broadcasting and Electronic Media* 45(1): 4–22.

Simpson, Ida Harper (1989) "The Sociology of Work: Where Have the Workers Gone?" *Social Forces* 67(3): 563–82.

Smith, Ryan A. (1997) "Race, Income, and Authority at Work: A Cross-Temporal Analysis of Black and White Men, 1972–1994." *Social Problems* 44: 701–19.

Smith, Ryan A. (2001) "Particularism in Control over Monetary Resources at Work: An Analysis of Racio-Ethnic Differences in the Authority Outcomes of Black, White, and Latino Men." *Work and Occupations* 28: 447–68.

Smith, Ryan A. and James R. Elliott (2002) "Does Ethnic Concentration Influence Employees' Access to Authority? An Examination of Contemporary Urban Labor Markets." *Social Forces* 81(1): 255–79.

Smith, Vicki (1990) *Managing in the Corporate Interest.* Berkeley, CA: University of California Press.

Smith, Vicki (1997) "New Forms of Work Organization." *Annual Review of Sociology* 23: 315–39.

Smith, Vicki (2001) *Crossing the Great Divide: Worker Risk and Opportunity in the New Economy*. Ithaca, NY: ILR Press.

Snyder, Karrie Ann and Adam Isaiah Green (2008) "Revisiting the Glass Escalator: The Case of Gender Segregation in a Female Dominated Occupation." *Social Problems* 55: 271–99.

Soule, S. (2006) "Divestment by Colleges and Universities in the United States: Institutional Pressures toward Isomorphism." In W. Powell and D. Jones (eds.), *How Institutions Change*. Chicago: University of Chicago Press.

Spenner, Kenneth (1979) "Temporal Changes in Work Content." *American Sociological Review* 44: 968–75.

Spenner, Kenneth (1983) "Deciphering Prometheus: Temporal Change in the Skill Level of Work." *American Sociological Review* 48: 824–37.

Stainback, Kevin and Donald Tomaskovic-Devey (2009) "Intersections of Power and Privilege: Long-Term Trends in Managerial Representation." *American Sociological Review* 74: 800–20.

Stark, David (2001) "Ambiguous Assets for Uncertain Environments: Heterarchy in Postsocialist firms." In P. DiMaggio (ed.), *The Twentieth Century Firm: Changing Economic Organization in International Perspective*. Princeton, NJ: Princeton University Press, pp. 69–104.

Sutton, John R., Frank Dobbin, John W. Meyer, and W. Richard Scott (1994) "The Legalization of the Workplace." *American Journal of Sociology* 99: 944–71.

Thomas, Robert J. (1994) *What Machines Can't Do: Politics and Technology in the Industrial Enterprise*. Berkeley, CA: University of California Press.

Thompson, James D. ([1967] 2003) *Organizations in Action: Social Science Bases of Administrative Theory*. New Brunswick, NJ: Transaction.

Tolbert, P. S. and L. G. Zucker (1983) "Institutional Sources of Change in the Formal Structure of Organizations: The Diffusion of Civil Service Reform, 1880–1935." *Administrative Science Quarterly* 28: 22–39.

Tomaskovic-Devey, Donald (1993) *Gender and Racial Inequality at Work: The Sources and Consequences of Job Segregation*. Ithaca, NY: ILR Press.

Tsui, A. S. and C. A. O'Reilly (1989) "Beyond Simple Demographic Effects: The Importance of Racial Demography in Superior-Subordinate Dyads." *Academy of Management Journal* 32: 402–23.

Vallas, S. P. (1999) "Re-thinking Post-Fordism: The Meaning of Workplace Flexibility." *Sociological Theory* 17: 68–101.

Vallas, S. P. (2003) "The Adventures of Managerial Hegemony: Ideology, Teams, and Worker Resistance." *Social Problems* 50: 204–25.

Vallas, S. P. (2006) "Empowerment Redux: Structure, Agency, and the Re-Making of Managerial Authority." *American Journal of Sociology* 111: 1677–717.

Vallas, S. P. and Daniel L. Kleinman (2008) "Contradiction, Convergence and the Knowledge Economy: The Confluence of Academic and Industrial Biotechnology." *Socio-Economic Review* 2.

Vidal, Matt (2010) "Lean Enough: The Postfordist Labor Process in U.S. Manufacturing." Unpublished paper. Department of Management, King's College London.

Warhurst, Chris and Dennis Nickson (2001) *Looking Good, Sounding Right: Style Counseling in the New Economy*. London: Industrial Society/Hyde House.

Warhurst, Chris and Dennis Nickson (2007) "Employee Experience of Aesthetic Labour in Retail and Hospitality." *Work, Employment and Society* 21(1): 103–20.

Waring, Amanda (2008) "Health Club Use and 'Lifestyle': Exploring the Boundaries between Work and Leisure." *Leisure Studies* 27(3): 295–309.

Weeks, Jon (2003) *Unpopular Culture: The Ritual of Complaint in a British Bank*. Chicago: University of Chicago Press.

Whyte, William H. (1956) *The Organization Man*. New York: Simon and Schuster.

Williams, Christine L. (1995) *Still a Man's World: Men Who Do Women's Work*. Berkeley, CA: University of California Press.

Wilson, George (1997) "Pathways to Power: Racial Differences in the Determinants of Job Authority." *Social Problems* 44: 38–54.

Wingfield, Adia Harvey (2009) "Racializing the Glass Escalator: Reconsidering Men's Experiences with Women's Work." *Gender and Society* 23: 5–26.

Zald, Mayer and Michael A. Berger (1978) "Social Movements in Organizations: Coup d'Etat, Insurgency, and Mass Movements." *American Journal of Sociology* 83: 823–61.

Zuboff, Shoshana (1988) *In the Age of the Smart Machine*. New York: Basic Books.

24

The Sociology of Consumption

P. J. REY AND GEORGE RITZER

Theorizing about consumption has been a part of the field of sociology since its earliest days, dating back, at least implicitly, to the work of Karl Marx in the mid- to late nineteenth century. However, Thorstein Veblen's (1899) *The Theory of the Leisure Class* is generally seen as the first major theoretical work to take consumption as its primary focus (although in the body of his work Veblen, like most other classic thinkers, focused on production – industry and business – not consumption). Despite these early roots, research on consumption began in earnest in the second half of the twentieth century in Europe, especially Great Britain. Interest in the topic among US sociologists was much slower to develop and it is still not a focal concern of many American sociologists. In fact, efforts have been underway for many years to form a Section in the American Sociological Association devoted to the study of consumption, but as yet those efforts have not succeeded. The irony of this is that the US is seen as the quintessential consumer society and has been a major exporter of its products, brands, and consumption sites (e.g., McDonald's, Wal-Mart) to the rest of the world. It may be that consumption is such a central part of American life that it seems unproblematic, not only to most Americans, but also to the majority of American sociologists. It also may be that the recipients of American consumption exports in other parts of the world are more troubled by them so that sociologists there are drawn more to the topic. American sociologists (and others) also continue to be locked into the productivist bias that dominated the discipline in its early years and, therefore, have been slow to recognize the importance of consumption.

While empirical sociological research on consumption has been slow to develop, it has been spurred in recent decades by the rise of consumerism, even "hyperconsumption." Beyond a number of important research monographs, several journals devoted to the topic have emerged including the *Journal of Consumer Behaviour* and the *International Journal of Consumer Research*. While some sociologists have published in those journals, it was the (2001) founding of the *Journal of Consumer Culture* that created a home for sociologists interested in consumption (although those from many other fields have published in the journal). Several books and articles offer an overview of academic, especially sociological, work on consumption in great detail (see, for example, Campbell 1995; Corrigan 1997; Slater 1999; Ritzer, Goodman & Wiedenhoft 2001; Sassatelli 2007). This chapter seeks to build on and update these texts by offering an overview of substantive and theoretical developments in the field over the last decade. However, we will go beyond such an overview to discuss the relevance of a sociological perspective on consumption to the rise, and continuation to this writing, of the Great Recession (or is it a more basic, structural change in the economy of the United States and other developed countries?). As with many other issues, those who have written on this recession have tended to have a productivist bias. Our aim in the final section of this chapter is to show the relevance of a sociology of consumption to this extremely important economic event.

SUBSTANTIVE STUDIES OF CONSUMPTION

In order to make this discussion manageable, we limit ourselves, primarily, to research published in the *Journal of Consumer Culture* (JCC) since its founding in 2001. While this is not fully representative of work in the field, it will give the reader a sense of some of its dominant concerns. The discussion is organized under several topic headings: identity, cultural appropriation, value and consumption, and risk and the environment. This reflects rather specific concerns in the field over the last decade. In comparison, Ritzer, Goodman, and Wiedenhoft (2001) argued that work in the field focused on consumers, the objects consumed, sites of consumption, and the processes of consumption. With these more general concerns in the back of our minds, we will focus in the remainder of this section on the four more specific topics mentioned above as dominant concerns in the JCC.

Identity

Much research has been done on how consumption shapes identity. The enveloping theoretical assumption of this work on identity is that who you are cannot (fully) be separated from what you consume, particularly in contemporary consumer culture. Moreover, identity theorists tend to assume that modern individuals are liberated from the constraints of consuming for "instrumental" (i.e., life-sustaining) purposes and can use consumption for other purposes such as identity work (Bauman 2001). Individuals are often driven to purchase unusual commodity objects (e.g., the Hummer H2 or expensive lingerie) in order to distinguish themselves from others (Jantzen, Østergaard & Vieira 2006; Shulz 2006). This trend begins at an early age. Consumption plays an important part in identity-formation processes for children socialized in contemporary society, so that who you are as an adult is linked to what you consumed as a child (Cook 2008; Tyler 2009).

Identity is not only linked to the content of what is consumed but also to the nature of the processes involved in producing and consuming that object. For example, Colin Campbell (2005) observed an increase in "craft consumption," where the same individual both designs and produces objects in order to consume them as a unique form of self-expression. Similarly, certain forms of ethical consumption (described further below) can be part of an individual's moral identity projects (Brace-Govan & Binay 2010). In fact, consumers may consciously or unconsciously engage in habitual consumption practices in order to maintain a consistent life-narrative regarding the type of person they are (Gaviria & Bluemelhuber 2010). More critical research has argued that the private processes of self-identity formation – "self-branding" – no longer have any meaningful distinction from broad public processes of capitalist production and consumption (Hearn 2008), or that consumers themselves are being manufactured as commodities (Zwick & Knott 2009).

Apart from the identity of individuals, consumption may produce, reinforce, or contradict collective identities. For example, contemporary young African Americans simultaneously convey racial distinctiveness and defy racist assumptions through consumption (Lamont & Molnár 2001; cf. Crockett 2008). Similarly, consumption became a means of maintaining social organization through identity politics as life rapidly changed in the early days of post-Soviet Russia (Shevchenko 2002; Caldwell 2004) and following the collapse of apartheid in South Africa (Laden 2003). Similarly, families use consumption habits such as homemade food to distinguish themselves and, simultaneously, to reinforce a collective family identity (Moisio, Arnould & Price 2004).

Consumption may also shape the dynamics between collective and group identities. Research demonstrates, for example, that consumption serves to refocus energy from collective identity or rebellion towards a more individualistic focus on lifestyle choices. Adam Arvidsson (2001) argues that this is precisely what occurred in the Italian youth market, as epitomized by the history of the Vespa scooter. Similarly, Jacqueline Botterill (2007) makes a broad historical argument that post-1950s consumption has largely been driven by a quest for freedom, autonomy, and individuality. The marketing of rebellion has had to become more sophisticated as traditionally iconic figures, such as the cowboy, the genius artist, and the outlaw, have become little more than parodied clichés. While much advertising is still driven by appeals to individualistic values, Botterill finds that a now popular alternative approach in advertising is to appeal to the ideology of athleticism (i.e., values such as hard work, achievement, discipline, and teamwork) and the still widely embraced image of the star athlete. In other cases, marketers have successfully fabricated new group identities (such as the "tween" [Cook & Kaiser 2004]) which serve as convenient new markets for their products.

However, some research calls into question the emphasis on consumption as a process of identity-formation, contending instead that group identification and social regulation still dominate identity-formation processes and mediate the effects of consumption practices (Warde 1994). Others argue that the net effect of the proliferation of individual and collective identities through consumption is that, ultimately, the consumer has become such a diverse and multifaceted entity that it is no longer easy to define. Instead, we are left with several competing accounts of the consumer. These accounts are not necessarily compatible or generalizable to all consumers (Gabriel & Lang 2008).

Cultural appropriation

The creation of a cultural identity may involve appropriation of, and playfulness with, other cultures. These appropriations might occur across class lines. A phenomenon labeled "Poor Chic" involves the appropriation of symbolically important lower-class commodity-objects (e.g., muscles, motorcycles, and tattoos) by the middle class (Halnon & Cohen 2006). Appropriated cultures may even be fictional, as illustrated by groups formed around the stories of H. P. Lovecraft, vampire tales, and various works of science fiction (Possamaï 2002).

Cultural appropriation can have grave consequences when patterns of consumption behavior are adopted by groups that lack sufficient resources to engage in them. Restated, we can say that as consumption patterns trickle down from the upper and middle classes to the lower class, they cause "collateral damage" to those who cannot hope to economically sustain such behaviors (Bauman 2007).

Value and consumption

Theorists of consumption (following in the footsteps of Pierre Bourdieu, who proposed the use of the concepts of economic, social, cultural, and symbolic capital) often expand the concept of value beyond the sphere of material economics. Aesthetic value, for example, describes the way culturally valued tastes are translated into monetary value through a network of institutions. Perhaps the most ubiquitous image in marketing is the thin, pale look of the female model's body (Entwistle 2002; Redmond 2003; Wissinger 2009), particularly if this body is presented as an object for male consumption (Amy-Chinn 2006). Holliday and Cairnie (2007) even propose the term "body capital" to explain the value that both men and women derive from labor (including surgery) to improve the state of their bodies relative to the prevailing social norms. Or, better yet, they can improve the state of future generations' bodies by purchasing Viking sperm for artificial insemination; these sperm are marketed with images centered on whiteness and purity (Kroløkke 2009). Other valued images that are widely used to promote products include youth and youthfulness (Langer 2004) and phallic symbols and masculinity (Thompson & Holt 2004). With respect to some hyper-rationalized industries, such as food service, consumers have gone so far as to assert aesthetic value as a right or cultural imperative (Sassatelli & Davolio 2010).

On the topic of brand value, Adam Arvidsson (2005, 2006) argues that consumers do much of the work involved in building brands and their value. The role played by companies, particularly marketing divisions, in contemporary consumer capitalism is to manage carefully the free and spontaneous activities of consumers so that they can be harnessed to create value for the companies. Because consumers are not compensated for this value they create through their branding "work," they can be seen as being exploited in the technical Marxian sense of the term.

Theorists of consumer culture have long understood that consumption can produce certain forms of capital for the consumer and researchers continue to elaborate upon this phenomenon. For example, Wright (2005) demonstrated that bookshop managers tend to hire preferentially workers who convey the message that leisurely reading is a respectable and worthwhile activity. Thus, implicitly, these managers are marketing cultural capital as much as the content of the books themselves. Similarly, another study found that women with high indicators of cultural capital modulated their selection of greeting cards on several axes (e.g., originality, simplicity, or irony) in order to convey tastes appropriate to a wider range of circumstances, while women with lower indicators of cultural capital generally only selected cards based on sentiment (West 2010).

What all of these new conversations about value have in common is that they tend to examine "immaterial" aspects of commodities, their production, and their consumption (Coté & Pybus 2007). This focus on the immaterial is, in no small way, influenced by the emergence of the internet.

Risk and the environment

Various forms of consumption are perceived as posing (sometimes unavoidable) risks to the individual and/or the environment. Under these circumstances, individual consumers are placed in the position of having to assess the potential risks and benefits and make decisions accordingly. Often the logic behind the cost-benefit analyses varies between cultural groups and is a source of profound ambivalence within them (Halkier 2001). The development of genetically modified foods is, for example, one field which poses new challenges for consumers. Such crops may be cheaper, fresher, or more nutritious, yet they come with the danger of unintended consequences for individuals and for the environment. Consumers report feeling capable of making the best decisions because they believe they are able to interpret various media sources and sort out the facts of the situation (Tulloch & Lupton 2002). However, they express doubts and insecurities regarding the efficacy of their actions in mediating environmental and personal risks (Connolly & Prothero 2008).

Within various cultures, the symbolic aspects of consumption are often tied to environmental factors. Often, environmentally-conscious consumption (whether primitive or modern) is coupled with discourses regarding purity or pollution. The symbolic value of the object of consumption is then derivative of such discourses (Neves 2004). The growth in sales of bottled water is one modern example of how the concept of purity is used to add value to a commodity (Wilk 2006). Similarly, consumption practices shape perception of the relationship between urban and natural environments (Wells 2002). The purity–pollution continuum is not, however, the only discourse that exists with respect to environmentally-conscious consumption.

Recently, there has been much discussion of "ethical consumption" (see Thompson & Coskuner-Balli 2007), one instantiation of which might involve consuming in such a way as to reduce one's overall impact on the environment (e.g., Schor

1999, 2010). Yet, consumers are now often compelled to consume more in order to maintain their "green subjectivities" (Connolly & Prothero 2008). Marketers have discovered a new sales base in these green consumers, and this, in turn, has led to accusations of corporate "greenwashing," whereby companies make a few very public gestures to give consumers the impression that they are being environmentally-friendly in order to add additional value to their product without necessarily incurring the cost of actually changing fundamental environmental practices (Laufer 2003).

The scope of ethical consumption is often larger than just the environment. It might also look at the social consequences of producing certain commodities. Images of child slaves and impoverished workers may dissuade consumers from purchasing commodities produced in certain regions of the world and may encourage them to seek more "just" alternatives (e.g., "fair trade" products) (Dolan 2005). Consumers use a variety of tactics to influence companies' decision-making, including boycotting (i.e., punishing business for unfavorable behavior) and "buycotting" (i.e., rewarding business for favorable behavior) (Neilson 2010). A prominent example of how discourses of social justice are increasingly being tied to consumption practices is the African diamond trade. Global outrage over the activities of violent militia groups funded by illegally produced diamonds led to a (voluntary) transnational accord on diamond verification standards called the Kimberley Process. The African diamond trade became such a public issue that it was made the subject of a 2006 Hollywood movie called *Blood Diamond*. Ethical consumption practices might even be characterized by an anti-consumption ethos that favors used or recycled products over new products (Brace-Govan & Binay 2010).

THEORIES OF CONSUMPTION

As in the case of the previous overview of substantive work on consumption, this section on theory will also be selective (there is simply too much theory to deal with in such a brief space) and focused on a limited number of themes, or problematics: (1) the separation and/or (re)integration of the socio-economic spheres of production and consumption; (2) understanding why dissatisfaction persists in an era of hyper-abundance; (3) the loss/maintenance of agency in a milieu of almost infinite choices. While we make no claims that this is the only or the best way to interpret the vast literature dealing with consumption, we believe that this schema will be useful to both scholars and students of these theories and of consumption.

The spheres of production and consumption

In many ways, the assumption that production and consumption exist as separate spheres, and, therefore, may be studied in isolation from one another, can be traced back to Marx's incalculable influence on the discipline of sociology. Marx observed a capitalist world where production and consumption occurred under a distinct set of conditions. Production was done mainly outside the home – in factories – because workers did not own the means of production and were forced to sell their labor in return for wages. Under such conditions, workers were both exploited and alienated, so that work was something to be avoided as much as possible. Consumption generally occurred in the home where workers were free to control their own activities; however, since workers' wages were so meager, they tended to consume relatively little. For this reason, consumption and production were divided across class lines, with the working class doing the bulk of the production and the capitalists doing the bulk of the consumption.

While this class division in the spheres of production and consumption is salient in Marx's work, his theory is certainly more nuanced, particularly in the *Grundrisse* ([1857–8] 1973: 83–94), where he outlines three relationships between production and consumption:

1   Factory workers clearly need to consume raw materials (and sometimes other commodities) in the process of production. In fact, Marx later elaborates on this process, calling it "productive consumption," which is defined by the fact that it results in "a commodity of more value than that of the elements composing it" ([1885] 1907: 31).

2   Production and consumption are also interdependent at a macro level insofar as production is required in order for there to be goods to consume and as long as consumption drives demand for production.

3   Each process – production and consumption – completes the other. Consumption marks the end-point of production, while consumption can only be materialized through the object created by production.

While Marx elaborates the three relations, he does so in passing, and they seem to remain only tangential to the overall theoretical development reflected in the *Grundrisse*.

Marx's most systematic (if largely implicit) treatment of the relationship between production and consumption occurs in his discussion of the crisis of overproduction. He predicted that productivity would eventually increase enough to meet all of the consumer demands of the bourgeoisie. At this point, the constant growth in production that political economists assumed was required for capitalism's continued existence would be hindered by a consumer base that was too small to create sufficient demand. As Marx explains, "The epochs in which capitalist production exerts all its forces are always periods of overproduction, because [...] the sale of commodities [...] is limited, not by the consumptive demand of society in general, but by the consumptive demand of a society in which the majority are poor and must always remain poor" ([1885] 1907: 636n.). Put simply, production cannot be greater than what a particular society can consume, and capitalist production is limited by the fact that such a small proportion of its constituents can afford to consume more than the minimum necessary for survival. Marx asks us to take as evidence:

> the commercial crises that by their periodical return put the existence of the entire bourgeois society on its trial, each time more threateningly. In these crises, a great part not only of the existing products, but also of the previously created productive forces, are periodically destroyed. In these crises, there breaks out an epidemic that, in all earlier epochs, would have seemed an absurdity – the epidemic of over-production. (Marx & Engels 1848: 14–15)

From this perspective, overproduction and its corollary, under-consumption, pose the greatest threat to capitalist production. Moreover, this demonstrates that even Marx, at least implicitly, understood that the separation under capitalism of the spheres of production and consumption was largely illusory and destined to be temporary.

Yet, despite these important insights into consumption, Marx's focus always remained firmly on production. Many theorists in the wake of Marx continue to wrestle with his characterization of consumption and production as separate spheres of activity – at least, insofar as Marx illustrated in his own work a belief that production could be studied largely separately from consumption.

Nevertheless, because Marx's theory of overproduction is so central to his conceptualization of the spheres of production and consumption, it is important to take a brief logical detour to consider how theorists of consumption have developed correctives to his theory of overproduction to account for why it never developed into the crisis that Marx had expected. We can organize these critiques into two categories: (1) those claiming that bourgeois (or any human) demand has never become saturated in the way that Marx expected; (2) those claiming that capitalism proved capable of adjusting for excess production by simply raising wages enough to create sufficient demand.

Natural vs. fabricated demand

Marx's assumption that humans have generated finite levels of demand stems from an essentialist theory of human nature, whereby human needs are predetermined and hard-wired into our very being, as opposed to things we learn and develop through our interaction with our environment. Many late nineteenth-century thinkers (e.g., Schopenhauer, Nietzsche, and Freud) offered opposing views of human needs as being fluid and emerging based on social context; however, Veblen (1899) was the first thinker to clearly articulate a theory of how the fluidity of desire is linked to consumption behavior. This relationship is, most prominently, captured in his concept of "conspicuous consumption," which describes consumption that is not engaged in to satisfy any immediate instinctual need, but, instead, is undertaken to communicate one's social status. Veblen argues that this behavior is particularly important for people who have high status (and, of course, the resources to communicate this status). Often, the most conspicuous forms of consumption are those which demonstrate that an individual has such ample resources that many of them can be wasted. Veblen observes that conspicuous consumption is so valued that people actually sacrifice gratification of more primal needs in order to engage in it – for example: "people will undergo a very considerable degree of privation in the comforts or the necessaries of life in order to afford what is considered a decent amount of wasteful consumption; so that it is by no means an uncommon occurrence, in an inclement climate, for people to go ill clad in order to appear well dressed" (1899: 168).

Similarly, Marcuse (1955) argued that capitalist society used marketing to fabricate demand amongst the masses, pacifying them and giving them a reason to continue working, even if they were perfectly capable of surviving without doing some or all of that work, and even if they hated the work they were doing. He explains:

We may distinguish both true and false needs. "False" needs are those which are superimposed upon the individual by particular social interests in his repression: the needs which perpetuate toil, aggressiveness, misery, and injustice. [...] Most of the prevailing needs to relax, to have fun, to behave and consume in accordance with the advertisements, to love and hate what others love and hate, belong to this category of false needs. [...] The only needs that have an unqualified claim for satisfaction are the vital ones – nourishment, clothing, lodging at the attainable level of culture. (Marcuse 1964: 50)

At the center of Marcuse's revolutionary vision is a world where we abandon all the desires which capitalism has created and use resources in the sole pursuit of our natural desires. This vision resonated with the anti-consumerist counter-culture of the 1960s, but was short-lived.

Erich Fromm complicates (and famously criticizes) Marcuse's theory of human desire, by arguing that it is natural for us to develop more culturally sophisticated desires. This claim, of course, begins to blur the lines between naturalism and social constructionism. He explains:

It is true that as long as the living standard of the population is below a dignified level of subsistence, there is a natural need for more consumption. It is also true that there is a legitimate need for more consumption as man develops culturally and more refined needs for better food, objects of artistic pleasure, books, etc. (Fromm 1955: 134)

Fromm's position is reconcilable, because he assumes humans have a natural need to be social and that civilization (along with all the sophisticated needs that it carries with it) is an extension of the need to be social.

By the 1970s, theorists – most notably, Baudrillard – were arguing that all desires were socially constructed (or, at least, socially mediated) and that the concept of natural desires was a Western fantasy – a grand narrative that, at best, was naïve, and, at worst, served to reinforce various regimes of social control. Skepticism that modern consumption is driven by natural needs persists today. Bauman (2001), for example, argues that it is our freedom to consume for non-instrumental, immaterial purposes (and not, for example, an increase in the amount we consume) that, primarily, differentiates postmodern consumers from their ancestors.

While few contemporary theorists retain the kind of rather naïve essentialism found in Marx, theorists also seldom endorse the opposite extreme of total constructionism represented by Baudrillard. In fact, in many ways, the conversation is shifting away from where our needs originate to how our needs are satisfied. Juliet Schor's (2010) recent book, *Plenitude*, for example, argues that many of our needs can be better satisfied through means other than the market, so that the social trend towards working longer hours is actually counter-productive.

Co-optation of the working class

Marx also assumed that capitalists would always pay the minimum possible wage to workers. As a result, workers could never be a significant part of the base for consumer demand. This assumption has simply been proven, empirically, to be false. While there are periods of exceptions, real wages in developed economies have generally risen over the last century. This fact, along with developments in mass production, has meant that the working class has come to form a central component of consumer-driven economies. In fact, the importance of the worker qua consumer has long been recognized by the public, including Henry Ford's famous statement of intent to produce a car that his workers could afford.

The emergence of mass consumer markets aroused a wave of critical theory (e.g., Benjamin, Adorno, Marcuse) that mourned the loss of the revolutionary moment in the West. That is, it marked the end of the moment when the working class could realize that the capitalist system had little to offer them and could overthrow it in favor of a system with a more equitable distribution of resources. These theorists believed that the working class had been co-opted by the capitalist system. That is, they had been given enough of a stake in the system so that, even though vast inequalities persisted, workers had a vested interest in keeping the system alive. In Marxian terms, workers now had something more to lose than their chains.

The consequence of co-optation is, as Adorno – the ardent pessimist – once eloquently stated, "[p]hilosophy, which once seemed obsolete, lives on because the moment to realize it was missed" ([1966] 1973: 3). Consumption is, in fact, at the heart of much analysis of the passing of the revolutionary moment in the West. Marcuse (1964) argued that as the working class became enamored with consumer goods, capitalist ideology achieved unquestionable dominance, and society could be described as "one-dimensional."

The co-optation of the working class has encouraged recent social theorists (Schutz 2004; Ritzer 2010b) to liken contemporary capitalism to a velvet cage (a direct spin-off of Max Weber's "iron cage" metaphor), where consumers may realize they are trapped in the system, but are content to remain that way. Still, other theorists (e.g., de Certeau [1980] 2002; Hall 1992) take a less pessimistic view, believing that workers qua consumers are the kings of the marketplace. We will explore this debate further in the third section.

Returning to the separation between the spheres of consumption and production, it should now be clear that the notion that these spheres are separated along class lines holds little sway in contemporary thought. Nevertheless, the two processes of production and consumption are still generally studied separately. Baudrillard, for example, criticizes Marx for having a productivist bias, yet, in *The Consumer Society*, turns all his attention in the other direction. One explanation is that researchers generally assume, like Marx, that the two spheres are largely separated spatially as well as temporally. While, perhaps, this separation was plausible in Marx's time, it is less so today. This is, in no small part, due to the fact that what is being produced and consumed has changed. Today, information and services constitute a much larger proportion of economic activity in developed countries.

Recent work argues for the need for a new concept that bridges production and consumption and represents them as interconnected processes. Several terms have been introduced to fill this gap, including "prosumption" (Toffler 1980; Kotler 1986; Humphreys & Grayson 2008; Ritzer 2010a; Ritzer & Jurgenson 2010), "co-creation" (Prahalad & Ramaswamy 2004; Tapscott & Williams 2006; Humphreys

& Grayson 2008; Zwick, Bonsu & Darmody 2008), and "produsage" (Bruns 2008). While all these terms have slightly different connotations, we will lump them all under the umbrella of "prosumption." Theorists of prosumption tend to endorse postmodern assumptions that old categories should be imploded and exist in varying intensities on a continuum (Baudrillard [1981] 1995). Ritzer (2010a), for example, claims that prosumption has always existed and that the spheres of production and consumption, which were separated out to a significant extent by early capitalism, are, in many instances, imploding once again (if they were ever separate) in late capitalism. The collapse of these two spheres is particularly clear with respect to newly emerging technologies (Green 2001; Coté & Pybus 2007; Ritzer & Jurgenson 2010) – most notably, the recent proliferation of user-generated content on the internet known as Web 2.0 (O'Reilly 2005). On social media like Facebook, for example, users are nearly always producing and consuming their profiles simultaneously. The implications of the reintegration of production and consumption in contemporary capitalism remain largely unexplored and will likely be a fertile ground for future research.

That said, we would not want to overlook the fact that certain theorists of consumption have long ago observed certain types of activity that might aptly be described as prosumption. Georg Simmel ([1911–12] 2000), for example, argues in "the tragedy of culture" that we use the objective culture of consumable products to produce ourselves as individuals. On this model, we produce objects so that we can consume them to produce ourselves. Thus, production and consumption are two sides of the same self-individuating coin. However, as Simmel clearly recognized, this relationship has become problematic in modernity because the proliferation of material goods has outstripped the productive capacities of the subjective culture through which we express ourselves.

We can read arguments of the Birmingham School, including those of Richard Hoggart (1998), Stuart Hall (1992), Raymond Williams (1995), Dick Hebdige (1981), and Paul Willis (1978), as arguing that people constantly prosume themselves and their environment through their interaction with cultural products. For example, Hall argues that media viewers can meaningfully be said to consume what they are watching if, and only if, they simultaneously engage in the production of meanings that ultimately influence individual attitudes and practice. He explains that media products must "be translated – transformed [...] – into social practices if the circuit is to be both completed and effective. If no 'meaning' is taken, there can be no 'consumption'"(Hall 1992: 107). Consumers are never just consumers of the various cultural scripts they encounter; instead, consumers use and modify scripts for their own purposes. Thus, consumption becomes an active, even productive, process. Similarly, de Certeau argues that consumers are "unrecognized producers, poets of their own affairs" ([1980] 2002: 34).

A more critical description of the productive consumer might be derived from Foucault's ([1975] 1995) concept of disciplinary power. This form of power is distinguished from other forms of power in Foucault's genealogy by its productivity. If discipline is carried out through consumption and consumption-oriented institutions, then the process can be viewed as both productive of the individual subject and reproductive of the social system. In both cases, prosumption appears to be implied.

DISSATISFACTION IN AN AGE OF ABUNDANCE

Related to the above conversation regarding natural versus socially constructed needs is the social-psychological question of how and why unhappiness persists in an age of abundance. Human happiness is related to the two theories of needs because happiness is generally considered to be the outcome of the satisfaction of needs. While it is possible to imagine nature as being so cruel as to have created humans with needs that are impossible to satisfy, theorists who affirm that needs are, at root, the product of human nature tend to assume that there are certain achievable conditions under which needs can be satisfied and happiness can be achieved.

Marx, for example, thought that human needs could be met in a society that created conditions under which all humans are able to labor freely without coercion or alienation. However, other essentialist thinkers were less optimistic. Freud thought that our natural needs – which fall into two categories, erotic and aggressive – are often in competition, both within ourselves and with the needs of others. This means that the best society can do is minimize conflict; however, there are better and worse ways of minimizing conflict. Freud saw repression as society's last resort. Repression occurs when society prevents its subjects from talking, or even thinking, about things that would otherwise produce conflict. Yet, implicit in Freud's ([1927] 1975) theory is the assumption that greater abundance would lead to a lessening of repression. For this reason, both Freudian (Adorno, Horkheimer, Fromm, and Marcuse) and post-Freudian (Foucault and Baudrillard) thinkers came to revise or reject Freud's theory of human needs in light of the post-World War II era of abundance.

Horkheimer and Adorno argued that Freud conflated true pleasure with mere gratification. The distinction they make between the two concepts is that while gratification is simply the fulfillment of basic erotic or aggressive needs, pleasure results from a struggle against certain obstacles to gratification. Or, in their words: "natural pleasure does not go beyond the appeasement of need. All pleasure is social. It originates in alienation" (Horkheimer & Adorno [1944] 1997: 105).

Pleasure cannot be given; it must be won. Because mass culture is essentially unidirectional, it can only produce gratification. In fact, pleasure is a threat to the capitalist system which relies on mass culture to breed passivity; this is because pleasure is a process and it must be active. Thus, to ensure its own flourishing, capitalism must restrict the pleasure process, thereby impinging on happiness. They explain: "Enjoyment becomes the object of manipulation, until, ultimately, it is entirely extinguished in fixed entertainments. The process has developed from the primitive festival to the modern vacation" (Horkheimer & Adorno [1944] 1997: 106). In this example, the festival – which interrupted the social order and always carried with it a risk that the order would never be re-established – is replaced by the vacation which no longer affords the experience of escaping frustrating social circumstances but, in fact, serves to strengthen the system.

Marcuse is similarly critical of consumer capitalism because he believes it uses the gratification of desire as a means of social control. Marketing has developed as a system to channel desire in directions that reinforce capitalism and serve its need for perpetual expansion, even if such desires are contrary to the rational best interests of individual consumers. In order to maximize the productivity of workers, capitalism must convince them that it is worthwhile to continue to spend vast portions of their life working. It does so by constantly channeling their desire toward new commodities that can only be purchased by earning more wages. Marcuse believes, however, that if the influence of marketing over human desire could be broken, workers would realize that society has already developed the capacity to meet all their needs without major conflict arising. Thus, for Marcuse, unhappiness emerges because the needs of the capitalist system are no longer in sync with the best interests of most members of society.

Fromm also attributes unhappiness to the nature of the capitalist system, specifically, its ideology of individualism. Rather than questioning the social conditions in which we are never really satisfied, we are told – and believe – that happiness is just one purchase away. Other people, we are encouraged to believe, are in competition with us and serve as barriers to our own satisfaction. As such, our consumption patterns are no longer consistent with our subsistence-based, or social, needs. Fromm explains: "our craving for consumption has lost all connection with the real needs of man. Originally, the idea of consuming more and better things was meant to give man a happier, more satisfied life. Consumption was a means to an end, that of happiness. It has now become an aim in itself" (1955: 134). Consumption is now fundamentally anti-social, and, therefore, makes us unhappy.

Foucault ([1976] 1990) breaks with the basic tenets of Freudian thought by attacking the concept of repression (and, by implication, the concept of natural desires) and instead argues that virtually every aspect of human subjectivity is the outcome of social processes. Foucault argues that, ironically, we have learned to take perverse pleasure in our own repression. Thus, instead of repression and happiness being disproportionately related, they have a far more complex, non-linear relationship. While Foucault seldom addresses consumption directly, the implication of his work is that repression may actually encourage consumption by creating desire for those things we feel we should not, or cannot, have (e.g., pornography, drugs, gambling, violent entertainment, etc.).

Not only does Baudrillard reject the idea that certain needs are universal to human nature, but, more radically, he dismisses the longstanding philosophical assumption (dating, at least, back to Socrates) that humans seek to be happy. He argues:

> The ideological force of the notion of happiness does not originate in a natural propensity on the part of each individual to realize that happiness for himself. It derives, socio-historically, from the fact that the myth of happiness is the one which, in modern societies, takes up and embodies *the myth of Equality*. All the political and sociological virulence with which that myth [i.e., the myth of Equality] has been charged since the industrial revolution and the revolutions of the nineteenth century has been transferred to Happiness. (Baudrillard [1970] 1998: 49)

Baudrillard goes on to explain that, in democratic society, material measures of inequality have been supplanted by measures of internal well-being as the foundation for discourses regarding justice. That is to say, there has been an ideological shift in society away from the belief that justice describes a set of circumstances where everyone has equal access to material wealth to one where "all men are equal before need and before the principle of satisfaction" ([1970] 1998: 50). Under such logic, an unequal distribution of wealth should not matter as long as the supposed basic needs of all members of society are met. The result, as Baudrillard sees it, is that the ideology of happiness/well-being has become a mechanism to legitimate material inequality.

CHOICE AND FREEDOM

The explosion of choices available to us is, of course, related, in no small part, to the great material wealth that emerged after World War II. While it is often assumed that happiness and freedom of choice are intimately related, it serves us well to remember the parable of the mule, who perished in indecision between which of two haystacks to eat first. Many social theorists are skeptical regarding the degree of freedom that emerges from all the ostensible choices brought about by great wealth. As a result, they are equally dubious about the relationship between those choices and happiness. So, while there may be implications for the previous discussion of happiness, let us shift our full attention to the issues of choice and freedom.

The debate over whether greater choice actually leads to greater freedom is, in many ways, an extension of the agency-structure debate, which has long been a major theme in the disciplinary discourse of (Continental) sociology. Of course, positions in such a complicated debate tend to be fairly sophisticated, so we can only loosely organize our discussion of various thinkers around this theme.

The thinkers associated with the Birmingham School are likely the best-known proponents of an agent-centered approach to understanding consumption and, as such, they tend to focus on individual experience. They conclude from this that individuals do, in fact, experience themselves as more free as a result of greater choice in the marketplace. As discussed above, the Birmingham School tends to view consumption as an active process of producing scripts for one's own experience. Thus, the more choices one has in the marketplace, the more tools one has in creating scripts for oneself. Or, as de Certeau puts it, these choices augment the consumer's freedom to become the "poets of their own affairs" ([1980] 2002: 34).

Structuralist thinkers, on the other hand, tend to examine the social forces which compel mass behavior. Marxists, for example, often argue that capitalism only provides the illusion of choice between various commodities, when the real and unthinkable choice is between the capitalist system and other systems of social organization. Brands, logos, and other features of a product just distract from the all-important question: through what set of social relations was this commodity produced? When we conceptualize choice only in terms of the qualities of a commodity, we fetishize it, forgetting that it is the labor that has gone into it which matters most. Taken to the extreme, the only relevant choice for a Marxist is the choice between alienated and unalienated labor.

Freudian theorists tend to focus on the manipulation of unconscious desire. A manipulated person might feel as though they are freely choosing to consume, while their decision to purchase a particular product has been directly influenced by a set of factors of which the person is completely unaware. This is particularly of concern when these unconscious influences are the product of marketing tactics which seek to influence the behavior of a person in a way that benefits a company, regardless of whether this is in the best interest of the individual in question. For a psychoanalytic theorist, true freedom is only achieved when people are consciously aware of all their (often conflicting) motivations and, thus, can make rational choices.

Weber's work is also relevant here insofar as rationalization has penetrated into our patterns of consumption, so that, even if we have choices between various commodities, we do not have the freedom to escape the process of rationalization; in fact, rational systems control those choices. In *The McDonaldization of Society*, Ritzer (2011) describes four dimensions of rationalization (i.e., efficiency, calculability, predictability, and control) and observes that each has become increasingly characteristic of consumer culture. However, Ritzer (2010b) also notes that the rationalization of consumption can be counter-productive for capitalism because too much of it causes consumers to become disenchanted. As a result, those who control the "cathedrals of consumption" (e.g., retailers) have employed a number of strategies to re-enchant consumption, including the production of spectacles (see Debord [1967] 1983), including dazzling (if inefficient) arrays of choices. Thus, ironically, through this irrational range of choices, consumers are actually more tightly bound in the iron cage of rationality.

Ideas in Foucault's work on sexuality are also applicable to the question of consumer freedom. Foucault ([1976] 1990, 1981) contrasts sexuality (which is a social construct) with pleasure (which can only fully be derived from "limit experiences" that produce ruptures in the experience of otherwise well-disciplined bodies). He is skeptical of sexuality because it cannot be separated from power and acts as a mechanism to discipline bodies and to regulate society by perpetuating coercive norms that tend to reinforce the status quo. The relationship between power and sexuality is complex. Individuals almost invariably take pleasure in both exercising and resisting pleasure. Foucault explains that pleasure and power operate as a double spiral: "The pleasure that comes from exercising a power that questions, monitors, watches, spies, searches out, palpates, brings to light; and on the other hand the pleasure that kindles at having to evade this power, flee from it, fool it, or travesty it" ([1976] 1990: 45). Consumption exhibits a similar relationship to power: marketers continuously capitalize on consumers' conflicting desires to be both normal and rebellious. When consumers purchase and enjoy commodities, they may be achieving happiness, but they are simultaneously reinforcing a system of social norms that produces and controls them.

Baudrillard also sees consumer society as a sort of trap. Choice is not synonymous with freedom insofar as we are never free to escape constant imperatives to make choices as consumers or to escape consumer society altogether. He says: "The carefully sustained mystique [...] of individual satisfaction and choice [...] is the very ideology of the industrial system, justifying all its arbitrary power and all the collective nuisances it generates: dirt, pollution, deculturation. In fact, the consumer is sovereign in a jungle of ugliness where *freedom of choice has been thrust upon him*" (Baudrillard [1970] 1998: 72).

Moreover, Baudrillard believes that even those who resist the dominant forms of consumption are instrumental in producing new forms of consumption that ultimately serve to reinforce the overarching system (what he calls "the code"). For example, the green movement, which began by claiming that human consumption patterns were detrimental to the environment, has led to entire green industries which market eco-friendly or sustainable products to Earth-conscious consumers. However, this paradox of resistance serving to reinforce the system is, perhaps, clearest in the case of fashion. Traditionally, fashion has established a set of norms from which only those with the highest status can afford to deviate, yet those deviations carried out by elites form the basis of future fashions (Simmel [1904] 2000; Bourdieu [1979] 1984). More recently, it has been argued that contemporary fashion is championed as the primary method through which people individuate themselves from one another, yet they are simultaneously united by the common purpose of self-individuation (Lipovetsky [1987] 2002). In such postmodern conceptions, desire is a moving target; thus happiness is ephemeral at best.

Bourdieu, in his *magnum opus*, *Distinction* ([1979] 1984), develops a complex account of the relationship between agency and structure, and, as a result, produces a very nuanced view of human choice that merits significant attention. Rather than "choice," Bourdieu prefers the term "taste." Taste is neither a spontaneous impulse, nor a hard-wired instinctual response; instead, taste describes a series of habits that are the unique product of experiences in a particular social milieu. When these habits – what Bourdieu calls habitus – are carried into a new social field, they determine how an actor will respond to the field. For Bourdieu, choice has little to do with freedom. Instead, choice is a mechanism through which members of certain classes can demonstrate their status and, as such, distinguish themselves from members of other classes.

THE SOCIOLOGY OF CONSUMPTION AND THE "GREAT RECESSION"

In our penultimate section, we now turn to a discussion of the continued relevance of consumption theory to current events, namely, the "Great Recession" that continues to unfold at the time of this chapter's writing. Consumers certainly bear some of the responsibility for the Great Recession that began in late 2007. However, to focus only on what we, the consumers, did is, at least to some degree, to "blame the victim" (Ryan 1976). We are not saying that consumers are innocent; that they did not play a significant role in creating their own economic problems (greed manifested in too much consumption and debt; naïveté about the problems they were creating for themselves). However, there *is* another side to this and that is what "they" did to consumers. They, in this case, are the financial wizards, the bankers, the loan officers, the real estate tycoons and brokers, marketers and advertisers, what is left of our "captains of industry" (Veblen 1899), and the "captains of commerce" (e.g., those who run the thriving Wal-Mart, as well as those who ran the defunct Circuit City). Of course, a focus on what "they" did is as one-sided as concerning ourselves only with what consumers did. However, there are good reasons to deal with what they did. After all, it was they who:

- created the shiny new financial tools (derivatives, credit default swaps);
- created the innovative new mortgages (interest-only payments – and even those payments could be waived from month to month and added to the principal – no down payments, adjustable loans, "liar loans" – encouraging people to lie about their financial status, especially their income);
- created the marketing and advertising campaigns designed to lead us to buy all sorts of things (the George Foreman grill, Viagra) we don't need and often don't use;
- managed great corporations (GM, Chrysler, AIG, Lehman Brothers) into the ground;
- designed cathedrals of consumption such as Wal-Mart, IKEA, and Carrefour to lead us into hyperconsumption by, for example, using loss leaders and the illusion of low price ("the high cost of low price," of "cheap");
- designed other cathedrals of consumption – Las Vegas casino-hotels, great cruise ships (the newest can handle 6,000 passengers), Disney Worlds, mega-malls – luring us to them (to spend large sums of money) by offering great spectacles;
- were, and are, integral parts of a capitalist system, especially the extremes of the American capitalist system, whose greed and rapaciousness very nearly led to its self-destruction.

Thus, we want to focus here on what "they" did to consumers, although it needs to be clear that consumers also bear a significant amount of responsibility for the Great Recession.

Even though the American economy is increasingly dominated by consumption (roughly 70 percent of the economy is accounted for by consumption), most popular, journalistic, and scholarly attention to it focuses on issues relating to production (productivity, factories, manual workers, labor unions, unemployment rates, and the like). Yet, consumers rather than factory workers are at the heart of the American economy. Thus, if we want to truly understand the Great Recession, or much else about the American economy, we cannot rely solely or even primarily on explanations that relate to production; we also need to look at the role of consumption in the near-total collapse of the economy.

What are some of the major consumer-related causes of the Great Recession?

For decades the US market has been inundated with cheap products (e.g., shiny electronic gadgets from Asia) that are often far more expensive in their countries of origin. These have proven hard, even foolish, to resist. As many have demonstrated, most recently Ellen Shell (2009) in *Cheap*, there is a high cost to low price (an idea most often associated with Wal-Mart) and one of those costs is its role in spurring hyperconsumption.

Then there is the seemingly low-priced (but nonetheless highly profitable) industrial food (see the documentary, *Food Inc.* [Kenner 2009]) that increasingly dominates our supermarket shelves and lies at the heart of the success of fast-food restaurants, as well as higher-end restaurant chains. Inexpensive industrial food (an orange likely costs more than a hamburger at McDonald's) also has the same high costs, as well as its devastating effect on the health of consumers (obesity, diabetes, especially in children).

There are the billions, probably trillions, of dollars all sorts of companies have invested to make products alluring, even impossible to resist. Marketing and advertising are the obvious villains (see the TV series, *Mad Men*) here in leading consumers, usually unwittingly, in the direction of the consumption of the wrong products (e.g., cigarettes in the era of *Mad Men*) and hyperconsumption.

We must not forget the role played by the US government (and others) in inducing Americans, especially those in the middle class, to consume. There are, for example, the long-running tax breaks such as deductions for mortgage payments (interest, taxes) that help fuel home-building and -buying. Then, there are the post-9/11 pronouncements by New York Mayor Rudy Giuliani and President George Bush that we needed to get out and shop (and Robert Reich's response asking when it had become our public duty to consume – of course, it had and that responsibility continues). Pronouncements and policies after the onset of the Great Recession and to this day include:

- stimulus packages, tax rebates, as well as fears about the latter that people would save the money and not spend it on consumption;
- worry over the continuing unwillingness to consume and the *increase* in the savings rate (after decades worrying about our minuscule savings rate);
- the government sponsored vehicle trade-in program, "Cash for clunkers"; $8,000 rebates for first-time home buyers, etc.

There is clearly a fundamental contradiction here: the government abhors and critiques the causes of the Great Recession (at least publicly) – especially hyperconsumption and hyperdebt – but it cannot countenance a slow-growing, let alone a smaller, economy and the lower tax revenues associated with less consumption. The government feels the need to stimulate the economy in general, and consumption in particular, leading to at least the eventual possibility of renewed hyperconsumption and hyperdebt.

Then there is the fact that great efforts are made to lure consumers to consume, often excessively. Our great "cathedrals of consumption" (Ritzer 2010b) – shopping malls, casino-hotels, theme parks, and cruise ships – are designed to do just that. However, this process can be seen in broader, more global terms.

The consumer represents a different challenge to the capitalist than the worker since consumers cannot be forced into behaving in desired ways; rather, they need to be cajoled into such behaviors. In this context, Walt Disney believed that what was needed was the construction of "weinies" in order to attract consumers and to lead them in the directions that you want them to go. In the context of Disney World, weinies are highly visible attractions (mountains, castles, and the like) to which virtually all visitors will find themselves drawn. Thus, they move in the way that Disney management wants them to move and they do so without anyone telling them where they should go and how they should get there. This allows for the efficient movement of large numbers of visitors who pay a high price of admission to the park. Furthermore, they are led to pass many kiosks, shops, restaurants, and the like, where they can spend even more money.

At a broader, more global level, we want to argue that cities, even countries, have long built weinies in order to draw people – people who, once they are there, are likely to spend large sums of money consuming all sorts of goods and services. This is a key aspect of what Hannigan (1998) called the "fantasy city." People are drawn to geographic locales, even specific cathedrals of consumption, because of the fantasy that they seem to offer.

It could be argued that the Eiffel Tower, built for the 1889 World's Fair and just over 1,000 feet high, was such a weinie. (Of course, the fairs themselves are created to draw tourists and, as consumption sites, and are forerunners of today's theme parks and shopping malls. It is often the case, as was true of the Eiffel Tower, that the weinies remain after the fair ends and serve as continuing magnets for later tourists – another example is the Space Needle in Seattle built for the 1962 World's Fair.) The Eiffel Tower was the tallest structure in the world until it was surpassed in 1930 by the Chrysler Building in New York City and within a year by the Empire State Building (at 1,250 feet). The "arms race" to have the world's tallest building (and tourist and consumer magnet) heated up in the ensuing years, both in New York City (with the ill-fated World Trade Center being taller than the Empire State Building) and in other major cities – Taipei 101 in Taipei, Taiwan (1,441 feet), the Petronas Twin Towers in Kuala Lumpur, Malaysia (1,482 feet), and the Shanghai World Financial Center (1,555 feet).

However, the weinie (to end all weinies? – probably not) has reached new heights in Dubai, the society that brought, or at least attempted to bring, consumer society as a whole to heights that exceeded even those of the home (and still the center) of consumer culture, the US. The tallest weinie of them all is now Burj Khalifa which is 2,717 feet tall, has 160 stories, and is taller than the Chrysler Building placed on top of the Empire State Building. (Burj Khalifa is modeled after Frank Lloyd Wright's proposed [fanciful, never built] pencil-thin Mile High Illinois which was to have been 528 stories.) Why was such a tall structure built in an area in which there was plenty of desert on which to build? It is not as if it was being squeezed into limited and costly space on the island of Manhattan. Dubai was asserting its arrival on the world stage in much the same way as other cities (Paris, New York, Seattle) had done in the past. This weinie was built to be a very visible and widely publicized symbol of the fact that Dubai had arrived as a fantasy city, and, more importantly, to help lure large numbers of visitors and consumers to Dubai.

Consumers lured into hyperconsumption in these and many other ways spent too much, went too far into debt (see below), and thereby contributed to the Great Recession. This was clear not only in the US, but globally. It was especially clear in Dubai. At the end of 2009, Dubai World, the state-owned company that was behind the development of many of Dubai's cathedrals of consumption, announced that it was unable to make payments due on its estimated $60–$100 billion debt and was negotiating with its creditors for at least a six-month extension. In fact, the Burj Dubai was quickly renamed the Burj Khalifa when the emir of nearby Abu Dhabi bailed out Dubai World, at least in the short run, with a loan of $10 billion (later increased to $20 billion).

Many, if not all, of Dubai's cathedrals of consumption are in trouble and their current value is likely much less than the amount owed on each of them; they are, in the parlance of the ongoing mortgage crisis in the US, "underwater." More generally, as the crisis in Dubai unfolds, it may be possible to think of it as an entire landscape of consumption that has acquired the dubious status of perhaps being the largest "dinosaur of consumption" in a world of consumption increasingly characterized by them (Ritzer 2010b).

Dubai's future is cloudy and depends, as do the futures of all the fantasy cities, on the ability of the global economy to emerge from the recession and boom once again. A specific factor in Dubai's case is the willingness of oil-rich neighbors such as Abu Dhabi (Dubai has little oil) to continue to bankroll it, and, more generally, another (very likely) spike in oil prices.

Finally, the Great Recession was, to a large degree, brought about by excesses in the credit market (for example, for home mortgages), and those excesses are important not only economically but because of their social and cultural nature and impact. Furthermore, that recession (if that is what it is) and its impact are, as we write, not merely of historical interest, but they are likely to continue to affect the economic, social, and cultural world for decades to come.

As in most other areas related to consumption, the United States took the lead in many aspects of the credit industry (especially the invention of the modern credit card). Credit is an integral part of consumer culture. The latter, like credit, is an area in which the United States has been in the forefront globally. However, just as they have not done much work on credit, American sociologists have also not been major contributors to the literature on consumer culture and consumption.

Similar to the concept of behavior-manipulating 'weinies' discussed above with respect to architecture, the credit industry also created irresistible incentives to lure consumers into debt. This was clear, for example, in the provision of low-interest, or even no-interest, mortgage loans in order to lure consumers into buying homes that, in many cases, they could not afford. Millions of people who bought homes under such conditions are "underwater," and in many cases they have walked away from their homes or lost them due to foreclosure.

In this context, the credit card is an especially important phenomenon (see, for example, Ritzer 1995; Klein 1999; Calder 2001; Manning 2001; Warren & Tyagi 2004). Various efforts have been made to lure people into acquiring and using credit cards. Those cards, in turn, have played a great role in what Simmel ([1907] 1978) in his analysis of money called the "temptation to imprudence" (see Ritzer 1995 for an application of this idea to credit cards).

Much insight into how the credit card industry controls its users, and leads them to be imprudent, is found in Doncha Marron's (2009) *Consumer Credit in the United States: A Sociological Perspective from the 19th Century to the Present*. In this analysis Marron relies heavily on the theories of Michel Foucault, especially his notion of governmentality. This is how Marron defines this often elusive concept: "Governmentality emphasizes the continuous inventiveness and resourcefulness of authorities, whether individuals, institutions, or diverse actors acting under the power rubric of the state, toward understanding and framing the actions of others, economic processes, or the course of perceived problems and issues" (2009: 9).

Marron offers a "grand narrative" (contra Foucault's idea of a genealogy) which deals with a transition from government of credit by external forces (especially the state) to self-government; to the government of the self as far as credit is concerned. This, too, connects with Foucault's thinking, especially his later work on the "care of the self." It is also tied to the work of a number of other contemporary European theorists – Giddens, Beck, and Bauman. They argue that people are increasingly required to create and re-create themselves. In recent years the burden for much of life has shifted away from the state and other larger social structures and now falls increasingly on individuals; this is, or at least was, as true in the realm of credit as anywhere else.

Consistent with the Foucauldian roots of his work, Marron argues that this process of self-control has a much more pernicious effect than external forms of control (such as through the Panopticon in the prisons analyzed by Foucault); it penetrates deep into the individual: "formal mechanisms of government are embedded in the very 'soul' of the consumer. Such control over credit use *penetrates deep into the subjective state* of the individual; individualized and internalized, it embodies not only the individual's generalized injunction to self-government but an increasing reflexivity over the means by which they are assessed and judged by lenders" (Marron 2009: 216–17).

Marron connects this argument to another grand narrative of the shift from "welfare-interventionism" to "neoliberalism." In the former, the state intervened in many sectors of society, including credit, through the creation and enforcement of various laws and agencies. The goal, at least ostensibly, was to help individuals by controlling forces and structures that might do them harm. Of course, in the process, and also often directly, the state exerted control over individuals as well. However, in recent years, and very much related to the conditions that gave rise to the Great Recession, we have seen the decline of the welfare state and the hegemony of neoliberalism (Harvey 2005). In this context, issues that relate to credit are increasingly the responsibility of those who receive the credit. They are to manage their credit, as well as the agencies that offer it, on their own with little or no help from the state. Marron calls this the "*new prudentialism*" and links it directly to neoliberalism. The new prudentialism "emphasizes the responsibility of individuals, households, and communities for their own risks" (Marron 2009: 175).

In the process, and in line with neoliberalism, control over the structures that dominate the credit business (e.g., the banks) was loosened or eliminated. This, of course, was another huge factor in the Great Recession since these businesses were free to do pretty much as they wanted; to take risks that very nearly sank the global economy. In terms of the issue of credit, neoliberalism freed up financial institutions to use all sorts of questionable methods in order to lure people into debt – into levels of debt many clearly could not handle and would never be able to repay. Thus, individuals were "made to be free" and as such were free to be lured into – and in fact rushed out to gobble up – huge amounts of credit. They were, in effect, both allowed and eager to ruin their own lives in much the same way that the national and global economies were wrecked by, among other things, excessive borrowing by many countries, including the United States. This reminds us of C. Wright Mills's thinking on "private troubles" (here, personal debt) and "public issues" (the recklessness of American – and other – financial institutions and of national governments), as well as their relationship to one another (in this case the way they worked in tandem to produce disastrous economic consequences for almost everyone in many places throughout the world).

What mattered most in the credit industry in earlier epochs was the "character" of the individual seeking credit. Over time, however, individuals increasingly became more abstract entities. They were eventually reduced to a series of numbers (especially their credit, or FICO, score), which determined their risk level, their credit-worthiness, and eventually whether or not they received credit, as well as how much credit they received. For their part, the financial institutions also created all sorts of abstract financial instruments (e.g., derivatives). More specifically, banks no longer created mortgage loans that they held themselves, but rather immediately sold them off to other financial institutions to be sliced and diced, combined with many other mortgages, and sold off as financial instruments that had little relationship to any concrete piece of real estate. It was the abstraction of this system, the fact that it was so detached from real consumers and real estate properties, that made it so easy for the entire system to spin out of control with so many wide-ranging and devastating consequences.

CONCLUSION

We have organized this overview of the sociology of consumption under three broad headings. First, we discussed recent substantive developments in the sociology of consumption as they relate to identity, cultural appropriation, value, and risk and the environment. Second, we laid out three central issues in the history of social theory pertaining to consumption – the relation between production and consumption, whether happiness is the product of desires that are natural or whether it is the result of desires that are socially constructed, and whether choice is agentic or structured. Third, we discussed the applicability of a consumption-oriented perspective to the development and continuation of the Great Recession. The motivation behind this last section is to dispel the view that the sociology of consumption deals, in the main, with trivial issues. The fact that it can be related in such a meaningful way to such a monumentally important issue as the recession demonstrates, we think, the power of this often underestimated and under-utilized type of sociology.

Whether or not the reader is convinced by the application to the Great Recession, the fact remains that the sociology of consumption is destined to become increasingly important because consumption can only grow in importance. The US may become a smaller player in this area in the future, but the emerging global economic powerhouses – China and India – are likely to shift, and to some degree already are shifting, at least some attention from production to how to spend some of their new-found wealth on consumption.

References

Adorno, T. W. ([1966] 1973) *Negative Dialectics*. New York: Continuum.
Amy-Chinn, D. (2006) "This Is Just for Me(n)." *Journal of Consumer Culture* 6(2): 155–75.
Arvidsson, A. (2001) "From Counterculture to Consumer Culture." *Journal of Consumer Culture* 1(1): 47–71.
Arvidsson, A. (2005) "Brands." *Journal of Consumer Culture* 5(2): 235.
Arvidsson, A. (2006) *Brands: Meaning and Value in Media Culture*. London: Routledge.
Baudrillard, J. ([1970] 1998) *The Consumer Society: Myths and Structures*. London: Sage.

Baudrillard, J. ([1981] 1995) *Simulacra and Simulation*. Ann Arbor, MI: University of Michigan Press.

Bauman, Z. (2001) "Consuming Life." *Journal of Consumer Culture* 1(1): 9–29.

Bauman, Z. (2007) "Collateral Casualties of Consumerism." *Journal of Consumer Culture* 7(1): 25–56.

Botterill, J. (2007) "Cowboys, Outlaws and Artists." *Journal of Consumer Culture* 7(1): 105.

Bourdieu, P. ([1979] 1984) *Distinction: A Social Critique of the Judgement of Taste*. London: Routledge and Kegan Paul.

Brace-Govan, J. and I. Binay (2010) "Consumption of Disposed Goods for Moral Identities: A Nexus of Organization, Place, Things and Consumers." *Journal of Consumer Behaviour* 9(1): 69–82.

Bruns, A. (2008) *Blogs, Wikipedia, Second Life, and Beyond: From Production to Produsage*. New York: Peter Lang.

Calder, L. (2001) *Financing the American Dream: A Cultural History of Consumer Credit*. Princeton, NJ: Princeton University Press.

Caldwell, M. L. (2004) "Domesticating the French Fry." *Journal of Consumer Culture* 4(1): 5–26.

Campbell, C. (1995) "The Sociology of Consumption." In D. Miller (ed.), *Acknowledging Consumption: A Review of New Studies*. London: Psychology Press, pp. 95–124.

Campbell, C. (2005) "The Craft Consumer." *Journal of Consumer Culture* 5(1): 23–42.

Chen, K. and D. Morley (1996) *Stuart Hall: Critical Dialogues in Cultural Studies*. London: Routledge.

Connolly, J. and A. Prothero (2008) "Green Consumption." *Journal of Consumer Culture* 8(1): 117–45.

Cook, D. T. (2008) "The Missing Child in Consumption Theory." *Journal of Consumer Culture* 8(2): 219–43.

Cook, D. T. and S. B. Kaiser (2004) "Betwixt and Be Tween." *Journal of Consumer Culture* 4(2): 203–27.

Corrigan, P. (1997) *The Sociology of Consumption: An Introduction*. London: Sage.

Coté, M. and J. Pybus (2007) "Learning to Immaterial Labour 2.0: MySpace and Social Networks." *Ephemera Theory and Politics in Organizations* 7(1): 88–106.

Crockett, D. (2008) "Marketing Blackness." *Journal of Consumer Culture* 8(2): 245–68.

Debord, G. ([1967] 1983) *Society of the Spectacle*. London: Rebel Press.

De Certeau, M. ([1980] 2002) *The Practice of Everyday Life*. Berkeley, CA: University of California Press.

Dolan, C. S. (2005) "Fields of Obligation." *Journal of Consumer Culture* 5(3): 365–89.

Entwistle, J. (2002) "The Aesthetic Economy." *Journal of Consumer Culture* 2(3): 317–39.

Foucault, M. ([1975] 1995) *Discipline and Punish: The Birth of the Prison*. New York: Vintage.

Foucault, M. ([1976] 1990) *The History of Sexuality, Vol. 1, An Introduction*. New York: Vintage.

Foucault, M. (1981) "How an 'Experience-Book' Is Born." In *Remarks on Marx: Conversations with Duccio Trombadori*. Trans. R. J. Goldstein and J. Cascaito. New York: Semiotext(e), pp. 25–42.

Freud, S. ([1927] 1975) *The Future of an Illusion*, Standard edn. New York: W. W. Norton.

Fromm, E. (1955) *The Sane Society*. Greenwich, CT: Fawcett Publications.

Gabriel, Y. and T. Lang (2008) "New Faces and New Masks of Today's Consumer." *Journal of Consumer Culture* 8(3): 321–40.

Gaviria, P. R. and C. Bluemelhuber (2010) "Consumers' Transformations in a Liquid Society: Introducing the Concepts of Autobiographical-Concern and Desire-Assemblage." *Journal of Consumer Behaviour* 9(2): 126–38.

Green, N. (2001) "How Everyday Life Became Virtual." *Journal of Consumer Culture* 1(1): 73–92.

Halkier, B. (2001) "Consuming Ambivalences." *Journal of Consumer Culture* 1(2): 205–24.

Hall, S. (1992) "Encoding/Decoding." In S. Hall, Dorothy Hobson, Andrew Lowe, and Paul Willis (eds.), *Culture, Media, Language: Working Papers in Cultural Studies, 1972–79.* London: Routledge, pp. 128–38.

Halnon, K. B. and S. Cohen (2006) "Muscles, Motorcycles and Tattoos." *Journal of Consumer Culture* 6(1): 33–56.

Hannigan, J. (1998) *Fantasy City: Pleasure and Profit in the Postmodern Metropolis.* London: Routledge.

Harvey, D. (2005) *A Brief History of Neoliberalism.* Oxford: Oxford University Press.

Hearn, A. (2008) "Meat, Mask, Burden." *Journal of Consumer Culture* 8(2): 197–217.

Hebdige, D. (1981) *Subculture: The Meaning of Style.* London: Routledge.

Hoggart, R. (1998) *The Uses of Literacy.* New Brunswick, NJ: Transaction.

Holliday, R. and A. Cairnie (2007) "Man Made Plastic." *Journal of Consumer Culture* 7(1): 57–78.

Horkheimer, M. and T. W. Adorno ([1944] 1997) *Dialectic of Enlightenment.* London: Verso.

Humphreys, A. and K. Grayson (2008) "The Intersecting Roles of Consumer and Producer: A Critical Perspective on Co-Production, Co-Creation and Prosumption." *Sociology Compass* 2(3): 963–80.

Jantzen, C., P. Østergaard, and C. M. S. Vieira (2006) "Becoming a 'Woman to the Backbone'." *Journal of Consumer Culture* 6(2): 177–202.

Kenner, R. (2009) *Food, Inc.* Magnolia Home Entertainment.

Klein, L. (1999) *It's in the Cards: Consumer Credit and the American Experience.* New York: Praeger.

Kotler, P. (1986) "Prosumers: A New Type of Consumer." *Futurist* 20(5): 24–8.

Krol0kke, C. (2009) "Click a Donor." *Journal of Consumer Culture* 9(1): 7–30.

Laden, S. (2003) "Who's Afraid of a Black Bourgeoisie?" *Journal of Consumer Culture* 3(2): 191–216.

Lamont, M. and V. Molnár (2001) "How Blacks Use Consumption to Shape Their Collective Identity." *Journal of Consumer Culture* 1(1): 31–45.

Langer, B. (2004) "The Business of Branded Enchantment." *Journal of Consumer Culture* 4(2): 251–77.

Laufer, W. S. (2003) "Social Accountability and Corporate Greenwashing." *Journal of Business Ethics* 43(3): 253–61.

Lipovetsky, G. ([1987] 2002) *The Empire of Fashion: Dressing Modern Democracy.* Princeton, NJ: Princeton University Press.

Manning, R. D. (2001) *Credit Card Nation: The Consequences of America's Addiction to Debt.* New York: Basic Books.

Marcuse, H. (1955) *Eros and Civilization: A Philosophical Inquiry into Freud,* 8th edn. Boston: Beacon Press.

Marcuse, H. (1964) *One-Dimensional Man: Studies in the Ideology of Advanced Industrial Society.* Boston: Beacon Press.

Marron, D. (2009) *Consumer Credit in the United States: A Sociological Perspective from the 19th Century to the Present.* New York: Palgrave Macmillan.

Marx, K. ([1857–8] 1973) *Grundrisse: Foundations of the Critique of Political Economy.* New York: Random House.

Marx, K. ([1885] 1907) *Capital: A Critique of Political Economy*. Chicago: C. H. Kerr and Company.

Marx, K. and F. Engels (1948) *The Communist Manifesto*, new edn. New York: International Publishers.

Moisio, R., E. J. Arnould, and L. L. Price (2004) "Between Mothers and Markets." *Journal of Consumer Culture* 4(3): 361–84.

Neilson, L. A. (2010) "Boycott or Buycott? Understanding Political Consumerism." *Journal of Consumer Behaviour* 9(3): 214–27.

Neves, L. M. P. (2004) "Cleanness, Pollution and Disgust in Modern Industrial Societies." *Journal of Consumer Culture* 4(3): 385–405.

O'Reilly, T. (2005) "What is Web 2.0: Design Patterns and Business Models for the Next Generation of Software." September 30. http://oreilly.com/web2/archive/what-is-web-20.html

Possamaï, A. (2002) "Cultural Consumption of History and Popular Culture in Alternative Spiritualities." *Journal of Consumer Culture* 2(2): 197–218.

Prahalad, C. and V. Ramaswamy (2004) "Co-creation Experiences: The Next Practice in Value Creation." *Journal of Interactive Marketing* 18(3): 5–14.

Redmond, S. (2003) "Thin White Women in Advertising." *Journal of Consumer Culture* 3(2): 170–90.

Ritzer, G. (1995) *Expressing America: A Critique of the Global Credit Card Society*. Thousand Oaks, CA: Pine Forge Press.

Ritzer, G. (2010a) "Focusing on the Prosumer: On Correcting an Error in the History of Social Theory." In *Prosumer Revisited*. VS Verlag für Sozialwissenschaften, pp. 61–79.

Ritzer, G. (2010b) *Enchanting a Disenchanted World: Continuity and Change in the Cathedrals of Consumption*, 3rd edn. Thousand Oaks, CA: Pine Forge Press.

Ritzer, G. (2011) *The McDonaldization of Society*, 6th edn. Thousand Oaks, CA: Pine Forge Press.

Ritzer, G. and N. Jurgenson (2010) "Production, Consumption, Prosumption: The Nature of Capitalism in the Age of the Digital 'Prosumer'." *Journal of Consumer Culture* 10(1): 13–36.

Ritzer, G., D. Goodman, and W. Wiedenhoft (2001) "Theories of Consumption." In G. Ritzer and B. Smart (eds.), *Handbook of Social Theory*. London: Sage, pp. 410–27.

Ryan, W. (1976) *Blaming the Victim*. New York: Vintage.

Sassatelli, R. (2007) *Consumer Culture: History, Theory and Politics*. London: Sage.

Sassatelli, R. and F. Davolio (2010) "Consumption, Pleasure and Politics." *Journal of Consumer Culture* 10(2): 202–32.

Schor, J. B. (1999) *The Overspent American: Why We Want What We Don't Need*. New York: Harper Perennial.

Schor, J. B. (2010) *Plenitude: The New Economics of True Wealth*. New York: Penguin.

Schulz, J. (2006) "Vehicle of the Self." *Journal of Consumer Culture* 6(1): 57–86.

Schutz, A. (2004) "Rethinking Domination and Resistance: Challenging Postmodernism." *Educational Researcher* 33(1): 15–23.

Shell, E. R. (2009) *Cheap: The High Cost of Discount Culture*. New York: Penguin.

Shevchenko, O. (2002) "In Case of Fire Emergency." *Journal of Consumer Culture* 2(2): 147–70.

Simmel, G. ([1904] 2000) "The Philosophy of Fashion." In D. Frisby and M. Featherstone (eds.), *Simmel on Culture: Selected Writings*. London: Sage, pp. 187–218.

Simmel, G. ([1907] 1978) *The Philosophy of Money*. London: Routledge and Kegan Paul.

Simmel, G. ([1911–12] 2000) "The Concept and Tragedy of Culture." In D. Frisby and M. Featherstone (eds.), *Simmel on Culture: Selected Writings*. London: Sage, pp. 55–74.

Slater, D. (1999) *Consumer Culture and Modernity*. Cambridge: Polity.

Tapscott, D. and A. D. Williams (2006) *Wikinomics: How Mass Collaboration Changes Everything*. New York: Portfolio.

Thompson, C. J. and G. Coskuner-Balli (2007) "Enchanting Ethical Consumerism." *Journal of Consumer Culture* 7(3): 275–303.

Thompson, C. J. and D. B. Holt (2004) "How Do Men Grab the Phallus?" *Journal of Consumer Culture* 4(3): 313–38.

Toffler, A. (1980) *The Third Wave*. New York: Bantam.

Tulloch, J. and D. Lupton (2002) "Consuming Risk, Consuming Science." *Journal of Consumer Culture* 2(3): 363–83.

Tyler, M. (2009) "Growing Customers." *Journal of Consumer Culture* 9(1): 55–77.

Veblen, T. (1899) *The Theory of the Leisure Class*. Reissue. Oxford: Oxford University Press.

Warde, A. (1994) "Consumption, Identity-Formation and Uncertainty." *Sociology* 28(4): 877–98.

Warren, E. and A. W. Tyagi (2004) *The Two-Income Trap: Why Middle-Class Parents Are Going Broke*. New York: Basic Books.

Wells, K. (2002) "Reconfiguring the Radical Other." *Journal of Consumer Culture* 2(3): 291–315.

West, E. (2010) "Expressing the Self through Greeting Card Sentiment." *International Journal of Cultural Studies* 13(5): 451.

Wilk, R. (2006) "Bottled Water." *Journal of Consumer Culture* 6(3): 303–25.

Williams, R. (1995) *The Sociology of Culture*. Chicago: University of Chicago Press.

Willis, P. E. (1978) *Profane Culture*. London: Routledge and Kegan Paul.

Wissinger, E. (2009) "Modeling Consumption." *Journal of Consumer Culture* 9(2): 273–96.

Wright, D. (2005) "Commodifying Respectability." *Journal of Consumer Culture* 5(3): 295–314.

Zwick, D. and J. D. Knott (2009) "Manufacturing Customers: The Database as New Means of Production." *Journal of Consumer Culture* 9(2): 221–47.

Zwick, D., S. K. Bonsu, and A. Darmody, (2008) "Putting Consumers to Work." *Journal of Consumer Culture* 8(2): 163.

25

Population

SUZANNE M. BIANCHI AND VANESSA WIGHT

In the 1960s, the overriding population concern was the high rates of fertility in many parts of the world. There was much hand-wringing about the "population explosion," with Paul Ehrlich's (1968) *The Population Bomb* required reading in many social problems courses. Although Ehrlich's rendition of the population problem was always a bit too alarmist for the trained demographer, the 1972 report of the Commission on Population Growth and the American Future was required reading for serious students of demography. The US had just witnessed an unprecedented two-decade interruption in its path toward lower fertility, with the large number of baby boom births that extended from 1946 to 1964. Although fertility rates were plunging again in the 1970s in the US, population growth in developing countries showed no signs of slowing. There were scholars like Julian Simon who suggested that concerns about overpopulation were overblown. But these views were in the minority and many governmental and non-governmental organizations were focused on increasing family planning services and lowering fertility.

What a different picture of world population growth we have today. Population growth continues, with the world population estimated at 6.8 billion in 2009 and projected to increase to 9.4 billion by 2050 (Population Reference Bureau 2009). Yet fertility has declined in all parts of the world, and though it is still well above replacement in many countries in Africa and the Middle East, countries throughout Southeast and East Asia have made the "demographic transition" from high to low fertility. Currently in China, the largest country in the world, after decades of more or less adherence to a one-child policy, the total fertility rate (average births per mother) stands at 1.6 – well below the level it would take to replace China's popu-

The Wiley-Blackwell Companion to Sociology, First Edition. Edited by George Ritzer.
© 2012 Blackwell Publishing Ltd. Published 2012 by Blackwell Publishing Ltd.

lation. In fact, India is projected to surpass China as the most populous country in the world by 2030 – although even in India the total fertility rate has fallen to a little above replacement at 2.7 births per woman, on average, in 2009 (Population Reference Bureau 2009). The population "problem" that often receives the most attention in demography journals currently is the very low levels of fertility in much of Southern and Eastern Europe and countries like Japan where there are major concerns about population decline and rapid population aging.

Today, the issues of mortality (and population aging) and international migration are far more likely to take center stage in population discussions than is (high) fertility. Many developing countries are currently in a window of opportunity – often referred to as the period of the "demographic dividend" (Lee 2007). They have large working-age populations (a result of earlier high fertility), relatively few children due to reduced fertility, and a small (but growing) elderly population, making for a ratio of dependents to workers that is quite favorable for economic growth.

Studying the interplay among the population processes of fertility, mortality, and migration is exciting because these processes are integral to our quality of life and standard of living. Many of the debates that consume US policy analysts are topics central to demographic study. How will we care for our growing older population? What will stop the flow of unauthorized immigrants into the country? How will we ensure the well-being of future generations when many parents do not marry before bearing children and relationships seem fragile? In this chapter, we describe some of the questions demographers and population scientists seek to answer, highlighting the "demographic perspective" and the processes of population change. We begin with the classic debate about whether population growth hinders economic development and wreaks havoc on the environment. We chart demographers' classic theory: the theory of the demographic transition. We delve into the processes of population change: fertility, mortality, and migration. We conclude with how these changes have altered our family lives.

THE DEBATE ABOUT POPULATION GROWTH AND ITS CONSEQUENCES

The study of human population size and growth has captured the popular imagination of societies for centuries (Weeks 2008). Livi-Bacci (2007) begins his text on historical populations with the statement, "Throughout human history, population has been synonymous with prosperity, stability, and security." One of the ways in which the US is powerful is that it is big – both in terms of land and also in terms of population size, ranking as the third largest country in the world.

Throughout most of human history, population growth rates were close to zero and for particular groups, underpopulation was a more serious problem than overpopulation. Population growth was limited until about 10,000 BC when humans began to settle in communities and cultivate the surrounding area, which allowed for higher population density. There is debate about whether mortality increased with settled agriculture – the clustering of populations in communities may have allowed diseases to spread more easily (Livi-Bacci 2007).

Rapid population growth is only a phenomenon of the past two centuries. Economic change beginning in the late eighteenth century relaxed or eliminated resource constraints on population growth. With enormous improvements in agricultural productivity, and with industrialization and the rise of wage labor, came improvement in public health and new sources of energy that made rapid population growth possible. Perhaps it is not surprising that this period ushered in the beginnings of what is until this day the classic population debate: is population growth the villain or the savior? Does rapid population growth retard economic development or does it spur the technological development that catapults societies to ever higher standards of living? More recently, how is population growth linked to the environment?

The classic pessimist: Malthus

The classic perspective on the dangers of population growth is the Malthusian perspective. Thomas Malthus, in his *Essay on the Principle of Population* (1798), argued that "population, when unchecked, increases in a geometrical ratio. Subsistence increases only in an arithmetical ratio" (Malthus 1798: 4). According to Malthus, the world was expected to expand at a rate that could not be supported by the environment – population growth was projected to outstrip the earth's resources. At the time Malthus was writing, living standards in England appeared to be declining. Malthus was a pessimist who believed that natural urges to procreate would overwhelm rational calculations about reproduction. Population growth would always outstrip resource growth – until some check operated to balance population and the economy. Checks could be things that increased the death rate and lowered living standards like poorer nutrition and starvation and increased susceptibility to disease. Or checks could be "preventative," which included things that would reduce the birth rate such as delayed marriage.

Although Malthus was wrong about arithmetic growth of the food supply and he tended to mix moralistic and scientific thinking, his ideas about the consequences of population growth remain in the debates today. Concern over resource shortages has been replaced with concern over environmental impact. Because Malthus set the terms of the debate about population growth, one cannot discuss population without referring to him. His perspective about the negative aspects of population growth has to some extent been echoed in arguments to the present day and his emphasis on empiricism (e.g., his study of crop yields to arrive at his conclusion about arithmetic growth in agricultural productivity) is a hallmark of demographic analysis today.

The optimists: Boserup and Simon

What is the other side of the debate? One argument is that technological developments can expand resources and it often takes the pressure of population growth to spur this technological development (Boserup 1976). It can be argued that inertia settles in and humans are not motivated to abandon an existing technology until there is a need – population growth is one factor that can create that need. Agricultural productivity increases when population pressures necessitate it.

Julian Simon (1977, 1981) was perhaps the most well-known proponent of the view that population growth can drive economic growth. In a series of works, beginning with *The Economics of Population Growth*, he argued that there are fundamentally no limits to growth: technology and human ingenuity will always rise to the challenge of finding a solution to new problems associated with population growth. Rising prices spur the development of new technology and exploration for additional resources.

The situation today

What seems to be the consensus today? Population growth by itself has at best mild direct effects on economic growth, with other factors (e.g., political stability) more important for determining whether countries prosper or not. Demographic evidence today indicates that the world has not experienced the geometric growth rate in the population that Malthus originally proposed. Furthermore, global society has managed to make progress in producing food at a tempo far above that projected by Malthus (Weeks 2008). There is much greater acceptance now than in the past of Simon's arguments about humans' capacity for innovation as a protective agent against the dangers of rampant population growth.

Nonetheless, mild population growth is generally believed preferable to rapid population growth. Since the 1980s, most developing countries have promoted family planning. Population growth is slowing everywhere, and in some countries the major concern is now over the prospect of zero or negative growth. This prospect of negative growth is challenging the major theory in the study of population, that of the demographic transition.

DEMOGRAPHIC THEORY OF POPULATION CHANGE AND DEMOGRAPHIC TRANSITION

More than a century after Malthus, the field of demography was the proving ground for another perspective on population growth – that of the *theory of demographic transition*. The first formulation of the theory was a description of demographic processes that evolved into a typology of a group of countries that by today's standards would be considered developed (Thompson 1929). Additional expansion on the themes originally advanced by Thompson launched the demographic transition theory – a broad framework that has had a predominant influence on demographers and their preoccupation with the determinants of population change (Kirk 1996; Weeks 2008).

Classic demographic transition theory

Demographic transition theory argues that societies typically move through three stages of growth patterns. First, societies are characterized by levels of high mortality and high fertility and exhibit either stable or low rates of population growth. Under this demographic regime, high levels of mortality promote high levels of fertility. Economic organization in pretransitional societies is largely structured around the family and the family's survival is essential to the long-term functioning of society (Coale 1973). Thus high levels of fertility are necessary to balance high rates of mortality.

During the second stage of the transition, mortality declines as the standard of living improves. Declines in fertility typically lag behind declines in mortality. This lag occurs because social norms and values are in place that support high levels of fertility and it takes time for these to change. People do not immediately recognize that more children are surviving and that the need to produce so many children (e.g., for their labor or as insurance in old age) no longer exists. While norms and values recalibrate, there is a period of rapid population growth.

The third stage of the transition is marked by declines in fertility. Technological advances, especially with industrialization and urbanization, change parents' conscious calculus about having children. For example, the value of children changes as education requirements increase and attending school removes children from supplying labor to family enterprises. Decreases in infant mortality mean that fewer births are necessary to achieve a given desired family size. Hence, fertility declines as the result of an increasing economic advantage to limiting family size (Coale 1973; Kirk 1996; Weeks 2008).

There is a fundamentally different world before and after the transition. Before undergoing the demographic transition, married women have many children and they spend their short adult life span having and caring for children, with many of those children dying in infancy and childhood. Because of high death rates, families are not particularly large. People only live into their thirties, on average, survival to old age is uncommon, and most people lose one or both of their parents by the time they are adults. Married people are likely to be widowed early and they also tend to lose their siblings. People live in a fragile world where the future is always uncertain.

After the transition, women have fewer children and they spend a much smaller proportion of their adult years having or caring for children. People live longer and most children survive to adulthood. Most individuals have living parents, at least in the early stages of adulthood. People become as likely to lose a spouse via divorce as by being widowed. In many ways, life is more predictable.

Reformulations of the demographic transition theory

The subtle assumption of demographic transition theory is that economic development creates the necessary preconditions for declines in mortality and subsequent declines in fertility. Findings from the European Fertility Project organized by Ansley Coale in 1963 challenged this theory. Re-examination of fertility and mortality declines in approximately 600 administrative divisions in Europe revealed a high level of regional variation in *when* fertility declined. As Coale stated, "the demographic transition correctly . . . predicted that mortality would decline before fertility . . . In neither instance does it specify . . . the circumstances under which the decline of fertility begins" (Coale 1973). In short, the demographic transition theory could not reliably identify a threshold at which fertility declined. The evidence suggested that economic development was important. However, given variation across regions in the timing of fertility declines, critics argued that economic development was not enough.

Thus began a series of reformulations aimed at explaining the conditions under which fertility fell in the wake of declines in mortality. The economic determinism of the classic demographic transition theory spawned a series of reformulations in which cultural and social context were thought to moderate the economic factors that influence fertility behavior.

For example, some critics argued that despite the increasing importance of material conditions in explaining fertility decline, ideational components that give meaning to the various costs and benefits of children are also important. In other words, the examination of fertility behavior should consider both the decision-making process (the cost-benefit framework) and the context within which fertility decisions are made (Lesthaeghe 1983; Lesthaeghe & Surkyn 1988). Similarly, John Caldwell argued that what mattered was what people thought about children – both the economic and social value placed on having them (Caldwell 1976).

Central to Caldwell's restatement of the demographic transition theory was the idea that fertility would only decline when wealth flows from children to parents reversed and flowed from parents to children. In the process of modernization, large family networks collapsed and were replaced by smaller families that were both economically and emotionally independent and self-sufficient. In the midst of familial and emotional nucleation, wealth flows from children to parents changed direction. As a result, people changed their ideas and attitudes about how many children to have. The economic value of (additional) children declined as they became the financial beneficiaries of substantial investments by their parents – thereby increasing the cost to parents of having them. Therefore fertility declined as families decreased their family size to adjust to changes in wealth flows (Caldwell 1976). Yet, Caldwell argued that the economically rational behavior influencing fertility decisions was also determined by non-economic factors, such as social and cultural conditions that exist in societies. It is these conditions that influence the social value of children and prevent fertility in societies from falling below replacement level, even when this may be at odds with the economic benefits of remaining child-free (van de Kaa 1996).

In a further elaboration, and in response to demography's failure to foresee the high levels of fertility resulting in the baby boom birth cohort of the 1950s and early 1960s, Richard Easterlin (1978) argued that the standard of living experienced as a child becomes the foundation or "yardstick" by which adults evaluate whether or not their current level of economic well-being is sufficient. Therefore, if individuals are able to achieve a level of economic well-being similar to the level they experienced in their parents' household, they will marry earlier and exhibit higher birth rates. If, however, economic prospects appear bleak and adults perceive it to be more difficult to achieve a standard of living similar to that they experienced growing up, they may delay marriage and childbearing.

According to Easterlin (1978), the age structure of a population interacts with the economy to influence marriage and fertility decisions. When the number and proportion of people entering working age is small in the presence of a burgeoning economy, their labor will be in high demand and well compensated. If this compensation provides a lifestyle similar to that they experienced as children, this will exert an upward pressure on fertility. People will feel comfortable assuming the increased financial burden of having children. If, however, there is a glut in the number of young adults entering the labor force, regardless of the state of the economy, their overabundance will increase the competition for jobs and lower wage rates. This makes it more difficult for individuals to achieve a standard of living comparable to that of their parents at the same age and will thus exert a downward pressure on fertility. In short, people will be reluctant to have children, or at least a large number of them (Easterlin 1978; Weeks 2008).

The second demographic transition

Classic demographic transition theory and its reformulations were preoccupied with explaining either high fertility or the transition from high to low fertility. Recent trends suggest that we are witnessing a deceleration in population growth on a global scale and most of this is due to widespread declines in fertility rates. So while the level of fertility still remains high in some areas of the world, the average number of children born to women has declined, resulting in a reduction in the overall rate of growth. This has led many in the field to shift their focus from an overwhelming concern about high fertility to a concern about low fertility. Some have argued that these demographic changes since the 1960s warrant the label "second demographic transition" (Lesthaeghe 1995).

Like the first demographic transition, this second demographic transition is also described in three stages. The first stage, which took place between 1955 and 1970, was characterized by an acceleration in divorce rates, the end of the baby boom, and an increase in the age of marriage. During the second stage, around 1975–80, cohabitation and childbearing outside of marriage increased. In the third stage, which marks the mid-1980s and onwards, divorce rates are flattened, remarriage is largely replaced with cohabitation, and delays in fertility characteristic at younger ages are recouped after age 30 (Lesthaeghe 1995).

The motivations for the second demographic transition are notably different than for the first demographic transition. Fertility declines in the first transition are linked to economic development and changes in the value of children, with an increased focus on child quality (i.e., investing more resources in fewer children with the expectation of improving the overall level of child well-being). The second demographic transition is inspired by an increase in secularization, rising individualism, and an increased focus on the quality of adult relationships. Low or below-replacement fertility, linked to delays in marriage and increased use of contraception, is now a function of increasing individual autonomy, a move toward gender symmetry, and a greater focus on the relationship between adult partners than was previously the case. Given these shifts, there is no reason to expect that fertility decline will end at replacement levels, as assumed in the (first) demographic transition theory. It may fall even lower – indeed has – in many parts of Europe.

POPULATION PROCESSES OF FERTILITY, MORTALITY, AND MIGRATION

These overarching theoretical perspectives on demographic change form the backdrop for what demographers deem important to study. The field of demography, the scientific study of human population, typically has had two strands of scholarship. *Formal demography* focuses on the conceptualization and measurement of population processes. This area within the field emphasizes the methods by which to measure fertility, mortality, and migration, how these processes operate across different populations and within the same population over time, and mathematical modeling for estimating population growth and structure. Yet demography is also interested in the relationship between demographic behavior and the larger social context. Thus *social demography* not only measures and quantifies population processes, but it also seeks to understand more broadly the context within which demographic behavior takes place, how this context influences demographic patterns, and the relationship between this behavior and subsequent social, economic, and biological processes. Hence, family and labor force patterns that are related to key demographic events, such as union formation and dissolution, household transitions and living arrangements, inter-generational relationships and exchanges, and employment status, become important objects of consideration.

Populations change under a limited number of conditions (Hinde 1998). Fertility, mortality, and migration processes change over time and affect population size, growth, structure, and composition. That is, the change observed in any given population over a period of time (e.g., from time t to $t+1$) is a function of the difference in the number of births ($B_{(t)}$) and deaths ($D_{(t)}$) experienced by a population plus the difference in the number of people moving into ($IM_{(t)}$) and out of ($OM_{(t)}$) the population. Thus, population change over time can be expressed in the following *basic demographic balancing equation*:

$$P_{(t+1)} = P_{(t)} + B_{(t)} - D_{(t)} + IM_{(t)} - OM_{(t)}$$

The main demographic processes that account for population change are *fertility*, *mortality*, and *migration*. Thus, much demographic work focuses on understanding these processes.

Fertility

One of the things that has intrigued formal demographers historically is the difference between fertility and fecundity. *Fertility* refers to actual reproduction (e.g., number of births), which is substantively different from *fecundity* or the capacity of an individual to bear children. (Box 25.1 discusses fertility measures.)

Demographers, with the help of biologists, calculate that populations of childbearing-age women, in the absence of substantial mortality, could average as many as 16 births over their reproductive years (25 reproductive years/1.5-year birth intervals) – yet no society approaches this level of fertility (McFalls 2007). The closest is the Hutterites of the 1930s, who averaged 11 births per woman, but most societies have averaged eight or fewer births per woman (Livi-Bacci 2007). This

---

Box 25.1: Measuring Fertility

Fertility can be measured by estimating a *crude birth rate*, which is the number of births per 1,000 people in the population. However, this rate includes people who cannot bear children, such as men, girls, and older women. Thus, *age-specific fertility rates* (ASFR) and the *total fertility rate* (TFR) are generally used to estimate fertility behavior. The ASFR is the number of births to women of a specific age per 1,000 women who are that age. The TFR is estimated using a *life table*, which is a method widely used by demographers to calculate variation in such vital events as births and deaths, as well as migration. Life table estimates are derived by subjecting a birth cohort to a set of fixed age-specific rates. It is a mathematical exercise that allows demographers to make inferences about future demographic behavior in a given population (e.g., the probability that a childless woman at age 30 will have a child by age 35, or the number of years a child born in 2000 can expect to live). The total fertility rate, thus, is a measure of completed fertility and represents the average total number of births a woman can expect to have provided the age-specific fertility rates remain constant over her reproductive life span. It is derived by summing the age-specific fertility rates.

The various fertility rates can be expressed as:

$$CBR = \frac{\# \ of \ births}{Total \ Pop} \times 1000 \quad ASFR = \frac{\# \ of \ births \ W_i}{Total \ W_i} \times 1000 \quad TFR = \sum ASFR$$

---

leaves a large role for factors other than biological capacity in explaining fertility levels and has led demographers to focus not only on biological factors but also on the larger cultural, social, and economic factors that influence the "proximate determinants of fertility." These proximate determinants include the proportion of women who are married (or in a sexual union), the proportion who use contraception, the proportion who are infecund (e.g., due to lengthy breastfeeding or other conditions that cause more permanent sterility), and the level of induced abortion (McFalls 2007). To understand what alters fertility requires understanding what influences each of these proximate determinants of childbearing. This is also where social demography conjoins with formal demography to provide a more complete understanding of fertility behavior.

Many of the theories originally aimed at explaining changes in fertility focused largely on developed countries. The fertility behavior and demographic transitions of developing countries, however, differ somewhat from those of their developed counterparts. For example, while the timing of the transition from high to lower fertility in developed countries was compatible with theories of economic development, the pace of transition has been so fast in many developing countries that it suggests other factors are at play (Watkins 1987). Some demographers argue for the importance of factors such as the control and distribution of family planning funds and methods. Diffusion of Western ideas about the advantages of smaller family size and contraception is also thought to be an important explanation of the pace with which developing countries moved through the transition (Watkins 2000;

Thornton 2001). The diffusion of Westernized family values, which typically accompanies modernization, is thought to be one of the most important social exports to developing countries. With an emphasis on smaller, emotionally nucleated families and increased attention and expenditures on children, the export and diffusion of Westernized social values, according to Caldwell (1976), eclipses the role of economic modernization in explaining fertility change.

Philip Morgan (1996) documents the components of a "modern" fertility regime – the regime that many countries have either achieved or seem to be moving toward. High-parity births (four or more) become rare and a sizable minority of women remains childless. Women tend to have one or two children, sometimes three, and have those children sometime between their late teens and late thirties (with the average age at first birth shifting upward). There are relatively large proportions of births to unmarried mothers (though this is not universal), with substantial race, ethnic, and socioeconomic variation in childbearing patterns. Period conditions/ events affect variability, especially in first-birth timing. Contraception and abortion are the key "proximate determinants" – this is certainly the case in the contemporary United States and other developed countries (McFalls 2007).

The new development that goes beyond this "modern" fertility scheme is the emergence of what has been labeled "lowest low fertility" – total fertility rates below an average of 1.3 children per woman – in countries of Southern and Eastern Europe and parts of Asia (Billari & Kohler 2004). Indications, at least in Europe, are that fertility levels may have reached their lowest and are now rebounding somewhat. In all countries except Moldova, levels are now above 1.3 (Goldstein, Sobotka & Jasilioniene 2009), although sometimes not much above this level. This low level of fertility is of great concern because most of the countries with such low fertility also have very low mortality levels and hence rapid population aging, imminent population decline, and a high percentage of the population in the older ages. They will have difficulty supporting their generous packages of old-age assistance in the future without an increase in fertility, substantial immigration, or both.

What has driven fertility to such low levels? One issue is that current rates may be artificially low because the timing of fertility is changing in Europe and elsewhere. When the timing of childbearing is shifting to older ages – as seems likely in these countries – there is a period of very low fertility, but then fertility rises as women eventually have their children but at older ages. Still, there is no getting around the fact that fertility rates have fallen to very low levels in the South of Europe while rebounding in the North in Scandinavia and France. One hypothesis is that gender roles have changed to be more egalitarian in Northern Europe and this is fertility-enhancing. In Southern Europe, the family system where women shoulder virtually all of the domestic tasks is "out of sync" with the increase in women's labor force participation and hence women are postponing or forgoing motherhood (McDonald 2000). Other cultural explanations draw on the second demographic transition theory and the rise in individualism as explanations of "lowest low" fertility. More structural explanations suggest that high unemployment of youth and young adults and high housing costs in these countries depress fertility.

What are the fertility trends and issues that garner greatest attention in the US? Because US fertility is around replacement level – and has been at that level since the late 1970s – the concerns about low levels of fertility are not an issue in the US as they are in Europe. Teenage childbearing rates, which declined in the US between the mid-1990s and 2005 but have since risen, remain much higher than in Europe (Hamilton, Martin & Ventura 2009). As in Europe, childbearing is being delayed by a significant proportion of US women, particularly highly-educated women, although the average age of childbearing is not as late in the US as in Europe. Childlessness is also on the increase (Biddlecom & Martin 2006). Currently in the US, among women aged 40 to 44, 20 percent have never had a child, double the percentage 30 years ago (Dye 2008).

A high proportion of US births – 40 percent – occur outside marriage (Hamilton, Martin & Ventura 2009), although a sizable share are to couples who are cohabiting. Much of the increase in the proportion of births to unmarried women is a result of lower proportions of women marrying and falling fertility rates within marriage. Only recently have the fertility rates of the unmarried actually begun to rise. Larry Wu (2008) provides recent estimates for birth cohorts and shows that births outside marriage were higher than we might have guessed for earlier cohorts: 10 percent of women born between 1925 and 1929 had a birth outside marriage (29 percent of blacks; 16 percent of Hispanics). However, across birth cohorts of women, there has been a large increase in the likelihood of having a birth outside marriage. We usually think of births to unmarried women as births to teens but Wu shows that a sizable fraction occur later in life – the percentage of women with an unmarried birth doubles between age 20 and 30. Whites have a larger share of unmarried births after divorce/separation (rather than before a first marriage) than is the case for blacks and Hispanics.

The high percentage of births outside marriage has focused attention on a phenomenon called "multi-partner fertility" – the likelihood that a woman has children by more than one partner (and vice versa, the likelihood that a man fathers children with more than one woman). While not a "new" phenomenon – divorced fathers have frequently had children by a new partner – the current concern in the US stems from the fragility of unmarried cohabitation, the high rate of nonmarital fertility, and the much higher likelihood that children potentially lose paternal investments (of time and money) when partnerships that were never formalized by marriage break up.

Mortality

Mortality is the study of deaths within a population. In the theory of the demographic transition, mortality falls first and is followed by the decline in fertility. Life expectancy has expanded greatly, particularly over the past century. McFalls notes that "average life expectancy in the world around 1900 was less than 30 years of age" (2007: 10). In 2009, it was 69 years of age, according to the World Data Sheet of the Population Reference Bureau (2009). What does a life expectancy of 69 mean? Life expectancy is a hypothetical measure – if an individual born today were to go through life experiencing the age-specific likelihood of death that is currently in place, this is the predicted average years of life for that infant. Life table techniques are used to calculate life expectancies (see Box 25.2 for more detail on measures of mortality).

Box 25.2: Measuring Mortality

Like fertility, the extent of mortality can be estimated using a crude death rate (i.e., the number of deaths per 1,000 people in a given population at a particular point in time). However, because the risk of death can vary by age, demographers typically use age-specific death rates to estimate mortality. As discussed above, age-specific rates provide the number of events, in this case deaths, to people of an exact age or age group per 1,000 people who are of the exact age or age group. A commonly used age-specific death rate among demographers is the *infant mortality rate* (IMR). The IMR is an estimate of the number of deaths to children less than 1 year old per 1,000 live births at a particular point in time. It is expressed as:

$$\text{IMR} = \frac{\textit{\# of deaths to children under age one in a given year}}{\textit{\# of live births in the given year}} \times 1000$$

Life expectancy is also commonly used to assess the degree of mortality within a particular population. Like the total fertility rate, life expectancy is estimated using a life table and the measure represents the average number of years, typically measured at birth, that a person can be expected to live, assuming that the rate of mortality at each age remains fixed.

When mortality declines, it typically first drops because infectious diseases are controlled. This tends to benefit the young the most and hence there is a drop in infant and child mortality. Paradoxically, populations grow younger in the early stages of mortality decline. Currently, the more developed countries of the world have an average life expectancy of 77 years, compared with a life expectancy of 67 years for less developed countries and only 56 in the least developed countries (Population Reference Bureau 2009). A large share of this gap could be closed if diseases that weaken children's survival probabilities could be better controlled – diarrhea, respiratory infections, measles, tetanus. Antibiotics, immunizations, and clean drinking water have dramatically reduced these diseases in the US and other developed countries and have brought mortality rates down in developing countries, though not to the level of developed countries (McFalls 2007). Cutler and Miller (2005) show the importance of the introduction of clean water technologies in the early twentieth century for the reduction in mortality in US cities. Countries that make this type of public infrastructure investment dramatically reduce mortality of the young.

Life expectancy in the US is currently 78 years, an increase from only 47 years in 1900 (McFalls 2007; Population Reference Bureau 2009). Gains in life expectancy – and in something researchers call "healthy life expectancy" – have come from improvements in the treatment of later life conditions such as high blood pressure and treatments for chronic diseases aimed at reducing mortality from the two leading causes, heart disease and cancers. As life expectancy increases, an interesting debate has emerged about just how long we can live.

The oldest documented person in history was a French woman, Jeanne Louise Calment (born February 21, 1875, died August 4, 1997), who lived to be 122 years old (McFalls 2007). Traditionalists (and pessimists) suggest that 85 years is a maximum life expectancy, a maximum already surpassed by some groups of women today – Japanese women and Chinese women in Hong Kong currently have life expectancies at birth of 86 years (Population Reference Bureau 2009). A group of "Visionary/Optimists" suggest that life expectancy at birth could increase to 100 to 125 years (or more). Based on recent work, the optimists may be correct; there are likely to be continued gains (Vaupel 2009).

In the US, as elsewhere, women outlive men. Average life expectancy at birth was 75 years for men in 2009 but 80 years for women (Population Reference Bureau 2009). US female life expectancy at older ages has been static in recent years, however, while still improving in other countries like Japan and France. Also, the gender gap in life expectancy has been narrowing. In 1900, women lived only two years longer than men, on average, but this gap widened to almost eight years in 1975. Currently it has narrowed to five years. Research by Preston and Wang (2006) shows that US women's smoking rates increased substantially across birth cohorts and this is a likely cause of the narrowing of the gender gap in life expectancy and perhaps also one of the reasons that US women have not experienced the same increases in life expectancy in recent years as have women in Japan.

An interesting paradox in the US is that Hispanics appear to have lower mortality than whites, in spite of their relative socioeconomic disadvantage. Efforts to measure and account for this Hispanic advantage (or lack of disadvantage) have yielded complex results. There are a number of hypotheses, with one being that migration is selective of the healthy and that the unhealthy return home. Since Hispanics have a high proportion who are immigrants, this may at least partially explain their mortality advantage. But there are also cultural hypotheses – for example, that Hispanics have large family and social networks that confer a health advantage by providing social support. Work by Palloni and Arias (2004) supports the return migration hypothesis: they found that the advantage of foreign-born Mexicans was attributable to return migration, with the less healthy more likely to return to Mexico. However, the verdict is still out because there is also evidence that immigrants have healthier behaviors (e.g., less smoking), which then get eroded in the second generation as their children behave more like long-term natives, increasing their health risk-taking behaviors. One thing is clear: the advantage for foreign-born Mexicans and 'Other Hispanics' is substantial – perhaps as much as eight more years of life expectancy at age 45 (Palloni & Arias 2004).

It is difficult to definitively explain differences in health and mortality because of what demographers call "selection issues" and also the possibility of reverse causality. Many of the variables that influence health status may be *influenced by* it. For example, does income enhance health or are the healthy merely able to earn more income? Does marriage protect against poor health or are the healthy just more likely to marry? In addition, mounting evidence suggests that health in childhood may have long-term effects – but it remains very difficult to trace these long-term consequences.

Migration

The Hispanic paradox in mortality highlights the importance of migration in the study of population change. Demographers who study *migration* focus on the movement of people and the effect of migration on societies (both senders and receivers). On the positive side, migration can act as a safety valve, alleviating social and economic pressures associated with overpopulation. People can also benefit from remittances received from family members who have migrated. Furthermore, migration can help some countries meet labor shortages that may be the result of declines in fertility. However, out-migration can also lead to labor shortages. Furthermore, some of the loss in labor can be among the most highly skilled (i.e., a "brain drain").

The challenges to studying migration are tremendous and most of this is related to the paucity of data available on the global movement of people. Thus, migration is typically estimated as a residual (using an *intercensal component method*) rather than measured directly. That is, if the size of the population at two points in time is known, as well as the number of births and deaths occurring during this time period, then the amount of net migration can be estimated as the residual.

Probably the "hottest" area of study is international migration, both unauthorized as well as legal flows from one country to another. In the US, there was a huge increase in immigration, especially from Latin America and Asia, in the later decades of the twentieth century. This makes the twentieth-century immigration picture resemble "bookends," according to Charles Hirschman (2005). The US had mass migration from Southern/Eastern Europe at the beginning of the twentieth century, with these "new immigrants" – Jews, Italians, Poles, Greeks, Slavs – often considered "nonwhite." After 1965 and up to the present, there have been sizable waves of immigrants from Latin America and Asia. Between these two periods of high immigration, the US essentially closed its doors to immigrants. Hence, the end of the twentieth century looked more like the beginning than the middle.

Hirschman (2005) notes that the US founding fathers did not intend that the US become a nation of immigrants – but it did. America's image as a land of opportunity/refuge has become to some extent part of its national identity – both for those inside and for those outside, seeking to come. It is an identity not rooted in nationhood, but rather one welcoming of strangers. Concerns about unauthorized immigration notwithstanding, the US remains one of the main "immigrant-receiving" countries of the world, with something like 800,000 residents legally admitted each year (Desai 2004) and estimates of around 8 million unauthorized migrants living in the US (Bean, Corona, Tuiran, Woodrow-Lafield & Van Hook 2001).

EXPANDING BEYOND FERTILITY, MORTALITY, AND MIGRATION

Earlier we differentiated between formal demography, which has concentrated on the core processes of fertility, mortality, and migration, and social demography, which expands the focus to include a broader context of demographic change. Even formal demography has typically paid attention to nuptiality or marriage patterns, in part because they tend to be so important for the study of fertility. To some extent, this interest in marriage patterns blends into the large area of study in social demography called family demography. This area has seen tremendous growth in the past few decades, with examination of a number of important topics spanning the life course.

Life-course living arrangements and transitions

Before 1850 in the US, parents and young adult children tended to live together on farms, with much of the population rural. Children were sometimes sent to work elsewhere as servants but were usually still under adult supervision. After 1850, up to a low point around 1970, parents and young adult children "uncoupled." Ruggles (2007) argues that an important factor was the growing economic independence of the younger generation. The decline in household-based production on farms and the rise of wage labor, in urban places, took young people away from family farms. The spread of mass education reinforced these trends. Children who spent more days in school reduced their economic contributions to the family enterprise. The rise of secondary education helped to erode the authority of family at the same time that families were investing more in the education of their children, because increasingly more education was needed to get good wage-labor jobs.

This increased independent living of the younger generation continued until about 1970 and then living in the parental home in the US began to increase. This occurred in part because adult transitions have been increasingly delayed (Furstenberg, Kennedy, McLoyd, Rumbaut & Settersten 2004). Young adults are taking longer to complete school, taking longer to settle into a "career," marrying later, and having children later (or having them outside marriage when they have them early). Many of these trends increase the likelihood of returning to the parental home between transitions.

Trends in marriage in the US have undergone a radical change and there are growing socioeconomic differences in marriage and fertility transitions. There is later marriage and more nonmarriage. There is more interracial marriage but less intermarriage across educational levels. First co-residential unions are increasingly cohabitations, not marriages. More childrearing is occurring outside of marriage – in single-parent households and cohabiting households. But this is much more true of those with only a high school education or less than it is of the college-educated, who still marry first, then have children, and tend to stay married as they raise those children.

Why do demographers care so much about marriage and cohabitation? Traditionally the percentage of the population who were married was important in assessing fertility. Marriage and childbearing were tightly connected. Today in Europe and the US, there is a decoupling of marriage and fertility which raises concerns about the well-being of children. In his book *The Marriage Go-Round*, Andrew Cherlin (2009) argues that the US is exceptional among developed countries for its high rates of marrying and divorcing, and its pattern of cohabitation. Whereas in Europe, cohabitations are often very "marriage-like," lasting for years, in the US cohabitations tend to be short-lived. Cherlin notes that 10 percent of US women have had three or more husbands or cohabiting partners by the time they reach age

35, more than twice the percentage for countries in Europe with the highest rates of union dissolution (Cherlin 2009: 19).

Debate continues about why these trends have occurred. There are at least three different hypotheses. Harking back to the theory of the second demographic transition, one account focuses on changes in values and attitudes. We have become more individualistic and less willing to sacrifice for the good of others and are therefore less likely to marry or remain in a bad union. A second account focuses on women's increased opportunities and the declining returns on marriage for women. In this account, marriage used to reflect a division of labor, with each partner gaining from trading with the other. Women specialized in the home and men in the market. This division of labor makes less sense today, but without it women gain less from marriage (they can support themselves) and men also gain less (they have lost the services of a "housewife"). Hence, a more egalitarian division of labor erodes the benefits of marriage (Becker 1991). The third account focuses on the deteriorating economic circumstances of young men. Recent changes in the economy have adversely affected the economic opportunities available to young men. Without stable jobs, men are reluctant to marry, and women perceive themselves as better off not married to such men (Oppenheimer 1997, 2003).

CONCLUSION

The population issues of the twenty-first century have both continuities and discontinuities with the past. There is far less concern about rapid population growth, though concerns about population have not disappeared from the discussions about the environment. There is currently more attention on very low fertility than on high fertility. Increasingly mortality issues center on population aging and the diseases of old age in developed countries, while many developing countries, particularly in Sub-Saharan Africa, continue to battle infectious diseases that keep infant and child mortality high and the HIV/AIDs epidemic. International migration is on the increase globally, with the situation in the US at the beginning of the twenty-first century reminiscent of the beginning of the twentieth century. Families have undergone profound changes as country after country has made the transition from high mortality and high fertility to low mortality and low fertility, sometimes very low fertility, with increased rates of late marriage or nonmarriage and marital dissolution.

In today's interconnected world, the study of population processes and change remains vibrant. Understanding the complex interweaving of demographic processes and social, cultural, and economic opportunities and constraints undergirds effective policy at the global, national, and local levels.

References

Becker, G. S. (1991) *A Treatise on the Family*, rev. edn. Cambridge, MA: Harvard University Press.

Bean, F. D., R. Corona, R. Tuiran, K. A. Woodrow-Lafield, and J. Van Hook (2001) "Circular, Invisible, and Ambiguous Migrants: Components of Difference in Estimates of the Number of Unauthorized Mexican Migrants in the United States." *Demography* 38: 411–22.

Biddlecom, A. and S. Martin (2006) "Childless in America." *Contexts* 5: 54.

Billari, F. and H. P. Kohler (2004) "Patterns of Low and Lowest-Low Fertility in Europe." *Population Studies* 58(2): 161–76.

Boserup, E. (1976) "Environment, Population, and Technology in Primitive Societies." *Population and Development Review* 2(1): 21–36.

Caldwell, J. C. (1976) "Toward a Restatement of Demographic Transition Theory." *Population and Development Review* 2(3/4): 321–66.

Coale, A. J. (1973) "The Demographic Transition." Paper presented at the IUSSP International Population Conference, Liège.

Cherlin, A. (2009) *The Marriage-Go-Round*. New York: Vintage Books.

Cutler, D. and G. Miller (2005) "The Role of Public Health Improvements in Health Advances: The Twentieth-Century United States." *Demography* 42: 1–22.

Desai, S. (2004) "Population Change." In G. Ritzer (ed.), *Handbook of Social Problems: A Comparative International Perspective*. Thousand Oaks, CA: Sage, pp. 69–86.

Dye, J. L. (2008) "Fertility of American Women 2006." *Current Population Reports, P20–558*. Washington, DC: US Census Bureau.

Easterlin, R. (1978) "What Will 1984 Be Like? Socioeconomic Implications of Recent Twists in Age Structure." *Demography* 15: 397–432.

Ehrlich, P. R. (1968) *The Population Bomb*. New York: Ballantine Books.

Furstenberg, F. F., Jr., S. Kennedy, V. C. McLoyd, R. G. Rumbaut, and R. A. Settersten, Jr. (2004) "Growing Up Is Harder to Do." *Contexts* 3(3): 33–41.

Goldstein, J. R., T. Sobotka, and A. Jasilioniene (2009) "The End of 'Lowest-Low' Fertility?" *Population and Development Review* 35(4): 663–99.

Hamilton, B. E., J. A. Martin, and S. J. Ventura (2009) "Births: Preliminary Data for 2007." *National Vital Statistics Reports*, Vol. 57, No. 12. Hyattsville, MD: National Center for Health Statistics.

Hinde, A. (1998) *Demographic Methods*. London: Arnold.

Hirschman, C. (2005) "Immigration and the American Century." *Demography* 42: 595–620.

Kirk, D. (1996) "Demographic Transition Theory." *Population Studies* 50(3): 361–87.

Lee, R. (2007) *Global Population Aging and Its Economic Consequences*. Washington, DC: American Enterprise Institute Press.

Lesthaeghe, R. (1983) "A Century of Demographic and Cultural Change in Western Europe: An Exploration of Underlying Dimensions." *Population and Development Review* 9(3): 411–35.

Lesthaeghe, R. (1995) "The Second Demographic Transition in Western Countries: An Interpretation." In K. Mason and A. Jensen (eds.), *Gender and Family Change in Industrialized Countries*. Oxford: Clarendon Press, pp. 17–62.

Lesthaeghe, R. and J. Surkyn (1988) "Cultural Dynamics and Economic Theories of Fertility Change." *Population and Development Review* 14(1): 1–45.

Livi-Bacci, M. (2007) *A Concise History of World Population*, 4th edn. Oxford: Blackwell.

Malthus, T. (1798) *An Essay on the Principle of Population*. London: J. Johnson.

McDonald, P. (2000) "Gender Equity in Theories of Fertility Transition." *Population and Development Review* 26(3): 427–39.

McFalls, J. (2007) "Population: A Lively Introduction. Fifth Edition." *Population Bulletin* 62(1).

Morgan, S. P. (1996) "Characteristic Features of Modern American Fertility." In John B. Casterline, Ronald D. Lee, and Karen A. Foote (eds.), *Fertility in the United States: New Patterns, New Theories*. New York: Population Council, pp. 19–63.

Oppenheimer, V. K. (1997) "Men's Career Development and Marriage Timing During a Period of Rising Inequality." *Demography* 34: 311–30.

Oppenheimer, V. K. (2003) "Cohabiting and Marriage During Young Men's Career-Development Process." *Demography* 40: 127–49.

Palloni, A. and E. Arias (2004) "Paradox Lost: Explaining the Hispanic Adult Mortality Advantage." *Demography* 41: 385–415.

Population Reference Bureau (2009) *World Population Data Sheet*. Washington, DC: Population Reference Bureau.

Preston, S. H. and H. Wang (2006) "Sex Mortality Differences in the United States: The Role of Cohort Smoking Patterns." *Demography* 43: 631–46.

Ruggles, S. (2007) "The Decline of Intergenerational Coresidence in the United States, 1850–2000." *American Sociological Review* 72: 964–89.

Simon, J. (1977) *The Economics of Population Growth*. Princeton, NJ: Princeton University Press.

Simon, J. (1981) *The Ultimate Resource*. Princeton, NJ: Princeton University Press.

Thompson, W. (1929) "Population." *American Journal of Sociology* 34: 959–75.

Thornton, A. (2001) "The Development Paradigm, Reading History Sideways, and Family Change." *Demography* 38: 449–65.

Van de Kaa, D. J. (1996) "Anchored Narratives: The Story and Findings of Half a Century of Research into the Determinants of Fertility." *Population Studies* 50(3): 389–432.

Vaupel, J. W. (2009) "Lively Questions for Demographers about Death at Older Ages." *Population and Development Review* 35(2): 347–56.

Watkins, S. C. (1987) "The Fertility Transition: Europe and Third World Compared." *Sociological Forum* 2(4): 645–73.

Watkins, S. C. (2000) "Local and Foreign Models of Reproduction in Nyanza Province, Kenya." *Population and Development Review* 26(4): 725–59.

Weeks, J. R. (2008) *Population: An Introduction to Concepts and Issues*, 10th edn. Belmont, CA: Wadsworth.

Wu, L. (2008) "Cohort Estimates of Nonmarital Fertility for U.S. Women." *Demography* 45: 193–207.

26

Urbanization

KEVIN FOX GOTHAM

Urbanization refers to the physical, demographic, and economic growth of cities. The term also implies the concentration of people and social activities into settlement patterns characterized by high-density land development. Urbanization results in part from population increase, due to both natural causes and immigration, as well as economic, social, and technological changes that spur people to move to areas of job growth and expanded opportunities. Generally, market forces and government policies drive urbanization processes and associated changes in livelihoods, land use, health, and natural resources management including water, soil, and forests. Employer location decisions, transformations in urban agriculture and production systems, and government development policies and budget allocations often generate intense urban in-migration and concentrate socio-economic activities in cities.

The most fundamental source of potential confusion in the study of urbanization and city growth is the conceptualization and measurement of "urban" itself. There are no clear answers to what defines an urban area. In the United States, federal government agencies have been central in defining cities, city boundaries, and urbanization trends. In 1910, the Census Bureau devised the term *metropolitan district* to describe and measure urban growth occurring beyond the city. As originally defined, a metropolitan district consisted of a central city with a population of at least 200,000, plus adjacent townships with a density of at least 150 persons per square mile. As the US population continued to grow outside central cities and economic relations increasingly shifted over established administrative boundaries,

The Wiley-Blackwell Companion to Sociology, First Edition. Edited by George Ritzer.
© 2012 Blackwell Publishing Ltd. Published 2012 by Blackwell Publishing Ltd.

the idea of a metropolitan district became less useful. In 1949, the Census Bureau introduced a new measure, the *standard metropolitan statistical area* (SMSA), consisting of the whole county containing a city of at least 50,000 plus surrounding counties which had a high degree of economic and social integration with the population nucleus (Bogue 1953).

By the 1970s, the US federal government had formulated three types of metropolitan area to measure urbanization trends and processes. Metropolitan Statistical Areas (MSAs) are metropolitan areas with populations of less than 1 million, regardless of the number of counties they may contain. If the metropolitan area exceeds 1 million, it is designated a Consolidated Metropolitan Statistical Area (CMSA). Primary Metropolitan Statistical Areas (PMSAs) are multi-centered constellations of CMSAs that spread across hundreds of square miles. These new designations suggest a fundamental transformation of cities from a dense, bounded, single-core city to extended multi-nucleated urban regions containing many centers of work, residence, and shopping encompassing an enormous population and crossing multiple administrative boundaries.

Urbanization is increasing in both developed and developing countries. In the United States, for example, about 80 percent of the nation's population live in metropolitan areas. From 1945 to 2002, urban land area in the US increased from around 15 million acres to roughly 60 million acres, almost twice the rate of US population growth. Urban growth during just the last 10 years of this period was 7.8 million acres or 13 percent (Brown, Johnson, Loveland & Theobald 2005). Yet urbanization trends are slower in the United States than in the developing world where rapid urbanization, particularly the growth of large cities, poses a formidable challenge in developing countries. In many developing cities, urbanization is associated with the problems of chronic unemployment, intense poverty, poor access to quality health care, poor sanitation, urban slums, and environmental degradation.

In 2008, the United Nations announced that 50 percent of the world's population now live in urban areas, a milestone in human history since human societies and communities have in the past been rural-based. The UN projects that the world's urban population will grow by 1.8 percent per year and by 2.3 percent per year in developing countries from 2007 to 2025. By 2020, the world's rural population will cease growing altogether and begin to decline (United Nations Population Division 2009). In part, the world's urban population will continue to increase because towns and villages not considered urban today will grow over time. Importantly, researchers and scholars expect migration to urban areas to increase as people migrate to areas of job growth, and prospects for higher income and higher standards of living. In addition, one of the most important features of rapid urbanization is the massive population growth and development in coastal cities. Globally, more than 1 billion of the world's population live within 100 km of the coast and current trends suggest that roughly half of the world's population will do so by 2030 (Cohen 2003). The implications of urbanization are broad and span the natural, physical, and social sciences. While scholars recognize that urbanization is a global trend, they disagree over the causes and impacts of urbanization, the development trajectories of urbanization, and the implications of urbanization for environmental sustainability.

THEORIES OF URBANIZATION

The study of cities and urbanization has a rich tradition in the arts, humanities, and social and natural sciences. To Lewis Mumford, the city is "primarily a storehouse, a conservator and accumulator" (1961: 97) of culture and human creativity. Diverse groups and organizations, along with a heterogeneity of abstract designs, scripts, and verbal signs contribute to the notion of the city as a container of human culture and a magnet for attracting people and ideas. One important concern in Mumford's work was to understand the reflexive relationship between cemeteries and cultural creation. The "necropolis," the "city of the dead," Mumford argued, "is the forerunner, almost to the core, of every living city" (1961: 7). Every culture's respect for the dead is a cultural expression of the human desire for a "fixed meeting place and eventually a continuous settlement" (1961: 6–7). Cemeteries, sacred caves, and shrines gave people their first conception of architectural space and their first glimpse of the power of a territory and space to intensify spiritual receptivity and emotional exaltation, a view closely shared by sociologist Emile Durkheim in his studies of the *Elementary Forms of Religious Life*. More broadly, Mumford's insight on the evolution of cities drew attention to the formative role of cemeteries and other sacred places in the development of Western culture. As he put it, "in the earliest gathering about a grave or a painted symbol, a great stone or sacred grove, one has the beginning of a succession of civic institutions that range from the temple to the astronomical observatory, from the theatre to the university" (1961: 9).

Modern theories of urbanization emerged in Europe during the eighteenth and nineteenth centuries as the industrial revolution transformed working, settlement, and lifestyle patterns throughout the continent. As hundreds of thousands of agrarian peasants and serfs left the countryside and flocked to work in the urban factories, a new breed of social observers sought to analyze the altered forms of social organization. The German sociologist Ferdinand Tönnies described the contrasting elements of urban and rural life. His concept of *Gemeinschaft* (community) characterized the small country village and its surrounding area in which people – united by close ties of family and neighborhood – shared similar traditional values and worked together for the common good. In contrast to this "we-ness," *Gesellschaft* (association or society) denoted the "me-ness" found in the city, where a future-looking orientation among a heterogeneous population replaced tradition, leading Tönnies to a pessimistic view of the city as characterized by atomized disunity, rampant individualism, and selfishness.

Other Europeans such as Karl Marx and Friedrich Engels, Max Weber, and Georg Simmel devoted much thought to the importance of the city, for example, as a seat of the emerging capitalist economy, a site of political and economic power, and a force of cultural change that affects mental life. Karl Marx and Friedrich Engels were among the first to describe the excesses of industrialization and the appalling lifestyle of exploited urban workers. Marx and Engels depicted the modern metropolis as expressing most vividly the peculiarities of capitalism including, for example, the antithesis between wage labor and capital, the valorization/realization of exchange-value, and the proletarianization of the populace. For Max Weber (1958), the European medieval city and its institutions were crucial links in the development of economic rationality and modern capitalism. The city, as Weber notes, expresses in concentrated form the peculiarities of formal rationality including the emphasis on calculation, efficiency, and predictability in the conduct of social relations and activity. In his famous essay, "Metropolis and Mental Life," Georg Simmel ([1903] 1950) drew attention to the intensity of nervous stimuli and the pervasiveness of money relations in forming an urban personality that is reserved, detached, and blasé. In other general writings, Simmel attempted to move theorizing away from viewing cities as containers or contexts of action to examining cities as forms and products of meaningful sociation.

In the United States, the early Chicago School urban sociologists focused their empirical attention on the spatial distribution of people and organizations, the causes and consequences of neighborhood racial succession, and ethnic and racial group adaptation to the urban environment. Robert Park, Ernst Burgess, Lewis Wirth, all commented on the impact of the immense size, density, and diversity of cities on society. From their writings emerged a theory of urbanization as following a series of stages based on changes in population, organization, environment, and technology. By the 1930s, social scientists around the nation were employing the insights and models developed by the Chicago School to examine urbanization and identify the processes of urban growth and development. The concentric ring model developed by Burgess was the first model of urbanization to explain the distribution of social groups within cities. This model depicts urban land use in concentric rings: the central business district (or CBD) was in the middle of the model, and the city expanded in rings with different land uses. In 1939, Homer Hoyt developed the sector model showing zones expanding outward from the city center along railroads, highways, and other transportation arteries. Later, in 1945, Chancy Harris and Edward Ullman put forward the multiple nuclei model which posits that urbanization can occur without a clear CBD. In this model, the number and kinds of nuclei characterize a city's urbanization pattern.

In the 1970s, several Marxian social scientists, including Manuel Castells (1977), David Harvey (1973), and Henri Lefebvre ([1970] 2003, 1991), popularized the concept of uneven development to direct theoretical and analytical attention to the impact of the political economy on urbanization trends. Uneven development refers to the inequitable spatial distribution of wealth and/or economic growth within a city or metropolitan area. The term also refers to the simultaneous occurrence of economic and wealth expansion in one area accompanied by disinvestment and/or expanding poverty in another area.

For Lefebvre (1991), urbanization reflects a basic conflict and struggle between abstract space and social space. According to Lefebvre, "abstract space" is constituted by the intersection of knowledge and power. It is the use of space by capitalists and state actors who are interested in the abstract qualities of space, including size, width, area, location, and profit. Abstract space is characterized by both fragmentation and homogenization of space, and both processes are the result of the commodification of space. In contrast, "social space" is the space of everyday lived experience, an environment as a place to live and to call home. For Lefebvre, the uses proposed by government and business for abstract space, such as planning a new highway or redeveloping older areas of the city, may conflict with existing social space, the way residents think about and use space. This conflict between abstract and social space is a basic one in modern society, according to Lefebvre, and involves spatial practices (externalized, material environments), representations of space (conceptual models used to direct social practice and land-use planning), and spaces of representation (the lived social relation of users to the built environment) (1991: 33, 38–9).

Castells proposed that urban scholars focus on the collective consumption characteristic of urbanized nations and the way in which political and economic conflicts within cities generate urban social movements for change. David Harvey, in contrast, argued that the central issue in understanding urbanization was not collective consumption but the more basic Marxist concern with capital accumulation. Influenced by Lefebvre, Harvey (1973) argued that investment in land and real estate is an important means of accumulating wealth and a crucial activity that pushes the growth of cities in specific ways. Urbanization and related processes reflect the continuous reshaping of the built environment to create a more efficient arena for profit making.

According to Harvey, powerful real estate actors invest, disinvest, and reshape land uses in a process of "creative destruction" that is continually accelerating, destroying communities and producing intense social conflicts and struggles over meanings and uses of urban space. Despite their different emphases, the work of Castells, Harvey, and Lefebvre helped focus scholarly attention on the capitalist system of for-profit production generally, and class struggle and capital accumulation specifically, as analytical starting points for understanding the nature of urbanization.

By the late 1970s and continuing into the 1980s, a new critical approach to the study of cities and urbanization had developed in Europe and the United States. Usually called the "critical political economy" or "socio-spatial approach," this perspective emphasized several major dimensions of cities: (1) the importance of class and racial domination (and, more recently, gender) in shaping urbanization; (2) the primary role of powerful economic actors, especially those in the real estate industry, in building and redeveloping cities; (3) the role of growth-assisted government actors in urban development; (4) the importance of symbols, meanings, and culture to the shaping of cities; (5) attention to the global context of urbanization (for overviews see Gottdiener & Feagin 1988; Feagin 1998). Gottdiener (1994) prefers the term "sociospatial" perspective to describe the critical political economy paradigm, a term that accents the society/space synergy, and emphasizes that cities are multifaceted expressions of local actions and macrostructural processes.

Influenced by the critical political economy paradigm, John Logan and Harvey Molotch (1987) have developed their own "growth machine" theory to explain urbanization. The growth machine approach argues that a powerful political coalition made up of an array of real estate and banking interests dominates and controls the urban redevelopment process. The desire for "growth" creates a consensus among a wide array of actors and elite groups, no matter how divided they may be on a specific issue or policy. Proponents of the growth machine approach suggest that growth coalitions are prevalent throughout local government because (1) city leaders seek to sustain growth to maintain governmental services and fiscal health, and (2) local businesses become involved in local policies to maintain and increase their profitability by influencing and shaping the city's regulation of land use, tax and employment policy, and provision of services. The formation of coalitions in pursuit of growth permeates all facets of the urbanization process, including the political system, as well as local utility companies, unions, media, and cultural institutions such as professional sports teams, theaters, symphony orchestras, and universities (for an overview, see Jonas & Wilson 1999).

URBANIZATION AND SUBURBANIZATION

One major point of debate in urban scholarship focuses on issues of conceptualization and addresses questions about when, where, why, and how urbanization developed. Early work by Childe (1950) located the beginnings of urbanization in early communities in Mesopotamia. The first cities were dense human agglomerations with up to 20,000 residents and dominated by the production of an agricultural surplus. A surplus of food and resources generated several other changes including the establishment of specialized groups including craftsmen, transport workers, merchants, officials, and priests. Over time, a system of taxation developed to support government activity, raise money for public works and standing armies, regulate marketplaces, and define a system of cultural relations. The production of an agricultural surplus created problems over the allocation and control of wealth, leading to the emergence of social stratification. Priests, military leaders, and other elites formed a "ruling class" who exempted themselves from physical labor and pursued "intellectual tasks." To control and regulate the growth of surplus, the ruling classes invented systems of recording, numerical calculation, and writing. In addition, Childe's thesis suggests that the first cities were the birthplaces of modern science as the invention of writing allowed early clerks, bureaucrats, and political officers to develop rational systems of knowledge to control investment. The concentration of surplus also provided a cultural foundation for artists and craftspeople to cultivate sophisticated styles and traditions, a development that led to the specialization of art and culture. Finally, for Childe, the rise of the first cities helped encourage and expand trade, a development that transformed relatively culturally homogeneous and isolated towns into cosmopolitan metropolises. As different kinds of people came into contact with one another, the increasing frequency of contact catalyzed the growth of new forms of cultural exchange and reciprocity.

The industrial revolution transformed Europe, generating rapid urban growth, destabilizing agrarian economies, and setting in motion major social and spatial changes. The economy, physical form, and culture of cities changed dramatically as feudal power broke down and trade and travel increased. The increasing size, density, and diversity of cities, combined with the growth of commerce, made urban life more rational, anonymous, and depersonalized. During the nineteenth century, London's population grew to 6 million, making it then the largest city ever known, and confounding all notions that there was a natural upper limit to the size of even the richest cities. In the United States, industrialization not only brought about a fundamental transformation in the nature of work, but also in systems of transportation, the structure and operations of city government, the experience of poverty, and the demographic movement of racial and ethnic groups on an unprecedented scale. In the first half of the twentieth century, the fastest urban growth around the world was in Europe and the United States. New York, London, and other First World capitals were magnets for immigration and job opportunity. In 1950, New York, London, Tokyo, and Paris boasted of having the world's largest metropolitan populations.

In the United States, during the early period of industrial expansion and national growth, the pace of urbanization accelerated to a mid-nineteenth-century peak. By the late nineteenth century, urban, rural, and national growth rates had stabilized. Cyclical downturns reduced the tempo to zero in the decades 1810–20 and 1830–40 and halved it in the period 1870–80, but in each case these perturbations were followed by post-recession recoveries under still-urbanizing conditions (Berry 1980). By the 1920s, however, the population of US central cities essentially stopped growing and the collapse of the economy during the Great Depression spotlighted a series of intense social problems facing cities, including increasing physical deterioration of core neighborhoods and commercial districts, forced concentration of inner-city blacks into crowded areas, and loss of industry (Gotham 2001). In the 1930s and later, US cities began to experience population and industrial deconcentration as people, industries, and jobs moved away from cities toward the suburbs, a process that accelerated after World War II.

The main factor pulling people out of central cities was a series of federal housing policies passed during the 1930s and later which provided mortgage insurance guarantees to encourage banks to make loans for single-family homes for middle-income people. Federal housing policies transformed the home-building and loan-lending industries by promoting economies of scale through suburban housing construction, a development related to federal efforts to promote suburbanization (Gotham 2002). The federal government's home-building subsidies, underwriting standards, and land-planning policies encouraged large builders to expand their scope of operations and market share by enhancing the financial feasibility of single-family homes. Community developers and large builders whose housing plans conformed to federal standards were able to get a government-insured mortgage for all homes they built (Weiss 1987). Once the Federal Housing Administration (FHA) subsidy was obtained, builders rapidly increased the size of their operations, producing a high volume of quality, moderately priced dwellings in suburban areas. In Long Island, New York, the William Levitt and Son Company was able to get federal subsidies to finance 4,000 houses before clearing the land to build Levittown (Checkoway 1984: 158–9). Overall, the level of suburban housing production rose significantly after World War II, from 209,000 units in 1945, to more than 1 million units by the end of the decade, to as many as 2,379,000 units by the early 1970s. On an annual basis, production levels during the 1950s, 1960s, and the early 1970s were equally impressive, remaining above 7 dwelling units per 1,000 population during these years, reaching a peak of 11.4 in 1972 (Rowe 1995: 184).

In *Race, Real Estate, and Uneven Development*, Gotham (2002) draws attention to the central impact of real estate activities and federal housing policies on the pace and development of urbanization and suburbanization during the twentieth century. Racially discriminatory government actions and real estate practices promulgated racial residential segregation that contributed to racialized urban development. The Federal Housing Administration, for example, recommended that private banks only make loans in racially homogeneous areas, thus severely limiting the housing opportunities of blacks, other minorities, and the poor. These segregative practices served to exacerbate existing racial and class polarization in cities and metropolitan areas, and contributed to disinvestment in many inner-city neighborhoods, through restrictive covenants and bank redlining (e.g., the refusal of banks to loan money in certain urban neighborhoods because of the racial composition of these areas). The totality of these events dramatically heightened inter-racial animosity in the 1960s, especially in the industrial North. Violent demonstrations in many cities accelerated central-city white flight during the next decade (Harris & Wilkins 1988). By the 1980s, hundreds of thousands of middle-class jobs had also left for suburban areas. The net result was rapid ex-urban growth accompanied by massive fiscal shortages in the urban core, place/spatial stratification by race and income, and spiraling racial and class inequalities within US metropolitan areas.

Since the 1960s, urban areas in the United States have been subjected to a series of unprecedented socio-spatial changes, including a decrease of population and employment in the "rustbelt," gentrification and redevelopment of the inner core of some older metropolitan areas, an increase in minority populations in central cities, rapid growth of "edge cities" on the metropolitan fringe, and the economic decline of older suburban communities. Moreover, urban politics has moved away from the days of generous federal funding through fiscal austerity to the present period of limited resources, federal retrenchment, privatization of services, and combined public/private partnerships in pursuit of growth. Since 1970, employers and firms have been creating more jobs in the suburbs than in the central cities, and employment growth has been greater for the areas outside central cities than for the inner cities in metropolitan areas. Detroit lost 800,000 people between 1950 and 1996, and its population declined by 33.9 percent between 1970 and 1996. Midwestern cities were particularly hard-hit by the twin problems of population decline and deindustrialization. St. Louis, for instance, lost more than half its population in the same period, as did Pittsburgh. Cleveland precipitously declined, as did Buffalo, Cincinnati, Minneapolis, and many other large US cities.

After shedding residents for decades, many US cities revived in the 1990s, with population trends stabilizing due to immigration and revitalization of downtown cores. By the 2000s, however, US Census Bureau figures revealed that suburbs had eclipsed central cities as the main locus of population growth. The collapse of the high-tech industry, eroding wealth and income, and the lack of urban job growth, combined with more affordable suburban housing and employment opportunities, attracted tens of thousands of foreign-born residents and others to the suburbs during the 2000s. Among the nation's 251 cities with at least 100,000 people, 68 lost population between 2000 and 2004. As Frey, Berube, Singer, and Wilson (2009) have found, racial and ethnic minorities are driving the nation's population growth and increasing diversity among its younger residents. In addition, the US exhibits wide regional and racial/ethnic disparities. While 56 percent and 38 percent of Asian and white adults, respectively, held post-secondary degrees in 2007, only 25 percent and 18 percent of blacks and Hispanics did so. These deep divides by race and ethnicity coincide with growing disparities across metropolitan areas owing to economic and demographic change. Both urban and suburban poverty rates rose during the 2000s. Today, working-age Americans account for a larger share of the poor than at any other point in the last 30 years. The number of suburban poor surpassed the number of central-city poor during this decade, and now outnumber them by more than 1.5 million. Yet even as poverty spreads throughout the metropolis, the concentration of poverty in highly distressed communities – after dropping in the 1990s – has been rising once again in the first decades of the twenty-first century.

Today, in virtually all US cities, policy-makers and elites have perceived their economic base as endangered by competition from other cities and have struggled to develop various programs, fiscal policies, and other subsidies to attract businesses. In this context of escalating competition for capital, cities have become important spatial targets and arenas for a variety of consumption-based economic development strategies to enhance the "fun factor" of cities – e.g., place marketing, tourism spectacles, sports mega-events, urban entertainment districts, and other attractions. Hannigan's (1998) work on the rise of fantasy cities, Chatterton and Hollands' (2003) investigation of urban nightscapes, Gottdiener's (2001) analysis of the ubiquity of theming, and Greenberg's (2007) examination of urban branding suggest that entertaining attractions and spectacles now dominate the political economy of urbanization. Throughout the United States, local governments and elites thus view entertainment spectacles as playing an important role in recasting cities as sites for leisure activities and consumption, typically through the development of sports stadiums, hotels, and tourist attractions (for an overview, see Hoffman, Fainstein & Judd 2003).

Megalopolis, Exurbia, and the Multinucleated Metropolitan Region

In the early 1950s, Jean Gottmann coined the term *megalopolis* to describe continuous zones of urbanization spreading along the Boston–Washington corridor in the United States, which he more positively characterized as the new "Main Street of the nation" (Gottmann 1961). Gottmann urged researchers to view the megalopolis as a novel urban form that is multi-nucleated and multi-functional. Population growth fueled suburbanization and suburbs later became their own independent and autonomous regions that merged with the central city to form an extensive metropolitan region on the United States East Coast. In 1950, the megalopolis had a population of 32 million inhabitants. Today, the megalopolis includes more than 44 million people, 16 percent of the entire United States population. Four of the largest CMSAs (Consolidated Metropolitan Statistical Areas) in the United States overlap with the megalopolis and account for over 38 million of the megalopolis population. The four CMSAs are New York–Northern New Jersey–Long Island, Washington–Baltimore, Philadelphia–Wilmington–Atlantic City, and Boston–Worcester–Lawrence. The implication of Gottmann's study of the megalopolis was that

> [w]e must abandon the idea of the city as a tightly settled and organized unit in which people, activities, and riches are crowded into a very small area clearly separated from its nonurban surroundings. Every city in this region spreads out far and wide around its original nucleus; it grows amidst an irregularly colloidal mixture of rural and suburban landscapes; it melts on broad fronts with other mixtures, of somewhat similar

though different texture, belonging to the suburban neighborhoods of other cities. (Gottmann 1961: 5)

Today, central cities and rural areas continue to lose population while metropolitan areas continue to grow and expand. Urban deconcentration and rural population loss signify the rise of the *multinucleated metropolitan region* characterized by the massive, regional scale of sprawl and the presence of multiple, specialized activity centers outside the downtown central business district (Gottdiener 1994). Traditionally, scholars have portrayed the city as a magnet that attracted people and activities within its boundary and a center that dominated its surrounding urbanized areas. This image is no longer relevant to urbanization in the US. Whereas the central business district or downtown was the focal point of urban life and the center of dominance in the past, there are now many separate and specialized centers dispersed across the entire metropolitan region. The notion of the multinucleated metropolitan region is useful for understanding changes in metropolitan spatial structure and dynamics of metropolitan life. The concept suggests a networked, interactive character of the metropolitan region tied together by the complex webs of communications and traffic flows. As a pattern of settlement space, the multinucleated metropolitan region organizes social life into multiple centers and segregated settlement spaces spreading across an extensive metropolitan region. Both population deconcentration and deindustrialization have helped transform metropolitan areas into polycentric regions that contain a diversity of economic and cultural activities, agglomeration patterns, and socio-spatial hierarchies. Overall, the multinucleated spatial formation has become the focus of urban studies in North America, Europe, and Japan. A variety of terms have been used interchangeably with the term multinucleated metropolitan region: the multicentered metropolitan region, the multimodal metropolitan area, the polycentric urban region, and the polynucleated urban field.

More recently, scholars have used the concept *exurbanization* to refer to a form of residential development that straddles an often ill-defined zone between densely packed suburbs and rural and small town locations. Although its boundaries are usually indistinct, exurban development begins somewhere beyond the sprawling suburbs and lies outside easy commuting distance to the central city. At its far reaches, exurbia does not so much end as blend into the surrounding agricultural countryside. Residents of exurbia occupy an uneasy middle ground between the perceived ills of the city and adjoining suburbs and rural places where it is believed that people live in harmony with the bucolic rural landscape. In her book *Building Suburbia*, Dolores Hayden (2003) develops a three-way classification of exurban development: reluctant suburbs, hot towns, and Valhallas. Reluctant suburbs are rural towns that often find themselves overwhelmed by population growth. Hot towns are affluent locations that attract telecommuters, sometimes termed "Lone Eagles." In Valhallas, places that are located in environmentally attractive areas become exclusive communities with access to nature's bounty restricted to those with the income needed to breach the gates of closed, high-security enclaves. Joel Garreau's (1991) fashionable term "edge cities" draws attention to the proliferation of satellite business and retail centers that now characterize the freeway interchanges on the fringes of metropolitan areas.

Urbanization in Less Developed Countries

One dominant trend in less developed countries is the formation of gigantic cities or primate cities that are disproportionately large in terms of population size relative to other cities contained within a given geographically bounded area, such as a region or a nation. Many scholars define urban primacy at the national level. Studies have shown that, in general, higher-income countries tend to have city-size distributions that are closer to the rank-size rule than lower-income countries, and in many of the latter, abnormally large primate cities are not unusual (Timberlake 1985). For example, Bangkok in Thailand is many times larger than the second largest city in the country, and Mexico City is nearly nine times more populous than Guadalajara. London and Paris, however, are also significantly larger than the rank-size rule would predict. Nevertheless, most cases of extreme urban primacy are in less developed countries rather than in wealthy, core countries. While cities such as Mexico City, Seoul, Jakarta, and Bangkok have grown recently to rival or exceed those in the developed world, interior regions remain relatively under-urbanized. China is an exception: its 12 largest cities have a combined population of over 111 million. As a result of rapid growth, many such cities face formidable economic, social, and ecological problems. In Mumbai (Bombay), where population density often exceeds 1 million people per square mile, people cluster in very compact living quarters without adequate food, water, health care, or education. São Paulo has been described as a "colossus" (its population approaches 20 million) where "every notion about planning and architecture evaporates" and "every municipal organization is powerless against the proliferation of the city" (Nijenhuis & De Vriers 2000).

Overall, scholars view abnormally large primate cities as symptomatic of a poorly integrated national or regional economy, one in which developmental advances in the primate city lack mechanisms to benefit the country or region. Interestingly, while early work by Hawley (1981) argued that primate cities perform "key functions" for the reproduction of society, other scholars argued that primate cities are "parasites" that siphon socio-economic resources from the rest of the country and generate little benefit in return (for an overview, see Timberlake 1985).

Scholars have suggested several explanations for the emergence and development of primate cities. One theory argues that urban primate growth is due to state policies that encourage disinvestment in rural areas and promote investment in cities, especially the largest and fastest-growing city in the country. Thus the largest city in the country, often the capital city, receives a disproportionate share of central government expenditures for social and economic infrastructure. Investment results in greater opportunities for employment, housing, education, and health care, thereby making these cities more attractive destinations for rural migrants. This understanding emphasizes the role of demographic factors in sustaining the primate city, and relates urban primacy to the broader phenomenon of "hyperurbanization" or "overurbanization."

Other scholars have suggested that the primate city is often a socio-spatial outcome of internal social and political inequality, particularly in countries in which geographically distinct ethnic groups compete for economic opportunity and access to political power. The dominant ethnic groups typically implement policies that favor "their" region and the leading city therein. A third explanation identifies the primate city as a historical vestige of past colonialism that exploited the people and natural resources of the country and region. Many scholars note that primate cities have often been the administrative headquarters of a former colonial power, maintaining, after independence, stronger ties with the former imperial country than with their own national hinterland. A fourth explanation, popular among dependency theorists, contends that primate cities are structural linchpins in a global network whereby asymmetrical forms of wealth flow out of former colonies or neocolonies back to the "metropole," thus contributing to the "development of underdevelopment" (Frank 1967; Timberlake 1985; Cohen 2003).

CONTEMPORARY URBANIZATION TRENDS: MEGA-CITIES AND GLOBAL CITIES

Today, over half the world's population live in urban areas and the number of mega-cities – metropolitan areas with a population of more than 10 million people – has grown from one in 1950 to more than 25 today. The huge scale of mega-cities presents us with new complexities, new dynamics, new opportunities, and new socio-economic, physical, and environmental problems. On the one hand, mega-cities express intense and complex interactions between different demographic, social, political, economic, and ecological processes. On the other hand, inadequate education and health-care systems, inefficient transportation systems, high concentrations of industrial production, ecological devastation, unregulated land development, lack of affordable housing development, and low wages and high poverty are a few of the many social problems that face mega-cities (Davis 2006).

Mega-cities are also major sites and expressions of global risk and disaster vulnerability. Much research has documented the increasing frequency and destructive tendencies of disasters, a development that correlates with increased urbanization thus making mega-cities "crucibles of hazard" (Mitchell 1999). As the United Nations (2009) has recently pointed out, more people than ever live in harm's way, at risk from earthquakes, droughts, floods, and other disasters, largely because of a surge in urban populations in both developing and developed nations. Thus, the pervasiveness and ubiquity of disaster reflects urbanization processes including growing urban poverty and rapid uneven development that can concentrate poverty and increase vulnerability to hazards and catastrophe. In addition, spreading urban development expands the target of vulnerability for hurricanes, earthquakes, and other catastrophes, thus making disasters a major urban problem.

The rise of mega-cities and the attendant socio-spatial transformations have caused researchers to focus attention on the development of *global cities* – i.e., cities that perform commanding roles in a globalizing economic system (Brenner & Keil 2006). Global cities are those urban areas consisting of a disproportionate number of major economic headquarters and services including corporate management, banking, finance, legal services, accounting, technical consulting, telecommunications, computing, international transportation, research, and higher education (Friedmann & Wolff 1982: 320). These cities express the growing extension, intensification, and velocity of global flows and networks of activity through economic globalization. The emergence of global cities signals the shift in the organization of capital accumulation and economic production since the late 1970s and a corresponding shift in the articulation functions of some cities away from local, regional, or national contexts to more varied and uneven connections to other cities and regions in the world.

Extending Immanuel Wallerstein's world systems approach to the study of cities, the global city concept suggests that the continued globalization of economic functions has created an international division of labor among cities and metropolitan areas. According to this view, expounded by John Friedmann, Saskia Sassen, and others, this international division of labor reflects and expresses inequities between core and periphery areas, between transnational elites and low-skilled workers, and between dominant groups and racial minorities. In addition, the international division of labor has led to an expansion of inner-city ghettos, to the development of a dual labor market within world cities, and to excessive rural–urban migration, and periphery–core immigration. In contrast to global city theorists, Richard Child Hill, Kuniko Fujita, and other proponents of the "nested city" hypothesis have asserted that national and local political-economic contexts, rather than global capitalism, remain the decisive factors determining spatial configurations.

Saskia Sassen's (2001) work has provided key empirical data corroborating some of the assertions about an emergent series of pre-eminent global cities as sites of concentrated global economic activity. Friedmann, Sassen, and other proponents of the global cities thesis argue that the emergent urban order is *hierarchical* and *polarized*. A small number of elite cities have become concentrated sites of global capital accumulation and control while inequalities within these cities have become very polarized. This polarization reflects the command-and-control function of global cities. On the one hand, these cities serve as a major locus for those elite organizations and institutions that have been able to attract an 'elite' professional class who are well-educated, footloose, and cosmopolitan in origin and outlook. The concentration of global finance, insurance, and real estate activities in the downtowns of global cities becomes a key driving force in the formation of a corresponding economy of low-waged and low-skilled employment which inadequately fills the void of lost manufacturing and other forms of economic activity. Or as Sassen's work (2001) argues in the cases of London, Tokyo, and New York, the growth in elite professions and services creates the need for a vast supply of low-skilled workers. The formation of this floating mass of migrants, the contemporary "industrial reserve army," in Karl Marx's famous thesis, expresses massive displacements and accelerated flows of people, capital, commodities, and technologies caused by the decline of manufacturing employment and global economic restructuring.

The massive restructurings associated with the rise of mega-cities, global cities, and other urban forms have generated much scholarly interest in theorizing and examining the growing significance of urbanization on the health and well-being of human populations and ecosystems. Scholars have long portrayed urbanization as a major threat to global ecology and biodiversity, causing the elimination of the large majority of native species and impoverishing natural ecosystems (Czech 2005). In their examination of the biodiversity of urban habitats in Birmingham (England), Angold (2006) and colleagues found that cities provide habitats for a rich and diverse range of plants and animals, which sometimes occur in unlikely recombinant communities. Pickett and colleagues' (Pickett, Cadenasso, Grove, et al. 2001) work in Baltimore and other urban areas suggests that cities can support important pools of biodiversity, representing surprisingly large fractions of the regional fauna. Indeed, Wania and colleagues (Wania, Kühn & Klotz 2004) found that native plant diversity was greater in urban than in nearby rural areas in central Germany. In short, scholars disagree over whether urbanization destroys the ecosystems, creates new habitats for diverse species, or can have simultaneous negative and positive effects on the natural environment.

In sum, urbanization is a global trend that is taking place at different speeds on different continents. The pace and degree of urbanization vary by geographic region, level of development, and size of country. Cities face many environmental and ecological problems associated with urbanization including substandard housing, pollution, crime, and overcrowding. At the same time, urbanization offers immense opportunities for economic and institutional innovation and cultural development. Thus, identifying the positive effects and negative consequences of urbanization is contested terrain. Particularly for mega-cities, urbanization anticipates trends with regional and global consequences that are difficult to predict. Large cities are the world's most important consumers of resources and generators of waste. At the same time, they are more and more the engines of national and regional economic growth. Thus, while urban areas present fundamental and pressing challenges to the foundations of ecological, social, and economic development, they carry the promise and the potential to overcome them.

References

Angold, B. (2006) "Biodiversity in Urban Habitat Patches." *Science of the Total Environment* 360: 196–204.

Berry, Brian J. L. (1980) "Urbanization and Counterurbanization in the United States." *Annals of the American Academy of Political and Social Science* 451: 13–20.

Bogue, D. (1953) *Population Growth in Standard Metropolitan Areas, 1900–1950.* Washington, DC: Housing and Home Finance Agency.

Brenner, Neil and Roger Keil (eds.) (2006) *Global Cities Reader.* New York: Routledge.

Brown, D. G., K. M. Johnson, T. R. Loveland, and D. M. Theobald (2005) "Rural Land-Use Trends in the Conterminous United States." *Ecological Applications* 15: 1851–63.

Castells, Manuel (1977) *The Urban Question: A Marxist Approach.* Cambridge, MA: MIT Press.

Chatterton, Paul and Robert Hollands (2003) *Urban Nightscapes: Youth Cultures, Pleasure Spaces, and Corporate Power.* London: Routledge.

Checkoway, Barry (1984) "Large Builders, Federal Housing Programs and Postwar Suburbanization." In William K. Tabb and Larry Sawyers (eds.), *Marxism and the Metropolis: New Perspectives in Urban Political Economy,* 2nd edn. New York: Oxford University Press, pp. 152–73.

Childe, V. Gordon (1950) "The Urban Revolution." *Town Planning Review* 21: 3–17.

Cohen, Barry (2003) "Urban Growth in Developing Countries: A Review of Current Trends and a Caution Regarding Existing Forecasts." *World Development* 32(1): 23–51.

Czech, Brian (2005) "Urbanization as a Threat to Biodiversity: Trophic Theory, Economic Geography, and Implications for Conservation Land Acquisition." In David N. Bengston (ed.), *Policies for Managing Urban Growth and Landscape Change: A Key to Conservation in the 21st Century*. St. Paul, MN: US Department of Agriculture, Forest Service, North Central Research Station.

Davis, Mike (2006) *Planet of Slums*. New York: Verso.

Feagin, Joe (1998) *The New Urban Paradigm*. New York: Rowman and Littlefield.

Frank, Andre Gunder (1967) *Capitalism and Underdevelopment in Latin America*. New York: Monthly Review Press.

Frey, William H., Alan Berube, Audrey Singer and Jill H. Wilson (2009) "Getting Current: Recent Demographic Trends in Metropolitan America." Brookings Research Report, March, Washington, DC.

Friedmann, John and Goetz Wolff (1982) "World City Formation: An Agenda for Research and Action." *International Journal of Urban and Regional Research* 6: 309–44.

Garreau, Joel (1991) *Edge Cities: Life on the New Frontier*. New York: Doubleday.

Gotham, Kevin Fox (ed.) (2001) *Critical Perspectives on Urban Redevelopment*. New York: Elsevier Press.

Gotham, Kevin Fox (2002) *Race, Real Estate, and Uneven Development: The Kansas City Experience, 1900–2000*. Albany, NY: State University of New York Press.

Gottdiener, Mark (1994) *The Social Production of Urban Space*. Austin, TX: University of Texas Press.

Gottdiener, Mark (2001) *Theming of America: Dreams, Visions, and Commercial Spaces*, 2nd edn. Boulder, CO: Westview Press.

Gottdiener, Mark and Joe Feagin (1988) "The Paradigm Shift in Urban Sociology." *Urban Affairs Review* 24(2): 163–87.

Gottmann, Jean (1961) *Megalopolis: The Urbanized Northeastern Seaboard of the United States*. New York: Twentieth Century Fund.

Greenberg, Miriam (2007) *Branding New York: How a City in Crisis Was Sold to the World*. New York: Routledge.

Hannigan, John (1998) *Fantasy City: Pleasure and Profit in the Postmodern Metropolis*. New York: Routledge.

Harris, Fred R. and Roger W. Wilkins (eds.) (1988) *Quiet Riots: Race and Poverty in the United States. The Kerner Report Twenty Years Later*. New York: Pantheon.

Harvey, David (1973) *Social Justice and the City*. London: Edward Arnold.

Hawley, Amos (1981) *Urban Society: An Ecological Approach*, 2nd edn. New York: Ronald.

Hayden, D. (2003) *Building Suburbia*. New York: Pantheon Books.

Hoffman, Lily M., Susan S. Fainstein, and Dennis R. Judd (eds.) (2003) *Cities and Visitors: Regulating People, Markets, and City Space*. New York: Blackwell.

Jonas, Andrew and David Wilson (eds.) (1999) *The Urban Growth Machine: Critical Perspectives Two Decades Later*. Albany, NY: State University of New York Press.

Lefebvre, Henri ([1970] 2003) *The Urban Revolution*. Trans. Robert Bononno. Minneapolis: University of Minnesota Press.

Lefebvre, Henri (1991) *The Production of Space*. New York: Routledge.

Logan, John and Harvey Molotch (1987) *Urban Fortunes: The Political Economy of Place*. Berkeley, CA: University of California Press.

Mitchell, James (ed.) (1999) *Crucibles of Hazard: Mega-Cities and Disasters in Transition*. New York: United Nations University Press.

Mumford, Lewis (1961) *The City in History: Its Origins, Its Transformations, and Its Prospects*. New York: Random House.

Nijenhuis, W. and N. De Vries (2000) *Eating Brazil*. Rotterdam: 010 Uitgeverij Publishers.

Pickett, S. T. A., M. L. Cadenasso, J. M. Grove, C. H. Nilon, R. V. Pouyat, W. C. Zipperer, and R. Costanza (2001) "Urban Ecological Systems: Linking Terrestrial, Ecological, Physical, and Socioeconomic Components of Metropolitan Areas." *Annual Review of Ecological Systems* 32: 127–57.

Rowe, Peter (1995) *Modernity and Housing*. Cambridge, MA: MIT Press.

Sassen, Saskia (2001) *The Global City: New York, London, Tokyo*. Princeton, NJ: Princeton University Press.

Simmel, Georg ([1903] 1950) "Metropolis and Mental Life." Trans. and ed. D. Weinstein. In Kurt Wolff, *The Sociology of Georg Simmel*. New York: Free Press, pp. 409–42.

Timberlake, Michael (ed.) (1985) *Urbanization in the World-Economy*. Orlando, FL: Academic Press.

United Nations International Strategy for Disaster Reduction (UNISDR) (2009) *Global Assessment Report on Disaster Risk Reduction*. Geneva: United Nations.

United Nations Population Division (2009) *World Urbanization Prospects: The 2007 Revision Population Database*. http://esa.un.org/unup/index.asp (accessed September 28, 2009).

Wania, A., I. Kühn, and S. Klotz (2004) "Plant Richness Patterns in Agricultural and Urban Landscapes in Central Germany – Spatial Gradients of Species Richness." *Landscape and Urban Planning* 75: 97–110.

Weber, Max (1958) *The City*. Trans. and ed. Don Martindale and Gertrud Neuwirth. New York: Free Press.

Weiss, Marc A. (1987) *Rise of the Community Builders: The American Real Estate Industry and Urban Land Planning*. New York: Columbia University Press.

27

Environmental Sociology

Richard York and Riley E. Dunlap

Although all societies have had impacts on the natural environment, modern societies have proven particularly prone to generating environmental problems on a large and ever-growing scale. The result is that we are now facing global-level problems of potentially catastrophic magnitude. It has become common in the twenty-first century to acknowledge the existence of human-generated (or anthropogenic) environmental problems. However, it is important to recognize that not long ago, particularly in the mid-twentieth century, there was pervasive exuberance in the United States that led the general public, politicians, and scholars alike to believe that modern societies had overcome natural constraints and that societies would "progress" into a continually brighter future free from the scarcity that had beset societies in the past (Catton & Dunlap 1980).

The discipline of sociology suffered from the same ecological blinders that characterized society in general. Early sociologists commonly made efforts to distance sociology from the natural sciences, insisting that social facts were principally explained by other social facts rather than by biological and physical phenomena. Over the course of the twentieth century, most sociologists largely ignored the natural environment, embracing a "human exemptionalism" viewpoint that implicitly (and sometimes explicitly) denied that modern societies were substantially influenced by their biophysical context. This began to change in the 1970s following rising concern among natural scientists, policy-makers, and the general public about pollution and other environmental problems, and particularly after the 1973 energy crisis which highlighted societies' dependence on natural resources (Catton & Dunlap 1980).

The Wiley-Blackwell Companion to Sociology, First Edition. Edited by George Ritzer.
© 2012 Blackwell Publishing Ltd. Published 2012 by Blackwell Publishing Ltd.

The year 1976 saw the founding of the Section on Environmental Sociology (subsequently renamed the "Section on Environment and Technology") of the American Sociological Association, marking the field's formal debut in the discipline. However, what some consider the field's founding statement came two years later with Catton and Dunlap's (1978) argument that environmental sociology represented a new paradigm in that it challenged the larger discipline's anthropocentric orientation by recognizing that all societies are fundamentally embedded in and dependent on the natural environment. Not only was environmental sociology defined as the study of societal-environmental interactions, but it was portrayed as having the potential to transform the larger discipline by infusing it with insights from ecology (Dunlap & Catton 1979; Catton & Dunlap 1980). While sociology has to some degree shed its exemptionalist orientation,[1] it continues to give environmental problems limited attention. Nonetheless, environmental sociology is now firmly established as a field of inquiry, the empirical examination of societal-environmental interactions is commonplace, and this research is being published in core disciplinary journals.

Environmental sociology has come to be sufficiently large and diverse, particularly as it has taken root internationally, that its contents cannot be easily summarized. In this chapter we cover some of the main research emphases and related theoretical debates that have been and are currently central to the field. We begin by examining the divide between realist and constructivist perspectives on environmental problems and how these perspectives have evolved. Then we examine debates over the causes of environmental problems, the social impacts of these problems, and potential solutions to them.

FROM CONSTRUCTIVISM AND REALISM TO AGNOSTICISM AND PRAGMATISM

Historically, the divide between social-constructivist and realist perspectives on environmental problems has been a fundamental schism within environmental sociology. Although this divide is common in many fields of sociology, it has been particularly prominent in environmental sociology. This is because a *strong* constructivist position essentially denies the materialistic foundation of the field – environmental problems are real and pose challenges for human societies – and replaces it with the view that such "problems" are contingent upon human knowledge and beliefs which are constructed through social processes, rather than reflecting objective biophysical conditions (Dunlap & Catton 1994; Murphy 1997). However, although some advocates of social constructivism seemed to question the reality of environmental problems (Macnaghten & Urry 1998), most constructivists have come to adopt moderate forms that do not deny the material existence of environmental problems but simply emphasize the processes by which they are socially constructed and contested (Burningham & Cooper 1999; Yearley 2005).

In addition, after early constructivist analyses of issues like anthropogenic climate change came under criticism for emphasizing that such problems remained "highly contested" while ignoring the powerful interests behind such contestation (Dunlap & Catton 1994), a body of realist-constructivist work has begun to emerge that analyzes the efforts of corporations and the conservative movement to manipulate societal perceptions and deny the severity of environmental problems. This work seeks to shed light on the efforts of those attempting to "deconstruct" such problems (McCright & Dunlap 2000, 2003; Freudenburg, Gramling & Davidson 2008; Bell & York 2010; Dunlap & McCright 2010; McCright & Dunlap 2010). Currently, most environmental sociologists appear to appreciate the importance of both constructivist and realist perspectives and possibilities for integrating them (Rosa 1998; Carolan 2005; Hannigan 2006; Foster & Clark 2008; York & Clark 2010).

More recently, the constructivist/realist divide in environmental sociology has evolved into a related but broader pair of stances termed "agnosticism" and "pragmatism" based on analysts' treatment of environmental conditions in their research (Dunlap 2010). Specifically, those adopting an agnostic stance (particularly prevalent among but not confined to European scholars) toward environmental problems are reluctant to employ scientific indicators of these phenomena, preferring instead to problematize, contextualize, and sometimes deconstruct scientific evidence regarding issues such as anthropogenic climate change (Wynne 2010). Their analyses offer valuable insights into the complexities and contingencies of climate science, but because they are hesitant about granting ontological standing to the claims of climate scientists they avoid examining the causes and likely impacts of rising greenhouse gas emissions (Yearley 2009).

In contrast, the pragmatic approach, which is popular with American scholars, employs scientific data on a wide range of environmental conditions (carbon dioxide and other greenhouse gas emissions, deforestation, fisheries' yields, toxic wastes, etc.) in empirical analyses to investigate their relationships with an array of social phenomena. While many of these analyses of societal-environmental interactions involve rigorous statistical analyses of large, quantitative data sets (see Dunlap 2010 and below for examples), pragmatists also perform more qualitative, in-depth case studies that provide rich insights into the evolution of such interactions over long periods of time (Freudenburg & Gramling 1994; Freudenburg, Gramling, Laska & Erikson 2009; Murphy 2009; Bell & York 2010).

The agnosticism about the state of environmental conditions which has roots in the postmodernist turn of the larger discipline and the popularity of constructivist analyses within environmental sociology so prevalent in the 1990s continues to have pervasive effects on sociological theorizing about societal-environmental interactions. This seems particularly true among European scholars, where even theorists of an ostensibly realist bent have taken agnostic positions toward the utility of scientific epistemology for the study of environmental phenomena. Most notably, proponents of ecological modernization theory (the substance of which we will discuss in a subsequent section) have come to advocate skepticism toward rigorous empirical analyses of environmental conditions in favor of methods that are more interpretive and subjective. Leading ecological modernization theorists Mol and Spaargaren, for example, declare "the limitations of empirical studies in closing larger theoretical debates" (2005: 94–5) and largely reject the use of empirical methods and hypothesis testing in analyses of the environmental consequences of modernization. They further question the validity of using "natural science 'empirical facts'" and mathematics to assess socially generated environmental problems (Mol & Spaargaren 2004: 262). This ambivalence toward scientific data has even led Mol and Spaargaren to declare "the irrelevance of 'more' or 'less'" (2004: 261) regarding the scale of production and consumption, countering the eminently realist recognition of ecological limits.

Such a stance (by no means unique to Mol and Spaargaren) is at odds with the large and growing body of research that analyzes in empirically rigorous fashion alternative theoretical explanations of the driving forces of environmental degradation (e.g., York, Rosa & Dietz 2003) and mechanisms of environmental reform (e.g., Roberts, Parks & Vasquez 2004). While empirically oriented pragmatists within environmental sociology can benefit from the cautions raised by agnostics concerning the pitfalls of employing imperfect data on environmental conditions, the broader gulf between the two "camps" concerning the utility of empirical evidence for adjudicating debates between theoretical perspectives clearly poses a challenge for the field.

ANTHROPOGENIC CAUSES OF ENVIRONMENTAL PROBLEMS

Perhaps the most fundamental and important justification for environmental sociology is that, at base, environmental problems are *social* problems in that they are caused by humans and have effects on humans (Dunlap & Marshall 2007). Clearly the natural sciences are essential for understanding what is happening in the natural world, but it is not the natural sciences that hold the key to explaining the social processes that lead to resource consumption and pollution emissions. When we discuss environmental problems, it is typically implicit that we mean *anthropogenic* conditions. Thus, it is clear that we need to understand the social processes affecting the types and scale of environmental problems that societies create. A major focus of environmental sociology, particularly in the United States, has been to assess the driving forces behind environmental degradation. Although there is a considerable diversity of views about the forces that lead to degradation of the environment, two major perspectives stand out: human ecology and Marxian political economy.

The human ecological perspective was at the heart of the founding of environmental sociology, as exemplified in the works of Catton and Dunlap (1978, 1980; Catton 1980).[2] This perspective represented a new version of human ecology by breaking from the human exemptionalism and neglect of the biophysical environment that had come to characterize mainstream sociological human ecology in the 1970s (Dunlap & Catton 1979, 1983). The "new human ecologists," as Buttel (1987) termed them, drew upon the work of ecologists in the natural sciences to emphasize the importance of environmental problems and identify the basic material conditions of societies – particularly their demographic features (e.g., population size and growth), scale of production and consumption, and mode of production (e.g., technology) – as the fundamental forces creating them.

This tradition has evolved into an extensive literature of quantitative cross-national research examining the effects of population, affluence, and technology on the environment, most notably based on the STIRPAT model developed by Dietz and Rosa (1994, 1997). STIRPAT is a stochastic version of the venerable I=PAT model (environmental Impacts are a multiplicative function of Population size, Affluence [per capita consumption or production], and Technology [the impact per unit of production or consumption]) which allows for hypothesis testing and is amenable to the addition of other causal forces and non-linear specification. STIRPAT has been used to analyze a variety of environmental impacts, including ecological footprints, carbon dioxide emissions, methane emissions, sulfur dioxide emissions, CFC emissions, fertilizer consumption, and pesticide use (York, Rosa & Dietz 2003; Cole & Neumayer 2004; Rosa, York & Dietz 2004; Longo & York 2008; York 2008b). The findings from this research program have consistently provided support for the fundamental arguments of human ecologists, showing that population and affluence (as typically measured by GDP per capita) are the primary driving forces behind environmental degradation, at least at the national level.

The Marxian political economy perspective was also represented in environmental sociology early on, and in many ways is complementary to the human ecological perspective (York & Mancus 2009). Schnaiberg's (1980) foundational book, *The Environment: From Surplus to Scarcity*, laid out the argument that there was a "treadmill of production" that drove modern industrialized economies, particularly capitalist ones, to endlessly expand production, so as to generate more profits for producers (see also Schnaiberg & Gould 1994).[3] The "treadmill" refers to the pattern whereby the profit-seeking of producers creates job losses due to technological innovation, as mechanization means that fewer workers are needed per unit of production, but these innovations entail higher levels of resource consumption and pollution – generating environmental degradation as well as unemployment. The "solution" to these problems in treadmill-dominated societies is typically to further expand production so as to create jobs and provide more money for government (via taxes on both workers and employers) to clean up the escalating environmental problems as well as to provide necessary social services for workers. But this further expansion, in turn, generates another round of mechanization, unemployment, and environmental degradation – hence the analogy of the treadmill, where one keeps moving yet stays in the same place.

O'Connor's (1988, 1991) second contradiction of capitalism thesis makes an argument similar to that of Schnaiberg's treadmill of production, in that it stresses the problems and contradictions inherent in the escalation of production in capitalist systems. The second contradiction thesis argues that increasing the scale of production increases the costs of production and expands environmental problems. This happens because initially natural resources are extracted that are of the highest quality and closest to the sites of production, but as these are depleted, further expansion of production requires accessing lower-quality resources (e.g., shifting from old-growth timber to new-growth, or high-concentration mineral ores to low-concentration ones) and/or those farther from the sites of production (e.g., extracting resources from "less developed" countries, or drilling for oil in the Arctic or deep seas). Thus, both the treadmill and the second contradiction emphasize the fundamentally unsustainable nature of economic growth.

One of the more active areas of theorizing in Marxian analyses of environmental problems over the past decade has centered on developing the implications of Marx's own theory of "metabolic rift," as explicated and elaborated by Foster (1999, 2000). As Foster has explained, a central feature of Marx's materialism was his recognition that all societies are dependent on a metabolic interaction with the natural world. Marx saw an emerging ecological crisis stemming from the degradation of soil driven by the exploitative practices of capitalist agriculture, which served to rob the soil as it did the workers in order to maximize profits. In particular, Marx argued that rapid urbanization driven by capitalist-industrial development separated people from the land, creating a rift in the metabolic exchange between people and nature that had typically sustained the soils in pre-industrial times. Whereas in pre-urbanized societies nutrients taken from the land in agricultural production were recycled back into the soil, in urbanized societies these nutrients were shipped to the city, in the form of food and fiber, where they became a waste problem. Instead of enriching the soil, waste in cities went into sewers or to dumps, subsequently polluting rivers and streams. Thus, Marx saw the emerging capitalist urban-industrial society as fundamentally unsustainable, which is one of the reasons he advocated a more even distribution of people across the landscape.

One important aspect of what Foster (1999, 2000), in developing the theory of metabolic rift, brings to Marxian political economy is an appreciation for the qualitative aspects of the environmental crisis. Whereas Schnaiberg's treadmill of production and O'Connor's second contradiction thesis emphasized the quantitative aspect of environmental impacts – the *scale* of production and consumption and the attendant quantity of withdrawals from and additions to the environment – Foster's metabolic rift emphasizes qualitative aspects of how the system of production and consumption is organized with respect to ecological processes. The metabolic rift theory highlights how societal-environmental relationships can be unsustainable even before they push up against limits of scale.

Foster's work has inspired others to generalize the metabolic rift thesis, using its conceptual apparatus to examine the global carbon cycle and climate change (Clark & York 2005), the oceanic crisis stemming from degradation of fisheries (Clausen & Clark 2005), and the nitrogen cycle (Mancus 2007), among other applications (e.g., Moore 2000; Dickens 2004). Metabolic rift and the treadmill of production are complementary perspectives, each highlighting different ways in which modern societies contribute to environmental degradation. Along with O'Connor's second contradiction thesis, they emphasize that capitalism has inherently unsustainable features.

Researchers examining the political economy of the world-system have also made important contributions to analyses of environmental problems (Roberts & Grimes 2002), producing a substantial and growing literature using increasingly sophisticated quantitative methods to assess the effects of various world-system factors on environmental conditions. For example, Jorgenson and Clark's (2009) analysis, using time-series data, of factors influencing national ecological footprints illustrates how the modern world-system structures a dynamic of ecologically unequal exchange: core nations consume the bulk of natural resources in the world and produce the greatest pollution, but most of the environmental impacts associated with this exploitation of nature occur in peripheral and semi-peripheral nations. This work builds on a tradition that has highlighted a variety of unequal exchanges in the global economy, such as the export of hazardous waste to the global periphery (Frey 1998) and the manner in which foreign direct investment in non-core nations often leads to environmentally destructive practices (Kentor & Grimes 2006; Jorgenson & Kuykendall 2008; Jorgenson 2009).

In addition to quantitative research, there is also a well-established tradition of historical analysis grounded in the world-systems perspective which aims to assess how environmental crises have emerged at different times and places and how these crises are related to specific political and economic conditions. Bunker (1984) presents a classic study in this tradition, showing how over the centuries the Brazilian Amazon was used as a source of raw materials for the world economy, creating wealth for those in core nations while locals gained little from the natural richness of the region. Taking a broader perspective, Moore (2000, 2003), who draws on metabolic rift theory, has analyzed the ecological regime that emerged as part of the rise of capitalism from the fifteenth century to the present, showing both the generally destructive nature of capitalism from its origins and the specific ways in which this has played out at different times and places. Examining an even more sweeping scope of time, Chew (2001) investigates how the dynamics of ancient world-systems led to unsustainable exploitation of the environment, often contributing to the decline of civilizations. This historical tradition adds important depth to contemporary debates over environmental crises, showing that the factors leading to environmental degradation are not entirely unique to modern societies.

SOCIAL IMPACTS OF ENVIRONMENTAL PROBLEMS

Changes in environmental conditions become identified as "problems" typically because of their impacts on human societies, and these impacts are another major focus of environmental sociology (Dunlap & Marshall 2007). A particular interest of environmental sociologists has been in assessing how social impacts are distributed unequally across various sectors of society, especially in terms of race and class (Brulle & Pellow 2006; Mohai, Pellow & Roberts 2009). Research in this area was spurred by a famous report by the United Church of Christ's Commission for Racial Justice (1987) which found pervasive evidence of minorities being disproportionately exposed to environmental hazards. Following this report an extensive literature on environmental justice developed, and case studies of environmental inequities have been an important part of this literature. A foundational work in this tradition is Bullard's (1990) *Dumping in Dixie*, which documented how waste storage and hazardous facilities frequently are located in areas where there are a high proportion of low-income and minority residents. Likewise, Roberts and Toffolon-Weiss (2001) and Pellow (2002) found minorities and the poor to be more likely to live in proximity to hazardous sites. More recently, Taylor (2009) has shown a long history of environmental injustice in American cities, where minorities and the poor frequently experience the worst aspects of environmental problems.

There has also been a great deal of quantitative research aimed at assessing the extent to which hazardous or other undesirable facilities are likely to be spatially associated with minority and low-income neighborhoods. Although some early work suggested that the location of hazardous facilities was not race- or class-based (Anderton, Anderson, Oakes & Fraser 1994), a substantial body of subsequent work has found that the race and class characteristics of neighborhoods are associated with the likelihood of close proximity to hazardous facilities (Brulle & Pellow 2006; Mohai, Pellow & Roberts 2009). This area of research has long been characterized by debates over methodology, particularly regarding how proximity to hazardous facilities should be measured, but has become increasingly refined with the application of geographic information systems (GIS) data (Downey 2006a). Researchers using GIS data have shown that, in addition to the location of hazardous facilities (Downey 2006b), vulnerability to heat exposure, stemming in part from the urban heat island effect, is also connected with race and class (Harlan, Brazel, Prashad, et al. 2006; Harlan, Brazel, Jenerette, et al. 2008; see also Zahran, Brody, Vedlitz, Grover & Miller 2008).

Work on environmental justice/inequalities has taken many forms, and there is no single theoretical perspective uniting it. However, there are some important efforts to give unity to this field. Taylor's (2000) environmental justice paradigm represents a noteworthy effort to give a larger framing to research in this area, recognizing the ecological embeddedness of societies as well as the social inequality that is rife in the modern world. Thus, Taylor argues that environmental justice is not simply a topic of research or a distinct area of theorization, but, rather, represents novel paradigmatic elements. Focusing on theory, rather than paradigms, Pellow's (2000) theory of environmental inequality formation explains how environmental inequities have multiple sources that play out over time and in diverse dimensions. This important work helps move beyond some of the simpler debates over whether race or class is "more" important, helping clarify how different forces operating at differing places and times have led to a variety of inequalities in the present.

Related to research on inequalities, sociologists have shown how environmentally destructive practices undermine overall community cohesion and generate an array of social problems (Freudenburg 1997). For example, a longstanding research project following the *Exxon Valdez* oil spill in Prince William Sound in 1989 has shown dramatic impacts on communities in the area, stemming in part from the high levels of stress generated by the accident, the subsequent economic decline, and the drawn-out litigation process (Gill & Picou 1998; Picou, Marshall & Gill 2004). Similarly, Bell's (2009) research on coal-mining communities in southern West Virginia found that the coal industry, by generating conflicts over environmental degradation and union loyalties and by cutting jobs (all of which are connected to the shift to the more mechanized and more environmentally destructive practice of mountain-top-removal mining), undermined social capital in the region, creating widespread emotional distress among residents and breaking down social ties.

THE WAY FORWARD: SOLUTIONS

How to address environmental problems and transform societies so that they do not consume resources and degrade the environment at unsustainable levels is a central question of our times. Based on the theories and research discussed earlier on causes of environmental problems, certain major issues stand out. Curtailing both economic and population growth appears to be the combined prescription of human ecologists and Marxian-oriented political economists. It is clear that capitalist-industrialization over the past two centuries has generated environmental problems on a scale and of a kind not previously seen in human history (Antonio

2009). Political economists suggest that in order to overcome the modern environmental crisis, societies need to halt the treadmill of production and the demand for endless growth of private profits, and move to an economy that provides for human needs. This would require a fundamental change in the structure of the global economy and a move to something along the lines of Daly's (1991) vision of a steady-state economy, one not based on endless growth (see also Schor 2010). However, efforts to achieve such a change face extraordinary political barriers, and many believe that it is simply not possible to so fundamentally alter the structure of the modern world.

Offering an alternative perspective to the founding traditions in the field, ecological modernization theory – which aimed to study environmental reform rather than the causes of environmental degradation *per se* – emerged in environmental sociology in the 1990s (Spaargaren & Mol 1992) as a counter to many of the arguments made by human ecologists and those in the political economy tradition. Ecological modernization theorists claim that it is neither possible nor desirable to abandon the capitalist-driven modernization project, and that further modernization holds the potential to overcome the ecological challenges created in its earlier phases (Mol 1995, 2001). They argue that a central feature of modernity is a percolation of rationality into all aspects of life, and that in the contemporary world an ecological rationality is emerging that will reform the institutions of modernity from within, without requiring radical social or economic change. Mol notes that "ecological modernization theory identifies modern science and technology as central institutions for ecological reform (and not in the first place as the culprits of ecological and social disruption)" (1996: 313).[4]

Despite the bold claims of ecological modernization theorists, systematic analyses have generally failed to confirm their assertion that the modernization process yields an overall amelioration of environmental problems. As York and Rosa (2003) have noted, evidence of ecological modernization relies heavily on case studies (Mol 1995, 2001; Mol, Sonnefeld & Spaargaren 2009), which are prone to highlighting particular instances of reform, but which do not address the general claim that improvement in environmental conditions is a consequence of modernization. Rigorous quantitative empirical work finds that societal modernization, as typically measured by GDP per capita, urbanization, and measures of connectedness to the global economy, consistently escalates a substantial variety of environmental problems such as greenhouse gas emissions and total resource consumption (York, Rosa & Dietz 2003; Rosa, York & Dietz 2004; York 2008b; Jorgenson & Clark 2009).

In fact, apparent cases of ecological reform in affluent nations often occur because polluting industries and resource extraction are shifted to poor nations through unequal exchange relationships, not because affluent nations actually reduce the demands they place on the environment (York & Rosa 2003; Jorgenson & Clark 2009; Dunlap 2010). The focus of ecological modernization theory on the production process in modernized nations has often made it blind to the overall scale of resource consumption and the environmental impacts that are spread around the world to meet the demands of the affluent (York & Rosa 2003; Carolan 2004). Thus, the evidence to date does not suggest that further modernization is likely to lead to improved environmental conditions, particularly at the global level. Furthermore, the continued weakening of environmental regulations and assaults on environmental science begun in the United States under the Reagan administration – reflecting the success of the Right in promoting an anti-environmental agenda – suggest that the world's most influential nation and continuing impediment to international climate policy-making may be undergoing a process of distinctly *unecological* modernization (Dunlap & Marshall 2007: 339; McCright & Dunlap 2010).

Others have suggested that the emergence of a world polity based on the principles of civil society, where environmental protection is seen as a key obligation of the nation-state, is helping to bring about ecological improvements around the world (Frank, Hironaka & Schofer 2000). Empirical cross-national research has found some support for this proposition (Schofer & Hironaka 2005), but it also affirms the ecologically destructive role played by unequal exchange in the current world-system (Jorgenson 2009; Shandra, Leckband, McKinney & London 2009). Therefore, it seems unlikely that the rise of international institutions aimed at curtailing environmental problems will make a substantial dent in our current ecological crises, unless more fundamental changes are made in the global economic system.

One of the emerging areas in environmental sociology is an assessment of the effects of women's status and gender inequality on environmental policy. Even though there is a body of theorizing and research about connections between environmental crises and gender relationships outside of environmental sociology (Merchant 1980; Shiva 1989; Rocheleau, Thomas-Slayter & Wangari 1996), there is only a limited amount of work in the field (Dunaway & Macabuac 2007; Salleh 2009), pointing to an important lacuna to be addressed by future research. Recently, cross-national research has begun to assess the extent to which women's status affects national support for environmental policies, with initial indications being that support for environmental protection is higher in nations where women have greater political status than in nations where they have low status, even controlling for a variety of indicators of "development" and "modernization" (Norgaard & York 2005; Nugent & Shandra 2009). There is also a growing body of research finding that women express more concern over environmental problems and risks than do men (Stern, Dietz & Kalof 1993; Davidson & Freudenburg 1996; McCright 2010). Taken together, these studies suggest that improving the status of women may benefit efforts to address environmental problems.

There has been a gradual rise of research on anti-consumerism and voluntary simplicity movements which explores how people are making efforts to move away from environmentally destructive lifestyles (Hinton & Goodman 2010; Schor 2010). For example, Zavestoski (2002) has examined anti-consumption attitudes among practitioners of voluntary simplicity, while Ergas (2010) has studied the ecovillage movement and examined how the members of one ecovillage work to live in a way that does not contribute to the ecological destruction associated with the larger global economy. More micro-level research such as this is an important complement to the macro-level focus of the Marxian political economy theories, which examine the larger contradictions of capitalism but which do not investigate in detail the changes in the everyday lives of people that will be necessitated by a transformation of the treadmill of production.

The anti-consumerism and political economy literatures collectively point to the need to re-envision the meaning of "develop," "wealth," "standard of living," and other concepts used in evaluating societies. Important efforts to reorient how social "progress" is measured are being made by a variety of scholars and activist organizations, two of which are particularly noteworthy. Redefining Progress aims to replace the standard measure of economic development – the gross domestic product (GDP) – with an alternative measure – the Genuine Progress Indicator (GPI) – which takes into account the damage caused to the environment by industry, the costs of crime, the value of unpaid labor, and other factors that the GDP neglects (Talberth, Cobb & Slattery 2007).

In the same spirit, the New Economics Foundation (2009) has developed the "happy planet index" which uses as its measure of societal well-being the degree to which nations produce happiness (as indicated by surveys of people's subjective self-assessment), and life expectancy relative to per capita ecological footprint. Societies in which people are happy and live long, while having a relatively small impact on the environment (such as Costa Rica, Jamaica, and Cuba), are considered to be doing well, whereas societies which have a large impact on the environment without having proportionately high levels of happiness and life expectancy (e.g., the United States and the United Arab Emirates) are not. These findings clearly challenge the widespread assumption that traditional patterns of economic growth are necessary for personal and societal well-being, and suggest the need for imagining alternative and more ecologically sustainable futures.

CONCLUSION

In the 35 years since its formal birth via the ASA Section, environmental sociology has come a long way. The Section is prospering, as is the International Sociological Association's Research Committee on Environment and Society (formally established in 1994), reflecting the rapid and successful internationalization of the field. Numerous environmental sociology texts have been published in several nations, and in the United States courses in the field have become commonplace and a growing number of positions are advertised for faculty who can teach them. But perhaps most importantly, the field has made considerable progress intellectually, as work by environmental sociologists is regularly published (and cited) in core, and increasingly in elite, journals in the discipline.

The growth and internationalization of environmental sociology, along with trends in the larger discipline, have generated differing approaches and major debates within the field, reflecting both its growing diversity and intellectual vitality. One finds within environmental sociology not only constructivism and realism, but agnostic versus pragmatic approaches to the use of environmental data – which in turn is related to the employment of qualitative and quantitative methods. Add in micro-level and macro-level (up to the world-system) foci, and differing approaches stemming from the varying sociological traditions in different regions of the world, and it becomes clear why the field is now far more diverse than in its early days (Dunlap 2010).

Yet, the key concerns of understanding the causes, impacts, and potential solutions of environmental problems remain central to the field, and our review has highlighted major research trends and methodological/theoretical divides on these core topics. The two most significant divisions occur over the utility of scientific data on environmental phenomena in empirical analyses and the (in)ability of ecological modernization processes to halt mounting ecological degradation at the global level. Debates over these two fundamental and interrelated issues will likely continue for some time.

It is apparent that environmental challenges such as climate change raise fundamental questions for the entire discipline of sociology, such as the necessity of and potential for altering the trajectory of economic growth endemic to industrialized capitalism and the possibilities of creating alternative forms of social and economic organization that are both economically and ecologically sustainable. If environmental sociology can help lead the way in addressing such questions it will enhance its standing in the larger discipline, and more importantly in society at large.

Notes

1 For a retrospective examination and clarification of Catton and Dunlap's plea for sociology to replace its "human exemptionalism paradigm" with a more ecologically sound one, and an assessment of disciplinary progress in overcoming exemptionalist thinking, see Dunlap (2002).

2 See the symposium on the foundational work of Catton and Dunlap in the journal *Organization and Environment* (York 2008a).

3 See the two special issues of the journal *Organization and Environment* focusing on the treadmill of production (Foster & York 2004; York & Foster 2005).

4 This is somewhat ironic, since, as noted above, ecological modernization theorists are critical of scientific methods when applied to analyses of the social drivers of environmentally negative consequences of modernity. Thus, ecological modernization theorists contradictorily question whether scientific methodology should be used for analyzing the causes and severity of environmental problems while claiming that techno-science can help us overcome the modern environmental crisis.

References

Anderton, Douglas L., Andy B. Anderson, John Michael Oakes, and Michael R. Fraser (1994) "Environmental Equity: The Demographics of Dumping." *Demography* 31: 229–48.

Antonio, Robert (2009) "Climate Change, the Resource Crunch, and the Global Growth Imperative." *Current Perspectives in Social Theory* 26: 3–73.

Bell, Shannon Elizabeth (2009) "'There Ain't No Bond in Town Like There Used to Be': The Destruction of Social Capital in the West Virginia Coalfields." *Sociological Forum* 24: 631–57.

Bell, Shannon Elizabeth and Richard York (2010) "Community Economic Identity: The Coal Industry and Ideology Construction in West Virginia." *Rural Sociology* 75: 111–43.

Brulle, Robert J. and David Naguib Pellow (2006) "Environmental Justice: Human Health and Environmental Inequalities." *Annual Review of Public Health* 27: 103–24.

Bullard, Robert D. (1990) *Dumping in Dixie: Race, Class, and Environmental Quality.* Boulder, CO: Westview Press.

Bunker, Stephen G. (1984) "Modes of Extraction, Unequal Exchange and the Progressive Underdevelopment of an Extreme Periphery: The Brazilian Amazon, 1600–1980." *American Journal of Sociology* 89: 1017–64.

Burningham, Kate and Geoff Cooper (1999) "Being Constructive: Social Construction and the Environment." *Sociology* 33: 297–316.

Buttel, Frederick H. (1987) "New Directions in Environmental Sociology." *Annual Review of Sociology* 13: 465–88.

Carolan, Michael S. (2004) "Ecological Modernization Theory: What About Consumption?" *Society and Natural Resources* 17: 247–60.

Carolan, Michael S. (2005) "Society, Biology and Ecology: Bringing Nature Back into Sociology's Disciplinary Narrative through Critical Realism." *Organization and Environment* 18: 393–421.

Catton, William R., Jr. (1980) *Overshoot: The Ecological Basis of Revolutionary Change.* Chicago: University of Illinois Press.

Catton, William R., Jr. and Riley E. Dunlap (1978) "Environmental Sociology: A New Paradigm." *American Sociologist* 13: 41–9.

Catton, William R., Jr. and Riley E. Dunlap (1980) "A New Ecological Paradigm for Post-Exuberant Sociology." *American Behavioral Scientist* 24: 15–47.

Chew, Sing C. (2001) *World Ecological Degradation: Accumulation, Urbanization, and Deforestation 3000 B.C. – A.D. 2000.* New York: Rowman and Littlefield.

Clark, Brett and Richard York (2005) "Carbon Metabolism: Global Capitalism, Climate Change, and the Biospheric Rift." *Theory and Society* 34: 391–428.

Clausen, Rebecca and Brett Clark (2005) "The Metabolic Rift and Marine Ecology: An Analysis of the Oceanic Crisis in Capitalist Production." *Organization and Environment* 18: 422–44.

Cole, Matthew A. and Eric Neumayer (2004) "Examining the Impact of Demographic Factors on Air Pollution." *Population and Environment* 26: 5–21.

Daly, Herman (1991) *Steady-State Economics*, 2nd edn. Washington, DC: Island Press.

Davidson, Debra J. and William Freudenburg (1996) "Gender and Environmental Risk Concerns: A Review and Analysis of Available Research." *Environment and Behavior* 28: 302–39.

Dickens, Peter (2004) *Society and Nature: Changing Our Environment, Changing Ourselves.* Cambridge: Polity Press.

Dietz, Thomas and Eugene A. Rosa (1994) "Rethinking the Environmental Impacts of Population, Affluence and Technology." *Human Ecology Review* 1: 277–300.

Dietz, Thomas and Eugene A. Rosa (1997) "Effects of Population and Affluence on CO2 Emissions." *Proceedings of the National Academy of Sciences of the USA* 94: 175–9.

Downey, Liam (2006a) "Using Geographic Information Systems to Reconceptualize Spatial Relationships and Ecological Context." *American Journal of Sociology* 112: 567–612.

Downey, Liam (2006b) "Environmental Racial Inequality in Detroit." *Social Forces* 85: 771–96.

Dunaway, Wilma A. and M. Cecilia Macabuac (2007) " 'The Shrimp Eat Better Than We Do': Philippine Subsistence Fishing Households Sacrificed for the Global Food Chain." *Review of the Fernand Braudel Center* 30: 313–37.

Dunlap, Riley E. (2002) "Paradigms, Theories and Environmental Sociology." In R. E. Dunlap, F. H. Buttel, P. Dickens, and A. Gijswijt (eds.), *Sociological Theory and the*

Environment: Classical Foundations, Contemporary Insights. Boulder, CO: Rowman and Littlefield, pp. 329–50.

Dunlap, Riley E. (2010) "The Maturation and Diversification of Environmental Sociology: From Constructivism and Realism to Agnosticism and Pragmatism." In M. Redclift and G. Woodgate (eds.), *The International Handbook of Environmental Sociology*, 2nd edn. Cheltenham: Edward Elgar, pp. 15–32.

Dunlap, Riley E. and William R. Catton, Jr. (1979) "Environmental Sociology." *Annual Review of Sociology* 5: 243–73.

Dunlap, Riley E. and William R. Catton, Jr. (1983) "What Environmental Sociologists Have in Common (Whether Concerned with 'Built' or 'Natural' Environments)." *Sociological Inquiry* 53: 113–35.

Dunlap, Riley E. and William R. Catton, Jr. (1994) "Struggling with Human Exemptionalism: The Rise, Decline and Revitalization of Environmental Sociology." *American Sociologist* 25: 5–30.

Dunlap, Riley E. and Brent K. Marshall (2007) "Environmental Sociology." In C. D. Bryant and D. L. Peck (eds.), *21st Century Sociology: A Reference Handbook*, Vol. 2. Thousand Oaks, CA: Sage, pp. 329–40.

Dunlap, Riley E. and Aaron M. McCright (2010) "Climate Change Denial: Sources, Actors and Strategies." In Constance Lever-Tracy (ed.), *Routledge Handbook of Climate Change and Society*. London: Routledge, pp. 240–59.

Ergas, Christina (2010) "A Model of Sustainable Living: Collective Identity in an Urban Ecovillage." *Organization and Environment* 23: 32–54.

Foster, John Bellamy (1999) "Marx's Theory of Metabolic Rift: Classical Foundation for Environmental Sociology." *American Journal of Sociology* 105: 366–405.

Foster, John Bellamy (2000) *Marx's Ecology: Materialism and Nature*. New York: Monthly Review Press.

Foster, John Bellamy and Brett Clark (2008) "The Sociology of Ecology: Ecological Organicism versus Ecosystem Ecology in the Social Construction of Ecological Science, 1926–1935." *Organization and Environment* 21: 311–52.

Foster, John Bellamy and Richard York (2004) "Political Economy and Environmental Crisis: Introduction to the Special Issue on the Treadmill of Production." *Organization and Environment* 17: 293–5.

Frank, David John, Ann Hironaka, and Evan Schofer (2000) "The Nation-State and the Natural Environment over the Twentieth Century." *American Sociological Review* 65: 96–116.

Freudenburg, William R. (1997) "Contamination, Corrosion and the Social Order: An Overview." *Current Sociology* 45: 41–57.

Freudenburg, William R. and Robert Gramling (1994) *Oil in Troubled Waters*. Albany, NY: State University of New York Press.

Freudenburg, William R., Robert Gramling, and Debra J. Davidson (2008) "Scientific Certainty Argumentation Methods (SCAMs): Science and the Politics of Doubt." *Sociological Inquiry* 78: 2–38.

Freudenburg, William R., Robert Gramling, Shirley Laska, and Kai T. Erikson (2009) *Catastrophe in the Making*. Washington, DC: Island Press.

Frey, R. Scott (1998) "The Export of Hazardous Industries to the Peripheral Zones of the World-System." *Journal of Developing Societies* 14: 66–81.

Gill, Duane A. and J. Steven Picou (1998) "Technological Disaster and Chronic Community Stress." *Society and Natural Resources* 11: 795–815.

Hannigan, John A. (2006) *Environmental Sociology: A Social-Constructionist Perspective*, 2nd edn. London: Routledge.

Harlan, Sharon L., Anthony J. Brazel, G. Darrel Jenerette, Nancy S. Jones, Larissa Larsen, Lela Prashad, and William L. Stefanov (2008) "In the Shade of Affluence: The Inequitable Distribution of the Urban Heat Island." *Research in Social Problems and Public Policy* 15: 173–202.

Harlan, Sharon L., Anthony J. Brazel, Lela Prashad, William L. Stefanov, and Larissa Larsen (2006) "Neighborhood Microclimates and Vulnerability to Heat Stress." *Social Science and Medicine* 63: 2847–63.

Hinton, Emma D. and Michael K. Goodman (2010) "Sustainable Consumption: Developments, Considerations, and New Directions." In M. Redclift and G. Woodgate (eds.), *The International Handbook of Environmental Sociology*, 2nd edn. Cheltenham: Edward Elgar, pp. 245–61.

Jorgenson, Andrew K. (2009) "Foreign Direct Investment and the Environment, the Mitigating Influence of Institutional and Civil Society Factors, and Relationships between Industrial Pollution and Human Health: A Panel Study of Less-Developed Countries." *Organization and Environment* 22: 135–57.

Jorgenson, Andrew K. and Brett Clark (2009) "The Economy, Military, and Ecologically Unequal Relationships in Comparative Perspective: A Panel Study of the Ecological Footprints of Nations, 1975–2000." *Social Problems* 56: 621–46.

Jorgenson, Andrew K. and Kennon Kuykendall (2008) "Globalization, Foreign Investment Dependence, and Agriculture Production: A Cross-National Study of Pesticide and Fertilizer Use Intensity in Less-Developed Countries, 1990–2000." *Social Forces* 87: 529–60.

Kentor, Jeffrey and Peter Grimes (2006) "Foreign Investment Dependence and the Environment: A Global Perspective." In Andrew Jorgenson and Edward Kick (eds.), *Globalization and the Environment*. Leiden: Brill, pp. 61–77.

Longo, Stefano and Richard York (2008) "Agricultural Exports and the Environment: A Cross-National Study of Fertilizer and Pesticide Consumption." *Rural Sociology* 73: 82–104.

Macnaghten, Phil and John Urry (1998) *Contested Natures*. Thousand Oaks, CA: Sage.

Mancus, Philip (2007) "Nitrogen Fertilizer Dependency and Its Contradictions: A Theoretical Explanation of Socio-Ecological Metabolism." *Rural Sociology* 272: 269–88.

McCright, Aaron M. (2010) "The Effects of Gender on Climate Change Knowledge and Concern in the American Public." *Population and Environment* 32: 66–87.

McCright, Aaron M. and Riley E. Dunlap (2000) "Challenging Global Warming as a Social Problem: An Analysis of the Conservative Movement's Counter-Claims." *Social Problems* 47: 499–522.

McCright, Aaron M. and Riley E. Dunlap (2003) "Defeating Kyoto: The Conservative Movement's Impact on U.S. Climate Change Policy." *Social Problems* 50: 348–73.

McCright, Aaron M. and Riley E. Dunlap (2010) "Anti-Reflexivity: The American Conservative Movement's Success in Undermining Climate Science and Policy." *Theory, Culture and Society* 26: 100–33.

Merchant, Carolyn (1980) *The Death of Nature: Women, Ecology, and the Scientific Revolution*. New York: Harper and Row.

Mohai, Paul, David Pellow, and J. Timmons Roberts (2009) "Environmental Justice." *Annual Review of Environment and Resources* 34: 405–30.

Mol, Arthur P. J. (1995) *The Refinement of Production: Ecological Modernization Theory and the Chemical Industry*. Utrecht: Van Arkel.

Mol, Arthur P. J. (1996) "Ecological Modernisation and Institutional Reflexivity: Environmental Reform in the Late Modern Age." *Environmental Politics* 5: 302–23.

Mol, Arthur P. J. (2001) *Globalization and Environmental Reform*. Cambridge, MA: MIT Press.

Mol, Arthur P. J. and Gert Spaargaren (2004) "Ecological Modernization and Consumption: A Reply." *Society and Natural Resources* 17: 261–5.

Mol, Arthur P. J. and Gert Spaargaren (2005) "From Additions and Withdrawals to Environmental Flows: Reframing Debates in the Environmental Social Sciences." *Organization and Environment* 18: 91–107.

Mol, Arthur P. J., David Sonnefeld, and Gert Spaargaren (eds.) (2009) *The Ecological Modernization Reader: Environmental Reform in Theory and Practice*. New York: Routledge.

Moore, Jason W. (2000) "Environmental Crises and the Metabolic Rift in World-Historical Perspective." *Organization and Environment* 13: 123–57.

Moore, Jason W. (2003) "The Modern World-System as Environmental History? Ecology and the Rise of Capitalism." *Theory and Society* 32: 307–77.

Murphy, Raymond (1997) *Sociology and Nature: Social Action in Context*. Boulder, CO: Westview Press.

Murphy, Raymond (2009) *Leadership in Disaster*. Montreal: McGill-Queen's University Press.

New Economics Foundation (2009) *The Happy Planet Index 2.0*. London: New Economics Foundation.

Norgaard, Kari and Richard York (2005) "Gender Equality and State Environmentalism." *Gender and Society* 19: 506–22.

Nugent, Colleen and John M. Shandra (2009) "Women's Political Participation and Protected Land Area: A Cross-National Analysis." *Organization and Environment* 22: 208–29.

O'Connor, James (1988) "Capitalism, Nature, Socialism: A Theoretical Introduction." *Capitalism, Nature, Socialism* 1: 11–38.

O'Connor, James (1991) "On the Two Contradictions of Capitalism." *Capitalism, Nature, Socialism* 2: 107–9.

Pellow, David N. (2000) "Environmental Inequality Formation: Toward a Theory of Environmental Injustice." *American Behavioral Scientist* 43: 581–601.

Pellow, David N. (2002) *Garbage Wars: The Struggle for Environmental Justice in Chicago*. Cambridge, MA: MIT Press.

Picou, J. Steven, Brent K. Marshall, and Duane A. Gill (2004) "Disaster, Litigation, and the Corrosive Community." *Social Forces* 82: 1493–522.

Roberts, J. Timmons and Peter E. Grimes (2002) "World-System Theory and the Environment: Toward a New Synthesis." In Riley E. Dunlap, Frederick H. Buttel, Peter Dickens, and August Gijswijt (eds.), *Sociological Theory and the Environment*. Boulder, CO: Rowman and Littlefield, pp. 167–94.

Roberts, J. Timmons and Melissa M. Toffolon-Weiss (2001) *Chronicles from the Environmental Justice Frontline*. Cambridge: Cambridge University Press.

Rosa, Eugene A. (1998) "Meta-Theoretical Foundations of Post-Normal Risk." *Journal of Risk Analysis* 1: 15–44.

Roberts, J. Timmons, Bradley C. Parks, and Alexis Vasquez (2004) "Who Signs Environmental Treaties and Why? Institutionalism, Structuralism and Participation by 192 Nations in 22 Treaties." *Global Environmental Politics* 4(3): 22–64.

Rocheleau, Dianne, Barbara Thomas-Slayter, and Esther Wangari (eds.) (1996) *Feminist Political Ecology: Global Issues and Local Experiences*. New York: Routledge.

Rosa, Eugene A., Richard York, and Thomas Dietz (2004) "Tracking the Anthropogenic Drivers of Ecological Impacts." *Ambio* 33: 509–12.

Salleh, Ariel (ed.) (2009) *Eco-Sufficiency and Global Justice: Women Write Political Ecology*. London: Pluto Press.

Schnaiberg, Allan (1980) *The Environment: From Surplus to Scarcity*. New York: Oxford University Press.

Schnaiberg, Allan and Kenneth Gould (1994) *Environment and Society: The Enduring Conflict*. New York: St. Martin's Press.

Schofer, Evan and Ann Hironaka (2005) "The Effects of World Society on Environmental Protection Outcomes." *Social Forces* 84: 25–45.

Schor, Juliet (2010) *Plentitude: The New Economics of True Wealth*. New York: Penguin.

Shandra, John M., Christopher Leckband, Laura McKinney, and Bruce London (2009) "Ecologically Unequal Exchange, World Polity, and Biodiversity Loss: A Cross-National Analysis." *International Journal of Comparative Sociology* 50: 285–310.

Shiva, Vandana (1989) *Staying Alive: Women, Ecology and Development*. London: Zed Books.

Spaargaren, Gert and Arthur P. J. Mol (1992) "Sociology, Environment and Modernity: Ecological Modernization as a Theory of Social Change." *Society and Natural Resources* 5: 323–44.

Stern, Paul C., Thomas Dietz, and Linda Kalof (1993) "Value Orientations, Gender, and Environmental Concern." *Environment and Behavior* 25: 322–48.

Talberth, John, Clifford Cobb, and Noah Slattery (2007) *The Genuine Progress Indicator 2006: A Tool for Sustainable Development*. Oakland, CA: Redefining Progress.

Taylor, Dorceta (2000) "The Rise of the Environmental Justice Paradigm: Injustice Framing and the Social Construction of Environmental Discourses." *American Behavioral Scientist* 43: 508–80.

Taylor, Dorceta (2009) *The Environment and the People in American Cities, 1600s–1900s: Disorder, Inequality, and Social Change*. Durham, NC: Duke University Press.

United Church of Christ (1987) *Toxic Wastes and Race in the United States*. New York: United Church of Christ Commission for Racial Justice.

Wynne, Brian (2010) "Strange Weather, Again: Climate Science as Political Art." *Theory, Culture and Society* 27: 289–305.

Yearley, Steven (2005) *Cultures of Environmentalism*. Basingstoke: Palgrave Macmillan.

Yearley, Steven (2009) "Sociology and Climate Change after Kyoto: What Roles for Social Science in Understanding Climate Change?" *Current Sociology* 57: 389–405.

York, Richard (2008a) "Introduction to the Symposium on Catton and Dunlap's Foundational Work Establishing an Ecological Paradigm." *Organization and Environment* 21: 446–8.

York, Richard (2008b) "De-Carbonization in Former Soviet Republics, 1992–2000: The Ecological Consequences of De-Modernization." *Social Problems* 55: 370–90.

York, Richard and Brett Clark (2010) "Critical Materialism: Science, Technology, and Environmental Sustainability." *Sociological Inquiry* 80: 475–99.

York, Richard and John Bellamy Foster (2005) "The Treadmill of Production: Extension, Refinement, and Critique: Introduction to Part II of the Special Issue on the Environment and the Treadmill of Production." *Organization and Environment* 18: 5–6.

York, Richard and Philip Mancus (2009) "Critical Human Ecology: Historical Materialism and Natural Laws." *Sociological Theory* 27: 122–49.

York, Richard and Eugene A. Rosa (2003) "Key Challenges to Ecological Modernization Theory: Institutional Efficacy, Case Study Evidence, Units of Analysis, and the Pace of Eco-Efficiency." *Organization and Environment* 16: 273–88.

York, Richard, Eugene A. Rosa, and Thomas Dietz (2003) "Footprints on the Earth: The Environmental Consequences of Modernity." *American Sociological Review* 68: 279–300.

Zahran, Sammy, Samuel D. Brody, Arnold Vedlitz, Himanshu Grover, and Caitlyn Miller (2008) "Vulnerability and Capacity: Explaining Commitment to Climate-Change Policy." *Environment and Planning C: Government and Policy* 26: 544–62.

Zavestoski, Stephen (2002) "The Social-Psychological Bases of Anti-Consumption Attitudes." *Psychology and Marketing* 19: 149–66.

28

Social Movements

Remy Cross and David A. Snow

Conceptualization and Significance

Social movements make diverse claims and can assume various forms. At their core, however, they all seek to effect some degree of individual, social, political, and/or cultural change. In some cases, the change sought is proactive and progressive in the sense of moving beyond the status quo or extant social and cultural currents, as in the case of the civil rights and women's movements in the United States; in other cases, the change may be more reactive or regressive in the sense of seeking to preserve the status quo by resisting currents of change or by returning to an earlier idealized order, as with the Taliban movement in Afghanistan in the early part of the current century. Whether progressive or regressive, forward- or backward-looking, skewed to the "left" or the "right" or anchored in the "center," all social movements share a number of characteristics that together define them as such. First, they are challengers to or defenders of existing institutional structures or systems of authority; second, they are collective rather than individual enterprises; third, they act outside of existing institutional or organizational arrangements, although in varying degrees, with some movements employing only extra-institutional tactics and others working within institutional channels while also engaging in some extra-institutional collective action; fourth, they operate with some degree of organization, ranging from a single social movement organization to a network or coalition of movement organizations that may vary in the degree to which they are tightly or loosely coupled; and fifth, they typically do so with some degree of temporal continuity.[1]

The sociological study of social movements and the various collective actions they sponsor or with which they are associated, such as protest events, sit-ins, blockades, and boycotts, is one of the most vibrant areas of sociological research within the US, and arguably within Europe as well. And for good reason. Social movements and their kindred collective actions are recurrent and conspicuous features of the social landscape, in part because they are phenomenologically note-worthy, involving relatively large numbers of people marching or rallying together in public places intended for other activities, and in part because they are typically associated with one or more of the hotly contested issues of the time. Partly because of such considerations, hardly a day goes by when some kind of social movement activity or related protest event does not receive some media attention, with some such events becoming major media stories across the globe. Were it otherwise, then there would not be such an escalating number of social movement studies that rely on media coverage of movements and protest events as their primary data base (see, for example, McAdam & Su 2002; Snow, Vliegenhart & Corrigall-Brown 2007; Amenta, Caren, Olasky & Stobaugh 2009).

The abundance of movement news stories and the protest events chronicled suggest that social movement activity and related protest events are indeed conspicuous features of the social landscape. And this is especially so when it is considered that much social movement activity occurs beneath the radar of the various media, and that there are few major social issues in which social movements are not involved on one side or the other. Because of such considerations, Meyer and Tarrow (1998) have argued that we live in a "movement society." If so, then understanding our own society, as well as the larger social world in which it is embedded, requires some knowledge and understanding of social movements and the activities with which they are associated. And this is especially so when it is considered that social movements play a major role in highlighting distributional and procedural inequalities and challenging the relevant institutional authorities to redress these inequities, are often the organizational carriers of constituent concerns regarding various "social problems," frequently function as visible indicators or outcroppings of emerging social and cultural concerns, and generally provide a "voice" for their adherents and bind them together into highly salient collective identities.

In the following pages, we address four sets of issues that are generally regarded as fundamental to understanding the emergence, operation, and impact of social movements as conceived above: (1) generating and facilitating conditions, (2) par-ticipation, (3) dynamics, and (4) outcomes. We then end with consideration of several new frontiers of social movement research.

GENERATING AND FACILITATING CONDITIONS

The desire for social change alone, no matter its source or intensity, is insufficient to generate organized movement campaigns. Rather, collective action that takes the form of social movements seeking to effect some kind of social change emerges from the confluence and interaction of a number of facilitating conditions: shared, mobi-lizing grievances; some degree of political opportunity; resource mobilization; and a favorable ecological context.

Mobilizing grievances

Initial explorations into the causes of social movements came to be called strain theories, grounding the genesis of movements in grievances that arose from social strains, such as racial discrimination, widespread unemployment, and extreme poverty. Because of its hydraulic-engine approach to movement emergence – a slow build-up of social pressures eventually leading to the eruption of a movement – strain theory came to be seen as a simplistic theory and was discarded as being the primary cause of movement activity (Tilly, Tilly & Tilly 1975; Snow, Cress, Downey & Jones 1998; Buechler 2004).

However the emphasis of strain theories on grievances is still relevant for understanding the root causes of many movements. After all, when individuals collectively challenge authorities via social movements, they typically do so over conditions about which they are deeply troubled and often feel passionately. These troublesome conditions, and the feelings associated with them – such as dissatisfaction, fear, indignation, resentment, and moral shock – can be thought of as grievances. They provide the primary motivational impetus for organizing social movement campaigns and for engaging in social movement activities. Consequently, none of the other various sets of conditions necessary for the emergence and operation of social movements matters much in the absence of *mobilizing grievances*. Unlike ubiquitous individual grievances, mobilizing grievances "are shared among some number of actors, be they individuals or organizations, and . . . are felt to be sufficiently serious to warrant not only collective complaint but also some kind of corrective, collective action" (Snow & Soule 2010: 24). However, mobilizing grievances do not arise spontaneously in response to material privation and distributional or procedural inequities. If they did, then, to paraphrase Leon Trotsky, one of the leaders of the Russian revolution, "the masses would be always in revolt" (Trotsky 1959: 249). But we know that is not the case, as history is replete with examples of aggregations of individuals who are exploited economically, who are deprived relative to their neighbors, and who are objects of stigmatization and differential treatment, but who have not mobilized in order to collectively challenge the responsible agents, or even some scapegoat, for their situation. This is due in no small part to the fact that such conditions are themselves subject to differential interpretation and framing. Whether some conditions or others become animating mobilizing grievances, then, is partly contingent on how they are framed (Snow, Rochford, Worden & Benford 1986; Gamson 1992; Benford & Snow 2000; Snow & Soule 2010).

Other contextual conditions

The generation of mobilizing grievances alone does not guarantee the emergence of a social movement or affiliated protest activity. In the language of causal analysis, mobilizing grievances constitute a necessary rather than sufficient condition for movement emergence. Also necessary is the opportunity to redress those grievances through various means of strategic action that involve their articulation to relevant audiences and the capacity to pressure the appropriate authorities to remedy those grievances. Such opportunity is not a simple, one-dimensional phenomenon, however. Rather, it is multi-dimensional in the sense that the opportunity to press one's claims collectively is based on the confluence of a number of overlapping conditions: the opportunity or freedom to express one's grievances publicly and to relevant authorities, whether through the media or by assembling and protesting in various public places; access to sufficient resources to organize and mount a campaign to address those grievances; and relatively safe, spatial enclaves in which the aggrieved can associate in absence of the curious and perhaps watchful eye of their targets or government officials.

Political opportunities

The opportunities approach to mobilization emphasizes the role played by both cycles or waves of contention (Tarrow 1998; Koopmans 2004) and structural opportunities in the political system in which the movement is embedded (Tilly 1978; McAdam 1996; Meyer 2004). The core idea is that movement mobilization is most likely to occur when there are opportunistic openings in the political system. Tarrow (1998) contends that these openings are cyclical in nature and that movements are more likely to experience success when they are able to take advantage of periodic openings in the political process that are more favorable to the claims they are making. The presence or absence of these openings may be signaled by shifting political alignments, the coming and going of allies, and by variation in the repressive behavior of authorities (McAdam 1996; Tarrow 1998). But there is no automatic relationship between these signals and mobilization, as signals, like all signs, must be noticed, which means that they can be missed or ignored. Additionally, signals have to be read or interpreted, which means that they are subject to differential interpretation and framing (Gamson & Meyer 1996). So while the actual presence or absence of political opportunity matters, it is arguable that it matters less than its perception, which is affected by threat-based grievances, moral shock or outrage, the perceived strength of the movement, and the passion generated by these factors, and, thus, how the structure of opportunity is read and framed. Moreover, challengers may sometimes define opportunities in terms of other factors, such as the perceived strength of their oppositional allies, as Kurzman (1996) found in his study of structural and perceived opportunity associated with the Iranian revolution of 1979.

Resources and organization

However important some degree of political opportunity to the prospects of movement mobilization, movements may not always be in a position to take advantage of political openings, even if they read them correctly, in the absence of a supportive organizational infrastructure and associated resources. As Almeida (2003) found in studying protest waves in El Salvador, the most successful groups were those that mobilized around grievances and threats and then built durable organizational resources which allowed them to better mobilize the next time an opportunity for mobilization came around. This and numerous other studies (see Edwards & McCarthy 2004) provide compelling support for the orienting premise of the resource mobilization perspective formulated by McCarthy and Zald (1977): the emergence and persistence of social movement activity is contingent on the availability of resources (e.g., money, labor, equipment, legitimacy) that can be accumulated and channeled by social movement organizations into movement mobilization and campaigns. Given the wide-ranging empirical support this general proposition has received, it is not surprising that Tilly and Tarrow (2007) regard resources/organization as foundational requisites necessary for successful and sustained movement action.

Ecological factors and free spaces

Along with some degree of political opportunity and the accumulation of some variety of resources, various ecological factors can affect the prospect and character of movement emergence and mobilization. Within the context of social movements, ecological factors refer to the spatial arrangement of movement-relevant populations and physical places, often called "free spaces," conducive to facilitating or sustaining collective challenges to authority. Although the role of ecological factors in relation to movement mobilization has not received as much attention as the aforementioned, there is compelling research that accents the importance of ecological factors. For example, Zhao's (2001) analysis of the 1989 Beijing student movement shows that the close proximity of Beijing's 67 universities in relation to each other and the dense campus living conditions significantly affected student mobilization. These observations are not peculiar to Beijing, as several ecological factors have been noted to affect on-campus mobilization of student movements worldwide: the spatial segregation of students, and spatial arrangements that channel student routines and aggregate them in particular places at particular times, such as student unions and administratively designated "free speech" areas.

In addition to the facilitative and constraining effects of such spatial arrangements, scholars have noted the importance of so-called "free spaces" (Evans & Boyte 1986; Polletta 1999). Such spaces are typically constituted by "small scale community or movement settings beyond the surveillance and control of institutionalized authorities that are voluntarily frequented by dissidents and system complainants . . . (and in which) various forms of cultural challenge, such as adversarial narratives and frames, that precede or accompany mobilization are generated or nurtured" (Snow & Soule 2010: 101–2). These "free spaces" have been found to nurture adversarial sentiments and mobilization in various movements, such as in the civil rights movement (Morris 1981) and in racist and white power movements (Blee 2002; Futrell & Simi 2004) in the US, and in Soviet oppositional movements in Estonia (Johnston & Snow 1998).

As complex social enterprises, movements require multiple factors to coalesce into a viable collective actor, much less a successful one. Being able to mobilize grievances and resources within a favorable political context, and having the spatial elbow-room to do so, are all necessary contextual elements that facilitate movement emergence and mobilization.

PARTICIPATION

Movements, it is important to remember, are made up of people willing to dedicate varying degrees of time and energy, as well as other resources, to altering or remedying some issue about which they are deeply and passionately concerned. But cognitive and emotional alignment with a movement does not guarantee participation. As Klandermans and his colleagues have emphasized with their distinction between "consensus mobilization" (shared grievances and goals) and "action mobilization" (actual participation), the former does not necessarily guarantee the latter (Klandermans 1984; Klandermans & Oegema 1987). Additionally, once some level of participation has occurred, there is no guarantee that it will be repeated or persistent. As Corrigall-Brown (2011) found in her comparative case study of trajectories of participation in four movements that differed in terms of goals and organizational structure, persistent participation was relatively infrequent among the 60 participants interviewed in-depth, with the majority either disengaging entirely from movement participation or at least dropping out for a period of time.

These observations suggest that a thorough understanding of movement participation requires consideration not only of what accounts for *differential recruitment* – why some individuals rather than others who are similarly situated socially and/or culturally – but also of what accounts for *differential participation and disengagement*. We cannot address these questions adequately given the limited space at our disposal and the extensive literature on the topic; so we will highlight four sets of factors that often interact and combine to account for differential recruitment and initial participation. They include structural, social psychological, and biographical factors, and the generation of selective incentives to participate.

Network-embedded invitations to participate

Over 30 years ago, Snow, Zurcher, and Ekland-Olson (1980) noted that hypothesized psychological and social psychological precipitants of movement participation matter little, if at all, in the absence of personal invitations to participate. Subsequent research has not only substantiated that contention but suggests that "being asked" may well be the most significant determinant of participation (Schussman & Soule 2005). But research has also shown repeatedly that the probability of being asked is generally a function of being embedded in networks linking those asked to participate to one or more movement members (for a summary, see Diani & McAdam 2003; Diani 2004).

It is not just interpersonal networks that are salient facilitators of differential recruitment, however, as many, and perhaps most, such networks are embedded in community and organizational contexts that may be variably facilitative of recruitment and participation (see, for example, Morris 1981; McAdam & Paulsen 1993; Dixon & Roscigno 2003). This fact of "embeddedness" has prompted other researchers to go beyond assaying the presence or absence of network ties to examine their structure and multiplexity. In research on the predictors of recruitment to the Mississippi Freedom Summer campaign of 1964, for example, it was found that some universities not only contributed a disproportionate share of student volunteers, but it was those students who were in positions of network centrality in a number of the university's organizations who were most likely to be recruited (Fernandez & McAdam 1988). Similarly, Gould's (1991) study of mobilization in the Paris Commune revealed that the key to explaining participation resided in overlapping neighborhood and National Guard networks.

Although the foregoing would appear to suggest that network-embedded invitations are a necessary condition for movement participation, such a conclusion would be overdrawn in light of instances of movement participation in the absence of prior network linkages. Some people, for example, are "seekers" or "searchers" in the sense that they are on the lookout for movements that share their lifestyle and/or worldview (Straus 1976; Balch & Taylor 1978) or provide an opportunity to realize a particular identity (Friedman & McAdam 1992; Kaplan & Liu 2000). It has also been shown that some events or situations may be so morally and emotionally shocking that individuals will be inclined to join the cause irrespective of the presence or absence of ties to movement members (Jasper & Poulsen 1995). Clearly such observations temper the inclination to treat social network ties as a necessary condition for participation.

It is also the case that network-embedded invitations and alignment with a movement's cause are not sufficient to account for differential recruitment and participation, as not all individuals who receive invitations from acquaintances, friends, or family will participate. Illustrating this point is research on a Dutch peace movement revealing that only one-sixth of those citizens who received invitations to participate in a movement event were motivated to do so, and only one-third of those actually did so (Klandermans & Oegema 1987). Of course, variation in receipt of network-based invitations to participate in a movement event and actual participation can be explained by a number of factors, including the strength of the network ties (McAdam & Paulsen 1993). But the fact remains that many, and probably most, recipients of network-based invitations fail to participate. Thus, factors other than network ties are necessary in order to account for differential recruitment.

Social psychological factors

In addition to seekership, there are other factors that fall under the social psychological canopy which can also influence the likelihood of initial and continuing participation. The literature on the range of relevant social psychological factors, such as collective efficacy and socialization, is too extensive to discuss here (but see Rohlinger & Snow 2003; Klandermans 2004; Snow & Soule 2010), so we will accent only two such factors: collective identity and emotion.

Collective identity

Few if any social psychological concepts or processes have received as much attention over the last 20 years in the study of social movements as collective identity, conceptualized as a sense of "we-ness" or "one-ness" that derives from perceived shared attributes or experiences among those who comprise a group, often in contrast to one or more perceived or imagined sets of others (Melucci 1989; Taylor & Whittier 1992; Polletta & Jasper 2001; Hunt & Benford 2004). Numerous studies conducted over the past 15 years have shown a strong relationship between identification with a particular group or collectivity and movement participation and activism (for a summary, see Stryker, Owens & White 2000; Klandermans 2004; Snow & Soule 2010).

When we consider these studies together with the previously mentioned observation that some individuals seek out movements that provide them with an opportunity to affirm their existing identities, it is clear that a relatively strong sense of identification with a particular social movement can be a significant determinant of some level of participation in support of that movement. Furthermore, work dating back to Blumer's (1951) discussion of *esprit de corps*, through Kanter's (1972) examination of commitment-building mechanisms in nineteenth-century communes, to recent work on the relationship between collective identity, solidarity, and commitment (Hunt & Benford 2004), indicates not only the importance of collective identity in relation to sustained participation, but also how it can be enhanced tactically and organizationally through shared rituals, mandated personal sacrifices, and engagement in collective events.

Emotions

Following on the heels of the increasing interest in collective identity in the 1990s came renewed interest in the link between emotions and social movements in the first decade of the 2000s. At the forefront of reigniting this interest in the role that emotions play in social movements was the work of Goodwin, Jasper, and Polletta (2001, 2004). They distinguish between reactive or reflex emotions and more enduring emotions, both of which are relevant to aspects of movement participation. Reflex emotions are involuntary and do not require cognitive processing. Examples include surprise, anger, disgust, joy, sadness, fear, and joy. When afraid of something, people may be more likely to join a movement that aims to do something about the perceived source of that fear, especially when the fear is collectively shared, as appears to be the case with NIMBY (not-in-my-backyard) movements.

Goodwin et al. (2001, 2004) do not discount the relevance of reflex emotions to initial movement participation, but they shift attention to the more enduring emotions that are more likely to sustain participation – such as affective emotions connected to positive or negative commitments to people, places, ideas, and things – and that form the backbone for understanding how emotions undergird more persistent participation. Affective emotions can also form the basis for collective identity and engender trust by creating bonds that underlie the rational core of self-interest. Finally, Goodwin et al. note that emotions need not always be on immediate display, and that they can be low-key or managed organizationally.[2]

Biographical availability

Another set of factors theorized to affect the probability of participation includes various life-cycle and lifestyle characteristics that may alter the costs and risks of participation, such as being married, having children, and being employed full-time. The absence of such factors, conceptualized as "personal constraints," has been hypothesized to render individuals biographically available for movement participation, while their presence supposedly makes them biographically unavailable (McAdam 1986). Yet, empirical research on the effects of various hypothesized indicators of biographical availability has been mixed at best (Nepstadt & Smith 1999; Schussman & Soule 2005; Corrigall-Brown, Snow, Smith & Quist 2009).

What accounts for this apparent disjunction in what makes good sense theoretically but lacks empirical affirmation? The answer resides, in part, in the failure to
assess biographical availability or unavailability in relation to the different stages
of participation noted earlier: one entails being informed about the occurrence of
an event and being willing to participate (consensus mobilization); the other involves
actual participation (action mobilization). This oversight was made clear in
Beyerlein and Hipp's research, based on a cross-sectional sample of 1,332 non-
institutionalized US adults aged 18 years and older, wherein they found that standard measures of unavailability (marriage, particularly for women, and work)
"generally had significant negative effects on *willingness* to participate in protest
action, but no effect on actual protest participation" (2006: 234).

Thus, biographical availability or unavailability appears to matter in relation to
one's willingness to participate but not so much in determining actual participation,
which is likely to be affected by commitment to the cause and the generation of
various participatory incentives through motivational framing.

Generating participatory incentives and motivational frames

The final factor we consider relevant to understanding differential recruitment and
participation concerns the issue of participation incentives. From the vantage point
of rational choice theory, most prospective participants who are part of a movement's constituency or mobilization potential would need added incentive because
of two considerations. One is that the perceived benefits or gains from participation
may not outweigh the perceived costs and risks. The other consideration is Olson's
(1965) "free rider" thesis, which holds that non-participation is highly rational
when the desired benefit is a "public good" that is available to everyone irrespective
of whether they contribute to its attainment, as is the case with clean air and water.
Certainly environmental activists would not be the sole beneficiaries of legislation
improving air and/or water quality. This simple fact raises the question of why not
"free ride" on the efforts of environmental activists. And even for those who may
not be inclined to free ride, they still may not be sufficiently motivated to participate
in movement activities, even though they share the movement's grievances and
subscribe to its aims. Thus, social movement leaders and activists are confronted
with the challenge of neutralizing the inclination to free ride and/or providing additional motivation for participation. This is the challenge referred to earlier as the
dilemma of "action mobilization" – that is, of moving willing sympathizers from
the sidelines to the playing field.

There are various sorts of incentives that increase the odds of participation.
They cluster into three sets: selective, solidary, and moral. *Selective incentives*,
unlike collective goods, are divisible and excludable in the sense that they benefit
only those who contribute their time, energy, and/or resources to the cause. *Solidary
incentives* are rooted in the previously discussed affective and emotional attachments that make one feel part of a collectivity. Last, *moral incentives* derive from
the principles and values that heighten one's sense of conviction, obligation, and
responsibility.

These incentives can be generated through a number of different processes. Some
are clearly matching processes, as with the provision of tangible material induce-

ments as a selective incentive for participation. Illustrative are the free meals and beverages that are sometimes given to those who attend a demonstration event at the end of a march. But these sorts of tangible things are far from being potent inducements except perhaps in the case of the most economically marginalized citizens. Far more compelling participatory inducements are solidary and moral incentives because passionate identification with a movement's cause is more likely to be based on affective ties to a group and its moral principles than on instrumental considerations. In other words, a sense of solidarity and moral convictions regarding distributional and procedural justice and injustice are the stuff that stirs the emotions and helps to forge the "iron in the soul" (Moore 1978). So how are solidaristic and moral incentives embellished or generated?

One potent mechanism for generating such incentives is *motivational framing*, which provides a "call to arms" or rationale for engaging in movement-sponsored collective action that goes beyond diagnostic and prognostic framing (Snow & Benford 1988). More concretely, motivational framing entails the construction of "vocabularies of motive" that provide prods to action by amplifying reasons for participation that override feared risks and the free rider problem. Benford (1993) outlines six sets of vocabularies of motive, the first four of which seem to be evident in the framing discourse of most movements (severity, urgency, collective efficacy, and moral propriety and obligation); but the last two (greater tangible benefit and status enhancement) appear to be associated primarily with religious, revolutionary, and terrorist movements, as with the "72 black-eyed virgins" promised to Palestinian suicide bombers (Snow & Byrd 2007).

We have highlighted in this section a number of factors that affect differential recruitment and participation. It is likely that all of these factors, and perhaps other ones, interact and combine to push or pull a person towards social movement participation. It is also the case that some of these factors matter differently depending on the character or degree of participation. For example, it may be the case that biographical availability or structural connections matter differently in relation to different kinds of movement activity, perhaps depending on the level of cost or risk associated with the activity. As well, it may be that some of these factors matter at different stages of the mobilization process. It is also probably the case that these factors interact with contextual factors discussed earlier. The point, then, is that differential recruitment and participation are complicated processes that involve the concatenation of a complex of factors.

DYNAMICS

While understanding the genesis of movements is important for pinpointing the conditions giving rise to their emergence, focusing on those conditions alone provides an incomplete picture of the dynamics of social movements – that is, how they operate and ebb and flow over time, and the various factors that influence their life course and character. During the past decade there has been increasing interest in movement dynamics, due in part to McAdam, Tarrow, and Tilly's 2001 book, *Dynamics of Contention*, which sought to identify the array of mechanisms and processes that affect the course and character of various forms of collective action cross-nationally. Some of these factors are external, such as the presence or absence of allies, public or bystander support, and counter-movements; other factors are internal, such as organizational structure and leadership (see Staggenborg 1988). But none of these factors operate independently. Rather, they can be best understood in terms of the principle of interactive determination, which "holds that understanding of focal objects of analysis cannot be fully achieved by attending only to qualities presumed to be intrinsic to them or to external factors that impinge on them; rather, it requires consideration of the interactional contexts or webs of relationships in which they are ensnared and embedded" (Snow & Soule 2010: 149–50). Thus, rather than attempt to summarize all of the factors relevant to understanding movement dynamics, we will discuss a number of factors that highlight the interactive character of movement dynamics.

Organizational and discursive fields

A central tenet of the resource mobilization perspective is that the viability of movement organizations, and thus social movements, is partly dependent on the existence of allied organizations that function as benefactors via the provision of resources (McCarthy & Zald 1977; Edwards & McCarthy 2004). But the life course of a movement is also affected by other kinds of organizations or collective actors. As Rucht notes succinctly in an analysis of movement allies, adversaries, and third parties, "social movements can be understood only in *relational* terms" (2004: 197).

This relational connection among various organizations and collectivities whose actions impinge on those of a movement has been variously conceptualized in terms of multi-organizational fields (Curtis & Zurcher 1973; Klandermans 1992; Rucht 2004), identity fields (Hunt, Benford & Snow 1994), and organizational fields (McAdam & Scott 2005). The concept of organizational fields is the most general of these embedding concepts, including any relatively organized "system of actors, actions, and relations . . . whose participants take one another into account as they carry out interrelated activities" (McAdam & Scott 2005: 10), including social movement activity. The analytic utility of the concept for the study of social movements is that it focuses attention on the array of actors relevant to the operation of a movement, and on the relationships among those actors and the consequences of their interaction. This can be seen in Armstrong's (2005) study of the field of lesbian/gay organizations in San Francisco which showed not only how the field had changed rather quickly in a short span of time, but also how that change impacted the movement. In the late 1960s the movement was dominated by organizations emphasizing societal transformation and anti-identity goals; by 1973, these goals had been replaced by the celebration of diversity and gay identity. This transformation was due in large part to field settlement or crystallization, involving movement from inter-organizational conflict and fractionation to convergence and coalescence.

Just as the concept of organizational fields provides analytic purchase for understanding movement dynamics, so does the concept of discursive fields, which conceptualizes an aspect of the context in which discourse and meaning-making processes, such as framing and narration, are generally embedded. Discursive fields evolve during the course of discussion and debate, sometimes but not always contested, about relevant events and issues, and encompass cultural materials (e.g., beliefs, values, ideologies, myths) of potential relevance and various sets of actors (e.g., targeted authorities, social control agents, counter-movements, media) whose interests are aligned, albeit differently, with the issues or events in question, and who thus have a stake in how those events and issues are framed and/or narrated (Snow 2008). Given that social movements almost always involve discussion and debate with one or more sets of actors about some pressing issue, it follows that most movements are embedded in a discursive field. Examples are wide-ranging, as with the discursive fields entailing the debates over abortion, creationism or intelligent design versus evolution, and global warming, among others. The point is that the discursive, meaning-making activity of movements cannot be fully apprehended apart from the discursive field in which that activity is nested.

Goals, strategy, and tactics

Although movement goals, strategy, and tactics are recognized as salient features of social movements, they are rarely treated equally in terms of the attention they receive: goals receive little attention because they are typically taken as given; strategy receives a bit more attention because of its connection to tactics; and tactics receive a good deal of attention (see McAdam 1983; Taylor & Van Dyke 2004; Snow & Soule 2010) because they typically are the public face of social movements. Yet, tactics cannot be fully understood apart from movement goals and strategy, and all three concepts are linked to the field in which the movement operates and how its goals and scope capabilities fit into that field.

A movement's *scope* is a way of analyzing the goal orientation of a movement. Scope is a method of placing any given social movement organization, coalition, or even field in comparison to the wider range of all possible movement permutations by considering what the movement hopes to accomplish and how it plans to do so. Scope can most easily be measured in terms of two variables: issue scope and organizational scope (Clemens 2005).

Issue scope refers to the reach and complexity of the issues pursued by the movement and how resonant they are in attracting a large audience. It provides a way of assessing the salience and reach of an issue for potential new recruits, media outlets, and other third party groups. Issue scope encompasses issues that are unlikely to appeal to a large audience because they are local or lack resonance with wider issues, as happens with NIMBY movements. At the other end of the spectrum, the most visible of movement goals, such as nuclear disarmament or reducing global warming, have a scope that can be of salience to billions.

Organizational scope measures the reach and perceived effectiveness of the organizations involved in an issue. For organizational scope, the salience of the movement's cause is secondary to the organization's capacity to mobilize around the issue. Movements with greater organizational capacity are, all other things being equal, better equipped to mobilize large numbers of constituents on behalf of movement-relevant issues and goals than those movements with a limited organizational capacity.

Returning to the matter of overall dynamics, both types of scope are tightly linked movement goals. Organizationally, goals refer to the changes desired by the movement or coalition. While they can be mediated by outside forces, such as by the actions of those organizations or groups that comprise the encompassing field, they are still primarily determined internally. Movement goals can literally be anything, but their success is bounded by their organizational scope as well as the strategy and tactics employed to further those goals.

While goals establish the aspirations of the group, it is the strategy that defines how they will be achieved. As Ganz notes, strategy represents the "relationship between intention, action, and outcome" (2000: 1010). The strategy is the plan, it is the cognitive scheme that pieces together resources and tactics and attempts to make them work in a manner that will facilitate goal attainment. While it is tempting to say that a movement has a goal and uses tactics as a means of accomplishing this goal, it is also vital to remember that these tactics, taken alone, do not materialize in a haphazard way and are usually marshaled in a strategic fashion pursuant to that goal. Goals are framed by strategies and then executed by the tactics used to enact those strategies.[3]

Tactics are the short-term, proximate methods by which a strategy is advanced in pursuit of a goal. The most common understanding of how movements choose tactics is that they do so by borrowing from similar movements (Soule 2004) or by entanglement in a shifting dance between a movement and its adversaries (McAdam 1983). McAdam indicates that this leads to strategies being the longer-term plan of a movement while tactics are more fluid and quick-changing due to the need to adapt to the actions of either counter-movements or authorities.

Tactics also give us insight into another important dynamic of movements, the diffusion of tactics within and across movement fields. Soule's (1997) examination of the movement to divest from the apartheid regime in South Africa among college campuses in the United States traced the diffusion not only of the tactics used by the movement organizations but also of the movement itself as it spread across campuses (see also Soule 2004; Tarrow 2005).

Recent scholarship (Taylor & Van Dyke 2004) has sought to expand the traditional "repertoires of contention" (Tilly 1995) view of tactics and allow for a broader reading of what constitutes tactical action and choice by movement actors. Taylor and Van Dyke stress that tactics can take on a variety of forms in addition to the commonly associated practices of street protest. In particular, more recent movements have attempted to shift towards tactics that are more performative or participatory and which make for protests that are strategically viable but also engaging and highly visible to bystanders.

Movement dynamics span a wide array of forms and influence all major dimensions of movement activity from the initial scope to the types of tactics that get deployed at protests and rallies. Only by securing a greater understanding of the organizational and discursive fields in which movements operate do we gain a complete view of the context in which movements operate. And it is this context that helps to shape the goals of the movement, affects the strategies that a movement follows to achieve these goals, and affects the kinds of tactics available and utilized to propel a movement forward towards its goals.

Outcomes

How do we assess the consequences of a movement's campaign? What constitutes "success" as opposed to "failure"? And are there different metrics for assessing movement outcomes and reaching a conclusion about their relative success or failure? From Gamson's (1990) seminal investigation of movement outcomes to the present, movement scholars have increasingly asked such questions about movement consequences (see Cress & Snow 2000; Amenta & Caren 2004; Earl 2004; Giugni 2004; Whittier 2004).

Analysis of movement outcomes has tended to focus on movements whose goals are aimed at policy and state-level changes (e.g., Amenta & Caren 2004; Andrews 2004; Amenta 2006), with the civil rights movement being perhaps the most notable example with the passage of landmark legislation. These types of outcomes favor movements with established histories and relatively well-financed organizations that are able to leverage their organization and resources to gain the passage of laws as a result of electing favorable candidates or by winning important court decisions (Boutcher 2011).

While political influence and change may well be the most conspicuous outcomes for many movements, there are also those that seek or achieve less obvious "cultural" outcomes. Earl (2004) points to three clusters of cultural consequences: social psychological consequences such as changes in cultural values and beliefs; changes in cultural products and practices, encompassing literature, music, and language; and changes in worldview and the basis of community, as reflected in movement-based subcultures and collective identities. There are also personal and biographic consequences of movement participation, ranging from changes in personal identity to changes in political or religious orientation, to changes in lifestyle practices, such as diet, dress, and childrearing practices (McAdam 1988; Klatch 1999; Giugni 2004; Corrigall-Brown 2011).

These types of personal cultural outcomes are also the purview of many religiously oriented movements which promise and/or generate individual-level consequences not normally associated with a clear-cut political agenda. For participants in such movements, the promised or actual outcome may be a dramatic lifestyle and/or personal change, presumed salvation, or even an afterlife more glorious than the here-and-now (Berger 1981; Hall 1987; Balch 1995). Clearly such actual or anticipated outcomes can motivate participants every bit as much as the prospect of legislative or electoral success. But even within the political arena, outcomes other than policy-oriented ones can be galvanizing, as Polletta (2006) found when examining stories told by activists in different contexts: it is often the process of seeking change that is especially meaningful and memorable for activists.

Finally, even movements that fail to achieve their goals can have significant effects in the way they influence other movements or make the transition from one field of activism to another, by creating spin-off movements or laying the groundwork in the form of networks of mobilization used by future movements (Meyer & Whittier 1994; Oliver & Meyers 2003). The failure of the conservative libertarian Goldwater campaign in the 1960s laid the groundwork for much of the modern American conservative movement's resurgence (Micklethwaite & Wooldridge 2004).

The realm of social movement outcomes remains an area where there is still fertile ground to till. Differing conceptions of success make objective assessments difficult and often lead to hesitation in declaring a movement successful or not. Further complicating outcome assessment is the fact that some movements thought moribund or defunct become viable again after a period of abeyance (Taylor 1989). And finally, we have said nothing about the unintended effects of social movement activity (see Snow & Soule 2010: 205–12), such as schism and factionalization within and the generation of counter-movements and varying degrees of repression externally, which adds a further complicating dimension to understanding movement consequences.

NEW FRONTIERS IN SOCIAL MOVEMENTS

The field of social movements is constantly changing and evolving, not only because of internal debates and theoretical reshuffling but also because of contextual factors like technological innovations, dynamic political landscapes, and the ebb and flow of contentious social issues. Because of such factors, we cannot say where the field will be in 10 or 20 years, but we do see the following topic areas as good candidates for future research and theorizing.

Advances in media technology

The emergence of new technologies has long been used by creative challengers to further their goals (Roscigno & Danaher 2001; Edwards 2005). Recent advances in media technology have had a discernible impact on the way some movements operate (Earl & Schussman 2003; Earl & Kimport 2008, 2009; Carty 2010), particularly in terms of resource accumulation and recruitment. Technologies such as the internet, cell phones, wireless networks, and personal video applications have become cheaper, more widely available, and more portable at a dramatic pace, putting them in the hands of activists who have found novel ways of adapting this technology for their own means (Horst & Miller 2009).

Additionally there is evidence that technology has enabled certain types of groups to become more viable (Robb 2007; Earl & Kimport 2009), while allowing others to become more efficient and effective (Earl & Kimport 2008). The ability of technology to create a truly two-directional mass communication medium allows once small or isolated groups to proffer messages that can reach millions, and bring together once scattered prospective recruits into virtual organizations that are not dependent on physical proximity (Robb 2007). However, others caution reading too much into the effectiveness of new technologies, pointing out that the basis for much of the excitement is as yet unsubstantiated empirically (Hindman 2009), or that such claims are overstated and even prove incorrect when analyzed (Butts & Cross 2009).

Such caveats notwithstanding, the potential of these new technologies seems considerable, especially for expanding existing repertoires of contention and generating new forms of collective action because of the ease of accessibility and minimal participation costs. Because of the nature of these advances, the networks used for activism can piggyback on those used by email, internet, and cell-phone applications. This allows for smaller groups to be more mobile and have greater access to resources (Robb 2007). Finally, while these communication technologies allow members to operate at some distance, they may still allow for members to feel fully emotionally engaged as part of a collective community (Polletta, Chen, Gardner & Motes 2009).

Transnational movements and activism

The focus of much movement scholarship has been geographically skewed, focusing inordinately on movements within Western democracies. Although the openness of Western democracies may invite movement activity, movements are hardly peculiar to democratic regimes, much less Western ones. Additionally, contemporary movements are less constrained by national borders; concerns over human rights or the right to a free press do not stop at national boundaries, but flow, in large measure, freely back and forth around the globe (Smith 2005). This has led to a rise in transnational activism and the creation of truly transnational protest movements (Thomas 2000; Smith 2004; Tarrow 2005).

One example that has become increasingly salient for scholars across the globe is the rise in militant extremist groups, particularly those that engage in terrorist attacks. The idea that activists are faced with the options of exit, voice, or remaining loyal to their organization or state (Hirschman 1970) has been a scheme that many movement scholars embrace. However, we may have focused too much on the second and third options in Hirschman's formulation, while ignoring the exit option, a concern which Hirschman later recognized (1993). The question of what happens to activists who find themselves unable to reconcile their grievances and beliefs within the system, and thus exit, may have an answer in the appeal of extremist ideologies and associated movements such as Al Qaeda. But it is not only that the relationship between system exit and the turn towards violence is poorly understood. Rather, it is arguable that our understanding of movement strategic violence in general is poorly understood (but see della Porta 1995), in part because of the field's focus on the strategy of non-violence among movements and violence and repression among social control agents. However, the rise of terrorist movements over the past 20 years provides good reason to reconsider that imbalanced focus.

CONCLUDING COMMENT

Our aim herein has been to identify and elaborate salient aspects of social movements and their dynamics for the non-specialist, while also accenting the importance of the study of social movements within sociology. Social movements are one avenue through which quite ordinary people are able to make their voices heard and try to change aspects of their social worlds they find troubling and often unjust. Movements and their participants are often the agency through which social wrongs are righted and, occasionally, institutions are toppled. But they can also be the agency

through which social wrongs are perpetrated. Either way, they represent, to paraphrase a bumper sticker popular with many activists, the ability of people to become
the change they wish to see in the world. Why and how that happens, the dynamics involved, and the resultant outcomes are the scholarly concerns that have animated, and will continue to animate, the study of social movements.

Notes

1   For more concrete conceptualizations of social movements which incorporate all or most
    of the elements in varying degrees, see McAdam, Tarrow, and Tilly (2001), Snow (2004),
    Snow and Soule (2010), and Tarrow (1998).
2   For more recent work on the role of emotions in relation to movement participation and
    persistence, see Flam and King (2005), Gould (2009), and Summers-Effler (2010).
3   For an expanded discussion of strategy, see Jasper (2006), Snow and Soule (2010: 165–
    71), and Turner (1970).

References

Almeida, Paul (2003) "Opportunity Organizations and Threat-Induced Contention: Protest
    Waves in Authoritarian Settings." *American Journal of Sociology* 109: 345–400.
Amenta, Edwin (2006) *When Movements Matter: The Townsend Plan & The Rise of Social
    Security*. Princeton, NJ: Princeton University Press.
Amenta, Edwin and Neal Caren (2004) "The Legislative, Organizational, and Beneficiary
    Consequences of State-Oriented Challengers." In David A. Snow, Sarah A. Soule, and
    Hanspeter Kriesi (eds.), *The Blackwell Companion to Social Movements*. Oxford: Black-
    well, pp. 461–88.
Amenta, Edwin, Neal Caren, Sheera Joy Olasky, and James E. Stobaugh (2009) "All the
    Movements Fit to Print: Who, What, When, Where, and Why SMO Families Appeared
    in the *New York Times* in the Twentieth Century." *American Sociological Review* 74:
    636–56.
Andrews, Kenneth T. (2004) *Freedom Is a Constant Struggle: The Mississippi Civil Rights
    Movement and Its Legacy*. Chicago: University of Chicago Press.
Armstrong, Elizabeth A. (2005) "From Struggle to Settlement: The Crystallization of a Field
    of Lesbian/Gay Organizations in San Francisco, 1969–1973." In G. Davis, D. McAdam,
    W. R. Scott, and M. N. Zald (eds.), *Social Movements and Organization Theory*. New
    York: Cambridge University Press, pp. 161–87.
Balch, Robert W. (1995) "Waiting for the Ships: Disillusionment and the Revitalization of
    Faith in Bo and Peep's UFO Cult." In James R. Lewis (ed.), *The Gods Have Landed:
    New Religious from Other Worlds*. Albany, NY: State University of New York Press,
    pp. 137–66.
Balch, Robert W. and David Taylor (1978) "Seekers and Saucers: The Role of Cultic Milieu
    in Joining a UFO Cult." In James Richardson (ed.), *Conversion Careers*. Beverly Hills,
    CA: Sage, pp. 43–65.
Benford, Robert D. (1993) "'You Could Be the Hundredth Monkey': Collective Action
    Frames and Vocabularies of Motive within the Nuclear Disarmament Movement."
    Sociological Quarterly 34: 195–216.

Benford, Robert D. and David A. Snow (2000) "Framing Processes and Social Movements: An Overview and Assessment." *Annual Review of Sociology* 26: 611–39.

Berger, Bennett (1981) *The Survival of a Counterculture: Ideological Word and Everyday Life among Rural Communards*. Los Angeles: University of California Press.

Beyerlein, Kraig and John R. Hipp (2006) "A Two-Stage Model for a Two-Stage Process: How Biographical Availability Matters for Social Movement Mobilization." *Mobilization* 11: 219–40.

Blee, Kathleen M. (2002) *Inside Organized Racism: Women in the Hate Movement*. Berkeley, CA: University of California Press.

Blumer, Herbert (1951) "Collective Behavior." In Alfred McClung Lee (ed.), *Principles of Sociology*. New York: Barnes and Noble.

Boutcher, Steven A. (2011) "Mobilizing in the Shadow of the Law: Lesbian and Gay Rights in the Aftermath of Bowers v. Hardwick." *Research in Social Movements, Conflict and Change* 31: 175–205.

Buechler, Steven M. (2004) "The Strange Career of Strain and Breakdown Theories of Collective Action." In David A. Snow, Sarah A. Soule, and Hanspeter Kriesi (eds.), *The Blackwell Companion to Social Movements*. Oxford: Blackwell, pp. 47–66.

Butts, Carter and Remy Cross (2009) "Change and External Events in Computer-Mediated Citation Networks: English Language Weblogs and the 2004 U.S. Electoral Cycle." *Journal of Social Structure* 10.

Carty, Victoria (2010) *Wired and Mobilizing: Social Movements, New Technology, and Electoral Politics*. New York: Routledge.

Clemens, Elizabeth (2005) "Two Kinds of Stuff: The Current Encounter of Social Movements and Organizations." In Gerald Davis, Doug McAdam, W. Richard Scott, and Mayer N. Zald (eds.), *Social Movements and Organization Theory*. New York: Cambridge University Press, pp. 351–65.

Corrigall-Brown, Catherine (2011) *Patterns of Protest: Trajectories of Participation in Social Movements*. Palo Alto, CA: Stanford University Press.

Corrigall-Brown, Catherine, David A. Snow, Kelly Smith, and Theron Quist (2009) "Explaining the Puzzle of Homeless Mobilization: An Examination of Differential Participation." *Sociological Perspectives* 52: 309–35.

Cress, Daniel and David A. Snow (2000) "The Outcomes of Homeless Mobilization: The Influence of Organization, Disruption, Political Mediation, and Framing." *American Journal of Sociology* 105: 1063–104.

Curtis, Russell L. and Louis A. Zurcher (1973) "Stable Resources of Protest Movements: The Multi-Organizational Field." *Social Forces* 52: 53–61.

Davis, Gerald, Doug McAdam, W. Richard Scott, and Mayer N. Zald (eds.) (2005) *Social Movements and Organization Theory*. New York: Cambridge University Press.

Della Porta, Donatella (1995) *Social Movements, Political Violence, and the State: A Comparative Analysis of Italy and Germany*. New York: Cambridge University Press.

Diani, Mario (2004) "Networks and Participation." In David A. Snow, Sarah A. Soule, and Hanspeter Kriesi (eds.), *The Blackwell Companion to Social Movements*. Oxford: Blackwell, pp. 339–59.

Diani, Mario and Doug McAdam (eds.) (2003) *Social Movements and Networks: Relational Approaches to Collective Action*. New York: Oxford University Press.

Dixon, Marc and Vincent J. Roscigno (2003) "Status, Networks, and Social Movement Participation: The Case of Striking Workers." *American Journal of Sociology* 108: 1292–327.

Earl, Jennifer (2004) "Cultural Consequences of Social Movements." In David A. Snow, Sarah A. Soule, and Hanspeter Kriesi (eds.), *The Blackwell Companion to Social Movements*. Oxford: Blackwell, pp. 508–30.

Earl, Jennifer and K. Kimport (2008) "The Targets of Online Protest: State and Private Targets of Four Online Protest Tactics." *Information, Communication and Society* 11: 449–72.

Earl, Jennifer and K. Kimport (2009) "Societies and Digital Protest: Fan Activism and Other Nonpolitical Protest Online." *Sociological Theory* 27: 3.

Earl, Jennifer and Alan Schussman (2003) "The New Site of Activism: On-Line Organizations, Movement Entrepreneurs, and the Changing Location of Social Movement Decision-Making." *Research in Social Movements, Conflicts and Change* 24: 155–87.

Edwards, Mark U., Jr. (2005) *Printing, Propaganda, and Martin Luther*. Minneapolis: Fortress Press.

Edwards, Robert and John McCarthy (2004) "Resources and Social Movement Mobilization." In David A. Snow, Sarah A. Soule, and Hanspeter Kriesi (eds.), *The Blackwell Companion to Social Movements*. Oxford: Blackwell, pp. 116–52.

Evans, Sara M. and Harry C. Boyte (1986) *Free Spaces: The Sources of Democratic Change in America*. New York: Harper and Row.

Fernandez, Roberto M. and Doug McAdam (1988) "Social Networks and Social Movements: Multiorganizational Fields and Recruitment to Mississippi Freedom Summer." *Sociological Forum* 3: 357–82.

Flam, Helena and Debra King (eds.) (2005) *Emotions and Social Movements*. Abingdon: Routledge.

Friedman, Debra and Doug McAdam (1992) "Identity Incentives and Activism: Networks, Choices and the Life of a Social Movement." In Carol Mueller and Aldon Morris (eds.), *Frontiers in Social Movement Theory*. New Haven: Yale University Press, pp. 156–73.

Futrell, Robert and Pete Simi (2004) "Free Spaces, Collective Identity, and the Persistence of U.S. White Power Activism." *Social Problems* 51: 16–42.

Gamson, William A. (1990) *The Strategy of Social Protest*, 2nd edn. Belmont, CA: Wadsworth.

Gamson, William A. (1992) *Talking Politics*. New York: Cambridge University Press.

Gamson William and David Meyer (1996) "Framing Political Opportunity." In Doug McAdam, John McCarthy, and Mayer N. Zald (eds.), *Comparative Perspectives on Social Movements: Political Opportunities, Mobilizing Structures, and Cultural Framing*. Cambridge: Cambridge University Press, pp. 275–90.

Ganz, Marshall (2000) "Resources and Resourcefulness: Strategic Capacity in the Unionization of California Agriculture, 1959–1966." *American Journal of Sociology* 105: 1003–62.

Giugni, Marco (2004) "Personal and Biographical Consequences." In David A. Snow, Sarah A. Soule, and Hanspeter Kriesi (eds.), *The Blackwell Companion to Social Movements*. Oxford: Blackwell, pp. 489–507.

Goodwin, Jeff, James M. Jasper, and Francesca Polletta (eds.) (2001) *Passionate Politics: Emotions and Social Movements*. Chicago: University of Chicago Press.

Goodwin, J., J. Jasper, and F. Polletta (2004) "Emotional Dimensions of Social Movements." In David A. Snow, Sarah A. Soule, and Hanspeter Kriesi (eds.), *The Blackwell Companion to Social Movements*. Oxford: Blackwell, pp. 413–32.

Gould, Deborah (2009) *Moving Politics: Emotion and ACT UP's Fight Against AIDS*. Chicago: University of Chicago Press.

Gould, Roger V. (1991) "Multiple Networks and Mobilization in the Paris Commune, 1871." *American Sociological Review* 56: 716–29.

Hall, John R. (1987) *Gone from the Promised Land: Jonestown in American Cultural History*. New Brunswick, NJ: Transaction.

Hindman, Matthew (2009) *The Myth of Digital Democracy*. Princeton, NJ: Princeton University Press.

Hirschman, Albert O. (1970) *Exit, Voice, and Loyalty: Responses to Decline in Firms, Organizations, and States*. Cambridge, MA: Harvard University Press.

Hirschman, Albert O. (1993) "Exit, Voice, and the Fate of the German Democratic Republic – An Essay in Conceptual History." *World Politics* 45: 173–202.

Horst, Heather and Daniel Miller (2009) *The Cell Phone: An Anthropology of Communication*. New York: Berg.

Hunt, Scott and Robert D. Benford (2004) "Collective Identity, Solidarity and Commitment." In David A. Snow, Sarah A. Soule, and Hanspeter Kriesi (eds.), *The Blackwell Companion to Social Movements*. Oxford: Blackwell, pp. 453–7.

Hunt, Scott, Robert D. Benford, and David A. Snow (1994) "Identity Fields: Framing Processes and the Social Construction of Movement Identities." In E. Larana, H. Johnson, and J. R. Gusfield (eds.), *New Social Movements: From Ideology to Identity*. Philadelphia, PA: Temple University Press, pp. 185–208.

Jasper, James (2006) *Getting Your Way: Strategic Dilemmas in the Real World*. Chicago: University of Chicago Press.

Jasper, James and Jane Poulsen (1995) "Recruiting Strangers and Friends: Moral Shocks and Social Networks in Animal Rights and Animal Protest." *Social Problems* 42: 493–512.

Johnston, Hank and David A. Snow (1998) "Subcultures and the Emergence of the Estonian Nationalist Opposition, 1945–1990." *Sociological Perspectives* 41: 473–97.

Kanter, Rosabeth (1972) *Commitment and Community: Communes and Utopias in Sociological Perspective*. Cambridge, MA: Harvard University Press.

Kaplan, Howard and X. Liu (2000) "Social Movements as Collective Coping with Spoiled Identities: Intimations from a Panel Study of Changes in the Life Course between Adolescence and Adulthood." In Sheldon Stryker, Timothy Owens, and Robert White (eds.), *Self, Identity and Social Movements*. Minneapolis: University of Minnesota Press, pp. 215–38.

Klandermans, Bert (1984) "Mobilization and Participation: Social Psychological Expansions of Resource Mobilization Theory." *American Sociological Review* 49: 583–600.

Klandermans, Bert (1992) "The Social Construction of Protest and Multiorganizational Fields." In Aldon D. Morris and Carol M. Mueller (eds.), *Frontiers in Social Movement Theory*. New Haven, CT: Yale University Press, pp. 77–103.

Klandermans, Bert (2004) "The Demand and Supply of Participation: Social-Psychological Correlates of Participation in Social Movements." In David A. Snow, Sarah A. Soule, and Hanspeter Kriesi (eds.), *The Blackwell Companion to Social Movements*. Oxford: Blackwell, pp. 360–79.

Klandermans, Bert and Dirk Oegema (1987) "Potentials, Networks, Motivations and Barriers: Steps towards Participation in Social Movements." *American Sociological Review* 52: 519–31.

Klatch, Rebecca E. (1999) *A Generation Divided: The New Left, The New Right, and the 1960s*. Berkeley, CA: University of California Press.

Koopmans, Ruud (2004) "Protest in Time and Space: The Evolution of Waves of Contention." In David A. Snow, Sarah A. Soule, and Hanspeter Kriesi (eds.), *The Blackwell Companion to Social Movements*. Oxford: Blackwell, pp. 19–46.

Kurzman, Charles (1996) "Structural Opportunity and Perceived Opportunity in Social Movement Theory: The Iranian Revolution of 1979." *American Sociological Review* 61: 153–70.

McAdam, Doug (1983) "Tactical Innovation and the Pace of Insurgency." *American Sociological Review* 48: 735–54.

McAdam, Doug (1986) "Recruitment to High-Risk Activism: The Case of Freedom Summer." *American Journal of Sociology* 92: 64–90.

McAdam, Doug (1988) *Freedom Summer*. Oxford: Oxford University Press.

McAdam, Doug (1996) "Political Opportunities: Conceptual Origins, Current Problems, and Future Directions." In Doug McAdam, John D. McCarthy, and Mayer N. Zald (eds.), *Comparative Perspectives on Social Movements: Political Opportunities, Mobilizing Structures, and Cultural Framings*. New York: Cambridge University Press, pp. 23–40.

McAdam, Doug and Ronnelle Paulsen (1993) "Specifying the Relationship between Social Ties and Activism." *American Journal of Sociology* 99: 640–67.

McAdam, Doug and W. Richard Scott (2005) "Organizations and Movements." In G. Davis, D. McAdam, W. R. Scott, and M. N. Zald (eds.), *Social Movements and Organization Theory*. New York: Cambridge University Press, pp. 4–40.

McAdam, D. and Yang Su (2002) "The War at Home: Antiwar Protests and Congressional Voting, 1965–1973." *American Sociological Review* 67: 696–721.

McAdam, Doug, Sidney Tarrow, and Charles Tilly (2001) *Dynamics of Contention*. New York: Cambridge University Press.

McCarthy, John and Mayer Zald (1977) "Resource Mobilization and Social Movements: A Partial Theory." *American Journal of Sociology* 82: 1212–41.

Melucci, Alberto (1989) *Nomads of the Present*. Oxford: Hutchinson Radius.

Meyer, David (2004) "Protest and Political Opportunities." *Social Forces* 30: 125–45.

Meyer, David S. and Sidney Tarrow (eds.) (1998) *The Social Movement Society: Contentious Politics for a New Century*. Boulder, CO: Rowman and Littlefield.

Meyer, David S. and Nancy Whittier (1994) "Social Movement Spillover." *Social Problems* 41: 277–98.

Micklethwaite, John and Adrian Wooldridge (2004) *The Right Nation: Conservative Power in America*. New York: Penguin.

Moore, Barrington, Jr. (1978) *Injustice: The Social Basis of Obedience and Revolt*. White Plains, NY: M. E. Sharpe.

Morris, Aldon D. (1981) "Black Southern Sit-in Movement: An Analysis of Internal Organization." *American Sociological Review* 46: 744–67.

Nepstadt, Sharon Erickson and Christian Smith (1999) "Rethinking Recruitment to High Risk/Cost Activism: The Case of the Nicaragua Exchange." *Mobilization* 4: 25–40.

Oliver, Pamela E. and Daniel J. Meyers (2003) "Networks, Diffusion, and Cycles of Collective Action." In Mario Diani and Doug McAdam (eds.), *Social Movements and Networks: Relational Approaches to Collective Action*. New York: Oxford University Press pp. 173–204.

Olson, Mancur (1965) *The Logic of Collective Action: Public Goods and the Theory of Groups*. Cambridge, MA: Harvard University Press.

Polletta, Francesca (1999) " 'Free Spaces' in Collective Action." *Theory and Society* 28: 1–38.

Polletta, Francesca (2006) *It Was Like a Fever: Storytelling in Protest and Politics*. Chicago: University of Chicago Press.

Polletta, Francesca and James Jasper (2001) "Collective Identity and Social Movements." *Annual Review of Sociology* 27: 283–305.

Polletta, Francesca, Pang Ching Chen, Beth Gardner, and Alice Motes (2009) "Is the Web Creating New Reasons to Protest?" Paper presented at Advances in Social Movement Research Conference, Dutch Royal Academy of Sciences, September 30–October 2.

Robb, John (2007) *Brave New War: The Next Stage of Terrorism and the End of Globalization*. New York: John Wiley and Sons.

Rohlinger, Deana A. and David A. Snow (2003) "Social Psychological Perspectives on Crowds and Social Movements." In John DeLamater (ed.), *Handbook of Social Psychology: Sociological Perspectives*. New York: Kluwer/Plenum, pp. 503–27.

Roscigno, Vincent J. and William F. Danaher (2001) "Media and Mobilization: The Case of Radio and Southern Textile Worker Insurgency." *American Sociological Review* 66: 21–48.

Rucht, Dieter (2004) "Movement Allies, Adversaries, and Third Parties." In David A. Snow, Sarah A. Soule, and Hanspeter Kriesi (eds.), *The Blackwell Companion to Social Movements*. Oxford: Blackwell, pp. 197–216.

Schussman, Alan, and Sarah Anne Soule (2005) "Process and Protest: Accounting for Individual Protest Participation." *Social Forces* 84: 1083–108.

Smith, Jackie (2004) "Transnational Processes and Movements." In David A. Snow, Sarah A. Soule, and Hanspeter Kriesi (eds.), *The Blackwell Companion to Social Movements*. Oxford: Blackwell, pp. 311–35.

Smith, Jackie (2005) "Building Bridges or Building Walls? Explaining Regionalization among Transnational Social Movement Organizations." *Mobilization* 10: 251–70.

Snow, David A. (2004) "Social Movements as Challenges to Authority: Resistance to an Emerging Conceptual Hegemony." In Daniel J. Meyers and Daniel M. Cress (eds.), *Authority in Contention: Research in Social Movements, Conflict, and Change*. London: Elsevier, pp. 3–25.

Snow, David A. (2008) "Elaborating the Discursive Contexts of Framing: Discursive Fields and Spaces." *Studies in Symbolic Interaction* 30: 3–28.

Snow, David A. and Robert D. Benford (1988) "Ideology, Frame Resonance, and Participant Mobilization." *International Social Movement Research* 1: 197–217.

Snow, David A. and Scott Byrd (2007) "Ideology, Framing Processes, and Islamic Terrorist Movements." *Mobilization* 12: 119–36.

Snow, David A. and Sarah A. Soule (2010) *A Primer on Social Movements*. New York: Norton.

Snow, David A., Daniel Cress, Liam Downey, and Andrew Jones (1998) "Disrupting the Quotidian: Reconceptualizing the Relationship between Breakdown and the Emergence of Collective Action." *Mobilization* 3: 1–22.

Snow, David A., Burke Rochford, Jr., Steven Worden, and Robert D. Benford (1986) "Frame Alignment Processes, Micromobilization, and Movement Participation." *American Sociological Review* 51: 464–81.

Snow, David A., Rens Vliegenhart, and Catherine Corrigall-Brown (2007) "Framing the French 'Riots': A Comparative Study of Frame Variation." *Social Forces* 86: 385–415.

Snow, David A., Louis A. Zurcher, and Sheldon Ekland-Olson (1980) "Social Networks and Social Movements: A Microstructural Approach to Differential Recruitment." *American Sociological Review* 45: 787–801.

Soule, Sarah A. (1997) "The Student Divestment Movement in the United States and Tactical Diffusion: The Shantytown Protest." *Social Forces* 75: 855–82.

Soule, Sarah A. (2004) "Diffusion Processes within and across Social Movements." In David A. Snow, Sarah A. Soule, and Hanspeter Kriesi (eds.), *The Blackwell Companion to Social Movements*. Oxford: Blackwell, pp. 294–310.

Staggenborg, Suzanne (1988) "The Consequences of Professionalization and Formalization in the American Labor Movement." *American Sociological Review* 53: 585–605.

Straus, Roger (1976) "Changing Oneself: Seekers and the Creative Transformation of Life Experience." In John Lofland (ed.), *Doing Social Life*. New York: John Wiley, pp. 252–72.

Stryker, Sheldon, Timothy Owens, and Robert White (eds.) (2000) *Self, Identity and Social Movements*. Minneapolis: University of Minnesota Press.

Summers-Effler, Erika (2010) *Laughing Saints and Righteous Heroes: A Theory of Persistence and Transformation in Social Movement Groups*. Chicago: University of Chicago Press.

Tarrow, Sidney (1998) *Power in Movement: Collective Action, Social Movements and Politics*. Cambridge: Cambridge University Press.

Tarrow, Sidney (2005) *The New Transnational Activism*. New York: Cambridge University Press.

Taylor, Verta (1989) "Social Movement Continuity: The Women's Movement in Abeyance." *American Sociological Review* 54: 761–75.

Taylor, Verta and Nella Van Dyke (2004) "Get up, Stand up': Tactical Repertoires of Social Movements." In David A. Snow, Sarah A. Soule, and Hanspeter Kriesi (eds.), *The Blackwell Companion to Social Movements*. Oxford: Blackwell, pp. 262–93.

Taylor, Verta and Nancy Whittier (1992) "Collective Identity in Social Movement Communities: Lesbian Feminist Mobilization." In Aldon D. Morris and Carol McClurg Mueller (eds.), *Frontiers in Social Movement Theory*. New Haven, CT: Yale University Press, pp. 104–29.

Thomas, Janet (2000) *The Battle in Seattle: The Story Behind and Beyond the WTO Demonstrations*. Boulder, CO: Fulcrum Publishing.

Tilly, Charles (1978) *From Mobilization to Revolution*. Reading, MA: Addison-Wesley.

Tilly, Charles (1995) *Popular Contention in Great Britain, 1758–1834*. Cambridge, MA: Harvard University Press.

Tilly, Charles and Sidney Tarrow (2007) *Contentious Politics*. Boulder, CO: Paradigm.

Tilly, Charles, Louise Tilly, and Richard Tilly (1975) *The Rebellious Century, 1830–1930*. Cambridge, MA: Harvard University Press.

Trotsky, Leon ([1932] 1959) *The History of the Russian Revolution*. Ed. F. W. Dupre. New York: Doubleday.

Turner, Ralph H. (1970) "Determinants of Social Movement Strategies." In T. Shibutani (ed.), *Human Nature and Collective Behavior: Papers in Honor of Herbert Blumer*. New Brunswick, NJ: Transaction, pp. 145–64.

Whittier, Nancy (2004) "The Consequences of Social Movements for Each Other." In David A. Snow, Sarah A. Soule, and Hanspeter Kriesi (eds.), *The Blackwell Companion to Social Movements*. Oxford: Blackwell, pp. 531–52.

Zhao, Dingxin (2001) *The Power of Tiananmen: State-Society Relations and the 1989 Beijing Student Movement*. Chicago: University of Chicago Press.

29

Globalization

PAUL DEAN AND GEORGE RITZER

Globalization is transforming how we think about the social world and has emerged as one of the most interesting, contentious, and important topics within contemporary scholarship. This academic interest is motivated, in part, by the popular concern over globalization and its impact on our everyday lives, including our own mobility, access to economic opportunity, the status of our jobs, accessibility to families, environmental sustainability, the prospects of democracy and governance, and issues of safety and terrorism. Its importance is seen everywhere and felt by the billions of people throughout the world. It is no coincidence then that the magnitude of these issues is reflected in the proliferation of scholarly work on globalization and its contentiousness is seen in even the most basic questions including what globalization is and when it started. This chapter surveys these basic issues and the major theories, methodologies, and topics within globalization from a sociological perspective.

Sociological definitions of globalization generally view it as a process or condition. For example, Ritzer defines globalization as a "transplanetary process or set of processes involving increasing liquidity and the growing multidirectional flows of people, objects, places, and information as well as the structures they encounter and create that are barriers to, or expedite, those flows" (2010: 2). Giddens (1990) also emphasizes globalizing processes, including capitalism (economic), the interstate system (political), militarism (security), and industrialism (international division of labor).

For others, globalization is a condition, or an effect of cultural, political, and economic processes, such as imperialism and post-Fordism (Rosenberg 2000). This condition of "globality" is seen as a "global consciousness" (Robertson 1992) or "world culture" (Boli & Lechner 2005) in which people share a similar set of practices and values using the same organizational and economic forms, and are aware

The Wiley-Blackwell Companion to Sociology, First Edition. Edited by George Ritzer.
© 2012 Blackwell Publishing Ltd. Published 2012 by Blackwell Publishing Ltd.

of themselves living in such a world. Whether globalization is defined as a process or condition, the common strand is its connectedness across space and time. This is not to say that global connectedness is balanced; to the contrary, this connectedness favors some groups at the expense of others, with barriers erected that restrict and redirect inter-connected flows of people, trade, and ideas. Nevertheless, the process and condition of globalized connectivity is unparalleled in our current world.

A related definitional issue is whether we see globalization as singular or plural (Hoffman 2002). On the one hand, globalization is treated by some as a single "world culture" or simply in economic terms (O'Rourke & Williamson 2002). But if we accept that globalization encompasses multiple attributes, and multiple differentiated and uneven economic, political, and cultural processes, then it may make more sense to speak in terms of globalizations (in the plural form), or globalization as multi-dimensional.

There are also many perspectives on when globalization began. While some scholars (Chanda 2007) suggest globalization began thousands of years ago, most commentators date the beginning of globalization to one of three periods. Some commentators, such as world-systems scholars (Wallerstein 1974), view globalization as nothing new, connecting it to the emergence of capitalism and modernity (early 1500s). An intermediary view dates its roots to the late 1800s with the expansion of international relations and trade (Robertson 1992). A third view locates globalization as starting some time between 1945 and the 1970s. Following World War II, international trade rapidly expanded with the founding of new global economic institutions (the Bretton Woods institutions), the emergence of multinational corporations, and technological advances. Globalization exploded in the 1970s with post-industrialization and global capitalist restructuring, the spread of neoliberal ideology, and the development of computer technologies. An alternative view documents these various "waves" (and other periodical waves) of globalization and their interim periods of de-globalization (Therborn 2000).

The remainder of this chapter is divided into three sections. The first section surveys several of the main globalization theories, including cultural and political economic theories. Next, we explore methodological considerations in the study of globalization. We focus specifically on methodological approaches, the different levels of analysis, and dimensions for operationalizing globalization. We then introduce several of the major topics in globalization today. While the major topics cannot be adequately addressed in a single chapter, we briefly introduce several of the most discussed topics in contemporary globalization scholarship. In addition to the topics of cultural convergence and divergence (discussed in the section on globalization theories), we focus on the role of the nation-state, the multinational corporation, the environment, global inequalities, technology, and alter-globalization movements. We conclude by suggesting several possibilities for the futures of globalization.

THEORIZING GLOBALIZATION

The theories used to understand globalization shape how we explain and interpret global processes and outcomes. Cultural theories of globalization tend to focus on the relationship between the global and the local and whether those interactions are producing cultural homogeneity or heterogeneity (Ritzer 2010). In this section, we begin by exploring representative theories from each perspective, then move on to several important political economic theories of globalization.

Cultural theories

Cultural theories that emphasize homogenization include Ritzer's (2004, 2006) complementary theories of McDonaldization and grobalization. McDonaldization is a force of cultural imperialism and is "the process by which the principles of the fast-food restaurant are coming to dominate more and more sectors of American society as well as of the rest of the world" (Ritzer 2004: 1). In this perspective, McDonald's is used as a paradigmatic example because of its four rationalizing principles that increasingly characterize cultural practices around the planet (in this, it draws from and builds upon Weber's theory of bureaucracy). The first principle is efficiency, in which organizations systematically seek the best method to achieve their goals. Second, there is an emphasis on calculability that focuses on the quantitative (rather than qualitative) dimensions of goods and services. Third, predictability ensures that everything is done the same across space and time. Fourth, greater and greater control is sought over workers and clients through increasing use of nonhuman technology. The paradox is that while these principles are meant to increase rationality, they also increase irrationality simultaneously (including negative environmental effects and the dehumanization of work and consumption practices). As exhibited by McDonald's (e.g., most of their new restaurants are opened overseas) and other fast-food chains (and corporations), these cultural practices have become increasingly global.

McDonaldization is one driving force (in addition to capitalism and Americanization) of grobalization, or "the imperialistic ambitions of nations, corporations, organizations, and the like and their desire, indeed need, to impose themselves on various geographic areas" (Ritzer 2006: 15). The main objective for these entities is to grow (hence, *gro*balize) their power, influence, and/or profits throughout the world. Like McDonaldization, it implies cultural convergence as social forms are increasingly characterized by nothing – that is, they are centrally conceived and controlled forms that are lacking in distinctive content (e.g., shopping malls, credit cards). However, these grobalizing forces are not totalizing; local (or glocal – defined below) forces continue to exert influence through the production of something, a "social form that is generally indigenously conceived, controlled, and comparatively rich in distinctive substantive content" (Ritzer 2006: 38). Through grobalizing processes, forms of nothing may conflict with, or even be rejected by, local cultures and societies. Nonetheless, Ritzer emphasizes the uni-directional flows from the grobal to the local/particular because forms of nothing are easy and cheap to replicate. The global media and commodities are particularly important in these flows because of their relatively coercive power over local forces.

Other theories of cultural convergence include neo-institutionalist theories of the world society (Meyer, Boli, Thomas & Ramirez 1997) and world culture (Boli & Thomas 1999; Boli & Lechner 2005). Like McDonaldization and grobalization, the neo-institutional approach identifies a diffusion of worldwide models (e.g., the nation-state, medicine, business) spread through global culture and associational processes. However, unlike Ritzer who emphasized capitalism, rationality, and Americanization as driving grobalization, neo-institutionalists do not locate this process as being driven by power relations or functionalist rationality. Instead, they explain cultural convergence (and "institutional isomorphism") in terms of the adoption of models because they are seen to be "universally applicable" and have been accorded legitimacy (Meyer, Boli, Thomas & Ramirez 1997). For example, specific economic policies and educational programs, whose successes are locally contingent, have been spread around the world not because they have been evaluated to rationally work or forced upon localities, but because they are universally and consensually accepted as legitimate cultural forms.

A second paradigm of cultural globalization suggests that the proliferation of local-global interactions leads to greater cultural variations that are not reducible to either local or global culture. The leading theory in this paradigm is Roland Robertson's (1992, 1995) theory of glocalization. Like Ritzer (2006), Robertson notes that globalization is a combination of both homogenization and heterogenization (and of something and nothing), but he believes that grobalization drastically underestimates the power of the local within these processes. Individuals and localities have the potential to reject, or creatively modify and adapt to, external forces. These various reactions to global processes depend on local conditions. For example, McDonald's in Russia advertises the local origins of its foods and its consumers integrate McDonald's menu items into domestic meals in creative ways (Caldwell 2004). As such, glocalization is sensitive to local and national differences and views globalization as resulting in cultural heterogenization.

Theories of hybridization and creolization also emphasize cultural heterogenization in ways that are very similar to glocalization. Hybridization refers to the unique mixing of two or more elements of different cultures (Canclini 1995; Nederveen Pieterse 2004), such as the adaptation of a beauty pageant (a US cultural phenomenon) to local Belizian practices and conceptions of beauty (Wilk 1995). Creolization, which comes from the term "creole" referring to people of mixed race, has been applied to the blending of language and culture (Hannerz 1987). These new cultural forms, like those discussed in terms of hybridization and glocalization, are argued to result in a greater degree of cultural heterogeneity.

Political economic theories

A second set of globalization theories has given centrality to political and economic features of globalization. These include world-systems theory (Wallerstein 1974), global capitalism (Sklair 2002), empire (Hardt & Negri 2000, 2004), and network society (Castells 1996).

One of the earliest theories of globalization is the world-system paradigm, which really emerged before globalization *per se* became a significant subject of academic inquiry (Arrighi 2005). It takes the global historical system as its unit of analysis (Wallerstein 1974). From this view, globalization started 500 years ago when the capitalist world economy emerged in Europe and gradually spread to incorporate all mini-societies (culturally, politically, and economically) within the global market. A key feature of this approach is the division of the world into dominant core societies (Western Europe, North America, Japan) and the dependent periphery (nations made dependent through, for example, colonialism) and semi-periphery. This represents an international division of labor, with value flowing from periphery to core. The development of this world system is driven by capitalist development and geopolitics, with nations and regions competing with each other to maintain or improve their position in the world system, and unfolding through cycles of growth and crisis.

In *Globalization: Capitalism and Its Alternatives*, Sklair (2002) distinguishes between capitalist globalization (the predominant form of globalization now) and a socialist form of globalization that does not yet exist but is foreshadowed by various alter-globalization movements. He argues that capitalist globalization consists of three types of transnational practices. First, economic practices of transnational corporations (TNC) include their cross-border linkages within systems of production and circulation. Second, there exists a transnational capitalist class (TCC) who act on common interests in expanding global capitalism and whose political practices seek to control and govern globalization through political parties and international associations. The transnational capitalist class consists of four fractions including TNC executives (corporate fraction), state and inter-state bureaucrats and politicians (state fraction), globalizing professionals (technical fraction), and merchants and media executives (consumerist fraction). Finally, Sklair outlines the culture-ideology practices of consumerism, which use global media to create artificial desires to be satisfied through commodity consumption. Working within a Marxist paradigm, Sklair also sees this system as sowing the seeds of its own destruction (for example, through environmental degradation and class polarization), with social movements challenging and proposing alternatives to global capitalism. These social movements, such as those supporting the culture-ideology of human rights, may ultimately lead to a form of socialist globalization.

The most ambitious and debated Neo-Marxian theory of globalization is Hardt and Negri's (2000, 2004) Empire. In contrast to earlier modernist imperialism, Empire is not associated with any single nation (e.g., the US) or any other single entity. Influenced by postmodernism, Hardt and Negri see Empire as a deterritorialized form of global capitalist power that lacks boundaries or a center. It is characterized by a new juridical power that simultaneously asserts a new form of order, norms, and ethical truths. This is the basis of power in Empire (which is not in the form of capitalist nations or a capitalist class), which is much more nebulous in that it penetrates (in a Foucauldian fashion) the individual psyche and biology. Through this biopolitical control, it claims to operate in the name of what is "right" and can intervene anywhere in the world at any time regarding humanitarian issues, war, or peace. This nebulous power leads to many conflicts between Empire and its subjects, the multitude. Rather than potential for resistance in a proletariat, Hardt and Negri see it in this group of people who produce social life in all its forms. Like the multitude, all of social life is subsumed under Empire, increasing the likelihood of resistance. Through global connectivity, there is utopian potential in the multitude that can ultimately overthrow Empire and construct an alternative (yet-to-be-named) social system.

Another important theory of globalization is Manuel Castells' (1996) theory of the network society. Castells argues that global forces, the most important of which is information technology, are transforming all of society – and network society is its new social structure. These information technologies have given rise to a "new economy" characterized by "informational capitalism," which is driven by the "networked enterprise" and coordinated through highly flexible and interdependent global networks of production and competition. Conflicts are always present in this new economic system, with power congealing through these networks and within knowledge production. Information technology has just as much influence over a radically new cultural life, where "virtuality becomes a fundamental component of our symbolic environment"; this culture is both real and virtual, constructed through electronic-based communication. This mediated environment has compressed time and space, facilitating decentralized networks operating in real-time not only for production systems but for social movements as well (e.g., women's movements and gay and lesbian movements). These have rendered political boundaries less controllable, therefore lessening the sovereignty and legitimacy of the nation-state. Unlike the theories identified above, Castells attributes causal determinacy to this information technology (rather than capitalist logic or cultural principles), and interprets changes in capitalism, culture, and politics as effects of this technology.

METHODOLOGICAL CONSIDERATIONS IN THE STUDY OF GLOBALIZATION

A variety of methodologies and data sources are used in the study of globalization. The basic (overlapping) considerations in these studies are methodological approaches (qualitative versus quantitative); level of analysis (from the individual to the entire world); and dimensionality of globalization, including economic, political, and/or cultural, and single versus multi-dimensional measures of globalization.

Methodological approaches to globalization are highly related to their level of analysis. Specifically, qualitative approaches tend to focus either at the micro level using ethnographic data, or at the world-systemic level using comparative historical methods (Wallerstein 1974). For example, ethnographic approaches analyze globalization through in-depth interviews and observations. These studies tend to analyze individuals and communities in order to understand the relationship between global and local phenomena, such as how globalization is affecting local culture (Caldwell 2004). This type of qualitative research is rarely used to measure globalization itself (Babones 2011). In contrast, the world-systems approach takes the world as its unit of analysis because it views the world system as a distinct entity, distinguishable from those smaller entities with which it interacts.

On the other hand, quantitative methodologies generally use national-level data for pragmatic purposes (the nation is typically the primary unit for administering quantitative surveys, therefore limiting the data to this level). One major issue regarding the level of analysis is how globalization is conceptualized: is globalization equal to the total of national-level processes (or outcomes) or are globalization processes (or outcomes) greater than the sum of its parts? This tension can be seen in the differing theoretical approaches of world-systems and world society (Babones 2007). World-systems theorists argue that globalization functions as broad structural processes that affect nations (or regions) in similar ways simultaneously.

Therefore, they are interested in focusing on the world system and the interaction between it and its constituent parts, rather than focusing on nations individually. World society theory stipulates that individual nations are an appropriate unit of analysis because they emulate cultural practices in successful nations, leading to the piecemeal construction of a singular global society and culture. One problem with the national approach, however, is that it may not be realistic to treat nations as independent cases in globalization studies, particularly given the assumptions made when utilizing certain statistical procedures (Babones 2007).

Beyond the unit of analysis, questions of operationalizing globalization must also consider what dimensions it entails. Globalization is most commonly reduced to its economic dimensions and measured by foreign trade or foreign direct investment (e.g., foreign trade as a proportion of GDP). It may also be measured in its cultural dimensions, which, in addition to qualitative data, may be captured through the World Values Survey (which now includes data on over 80 nations gathered across five waves in 20 years). Political globalization may be measured using sources such as the *Europa World Year Book* or the International Institute of Strategic Studies' annual volume *The Military Balance* (Babones 2007). It has also been measured using tourist arrivals, migration statistics, treaty memberships (Guillen 2001), and cutting-edge satellite imagery looking at rural areas (Babones 2011). Multi-dimensional indices include the Maastricht Globalisation Index (MGI, 11 indicators), the Konjunkturforschungsstelle (KOF, 24 indicators), or GlobalIndex (31 indicators).

MAJOR TOPICS IN GLOBALIZATION

A great variety of topics are involved in, and affected by, the processes and conditions of globalization. Indeed, there are far too many important topics to cover in a single chapter (for more comprehensive reviews, see Ritzer 2007). Two of the most important topics – whether globalization is producing greater cultural convergence or divergence and the relationship between the global and local – were discussed at length in the globalization theories section above and will not, therefore, be addressed here. We will focus, rather, on six topics that have emerged as some of the most debated and pressing topics within globalization studies today. These include the role of the nation-state, the multinational corporation, the environment, global inequalities, technology, and alter-globalization movements.

The role and authority of the nation-state

One of the most central topics within globalization concerns the role and authority of the nation-state, and whether its authority is decreasing in the current era of globalization. The nation-state system was institutionalized with the Treaty of Westphalia (1648) which established sovereign states as its primary organizing principle. Scholars, therefore, have viewed the nation-state as preeminent in our modern era, but many observers now argue that its privileged position is eroding with current globalizing processes (Hayman & Williams 2006).

One of the greatest threats to the nation-state is the global economy and global economic flows. For example, Strange argued that technological and financial changes have led to "the accelerated integration of national economies into one single global market economy" (1996: 13–14), with power shifting from the state to the market. States compete to attract capital, which is increasingly mobile and uses its mobility to extract concessions from states. As transnational corporations (Sklair 2002) and global economic institutions (McMichael 2008) have become increasingly powerful, states have not been able to control these movements, especially financial flows (Strange 1996). Evans (1997) argued that because most states have adopted neoliberal ideology, which itself dictates a weak role for the state, the declining authority of the nation-state is more a result of ideology than globalization *per se*.

Cultural and political factors have also challenged the authority of the state. For example, human rights have become a significant global political issue, with advocates seeking to define and enforce *universal* human rights (Elliott 2007; Chatterjee 2008). As a result, these advocates argue that it is not exclusively a state concern (Levy & Sznaider 2006) and assert that it is the right of global organizations to intervene in nation-states where universal human rights have been violated. Such interventions generally take place through international nongovernmental organizations (e.g., Amnesty International) (Boli & Lechner 2005), or the transnational (European Union) and global political agencies (United Nations) which now facilitate more "fluid" international relations (Waters 1995). In short, the nation-state is a highly "porous" entity unable to fully control its borders (Bauman 1992: 57). Furthermore, these processes, perhaps only accelerating in recent years, have led some critics to argue that our conception of the nation-state as autonomous and self-controlled has always been exaggerated.

However, there are still some analysts who argue that the nation-state has maintained its authority, and remains the most important actor in globalization (Gilpin 2001). One extreme argument made by Beland asserts that "the role of the state is enduring – even increasing – in advanced industrial societies" (2008: 48) due to collective security responses to terrorism, economic crisis, immigration, and the spread of disease. From the world-system perspective, globalization actually fosters nation-states (Wallerstein 1974). Most scholars who argue for the continued significance of the state, however, tend to view the role of the nation-state as changing in some ways (Sassen 1996). For example, Meyer et al. view states as "identifying and managing" (Meyer, Boli, Thomas & Ramirez 1997: 157) the problems of adopting and adapting world-cultural principles. From a Neo-Marxist perspective, Robinson argues that the role of nation-states has transformed and is being "absorbed into the larger structure of a Transnational State" (2004: 88). Nation-states are vital in serving the interest of a transnational capitalist class, which functions as a loose supranational network, but requires nation-states to institute policies necessary for global capitalist accumulation. From these perspectives, states function as very important meso-level structures that are integrated within, but also shape, broader global structures.

The multinational (or transnational) corporation

As mentioned above, if the power and authority of the nation-state has declined, it is the multinational (or transnational) corporation that has replaced it. A multinational corporation (MNC) "is a firm that has the power to *coordinate* and *control* operations" in more than two countries "even if it does not own them" (Dicken 2007: 106). While such companies have a history reaching back to at least 1867 (Sklair 2002), they have grown dramatically in number, scope, and significance in the period of globalization following World War II. There are now about 61,000 MNCs, with production operations involving over 900,000 affiliates, which account for about 10 percent of the world's gross national product (GNP) (Ritzer 2010). Nonetheless, a fairly small number of "global corporations" (e.g., Toyota, General Electric, and others on the Fortune 500 list) are dominant, most of which are head-quartered in the most industrialized countries (Dicken 2007).

Corporations have expanded their operations multinationally for a variety of reasons. For example, corporations may have saturated their domestic market and so they expand geographically to reach new markets, or they may find that cultural and political differences in accessing a market require that they have a presence in that market. They may also utilize price advantages of different countries, such as drawing upon cheap labor in less developed countries but research and development capacities in more developed countries. As such, their production and distribution systems may be integrated into a "global value chain," where the value added to a good or service occurs through different phases of production spread around the globe (Gereffi 2005). These value chains function as dispersed networks (Castells 1996) that may include their own operations, partnerships with affiliates, or relationships with independent suppliers and buyers.

As suggested above, these corporations have attained a new level of power within globalization. Many of the largest corporations have economies larger than most nation-states (Sklair 2002), but, unlike nation-states, are not bound to a geographic area. If policies in one nation impinge upon the profits of a corporation (e.g., environmental regulations or strong labor protections), then they may move to a nation with more favorable policies. This has created a "race to the bottom," where states compete for capital and jobs (at the expense of the environment and workers). The vast economic resources of these corporations also give them more direct influence over national and regional policy, as exhibited through global economic institutions (e.g., the World Economic Forum) and direct relationships with state bureaucrats and politicians (Sklair 2002). On the one hand, states have much less power over corporations; on the other hand, they have willingly worked with corporations to spread capitalist globalization into further areas of social life (Hardt & Negri 2000; Sklair 2002).

Contrary to these arguments, Dicken (2007) refutes the claim that corporations have grown more powerful than nation-states and notes the ways in which they remain anchored to specific locations. For example, he states that MNCs demonstrate a variety of cultural, political, social, and economic characteristics unique to their original location. He further argues that these differences represent diversity, rather than homogeneity, in organizational forms.

One of the ways in which the struggle over power has played out is in the regulation of corporations. After early attempts to create a global legal regulatory system through the UN Commission on Transnational Corporations failed (Rowe 2005), global policy with respect to corporations has taken a new form. This emergent form, focused on promoting "corporate social responsibility" (Dean 2009) on a global level, is most notable in the UN Global Compact. The aims of this Global Compact have been to construct minimum standards of "good corporate conduct," and to facilitate sustainable development. On the one hand, it signifies a global governance structure (transcending other state-centric approaches) to shape corporate activity through a diverse network of social actors (Fritsch 2008). On the other hand, this new effort represents a paradigm shift within the UN, which now seeks active engagement with MNCs, "thereby opening the UN system to private business interests" (Fritsch 2008: 1). Critics note that it is not only voluntary (therefore lacking any enforcement mechanism), but it reinforces corporate hegemony through the rule-making interests of the transnational capitalist class (Rowe 2005).

Globalization and the environment

Scholars are increasingly aware that one of the most important issues in globalization studies is the environment (Stevis 2005). While the environment is, and always has been, inherently global (people share the same atmosphere, waterways, and, literally, the earth), early globalization studies tended to ignore the environment (Yearley 2007). Partially as a result of the environmental movement's efforts since the 1970s, including the publicizing of known dangers of nuclear testing and acid rain, its importance can no longer be ignored. Important global environmental problems include habitat destruction, decline in biodiversity, decline in arable farmland, decline in fresh water, population growth, and the spread of toxic chemicals (Diamond 2006).

The shift in consciousness about the environment as a global issue has been most notable with the depletion of the ozone layer and global climate change. The ozone layer, which is a stratum in the atmosphere that blocks out radiation that is harmful to humans and other forms of life, has been depleted at a rapid rate in the last several decades. Manufactured chemicals, especially chlorofluorocarbons (CFCs), common in appliances such as refrigeration and air-conditioning systems, are the main cause of ozone depletion. As Yearley (2007: 242) notes, there are two main dimensions that make this a global issue. First, the ozone layer is literally a protective gaseous casing around the globe, and is not owned by any single group or nation-state. Second, there is almost no relationship between the physical source of ozone-depleting chemicals and where these environmental consequences and flows end up. These chemicals may remain in the atmosphere for years, drifting to any area of the world (i.e., away from their source), before finally unleashing their destructive effects.

While the issue of ozone depletion was most salient in the 1980s, global climate change is the most pressing environmental issue today. Global climate change refers most generally to changes in weather patterns over time, and typically refers to global warming, or the "greenhouse effect." The primary cause behind climate change is an increase in carbon dioxide in the atmosphere, brought about by the burning of fossil fuels, other industrial activity, and deforestation. It leads to a rise in the Earth's average temperatures, affecting a variety of ecosystems (sometimes in irreversible ways). Like ozone depletion, it is global because, regardless of its local or national sources, it has global implications (Yearley 2007). Furthermore, different geographic regions emit varying levels of carbon dioxide, contributing disproportionately to climate change; and different regions will experience different impacts (e.g., coastal areas will lose land mass to rising sea levels).

As should be apparent from the examples above, global environmental problems are closely linked to economic globalization and development. In particular, one form of economic globalization – neoliberal globalization – often exacerbates environmental problems because it sees environmental regulations as barriers to further economic development (Antonio 2007). Neoliberal economists and capitalists generally seek to expand manufacturing (and its associated pollutants) to less developed countries, and oppose environmental safeguards on the grounds that they lead to slower economic growth, which, from their point of view, takes precedence over environmental issues (Ritzer 2010). This was precisely the logic that led George W. Bush to withdraw US involvement (in 2001) in the Kyoto Protocol, an international agreement which sought to address climate change by reducing carbon emissions (Zedillo 2008). The environmental movement, on the other hand, argues that the environment should take priority because, without a livable environment, there can be no economic growth.

Despite resistance from many capitalists, neoliberal economists, and some governments, there have been a variety of worldwide responses to deal with these common issues. In addition to the Kyoto Protocol, one of the most important efforts is the Intergovernmental Panel on Climate Change (IPCC) which has produced several scientific reports documenting climate change and has fostered coordinated efforts to address them. Possible solutions include carbon taxes, carbon neutrality, renewable energy sources, and, most politically volatile, lower consumption levels. Since 1987, the UN has promoted sustainable development (though the term remains notoriously hard to define) programs that consider environmental (and sometimes social) factors in economic development projects. While some corporations have sought positive public relations by making themselves appear to help the environment (i.e., "greenwashing"), others have found great economic potential in environmental reform, such as the production of alternative energy sources (e.g., wind turbines, solar panels). Finally, a number of economists have actually sought to redefine the field of economics by treating the economy as a subsystem of the ecosystem and its limited carrying capacity (Daly & Townsend 1993).

Global inequalities

Understanding social inequalities is a fundamental part of sociology, and it is no different in the sociological study of globalization. Studies of global inequality are unique in that they look at inequality between nations or regions. Global inequalities are perhaps most often conceived of between the highly developed and wealthier "core" countries (the global North), and the less developed "peripheral" countries (the global South). This section evaluates trends of rising or falling inequality and explores class, race, and gender inequalities, but other striking global inequalities exist in health, between rural and urban areas, across sexual orientation, and across a reconfigured digital divide (Ritzer 2010).

A central question (and the most heated debate) concerning global inequality is whether inequality is increasing or decreasing (McGrew 2007). On the one hand,

Firebaugh and Goesling (2007) focused on income inequality (they also considered health and education inequalities), and found that while income inequality increased from the beginning of industrialization until about the 1950s, it stabilized in the 1960s through the 1980s, and is gradually decreasing today. They conceptualize differences in income between groups as "relative access to welfare" and theorize that spreading industrialization improves access to welfare in poorer parts of the world. This industrialization process is especially important for highly populous areas such as China and India (and their 2.5 billion citizens), whose disproportionately large populations are experiencing income growth. They argue that this ultimately reduces the gap between the North and South, thereby decreasing global inequality (at least in the short term).

On the other hand, Korzeniewicz and Moran (2007) considered several measures of income inequality but found a steady increase over time, which was most pronounced during the 1980s, and continues today. The competing perspectives on this issue rely on different measures and methods of analyzing inequality. Firebaugh and Goesling use a method of purchasing power parity (PPP) that considers inflation and local cost of living to determine the relative purchasing power of local earnings. Korzeniewicz and Moran compared incomes in their study by converting all currencies to US dollars using official exchange rates (FX), which better reflects changing flows such as trade.

As Korzeniewicz and Moran argue, at the heart of this dispute is "the meaning of income as an indicator" (2007: 2). By taking the relative price differences of goods and services at the local level, incomes standardized by PPP are thought to approximate local welfare conditions (however, historical PPP data are somewhat crude estimates). Korzeniewicz and Moran, on the other hand, view income distribution as indicative of relations between populations that reflect differentials in power and command over resources, products, and labor. This is an inherently relational perspective that is consistent with their world-systems approach. The interpretation of income as a measure of welfare, however, is more consistent with the modernization theory driving the PPP approach.

The class inequalities explored above are also highly related to various other forms of inequality, such as race and ethnicity. Winant argues that "Globalization is a re-racialization of the world. What have come to be called 'North-South' issues are also deeply racial issues. The disparities . . . between the (largely white and wealthy) global North and the (largely dark-skinned and poor) global South have always possessed a racial character" (2004: 131). The global flows of people (including forced flows from the slave trade) can also help us understand persistent racial inequalities within nations, such as the US.

These global flows of people are also decoupling ethnic identities from national boundaries, sometimes exacerbating inequality and conflict. For example, the Kurds lack a nation-state of their own and are spread out over several geographic areas (e.g., Iran, Iraq, Syria, Turkey). Steady Hispanic immigration into the US has provoked xenophobia and intensified debates over immigration policy (this debate will certainly change shape as racial minorities are projected to become the statistical majority in the US by mid-century). Similar patterns have also led to recent riots by working-class immigrants (mostly Arabs and Africans) in France, who were reacting to persistent racism, lending further evidence to racism as a global problem (Ritzer

2010). Where globalization facilitates rapidly changing cultural landscapes and shifting economic opportunity from some racial and ethnic groups to others, such reactions have become more common.

Global capitalism has also reinforced many gender inequalities. In particular, women often fill the jobs created by MNCs that have shifted their production facilities to developing countries and flexible labor regimes characterized by part-time or temporary work, low security, and no benefits. Women are preferred in these types of jobs because they typically have fewer economic options and are willing to work for lower wages, are believed to be more docile, and demonstrate greater dexterity in standardized, menial, and repetitive labor. This is especially true in Export Processing Zones (EPZs), where women make up the vast majority of workers and are subject to unpaid overtime, exploitative working conditions, and often must undergo pregnancy testing to obtain or keep a job (Pearson 1992). This feminization of labor (Standing 1989) also extends to global care chains (Hochschild 2000), or the series of personal relationships between people across the globe based on the paid or unpaid work of caring. Women in global care chains supply their own labor (including social, health, and sexual care services through menial tasks) while relying upon the paid and unpaid care work of other women. Such work reflects traditional gender ideology, and disproportionately draws women into domestic work and even sex trafficking.

Globalization and technology

As Castells (1996) discussed in his theory of the network society, technology has played an important role within globalization. But even before the recent information technologies of the network society, earlier communication and transportation technologies facilitated globalization processes. For example, the world's first container ship was constructed in 1956, allowing much more rapid loading, unloading, and shipment of commodities and other cargo. Advanced aviation technologies decreased the cost of moving both people and cargo quickly through the air. And of course, today, cell phones, the internet, mass media, and social media have connected people in unprecedented ways through interpersonal communication and the instantaneous flows of information and ideas.

While many technologies have gradually diffused across geographic borders (especially in the North), it is also very common for technological adoption in developing countries to be erratic and irregular. Specifically, technological advances often "hop" over less developed areas (skipping them entirely) and end up in other areas (Ritzer 2010). In a process known as leapfrogging, these developing areas will often go directly to later, more advanced technologies. For example, countries that have not had access to widespread electrical grids or fixed phone lines (i.e., "landlines") have often moved directly to solar panels and cell phones. These later technological advances have made it cheaper and more feasible to integrate certain technologies, improving people's quality of life and productivity. In many cases, this has led to local, direct economic gains, or it has facilitated transfer of cross-border funds through remittances (Corbett 2008). Nonetheless, technological advances are no panacea for many global problems such as illiteracy, and a digital divide still remains.

Regardless of uneven technological adoption, telecommunications have connected the world in unprecedented ways. Mass media was perhaps the first example of this, albeit early mass media tended to come from Western sources (e.g., CNN, BBC, Hollywood) and was linked to a structure of media imperialism. Recent mass media outlets, such as Al Jazeera, Bollywood, and a variety of local media sources, have grown quickly and now compete globally with Western media. Furthermore, independent media ("Indymedia") have also grown in significance (Juris 2005), especially in terms of the alter-globalization movement (see below).

Nowhere are these telecommunications more striking than the internet. The internet is a decentralized global phenomenon, controlled by no single nation or set of organizations, and linking people across all geographic and social boundaries (although some barriers have been erected – e.g., within China). Its significance has only grown with the ascendancy of Web 2.0, social media sites where users (or prosumers) both produce and consume online content (Ritzer & Jurgenson 2010) (see Chapter 33). This includes social networking sites (e.g., Facebook, Orkut), virtual worlds such as *Second Life*, and various other deterritorialized web-based networks. On the negative side, these global technologies have simultaneously facilitated new social problems including spam and computer viruses.

Resistance to, and producing alternatives within, globalization

As suggested throughout this chapter, globalizing processes have created winners and losers, which has provoked a variety of responses ranging from the conservative to the progressive (Kahn & Kellner 2007). These struggles have often transformed into sustained social movements, and have been typically referred to as "anti-globalization" movements. Conservative anti-globalization movements include nationalists (e.g., the Scottish National Party), isolationists (e.g., the America First Party), and religious fundamentalists (e.g., the Taliban), who seek to maintain or strengthen cultural and economic boundaries between nations (or localities) and globalization (Ritzer 2010). Alternatively, a progressive, global justice movement (which may have initially accepted the "anti-globalization" label but now rejects it) is often believed to have begun at the 1999 protests against the World Trade Organization (WTO) in the "Battle for Seattle" (however, Boli and Thomas [1999] argue that it can be traced back much further), which included a broad coalition of religious organizations, trade unions, and radical leftists.

Because few groups reject globalization in and of itself, Kellner (2002) argues that it is more fruitful to think about such resistance as globalization from below, as opposed to globalization from above. Globalization from above is characterized as the growing centralization and organization of power, which serves the interests of economic and political elites, and includes the WTO, International Monetary Fund, MNCs, or the "Washington Consensus." Globalization from below refers to the marginalized individuals and social movement groups that resist centralization of power, seek to preserve specific forms of society and culture, and resist attacks on rights and benefits. They seek to shape globalization democratically and uphold progressive values such as autonomy, peace, democracy, ecological sustainability, and social justice. These include movements directed at the global political economy, including Fair Trade and "anti-corporate globalization" (Juris 2005), and culture (e.g., the slow food movement). Not only are they global in the sense that they seek to shape globalization, but they are organized globally in trans-national networks (Castells 1996).

Perhaps the most well known example of globalization from below is the World Social Forum, which originated in Porto Allegre, Brazil, in 2001. As an alternative to the annual World Economic Forum in Davos, Switzerland, it serves as a demo-cratic platform (as opposed to a social movement *per se*) to discuss and create concrete proposals for shaping globalization. It facilitates the exchange of ideas and experiences, and the construction of new networks of cross-national solidarity, based on common problems. With the slogan "Another World is Possible," it attracts members from around the world each year, drawing 155,000 participants in 2005. However, with tremendous diversity of participants and viewpoints, it has proven difficult to develop specific proposals and actions.

The role of technology and Indymedia has been especially important in facilitat-ing and organizing globalization from below. Communication technologies, such as the internet and cell phone, were particularly important for the "Battle for Seattle" and the use of Indymedia to broadcast coverage of the protests that countered mainstream media's focus on the clashes with police and limited episodes of violence. These technologies now play central roles in coordinating decentralized global justice networks through free and open communication, distributing informa-tion, and facilitating direct democratic participation (Hardt & Negri 2000, 2004; Juris 2005). On the negative side, they simultaneously facilitate the spread of racist and xenophobic messages in neo-fascist reactions to globalization (Kellner 2002).

CONCLUSION

It should be clear from this chapter that the globalizations discussed here are highly complex, multi-dimensional phenomena and that sociologists (and other social scientists) continue to debate their various processes and effects. Their multi-dimensional and highly contentious character makes it very difficult to predict the future of globalization, but we feel confident making at least one prediction: glo-balization will continue, and will most likely grow and expand. But how will the role of the nation-state and MNCs change as these processes unfold? Will globaliza-tion continued to be controlled from above (e.g., the World Economic Forum), or will social movements and civil society demand greater control from below (e.g., the World Social Forum)? Will global inequality increase or can the power and welfare of the world's poor be improved, thus decreasing inequality? What will happen to local cultures and indigenous ways of life as globalization deepens its reach?

In terms of the global political economy, Wallerstein (2005) explores three possible scenarios. First, he explores the notion that every part of the world could achieve similar economic welfare, and similar cultural and political institu-tions, to those of the most developed and progressive nations (e.g., Denmark). Wallerstein argues that such a level of equality is impossible because it would require that certain nations and industries not monopolize productive activity, and that would undermine the entire capitalist system. Second, he explores the possibility of the world persisting with its current level of inequality. Again, he does not see this as possible because the rate of capital accumulation is already declining, thus weakening political structures reliant on this accumulation, and giving rise to the "dangerous classes" that could challenge this system of inequality. Wallerstein is optimistic about a third option – the collapse of the current world system – although he is unsure of what would replace it. He does, however, see great hope in globalization from below, especially the World Social Forum and various social movements.

An extreme and negative possibility is Turner's (2007) "Mad Max" scenario. This reference is from an Australian movie that depicts an apocalyptic vision of the future where people live a very primitive and violent existence. The trends that suggest such a gruesome scenario is indeed possible include the accelerating crises of the capitalist economy, diminishing oil supplies and rising costs, struggles over food security in developing countries, water wars, rising sea levels, nuclear proliferation, and global terrorism. One could even argue that we are already seeing such scenarios in Iraq, Afghanistan, Pakistan, and Somalia.

Ultimately, we cannot predict which of the above scenarios, if any, are likely to play out in the future(s) of globalization(s). Indeed, the fluidity of these complex global processes makes it difficult to evaluate these various outcomes. But as these globalizing processes expand and transform further local and national troubles into global issues, our need for sophisticated sociological analyses of these processes and outcomes will only increase.

References

Antonio, Robert (2007) "The Cultural Construction of Neoliberal Globalization." In George Ritzer (ed.), *The Blackwell Companion to Globalization*. Malden, MA: Blackwell, pp. 67–83.

Arrighi, Giovanni (2005) "Globalization in World-Systems Perspective." In Richard Applebaum and William Robinson (eds.), *Critical Globalization Studies*. New York: Routledge.

Babones, Salvatore (2007) "Studying Globalization: Methodological Issues." In George Ritzer (ed.), *The Blackwell Companion to Globalization*. Malden, MA: Blackwell, pp. 144–61.

Babones, Salvatore (2011) "Methods in the Study of Globalization." In George Ritzer (ed.), *The Encyclopedia of Globalization*. Malden, MA: Blackwell.

Bauman, Zygmunt (1992) *Intimations of Postmodernity*. New York: Routledge.

Beland, Daniel (2008) *States of Global Insecurity: Politics, Policy, and Society*. New York: Worth.

Boli, John and Frank Lechner (2005) *World Culture: Origins and Consequences*. Malden, MA: Blackwell.

Boli, John and George Thomas (1999) *Constructing World Culture: International Nongovernmental Organizations Since 1875*. Stanford, CA: Stanford University Press.

Caldwell, Melissa (2004) "Domesticating the French Fry: McDonald's and Consumerism in Moscow." *Journal of Consumer Culture* 4(1): 5–26.

Canclini, Nestor Garcia (1995) *Hybrid Cultures: Strategies for Entering and Leaving Modernity*. Minneapolis: University of Minnesota Press.

Castells, Manuel (1996) *The Rise of the Network Society*. Malden, MA: Blackwell.

Chanda, Nayan (2007) *Bound Together: How Traders, Preachers, Adventurers, and Warriors Shaped Globalization*. New Haven, CT: Yale University Press.

Chatterjee, Deen (2008) *Democracy in a Global World: Human Rights and Political Participation in the 21st Century*. Lanham, MD: Rowman and Littlefield.

Corbett, Sara (2008) "Can the Cellphone Help End Global Poverty?" *New York Times Magazine*, April 13.

Daly, Herman and Kenneth Townsend (eds.) (1993) *Valuing the Earth: Economics, Ecology, Ethics*. Cambridge, MA: MIT Press.

Dean, Paul (2009) "Corporate Social Responsibility." In George Ritzer (ed.), *Blackwell Encyclopedia of Sociology*. Malden, MA: Blackwell.

Diamond, Jared (2006) *Collapse: How Societies Choose to Fail or Succeed*. New York: Penguin.

Dicken, Peter (2007) *Global Shift: Mapping the Changing Contours of the World Economy*, 5th edn. New York: Guilford Press.

Elliott, Michael (2007) "Human Rights and the Triumph of the Individual in World Culture." *Cultural Sociology* 1(3): 343–63.

Evans, Peter (1997) *Governments, Globalization, and International Business*. New York: Oxford University Press.

Firebaugh, Glenn and Brian Goesling (2007) "Globalization and Global Inequalities: Recent Trends." In George Ritzer (ed.), *The Blackwell Companion to Globalization*. Malden, MA: Blackwell, pp. 549–64.

Fritsch, Stefan (2008) "The UN Global Compact and Global Governance of Corporate Social Responsibility: Complex Multilateralism for More Human Globalisation?" *Global Society* 22(1): 1–26.

Gereffi, Gary (2005) "The Global Economy: Organization, Governance, and Development." In Neil Smelser and Richard Swedberg (eds.), *Handbook of Economic Sociology*. Princeton, NJ: Princeton University Press, pp. 160–82.

Giddens, Anthony (1990) *The Consequences of Modernity*. Stanford, CA: Stanford University Press.

Gilpin, Robert (2001) *Global Political Economy*. Princeton, NJ: Princeton University Press.

Guillen, Mauro (2001) "Is Globalization Civilizing, Destructive, or Feeble? A Critique of Five Key Debates in the Social Science Literature." *Annual Review of Sociology* 27: 235–60.

Hannerz, Ulf (1987) "The World in Creolisation." *Africa* 57: 546–59.

Hardt, Michael and Antonio Negri (2000) *Empire*. Cambridge, MA: Harvard University Press.

Hardt, Michael and Antonio Negri (2004) *Multitude*. New York: Penguin.

Hayman, P. A. and John Williams (2006) "Westphalian Sovereignty: Rights, Intervention, Meaning, and Context." *Global Society* 20(4): 521–41.

Hochschild, Arlie (2000) "Global Care Chains and Emotional Surplus Value." In N. W. Hutton and Anthony Giddens (eds.), *On the Edge: Living with Global Capitalism*. London: Jonathan Cape, pp. 130–46.

Hoffman, Stanley (2002) "Clash of Globalizations." *Foreign Affairs* 81(4): 104–15.

Juris, Jeffrey (2005) "The New Digital Media and Activist Networking within Anti-Corporate Globalization Movements." In Jonathan Xavier Inda and Renato Rosaldo (eds.), *The Anthropology of Globalization: A Reader*, 2nd edn. Malden, MA: Blackwell, pp. 352–70.

Kahn, Richard and Douglas Kellner (2007) "Resisting Globalization." In George Ritzer (ed.), *The Blackwell Companion to Globalization*. Malden, MA: Blackwell, pp. 662–74.

Kellner, Douglas (2002) "Theorizing Globalization." *Sociological Theory* 20(3): 285–305.

Korzeniewicz, Patricio and Timothy Moran (2007) "World Inequality in the Twenty-First Century: Patterns and Tendencies." In George Ritzer (ed.), *The Blackwell Companion to Globalization*. Malden, MA: Blackwell, pp. 565–92.

Levy, Daniel and Natan Sznaider (2006) "Sovereignty Transformed: A Sociology of Human Rights." *British Journal of Sociology* 57(4): 657–76.

McGrew, Anthony (2007) "Globalization in Hard Times: Contention in the Academy and Beyond." In George Ritzer (ed.), *The Blackwell Companion to Globalization*. Malden, MA: Blackwell, pp. 29–53.

McMichael, Philip (2008) *Development and Social Change: A Global Perspective*, 4th edn. Thousands Oaks, CA: Pine Forge Press.

Meyer, John, John Boli, George Thomas, and Francisco Ramirez (1997) "World Society and the Nation-State." *American Journal of Sociology* 103: 144–81.

Nederveen Pieterse, Jan (2004) *Globalization and Culture: Global Melange*. Lanham, MD: Rowman and Littlefield.

O'Rourke, Kevin and Jeffrey Williamson (2002) "When Did Globalisation Begin?" *European Review of Economic History* 6(1): 23–50.

Pearson, Ruth (1992) "Gender Issues in Industrialisation." In T. Hewitt, J. Johnson, and D. Wield (eds.), *Industrialisation and Development*. Oxford: Oxford University Press, pp. 222–47.

Ritzer, George (2004) *The McDonaldization of Society*. Thousand Oaks, CA: Pine Forge Press.

Ritzer, George (2006) *The Globalization of Nothing 2*. Thousand Oaks, CA: Pine Forge Press.

Ritzer, George (ed.) (2007) *The Blackwell Companion to Globalization*. Malden, MA: Blackwell.

Ritzer, George (2010) *Globalization: A Basic Text*. Malden, MA: Wiley-Blackwell.

Ritzer, George and Nathan Jurgenson (2010) "Production, Consumption, Prosumption. The Nature of Capitalism in the Age of the Digital 'Prosumer'." *Journal of Consumer Culture* 10(1): 13–36.

Robertson, Roland (1992) *Globalization*. London: Sage.

Robertson, Roland (1995) "Glocalization: Time-Space and Homogeneity-Heterogeneity." In Mike Featherstone, Scott Lash, and Roland Robertson (eds.), *Global Modernities*. London: Sage, pp. 25–44.

Robinson, William (2004) *A Theory of Capitalist Globalization: Production, Class, and State in a Transnational World*. Baltimore, MD: Johns Hopkins University Press.

Rosenberg, Justin (2000) *Follies of Globalization Theory: Polemical Essays*. London: Verso.

Rowe, James (2005) "Corporate Social Responsibility as Business Strategy." In R. Lipschutz (ed.), *Globalization, Governmentality, and Global Politics*. New York: Routledge, pp. 130–70.

Sassen, Saskia (1996) *Losing Control? Sovereignty in an Age of Globalization*. New York: Columbia University Press.

Sklair, Leslie (2002) *Globalization: Capitalism and Its Alternatives*. Oxford: Oxford University Press.

Standing, Guy (1989) "Global Feminization through Flexible Labor." *World Development* 17: 1077–95.

Stevis, Dimitris (2005) "The Globalizations of the Environment." *Globalizations* 2(3): 323–33.

Strange, Susan (1996) *The Retreat of the State: The Diffusion of Power in the World Economy*. Cambridge: Cambridge University Press.

Therborn, Goran (2000) "Globalizations: Dimensions, Historical Waves, Regional Effects, Normative Governance." *International Sociology* 15: 151–79.

Turner, Bryan (2007) "The Futures of Globalization." In George Ritzer (ed.), *The Blackwell Companion to Globalization*. Malden, MA: Blackwell, pp. 675–92.

Wallerstein, Immanuel (1974) *The Modern World-System*. New York: Academic Press.

Wallerstein, Immanuel (2005) "After Developmentalism and Globalization, What?" *Social Forces* 83(3): 1263–78.

Waters, Mary (1995) *Globalization*. New York: Routledge.

Wilk, Richard (1995) "Learning to Be Local in Belize: Global Systems of Common Difference." In Daniel Miller (ed.), *Worlds Apart: Modernity through the Prism of the Local*. New York: Routledge, pp. 110–33.

Winant, Howard (2004) *The New Politics of Race: Globalism, Difference, Justice*. Minneapolis: University of Minnesota Press.

Yearley, Steve (2007) "Globalization and the Environment." In George Ritzer (ed.), *The Blackwell Companion to Globalization*. Malden, MA: Blackwell, pp. 239–53.

Zedillo, Ernesto (ed.) (2008) *Global Warming: Looking Beyond Kyoto*. Washington, DC: Brookings.

Part III

Cutting Edge Issues in Sociology

30

After Neoliberalism

Whither Capitalism?

Robert J. Antonio

Hegel remarks somewhere that all facts and personages of great importance in world history occur, as it were, twice. He forgot to add: the first time as tragedy, the second as farce.

Karl Marx (1963: 18)

Attacking entitlements and championing personal responsibility, Prime Minister Margaret Thatcher declared that there is no such thing as "society," but only "individual men and women and their families." She held that "society" is invoked to signify mythical collective interests and justify dependence on state welfare provision, which short-circuits individual initiative and voluntarism. This 1987 declaration punctuated her largely successful effort to undercut the "social solidarities" (e.g., trade unions, professional associations, public employees' groups) that resisted her neoliberal agenda of cutting the welfare state, privatizing public goods, expanding private property rights, and promoting "personal responsibility" to cope with social ills. Thatcher also famously popularized the neoliberal war cry – "There Is No Alternative!" She aimed "to change the soul," or culture, not merely the economic and political surface of daily life, so that neoliberal sensibilities would be forged into a taken-for-granted worldview and reflex habits that would color individual values, opinions, and choices (Harvey 2005: 22–3). President Reagan espoused similar views in the 1980s, and considered Prime Minister Thatcher his staunch ally. As I write, British Prime Minister David Cameron is attempting to recycle Thatcherism under the ironic logo of "The Big Society" and to cut the social state more drastically than she was able to do. American neoliberals concur – a tougher version of their policies is the only road to prosperity.

The Wiley-Blackwell Companion to Sociology, First Edition. Edited by George Ritzer.
© 2012 Blackwell Publishing Ltd. Published 2012 by Blackwell Publishing Ltd.

England was the original homeland of liberal individualism, but it found fertile soil in the nineteenth-century US; some new, distinctive features were developed in the US and exported. Since the late 1970s, neoliberal ideas, reforms, and power have reshaped American political imagination about what is right, what is possible, and by what means. This major political and cultural shift makes it hard to fathom, today, how President Johnson could have mounted his mid-1960s "War on Poverty" and advocated "equality of condition," how Republican President Nixon could have proposed a "Family Assistance Plan," in 1969, to provide a minimum income for poor families and, in 1971, employed wage and price controls, or how *public* higher education was then nearly free or very inexpensive in almost every state. In recent decades, neoliberal views on free enterprise, small government, reduced taxation, and personal responsibility have dominated American political discourse about "economic" issues. Even a Democratic, African American President and Democratic Congress have stressed the plight of the "middle class," not of the poor, and generally have been silent about much increased economic inequality. Similar sharp swings between divergent visions and regimes of capitalism have occurred before in American history (e.g., between the Gilded Age and the Progressive Period and between the Roaring '20s and the New Deal Era), driven by efforts to cope with severe economic crises and their social impacts.

The 2008 financial meltdown[1] and "Great Recession" ended neoliberals' certainty about continuing hegemony of the "Washington Consensus," or US-led, global neoliberalism.[2] Nobel Prize-winning economist Joseph Stiglitz (2010) pronounced neoliberalism "dead," arguing for much expanded government regulation of economic affairs. Capitalism faces major "structural crises" and "systemic gridlock," warned sociologist Immanuel Wallerstein (2010), and social theorist Slavoj Žižek (2010) declared that we are in "a permanent economic crisis." Many more critics of neoliberalism held that decades of debt-driven, speculative financial growth, ensured by periodic government bailouts, cannot be sustained and that the conditions *ex ante* that spurred financial growth cannot be restored. Conservative pundits countered that the failure of President Obama's stimulus package to generate substantial job growth proved that Keynesian and New Deal statism is bankrupt. They insisted that more stringent neoliberalism than before the crisis, with even less state regulation of economic affairs, permanent institution of the Bush tax cuts for the rich, and more sharply reduced entitlements, provides the only route out of the downturn to renewed financial stability and growth. The outcome of the crisis is uncertain as I write. Despite modest re-regulation and proposals for more comprehensive reform, a substantially restructured policy regime is unlikely in the current climate; most Republicans and some Democrats have called for more single-minded, austere, neoliberal political rule and have expressed staunch opposition to re-regulation of the finance sector and to increased taxation to reduce large deficits at the local, state, and federal levels. Draconian cuts of social services and education have been proposed or have already been instituted in many states and localities across the nation.

In the immediate wake of the 2008 economic meltdown, it appeared that the ensuing crisis would regenerate fresh versions of earlier policy debates over *market liberalism*, or still hegemonic, but embattled "neoliberalism," and *social liberalism*, re-emergent, yet under attack and still ill-defined. As I write, this debate has been restricted mostly to intellectual circles – elected officials and policy-makers from both major parties have opposed or lacked the political will to frame an alternative to neoliberalism. Both approaches have deep historical roots in Anglo-American political culture, have dominated in different historical moments, and have had different historical forms (e.g., Dewey [1935] 1987; Foner 1998). The fresh debates over them present polar views of the past and present. For example, former Clinton Administration Secretary of Labor, social liberal Robert Reich (2007), contrasts "democratic capitalism" (circa 1945–75) with today's unequal, undemocratic "supercapitalism." Conversely, President of the conservative American Enterprise Institute, market liberal Arthur C. Brooks (2010), pits "free enterprise," or "America's DNA," against "big government," typified by the defunct Soviet Union's "socialism," Lyndon Johnson's moribund "Great Society," and "Obamacare." Similar polarized views and conflictive portrayals of history and policy suffuse debates about contemporary capitalism. My intention is to provide analytical resources to help make sense of the split and to entertain critically capitalism's future.

CLASHING MODELS OF CAPITALISM: HAYEK VS. POLANYI

> It is necessary now to state the unpalatable truth that it is Germany whose fate we [England and the United States] are in some danger of repeating . . . Only if we recognize the danger in time can we hope to avoid it. (Hayek 1944: 2)

> Market society was born in England – yet it was on the Continent that its weaknesses engendered the most tragic complications. In order to comprehend German fascism, we must revert to Ricardian England. (Polanyi [1944] 1957: 30)

Important in their day, and specters in our times, Hayek and Polanyi theorized the relationship between capitalism and totalitarianism in diametrically opposed ways in texts aimed at influencing the emerging wartime debate over post-World War II reconstruction. They feared that transition to a peacetime economy would lead back to depression and dictatorship. Both thinkers have been revived in current debates about market liberalism and social liberalism, which they have already influenced (having long been absorbed into the atmospherics of this discourse). Many other thinkers have impacted these debates, but Hayek's and Polanyi's classic texts, framed in a deeply uncertain time, or moment of decision, provide lucid conceptual frames for two conflictive policy regimes.

Hayek's *The Road to Serfdom* (1944) was a touchstone for conservative and libertarian thinkers long before our neoliberal era. Influenced by Hayek's earlier work, Walter Lippmann (1937) held that "collectivism" was the wellspring of 1930s totalitarianism as well as the New Deal and that the latter's social liberalism might likely turn totalitarian in "gradual" steps. Fearing the same, Joseph Schumpeter ([1942] 1962: 61) warned, in a now classic work, that capitalism would not survive. Received in a climate of economic insecurity and fear of fascism and communism, these widely read books prepared the way for Hayek. Providing a lucid small-government, anti-New Deal argument, his book was embraced instantly by the

American right. His market liberalism resonated with deeply rooted "rugged indi-vidualist" facets of American culture, which had been re-articulated as "economic freedom," or "free enterprise" in the late nineteenth century and flourished in the financial bubble of the "Roaring '20s." In 1945, *Reader's Digest* published a con-densed version of Hayek's book as a lead article; the Book-of-the-Month Club sold reprints; General Motors distributed it to all its workers; and *Look Magazine* published a cartoon version. The *Reader's Digest* piece alone reached 8,750,000 subscribers. Causing a stir, Winston Churchill drew on the book in a major 1945 speech that equated socialism with totalitarianism. Prime Minister Thatcher and President Reagan later claimed to have been inspired by Hayek and met with him (Nash 1976: 5–10; Foner 1998: 235–6; Shearmur 2006; Caldwell 2007). And Hayek's iconic text has been invoked anew against the post-2008 "Keynesian revival," myriad calls for increased regulation, and President Obama's alleged "socialism." After Glenn Beck touted Hayek's classic on his Fox TV show, in mid-June 2010, the work shot up to number one on Amazon.com's bestseller list (*Inde-pendent* 2010; Lahart 2010; Roberts 2010).

Writing for the conservative *New York Sun*, economist Gregory Clark (2008) asserted: "Karl Polanyi's *The Great Transformation* (1944), published the same year as Friedrich Hayek's *The Road to Serfdom*, is as sacred a text to the opponents of free-market capitalism as Hayek's is to the Chicago School." Written when the 2008 financial crisis was deepening, Clark's scathing "reconsideration" of Polanyi's text and Polanyian Fred Block's (2008) response shed light on the book's current rele-vance.[3] Polanyi's ([1944] 1957) incisive critique of market liberalism elucidated views of society and capitalism that contradict almost every major theme of Hayek's text. Polanyi likely framed his work, at least in part, with Hayek and his teacher Ludwig von Mises in mind. Polanyi was long familiar with their arguments about market liberalism and the collectivist threat to capitalism and democracy. Polanyi's brother Michael operated in common intellectual circles with Hayek and contributed to market liberal thought, elaborating the core Hayekian concepts of "spontaneous order" and "tacit knowledge." A difficult read, *The Great Trans-formation* did not reach nearly as many readers as Hayek's classic, or have its immediate impact. But Polanyi's text is still one of the twentieth century's most important works in heterodox economic history and a "message in a bottle" that has been recovered and pitted against the Hayek revival and neoliberalism. Many of its core themes have been incorporated into economic sociology and insti-tutionalist economics, especially in arguments about the economy's socio-cultural "embeddedness."[4] Polanyi's counterpoints against market liberalism illuminate the conceptual basis for social liberalism and can be employed, along with Hayek's book, to make sense of core facets of contemporary political polarization (Harvey 2005: 37; Dale 2010: 207–34).

Hayek averred that "collectivism" (or "socialism") was the common thread that animated Nazism, fascism, and Stalinism and that, via possible or even likely postwar central planning, capitalist democracies could become totalitarian regimes. He asserted that all our freedoms depend on economic freedom (especially on nearly absolute property rights) and that regulation, redistribution, and socialization violate these rights and pave the way to "serfdom" (Hayek 1944: 70–1, 100). Hayek thought that the state's role should be limited to protecting private property, contracts, and liberal freedoms (e.g., association, religion, speech, press) and ensuring adequacy of capitalist infrastructure and necessary forms of intercourse. Ideas that broader state planning serves "common purposes," he held, justify elite rule and collectivist, totalitarian drift. Like Herbert Spencer, he saw the state to be the almost exclusive source of social coercion and main threat to freedom and democracy. By contrast, he envisaged competitive markets as constituting the freest, most efficient, most democratic organization. He held that market liberalism gives rise to plural values and social complexity, which can be meshed effectively and perpetuated only by a competitive market's "spontaneous order," based on free choice and uncoerced cooperation.

Hayek held that modern civilization and, paradoxically, individual freedom depend on our "submission to the impersonal forces of the market" (1944: 204). He saw competitively set prices as manifesting dispersed information from multitudinous individual choices and providing effective signals that voluntarily coordinate consumers and producers. For Hayek, the free market's supraindividual, tacit knowledge and systemic rationality are instrumentally and ethically superior to collectivist planners' and socialist politicians' rationally calculated choices and coercive governance, reflecting constricted knowledge, narrow interests, and elitist culture. In his view, state interference undermines the price system and thereby economic efficiency and rationality and ultimately individual freedom, initiative, and responsibility. Collectivism saps our autonomy and makes us vulnerable to political manipulation, Hayek alleged, while capitalism cultivates "independence," "self-reliance," "voluntary cooperation," and "willingness to bear risks" and to uphold our "convictions against the majority" (Hayek 1944: 212–15).

Hayek saw free-market provision of handsome rewards for able people in demanding roles and just deserts for less qualified, less able, and less willing workers to be chief drivers of capitalist efficiency. He considered steep economic inequalities to inhere in capitalism's normal workings; meddling with wage rates and provision for the sake of equality would distort price signals. Hayek acknowledged that good or bad fortune (including the station one is born into) as well as ability and motivation shape individual outcomes. However, he rejected emphatically statist efforts to increase fairness by egalitarian reforms, holding that capitalism and democracy must depend strictly on "formal equality" before the law, or procedural justice.[5] He believed that redistribution's detrimental socio-economic consequences constitute a far greater threat than the perceived unfairness posed by inherited wealth and advantage and by possible torpor of some fortunate persons. Creating "substantive law" to enforce distributive justice and reduce economic inequality, Hayek argued, violates property rights, mandates expansive and intrusive government, destroys rule of law, and lapses toward totalitarianism. On the contrary, he declared, market liberalism offers unparalleled opportunities for social mobility, individual freedom, and general affluence, which are all precluded by egalitarian socialization and redistribution and consequent collectivist state inefficiency, lawless power, and unfreedom (Hayek 1944: 79–87, 101–18).

Although touting capitalism's inherently democratic nature, Hayek distrusted democracy, warning against making it "a fetish" and berating "fashionable concentration" on it as "the main value threatened" (Hayek 1944: 70–1). He feared that hegemonic, New Deal political culture's emphases on state intervention and

572   ROBERT J. ANTONIO

redistribution and receptivity to arguments for increased substantive equality and economic security would grow stronger and become more popular when troops returned home, state military outlays shrunk, and peacetime reconstruction commenced. Hayek held that preserving capitalism and "democracy" requires "fixed laws" to secure property rights (and limited government) against undue restriction or abrogation by interventionist state policy-makers or by direct votes of the citizenry. As stated above, Hayek considered stable and nearly unlimited property rights to be the keystone of economic freedom and thereby of all individual liberties. Opposing "dogmatic laissez faire" views, Hayek (1944: 36–7) endorsed use of the state's strong hand when it is needed to uphold market society and stem totalitarian collectivization by "democratic" plebiscites. He reminded readers that Hitler came to power via promises of substantive justice. Hayek later held that transitional dictatorship is sometimes necessary to create or preserve economic freedom. He visited Chile's Augusto Pinochet dictatorship, and advised its leaders about their new constitution. Hayek and his colleagues from the market liberal Mont Pèlerin Society and Chicago School engineered the regime's market liberalization, later touted as the exemplar "economic miracle" of neoliberal restructuring. Hayek was untroubled by General Pinochet's violent overthrow of democratically elected Salvador Allende's socialist regime. Distinguishing authoritarianism from collectivist totalitarianism, Hayek saw the brutal Chilean dictatorship to be more liberal than "democracies" that violate economic freedom.[6] In his view, moreover, authoritarian regimes committed to "economic freedom" can become democracies. Famously championed by Jean Kirkpatrick (1992), a Reagan Administration Cabinet member who admired Hayek, this polarity has been an important principle in much US foreign policy; it gives primacy to market liberal reform, equates it with democratization, and justifies military interventions in behalf of US economic and geopolitical interests as serving freedom *per se*.

Karl Polanyi's historical sociology of capitalist development, *The Great Transformation* ([1944] 1957), poses a normative argument supporting social democracy. Drawing from social anthropology and sociology, he held that, in pre-modern societies, "economic" activities are so "submerged" or "embedded" in everyday social relations and routines that they are not visible as an "economy"; norms of "reciprocity" and "redistribution" prevail, not individual self-interest and economic rationality (e.g., exchange rates governed by supply and demand). Although market exchange was common in much of Europe by the sixteenth century, Polanyi explained, it was regulated comprehensively by mercantilist states. He held that the concepts of "self-regulating markets" and "market society" emerged during the nineteenth-century industrial revolution, when new capitalist elites and institutions and liberal democratic states made the price system, supply and demand, and other rules of the market hegemonic. By "great transformation" Polanyi meant a world-historical reversal of the pre-modern condition; capitalist social differentiation organized production and exchange into a distinct economic system and subordinated the rest of "society" to it. For example, he held that labor activity was narrowed into a contract between individual workers and capitalist employers, severed from family, community, craft, and religious relations, in which it had been enmeshed and by which it had been regulated. He did not suggest that these and other social relations and influences were removed entirely, but that they were subordinated to hegemonic economic rules. Polanyi saw the self-regulating market to be a fiction; a mythical, austere "utopia" that justifies social disembedding by hypostatizing economic freedom, masking capitalist control and unfreedom, and countering efforts to resist or regulate sources of damages.

Polanyi claimed that market society was created by the state and that public investment, regulation, and control in behalf of capitalism has been the norm thereafter. Portraying a "double movement," however, he argued that sharply reducing social regulation and extending market society hegemony causes "catastrophic dislocation of the lives of the common people," and thus generates social responses to limit the damages (Polanyi [1944] 1957: 33). For example, Polanyi held that states, pressed by unions and other groups, instituted minimum wages, safety standards, social insurance, and other forms of social regulation to mitigate harsh nineteenth-century factory regimes. While capitalist elites employed the state to extend market society and block regulation, Polanyi noted, other citizens, empowered by extended suffrage and representation, pressed the state for protective measures. Polanyi (1944] 1957: 130) argued that, by 1914, expansionary capitalism "engulfed space and time" and reached "every part of the globe," stirring highly varied defensive responses, often reflexes to crises, by myriad organizations, groups, and individuals in diverse locales under divergent conditions. Rebuking reduction of these multifarious reactions to a "collectivist conspiracy," he contended that this "liberal mythology" directs attention away from market liberalism's harsh impacts, blames political democracy for the wreckage, justifies state intervention (including coercion and violence) for capitalist elites, and devalues substantive democratization (Polanyi [1944] 1957: 144–51). He held that market liberals' fanatical faith that self-regulating markets will eventually provide "secular salvation" insulates them from coming to terms with contrary social facts and the human costs of their obdurateness, especially when alternative strategies are most needed to curtail damages (Polanyi [1944] 1957: 135).[7]

Polanyi contended that the dominant free-market policies of the 1920s proved to be a spectacular failure by the early 1930s, but that true-believing market liberals attributed the Great Depression and consequent disastrous, misguided "protective" responses (fascist movements and dictatorships), which followed in its wake, to the character defects of pliant social liberal policy-makers, who failed to enforce the rules of the "self-regulating market" stringently enough (Polanyi [1944] 1957: 141–2, 257–8b). Polanyi declared that for market liberals:

> no private suffering, no infringement of sovereignty, was deemed too great a sacrifice for the recovery of monetary integrity. The privations of the unemployed made jobless by deflation; the destitution of public servants dismissed without a pittance; even the relinquishment of national rights and loss of constitutional liberties were judged a fair price to pay for the fulfillment of the requirement of sound budgets and sound currencies, these *a priori* of economic liberalism. (1944: 142)

Polanyi saw fascism, socialism, and the New Deal to be the most consequential, organized currents in a veritable flood of defensive responses to the total breakdown of market society and governance by unyielding market liberal policy-makers. In his view, however, these major currents were alike *only* in rejecting self-regulating markets. Polanyi held that fascism and socialism are profoundly divergent types of regime; fascism opposes political democracy as emphatically as it does market liberalism, while socialism is "essentially, the tendency inherent in an industrial civilization to transcend the self-regulating market by consciously subordinating it to a democratic society" (Polanyi [1944] 1957: 234). Ironically, like Hayek, Polanyi treated socialism as a broad collectivist current, but held that its historical realization would be the type of socially embedded democratic, egalitarian regime that Hayekian market liberals demonized. Yet Polanyi appreciated historical contingency, and he did not turn socio-cultural tendencies into iron laws of political development. Thus, he did not hesitate identifying the USSR as a dictatorship that did not permit its citizens freedoms guaranteed by its constitution. Also, he stressed the importance of class inequality and class conflict, but rejected "popular Marxism's" theory of class interest and overall class theory. By contrast to market liberals and orthodox Marxists, Polanyi did not attribute the economy epistemic or normative primacy (Polanyi [1944] 1957: 151–2, 234, 244–8, 257).

Polanyi feared that free-market policies would be reasserted after the war and generate another round of economic crises and virulent anti-liberal, anti-democratic responses. Thus, he advocated social re-embedding of the economy by means of government planning, regulation, and redistribution. Arguing against limiting "freedom" to formal equality, he held that every individual, "irrespective of his or her political views, or color or race," should have the right to a decent job and to a fair share of "industrial society's" fruits – "income, leisure, and security." He also called for protections against the abuses of "arbitrary power" and social "victimization" (Polanyi [1944] 1957: 256–8). Charging that market liberalism savages the "soil," "resources," and "climate," Polanyi asserted that nature and social institutions are "inextricably interwoven," and presciently called for protection of the land and natural world (Polanyi [1944] 1957: 73, 178–91). Polanyi acknowledged that state bureaucracy threatens individual freedom, but also implied that portrayal of market society as a self-regulated order constituted by myriad uncoerced individual choices is a "radical illusion" that puts a halo around concentrated wealth and power. He held that all societies must employ "power" and "compulsion," that they suffuse "industrial society's" public *and* private bureaucracies and mass associations, and that substantive freedom and social protection for the many are not possible without such constraints on individual action (Polanyi [1944] 1957: 255–8b). In his view, coming to terms with this sociological reality makes possible what market liberals forgo: striving "to remove all removable injustice and unfreedom." Polanyi saw this aim to be the regulative ideal of a genuinely democratic society and always a work in progress.

Hayek and Polanyi employed the terms freedom and democracy in contrary ways, and had opposed views of the economy–society relationship. Hayek's freedom means free enterprise and formal legal equality, unburdened by social regulation and redistribution. His idea of democracy is ultimately reducible to "economic freedom," or property rights, contracts, and consumer choice. He embraced liberal institutions and formally democratic electoral processes as long as they do not truncate economic freedom. Polanyi rejected market liberalism's view that liberty and equality and formal law and substantive law are inherently contradictory and mutually exclusive. Although insufficiently elaborated, he implied that freedom, if it is to be more than a deceptive slogan and abstraction, requires means to activate formal rights and that democracy demands just distribution of the means for competitive struggles over desired roles and for wider cultural participation. This substantive equality of opportunity calls for egalitarian or collectivist institutions and practices to secure it. Polanyi advocated re-embedding the economy in society by countering market liberal hegemony and employing public planning, regulation, and redistribution to achieve substantive democracy and avert dictatorship. Avoiding abstract formulaic balancing of liberty and equality, Polanyi held that achievement of social justice and social democracy depends on contingent social practices adjusted to locale, time, and culture. For Hayek, Polanyi plotted a path to despotism.

MARKET LIBERALISM'S RETURN: FROM THE "NOT QUITE GOLDEN AGE" TO THE "GREAT U-TURN"

Many thinkers have narrated the economic growth, expanded middle class, and upgraded standard of living of the long postwar boom in the US.[8] Social liberalism was hegemonic, but the postwar-era US never realized Polanyi's high hopes for social democracy. Cold War social liberals wed Keynesianism to a permanent war economy and anti-communism, which impacted strongly on domestic politics and limited social reform and redistribution. Hayekian fear of creeping socialism at home and abroad was integrated into social liberalism and was a root of its later defeat. Still social liberals described a fundamental democratic transformation, seeing the US as a new type of affluent middle-class society that had overcome classical capitalism's cyclical economic crises and class conflicts and that ended ideological debate about socialist alternatives. Announcing a new, higher phase of modernization, social theorists portrayed the US as an "advanced industrial society" or "post-industrial society," rather than a capitalist one. Even left-leaning critics used the new terms in critiques of conformist consumerism and welfare-state complacency. Their emphasis on the primacy of "society" and claim that free-market and Marxist materialism were moribund implied Polanyian social re-embedding of the economy. Leading postwar social theorist Talcott Parsons declared, before the war, that Spencer and Marx were irrelevant and that social theorists converged around the view that inclusive social values are the decisive organizing force in modern societies. In the postwar era, he held that the market was a "subsystem of society" and that "evolutionary breakthroughs" made America the globe's "lead society." He implied that social liberalism ruled and was nearly complete in the US and that other parts of the globe would converge with the American model (even the USSR). Parsons and other social liberals held that progressive modernization favored social justice; class and minority movements and legislation would soon realize substantive equal opportunity. They also believed, albeit sometimes tacitly, that the new societal regime, aided by enormous, ever progressing scientific-technological knowledge and application, would sustain economic growth *ad infinitum* and thereby evolve toward a post-scarcity society and world (Parsons 1971: 86–143; Hodgson 1978: 67–98; Brick 2006: 121–85).

Scuttling New Deal "freedom from want," postwar market liberals championed "free enterprise" as the driver of economic growth, cornerstone of democracy, and bulwark against communism. Hayek's ideas provided inspiration for this rising segment of the resistant right. As the middle class prospered, "consumer freedom" became the hegemonic lived reality of American life, but liberals of different persuasions argued that "free enterprise" made it possible. The youth counterculture and new social movements offered alternative justice-oriented ideals of freedom, but market liberalism surged in the mid- and later 1970s climate of political crisis and stagflation. Well-funded right-wing think tanks proliferated, and skillfully diffused market liberal ideas. Upset by "excesses" of 1960s youth culture and welfare state social policy and fearful that the "American Century" was ending, many halting social liberals joined growing neoconservative and neoliberal forces. Stagnant wages, economic insecurity, and increased taxes led many average Americans to embrace the right, especially its anti-tax rhetoric, given impetus by California's Prop 13 property tax revolt and rollback. Realignment in white parts of the sunbelt, and evangelical Christian alliance with the neoliberal gospel fortified already intense attacks on "liberalism" (also known as social liberalism) as *the* cause of all evils. Populist backlash against youth revolt, class legislation, and alleged perfidies of minorities, women, and immigrants also fueled the "great reversal," or return of market liberal hegemony (Foner 1998: 307–32; Brick 2006: 219–46; Judt 2010: 81–135).

The Thatcher and Reagan elections empowered the new generation of market liberals, but they met resistance from well-entrenched social liberal organizations and legislators. Also, a new (post-New Left) social liberal left posed alternative policy frameworks. French "regulationist" and American "social structure of accumulation" theorists fused institutional economics with neo-Marxian ideas in opposition to market liberal thought. They considered the economy to be an interdependent complex of social and cultural institutions bearing the imprint of "society" and relying upon it. Convergent with Polanyi, they argued that capital accumulation depends on organizational and cultural complexes and that this institutional embedding becomes a focal point of political debate and social struggle in socio-economic crises. They held that political and social regime shifts occur when profit squeezes and related social problems become serious enough to generate decisive struggles between hegemonic and counter-hegemonic blocs. From this vantage point, recurrent shifts between market liberalism and social liberalism manifest capitalism's periodic adjustments to its changing socio-economic limits. In the late 1970s and 1980s, these left-leaning critics advocated a much more robust social liberalism than the Cold War version and a decisive alternative to market liberalism (e.g., Bowles & Gintis 1986: 176–213). At this time, Polanyi's work and especially his ideas about embeddedness were being absorbed into economic sociology and institutional economics and employed to criticize the market liberal resurgence.

Representing this liberal-left current of thought, Bennett Harrison and Barry Bluestone's classic, *The Great U-Turn* (1988), was one of the most incisive, influential critiques of ascendant neoliberalism, portraying its sharp departure from post-World War II "Fordism" and connecting it to "globalization." They first formulated the book's core ideas about the eroded quality of jobs, shrunken middle class, and need to intervene in behalf of labor in a 1986 report to the US Congress Joint Economic Committee, which was savaged by Reaganite neoliberals. Facing increased international competition, Harrison and Bluestone contended, US corporations adopted short-term financial strategies, reduced investment in domestic production and innovation, sent capital and jobs abroad, employed anti-union tactics, and embraced free-market ideology and related "casino society" deregulation, privatization, financialization, and upper-bracket tax reduction, which reversed postwar trends toward reduced economic inequality and an expanded middle class. Harrison and Bluestone (1988: 169–96) advocated global reflation and opposed World Bank and International Monetary Fund austerity programs. They called for industrial policy and workplace democracy – increased unionization, public infrastructure investment, and an expanded social safety net. Other budding liberal-left social democrats articulated similar ideas, but neoliberals routed them. The liberal-left did not win much support in the Democratic Party or with the general public, and with the late 1980s rise of the "New Democrats" and "Democratic Leadership Council" and their dominance in the Clinton Administration, market liberals captured both major political parties and dominated political media culture in the US. The rise of "New Labour" and Prime Minister Tony Blair marked a similar shift in the UK.

HEGEMONIC NEOLIBERALISM: FROM CREST TO CRISIS TO EMPHATIC REASSERTION(?)

David Harvey's *The Condition of Postmodernity* (1989) analyzed the restructured firms and labor markets, weakened unions and working-class political parties, diminished welfare rights, financial emphasis, and market liberal ideology. Attending especially to globalization's spatial-temporal reconfiguration of capitalism, Harvey held that the new regime made the world faster and smaller and accelerated capital's "turnover time" (realization of profit and reinvestment), solving the profit squeeze and generating speculative bubbles. Deregulation and new communications and information technologies, he argued, diminish social, political, and geographical constraints on capital. The enhanced "flexibility" he portrayed amounts to Polanyian disembedding – the rules of unfettered capitalism attained primacy in the US and UK and were ascendant globally. He contended that globalization and postmodern cultural fragmentation blunted organized resistance to neoliberalism so decisively that determinate alternatives were not visible on the horizon. From the right, Francis Fukuyama's (1989) "end of history" thesis portrayed Reagan-reformed, US-style capitalism as the ultimate form of liberal democracy, which cannot be superseded. Believing communism and socialism to be in terminal decline and liberal democracies to be convergent around market liberal strategies, critics as well as supporters of neoliberalism declared an "end to left and right" and "end of alternatives." The collapsed Soviet bloc, the Tiananmen Square protests, and the US-led first Iraq war also seemed to affirm that Prime Minister Thatcher's dream was coming true. In the neoliberal era, most Republicans and many Democrats treat market liberalism as if it were a primary root and driver of "American exceptionalism."

In the wake of meteoric stock market gains, Clinton Democrat Thomas L. Friedman (2000) gushed, in his best-selling, globalization book, that American-style capitalism's "golden straitjacket" frees markets from regulation, limits political choice to "Pepsi or Coke," forges a global stockholder and financial trader "democracy," stirs breakthrough technical innovations, speeds economic growth, and thereby "blows away" all competing policy regimes. Surviving the "New Economy" requires all participants to don this neoliberal garb, insisted Friedman and other globalization advocates. In their view, the tilt toward deregulated neoliberalism and a sharply scaled-back social and regulatory state is inevitable. European-style social democracies and Asian-style developmental states must eventually give way to market liberalism. Although creating a highly unequal "winners take all" society, Friedman argued, neoliberal "fast capitalism" yields unparalleled affluence and drives progressive modernization. His claims about "Americanization-globalization" echoed Parsons' evolutionary certainty, but the lead society was now the prototype market liberal regime. Even after the 2000 dot-com bust, the post-9/11 contraction, the huge wave of corporate accounting scandals (e.g., Enron, WorldCom), and China's and India's ascent to great economic power, hardcore believers in the neoliberal "Washington Consensus" still asserted its indubitable supremacy and certain advance in all forward-looking nations (e.g., Friedman 2005).

The 2008 financial meltdown and recession, for a moment, suddenly ended neoliberal triumphalism, and stimulated calls for a social liberal renewal. President Obama's successful campaign trope of "change" played on social liberal hopes for substantial reform. Joseph Stiglitz's (2010: 184–209, 275–97) portrayal of a "new capitalist order" and "new society" and Tony Judt's (2010) call for revived social democracy outlined social re-embedding of Polanyian proportions. Related arguments abounded in the recession's immediate wake. The roles of market liberalism and social liberalism were the reverse of when Hayek and Polanyi wrote their classics. The Hayek revival came after more than three decades of neoliberal hegemony, when critics claimed that the regime was in terminal crisis, whether it survived politically or not (Kotz & McDonough 2010: 116–18; Stiglitz 2010). Fearing a Keynesian or social democratic revival, neoliberals warned about the imminent collectivist threat and Obaman "socialism." Aiming to stem such fear, Judt (2010: 229) argued that social democrats seek "a compromise," a fusion of capitalism and democracy, not "transformative" change. Stiglitz and other left-leaning social liberals have implied the same; updated social liberalism of the Polanyian sort can restore growth, increase socio-economic justice, and establish a more balanced relation to nature and other cultures. However, sufficient support was sorely lacking, in the major parties and general citizenry, for comprehensive reform or any reform that incurs substantial *costs*. The historic gains made by Republicans (especially those with conservative libertarian "Tea Party" sympathies), in the 2010 mid-term congressional elections, repudiated directly and emphatically social liberal aspirations. Effective market liberal and neo-populist counterattacks on the Obama Administration's modest reforms called for more stringent, disciplined neoliberal political rule, and made it a distinct possibility. Polanyian-like ideas have never held full sway in American life, while Hayekian conceptions and sensibilities now constitute a habitus supported by an entrenched policy regime and its structures.

CAPITALISM AT THE POINT OF INFLECTION: NEOLIBERALISM'S WAKE

We need new mental conceptions to understand the world. What might these be and who will produce them, given the sociological and intellectual malaise that hangs over knowledge production more generally?

(Harvey 2010a: 237)

At the 2010 annual meeting of the American Sociological Association, in the largest ballroom before a packed audience, noted critics of neoliberalism analyzed the 2008 financial crisis, related crisis tendencies, and possibilities for reform. David Harvey (2010b) argued that capitalism had reached its "inflection point" – it cannot sustain growth. The other participants seemed bemused by Harvey's claim, especially his passing reference to "revolution."[9] They did not engage his core point that the growth imperative, essential to capitalism *per se*, can no longer be sustained. By revolution, he meant, *contra* Judt and Stiglitz, that today's conditions demand transformative thought and radical reconstruction – that liberal reform is not enough. Harvey made no mention of an alternative system nor did he identify a collective agent of change. The prospects for a possible alternative to capitalism as we know it are uncertain and purely speculative. Even minor reform depends on the highly uncertain battle over market liberalism and social liberalism that conjured up the spirits of Hayek and Polanyi. Regardless of that outcome, however, certain major trends make *possible* the systemic crisis of capitalism or inflection point suggested by Harvey.

Environment

Neoliberal globalization's enormous expansion of capitalism has greatly accelerated the speed and volume of the throughput of natural resources and creation of wastes. Extremely rapid development of massive new built environments and integration of hundreds of millions (soon to be billions) of people into global capitalism generated, with lightning speed, huge spikes in resource usage and waste production, human development setbacks in vulnerable parts of the world, and profound risks for all humanity and life on the planet. Since the late 1980s we have been exceeding the biosphere's carrying capacity at an accelerating rate. As car and consumer culture spreads globally, as it has to China, the prospects for eco-catastrophe increase. Neoliberals attacked the veracity of the 2007 UN Intergovernmental Panel on Climate Change (IPCC) *Fourth Assessment Report* (*AR4*), but most recent science suggests that the report was overly optimistic and that *AR5* (2014) will offer more dire scenarios. *AR4* held that the current pace of greenhouse gas emissions promises substantially diminished life conditions by the end of this century for much of the planet, especially for peoples who lack adequate resources to adapt to changes. Feedback effects and other serious problems (e.g., land-use issues, biodiversity loss, overharvesting, fresh water loss, invasive species, nitrogen overfertilization, toxic pollution), all spiking sharply, greatly increase ecological costs and risks. Yet the "bottom billion" poorest people and many more await integration into global capitalism. How can they be brought out of poverty without worsening the ecological crisis? We are caught in a pincer between economic growth and ecological crisis. During the recessionary slowdown, the aim has been to restore growth as we have known it, without entertaining planetary overshoot or ecological devastation. Increased numbers of Americans surveyed said that they do *not* believe in climate change or they do *not* believe that it is a consequence of human actions. The percentage of people who consider it a very serious problem also declined sharply (Pew Research Center 2009b). Neoliberal think tanks have expended enormous resources to blunt concern about ecological risks. As George Will (2008) alleged, invoking Hayek, such environmental concerns provide "license to intrude" everywhere, expand government, and curtail individual freedom (to build a "power plant" or drive an "SUV"). Neoliberalism's growth imperative was formulated when hinterlands were abundant and far less of the globe was integrated into capitalism. By making the world smaller and faster, globalization makes it fuller, magnifying greatly the contradiction of unplanned, exponential growth with the biophysical world. Modern social and economic theories did not address sufficiently social life's embeddedness in the biosphere and dependence upon it. Polanyi presciently hinted at this issue, but did not entertain its consequences in a full world. Market liberalism and social liberalism have presumed the growth imperative in some form, as has socialism as we have known it. Transformative thought is clearly necessary here (e.g., see Speth 2008; Antonio 2009a, 2009b).

Finance

Diverse analysts have long stressed "financialization," entailing securitization and new forms of highly complex, very risky financial products, as a central facet or motor of neoliberal globalization (finance accounted for 40 percent of all corporate profits at its peak in the US [Tabb 2010: 151]). The new products have been sold in deregulated, global financial markets. Goods- and service-producing firms as well as the big banks have substantial financial wings and investments. In the US, the walls separating commercial banks and investment banks and between accounting firms that vet and those that make deals have been eliminated. The financial meltdown nearly brought global capitalism to a halt, and caused serious damage to the "real economy" as well as to finance. Globalized finance spread the crisis quickly in international markets. For nearly three decades the US federal government has served as the investor of last resort, bailing out the big banks and big investors who engage in risky speculative practices until the bubbles have burst. Neoliberal state activism in financial markets confirms Polanyi's arguments about the actual role of the state and the myth of self-regulating markets. The neoliberal pattern of privatizing gains and socializing losses has created a "moral hazard" that invites ever more risky speculative activity. Critics hold that debt-driven, speculative financial growth cannot be sustained and that the series of bubbles and bailouts, which have plagued the neoliberal regime and peaked with the huge losses from the last wave of derivatives trading, based on highly leveraged mortgage-backed assets, are over. A more fundamental issue than these obvious excesses is the possibility that finance's function has changed, no longer largely serving growth in the "real economy," or production of goods and non-financial services. Many analysts have pointed to low capacity utilization in the real economy, which results in substantially slower, lower profit-taking in the most impacted sectors. Thus, investors seek new financial outlets that speed the turnover time of investment and offer much higher profits. Critics argue that much of the new financial economy has operated like a Ponzi scheme, imposing exorbitant transaction costs, making the middle class dependent on the increasingly finance-driven stock market, appropriating resources from middling and poorly paid workers, failing to grow the real economy, and animating the transition of the US into a finance-based plutocracy (e.g., Morris 2008; Foster & Magdoff 2009; Stiglitz 2010; Tabb 2010).

Employment/inequality

Neoliberal globalization has created a transnational division of labor, and expanded exponentially the global capitalist workforce. Capitalist transformation of peasantry into wage workers, overall shift of productive and property relations, and consequent disembedding, as described by Polanyi, which took centuries in Europe, now occurs exceptionally fast, aided by the state's much enhanced capacity to create capitalism's legal, social, and material infrastructure and by rapid diffusion of technologies (e.g., China's stunning ascent to becoming a leading producer of advanced technologies and a global economic powerhouse). Marx argued presciently that scientific and technological knowledge continually revolutionizes modern industry and that the "reserve army" of unemployed and underemployed will grow massively with globalized capitalism. Employment problems and the vicissitudes of contingent and informal labor are rife today across the world. Even in wealthy countries, substantial segments of the populace suffer underemployment and economic insecurity. Mainstream economists warn that the US may be in a long or permanent period of "jobless growth." However, neoclassical economists lack the analytical tools and political will to address structural unemployment (Stiglitz 2010: 245–8). As the global wage labor force expands and technologies continue to be diffused and rationalized, increased employment problems will grow already steep economic inequalities. Neoliberal-era income gains have gone largely to the wealthiest 1 percent of Americans, and especially to a tiny fraction at the very top.[10] Hayekian procedural equality and anti-redistribution tax and social policies have been *the* rule in the neoliberal-era US, which many analysts portray as a "New Gilded Age."[11] Still neoliberal policy-makers have held that the American retirement age ought to be raised to 70, which would flood labor markets with elderly workers, or more likely, if current trends hold, simply impoverish them. However, those social liberals who decry increased class inequalities have not yet come to terms with the structural nature of global employment problems, which will likely accelerate substantially with continued globalization and technological rationalization. Economic inequality is increasing *within* countries globally, and employment and income problems impact negatively already low capacity utilization. However, solving the global employment problem, under capitalism as we have known it, would sharply increase the throughput of resources and production of waste.

Civil society

Karl Mannheim ([1936] 1955: 40) said that ruling groups could become "so intensively interest bound to a situation" that they *cannot see* conditions that might undermine their regime. This is arguably the case with neoliberalism, and this unconsciousness extends far beyond the leadership strata. Liberals of all stripes usually portray civil society in glowingly hopeful terms and as the chief counterforce to the ideological blinders intimated by Mannheim. However, this public space has divergent, competing interests, voices, and organizations. The neoliberal era has expanded the power of money culture and corporate lobbyists. Populists, diverse hate groups, and multifarious other parties participate in cyberspace and on airwaves. The sports-entertainment complex has reshaped the delivery and even the form of news and political conversation, contributing to postmodern fragmentation decried by critics left and right. Political polarization and related media posturing undercut sober discussion of complex issues, such as climate change or structural unemployment. Powerful interests, often with considerable support from below, employ their resources to keep pressing matters off the national agenda. Civil society and its media are rich in information and democratic actors and voices, but it takes disciplined attention and critical capacities to separate serious arguments and valuable information from the cacophony. A well-educated, well-informed majority is needed to develop a substantively democratic civil society or even a formal democratic order capable of addressing major problems. However, privatization and standardization of public education undercut the cultivation needed by either regime. The increased intensity and insecurity and eroded wages and benefits of many jobs makes matters worse. Economic inequalities, harshest at the intersections with other subaltern social statuses, also diminish the cultural capacity and political will to address major problems. In the US, inequalities are boldly inscribed in built environments and social ecologies that isolate classes and races and make plutocratic trends a highly visible part of the cultural landscape. Such problems are multiplied in the case of global civil society. Pressing issues, like climate change, call for transnational cooperation, which adds another layer of complexity to the above. How do we generate reasoned public conversation about crisis tendencies given these conditions? And how do we cope with the populist responses to the disembedding of which Polanyi warned?

CONCLUSION

The future of capitalism is an open question, as is the direction of change. It is possible that reform will be insubstantial and that the problems mentioned above will fester, but the intensity, speed, and multifaceted nature of rapidly mounting environmental damages, under a regime of unplanned, exponential growth, risks global catastrophe. The costs of inattention are already high. Embraced by social liberals as well as market liberals, growth has animated modern capitalism since its inception; its "treadmill of production" makes our jobs, retirement incomes, social services, and children's education dependent on continuous growth *ad infinitum*. The growth imperative is not merely an ideology and the presumed yardstick of societal well-being; it is a habitual, taken-for-granted way of life. That restored growth is the top priority for most people, whatever the costs, is no surprise; because the costs of change are high, the magical belief that science and the market solve all such problems rules. But the contradiction of global capitalism and biophysical limits of a much fuller world will grow worse without concerted collective action and major sacrifices. The other pressing problems mentioned above need to be at least recognized, engaged, and tackled, if not solved, to gain traction for addressing the environmental crisis. Thus, my argument above is *not* against reform and partial mitigation; such change can reduce the pain and create a climate for more prudent consideration of all the longer-term problems we face.

We live in a climate of uncertainty. Slow growth could provide time to re-think and re-engineer capitalism as we have known it, but the conditions may generate the type of populist revolt that both Hayek and Polanyi feared. Rapidly restored growth might reduce unemployment, but will certainly intensify mounting ecological crises. Whatever the outcome of the recessionary downturn, the problems outlined above will likely persist and grow worse without a major transformation of capitalism. Neoliberalism may continue to rule politically and culturally, but its persistence will hasten and deepen the crisis. Revived social liberalism would still have to come to terms with its unsustainable growth imperative, which requires more substantial change than a new regime of accumulation. Slavoj Žižek says: "Today we do not know what we have to do, but we have to act now, because the consequence of non-action could be disastrous" (2010: 95). Yet we do know that a serious action plan must address the growth imperative critically and entertain alternatives to it. Harvey is right about the need for transformative thinking about our normative and substantive directions – about what type of economy and society we want to become in light of where we have been and the constraints we now face. Renewed political and ethical imagination and critical thought, grounded in the moving realities of increasingly global culture, are required to preserve democracy and perhaps the planet. Re-engineered, re-designed capitalism or a genuine alternative, which supersedes the growth imperative and frenetic work and consumption it demands, could improve our well-being and that of future generations, and cultivate a more pacified relation to nature and each other. Such change will entail big costs and sacrifices, but the prospects for crisis and catastrophe facing us on the current course leave no alternative, but to craft new ways of life.

Acknowledgments

My friends Bob Kent, Tom Skrtic, and Bill Staples provided incisive criticism of this essay.

Notes

1 I refer to the 2008 financial meltdown for brevity's sake; imminent financial collapse in the fall of that year led to the first phase of the federal bailout. The crisis began in 2007, but the related economic slowdown, the worst since the Great Depression, goes on as I write.

2 Pew Research Center (2009a, 2010) studies indicated shifting views about the US's leading role in the world after the crisis began. Americans surveyed held that the US should "mind its own business," and more of them thought that China, rather than the

584 ROBERT J. ANTONIO

US, was the globe's leading economic power. Global respondents also tended to identify China as the top economic power.

3 Assuring conservative readers that free-market capitalism is "resilient and stable" (especially in English-speaking nations) and that "radical alternatives no longer beckon," Clark trashed Polanyi's work and said that, while it has classic status in sub-areas of sociology, political science, and anthropology, economists ignore or deride it. Sociologist Block refutes Clark's claims.

4 See, for example, Stanfield 1980; Block 2003; Harvey 2005; Ozveren 2007; Kurtuluş 2008; Dale 2010. Nobel Prize-winning economist Joseph Stiglitz ([1944] 2001) wrote the foreword and Fred Block ([1944] 2001) penned the introduction to the most recent edition of *The Great Transformation*.

5 Hayek (1944: 119–22) conceded that states should protect "against severe physical privation," assist victims of "acts of God" (natural disasters), and cope with mass unemployment (albeit by monetary policy and other methods that would be consistent with classical liberalism). Yet, he did not object to states helping "organize a comprehensive system of social insurance."

6 See Fischer 2009: 326–9; Mirowski 2009: 440–6. Hayek's (1967: 161) distinction between authoritarian versus totalitarian regimes and their relation to democracy appears as the third of 61 principles in his succinct, systematic statement of his overall vision of "liberal social order," which he had originally presented, in 1966, at the Mont Pèlerin Society.

7 Denouncing *The Great Transformation* as a "vicious" and "fallacious" work, Hayekian Murray Rothbard (2004) charged that Polanyi is a typical "collectivist" who believes freedom can be preserved even when its "*cause*" (self-regulating market society) is destroyed.

8 Robert Reich (2007) described this conjuncture as a "not quite golden age," because of its exclusions (e.g., African Americans and women) and other problems. Still much of today's urban ecology, built environments, creature comforts, and forms of leisure and consumption have roots in this period. US manufacturing firms dominated their huge home market and world markets. New mass media and mass entertainment, especially TV, and a revolutionized retail sector and federally subsidized suburbs forged a mass consumer society. Union membership peaked and labor cooperated with management, trading aspirations for shared control of the labor process for higher wages and benefits and stable employment. This postwar "capital-labor accord" increased affluence, security, and opportunity. Keynesian management of aggregate demand balanced production and consumption and maintained nearly full employment, steady accumulation, and high profit rates. Mass higher education facilitated the rise of an affluent professional middle class, provided unparalleled educational access to workers, and promised the substantive equality of opportunity that Polanyi called for. This hope was also served by civil rights struggles, Great Society legislation, and nascent women's, gay and lesbian, and disability rights movements.

9 The other participants were economist James Galbraith and sociologists Fred Block, Miguel Centano, Frances Fox Piven, Michael Schwartz, and Clarence Lo.

10 Charles Morris (2008: 152–3) states that between 1980 and 2006 (the height of neoliberal dominance): "Almost *all* the top tenth's share gains . . . went to the top 1 percent, or the 'top centile,' who more than doubled their share of national cash income from 9 percent to 20 percent. Even within the top centile, however, the distribution of gains was radically skewed. Nearly 60 percent of it went to the top *tenth* of 1 percent of the population, and more than a fourth of it to the top one-hundredth of

1 percent of the population." Congress, and especially Republicans, are generally most responsive to high-income people, but neither party has been responsive to low-income people. Their views have had negligible impact on elected officials and are absent in political discourse. The general public in the US appear to care little about abuse of wealth, and reject European social democracy. These views *may* erode if, as expected, employment problems worsen and more retirees suffer from inadequate savings (Bartels 2008: 252–82, 294–8).

11 In Bartels' (2008: 129, 131, 149, 155–61) research, about half the interviewees did not acknowledge that inequality had increased or said they had not thought about it. Nearly half of the people believed that the country would be better off if we worried less about inequality. Reflecting the political polarization, the more informed the "extreme conservative," the more likely that he or she will deny increasing inequality and less likely he or she will say that inequality is bad. However, other researchers have found that Americans greatly underestimate the degree of economic inequality, yet also aspire to a much more equitable society than currently exists in the US. They found this to hold across all demographic groups, even the wealthy and Republicans (Norton & Ariely 2011).

References

Antonio, R. J. (2009a) "Climate Change, the Resource Crunch, and the Global Growth Imperative." In H. F. Dahms (ed.), *Nature, Knowledge, and Negation: Current Perspectives in Social Theory*, Vol. 26. Bingley: Emerald, pp. 3–74.

Antonio, R. J. (2009b) "Reply to Critics: Choosing Life." In H. F. Dahms (ed.), *Nature, Knowledge, and Negation: Current Perspectives in Social Theory*, Vol. 26. Bingley: Emerald, pp. 115–28.

Bartels, L. M. (2008) *Unequal Democracy: The Political Economy of the New Gilded Age*. Princeton, NJ: Princeton University Press.

Block, F. ([1944] 2001) "Introduction." In K. Polanyi, *The Great Transformation: The Political and Economic Origins of Our Time*. Boston: Beacon Press, pp. xviii–xxxviii.

Block, F. (2003) "Karl Polanyi and the Writing of *The Great Transformation*." *Theory and Society* 32: 275–306.

Block, F. (2008) "No Such Thing as a Free Market." Longview Institute for the Public Good, June 11. www.longviewinstitute.org/nosuchthing (accessed August 21, 2010).

Bowles, S. and H. Gintis (1986) *Democracy and Capitalism: Property, Community, and the Contradictions of Modern Social Thought*. New York: Basic Books.

Brick, H. (2006) *Transcending Capitalism: Visions of a New Society in Modern American Thought*. Ithaca, NY: Cornell University Press.

Brooks, A. C. (2010) *The Battle: How the Fight between Free Enterprise and Big Government Will Shape America's Future*. New York: Basic Books.

Caldwell, B. (2007) "The Publication History of *The Road to Serfdom*" [excerpted from the author's Introduction]. In F. A. Hayek, *The Road to Serfdom*. Chicago: University of Chicago Press. www.press.uchicago.edu/Misc/Chicago/320553.html (accessed August 4, 2010).

Clark, G. (2008) "Reconsiderations: '*The Great Transformation*' by Karl Polanyi." *New York Sun*, June 4. www.nysun.com/arts/reconsiderations-the-great-transformation-by-karl/79250/ (accessed August 21, 2010).

Dale, G. (2010) *Karl Polanyi: The Limits of the Market*. Cambridge: Polity Press.

Dewey, J. ([1935] 1987) *Liberalism and Social Action*. In J. A. Boydston (ed.), *John Dewey, The Later Works, 1925–1953, Vol. 11, 1935–1937*. Carbondale, IL: Southern Illinois University Press, pp. 1–65.

Fischer, K. (2009) "The Influence of Neoliberals in Chile Before, During, and After Pinochet." In P. Mirowski and D. Plehwe (eds.), *The Road from Mont Pèlerin: The Making of the Neoliberal State*. Cambridge, MA: Harvard University Press, pp. 305–46.

Foner, E. (1998) *The Story of American Freedom*. New York: W. W. Norton.

Foster, J. B. and F. Magdoff (2009) *The Great Financial Crisis: Causes and Consequences*. New York: Monthly Review Press.

Friedman, T. L. (2000) *The Lexus and the Olive Tree*. New York: Anchor Books.

Friedman, T. L. (2005) *The World Is Flat: A Brief History of the Twenty-First Century*. New York: Farrar, Straus and Giroux.

Fukuyama, F. (1989) "The End of History?" *National Interest* 16: 3–18.

Harrison, B. and B. Bluestone (1988) *The Great U-Turn: Corporate Restructuring and the Polarizing of America*. New York: Basic Books.

Harvey, D. (1989) *The Condition of Postmodernity: An Enquiry into the Origins of Cultural Change*. Oxford: Blackwell.

Harvey, D. (2005) *A Brief History of Neoliberalism*. Oxford: Oxford University Press.

Harvey, D. (2010a) *The Enigma of Capital and the Crises of Capitalism*. Oxford: Oxford University Press.

Harvey, D. (2010b) "The Enigma of Capital and the Crisis This Time." Paper presented at the 105th Annual Meeting of the American Sociological Association, Atlanta, GA, August 16.

Hayek, F. A. (1944) *The Road to Serfdom*. Chicago: University of Chicago Press.

Hayek, F. A. (1967) *Studies in Politics, Philosophy, and Economics*. New York: Clarion.

Hodgson, G. (1978) *America in Our Time*. New York: Vintage.

Independent (2010) "Friedrich Hayek: Darling of the Right Reborn in the USA." *The Independent*, July 3. www.independent.co.uk/news/world/americas/friedrich-hayek-darling-of-the-right-is-reborn-in-the-usa-2017267.html (accessed July 21, 2010).

Judt, T. (2010) *Ill Fares the Land*. New York: Penguin.

Kirkpatrick, J. (1992) "Toward Human Governance." *Religion and Liberty* 2(2). www.acton.org/publications/randl/rl_interview_34.php (accessed August 4, 2010).

Kotz, D. M. and T. McDonough (2010) "Global Neoliberalism and the Contemporary Social Structure of Accumulation." In T. McDonough, M. Reich, and D. M. Kotz (eds.), *Contemporary Capitalism and Its Crises: Social Structure of Accumulation Theory for the 21st Century*. Cambridge: Cambridge University Press, pp. 93–120.

Kurtuluş, G. (2008) "Karl Polanyi and the Antinomies of Embeddedness." *Socio-Economic Review* 6: 5–33.

Lahart, J. (2010) "The Glen Beck Effect: Hayek Has a Hit." *The Wall Street Journal*, June 17. http://blogs.wsj.com/economics/2010/06/17/the-glenn-beck-effect-hayek-has-a-hit/ (accessed August 1, 2010).

Lippmann, W. (1937) *The Good Society*. Boston: Little, Brown, and Co.

Mannheim, K. ([1936] 1955) *Ideology and Utopia*. New York: Harvest Books.

Marx, Karl (1963) *The 18th Brumaire of Louis Bonaparte*. New York: International Publishers.

Mirowski, P. (2009) "Postface: Defining Neoliberalism." In P. Mirowski and D. Plehwe (eds.), *The Road from Mont Pèlerin: The Making of the Neoliberal State*. Cambridge, MA: Harvard University Press, pp. 417–55.

Morris, C. R. (2008) *The Two Trillion Dollar Meltdown: Easy Money, High Rollers, and the Great Credit Crash*. New York: Public Affairs.

Nash, G. H. (1976) *The Conservative Intellectual Movement in America Since 1945*. New York: Basic Books.

Norton, Michael I. and Dan Ariely (2011) "Building a Better America – One Wealth Quintile at a Time." *Perspectives on Psychological Science* 6(1): 9–12.

Ozveren, E. (2007) "Karl Polanyi and Return of the 'Primitive' in Institutional Economics." *Journal of Economic Issues* 41(3): 783–808.

Parsons, T. (1971) *The System of Modern Societies*. Englewood Cliffs, NJ: Prentice Hall.

Pew Research Center (2009a) "U.S. Seen as Less Important, China as More Powerful." December 3. http://pewglobal.org/2010/06/17/obama-more-popular-abroad-than-at-home/ (accessed July 15, 2010).

Pew Research Center (2009b) "Fewer Americans See Solid Evidence of Global Warming." October 22. http://pewresearch.org/pubs/1386/cap-and-trade-global-warming-opinion (accessed July 18, 2010).

Pew Research Center (2010) "Obama More Popular Abroad Than at Home, Global Image of U.S. Continues to Benefit." June 17. http://pewresearch.org/pubs/1630/obama-more-popular-abroad-global-american-image-benefit-22-nation-global-survey (accessed July 14, 2010).

Polanyi, K. ([1944] 1957) *The Great Transformation: The Political and Economic Origins of Our Time*. Boston: Beacon Press.

Reich, R. B. (2007) *Supercapitalism: The Transformation of Business, Democracy, and Everyday Life*. New York: Alfred A. Knopf.

Roberts, R. (2010) "Why Friedrich Hayek Is Making a Comeback." *The Wall Street Journal*, June 28. http://online.wsj.com/article/SB10001424052748704911704575326500718166146.html (accessed August 1, 2010).

Rothbard, M. R. (2004) "Down with Primitivism: A Thorough Critique of Polanyi." Ludwig von Mises Institute, September 17. http://mises.org/daily/1607 (accessed July 31, 2010).

Schumpeter, J. A. ([1942] 1962) *Capitalism, Socialism, and Democracy*, 3rd edn. New York: Harper Torchbooks.

Shearmur, J. (2006) "Hayek, *The Road to Serfdom*, and the British Conservatives." *Journal of the History of Economic Thought* 28(3): 309–14.

Speth, J. G. (2008) *The Bridge at the End of the World: Capitalism, the Environment, and Crossing from Crisis to Sustainability*. New Haven, CT: Yale University Press.

Stanfield, J. R. (1980) "The Institutional Economics of Karl Polanyi." *Journal of Economic Issues* 14(3): 593–614.

Stiglitz, J. E. ([1944] 2001) "Foreword." In K. Polanyi, *The Great Transformation: The Political and Economic Origins of Our Time*. Boston: Beacon Press, pp. vii–xvii.

Stiglitz, J. E. (2010) *Freefall: America, Free Markets, and the Sinking of the World Economy*. New York: W. W. Norton.

Tabb, W. K. (2010) "Financialization in the Contemporary Social Structure of Accumulation." In T. McDonough, M. Reich, and D. M. Kotz (eds.), *Contemporary Capitalism and Its Crises: Social Structure of Accumulation Theory for the 21st Century*. Cambridge: Cambridge University Press, pp. 145–67.

Wallerstein, I. (2010) "Structural Crises." *New Left Review* 62(April): 133–42.

Will, G. (2008) "An Environmental 'License to Intrude'." *Lawrence Journal World* 23(May). www2.ljworld.com/news/2008/may/23/environmental_license_intrude/ (accessed May 23, 2008).

Žižek, S. (2010) "A Permanent Economic Emergency." *New Left Review* 64(July): 85–95.

31

Organized Coercion and Political Authority

Armed Conflict in a World of States

MEYER KESTNBAUM

How can we bring together interstate and civil war, insurgency, revolt, and terror under a single framework and make sense of them as part of a single domain? The point of departure for such an effort lies in two elements of Carl von Clausewitz's analysis of warfare in *On War* ([1832] 1976). Clausewitz initially defines war as the use of force to compel an opponent to do one's will. Not only is war always about coercion, it is fundamentally relational such that the use of force constitutes the tie between two (or more) actors. A critical relational quality emerges again when Clausewitz looks within each of the warring parties, which at least for the purposes of general analysis he conceives of as more or less modern territorial states. Unpacking the warring party, Clausewitz identifies its trinitary structure: the state, offering political direction; the armed forces, comprising the organized coercive force directed by the state; and society, those under the rule of the state who may be drawn upon to constitute or support the armed forces.

Taken together, Clausewitz's focus on relations among and within belligerents has several broad implications. First, if our goal is to make sense of the domain of armed conflict, then our analytic attention needs to fall squarely on how war is actually made – on how war works from the inside, as parties to a conflict form and direct coercive force (see Kestnbaum 2005). Rather than focus on why any particular war is fought, this approach highlights the logic of armed conflict *per se*, allowing the analyst to identify regularities in the way such conflicts are shaped by and serve to remake belligerents. Second, any attempt to examine how war is made requires we pay explicit attention to the political authority of the state. The state

The Wiley-Blackwell Companion to Sociology, First Edition. Edited by George Ritzer.
© 2012 Blackwell Publishing Ltd. Published 2012 by Blackwell Publishing Ltd.

raises and directs force in its service, rendering the use of coercion fundamentally political. This is what is meant by Clausewitz's often quoted claim that war is the continuation of politics by other means.

Powerfully suggestive in itself, Clausewitz expands the implications of his relational understanding of war by explicitly historicizing this abstract presentation (see Clausewitz [1832] 1976: 585–94; Paret 1992). Examining the sweep of armed conflict over the millennium preceding the French revolutionary and Napoleonic Wars and their aftermath, Clausewitz makes clear that his initial characterization of the trinity captures a particular historical moment in which interstate war is dominated by centralized states raising standing military forces, while differently composed political authorities both raise and contend with a range of other types of organized coercion at other junctures. In doing so, Clausewitz underscores that his relational approach revolves around paying careful attention to the precise ways in which coercive force is organized on the ground and to the way these set the terms for armed conflict. Explicit focus on organized coercion, its particular forms and their specific relations to political authority, then, comprises the third element of Clausewitz's relationalism.

It was to take another three-quarters of a century, however, for Max Weber fundamentally to recast the relational characterization of the warring party in a manner that lets us specify the broad domain of armed conflict, from interstate war to terror. The key can be found in Weber's seminal formulation that the distinguishing feature of the modern state lies in its claim of a monopoly over the legitimate use of force (Weber 1978, 1: 50–6, 2: 901–4). Articulated in these terms, Weber affirms the centrality of the political authority–coercive force relationship within the territorial extent of the polity, making it the defining feature of political association, as well as the analytic focus on concrete forms of organized coercion. But what is especially important for our purposes is an added element: Weber's emphasis not only on a monopoly of force but just as importantly on the *claim* of monopoly over its *legitimate use*. Although proposed in sweeping and definitional terms, Weber's formulation points to the contingent and contested relationship between political authority on the one hand and organized coercion on the other, where state control over particular forms of organized coercion within a given territory must be accomplished and maintained. If all modern states claim a monopoly over the legitimate use of force, by no means do all in fact achieve or retain such a monopoly. Weber's formulation demands we treat the political authority–organized coercion relationship as problematic and variable, and adds a dynamic and developmental component, spurring us to examine the processes by which organized coercion and political control over force shift across time and space.

With these tools in place, we are in a position to bring together interstate and civil war, insurgency, revolt, and terror in a single analytic framework. All of the forms of armed conflict considered here involve the use of force by two or more organized coercive bodies on a continued basis. It is not strictly speaking necessary that the state be a party to the conflict, but since the emergence of a globe more or less organized into territorially exclusive and competing states, the state is implicated in all uses of organized coercion, within or across its borders. As a consequence, without too much slippage, one may refer collectively to interstate and civil war, revolt, insurgency, and terror as forms of warfare, and to the action involved as war making. What defines the variety of warfare, then, is the alignment of the particular use of organized coercion with respect to the state or states involved.[1]

Political alignment of the use of force immediately directs our attention to the issue of central state control over any particular pattern of organized coercion. Approaching it in these terms is particularly useful, since it allows us to identify distinct types of coercive organizations across a wide range of settings and to situate them politically. State control can be understood to vary along two dimensions. On the first, the question is to what extent does the state raise, supply, pay, and otherwise administer a coercive organization. On the second, the question is to what extent does the state authorize a coercive organization, indicating that body acts with its mandate. These analytic dimensions can be seen as inscribing a two-dimensional space where at one corner, for example, lie standing armed forces raised as well as paid for by the state and duly constituted under its authority.[2] At the opposite corner of this space lie forms of what may be called militarized self-help (see Crone & Cook 1980), neither raised nor sanctioned by the state, such as militants and armed bands, local militias and self-defense forces, and guerrillas and some paramilitaries. Despite the absence of multiple administrative ties, forms of militarized self-help may acquire state recognition, forming perhaps in response to state appeals for local involvement or working as *de facto* agents of the state, and by such means operate with the state's permission and even license. Some militias and paramilitaries, particularly, may move toward the middle of this space between the broad range of militarized self-help and state military forces, insofar as they come to be regulated under national law (or further, are formed into part of an overarching national military force), enter into partnerships with state agencies or the armed forces, or are formed as military wings of political associations such as mass political parties and are bound to the regime in power (see Ahram 2011). State control, of course, does not dictate how a particular form of organized coercion will act relative to political authority. To underscore the point, one need only think of a standing army collapsing and turning to support revolutionary challengers (see Chorley 1973; Skocpol 1979), or local self-defense forces rising up to wage a people's war against a foreign invader (Clausewitz [1832] 1976: 479–83; Geyer 2002). Rather, ties of administration and authorization give the analyst purchase on why at any particular historical conjuncture a specific form of organized coercion may act in accord with the state, may take up an oppositional stance and challenge the state, or may act more or less orthogonally to the state.

If alignment and state control help illuminate what holds together the breadth of the domain of war making, we must look further inside the actual use of force to appreciate fully the structure and dynamics of any particular struggle. Analytically, the use of coercive force can be resolved into two distinct components: mobilization for war and the definition and treatment of the enemy. The first is an issue of how belligerents produce force. It includes the formation of coercive organization itself, as well as the mobilization of the human, material, and moral or political resources behind conflict that afford the capacity to bring force to bear. The second is an issue of how belligerents apply force versus a foe. It includes the designation of whom that force is directed against, what form that force takes, and to what effect. Both may vary in scope and intensity. The former brings into relief relations among the state, organized coercion, and society, as we have already described, and may draw attention to linkages across state borders in terms of people, material resources, or political support that feed into a particular pattern of mobilization. The latter highlights relations among warring parties as well as the way in which the actual incidence of force serves to reinforce or blur distinctions between combatants and noncombatants among those subject to coercion, intentional or otherwise. It is tempting, perhaps, to collapse the two or to focus only on one dimension. Attending to the two distinct component parts of the use of force, however, ensures the analyst can trace coercion from the assembling of its many elements through to its employment against concrete persons and things, allowing the analyst to identify and begin to explain why mobilization or treatment of the enemy may look rather different for opponents in an armed struggle, or why either may shift over time for any particular belligerent.

LOGICS OF CHANGE IN THE DOMAIN OF WAR

Following from the toolkit developed here, our analysis of war making aims to shed light on how mobilization (including the actual pattern of organized coercion) as well as definition and treatment of the enemy shift and change, in armed conflicts defined with respect to the authoritative claims of states. Given the tremendous range of settings under examination – from stable states at war, to insurgencies and revolts within such states, to imperial expansions and colonial challenges, wars of independence and social revolutions, civil wars arising in all such environments including those that draw involvement from across borders, as well as national and transnational forms of terrorism – it is useful to join the recent call in macroscopic and historical analysis and to focus on the central processes that can be said to structure and give coherence to the domain as a whole (Adams, Clemens & Orloff 2005; Clemens 2007). Three such processes stand out: how state formation shapes the way war is waged; how war making shapes the formation of the state; and how making war reshapes the way war is waged. Full causal explanations either of state formation or changes in ways of making war may take account of a vast array of additional elements, from geopolitical structure to technology to language, for example; however, to elucidate the core of what holds this domain together I will limit myself to these three. In doing so, I hope not only to highlight the central dynamics and particular mechanisms through which notable transformations arise in armed conflict, but also to reshape how we think about the logic of state formation and its relation to war.

Before looking further into each of the central processes, I need to make several analytic distinctions clear. First, when I talk of state formation, I mean more than simply the organizational structure of the state apparatus and the capacity of the state to penetrate its territory down to the locality and to control those residing within. I am also talking about the extent to which organized coercion within its territory may fall beyond the control of the state, and furthermore about the way in which differently situated people under the rule of the state are included or alternately excluded or marginalized in the polity as well as how such people are categorized relative to the state, that is, in what idiom they are cobbled together or differentiated. Second, when I talk of ways of making war I mean both *how states and non-state groups mobilize for war* – the way in which coercive force is orga-nized, the concrete organizational and network structures through which the polity (or another collectivity) mobilizes, and under what social categories or in terms of what identities they mobilize – as well as *whom they define as the enemy, in what terms, and how they direct organized coercion at that enemy*. Third, when talking about how state making influences war making, or vice versa, the focus is on dynam-ics – hence, attention turns to how shifts in the way the state is formed or the actual process of mobilizing for war and using force against an enemy induce change in the state or in war making. And fourth, in any such discussion, it is necessary to recognize that we are talking about both state-led war and non-state actors engaged in armed conflict, directed variously at what can be called their own state, another state, or other identified groups. Hence, these relationships need to be traced out with sensitivity to how they form or reform relationships among state and non-state coercion and its use.

FROM STATE MAKING TO WAR MAKING

The recent passing of Charles Tilly has spurred widespread effort to consider his legacy for sociological inquiry. As part of this assessment, it has become increasingly clear that a great deal of what is going on in the domain of armed conflict can be captured by focusing on the subordinate of the two clauses in his much cited formula, "war made states, and vice versa" (Tilly 1992: 67). Here, the notion is that the way in which the state has been made powerfully shapes how war making proceeds. We can look at this in three parts: state mobilization, state and the defini-tion of the enemy, and the formation and mobilization of non-state force against the state.

The manner in which the state has been made – notably in terms of who is armed and who is not, and how coercive force is organized relative to the state as well as who is mobilized into politics and how – sets the terms for how the state organizes and mobilizes for war. These relationships become central (and are most readily observed) at decisive moments in the history of national states undergoing signifi-cant political change – moments of founding or re-founding, when for example independence is achieved or a new form of political rule is installed, collapse is averted or the state brings itself back from collapse (cf. Wimmer & Minn 2006). At such moments, the organization of politics within states fundamentally alters the conditions under which state-led force is organized. Two things are going on here. First is the proposition that states reorganize or reconstitute coercion under their control only when spurred to do so by perceived threats and opportunities that in turn create substantial pressures or attractive alternatives that induce reform. Second is the observation that significant shifts in the relationship between the state and organized coercion – as in the collapse of the armed forces or the emergence of new forms of organized coercion beyond state control – as well as shifts in the relation between the state and society – as in the remaking of the social composition of a ruling coalition, or the incorporation of previously excluded social classes into national politics – offer two of the more compelling sets of pressures *and* opportunities for the reorganization of force and, furthermore, influence the direction of reform. Why? Singly or together, changes in these dimensions of state formation shift the logic of military reform, in conjunction with state structures, coercive organizations, and other institutions in place, altering what is politically desirable, militarily practical, and organizationally possible when mobilizing for war.

One need only look at the range of examples of Latin American states acquiring independence from Spain in the early nineteenth century, drawn together by Miguel Centeno (2002), in contrast to cases of political or social revolution in Europe and North America around the end of the eighteenth century (Skocpol 1979, 1994; Kestnbaum 2000, 2002) and Southeast Asian states formed in the aftermath of post-Word War II decolonization (see Slater 2010; Ahram 2011), to discern a central pattern. In those Latin American states that had been built with a relatively weak administrative core and were based on exclusion of indigenous populations and whose armed force was provided by colonial rulers (whether or not augmented by some number of locals), since independence did not involve the mobilization of the masses there was neither political impetus to mobilize the popular classes into politics behind the cause of independence nor call to mobilize those masses into the armed forces to secure independence, nor was there organizational capacity to do so. As a consequence, political exclusion and relatively narrow-based, weak armed forces not rooted in the populace were reinforced. Alternatively, where political independence or social revolution involved the mobilization of the popular classes into national politics, and the pressure to secure a newly mass-based polity emerged – whether to defend independence or the new pattern of republican governance in war – as in the revolutionary United States, or the French Revolution – then the reshaping of politics precipitated a dramatic reorganization of coercive force. The result was the formation of a broad-based military rooted in the popular classes that formed the cornerstone of state-led mass military mobilization. Institutionally, this was accomplished first by organizing politics around the person of the national citizen, and second by reorganizing the armed forces around the citizen-soldier. In this model, the nation was mobilized as one polity behind war making, in which every man, woman, and child had a role in principle, but some would serve their nation in war by bearing arms for the state. As I will examine further below, this route to the construction of coercive force generally involved the state's absorption of coercive forms – citizen militias or local self-defense forces, for example – that emerged at least originally as independent of governing political authority, and perhaps in the course of revolution stood even in opposition. However, under the new regime they were subsequently incorporated into the formal structure of state-led forces and, as it were, "regularized" – formally brought under central state control, bound to if not subsumed within the regular, standing armed forces (cf. Ahram 2011). In some instances, notably those in which a mass party state was the result of the politics of popular mobilization, the party itself (or potentially other central political institutions created as part of the new politics) may become militarized, in which for example the party develops an organizationally separate armed wing, forming a paramilitary force. Examples include the Nazi Brownshirts or SA and later the SS, and the Baath party paramilitary forces in Iraq under Saddam Hussein. By contrast to such popular incorporating reconstructions of armed force, among Southeast Asian authoritarian regimes formed after World War II, coercive force was reorganized in response to patterns of popular political mobilization, but in part because of the regime's resistance to political inclusion, it involved neither the thoroughgoing reconstruction of central state forces around formerly rebellious local coercive forms nor the elimination or absorption of quasi-official forces formed at the local level. Instead, the reorganization of coercion in response to popular political mobilization amounted to the retention of a measure of coercive force controlled by communal elites, typically organized as militias or paramilitaries, coordinated with authoritarian rule at the center through elite pacts.

In the domain of state-organized force, the organization of the polity also has a definite impact on how the enemy in war is defined, against whom coercion is employed as a matter of design. Insofar as particular understandings of the "us" from whom sovereign authority derives and in whose name that state rules are articulated in policy and reinforced in practice, that categorical delineation of membership serves to define not merely who it is that is "not us," but more importantly, perhaps, the principle of differentiation from which follows the political authority to use coercive force (see Schmitt [1927] 1976). To take but one example, to the extent that membership is national in character, as emerged out of the French Revolution in Europe, then the constitution of those whom state force is to serve is national in form and their enemy is nationalized, where nationality is taken as a difference politically significant enough that it may constitute the basis for the use of deadly force (see Brubaker 1992; Scarry 1996; Horne 2002). Insofar as the crucial difference between us and them is further rendered in ethnic, religious sectarian, or kinship terms, the perception of difference may deepen, intensifying conflict. Furthermore, the prospect of salient difference cutting across political boundaries – both within and among states – grows dramatically, and with it comes an increasing complexity in patterns of differentiating between friend and enemy and mapping that distinction onto state boundaries, where internal enemies may clearly emerge and populations beyond state borders may be gathered together into an extension of the "us" who are at war (see Brubaker 1996). Such dynamics of overlaying, in turn, can be further naturalized and rendered fundamental insofar as differences are additionally racialized, whether the difference is conceived primarily in racial terms or rather acquires a racialized cast. Such observations regarding race, in turn, underscore the extent to which ethnicity, religion, or clan – in addition to race *per se* – may displace nation, taken here simply as a point of departure, either supplanting nation through this process of overlaying or forming the primary understanding of salient difference in the first instance.

For each of these broad categorical bases of defining the distinctiveness of those ruled by one state, of significance for our purposes is the extent to which this principle cuts across the longstanding organizationally based and normatively elaborated distinction between combatants and noncombatants in war (Walzer 1977; Best 1980, 1994). This has two implications with respect to persons intentionally targeted in armed conflict. The first has to do with when force is directed not at those armed by a state but rather at others identified as part of a larger collective. Here, we are talking about a process where the politically salient distinction between us and them supplants other meaningful distinctions in war, such that states intentionally direct armed force against noncombatants and especially civilians as a matter of design (see Downes 2008; Kestnbaum 2009). The second brings into relief the issue of those who bear arms without a state's authority, where they – and those who offer support or haven – are formed into an enemy to be targeted and attacked (see McPherson 1997; Horne 2002; Valentino, Huth & Balch-Lindsay 2004). The importance of such categorical differentiation is twofold: it serves to form the opponent into a more or less homogeneous enemy against whom coercion may be used legitimately, identified with nation, perhaps, or race; and it readily coexists with aggressive and thoroughgoing efforts by states at war to distinguish in minute ways among their own populations, assigning radically different tasks as well as rewards or burdens in war, yet drawing them all together ostensibly as part of one political community set in motion together to wage war.

The structure of the state also influences war making by another route, highlighted in the emergence of non-state coercive organizations behind which people mobilize into armed conflict. In the formation of such militarized self-help, the organization of the polity has a dual effect: it provides a crucial impetus and even wherewithal to organize force beyond the state at the same time as it galvanizes and sharpens the sense of whom this very force is to be employed against, how it is to be used, and under what conditions. All varieties of militarized self-help are formed by sets of people who might be called coercive entrepreneurs (Tilly 2003). But they emerge through several different processes as a result of distinct mechanisms and may be aligned variously with the regime in power, against that regime, or orthogonal to the regime, with either a domestic or transnational focus.

Among the least clearly delineated, perhaps, is a process that can be understood as a form of popular appropriation of armed conflict. What is crucial is the extent to which ordinary people appropriate an armed conflict for themselves, identifying such fights as fundamentally their own. In terms of self-armed fighters aligned with the state, while not limited to moments when the state's forces are in dire circumstances, notable examples have occurred historically when states are severely under duress, facing collapse or having just collapsed, emerging perhaps in response to an appeal to take up arms and wage "people's war" as in Prussia or Spain during the Napoleonic Wars. Among this group, we are talking about a broad, somewhat heterogeneous class of pro-regime guerrillas or partisans, including the so-called raiders in the US Civil War (and others identified as guerrillas on both the Union and Confederate sides) as well as the *francs-tireurs* of the Franco-Prussian War. By the same token, the popular appropriation of war – whether the conflict is ongoing, about to emerge, or even where open hostilities have ceased – may also produce militant challenges or counter-regime insurgents, insofar as the armed conflict itself is one that divides the polity meaningfully, as can be seen in both Iraq and Afghanistan currently. Furthermore, the mechanism of popular appropriation (in conjunction with others I will discuss) is central to the transformation of militancy into terrorist organizations targeting both states in which they reside and states other than the ones in which they organize, train, and so forth – where the avowed political cause and actions of the terrorist organization are taken to be one's own. Few more striking examples can be offered than the conversion of Islamist political challenge and anti-Americanism into large-scale terror employed against the United States on September 11, 2001 (see Ajami 2001; Friedman 2002).

At largely the opposite end of the spectrum, where states alienate control or never acquire control over localities or particular regions, lies a distinct alternative logic that might be identified with the emergence of a localist politics and administration. Such localism is characteristic of states that have not elaborated an administrative and coercive structure allowing them to rule directly from the center to the locality, or which lack the capacity to exert central control territorially for other reasons (see Goodwin & Skocpol 1994; Goodwin 2001). It also describes a range of political bargains struck in the course of state making in which central authority grants autonomy to a locality or acquires formal control over an otherwise autonomous district or region, allowing it to organize coercive force independently in the form of local militias, paramilitaries, or security forces in exchange for maintaining order there and typically staying out of national politics (see Slater 2010). These local governance and coercive arrangements are frequently organized along agrarian landholding, ethnic, religious, or clan lines locally, and by virtue of their local focus and distinctive social bases may diverge strongly in their concerns from central authority. In rather less common but notable instances, for example in North Africa and parts of the Middle East currently, such localism may involve the formal political institutionalization of religious or kinship membership organizations – neither part of the state nor formed to manage politics *per se* – bringing a form of political self-help expressly into institutional politics and transforming whatever armed wing it develops into an independent basis of military organization normalized in politics but beyond the control of the central state (see Crone & Cook 1980; Charrad 2001). In a notable variant characteristic of some contemporary authoritarianisms facing strong internal political challenges, rather than allowing local religious or clan leaders to organize force independently, such localism may encompass civil administrative and judicial concerns, involve religious or ethno-cultural education, and include the acceptance of armed militant activity at the locality as long as that activity is directed explicitly away from the regime in power (Friedman 2002).

While the former set of logics does not typically give rise to insurgency or civil war, another set highlighting the way state policy or practice marginalizes or subordinates persons based on ethnicity, religion, kinship, or class may do precisely that. The effect is intensified when the state additionally acts in a corrupt or predatory manner – notably when it appropriates property or other wealth without consent (Bates 2008), strips people of political rights or excludes them from the political process (Goodwin & Skocpol 1994), or aggressively attempts to assimilate ethno-culturally or religiously differentiated groups (Brubaker 1996). The result of such state action is to galvanize the targeted group's sense of collective identity and to spur them to form local militias or paramilitary forces for the purposes of ensuring they are not trampled by state policy. It may even spur the formation of a broader movement supporting a guerrilla force. In parallel, such action may signal a willingness on the part of the state to tolerate or even embrace the formation of militia and paramilitary organizations willing to carry out precisely these policies, but which remain only loosely aligned with the state itself. The longstanding situation in Colombia illustrates many of these dynamics (see Davis & Pereira 2003). Perhaps the most extreme form of this unfolding process may be observed in instances of ethnic cleansing, such as in the former Yugoslavia or, more recently, in Sudan (Mann 2005).

Both the localism and state policy arguments are closely related to another set of contentions, typically identified with the weakness of the state rather than its actions or the structured bargains it is able to put in place and maintain. Importantly, such weakness – in its more extreme forms involving state failure or collapse – produces two distinct routes by which independent force emerges and people are mobilized behind that force. On the first, where the state effectively withdraws and is unable to provide for local security, local self-defense forces or militias may form in response, filling the void left by the state. On the second, recognizing the inability of the state effectively to prevent their independent organization, opportunists organize coercively, forming militias, paramilitaries, or bands loyal to particular warlords as part of their effort to secure material gain and even political voice if not local control. In many ways, the situation in Somalia especially during the 1990s exemplifies the conjunction of these two routes to the formation of non-state organized coercion. It is in such environments that we may see foreign states supporting the emergence or persistence of militarized self-help, through the provision of resources and training or even the channeling of willing participants across borders, as is the case with elements in Pakistan supporting insurgents in Afghanistan in the present moment, or the United States (among other countries) supporting the Mujahideen resistance in Afghanistan during the 1980s war with the Soviet Union. And it is frequently in conjunction with such state weakness that we see the independent organization of terrorist groups whose actions are likely directed against the regime in power, perhaps as a response to social marginalization and state predation or assimilation, or involving popular appropriation of a conflict in which the target may shift away from the regime in power.

Across each of these logics and their conjunction, however, it would be erroneous to assume that militarized self-help, especially those forms not explicitly aligned with the regime in power, emerges primarily out of state weakness or the state's inability to suppress such forces. Instead, regimes may accept and even invite the formation of local militias, paramilitary organizations, and perhaps bands of thugs over whom they have little or no direct control, precisely because they form a politically useful complement to state-raised and authorized forces (see Slater 2010; Ahram 2011). What is important here is what may be gained at the expense of central political direction, domestically or internationally – notably potential allies and supporters as well as a shift in accountability and therefore in the political limits on the use of coercion.

FROM WAR MAKING TO STATE MAKING

When we turn to how war making transforms the state, we observe a range of effects that move beyond the now hallowed observation advanced by Tilly (1985, 1992) and others that war making precipitates state making, both in terms of political subordination to central rule and organizational elaboration of the state apparatus, but only when a sufficiently elaborated administrative core is already in place (Centeno 2002). To move beyond such formulations, I make the following argument: that the way the state organizes and mobilizes for war helps create, elaborate, or affirm social group memberships, forging a link between those group memberships, the state, and war in particular terms that render those memberships politically salient; and that military mobilization may induce both state controls over coercive organizations and the construction of administrative structures peculiar to the state that mirror the armed forces themselves, depending on political circumstances, or alternately may precipitate the weakening or collapse of state organizations.

The capacity of military mobilization to alter the political salience of social group memberships lies in the fundamentally political nature of war from the perspective of the state. Following Weber, insofar as coercive force guarantees political authority, internally and externally, and the state claims to monopolize its legitimate use, the use of force is rendered a political act and the group membership(s) in terms of which people are mobilized into war and differentiated from an enemy acquire a peculiar resonance and political significance. This can be viewed in terms of the constitution of the political community in a unitary sense, as what putatively binds the community together and distinguishes it from others (amidst its perhaps less explicitly acknowledged exclusions), getting at the way in which the polity understands itself and is understood by others. But it can also be viewed in terms that cut across such overarching identifications of the political community, highlighting politically meaningful distinctions drawn among its members.

Taking up the first view, the point of departure lies in the way the state mobilizes for war, through what set of institutions and in terms of what understanding of group membership, which powerfully shapes not only how those mobilized understand membership in the polity but also warfare itself. Among the more notable examples is the nationalization of war around the turn of the nineteenth century in Europe and North America. At that conjuncture, mobilizing the popular as well as the respectable classes into war as national citizens – recharging and redeploying the institution of the citizen-soldier, appealing to the breadth of the polity in terms of their common membership in a single community of nationals, enunciating an obligation to play some active role in ongoing war in terms of an individual's national citizenship, even if it is not to bear arms – and presenting to foes the reality of a mobilized nation had the effect of reorganizing war among states in national terms (Kestnbaum 2005). This was the case both with respect to how states undertook to make war and characterized the conflict as well as how ordinary people made sense of war and their place in it. In the emergence of these new shared meanings, the way in which the newly emergent institution of the national citizen was bound to soldiering in socially consequential terms through authoritative policy implemented by the state – for example, in the formation of a centralized system of conscription based on national citizenship – formed a critical mechanism (Kestnbaum 2002). Defining the enemy with regard to the same principle of differentiation as the "us" mobilized together into war, then, serves primarily to reinforce the centrality of that axis of differentiation and to affirm its political primacy. Of course, the effects of mobilization and defining the enemy in a particular manner are not limited to "the nation" – as noted above, religious, ethnic, kinship, and racial membership stand out. From an institutional perspective, what is important is that citizenship itself may be linked variously to ethnic, religious, kinship, and even racial membership, such that it forms the institutional matrix through which each of these forms of boundary making and collective identification may be mobilized into war and rendered politically as well as militarily salient.

Following the broad logic of this kind of analysis is a complementary one emphasizing not the collective membership potentially unifying a polity but rather the way groups constructed along alternative lines are incorporated into the wider polity, and under what conditions. Here, the mobilization of previously excluded social class and gender groups alongside racial, religious, and ethnic distinctions stands out (see Marwick 1974). It is the social fact of bearing arms (or potentially some other form of active participation) in a state-led war effort that establishes the place of such differentiated and newly included people in the polity (see Elshtain 1995). Or at least, participation forms the basis for a claim of recognition, whether or not that claim is accepted and institutionalized on fully equal terms, as can be seen for example among freed former slaves who fought for the Union in the US Civil War (Berlin et al. 1979). Such claims to recognition as full members, in particular, play out according to rather different logics, however, within differently constructed empires or colonial environments, where ethnicity, religion, clan, or race, for example, may constitute the basis for formal political distinctions yielding greater or lesser self-rule.

The prospect, and indeed the likelihood, that such incorporation is partial opens the door to the counter line of analysis, in which mobilization into war serves rather to differentiate among persons in new or newly salient terms, playing out alongside the potential unifying effects of going to war. State-led mobilizations that involve exclusions, marginalizations, dissimilations, or (forced) assimilations that adversely affect the groups in question, especially mobilizations that place identifiable burdens on some or visibly deny potential benefits of war to others, sensitize those affected to the grounds on which they are differentiated and may lead to politicization of that inequality and potentially radicalization (see Blum 1982; Winter & Prost 2005). Furthermore, state practices in war or responses to the fiscal or security pressures of war and its aftermath may alienate critical constituencies, among them elites forming part of the state apparatus itself as well as members of the armed forces (see Chorley 1973; Skocpol 1979). Beyond eroding the capacity of a war emergency to unify a polity, both of these processes can play a part in precipitating revolt and in unmaking the capacity of the state to put down such challenges, as can be seen for example in the Russian Revolution.

Such arguments regarding the role of war making in producing fault lines within polities at war lead to a series of special contentions concerning how incorporation in war produces differentiation based on distinct political configurations of struggle. State mobilization to put down an insurgency or revolutionary challenge, and even more clearly to wage a protracted civil war, has peculiar qualities: the cleavage within the polity can clearly be heightened, and a new relational dynamic created in which the subgroups forming the opposition coalesce more firmly together, as do those identified with the state. Furthermore, the line separating friend from enemy in such conflicts shapes how the polity may reunite afterward, creating a cleavage whose persistence outlasts the war *per se*. Colonial environments, others where the rule of the state is imposed by force from without, and even international protectorate or client relationships share certain features with actual or incipient civil war, even where there is not open revolt. There, incorporation in the state's war making or accepting its provisions renders such participation collaboration with an alien or occupying power, or complicity in foreign rule. Either way, the association with rule from outside imposed by force means that those associated are lumped in with the political opponent, whose rule may be challenged by force of arms.

Logics regarding newly salient group membership resulting from war can be linked back to the formation of non-state coercive organization and mobilization into conflict. We can see this in terms of overarching group memberships, where the nationalization of war, for example, leads to the popular appropriation of armed conflict and the creation of pro- or anti-regime guerrillas. And we can see this as well in terms of how internal divisions and the galvanizing of political opposition resulting from war making may be linked to the formation of both militants or guerrillas challenging the regime in power as well as potentially the formation of paramilitaries which may bend either toward or away from the regime, depending upon circumstances.

When we turn from how war shapes the complexity of group memberships to its impact on the organizational structure of the state apparatus, we are on somewhat more conventional ground perhaps. But I want to emphasize the distinctiveness of the mechanisms by which war making – both mobilization and treatment of the enemy – remakes states. Here the focus rests on the actual organizational elements that are brought together to form, organize, and raise coercive force; recruit and train personnel; equip and feed them; produce the necessities of war and deliver them where they need to go; and mobilize political support behind the conflict. Perhaps the clearest way to illustrate how mobilization for war may yield these effects is to focus on war in the midst of social revolution or the successful attempt to achieve political independence. There, for example in the French Revolution, we observe a threefold process in which temporary forms of coercive organization and of mobilization in support of those coercive organizations are created; newly emergent and residual coercive organizational elements are regularized as part of one standing military structure under central state control; and the use of the regularized military in war, including the mobilization it demands, drives the regularization of military and civil administration supporting war making. In this instance, the first two steps form the basis on which forces which emerged as counter-regime or orthogonal to the regime in power came to be incorporated into the state's military force, organized around the citizen-soldier. The chief instruments are recruitment reform, including conscription, and amalgamation, through which citizen militias are bound to and may even become critical elements of the standing armed forces. The construction of this regularized military depends, in turn, on a massive organizational infrastructure created by networks of voluntary associations and clubs, political committees, councils, and conventions which emerge as part of the mobilization of the popular classes into national politics, alongside citizen militias or guerrillas acting to recruit personnel or political support for revolution and war, in conjunction with those elements of the state apparatus that remain intact (see Skocpol 1994; Horne 1997; Kestnbaum 2000; Skocpol, Munson, Karch & Camp 2002; Kestnbaum 2005). Together, these constitute an improvised variant of direct rule, where networks of non-state organizations create critical linkages tying the center all the way down to the local community and are densely organized and rooted at the locality. Mobilizing for war through this far-flung apparatus cobbled together from temporary and re-purposed organizations and elements of state administration leads, over time, to explicit efforts to build up these organizational channels by rendering them formal administrative offices and agencies bound to the central state. Within state administration proper, the model presented by the hierarchical structure of the armed forces, with the delineation of tasks, jurisdiction, and conditions of service, may be emulated explicitly in the effort to bring the administration of war in-house, as it were. Where it touches on the organization of production, and even more so the mobilization of political support, such effects may be mediated by other prevailing organizational forms, drawing in the latter instance especially on the elaboration of organizational political networks, in the form of political clubs, parties, and so on.

We would be remiss, however, if we did not also highlight some of the ways in which mobilization for war and actually using force against an enemy may instead lead to the unmaking of the state in organizational terms. We can see this first where the entire process of regularization I have just laid out may be cut short after the first step. In such instances, where for example the state's call to raise up the countryside in arms by calling for a people's war to repel invasion or secure independence is met by either limited state capacity or political desire to bring newly emergent coercive organizations under central control (see Slater 2010; Ahram 2011), military mobilization instead leads to a proliferation of coercive organizations beyond the central state. But there is a larger issue as well, and that is the way in which mobilization may weaken or undermine the state. Mobilizing people, material resources, and political support into war places tremendous strains on the state. When the economic, political, or organizational challenges of making war stretch the state to its limits, we may see the erosion of a unifying sense of purpose, loss of support on which state capacity to mobilize depends in part, and defections among elites and state personnel as described above that compromise the integrity of the state apparatus itself (see also Collins 1999). In conjunction with attacks at the hands of the enemy that figure centrally below, such challenges may ultimately exceed the capacity of the state, precipitating its breakdown and collapse and leaving the state unable to defend itself.

FROM WAR MAKING TO NEW WAYS OF MAKING WAR

When we turn to how making war reshapes the manner in which war is waged, it is important to underscore two aspects of the analysis. First, whereas the processes involving state formation emphasize relationships and dynamics within particular states, and by this means offer purchase on how parties to a conflict organize and direct force, here armed relations among belligerents take center stage, and these relations frequently cut across state borders. Second, we are able to refine and specify arguments regarding how making war shapes the manner in which war is waged by focusing on particular ways in which mobilization for armed conflict and treatment of the enemy are intertwined.

Military mobilization and definition and treatment of the enemy may be seen as linked by several different logics of escalation and de-escalation in the scope or intensity with which coercive force is mobilized and employed, chiefly in terms of how deeply mobilization extends into the society mobilized and how broadly coercive force is directed against a designated foe. Arguments in this area focusing upon how expanded mobilization may precipitate expanded mobilization, or brutality may precipitate brutality, are more or less common, and typically take the same form. They emphasize spirals of response dominated by matching or exceeding the action of one's adversary; constraints imposed by resources, institutional structures within states, and potentially international organizations; and the breaking of such spirals due to shifts in how force is organized and projected, alliance structures, or the role of concerted international agreements in transforming backlashes into restraints on treatment of the enemy. Opportunities to clarify distinctive logics beyond the commonplace exist, instead, when we focus more tightly on how mobilization shapes treatment of the enemy, and how treatment of the enemy shapes mobilization. Let us look at the first.

Through what Geoffrey Parker (1994) has characterized as a logic of reciprocity, the organization of coercive force by the state establishes a kind of baseline of how established polities may go to war, and, in particular, how they define and treat the enemy. The organizational separation of combatant and noncombatant represented by the state's raising and maintaining of standing military forces has been mirrored historically in the normative granting of immunity from coercion by design to noncombatants, forming a centerpiece of the laws of war. By rendering noncombatant immunity central to expectations of how states may legitimately wage war, adherence to such norms acquires a self-enforcing quality. State makers break such norms only at their peril, recognizing they will bear tremendous costs in the form of retaliation, both at the hands of their foe in terms of coercive force directed against their own civilians and harsh treatment of their own soldiers, and politically from both groups at home due to the state's role in precipitating the brutal measures employed against them.

In a war-making environment regulated by reciprocity, when parties to a conflict discover that expanding or otherwise altering mobilization will not produce military victory, broadening the definition of the enemy against whom they intentionally direct coercive force opens as a way to seek military advantage. Such a broadening of the enemy represents a shift from exclusively or even primarily targeting those who bear arms against them to targeting an opponent's capacity to make war, including material or productive resources but also popular morale, political will to support war, or confidence in the capacities of the state prosecuting war. Overcoming the apparent military and political costs of broadening "the enemy" typically amounts to constructing such action as both necessary and justified, involving some combination of determining that such a course of action is worthwhile relative to alternatives and arguing that it is morally acceptable or legitimate (see Walzer 1977). For terrorist groups (and some militants), this results in part from asymmetries in coercive organization and capacity that imply conventional military means will not produce the desired response from the state or states they target, in conjunction with the moral and political imperative of achieving such an effect. But for state and non-state actors including militants and terrorists across the domain of armed conflict, arriving at a sense that intentionally targeting noncombatants and civilians is both necessary and justifiable draws attention to a shift in perception or understanding of the opponent in war. Ideological or other reconstructions of "the enemy" in which the opponent is understood as fundamentally different and deserving of little in the way of conventional protections in war, often emphasizing the brutal measures it employs or its willingness to target civilians, may play a role in such shifts in perception of the foe (see Dower 1986; Bartov 2000), and may feature prominently in terror – but such reworkings are the product of much more than just the way coercive force is produced by a particular belligerent. One feature of military mobilization, however, plays a pivotal role in shifting perceptions and constructions in a wide array of conflicts, from interstate wars involving guerrilla elements, to civil wars, to open revolts and revolutions – and that is the entry of coercive forces neither raised nor authorized by the state. The presence of militarized self-help precipitates a kind of homogenization of the enemy, where from the point of view of states as well as paramilitaries and even militias or guerrillas engaging forms of militarized self-help, the distinction between combatant and noncombatant loses its salience and is replaced instead by a broader foe whose very structure renders attack on civilians militarily useful (perhaps uniquely so) as well as legitimate, since the people themselves are mobilized directly into armed conflict (see McPherson 1997; Horne 2002; Valentino, Huth & Balch-Lindsay 2004). With such a homogenization of the enemy, unarmed civilians may readily become the targets of direct and intentional coercion, irrespective of what role they play in the actual hostilities.

How the enemy is defined and attacked, in turn, can have powerful effects on mobilization for armed conflict. The intentional use of force itself is radicalizing. Not only does it introduce violence *per se* into social relationships, but also subjecting any set of persons to coercion dramatizes the grounds on which such measures are taken, the particular collective membership those persons share that (putatively) explains and legitimates the use of coercion, and explicitly renders those who have used force an armed foe. This is the basis for what may broadly be called "blowback" from armed conflict, in which attack constitutes the animus for a response and sets the parameters within which it arises. To take an example, the state's or an ethnic group's use of coercion against ethnic minorities pushes those persons to identify more strongly as a particular minority while making them aware of the dangers they face as such, leading them to form militias to provide self-defense where patterns of state formation allow or even encourage it. Likewise, the use of mass terror on September 11, 2001 constructed a broad sense of America as a nation under attack on home soil that precipitated a particular pattern of mobilization in response, including popular refusal to let terror fundamentally bring routine life to a halt, stepping up of protection of the homeland, and military attacks against foreign states potentially or putatively linked to the spawning of such terror in the first place, with the object of replacing regimes in power.

Central to the way the use of force precipitates the organization of coercion and mobilization is the extent to which attacks serve to bound the groups against whom they are directed. They do so by rendering vivid what their victims share while at the same time obscuring what might be taken to distinguish among them. The key to such a transformation lies in how the use of coercion specifies a particular categorical group membership against which it is directed while being indiscriminate in its effects within that category. Treating the category as internally undifferentiated when it comes to force, lethal or otherwise, generalizes the risk as well as the insult, forging people together as those under attack and demanding a response organized along the same lines. Insofar as attacks are limited to those bearing arms, even among self-armed fighters, this process plays out in subtle ways often gaining little notice since it re-affirms the organizational as well as normative distinction between combatants and noncombatants in armed conflict. Where it stands out as most overtly transformative is when attack moves beyond those bearing arms, from intentional attack on property to the use of weapons of mass destruction, and in the case of much terror, where indiscriminate attack on civilians is the object. When attack includes noncombatants, the potential of coercion to form a group that arms itself where none had existed months or even weeks before, or to galvanize a powerful, concerted response from an expansive, diffuse populace and a government preoccupied with other concerns, is striking.

THINGS FALL APART?

Borrowing from William Butler Yeats, if the domain of war is frequently seen in terms of destruction and anarchy, where the center cannot hold, then specifying the three core processes linking war making and state making may go some way toward imposing order on the apparently chaotic, identifying regularities across a welter of different settings, patterns of conflict, and particular belligerents. To assemble concrete explanatory accounts for specific developments or transformations, it is necessary to bring these processes and their constitutive logics together. The preceding analysis points the way, for example, identifying how the revolutionary transformations of regimes alter the character of political inclusion and mobilization, and how this translates into re-organized state-raised military forces by means of reform in conjunction with the use and regularization of militarized self-help created as part of the revolutionary challenge in the first place.

We can go much further, however, than simply recognizing that state formation gives rise to new extra-state coercive organizations that through their use in war shape how the state reforms its armed forces and pattern of military mobilization. First, we must recognize that the three core processes are interwoven in more or less elongated sequential chains. This is most obvious, for example, where particular dimensions of war making lead to state formation which in turn induces change in war making, or where mobilization may yield changes in the enemy that then induce reorganizations of force or altered mobilization. Second, by including how mobilization and treatment of the enemy may shape one another, we are able more thoroughly to specify the domain and forge such sequenced processual chains. This works intensively, in the sense that we are able to work out how transformations of war making arise from within warfare itself. And it also works extensively, since the waging of war itself links belligerents to one another. Identifying how making war changes the way war is made lets us specify how state formation in one polity can shape how a second polity goes to war, or vice versa, by focusing upon the determinants of how each mobilizes and treats the enemy, and following from this upon how each belligerent responds to what the other does in armed conflict. In this sense, the actual practice of war making and the logics by which it changes provide the crucial nexus linking together the whole domain of war and the state more or less coherently.

Despite any appearance to the contrary, such an organizational understanding of armed conflict is profoundly historical in nature. From its attention to sequence and timing to its specification accommodating varied settings and parties to a conflict, this approach requires the analyst to situate any particular examination of war, insurgency, revolt, or the use of terror in its historical, institutional, cultural, and social context, to work out the historically particular configuration of coercive organizations and their relationships to the state, and to trace out the historically specific ways in which state formation and war making unfold in relation to one another. That is both its invitation and its demand.

Questions of temporality emerge in another sense, just below the surface, reinforcing the historical nature of this approach and drawing attention to two broad implications for the understanding of war. Although not explicitly drawn out in the focus on process, particular conflicts play a critical role in shaping how both war making and state formation proceed. They provide a focal point, where waging war and making the state come together in time. What is more, by virtue of the way they have variously shaped war making or state formation, *prior conflicts* are no less important. They leave a durable imprint. Related to this is a second issue about understanding war broadly. Change or transformation in this domain occurs at wildly different temporal rhythms. Alongside the durable impact of a mass war waged two centuries earlier, for example, in which the citizen-soldier became central to US war making, we can see the rapid emergence *in the midst of ongoing war* in Iraq and Afghanistan of new ways of organizing and directing force, as well as new ways of mobilizing support for ongoing war in the current conflicts. Such shifts in war making arising during war and as a product of how that war is being waged are not the exception, but rather the rule. A full understanding of armed conflict requires the ability to identify and reconcile change playing out at such different rhythms, within and across borders, during and away from shooting wars, taking account of legacies from the past and working out the unfolding of change through the analysis of clear, sequenced chains of causal linkages.

Acknowledgments

My thanks to Cynthia R. Cook, Sarah Wanenchak, and Molly Clever for their assistance with the formulation of this chapter as well as their insightful comments on the material it treats.

Notes

1 Terror, of course, need not be responded to by force to qualify as terror, but requires the breaching of coercive self-protections that imply at least the reasonable prospect of a coercive response. Furthermore, while it is defined by its relation to particular states and

the political ends it is hoped the use of force will achieve, terror is further defined in terms of specific means: the use of indiscriminate attack specifically targeting noncombatants.

2   For the formulation of armed forces duly constituted under the authority of the central state, I am indebted to Rothenberg (1994).

References

Adams, J., E. S. Clemens, and A. S. Orloff (2005) "Introduction: Social Theory, Modernity, and the Three Waves of Historical Sociology." In J. Adams, E. S. Clemens, and A. S. Orloff (eds.), *Remaking Modernity: Politics, History, and Sociology*. Durham, NC: Duke University Press, pp. 1–72.

Ahram, A. (2011) *Proxy Warriors: The Rise and Fall of State Sponsored Militias*. Stanford, CA: Stanford University Press.

Ajami, F. (2001) "The Sentry's Solitude." *Foreign Affairs*, November/December: 2–16.

Bartov, O. (2000) *Mirrors of Destruction: War, Genocide, and Modern Identity*. New York: Oxford University Press.

Bates, R. H. (2008) *When Things Fell Apart: State Failure in Late-Century Africa*. Cambridge: Cambridge University Press.

Berlin, I. et al. (1979) *The Black Military Experience in the Civil War*, Vol. 4. New York: Cambridge University Press.

Best, G. (1980) *Humanity in Warfare*. New York: Columbia University Press.

Best, G. (1994) *War and Law since 1945*. Oxford: Clarendon Press.

Blum, J. M. (1982) "United Against: American Culture and Society during World War II." In H. R. Borowski (ed.), *The Harmon Memorial Lectures in Military History, 1959–1987*. Washington, DC: Office of Air Force History, pp. 577–90.

Brubaker, R. (1992) *Citizenship and Nationhood in France and Germany*. Cambridge, MA: Harvard University Press.

Brubaker, R. (1996) *Nationalism Reframed: Nationhood and the National Question in the New Europe*. Cambridge: Cambridge University Press.

Centeno, M. A. (2002) *Blood and Debt: War and the Nation-State in Latin America*. University Park, PA: Pennsylvania State University Press.

Charrad, M. (2001) *States and Women's Rights: The Making of Postcolonial Tunisia, Algeria, and Morocco*. Berkeley, CA: University of California Press.

Chorley, K. (1973) *Armies and the Art of Revolution*. Boston: Beacon Press.

Clausewitz, C. von ([1832] 1976). *On War*. Ed. and trans. M. Howard and P. Paret. Princeton, NJ: Princeton University Press.

Clemens, E. (2007) "Toward a Historicized Sociology: Theorizing Events, Processes, and Emergence." *Annual Review of Sociology* 33: 527–49.

Collins, R. (1999) "The Geopolitical Basis of Revolution: The Prediction of the Soviet Collapse." In *Macrohistory: Essays in Sociology of the Long Run*. Stanford, CA: Stanford University Press, pp. 37–69.

Crone, P. and M. Cook (1980) *Hagarism: The Making of the Islamic World*. Cambridge: Cambridge University Press.

Davis, D. E. and A. W. Pereira (eds.) (2003) *Irregular Armed Forces and Their Role in Politics and State Formation*. Cambridge: Cambridge University Press.

Dower, J. W. (1986) *War without Mercy: Race and Power in the Pacific War*. New York: Pantheon Books.

Downes, A. B. (2008) *Targeting Civilians in War*. Ithaca, NY: Cornell University Press.

Elshtain, J. B. (1995) *Women and War*. Chicago: University of Chicago Press.

Friedman, T. L. (2002) *Longitudes and Attitudes: Exploring the World after September 11*. New York: Farrar, Straus and Giroux.

Geyer, M. (2002) "People's War: The German Debate about a Levée en Masse in October 1918." In D. Moran and A. Waldron (eds.), *The People in Arms: Military Myth and National Mobilization since the French Revolution*. Cambridge: Cambridge University Press, pp. 124–58.

Goodwin, J. (2001) *No Other Way Out: States and Revolutionary Movements, 1945–1991*. Cambridge: Cambridge University Press.

Goodwin, J. and T. Skocpol (1994) "Explaining Revolutions in the Contemporary Third World." In T. Skocpol (ed.), *Social Revolutions in the Modern World*. Cambridge: Cambridge University Press, pp. 259–78.

Horne, J. (1997) *State, Society and Mobilization in Europe during the First World War*. Cambridge: Cambridge University Press.

Horne, J. (2002) "Defining the Enemy: War, Law and the Levée en Masse from 1870 to 1945." In D. Moran and A. Waldron (eds.), *The People in Arms: Military Myth and National Mobilization since the French Revolution*. Cambridge: Cambridge University Press, pp. 100–23.

Kestnbaum, M. (2000) "Citizenship and Compulsory Military Service: The Revolutionary Origins of Conscription in the United States." *Armed Forces and Society* 27: 7–36.

Kestnbaum, M. (2002) "Citizen-Soldiers, National Service and the Mass Army: The Birth of Conscription in Revolutionary Europe and North America." *Comparative Social Research* 20: 117–44.

Kestnbaum, M. (2005) "Mars Revealed: The Entry of Ordinary People into War among States." In J. Adams, E. S. Clemens, and A. S. Orloff (eds.), *Remaking Modernity: Politics, History, and Sociology*. Durham, NC: Duke University Press, pp. 249–85.

Kestnbaum, M. (2009) "The Sociology of War and the Military." *Annual Review of Sociology* 35: 235–54.

Mann, M. (2005) *The Dark Side of Democracy: Explaining Ethnic Cleansing*. New York: Cambridge University Press.

Marwick, A. (1974) *War and Social Change in the Twentieth Century: A Comparative Study of Britain, France, Germany, Russia and the United States*. London: Macmillan.

McPherson, J. M. (1997) "From Limited War to Total War in America." In S. Förster and J. Nagler (eds.), *On the Road to Total War: The American Civil War and the German Wars of Unification, 1861–1871*. Cambridge: Cambridge University Press, pp. 295–309.

Paret, P. (1992) *Understanding War: Essays on Clausewitz and the History of Military Power*. Princeton, NJ: Princeton University Press.

Parker, G. (1994) "Early Modern Europe." In M. E. Howard, G. J. Andreopoulos, and M. R. Shulman (eds.), *The Laws of War: Constraints on Warfare in the Western World*. New Haven, CT: Yale University Press, pp. 40–58.

Rothenberg, G. E. (1994) "The Age of Napoleon." In M. E. Howard, G. J. Andreopoulos, and M. R. Shulman (eds.), *The Laws of War: Constraints on Warfare in the Western World*. New Haven, CT: Yale University Press, pp. 86–97.

Scarry, E. (1996) "The Difficulty in Imagining Other People." In J. Cohen (ed.), *For Love of Country: Debating the Limits of Patriotism*. Boston: Beacon Press, pp. 98–110.

Schmitt, C. ([1927] 1976) *The Concept of the Political*. New Brunswick, NJ: Rutgers University Press.

Skocpol, T. (1979) *States and Social Revolutions: A Comparative Analysis of France, Russia, and China*. Cambridge: Cambridge University Press.

Skocpol, T. (1994) "Social Revolutions and Mass Military Mobilization." In *Social Revolutions in the Modern World*. Cambridge: Cambridge University Press, pp. 279–98.

Skocpol, T., Z. Munson, A. Karch, and B. Camp (2002) "Patriotic Partnerships: Why Great Wars Nourished American Civic Voluntarism." In I. Katznelson and M. Shefter (eds.), *Shaped by War and Trade: International Influence in American Development*. Princeton, NJ: Princeton University Press, pp. 134–80.

Slater, D. (2010) *Ordering Power: Contentious Politics and Authoritarian Leviathans in Southeast Asia*. Cambridge: Cambridge University Press.

Tilly, C. (1985) "War-Making and State-Making as Organized Crime." In P. Evans, D. Rueschemeyer, and T. Skocpol (eds.), *Bringing the State Back In*. Cambridge: Cambridge University Press, pp. 169–91.

Tilly, C. (1992) *Coercion, Capital, and European States, AD 990–1992*. Cambridge, MA: Blackwell.

Tilly, C. (2003) *The Politics of Collective Violence*. New York: Cambridge University Press.

Valentino, B., P. Huth, and D. Balch-Lindsay (2004) " 'Draining the Sea': Mass Killing and Guerrilla Warfare." *International Organization* 58: 375–407.

Walzer, M. (1977) *Just and Unjust Wars: A Moral Argument with Historical Illustrations*. New York: Basic Books

Weber, M. (1978) *Economy and Society*. Ed. and trans. G. Roth and C. Wittich. Berkeley, CA: University of California Press.

Wimmer, A. and B. Minn (2006) "From Empire to Nation-State: Explaining Wars in the Modern World, 1816–2001." *American Sociological Review* 71: 867–97.

Winter, J. and A. Prost (2005) *The Great War in History: Debates and Controversies, 1914 to the Present*. Cambridge: Cambridge University Press.

32

Science and Technology

Now and in the Future

MARK ERICKSON AND FRANK WEBSTER

INTRODUCTION: PARADOX AND PUZZLE

It is difficult even to imagine our society without science and technology. Striving to do so results in a kind of reverse sci-fi: no telephones, cars, DVDs, or computers; no modern medicine; no knowledge of the origin of the earth and life on it; no understanding of celestial mechanics and the size and form of the universe we inhabit. That such a world defies the imagination tells us significant things about science and technology. First, science and technology are ubiquitous, *visible* in practically every part of our lives and society, from our individual lives relying on medical knowledge to prolong our life span through drugs, vaccines, and appropriate nutrition, to the way that global economic systems rely on complex networks of integrated computers, production facilities, and transport systems. Second, it shows that science and technology exhibit a peculiar kind of *invisibility*: we can find it difficult to see them in society precisely because they are so ubiquitous and distributed. Under our noses, as it were, we are often only dimly aware of their presence. Typically, we switch on the light, scarcely thinking about the electrical supply to the fitting; we turn on the tap without reflecting on the science that brings us potable water; and we draw cash from an ATM with hardly a thought for the technological apparatus enabling it. A new generation of cell phones may make an impact on us through advertising and through displaying new features, and we might comment on seeing such new devices in the hands of our friends and colleagues. But older-generation cell phones are rarely commented upon, noticed only

The Wiley-Blackwell Companion to Sociology, First Edition. Edited by George Ritzer.
© 2012 Blackwell Publishing Ltd. Published 2012 by Blackwell Publishing Ltd.

through their absence: we are even surprised when we find people who do not have ready access to such technologies, though they were strikingly new but a short while ago. Third, our inability to conceive of a world without science and technology tells us a great deal about how closely bound up they are with our understanding of how our world works: from our depiction of what a human self is – as a conscious being with special properties which derive from having a specific genetic code made from DNA – to our understanding of what our society is – a vastly complex network of interacting people, institutions, and technological artifacts such as transport systems and the internet. We use science and technology to explain how and why the world we see around us is the way that it is, telling ourselves that much of our world is determined by the technology that emerges in it, and that scientific knowledge is a better form of knowledge than others available and that there is an inevitability to scientific discovery and progress – a grouping of ideas that we may call *scientism*.

Despite their ubiquity and significance, sociology largely ignored technology and failed to examine critically the form and content of science until the mid-twentieth century. Indeed, the discipline continues to pay little attention to science and technology, if the neglect of current textbooks is a reliable guide.[1] Moreover, sociological accounts of science and technology offered during the nineteenth century often restate a form of technological determinism and a desire to emulate the "superior" natural sciences. Karl Marx, an admirer of the greatest natural scientist of the nineteenth century, Charles Darwin (so much so that he sent him an inscribed copy of *Capital* in 1873), provides a good example:

> Social relations are closely bound up with productive forces. In acquiring new productive forces men change their modes of production; and in changing their mode of production, in changing the way of earning a living, they change all their social relations. The hand-mill gives you society with the feudal lord; the steam-mill, society with the industrial capitalist. (Marx [1847] 1976: 166)

Not only does Marx present here an avowedly *technological determinist* argument – that the productive technology of a particular epoch will dictate the forms of social relations that exist – he also makes a bid throughout his work for the adoption of a scientific method and frame of reference to understand the social world.

Marx was little different in this respect from other founders of the discipline of sociology, particularly Emile Durkheim who strove to construct a scientific sociology. Even Max Weber, the preeminent sociologist of subjectivity, described sociology as "that science which aims at the interpretive understanding of social behaviour in order to gain an explanation of its causes, its course, and its effects" (Weber 1993: 29).

However, Weber does provide us with the first piece of sustained social scientific critique of science as a social institution, in a lecture delivered in 1918, in which he does three things. First, he describes the external conditions of science, concentrating primarily on the organization of science in contemporary Germany and offering some comparisons to the situation in North America. Here Weber focuses on the rationalization and institutionalization of science. Second, he goes on to discuss the inward "calling" (*beruf*) for science, his focus centered on the motivation towards a scientific career that scientists share. Finally, he offers a discussion of what science actually is and what role it fulfills in society, which is twofold: to provide value-free and legitimate knowledge and also to undermine continuously and progressively its own intellectual foundations through questioning and skepticism (Weber [1922] 1988).

Weber's account of science is different from previous social scientists' approaches in that he locates science firmly within society and regards scientists as fulfilling social roles in ways similar to other people, while relating these roles to factors external to the project of science. Weber thus gives us a social account of the scientific life and we can see this as the first step towards a sustained sociological treatment of not only the form, but also the content, of science.

Weber's focus on the social role, position, purpose, and effect of science in society delineates much of the contemporary project of sociology of science. Indeed, Weber's work provided a template for sociological studies of science and technology right up to the 1970s. Perhaps most influential here was the work of American functionalist Robert K. Merton ([1942] 1968). In examining how the scientific community organizes itself around shared norms and values of *universalism* (truth claims are judged by impersonal criteria), *disinterestedness* (impartiality and integrity), *communalism* (scientific knowledge is a common good), and *organized skepticism* (as a methodological and institutional mandate), Merton connects the ideal type of shared method of the natural sciences (the experiment) with the construction of value-free truths that emerge from the deployment of this method and the orientation of an entire community towards that single goal. It presents a rosy, though then pervasive, picture of what scientists were considered to be doing: producing truthful, progressive, and cumulative knowledge about the natural world.

The sociological accounts of science and technology that emerged up to the 1970s reflected, and reinforced, scientism and technological determinism. This is, perhaps, no surprise as social representations of science and technology in this period often presented similar views. Science fiction films of the 1950s and 1960s presented visions of a wholly technologized future where science had solved most if not all of the world's problems, such as energy and food shortages; cultural, political, and social commentators such as Alvin Toffler and Daniel Bell predicted post-industrial societies where technology and high-tech production would predominate in our lives with governments across the globe investing in science research and big-budget technological projects as ways of ensuring global and economic influence.

Common to these accounts is the idea that scientific knowledge is somehow separate, superior, and more truthful than other kinds of knowledge, that technologies are autonomous objects responsible for changing at least some aspects of the society they enter into, and that science and technology are a motor of progress in contemporary societies: "The nature of technology is that it is cumulative and it becomes diffused" (Bell 1967: xxiii).

The above discussion of technological determinism and scientism needs to be placed in some context if we are to avoid the charge that we are also applying a kind of deficit model where people are foolish for adopting these frames of reference. This would be quite wrong. Scientism is, *prima facie*, an appropriate response to adopt given the importance and intrusion of science into people's lives. Not only that, we must also recognize that large amounts of social scientific thought deploy forms of scientism: psychology appears particularly prone to this mode of explanation,[2] but so too is a good deal of sociology and political science, where quantitative methods and analysis are again ascendant and are core parts of undergraduate and postgraduate curricula. Similarly, technological determinism asks pertinent and often pressing questions of society, particularly in terms of our relationships to technologies (e.g., how has the internet changed our society? What impact will e-publishing technologies have on the management of libraries? What are mobile communications doing to interpersonal relationships?).

However, where these theories fall short is in their oversimplification of the issues surrounding science and technology, and in their construction of science and technology as essentially separate and neutral forms of knowledge that are impervious to human agency. Bluntly, they fail to acknowledge how science is actually practiced (as opposed to the ideal-typical formulation offered by Merton) and they mistakenly presume that science and technology, *qua* science and technology, are asocial practices (though their findings and innovations have enormous social effects). As such, they are meager theories to explain the complexity, richness, and indeed significance of science and technology, as MacKenzie and Wajcman argue:

> The view that technology just changes, either following science or of its own accord, promotes a passive attitude to technological change. It focuses our minds on how to adapt to technological change, not on how to shape it. It removes a vital aspect of how we live from the sphere of public discussion, choice, and politics. Precisely because technological determinism is partly right as a theory of society (technology matters not just physically and biologically, but also to our human relations to each other) its deficiency as a theory of technology impoverishes the political life of our societies ... As a vitally important part of "progress", technological change is a key aspect of what our societies need to actively shape, rather than passively respond to. (1999: 5–6)

TECHNOSCIENCE

For this reason we need to bear in mind that scientism and technological determinism are significant factors in the thought style of many people in our society, and this thought style has not emerged in a vacuum: it has been formed through experience and culture, both of which, in our society, are themselves suffused with ideas of science and technology. The coming together, indeed the inseparability, of science and technology has led some commentators to describe our present society as *technoscientific*.

This hybrid term is useful to us in that it conjures an image of the fusion of science and technology, and the penetration of science and technology into most, if not all, aspects of our social and personal lives. But it does more than that. As Donna Haraway points out (1997), it implies an extravagance and a modality that replaces other ways of being in the world. Instead of us being modern, Haraway argues we are now technoscientific, a state of affairs that transcends the modern categories of the world – breaking through the remaining barriers between nature and society, science and technology, natural and artificial, subject and object. We have become quite different people in this technoscientific world, and former categories for analysis and explanation appear no longer appropriate. For Haraway, we have transcended being human, have become "post-human" or, using her preferred term, "cyborgs" (1991). As such, we need no longer be bound by outmoded and oppressive dichotomous categories such as male/female and nature/society, but can see technoscience as a series of practices where categories are formed, emerge, and are deployed in much more fluid and relational ways. For instance, divisions between the natural body and society have become blurred in an era of spare part and cosmetic surgery (hip joint replacements, heart transplants, laser eye surgery, breast enhancements, prosthetic technologies), body-modifying drugs (Viagra, steroids, anti-depressants), interventions in biological reproduction (from birth control to artificial insemination, *in vitro* fertilization, and genetic screening), and carefully designed diet and exercise regimes aiming to reshape a given body (too many to mention). Just about everything becomes subsumed in this new way of being, and technoscience provides us with a grammar and language which we use to describe the world. Indeed, it can be contended that renewed adherence to scientism and technological determinism are features of technoscience and set the context for our research into science and technology. Our lives are now described by technoscientific language, our meanings are constructed around technoscientific viewpoints on the world.

A cognate term is *technocapitalism*, a concept that endorses the intimate connections of science and technology and their pervasive presence in our everyday lives and routines, while readily adopting the language of technological determinism, scientific progress, and the inevitability of progress. But technocapitalism insists too on the primacy of capitalism amidst all this, hence it lays stress on the importance of phenomena such as biotechnology, genomics, molecular computing, nanotechnology, and informatics to the continuation and consolidation of corporate expansion, commodification, and profitability (Kellner 1989; Suarez-Villa 2009).

SOCIAL CONSTRUCTIONISM

Contemporary analyses of technoscience are rooted in a fundamental challenge to mainstream sociological accounts of science and technology that dominated most of the twentieth century. What Weber, Merton, and their successors had done was to adopt a frame of reference that was, in key respects, uncritical of the method and content of science and technology. Their critics have insisted that science and technology in practice are nowhere so straightforward as these thinkers suggested: for instance, that the norms and values enunciated by Mertonians were either transgressed in the laboratory or were so open to interpretation as to be of little analytical use, or, again, that technologies in their design as well as application – *contra* the assertion that they stem immanently from scientific progress – could incorporate values and express interests. The changes in our understanding that the adoption of a social constructionist frame of reference for studies of science and technology makes are still being felt today and it is reasonable to describe *social constructionism* as the dominant paradigm for science and technology studies.

A number of classic laboratory-based sociological studies served to shatter the façade of a neutral and truthful account of nature being produced by scientists using their superior method. Influenced by the relativist account of the history of science produced by Thomas Kuhn (1962), and the anarchist theory of knowledge proposed by Paul Feyerabend (1981), the work of Steve Woolgar and Bruno Latour especially showed that, rather than laboratory scientists acting in concert to discover new facts about the world, the laboratory could be seen as a site for the *construction* of facts – and this process of construction was social: "Scientific activity is not 'about nature', it is a fierce fight to *construct* reality. The *laboratory* is the workplace, and the set of productive forces, which makes construction possible" (Latour & Woolgar 1979: 243, emphases in original). Other social constructionists picked up on this theme: "[T]he natural world has a small or nonexistent role in the construction of scientific knowledge" (Collins 1981: 3).

This radical change in perspective, one may say from realism to relativism, has had dramatic effects both socially and in terms of sociological analysis of science. Pioneers in this shift included David Bloor ([1976] 1991) whose "strong programme" insisted that science and technology might be examined sociologically or, put more provocatively, that science and technology ought not to be exempted – bracketed off, as if beyond the social world (though imposing often determining impacts on society) – from sociological study. Once science and technology were so included, then it followed that the practices of scientists and the processes of technological innovation would come in for scrutiny. On these premises developed the "sociology of scientific knowledge" (SSK) and, in later progeny, "science and technology studies" (STS) (Sismondo 2004). Within this field, some scholars presented interest-based accounts of science and technology, for example arguing that class or gender interests or researchers' ambitions and orientations were influences. Against this came a more interpretive approach, one that queried interest accounts and favored examining science and technology as "texts" that may be examined as "discourses" (Woolgar 1981).

ACTOR NETWORK THEORY

The social constructionist turn has consolidated itself as a hegemonic paradigm, and as a dominant method, that of Actor Network Theory (ANT). At the time of writing these dominate the landscape of social approaches towards science, although not completely, as we shall see. Originating in and driven on especially by the work of Bruno Latour (1987, 1996, 1999), with important contributions from Michel Callon (1987) and John Law (1986, 1991, 1994), ANT is now a heterogeneous set of approaches that coalesce around a post-positivist, post-structural perspective that takes seriously the relationships between humans and non-humans. ANT's roots in SSK and social constructionism are clearly strong. ANT is also the site from which a sustained analysis of technoscience emerged, as ANT argues strongly that "technology" and "science" are inextricably linked and cannot be separated. ANT starts from the point of challenging the general social theoretical idea that human social relations "were simply unmediated relationships between naked human beings, rather than being made possible and stable by artefacts and technologies" (Mac-

Kenzie [1996] 1998: 14). Starting from a "strong programme" position of seeing knowledge not as "true belief" but as whatever people choose to call knowledge, ANT uses the principle of symmetry – that beliefs and actions of all sorts need to be explained in a similar way – to examine how the products of technoscience emerge from the actions and interests of actors in networks. Actors' interests, be they human or non-human, need to be managed and deployed, and it is these processes that give rise to the construction of knowledge and technologies. In ANT studies, science, technology, social and political processes become fused and indivisible.

To achieve its aims, ANT proceeds through identifying case studies of interest, and then investigating the network of relations that emerge from given situations. For example, Bruno Latour's examination of a failed transport initiative (project Aramis) in France from the 1960s to the 1990s identifies a complex of network relations, and relations between humans and non-humans (Latour 1996). Latour uses primary interview material coupled to original documents to chart the rise of project Aramis – noting who the key actors are, and letting them speak. For Latour, non-human objects can also tell a story:

> Machines . . . are cultural objects worthy of . . . attention and respect. [Humanists will] find that if they add interpretation of machines to interpretations of texts, their culture will not fall to pieces; instead it will take on added density. I have sought to show technicians that they cannot even conceive of a technological object without taking into account the mass of human beings with all their passions and politics and pitiful calculations, and that by becoming good sociologists and good humanists they can become better engineers and better-informed decision makers. (1996: viii)

As the narrative progresses it becomes clear that the engineering aspects of the project are intertwined with the human interests of the human actors – and are sometimes displaced by these. Latour argues that meetings of various spokespersons bring together the different worlds of interests:

> The highly placed official speaks in the name of developing the French infrastructure and supports the project of the transportation minister – who speaks in the name of government, which speaks in the name of voters. The transportation minister supports Matra's project, and Matra speaks in the name of captive drivers, who support the project of the engineer, who speaks in the name of cutting edge technology. It is because these people translate all the divergent interests of their constituents, and because they meet together nevertheless, that the Aramis project can gain enough certainty, enough confidence, enough enthusiasm to be transformed from paper to prototype. (1996: 42–3)

Latour's case study focuses on large-scale and expensive public engineering projects. However, the small-scale also admits of ANT analysis. John Law's (1994) early ANT study of a single physics research laboratory identified the localized networks surrounding individuals and small groups of researchers involved in specific research projects and, in contrast to Latour, not responsible for making tangible "products" such as trains or submarines. Law's theoretical and conceptual framework has proved influential on subsequent studies as he reconfigures essentialist notions of what people are. Rather than maintaining a version of people as single and bounded entities, Law notes that: "People are networks. We are all artful arrangements of bits and pieces . . . We are composed of, or *constituted* by our props, visible, invisible, present and past" (1994: 33). In addition, Law notes that ANT's basis in a post-structural perspective means that social analysis is a process of telling stories, and he foregrounds the contingent nature of the narratives we tell about the world: "[ANT] tends to tell *stories*, stories that have to do with the processes of ordering that generate effects such as technologies, stories about how actor-networks elaborate themselves, and stories which erode the analytical status of the distinction between the macro and micro-social" (1994: 18).

FEMINISM

ANT and social constructionism are the outcome of one of the significant challenges to the standard, realist account of science, and the shift of focus from the structure to the content of science has fundamentally changed how sociology perceives science and technology. However, another major challenge to the received account of science and technology in the 1970s came from a different direction: feminism. Here science and technology are gendered, and this in multiple ways.

Second-wave feminist thought showed that in a society where the labor market and production are segregated by sex, technology becomes gendered. Cynthia Cockburn's (1983) pioneering account of the newspaper print industry underlined ways in which male power may be consolidated and justified *through* technology, in that sphere notably with the insistence that compositors' work with hot metal, platemaking, and linotype technologies required and expressed their inherent "masculinity." Perhaps not surprisingly, Cockburn found that the introduction of computerized typesetting systems in the 1980s would not only undermine justifications for the male monopoly of print jobs but would also leave the men feeling emasculated, reduced to the role of mere "typists" (cf. Martin 1981). In a subsequent study of the microwave oven, Cockburn and Susan Ormrod (1993) reveal how gender and technology are interlinked social processes that help to shape one another. Starting from an examination of gender prejudices and stereotypes in society and proceeding through an analysis of science and technology as culture they show how the gender hierarchy (where women are generally perceived as subordinate to men) and the technology hierarchy (where some technologies such as automobiles and computers are seen as superior to others such as microwave ovens and fridges) replicate one another. By examining the entire process surrounding the production of an artifact (the microwave oven) from design, through production, to consumption and use, Cockburn and Ormrod show how gender becomes inscribed on technology at each step. Notably, they maintain a focus on the material conditions and relations that surround the artifact and draw conclusions from these things.

A similar move in the examination of natural science revealed how science itself is a gendered social institution. If we take Merton at face value then the institution of science should be neutral and unbiased with the only beneficiary being "the truth." Yet the natural sciences are characterized by gender distinction and shot through with gender discrimination. Women in science have disproportionately lower pay and status, and face a wide range of challenges in the workplace and their careers. Sociologists in the 1970s identified the "triple penalty" that women in science face: science is defined as culturally inappropriate for women, women in science are seen as less competent than men, and women face actual discrimination in terms of their material conditions (Zuckerman & Cole 1975: 84). Little has changed in the last 30 years. Baroness Susan Greenfield's investigation into continued gender discrimination against women in science revealed a catalogue of problems facing women:

- Few visible role models and mentors
- Lack of transparency for pay and promotion procedures
- Gender imbalance in the decision-making process
- Slow setting-up and take-up of work-life balance policies
- Intangible cultural factors that seem to exclude them from the corridors of power
- Institutional sexism
- Stereotyping of careers advice
- The research-based career is predicated around publishing in refereed journals and raising one's profile at key conferences, leaving little time for gaining broader management knowledge and skills that can add value to the professional skills of the scientist or engineer
- The publication record is heavily compromised by a career break or a (more senior) partner relocating to a new institution
- Women having to work harder to convince and persuade their managers that they want and need more responsibility which they see being given to their male colleagues (Peters, Lane, Rees & Samuels 2002: 29).

CONVERGENCE

More recent feminist studies of science and technology have suggested a convergence with the ANT and social constructionist paradigm, and have also used the context of technoscience to frame their studies. For example, Judy Wajcman's (2004) technofeminism builds on the earlier work of Cockburn in seeing technology and gender as mutually shaping one another. However, Wajcman adopts an ANT approach to look at how processes of enrollment of machines into networks lead to localized effects of meaning construction. This is because, from the ANT perspective, technology and society are mutually constitutive as they are "made of the same stuff – networks linking human beings and non-human entities . . . [ANT theorists'] most controversial idea, that we cannot deny *a priori* that non-human actors or 'actants' can have agency, has helped us to understand the role of technology in producing social life" (Wajcman 2004: 38–9). This approach connects to the work of Donna Haraway, one of the architects of technoscience, who emphasizes the need to understand social categories such as gender as emerging from technoscience through its practices.

We have thus turned full circle, from the divergent critiques of science and technology that emerged in the 1970s from social constructionists and feminists, to the convergence of feminist and quite mainstream approaches through the uptake of ANT and the technoscientific frame of reference. There is not, of course, unanimity. For instance, more radical thinkers have embraced much of the constructivist point of view, but their unwillingness to abandon entirely the liberatory potential of science and technology leads some to hesitate to embrace a strongly relativist approach (cf. Noble 1977, 1984; Aronowitz 1988). Thus the likes of Andrew Feenberg and Langdon Winner, while they are eager to admit there is a social imprint on science and technology, express impatience with the inability of much constructivism to go beyond pointing that out to unpicking more precise power differentials (Winner 1977, 1986, 1993), and there is resistance to arguments that fail to acknowledge that science and technology may at once incorporate social interests *and* offer possibilities for social improvement (hence Feenberg [1991, 2002] accepts a degree of autonomy, even neutrality, for at least some science and technology). Furthermore, radicals' greater degree of concern for political consequences leads to an emphasis on disproportionate corporate power in scientific and technological innovation (Noble 1977; Dickson 1984; Noble 1984), while the journal *Science as Culture* has embraced a constructivist approach since its inception in 1987 yet has still maintained its distinctively political concerns.

Thus we can still discern a range of theoretical approaches and explanatory frameworks being deployed in spite of significant convergence. This is due, in large part, to the diversity of the subject matter. It is not the case that social studies of science and technology can be confined to observation and analysis of the emergence of scientific knowledge and technologies from research laboratories and design bureaus. Far from it. Our technoscientific world is characterized by the widespread distribution and pervasive effect of science and technology in most aspects of social and personal life. Given this, it is unsurprising that specific topics permit of local explanation.

THE ROLE OF EXPERTISE

Take, for example, the role of experts. Our relationship to and attitudes towards science and technology are mediated, facilitated, and sometimes obstructed by experts – people with specific expertise in a particular area of science or technology. But how do we define an expert? Formerly, this seemed straightforward: experts were accredited by formal institutions (universities, governments) and were presented as people who possessed specialist knowledge and could make definitive judgments about what constituted specialist knowledge. However, such a straightforward description of an expert is difficult to uphold in current society: expertise has become a much more widely distributed phenomenon (Finnegan 2005). We can see this in many places: medical patient support groups where those who have a particular condition may become as expert as those who treat them; environmental campaign groups where "lay people" such as farmers and fishermen use their local (and often tacit) knowledge to challenge and oppose the plans of developers or governments; amateur astronomers who scan the night skies and, occasionally, find new celestial bodies and objects of interest (and, of course, this example has roots very deep in modern society [Chapman 1982]).

Perhaps the most obvious place where we see expertise spreading out and changing its status is in the realm of information and communication technology. The internet has been a factor in major social change in recent years and its effects in commerce are obvious, as are the changes that have taken place in news media and entertainment. However, a distributed network of computers that allows individuals to host their own sites where they can express their own opinions has become a significant site of expertise in two major ways. The first is through lay experts designing and reconfiguring the internet itself: programmers, systems administrators, hackers, and beta testers distributed around the globe have amassed vast amounts of specialist knowledge that rival and surpass that of information technology professionals and computer designers. The second is through access to information and raw scientific data. Internet users, with some technical know-how, can access raw data for themselves and use this to construct their own analyses of experiments, studies, and research programs. The debates around the veracity and validity of climate change data are an example of this, where non-scientists have accessed scientific data on global warming and have come to significantly different conclusions from formal scientific bodies.

Collins and Evans (2002) use this shift in expertise as a starting point to reconfigure sociology of science and science studies. Formerly, science studies was concerned with the "Problem of Legitimacy," where argument would take place over just how far we could see legitimate knowledge being articulated. Such studies, particularly informed by the ANT paradigm, showed that technical decision-making was not solely the province of designated experts and professionals, but also included other actors and actants. But a problem remains, that of extension: "how far should participation in technical decision-making extend?" (Collins & Evans 2002: 237). This "Problem of Extension" takes us to the heart of discussions of science and technology in society: who is making decisions, on what basis, and who is being excluded and included?

Moving beyond debates about boundary maintenance, Collins and Evans propose that we reconfigure our understanding of expertise to include a much wider range of people operating at a number of different, sometimes overlapping, levels. This, in terms of a social science project, sets a range of different challenges and, in their terms, is a new, "third" wave. Our social scientific understanding of science and technology had a first wave, where scientists were seen as the legitimate arbiters of the truth and they distributed this to an excluded and separate laity – all expertise was thought to be located in the scientific community. In wave two a democratic rights model was promoted where the public/scientists boundary became permeable as part of a rights-based model. In the third wave, there are pockets of expertise amongst the lay public, and a rights-based model which leads to the boundary between scientists/technologists and the lay public disappearing. However, this model is precisely that – a proposal for a program of action that would "develop a discourse of expertise which will help to put citizens' expertise alongside scientists' expertise" (Collins & Evans 2002: 251). This shift in focus has led to a large amount of science studies literature moving towards analyses of expertise (the number of journal articles on this topic more than doubled between 1999 and 2009, from 416 to 971 in the Social Science Citation Index) – particularly expertise that is based upon experience (journal articles on this topic rose from 66 in 1999 to 142 in 2009).

But the idea that the lay public can also have expertise, or indeed need to have expertise, is not a particularly new one. It has been a feature of a long-running debate in science and technology studies concerning the public understanding of science (PUS). Writing in the late 1990s, Steve Fuller (1997) described the public understanding of science as "our latest moral panic," parodying the sometimes-shrill pronouncements of a perceived lack of public knowledge of science. Fuller's parody reveals something important about debates concerning the public understanding of science: that, in general, these are based on a deficit model where, it is assumed, the public have a lack of scientific knowledge, this is a bad thing, and that means to rectify this must be found. Hence national drives for improved science understanding, worries about the quality of school science education, and, increasingly, worries about public misunderstanding or even rejection of core scientific paradigms, notably Darwinian evolution. The PUS model remains prominent in public discussion, less so in academic discussion as the deficit model has been increasingly called into question by qualitative evidence-based studies which found significant levels of "lay" local knowledge of science (Irwin & Michael 2003).

But the relationship between the public and science and technology is still a difficult one, as evidenced by, for example, protests over genetic modification of crops in the UK. Increasingly academics have moved from PUS to PEST: public engagement with science and technology. This model examines dynamic relations between the public and science/technologies, where both "sides" have concerns and knowledge that is relevant. PEST projects and approaches focus on an interplay and interchange of ideas and different strategies, not just "standard" pedagogic models, to enhance public engagement. Yet, as many commentators point out, whilst a deficit model may not be the most appropriate, neither is a model that is based on an assumption of equality. Formal science remains an elite (and expensive) pursuit, and technologies are often owned and controlled by capitalist enterprises, which, whilst welcoming public input to promote sales of products, are unlikely to share commercially sensitive knowledge with potential competitors, or by government agencies such as defense departments whose public accountability is tenuous. The odds are still stacked against the public in technoscience.

CONCLUSION

Science and technology are indubitably crucial to the way we live nowadays. This much is easily agreed. However, how science and technology are studied – and how they are more widely regarded – has changed irrevocably. Since the 1960s at least, sociologists and cognate observers, starting from points as diverse as feminism and ethnomethodology, have assailed the defenders of science and technology who would have it that their forms of knowledge are superior in the evidence they adduce and in the conduct of inquiry they undertake and that the artifacts they produce are at once autonomous from society and yet a decisive key to social (and indeed other) changes. Sustained attacks on the presumptuousness of scientism and the oversimplifications of technological determinism have hit home. Science and technology have lost a good deal of their mystique even as they have moved still further to the center of human activities and everyday life. At the same time, scientists and technologists have lost a good deal of the trust, esteem, and deference they could once command. The wider public appears to have become markedly more skeptical and questioning of scientists and technologists, indeed of just about any claims to expertise.

To be sure, there has been resistance from scientists and technologists to this trend, even signs of a backlash manifest in the "science wars." Briefly stated, the science wars were a high-profile public debate between natural scientists, who staunchly defended the idea that science and its methods were objective, and STS academics (and others), who promoted a relativist conception of natural science, challenging its impartiality and "truthfulness." The debate was exemplified in the "Sokal affair," when physicist Alan Sokal successfully hoaxed the radical journal *Social Text* into publishing an article titled "Transgressing the Boundaries: Towards a Transformative Hermeneutics of Quantum Gravity" (Sokal 1996). Sokal's piece was a collection of jargon and theoretical abstraction that deployed a wide range of natural science concepts to construct a parodic STS article. The result was a furor in which battle lines became even more entrenched, but, notably, the status of science was raised in relation to its more extreme critics since an article that was demonstrably flawed and ignorant of basic mathematics and physics had been accepted for publication in a journal that subscribed to social constructionism. Sokal's subsequent book challenging the intellectual rigor of contemporary social and cultural theorists who adapt scientific concepts and terminology in their own theories provoked even more debate, not least due to its provocative title – *Fashionable Nonsense: Postmodern Intellectuals' Abuse of Science* (Sokal & Bricmont 1998). There can be no doubt that the Sokal affair was a body blow to constructivism and a salutary reminder of its wilder forms of reasoning. Nevertheless, it seems clear that there can be no return to the status quo ante. Social constructivism is today the new orthodoxy amongst social analysts, however implausible some of its arguments may be.

Yet this orthodoxy has its limitations. For all that social constructivism and ANT are good at identifying local conditions of the production of knowledge and technology, we have lost some significant themes from earlier sociological studies of science (Erickson 2005). Not the least of these is the relationship between science and other social institutions, something that was central to the work of Weber, Merton, and even Marx. ANT's focus on the politics of nature can be at the expense of understanding the social role and governance of science.

This is particularly clear if we look at current controversies, for example the debate about teaching evolutionary theory in schools, particularly in the USA. A number of high-profile court cases have brought to prominence the conflict between fundamentalist Christian, creationist, and standard scientific, evolutionary, accounts of the origins of life on earth. Such disagreements are, of course, not new, but, given the emergence of technoscience, the ongoing clash of science and religion seems all the more significant. The recent rise of "intelligent design theory" (Behe 1996), which claims a non-religious orientation but posits that life on earth could only have arisen due to some external, intelligent agent designing organisms, is making inroads into science curricula in US schools (Campbell & Meyer 2003), although the theory itself has been described as re-labeled creationism in a prominent trial (Kitzmiller v. Dover Area School District 2005: 33). For sociologist Steve Fuller (2007b), the arguments surrounding creationism and evolutionism are rooted in much deeper issues, notably the historical struggle between Church and State to be the source of legitimate authority in society. But ANT in particular struggles to get much purchase on these issues, focusing as it does on the objects that emerge from networks rather than the context that networks are located within.

FUTURE TRENDS

The future of science and technology can be summed up in one word: more. We will have more scientific knowledge in the coming years not least due to the fact that the formal institution of science is now geared up to producing huge amounts of data, conference papers, and journal articles. And we will have more technology as technocapitalism seeks to invigorate existing, and to construct new, markets through creating new technological products, and governments continue to seek technological solutions to societal problems. For sociology of science and technology the challenge is not to predict the future, but to understand why current trends are continuing and to provide frameworks for understanding what science and technology mean in society. This is a big challenge, touching upon issues ranging from the relationship between individuals and their personal technologies to the very nature of humanity itself (Fuller 2007a: ch. 6). Yet the range of theories available and the history of social analyses of science and technology should reassure us that this challenge can be surmounted, at least to some degree and in the confines of academic discourse.

The even greater challenge is to analyze and, perhaps, confront the wider context of scientism and technological determinism. Sociologists of knowledge have long realized that escaping from the clutches of dominant thought in society is no easy matter. This explains, at least in part, the continuing tension between the natural sciences and those who apply formal scientific methods, knowledge, and theory to the production of technologies, and those applying social theoretical frameworks to make sense of science and technology. This is a gap that, at least for the foreseeable future, will not be easily bridged.

Notes

1 Best-selling texts such as Giddens (2006), Marsh et al. (2009), and Fulcher and Scott (2007) offer no discrete or sustained discussion of science and technology.
2 The rise of evolutionary psychology is an example of this. See Rose and Rose (2001) for a critical treatment of this trend.

References

Aronowitz, Stanley (1988) *Science as Power: Discourse and Ideology in Modern Society.* Minneapolis, MN: University of Minnesota Press.

Behe, Michael J. (1996) *Darwin's Black Box: The Biochemical Challenge to Evolution*. New York: Free Press.

Bell, Daniel (1967) "Introduction." In H. Kahn and A. J. Wiener (eds.), *The Year 2000: A Framework for Speculation on the Next Thirty-Three Years*. New York: Macmillan.

Bloor, David ([1976] 1991) *Knowledge and Social Imagery*, 2nd edn. Chicago: University of Chicago Press.

Callon, Michel (1987) "Society in the Making: The Study of Technology as a Tool for Sociological Analysis." In Wieber Bijker et al. (eds.), *The Social Construction of Technological Systems: New Directions in the Sociology and History of Technology*. Cambridge, MA: MIT Press, pp. 83–103.

Campbell, John Angus and Stephen C. Meyer (2003) *Darwinism, Design, and Public Education*. East Lansing, MI: Michigan State University Press.

Chapman, Allan (1982) *Three North Country Astronomers*. Swinton: Neil Richardson.

Cockburn, Cynthia (1983) *Brothers: Male Dominance and Technological Change*. London: Pluto Press.

Cockburn, Cynthia and Susan Ormrod (1993) *Gender and Technology in the Making*. London: Sage.

Collins, Harry M. (ed.) (1981) "Stages in the Empirical Programme of Relativism." *Social Studies of Science* 11(1): 3–10.

Collins, Harry M. and R. Evans (2002) "The Third Wave of Science Studies: Studies of Expertise and Experience." *Social Studies of Science* 32: 235–96.

Dickson, David (1984) *The New Politics of Science*. New York: Pantheon.

Erickson, Mark (2005) *Science, Culture and Society: Understanding Science in the 21st Century*. Cambridge: Polity.

Feenberg, Andrew (1991) *Critical Theory of Technology*. New York: Oxford University Press.

Feenberg, Andrew (2002) *Transforming Technology: A Critical Theory Revisited*. Oxford: Oxford University Press.

Feyerabend, Paul (1981) *Realism, Rationalism and Scientific Method*. New York: Cambridge University Press.

Finnegan, Ruth (ed.) (2005) *Participating in the Knowledge Society: Researchers Beyond the University Walls*. Basingstoke: Palgrave Macmillan.

Fulcher, James and John Scott (2007) *Sociology*, 3rd edn. Oxford: Oxford University Press.

Fuller, Steve (1997) *Science*. Buckingham: Open University Press.

Fuller, Steve (2007a) *New Frontiers in Science and Technology Studies*. Cambridge: Polity Press.

Fuller, Steve (2007b) *Science vs. Religion? Intelligent Design and the Problem of Evolution*. Cambridge: Polity Press.

Giddens, Anthony (2006) *Sociology*, 5th edn. Cambridge: Polity Press.

Haraway, Donna J. (1991) *Simians, Cyborgs and Women: The Reinvention of Nature*. London: Free Association Books.

Haraway, Donna J. (1997) *Modest_Witness@Second_Millennium. FemaleMan©_Meets_OncoMouse™: Feminism and Technoscience*. New York: Routledge.

Irwin, Alan and Mike Michael (2003) *Science, Social Theory and Public Knowledge*. Maidenhead: Open University Press.

Kellner, Douglas (1989) *Critical Theory, Marxism and Modernity*. Cambridge: Polity Press.

Kitzmiller v. Dover Area School District (2005) *Memorandum Opinion*, December 20. www.talkorigins.org/faqs/dover/kitzmiller_v_dover_decision.html (accessed December 21, 2009).

Kuhn, Thomas (1962) *The Structure of Scientific Revolutions*. Chicago: University of Chicago Press.

Latour, Bruno (1987) *Science in Action*. Cambridge, MA: Harvard University Press.

Latour, Bruno (1996) *Aramis, or the Love of Technology*. Cambridge, MA: Harvard University Press.

Latour, Bruno (1999) *Pandora's Hope: Essays on the Reality of Science Studies*. Cambridge, MA: Harvard University Press.

Latour, Bruno and Steve Woolgar (1979) *Laboratory Life: The Social Construction of Scientific Facts*. Thousand Oaks, CA: Sage.

Law, John (ed.) (1986) *Power, Action and Belief: A New Sociology of Knowledge?* Sociological Review Monograph 32. London: Routledge.

Law, John (ed.) (1991) *A Sociology of Monsters: Essays on Power, Technology and Domination*. Sociological Review Monograph 38. London: Routledge.

Law, John (1994) *Organizing Modernity*. Oxford: Blackwell.

MacKenzie, Donald ([1996] 1998) *Knowing Machines: Essays on Technical Change*. Cambridge, MA: MIT Press.

MacKenzie, Donald and Judy Wajcman (eds.) (1999) *The Social Shaping of Technology*, 2nd edn. Buckingham: Open University Press.

Marsh, Ian et al. (2009) *Sociology: Making Sense of Society*. Harlow: Pearson.

Martin, Roderick (1981) *New Technology and Industrial Relations in Fleet Street*. Oxford: Clarendon Press.

Marx, Karl ([1847] 1976) "The Poverty of Philosophy." In Karl Marx and Friedrich Engels, *Collected Works*, Vol. 6. London: Lawrence and Wishart.

Merton, Robert K. ([1942] 1968) "Science and Democratic Social Structure." In *Social Theory and Social Structure*. New York: Free Press, pp. 604–15.

Noble, David F. (1977) *America by Design: Science, Technology, and the Rise of Corporate Capitalism*. New York: Knopf.

Noble, David F. (1984) *Forces of Production: A History of Industrial Automation*. New York: Knopf.

Peters, Jan, Nancy Lane, Teresa Rees, and Gill Samuels (2002) *Set Fair: A Report on Women in Science, Technology and Engineering from the Baroness Greenfield to the Secretary of State for Trade and Industry*. London: DTI.

Rose, Hilary and Steven Rose (eds.) (2001) *Alas, Poor Darwin: Arguments Against Evolutionary Psychology*. London: Vintage.

Sismondo, Sergio (2004) *An Introduction to Science and Technology Studies*. Oxford: Blackwell.

Sokal, Alan (1996) "Transgressing the Boundaries: Towards a Transformative Hermeneutics of Quantum Gravity." *Social Text* 46/47: 217–52.

Sokal, Alan D. and Jean Bricmont (1998) *Fashionable Nonsense: Postmodern Intellectuals' Abuse of Science*. New York: Picador.

Suarez-Villa, Luis (2009) *Technocapitalism: A Critical Perspective on Technological Innovation and Corporatism*. Philadelphia, PA: Temple University Press.

Wajcman, Judy (2004) *Techno-feminism*. Cambridge: Polity Press.

Weber, Max ([1922] 1988) *Science as a Vocation*. Ed. Peter Lassman, Irving Velody, and Herminio Martins. London: Routledge.

Weber, Max (1993) *Basic Concepts in Sociology*. Trans. and intro. H. P. Secher. New York: Citadel Press.

Winner, Langdon (1977) *Autonomous Technology: Technics-out-of-Control in Political Thought*. Cambridge, MA: MIT Press.

Winner, Langdon (1986) *The Whale and the Reactor*. Chicago: University of Chicago Press.

Winner, Langdon (1993) "Upon Opening the Black Box and Finding It Empty: Social Constructivism and the Philosophy of Technology." *Science Technology and Human Values* 18(3): 362–78.

Woolgar, Steve (1981) "Interests and Explanation in the Social Study of Science." *Social Studies of Science* 11: 365–94.

Zuckerman, Harriet and Jonathan R. Cole (1975) "Women in American Science." *Minerva* 13(1): 82–102.

33

The Internet, Web 2.0, and Beyond

NATHAN JURGENSON AND GEORGE RITZER

Technology changes rapidly, often transforming the social world in the process. The internet, Web 2.0 in particular, is a perfect, even an extreme, example of this fact. This chapter focuses on the changes in the last half-decade that have radically transformed the web, creating what many now describe as Web 2.0 (succeeding the largely earlier Web 1.0). This new version of the internet is defined by the explosion in user-generated content. Because so many people are actively involved in this, as well as in the internet in general, their social lives have changed, sometimes dramatically. Furthermore, new, very active, social worlds have been, and are being, created on the internet; users are actively creating a more richly social internet. Because of its impact on the larger social world, and because of the social worlds that it is creating, Web 2.0, as well as whatever form the web takes in the future (Web 3.0), should (must) be of increasing concern to sociologists.

TECHNOLOGY IS SOCIAL: AN INTRODUCTION TO SOCIAL TECHNOLOGIES ONLINE

Barry Wellman (Wellman, Salaff, Dimitrova, Garton, Gulia & Haythornthwaite 1996; Wellman & Gulia 1999a, 1999b; Wellman, Haase, Witte & Hampton 2001; Wellman & Haythornthwaite 2002) has argued that *computer networks can be social* (see especially Wellman et al.'s [1996] article, "Computer Networks as Social Networks: Collaborative Work, Telework, and Virtual Community"). One of his early insights is that virtual communities are based more on shared interests

The Wiley-Blackwell Companion to Sociology, First Edition. Edited by George Ritzer.
© 2012 Blackwell Publishing Ltd. Published 2012 by Blackwell Publishing Ltd.

than on shared characteristics of individuals. Following Castells' (1996) influential ideas on "the network society," Wellman and Hampton (1999) argue that we have moved from "little boxes" of shared characteristics and geographical limitations to a world of networks. They deal with the then-emerging web and ask whether it will connect us to each other or disconnect us from "real life" communities. They state that while there "is no technological determinism, there are technological implications" (Wellman & Hampton 1999: 649). Wellman and Haythornthwaite (2002) wrote important early articles discussing the social nature of computing at a time when the internet was just becoming an important part of everyday life. Wellman and Haythornthwaite's interest in social capital carries on, as we will see below, through future research, even though most current work has moved away from this topic. Ackerman, Halverson, Erickson, Kellogg, and Orlikowski (2008) also published an influential early article discussing technology in the workplace as process-situated and enacted within social interaction.

Web 1.0 versus Web 2.0

Web 2.0 is a term coined by Tim O'Reilly (2005) as part of "The Web 2.0 Conference" held in 2004. His early description of the concept was not fully coherent. As a result, the term came to be used in various ways. One could simply see Web 1.0 and 2.0 as involving different time periods. That is, Web 1.0 describes the internet that existed in the five, or so, years before the dot-com bubble burst in 2000, or more generally the first decade of the internet (the 1990s). In contrast, that which exists at the present, or the internet's second decade (from 2000 to the time of this writing in early 2011), is Web 2.0. Another way to contrast the two is by the change in connectivity speed. Web 1.0 was most likely to be experienced through dial-up connections and Web 2.0 through high-speed broadband connections. Yet another view of this move from Web 1.0 to Web 2.0 focuses on the shift of the internet from existing exclusively on computer screens towards other, often mobile, platforms, such as laptops (and net books), cell phones (i.e., "smart phones"), and other internet-capable devices (such as the iPad).

However, we reject the view that Web 1.0 and 2.0 can be completely distinguished from one another. Instead, we see them as overlapping and coexistent (Jurgenson & Ritzer 2009; Jurgenson 2010; Ritzer & Jurgenson 2010). Not only have Web 1.0 and 2.0 coexisted, they continue to coexist to this day. Corporate sites characteristic of Web 1.0 continue to populate the web and there has been at least some user-generated content, in the form of email, chatrooms (Usenet), MUDs, and MOOs, for as long as the internet has been in existence.[1] However, *it is the explosion of user-generated content that defines Web 2.0 and differentiates it from the provider-generated content of Web 1.0.* Put somewhat differently, Web 2.0 is a more locally conceived, bottom-up system while Web 1.0 is more centrally conceived and top-down. Web 1.0 encompasses older websites that had not yet taken advantage of the user-generated content as well as today's sites that remain top-down. Examples of Web 1.0 include the following:

- Switchboard.com and YellowPages.com, which centrally conceive how users find people and businesses through the framework of the sites.

- The Apple Store and other shopping sites that dictate the content and users' browsing (i.e., shopping).
- Online consumption of news on Web 1.0 is more centrally conceived than today's more popular news sites which often allow users to "comment," or allow communities to direct user searches through the use of "most emailed," "most blogged," or "most searched" lists. News sites in the past that did not have these features, as well as those news sites that have not incorporated them to this day, are examples of Web 1.0.
- The creators of Fodors.com use their own tastemakers to point tourists to various hotels, restaurants, activities, and so forth. More general information is searched for on sites like about.com, whose creators employ "experts" to help users find information, again, exemplifying the centrally conceived nature of Web 1.0.

It is very tempting to offer a "grand narrative" (Lyotard 1984) of a shift over time from a top-down Web 1.0 to a bottom-up Web 2.0. However, not only are such grand narratives passé, but like all grand narratives, this one would be far too simplistic. We should recognize that the degree to which users produce content on a site is not a dichotomous variable, but rather represents a continuum where some sites are further towards one end or the other of the 1.0–2.0 spectrum than other sites. At least some user-generation occurs on many Web 1.0 sites and some top-down structures exist on Web 2.0 (e.g., the format of articles on Wikipedia or the profile pages on Facebook). Thus, we define Web 1.0 by the high degree to which it is centrally conceived – a top-down creation. Web 2.0 is defined by the great extent to which it is user-generated and bottom-up.

There is a clear and strong "cyber-libertarian" ideology behind Web 2.0 that seeks to keep the internet free and open (including to inputs by users). The idea is that "information should be free." This is to be made possible by limiting or removing structures online that limit that freedom. Cyber-libertarianism privileges the power and wisdom of "the crowd." However, this ideology was also present in Web 1.0. Indeed, it was present at the very beginning of all thinking about the internet and its possibilities. The internet, much like many other technologies, was conceived by some as a revolutionary, if not utopian, development that would bring great increases in freedom for those involved (as will be seen later in this chapter). In spite of such great hopes and grand ambitions, the internet has not been able to fully resist corporate structures, hierarchies, and control. Lawrence Lessig (1999, 2006) discusses this in his influential book, *Code*, where he looks at how the internet is regulated by legal and computer code. Indeed, the legal regulation of the internet has been a hotly contested topic surrounding what has come to be known as the "net-neutrality" debate that pits the cyber-libertarians against the corporate and legal efforts to restrict the use of the internet. Companies like AOL and Microsoft have sought to control many internet technologies with their own products and to purchase online real estate much in the way this occurs in the material world. In this way, Web 1.0 came to be in conflict with cyber-libertarian ideals. Corporate entities sought, sometimes successfully, to control the ways users interacted with the web. They also created centrally conceived internet products that structured and greatly limited the ways in which individuals used the internet. While the internet itself was never under complete corporate control, companies controlled much of how individuals encountered the web.

Of course, in its early years, this was not how many saw the internet. It is with the benefit of hindsight that we can conceive of the internet as once having been a more top-down system. In other words, Web 1.0 is a largely retrospective label created and used in order to contrast it to the technologies that became more popular later (remembering the general point that remnants of Web 1.0 continue to exist today). While the internet today is increasingly a place where more and more users are able to produce content, it was not always this way. For instance, the easy-to-create social networking sites of today stand in contrast to the personal web pages of the early days of the web that were primarily created by experts who were technologically advanced. Web 1.0 was an attempt to reposition online traditional business and organizational models. At the time, this did not seem overly top-down or constraining to much of the business community or to many users.

However, the cyber-libertarian ideals that predated Web 1.0 had not disappeared. Those who bought into these ideals saw the bursting of the Web 1.0 bubble as an opportunity, as offering the potential for "creative destruction" (Schumpeter 1942). In this case, the destruction of Web 1.0 (or at least some aspects of it) was seen as necessary for the emergence of Web 2.0. To put it in other terms, the possibility of the emergence of a "flat world" (Friedman 2005) free of competitive advantage was to be found under the ruins of hierarchies that dominated Web 1.0. Here was the opportunity to actualize the libertarian project online. This time it was fueled by, among other factors, the failure of the internet to produce the expected profits and, more positively, by the power of new high-speed technologies that enabled infinitely more users to interact online. A new kind of richly social and more humanized online experience was made possible by the fast, accessible, and much more user-friendly internet. Akin to other utilities, the internet was now always on.

In addition to the Web 1.0 experience of reading, browsing, and consuming content produced by others, Web 2.0 technologies have lowered the barriers to creation of content by, and socialization among, users. One way of describing this is to see the implosion of the consumer and the producer on Web 2.0 into the "prosumer." That is, on Web 2.0, users produce that which they consume (e.g., users both produce and consume the profiles and networks on Facebook).

Major examples of Web 2.0, and of the centrality of user-generation, of prosumers, on them, include:

- Wikipedia, where users generate articles and constantly edit, update, and comment on them;
- Facebook, MySpace, and other social networking websites, where users create profiles composed of videos, photos, and text, interact with one another, and build communities;
- Second Life, where users create the characters, communities, and the entire virtual environment;
- the blogosphere, blogs (web logs), microblogging (e.g., Twitter), and the comments on them produced by those who consume them;
- eBay and Craigslist, where consumers rather than retailers create the market;

- YouTube and Flickr, where mostly amateurs upload and download videos and photographs;
- Current TV, where viewers create much of the programming, submit it via the internet, and decide which submissions are aired;
- Linux, a free, collaboratively-built open-source operating system, and other open-source software applications, like Mozilla Firefox, created, maintained, customized, and enhanced by those who use them;
- Amazon.com, whose consumers do all the work involved in ordering products and write the reviews;
- Yelp, whose users create an online city guide by ranking, reviewing, and discussing various locations and activities in an area;
- Chatroulette, where the entire experience of video-chatting with random strangers is produced by the users;
- Formspring.me, where users answer questions asked anonymously about themselves;
- the GeoWeb, which consists of online maps where, increasingly, users are creating and augmenting content with Google, Microsoft, and Yahoo tools (Helft 2007). Google Maps users, for example, can fix errors; add the locations of businesses; upload photos; link Wikipedia articles to, and blog about their experiences with, or reviews of, places on the map, thereby creating social communities.

In sum, the Web 1.0 user experience was best characterized as "looking stuff up" preset by others using revolutionary new search engine technology,[2] whereas on Web 2.0 users are producing in addition to consuming (prosuming), making possible an increasingly humanized and social web.

We can reaffirm Wellman et al.'s (1996) view that computers are social by looking at *how* sociality is enacted in new and exciting ways on the social networking sites that are so central to Web 2.0.

SOCIAL NETWORKING SITES

A "virtual community" is defined as "an aggregation of individuals or business partners who interact around a shared interest, where the interaction is at least partially supported and/or mediated by technology and guided by some protocols or norms" (Porter 2004: 2). However, the term "virtual community" is of diminishing utility in describing socialization online given the emergence of social networking sites (often shortened to "SNS"). While we can think of social networking sites as leading to the formation of virtual communities, the interaction that takes place is not completely "virtual." It is often enacted with those one is connected to in one's material world, in one's everyday life.

SNS sites such as MySpace and Facebook[3] have become, for many, the dominant way in which socialization, interaction, and identity performance are enacted online (however, virtual communities such as Ravelry,[4] listservs, discussion forums, etc. continue to exist). Boyd and Ellison define social networking sites as "web-based services that allow individuals to (1) construct a public or semi-public profile within a bounded system, (2) articulate a list of other users with whom they share a connection, and (3) view and traverse their list of connections and those made by others within the system" (2008: 211).

A social networking site is predicated on users constructing or "filling in" profiles themselves. It is this that makes these sites defined by prosumption, as well as part of Web 2.0. In the definition of social networking sites above, the phrase "public or semi-public" indicates that the profile is available to some, and perhaps all, web users. The "shared connections" are often called "friends" on these sites, which is the way the system (e.g., Facebook) interconnects profiles. The term "networking" in this definition can be misleading because it is not always the primary function of these sites, and is not what distinguishes them from other forms of digital socialization (email, chat, texting, media sharing, etc.). What makes social networking sites unique is that they allow users to display and interact with their social networks. In this way, the most important feature of a social networking site is a profile page that displays one's friends. Information is also displayed about the user, often including a photo. Additionally, users can sometimes customize the look/feel of the page. MySpace pages are highly customizable, and Facebook allows some customization in applications (third-party add-ons that have functions not always built into the site by Facebook) users can choose. Often they can choose how visible their profile is and to whom it is visible.

This brings us to the key differences between social networking sites and face-to-face interaction. Because the former is digital, it is comprised mainly of text, photos, and videos. This digital communication is thus searchable (that is, others can find the profile or information in it using the site's – or a general – search engine [Watts, Dodds & Newman 2002; boyd 2006, 2008]), persistent (the sites continue to exist even when the user is not online), replicable (others can view and even copy or save information on the profile), and the audience is largely invisible (users do not know who is looking at their profiles and when [boyd 2006, 2008]). While face-to-face interaction typically happens synchronically in real-time, social networking sites allow asynchronous interaction. This means that all participants do not have to be involved at the same time. For instance, one does not usually experience the photos uploaded to a friend's Facebook page at the moment they are added, but at a later time when one checks the site.

The very brief history of social networking sites begins with the 2002 founding of Friendster as a competitor to Match.com. Match.com sought to link strangers for the purpose of dating, and Friendster tried to better help people find dates by linking friends-of-friends (boyd & Ellison 2008). Friendster had technical trouble handling the growth of the site and often deleted profiles that did not meet its strict regulations. Because of this, many users switched to another social networking site, MySpace.

MySpace was initially fueled by "indie" and hip-hop bands in the Los Angeles area, and their fans. MySpace allowed users to customize their pages to a large degree and by 2004 was experiencing substantial growth in membership. News Corporation bought MySpace in 2005 for $580 million. By this time, another social networking site, Facebook, had been created, initially only for Harvard students. It eventually opened up to all college students as long as they registered using email addresses associated with universities. This gave users the sense that it was an intimate and private community (boyd & Ellison 2008: 218). Still later, Facebook opened to everyone and then globalized; as of this writing it has over 750 million members and has long since surpassed MySpace as the most popular social networking site.

Social networking sites have become "essential" to young people (boyd 2008). Hargittai (2008: 284) found that females are slightly, but statistically significantly, more likely to use social networking sites than males. Nonwhites are more likely to use MySpace, whereas whites prefer Facebook (more on this below). Similarly, Zhao (2009) found that inner-city youth typically use MySpace and suburban youth prefer Facebook.

"Friending" is the way in which users make connections with others on social networking sites. Boyd (2006) discusses how "friending" is different from actually being friends. Indeed, users of social networking sites understand the distinction between the term "friend" on these sites and the traditional meaning of "friendship." The notion that "friending" only includes one's closest buddies fails to understand the online culture of friending. Livingstone (2008) shows that teenagers have a graduated conception of friends as opposed to the binary definition found on social networking sites. Thus, a "friend" on Facebook simply describes an individual who one chooses to interact with (e.g., send a message). It also describes those who can view each other's information.

Boyd states that the most common reasons for being listed as a friend on a social networking site are:

1) Actual friends
2) Acquaintances, family members, colleagues
3) It would be socially inappropriate to say no because you know them
4) Having lots of Friends makes you look popular
5) It's a way of indicating that you are a fan (of that person, band, product, etc.)
6) Your list of Friends reveals who you are
7) Their Profile is cool so being Friends makes you look cool
8) Collecting Friends lets you see more people (Friendster)
9) It's the only way to see a private Profile (MySpace)
10) Being Friends lets you see someone's bulletins and their Friends-only blog posts (MySpace)
11) You want them to see your bulletins, private Profile, private blog (MySpace)
12) You can use your Friends list to find someone later
13) It's easier to say yes than no. (boyd 2006: 8)

OTHER FORMS OF DIGITAL SOCIALIZATION

Much attention is paid to social networking sites, but other sorts of digital socialization occur online.

Instant Messaging is a quasi-synchronous (quasi because of typing time), computer-based, one-on-one method of communication characterized by the rapid exchange of short text messages (Nardi, Whittaker & Bradner 2000; see Cho, Trier & Kim [2005] for a discussion of instant messaging in the workplace).

Virtual Worlds are fully-realized digital environments. Early versions were text-based; they now can take the form of three-dimensional worlds. Some are games, such as *World of Warcraft*. Others are simply spaces of interaction such as Second Life and, especially, worlds targeted at younger age groups such as Webkinz, Club Penguin, and others. In these worlds, users inhabit digital representations of themselves, called "avatars." Steinkuehler and Williams (2006) discuss online games as "third places," a place for sociability outside of the workplace and the home. Herman, Coombe & Kaye (2006) discuss the relationship between the players of massive multiplayer online games and the corporations that host them as involving a sort of "goodwill" between the two, making the point that sociality is negotiated between both those creating and those operating within these worlds.

The *blogosphere* is comprised of individual blogs, a shortened term for "web log." *Blogs* are websites that offer users a simple way of producing content. One simply types into a form and the content is available on the internet. Maratea (2008) views blogging as a powerful tool opening the public sphere to a large number of people. Guadagno, Okdie & Eno (2007) discuss the personality predictors of blogging, showing that those high in openness to new experiences are more likely to be bloggers. Bortree (2005) finds that blogs are an important tool for the construction of identities by teenage girls. A new trend is what has come to be known as "micro-blogging," with the most popular example being Twitter, where each microblog post (or "tweet") is limited to 140 characters (so, shorter than this full sentence). The series of tweets of those one chooses to follow are displayed as a stream of content for the user.

Wikis are web pages that can be edited by potentially large audiences. The most famous, of course, is Wikipedia, the world's largest encyclopedia, which is produced entirely by users creating and editing the articles.

Our next task is to look at some of the main sociological concerns in the literature on digital socializing online. We will discuss the web as community with respect to the self and subjectivity, inequalities, and labor online.

THE SELF, SUBJECTIVITY, AND IDENTITY

It comes as no surprise that a major focus of discussions on digital socializing deals with identity and subjectivity, specifically with respect to social networking sites. These sites are aimed specifically at the online presentation of the self. Thus, much of this discussion is based on Goffman's (1959) work on self-presentation and impression management. While social capital dominated earlier thinking about digital socialization, the explosive popularity of social networking sites (e.g., MySpace and Facebook) has, rightly, shifted concern towards subjectivity and identity.

One trend essential to understanding the presentation of self online is that, given the interconnectedness of the material and digital worlds, individuals do this to exist both online and offline. Sundén (2003) argues that in order to exist online, we must write ourselves into being. Liu (2008) describes social networking site profiles as "taste performances," drawing on Veblen and Banta (2007) and Bourdieu and Nice (1984) and their view that taste is often linked to class hierarchies. Coté and Pybus (2007) discuss "immaterial labor 2.0" as the production of online subjectivities through an open-ended process of becoming. Boyd (2007) discusses how social networking sites are places where youth can write themselves and their communities into being.

It is important to discuss whether or not digital self-presentation makes new identities possible. One debate with respect to self-presentation online is between those who view it as engendering an open-ended process of immense possibilities and those who see it as a more constrained, but still largely honest, portrait of oneself than that which exists in everyday life. Internet-dating sites have been used to demonstrate that people typically do not create fantasy selves online, but, instead, build an accurate digital identity as a way of building trust with those they will eventually meet offline (Toma, Hancock & Ellison 2008; Hancock & Toma 2009).[5] Since the dating profiles are created with the intent to meet others in the material world, a high degree of honesty is required. As opposed to Dery's (1994) earlier discussion of cyber-selves being disengaged from cultural or biological factors, Hardey (2002) views the material world as a "casing for the virtual media." While the internet allows the possibility of what Haraway (1995) called "multiple identities" or an explosion of different "possible selves" (Markus & Nurius 1986), the internet for many is another environment in which to act out the same self as one does in the material world.

As opposed to the views of users as god-like creators of online identities,[6] recent work has indicated that subjectivity is co-constructed by others, especially on Facebook. That is, people reveal who they are through their connections (friends) (Donath & boyd 2004). Zhao, Grasmuck, and Martin (2008) demonstrate that on Facebook (as a non-anonymous network, as opposed to more anonymous ones), individuals claim their identities by showing rather than telling; through friends, groups, networks, or consumer choices rather than narratives. As such, the presentation of self on, say, Facebook is, in part, a function of the others with whom one is interacting. Thus, profiles are not simply self-constructions, but co-creations. Facebook users tend to show their "true selves" because they have to display their real names and their real institutional settings.[7]

It is difficult to think of the digital self as something wholly new and limitless because of the fact that the most common digital identity tasks involve, as we saw in the case of online dating profiles, socialization with those one interacts with in the material world. The notion of a "real-physical" and "virtual-digital" self as separate and distinct should be rejected in favor of looking at the self (and identity) as an augmented realization of *both* the digital and the physical. This suggests the existence of an "augmented self" that allows for the conceptualization of the ways in which (1) our physical self is influenced by digital representations (e.g., our Facebook profiles), as well as (2) the ways in which our digital selves are anchored and influenced by the realities of our physical worlds. For example, when individuals attach their physical location to their Facebook status update, they are anchoring their digital selves in physical geography, often with the intent to meet other Facebook friends in this material world location. When doing this, they are also choosing their physical location based on the digital self-presentation they want to display. This means that one's digital documentation can influence one's physical appearance, even one's body. Similar to Haraway's (1995) "cyborg thesis" of bodies entangled with technology, subjectivity with respect to social networking online has clearly produced an "augmented self" of entangled digitality and materiality.

As stated above, it is the idea that the digital self is augmented by one's material self that causes self-presentation to be more honest than early internet researchers anticipated. Pecora (2002) states that the movie *The Truman Show* (1998) gets things only half right: we are the stars of media realities, but we are *also the producers* of those realities in the case of self-presentation online. Lewis and George (2008) discuss deception online as compared to face-to-face interaction. Individuals, across American and Korean cultures, were *more* likely to be deceptive in face-to-face interaction than they were on the internet. Livingstone (2008) states that, in deciding what *not* to say about themselves, users are engaging in "an agentic act to protect their identity and their spaces of intimacy." In addition, Ellison, Steinfield, and Lampe (2007) argue that the trend in the virtual community literature has shifted away from forging new online relationships to looking at how offline relationships have moved online. Thus, the trend is toward honesty and away from a view of the self as one of infinite possibilities because those being interacted with online are also interacted with on a face-to-face basis. In sum, we have reason to view the online presentation of the self as having truth-telling, falsification, and strategic impression management components; and different sites might privilege these different trajectories differently (as is also the case with material-world self-presentation). For instance, in a virtual world like Second Life, users can choose to be anonymous and de-linked from the material world and thus can portray almost any identity they can dream up. The avatar and the material-body, the self-of-bits and the self-of-atoms, can be largely divergent, even if they are always linked to some degree. On social networking sites, users "friend" those they know in their everyday material-world lives. This allows the avatar and the body to become reciprocally augmented to a much greater degree.

While the trend is towards viewing digital socializing as more honest, there are still many opportunities to be strategic in one's self-presentation. When self-presentation is mediated by technology, as is the case with Facebook, users are offered additional control not found to the same degree in the physical world. Goffman (1959) differentiated between expressions that are "given" and those that are "given off." As opposed to intentionally "given" expressions, "given off" expressions are unintentional. Unintentional expressions can be limited on social networking sites to a far greater degree than in the material world. Thus intentional "given" behaviors are relatively more common on social networking sites than in the physical world.

Sessions (2009) deals with users' "MySpace Angles," or profile pictures that give the impression that the person who posted them is more attractive than they actually are. Some view this as dishonest. Sessions discusses three main themes regarding MySpace Angles: (1) users are conforming to the social trend and not expressing their individuality or "true self"; (2) the presentation of these photographs is narcissistic; and (3) the photographs purposely conceal the body. Hancock and Toma (2009) add to this discussion by making the point that there is pressure for females to portray a body online that is more conventionally attractive than the one they actually possess. At the same time, honesty leads them to minimize the discrepancy between their digital and material selves, leading to difficulties in maintaining these contradictory motives. Again, these points also reflect the degree to which the digital self is an "augmented self." Social networking sites need to be viewed as part of an "embodied internet," or what has been called "the Internet of things."[8]

It is in the degree to which digital selves become augmented by physicality that online socializing becomes anchored by material bodies and material-world connections. In this sense, the new focus on Facebook as a relatively honest environment is justified. Mark Zuckerberg, founder and CEO of Facebook, states: "I think Facebook is who people really are."[9]

Coupled with honesty is the issue of surveillance and privacy on social networking sites. As demonstrated above, profiles that contain detailed information about users are often visible to many others, sometimes people the users do not know. Boyd (2007: 134) acknowledges the invisible audiences on social networking sites that do not exist in face-to-face interaction. Barnes (2006) discusses the "privacy paradox" as, for example, the situation where teens simultaneously wish to make themselves visible *and* they also want to retain some privacy. Gross and Acquisti (2005) discuss privacy and the risk of identity theft and stalking due to the sheer amount of information displayed by users. Hinduja and Patchin (2008) conclude that, for the most part, youths behave responsibly in disclosing personal information on MySpace. Lewis, Kaufman, and Christakis (2008) discuss the factors that determine whether a student has a private versus a public profile. Findings include the fact that people are more likely to have a private profile if their friends do; women are more likely to have a private profile than men; and having a private profile is associated with greater amounts of online activity.

Lange (2008) uses YouTube data to make the distinction between "publicly private" and "privately public" displays of information. "Publicly private" displays of information are those where personal information is revealed, but the content is not widely disseminated. "Privately public" displays are those where little personal information is shared with a far larger potential audience. We can go further and note that Lange's formulation suggests two additional categories: "privately private," where little information is disseminated to a small audience, and "publicly public," where large amounts of information are shared with a large audience.

What these ideas about publicity and privacy suggest is that privacy and publicity online have a very complicated relationship with one another. When social networking is done in quasi-public spaces like Facebook, one is always concerned with both privacy and publicity, often at the same time. Users want their digital documentation to be successful. To be successful, they have to learn how to reveal successfully. It follows that they are also very interested in when (and what) not to reveal, or when (and what) to conceal altogether. In other words, they need to also learn how to conceal successfully. In this way, privacy and publicity imply each other, and are increasingly interwoven.

Another aspect of the digital online presentation of the self is that of self-documentation. Pecora (2002) argues that the digital documenting of lives with home movies is due to narcissism (see Lasch 1978). He likens reality TV to psychology experiments because they emanate from the same drive: to make clear human norms and patterns of behavior. Pecora quipped that we might, in a decade, lose our will to be surveilled. He has been shown to be exactly wrong as the new home movies (i.e., on sites like YouTube) and social networking sites that follow the same self-disclosing trend have exploded in popularity.[10]

Adamic and Adar (2003) discuss the emerging amount of information documented about people on the web as a reflection of the users in the real world. As digitality becomes increasingly important in individuals' lives (as it has especially for youth), documentation becomes central to existence. Boyd quotes an 18-year-old saying, "If you're not on MySpace, you don't exist" (2008: 119). Boyd discusses how social networking sites are opportunities for youths to write themselves and their communities into being. Boyd also states that "there is an ethos that if it is possible to access a public expression, one should have the right to do so" (2008: 138). On social networking sites, users are documenting their lives in order to exist in the digital world. Not discussed at length in the literature reviewed, but something that can be deduced from it, is that, given the interconnectedness of the two, one documents oneself online to exist in the material world as well.

Indeed, the opportunities to document oneself online are proliferating. It seems that Pecora was correct to reference Lasch's (1978) *The Culture of Narcissism* because this book argues that we are increasingly afraid of being nothing, or of being unimportant, so we develop narcissistic impulses to become real. The explosion of new ways to document ourselves online allows new outlets for importance, existence, and perhaps even an immortality that living only in the material world simply does not permit. The logic is that increased digital documentation means increased digital existence. Beyond social networking sites, we document ourselves on Twitter, YouTube, Flickr, and even increasingly with services that track, geographically, where we are at all times, often via "smart" phone (e.g., Loopt, Fire Eagle, Google Latitude, etc.). These new technologies mean that more and more areas of our lives become part of this performance because new parts of our lives can now be documented (e.g., our geographic locations at every moment).

Missing from much of this literature are discussions of those who do *not* use these technologies at all, not because of a digital divide (related to social class), but because they choose not to, even if access is possible. While social networking site usage for college-aged youth is ubiquitous, others have never begun or have stopped[11] digital socializing to a large degree.

INEQUALITIES

There are tensions between the trends towards thinking about internet technology as utopian and the research that points to continuing online social inequalities. Some technology experts take an optimistic view regarding technological changes, linking new technologies to increased freedom, democratization, and a more utopian future. Fisher and Wright (2001) discuss Ogburn's (1922) theory of cultural lag which states that the effects of technological change will not become apparent to social actors for some time after its introduction to a society. Concerns about the internet are often ideologically charged and are filled as much with the hopes and fears of individual commentators as with the actual effects of the technology. Some thinkers (Haraway 1995; Sclove 1995; Fisher 1998; Haraway & Proctor 1998; Fisher & Wright 2001), on the one hand, view technology as the big fix for society. On the other hand, Simmel ([1907] 1982), Baudrillard (1983), and Gergen (1991) view technology in far more dystopian terms.

While some discuss the internet as inherently democratizing – or "flattening" (Friedman 2005) – it is important to note that those who best learn to navigate the world of social networking sites create special advantages for themselves. For example, Harp and Tremayne (2006) discuss the gendered blogosphere and find that women are severely under-represented in the top blogs. The authors argue that top bloggers hyper-linking with each other, gain concentrated power to choose who will be the other top bloggers. Mackenzie (2005), using Linux programming as an example, discusses how computer code, far from being neutral, tends to become cultural because of the "authorizing contexts" in which coding occurs. In discussing Castells' (1996) "network societies" and Lash's (2002) "information order," she shows how Linux (a free and "open source" operating system that is "open" to edits and revisions) has its own collective agency and cultural norms, evidenced by the fact that it is nearly all male. Thus, this is not a "flattened" world, but one where power begets power. Even in open-source communities, it is important to note how power hierarchies emerge (Stewart 2005). Fred Turner (2009) has also shown how the rhetoric of the "commons" is supposedly centered on democratization, but is enacted as a form of professional networking in an effort to move up in a hierarchy. Turner (2006) recognizes that early "cyber-libertarians," "cyber punks," and hackers believed they could tear down hierarchies and undermine corporations and governments. However, as we will see, this has not come to be because digital socialization has recreated many of the same structural inequalities well known in the material world. And this is not surprising given the theoretical point made earlier that the material and physical worlds should not be seen as separate. Early technologists mistakenly looked at the digital order in isolation from the rest of the social world, whereas today we should be mindful that sociality is an augmented reality that exists as a result of the implosion of atoms and bits.

We will now look at how material-world demographic differences play out online, beginning with the idea that males and females use the internet differently. Guadagno, Okdie, and Eno (2007) discuss the personality predictors of blogging and found that for women, opposed to men, being high in neuroticism was associated with blogging. Manago et al. discuss the different ways males and females portray themselves online, such as the way that females are rewarded for posting sexualized photos of themselves (while in the same breath promiscuity is criticized by peers and society in general [Manago, Graham, Greenfield & Salimkhan 2008: 454]). Lewis, Kaufman, and Christakis (2008) discuss the factors that predict whether a student has a private or a public profile and found that women are more likely to have a private profile than men. Thelwall (2008) found that more men than women use MySpace, women tend to maintain private profiles, and both men and women prefer to list women as their closest friends on the site. Magnuson and Dundes (2008) found that women report significant others across their profiles more than do men.

Remember Hancock and Toma's (2009) point that there is pressure for females to portray a body online that is more conventionally attractive than the one they actually possess. Indeed, there has been much attention paid to women's (especially young women's) bodies as potentially overexposed on social networking sites.

Far less research has focused on race and internet usage than on gender, although danah boyd consistently uses BlackPlanet – an African American-centered early social networking site – in her examples and data. The most frequently made point about race and social networking site usage is, as we have seen, that whites prefer Facebook and nonwhites MySpace. This finding serves to locate social networking site usage as not being separate from material-world differences, but as part of how race is enacted within society writ large. Boyd's (forthcoming) paper, "White Flight in Networked Publics," takes on a spatial metaphor when discussing how white youth moved away from MySpace to Facebook as a "white flight" similar to the white exodus from the cities to the suburbs. The "suburbs of Facebook" are fenced in, walled, and gated like suburbs in that they are typically more private than MySpace profiles. Meanwhile, the more open nature of MySpace means that the unattended profiles that the whites left behind become littered with spam ("digital graffiti"), turning MySpace into a "digital ghetto."

Blacks and Hispanics have been found to be more likely than whites to use cell phones for a variety of purposes – to take pictures, send emails, access the internet, play music or videos, or use many of the other features modern "smart" phones possess (Horrigan 2009). In a February 2010 survey of 1,753 Americans, Edison Research found that blacks are twice as likely to use Twitter as whites.[12]

Age is important in this discussion because nearly all American youth use social networking sites. However, older users are rapidly moving to sites like Facebook and in the process becoming the site's fastest-growing demographic. Livingstone (2008) contends that the youngest users of social networking sites prefer flashy, stylistic, identity-centered pages, while older teenagers prefer subtler pages that highlight their relationships with others. Blogs, the blogosphere, and the "micro-blogging" service Twitter ("teens don't tweet"[13]) are used primarily by adults for news and as tools for self-marketing and promotion.

One important topic regarding age and socializing online is the debate over "digital natives" versus "digital immigrants." Prensky (2001) wrote a well-known article arguing that older individuals are "digital immigrants" who have had to migrate to digital platforms and learn how to incorporate these new technologies into their previous understandings. This is contrasted with youths, who are said to be "digital natives" and who have never had to learn how to incorporate the digital into previously-created analogue understandings (or at least they were very young when they began using digital technologies). However, others have subsequently argued that digital natives are just a small subset of youths, and are not indicative of an entire generation (Hargittai 2010). Indeed, many youths, especially the disadvantaged, are not "digital natives."

Discussion of digital inequalities often takes place under the heading of the "digital divide." Traditionally, the digital divide has referred to differences in the degree of physical access to communication technologies. There is a large literature discussing this issue that remains quite important, especially with respect to new concerns over global inequalities and global connectivity. However, this issue does not fall within the scope of this literature review. Instead, as internet access has become more diffuse, what has increasingly become the focus is the different ways in which individuals learn to *use* these technologies. Much of boyd and Ellison's work concludes with the general point that social networking sites are important socialization tools for youths and will be important for the worlds they will inhabit as adults. They argue that those who do not learn to use social networking sites effectively will be the victims of a new digital divide based on *how* the web is used rather than simple access to it (boyd 2008: 137; Hargittai 2008). This follows Haythornthwaite's (2001) earlier point that the digital divide should not simply deal with *who* is online, but also with what they are there for, how much time they are spending online, and what they are doing there. Eszter Hargittai (2002) labels this a "second order digital divide." For example, a major study conducted by the MacArthur Foundation (Lewin 2008) on the way teens use social networking sites suggests that, "their participation is giving them the technological skills and literacy they need to succeed in the contemporary world. They're learning how to get along with others, how to manage a public identity, how to create a home page."

It is best to think of this second-order digital divide as a *post-structural* digital divide. The digital divide typically refers to structural access and structural inequalities. This new digital divide is habit-based, between those who have and those who have not learned the important skills of online social networking and content production. Pierre Bourdieu (Bourdieu & Nice 1984), in his landmark, post-structural analysis, describes the way things like skills, habits, and tastes are often learned outside the education system. That is, those habits that the upper class learn that reproduce their status as upper class are not simply the product of access to education but are also learned more informally. Similarly, in the case of the internet, a different sort of digital divide could be based on computer usage behaviors that have little to do with (structural) material access. Much like the rest of the social world, adolescents, even those *with access*, are learning the skills online essential for future success, and they are learning these skills unequally.

LABOR AND PROSUMPTION

As mentioned above, "prosumption" is implosion of the processes of production and consumption into one another. Prosumption involves both production and consumption rather than focusing on either one (production) or the other (consumption) (Ritzer & Jurgenson 2010). The concepts of prosumption and the prosumer were first discussed in Toffler's (1981) *The Third Wave*. Toffler made the point that the prosumer is not a new phenomenon because, for example, those on a pre-industrial farm produced that which they consumed.[14] He states that it was the industrial revolution that divided the spheres of production and consumption. However, Toffler goes on to argue that the prosumer was of increasing relevance in his day. "The rise of the prosumer" is evidenced by consumers increasingly self-assembling and repairing goods in a do-it-yourself (DIY) fashion. Self-service trends in electronic banking, grocery stores, and even the explosion of self-help books drove the idea that consumers increasingly are active producers. ATMs and other electronic kiosks such as those at movie theaters, hotels, airports, and in the self-checkout lanes in grocery stores have proliferated since Toffler's writings on the topic. Ritzer (2011), in *The McDonaldization of Society*, also looked at the way in which customers are "put to work" as unpaid employees in systems focused on efficiency. Additionally, through market research, consumers, in part, create the products they consume. Arvidsson (2006) discusses this process via branding, and Zwick and Knott (2009) via electronic databases. In the media, reality television, amateur pornography, citizen journalism, and many other aspects highlight the increasing role of consumers as producers of content.

The prosumer is of increasing relevance online through user-generated content on Web 2.0 (as described at the beginning of this chapter). Remember that consumers are producing open-source software (e.g., Linux, Mozilla Firefox) and Wikipedia, the world's largest encyclopedia. They are producing content on social networking sites (e.g., Facebook, MySpace), the blogosphere, the microblogging tool Twitter, and in many other places. Comments and reviews on sites such as Amazon.com and Yelp, as well as the videos on YouTube and photos on Flickr, are also "user-generated." The virtual world of Second Life is almost entirely "crowd-sourced"; that is, produced by those who consume it.

Ritzer (2010) argues that prosumption is the mid-point between pure consumption and pure production, and differentiates between two types of prosumers: (1) the producer as consumer, and (2) the consumer as producer. For instance, producers consume raw materials in the process of production, and consumers can produce a product's design, as well as their own identities, through their consumption – what Coté and Pybus (2007) call "immaterial labor 2.0."

One trajectory of prosumption online has been towards what has come to be known as the "commons-based peer-production" of not-for-profit resources (e.g., Linux, Wikipedia, Creative Commons licensing) (Benkler 2002). However, much prosumption takes place within profit-oriented sites such as Flickr and Facebook, and debate exists on whether the prosumer is ultimately empowered or exploited by the implosion of production and consumption on these sites (Zwick, Bonsu & Darmody 2008). Toffler (1981) viewed the prosumer as active and as questioning the role of markets; Tapscott and Williams (2006) state that calling prosumption exploitation "goes too far." Zwick, Bonsu, and Darmody (2008) and Humphreys and Grayson (2008) acknowledge the debate and the ethical issues surrounding unpaid labor, but do not strongly focus on the potential exploitation of the prosumer in the way that Ritzer (2011) does when he describes prosumption as "unpaid labor."

Christian Fuchs (2010) is perhaps the strongest critic of the exploitation that occurs with prosumption online. From a Marxist framework, he argues that users are producing material profits for companies like Facebook and are paid no material wages in return. If exploitation from a Marxist perspective is the ratio between profit produced and wages earned, the exploitation here is "infinite." Coté and Pybus's (2007) article can be read as a rebuttal to Fuchs, even if they do not take him on specifically in their arguments. They focus on more than just material wages when discussing the value that users gain from this "unpaid labor." They describe this prosumptive labor (they call it "labor 2.0") as biopolitical and as part of the larger post-Fordist re-imagining of production. This is "profitable" for, say, Facebook users, because it builds valuable social relationships and networked subjectivities. Thus we cannot see producers online as a crowd of "unwitting immaterial apprentices," but rather as individuals producing social relations and affect. They argue that MySpace is "intensely gratifying" because it "allows users to feel a part of something larger" (Coté & Pybus 2007: 95). We are no longer passive "couch potatoes," but web surfers and bloggers (2007: 99).

Thus, the view of labor has changed from the Marxist image of a worker in a factory. This new labor can be seen as part of everyday life; indeed, it can also be thought to be playful. The idea that play and labor have imploded online has led to some discussion of "playbor" (Kücklich 2005), or, similarly, how work and leisure can be combined into "weisure" (Conley 2009).[15]

Poole (2008) takes this issue on forcibly in "Working for the Man: Against the Employment Paradigm in Videogames."[16] He argues that video games are about work as much as they are about play. To "play" the game is to be obedient to the game in completing its tasks, what he calls "system[s] of coercion, freely entered into." He utilizes Adorno, who stated, "[a]musement under late capitalism is the prolongation of work." We can use Poole's analysis of video games with respect to socialization online to criticize the notion that amusement is simply a value gained, as Coté and Pybus (2007) state above; it is also a tool of capitalism. This is just the awareness that some AOL users in the 1990s had when they came to learn that their prosumptive activities were making profits for the company and subsequently sued AOL for a share of the earnings (the users lost this case). Niedzviecki states that, regarding online prosumption, "we don't think of it as work" (2009: 242). Niedzviecki contends that while many users are not interested in where the information that they submit to Facebook goes, they (we) should be aware that their everyday lives – gestures, actions, choices, locations, thoughts – have become valuable commodities (2009: 249); indeed, we have produced ourselves as commodities from which others profit.

CONCLUSIONS, INSIGHTS, AND FUTURE DIRECTIONS

This chapter reaffirms the sometimes counter-intuitive idea that technology in general and the internet in particular are social. The internet is therefore of inherent concern to sociologists and this is especially the case with Web 2.0 where the vast majority of the content is created, often collaboratively, by the users of the sites. Beyond that, people do a great deal of communicating, socializing, interacting, and self-expression and presentation on these sites. While these new social media are certainly important to many people, their very immersion and seeming control may serve to obscure or conceal the various problems that social media create. For example, in spite of their seeming control, users of Web 2.0 and social media may be alienated from and, more importantly, exploited by those who control and profit from these sites. This is especially the case because, as prosumers, users are doing much of the work associated with creating content on Web 2.0 sites like Facebook or YouTube, work for which they are certainly not being paid. In a sense, they are being exploited to a greater degree than wage workers who are at least being (under) paid for their work. Does the power and the pleasure of doing the work associated with being a social media prosumer serve to obscure this exploitation? Or are these unpaid digital laborers compensated in the often immaterial, non-monetary value they gain from sites like Facebook, sites that are used free of charge?

Next, there is a tendency to see social networking sites as purely "virtual" worlds set apart from a "real" world that is physical. However, instead of looking at reality in modern binary terms, it is better to see the digital and physical worlds as tightly intertwined and increasingly difficult to differentiate from one another. In other words, they are creating an augmented reality that is some combination of the physical and the digital, of atoms and bits. Thus, our physical reality is increasingly augmented by technologies such as the cell phones in the pockets of our jeans, or by our bedsides, that give us access to Facebook (and other social networking sites). And, our online worlds are increasingly physical in the sense that our Facebook lives are linked to our offline lives, even to our bodies.

Last, in its early days, and to some extent to this day, a major concern associated with the internet has been the "digital divide," especially the distinction between those who do and do not have access to it. While this concern persists, there is now also the matter of the differences in the way in which groups of people (differentiated by, for example, race and gender) *use* the technology. As access to the internet becomes more diffuse and perhaps ubiquitous, other issues, such as how people learn to use social networking sites, are likely to attract increasing attention from sociologists interested in, and concerned about, the inequalities associated with the internet.

Notes

1 MUD refers to "Multi-User Dungeon" and a MOO is a "MUD, Object Oriented." These are both early text-based virtual communities where users could interact with each other.

2 The development of effective search engines, especially the one developed by Google, made the web far more usable and defines a Web 1.0 era of users as consumers of content.

3 Other popular social networking sites include, but are not limited to, LinkedIn (aimed at professionals), BlackPlanet (aimed at African Americans), Badoo (European), Couch Surfing (for travelers), hi5 (popular outside of the US), Mixi (Japanese), Orkut (popular in Brazil, India, and elsewhere), Vkontakte (Russian), and Qzone and Renren (both popular in China).

4 Ravelry is a social networking site not based as much on people's material-world lives, but on shared interests (here, the fiber arts).

5 However, these studies do find slight differences between users and their profiles on dating sites, and these differences are distinct for men and women. Men tend to slightly overestimate their height while women slightly underestimate their weight, and women choose profile pictures that misrepresent their actual appearance more than their male counterparts.

6 The term "avatar" comes from the idea of god-like creation in a more literal sense.

7 However, some people do construct fake Facebook pages, or "fakebooks."

8 See the *New York Times* article, "Connecting Your Car, Socks and Body to the Internet," where bodies can be used as input devices, what has come to be known as "skinput." http://bits.blogs.nytimes.com/2010/03/01/connecting-your-car-socks-and-body-to-the-Internet/

9   www.newsweek.com/id/207897/
10 Reminiscent of Andy Warhol's comment that everyone has 15 minutes of fame; or as internet pioneer Josh Harris states in the movie *We Live in Public* (2009) as a correction to Warhol, on the web, everyone has 15 minutes of fame every day.
11 Suicidemachine.org is a service that kills all of your social networking profiles.
12 www.edisonresearch.com/twitter_usage_2010.php
13 "Stats Confirm It: Teens Don't Tweet." http://mashable.com/2009/08/05/teens-dont-tweet/
14 Of course, there *is* a division of labor on a pre-industrial farm, meaning that one consumed many things one did not directly produce. However, on this farm, one would likely consume that which one produced, and, further, the farm itself can be seen as a prosumptive system.
15 One's choice of terms here depends on whether one views, for example, Facebook as play or leisure.
16 http://stevenpoole.net/trigger-happy/working-for-the-man/

References

Ackerman, M. S., C. A. Halverson, T. Erickson, W. A. Kellogg, and W. J. Orlikowski (2008) "Using Technology and Constituting Structures: A Practice Lens for Studying Technology in Organizations." In *Resources, Co-Evolution and Artifacts, Computer Supported Cooperative Work*. London: Springer, pp. 255–305.

Adamic, L. A. and E. Adar (2003) "Friends and Neighbors on the Web." *Social Networks* 25: 211–30.

Arvidsson, A. (2006) *Brands. Meaning and Value in Media Culture*. London: Routledge.

Barnes, S. B. (2006) "A Privacy Paradox: Social Networking in the United States." *First Monday* 11.

Baudrillard, J. (1983) *Simulations*. New York: Semiotext(e).

Benkler, Y. (2002) "Coase's Penguin, or, Linux and the Nature of the Firm." *Yale Law Journal* 112: 367–445.

Bortree, D. S. (2005) "Presentation of Self on the Web: An Ethnographic Study of Teenage Girls' Weblogs." *Education, Communication and Information* 5: 25–39.

Bourdieu, P. and R. Nice (1984) *Distinction: A Social Critique of the Judgment of Taste*. Cambridge, MA: Harvard University Press.

Boyd, D. (2006) "Friends, Friendsters, and MySpace Top 8: Writing Community into Being on Social Network Sites." *First Monday* 11(12).

Boyd, D. (2007) "Why Youth (Heart) Social Network Sites: The Role of Networked Publics in Teenage Social Life." In D. Buckingham (eds.), *Youth, Identity, and Digital Media*. MacArthur Foundation Series on Digital Learning. Cambridge, MA: MIT Press, pp. 119–42.

Boyd, D. (2008) "Taken out of Context: American Teen Sociality in Networked Publics." PhD dissertation, School of Information, University of California-Berkeley.

Boyd, D. (forthcoming) "White Flight in Networked Publics? How Race and Class Shaped American Teen Engagement with MySpace and Facebook." In Lisa Nakamura and Peter Chow-White (eds.), *Digital Race Anthology*. London: Routledge.

Boyd, D. M. and N. B. Ellison (2008) "Social Network Sites: Definition, History, and Scholarship." *Journal of Computer-Mediated Communication* 13: 210–30.

Castells, M. (1996) *Rise of the Network Society: The Information Age: Economy, Society and Culture*. Oxford: Wiley-Blackwell.

Cho, H. K., M. Trier, and E. Kim (2005) "The Use of Instant Messaging in Working Relationship Development: A Case Study." *Journal of Computer-Mediated Communication* 10(4).

Conley, D. (2009) *Elsewhere, USA*. New York: Pantheon.

Coté, M. and J. Pybus (2007) "Learning to Immaterial Labour 2.0: MySpace and Social Networks." *ephemera* 7: 88–106.

Dery, M. (1994) *Flame Wars: The Discourse of Cyberculture*. Durham, NC: Duke University Press.

Dijck, J. van (2009) "Users Like You? Theorizing Agency in User-Generated Content." *Media, Culture and Society* 31: 41.

Donath, J. and D. Boyd (2004) "Public Displays of Connection." *BT Technology Journal* 22: 71–82.

Ellison, N. B., C. Steinfield, and C. Lampe (2007) "The Benefits of Facebook Friends: Social Capital and College Students' Use of Online Social Network Sites." *Journal of Computer-Mediated Communication* 12: 1143–68.

Fisher, D. R. (1998) "Rumoring Theory and the Internet: A Framework for Analyzing the Grass Roots." *Social Science Computer Review* 16: 158.

Fisher, D. R. and L. M. Wright (2001) "On Utopias and Dystopias: Toward an Understanding of the Discourse Surrounding the Internet." *Journal of Computer-Mediated Communication* 6: 1–13.

Friedman, T. L. (2005) *The World Is Flat: A Brief History of the Twenty-First Century*. New York: Farrar, Straus and Giroux.

Fuchs, C. (2010) "Class, Knowledge and New Media." *Media, Culture and Society* 32: 141.

Gergen, K. J. (1991) *The Saturated Self: Dilemmas of Identity in Contemporary Life*. New York: Basic Books.

Goffman, E. (1959) *The Presentation of Self in Everyday Life*. New York: Doubleday/Anchor Books.

Gross, R. and A. Acquisti (2005) "Information Revelation and Privacy in Online Social Networks." WPES '05: Proceedings of the 2005 ACM Workshop on Privacy in the Electronic Society.

Guadagno, R. E., B. M. Okdie, and C. A. Eno (2007) "Who Blogs? Personality Predictors of Blogging." *Computers in Human Behavior*. doi:10.1016/j.chb.2007.09.001.

Hancock, J. T. and C. L. Toma (2009) "Putting Your Best Face Forward: The Accuracy of Online Dating Photographs." *Journal of Communication* 59: 367–86.

Haraway, D. (1995) "A Manifesto for Cyborgs: Science, Technology, and Socialist Feminism in the 1980s." In Steven Seidman (ed.), *The Postmodern Turn: New Perspectives on Social Theory*. New York: Cambridge University Press, pp. 82–115.

Haraway, D. J. (1997) *Modest_Witness@Second_Millennium. FemaleMan©_Meets_ OncoMouse™: Feminism and Technoscience*. New York: Routledge.

Hardey, M. (2002) "Life Beyond the Screen: Embodiment and Identity through the Internet." *Sociological Review* 50: 570–85.

Hargittai, E. (2002) "Second Level Digital Divide." *First Monday* 7(4).

Hargittai, E. (2008) "Whose Space? Differences among Users and Non-Users of Social Network Sites." *Journal of Computer-Mediated Communication* 13: 276–97.

Hargittai, E. (2010) "Digital Na(t)ives? Variation in Internet Skills and Uses among Members of the 'Net Generation'." *Sociological Inquiry* 80(1): 92–113.

Harp, D. and M. Tremayne (2006) "The Gendered Blogosphere: Examining Inequality Using Network and Feminist Theory." *Journalism and Mass Communication Quarterly* 83: 247.

Haythornthwaite, C. (2001) "Introduction: The Internet in Everyday Life." *American Behavioral Scientist* 45: 363–82.

Helft, M. (2007) "With Simple New Tools on Web, Amateurs Reshape Mapmaking." *New York Times*, July 27: A1, A16.

Herman, A., R. J. Coombe, and L. Kaye (2006) "Your Second Life?" *Cultural Studies* 20: 184–210.

Hinduja, S. and J. W. Patchin (2008) "Personal Information of Adolescents on the Internet: A Quantitative Content Analysis of MySpace." *Journal of Adolescence* 31: 125–46.

Horrigan, J. (2009) *Wireless Internet Use*. Washington, DC: Pew Internet & American Life Project 2009–07.

Humphreys, A. and K. Grayson (2008) "The Intersecting Roles of Consumer and Producer: A Critical Perspective on Co-Production, Co-Creation and Prosumption." *Sociology Compass* 2: 963–80.

Jurgenson, N. (2010) "The De-McDonaldization of the Internet." In G. Ritzer (ed.), *McDonaldization: The Reader*, 3rd edn. Thousand Oaks, CA: Pine Forge Press, pp. 159–71.

Jurgenson, N. and G. Ritzer (2009) "Efficiency, Effectiveness, and Web 2.0." In Sharon Kleinman (ed.) *The Culture of Efficiency*. New York: Peter Lang, pp. 51–67.

Kücklich, J. (2005) "Precarious Playbour: Modders and the Digital Games Industry." *Fibreculture 5*.

Lange, P. G. (2008) "Publicly Private and Privately Public: Social Networking on YouTube." *Journal of Computer-Mediated Communication* 13: 361–80.

Lasch, C. (1978) *The Culture of Narcissism: American Life in an Age of Diminishing Expectations*. New York: Norton.

Lash, S. (2002) *Critique of Information*. London: Sage.

Lessig, L. (1999) *Code and Other Laws of Cyberspace*. New York: Basic Books.

Lessig, L. (2006) *Code: Version 2.0*. New York: Basic Books.

Lewin, T. (2008) "Teenagers' Internet Socializing Not a Bad Thing." *The New York Times*, November 20. www.nytimes.com/2008/11/20/us/20internet.html (accessed November 16, 2010).

Lewis, C. C. and J. F. George (2008) "Cross-Cultural Deception in Social Networking Sites and Face-to-Face Communication." *Computers in Human Behavior* 24: 2945–64.

Lewis, K., J. Kaufman, and N. Christakis (2008) "The Taste for Privacy: An Analysis of College Student Privacy Settings in an Online Social Network." *Journal of Computer-Mediated Communication* 14: 79–100.

Lewis, K., J. Kaufman, M. Gonzalez, A. Wimmer, and N. Christakis (2008) "Tastes, Ties, and Time: A New Social Network Dataset Using Facebook.com." *Social Networks* 30: 330–42.

Liu, H. (2008) "Social Network Profiles as Taste Performances." *Journal of Computer-Mediated Communication* 13: 252–75.

Livingstone, S. (2008) "Taking Risky Opportunities in Youthful Content Creation: Teenagers' Use of Social Networking Sites for Intimacy, Privacy and Self-Expression." *New Media and Society* 10: 393–411.

Lyotard, J. F. (1984) *The Postmodern Condition: A Report on Knowledge*. Minneapolis, MN: University of Minnesota Press.

Mackenzie, A. (2005) "The Performativity of Code: Software and Cultures of Circulation." *Theory, Culture and Society* 22: 71–92.

Magnuson, M. J. and L. Dundes (2008) "Gender Differences in 'Social Portraits' Reflected in MySpace Profiles." *CyberPsychology and Behavior* 11: 239–41.

Manago, A. M., M. B. Graham, P. M. Greenfield, and G. Salimkhan (2008) "Self-Presentation and Gender on MySpace." *Journal of Applied Developmental Psychology* 29: 446–58.

Maratea, R. (2008) "The E-Rise and Fall of Social Problems: The Blogosphere as a Public Arena." *Social Problems* 55(1): 139–60.

Markus, H. and P. Nurius (1986) "Possible Selves." *American Psychologist* 41: 954–69.

Nardi, B. A., S. Whittaker, and E. Bradner (2000) "Interaction and Outeraction: Instant Messaging in Action." In *Proceedings of the 2000 ACM Conference on Computer Supported Cooperative Work*. New York: ACM, pp. 79–88.

Niedzviecki, H. (2009) *The Peep Diaries*. San Francisco: City Lights Books.

Ogburn, W. F. (1922) *Social Change*. New York: Viking Press.

O'Reilly, T. (2005) "What Is Web 2.0." O'Reilly Media – Technology Books, Tech Conferences, IT Courses, News. http://oreilly.com/web2/archive/what-is-web-20.html (accessed July 8, 2011).

Pecora, V. P. (2002) "The Culture of Surveillance." *Qualitative Sociology* 25: 345–58.

Porter, C. E. (2004) "A Typology of Virtual Communities: A Multi-Disciplinary Foundation for Future Research." *Journal of Computer-Mediated Communication* 10(1).

Prensky, M. (2001) "Digital Natives, Digital Immigrants." *On the Horizon* 9: 1–6.

Ritzer, G. (2010) "Focusing on the Prosumer." In *Prosumer Revisited*. VS Verlag für Sozialwissenschaften, pp. 61–79. http://dx.doi.org/10.1007/978-3-531-91998-0_3

Ritzer, G. (2011) *The McDonaldization of Society*, 6th edn. Thousand Oaks, CA: Pine Forge Press.

Ritzer, G. and N. Jurgenson (2010) "Production, Consumption, Prosumption: The Nature of Capitalism in the Age of the Digital 'Prosumer'." *Journal of Consumer Culture* 10: 13–36.

Schumpeter, J. A. (1942) "Capitalism." In *Socialism and Democracy*. New York: Harper.

Sclove, R. (1995) *Democracy and Technology*. New York: Guilford Press.

Sessions, L. F. (2009) "'You Looked Better on MySpace': Deception and Authenticity on the Web 2.0." *First Monday* 14.

Simmel, G. ([1907] 1982) *The Philosophy of Money*. London: Routledge.

Steinkuehler, C. A. and D. Williams (2006) "Where Everybody Knows Your (Screen) Name: Online Games as Third Places." *Journal of Computer-Mediated Communication* 11: 885–909.

Stewart, D. (2005) "Social Status in an Open-Source Community." *American Sociological Review* 70: 823–42.

Sundén, J. (2003) *Material Virtualities: Approaching Online Textual Embodiment*. New York: Peter Lang.

Tapscott, D. and A. D. Williams (2006) *Wikinomics: How Mass Collaboration Changes Everything*. New York: Portfolio.

Thelwall, M. (2008) "Social Networks, Gender, and Friending: An Analysis of MySpace Member Profiles." *Journal of the American Society for Information Science and Technology* 59: 1321–30.

Toffler, A. (1981) *The Third Wave*. New York: Bantam Books.

Toma, C. L., J. T. Hancock, and N. B. Ellison (2008) "Separating Fact from Fiction: An Examination of Deceptive Self-Presentation in Online Dating Profiles." *Personality and Social Psychology Bulletin* 34: 1023–36.

Turner, F. (2006) *From Counterculture to Cyberculture: Stewart Brand, the Whole Earth Network, and the Rise of Digital Utopianism.* Chicago: University of Chicago Press.

Turner, F. (2009) "Burning Man at Google: A Cultural Infrastructure for New Media Production." *New Media and Society* 11: 73–94.

Veblen, T. and M. Banta (2007) *The Theory of the Leisure Class.* New York: Oxford University Press.

Watts, D. J., P. S. Dodds, and M. E. J. Newman (2002) "Identity and Search in Social Networks." *Science* 296(5571): 1302–5.

Wellman, B. and M. Gulia (1999a) "Net-Surfers Don't Ride Alone: Virtual Communities as Communities." In B. Wellman (ed.), *Networks in the Global Village: Life in Contemporary Communities.* Boulder, CO: Westview Press, pp. 331–66.

Wellman, B. and M. Gulia (1999b) "Virtual Communities as Communities: Net Surfers Don't Ride Alone." In B. Wellman (ed.), *Networks in the Global Village: Life in Contemporary Communities.* Boulder, CO: Westview Press, pp. 167–94.

Wellman, B. and K. Hampton (1999) "Living Networked On and Offline." *Contemporary Sociology* 28: 648–54.

Wellman, B. and C. A. Haythornthwaite (2002) *The Internet in Everyday Life.* Oxford: Blackwell.

Wellman, B., J. Salaff, D. Dimitrova, L. Garton, M. Gulia, and C. Haythornthwaite (1996) "Computer Networks as Social Networks: Collaborative Work, Telework, and Virtual Community." *Annual Review of Sociology* 22: 213–38.

Wellman, B., A. Q. Haase, J. Witte, and K. Hampton (2001) "Does the Internet Increase, Decrease, or Supplement Social Capital." *American Behavioral Scientist* 45: 436–55.

Zhao, S. (2009) "Teen Adoption of MySpace and IM: Inner-City versus Suburban Differences." *CyberPsychology and Behavior* 12(1): 55–8.

Zhao, S., S. Grasmuck, and J. Martin (2008) "Identity Construction on Facebook: Digital Empowerment in Anchored Relationships." *Computers in Human Behavior* 24: 1816–36.

Zwick, D. and D. Knott (2009) "Manufacturing Customers: The Database as New Means of Production." *Journal of Consumer Culture* 9: 221–47.

Zwick, D., S. K. Bonsu, and A. Darmody (2008) "Putting Consumers to Work: Co-Creation and New Marketing Govern-Mentality." *Journal of Consumer Culture* 8: 163–96.

Index

abortion 479
academic achievement 355–6
academic performance 349
Actor-Behavior-Object (ABO) 124
Actor Network Theory (ANT) 104,
    614–16, 617
adolescence 238, 372
affect, and class 269–70, 279–82
affect control theory 122–4, 125,
    126–7, 128
Afghanistan, and women 318
African Americans 298–99, 371
Agamben, Giorgio 108, 109–10
age 198, 338, 394, 428–9, 475–6
agency, and life course 200
agency–structure theory 100, 111,
    423, 457, 459
age-specific fertility rate (ASFR) 478
aggregation rules 140
AIDS 246, 256
alternative theories, scope 17
American Journal of Sociology 40, 41
Americans, Native 290–1, 313,
    314, 315, 397

American Sociological Association
    42, 43, 444
  sections 4, 319, 388, 505
ancient world 26, 83–4, 272
anti-Apartheid movement 374
anti-consumerism 513, 514
anti-globalization movement 558
anti-Vietnam war movement 374
Aramis, project 615
Aristotle 27
artificial groups 141
Asian Americans 292–4, 299
Aston School 164
athletics, and gender 304

baby boom 475, 476
Battle for Seattle 558, 559
Baudrillard, Jean 104, 112
Bauman, Zygmunt 100–1
Beccaria, Cesare 229, 230
Beck, Ulrich 101, 105
behavioral control 123
behavioral display 309
Bentham, Jeremy 108

The Wiley-Blackwell Companion to Sociology, First Edition. Edited by George Ritzer.
© 2012 Blackwell Publishing Ltd. Published 2012 by Blackwell Publishing Ltd.